THROUGH TIME AND CULTURE

THROUGH TIME AND CULTURE

Introductory Readings in Philosophy

A. Pablo Iannone
Central Connecticut State University

Prentice Hall, Englewood Cliffs, New Jersey 07632

Library of Congress Cataloging-in-Publication Data

Iannone, A. Pablo.
    Through time and culture : introductory readings in philosophy /
  A. Pablo Iannone.
       p. cm.
    Includes bibliographical references.
    ISBN 0-13-920620-5
    1. Philosophy –Introductions. I. Title.
  BD21.I26 1994   93-23864
  100–dc20   CIP

Acquisitions editor: Ted Bolen
Editorial/production supervision and interior design: Serena Hoffman
Production Coordinator: Kelly Behr
Copy editor: Carol Freddo
Cover design: Robert Ferrar-Wagner
Cover art: *In the Cactus Grove* by Pedro Figari (1861–1938),
          Private Collection/Art Resource.

© **1994 by Prentice-Hall, Inc.**
A Paramount Communications Company
Englewood Cliffs, New Jersey 07632

Printed in the United States of America
10 9 8 7 6 5 4 3 2 1

ISBN 0-13-920620-5

Prentice-Hall International (UK) Limited, *London*
Prentice-Hall of Australia Pty. Limited, *Sydney*
Prentice-Hall Canada Inc., *Toronto*
Prentice-Hall Hispanoamericana, S.A., *Mexico*
Prentice-Hall of India Private Limited, *New Delhi*
Prentice-Hall of Japan, Inc., *Tokyo*
Simon & Schuster Asia Pte. Ltd., *Singapore*
Editora Prentice-Hall do Brasil, Ltda., *Rio de Janeiro*

To my wife, Mary Kay Garrow,
and to our daughters, Alejandra Emilia and Catalina Patricia—
all sources of hope and reassurance
in the everyday task
of dealing with fact, memory, and fantasy
in a diverse and changing world.

Contents

Preface   xiii

General Introduction   1

Senses of the Term "Philosophy"   1
Philosophy's Aims and Philosophers' Motives   2
Problems and Branches of Philosophy   3
Philosophy, Philosophies, and Philosophical Traditions   5
Philosophical Traditions and Fields Other Than Philosophy   5

PART I
What Is Philosophy?   *9*

A.   How Did Philosophy Begin?

1.   Traditional Veda Text   *The Upanishads*   21
2.   Plato   *Apology*   28
3.   Aristotle   Wisdom and Philosophy   42

B.   How Has Philosophy Come to Be Conceived?

4.   Alfred North Whitehead   The Aims of Education   49
5.   Arthur E. Murphy   The Philosophic Mind and the Contemporary World   56
6.   John Dewey   Changing Conceptions of Philosophy   62

C.   What Are Philosophy's Logical Tools?

7.   Robert P. Churchill   Analyzing Arguments   69

Questions for Review and Further Thought   78

PART II
What Are Truth, Knowledge, and Faith, and How Are They Related?   80

A.   What Is Truth?

8.   Satischandra Chatterjee   Indian and Western Theories of Truth   94
9.   W. P. Montague   Pragmatism as Relativism   99

B.   What Can We Know?

10.   Vasubandhu   All Is Representation   106
11.   René Descartes   Meditations of First Philosophy   113
12.   George Berkeley   Of the Principles of Human Knowledge   120
13.   Charles Sanders Peirce   The Fixation of Belief   128
14.   Ernest Nagel   Science and Common Sense   134

C.   Is Faith Justified?

15.   Traditional Buddhist Text   The Five Cardinal Virtues and the Definition of Faith   142
16.   W. K. Clifford   The Ethics of Belief   143
17.   William James   The Will to Believe   147
18.   Annette Baier   Secular Faith   152

Questions for Review and Further Thought   162

PART III
What Is the Universe Really Like?   164

A.   Is There a God?

19.   St. Anselm   Proslogium   182
20.   Gaunilon de Marmoutier   In Behalf of the Fool   185
21.   St. Thomas Aquinas   The Existence of God   188
22.   David Hume   Design, Evil, and God's Existence   192
23.   Ernest Nagel   Philosophical Concepts of Atheism   203

B.   Are There Minds Beside Matter?

24.   Rhazes   From *Spiritual Physick*   211
25.   Gilbert Ryle   The Ghost in the Machine   216

C.   Do All Events Have Causes?

26.   Averroes   From *The Incoherence of the Incoherence*   223
27.   David Hume   Of Probability; and the Idea of Cause and Effect   235
28.   Mario Bunge   Induction in Science   239

D.   Are We Ever Free to Do as We Choose?

29.   Lorenzo Valla   Dialogue on Free Will   246
30.   Roderick W. Chisholm   Responsibility and Avoidability   257

E.   What Is It to Be a Person?

31.   John Locke   Personal Identity   259
32.   Risieri Frondizi   The Nature of the Self   269

Questions for Review and Further Thought   276

PART IV
What Is Morally Justified?   278

A.   What Is the Moral Significance of Living in a Community?

33.   Mo Tzu   Universal Love   303
34.   Plato   From *The Republic*   307
35.   Aristotle   From the *Nicomachean Ethics*   310

B.   What Is the Moral Significance of Human Nature?

36.   St. Thomas Aquinas   On Happiness, the Virtues, and the Natural Law   314
37.   Ibn Khaldûn   Of Natural Groups, Group Feeling, Civilization, and Justice   323
38.   Thomas Hobbes   From *Leviathan*   335
39.   David Hume   Of the Influencing Motives of the Will   351

C.   How Can the Demands of Justice, Utility, and Culture Be Balanced Against One Another?

40. Immanuel Kant   The Categorical Imperative   354
41. John Stuart Mill   On the Connection Between Justice and Utility   357
42. Karl Marx   Labor Power, Exchanges, Surplus Value, and Exploitation   369
43. Mohandas K. Gandhi   Through Non-Violence to God   379
44. Simone de Beauvoir   The Ethics of Ambiguity   380
45. María C. Lugones and Elizabeth V. Spelman   Have We Got a Theory for You! Feminist Theory, Cultural Imperialism, and the Demand for "The Woman's Voice"   389

Questions for Review and Further Thought   399

PART V
What Is Aesthetically Valuable?   401

46. Monroe C. Beardsley   In Defense of Aesthetic Value   410
47. Innocent C. Onyewuenyi   Traditional African Aesthetics: A Philosophical Perspective   422
48. William K. Wimsatt and Monroe C. Beardsley   The Intentional Fallacy   428
49. José Ortega y Gasset   The Dehumanization of Art   435

Questions for Review and Further Thought   450

PART VI
What Are Philosophy's Prospects Today?   452

50. Marjorie Grene   Puzzled Notes on a Puzzling Profession   462
51. Kai Nielsen   Philosophy as Critical Theory   465
52. Leopoldo Zea   The Actual Function of Philosophy in Latin America   476
53. María Lugones   Playfulness, "World"-Travelling, and Loving Perception   484
54. K. C. Anyanwu   Cultural Philosophy as a Philosophy of Integration and Tolerance   493

Questions for Review and Further Thought   505

Glossary   507

Selected Bibliography   511

Preface

In our fragmented twentieth century, diversity and growing cultural self-assertion elicit romantic enthusiasm among some and cautious skepticism—if not outright fear—among others. There are those who hail pluralism as a way out of ethnocentric parochialism and see in it a new freedom for long-oppressed ethnic groups. Others argue that pluralism is just another name for confusion and that this confusion is undermining the foundations of Western culture.

Philosophy has not remained impervious to this controversy. Some traditionalists are determined to uphold the intellectual values embodied in the works of Plato, Aristotle, and other Western philosophical classics against non-Western influences. Some multiculturalists are equally determined to demonstrate that the Western philosophical classics embody values that are detrimental to non-Westerners and all women.

This situation poses a variety of philosophical questions, not the least of which is: Can the philosophical traditions embodied in the works of Plato, Aristotle, and other Western philosophical classics be sensitively and fruitfully applied across cultural boundaries? Philosophy would stand to gain from reflection on this and related questions in three ways. First, such reflection would lead to greater understanding of the nature, scope, and purposes of philosophy, and attaining this understanding is an important aim of philosophy. Second, such reflection would help us to better assess philosophy's present condition and future prospects. Finally, this kind of reflection would help philosophy students develop open and inquiring minds. Indeed, in this age of growing cross-cultural interactions, it is urgent that we all become more open-minded. As history and current events make plain, cultural parochialism often creates devastating conflicts.

Through Time and Culture aims to provide a basis for such reflection. It has three main objectives: to introduce English-speaking readers to philosophy through a cross-cultural approach; to facilitate cross-cultural philosophical dialogue; and to investigate to what extent Western philosophical language and categories can play a useful role in such dialogue. In pursuing these goals, the book points to the political aspects of the relations between philosophical traditions and the ways in which knowledge claims are established within these traditions, especially at the cross-cultural level. The thorough elucidation of the nature and significance of such political aspects, however, falls outside the scope of this book.

Through Time and Culture covers European and Anglo-American traditions and examines recurrent problems within these traditions. It seeks to apply the discussions and the categories used in Western traditions to philosophical problems arising in other cultures. It also examines the contributions of philosophers from other cultures to the discussion of the problems. In carrying out this task, our aim is to find a balance between two extreme forms of misunderstanding characteristic of cultural parochialism. One is the failure to recognize resemblances—or differences—between the works of philosophers in different traditions. The other is the tendency to draw false analogies—or false contrasts—between those traditions.

Though this book does not adopt an advocacy stance, neither is its position exactly neutral. One of its presuppositions is that philosophy is not a strictly Western phenomenon. On the other hand, it does not deny that Western philosophical categories have any sound application to philosophical problems arising in other cultures. This is not a blandly pluralistic position, since *Through Time and Culture* does not presuppose that Western categories are applicable to all philosophical problems across the range of human cultures. Instead, it tests these categories by applying them to philosophical problems arising in different cultures in order to discover where such application is useful and where it misconstrues the problem.

This book has six interconnected parts, the first four of which are divided into sections. The organizational categories are those widely used in Western philosophy—epistemology, metaphysics, ethics and sociopolitical philosophy, and aesthetics—but these terms do not appear in the titles. Instead, questions central to these categories are used to introduce each part and its sections. Part I contains discussions of the nature, conceptions, and tools of philosophy. It has three sections. The first presents some ancient beginnings of philosophy and the conceptions of philosophy they involved. The second presents reflections on the nature and conceptions of philosophy formulated after philosophy had been developing for more than two millennia. The third section focuses on logical tools for doing philosophy. Part II contains epistemological discussions of truth, perception, knowledge, and faith. Part III deals with metaphysical problems about the existence of God, mind and matter, causality, free will, and personal identity. Part IV presents discussions of ethics and sociopolitical philosophy, ranging from those found in Plato and Aristotle to those found in today's feminist writings. Part V deals with problems in aesthetics, especially in the philosophy of art, such as the problem of identifying a work of art and the role of the author's intentions in this identification. The book closes with discussions of philosophy's present state and prospects in Part VI.

Through Time and Culture is of interest to the initiated because it integrates philosophical discussions from a variety of cultural traditions on topics of common concern. At the same time, it is accessible to the uninitiated because philosophical language and categories are introduced by reference to problems raised—and language and categories used—in ordinary life. This approach helps to clarify how applicable particular philosophical positions and categories are to different cultural environments.

Three criteria were used to choose the selections for this book. The first was whether a selection would be useful for teaching philosophy as it is actually practiced rather than a watered-down version of philosophy. The second was whether a selection has been significantly influential in the history of philosophy or is significantly influential in philosophy today. The third was whether, if the selection has not been significantly influential historically and is not so today, it is nonetheless likely to facilitate cross-cultural philosophical dialogue. However, there is no effort to represent *every* philosophical perspective or even *every* culture here, because this is intended to be a *cross-cultural*, not a multicultural, introduction to philosophy.

This approach is in accordance with the purpose of facilitating cross-cultural philosophical dialogue. Such a purpose is hindered rather than helped by including selections merely because they represent this or that philosophical perspective or culture, even though they are not influential and do not facilitate the dialogue. The approach is also in accordance with the book's pedagogical aim, which is to lead to engaged cross-cultural philosophical dialogue. A collection of largely unrelated samples of what philosophers have said in this or that culture would have historical or anthropological worth. But the aim here is different: to introduce readers *philosophically* to the practice of philosophy.

Though the selections do not exhaust the gamut of philosophical perspectives and cultures, they are quite wide-ranging. Some embody ancient positions that are still current in philosophy; others convey more recently developed positions. Some are traditional European or Anglo-American pieces; others were written by philosophers from such places as India, China, Africa, and Latin America. Some of these philosophers are our contemporaries; others lived long ago.

In accordance with the book's purposes of facilitating cross-cultural philosophical dialogue and investigating the overlap between philosophical problems and discussions from various cultural traditions, a number of the selections are presented in full rather than in an edited version. This has the pedagogical advantage of letting readers encounter philosophical works as they were actually presented by their authors rather than as slanted condensations. It also helps bring out the philosophical and cultural context of an author's reflections and the connections between one author's reflections and another's.

Introductory essays in each part help focus reader's attention on these connections. These essays are meant to perform different functions, depending on the pedagogical needs and philosophical topic at that point. Sometimes their function is to tie selections to each other or into larger discussions that cannot be represented by selections. At other times the essays are meant to elucidate points raised in the selections or related to them. At still other times, the essays simply raise questions for further thought. The general intention of these introductory essays is to encourage readers to engage in fruitful critical scrutiny of the ideas discussed.

Specific passages from the selections themselves are used as evidence for the interpretations advanced in the essays. This is not only sound philosophical practice but also a running example of how to use philosophical texts as evidence for interpretations of them. The interpretations should be particularly helpful for readers doing independent study. For those who are taking a course, they should serve as a supplement to the instructor's interpretive work.

To facilitate an integrated and critical study of the problems raised by the book's selections and discussions, sets of questions are included in the General Introduction and in the introductions to the parts—that is, in the context of the discussions that prompt them. In addition, reading questions are provided in each selection's head-note and global questions for review and further thought are provided at the end of each part. A Glossary appears at the end of the book to enable readers to understand terms used in the selections without having to go to a specialized dictionary. Also included at the end of the book is an interdisciplinary and cross-cultural Selected Bibliography to direct those who want to do further reading on a given topic.

Although *Through Time and Culture* is designed primarily for introductory philosophy courses, it is also useful for people in other disciplines. It meets some of the teaching needs in courses on the history of ideas and cultural history. Students in journalism and sociology can also benefit from reading this book. Indeed, it is not a single-discipline book. Neither is it just an academic book. Its potential readership includes people working in business and government, especially at the international level, as well as anyone who wants to be informed about philosophical problems and traditions and their cross-cultural significance.

A NOTE TO THE INDEPENDENT READER

Though designed primarily to be used in college courses, this book should also be very helpful to those undertaking independent introductory study in philosophy. This note is addressed especially to such readers.

The General Introduction and the part introductions aim to guide you to think critically and fruitfully about the philosophical problems raised by the selections. They do not try to suggest solutions, but rather to provide some basic elements for better dealing with the problems. This is done in two main steps. First, conflicting claims concerning topics addressed by the selections are presented. Then questions that pose philosophical problems about these topics are formulated.

This approach is meant to develop your reasoning and value-appraising skills by encouraging a critical discussion of a variety of philosophical problems. Thus you may be helped to develop habits of mind that will enable you to deal better, not only with the problems discussed here, but also with others that might arise in your life.

I suggest that you read the General Introduction before tackling any of the sections, and likewise that you read each part's introduction before reading any section in that part. The parts themselves do not have to be read in order, nor is it necessary to read the whole book in order to understand a section of it. You will gain greater understanding from reading the whole book, however, because its parts are interrelated.

It is most essential to read the sections in this book actively—that is, with questions in mind—rather than just letting the words pass before your eyes. Some basic questions you should find yourself asking are:

What does the author maintain in this selection?

What reasons does the author state in support of this position?

Are they good reasons?

What common opinions go against what the author maintains?

Are there any plausible reasons behind those common opinions?

Are these reasons better than those the author offers in support of what he or she maintains?

Are there even better reasons for still another opinion, which goes against both common opinions and that of the author?

If so, what is this opinion and what are its supporting reasons?

To what problems are all of these opinions and reasons relevant, and what is the significance of these problems?

To facilitate your task, reading questions are provided at the beginning of each selection and global questions for review and further thought at the end of each part. These questions may be dizzying to the novice. However, this is no reason to be discouraged. Thinking well, like singing well, is not something most of us can readily do. To develop the ability to think well about philosophical matters takes a great deal of practice and reflection. This book is meant to provide conditions conducive to such practice and reflection.

ACKNOWLEDGMENTS

Through Time and Culture developed out of my teaching of introductory philosophy and other courses in the United States, at the University of Wisconsin at Madison, the University of Texas at Dallas, Iowa State University, the University of Florida, and Central Connecticut State University; and in Canada, at Dalhousie University. It was partly prompted by my experiences as a student in Argentina and the United States, and greatly stimulated by my students' interest in philosophical problems that cut across cultural boundaries. It also benefited from my many discussions about philosophy and the teaching of philosophy, as well as my cross-cultural experiences with teachers, friends, and colleagues over the past two decades or so. In particular, I thank María Lugones, with whom I have had a dialogue for thirty-some years now on the subjects addressed in this book; Marcus G. Singer and Jon N. Moline, from whose philosophical practice and classroom example I learned much about philosophy and about the teaching of introductory philosophy; and those people with whom, in various capacities during the past decade or so, I have had informal discussions on topics addressed in this book: Geoff Bryce, Claudia Card, Margaret Carter, John Jakovina, David Kline, Richard Lippke, Elizabeth Díaz Herrera, and Don Kanel at the University of Wisconsin-Madison; Robert B. Louden at Iowa State University; Tom Auxter, Robert Baum, Kurt Baier, Annette Baier, Richard Haynes, and Tom Simon at the University of Florida; David Braybrooke and the other members of the Department of Philosophy at Dalhousie University; and Mario Bunge at McGill University.

Among my colleagues at Central Connecticut State University, I thank the librarians at the Elihu Burrit Library, who gave me invaluable help in putting together this book's selections. I am also grateful to those members of the Department of Philosophy with whom, during the past eight years, I have had discussions about the teaching of philosophy, cross-cultural problems, the philosophy of history, and the philosophy of culture: David Blitz, Lee Creer, Eleanor Godway, Judith McBride, Joe

McKeon, and Stephen Morris. I also thank Connecticut State University for various grants that provided significant support—not the least of which has been access to the Yale University libraries—and the Prentice Hall readers and editors, especially Ted Bolen, Nicole Gray, Serena Hoffman, and Diane Schaible, who helped with the final stages of manuscript preparation and book production.

What I owe my wife, Mary Kay Garrow, for her unfaltering encouragement and sound editorial suggestions for this and my previous philosophy books, I cannot possibly repay. Our daughters, Alejandra Emilia and Catalina Patricia—bilingual and fascinating members of a multicultural home—have played an essential part in this book by filling my task with happiness. Who they are, together with their joy in life, curiosity about other cultures, and incipient love of learning, has given concrete meaning to this book's aspirations.

A. Pablo Iannone

Certainly everything in Europe has become questionable. But I need immediately to add something so that you will not twist my diagnosis of the situation through which Europe is passing. . . . The fact that our civilization has become problematic for us, that all its principles are *without exception* questionable, is not necessarily sad or lamentable or the danger of death agony, but perhaps signifies on the contrary that a new form of civilization is germinating in us; that therefore under the apparent catastrophes . . . a new form of human existence is being born.

José Ortega y Gasset, *"De Europa meditatio quaedam"*

General Introduction

SENSES OF THE TERM "PHILOSOPHY"

I know that you, ladies and gentlemen, have a philosophy, each and all of you, and that the most interesting and important thing about you is the way in which it determines the perspective in your several worlds. You know the same of me. And yet I confess to a certain tremor at the audacity of the enterprise which I am about to begin. For the philosophy which is so important in each of us is not a technical matter; it is our more or less dumb sense of what life deeply and honestly means. It is only partly got from books; it is our individual way of just seeing and feeling the total push and pressure of the cosmos.

William James, *Pragmatism*

In this passage, James uses the term "philosophy" in the *personal* sense—as a particular person's beliefs and presuppositions about the world. It is that person's outlook on things and does not entirely coincide with any other person's philosophy. Some believe, for example, that the universe had a beginning and will have an end. Others hold that it always was and always will be. This kind of difference in personal philosophies prompts the question: Who is right?

In attempting to resolve personal differences in outlook, people sometimes appeal to the beliefs and presuppositions predominant in their particular group— say, a church, an ethnic group, a society, or a group of societies. Thus, in trying to resolve the question of whether the universe had a beginning, Christians may say that it did because one of the tenets of their church says so. Hopi Indians in the United States or Aymara Indians living around Lake Titicaca in Bolivia may very well respond that, as everyone in their culture knows, time is circular: the universe has neither a beginning nor an end, but repeats itself. In making these statements, these individuals would be supporting their personal philosophies by appealing to their group's philosophy. In this social sense, "philosophy" is a particular *group's* predominant beliefs and presuppositions about the world, its predominant outlook on things. Typically, the group has explicitly formulated its philosophy in traditional sayings, legends, or beliefs; at the very least, it presupposes it in its customs. In this social sense, one can talk of Western European philosophy by contrast with, say, East Asian philosophy, or at a greater level of differentiation, one can contrast the philosophies of cultural subgroups in Western Europe or East Asia.

A group's philosophy can be criticized by members of that group or by people from other groups. Such criticism can take more than one form. Most commonly, it expresses opposition to the ideas of the philosophy. Thus, critics who think the universe had no beginning might oppose a philosophy that says the universe had a beginning. Or the criticism may not involve opposition to the ideas, but simply state that, concerning a certain problem, the group's philosophy is silent or unclear. For example, critics may argue that the Aymara Indians' philosophy is limited because it says nothing about the problem of whether human beings are complex physical and chemical systems. In either case, the criticisms indicate the philosophical problem formulated by the question: What is the right view on these matters?

One might reject this question, and criticize the philosophies just mentioned and any other attempts at resolving philosophical puzzlements as irrelevant, a waste of time, or a pointless exercise. However, this in itself would be to formulate a philosophy. So, unless one refuses to think about these matters at all, having a philosophy is inescapable.

To say that philosophy is inescapable is to formulate a philosophical view that is part of a philosophy. And like any other philosophical view, this one is open to question. To subject a view to critical scrutiny and to try to resolve the matter by appealing to reason (as I just did by pointing out features of the act of rejecting philosophies) is to engage in philosophical inquiry. When people engage in such inquiry, they *do* philosophy rather than simply *have* a philosophy in the personal and social senses. In this sense, philosophy is an activity, not simply a set of beliefs and presuppositions. The activity is *about* beliefs and presuppositions. It is often prompted by disagreements about these beliefs and presuppositions between individuals, between groups, or between individuals and groups. It can also be motivated by the incompleteness or lack of clarity of existing philosophies. Finally, it can arise out of sheer curiosity about the world. Thus, *philosophy as a branch of inquiry* is a critical and comprehensive study of the various aspects of the world: reality, knowledge, reasoning, norms, and values. It deals with puzzles about these aspects that arise in science, morality, art, literature, religion—that is, in the social and natural worlds.

PHILOSOPHY'S AIMS AND PHILOSOPHERS' MOTIVES

To say that philosophy is inescapable to anyone who thinks about these puzzlements is not to say that everyone is a philosopher. Many people pursue philosophical inquiry only a short distance and then stop, out of simple satisfaction with everyday answers, lack of curiosity, or boredom. Though these people engage in philosophy as a branch of inquiry, they are not philosophers but, at best, proto-philosophers. By contrast, philosophers are not satisfied with everyday answers but are motivated by curiosity or concern to seek good answers to philosophical questions, sometimes to the point of personal hardship.

Out of curiosity, puzzlement, or wonder, some philosophers ask questions ranging from Is time dependent on clocks or are clocks dependent on time? and Did the universe ever begin? to Are humans nothing but complex physical and chemical systems? Others, engaging in philosophy as a branch of inquiry out of concern, ask such questions as: Is the abortion of a human fetus murder? and Is there an obligation to care for the environment and future generations?

Philosophers engage in philosophy as a branch of inquiry in a sustained manner and are guided by various aims. One aim is to make ideas clear and explicit. Another is to examine and evaluate the reasons for holding ideas. A third is to establish how ideas and reasons for holding them are interrelated. A fourth aim is to establish the theoretical or practical significance of ideas. In pursuing these aims, philosophers formulate, or contribute criticisms and suggestions that lead to the eventual formulation of, a reasoned body of beliefs about reality, knowledge, reasoning, norms, and values. In this *philosophical theory* sense of "philosophy," a philosophy—say, Aristotle's or Confucius'—is a *product* of philosophy as a branch of inquiry.[1]

This book aims to provide introductory guidance to philosophy as a branch of inquiry and its products. As stated in the Preface, it also aims to facilitate cross-cultural philosophical dialogue and to provide material for investigating the degree of overlap between philosophical discussions and categories in quite disparate cultures and at quite different times. In this regard, it is also a book of evidence. The selections it includes provide a starting point and a common ground for integrating philosophical discussions taking place in today's multicultural world.[2]

PROBLEMS AND BRANCHES OF PHILOSOPHY

There can be a philosophical inquiry about anything, for philosophy deals with everything. In order to focus inquiry, however, Western philosophy has been traditionally divided into branches. The most frequently used classification is: *metaphysics, epistemology, logic, ethics and socio-political philosophy,* and *aesthetics.*[3] This system is a matter of emphasis rather than of mutually exclusive categories. In fact, the branches often overlap. Further, they do not cover the entire subject. These categories, for example, do not cover higher-level philosophical problems about the nature of philosophy (presented in Part I of this book) or philosophy's prospects for the future (discussed in Part VI). Finally, these are categories developed in Western philosophy, and for that reason, uncritical acceptance of them is likely to lead to a parochial way of doing philosophy. Yet these branches have the advantage of making philosophy accessible to this book's intended readers. For though you may not know such technical terms as "epistemology" and "metaphysics," you are largely familiar with Western culture and fluent in English, and are therefore familiar with the kind of thinking that fits these categories. In addition, using such a classification helps test how and to what extent Western philosophical categories are applicable to the philosophical problems and discussions exemplified in the African, Asian, and Latin American selections included here. So with an awareness of its limitations, we have used this classification system to organize our readings and discussions. Let us now roughly characterize it.

Consider two questions proposed earlier: Is time dependent on clocks or are clocks dependent on time? and Did the universe ever begin? These questions belong to *cosmology,* a subdivision of *metaphysics* that studies the universe as a whole and the laws, causes, or purposes that give it structure. Another subdivision of metaphysics is *ontology,* which studies what there is. It asks such questions as: What is ultimately real?

and What grounds distinguish appearance from reality? In general, *metaphysics* is the study of the nature and structure of reality, of being, of existence as such, and of the essences of things.

One might hold, as St. Thomas Aquinas did in the late Middle Ages, the cosmological view that the universe had a beginning. Or one might hold, as Thales, one of the first Western philosophers, did, the ontological view that water and only water is ultimately real.

Views such as those just mentioned often prompt questions about knowledge. They range from How can one know whether the universe had a beginning? to What is knowledge?, What, if anything, can be known?, and On what basis can it be known? These are questions of *epistemology*, also called *gnoseology* and *theory of knowledge*. This branch of philosophy studies knowledge; its relations to truth, experience, belief, and doubt; its kinds, basis, and scope; and the nature of truth.

In investigating these and other philosophical topics, reasons are used and criticized. This raises the question: What instances of reasoning are good and why? *Logic* is the branch of philosophy that discusses this and such related questions as: What kinds of reasoning are there? and What are the criteria for assessing instances of reasoning of a given kind? It studies the nature, scope, and kinds of reasoning and the criteria for telling good reasoning from bad. It also studies the relation of these criteria to ordinary languages, such as English and Spanish, by contrast with artificial languages, such as those of mathematics and symbolic logic, which replace words and complex expressions with symbols. Further, it studies the nature and kinds of meaning, the types and functions of definitions, and the relative adequacy of symbolic and ordinary languages for dealing with philosophical problems.

Instances of reasoning can be found in discussions of practically any topic. In philosophy, they can be found in metaphysical, epistemological, and logical discussions, as well as in discussions falling outside these areas. Philosophers use reasoning to deal with such questions as: Is it ever right for a woman to have an abortion? and Should any abortions be permitted by law? These kinds of questions are addressed by *ethics and socio-political philosophy*, which is also called *moral philosophy* and *moral theory*. This branch of philosophy is concerned with problems of conduct; the nature of right and wrong; institutional problems concerning whether policies, practices, or entire social arrangements are justified; the nature of obligations and justice; problems of character; and the nature of good and bad.

As the preceding paragraph makes plain, moral philosophy is concerned with values that need to be upheld or respected. For example, one view of moral philosophy holds that we should avoid inflicting wanton harm and indignity not only on humans but also on nonhuman animals, plants, ecosystems, and Planet Earth.

The delight or insightful excitement that a variety of objects, from works of art to natural landscapes and events, can cause is part of the subject of *aesthetics*. This branch of philosophy studies the experiences and activities related to such objects and asks: Can something have aesthetic value even if one does not like it? Is beauty always in the eye of the beholder? What is a work of art?

PHILOSOPHY, PHILOSOPHIES,
AND PHILOSOPHICAL TRADITIONS

There is more than one philosophical theory or philosophy, and often one philosophy contradicts another. This raises a further philosophical question: Which philosophy is better and why? In this book, an introduction to philosophical problems and to various ways philosophers have attempted to resolve them is provided in the introductory essay to each part. In discussing the particular philosophical problems addressed by the selections in a part, the introductory essay has three main functions. First, it formulates the various philosophical views embedded in the selections. Second, it suggests approaches for the critical scrutiny of these views. Third, it provides examples of how to approach points of difference between these views in order to intelligently handle the problems addressed in the selections.

The selections are not simplistic opposing pairs; actual philosophical disagreements are more complex than that. Some selections do explicitly oppose each other, but more often, selections only implicitly make presuppositions contrary to those of other selections or simply indicate disagreements not addressed in other selections. This reflects the ways in which philosophical disagreements actually develop, which should help you to deal with philosophical problems and disagreements as they actually exist. A careful reading of each part's introductory section will give you a greater understanding of these matters and put you in a better position to develop sound philosophical theories and apply them to the philosophical problems discussed, as well as to any other philosophical problems you may pose yourself.

Philosophical problems have been formulated both within the Western philosophical tradition (initially in ancient Greece) and outside it. Non-Western traditions include those of China and India, as well as those of Africa and Latin America, which, however affected by Western influences, have significant non-Western features.[4] These various traditions are as different from one another as their cultures are. Yet they have significant similarities that are worth investigating. For these similarities raise the fascinating philosophico-anthropological question: Does the fact that similar philosophical ideas were formulated at about the same time within cultures that had little if any communication with each other show that there is a common human nature? And this question gives rise to others: What is human nature? How common is it? Can it explain the similarity of views developed in highly different cultures that had no intercommunication? Or can this similarity be better explained by other notions?

PHILOSOPHICAL TRADITIONS
AND FIELDS OTHER THAN PHILOSOPHY

Another philosophical question posed by the study of philosophy through different cultures and historical periods concerns the relation of philosophy to other fields. Is philosophy a science, a branch of literature, an extension of religion, a form of education, or something else? Even within the Western tradition, views on this matter are far from unanimous. Some philosophers, especially in the twentieth century, have thought of philosophy as a science. Hans Reichenbach, for example, espoused this position in *The Rise of Scientific Philosophy.*[5] Others have conceived of philosophy as analogous, if not identical, to literature. R. G. Collingwood formulated this position in "Philosophy as a Branch of Literature."[6] Still others think of it as an extension of religion, providing consolation to those faced with misfortunes. An outstanding exponent of this view is Boethius, a sixth-century Roman consul who wrote *The Consolation of Philosophy.*[7] Earlier, the great philosophers of ancient Greece—Socrates, Plato, and Aristotle—believed that philosophy was a form of education leading to the good life. For them, it was (and for some, it still is) a way to wisdom. Indeed, the term "philosophy" is derived from two Greek words: *philein,* meaning "to love," and *sophia,* meaning "wisdom." Hence, "philosophy" means "the love of wisdom," and in this conception, the philosopher is a lover of wisdom.

These various conceptions of philosophy are cross-cultural. Take the conception of philosophy as a form of education. In ancient Greece, Socrates, who wrote nothing, was a sage whose philosophy was exemplified in his personal history and formulated in his conversations with the youth of Athens. Analogously, the sages and gurus of the Indian and Chinese traditions used to (and some still do) lead the young to self-knowledge through conversations and example.

Other conceptions of philosophy are represented in different cultures during different historical periods. Arguably, the conception of philosophy as literature is incipient in the work of Plato, who wrote at a time when the distinction between philosophy and literature had not yet been sharply drawn. It is clearly present, along with the idea that philosophy is an extension of religion, in the work of Boethius. His *Consolation of Philosophy* is written in alternating rhyme and prose sections. The idea of philosophy as literature is also found in various works of Spanish-speaking writers—for example, in those of Jorge Luis Borges[8]—as well as in the Hindu and Chinese traditions.[9]

The conception of philosophy as science is found long before Reichenbach in the work of the medieval Persian philosopher and scientist Rhazes.[10] And philosophy as an extension of religion was a common conception throughout the Middle Ages, in both Christian and Muslim cultures, and can still be found practically everywhere today. After all, philosophy's origins can be traced to religious convictions and rituals concerning life, death, the relation of human beings to superhuman powers, and the relation of the living to their ancestors.

Whatever the underlying conception of philosophy, the questions raised within its scope at different times and in different cultures are often similar: What am I? Is the world I perceive real or merely an appearance of some other reality? Am I real or an appearance? How can I come to know the right answer to these questions or, for that matter, to any question? Can I ever, with good reason, be certain of my answer? Is wisdom achievable? Is happiness attainable? How? Is there a god? Are there many gods? And if there is a god, is that god a person? If so, could that person be perfectly knowledgeable, powerful, benevolent, and just, even though it appears there is evil in the world? Are we ever responsible for our actions? What is the basis, if any, of good and bad, right and wrong, justified and unjustified? In order to build a common ground between various culturally delineated philosophical traditions (though not, of course, a systematic unity or totality), this book focuses on such questions.

That is not to say that this book is philosophically neutral. For one thing, since it is a philosophy book, it relies on reason rather than blind faith or mere tenacity.

Besides, it espouses a conception of philosophy that takes traditional ideas seriously, but does not address them in a vacuum, for it also takes seriously the constraints and procedures for building common ground among various philosophical traditions in discussing those ideas. In doing so, the book points to, though it does not pursue, the parallel program of examining the political aspects of the relations between philosophical traditions and of establishing knowledge claims, especially at the cross-cultural level. Philosophy, in this approach, is not simply a science, an extension of religion, a branch of literature, or a form of education. Nor is it the handmaiden of the sciences. Rather, philosophy is pragmatically conceived as a form of intellectual diplomacy that includes a spur to action. *Through Time and Culture* seeks to find—and, where necessary, to build—enough common ground among different philosophical and cultural traditions to better address the kinds of questions noted in this General Introduction and to advance communication, understanding, and meaningful philosophical dialogue among these traditions.

This volume is not a work of advocacy, as I have said, but neither does it make any pretense to philosophical neutrality. It uses a philosophy-as-diplomacy approach to problems. The part introductions provide grounds for deciding whether this approach is preferable to alternative approaches that address philosophical problems entirely from within a culture, a philosophical tradition, or (more parochially) a school of thought. Full-fledged arguments for this approach belong elsewhere.[11] You should keep in mind, however, that this book encourages critical examination not only of the philosophical problems treated but also of the very approach it uses regarding these problems. Dogmatism is out of place in philosophy as a branch of inquiry. So is parochialism. Both are barriers to the attainment of wisdom that all genuine philosophy seeks.

NOTES

[1] The distinctions discussed here are examined with regard to the specific branch of philosophy known as moral philosophy in Iannone, *Contemporary Moral Controversies in Technology* (New York and London: Oxford University Press, 1987), pp. 3–4; and *Contemporary Moral Controversies in Business* (New York and London: Oxford University Press, 1989), pp. 3–4.

[2] This double purpose—introductory text and book of evidence for integrating current, quite disparate, discussions—also guided the writing of my *Contemporary Moral Controversies in Technology* and *Contemporary Moral Controversies in Business*. For very useful discussions of the need for such integration and the forms that it could take, see the articles by Martin Benjamin, Lawrence Blum, Linda H. Damico, Grant H. Cornwell, Michael Goldman, Nalini Bhushan, Michael Taber, and Thomas Auxter in *Teaching Philosophy*, Vol. 14, No. 2 (June 1991). The present book seeks a workable balance between various philosophical concerns formulated by these authors.

[3] See, for example, Marcus G. Singer's entry in *The World Book Encyclopedia*, ed. Robert O. Celeny (Chicago: World Book, Inc., 1986), Vol. 15, pp. 345–353. This classification system is used to organize philosophy programs in many English-speaking and non–English-speaking universities. Other classification systems are possible. For example, philosophy is sometimes classified by reference to fields (such as philosophy of knowledge, of religion, of morals, of language, and of art) or, less frequently, by the tripartite division of metaphysics, methodology, and axiology. Both classification systems are compatible with the one used in this book, but the first is too focused and the second too general to provide the overall articulation of specific areas our purposes require.

[4] For an instructive discussion of the use and limitations of the Western-Eastern distinction, see Paul Masson-Oursel, *Les philosophies orientales* (Paris: Hermann, 1941). See also Paul Masson-Oursel, the introduction to "La filosofia en Oriente," ed. Emile Bréhier, *Historia de la Filosofia* (Buenos Aires: Editorial Sudamericana, 1944).

5   Hans Reichenbach, *The Rise of Scientific Philosophy* (Berkeley: University of California Press, 1951).

6   R. G. Collingwood, "Philosophy as a Branch of Literature," Chapter X in *An Essay on Philosophical Method* (Oxford: Oxford University Press, 1933). See also his *The Principles of Art* (New York: Oxford University Press, 1958), pp. 292–299: "Art and Intellect."

7   Boethius, *The Consolation of Philosophy,* trans. and rev. H. F. Stewart (Cambridge, MA: Harvard University Press, 1936).

8   See, for example, Jorge Luis Borges, *Labyrinths* (New York: New Directions, 1962, 1964).

9   See, for example, Louis Renou (ed.), *Hinduism* (New York: George Braziller, 1962), pp. 61–81: "The Vedic Hymns" and pp. 86–1105: "The Upanishads." For the Chinese tradition, see Lao Tzu, *Tao Te Ching* (New York: Penguin, 1963).

10   Rhazes, *The Spiritual Physick of Rhazes,* trans. A. J. Arberry (London: John Murray, 1950).

11   A beginning in the suggested direction can be found in my *Philosophy as Diplomacy: Essays in Ethics and Policy Making* (Atlantic Highlands, NJ: Humanities Press International, 1993).

I

What Is Philosophy?

A. HOW DID PHILOSOPHY BEGIN?

There is no record indicating that philosophical reflection had an abrupt and single beginning on Earth. However naive and fragmentary, such reflection is evident throughout preliterate storytelling and traditions concerning the creation of the universe and other cosmological matters. It is also evident in ethical codes of conduct embedded in tribal customs and handed down orally. Philosophical reflection is further evidenced in early written works. An example of the latter is the *Upanishads* ("Approaches"), which appeared in India in the sixth century B.C. They formulate ritual or cosmogonic information in highly speculative fashion and reflect the equivalence felt in ancient India between the human and divine worlds. We will examine the *Upanishads*, as well as the other selections in Part I, with a view to gaining an overall understanding of the nature of philosophy, some of its crucial constituents, and the logical tools used in philosophical practice.

The first of the *Upanishads*, "Unity and Diversity," describes the tension between these notions and presupposes the metaphysical question: Is there basically only one thing, or is there more than one, perhaps many? It postulates the existence of the One (also translated as the Absolute). This is supposed to be something that never changes, involves and surpasses all differences, is in each and every thing, and cannot be grasped through the senses. In fact, the One cannot be grasped with the mind: "Unmoving, the One is swifter than the mind." This prompts the questions: Can the One be known at all? If so, in what way?

In the Western tradition, there are various ways of knowing something. For example, one can know something *by acquaintance*. This is a form of immediate knowledge of something by being confronted with it. It is the way in which one knows his or her closest relatives or friends, in which one knows the place where one grew up, the excitement and anxiety of going to college, the loneliness and mixed feelings of exile. One has seen, heard, and talked with people one knows by acquaintance. One has seen, smelled, and heard the sounds of places one is acquainted with. And having felt the emotions of going to college or living in a foreign land, one knows them by acquaintance. As these examples indicate, knowledge by acquaintance need not be of physical objects or events. It can also be of mental events such as feelings of anxiety, fear, or nostalgia. This prompts a further question: Can the One mentioned in the *Upanishads* somehow be known by acquaintance? Such acquaintance cannot take place through the senses, for these discern only diversity and change, and the One is something that never changes. Nor can it take place through the mind, for, as stated in the first of the *Upanishads,* the mind is unable to grasp the One.

Another alternative suggests itself. By contrast with—but not to the exclusion of—knowledge by acquaintance, one can know facts about what one has never become acquainted with. For example, one can *know that* one's friends have parents without having met those parents. Analogously, someone who has never lived in exile can *know that* some people in this situation feel special mixed emotions. Mathematicians hold that we can *know that* numbers are infinite without being acquainted with each of the numbers. Similarly, in matters of religion, some (e.g., St. Thomas Aquinas) have held that finite and imperfect human beings can *know that* God exists without—given their finitude and imperfections—being able to become acquainted with God. Is this type of knowledge, *knowledge that* or *knowledge of facts,* the type of knowledge human beings can have of the One the *Upanishads* postulate?

In pursuing this question, it is crucial to ask: What role, if any, are language and reasoning supposed to play in attaining knowledge of the One? The third of the *Upanishads,* "The Creation of the World from the Soul," includes some cautionary remarks. The world "became differentiated just by name and form. . . . Even today this world is differentiated just by name and form." If this is so, words may hinder rather than help us attain knowledge of the One because they refer or describe and, in either case, seem to differentiate. When they refer, as the term "it" does in the sentence "It is a dog," words point to one or more particular items instead of to others. In doing so, they seem to differentiate. When they describe, as the term "dog" does in the sentence "It is a dog," they ascribe certain features (here, those of being a dog) to given items rather than ascribing other features (say, those of being a cat) to them. Here again, words seem to differentiate.

One could respond that in these examples "it" is a pronoun, not a name, and "dog" is a noun, not a name. But consider "Mago is a dog." Here the term "Mago" is a name that both refers to some item instead of others and describes it as being called "Mago" rather than something else. Hence, it appears to differentiate on two counts. Must this be the case? Or is there a way of using words that will avoid the pitfall of differentiation? Is differentiation a pitfall after all?

These philosophical questions are also presupposed in the *Upanishads,* especially in the view upheld in the eighth section, "Allegory of the Vedic Gods' Ignorance of Brahman." This is the view that the One or "Brahman" is known by intuition. It is not described by saying *what* it is, because description would introduce differentiation, and hence, only partial and slanted knowledge. Instead, it is denoted by a linguistic expression that has no descriptive meaning: "Ah!" This is the cry of astonishment with which we react to the sudden appearance of lightning or to a memory that suddenly flashes through our minds. The text reads: " . . . in the lightning which flashes forth, which makes one blink, and say "Ah!"—that "Ah!" refers to divinity."

Given the *Upanishads'* position, this intuition, as well as the knowledge it supposedly provides, is not open to assessment by appeal to reason. For by their very nature, reasons involve description—hence, differentiation, which, according to the *Upanishads,* is bound to convey a slanted and partial picture, thus hindering the knowledge of the One. Of course, one might argue that it is not obvious that differentiation is or leads to partial knowledge. Indeed, many think otherwise. If they are mistaken in thinking so, reasons should be formulated to establish their error.

But let us turn to another point: Can one, consistent with the philosophy of the *Upanishads,* ever offer reasons on any subject? One can. For to say that only through intuition can one realize that the One exists is not to say that reasons and description are not useful for drawing practical inferences from the One's existence. Indeed, such inferences are drawn at the end of the third *Upanishad,* "The Creation of the World from the Soul":

> If of one who speaks of anything else than the Self as dear, one should say, "He will lose what he holds dear," he would indeed be likely to do so. One should reverence the Self alone as dear. He who reverences the Self alone as dear—what he holds dear, verily, is not perishable.

That one should hold only the Self dear is a practical conclusion drawn on the grounds that the Self is not perishable.

The ideas formulated in the *Upanishads* display both startling similarities to and significant differences from those in Part I's second selection, the *Apology* by Plato (428–348 B.C.). The differences concern the uses of reason. By contrast with the *Upanishads,* which hold that intuition is the central component of the search for truth and wisdom, the *Apology* insists that reason is central to the search. This work makes plain the method of Socrates, Plato's teacher, who left no writings.[1] Through dialogue, Socrates cross-examines people who appear to be wise or who are claimed to be so—by others or themselves—in an attempt to establish whether they are indeed wise. For if they are, they might be of help in Socrates' task: seeking truth and wisdom. Socrates' cross-examination involves relentlessly asking such questions as What do you mean? and How do you know? and prompting the respondent to formulate the implications of vague ordinary opinions so that clear ideas can take their place. An appeal to intuition or mere declamation and lecturing will not do in this enterprise. Socrates says:

> I shall never stop practicing philosophy and exhorting you and elucidating the truth for everyone that I meet. I shall go on saying . . . Are you not ashamed that you give your attention to acquiring as much money as possible, and similarly with reputation and honor, and give no attention or thought to truth and understanding and the perfection of your soul?
>
> And if any of you disputes this . . . I shall question him and examine him and test him. . . . I shall do this to everyone that I meet. . . .

As for the similarities between the *Apology* and the *Upanishads,* both display a concern with death, the possibility of an afterlife, the possibility of something enduring beyond the diversity and change typical of our world, and personal improvement. In the *Upanishads'* last section, Naciketas tells the god Yama (death) that long life, wealth, and earthly pleasures are transient and "wear out . . . the vigor of all the senses of men." He adds:

> Having approached the undecaying immortality, what decaying mortal on this earth below who now knows and meditates on the pleasures of beauty and love, will delight in an over-long life?

Socrates also deals with death in the *Apology*. He does not claim to know that there is an afterlife or even what death actually is. He simply claims that "nothing can harm a man either in life or after death." He reasons as follows:

> Death is one of two things. Either it is annihilation, and the dead have no consciousness of anything, or, as we are told, it is really a change—a migration of the soul from this place to another. Now if there is no consciousness but only a dreamless sleep, death must be a marvelous gain. . . . If death is like this, then, I call it gain, because the whole of time . . . can be regarded as no more than one single night. If on the other hand death is a removal from here to some other place, and if . . . all the dead are there, what greater blessing could there be than this, gentlemen? . . . And above all I should like to spend my time there, as here, in examining and searching people's minds, to find out who is really wise among them, and who only thinks that he is.

Socrates' position raises a number of questions: What is wisdom? What is understanding? Does philosophy help attain either of these? Does philosophy help establish what they are? His words indicate that in his view wisdom is primarily a matter of personal worth, which can be improved through education—crucially, self-education—in the activity of philosophy. As a result of pursuing this activity, one becomes wiser in that one grows more knowledgeable about one's ignorance and related limitations. This knowledge is supposed to improve character so that one becomes a better person. But is this true? Or do wisdom and personal improvement require knowledge that goes beyond the negative recognition that we are ignorant concerning the definitions of wisdom, virtue, and other human characteristics?

In the next selection, "Wisdom and Philosophy," Aristotle (384–322 B.C.), explores these questions. He distinguishes between practical wisdom, by which we make sound particular decisions, and theoretical wisdom, by which we know why sound decisions are sound. Aristotle is often interpreted as judging theoretical wisdom superior to practical wisdom. He states that "Wisdom is knowledge about certain principles and causes" and the branch of inquiry that seeks this knowledge "investigates the first principles and causes." This branch of inquiry is philosophy. He adds:

> That it is not a science of production is clear even from the history of the earliest philosophers. For it is owing to their wonder that men both now begin and at first began to philosophize. . . . And a man who is puzzled and wonders thinks himself ignorant . . .; therefore since they philosophized in order to escape from ignorance, evidently they were pursuing science in order to know, and not for any utilitarian end. And this is confirmed by the facts; for it was when almost all necessities of life and the things that make for comfort and recreation had been secured, that such knowledge began to be sought.

For Aristotle, then, philosophy originates in wonder and puzzlement and seeks knowledge of first principles for its own sake, not for the sake of utility or advantage.

In response, Socrates might ask: Is such knowledge attainable? And supposing knowledge of some first principles is attainable, is it relevant to wisdom? Concerning its attainability, Aristotle sets out to investigate the claims previous philosophers made concerning first principles. Accordingly, he summarizes the philosophical views of various Greek philosophers who preceded Socrates and are accordingly called Pre-Socratic.

As his discussion makes plain, except for the Sophists (e.g., Protagoras and Gorgias), whom Aristotle does not discuss in the selection, the Pre-Socratics were primarily concerned with cosmological questions. These included the nature and origin of the universe, the nature of reality, and the basic stuff that underlies all appearances and on whose basis all appearances can be explained.

Among the Pre-Socratics Aristotle mentions are Thales, who thought the basic stuff was water, and Anaximenes, who thought it was air. He does not mention Anaximander, who together with Thales, his teacher, and Anaximenes, Thales' student, constituted the Milesian school. Anaximander stated that the basic underlying stuff was imperceptible and could neither be destroyed nor created. One modern interpretation of these statements is that Anaximander was talking of energy and anticipating the law of conservation of energy. At any rate, Anaximander's idea that the basic substance was imperceptible was new and significant. For it involved the novel and, since then, influential concept that the world of appearances may be simply a manifestation of something else that is both imperceptible and more basic.

In passing, Aristotle mentions Hippasus of Metapontium and Heraclitus of Ephesus as those who held that the basic stuff was fire. This is true, but Heraclitus associated fire not only with permanence but also with change. He stated that all things change, which raised problems of identity. In this regard, he is famous for having written: "In the same river we both step and do not step, we are and are not."[2] Such an emphasis on change has led people to contrast Heraclitus sharply with the Milesian philosophers.

Aristotle, however, does not make this contrast in the selection being discussed. Instead, he draws a contrast between the Milesians and the *pluralists*. He says that two of these pluralists, Empedocles and Anaxagoras, postulated more than one basic substance or cause, but did not quite explain how these yielded all other things. He credits the *atomists* Leucippus and Democritus with having developed such an explanation. For they held that the basic elements were the full and the void, that the differences in the basic elements were the causes of all other qualities, and that these differences were only in "shape, order, and position."

Aristotle also mentions Pythagoras and the Pythagoreans, who held that the principles of numbers were the elements of all things. He notes the significance of their concern with keeping their theory coherent. This relates to a frequently used philosophical and scientific method that consists in postulating the existence of entities without which a theory would be incoherent or could not explain what it is meant to explain. For the sake of coherence in their theory, the Pythagoreans postulated the existence of subatomic particles.

Aristotle makes special mention of those who "spoke of the universe as if it were one entity." This is an idea we discussed when we considered the *Upanishads*. Aristotle lists three such philosophers:

> Parmenides seems to fasten on that which is one in definition; Melissus on that which is one in matter . . . while Xenophanes, the first of these partisans of the One . . . says the One is God.

Parmenides, as Aristotle indicates, gave arguments for his views. The statement "All is one" was a conclusion from reason. In outline, Parmenides reasoned thus: Whatever is an object of thought exists. If nonbeing is an object of thought, then it exists and therefore must both be and not be. But this is a contradiction. Hence, nonbeing cannot be thought and there is only being. From this, Parmenides concluded that change and diversity are mere appearances.

One might respond that Parmenides' argument involves an equivocal use of the verb "to be." Let us grant that if nonbeing is an object of thought (whether as the content of thought or as something distinct from thought), then it must exist, because otherwise we could not meaningfully talk about it. What is it, however, that in this case is said to exist? One interpretation is that it is the collection of all things other than those that exist—or, as some would put it today, the "empty class."

Using this interpretation, one could argue as follows: To say that the class is empty is to say that it has no members—in other words, that no members of this class are, or exist. So from the assumption that nonbeing is an object of thought, Parmenides could at best infer that it—the collection of things other than those that exist—must be, and its members must not be. But this is not a contradiction. One might accordingly conclude that Parmenides' argument is unsound, just as it would be unsound to argue that the number zero cannot be thought, because if zero were an object of thought, then it would both have to be and not be. Is this a good response to Parmenides' argument? Could Parmenides soundly answer that he was raising questions about the members of the empty class that, as soon as they are said not to exist, are an object of thought and must therefore exist?

By contrast with Parmenides' reliance on argument, Xenophanes appears to have believed that the One is God on the basis of intuition. In this regard, his position is closer to that formulated in the *Upanishads*.

This is all that, according to Aristotle, the Pre-Socratics had to teach by way of first principles. As stated, his interest in these teachings was prompted by his characterization of wisdom as knowledge of basic principles and causes, namely, those studied by philosophy. Yet Socrates' questions remain. He might argue that Aristotle has not shown that knowledge of first principles is attainable. For the principles Aristotle examined are hypotheses that, at best, we can have good probabilistic reasons to believe; we can not know them as certain and definitive. Further, he might argue that, as Aristotle himself acknowledged, the principles he reviewed were largely cosmological, and hence irrelevant to wisdom, which, presumably, concerns practice. This difference has informed many a philosophical discussion throughout the centuries and affected the manner in which philosophy has come to be conceived, a matter we now turn to.

B. HOW HAS PHILOSOPHY COME TO BE CONCEIVED?

Aristotle's conception of wisdom puts the emphasis on theoretical wisdom, hence on knowledge; not—or at least not as much as Socrates' conception—on practice and a way of life. This raises the question: Are Aristotle's conceptions of wisdom and philosophy well taken? There are some reasons to think that they are not. For today, as in Aristotle's time, a wise person is not one who is simply very well informed, even if this information is about some first principles. Rather, as Socrates himself might have said, a wise person uses his or her information well to live a good life, and this goes beyond mere contemplation into practical matters. Indeed, this ability to use information to live a good life, rather than the mere acquisition of expert knowledge on some subject or another, is the mark of a good education, according to Alfred North Whitehead (1861–1947). In "The Aims of Education," he discusses this contrast:

> Culture is activity of thought, and receptiveness to beauty and humane feeling. Scraps of information have nothing to do with it. A merely well-informed man is the most useless bore on God's earth.

Whitehead explains the nature of the education to be imparted and the culture to be acquired:

> What education has to impart is an intimate sense for the power of ideas, for the beauty of ideas, and for the structure of ideas, together with a particular body of knowledge which has peculiar reference to the life of the being possessing it.

The powers thus attained include the "evocation of curiosity, of judgment, of the power of mastering a complicated tangle of circumstances, the use of theory in giving foresight in special cases." And he adds: "There is only one subject-matter for education, and that is Life in all its manifestations."

This prompts the question: Is wisdom the result of education as Whitehead understands it? If it is not, what is the difference? And if it is, can philosophy make any special contribution toward attaining wisdom? Is, for example, the knowledge of certain basic principles crucial to its attainment, as Aristotle thought? Whitehead comments:

> . . . there is not one course of study which merely gives general culture, and another which gives special knowledge. . . . You may not divide the seamless coat of learning.

Since philosophy has no circumscribed subject matter, it is best characterized as interdisciplinary, which tends to make it central to imparting an education in Whitehead's sense. The present book evidences the interdisciplinary nature of philosophy.

For greater specification of the characteristics of a philosophical education, we turn to the next selection, "The Philosophic Mind and the contemporary World" by Arthur E. Murphy (1901–1962). Murphy says:

> In philosophy . . . information is not enough. . . . Here the student must not only acquire some information about thinking, he must actually participate in the activity of thinking for himself.
>
> . . . To understand an idea of Aristotle's it is not enough to know that Aristotle had it and where he wrote it down and what somebody else said about it afterward. To grasp it as an idea one must think it for oneself, and that means actually to participate in the activity of problem solving in which it is offered as an answer and to see what the conditions of the problem are and to what extent it really *is* an answer.

Murphy's statement echoes some of the points made in the preceding discussion and in the General Introduction. Yet, though it may help to distinguish philosophy from history, it does not clearly distinguish it from other studies—say, from cultural anthropology. To be sure, Murphy further clarifies his position, explaining that

"In philosophy it is not only a question of what is believed but of the way in which and the grounds on which it is accepted." What are the ways in which and the grounds on which something is accepted in philosophy? Murphy answers by referring to characteristic features of what he calls "the philosophic mind." Individuals who possess the philosophic mind are curious, seek as comprehensive an understanding of things as can be attained, attempt to improve our understanding of the distinction between appearance and reality, try to examine things in perspective, and presuppose that human beings can attain the wisdom thus sought.

Are these features indeed characteristic of philosophically minded individuals? And are they crucial for philosophy? Is, for example, the inclination to search for comprehensiveness crucial to philosophy as a collective enterprise or to individual philosophical inquiry? Can it help distinguish philosophy from all other studies? How? What else could? In any case, is Murphy's position closer to Socrates' or to Aristotle's? Why? Finally, how crucial is it for philosophy to have the uses Murphy mentions? Can it help us overcome poverty of spirit, intellectual stagnation, fanaticism, and chauvinism? Can it at least help us overcome the narrow parochialism of philosophical schools and traditions? In this book, we are attempting to lay the groundwork for this enterprise as well as to test philosophy's ability to overcome these obstacles.

In trying to overcome parochialism, it is as futile to look for common characteristics in non-Western philosophy in general as to try to characterize the entire spectrum of Western philosophy. In both cases, there is much internal diversity. A more promising approach—and the one this book adopts—is to look into specific problem areas and specific concepts and to study the thoughts of specific individual philosophers rather than the views ascribed to schools. This concern with *philosophical diversity* guides our approach as much as a concern with *philosophical overlaps*. For, in fact, individual philosophical discussions in two or more philosophical traditions—say, Indian, Chinese, African, or Western—often have a family resemblance. Indeed, as the selections in this book demonstrate, cross-cultural influences in philosophy have become more and more apparent in our highly interdependent twentieth-century world, and as a consequence, different philosophical traditions have become less dissimilar. At this point, we must ask: Are the various conceptions of philosophy changing in a convergent manner? If so, toward what? Would such convergence be a good thing?

The next selection in Part I, "Changing Conceptions of Philosophy" by John Dewey (1859–1952), provides a vantage point from which to address these questions. Dewey begins by discussing the origins of philosophy in a manner consonant with our discussion of philosophy's beginnings in Section A of this essay. Then he outlines a process explaining those beginnings:

> It is enough for our purposes that under social influences there took place a fixing and organizing of doctrines and cults which gave general traits to the imagination and general rules to conduct, and that such a consolidation was a necessary antecedent to the formation of any philosophy as we understand that term.

But, though necessary, these features did not suffice to generate philosophy. The "motive for logical system and intellectual proof" also had to be present. Dewey supposes its appearance was brought about "by the need of reconciling the moral rules and ideals embodied in the traditional code with the matter of fact positivistic knowledge which gradually grows up."

In other words, the growth of factual knowledge provided by science, which is largely based on observation and experiment and which is testable by reference to its predictions, poses a problem for morality. For it is at least questionable that morality—widely speaking, whatever is traditionally believed to be crucial to people's lives—is based on observation and experiment and is testable by reference to any predictions it might make. The problem is to find a method of inquiry capable of providing a firm basis for morality.

According to Dewey, philosophy's role from the outset was shaped by this problem. That is, it had an apologetic role. Dewey argues that there are two features of philosophy, traceable to its origins, that have prevented it from effectively addressing the need to find a method of inquiry capable of providing a sound basis for morality. One is "an overdeveloped attachment to system for its own sake, and an over-pretentious claim to certainty." The other is the presupposition that reflective thought, like the mere reliance on authority it opposed, is both universal and comprehensive. According to Dewey, philosophy's commitment to both these features led it to distinguish between two realms of reality: the ordinary, empirical, everyday world and the world of ultimate reality. Philosophy saw its role as proving the existence of ultimate reality and providing clarification of it.

Arguably, this was largely a problem in Western philosophy—more specifically, Western academic philosophy. It was probably exacerbated by the advent of literacy and, later, the development of philosophy as a profession. Against this background, Dewey advances a modern conception of philosophy that is supposed to arise out of social and emotional rather than intellectual material. Its main concern is not: What is the nature of reality? Instead, it addresses such questions as: What aspects of human experience are human beings most deeply and passionately attached to? Given this, how should human beings shape their intelligent activities and social institutions? In this conception, philosophy's role is not to prove the existence of some other world ("ultimate reality") and to explain it, but rather to clarify our ideas concerning moral and social conflicts in this world.

It can be argued that Dewey's conception of philosophy is not as new as he makes it out to be, but simply a modern version of Socrates' conception, which focused on wisdom as practice. Actually, Dewey's conception is in contrast with the conception of philosophy prevalent today, which is Aristotelian: that is, wisdom is considered to be largely a matter of contemplating first principles so that a wise person can use the information thus acquired to live a good life. Perhaps both these conceptions should be superseded. For as the selections in this book demonstrate, pure curiosity and puzzlement are no more—and no less—crucial than social, moral, and other practical concerns to philosophy.

Whatever one's position on this (or any other) matter of philosophical interest, reasoning should play some role in addressing it. This is why arguments are central to philosophical inquiry, and logic, which studies argument and methods of philosophical reasoning, is central to philosophy. We will now examine some of the intellectual tools of philosophy.

C. WHAT ARE PHILOSOPHY'S LOGICAL TOOLS?

The last selection in Part I, Robert P. Churchill's "Analyzing Arguments," provides some introductory guidance in logic, that discipline which studies the tools used in philosophical and other forms of reasoning. Logic presupposes a distinction between statements, which are anything capable of being true or false, and other linguistic expressions, which are not capable of being true or false. Examples of statements are "2 + 2 = 4," which is true, and "cats are canines," which is false. Linguistic expressions incapable of being true or false include commands (e.g., "Come to the door!"), requests (e.g., "Please bring candy"), and expressions of emotion or feelings (e.g., "Ouch!"). Questions, which are requests for information (e.g., "Did you bring candy?"), are also incapable of being true or false.

Churchill contrasts *necessary* with *empirical* statements. A necessary statement is one that is true or false just by virtue of the meaning of its terms or just by virtue of its form. For example, "All bachelors are unmarried" is true, but not just by virtue of its form (All A's are M's), for "All husbands are unmarried" has the same form but is not true. "All bachelors are unmarried" is true because of the meaning of its terms alone. "All cats are not cats," on the other hand, is false by virtue of its form (All A's are not A's), for if any other term—say, "dogs" or "revolutions"—were to be substituted for "cats" in the statement (i.e., "All dogs are not dogs" or "All revolutions are not revolutions"), the statement would remain false. By contrast, the truth or falsity of empirical statements such as "There is a chair in this room" and "José was born in Venezuela" cannot be settled simply by virtue of their form or the meaning of their terms.

Reflect for a moment on the statements "All propositions are false," "All universalizations have exceptions," "I'm not denying anything right now," and "I'm not uttering anything right now." We can treat the second of these as an empirical statement and argue that it is false because at least one universalization—"All cats are felines"—has no exceptions. Arguing this way is fine, but it requires ingenuity to find a universalization without exceptions.

Let us consider another, more formal, approach to establishing the truth or falsity of this statement. The statement has a shortcoming that does not require coming up with a particular universalization to prove it false: it is self-refuting. To see this, first assume that the statement "All universalizations have exceptions" is true. If so, this statement itself—which is a universalization—must have an exception. But since an exception to this statement would be a universalization without any exceptions, it follows that at least one universalization has no exceptions. This conclusion, which logically follows from "All universalizations have exceptions," contradicts it. In other words, the statement is self-refuting: it leads to a contradiction through what it says or implies and the description of what it is. This can be established without having to use our imagination to formulate a particular universalization without exceptions.

In discussing "All-generalizations have exceptions," we have just given an argument. Arguments are lists of statements, some of which—the premises or reasons—are regarded as a basis for accepting one of them—the conclusion. These lists are bounded—that is, they have a beginning and an end—and the steps are countable—that is, they can be paired up with the natural numbers 1, 2, 3, and so on until the last step.

Churchill also discusses the crucial distinction between *deduction* and *induction*. Informally speaking, a deductive argument is one whose premises are regarded as providing a conclusive basis for accepting the conclusion; while an inductive argument is one whose premises are regarded as providing a basis, but not a conclusive basis, for accepting the conclusion.

Validity and *soundness* are crucial for assessing deductive arguments. Validity concerns the form of the argument. An argument is valid if it has a form such that, if all the premises of a particular instance of this form are true, its conclusion must also be true. An example is:

> *If Jimmy is an infant, then he is messy.*
> *Jimmy is an infant.*
> *Hence, Jimmy is messy.*

Soundness concerns not only the form of an argument but also the truth of its premises. An argument is sound whenever it is valid *and* has only true premises. The preceding argument, for example, is sound if Jimmy is indeed an infant and if it is also true that if he is an infant, then he is messy. Otherwise it is valid but not sound. Indeed, valid arguments can have false premises and a false conclusion. For example:

> *All horses are reptiles.*
> *Caligula's horse was human.*
> *Hence, Caligula's horse was a reptile.*

Just as there are statements that are self-refuting, so there are entire arguments that are self-defeating. These are arguments in which if the conclusion were true, then one or more of the premises used to arrive at that conclusion would have no basis. These kinds of arguments may have a valid form. In addition, they may have some true premises and some other premises whose falsity is difficult to establish. (Ask yourself: Could they have *only* true premises?) Yet it is easy to show that they are self-defeating. Consider the following argument:

> *Some of our sense perceptions sometimes deceive us.*
> *If so, then we may not rely on any of them as a basis for our statements.*
> *Hence, we may not rely on any of them as a basis for our statements.*

This is a self-defeating argument because if the conclusion were true, then the argument's first statement would be undermined—that is, there would be no basis for it. For we rely on some sense perceptions in order to establish that our sense perceptions sometimes deceive us—say, when we see upon turning on the light in a dark room that what we thought was a man is, after all, a broom. Reflect critically on the logical notions just discussed and, when appropriate, use them in evaluating arguments offered in this book.

NOTES

[1]   For our sources concerning Socrates' philosophy, see A. R. Lacey, "Our Knowledge of Socrates," in Gregory Vlastos (ed.), *The Philosophy of Socrates* (Garden City, NY: Doubleday, 1971), pp. 22–49. For a good brief discussion of some of the points made about ancient philosophy in Part I, see the entry entitled "Philosophy" by Marcus G. Singer in *The World Book Encyclopedia*, ed. Robert O. Celent (Chicago: World Book, 1986), Vol. 15, pp. 345–353, esp. pp. 348–349.

[2]   Walter Kauffman, *Philosophic Classics* (Englewood Cliffs, NJ: Prentice Hall, 1961), p. 19.

Traditional Veda Text (Sixth Century B.C.)
THE UPANISHADS

The Upanishads, *which appeared in India in the sixth century B.C., are treatises containing ritual or cosmogonic information. They also address various philosophical questions, such as: Is all reality basically one individual thing? and How can this be known? These and related questions are discussed in Section A of the introductory essay to Part I.*

READING QUESTIONS

In reading the selection, try to answer the following questions and identify the passages that support your answers:

1. What question can the first *Upanishad* be interpreted to answer?
2. What answer does it give to this question?
3. In what way is this answer supposed to be known?
4. What role, if any, are knowledge and reasoning supposed to play in attaining this knowledge?
5. Does the differentiation involved in using language lead to a partial picture of the world?

1. UNITY AND DIVERSITY

By the Lord enveloped must this all be—
Whatever moving thing there is in the moving world.
With this renounced, thou mayest enjoy.
Covet not the wealth of anyone at all.

Even while doing deeds here,
One may desire to live a hundred years.
Thus on thee—not otherwise than this is it—
The dead adheres not on the man.

Devilish are those worlds called,
With blind darkness covered o'er!
Unto them, on deceasing, go
Whatever folk are slayers of the Self.

Unmoving, the One[1] is swifter than the mind.
The sense-powers reached not It, speeding on before.

Past others running, This goes standing.
In It Mātariśvan[2] places action.

It moves. It moves not.
It is far, and It is near.
It is within all this,
And It is outside of all this.

Now, he who on all beings
Looks as just in the Self,
And on the Self as in all beings—
He does not shrink away from Him.

In whom all beings
Have become just the Self of the discerner—
Then what delusion, what sorrow is there,
Of him who perceives the unity!

Into blind darkness enter they
That worship ignorance;
Into darkness greater than that, as it were, they
That delight in knowledge.

---

[1] The Absolute (as a neuter form).

[2] The god of the wind

Knowledge and non-knowledge—
He who this pair conjointly knows,
With non-knowledge passing over death,
With knowledge wins the immortal.

Into blind darkness enter they
Who worship non-becoming;
Into darkness greater than that, as it were, they
Who delight in becoming.

Becoming and destruction—
He who this pair conjointly knows,
With destruction passing over death,
With becoming wins the immortal.

(Īśā)

2. THE UNITARY WORLD-SOUL

As the one fire has entered the world
And becomes corresponding in form to every
     form,
So the one Inner Soul of all things
Is corresponding in form to every form, and yet is
     outside.

As the one wind has entered the world
And becomes corresponding in form to every
     form,
So the one Inner Soul of all things
Is corresponding in form to every form, and yet is
     outside.

As the sun, the eye of the whole world,
Is not sullied by the external faults of the eyes,
So the one Inner Soul of all things
Is not sullied by the evil in the world, being
     external to it.

The Inner Soul of all things, the One Controller,
Who makes his one form manifold—
The wise who perceive Him as standing in oneself,
They, and no others, have eternal happiness!

Him who is the Constant among the inconstant,
     the Intelligent among intelligences,
The One among many, who grants desires—
The wise who perceive Him as standing in oneself,
They, and no others, have eternal peace!

(Katha, 5.9–13)

3. THE CREATION OF THE WORLD FROM THE SOUL

In the beginning this world was Soul alone in the form of a Person. Looking around, he saw nothing else than himself. He said first: "I am." Thence arose the name "I." Therefore even today, when one is addressed, he says first just "It is I" and then speaks whatever name he has. Since before all this world he burned up all evils, therefore he is a person. He who knows this, verily, burns up him who desires to be ahead of him.

He was afraid. Therefore one who is alone is afraid. This one then thought to himself: "Since there is nothing else than myself, of what am I afraid?" Thereupon, verily, his fear departed, for of what should he have been afraid? Assuredly it is from a second that fear arises.

Verily, he had no delight. Therefore one alone has no delight. He desired a second. He was, indeed, as large as a woman and a man closely embraced. He caused that self to fall into two pieces. Therefrom arose a husband and a wife. Therefore this is true: "Oneself is like a half-fragment," as Yājñavalkya used to say. Therefore this space is filled by a wife. He copulated with her. Therefrom human beings were produced.

And she then bethought herself: "How now does he copulate with me after he has produced me just from himself? Come, let me hide myself." She became a cow. He became a bull. With her he did indeed copulate. The cattle were born. She became a mare, he a stallion. She became a female ass, he a male ass; with her he copulated, of a truth. Thence were born solid-hoofed animals. She became a she-goat, he a he-goat; she a ewe, he a ram. With her he did verily copulate. Therefrom were born goats and sheep. Thus, indeed, he created all, whatever pairs there are, even down to the ants.

He knew: "I, indeed, am this creation, for I emitted it all from myself." Thence arose creation. Verily, he who has this knowledge comes to be in that creation of his.

Then he rubbed thus. From his mouth as the fire-hole and from his hands he created fire. Both the hands and the mouth are hairless on the inside, for the fire-hole is hairless on the inside.

This that people say, "Worship this god! Worship that god!"—one god after another—this is his creation indeed! And he himself is all the gods.

Now, whatever is moist, that he created from semen, and that is Soma. This whole world, verily, is just food and the eater of food.

That was Brahman's super-creation: namely, that he created the gods, his superiors; likewise, that, being mortal, he created the immortals. Therefore was it a super-creation. Verily, he who knows this comes to be in that super-creation of his.

Verily, at that time the world was undifferentiated. It became differentiated just by name and form, as the saying is: "He has such a name, such a form." Even today this world is differentiated just by name and form, as the saying is: "He has such a name, such a form."

He entered in here, even to the fingernail-tips, as a razor would be hidden in a razor-case, or fire in a fire-holder. Him they see not, for as seen he is incomplete. When breathing, he becomes breath by name; when speaking, the voice; when seeing, the eye; when hearing, the ear; when thinking, the mind: these are merely the names of his acts. Whoever worships one or another of these—he knows not; for he is incomplete with one or another of these. One should worship with the thought that he is just one's self, for therein all these become one. That same thing, namely this self, is the trace of this All, for by it one knows this All. Just as, verily, one might find by a footprint, thus. He finds fame and praise who knows this.

That Self is dearer than a son, is dearer than wealth, is dearer than all else, since this self is nearer.

If of one who speaks of anything else than the Self as dear, one should say, "He will lose what he holds dear," he would indeed be likely to do so. One should reverence the Self alone as dear. He who reverences the Self alone as dear—what he holds dear, verily, is not perishable.

(*Bṛhad-Āraṇyaka*, 1.4, 1–8)

4. THE CONVERSATION BETWEEN YĀJÑAVALKYA AND MAITREYĪ

"Maitreyī!" said Yājñavalkya, "lo, verily, I am about to go forth from this state. Behold! let me make a final settlement for you and that Kātyāyanī."

Then said Maitreyī: "If now, sir, this whole earth filled with wealth were mine, would I be immortal thereby?"

"No," said Yājñavalkya. "As the life of the rich, even so would your life be. Of immortality, however, there is no hope through wealth."

Then said Maitreyī: "What should I do with that through which I may not be immortal? What you know, sir—that, indeed, tell me!"

Then said Yājñavalkya: "Ah! Lo, dear as you are to us, dear is what you say! Come, sit down. I will explain to you. But while I am expounding, do you seek to ponder thereon."

Then said he: "Lo, verily, not for love of the husband is a husband dear, but for love of the Soul a husband is dear.

"Lo, verily, not for love of the wife is a wife dear, but for love of the Soul a wife is dear.

"Lo, verily, not for love of the sons are sons dear, but for love of the Souls sons are dear.

"Lo, verily, not for love of wealth is wealth dear, but for love of the Soul wealth is dear.

"Lo, verily, not for love of Brahmanhood is Brahmanhood dear, but for love of the Soul Brahmanhood is dear.

"Lo, verily, not for love of the worlds are the worlds dear, but for love of the Soul the worlds are dear.

"Lo, verily, not for the love of the gods are the gods dear, but for love of the Soul the gods are dear.

"Lo, verily, not for love of beings are beings dear, but for love of the Soul beings are dear.

"Lo, verily, not for love of all is all dear, but for love of the Soul all is dear.

"Lo, verily, it is the Soul that should be seen, that should be hearkened to, that should be thought on, that should be pondered on, O Maitreyī Lo, verily, with the seeing of, with the hearkening to, with the thinking of, and with the understanding of the Soul, this world-all is known.

"Brahmanhood has deserted him who knows Brahmanhood in aught else than the Soul.

"The worlds have deserted him who knows the worlds in aught else than the Soul.

"The gods have deserted him who knows the gods in aught else than the Soul.

"Beings have deserted him who knows beings in aught else than the Soul.

"Everything has deserted him who knows everything in aught else than the Soul.

"It is—as, when a drum is being beaten, one would not be able to grasp the external sounds, but by grasping the drum or the beater of the drum the sound is grasped.

"It is—as, when a conch-shell is being blown, one would not be able to grasp the external sounds, but by grasping the drum or the beater of the drum the sound is grasped.

"It is—as, when a lute is being played, one would not be able to grasp the external sounds, but by grasping the lute or the player of the lute the sound is grasped.

"It is—as, from a fire laid with damp fuel, clouds of smoke separately issue forth, so, lo, verily, from this great Being has been breathed forth that which is *Ṛg-Veda, Yajur-Veda, Sāma-Veda,* Hymns of the Atharvans and Angiras', Legend, Ancient Lore, Sciences, Mystic Doctrines, Verses, Aphorisms,

Explanations, and Commentaries. From it, indeed, are all these breathed forth.

"It is—as of all waters the uniting-point is the sea, so of all touches the uniting-point is the skin, so of all tastes the uniting-point is the tongue, so of all smells the uniting-point is the nostrils, so of all forms the uniting-point is the eye, so of all sounds the uniting-point is the ear, so of all intentions the uniting-point is the mind, so of all knowledges the uniting-point is the heart, so of all acts the uniting-point is the hands, so of all pleasures the uniting-point is the generative organ, so of all evacuations the uniting-point is the anus, so of all journeys the uniting-point is the feet, so of all the Vedas the uniting-point is speech.

"It is—as a lump of salt cast in water would dissolve right into the water; there would not be any of it to seize forth, as it were, but wherever one may take, it is salty indeed—so, lo, verily, this great Being, infinite, limitless, is just a mass of knowledge.

"Arising out of these elements, into them also one vanishes away. After death there is no consciousness. Thus, lo, say I." Thus spake Yājñavalkya.

Then spake Maitreī: "Herein, indeed, you have bewildered me, sir—in saying: "After death there is no consciousness!"

Then spake Yājñavalkya: "Lo, verily, I speak not bewilderment. Sufficient, lo, verily is this for understanding.

"For where there is a duality, as it were, there one sees another; there one smells another; there one hears another; there one speaks to another; there one thinks of another; there one understands another. Where, verily, everything has become just one's own self, then whereby and whom would one smell? then whereby and whom would one see? then whereby and whom would one hear? then whereby and to whom would one speak? then whereby and on whom would one think? then whereby and whom would one understand? Whereby would one understand him by whom one understands this All? Lo, whereby would one understand the understander?"

(*Ibid.*, 2.4)

5. THE SOUL IN DREAMLESS SLEEP

"As a falcon, or an eagle, having flown around here in space, becomes weary, folds its wings, and is borne down to its nest, just so this person hastens to that state where, asleep, he desires no desires and sees no dream.

"Verily, a person has those channels called hitā; as a hair subdivided a thousandfold, so minute are they, full of white, blue, yellow, green, and red. Now when people seem to be killing him, when they seem to be overpowering him, when an elephant seems to be tearing him to pieces, when he seems to be falling into a hole—in these circumstances he is imagining through ignorance the very fear which he sees when awake. When, imagining that he is a god, that he is a king, he thinks 'I am this world-all,' that is his highest world.

"This, verily, is that form of his which is beyond desires, free from evil, without fear. As a man, when in the embrace of a beloved wife, knows nothing within or without, so this person, when in the embrace of the intelligent Soul, knows nothing within or without. Verily, that is his true form in which his desire is satisfied, in which the Soul is his desire, in which he is without desire and without sorrow.

"There a father becomes not a father; a mother, not a mother; the worlds, not the worlds; the gods, not the gods; the Vedas, not the Vedas; a thief, not a thief. He is not followed by good, he is not followed by evil, for then he has passed beyond all sorrows of the heart.

"An ocean, a seer alone without duality, becomes he whose world is Brahman, O King!"—thus Yājñavalkya instructed him. "This is a man's highest path. This is his highest achievement. This is his highest world. This is his highest bliss. On a part of just this bliss other creatures have their living.

"If one is fortunate among men and wealthy, lord over others, best provided with all human enjoyments—that is the highest bliss of men. Now a hundredfold the bliss of men is one bliss of those who have won the fathers' world. Now a hundredfold the bliss of those who have won the fathers' world is one bliss in the Gandharva-world. A hundredfold the bliss in the Gandharva-world is one bliss of the gods who gain their divinity by meritorious works. A hundredfold the bliss of the gods by works is one bliss of the gods by birth and of him who is learned in the Vedas, who is without crookedness, and who is free from desire. A hundredfold the bliss of the gods by birth is one bliss in the Prajāpati-world and of him who is learned in the Vedas, who is without crookedness, and is free from desire. A hundredfold the bliss in the Prajāpati-world is one bliss in the Brahman-world and of him who is learned in the Vedas, who is without crookedness, and who is free from desire. This truly is the highest world. This is the Brahman-world, O King."—Thus spake Yājña-valkya.

(Ibid., 4.3, 19–33, passim)

6. THE INDIVIDUAL SOUL IDENTICAL WITH BRAHMAN

Verily, this whole world is *Brahman*. Tranquil, let one worship It as from which he came forth, as that into which he will be dissolved, as that in which he breathes.

Now, verily, a person consists of purpose. According to the purpose which a person has in this world, thus does he become on departing hence. So let him form for himself a purpose.

He who consists of mind, whose body is life, whose form is light, whose conception is truth, whose soul is space, containing all works, containing all desires, containing all odors, containing all tastes, encompassing this whole world, the unspeaking, the unconcerned—this Soul of mine within the heart is smaller than a grain of rice, or a barley-corn, or a mustard seed, or a grain of millet, or the kernel of a grain of millet; this Soul of mine within the heart is greater than the earth, greater than the atmosphere, greater than the sky, greater than these worlds.

Containing all works, containing all desires, containing all odors, containing all tastes, encompassing this whole world, the unspeaking, the unconcerned—this is the Soul of mine within the heart, this is *Brahman*. Into him I shall enter on departing hence.

If one would believe this, he would have no more doubt.—Thus used Sāndilya to say—yea, Sāndilya!

(Chandogya, 3.14)

7. THE RIVALRY OF THE FIVE BODILY FUNCTIONS, AND THE SUPERIORITY OF BREATH

Om! Verily, he who knows the chiefest and best, becomes the chiefest and best. Breath, verily, is the chiefest and best.

Verily, he who knows the most excellent, becomes the most excellent of his own people. Speech, verily, is the most excellent.

Verily, he who knows the firm basis, has a firm basis both in this world and in the yonder. The eye, verily, is a firm basis.

Verily, he who knows attainment—for him wishes are attained, both human and divine. The ear, verily, is attainment.

Verily, he who knows the abode, becomes an abode of his own people. The mind, verily, is the abode.

Now, the Vital Breaths disputed among themselves on self-superiority, saying in turn: "I am superior!" "I am superior!"

Those Vital Breaths went to Father Prajāpati, and said: "Sir! Which of us is the most superior?"

He said to them: "That one of you after whose going off the body appears as if it were the very worst off—he is the most superior of you."

Speech went off. Having remained away a year, it came around again, and said: "How have you been able to live without me?"

"As the dumb, not speaking, but breathing with the breath, seeing with the eye, hearing with the ear, thinking with the mind. Thus."

Speech entered in.

The Eye went off. Having remained away a year, it came around again, and said: "How have you been able to live without me?"

"As the blind, not seeing, but breathing with the breath, speaking with speech, hearing with the ear, thinking with the mind. Thus."

The Eye entered in.

The Ear went off. Having remained away a year, it came around again, and said: "How have you been able to live without me?"

"As the deaf, not hearing, but breathing with the breath, speaking with speech, seeing with the eye, thinking with the mind. Thus."

The Ear entered in.

The Mind went off. Having remained away a year, it came around again, and said: "How have you been able to live without me?"

"As simpletons, mindless, but breathing with the breath, speaking with speech, seeing with the eye, hearing with the ear. Thus."

The mind entered in.

Now when the Breath was about to go off—as a fine horse might tear out the pegs of his foot-tethers all together, thus did it tear out the other Breaths all together. They all came to it and said: "Sir! Remain. You are the most superior of us. Do not go off."

The Speech said unto that one: "If I am the most excellent, so are you the most excellent."

Then the Eye said unto that one: "If I am a firm basis, so are you a firm basis."

Then the Ear said unto that one: "If I am attainment, so are you attainment."

Then the Mind said unto that one: "If I am an abode, so are you an abode."

Verily, they do not call them "Speeches," nor "Eyes," nor "Ears," nor "Minds." They call them "Breaths," for the vital breath is all these.

(*Ibid.*, 5.1)

8. ALLEGORY OF THE VEDIC GODS' IGNORANCE OF BRAHMAN

Now, Brahman won a victory for the gods. Now, in the victory of this Brahman the gods were exulting. They bethought themselves: "Ours indeed is this victory! Ours indeed is this greatness!"

Now, Brahman understood this of them. It appeared to them. They did not understand it. "What wonderful being is this?" they said.

They said to Fire: "All-possessor, find out this—what this wonderful being is."

"So be it."

He ran unto It.

Unto him It spoke: "Who are you?"

"Verily, I am Fire," he said. "Verily, I am All-possessor."

"In such as you what power is there?"

"Indeed, I might burn everything here, whatever there is here in the earth!"

It put down a straw before him. "Burn that!"

He went forth at it with all speed. He was not able to burn it. Thereupon indeed he returned, saying: "I have not been able to find out this—what this wonderful being is."

Then they said to Wind: "Wind, find out this—what this wonderful being is."

"So be it."

He ran unto It.

Unto him It spoke: "Who are you?"

"Verily, I am Wind," he said. "Verily, I am Mātariśvan."

"In such as you what power is there?"

"Indeed, I might carry off everything here, whatever there is here in the earth."

It put down a straw before him. "Carry that off!"

He went at it with all speed. He was not able to carry it off. Thereupon indeed he returned, saying: "I have not been able to find out this—what this wonderful being is."

Then they said to Indra: "O Liberal, find out this—what this wonderful being is."

"So be it."

He ran unto It. It disappeared from him.

In that very space he came upon a woman exceedingly beautiful, Umā daughter of the Snowy Mountain.

To her he said: "What is this wonderful being?"

"It is Brahman," she said. "In that victory of Brahman, verily, exult ye."

Thereupon he knew it was Brahman.

Therefore, verily, these gods, namely Fire, Wind, and Indra, are above the other gods, as it were; for these touched It nearest, for these and specially Indra first knew It was Brahman.

Therefore, verily, Indra is above the other gods, as it were; for he touched It nearest, for he first knew It was Brahman.

Of It there is this teaching.—

That in the lightning which flashes forth, which makes one blink, and say "Ah!"—that "Ah!" refers to divinity.

Now with regard to oneself.—

That which comes, as it were, to the mind, by which one repeatedly remembers—that conception is Brahman!

(*Kena*, 3.1–12, 4.1–5)

9. A DYING FATHER'S BEQUEST OF HIS VARIOUS POWERS TO HIS SON

Now next, the Father-and-Son Ceremony, or the Transmission, as they call it.—

A father, when about to decease, summons his son. Having strewn the house with new grass, having built up the fire, having set down near it a vessel of water together with a dish, the father, wrapped around with a fresh garment, remains lying. The son, having come, lies down on top, touching organs with organs. Or he may, even, transmit to him seated face to face. Then he delivers over to him thus:—

Father: "My speech in you I would place!"

Son: "Your speech in me I take."

Father: "My breath in you I would place!"

Son: "Your breath in me I take."

Father: "My eye in you I would place!"

Son: "You eye in me I take."

Father: "My ear in you I would place!"

Son: "Your ear in me I take."

Father: "My tastes in you I would place!"

Son: "Your tastes in me I would take."

Father: "My deeds in you I would place!"

Son: "Your deeds in me I take."

Father: "My pleasure and pain in you I would place!"

Son: "Your pleasure and pain in me I take."

Father: "My bliss, delight, and procreation in you I would place!"

Son: "Your bliss, delight, and procreation in me I take."

Father: "My goings in you I would place!"

Son: "Your goings in me I take."

Father: "My mind in you I would place!"

Son: "Your mind in me I take."

Father: "My intelligence in you I would place!"

Son: "Your intelligence in me I take."

If, however, he should be unable to speak much, let the father say summarily: "My vital breaths in you I would place!" and the son reply: "Your vital breaths in me I take."

Then, turning to the right, he goes forth toward the east.

The father calls out after him: "May glory, sacred luster, and fame delight in you!"

Then the other looks over his left shoulder. Having hid his face with his hand, or having covered it with the edge of his garment, he says: "Heavenly worlds and desires do you obtain!"

If he should become well, the father should dwell under the lordship of his son, or he should wander around as a religious mendicant. If, however, he should decease, so let them furnish him as he ought to be furnished.

(*Kausītaki*, 2.15)

10. NACIKETAS AND GOD YAMA (DEATH)

[A poor and pious Brahmana, Vājaśravasa, performs a sacrifice and gives as presents to the priests a few old and feeble cows. His son, Naciketas, feeling disturbed by the unreality of his father's observance of the sacrifice, proposes that he himself may be offered as offering to a priest. When he persisted in his request, his father in rage says, "Unto Yama, I give thee." Naciketas goes to the abode of Yama, and finding him absent, waits there for three days and nights unfed. Yama, on his return, offers three gifts in recompense for the delay and discomfort caused to Naciketas. For the first, Naciketas asked, "Let me return alive to my father." For the second, "Tell me how my good works may not be exhausted"; and for the third "Tell me the way to conquer re-death."]

Naciketas and His Father

Desirous of the fruit of the sacrifice, Vājaśravasa, they say, gave away all that he possessed. He had a son by name Naciketas.

As the gifts were being taken to the priests, faith entered him, although but a mere boy; he thought.

Their water drunk, their grass eaten, their milk milked, their strength spent, joyless, verily, are those worlds, to which he, who presents such cows goes.

He said to his father, "O Sire, to whom wilt thou give me?" For a second and a third time he repeated, when the father said to him, "Unto Death shall I give thee."

Naciketas, "Of many sons or disciples I go as the first; of many, I go as the middling. What duty towards Yama that my father has to accomplish today, does he accomplish through me?

"Consider how it was with the forefathers; behold how it is with the later men; a mortal ripens like corn, and like corn is born again."

Naciketas in the House of Death

As a very fire a Brahmana guest enters into houses and the people do him this peace-offering; bring water, O Son of the Sun!

Hopes and expectation, friendship and joy, sacrifices and good works, sons, cattle and all are taken away from a person of little understanding in whose house a Brahmana remains unfed.

Yama's Address to Naciketas

"Since thou, a venerable guest, hast stayed in my house without food for three nights, I make obeisance to thee, O Brahmana. May it be well with me. Therefore, in return, choose thou three gifts."

Naciketas's First Wish

"That my father will allayed anxiety, with anger gone, may be gracious to me, O Death, and recognising me, greet me, when set free by you and this, I choose as the first gift of the three."

Yama said: "As of old through my favour will he sleep peacefully through nights, his anger gone, seeing thee released from the jaws of death."

Naciketas's Second Wish

Naciketas said: "In the world of heaven there is no fear whatever; thou are not there, nor does one fear old age. Crossing over both hunger and thirst, leaving sorrow behind, one rejoices in the world of heaven.

"Thou knowest, O Death, that fire sacrifice which is the aid to heaven. Describe it to me, full of faith, how the dwellers in heaven gain immortality. This I choose, as my second boon."

Yama said: "Knowing well as I do, that fire sacrifice which is the aid to heaven, I shall describe it to thee—learn it of me, O Naciketas. Know that fire to be the means of attaining the boundless world, as the support of the universe and as abiding in the secret place of the heart."

Yama described to him that the fire sacrifice which is the beginning of the world as also what kind of bricks are to be used in building the sacrificial altar, how many and in what manner. And Naciketas repeated all that just as it had been told: then, pleased with him, Death spoke again.

Yama, the great soul, extremely delighted, said to Naciketas: "I give thee here today another boon. By thine own name will this fire sacrifice become known. Take also this many-shaped chain.

"He who has lit the Naciketas fire thrice, associating with the three, performs the three acts, crosses over birth and death. Knowing the son of Brahma, the omniscient, resplendent and adorable and realising him, one obtains this everlasting peace.

"The wise man who has sacrificed thrice to Naciketas and who knows this three, and so knowing, performs meditation on fire throwing off first the bonds of death and overcoming sorrow, rejoices in the world of heaven.

"This is thy fire sacrifice, O Naciketas, which leading to heaven, which thou hast chosen for thy second boon. This first sacrifice people will call by thy name only. Choose now, O Naciketas, the third boon."

Naciketas's Third Wish

Naciketas said: "There is this doubt in regard to a man who has departed, some holding that he is and some that he is not. I would be instructed by thee in this knowledge. Of the boons, this is the third boon."

Yama said: "Even the gods of old had doubt on this point. It is not, indeed, easy to understand; so subtle in this truth. Choose another boon, O Naciketas. Do not press me. Release me from this."

Naciketas said: "Even the gods had doubt, indeed, as to this, and thou, O Death, sayest that it is not easy to understand. Instruct me for another teacher of it, like thee, is not to be got. No other boon is comparable to this at all."

Yama said: "Choose sons and grandsons that shall live a hundred years, cattle in plenty, elephants, gold and horses. Choose vast expanses of land and life for thyself as many years as thou wilt.

"If thou deemest any boon like unto this, choose that as also wealth and long life. O Naciketas, prosper then on this vast earth. I will make thee the enjoyer of thy desires.

"Whatever desires are hard to attain in this world of mortals, ask for all those desires at thy will. Here are noble maidens with chariots and musical instruments: the like of them cannot be won by men. Be served by these whom I give to thee. O Naciketas, pray ask not about death."

Naciketas said: "Transient are these and they wear out, O Yama, the vigour of all the senses of men. All life, moreover, is brief. Thine be the chariots, thine the dance and song.

"Man is not to be contented with wealth. Shall we enjoy wealth when we have seen thee? Shall we live as long as thou are in power? That alone is still the boon chosen by me.

"Having approached the undecaying immortality, what decaying mortal on this earth below who now knows and meditates on the pleasures of beauty and love, will delight in an over-long life?

"Tell us that about which they doubt, O Death, what there is in the great passing-on. This boon which penetrates the mystery, no other than that does Naciketas choose."

Plato (428–348 B.C.)
APOLOGY

In this work, Socrates, Plato's teacher, defends himself against various charges leveled against him by the citizens of Athens. In the process, he describes and exemplifies the use of his philosophical method and addresses various philosophical questions, from What is wisdom? to What is the significance of death? A discussion of these and related questions can be found in Section A of the introductory essay to Part I.

READING QUESTIONS

As you read the selection, try to answer the following questions and identify the passages that support your answers:

1. What is Socrates' aim in the dialogue?
2. What is his method for attaining this aim?
3. Does Socrates claim to know what death is or that there is an afterlife?
4. Does Socrates claim to know what wisdom is?
5. Can Socrates' method lead to knowledge?

I do not know what effect my accusers have had upon you, gentlemen, but for my own part I was almost carried away by them—their arguments were so convincing. On the other hand, scarcely a word of what they said was true. I was especially astonished at one of their many misrepresentations; I mean when they told you that you must be careful not to let me deceive you—the implication being that I am a skillful speaker. I thought that it was peculiarly brazen of them to tell you this without a blush, since they must know that they will soon be effectively confuted, when it becomes obvious that I have not the slightest skill as a speaker—unless, of course, by a skillful speaker they mean one who speaks the truth. If that is what they mean, I would agree that I am an orator, though not after their pattern.

My accusers, then, as I maintain, have said little or nothing that is true, but from me you shall hear the whole truth—not, I can assure you, gentlemen, in flowery language like theirs, decked out with fine words and phrases. No, what you will hear will be a straightforward speech in the first words that occur to me, confident as I am in the justice of my cause, and I do not want any of you to expect anything different. It would hardly be suitable, gentlemen, for a man of my age to address you in the artificial language of a schoolboy orator. One thing, however, I do most earnestly beg and entreat of you. If you hear me defending myself in the same language which it has been my habit to use, both in the open spaces of this city—where many of you have heard me—and elsewhere, do not be surprised, and do not interrupt. Let me remind you of my position. This is my first appearance in a court of law, at the age of seventy, and so I am a complete stranger to the language of this place. Now if I were really from another country, you would naturally excuse me if I spoke in the manner and dialect in which I had been brought up, and so in the present case I make this request of you, which I think is only reasonable, to disregard the manner of my speech—it may be better or it may be worse—and to consider and concentrate your attention upon this one question, whether my claims are fair or not. That is the first duty of the juryman, just as it is the pleader's duty to speak the truth.

The proper course for me, gentlemen of the jury, is to deal first with the earliest charges that have been falsely brought against me, and with my earliest accusers, and then with the later ones. I make this distinction because I have already been accused in your hearing by a great many people for a great many years, though without a word of truth, and I am more afraid of those people than I am of Anytus and his colleagues, although they are formidable enough. But the others are still more formidable. I mean the people who took hold of so many of you when you were children and tried to fill your minds with untrue accusations against me, saying, There is a wise man called Socrates who has theories about the heavens and has investigated everything below the earth, and can make the weaker argument defeat the stronger.

It is these people, gentlemen, the disseminators of these rumors, who are my dangerous accusers, because those who hear them suppose that anyone who inquires into such matters must be an atheist. Besides, there are a great many of these accusers, and they have been accusing me now for a great many years. And what is more, they approached you at the most impressionable age, when some of you were children or adolescents, and they literally won their case by default, because there was no one to defend me. And the most fantastic thing of all is that it is impossible for me even to know and tell you their names, unless one of them happens to be a playwright. All these people, who have tried to set you against me out of envy and love of slander—and some too merely passing on what they have been told by others—all these are very difficult to deal with. It is impossible to bring them here for cross-examination: one simply has to conduct one's defense and argue one's case against an invisible opponent, because there is no one to answer. So I ask you to accept my statement that my critics fall into two classes, on the one hand my immediate accusers, and on the other those earlier ones whom I have mentioned, and you must suppose that I have first to defend myself against the latter. After all, you heard them abusing me longer ago and much more violently than these more recent accusers.

Very well, then, I must begin my defense, gentlemen, and I must try, in the short time that I have, to rid your minds of a false impression which is the work of many years. I should like this to be the result, gentlemen, assuming it to be for your advantage and my own; and I should like to be successful in my defense, but I think that it will be difficult, and I am quite aware of the nature of my task. However, let that turn out as God wills. I must obey the law and make my defense.

Let us go back to the beginning and consider what the charge is that has made me so unpopular, and has encouraged Meletus to draw up this indictment. Very well, what did my critics say in attacking my character? I must read out their affidavit, so to speak, as though they were my legal accusers: Socrates is guilty of criminal meddling, in that he inquires into things below the earth and in the sky, and makes the weaker argument defeat the stronger, and teaches others to follow his example. It runs something like that. You have seen it for yourselves in the play by Aristophanes, where Socrates goes whirling round, proclaiming that he is walking on air, and uttering a great deal of other nonsense about things of which I know nothing whatsoever. I mean no disrespect for such knowledge, if anyone really is versed in it—I do not want any more lawsuits brought against me by Meletus—but the fact is, gentlemen, that I take no interest in it. What is more, I call upon the greater part of you as witnesses to my statement, and I appeal to all of you who have ever listened to me talking—and there are a great many to whom this ap-

plies—to clear your neighbors' minds on this point. Tell one another whether any one of you has ever heard me discuss such questions briefly or at length, and then you will realize that the other popular reports about me are equally unreliable.

The fact is that there is nothing in any of these charges, and if you have heard anyone say that I try to educate people and charge a fee, there is no truth in that either. I wish that there were, because I think that it is a fine thing if a man is qualified to teach, as in the case of Gorgias of Leontini and Prodicus of Ceos and Hippias of Elis. Each one of these is perfectly capable of going into any city and actually persuading the young men to leave the company of their fellow citizens, with any of whom they can associate for nothing, and attach themselves to him, and pay money for the privilege, and be grateful into the bargain.

There is another expert too from Paros who I discovered was here on a visit; I happened to meet a man who has paid more in Sophists' fees than all the rest put together—I mean Callias, the son of Hipponicus. So I asked him—he has two sons, you see—Callias, I said, if your sons had been colts or calves, we should have had no difficulty in finding and engaging a trainer to perfect their natural qualities, and this trainer would have been some sort of horse dealer or agriculturalist. But seeing that they are human beings, whom do you intend to get as their instructor? Who is the expert in perfecting the human and social qualities? I assume from the fact of your having sons that you must have considered the question. Is there such a person or not?

Certainly, said he.

Who is he, and where does he come from? said I. And what does he charge?

Evenus of Paros, Socrates, said he, and his fee is five minas.

I felt that Evenus was to be congratulated if he really was a master of this art and taught it at such a moderate fee. I should certainly plume myself and give myself airs if I understood these things, but in fact, gentlemen, I do not.

Here perhaps one of you might interrupt me and say, But what is it that you do, Socrates? How is it that you have been misrepresented like this? Surely all this talk and gossip about you would never have arisen if you had confined yourself to ordinary activities, but only if your behavior was abnormal. Tell us the explanation, if you do not want us to invent it for ourselves.

This seems to me to be a reasonable request, and I will try to explain to you what it is that has given me this false notoriety. So please give me your attention. Perhaps some of you will think that I am not being serious, but I assure you that I am going to tell you the whole truth.

I have gained this reputation, gentlemen, from nothing more or less than a kind of wisdom. What kind of wisdom do I mean? Human wisdom, I suppose. It seems that I really am wise in this limited sense. Presumably the geniuses whom I mentioned just now are wise in a wisdom that is more than human. I do not know how else to account for it. I certainly have no knowledge of such wisdom, and anyone who says that I have is a liar and willful slanderer. Now, gentlemen, please do not interrupt me if I seem to make an extravagant claim, for what I am going to tell you is not my own opinion. I am going to refer you to an unimpeachable authority. I shall call as witness to my wisdom, such as it is, the god at Delphi.

You know Chaerephon, of course. He was a friend of mine from boyhood, and a good democrat who played his part with the rest of you in the recent expulsion and restoration. And you know what he was like, how enthusiastic he was over anything that he had once undertaken. Well, one day he actually went to Delphi and asked this question of the god—as I said before, gentlemen, please do not interrupt—he asked whether there was anyone wiser than myself. The priestess replied that there was no one. As Chaerephon is dead, the evidence for my statement will be supplied by his brother, who is here in court.

Please consider my object in telling you this. I want to explain to you how the attack upon my reputation first started. When I heard about the oracle's answer, I said to myself, What does the god mean? Why does he not use plain language? I am only too conscious that I have no claim to wisdom, great or small. So what can he mean by asserting that I am the wisest man in the world? He cannot be telling a lie; that would not be right for him.

After puzzling about it for some time, I set myself at last with considerable reluctance to check the truth of it in the following way. I went to interview a man with a high reputation for wisdom, because I felt that here if anywhere I should succeed in disproving the oracle and pointing out to my divine authority, You said that I was the wisest of men, but here is a man who is wiser than I am.

Well, I gave a thorough examination to this person—I need not mention his name, but it was one of our politicians that I was studying when I had this experience—and in conversation with him I formed the impression that although in many people's opinion, and especially in his own, he appeared to be wise, in fact he was not. Then when I began to try to show him that he only thought he was wise and was not really so, my efforts were resented both by him and by many of the other people present. However, I reflected as I walked away, Well, I am certainly wiser than this man. It is only too likely that neither of us has any knowledge to boast of, but he thinks that he knows something which he does not know, whereas I am quite conscious of my ignorance. At any rate it seems that I am wiser than he is to this small extent, that I do not think that I know what I do not know.

After this I went on to interview a man with an even greater reputation for wisdom, and I formed the same impression again, and here too I incurred the resentment of the man himself and a number of others.

From that time on I interviewed one person after another. I realized with distress and alarm that I was making myself unpopular, but I felt compelled to put my religious duty first. Since I was trying to find out the meaning of the oracle, I was bound to interview everyone who had a reputation for knowledge. And by dog, gentlemen, for I must be frank with you, my honest impression was this. It seemed to me, as I pursued my investigation at the god's command, that the people with the greatest reputations were almost entirely deficient, while others who were supposed to be their inferiors were much better qualified in practical intelligence.

I want you to think of my adventures as a sort of pilgrimage undertaken to establish the truth of the oracle once for all. After I had finished with the politicians I turned to the poets, dramatic, lyric, and all the rest, in the belief that here I should expose myself as a comparative ignoramus. I used to pick up what I thought were some of their most perfect works and question them closely about the meaning of what they had written, in the hope of incidentally enlarging my own knowledge. Well, gentlemen, I hesitate to tell you the truth, but it must be told. It is hardly an exaggeration to say that any of the bystanders could have explained those poems better than their actual authors. So I soon made up my mind about the poets too. I decided that it was not wisdom that enabled them to write their poetry, but a kind of instinct or inspiration, such as you find in seers and prophets who deliver all their sublime messages without knowing in the least what they mean.

It seemed clear to me that the poets were in much the same case, and I also observed that the very fact that they were poets made them think that they had a perfect understanding of all other subjects, of which they were totally ignorant. So I left that line of inquiry too with the same sense of advantage that I had felt in the case of the politicians.

Last of all I turned to the skilled craftsmen. I knew quite well that I had practically no technical qualifications myself, and I was sure that I should find them full of impressive knowledge. In this I was not disappointed. They understood things which I did not, and to that extent they were wiser than I was. But, gentlemen, these professional experts seemed to share the same failing which I had noticed in the poets. I mean that on the strength of their technical proficiency they claimed a perfect understanding of every other subject, however important, and I felt that this error more than outweighed their positive wisdom. So I made myself spokesman for the oracle, and asked myself whether I would rather be as I was—neither wise with their wisdom nor stupid with their stupidity—or possess both qualities as they did. I replied through myself to the oracle that it was best for me to be as I was.

The effect of these investigations of mine, gentlemen, has been to arouse against me a great deal of hostility, and hostility of a particularly bitter and persistent kind, which has resulted in various malicious suggestions, including the description of me as a professor of wisdom. This is due to the fact that whenever I succeed in disproving another person's claim to wisdom in a given subject, the bystanders assume that I know everything about that subject myself. But the truth of the matter, gentlemen, is pretty certainly this, that real wisdom is the property of God, and this oracle is his way of telling us that human wisdom has little or no value. It seems to me that he is not referring literally to Socrates, but has merely taken my name as an example, as if he would say to us, The wisest of you men is he who has realized, like Socrates, that in respect of wisdom he is really worthless.

That is why I still go about seeking and searching in obedience to the divine command, if I think that anyone is wise, whether citizen or stranger, and when I think that any person is not wise, I try to help the cause of God by proving that he is not. This occupation has kept me too busy to do much either in politics or in my own affairs. In fact, my service to God has reduced me to extreme poverty.

There is another reason for my being unpopular.

A number of young men with wealthy fathers and plenty of leisure have deliberately attached themselves to me because they enjoy hearing other people cross-questioned. These often take me as their model, and go on to try to question other persons. Whereupon, I suppose, they find an unlimited number of people who think that they know something, but really know little or nothing. Consequently their victims become annoyed, not with themselves but with me, and they complain that there is a pestilential busybody called Socrates who fills young people's heads with wrong ideas. If you ask them what he does, and what he teaches that has this effect, they have no answer, not knowing what to say. But as they do not want to admit their confusion, they fall back on the stock charges against any philosopher, that he teaches his pupils about things in the heavens and below the earth, and to disbelieve in gods, and to make the weaker argument defeat the stronger. They would be very loath, I fancy, to admit the truth—which is that they are being convicted of pretending to knowledge when they are entirely ignorant. So, jealous, I suppose, for their own reputation, and also energetic and numerically strong, and provided with a plausible and carefully worked-out case against me, these people have been dinning into your ears for a long time past their violent denunciations of myself.

There you have the causes which led to the attack upon me by Meletus and Anytus and Lycon, Meletus being aggrieved on behalf of the poets, Anytus on behalf of the professional men and politicians, and Lycon on behalf of the orators. So, as I said at the beginning, I should be surprised if I were able, in the short time that I have, to rid your minds of a misconception so deeply implanted.

There, gentlemen, you have the true facts, which I present to you without any concealment or suppression, great or small. I am fairly certain that this plain speaking of mine is the cause of my unpopularity, and this really goes to prove that my statements are true, and that I have described correctly the nature and the grounds of the calumny which has been brought against me. Whether you inquire into them now or later, you will find the facts as I have just described them.

So much for my defense against the charges brought by the first group of my accusers. I shall now try to defend myself against Meletus—high-principled and patriotic as he claims to be—and after that against the rest. Let us first consider their deposition again, as though it represented a fresh prosecution. It runs something like this: Socrates is guilty of corrupting the minds of the young, and of believing in deities of his own invention instead of the gods recognized by the state. Such is the charge. Let us examine its points one by one.

First it says that I am guilty of corrupting the young. But I say, gentlemen, that Meletus is guilty of treating a serious matter with levity, since he summons people to stand their trial on frivolous grounds, and professes concern and keen anxiety in matters about which he has never had the slightest interest. I will try to prove this to your satisfaction.

Come now, Meletus, tell me this. You regard it as supremely important, do you not, that our young people should be exposed to the best possible influence?

I do.

Very well, then, tell these gentlemen who it is that influences the young for the better. Obviously you must know, if you are so much interested. You have discovered the vicious influence, as you say, in myself, and you are now prosecuting me before these gentlemen. Speak up and inform them who it is that has a good influence upon the young. . . . You see, Meletus, that you are tongue-tied and cannot answer. Do you not feel that this is discreditable, and a sufficient proof in itself of what I said, that you have no interest in the subject? Tell me, my friend, who is it that makes the young good?

The laws.

That is not what I mean, my dear sir. I am asking you to name the *person* whose first business it is to know the laws.

These gentlemen here, Socrates, the members of the jury.

Do you mean, Meletus, that they have the ability to educate the young, and to make them better?

Certainly.

Does this apply to all jurymen, or only to some?

To all of them.

Excellent! A generous supply of benefactors. Well, then, do these spectators who are present in court have an improving influence, or not?

Yes, they do.

And what about the members of the Council?

Yes, the councilors too.

But surely, Meletus, the members of the Assembly do not corrupt the young? Or do all of them too exert an improving influence?

Yes, they do.

Then it would seem that the whole population of Athens has a refining effect upon the young, except

myself, and I alone demoralize them. Is that your meaning?

Most emphatically, yes.

This is certainly a most unfortunate quality that you have detected in me. Well, let me put another question to you. Take the case of horses. Do you believe that those who improve them make up the whole of mankind, and that there is only one person who has a bad effect on them? Or is the truth just the opposite, that the ability to improve them belongs to one person or to very few persons, who are horse trainers, whereas most people, if they have to do with horses and make use of them, do them harm? Is not this the case, Meletus, both with horses and with all other animals? Of course it is, whether you and Anytus deny it or not. It would be a singular dispensation of fortune for our young people if there is only one person who corrupts them, while all the rest have a beneficial effect. But I need say no more. There is ample proof, Meletus, that you have never bothered your head about the young, and you make it perfectly clear that you have never taken the slightest interest in the cause for the sake of which you are now indicting me.

Here is another point. Tell me seriously, Meletus, is it better to live in a good or in a bad community? Answer my question, like a good fellow; there is nothing difficult about it. Is it not true that wicked people have a bad effect upon those with whom they are in the closest contact, and that good people have a good effect?

Quite true.

Is there anyone who prefers to be harmed rather than benefited by his associates? Answer me, my good man; the law commands you to answer. Is there anyone who prefers to be harmed?

Of course not.

Well, then, when you summon me before this court for corrupting the young and making their characters worse, do you mean that I do so intentionally or unintentionally?

I mean intentionally.

Why, Meletus, are you at your age so much wiser than I at mine? You have discovered that bad people always have a bad effect, and good people a good effect, upon their nearest neighbors. Am I so hopelessly ignorant as not even to realize that by spoiling the character of one of my companions I shall run the risk of getting some harm from him? Because nothing else would make me commit this grave offense intentionally. No, I do not believe it, Meletus, and I do not suppose that anyone else does. Either

I have not a bad influence, or it is unintentional, so that in either case your accusation is false. And if I unintentionally have a bad influence, the correct procedure in cases of such involuntary misdemeanors is not to summon the culprit before this court, but to take him aside privately for instruction and reproof, because obviously if my eyes are opened, I shall stop doing what I do not intend to do. But you deliberately avoided my company in the past and refused to enlighten me, and now you bring me before this court, which is the place appointed for those who need punishment, not for those who need enlightenment.

It is quite clear by now, gentlemen, that Meletus, as I said before, has never shown any degree of interest in this subject. However, I invite you to tell us, Meletus, in what sense you make out that I corrupt the minds of the young. Surely the terms of your indictment make it clear that you accuse me of teaching them to believe in new deities instead of the gods recognized by the state. Is not that the teaching of mine which you say has this demoralizing effect?

That is precisely what I maintain.

Then I appeal to you, Meletus, in the name of these same gods about whom we are speaking, to explain yourself a little more clearly to myself and to the jury, because I cannot make out what your point is. Is it that I teach people to believe in some gods—which implies that I myself believe in gods, and am not a complete atheist, so that I am not guilty on that score—but in different gods from those recognized by the state, so that your accusation rests upon the fact that they are different? Or do you assert that I believe in no gods at all, and teach others to do the same?

Yes, I say that you disbelieve in gods altogether.

You surprise me, Meletus. What is your object in saying that? Do you suggest that I do not believe that the sun and moon are gods, as is the general belief of all mankind?

He certainly does not, gentlemen of the jury, since he says that the sun is a stone and the moon a mass of earth.

Do you imagine that you are prosecuting Anaxagoras, my dear Meletus? Have you so poor an opinion of these gentlemen, and do you assume them to be so illiterate as not to know that the writings of Anaxagoras of Clazomenae are full of theories like these? And do you seriously suggest that it is from me that the young get these ideas, when they can buy them on occasion in the market place for a drachma at most, and so have the laugh on Socrates

if he claims them for his own, to say nothing of their being so silly? Tell me honestly, Meletus, is that your opinion of me? Do I believe in no god?

No, none at all, not in the slightest degree.

You are not at all convincing, Meletus—not even to yourself, I suspect. In my opinion, gentlemen, this man is a thoroughly selfish bully, and has brought this action against me out of sheer wanton aggressiveness and self-assertion. He seems to be devising a sort of intelligence test for me, saying to himself, Will the infallible Socrates realize that I am contradicting myself for my own amusement, or shall I succeed in deceiving him and the rest of my audience?

It certainly seems to me that he is contradicting himself in this indictment, which might just as well run: Socrates is guilty of not believing in the gods, but believing in the gods. And this is pure flippancy.

I ask you to examine with me, gentlemen, the line of reasoning which leads me to this conclusion. You, Meletus, will oblige us by answering my questions. Will you all kindly remember, as I requested at the beginning, not to interrupt if I conduct the discussion in my customary way?

Is there anyone in the world, Meletus, who believes in human activities, and not in human beings? Make him answer, gentlemen, and don't let him keep on making these continual objections. Is there anyone who does not believe in horses, but believes in horses' activities? Or who does not believe in musicians, but believes in musical activities? No, there is not, my worthy friend. If you do not want to answer, I will supply it for you and for these gentlemen too. But the next question you must answer. Is there anyone who believes in supernatural activities and not in supernatural beings?

No.

How good of you to give a bare answer under compulsion by the court! Well, do you assert that I believe and teach others to believe in supernatural activities? It does not matter whether they are new or old. The fact remains that I believe in them according to your statement; indeed you solemnly swore as much in your affidavit. But if I believe in supernatural activities, it follows inevitably that I also believe in supernatural beings. Is not that so? It is. I assume your assent, since you do not answer. Do we not hold that supernatural beings are either gods or the children of gods? Do you agree or not?

Certainly.

Then if I believe in supernatural beings, as you assert, if these supernatural beings are gods in any sense, we shall reach the conclusion which I mentioned just now when I said that you were testing my intelligence for your own amusement, by stating first that I do not believe in gods, and then again that I do, since I believe in supernatural beings. If on the other hand these supernatural beings are bastard children of the gods by nymphs or other mothers, as they are reputed to be, who in the world would believe in the children of gods and not in the gods themselves? It would be as ridiculous as to believe in the young of horses or donkeys and not in horses and donkeys themselves. No, Meletus, there is no avoiding the conclusion that you brought this charge against me as a test of my wisdom, or else in despair of finding a genuine offense of which to accuse me. As for your prospect of convincing any living person with even a smattering of intelligence that belief in supernatural and divine activities does not imply belief in supernatural and divine beings, and vice versa, it is outside all the bounds of possibility.

As a matter of fact, gentlemen, I do not feel that it requires much defense to clear myself of Meletus' accusation. What I have said already is enough. But you know very well the truth of what I said in an earlier part of my speech, that I have incurred a great deal of bitter hostility, and this is what will bring about my destruction, if anything does—not Meletus nor Anytus, but the slander and jealousy of a very large section of the people. They have been fatal to a great many other innocent men, and I suppose will continue to be so; there is no likelihood that they will stop at me. But perhaps someone will say, Do you feel no compunction, Socrates, at having followed a line of action which puts you in danger of the death penalty?

I might fairly reply to him, You are mistaken, my friend, if you think that a man who is worth anything ought to spend his time weighing up the prospects of life and death. He has only one thing to consider in performing any action—that is, whether he is acting rightly or wrongly, like a good man or a bad one. On your view the heroes who died at Troy would be poor creatures, especially the son of Thetis. He, if you remember, made light of danger in comparison with incurring dishonor when his goddess mother warned him, eager as he was to kill Hector, in some such words as these, I fancy: My son, if you avenge your comrade Patroclus' death and kill Hector, you will die yourself—'Next after Hector is thy fate prepared.' When he heard this warning, he made light of his death and danger, being much more afraid of an ignoble life and of failing to avenge his friends. 'Let me die forthwith,' said he, 'when I have requited

the villain, rather than remain here by the beaked ships to be mocked, a burden on the ground.'[1] Do you suppose that he gave a thought to death and danger?

The truth of the matter is this, gentlemen. Where a man has once taken up his stand, either because it seems best to him or in obedience to his orders, there I believe he is bound to remain and face the danger, taking no account of death or anything else before dishonor.

This being so, it would be shocking inconsistency on my part, gentlemen, if, when the officers whom you chose to command me assigned me my position at Potidaea and Amphipolis and Delium, I remained at my post like anyone else and faced death, and yet afterward, when God appointed me, as I supposed and believed, to the duty of leading the philosophical life, examining myself and others, I were then through fear of death or of any other danger to desert my post. That would indeed be shocking, and then I might really with justice be summoned into court for not believing in the gods, and disobeying the oracle, and being afraid of death, and thinking that I am wise when I am not. For let me tell you, gentlemen, that to be afraid of death is only another form of thinking that one is wise when one is not; it is to think that one knows what one does not know. No one knows with regard to death whether it is not really the greatest blessing that can happen to a man, but people dread it as though they were certain that it is the greatest evil, and this ignorance, which thinks that it knows what it does not, must surely be ignorance most culpable. This, I take it, gentlemen, is the degree, and this the nature of my advantage over the rest of mankind, and if I were to claim to be wiser than my neighbor in any respect, it would be in this— that not possessing any real knowledge of what comes after death, I am also conscious that I do not possess it. But I do know that to do wrong and to disobey my superior, whether God or man, is wicked and dishonorable, and so I shall never feel more fear or aversion for something which, for all I know, may really be a blessing, than for those evils which I know to be evils.

Suppose, then, that you acquit me, and pay no attention to Anytus, who has said that either I should not have appeared before this court at all, or, since I have appeared here, I must be put to death, because if I once escaped your sons would all immediately become utterly demoralized by putting the

---

[1]   *Iliad* 18.96 sq.

teaching of Socrates into practice. Suppose that, in view of this, you said to me, Socrates, on this occasion we shall disregard Anytus and acquit you, but only on one condition, that you give up spending your time on this quest and stop philosophizing. If we catch you going on in the same way, you shall be put to death.

Well, supposing, as I said, that you should offer to acquit me on these terms, I should reply, Gentlemen, I am your very grateful and devoted servant, but I owe a greater obedience to God than to you, and so long as I draw breath and have my faculties, I shall never stop practicing philosophy and exhorting you and elucidating the truth for everyone that I meet. I shall go on saying, in my usual way, My very good friend, you are an Athenian and belong to a city which is the greatest and most famous in the world for its wisdom and strength. Are you not ashamed that you give your attention to acquiring as much money as possible, and similarly with reputation and honor, and give no attention or thought to truth and understanding and the perfection of your soul?

And if any of you disputes this and professes to care about these things, I shall not at once let him go or leave him. No, I shall question him and examine him and test him; and if it appears that in spite of his profession he has made no real progress toward goodness, I shall reprove him for neglecting what is of supreme importance, and giving his attention to trivialities. I shall do this to everyone that I meet, young or old, foreigner or fellow citizen, but especially to you, my fellow citizens, inasmuch as you are closer to me in kinship. This, I do assure you, is what my God commands, and it is my belief that no greater good has ever befallen you in this city than my service to my God. For I spend all my time going about trying to persuade you, young and old, to make your first and chief concern not for your bodies nor for your possessions, but for the highest welfare of your souls, proclaiming as I go, Wealth does not bring goodness, but goodness brings wealth and every other blessing, both to the individual and to the state.

Now if I corrupt the young by this message, the message would seem to be harmful, but if anyone says that my message is different from this, he is talking nonsense. And so, gentlemen, I would say, You can please yourselves whether you listen to Anytus or not, and whether you acquit me or not. You know that I am not going to alter my conduct, not even if I have to die a hundred deaths.

Order, please, gentlemen! Remember my request to give me a hearing without interruption. Besides, I believe that it will be to your advantage to listen. I am going to tell you something else, which may provoke a storm of protest, but please restrain yourselves. I assure you that if I am what I claim to be, and you put me to death, you will harm yourselves more than me. Neither Meletus nor Anytus can do me any harm at all; they would not have the power, because I do not believe that the law of God permits a better man to be harmed by a worse. No doubt my accuser might put me to death or have me banished or deprived of civic rights, but even if he thinks—as he probably does, and others too, I dare say—that these are great calamities, I do not think so. I believe that it is far worse to do what he is doing now, trying to put an innocent man to death. For this reason, gentlemen, so far from pleading on my own behalf, as might be supposed, I am really pleading on yours, to save you from misusing the gift of God by condemning me. If you put me to death, you will not easily find anyone to take my place. It is literally true, even if it sounds rather comical, that God has specially appointed me to this city, as though it were a large thoroughbred horse which because of its great size is inclined to be lazy and needs the stimulation of some stinging fly. It seems to me that God has attached me to this city to perform the office of such a fly, and all day long I never cease to settle here, there, and everywhere, rousing, persuading, reproving every one of you. You will not easily find another like me, gentlemen, and if you take my advice you will spare my life. I suspect, however, that before long you will awake from your drowsing, and in your annoyance you will take Anytus' advice and finish me off with a single slap, and then you will go on sleeping till the end of your days, unless God in his care for you sends someone to take my place.

If you doubt whether I am really the sort of person who would have been sent to this city as a gift from God, you can convince yourselves by looking at it in this way. Does it seem natural that I should have neglected my own affairs and endured the humiliation of allowing my family to be neglected for all these years, while I busied myself all the time on your behalf, going like a father or an elder brother to see each one of you privately, and urging you to set your thoughts on goodness? If I had got any enjoyment from it, or if I had been paid for my good advice, there would have been some explanation for my conduct, but as it is you can see for yourselves that although my accusers unblushingly charge me with all sorts of other crimes, there is one thing that they have not had the impudence to pretend on any testimony, and that is that I have ever exacted or asked a fee from anyone. The witness that I can offer to prove the truth of my statement is, I think, a convincing one—my poverty.

It may seem curious that I should go round giving advice like this and busying myself in people's private affairs, and yet never venture publicly to address you as a whole and advise on matters of state. The reason for this is what you have often heard me say before on many other occasions—that I am subject to a divine or supernatural experience, which Meletus saw fit to travesty in his indictment. It began in my early childhood—a sort of voice which comes to me, and when it comes it always dissuades me from what I am proposing to do, and never urges me on. It is this that debars me from entering public life, and a very good thing too, in my opinion, because you may be quite sure, gentlemen, that if I had tried long ago to engage in politics, I should long ago have lost my life, without doing any good either to you or to myself. Please do not be offended if I tell you the truth. No man on earth who conscientiously opposes either you or any other organized democracy, and flatly prevents a great many wrongs and illegalities from taking place in the state to which he belongs, can possibly escape with his life. The true champion of justice, if he intends to survive even for a short time, must necessarily confine himself to private life and leave politics alone.

I will offer you substantial proofs of what I have said—not theories, but what you can appreciate better, facts. Listen while I describe my actual experiences, so that you may know that I would never submit wrongly to any authority through fear of death, but would refuse even at the cost of my life. It will be a commonplace story, such as you often hear in the courts, but it is true.

The only office which I have ever held in our city, gentlemen, was when I was elected to the Council. It so happened that our group was acting as the executive when you decided that the ten commanders who had failed to rescue the men who were lost in the naval engagement should be tried en bloc, which was illegal, as you all recognized later. On this occasion I was the only member of the executive who insisted that you should not act unconstitutionally, and voted against the proposal; and although your leaders were all ready to denounce and arrest me, and you were all urging them on at the top of your voices, I thought that it was my duty to face it out on the side of law and justice rather than support you, through fear of prison or death, in your wrong decision.

This happened while we were still under a democracy. When the oligarchy came into power, the Thirty Commissioners in their turn summoned me and four others to the Round Chamber and instructed us to go and fetch Leon of Salamis from his home for execution. This was of course only one of many instances in which they issued such instructions, their object being to implicate as many people as possible in their wickedness. On this occasion, however, I again made it clear not by my words but by my actions that death did not matter to me at all—if that is not too strong an expression—but that it mattered all the world to me that I should do nothing wrong or wicked. Powerful as it was, that government did not terrify me into doing a wrong action. When we came out of the Round Chamber, the other four went off to Salamis and arrested Leon, and I went home. I should probably have been put to death for this, if the government had not fallen soon afterward. There are plenty of people who will testify to these statements.

Do you suppose that I should have lived as long as I have if I had moved in the sphere of public life, and conducting myself in that sphere like an honorable man, had always upheld the cause of right, and conscientiously set this end above all other things? Not by a very long way, gentlemen; neither would any other man. You will find that throughout my life I have been consistent in any public duties that I have performed, and the same also in my personal dealings. I have never countenanced any action that was incompatible with justice on the part of any person, including those whom some people maliciously call my pupils. I have never set up as any man's teacher, but if anyone, young or old, is eager to hear me conversing and carrying out my private mission, I never grudge him the opportunity; nor do I charge a fee for talking to him, and refuse to talk without one. I am ready to answer questions for rich and poor alike, and I am equally ready if anyone prefers to listen to me and answer my questions. If any given one of these people becomes a good citizen or a bad one, I cannot fairly be held responsible, since I have never promised or imparted any teaching to anybody, and if anyone asserts that he has ever learned or heard from me privately anything which was not open to everyone else, you may be quite sure that he is not telling the truth.

But how is it that some people enjoy spending a

great deal of time in my company? You have heard the reason, gentlemen; I told you quite frankly. It is because they enjoy hearing me examine those who think that they are wise when they are not—an experience which has its amusing side. This duty I have accepted, as I said, in obedience to God's commands given in oracles and dreams and in every other way that any other divine dispensation has ever impressed a duty upon man. This is a true statement, gentlemen, and easy to verify. If it is a fact that I am in process of corrupting some of the young, and have succeeded already in corrupting others, and if it were a fact that some of the latter, being now grown up, had discovered that I had ever given them bad advice when they were young, surely they ought now to be coming forward to denounce and punish me. And if they did not like to do it themselves, you would expect some of their families—their fathers and brothers and other near relations—to remember it now, if their own flesh and blood had suffered any harm from me. Certainly a great many of them have found their way into this court, as I can see for myself—first Crito over there, my contemporary and near neighbor, the father of this young man Critobulus, and then Lysanias of Sphettus, the father of Aeschines here, and next Antiphon of Cephisus, over there, the father of Epigenes. Then besides there are all those whose brothers have been members of our circle—Nicostratus, the son of Theozotides, the brother of Theodotus, but Theodotus is dead, so he cannot appeal to his brother, and Paralus here, the son of Demodocus, whose brother was Theages. And here is Adimantus, the son of Ariston, whose brother Plato is over there, and Aeantodorus, whose brother Apollodorus is here on this side. I can name many more besides, some of whom Meletus most certainly ought to have produced as witnesses in the course of his speech. If he forgot to do so then, let him do it now—I am willing to make way for him. Let him state whether he has any such evidence to offer. On the contrary, gentlemen, you will find that they are all prepared to help me—the corrupter and evil genius of their nearest and dearest relatives, as Meletus and Anytus say. The actual victims of my corrupting influence might perhaps be excused for helping me; but as for the uncorrupted, their relations of mature age, what other reason can they have for helping me except the right and proper one, that they know Meletus is lying and I am telling the truth?

There, gentlemen, that, and perhaps a little more to the same effect, is the substance of what I can say in my defense. It may be that some one of you, re-

membering his own case, will be annoyed that whereas he, in standing his trial upon a less serious charge than this, made pitiful appeals to the jury with floods of tears, and had his infant children produced in court to excite the maximum of sympathy, and many of his relatives and friends as well, I on the contrary intend to do nothing of the sort, and that, although I am facing, as it might appear, the utmost danger. It may be that one of you, reflecting on these facts, will be prejudiced against me, and being irritated by his reflections, will give his vote in anger. If one of you is so disposed—I do not expect it, but there is the possibility—I think that I should be quite justified in saying to him, My dear sir, of course I have some relatives. To quote the very words of Homer, even I am not sprung 'from an oak or from a rock,'[2] but from human parents, and consequently I have relatives—yes, and sons too, gentlemen, three of them, one almost grown up and the other two only children—but all the same I am not going to produce them here and beseech you to acquit me.

Why do I not intend to do anything of this kind? Not out of perversity, gentlemen, nor out of contempt for you; whether I am brave or not in the face of death has nothing to do with it. The point is that for my own credit and yours and for the credit of the state as a whole, I do not think that it is right for me to use any of these methods at my age and with my reputation—which may be true or it may be false, but at any rate the view is held that Socrates is different from the common run of mankind. Now if those of you who are supposed to be distinguished for wisdom or courage or any other virtue are to behave in this way, it would be a disgrace. I have often noticed that some people of this type, for all their high standing, go to extraordinary lengths when they come up for trial, which shows that they think it will be a dreadful thing to lose their lives—as though they would be immortal if you did not put them to death! In my opinion these people bring disgrace upon our city. Any of our visitors might be excused for thinking that the finest specimens of Athenian manhood, whom their fellow citizens select on their merits to rule over them and hold other high positions, are no better than women. If you have even the smallest reputation, gentlemen, you ought not to descend to these methods; and if we do so, you must not give us license. On the contrary, you must make it clear that anyone who stages these pathetic scenes and so brings ridicule upon our city is

---

[2]   *Odyssey* 19.163.

far more likely to be condemned than if he kept perfectly quiet.

But apart from all question of appearances, gentlemen, I do not think that it is right for a man to appeal to the jury or to get himself acquitted by doing so; he ought to inform them of the facts and convince them by argument. The jury does not sit to dispense justice as a favor, but to decide where justice lies, and the oath which they have sworn is not to show favor at their own discretion, but to return a just and lawful verdict. It follows that we must not develop in you, nor you allow to grow in yourselves, the habit of perjury; that would be sinful for us both. Therefore you must not expect me, gentlemen, to behave toward you in a way which I consider neither reputable nor moral nor consistent with my religious duty, and above all you must not expect it when I stand charged with impiety by Meletus here. Surely it is obvious that if I tried to persuade you and prevail upon you by my entreaties to go against your solemn oath, I should be teaching you contempt for religion, and by my very defense I should be accusing myself of having no religious belief. But that is very far from the truth. I have a more sincere belief, gentlemen, than any of my accusers, and I leave it to you and to God to judge me as it shall be best for me and for yourselves.

There are a great many reasons, gentlemen, why I am not distressed by this result—I mean your condemnation of me—but the chief reason is that the result was not unexpected. What does surprise me is the number of votes cast on the two sides. I should never have believed that it would be such a close thing, but now it seems that if a mere thirty votes had gone the other way, I should have been acquitted. Even as it is, I feel that so far as Meletus' part is concerned I have been acquitted, and not only that, but anyone can see that if Anytus and Lycon had not come forward to accuse me, Meletus would actually have forfeited his one thousand drachmas for not having obtained one fifth of the votes.

However, we must face the fact that he demands the death penalty. Very good. What alternative penalty shall I propose to you, gentlemen? Obviously it must be adequate. Well, what penalty do I deserve to pay or suffer, in view of what I have done?

I have never lived an ordinary quiet life. I did not care for the things that most people care about—making money, having a comfortable home, high military or civil rank, and all the other activities, political appointments, secret societies, party organizations, which go on in our city. I thought that I was really too strict in my principles to survive if I went in for this sort of thing. So instead of taking a course which would have done no good either to you or to me, I set myself to do you individually in private what I hold to be the greatest possible service. I tried to persuade each one of you not to think more of practical advantages than of his mental and moral well-being, or in general to think more of advantage than of well-being in the case of the state or of anything else. What do I deserve for behaving in this way? Some reward, gentlemen, if I am bound to suggest what I really deserve, and what is more, a reward which would be appropriate for myself. Well, what is appropriate for a poor man who is a public benefactor and who requires leisure for giving you moral encouragement? Nothing could be more appropriate for such a person than free maintenance at the state's expense. He deserves it much more than any victor in the races at Olympia, whether he wins with a single horse or a pair or a team of four. These people give you the semblance of success, but I give you the reality; they do not need maintenance, but I do. So if I am to suggest an appropriate penalty which is strictly in accordance with justice, I suggest free maintenance by the state.

Perhaps when I say this I may give you the impression, as I did in my remarks about exciting sympathy and making passionate appeals that I am showing a deliberate perversity. That is not so, gentlemen. The real position is this. I am convinced that I never wrong anyone intentionally, but I cannot convince you of this, because we have had so little time for discussion. If it was your practice, as it is with other nations, to give not one day but several to the hearing of capital trials, I believe that you might have been convinced, but under present conditions it is not easy to dispose of grave allegations in a short space of time. So, being convinced that I do no wrong to anybody, I can hardly be expected to wrong myself by asserting that I deserve something bad, or by proposing a corresponding penalty. Why should I? For fear of suffering this penalty proposed by Meletus, when, as I said, I do not know whether it is a good thing or a bad? Do you expect me to choose something which I know very well is bad by making my counterproposal? Imprisonment? Why should I spend my days in prison, in subjection to the periodically appointed officers of the law? A fine, with imprisonment until it is paid? In my case the effect would be just the same, because I have no money to pay a fine. Or shall I suggest banishment? You would very likely accept the suggestion.

I should have to be desperately in love with life to do that, gentlemen. I am not so blind that I cannot see that you, my fellow citizens, have come to the end of your patience with my discussions and conversations. You have found them too irksome and irritating, and now you are trying to get rid of them. Will any other people find them easy to put up with? That is most unlikely, gentlemen. A fine life I should have if I left this country at my age and spent the rest of my days trying one city after another and being turned out every time! I know very well that wherever I go the young people will listen to my conversation just as they do here, and if I try to keep them off, they will make their elders drive me out, while if I do not, the fathers and other relatives will drive me out of their own accord for the sake of the young.

Perhaps someone may say, But surely, Socrates, after you have left us you can spend the rest of your life in quietly minding your own business.

This is the hardest thing of all to make some of you understand. If I say that this would be disobedience to God, and that is why I cannot 'mind my own business,' you will not believe that I am serious. If on the other hand I tell you that to let no day pass without discussing goodness and all the other subjects about which you hear me talking and examining both myself and others is really the very best thing that a man can do, and that life without this sort of examination is not worth living, you will be even less inclined to believe me. Nevertheless that is how it is, gentlemen, as I maintain, though it is not easy to convince you of it. Besides, I am not accustomed to think of myself as deserving punishment. If I had money, I would have suggested a fine that I could afford, because that would not have done me any harm. As it is, I cannot, because I have none, unless of course you like to fix the penalty at what I could pay. I suppose I could probably afford a mina. I suggest a fine of that amount.

One moment, gentlemen, Plato here, and Crito and Critobulus and Apollodorus, want me to propose thirty minas, on their security. Very well, I agree to this sum, and you can rely upon these gentlemen for its payment.

Well, gentlemen, for the sake of a very small gain in time you are going to earn the reputation—and the blame from those who wish to disparage our city—of having put Socrates to death, 'that wise man'—because they will say I am wise even if I am

not, these people who want to find fault with you. If you had waited just a little while, you would have had your way in the course of nature. You can see that I am well on in life and near to death. I am saying this not to all of you but to those who voted for my execution, and I have something else to say to them as well.

No doubt you think, gentlemen, that I have been condemned for lack of the arguments which I could have used if I had thought it right to leave nothing unsaid or undone to secure my acquittal. But that is very far from the truth. It is not a lack of arguments that has caused my condemnation, but a lack of effrontery and impudence, and the fact that I have refused to address you in the way which would give you most pleasure. You would have liked to hear me weep and wail, doing and saying all sorts of things which I regard as unworthy of myself, but which you are used to hearing from other people. But I did not think then that I ought to stoop to servility because I was in danger, and I do not regret now the way in which I pleaded my case. I would much rather die as the result of this defense than live as the result of the other sort. In a court of law, just as in warfare, neither I nor any other ought to use his wits to escape death by any means. In battle it is often obvious that you could escape being killed by giving up your arms and throwing yourself upon the mercy of your pursuers, and in every kind of danger there are plenty of devices for avoiding death if you are unscrupulous enough to stick at nothing. But I suggest, gentlemen, that the difficulty is not so much to escape death; the real difficulty is to escape from doing wrong, which is far more fleet of foot. In this present instance I, the slow old man, have been overtaken by the slower of the two, but my accusers, who are clever and quick, have been overtaken by the faster—by iniquity. When I leave this court I shall go away condemned by you to death, but they will go away convicted by truth herself of depravity and wickedness. And they accept their sentence even as I accept mine. No doubt it was bound to be so, and I think that the result is fair enough.

Having said so much, I feel moved to prophesy to you who have given your vote against me, for I am now at that point where the gift of prophecy comes most readily to men—at the point of death. I tell you, my executioners, that as soon as I am dead, vengeance shall fall upon you with a punishment far more painful than your killing of me. You have brought about my death in the belief that through it you will be delivered from submitting your conduct to criticism, but I say that the result will be just the opposite. You will have more critics, whom up till now I have restrained without your knowing it, and being younger they will be harsher to you and will cause you more annoyance. If you expect to stop denunciation of your wrong way of life by putting people to death, there is something amiss with your reasoning. This way of escape is neither possible nor creditable. The best and easiest way is not to stop the mouths of others, but to make yourselves as good men as you can. This is my last message to you who voted for my condemnation.

As for you who voted for my acquittal, I should very much like to say a few words to reconcile you to the result, while the officials are busy and I am not yet on my way to the place where I must die. I ask you, gentlemen, to spare me these few moments. There is no reason why we should not exchange fancies while the law permits. I look upon you as my friends, and I want you to understand the right way of regarding my present position.

Gentlemen of the jury—for *you* deserve to be so called—I have had a remarkable experience. In the past the prophetic voice to which I have become accustomed has always been my constant companion, opposing me even in quite trivial things if I was going to take the wrong course. Now something has happened to me, as you can see, which might be thought and is commonly considered to be a supreme calamity; yet neither when I left home this morning, nor when I was taking my place here in the court, nor at any point in any part of my speech did the divine sign oppose me. In other discussions it has often checked me in the middle of a sentence, but this time it has never opposed me in any part of this business in anything that I have said or done. What do I suppose to be the explanation? I will tell you. I suspect that this thing that has happened to me is a blessing, and we are quite mistaken in supposing death to be an evil. I have good grounds for thinking this, because my accustomed sign could not have failed to oppose me if what I was doing had not been sure to bring some good result.

We should reflect that there is much reason to hope for a good result on other grounds as well. Death is one of two things. Either it is annihilation, and the dead have no consciousness of anything, or, as we are told, it is really a change—a migration of the soul from this place to another. Now if there is no consciousness but only a dreamless sleep, death must be a marvelous gain. I suppose that if anyone were told to pick out the night on which he slept so soundly as not even to dream, and then to compare it with all the other nights and days of his life, and then were told to say, after due consideration, how many better and happier days and nights than this he had spent in the course of his life—well, I think that the Great King himself, to say nothing of any private person, would find these days and nights easy to count in comparison with the rest. If death is like this, then, I call it gain, because the whole of time, if you look at it in this way, can be regarded as no more than one single night. If on the other hand death is a removal from here to some other place, and if what we are told is true, that all the dead are there, what greater blessing could there be than this, gentlemen? If on arrival in the other world, beyond the reach of our so-called justice, one will find there the true judges who are said to preside in those courts, Minos and Rhadamanthus and Aeacus and Triptolemus and all those other half-divinities who were upright in their earthly life, would that be an unrewarding journey? Put it in this way. How much would one of you give to meet Orpheus and Musaeus, Hesiod and Homer? I am willing to die ten times over if this account is true. It would be a specially interesting experience for me to join them there, to meet Palamedes and Ajax, the son of Telamon, and any other heroes of the old days who met their death through an unfair trial, and to compare my fortunes with theirs—it would be rather amusing, I think. And above all I should like to spend my time there, as here, in examining and searching people's minds, to find out who is really wise among them, and who only thinks that he is. What would one not give, gentlemen, to be able to question the leader of that great host against Troy, or Odysseus, or Sisyphus, or the thousands of other men and women whom one could mention, to talk and mix and argue with whom would be unimaginable happiness? At any rate I presume that they do not put one to death there for such conduct, because apart from the other happiness in which their world surpasses ours, they are now immortal for the rest of time, if what we are told is true.

You too, gentlemen of the jury, must look forward to death with confidence, and fix your minds on this one belief, which is certain—that nothing can harm a good man either in life or after death, and his fortunes are not a matter of indifference to the gods. This present experience of mine has not come about mechanically. I am quite clear that the time had come when it was better for me to die and be released from my distractions. That is why my sign never turned me back. For my own part I bear no grudge at all against those who condemned me and accused me, although it was not with this kind intention that they did so, but because they thought that they were hurting me; and that is culpable of them. However, I ask them to grant me one favor. When my sons grow up, gentlemen, if you think that they are putting money or anything else before goodness, take your revenge by plaguing them as I plagued you; and if they fancy themselves for no reason, you must scold them just as I scolded you, for neglecting the important things and thinking that they are good for something when they are good for nothing. If you do this, I shall have had justice at your hands, both I myself and my children.

Now it is time that we were going, I to die and you to live, but which of us has the happier prospect is unknown to anyone but God.

Aristotle (384–322 B.C.)
WISDOM AND PHILOSOPHY

Aristotle argues that philosophy starts in wonder and puzzlement and seeks wisdom, which he characterizes as knowledge of first principles and causes. In seeking these principles, he reviews the philosophical ideas of various Pre-Socratic philosophers. Aristotle's views on wisdom are discussed at the end of Section A of the introductory essay to Part I.

READING QUESTIONS

While reading the selection, try to answer the following questions and identify the passages that support your answers:

1.   What is wisdom according to Aristotle?
2.   What reasons does he give in support of his views on wisdom?
3.   Does Aristotle's position entail the claim that knowledge makes us better persons? If so, how and why? If not, why not?
4.   Why was Aristotle interested in the doctrines of the Pre-Socratic philosophers?
5.   Does wisdom involve a practical element? Why or why not?

Reprinted from "Metaphysics," translated by W.D. Ross (ed.), *The Oxford Translation of Aristotle,* and included in Richard McKeon (ed.), *The Basic Works of Aristotle* (New York: Random House, 1966), pp. 689–700. Copyright © 1966 by Oxford University Press, Clarendon Press. Reprinted by permission of Oxford University Press.

BOOK A (1)

1 All men by nature desire to know. An indication of this is the delight we take in our senses; for even apart from their usefulness they are loved for themselves; and above all others the sense of sight. For not only with a view to action, but even when we are not going to do anything, we prefer seeing (one might say) to everything else. The reason is that this, most of all the senses, makes us know and brings to light many differences between things.

By nature animals are born with the faculty of sensation, and from sensation memory is produced in some of them, though not in others. And therefore the former are more intelligent and apt at learning than those which cannot remember; those which are incapable of hearing sounds are intelligent though they cannot be taught, e.g. the bee, and any other race of animals that may be like it; and those which besides memory have this sense of hearing can be taught.

The animals other than man live by appearances and memories, and have but little of connected experience; but the human race lives also by art and reasonings. Now from memory experience is produced in men; for the several memories of the same thing produce finally the capacity for a single experience. And experience seems pretty much like science and art, but really science and art come to men *through* experience; for 'experience made art', as Polus says,[1] 'but inexperience luck'. Now art arises when from many notions gained by experience one universal judgement about a class of objects is produced. For to have a judgement that when Callias was ill of this disease this did him good, and similarly in the case of Socrates and in many individual cases, is a matter of experience; but to judge that it had done good to all persons of a certain constitution, marked off in one class, when they were ill of this disease, e.g. to phlegmatic or bilious people when burning with fever—this is a matter of art.

With a view to action experience seems in no respect inferior to art, and men of experience succeed even better than those who have theory without experience. (The reason is that experience is knowledge of individuals, art of universals, and actions and productions are all concerned with the individual; for the physician does not cure *man*, except in an incidental way, but Callias or Socrates or some other called by some such individual name, who happens to be a man. If, then, a man has the theory without the experience, and recognizes the universal but does not know the individual included in this, he will often fail to cure; for it is the individual that is to be cured.) But yet we think that *knowledge* and *understanding* belong to art rather than to experience, and we suppose artists to be wiser than men of experience (which implies that Wisdom depends in all cases rather on knowledge); and this because the former know the cause, but the latter do not. For men of experience know that the thing is so, but do not know why, while the others know the 'why' and the cause. Hence we think also that the master-workers in each craft are more honourable and know in a truer sense and are wiser than the manual workers, because they know the causes of the things that are done (we think the manual workers are like certain lifeless things which act indeed, but act without

knowing what they do, as fire burns—but while the lifeless things perform each of their functions by a natural tendency, the labourers perform them through habit); thus we view them as being wiser not in virtue of being able to act, but of having the theory for themselves and knowing the causes. And in general it is a sign of the man who knows and of the man who does not know, that the former can teach, and therefore we think art more truly knowledge than experience is; for artists can teach, and men of mere experience cannot.

Again, we do not regard any of the senses as Wisdom; yet surely these give the most authoritative knowledge of particulars. But they do not tell us the 'why' of anything—e.g. why fire is hot; they only say *that* it is hot.

At first he who invented any art whatever that went beyond the common perceptions of man was naturally admired by men, not only because there was something useful in the inventions, but because he was thought wise and superior to the rest. But as more arts were invented, and some were directed to the necessities of life, others to recreation, the inventors of the latter were naturally always regarded as wiser than the inventors of the former, because their branches of knowledge did not aim at utility. Hence when all such inventions were already established, the sciences which do not aim at giving pleasure or at the necessities of life were discovered, and first in the places where men first began to have leisure. This is why the mathematical arts were founded in Egypt; for there the priestly caste was allowed to be at leisure.

We have said in the *Ethics*[2] what the difference is between art and science and the other kindred faculties; but the point of our present discussion is this, that all men suppose what is called Wisdom to deal with the first causes and the principles of things; so that, as has been said before, the man of experience is thought to be wiser than the possessors of any sense-perception whatever, the artist wiser than the men of experience, the master-worker than the mechanic, and the theoretical kinds of knowledge to be more of the nature of Wisdom than the productive. Clearly then Wisdom is knowledge about certain principles and causes.

2 Since we are seeking this knowledge, we must inquire of what kind are the causes and the principles, the knowledge of which is Wisdom. If one were to

---

[1] Cf. Pl. *Gorg.* 448 c, 462 B.C.

[2] 1139[b] 14–1141[b] 8.

take the notions we have about the wise man, this might perhaps make the answer more evident. We suppose first, then, that the wise man knows all things, as far as possible, although he has not knowledge of each of them in detail; secondly, that he who can learn things that are difficult, and not easy for man to know, is wise (sense-perception is common to all, and therefore easy and no mark of Wisdom); again, that he who is more exact and more capable of teaching the causes is wiser, in every branch of knowledge; and that of the sciences, also, that which is desirable on its own account and for the sake of knowing it is more of the nature of Wisdom than that which is desirable on account of its results, and the superior science is more of the nature of Wisdom than the ancillary; for the wise man must not be ordered but must order, and he must not obey another, but the less wise must obey *him*.

Such and so many are the notions, then, which we have about Wisdom and the wise. Now of these characteristics that of knowing all things must belong to him who has in the highest degree universal knowledge; for he knows in a sense all the instances that fall under the universal. And these things, the most universal, are on the whole the hardest for men to know; for they are farthest from the senses. And the most exact of the sciences are those which deal most with first principles; for those which involve fewer principles are more exact than those which involve additional principles, e.g. arithmetic than geometry. But the science which investigates causes is also *instructive*, in a higher degree, for the people who instruct us are those who tell the causes of each thing. And understanding and knowledge pursued for their own sake are found most in the knowledge of that which is most knowable (for he who chooses to know for the sake of knowing will choose most readily that which is most truly knowledge, and such is the knowledge of that which is most knowable); and the first principles and the causes are most knowable; for by reason of these, and from these, all other things come to be known, and not these by means of the things subordinate to them. And the science which knows to what end each thing must be done is the most authoritative of the sciences, and more authoritative than any ancillary science; and this end is the good of that thing, and in general the supreme good in the whole of nature. Judged by all the tests we have mentioned, then, the name in question falls to the same science; this must be a science that investigates the first principles and causes; for the good, i.e. the end, is one of the causes.

That it is not a science of production is clear even from the history of the earliest philosophers. For it is owing to their wonder that men both now begin and at first began to philosophize; they wondered originally at the obvious difficulties, then advanced little by little and stated difficulties about the greater matters, e.g. about the phenomena of the moon and those of the sun and of the stars, and about the genesis of the universe. And a man who is puzzled and wonders thinks himself ignorant (whence even the lover of myth is in a sense a lover of Wisdom, for the myth is composed of wonders); therefore since they philosophized in order to escape from ignorance, evidently they were pursuing science in order to know, and not for any utilitarian end. And this is confirmed by the facts; for it was when almost all the necessities of life and the things that make for comfort and recreation had been secured, that such knowledge began to be sought. Evidently then we do not seek it for the sake of any other advantage; but as the man is free, we say, who exists for his own sake and not for another's, so we pursue this as the only free science, for it alone exists for its own sake.

Hence also the possession of it might be justly regarded as beyond human power; for in many ways human nature is in bondage, so that according to Simonides 'God alone can have this privilege', and it is unfitting that man should not be content to seek the knowledge that is suited to him. If, then, there is something in what the poets say, and jealousy is natural to the divine power, it would probably occur in this case above all, and all who excelled in this knowledge would be unfortunate. But the divine power cannot be jealous (nay, according to the proverb, 'bards tell many a lie'), nor should any other science be thought more honourable than one of this sort. For the most divine science is also most honourable; and this science alone must be, in two ways, most divine. For the science which it would be most meet for God to have is a divine science, and so is any science that deals with divine objects; and this science alone has both these qualities; for (1) God is thought to be among the causes of all things and to be a first principle, and (2) such a science either God alone can have, or God above all others. All the sciences, indeed, are more necessary than this, but none is better.

Yet the acquisition of it must in a sense end in something which is the opposite of our original inquiries. For all men begin, as we said, by wondering that things are as they are, as they do about self-moving marionettes, or about the solstices or the incommensurability of the diagonal of a square with the side; for it seems wonderful to all who have not yet seen the reason, that there is a thing which cannot be measured even by the smallest unit. But we must end in the contrary and, according to the proverb, the better state, as is the case in these instances too when men learn the cause; for there is nothing which would surprise a geometer so much as if the diagonal turned out to be commensurable.

We have stated, then, what is the nature of the science we are searching for, and what is the mark which our search and our whole investigation must reach.

3 Evidently we have to acquire knowledge of the original causes (for we say we know each thing only when we think we recognize its first cause), and causes are spoken of in four senses. In one of these we mean the substance, i.e. the essence (for the 'why' is reducible finally to the definition, and the ultimate 'why' is a cause and principle); in another the matter or substratum, in a third the source of the change, and in a fourth the cause opposed to this, the purpose and the good (for this is the end of all generation and change). We have studied these causes sufficiently in our work on nature,[3] but yet let us call to our aid those who have attacked the investigation of being and philosophized about reality before us. For obviously they too speak of certain principles and causes; to go over their views, then, will be of profit to the present inquiry, for we shall either find another kind of cause, or be more convinced of the correctness of those which we now maintain.

Of the first philosophers, then, most thought the principles which were of the nature of matter were the only principles of all things. That of which all things that are consist, the first from which they come to be, the last into which they are resolved (the substance remaining, but changing in its modifications), this they say is the element and this the principle of things, and therefore they think nothing is either generated or destroyed, since this sort of entity is always conserved, as we say Socrates neither comes to be absolutely when he comes to be beautiful or musical, nor ceases to be when he loses these characteristics, because the substratum, Socrates himself, remains. Just so they say nothing else comes to be or ceases to be; for there must be some entity—either one or more than one—from which all other things come to be, it being conserved.

Yet they do not all agree as to the number and the nature of these principles. Thales, the founder of this type of philosophy, says the principle is water (for which reason he declared that the earth rests on water), getting the notion perhaps from seeing that the nutriment of all things is moist, and that heat itself is generated from the moist and kept alive by it (and that from which they come to be is a principle of all things). He got his notion from this fact, and from the fact that the seeds of all things have a moist nature, and that water is the origin of the nature of moist things.

Some[4] think that even the ancients who lived long before the present generation, and first framed accounts of the gods, had a similar view of nature; for they made Ocean and Tethys the parents of creation,[5] and described the oath of the gods as being by water,[6] to which they give the name of Styx; for what is oldest is most honourable, and the most honourable thing is that by which one swears. It may perhaps be uncertain whether this opinion about nature is primitive and ancient, but Thales at any rate is said to have declared himself thus about the first cause. Hippo no one would think fit to include among these thinkers, because of the paltriness of his thought.

Anaximenes and Diogenes make air prior to water, and the most primary of the simple bodies, while Hippasus of Metapontium and Heraclitus of Ephesus say this of fire, and Empedocles says it of the four elements (adding a fourth—earth—to those which have been named); for these, he says, always remain and do not come to be, except that they come to be more or fewer, being aggregated into one and segregated out of one.

Anaxagoras of Clazomenae, who, though older than Empedocles, was later in his philosophical activity, says the principles are infinite in number; for he says almost all the things that are made of parts like themselves, in the manner of water or fire, are generated and destroyed in this way, only by aggregation and segregation, and are not in any other sense generated or destroyed, but remain eternally.

From these facts one might think that the only cause is the so-called material cause; but as men thus advanced, the very facts opened the way for them and joined in forcing them to investigate the sub-

---

[3] *Phys.* ii. 3, 7.

[4] The reference is probably to Plato (*Crat.* 402 B, *Theaet.* 152 E, 162 D, 180 C).

[5] Hom. *Il.* xiv, 201, 246.

[6] *Ibid.* ii. 755, xiv. 271, xv. 37.

ject. However true it may be that all generation and destruction proceed from some one or (for that matter) from more elements, why does this happen and what is the cause? For at least the substratum itself does not make itself change; e.g. neither the wood nor the bronze causes the change of either of them, nor does the wood manufacture a bed and the bronze a statue, but something else is the cause of the change. And to seek this is to seek the second cause, as *we* should say—that from which comes the beginning of the movement. Now those who at the very beginning set themselves to this kind of inquiry, and said the substratum was one,[7] were not at all dissatisfied with themselves; but some at least of those who maintain it to be one[8]—as though defeated by this search for the second cause—say the one and nature as a whole is unchangeable not only in respect of generation and destruction (for this is a primitive belief, and all agreed in it), but also of all other change; and this view is peculiar to them. Of those who said the universe was one, then, none succeeded in discovering a cause of this sort, except perhaps Parmenides, and he only inasmuch as he supposes that there is not only one but also in some sense two causes. But for those who make more elements[9] it is more possible to state the second cause, e.g. for those who make hot and cold, or fire and earth, the elements; for they treat fire as having a nature which fits it to move things, and water and earth and such things they treat in the contrary way.

When these men and the principles of this kind had had their day, as the latter were found inadequate to generate the nature of things men were again forced by the truth itself, as we said,[10] to inquire into the next kind of cause. For it is not likely either that fire or earth or any such element should be the reason why things manifest goodness and beauty both in their being and in their coming to be, or that those thinkers should have supposed it was; nor again could it be right to entrust so great a matter to spontaneity and chance. When one man[11] said, then, that reason was present—as in animals, so throughout nature—as the cause of order and of all arrangement, he seemed like a sober man in contrast with the random talk of his predecessors. We know that Anaxagoras certainly adopted these views,

but Hermotimus of Clazomenae is credited with expressing them earlier. Those who thought thus stated that there is a principle of things which is at the same time the cause of beauty, and that sort of cause from which things acquire movement.

4 One might suspect that Hesiod was the first to look for such a thing—or some one else who put love or desire among existing things as a principle, as Parmenides, too, does; for he, in constructing the genesis of the universe, says:—

> Love first of all the Gods she planned.

And Hesiod says:—

> First of all things was chaos made, and then
> Broad-breasted earth, . . .
> And love, 'mid all the gods pre-eminent,

which implies that among existing things there must be from the first a cause which will move things and bring them together. How these thinkers should be arranged with regard to priority of discovery let us be allowed to decide later;[12] but since the contraries of the various forms of good were also perceived to be present in nature—not only order and the beautiful, but also disorder and the ugly, and bad things in greater number than good, and ignoble things than beautiful—therefore another thinker introduced friendship and strife, each of the two the cause of one of these two sets of qualities. For if we were to follow out the view of Empedocles, and interpret it according to its meaning and not to its lisping expression, we should find that friendship is the cause of good things, and strife of bad. Therefore, if we said that Empedocles in a sense both mentions, and is the first to mention, the bad and the good as principles, we should perhaps be right, since the cause of all goods is the good itself.

These thinkers, as we say, evidently grasped, and to this extent, two of the causes which we distinguished in our work on nature[13]—the matter and the source of the movement—vaguely, however, and with no clearness, but as untrained men behave in fights; for they go round their opponents and often strike fine blows, but they do not fight on scientific principles, and so too these thinkers do not seem to know what they say; for it is evident that, as a rule, they make no use of their causes except to a small

[7]   Thales, Anaximenes, and Heraclitus.
[8]   The Eleatics.
[9]   The reference is probably to Empedocles.
[10]   [2]18.
[11]   Anaxagoras.
[12]   The promise is not fulfilled.
[13]   *Phys.* ii. 3, 7.

extent. For Anaxagoras uses reason as a *deus ex machina* for the making of the world, and when he is at a loss to tell from what cause something necessarily is, then he drags reason in, but in all other cases ascribes events to anything rather than to reason.[14] And Empedocles, though he uses the causes to a greater extent than this, neither does so sufficiently nor attains consistency in their use. At least, in many cases he makes love segregate things, and strife aggregate them. For whenever the universe is dissolved into its elements by strife, fire is aggregated into one, and so is each of the other elements; but whenever again under the influence of love they come together into one, the parts must again be segregated out of each element.

Empedocles, then, in contrast with his predecessors, was the first to introduce the dividing of this cause, not positing one source of movement, but different and contrary sources. Again, he was the first to speak of four material elements; yet he does not *use* four, but treats them as two only; he treats fire by itself, and its opposites—earth, air, and water—as one kind of thing. We may learn this by study of his verses.

This philosopher then, as we say, has spoken of the principles in this way, and made them of this number. Leucippus and his associate Democritus say that the full and the empty are the elements, calling the one being and the other non-being—the full and solid being being, the empty non-being (whence they say being no more is than non-being, because the solid no more is than the empty); and they make these the material causes of things. And as those who make the underlying substance one generate all other things by its modifications, supposing the rare and the dense to be the sources of the modifications, in the same way these philosophers say the differences in the elements are the causes of all other qualities. These differences, they say, are three—shape and order and position. For they say the real is differentiated only by 'rhythm' and 'inter-contact' and 'turning'; and of these rhythm is shape, inter-contact is order, and turning is position; for A differs from N in shape, AN from NA in order, ⊞ from H in position. The question of movement—whence or how it is to belong to things—these thinkers, like the others, lazily neglected.

Regarding the two causes, then, as we say, the inquiry seems to have been pushed thus far by the early philosophers.

5 Contemporaneously with these philosophers and before them, the so-called Pythagoreans, who were the first to take up mathematics, not only advanced this study, but also having been brought up in it they thought its principles were the principles of all things. Since of these principles numbers are by nature the first, and in numbers they seemed to see many resemblances to the things that exist and come into being—more than in fire and earth and water (such and such a modification of numbers being justice, another being soul and reason, another being opportunity—and similarly almost all other things being numerically expressible); since, again, they saw that the modifications and the ratios of the musical scales were expressible in numbers;—since, then, all other things seemed in their whole nature to be modelled on numbers, and numbers seemed to be the first things in the whole of nature, they supposed the elements of numbers to be the elements of all things, and the whole heaven to be a musical scale and a number. And all the properties of numbers and scales which they could show to agree with the attributes and parts and the whole arrangement of the heavens, they collected and fitted into their scheme; and if there was a gap anywhere, they readily made additions so as to make their whole theory coherent. E.g. as the number 10 is thought to be perfect and to comprise the whole nature of numbers, they say that the bodies which move through the heavens are ten, but as the visible bodies are only nine, to meet this they invent a tenth—the 'counter-earth'. We have discussed these matters more exactly elsewhere.[15]

But the object of our review is that we may learn from these philosophers also what they suppose to be the principles and how these fall under the causes we have named. Evidently, then, these thinkers also consider that number is the principle both as matter for things and as forming both their modifications and their permanent states, and hold that the elements of number are the even and the odd, and that of these the latter is limited, and the former unlimited; and that the One proceeds from both of these (for it is both even and odd), and number from the One; and that the whole heaven, as has been said, is numbers.

Other members of this same school say there are ten principles, which they arrange in two columns of cognates—limit and unlimited, odd and even, one

[14] Cf. Pl. *Phaedo*, 98 BC., *Laws*, 967 B–D.

[15] *De Caelo*, ii. 13.

and plurality, right and left, male and female, resting and moving, straight and curved, light and darkness, good and bad, square and oblong. In this way Alcmaeon of Croton seems also to have conceived the matter, and either he got this view from them or they got it from him; for he expressed himself similarly to them. For he says most human affairs go in pairs, meaning not definite contrarieties such as the Pythagoreans speak of, but any chance contrarieties, e.g. white and black, sweet and bitter, good and bad, great and small. He threw out indefinite suggestions about the other contrarieties, but the Pythagoreans declared both how many and which their contrarieties are.

From both these schools, then, we can learn this much, that the contraries are the principles of things; and how many these principles are and which they are, we can learn from one of the two schools. But how these principles can be brought together under the causes we have named has not been clearly and articulately stated by them; they seem, however, to range the elements under the head of matter; for out of these as immanent parts they say substance is composed and moulded.

From these facts we may sufficiently perceive the meaning of the ancients who said the elements of nature were more than one; but there are some who spoke of the universe as if it were one entity, though they were not all alike either in the excellence of their statement or in its conformity to the facts of nature. The discussion of them is in no way appropriate to our present investigation of causes, for they do not, like some of the natural philosophers, assume being to be one and yet generate it out of the one as out of matter, but they speak in another way; those others add change, since they generate the universe, but these thinkers say the universe is unchangeable. Yet *this* much is germane to the present inquiry: Parmenides seems to fasten on that which is one in definition, Melissus on that which is one in matter, for which reason the former says that it is limited, the latter that it is unlimited; while Xenophanes, the first of these partisans of the One (for Parmenides is said to have been his pupil), gave no clear statement, nor does he seem to have grasped the nature of either of these causes, but with reference to the whole material universe he says the One is God. Now these thinkers, as we said, must be neglected for the purposes of the present inquiry—two of them entirely, as being a little too naïve, viz. Xenophanes and Melissus; but Parmenides seems in places to speak with more insight. For, claiming that,

besides the existent, nothing non-existent exists, he thinks that of necessity one thing exists, viz. the existent and nothing else (on this we have spoken more clearly in our work on nature),[16] but being forced to follow the observed facts, and supposing the existence of that which is one in definition, but more than one according to our sensations, he now posits two causes and two principles, calling them hot and cold, i.e. fire and earth; and of these he ranges the hot with the existent, and the other with the non-existent.

From what has been said, then, and from the wise men who have now sat in council with us, we have got thus much—on the one hand from the earliest philosophers, who regard the first principle as corporeal (for water and fire and such things are bodies), and of whom some suppose that there is one corporeal principle, others that there are more than one, but both put these under the head of matter; and on the other hand from some who posit both this cause and besides this the source of movement, which we have got from some as single and from others as twofold.

Down to the Italian school, then, and apart from it, philosophers have treated these subjects rather obscurely, except that, as we said, they have in fact used two kinds of cause, and one of these—the source of movement—some treat as one and others as two. But the Pythagoreans have said in the same way that there are two principles, but added this much, which is peculiar to them, that they thought that finitude and infinity were not attributes of certain other things, e.g. of fire or earth or anything else of this kind, but that infinity itself and unity itself were the substance of the things of which they are predicated. This is why number was the substance of all things. On this subject, then, they expressed themselves thus; and regarding the question of essence they began to make statements and definitions, but treated the matter too simply. For they both defined superficially and thought that the first subject of which a given definition was predicable was the substance of the thing defined, as if one supposed that 'double' and '2' were the same, because 2 is the first thing of which 'double' is predicable. But surely to be double and to be 2 are not the same; if they are, one thing will be many—a consequence which they actually drew. From the earlier philosophers, then, and from their successors we can learn thus much.

[16]   *Phys.* i.e.

Alfred North Whitehead (1861–1947)
THE AIMS OF EDUCATION

Whitehead argues that a certain degree of cultural sophistication, as opposed to mere expert knowledge, is the mark of a good education. But the aim of a good education, according to the Greek philosophers, is wisdom. Is culture, in Whitehead's sense, wisdom? Can philosophy make any special contribution toward acquiring culture? These and related questions are discussed in Section B of the introductory essay to Part I.

READING QUESTIONS

In reading the selection, try to answer the following questions and identify the passages that support your answers:

1. What is education according to Whitehead?
2. Is wisdom the result of education as Whitehead understands it?
3. Can philosophy make any special contribution toward education thus conceived or toward attaining wisdom?
4. Is philosophy simply another discipline, or is it an interdisciplinary branch of inquiry?
5. In fostering education, is philosophy conceived as interdisciplinary preferable to philosophy viewed as a self-contained discipline?

Reprinted with the permission of Macmillan Publishing Company from *The Aims of Education and Other Essays,* by A. N. Whitehead, pp. 1–23. Copyright 1929 by Macmillan Publishing Company, renewed © 1957 by Evelyn Whitehead.

Culture is activity of thought, and receptiveness to beauty and humane feeling. Scraps of information have nothing to do with it. A merely well-informed man is the most useless bore on God's earth. What we should aim at producing is men who possess both culture and expert knowledge in some special direction. Their expert knowledge will give them the ground to start from, and their culture will lead them as deep as philosophy and as high as art. We have to remember that the valuable intellectual development is self-development, and that it mostly takes place between the ages of sixteen and thirty. As to training, the most important part is given by mothers before the age of twelve. A saying due to Archbishop Temple illustrates my meaning. Surprise was expressed at the success in after-life of a man, who as a boy at Rugby had been somewhat undistinguished. He answered, "It is not what they are at eighteen, it is what they become afterwards that matters."

In training a child to activity of thought, above all things we must beware of what I will call "inert ideas"—that is to say, ideas that are merely received into the mind without being utilised, or tested, or thrown into fresh combinations.

In the history of education, the most striking phenomenon is that schools of learning, which at one epoch are alive with a ferment of genius, in a succeeding generation exhibit merely pedantry and routine. The reason is, that they are overladen with inert ideas. Education with inert ideas is not only useless: it is, above all things, harmful—*Corruptio optimi, pessima.* Except at rare intervals of intellectual ferment, education in the past has been radically infected with inert ideas. That is the reason why uneducated clever women, who have seen much of the world, are in middle life so much the most cultured part of the community. They have been saved from this horrible burden of inert ideas. Every intellectual revolution which has ever stirred humanity into greatness has been a passionate protest against inert ideas. Then, alas, with pathetic ignorance of human psychology, it has proceeded by some educational scheme to bind humanity afresh with inert ideas of its own fashioning.

Let us now ask how in our system of education we are to guard against this mental dryrot. We enunciate two educational commandments, "Do not teach too many subjects," and again, "What you teach, teach thoroughly."

The result of teaching small parts of a large number of subjects is the passive reception of disconnected ideas, not illumined with any spark of vitality. Let the main ideas which are introduced into a child's education be few and important, and let them be thrown into every combination possible. The child should make them his own, and should understand their application here and now in the circumstances of his actual life. From the very beginning of his education, the child should experience the joy of discovery. The discovery which he has to make, is that general ideas give an understanding of that stream of events which pours through his life, which is his life. By understanding I mean more than a mere logical analysis, though that is included. I mean "understanding" in the sense in which it is used in the French proverb, "To understand all, is to forgive all." Pedants sneer at an education which is useful. But if education is not useful, what is it? Is it a talent, to be hidden away in a napkin? Of course, education should be useful, whatever your aim in life. It was useful to Saint Augustine and it was useful to Napoleon. It is useful, because understanding is useful.

I pass lightly over that understanding which should be given by the literary side of education. Nor do I wish to be supposed to pronounce on the relative merits of a classical or a modern curriculum. I would only remark that the understanding which we want is an understanding of an insistent present. The only use of a knowledge of the past is to equip us for the present. No more deadly harm can be done to young minds than by depreciation of the present. The present contains all that there is. It is holy ground; for it is the past, and it is the future. At the same time it must be observed that an age is no less past if it existed two hundred years ago than if it existed two thousand years ago. Do not be deceived by the pedantry of dates. The ages of Shakespeare and of Molière are no less past than are the ages of Sophocles and of Virgil. The communion of saints is a great and inspiring assemblage, but it has only one possible hall of meeting, and that is, the present; and the mere lapse of time through which any

particular group of saints must travel to reach that meeting-place, makes very little difference.

Passing now to the scientific and logical side of education, we remember that here also ideas which are not utilised are positively harmful. By utilising an idea, I mean relating it to that stream, compounded of sense perceptions, feelings, hopes, desires, and of mental activities adjusting thought to thought, which forms our life. I can imagine a set of beings which might fortify their souls by passively reviewing disconnected ideas. Humanity is not built that way—except perhaps some editors of newspapers.

In scientific training, the first thing to do with an idea is to prove it. But allow me for one moment to extend the meaning of "prove"; I mean—to prove its worth. Now an idea is not worth much unless the propositions in which it is embodied are true. Accordingly an essential part of the proof of an idea is the proof, either by experiment or by logic, of the truth of the propositions. But it is not essential that this proof of the truth should constitute the first introduction to the idea. After all, its assertion by the authority of respectable teachers is sufficient evidence to begin with. In our first contact with a set of propositions, we commence by appreciating their importance. That is what we all do in after-life. We do not attempt, in the strict sense, to prove or to disprove anything, unless its importance makes it worthy of that honour. These two processes of proof, in the narrow sense, and of appreciation, do not require a rigid separation in time. Both can be proceeded with nearly concurrently. But in so far as either process must have the priority, it should be that of appreciation by use.

Furthermore, we should not endeavour to use propositions in isolation. Emphatically I do not mean, a neat little set of experiments to illustrate Proposition I and then the proof of Proposition I, a neat little set of experiments to illustrate Proposition II and then the proof of Proposition II, and so on to the end of the book. Nothing could be more boring. Interrelated truths are utilised *en bloc*, and the various propositions are employed in any order, and with any reiteration. Choose some important applications of your theoretical subject; and study them concurrently with the systematic theoretical exposition. Keep the theoretical exposition short and simple, but let it be strict and rigid so far as it goes. It should not be too long for it to be easily known with thoroughness and accuracy. The consequences of a plethora of half-digested theoretical knowledge are deplorable. Also the theory should not be muddled up with the practice. The child should have no doubt when it is proving and when it is utilising. My point is that what is proved should be utilised, and that what is utilised should—so far as is practicable—be proved. I am far from asserting that proof and utilisation are the same thing.

At this point of my discourse, I can most directly carry forward my argument in the outward form of a digression. We are only just realising that the art and science of education require a genius and a study of their own; and that this genius and this science are more than a bare knowledge of some branch of science or of literature. This truth was partially perceived in the past generation; and headmasters, somewhat crudely, were apt to supersede learning in their colleagues by requiring left-hand bowling and a taste for football. But culture is more than cricket, and more than football, and more than extent of knowledge.

Education is the acquisition of the art of the utilisation of knowledge. This is an art very difficult to impart. Whenever a text-book is written of real educational worth, you may be quite certain that some reviewer will say that it will be difficult to teach from it. Of course it will be difficult to teach from it. If it were easy, the book ought to be burned; for it cannot be educational. In education, as elsewhere, the broad primrose path leads to a nasty place. This evil path is represented by a book or a set of lectures which will practically enable the student to learn by heart all the questions likely to be asked at the next external examination. And I may say in passing that no educational system is possible unless every question directly asked of a pupil at any examination is either framed or modified by the actual teacher of that pupil in that subject. The external assessor may report on the curriculum or on the performance of the pupils, but never should be allowed to ask the pupil a question which has not been strictly supervised by the actual teacher, or at least inspired by a long conference with him. There are a few exceptions to this rule, but they are exceptions, and could easily be allowed for under the general rule.

We now return to my previous point, that theoretical ideas should always find important applications within the pupil's curriculum. This is not an easy doctrine to apply, but a very hard one. It contains within itself the problem of keeping knowledge alive, of preventing it from becoming inert, which is the central problem of all education.

The best procedure will depend on several factors, none of which can be neglected, namely, the genius of the teacher, the intellectual type of the pupils, their prospects in life, the opportunities offered by the immediate surroundings of the school, and allied factors of this sort. It is for this reason that the uniform external examination is so deadly. We do not denounce it because we are cranks, and like denouncing established things. We are not so childish. Also, of course, such examinations have their use in testing slackness. Our reason of dislike is very definite and very practical. It kills the best part of culture. When you analyse in the light of experience the central task of education, you find that its successful accomplishment depends on a delicate adjustment of many variable factors. The reason is that we are dealing with human minds, and not with dead matter. The evocation of curiosity, of judgment, of the power of mastering a complicated tangle of circumstances, the use of theory in giving foresight in special cases—all these powers are not to be imparted by a set rule embodied in one schedule of examination subjects.

I appeal to you, as practical teachers. With good discipline, it is always possible to pump into the minds of a class a certain quantity of inert knowledge. You take a text-book and make them learn it. So far, so good. The child then knows how to solve a quadratic equation. But what is the point of teaching a child to solve a quadratic equation? There is a traditional answer to this question. It runs thus: The mind is an instrument, you first sharpen it, and then use it; the acquisition of the power of solving a quadratic equation is part of the process of sharpening the mind. Now there is just enough truth in this answer to have made it live through the ages. But for all its half-truth, it embodies a radical error which bids fair to stifle the genius of the modern world. I do not know who was first responsible for this analogy of the mind to a dead instrument. For aught I know, it may have been one of the seven wise men of Greece, or a committee of the whole lot of them. Whoever was the originator, there can be no doubt of the authority which it has acquired by the continuous approval bestowed upon it by eminent persons. But whatever its weight of authority, whatever the high approval which it can quote, I have no hesitation in denouncing it as one of the most fatal, erroneous, and dangerous conceptions ever introduced into the theory of education. The mind is never passive; it is a perpetual activity, delicate, receptive, responsive to stimulus. You cannot postpone its life until you have sharpened it. Whatever interest attaches to your subject-matter must be evoked here and now; whatever powers you are strengthening in the pupil, must be exercised here and now; whatever possibilities of mental life your teaching should impart, must be exhibited here and now. That is the golden rule of education, and a very difficult rule to follow.

The difficulty is just this: the apprehension of general ideas, intellectual habits of mind, and pleasurable interest in mental achievement can be evoked by no form of words, however accurately adjusted. All practical teachers know that education is a patient process of the mastery of details, minute by minute, hour by hour, day by day. There is no royal road to learning through an airy path of brilliant generalisations. There is a proverb about the difficulty of seeing the wood because of the trees. That difficulty is exactly the point which I am enforcing. The problem of education is to make the pupil see the wood by means of the trees.

The solution which I am urging, is to eradicate the fatal disconnection of subjects which kills the vitality of our modern curriculum. There is only one subject-matter for education, and that is Life in all its manifestations. Instead of this single unity, we offer children—Algebra, from which nothing follows; Geometry, from which nothing follows; Science, from which nothing follows; History, from which nothing follows; a Couple of Languages, never mastered; and lastly, most dreary of all, Literature, represented by plays of Shakespeare, with philological notes and short analyses of plot and character to be in substance committed to memory. Can such a list be said to represent Life, as it is known in the midst of the living of it? The best that can be said of it is, that it is a rapid table of contents which a deity might run over in his mind while he was thinking of creating a world, and had not yet determined how to put it together.

Let us now return to quadratic equations. We still have on hand the unanswered question. Why should children be taught their solution? Unless quadratic equations fit into a connected curriculum, of course there is no reason to teach anything about them. Furthermore, extensive as should be the place of mathematics in a complete culture, I am a little doubtful whether for many types of boys algebraic

solutions of quadratic equations do not lie on the specialist side of mathematics. I may here remind you that as yet I have not said anything of the psychology or the content of the specialism, which is so necessary a part of an ideal education. But all that is an evasion of our real question, and I merely state it in order to avoid being misunderstood in my answer.

Quadratic equations are part of algebra, and algebra is the intellectual instrument which has been created for rendering clear the quantitative aspects of the world. There is no getting out of it. Through and through the world is infected with quantity. To talk sense, is to talk in quantities. It is no use saying that the nation is large,—How large? It is no use saying that radium is scarce,—How scarce? You cannot evade quantity. You may fly to poetry and to music, and quantity and number will face you in your rhythms and your octaves. Elegant intellects which despise the theory of quantity, are but half developed. They are more to be pitied than blamed. The scraps of gibberish, which in their school-days were taught to them in the name of algebra, deserve some contempt.

This question of the degeneration of algebra into gibberish, both in word and in fact, affords a pathetic instance of the uselessness of reforming educational schedules without a clear conception of the attributes which you wish to evoke in the living minds of the children. A few years ago there was an outcry that school algebra was in need of reform, but there was a general agreement that graphs would put everything right. So all sorts of things were extruded, and graphs were introduced. So far as I can see, with no sort of idea behind them, but just graphs. Now every examination paper has one or two questions on graphs. Personally, I am an enthusiastic adherent of graphs. But I wonder whether as yet we have gained very much. You cannot put life into any schedule of general education unless you succeed in exhibiting its relation to some essential characteristic of all intelligent or emotional perception. It is a hard saying, but it is true; and I do not see how to make it any easier. In making these little formal alterations you are beaten by the very nature of things. You are pitted against too skilful an adversary, who will see to it that the pea is always under the other thimble.

Reformation must begin at the other end. First, you must make up your mind as to those quantitative aspects of the world which are simple enough to be introduced into general education; then a schedule of algebra should be framed which will about find its exemplification in these applications. We need not fear for our pet graphs, they will be there in plenty when we once begin to treat algebra as a serious means of studying the world. Some of the simplest applications will be found in the quantities which occur in the simplest study of society. The curves of history are more vivid and more informing than the dry catalogues of names and dates which comprise the greater part of that arid school study. What purpose is effected by a catalogue of undistinguished kings and queens? Tom, Dick, or Harry, they are all dead. General resurrections are failures, and are better postponed. The quantitative flux of the forces of modern society is capable of very simple exhibition. Meanwhile, the idea of the variable, of the function, of rate of change, of equations and their solution, of elimination, are being studied as an abstract science for their own sake. Not, of course, in the pompous phrases with which I am alluding to them here, but with that iteration of simple special cases proper to teaching.

If this course be followed, the route from Chaucer to the Black Death, from the Black Death to modern Labour troubles, will connect the tales of the mediaeval pilgrims with the abstract science of algebra, both yielding diverse aspects of that single theme, Life. I know what most of you are thinking at this point. It is that the exact course which I have sketched out is not the particular one which you would have chosen, or even see how to work. I quite agree. I am not claiming that I could do it myself. But your objection is the precise reason why a common external examination system is fatal to education. The process of exhibiting the applications of knowledge must, for its success, essentially depend on the character of the pupils and the genius of the teacher. Of course I have left out the easiest applications with which most of us are more at home. I mean the quantitative sides of sciences, such as mechanics and physics.

Again, in the same connection we plot the statistics of social phenomena against the time. We then eliminate the time between suitable pairs. We can speculate how far we have exhibited a real causal connection, or how far a mere temporal coincidence. We notice that we might have plotted against the time one set of statistics for one country and another set for another country, and thus, with suitable choice of subjects, have obtained graphs which certainly exhibited mere coincidence. Also other graphs exhibit obvious causal connections. We won-

der how to discriminate. And so are drawn on as far as we will.

But in considering this description, I must beg you to remember what I have been insisting on above. In the first place, one train of thought will not suit all groups of children. For example, I should expect that artisan children will want something more concrete and, in a sense, swifter than I have set down here. Perhaps I am wrong, but that is what I should guess. In the second place, I am not contemplating one beautiful lecture stimulating, once and for all, an admiring class. That is not the way in which education proceeds. No; all the time the pupils are hard at work solving examples, drawing graphs, and making experiments, until they have a thorough hold on the whole subject. I am describing the interspersed explanations, the directions which should be given to their thoughts. The pupils have got to be made to feel that they are studying something, and are not merely executing intellectual minuets.

Finally, if you are teaching pupils for some general examination, the problem of sound teaching is greatly complicated. Have you ever noticed the zigzag moulding round a Norman arch? The ancient work is beautiful, the modern work is hideous. The reason is, that the modern work is done to exact measure, the ancient work is varied according to the idiosyncrasy of the workman. Here it is crowded, and there it is expanded. Now the essence of getting pupils through examinations is to give equal weight to all parts of the schedule. But mankind is naturally specialist. One man sees a whole subject, where another can find only a few detached examples. I know that it seems contradictory to allow for specialism in a curriculum especially designed for a broad culture. Without contradictions the world would be simpler, and perhaps duller. But I am certain that in education wherever you exclude specialism you destroy life.

We now come to the other great branch of a general mathematical education, namely Geometry. The same principles apply. The theoretical part should be clear-cut, rigid, short, and important. Every proposition not absolutely necessary to exhibit the main connection of ideas should be cut out, but the great fundamental ideas should be all there. No omission of concepts, such as those of Similarity and Proportion. We must remember that, owing to the aid rendered by the visual presence of a figure, Geometry is a field of unequalled excellence for the exercise of the deductive faculties of reasoning.

Then, of course, there follows Geometrical Drawing, with its training for the hand and eye.

But, like Algebra, Geometry and Geometrical Drawing must be extended beyond the mere circle of geometrical ideas. In an industrial neighbourhood, machinery and workshop practice form the appropriate extension. For example, in the London Polytechnics this has been achieved with conspicuous success. For many secondary schools I suggest that surveying and maps are the natural applications. In particular, plane-table surveying should lead pupils to a vivid apprehension of the immediate application of geometric truths. Simple drawing apparatus, a surveyor's chain, and a surveyor's compass, should enable the pupils to rise from the survey and mensuration of a field to the construction of the map of a small district. The best education is to be found in gaining the utmost information from the simplest apparatus. The provision of elaborate instruments is greatly to be deprecated. To have constructed the map of a small district, to have considered its roads, its contours, its geology, its climate, its relation to other districts, the effects on the status of its inhabitants, will teach more history and geography than any knowledge of Perkin Warbeck or of Behren's Straits. I mean not a nebulous lecture on the subject, but a serious investigation in which the real facts are definitely ascertained by the aid of accurate theoretical knowledge. A typical mathematical problem should be: Survey such and such a field, draw a plan of it to such and such a scale, and find the area. It would be quite a good procedure to impart the necessary geometrical propositions without their proofs. Then, concurrently in the same term, the proofs of the propositions would be learnt while the survey was being made.

Fortunately, the specialist side of education presents an easier problem than does the provision of a general culture. For this there are many reasons. One is that many of the principles of procedure to be observed are the same in both cases, and it is unnecessary to recapitulate. Another reason is that specialist training takes place—or should take place—at a more advanced stage of the pupil's course, and thus there is easier material to work upon. But undoubtedly the chief reason is that the specialist study is normally a study of peculiar interest to the student. He is studying it because, for some reason, he wants to know it. This makes all the difference. The general culture is designed to foster an activity of mind; the specialist course utilises this activity. But it does not do to lay too much stress on these neat antitheses. As we have already seen, in the general course foci of special interest will arise; and similarly in the special study, the external connections of the subject drag thought outwards.

Again, there is not one course of study which merely gives general culture, and another which gives special knowledge. The subjects pursued for the sake of a general education are special subjects specially studied; and, on the other hand, one of the ways of encouraging general mental activity is to foster a special devotion. You may not divide the seamless coat of learning. What education has to impart is an intimate sense for the power of ideas, for the beauty of ideas, and for the structure of ideas, together with a particular body of knowledge which has peculiar reference to the life of the being possessing it.

The appreciation of the structure of ideas is that side of a cultured mind which can only grow under the influence of a special study. I mean that eye for the whole chess-board, for the bearing of one set of ideas on another. Nothing but a special study can give any appreciation for the exact formulation of general ideas, for their relations when formulated, for their service in the comprehension of life. A mind so disciplined should be both more abstract and more concrete. It has been trained in the comprehension of abstract thought and in the analysis of facts.

Finally, there should grow the most austere of all mental qualities; I mean the sense for style. It is an aesthetic sense, based on admiration for the direct attainment of a foreseen end, simply and without waste. Style in art, style in literature, style in science, style in logic, style in practical execution have fundamentally the same aesthetic qualities, namely, attainment and restraint. The love of a subject in itself and for itself, where it is not the sleepy pleasure of pacing a mental quarter-deck, is the love of style as manifested in that study.

Here we are brought back to the position from which we started, the utility of education. Style, in its finest sense, is the last acquirement of the educated mind; it is also the most useful. It pervades the whole being. The administrator with a sense for style hates waste; the engineer with a sense for style economises his material; the artisan with a sense for style prefers good work. Style is the ultimate morality of mind.

But above style, and above knowledge, there is something, a vague shape like fate above the Greek gods. That something is Power. Style is the fashioning of power, the restraining of power. But, after all, the power of attainment of the desired end is fundamental. The first thing is to get there. Do not bother about your style, but solve your problem, justify the ways of God to man, administer your province, or do whatever else is set before you.

Where, then, does style help? In this, with style the end is attained without side issues, without raising undesirable inflammations. With style you attain your end and nothing but your end. With style the effect of your activity is calculable, and foresight is the last gift of gods to men. With style your power is increased, for your mind is not distracted with irrelevancies, and you are more likely to attain your object. Now style is the exclusive privilege of the expert. Whoever heard of the style of an amateur painter, of the style of an amateur poet? Style is always the product of specialist study, the peculiar contribution of specialism to culture.

English education in its present phase suffers from a lack of definite aim, and from an external machinery which kills its vitality. Hitherto in this address I have been considering the aims which should govern education. In this respect England halts between two opinions. It has not decided whether to produce amateurs or experts. The profound change in the world which the nineteenth century has produced is that the growth of knowledge has given foresight. The amateur is essentially a man with appreciation and with immense versatility in mastering a given routine. But he lacks the foresight which comes from special knowledge. The object of this address is to suggest how to produce the expert without loss of the essential virtues of the amateur. The machinery of our secondary education is rigid where it should be yielding, and lax where it should be rigid. Every school is bound on pain of extinction to train its boys for a small set of definite examinations. No headmaster has a free hand to develop his general education or his specialist studies in accordance with the opportunities of his school, which are created by its staff, its environment, its class of boys, and its endowments. I suggest that no system of external tests which aims primarily at examining individual scholars can result in anything but educational waste.

Primarily it is the schools and not the scholars which should be inspected. Each school should grant its own leaving certificates, based on its own curriculum. The standards of these schools should be sampled and corrected. (But the first requisite for educational reform is the school as a unit, with its approved curriculum based on its own needs, and evolved by its own staff.) If we fail to secure that, we simply fall from one formalism into another, from one dung-hill of inert ideas into another.

In stating that the school is the true educational unit in any national system for the safeguarding of efficiency, I have conceived the alternative system as being the external examination of the individual scholar. But every Scylla is faced by its Charybdis—or, in more homely language, there is a ditch on both sides of the road. It will be equally fatal to education if we fall into the hands of a supervising department which is under the impression that it can divide all schools into two or three rigid categories, each type being forced to adopt a rigid curriculum. When I say that the school is the educational unit, I mean exactly what I say, no larger unit, no smaller unit. Each school must have the claim to be considered in relation to its special circumstances. The classifying of schools for some purposes is necessary. But no absolutely rigid curriculum, not modified by its own staff, should be permissible. Exactly the same principles apply, with the proper modifications, to universities and to technical colleges.

When one considers in its length and in its breadth the importance of this question of the education of a nation's young, the broken lives, the defeated hopes, the national failures, which result from the frivolous inertia with which it is treated, it is difficult to restrain within oneself a savage rage. In the conditions of modern life the rule is absolute, the race which does not value trained intelligence is doomed. Not all your heroism, not all your social charm, not all your wit, not all your victories on land or at sea, can move back the finger of fate. To-day we maintain ourselves. To-morrow science will have moved forward yet one more step, and there will be no appeal from the judgment which will then be pronounced on the uneducated.

We can be content with no less than the old summary of educational ideal which has been current at any time from the dawn of our civilisation. The essence of education is that it be religious.

Pray, what is religious education?

A religious education is an education which inculcates duty and reverence. Duty arises from our potential control over the course of events. Where attainable knowledge could have changed the issue, ignorance has the guilt of vice. And the foundation of reverence is this perception, that the present holds within itself the complete sum of existence, backwards and forwards, that whole amplitude of time, which is eternity.

Arthur E. Murphy (1901–1962)
THE PHILOSOPHIC MIND
AND THE CONTEMPORARY WORLD

Murphy explains what philosophy is by evoking the philosophic mind. He argues that the philosophic mind is curious and comprehensive, tries to explain the distinction between appearance and reality, looks at things in perspective, and believes that human beings are capable of seeking and attaining wisdom. His views are discussed at some length in Section B of the introductory essay to Part I.

READING QUESTIONS

As you read the selection, try to answer the following questions and identify the passages that support your answers:

1. What does Murphy consider central for learning philosophy?
2. Explain how, in philosophy, it is not only what is believed that is important, but also why and how it is believed.
3. What qualities, according to Murphy, characterize philosophers?
4. How does he distinguish philosophy from other studies?
5. What else, if anything, could help distinguish philosophy from other studies?

Reprinted with the permission of Dr. Frederick H. Ginascol, Executor of Arthur E. Murphy Estate, from William H. Hay, Marcus G. Singer, and Arthur E. Murphy (eds.), *Reason and the Common Good* (Englewood Cliffs, NJ: Prentice Hall, 1963), pp. 365–375.

When the Humanities are afforded as handsome an opportunity as this Conference presents to explain themselves and their reason for being in an American University, the question that is at the back of nearly everybody's mind is a direct, if not a simple one. What is to be got out of humanistic studies—how many students who devote their time and effort to them expect to come away richer, or more skillful, or in some other assignable way better off than when they started? This question arises with particular urgency in the case of philosophy—a queer sort of subject in common repute, which seems to fit in nowhere and to lead to nothing in particular, and which yet, for some reason, men keep coming back to when they are deeply troubled and perplexed. What, within the general pattern of the humanistic studies, is to be got out of philosophy and for whom and under what conditions is it worth having? These are the questions which, without further preface, I propose to try to answer.

Read at the University of Rochester Conference on the Humanities, March 27, 1947.

The first thing one might normally expect to get out of the study of philosophy is information about what various men called "philosophers" have taught in the past and about the circumstances under which their doctrines were developed and the kind of influence they had in their own time, and beyond. Some of these men—Plato, Aristotle, Augustine, Descartes, Kant, Hegel, Nietzsche—have profoundly influenced the course of subsequent thought in all manner of interesting ways, and it is hardly possible to be well informed about the roots and meaning of contemporary culture without some knowledge of who they were and what they said. In the field of "general education," which tends in practice to be largely that of general information, they bulk large. A student at the University of Illinois who had elected a somewhat varied program told me a year or two ago that he was hearing about Plato's *Republic* in every course he was taking except plant pathology. Now Plato's *Republic* is indubitably philosophy, if anything is, and that some information about it should be considered important in so many different connections is to be accounted, I suppose, a tribute to the importance of our subject.

In philosophy, however, information is not enough. This is, for some students, a disquieting discovery. They come, notebook in hand, from classes in which they have faithfully recorded the material that the lecturer has got together on whatever subject, from geology to labor management, they have elected to study, and which they will be expected to remember and rewrite on examination papers. If the lecturer speaks slowly and clearly, and the student's pen, paper and memory are adequate to the demands made upon them, there is no reason why he should not, thus equipped, come well and bravely through the ordeal of very much of what is called a general education. But in philosophy the ordinary rules no longer hold. Here the student must not only acquire some information about thinking, he must actually participate in the activity of thinking for himself. And since it is notoriously hard to think and take notes at the same time, the novel exercise is likely to get in the way of what he takes to be the main business of the hour—the writing down of the information which, together with the grade which records his faithful memory of it at the right time, will quite literally be what he has "got out of" the course. To lose his notebook would be, for all practical educational purposes, to lose his mind. But this, as a little reflection will show, is not the philosophic mind that we are seeking.

Nor is this, as the troubled student sometimes suspects, just one more proof of the oddity of philosophers. It follows rather from the special nature of their subject, which is *ideas* considered not as events but as ideas. To understand an idea of Aristotle's it is not enough to know that Aristotle had it and where he wrote it down and what somebody else said about it afterward. To grasp it as an idea one must think it for oneself, and that means actually to participate in the activity of problem solving in which it is offered as an answer and to see what the conditions of the problem are and to what extent it really *is* an answer. In this field at least Santayana's aphorism applies: "We cannot cease to think and still continue to know." Or, to put the same point another way: in philosophy ideas must be known at first hand or by acquaintance and not merely by description if they are to be understood. The student who is not prepared to engage in this activity of thinking ought not to undertake the study of philosophy. If at any future time he needs to locate items of information about the great philosophers, he or his secretary or research

assistant will find in easily accessible encyclopedias everything that is relevant to his purpose.

But if something more than information is to be got out of philosophy, what is it? The answer currently popular among professional educators and moralists as well as with many students is that it is sound doctrine and right attitudes of belief on issues of ultimate importance. Philosophers discuss such issues—the reality of God and of the human soul— the moral order and its ground and sanctions—the nature of political obligation and the justifying reasons, if any, behind the claims of constituted authorities. A person's convictions on such matters may properly, in ordinary usage, be referred to as his "philosophy" and it is important to any well-constituted society that its members should have the right beliefs on these subjects rather than the wrong ones. To inculcate such beliefs, or to fortify and confirm them in those who, through their cultural heritage and political allegiance, already possess them is a part of the service which education is expected to render to the state, and where, if not in philosophy, is this work properly to be done? "Render unto Caesar the things that are Caesar's" is an admonition we are not likely in these times to forget. For it has been discovered that ideas are weapons, and in the struggle for power which now divides the world their importance will hardly be neglected.

Is this what is to be "got out" of philosophy and philosophers today? I hope and believe that it is not. Yet the request seems reasonable enough. If the philosophers *have* the right beliefs on these high matters, why should they be reluctant to teach their conclusions with authority? And if they should turn out to be the wrong kind of philosophers—if their conclusions are not unequivocally on our side in the ideological battle—why should they be allowed to teach at all? To see the answer to these questions is to have advanced a long way in the understanding of what philosophy is and what it is worth to those who are prepared to meet its standards.

The essential point is this. In philosophy it is not only a question of what is believed but of the way in which and the grounds on which it is accepted. Kierkegaard put the matter drastically when he said that one may be "in the truth" on ultimate issues even when what he believes is by any external or objective standard false, while an objectively true belief, accepted in the wrong way, is a lie in the soul of the believer. Men may indeed be "given" an accredited philosophy by state or church, or by educational philosophers duly responsive to the demands of both, but they will not become the wiser, better or more enlightened in the process of thus receiving it. They will become instead the readily manipulatable partisans of doctrines whose merits they are neither intellectually nor morally in a position to judge, but to which by indoctrination they are committed at all cost. Such a doctrine may be identical in content with what some of the greatest philosophers and sages have taught. But, for those who thus receive it, it is not philosophy for all that, in the sense in which philosophy is the love of wisdom or the effective possession and use of it.

Philosophy does have profoundly to do with our beliefs or commitments on ultimate issues of life, value and human destiny—and when we are asked to say *where we stand* on such issues we are being asked, in substance, for our philosophy. Philosophy in this sense, like the poor, we have always with us. For we all have such commitments, whether we are aware of them or not, and when they are challenged we become conscious of them and remain uneasy until in one way or another they have been reinforced or substantiated. To invoke them, thus supported, against those who disagree, is an inspiring and exhilarating experience and a stimulus to resolute action with an undivided mind. It is a natural confusion to suppose that the philosophers who are lovers of and seekers for wisdom, and whose works are often posthumously honored as literary and cultural monuments, are the men to whom we ought to look for this sort of ideological comfort and support.

It is a confusion, nonetheless. For in philosophy as a rational discipline such commitments are the beginning, not the end, of inquiry. We do indeed want to know where we stand with regard to them, and the philosopher's search is for just such a standpoint—for a way of judging and correcting them that can carry us beyond our starting point and out into the larger world of truth and meaning that lies beyond their partisan and parochial limitations. What develops in this process of inquiry and must be achieved if we are to pursue it successfully is a distinctive way of understanding such commitments— a philosophic habit or attitude of mind. It is this way of looking at the world and our own commitments within it which, borrowing from Wordsworth, I have called "the philosophic mind." This, I think, is what the student who is prepared to devote himself to its study can reasonably expect to get out of philosophy. It is time now to go on to say more explicitly what it is and why it is worth having.

The philosophic mind is, in the first place, an inquiring mind. It is right and illuminating to say, with Aristotle, that philosophy begins in wonder. But not just any kind of wonder. The marvelous, the occult, the merely freakish and "colossal," are objects of wonder for the popular mind and arouse an interest that illustrated weeklies, motion pictures, sideshows and various forms of commercialized superstition exist to satisfy. The wonder that generates a philosophical inquiry is of a different sort—it is elicited not by the marvelous but by the familiar, by the things that everybody "knows" and takes for granted. Socrates liked to describe himself as an ignorant man, and there are ill-furnished minds today that pride themselves on being, in this at least, his disciples. The point was, however, that Socrates knew that he did not know the things that his fellow citizens were sure about, not because he lacked some information that they possessed, but because he saw, as they did not, the dubiety of the obvious, the oddity of the commonplace, the insecurity of the preconceptions to which "right thinking men" unthinkingly subscribe. Whitehead made the same essential point when he said with penetrating brevity that philosophy is "an attitude of mind toward doctrines ignorantly entertained"—that attitude, specifically, in which an awareness of initial ignorance as to the ground and meaning of one's preconceptions is the beginning of the quest for the wisdom that will clarify and correct them. To have doubted one's preconceptions, said Justice Holmes, is the mark of a civilized mind. It is, at least, the mark of the philosophic mind and those who are not prepared to undergo its discipline, for whom philosophy is a cushion of ultimate ideological self-satisfaction on which to rest a tired mind, or a brickbat to hurl at those of a different faith, are ignorant men indeed, but they are not in the Socratic sense philosophers.

Such questioning, however, if it is philosophical, is never merely captious. The lover of wisdom is by no means unaware of the substantial store of that too rare commodity that is embedded in our preconceptions and in the traditions and loyalties that they represent. If he is dissatisfied with them as *ultimate* criteria of truth and value, it is because, as Plato's description of the true philosopher makes clear, he is a lover not of a part of wisdom only, but of the whole. He therefore takes the responsibility for relating the ultimate assurances of any special segment of experience, and of any limited perspective within it, to what lies outside that area or point of view. He can discount nothing that is humanly significant, for nothing human can be alien to his purpose, his sympathy and his understanding. This demand for inclusiveness, and consequent discontent with anything partial or partisan which claims an absoluteness and finality which, in a wider view, it cannot rationally maintain, is the second distinguishing mark of the philosophic mind.

There is something genial and easygoing in the picture which such a description naturally calls to mind. To see all sides of every question, and good in everything, is, it would seem, to be very good natured indeed. One thinks of William James, with his kindly hospitality to the ideas of cranks and his appreciation of all varieties of human aspiration and experience. Such generosity is indeed a mark of philosophic insight, but it would be a mistake to think of it as easily come by. The method of attaining it is more accurately, if allegorically, outlined in the Myth of the Cave in Plato's *Republic*. The truth at which philosophy is aiming in its quest for wisdom is as plain and public as the sunlight of that common world in which men live and work together when they understand each other and themselves. But to be a free man in that world one must first have turned his back on the illusions of perspective which are, as Spinoza memorably said, the instruments of human bondage. "When half gods go, the gods arrive," but we know today that the manner of their going is sometimes more like the casting out of demons than Emerson seems ever to have realized.

The intellectual process in which the partiality of every limited interest and idea is exposed in the interest of a more inclusive wisdom is called dialectic, and a philosophy that must cut its way through prejudice and special pleading toward wholeness of understanding will in this sense be dialectical in its method. The philosophic mind is one that tries to see such absolutistic pretensions for what they are and, without denying or disparaging the genuineness of the values they represent, to see through them to the further truth they have distorted or denied.

No human insight can assess the truth from other than a partial standpoint, and the lover of wisdom would sin against the very light he seeks if he were to forget or deny his own humanity. He sees the world from where he is, and he cannot see everywhere—the divine omniscience and ubiquity are not for him. Hence he must make his own selection among the facts and values that present themselves

for his interpretation, fixing on some as for his purposes fundamental, basic and real, and relegating others to the status of the apparent and peripheral. Everything that he can understand must have some sort of meaning and reality, but not everything will be real in the same way or on the same level. The ultimate or final things will be those which maintain themselves as genuine and reliable in the light of the most penetrating and comprehensive scrutiny he can bring to bear on them, and on these he will build his philosophy. Hence a third essential mark of the philosophic mind. The philosopher is the man who takes the responsibility for making the distinction between appearance and reality, which is inherent in all our thinking, wisely, from the standpoint of such wisdom as he has and for the sake of the further wisdom that in this way he can secure. A good philosophy is one that contributes to such understanding, that enables us to see more than we could have seen without it and to bring otherwise isolated or discrepant aspects of experiences into fruitful relation to the rest of what we know. A bad philosophy is one that blocks the path of understanding in just these ways.

It is notorious that philosophers, like other men, differ in their identifications of the realities by reference to which experience can most wisely be organized and understood. The way in which they agree among themselves and differ from others is that they are prepared to see this identification as a problem rather than a preconception and to justify their theories by reference to their contribution to the larger undertaking which is the quest for comprehensive wisdom. It is often taken as a matter of reproach that philosophers go on and on arguing with each other about the ultimate realities and seem to reach no final conclusions. It should rather be made an occasion for thankfulness and congratulation. For to achieve finality in a process in which all claims to finality are and must be partial and in which all partiality is subject to correction as we live and learn would be to reach a state of mind in which both living and learning had ceased to function as sources of wisdom. And to refuse to argue on such matters would be not to free ourselves from ultimate commitments, which are inescapable in all human thinking, but to withdraw them from the sphere of rational discussion and correction. It is by arguing and by changing our minds, not arbitrarily or blindly but with reasons, that we become as wise in these matters as at any time it is humanly possible to be. For the philosopher who has not confused himself, or his ecclesiastical superior, or the state, with God, and who knows his human limitations, a finality exempt from such criticism and correction would not be the fulfillment of his purpose but its negation. For he is a lover not only of that part of wisdom which his own particular doctrine or school of thought has selected for preferential attention, but of the whole, and he knows that it is only in the process of rational inquiry that the limitations inherent in every partial standpoint are corrected in the quest for the wider good he seeks.

A further characteristic of the philosophic mind—its "detachment"—appears directly as a consequence of the traits that we have so far been considering. The philosopher, just because he is concerned with the truth that is not exhausted in any human insight, will refuse to put all his eggs in one basket, even if that basket be his own. He will see each particular good against the background of a world in which there are other goods as well and possibilities of good not realized, and will strive to estimate the significance of all local enthusiasms and causes from a standpoint in which neither partisanship nor special pleading has the final word. This does not mean that he is without preferences and enthusiasms of his own; it does mean that he is prepared to see them in a perspective in which their limits and relativity are made plain and their immediate urgency thereby qualified and corrected.

Samuel Alexander, who philosophizing happily exemplified this coolness of judgment, offers a pleasing illustration of its working. "On a certain occasion Boswell had invited Johnson with some others to supper at his lodgings. But, the landlord having proved disagreeable, Boswell was obliged to change the place of meeting from his house to the Mitre, and waited on Johnson to explain his 'serious distress.' 'Consider, sir,' said Johnson, 'how insignificant this will appear a twelvemonth hence.' That was a philosophic answer, and Johnson had in practical conduct, though certainly not in speculation, the philosophic mind."[1]

It is not through levity or indifference that the philosopher has the temerity to view with some degree of detachment the claims and counterclaims in which the circumstances of his life involve him. He refuses to be wholly serious about some of the ma-

jor preoccupations of his contemporaries and in this may sometimes affront the common sense of his time and country. Common sense has had its revenge, from the story about the first Greek philosopher who fell into a well "in a fit of abstraction" while looking at the stars, to more recent and ill-natured gibes at those who seek refuge in an "ivory tower" of speculation from the "realities" of practical life. The genuine philosopher is not much bothered by that, nor should he be. He means to keep out of wells, where possible, and also to take his bearings by the stars where larger issues are at stake. As for "realities," he is pretty sure that his "practical" critic does not know one when he sees it and is constantly being cheated with second-rate and shoddy stuff in consequence. Like Thoreau, he does not propose to impoverish his life by paying the market price for goods which the values of the market place do not justly measure, and "practical" has therefore a somewhat different meaning for him than for his critics. Hence, without wishing to be at all unsociable, he sometimes finds himself going in one direction while the crowd is hurrying in another. He thinks, however, that he knows where he is going while the crowd does not and would not be greatly surprised to find that in the long run they have shifted their direction and were coming his way so that, in the larger perspective of history, he might even appear to have been leading a parade. Stranger things have happened. Meanwhile he must be about his business, which is not that of leading parades or of following them, and is glad to welcome to that enterprise all who have a mind to share it with him.

It would be a misconception of his work, however, to suppose that such detachment was the philosopher's final response to the problems of the world in which he finds himself. Rather is his detachment the consequence and expression of a different loyalty. He is committed to an undertaking in whose worth he believes, and it is this commitment which makes sense of all the rest. Since it is an attitude and an affirmation, a claim to the reality of things not seen as yet, it may properly be called a faith. The fifth and, for our purposes, final mark of the philosophic mind is the quality and object of its faith.

It is a faith in the capacity of the human mind to achieve in some rewarding measure the wisdom that it seeks, and to live, in the light of it, a juster and more generous life than would otherwise be attainable. This is not always the faith the professed philosopher professes, when called on to edify, instruct or entertain, but it is the faith he works by and

---

[1] Samuel Alexander, *Space, Time, and Deity* (London: Macmillan and Co., Limited, 1920), I, 3–4.

justifies to the extent that his work attains its goal. No man who remembers his human limitations will claim to have reached the end of his search for wisdom or to possess the wholeness of truth that he is seeking. But if, within the present situation in which, like the rest of us, he lives, he has achieved a standpoint from which a man may see something of the scope and greatness of the world beyond the end of his nose and the urgency of his appetites and suspicions and if, reporting what he sees, he can bring into the heat and clutter of contemporary life a range of insight, steadiness of purpose and magnanimity of spirit which can lift it somewhat above the routine, exclusiveness, and mediocrity into which, without such insight, it regularly tends to fall, then he has done his job as a philosopher. He thinks it is a job worth doing.

Such is the philosophic mind which those who undertake the study and discipline of philosophical inquiry may expect in some measure to achieve. What, now, does it offer that is pertinent to the needs and interests of the contemporary world and of those who wish to participate in it as fully and intelligently as possible? There is time for no more than a brief answer; I shall try to make it to the point. One thing that the contemporary world is deeply concerned about is "peace of mind." The sense of both personal and national insecurity is widespread. We are confronted by alien and apparently hostile forces in a world that is larger and less congenial than we had been led to suppose. We seek a form of faith or ideological security that will give us something to hold on to, that will put a sure foundation under our shaken and half-undermined conviction. And it is natural that we should do so.

The situation, however, has its dangers. An examination paper I read recently told me that what most people were looking for now-a-days was "piece" of mind. Even an unintended pun may have a moral for the philosophic mind, and this is a case in point. For it seems dangerously near the truth to say that that is exactly what many people today are after. They want to purchase peace of mind by retreating into some fragment or aspect of experience to which they can cling no matter what, and to shut out all those wider and disturbing meanings which might upset their meager absolutes. Thus Mr. Aldous Huxley tells us that we shall be philosophers indeed—"perennial philosophers"—if we become "poor in spirit" and thus find in the mystical immediacy of an unutterable experience the solution, which is also the negation, of our deepest problems.

Another instance of a somewhat similar poverty of spirit is that frightened nationalism which, finding its preconceptions challenged by "alien ideologies," seeks the protection of its own ideals in the exclusion of such dangerous doctrines from public hearing and those suspected of any sort of sympathy with them from the public pay roll. The alarm thus manifested is understandable. But those of us who wish not only to sympathize with but to put into practice the ideals of democracy will be blind indeed if we do not see that it is an unwholesome thing for free men to be afraid of ideas, even if they are radical and mistaken ideas. It sets up the defensive reaction appropriate to a closed and frightened mind. We dare not seek a basis of common understanding with nations with whose economic, political and religious ideals we differ for fear of giving aid and comfort to an ideological enemy. And yet it is only on the basis of such an understanding that any genuine international community can be established. Those who profess to honor the ideal of such a community and at the same time cut off that free competition of ideas in terms of which alone, as a great American jurist affirmed in a period of similar panic, the truth is reliably established, may mean well, but they do not think well or act wisely. And their country may pay a heavy price in the future for their meagerness of mind.

Finally, to make a long story short enough for present purposes, we should consider the practical men who think that they can find security in concentration on small aims and tangible goods, and who resent as "metaphysical" the introduction into their calculations of any question of the meaning in human terms of the instruments and accessories toward whose production and sale their effort is untiringly addressed. Mr Santayana's saying that "fanaticism is redoubling your effort when you have forgotten your aim" is well known. I doubt its applicability to many sorts of fanatics now abroad in the world. But it might well be modified to read "specialization is redoubling your effort when you have forgotten your aim." In that form the dictum would apply with justice to a good deal of contemporary American life, and not least to American universities. We all know this well enough, and have by now so far acquiesced in it that it seems both trite and impolite to refer to it. My point is that this "practicality" too is a kind of deliberate fragmentariness or poverty of spirit, a way of living with a piece of one's mind and securing, in this simplification, a partial respite from the claims of the larger world with which the specialist in his professional capacity is not prepared to deal. It is to be understood and judged as such.

As against such dubious and desperate expedients as these, it is surely the part of sanity and courage to insist once more that peace of mind is to be reliably secured only in wholeness and integrity of mind and that the business of a sound philosophy is not to protect our conceptions against the hazards of an uncertain world and a growing experience but rather to give us the means of growing up to the demands of that world and laying hold of and using its resources for all that they are worth. Clearly this is a risky business. The peace it promises is the steady assurance of a mind adequate to its business and not afraid in consequence to put its powers and ideals to the test of the widest experience that can be brought to bear on them. We shall need that sort of mind if America is to play its part cooperatively in the world community which our present situation makes both possible and necessary, but also tragically improbable, and if we are to do our part in America. Simple-mindedness may have been a virtue in simpler times than ours; it is a tragic misfit today, for it can only be the artificial and willful simple-mindedness that is also self-deception. Between such narrowness of mind and poverty of spirit on the one side and the full acceptance of our intellectual and moral responsibilities on the other we have now to choose. If we should choose the first alternative there will not in the near future be much place in America for the kind of philosophy of which I have been speaking. But if, as I believe, the spiritual resources of our country are great enough for choosing the second then we shall be called upon to make use of just the qualities of mind that have so far been described, not as an academic exercise but as a steady attitude of preference and sound judgment in the conduct of affairs. For we shall have to question and enlarge our traditional preconceptions from the standpoint of a more inclusive good, and to prefer the integrity of the process in which public understanding is won to the victory of our side in recurrent controversies and conflicts of interest. We shall have, in short, to be lovers not only of those parts of wisdom and goodness which we have come to regard as our peculiar possession but of the whole toward which, as partners in a common enterprise, all men may work together. And we shall have to learn to make that devotion decisive at crucial moments in our political behavior.

This is a large undertaking. I do not know that we shall succeed in it, or even that we shall be given any real chance to try. But of this I am sure. Nothing less than this is demanded of us by our situation in the contemporary world, and if we do not succeed at this level we shall fail no less surely and more ignominiously on the lower level to which the faint of heart and small of mind now ask us to retreat. This is the plain meaning of the task before us. It is not the business of education, if it is honest, to make hard things look easy, or to sell cheap the goods on which our civilization depends. It is its business to show them forth as the good they are and to invite those who see and honor them to share in the continuing work by which they are fostered and advanced. With such an invitation addressed, in customary fashion, "to whom it may concern," this discussion reaches its appropriate conclusion.

John Dewey (1859–1952)
CHANGING CONCEPTIONS OF PHILOSOPHY

Dewey argues for a modern conception of philosophy that arises out of social and emotional, not merely intellectual, material. According to this conception, philosophy does not aim at proving the existence of some other world, but rather at clarifying human ideas concerning moral and social conflicts in this world. A discussion of Dewey's views on philosophy can be found at the end of Section B of the introductory essay to Part I.

READING QUESTIONS

While reading the selection, try to answer the following questions and identify the passages that support your answers:

1. What problem has traditionally shaped philosophy's role according to Dewey?
2. What conception of philosophy does Dewey propose?
3. What reasons does he give for accepting this conception?
4. What is the role of knowledge in this conception of philosophy?
5. Does Dewey's conception of philosophy make room for problems motivated by sheer curiosity? Why or why not?

Reprinted from John Dewey, *Reconstruction in Philosophy* (Boston: Beacon, 1957), pp. 5–27.

It seems to me that the historic source of philosophies cannot be understood except as we . . . recognize that the ordinary consciousness of the ordinary man left to himself is a creature of desires rather than of intellectual study, inquiry or speculation. Man ceases to be primarily actuated by hopes and fears, loves and hates, only when he is subjected to a discipline which is foreign to human nature, which is, from the standpoint of natural man, artificial. Naturally our books, our scientific and philosophical books, are written by men who have subjected themselves in a superior degree to intellectual discipline and culture. Their thoughts are habitually reasonable. They have learned to check their fancies by facts, and to organize their ideas logically rather than emotionally and dramatically. When they do indulge in reverie and day-dreaming—which is probably more of the time than is conventionally acknowledged—they are aware of what they are doing. They label these excursions, and do not confuse their results with objective experiences. We tend to judge others by ourselves, and because scientific and philosophic books are composed by men in whom the reasonable, logical and objective habit of mind predominates, a similar rationality has been attributed by them to the average and ordinary man. It is then overlooked that both rationality and irrationality are largely irrelevant and episodical in undisciplined human nature; that men are governed by memory rather than by thought, and that memory is not a remembering of actual facts, but is association, suggestion, dramatic fancy. The standard used to meas-ure the value of the suggestions that spring up in the mind is not congruity with fact but emotional congeniality. Do they stimulate and reinforce feeling, and fit into the dramatic tale? Are they

consonant with the prevailing mood, and can they be rendered into the traditional hopes and fears of the community? If we are willing to take the word dreams with a certain liberality, it is hardly too much to say that man, save in his occasional times of actual work and struggle, lives in a world of dreams, rather than of facts, and a world of dreams that is organized about desires whose success and frustration form its stuff.

To treat the early beliefs and traditions of mankind as if they were attempts at scientific explanation of the world, only erroneous and absurd attempts, is thus to be guilty of a great mistake. The material out of which philosophy finally emerges is irrelevant to science and to explanation. It is figurative, symbolic of fears and hopes, made of imaginations and suggestions, not significant of a world of objective fact intellectually confronted. It is poetry and drama, rather than science, and is apart from scientific truth and falsity, rationality or absurdity of fact in the same way in which poetry is independent of these things.

This original material has, however, to pass through at least two stages before it becomes philosophy proper. One is the stage in which stories and legends and their accompanying dramatizations are consolidated. At first the emotionalized records of experiences are largely casual and transitory. Events that excite the emotions of an individual are seized upon and lived over in tale and pantomime. But some experiences are so frequent and recurrent that they concern the group as a whole. They are socially generalized. The piecemeal adventure of the single individual is built out till it becomes representative and typical of the emotional life of the tribe. Certain incidents affect the weal and woe of the group in its entirety and thereby get an exceptional emphasis and elevation. A certain texture of tradition is built up; the story becomes a social heritage and possession; the pantomime develops into the stated rite. Tradition thus formed becomes a kind of norm to which individual fancy and suggestion conform. An abiding framework of imagination is constructed. A communal way of conceiving life grows up into which individuals are inducted by education. Both unconsciously and by definite social requirement individual memories are assimilated to group memory or tradition, and individual fancies are accommodated to the body of beliefs characteristic of a community. Poetry becomes fixated and systematized. The story becomes a social norm. The original drama which re-enacts an emotionally important experience is institutionalized into a cult. Suggestions previously free are hardened into doctrines.

The systematic and obligatory nature of such doctrines is hastened and confirmed through conquests and political consolidation. As the area of a government is extended, there is a definite motive for systematizing and unifying beliefs once free and floating. Aside from natural accommodation and assimilation springing from the fact of intercourse and the needs of common understanding, there is often political necessity which leads the ruler to centralize traditions and beliefs in order to extend and strengthen his prestige and authority. Judea, Greece, Rome, and I presume all other countries having a long history, present records of a continual working over of earlier local rites and doctrines in the interests of a wider social unity and a more extensive political power. I shall ask you to assume with me that in this way the larger cosmogonies and cosmologies of the race as well as the larger ethical traditions have arisen. Whether this is literally so or not, it is not necessary to inquire, much less to demonstrate. It is enough for our purposes that under social influences there took place a fixing and organizing of doctrines and cults which gave general traits to the imagination and general rules to conduct, and that such a consolidation was a necessary antecedent to the formation of any philosophy as we understand that term.

Although a necessary antecedent, this organization and generalization of ideas and principles of belief is not the sole and sufficient generator of philosophy. There is still lacking the motive for logical system and intellectual proof. This we may suppose to be furnished by the need of reconciling the moral rules and ideals embodied in the traditional code

with the matter of fact positivistic knowledge which gradually grows up. For man can never be wholly the creature of suggestion and fancy. The requirements of continued existence make indispensable some attention to the actual facts of the world. Although it is surprising how little check the environment actually puts upon the formation of ideas, since no notions are too absurd not to have been accepted by some people, yet the environment does enforce a certain minimum of correctness under penalty of extinction. That certain things are foods, that they are to be found in certain places, that water drowns, fire burns, that sharp points penetrate and cut, that heavy things fall unless supported, that there is a certain regularity in the changes of day and night and the alternation of hot and cold, wet and dry:—such prosaic facts force themselves upon even primitive attention. Some of them are so obvious and so important that they have next to no fanciful context. Auguste Comte says somewhere that he knows of no savage people who had a God of weight although every other natural quality or force may have been deified. Gradually there grows up a body of homely generalizations preserving and transmitting the wisdom of the race about the observed facts and sequences of nature. This knowledge is especially connected with industries, arts and crafts where observation of materials and processes is required for successful action, and where action is so continuous and regular that spasmodic magic will not suffice. Extravagantly fantastic notions are eliminated because they are brought into juxtaposition with what actually happens.

The sailor is more likely to be given to what we now term superstitions than say the weaver, because his activity is more at the mercy of sudden change and unforeseen occurrence. But even the sailor while he may regard the wind as the uncontrollable expression of the caprice of a great spirit, will still have to become acquainted with some purely mechanical principles of adjustment of boat, sails and oar to the wind. Fire may be conceived as a supernatural dragon because some time or other a swift, bright and devouring flame called before the mind's eye the quick-moving and dangerous serpent. But the housewife who tends the fire and the pots wherein food cooks will still be compelled to observe certain mechanical facts of draft and replenishment, and passage from wood to ash. Still more will the worker in metals accumulate verifiable details about the conditions and consequences of the operation of heat. He may retain for special and ceremonial occasions traditional beliefs, but everyday familiar use will expel these conceptions for the greater part of the time, when fire will be to him of uniform and prosaic behavior, controllable by practical relations of cause and effect. As the arts and crafts develop and become more elaborate, the body of positive and tested knowledge enlarges, and the sequences observed become more complex and of greater scope. Technologies of this kind give that common-sense knowledge of nature out of which science takes its origin. They provide not merely a collection of positive facts, but they give expertness in dealing with materials and tools, and promote the development of the experimental habit of mind, as soon as an art can be taken away from the rule of sheer custom.

For a long time the imaginative body of beliefs closely connected with the moral habits of a community group and with its emotional indulgences and consolations persists side by side with the growing body of matter of fact knowledge. Wherever possible they are interlaced. At other points, their inconsistencies forbid their interweaving, but the two things are kept apart as if in different compartments. Since one is merely superimposed upon the other their incompatibility is not felt, and there is no need of reconciliation. In most cases, the two kinds of mental products are kept apart because they become the possession of separate social classes. The religious and poetic beliefs having acquired a definite social and political value and function are in the keeping of a higher class directly associated with the ruling elements in the society. The workers and craftsmen who possess the prosaic matter of fact knowledge are likely to occupy a low social status, and their kind of knowledge is affected by the social disesteem entertained for the manual worker who engages in activities useful to the body. It doubtless was this fact in Greece which in spite of the keenness of observation, the extraordinary power of logical reasoning and the great freedom of speculation attained by the Athenian, postponed the general and systematic employment of the experimental method. Since the industrial craftsman was only just above the slave in social rank, his type of knowledge and the method upon which it depended lacked prestige and authority.

Nevertheless, the time came when matter of fact knowledge increased to such bulk and scope that it came into conflict with not merely the detail but with the spirit and temper of traditional and imaginative beliefs. Without going into the vexed question of how and why, there is no doubt that this is just what happened in what we term the sophistic movement in Greece, within which originated philosophy proper in the sense in which the western world understands that term. The fact that the sophists had a bad name given them by Plato and Aristotle, a name they have never been able to shake off, is evidence that with the sophists the strife between the two types of belief was the emphatic thing, and that the conflict had a disconcerting effect upon the traditional system of religious beliefs and the moral code of conduct bound up with it. Although Socrates was doubtless sincerely interested in the reconciliation of the two sides, yet the fact that he approached the matter from the side of matter of fact method, giving its canons and criteria primacy, was enough to bring him to the condemnation of death as a contemner of the gods and a corrupter of youth.

The fate of Socrates and the ill-fame of the sophists may be used to suggest some of the striking contrasts between traditional emotionalized belief on one hand and prosaic matter of fact knowledge on the other:—the purpose of the comparison being to bring out the point that while all the advantages of what we call science were on the side of the latter, the advantages of social esteem and authority, and of intimate contact with what gives life its deeper lying values were on the side of traditional belief. To all appearances, the specific and verified knowledge of the environment had only a limited and technical scope. It had to do with the arts, and the purpose and good of the artisan after all did not extend very far. They were subordinate and almost servile. Who would put the art of the shoemaker on the same plane as the art of ruling the state? Who would put even the higher art of the physician in healing the body, upon the level of the art of the priest in healing the soul? Thus Plato constantly draws the contrast in his dialogues. The shoemaker is a judge of a good pair of shoes, but he is no judge at all of the more important question whether and when it is good to wear shoes; the physician is a good judge of health, but whether it is a good thing or not to be well or better to die, he knows not. While the artisan is expert as long as purely limited technical questions arise, he is helpless when it comes to the only really important questions, the moral questions as to values. Consequently, his type of knowledge is inherently inferior and needs to be controlled by a higher kind of knowledge which will reveal ultimate ends and purposes, and thus put and keep technical and mechanical knowledge in its proper place. Moreover, in Plato's pages we find, because of Plato's adequate dramatic sense, a lively depicting of the impact in particular men of the conflict between tradition and the new claims of purely intellectual knowledge. The conservative is shocked beyond measure at the idea of teaching the military art by abstract rules, by science. One does not just fight, one fights for one's country. Abstract science cannot convey love and loyalty, nor can it be a substitute, even upon the more technical side, for those ways and means of fighting in which devotion to the country has been traditionally embodied.

The way to learn the fighting art is through association with those who have themselves learned to defend the country, by becoming saturated with its ideals and customs; by becoming in short a practical adept in the Greek tradition as to fighting. To attempt to derive abstract rules from a comparison of native ways of fighting with the enemies' ways is to begin to go over to the enemies' traditions and gods: it is to begin to be false to one's own country.

Such a point of view vividly realized enables us to appreciate the antagonism aroused by the positivistic point of view when it came into conflict with the traditional. The latter was deeply rooted in social habits and loyalties; it was surcharged with the moral aims for which men lived and the moral rules by which they lived. Hence it was as basic and as comprehensive as life itself, and palpitated with the warm glowing colors of the community life in which men realized their own being. In contrast, the positivistic knowledge was concerned with merely physical utilities, and lacked the ardent associations of belief hallowed by sacrifices of ancestors and worship of contemporaries. Because of its limited and concrete character it was dry, hard, cold.

Yet the more acute and active minds, like that of Plato himself, could no longer be content to accept, along with the conservative citizen of the time, the old beliefs in the old way. The growth of positive knowledge and of the critical, inquiring spirit undermined these in their old form. The advantages in definiteness, in accuracy, in verifiability were all on the side of the new knowledge. Tradition was noble in aim and scope, but uncertain in foundation. The unquestioned life, said Socrates, was not one fit to be lived by man, who is a questioning being because he is a rational being. Hence he must search out the reason of things, and not accept them from custom and political authority. What was to be done? Develop a method of rational investigation and proof which should place the essential elements of traditional belief upon an unshakable basis; develop a method of thought and knowledge which while purifying tradition should preserve its moral and social values unimpaired; nay, by purifying them, add to their power and authority. To put it in a word, that which had rested upon custom was to be restored, resting no longer upon the habits of the past, but upon the very metaphysics of Being and the Universe. Metaphysics is a substitute for custom as the source and guarantor of higher moral and social values—that is the leading theme of the classic philosophy of Europe, as evolved by Plato and Aristotle—a philosophy, let us always recall, renewed and restated by the Christian philosophy of Medieval Europe.

Out of this situation emerged, if I mistake not, the entire tradition regarding the function and office of philosophy which till very recently has controlled the systematic and constructive philosophies of the western world. If I am right in my main thesis that the origin of philosophy lay in an attempt to reconcile the two different types of mental product, then the key is in our hands as to the main traits of subsequent philosophy so far as that was not of a negative and heterodox kind. In the first place, philosophy did not develop in an unbiased way from an open and unprejudiced origin. It had its task cut out for it from the start. It had a mission to perform, and it was sworn in advance to that mission. It had to extract the essential moral kernel out of the threatened traditional beliefs of the past. So far so good; the work was critical and in the interests of the only true conservatism—that which will conserve and not waste the values wrought out by humanity. But it was also precommitted to extracting this moral essence in a spirit congenial to the spirit of past beliefs. The association with imagination and with social authority was too intimate to be deeply disturbed. It was not possible to conceive of the content of social institutions in any form radically different from that in which they had existed in the past. It became the work of philosophy to justify on rational grounds the spirit, though not the form, of accepted beliefs and traditional customs.

The resulting philosophy seemed radical enough and even dangerous to the average Athenian because of the difference in form and method. In the sense of pruning away excrescences and eliminating factors which to the average citizen were all one with the basic beliefs, it was radical. But looked at in the perspective of history and in contrast with different types of thought which developed later in different social environments, it is now easy to see how profoundly, after all, Plato and Aristotle reflected the meaning of Greek tradition and habit, so that their writings remain, with the writings of the great dramatists, the best introduction of a student into the innermost ideals and aspirations of distinctively Greek life. Without Greek religion, Greek art, Greek civic life, their philosophy would have been impossible; while the effect of that science upon which the philosophers most prided themselves turns out to have been superficial and negligible. This apologetic spirit of philosophy is even more apparent when Medieval Christianity about the twelfth century sought for a systematic rational presentation of itself and made use of classic philosophy, especially that of Aristotle, to justify itself to reason. A not unsimilar occurrence characterizes the chief philosophic systems of Germany in the early nineteenth century, when Hegel assumed the task of justifying in the name of rational idealism the doctrines and institutions which were menaced by the new spirit of science and popular government. The result has been that the great systems have not been free from party spirit exercised in behalf of preconceived beliefs. Since they have at the same time professed complete intellectual independence and rationality, the result has been too often to impart to philosophy an element of insincerity, all the more insidious because wholly unconscious on the part of those who sustained philosophy.

And this brings us to a second trait of philosophy springing from its origin. Since it aimed at a rational justification of things that had been previously accepted because of their emotional congeniality and social prestige, it had to make much of the apparatus of reason and proof. Because of the lack of intrinsic rationality in the matters with which it dealt, it leaned over backward, so to speak, in parade of logical form. In dealing with matters of fact, simpler and rougher ways of demonstration may be resorted to. It is enough, so to say, to produce the fact in question and point to it—the fundamental form of all demonstration. But when it comes to convincing men of the truth of doctrines which are no longer to be accepted upon the say-so of custom and social authority, but which also are not capable of empirical verification, there is no recourse save to magnify the signs of rigorous thought and rigid demonstration. Thus arises that appearance of abstract definition and ultra-scientific argumentation which repels so many from philosophy but which has been one of its chief attractions to its devotees.

At the worst, this has reduced philosophy to a show of elaborate terminology, a hair-splitting logic, and a fictitious devotion to the mere external forms of comprehensive and minute demonstration. Even at the best, it has tended to produce an overdeveloped attachment to system for its own sake, and an over–pretentious claim to certainty. Bishop Butler declared that probability is the guide of life; but few philosophers have been courageous enough to avow that philosophy can be satisfied with anything that is merely probable. The customs dictated by tradition and desire had claimed finality and immutability. They had claimed to give certain and unvarying laws of conduct. Very early in its history philosophy made pretension to a similar conclusiveness, and something of this temper has clung to classic philosophies ever since. They have insisted that they were more scientific than the sciences—that, indeed, philosophy was necessary because after all the special sciences fail in attaining final and complete truth. There have been a few dissenters who have ventured to assert, as did William James, that "philosophy is vision" and that its chief function is to free men's minds from bias and prejudice and to enlarge their perceptions of the world about them. But in the main philosophy has set up much more ambitious pretensions. To say frankly that philosophy can proffer nothing but hypotheses, and that these hypotheses are of value only as they render men's minds more sensitive to life about them, would seem like a negation of philosophy itself.

In the third place, the body of beliefs dictated by desire and imagination and developed under the influence of communal authority into an authoritative tradition, was pervasive and comprehensive. It was, so to speak, omnipresent in all the details of the group life. Its pressure was unremitting and its influence universal. It was then probably inevitable that the rival principle, reflective thought, should aim at a similar universality and comprehensiveness. It would be as inclusive and far-reaching metaphysically as tradition had been socially. Now there was just one way in which this pretension could be accomplished in conjunction with a claim of complete logical system and certainty.

All philosophies of the classic type have made a fixed and fundamental distinction between two realms of existence. One of these corresponds to the religious and supernatural world of popular tradition, which in its metaphysical rendering became the world of highest and ultimate reality. Since the final source and sanction of all important truths and rules of conduct in community life had been found in superior and unquestioned religious beliefs, so the absolute and supreme reality of philosophy afforded the only sure guaranty of truth about empirical matters, and the sole rational guide to proper social institutions and individual behavior. Over against this absolute and noumenal reality which could be apprehended only by the systematic discipline of philosophy itself stood the ordinary empirical, relatively real, phenomenal world of everyday experience. It was with this world that the practical affairs and utilities of men were connected. It was to this imperfect and perishing world that matter of fact, positivistic science referred.

This is the trait which, in my opinion, has affected most deeply the classic notion about the nature of philosophy. Philosophy has arrogated to itself the office of demonstrating the existence of a transcendent, absolute or inner reality and of revealing to man the nature and features of this ultimate and higher reality. It has therefore claimed that it was in possession of a higher organ of knowledge than is employed by positive science and ordinary practical experience, and that it is marked by a superior dignity and importance—a claim which is undeniable *if* philosophy leads man to proof and intuition of a Reality beyond that open to day-by-day life and the special sciences.

This claim has, of course, been denied by various philosophers from time to time. But for the most part these denials have been agnostic and sceptical. They have contented themselves with asserting that absolute and ultimate reality is beyond human ken. But they have not ventured to deny that such Reality would be the appropriate sphere for the exercise of philosophic knowledge provided only it were within the reach of human intelligence. Only comparatively recently has another conception of the proper office of philosophy arisen. This course of lectures will be devoted to setting forth this different conception of philosophy in some of its main contrasts to what this lecture has termed the classic conception. At this point, it can be referred to only by anticipation and in cursory fashion. It is implied in the account which has been given of the origin of philosophy out of the background of an authoritative tradition; a tradition originally dictated by man's imagination working under the influence of love and hate and in the interest of emotional excitement and satisfaction. Common frankness requires that it be stated that this account of the origin of philosophies claiming to deal with absolute Being in a systematic way has been given with malice prepense. It

seems to me that this genetic method of approach is a more effective way of undermining this type of philosophic theorizing than any attempt at logical refutation could be.

If this lecture succeeds in leaving in your minds as a reasonable hypothesis the idea that philosophy originated not out of intellectual material, but out of social and emotional material, it will also succeed in leaving with you a changed attitude toward traditional philosophies. They will be viewed from a new angle and placed in a new light. New questions about them will be aroused and new standards for judging them will be suggested.

If any one will commence without mental reservations to study the history of philosophy not as an isolated thing but as a chapter in the development of civilization and culture; if one will connect the story of philosophy with a study of anthropology, primitive life, the history of religion, literature and social institutions, it is confidently asserted that he will reach his own independent judgment as to the worth of the account which has been presented today. Considered in this way, the history of philosophy will take on a new significance. What is lost from the standpoint of would-be science is regained from the standpoint of humanity. Instead of the disputes of rivals about the nature of reality, we have the scene of human clash of social purpose and aspirations. Instead of impossible attempts to transcend experience, we have the significant record of the efforts of men to formulate the things of experience to which they are most deeply and passionately attached. Instead of impersonal and purely speculative endeavors to contemplate as remote beholders the nature of absolute things-in-themselves, we have a living picture of the choice of thoughtful men about what they would have life to be, and to what ends they would have men shape their intelligent activities.

Any one of you who arrives at such a view of past philosophy will of necessity be led to entertain a quite definite conception of the scope and aim of future philosophizing. He will inevitably be committed to the notion that what philosophy has been unconsciously, without knowing or intending it, and, so to speak, under cover, it must henceforth be openly and deliberately. When it is acknowledged that under disguise of dealing with ultimate reality, philosophy has been occupied with the precious values embedded in social traditions, that it has sprung from a clash of social ends and from a conflict of inherited institutions with incompatible contemporary tendencies, it will be seen that the task of future philosophy is to clarify men's ideas as to the social and moral strifes of their own day. Its aim is to become so far as is humanly possible an organ for dealing with these conflicts. That which may be pretentiously unreal when it is formulated in metaphysical distinctions becomes intensely significant when connected with the drama of the struggle of social beliefs and ideals. Philosophy which surrenders its somewhat barren monopoly of dealings with Ultimate and Absolute Reality will find a compensation in enlightening the moral forces which move mankind and in contributing to the aspirations of men to attain to a more ordered and intelligent happiness.

Robert P. Churchill (contemporary)
ANALYZING ARGUMENTS

Churchill contrasts necessary with empirical statements, and deductive with inductive arguments. He also presents some notions central for assessing arguments: namely, form and content, validity, soundness, and reliable inductive inference. These and related notions are discussed in Section C of the introductory essay to Part I.

READING QUESTIONS

As you read the selection, try to answer the following questions and identify the passages that support your answers:

1. What is a statement?
2. What is, according to Churchill, the distinction between necessary and empirical statements?
3. What is an argument in the logician's sense of "argument"?
4. What is a valid argument?
5. What is a sound argument?

Reprinted from Robert P. Churchill, *Becoming Logical* (New York: St. Martin's, 1986), pp. 40–44, 46–54, 57–59. Copyright © 1986 by Robert P. Churchill. Reprinted by permission of St. Martin's Press, Inc.

When considering an argument from a logical point of view, we temporarily suspend interest in what its statements actually mean and focus exclusively on the relationship between the premises and the conclusion. That is, we distinguish the *form* of the argument—the connection between its parts—from its *content*. To increase our ability to understand and evaluate arguments, we must further investigate their formal properties. In addition, we must develop a clearer understanding of what counts as a "good" argument in logic. Particularly, we must consider the concepts of *deduction* and *induction* and *validity* and *soundness* as they apply to argumentation.

1. DEDUCTION AND INDUCTION

Logicians divide arguments into two basic types: *deductive* and *nondeductive*. This division marks a significant difference in the way we analyze and evaluate arguments. By far the largest number of nondeductive arguments are of a type called *inductive*, and an understanding of inductive reasoning is indispensable to an analysis of other nondeductive arguments. So this discussion will concern the kinds of arguing called *deduction* and *induction*.

In a deductive argument, the premises are intended to supply all the information needed to support the conclusion. The conclusion makes *explicit* a bit of information already *implicit* in the premises when they are brought together; it is said to be "contained in" the premises. Thus, one who presents a deductive argument believes the truth of the premises will guarantee the truth of the conclusion. Thus,

> A deductive argument is one that would be justified by claiming that if the premises are true, they necessarily establish the truth of the conclusion.

The premises of an inductive argument may supply good reasons for accepting the conclusion; they may even make its truth highly probable. But the truth of the premises cannot *insure* that the conclusion will be true as well. The conclusion of an inductive argument "goes beyond" the premises: it expresses a conjecture that can definitely be known to be true (or false) only after further observation—if ever.

> An inductive argument is one in which the premises provide evidence for believing the conclusion is true, but not conclusive evidence.

In accepting the conclusion of an argument, one is said to be making an inference.

> An inference is a mental act by which one comes to believe a conclusion because it is supported by premises that are accepted as true.

Depending on whether the argument under consideration is deductive or inductive, one is said to be making a *deductive inference* or an *inductive inference*. Deductive inference involves the rearranging of information; one starts with statements assumed to be true to see what other statements can be logically derived from them. But inductive inference is an information-extending process: one starts with a set of particular observations and infers from them some conclusion about an entity or event that has not yet been experienced. While deductive inference extracts the implications of what is already known, inductive inference moves from the known to the unknown. The following hypothetical case history contains examples of both deductive and inductive inferences.

Imagine that your life's ambition has been to become a first-rate entomologist, a scientist who studies insects. As a child, you had a prize-winning butterfly collection that was the pride of the neighborhood; in high school, you won a science-fair award for the breeding of praying mantises in captivity; and your enthusiasm has just seen you through four arduous years as a zoology major.

On your last exam as a senior you came across the following true-or–false statement:

> *Some scorpions have antennae.*

Given your knowledge of insects and related species, you quickly checked off "false" as the answer to the question. Your reasoning would have gone something like this:

> *All scorpions are arachnids.*
> *No arachnids have antennae.*
> *Therefore, no scorpions have antennae.*

Now on a vacation in Arizona, you notice what appears to be a new species of spider. Deciding to observe these spiders to see if they will spin webs, you reason as follows:

> *All the spiders I have observed in their natural habitats have spun webs.*
> *All the kinds of spiders studied in college zoology spin webs.*
> *All species of spiders so far discovered in the southwestern United States have been web spinners.*
> *Therefore, it is highly probable that this new species of spider spins webs.*

Your expectations are fulfilled; the spiders are fine web spinners.

You include the news of the discovery in a letter to an acquaintance who works at the Smithsonian Institution in Washington, D.C. Soon your friend sends you an announcement of an opening for an assistant curator at the Smithsonian's "bug museum"—the entomology division of the Museum of Natural History.

You drive your car to Washington, approach the museum, and search for a parking space. The only empty space is next to a fire hydrant. Should you park your car there? Quickly thinking over your past experience, you recall getting two traffic tickets—one in Chicago and one in Pittsburgh—for parking next to fire hydrants. You know someone in St. Louis who also got a ticket for parking next to a fire hydrant. So you decide to pass up this space.

After having safely parked your car in a pay lot, you hurry into the museum's employment office. There, while you fill out an application, you are told that the museum has adopted a new rule for zoologists seeking employment. To qualify for an appointment, an applicant must have either a B.S. and three years of experience, or a B.S. awarded in the last three years and a cumulative grade point average of 3.25 or better. You breathe a sigh of relief. You are fresh out of college with no employment record; you have a B.S.; and you graduated with a 3.57 average. "Wish me luck," you whisper softly to the mounted and displayed skeleton of a brontosaurus as you are ushered into the director's office for an interview.

This hypothetical case contains two illustrations each of deduction and induction. The reasoning that led you to conclude that no scorpions have antennae is an example of deductive inference. You realize this is true simply by seeing how the premises relate arachnids, scorpions, and the characteristic of having antennae. The reasoning concerning employment qualifications is a second example of deductive inference. Here again, the inference—that you meet the job requirements for an assistant curator of entomology—is based solely upon an understanding of the logical relations between the premises. The rule specifies *alternative* conditions for an appointment, and your own qualifications match one of those alternatives.

The two inductive inferences are the assumptions that the new species of spider will be web spinners and that it would be unwise to park near a fire hydrant. Your past experience of spiders—all that you have read about them and directly observed—leads you to infer that members of the new species, which you have not yet studied, will probably spin webs. Likewise, you reason from your past experiences of parking next to fire hydrants and from the experience of a friend who once did so that parking beside this fire hydrant will result in your being ticketed.

Besides occurring within the same discussion, deductive and inductive arguments can be interrelated. The conclusion of an inductive argument can be used as a premise of a deductive argument, and vice versa. Suppose, for example, that a long examination of every known species of spider in the Arizona deserts confirms that they all spin webs. This evidence would be the premise of an inductive argument that concluded "All spiders indigenous to the Arizona deserts are web spinners." This conclusion, in turn, can be used as a premise in a deductive argument:

All spiders indigenous to the Arizona deserts are web spinners.
This spider was found living naturally in the Arizona deserts.
Therefore, this spider is a web spinner.

Deductive and inductive inferences can be distinguished from each other according to the kind of claim being made. If the arguer believes that, given the truth of the premises, the conclusion is established beyond any reasonable doubt, then the argument is intended to be deductive. The arguer justifies the argument by claiming that someone who accepts the premises as true *must* also accept the conclusion as true. Someone, for example, who believes that all scorpions are arachnids and that no arachnids have antennae would be inconsistent in denying that no scorpions have antennae. To do so would be saying that it is both true and false that no scorpions have antennae. And a museum personnel director who accepts a B.S. and a grade point average of 3.25 or above as qualifying an applicant for consideration would be inconsistent in claiming that with a B.S. and a 3.57 average you do not satisfy the specified requirements.

While the premises of an inductive argument may provide very strong support for the conclusion, there would be no inconsistency in accepting the premises but rejecting the conclusion. For example, it could be the case that all species of spiders hitherto observed have been web spinners but still possible (although not probable) that the newly discovered species does not spin webs. Similarly, it is possible (although not probable) that cars parked next to fire hydrants in Washington, D.C., will not be ticketed, even though they have been ticketed in all other American cities and towns in which you have had any experience.

A clue to whether an argument is deductive or inductive can sometimes be found in its wording. If the speaker or writer says that the conclusion "must" follow or "necessarily" follows, then the argument is to be considered deductive. If the conclusion is referred to as "probable" or "likely," or in words to that effect, then the argument is intended to be inductive. It is often impossible to tell from the wording, though, whether an argument is intended to be deductive or inductive. In such cases, we must decide whether the argument makes better sense if interpreted as deductive or as inductive.

Another difference between deduction and induction concerns the kind of information contained in their premises and conclusions. Deduction often involves reasoning from the general to the specific—for example, from characteristics of the whole biological class of arachnids to those of one species—scorpions. And induction often involves making generalizations on the basis of particular instances. An example of such reasoning is as follows:

The new species of spiders discovered in Arizona spin webs.
The spiders I observed at college spin webs.
The spiders my roommate saw in Minnesota spin webs.
Therefore, probably all spiders spin webs.

By no means is all deduction reasoning from the general to the specific, however, nor is induction always from particular instances to a general rule. Here, for example, is a deductive argument in which the distinction between the "general" and "specific" does not even arise:

If the Flying Wallendas have no more accidents, they will revive the public's interest in circus acrobatics.
The Flying Wallendas will have no more accidents.
Therefore, the Flying Wallendas will revive the public's interest in circus acrobatics.

The inductive reasoning involving the parking tickets was an argument from experience of traffic regulations in two specific cities to a conjecture about traffic regulations in another specific city. It did not proceed to a generalization about traffic regulations throughout the world. Here is another inductive argument that does not proceed from specific instances to a general rule:

The wool suit I bought from the local tailor was poorly sewn.
The corduroy suit I bought from the local tailor was poorly sewn.
Therefore, the next suit I buy from the local tailor will be poorly sewn.

In common parlance *deduction* is used to mean almost any kind of inference, though often what is being referred to is an inductive argument. Dr. Watson, Sherlock Holmes's faithful companion, was given to describing Holmes's inferences as "brilliant deductions." However, many of those inferences were inductive, not deductive. For example, in "The Red-Headed League," Holmes "deduces" that a client has been in China by observing that a tattoo on the man's arm has a design peculiar to Chinese tattooers. But Holmes's reasoning is really inductive, for the evidence of the design does not guarantee that the man was in China. The design might have been made by a Chinese tattooer in London or even by a European tattooer copying a Chinese original.

2. VALIDITY, SOUNDNESS, AND RELIABLE INDUCTIVE INFERENCE

In the previous section, we made a distinction between deductive arguments and inductive arguments. We shall now see what it means for each kind of argument to be "good." In deduction, the acceptability of the conclusion depends entirely on the *form* of the argument. In induction, the conclusion is acceptable only if the premises provide sufficient *evidence* to make its truth probable.

To consider deductive arguments first, what, then, is the difference between form and content? And how are the form and content of an argument related to its *validity* and *soundness*—the qualities that make it a good argument?

Form and Content

. . . Whether statements about people, things, or events are true or not usually has to do with their relationship to factual situations. Thus, the statement "Ospreys inhabit the Chesapeake Bay" is true, while the statement "Wild orchids grow in Iceland" is false. Ospreys can indeed be found living wild in the tidewater inlets of Chesapeake Bay, but orchids cannot be found growing naturally in the countryside of Iceland. What is true or false, then, is the statement's *content.*

Form is that which remains the same throughout changes in content. It can be likened to the federal income-tax form, which is the same for everyone, even though the information written on it differs depending upon which taxpayer fills it out. The point is illustrated by comparing two statements:

New York City is smaller than Atlanta.
Atlanta is smaller than Chicago.

The first statement is false, the second true. The content of the first statement is different from the content of the second. But both have the same form, as can be seen by substituting letters—known as *variables,* because they have no fixed meaning—for the names of cities:

X *is smaller than* Y.

Although the truth or falsity of a statement usually depends upon its content, there are exceptions to this general rule. Some sentences express truthful statements just because of the meaning or the logical relationships of the words included in them. "It is either raining or it is not raining" belongs to this group. Regardless of the weather, this sentence will be true because its truth is a consequence of its form.

While truth is a property of statements, *validity and soundness are properties of an argument as a whole.* Premises and conclusions, being statements, are said to be true or false. But in evaluating an argument, we must consider the relationship, or connection, between its parts. Our purpose is to see whether it is possible to move from the truth of the premises to the truth or probable truth of the conclusion.

The speaker or writer who presents an argument is in effect claiming (1) that the premises are true, and (2) that because the premises are true, the conclusion is also true. Thus, two kinds of error can be made when advancing an argument. One can make a *factual error* by being mistaken in claiming that the premises are all true. Or one can make a *logical error* by misinterpreting the logical relation between the premises and the conclusion. If the error has to do with the logical relation between its parts, then the argument has an inadequate form and is said to be *invalid*. If one or more of the premises (and/or the conclusion) are false, the argument is said to be *unsound*. In either case, the argument is fallacious.

Validity

The concept of validity concerns the form of an argument. If the premises are linked to the conclusion in such a way that their truth would guarantee the truth of the conclusion, then the argument is called *valid*. Validity, therefore, pertains only to deductive arguments. For as shown in Section 1, in a deductive argument the conclusion makes explicit information that is implicit in the premises.

> A *valid argument is a deductive argument such that, if the premises were all true, the conclusion would have to be true.*

A standard example of a valid deductive argument is the following:

> *All human beings are mortal.*
> *Socrates is a human being.*
> *Therefore, Socrates is mortal.*

Now, if all human beings are in the group of mortal beings, and if Socrates is a human being, Socrates must be in the group of mortal beings. The truth of the premises guarantees the truth of the conclusion.

This argument is valid in virtue of its form; it really does not matter what the content of the argument is. To say that it has a *valid form* means that any

argument with exactly the same form will also be valid. Thus, a valid argument will still result if the name *Ronald Reagan* is substituted for *Socrates* in the original. In fact, one can substitute different words for all the terms in the original argument and still have a valid argument. For example, the argument

> *All cetaceans are marine mammals.*
> *A dolphin is a cetacean.*
> *Therefore, a dolphin is a marine mammal.*

has the same form as our argument about Socrates' mortality. Both have the form

> *All* X *are* Y.
> Z *is an* X.
> *Therefore,* Z *is* Y.

The validity of an argument depends entirely upon the formal relationship between the premises and conclusion or between the terms (for example, dolphins, cetaceans, marine animals) linked by the premises and conclusion. An argument, whose form is valid can guarantee the *truth* of a conclusion only when the premises are all true. Thus, it is possible to have a valid argument with a false conclusion. The following is one example:

> *All aquatic creatures have gills.*
> *A whale is an aquatic creature.*
> *Therefore, a whale has gills.*

Here we have an argument with the same valid form as the arguments about Socrates and dolphins. We saw that a valid deductive argument cannot have all true premises and a false conclusion. In the argument immediately preceding, the conclusion is false, *but so is the first premise.* This demonstrates that questions about the truth of the premises must be answered independently of questions about the validity of the argument.

Can an *invalid* argument have a true conclusion? Look at this example:

> *All cetaceans have fins.*
> *All dolphins have fins.*
> *Therefore, all dolphins are cetaceans.*

Here the premises are all true, and so is the conclusion. But the premises don't guarantee the conclusion, any more than the premises that all Swedes are Scandinavians and that all Norwegians are Scandinavians can guarantee that all Norwegians are Swedes.

The form of this argument is as follows:

All X *are* Y.
All Z *are* Y.
Therefore, all Z *are* X.

As further evidence that this form is invalid, we can substitute one or more terms to produce an argument with exactly the same form that has true premises and a false conclusion. Let's substitute *fish* for *dolphins:*

All cetaceans have fins.
All fish have fins.
Therefore, all fish are cetaceans.

An argument form cannot be valid if it allows us to deduce a false conclusion from true premises. The conclusion of the previous example, "All dolphins are cetaceans," happens to be true, but not because the premises insure its truth.

Soundness

At the beginning of this discussion it was stated that someone who presents a deductive argument is ordinarily claiming (1) that the premises are true, and (2) that because the premises are true, the conclusion is also true. In considering validity, we have been discussing the second point.

To accept a conclusion as justified, we need to know not only that the inference is *valid* but also that the premises are true. Premises are the foundations of an argument; any argument built on unreliable or shaky premises, like the proverbial house built upon sand, cannot be expected to stand.

If an argument is valid and also has true premises, then it is said to be *sound.*

A sound argument is a deductive argument that is justified because it is valid and has true premises.

TABLE 1   Conditions of Validity and Soundness for Deductive Arguments

If the Premises are:	And the Reasoning is:	Then the Argument is:
true	valid	sound
true	invalid	unsound
false	valid	unsound
false	invalid	unsound

The table shows that of the four possible combinations, only one yields an argument that is sound—that is, whose conclusion is justified. Such an argument has both valid form and true premises.

While valid arguments can be either sound or unsound, all sound arguments are valid. Table 1 summarizes these relations.

You might wonder whether anyone would be interested in deductive arguments that are unsound. Sometimes the subject of an argument is so important that adjusting the argument to make it sound is worthwhile. Suppose, for example, that the person presenting the argument has the facts right (true premises) but has reached the conclusion through faulty inference (invalid form). Here it is important to see whether the faulty inference can be replaced by a correct one or whether a conclusion with a similar impact can be reached. Suppose, on the other hand, that the inference is valid but the argument is unsound because the premises are in doubt. In this case, if you are inclined to reject the conclusion, you will want to show why at least one of the premises is false. But if you are inclined to accept the conclusion, you will want to obtain additional information to show that the premises are true.

Sometimes we cannot determine whether premises are true. In this case, being able validly to infer the consequences that would follow from such premises if they were true can help us judge whether they are in fact true. If, by a *deductive* inference, we arrive at a conclusion that we know is false, then we can be sure that at least one of the premises is false, because a false conclusion cannot validly be *deduced* from true premises.

Examples of this use of valid inference can be found in the history of science. Up until the eighteenth century, for example, many scientists believed in the existence of phlogiston. Phlogiston was thought to be a constituent of all combustible substances, and it was supposedly released as a flame during combustion. The French chemist Antoine Lavoisier (1743–1794) reasoned that if phlogiston escapes from a substance during combustion, then the product remaining after the combustion process would have less weight than the original substance. However, Lavoisier's experiments on the combustion of metals showed that the end product of the combustion process has *greater* weight than the original metal. This served to show that the initial assumption that combustible substances contain phlogiston was false.

Reliable Inductive Inference

The premises of an inductive argument can never guarantee the truth of the conclusion. As we saw in Section 1, no inconsistency is involved in accepting the truth of the premises but denying the truth of the conclusion. Strictly speaking, all inductive arguments are invalid if by valid we mean deductively valid. But to call inductive arguments invalid would be to misunderstand the spirit of inductive inference.

The concept of validity simply does not apply to induction because the purpose of inductive reasoning differs from that of deductive reasoning. Deductive reasoning depends upon the forms by which we move from statements taken to be true to other statements that must therefore be true. Inductive reasoning takes over when these formal relations cannot be established—when we must reason from statements, or propositions, we take to be true to conclusions that go beyond the range of our present knowledge. Consequently, even good inductive arguments can never be sound in the strict sense in which a valid deductive argument can be sound. They cannot fulfill all the requirements for soundness.

That inductive arguments are not strictly sound does *not* mean that we are never justified in accepting the conclusion of such an argument. But whether an inductive argument can be considered justified— or reliable—depends on both the amount and kind of evidence available to support the conclusion and on the extent to which we intend to rely on the conclusion. Thus, in analyzing inductive arguments, we must discover the *degree* to which the weight and relevance of the evidence warrants belief in the conclusion.

The conclusion of an inductive argument is properly stated in terms of some degree of probability. A conclusion that is claimed to be "highly probable" requires weightier and more pertinent evidence than one that is asserted to be only "probable" or "likely" or "possible." In evaluating the argument, one must determine whether the evidence presented in the premises is sufficient to the probability claimed of the conclusion. If the evidence in the relevant premises is sufficient for the degree of probability claimed for the conclusion, then the conclusion can be accepted as justified—even though we can never be sure it will not be proved false in the long run. Thus, while inductive arguments cannot be valid or sound in the same way that deductive inferences can be valid and sound, we can certainly tell the difference between good and bad, reliable and unreliable, inductive arguments.

3. NECESSARY AND EMPIRICAL, OR CONTINGENT, STATEMENTS

Some statements can be known to be true or false just by understanding the meaning of the words used to convey them. Examples are the statements expressed by the sentences "A bachelor is an unmarried male" and "A vixen is a female fox." That it would not be correct to call anyone a bachelor unless this person were an unmarried male shows that it is because of the meaning of *bachelor* that "A bachelor is an unmarried male" can be known to be true. Conversely, to say that a married male is a bachelor is to say something that can be known to be false from the meaning of the words involved. In the same way, it is because *vixen* means "female fox" that the sentence, "A vixen is a female fox," expresses a necessarily true statement and "A vixen is a male fox" expresses a necessarily false statement.

To say that one of these examples is *necessarily* true while the other is *necessarily* false is simply to say that its truth or falsity is determined by the meaning of the words and is not open to confirmation or disconfirmation through experience. We would not need to survey, study, or otherwise observe bachelors or vixens to know whether these sentences express true or false statements. Necessary statements can be known to be true or false without empirical evidence—that is, information obtained from observation or sense perception.

In some cases, the truth or falsity of a necessary statement depends on the logical form of the words used to express it as well as on the meaning of the words themselves. A necessarily true statement is expressed by "Roses are red or they are not red" because the terms *are red* and *are not red* are related by *or* to establish exhaustive categories. Likewise, "Roses are red and they are not red" is self-contradictory because the terms are joined by *and*. In these instances, we say that the statement is necessarily true or necessarily false because of its logical form.

> A necessary statement is one that can be known to be true or false either by understanding the meanings of the words used to express it, or by understanding its logical form.

In this section, we shall concentrate on necessary statements whose truth or falsity depends on the meanings of the words used to express them. . . . But whether the truth or falsity of a statement depends on the meanings of its words or on its form, a necessary statement can be known to be true or false without evidence supplied by observation.

By contrast, statements that are called *empirical*—a word derived from the Latin for "experience"—can be known to be true or false only with reference to the kind of evidence acquired through perception—sensory evidence regarding what has been seen or heard or felt or smelled or tasted. This evidence might consist of direct perceptions of one's own, or it might be indirect, consisting, for example, of what one has heard or read concerning the perceptions of others. Much of history and of the sciences consists of empirical information.

Empirical statements are also called *contingent* statements to emphasize that our knowledge of their truth or falsity is dependent, or contingent, on sensory experience. Thus, for instance, "Oranges are grown in southern California" cannot be known to be true just from a knowledge of the meaning of *oranges* and *southern California* or by understanding the relation indicated by the word *in*. We know it is true because oranges are seen to grow there.

This is not to deny that one can believe that an empirical statement—for example, "Laetrile cures cancer"—is true without having reliable evidence to support the belief. But one cannot know that such a statement is true (or entertain a reasonable belief in its truth) without having (or expecting to have) such evidence.

To some extent, experience is needed to know anything. We cannot even know that "If John is a bachelor, then he is unmarried" is necessarily true unless we have had the experience of learning the meanings of the words in the sentence. But this is a weak sense of "having experience." To say that empirical statements are based on experience means that they can be known to be true or false *only if* they are based on direct or indirect evidence obtained by use of the *senses*.

In addition, there are "borderline" cases in which the distinction between necessary and empirical statements is not clear. Some statements do not seem to belong in either category. Consider this example:

> If you eat a well-balanced diet, you will get all the vitamins your body needs.

Does this example express a necessarily true statement? It is tempting to say that it does, because a *well-balanced diet* is by definition one that provides the needed vitamins. We cannot be completely confident of this response, however, because *well-balanced diet* is indefinite in meaning. Suppose biochemists

discover that the common cold can be prevented only by ingesting massive doses of vitamin C—larger doses than can be acquired by a normal adult through the consumption of natural food. Should we then expand the meaning of *well-balanced diet* to include massive doses of vitamin C provided by pharmaceutical companies? Or should we decide that, under those hypothetical conditions, the statement would be empirical and false?

Although some statements cannot be definitely classified as either necessary or empirical, the distinction is still important. Many statements *do* fit into one category or the other. And with statements that do not fit neatly into either category, it is often useful to ask how they could be understood to be empirical and how they could be understood to be necessary. Answering these questions can bring about a fuller understanding of the meaning of a statement. And insofar as the statement can be understood to be empirical, the analysis can reveal the sort of evidence needed to show that it is true or false.

4. ARGUMENTATION AND ETHICS

As you become more adept at analyzing arguments, *your standards for reasonable and acceptable thinking will rise.* You will expect clearer and more consistent thought of yourself as well as of others. And when you find yourself in a debate over some compelling issue—say, abortion, the nuclear arms freeze, the Equal Rights Amendment, the reinstitution of the draft—you will find that you can help raise the level of the discussion by applying your logical skills. You may even begin to feel some responsibility for doing so. And insofar as clear and consistent thinking is generally conducive to finding the best solutions to problems, such contributions will not only be logical but also *ethical.*

What makes the use of logic ethical is not dissimilar to what makes the use of other kinds of special knowledge ethical. Those with special skills have a moral responsibility to use them in certain situations. Someone familiar with lifesaving techniques, for example, has a moral responsibility to use this knowledge to help a person who is drowning. Similarly, if you should voluntarily become involved in a disagreement over a matter that could have serious consequences, you in a sense have an obligation—a kind of *noblesse oblige*—to do what you can to make the dispute more rational.

The ethics of logical analysis can be formulated as four simple principles—the principles of *responsible expertise, fair play, charity,* and *tolerance.*

The Principle of Responsible Expertise

The responsibility, discussed above, to do what one can to raise the level of rational debate and to expose faulty reasoning is the *Principle of Responsible Expertise.* Having the skill to analyze and evaluate reasoning involves a moral obligation to apply that skill when one willingly engages in a dispute of some importance.

No logician has an obligation to interfere in a matter that is not of at least indirect concern. But once you have decided that you can and should contribute to a discussion, you have an obligation to reason as effectively as you can.

The Principle of Fair Play

. . . The *Principle of Fair Play* stipulates that you avoid taking unfair advantage of the adversary in a debate by using chicanery, sophistry, or other "underhanded" techniques. Fallacious argument was mentioned in Section 1, and you will learn to identify many kinds of fallacies as you study logic further. The objective of learning to detect fallacies is not only to avoid being victimized oneself. Equally important is to avoid fallacies in your own argumentation. It is far better to lose a dispute fairly than to win dishonorably.

The Principle of Fair Play is no ironclad rule, however. There may be times when the consequences of a dispute are so trivial that it does not matter whether one resorts to fallacious reasoning—and doing so may at least be entertaining.

The Principle of Charity

This principle requires that we try to make the best possible interpretation of the discourse being evaluated, whether we are trying to decide if an argument occurs in a passage, looking for the main point of an argument, attempting to clarify the meaning of questionable words or phrases, or formulating missing premises. The aim is to give the benefit of the doubt to the speaker or author. Rather than ridiculing someone for a remark that doesn't follow from what was said earlier or that isn't strictly true, it is more reasonable and responsible to try to reinterpret the passage so that it will make more sense.

It would frustrate attempts to communicate ideas and justify beliefs if arguments had to be perfectly expressed before they could be considered. So be charitable when what the speaker or writer intended requires some guesswork. But being charitable doesn't mean going to extremes to save defective arguments. Reject an argument when there are good reasons for doing so. The Principle of Charity is a reminder to attend to the main thrust of an argument and deal with it fairly.

The Principle of Charity also offers sound practical advice by telling us to avoid setting up a "straw man"—a weak imitation of the argument we are considering. It may be easy to break down a "straw man," but it will also be easy for an adversary to rebut an attack by reformulating the argument slightly to meet your objections. The arguer will simply claim, correctly, that you have misinterpreted the argument by making it seem weaker than it really is.

The Principle of Tolerance

The *Principle of Tolerance* is closely related to the Principle of Charity and the Principle of Fair Play, but it pertains more to your general outlook or frame of mind. In logic, to be tolerant is to recognize the fact that there are times and places when argument analysis just doesn't come into play.

Unfortunately, some people have the idea that the goal of logic is to score points over "opponents." They lose sight of its true purpose—to identify sound and reliable arguments—and they go out of their way to look for errors and to correct others. Sometimes called "logic-choppers," such people try to interpret most conversations as argumentative discourse. But language has many uses, only one of which is to convey information and justify beliefs. And there is an important difference between knowledge and wisdom: to be wise is to possess the understanding and skill to make mature judgments about the use of human knowledge in the context of daily life. We should not try to make an argument out of everything.

Life is not an argument

QUESTIONS FOR REVIEW AND FURTHER THOUGHT

1. What teachings are imparted in the *Upanishads,* and what methods are used to impart them? In what manner and to what extent, if any, do the teaching methods of the *Upanishads* encourage the use of reason? Do they have room for improvement? Why or why not?

2. What touched off Socrates' activities as described in Plato's *Apology?* What method did Socrates use to carry out these activities? In what manner and to what extent, if any, do Socrates' activities and method encourage the use of reason? Do they have room for improvement? Why or why not?

3. How are Aristotle's method and purposes in "Wisdom and Philosophy" different from those of Socrates in Plato's *Apology?* Do they involve a different conception of reason? If so, what is it? If not, why not?

4. How does Whitehead distinguish between culture and expert knowledge? How is this distinction relevant to education? Is it relevant to the attainment of wisdom? Why or why not?

5. What conception of philosophical inquiry would be likely to play a significant role in education understood in Whitehead's sense? Why? Would this conception have any shortcomings? What and why, or why not?

6. What conception of philosophy is elicited by Murphy's discussion? Does it have any shortcomings? If so, what are they, why are they shortcomings, and how could they be overcome? If not, why not?

7. What conception(s) of philosophy is (are) apparently practiced by the philosophers Aristotle discusses? Critically compare and contrast it (them) with other conceptions of philosophy described in Part I.

8. Is Dewey's conception of philosophy preferable to any of those previously mentioned? If so, which ones, and why? Specifically, how sound is Dewey's conception compared with Aristotle's? Give reasons for your assessment and suggest an alternative conception that would overcome whatever shortcomings you see in each of these.

9. Can philosophy conceived as the search for wisdom be parochial? Why or why not?

10. What are the uses of logic in philosophy? How crucial are these uses to philosophy? Given your answers to these two questions, does it follow that logic is a branch of philosophy? Why or why not?

11. Are any of the following statements self-refuting? Give reasons for your answers.
    a. I am lying.
    b. Nothing can possibly be said about anything.
    c. No statement can be taken seriously.
    d. I am not denying anything.
    e. I do not exist.
    f. "Rumors of my death have been highly exaggerated." (Mark Twain)
    g. "You're so vain.
       I bet you think this song is about you." (Carly Simon)

12. What shortcomings can you detect in the following argument? Why are they shortcomings?

> I know that any statement I claim to know might be false.
> I also know that if any statement I claim to know might be false, then I do not know any statement I claim to know.
> Hence, I do not know any statement I claim to know.

13. Explain what, if anything, is wrong with the following statement: "We know that the robbery was the work of thieves because, in the past, thieves and robberies have been highly correlated."

14. Do any of the authors in Part I engage in cross-cultural reflection and dialogue to any extent? Do they, for example, try to adapt categories used in other cultures to their own cultural context? Which authors do this, and how and how fruitfully do they do it? If you think that none engage in cross-cultural reflection, how could they have done this while remaining faithful to their own views?

II

What Are Truth, Knowledge, and Faith, and How Are They Related?

A. WHAT IS TRUTH?

Philosophy does not give us knowledge, as it lacks methods of verification (the discovery and use of these gives ipso facto *to all progress in the cognitive field the character of a specialized science). On the other hand, by coordinating cognitive values with other human values it can give rise to a "wisdom," but a wisdom presupposes an engagement and therefore several wisdoms nonreducible to each other can coexist, while a single truth is alone acceptable when we deal with a problem of knowledge in the strict sense.*

Jean Piaget, *Insights and Illusions of Philosophy*[1]

This passage raises questions addressed by selections in Part II, and of interest throughout the book: What is truth? What is knowledge? Is knowledge justified true belief? Is all justification of belief scientific? Or can belief be justified by reasons other than evidence or proof? At any rate, how does wisdom relate to belief, knowledge, and truth?

The first selection, "Indian and Western Theories of Truth," by Satischandra Chatterjee (1893–?), deals with some of the questions just formulated by focusing on the nature of, and the tests or criteria for, truth. It examines the nature of and criteria for truth by drawing parallels between Indian and Western theories of truth. The author holds that conceptions of truth are of two main types: those that come under the theory of the *intrinsic* validity of knowledge and those that come under the theory of the *extrinsic* validity of knowledge. According to the former theory, knowledge, whenever it exists, is both true and known to be true simply by virtue of its internal conditions. In this view, "truth is a self-evident character of all knowledge." This conception informs the Sāṅkhya, Mīmāṁsā, and Advaita Vedānta Indian philosophical systems. It has no exact parallels in Western philosophy. *Intuitionism* comes the closest, but Chatterjee argues that intuitionism fails to explain falsehood and confuses psychological certitude with logical certainty. As for the theory of the intrinsic validity of knowledge, she argues that self-evidence concerns only the self, because the self "is manifest even in any doubt or denial of its reality." But: Is the self indeed thus manifest? Supposing it is: Since the intrinsic validity theory strictly applies only to the self, it would seem to have the highly skeptical implication that nothing but the self can be known.

This threat of skepticism may lead to alternative conceptions of truth and knowledge, those that come under the theory of the extrinsic validity of knowledge. This theory holds that the validity of knowledge depends on something not inherent in it, that truth is both constituted and known by external conditions. These external conditions can take at least three forms, which we will roughly characterize as follows. First, according to the *correspondence* theory of truth, the external conditions are correspondences between that which is true—say, a declarative sentence, a belief, or a judgment—and that which makes it true—say, a fact, a state of affairs, or an event. There are more and less strict ways of interpreting this theory. In the stricter interpretation, correspondence theory is a picture theory of truth. That is, what is true—say, a declarative sentence—has a structure that pictures what makes it true: a section of the world.

The problem is that it is always difficult, and often impossible, to find a part of reality that corresponds to each part of a declarative sentence—that is, to such things as nouns, verbs, and adverbs. This problem has led people to propose weaker versions of the correspondence theory of truth. In one weaker interpretation of the theory, something is true if it can be correlated with a fact; and it is false if it cannot, or if its negation can be correlated with a fact. A still weaker version holds that something is true if it says what is the case. For example, to say that the declarative sentence "Some birds fly" is true is to say that it says what is the case: some birds fly. This interpretation of the theory is close to the commonsense notion of truth and to the common conception that truths are about something—that is, that they have referents in the world. At this point, however, the question arises: Is truth redundant when calling something true is merely shorthand for repeating what it says?

Some object that truth thus defined is redundant. They argue that the declarative sentence "It is true that some birds fly" adds no descriptive content to "Some birds fly." At most it adds emphatic content. It is like saying "Yeah! Some birds fly." If this objection is sound, however, it establishes not that truth itself but only truth *claims* are redundant. Moreover, it is doubtful that all or even most truth claims are thus redundant. For "It is true that some birds fly" is only one among various truth claims one can make about the declarative sentence "Some birds fly." Another is "The declarative sentence 'Some birds fly' is true." By contrast with "Some birds fly," this truth claim is not about birds and flying. It is about *the sentence* "Some birds fly." Hence, it is not redundant.

The difficulties inherent in the correspondence version have led some thinkers to adopt an alternative version of the theory of extrinsic validity that conceives of truth as constituted and known by some external condition(s). The *coherence* version of the theory holds that the external condition is the greater mutual consistency of all those things that are true—say, declarative sentences, beliefs, or judgments—compared with rival sets of things (declarative sentences, beliefs, or judgments). According to this theory, a single sentence such as "Some birds fly" is not by itself true. Rather, its truth depends on whether or not the system of sentences to which it belongs is more consistent than alternative systems. Indeed, some thinkers have gone so far as to state that only systems, not their component sentences, beliefs, or judgments, can be true.

This theory avoids the problems of the correspondence theory. Indeed, it is attractive wherever immediate verification is impossible and hypothetical reasoning is imperative. Yet, as an all-encompassing theory of truth, it has serious drawbacks. One is that it offends commonsense notions of truth, for on its basis, such commonsensically true sentences as "Some birds fly" and "The Soviet Union ceased to exist in December 1990" either cease to be true or false at all, or they are true only if they belong to an entire system of sentences whose consistency is greater than that of competing systems. But there is no conclusive proof that there is such a system, let alone a method for discovering it. And even if such a system could be demonstrated, those commonsensically true sentences—however obvious their truth—would be, at best, partially true because dependent on the system.

The third theory of extrinsic validity may escape some of these implications. According to the *pragmatic* conception of truth, the external conditions concern the presence of those things that are true—declarative sentences, beliefs, or judgments—in the eventual outcome of inquiry were this inquiry to be continued indefinitely, *whether or not it does continue.* In other words, to say that declarative sentences, beliefs, or judgments are true is to say that they would always withstand the critical scrutiny of inquiry. By contrast with the coherence theory of truth, this theory makes it possible for the sentence "Some birds fly" to be fully, not just partially, true. Further, such sentences as "Some birds fly" and "The desk on which I am writing is solid" are substantiated enough by previous inquiry to be known to be true *right now.*

As for the inquiry that, if indefinitely pursued, would show such sentences to be true, some pragmatists (e.g., Charles Sanders Peirce) thought it amounted to a strictly conceptual process. Others (e.g., William James) appear to be have thought that, at least in some contexts, it also involved the effect of beliefs on our senses and emotions.[2]

Chatterjee's characterization of the pragmatic theory of truth leans toward James's conception. She argues that "The Buddhists adopt the pragmatist theory of truth and reality." Against it, she advances the Nyāya criticisms of this theory:

> It is by no means the case that truth is only a matter of practical utility. The atomic and the electron theories of matter make very little difference in our practical life. Similarly, the different theories of truth involve no great difference in their practical consequences. But in the absence of any other test than that of practical utility we cannot say which one is true and which one is false. Further, there are certain beliefs which are admittedly wrong but which are otherwise useful for certain purposes of life. But no one would claim any truth for a wrong belief on account of its practical utility.

These are sound criticisms of the Buddhist theory of truth, at least as Chatterjee presents it. They do not affect Peirce's version of the pragmatic theory of truth, however, for that has nothing to do with practical utility. Whether or not they affect James's version of the same theory depends on the context in which, according to James, the effects of beliefs on our senses and emotions are tests for ascertaining the truth. We will look at James's version of the pragmatic theory of truth in Section C of this essay.

Other criticisms can be raised against the pragmatic theory of truth. What evidence do we have that if inquiry is pursued indefinitely, opinions will converge on each and every matter, so that a set of sentences (those the opinions upheld) will turn out to be true? Actually, there is plenty of evidence that unanimity, or even general agreement among reasonable people, on many subjects, from the nature of and relations between the sexes and ethnic groups to the sound conception of truth, is uncommon. Does that mean that the sentences upheld in these disagreements are neither true nor false? This criticism raises doubts about the soundness of an all-encompassing pragmatic theory of truth.

According to Chatterjee, the Nyāya theory of truth is a combined theory of truth. "It defines the truth of all knowledge as a correspondence of relations," very much like the weaker versions of the correspondence theory of truth. "The Nyāya view of correspondence is thus different from the new realistic idea of structural correspondence or identity of contents." Furthermore, although according to this theory truth is correspondence, the criterion of truth is coherence in a wide sense. First, it includes coherence with further observations. For example, we can test the judgment "That is the ship's light" by approaching the light and seeing if it is on the ship. Second, it includes coherence with other valid knowledge. For example, the judgment "I am seeing the Atlantic Ocean" can be tested by reliance on valid knowledge of geography, where I am located, and how the sea should appear from where I am seeing it. Third, the criterion of truth includes the pragmatic element of practical utility. For example, "This is the house where I live" can be tested by our living in it. Nonetheless, according to the Nyāya theory of truth, these three tests are just that: tests. They are not constituent features of truth.

Do all truths require testing according to the Nyāya theory of truth? Chatterjee points out that some do not. Necessary truths, such as "Either this is or is not a table" and "Robberies are the work of thieves," do not require testing to be known, nor do introspective truths, such as my knowing that I know I am hungry when I know I am hungry. But memories, sense perceptions of events, objects, or states of affairs external to us, and perceptions of other persons all need the tests of truth. We may ask: Is this so? Why? Consider such sentences as "Torture for torture's sake is always wrong" and "Lying for the sake of lying is always wrong." Do these need testing? Why or why not?[3]

Here, the further question arises: Are there any absolute truths in the sense that they hold for everyone and all time? Some will affirm the opposite: All truths are relative. The second selection in Part II, "Pragmatism as Relativism" by W. P. Montague (1873–1953), discusses this view in connection with the philosophy of pragmatism. After examining the background leading to this view, Montague says:

> The third of the reasons for the popularity of Epistemological relativism may be stated as follows: *All truth depends upon or is in part created by individuals. It is, therefore, inseparable from them and relative to them; and as such, it changes as they change.*

In criticizing this view, he holds that the strength of relativism rests on the ambiguity of the term "truth": "By 'truth' may be meant (1) whatever is believed, or (2) whatever is real or is a fact." He argues that when truth has the first meaning, epistemological relativism amounts to the truism that whatever is believed changes as people's minds change. When it has the second meaning, epistemological relativism becomes a paradox, for it then means that the facts or realities of the world change as people's minds change. That is, when people believed the Earth was flat, the Earth indeed was flat; but now that people believe the Earth is not flat, in fact it is not flat. This view entails believing either that a huge geological change has occurred or that the Earth can be both flat and not flat at the same time. This, Montague argues, shows the absurdity of epistemological relativism.

In response, an epistemological relativist might say "That is true for you, but not for me," meaning Montague's position is true relative to Montague, but not to the relativist. In that case, it is hard to imagine why the relativist would want to argue the matter. A serious relativist should simply be content to let Montague hold his nonrelativistic view, for as soon as the relativist tries to argue against positions such as Montague's, the presumption creeps in that there is a single truth for both relativists and nonrelativists concerning relativism. That is, epistemological relativism either has no quarrel with nonrelativism, and so ceases to be an alternative view, or it refutes itself.

B. WHAT CAN WE KNOW?

The next selection, "All Is Representation," by Vasubandhu (fourth century A.D.), advances the view that all objects thought to exist in the external world exist only in consciousness. This view, known as *idealism,* is opposed to *realism,* or the view that there is a world of objects external to our consciousness. Emphasizing mental activity rather than the passivity of impressions, Vasubandhu writes:

> V. If you grant that from the force of deeds
>   Special elements are born
>
>   . . .
>
>   Why not admit [the process to be] in consciousness?

> VI. The impression of the deed is in one place;
>   You assert its fruit to be in another;
>   That the consciousness which is impressed has the fruit
>   You deny. What is the reason?

This passage indicates how arguments for idealism traditionally start. They do so with the statement—or, as in the passage, with rhetorical questions implying the statement—that experience involves a strictly mental event and hence is interior to us. It is on this basis that idealists conclude that experience can only be of things interior to us.

Is such a starting point an accurate description of the situation? When we see a blue object, it is in no way obvious that we also experience our seeing it as a mental event. To say that it is a mental event is a hypothesis not warranted by our experience of the blue object.[4]

Though the unwarranted nature of the hypothesis with which arguments for idealism traditionally begin weakens them, this is not a conclusive reason for rejecting idealism. However, additional questions arise: Is idealism open to the criticism previously advanced against the coherence theory of truth? That is, do idealistic views confuse the reality of external objects with our evidence for them or ideas of them? (See Section A of this essay.) In fact, does idealism always presuppose a coherence theory of truth and therefore stand or fall with it? A defender of idealism might insist that its arguments be addressed for what they are in themselves, not for the theory of truth they commit idealists to. Yet one way of assessing theories is by the soundness of their implications. If idealism presupposes an unsound theory of truth, this is a reason to reject it.

No doubt, neither of the criticisms we just mentioned is by itself conclusive, but together they may constitute a case against idealism. We will return to this point when we discuss the selection by Berkeley.

Our next selection, "From *Meditations of First Philosophy*," was written by René Descartes (1596–1650), who upheld the doctrine of rationalism. The basic tenet of rationalism is that the nature of reality can be deduced from premises that are independent of experience, and therefore the knowledge thus acquired is necessary and certain.

Descartes, who wrote in the midst of a scientific revolution, was a scientist as well as a philosopher. He formulated analytic geometry, which was crucial for the development of infinitesimal calculus. He also formulated the laws of optics (which were independently arrived at by Fermat as well). Descartes was a contemporary of Harvey, who provided a new understanding of blood circulation and of the heart as a pump. Galileo's work on projectiles and falling bodies and Kepler's work on astronomy were already known when Descartes wrote, though neither Newton's work on physics nor Boyle's on gases had yet appeared.

In contrast with Dewey's notion of philosophical motivation (see Section B of the introductory essay to Part I), according to which philosophy has been recurrently driven by the need to justify crucial ordinary beliefs jeopardized by scientific development, Descartes saw science endangered by traditional philosophy. His main aim was to establish a firm and abiding basis for the sciences as old scientific theories collapsed and new ones took their place. This was largely a new motivation in philosophy.

Descartes thought that the basis for the sciences should be what could be known beyond the possibility of doubt. His method for finding this was *universal* and *systematic* doubt. Descartes' doubt was universal in that it applied to a wide range of opinions. He saw that, given his human limitations, he could not try to doubt every opinion one by one, but he could make his doubt systematic. That is, he could aim at doubting entire *kinds* of opinions: those based on sense experience, those based on memories, and those based on judgments about universal things such as numbers and figures. Like Descartes' motivation, his use of the method of universal and systematic doubt was something new in philosophy. Indeed, it was quite revolutionary because it was egocentric. It placed the individual thinker at the center of the philosophical enterprise by making this individual the touchstone of what could be judged to constitute the basis of science. This approach has been greatly influential in Europe, Anglo-America, and Latin America, and has prompted significant philosophical inquiry in other philosophical traditions. For this reason, we will examine the selection by Descartes more closely than other selections in this part.

In Meditation I, Descartes applies his method to the three kinds of opinions mentioned: those based on sense experience, those based on memories, and those based on judgments about universal things. His applications of the method can be interpreted as three arguments: that from illusion, that from dreaming, and that based on the demon hypothesis. The *argument from illusion* is an assault on the naive view that all sense experiences are accurate and provide a basis for true judgments. It could be interpreted as follows:

> *A significant number of our sense perceptions are illusory.*
> *If so, we cannot be sure of each and every one of them and should provisionally treat them all as illusory and the opinions based on them as false.*
> *Hence, we cannot be sure of each and every one of them and should provisionally treat them all as illusory and the opinions based on them as false.*

This argument is valid (see Selection 7 by Robert P. Churchill and the relevant discussion in Part I's introductory essay); its first premise is true, and its second premise is directly based on Descartes' method. A rule crucial to this method is: If one cannot be sure of a specific kind of source of opinions, then for the purpose of doing science, one should not rely on such a source or on the opinions based on it. It is not necessary to say that they are false, but only to proceed as if they were false. If this second premise is true, then the argument is sound. But is it true? If one tries to pursue this matter, one soon finds that one's disagreement is with Descartes' method, because the premise is based on the methodological rule just stated. One also finds that evaluating the premise thoroughly is a complicated matter because it involves evaluating the rule's implications for scientific inquiry.

An alternative, more promising line of criticism consists in pointing out that we can determine that some of our sense perceptions are illusory only on the basis of other sense perceptions. For example, we may look into a dark room and think we can see a man in a corner. Upon turning on the room's light, we can see that it is actually a broom, not a man, in the corner. On the basis of our perception of the broom, we determine that our initial perception was an illusion. Indeed, without our perception of the broom or some other relevant sense perception, we could not find our initial perception illusory. Yet, if the conclusion of the argument from illusion were true, we could not rely on *any* sense perception. Hence, we would have no good reason for assuming one of the argument's premises. In short, the argument, as formulated, is self-defeating.

In response, Descartes could say he never meant the argument from illusion to be formulated as we have put it. He could argue that it applies, not to all sense perceptions, but only to our sense perceptions of what is very small, far away, or otherwise hard to perceive. Then the argument would not be self-defeating. Still, it would not make the case for rationalism, for it does not rule out our relying on sense perceptions of things that are sufficiently large or close by, or otherwise positioned and constituted so that they are easy to perceive.

Descartes offers a second argument, the *argument from dreaming*, against the view that opinions based on memories and all sense perceptions can be relied on. It can be formulated as follows:

> *A significant number of our representations of material objects or events appear to us in dreams.*
> *The appearances of these representations are just like those we have while awake.*
> *If so, we cannot be sure that any of our representations of material objects and events are of existing objects or events, and should treat them all as if they appeared to us in dreams and the opinions based on them as false.*
> *Hence, we cannot be sure that any of our representations of materials objects and*

events are of existing objects and events, and should treat them all as if they appeared to us in dreams and the opinions based on them as false.

This argument is open to a criticism parallel to that formulated against the argument from illusion. For its first premise presupposes that we can, at least sometimes, tell which particular representations of particular objects or events we have in dreams and which ones we have while awake. But in doing so, we are not treating all such representations as if they appeared to us in dreams. This is precisely what the argument's conclusion precludes. Hence, the argument is self-defeating because its conclusion, if true, undermines its first premise. That is, it leaves us without any good reason for accepting the premise.

We will next discuss Descartes' third argument, against the reliability of opinions based on judgments about universal things, and its related *demon hypothesis.* It can be formulated as follows:

Whenever we are forming any judgment about universal things—e.g., whenever we add 2 + 3 or the sides of a square—a demon could be deceiving us.
If so, we cannot be sure of any judgments we form about universal things and should treat all such judgments as false.
Hence, we cannot be sure of any judgments we form about universal things and should treat all such judgments as false.

If this argument is sound, not just the natural and social sciences, but mathematics and logic as well, are open to Descartes' doubt. Here as before, however, if the argument's conclusion were true, its first premise would be undermined. For the premise is based on a judgment about something universal: namely, about all instances of judgment about universal things. And this is precisely the kind of judgment the conclusion says we should treat as false.

Does the previous discussion undermine Descartes' position? It would if he were giving arguments from a commonsense standpoint. But this is not necessarily what he was doing. He could have been formulating doubts from the standpoint of his own system as a whole. From this standpoint, the premises the arguments' conclusions appear to undermine would not rely on the reasons these conclusions rule out. For example, concerning the argument from illusion, Descartes could argue that we need not discover the first premise by means of the senses. Instead, we can discover by means of the intellect that our sense perceptions of things very small, far away, or otherwise hard-to-perceive sometimes deceive us. And he could make the same point concerning the first premise of the argument from dreaming. He could also appeal to the light of reason to defend the demon hypothesis. He could say that our intellectual intuition can help us *see that* we could be deceived by a demon. To say this is to say that seeing something is different from and prior to forming a judgment about it. Are these replies sound?

To answer this question fully would involve assessing Descartes' system as a whole by comparing it with other systems, a task that falls outside the scope of this book.[5] Here we simply note that in Meditation II Descartes proceeds to find that he cannot doubt that he exists. His formula is "I am, I exist." He says this proposition "is necessarily true each time that I pronounce it, or that I mentally conceive it." In the same manner, he reaches the proposition "I am . . . a thing that exists." A critic may here object that although Descartes reached doubtless propositions in this meditation, these fall far short of constituting a system. The real test of Descartes' philosophy is whether the whole system is clear, consistent, enlightening, and comprehensive enough to make sense of the physical, social, and personal worlds. Until we know this, we would have to suspend judgment on his three arguments.

The next selection in Part II, "Of the Principles of Human Knowledge" by George Berkeley (1685–1753) like Vasubandhu's, upholds idealism. Berkeley was an empiricist, not a rationalist like Descartes. That is, he sought to base knowledge on sense experience. Now, no idealist denies that external objects in some sense exist. What the idealist asks is: What *kind* of existence do external objects have? Berkeley answers that it is mental. As we saw, so does Vasubandhu.

Berkeley disparagingly characterizes the opposite view, realism, as follows:

> It is indeed an opinion strangely prevailing amongst men that houses, mountains, rivers, and, in a word, all sensible objects have an existence, natural or real, distinct from their being perceived by the understanding.

This characterization of realism is at least partially accurate. Realism holds, first, that physical objects have an *existence distinct from experience,* and second, that the existence of physical objects is *logically independent of experiences.* That is, no collections of statements about actual or specifiable experiences entail statements that one or more physical objects exist.

Immediately after characterizing realism, Berkeley indicates his arguments against this position and for idealism:

> But with how great an assurance and acquiescence soever this principle may be entertained in the world, yet whoever shall find in his heart to call it in question may, if I mistake not, perceive it to involve a manifest contradiction. For what are the forementioned objects but the things we perceive by sense? And what do we perceive besides our own ideas or sensations? And is it not plainly repugnant that any one of these, or any combination of them, should exist unperceived?

It is crucial to keep in mind here that, as Berkeley says, people ordinarily believe that "houses, mountains, rivers, and, in a word, all sensible objects have an existence . . . distinct from their being perceived by the understanding," because the very commonness of this belief places the burden of proof on the idealist. As we indicated when discussing Vasubandhu's views, traditional arguments for idealism use an unwarranted starting point—a hypothesis that defies our experience. In itself, however, this is not a conclusive reason for rejecting idealism. It is true that common belief supports realism, but such a support is decisive only in the absence of good arguments to the contrary.

Another philosopher who thought Descartes' philosophy quite misguided was Charles Sanders Peirce (1839–1914). In "The Fixation of Belief," he criticizes Descartes' notion of doubt as amounting to paper doubt rather than real doubt, which makes it suspect. Peirce argues that real doubt involves three main features. First, whoever doubts something experiences the "sensation of doubt," which is a feeling of uneasiness and dissatisfaction. Second, this feeling, like an itch, causes the person who doubts to try to get rid of it. Third, doubt has no action-guiding function. According to Peirce, the struggle to get rid of doubt is inquiry and its end point is belief, which also involves three main features. First, whoever believes something has a feeling of satisfaction or relief. Second, this feeling is accompanied by an absence of struggle, because the irritation of doubt no longer exists. Third, beliefs have action-guiding functions.

Peirce's conception of inquiry poses various questions. In what sense are all beliefs accompanied by a feeling of satisfaction? In what sense, for example, is the belief in bad—hence dissatisfying—news accompanied by a feeling of satisfaction? Or is Peirce talking about purely intellectual satisfaction? If so, what is that? Is it an attitude—perhaps that expressed in saying "yeah!" or in ceasing to wonder—about a declarative sentence? But one may come to assert a sentence out of lack of imagination or cease to wonder about it out of sheer exhaustion. What is proved by the fact that one believes it? Peirce says that "the settlement of opinion is the sole end of inquiry." But the fact that a belief has been fixed or an opinion settled to one's intellectual satisfaction hardly establishes that the belief or opinion is true. Peirce himself states that we should not belittle such methods of fixing belief as tenacity, authority, and the a priori method. Yet we should also recognize that we want our "opinions to coincide with the fact, and that there is no reason why the results of those first three methods should do so."

What is it, then, to fix belief? Peirce might respond that it is to make given declarative sentences free from *all*—not just from any one individual's or group's—actual doubt. In other words, a fixed belief is one that would survive the test of inquiry no matter how far inquiry is pursued. Then what Peirce calls "the fact" would be the set of all those sentences that, through such inquiry, end up being believed.[6] This brings up some of the points raised concerning the pragmatic theory of truth (see Selection 9 and the corresponding discussion in Section A of this essay). Why, for example, believe that, were inquiry to be pursued indefinitely, opinions would converge on each and every matter, so that a set of sentences—those the opinions upheld—would turn out to be true? On many a subject general agreement among reasonable people is quite uncommon, so why believe that it would become common if inquiry proceeded far enough? Besides, even if such common agreement were achieved, it might not be universal. In either case, would the sentences be neither true nor false?

Peirce might respond that current lack of agreement is hardly conclusive evidence that eventual unanimity or widespread agreement are unlikely. He points to the method of science as the only one that is self-correcting and capable of achieving such agreement. This raises the question: Is the foreseen eventual agreement one among scientists, or can it be reached by ordinary people at the level of common sense? Peirce could respond that this question presupposes too sharp a distinction between science and common sense, and argue that the agreement would be reached at the level of critical common sense.[7] But this response also raises questions: How, if at all, is scientific inquiry different from commonsense inquiry? And what special contribution does each make to the acquisition of knowledge?

Ernest Nagel (1901–1985) addresses these very questions in the next selection, "Science and Common Sense." He acknowledges that "no sharp line separates beliefs generally subsumed under the familiar but vague rubric of "common sense" from those cognitive claims recognized as "scientific." He adds, however, that despite these hazy boundaries, there is a core of features characteristic of science and sets out to describe them. According to Nagel, the crucial feature of science is "the desire for explanations which are at once systematic and controllable by factual evidence."

But what is an "explanation"? Are systematic explanations always better than nonsystematic ones? Should they always be controllable by factual evidence? These questions point up the tensions between common sense and science, and raise the further question: Should scientific reasoning guide all our thoughts and actions, or are there areas where nonscientific reasons or even blind faith may take precedence? We address this question in the next section.

C.   IS FAITH JUSTIFIED?

This section's first selection, "The Five Cardinal Virtues and the Definition of Faith," briefly characterizes the nature, objects, and function of faith in Buddhism. Whoever has faith has no doubts left concerning Buddhist teachings. These, from transmigration to a Buddha's qualities, are the objects of faith, which has the function of guiding the person to acquire and develop the qualities of a Buddha. This is done with the help of the remaining four Buddhist virtues: vigor, mindfulness, concentration, and wisdom.

Is faith thus understood—as having left behind all doubts concerning matters that cannot be settled on scientific grounds (e.g., transmigration)—a good thing? Are there other kinds of faith? What about the ordinary faith airline passengers generally have in pilots? Does every belief system involve faith? Is there, for example, such a thing as faith in science? The next selection, "The Ethics of Belief" by W. K. Clifford (1845–1879), questions the value of faith. Indeed, Clifford argues that "It is wrong in all cases to believe on insufficient evidence; and where it is presumption to doubt and to investigate, there it is worse than presumption to believe."

Clifford begins his argument for these conclusions by presenting cases. A shipowner sent out an emigrant ship after allowing himself to come to believe that it was seaworthy, not on the basis of evidence, "but by stifling his doubts." Whether or not the ship managed the journey safely, Clifford argues, the shipowner "*had no right to believe on such evidence as was before him.*" The same dictum applies to those who, in Clifford's next case, believed the charges made by agitators against the members of a religious sect accused of using unfair means to teach their doctrines to children.

One might object that Clifford's cases show *actions* to be wrong, not beliefs. But Clifford argues that "it is not possible so to sever the belief from the action it suggests as to condemn the one without condemning the other." He gives three reasons for this. First, fair inquiry is necessary to do one's duty. Second, no belief is ever insignificant, because beliefs affect our habits of thought, and hence our character. Third, no belief is merely a private matter, because every belief is interwoven with the believer's society and its past, and affects others. For the last reason, Clifford argues that the judgment passed concerning the specific cases he presented must be extended to all beliefs: "No simplicity of mind, no obscurity of station, can escape the universal duty of questioning all that we believe." He later adds: "To sum up: it is wrong always, everywhere, and for anyone, to believe anything upon insufficient evidence."

Note that the second thesis here is actually different from the first. It also differs from Clifford's additional thesis: that it is wrong to make oneself credulous by stifling doubts that arise about anything in one's mind. Are these theses true? What does Clifford mean by "sufficient evidence"? Is it proof? Or would he consider analogy and reliable testimony sufficient evidence?

Our next author takes the position that at times, though we do not have sufficient evidence (i.e., proof, analogies, or reliable testimony) to support our beliefs, we are nonetheless quite entitled to hold them. In "The Will to Believe," William James (1842–1910) presupposes a distinction between two main types of reasons for believing a statement—say, the statement "God exists." First are reasons that are either proofs or evidence *for the truth* of statements. Proofs are typically used in mathematics. For example, the proof of Pythagoras' theorem is a list of jointly conclusive reasons for the truth of the theorem. Evidence is typically used in the sciences, and it is often used in everyday life. For example, the doorbell's ringing is evidence (though not conclusive evidence) for the truth of the statement that someone is at the door.

The second type of reasons for believing statements are *emotive reasons*—that is, reasons other than proof or evidence. James writes:

> Our passional nature not only lawfully may, but must, decide an option between propositions, whenever it is a genuine option that cannot by its nature be decided on intellectual grounds; for to say, under such circumstances, "Do not decide, but leave the question open," is itself a passional decision,—just like deciding yes or no,—and is attended with the same risk of losing the truth.

James's position is that emotive reasons are good reasons for believing something whenever we are in a situation that satisfies three main conditions. First, we face a *genuine option;* that is, we face an option between alternative beliefs that is *forced, live, and momentous.* By "forced," James means that we have no uncommitted alternative concerning a series of statements: we must accept one of them and thereby disbelieve the others. By "live," he means that all alternatives have some value or disvalue for us: we are not neutral about them. Finally, a genuine option is "momentous" in that it would make a significant difference to our lives and is both unique and irreversible.

The second condition our situation must satisfy is that reasons for the truth of the alternative statements in our option be mixed or absent. This, to use James's phrase, makes them "undecidable on intellectual grounds."

The third condition is that the consequences to us depend on what we believe. This condition does not just pertain to believing in God. It also pertains to personal relations (e.g., do you love me or not?), societal arrangements (e.g., can we count on enough others to comply with sound environmental policies?), and personal activities (e.g., should I believe that I will be able to swim back to shore [win this game, get my degree], or should I take a wait-and-see attitude about it?). It is well to keep in mind here that though James refers to Pascal's wager in this selection, his position is different from Pascal's. Pascal's wager concerns eternal reward or punishment, while the consequences James refers to are consequences for us *here and now,* in our worldly life.

Is James's position sound? Is it complete? As we saw, James formulated three conditions meant to be jointly sufficient for judging emotive reasons to be good reasons for believing a given statement. One of them is the condition that a genuine option cannot be decided on intellectual grounds. Is this condition necessary? Consider the following case. Around 1942, the evidence overwhelmingly indicated that the Allies were bound to be defeated by the Third Reich. Was it nonetheless justified for them to believe, *on the face of the evidence,* that they were going to win World War II? One may be inclined to say that they were justified because had they taken a wait-and-see attitude, they would have been setting themselves up for certain defeat. James's conditions do not cover this case, so his account appears incomplete.[8]

James's account can be criticized on the grounds that it justifies too many beliefs. Consider the area of personal relations. Suppose two people just met and one of them has fallen in love with the other at first sight. The lover lacks, and cannot soon gather, any evidence to answer the question "Do you love me or not?" but cannot stand to have this question unanswered any longer. Having read James's statement "The previous faith on my part in your liking's existence is in such cases what makes your liking come," the lover calls the other, declares his or her love, and insists the love is mutual. Is the lover's belief justified? Does James's account entail that it is?

James describes the position of the denigrator of faith (like Clifford) in a nutshell: "*Better risk loss of truth than chance of error,*—that is your faith-vetoer's exact position." He argues for the opposite position—that it is better to risk error than loss of truth—on the grounds that "*a rule of thinking which would absolutely prevent me from acknowledging certain kinds of truth if those kinds of truth were really there, would be an irrational rule.*"

To this, Clifford could reply that his position does not prevent acknowledging any truths, but only points out the moral cost of rushing to hold them passionately: a sacrifice of wisdom, courage, and even faith itself. It would only take a bit of reflection to avoid such cost. Could James respond that such reflection is possible only when the options are not live to you? If so, can one have a live option without being fanatical about it?

In the last selection in Part II, "Secular Faith," Annette Baier discusses a type of faith that addresses these questions. She argues that "the secular equivalent of faith in God, which we need in morality as well as in science or knowledge acquisition, is faith in the human community and its evolving procedures—in the prospects for many-handed cognitive ambitions and moral hopes." Here faith converges with hope and trust in people, and is understood to involve belief on grounds other than deductive and inductive reasons. This amounts to rejecting Descartes' self-centered approach to knowledge and a "return to what Descartes spurned, the support of human tradition, of a cross-generational community."

In the process of arguing for her position, Baier focuses on matters of ethics and social and political philosophy discussed by James, Hobbes (see Part IV, Selection 38), and Kant (see Part IV, Selection 40). With Kant, she holds that the secular faith we live by is a faith in the possibility of a society in which our just actions would theoretically qualify us for membership. The question arises: For one's faith not to be futile, is it also necessary that one's actions, though unlikely to make *the* difference for actualizing a just society, at least give the actualization of such a society a chance? Is this a sufficient condition? What does this condition involve? We will return to moral justification in Part IV, after we discuss the nature of the universe through topics ranging from proofs concerning the existence of God to notions of personal identity in Part III.

NOTES

[1] Jean Piaget, *Insights and Illusions of Philosophy* (New York: The New American Library, 1971), p. 216.

[2] See Selections 13 (Peirce) and 17 (James) and the discussions of these selections in Sections B and C of this essay.

[3] Sentences such as these are sometimes called "moral laws." A good discussion of their epistemological status can be found in Marcus G. Singer, "Some Preliminary Observations on Truth in Ethics," *Philosophy in Context 16* (1986):11–16.

[4] G. E. Moore made this point in "The Refutation of Idealism," *Philosophical Studies* (London: Routledge & Kegan Paul, 1958), p. 20.

[5] An analogous position is suggested by Anthony Kenny, *Descartes: A Study of His Philosophy* (New York: Random House, 1968), pp. 36–39.

[6] Peirce actually advances this view in "How to Make Our Ideas Clear," in Philip P. Wiener (ed.), *Charles S. Peirce: Selected Writings (Values in a Universe of Chance)* (New York: Dover, 1958), pp. 113–136.

[7] See, for example, Peirce's "Critical Common-Sensism," in Justus Buchler (ed.), *Philosophical Writings of Peirce* (New York: Dover, 1955), pp. 290–301.

[8] If, however, the conditions are meant to be not just jointly sufficient but individually necessary, then James's account entails that it is always wrong to believe anything (as in the World War II case) merely on the face of overwhelming evidence.

Satischandra Chatterjee (1893–?)
INDIAN AND WESTERN THEORIES OF TRUTH

Chatterjee, who was born in West Bengal, India, distinguishes two main types of theories of truth, depending on whether they come under the theory of the intrinsic validity of knowledge or under that of the extrinsic validity of knowledge. After criticizing the former type of theory, she discusses the correspondence, coherence, and pragmatic theories of truth, and argues for a combined theory: the Nyāya theory of truth. Chatterjee's position and various theories of truth are discussed at the beginning of Section A of the introductory essay to Part II.

READING QUESTIONS

In reading the selection, try to answer the following questions and identify the passages that support your answers:

1.   What are intrinsic and extrinsic validity of knowledge?
2.   What theories of truth does the author mention?
3.   What is the correspondence theory of truth and how good is it?
4.   What is the coherence theory of truth and how good is it?
5.   What is the pragmatic theory of truth and how good is it?

Reprinted from Satischandra Chatterjee, *The Nyāya Theory of Knowledge* (Calcutta: University of Calcutta Press, 1950), pp. 100–112. Reprinted by permission of the University of Calcutta and Mrs. Purabi Chatterjee, daughter-in-law of the late Satischandra Chatterjee, executrix of the Estate of late Satischandra Chatterjee.

. . . Here we propose to examine the Indian theories of truth, . . . in the light of parallel Western theories. With regard to truth there are two main questions, namely, how truth is constituted, and how truth is known. The first question relates to the nature of truth and the answers to it give us the definitions of truth. The second question refers to the ascertainment of truth and the answers to it give us the tests or criteria of truth.

With regard to these two questions there seem to be two possible answers. Thus it may be said that truth is a self-evident character of all knowledge. Every knowledge is true and known to be true by its very nature. Knowledge does not depend on any external conditions either to be made true or to be known as true. This is the theory of the intrinsic validity (*svataḥ prāmāṇya*) of knowledge as advocated by the Sāṅkhya, Mīmāṁsā and Advaita Vedānta systems of Indian Philosophy. According to the last two schools, the truth of knowledge consists just in its being uncontradicted (*abādhita*). The absence of contradiction, however, is not a positive but a negative

condition of truth. Knowledge is both made true and known to be true by its own internal conditions. It is only falsehood that is externally conditioned. So truth is self-evident, while falsity requires to be evidenced by external grounds. The Sāṅkhya goes further than this. It maintains that both truth and falsehood are internally conditioned and immediately known, *i.e.* are self-evident.

There is no exact parallel to the above theory of truth in Western philosophy. It is true that in modern European philosophy knowledge, in the strict sense, is always taken to mean true belief. But truth or validity is not regarded as intrinsic to all knowledge, independently of all external conditions. It is in the writings of Professor L. A. Reid, a modern realist who owns no allegiance to the current schools of realism, that we find some approach to the view that truth is organic to knowledge. But even Reid makes it conditional on knowledge efficiently fulfilling its function, namely, the apprehension of reality as it is. He thinks that truth is nothing else but knowledge doing its job. Thus he says: "Truth is, indeed, simply, . . . the quality of knowledge perfectly fulfilling its functions." Again he observes: "If knowledge were not transitive, if we were not in direct contact, joined with reality, then all our tests, coherence, correspondence, and the rest, would be worthless."[1] Here truth is admitted to be a natural function of knowledge, but not as inherent and self-evident in all knowledge. In the theory of intuitionism, we find a close approach to the view of self-evident validity. To the question 'How do we know that a belief is true or valid?' intuitionism has a simple answer to give, namely, that we know it immediately to be such. As Hobhouse puts the matter: "Intuitionism has a royal way of cutting this, and indeed most other knots: for it has but to appeal to a perceived necessity, to a clear idea, to the inconceivability of the opposite, all of which may be known by simply attending to our own judgment, and its task is done."[2] Among intuitionists, Lossky has made an elaborate attempt to show that truth and falsity are known through an immediate consciousness of their objectivity and subjectivity respectively. For him, truth is the objective and falsity the subjective appearance of the object. But how do we know that the one is objective and the other is subjective? The answer given by Lossky as also by Lipps is that we have "an immediate consciousness of subjectivity" and "an immediate consciousness of objectivity". To quote Lossky's own words: "It is in this consciousness of objectivity and subjectivity, and not . . . in the laws of identity, contradiction, and excluded middle, that our thought has a real and immediate guide in its search for truth."[3]

It should be remarked here that the above theories of self-evident truth or intrinsic validity give us a rather jejune and untenable solution of the logical problem of truth. They leave no room for the facts of doubt and falsehood in the sphere of knowledge. But any theory of truth which fails to explain its correlate, namely, falsehood, becomes so far inadequate. Further, it makes a confusion between psychological belief and logical certainty. Psychologically a wrong belief may be as firm as a right one. But this does not mean that there is no distinction between the two. Subjective certitude, as such, cannot be accepted as a test of truth. It is true that the theory of intrinsic validity does not appeal to any test of truth other than the truth itself. It as-

sumes that the truth of knowledge is self-evident, and that we cannot think of the opposite. In fact, however, there is no such self-evident truth. It is only in the case of the self that we can speak of self-evidence in this sense. The self is a self-manifesting reality. It is manifest even in any doubt or denial of its reality. Hence self-evidence belongs really to the self only. It is on the analogy of the self that we speak of the self-evidence of any other truth. A truth is self-evident in so far as it has the evidence of the self or is evident like the self. But as we have just said, there is no such self-evident truth other than the self itself. In the case of any other truth, we can always think of the opposite in a sensible way. That 'two and two make five' is not as nonsensical as 'abracadabra'. Even if the opposite of a certain belief be inconceivable, it does not follow that the belief is infallible. What was once inconceivable is now not only conceivable but perfectly true. Hence we cannot say that self-evident validity is intrinsic to all knowledge.

The second answer to the question 'How is truth constituted and known?' leads us to the theory of extrinsic validity (*paratah prāmānya*). According to this, the truth of any knowledge is both constituted and known by certain external conditions. As a general rule, the validity of knowledge is due to something that is not inherent in it. So also the knowledge of validity depends on certain extraneous tests. Validity is thus assigned to one knowledge on the ground of some other knowledge. This is the theory of extrinsic validity as advocated by the Nyāya and the Bauddha systems. In Western philosophy, the correspondence, the coherence and the pragmatist theories of truth all come under the doctrine of extrinsic validity. In each of them the truth of knowledge is made to depend on certain external conditions other than the knowledge itself. According to almost all realists, old and new, it is correspondence to facts that constitutes both the nature and the test of truth.[4] Of course, some realists differ from this general position and hold a different view of the matter. Thus Alexander[5] makes coherence the ground of truth. But in speaking of coherence as determined by reality, he accepts indirectly the theory of correspondence. Reid,[6] on the other hand, treats correspondence to the given only as a test of truth. Russell[7] defines truth in terms of correspondence

[1] L. A. Reid, *Knowledge and Truth,* pp. 185, 199, 204.

[2] Hobhouse, *Theory of Knowledge,* p. 488.

[3] Lossky, *The Intuitive Basis of Knowledge,* pp. 227–29.

[4] *Vide The New Realism and Essays in Critical Realism.*

[5] *Space, Time and Deity,* Vol. II, pp. 251f.

[6] *Knowledge and Truth,* Chap. VIII.

[7] *The Problems of Philosophy,* Chaps. XII, XIII; *Our Knowledge of the External World,* p. 58; *The Analysis of Mind,* p. 165.

and accepts coherence as a test of some truths, while others are said to be self-evident. In the philosophy of objective idealism,[8] coherence in the sense of the systematic unity of all experiences is made both the ground and the test of truth. The truth consists in the coherence of all experiences as one self-maintaining and all-inclusive system. It is in this sense that Bosanquet[9] says that 'the truth is the whole and it is its own criterion. Truth can only be tested by more of itself.' Hence any particular knowledge is true in so far as it is consistent with the whole system of experience. On this view, the truth of human knowledge becomes relative, since coherence as the ideal of the completed system of experience is humanly unattainable. For pragmatism,[10] truth is both constituted and known by practical utility. The truth of knowledge consists in its capacity to produce practically useful consequences. So also the method of ascertaining truth is just to follow the practical consequences of a belief and see if they have any practical value. With this brief statement of the realistic, the idealistic and the pragmatist theories of truth, we proceed to examine the Buddhist and the Nyāya theories of extrinsic validity.

From what we have said before it is clear that the Buddhists adopt the pragmatist theory of truth and reality. For them, practical efficiency is the test of both truth and reality. The real is what possesses practical efficiency (*arthakriyā*) and the true is the useful and so practically efficient (*arthakriyāsāmarthya*). But the pragmatic conception of truth is embarrassed by serious difficulties. The Nyāya criticism of the Bauddha conception of *pramāṇa* has brought out some of these difficulties. Here we may note that to reduce the true to the useful is to make it almost meaningless. It is by no means the case that truth is only a matter of practical utility. The atomic and the electron theories of matter make very little difference in our practical life. Similarly, the different theories of truth involve no great difference in their practical consequences. But in the absence of any other test than that of practical utility we cannot say which one is true and which is false. Further, there are certain beliefs which are admittedly wrong but which are otherwise useful for certain purposes of life. But no one would claim any

truth for a wrong belief on account of its practical utility. Hence the Buddhist and the pragmatist theories of truth cannot be accepted as sound and satisfactory.

The Nyāya theory of truth, it will be seen, combines the correspondence, the coherence and the pragmatist theories with certain modifications. According to it, the truth of knowledge consists in its correspondence with objective facts, while coherence and practical utility are the tests of truth in such cases in which we require a test. It defines the truth of all knowledge as a correspondence of relations (*tadvati tatprakāraka*). To know a thing is to judge it as having such-and-such a character. This knowledge of the thing will be true if the thing has really such-and-such a character; if not, it will be false. The Nyāya view of correspondence is thus different from the new realistic idea of structural correspondence or identity of contents.[11] That knowledge corresponds to some object does not, for the Naiyāyika, mean that the contents of the object bodily enter into consciousness and become its contents. When, for example, I know a table, the table as a physical existent does not figure in my consciousness. This means only that I *judge* something as having the attribute of 'tableness' which really belongs to it. There is a subjective cognition of a physical object. The one corresponds to the other, because it *determines* the object as it is, and does not itself become what it is. If it so became the object itself, there would be nothing left on the subjective side that might correspond to the physical object. Nor again does the Nyāya follow the critical realist's idea of correspondence between character-complexes, referred to the object by the knowing mind, and the characters actually belonging to the object. When we know anything we do not first apprehend a certain logical essence or a character-complex and then refer it to the thing known. Our knowledge is in direct contact with the object. In knowing the object we judge it as having a relation to certain characters or attributes. Our knowledge will be true if there is correspondence between the relation asserted in knowledge, and that existing among facts. Thus my knowledge of a conch-shell as white is true because there is a real relation between the two corresponding to the relation affirmed by me. On the other hand, the perception of silver in a shell is false because it asserts a relation

[8]   *Vide* Joachim, *The Nature of Truth*, Chap. III.

[9]   *Logic*, Vol. II, pp. 265–67.

[10]   James, *Pragmatism*, Lect. VI; Perry, *Present Philosophical Tendencies*, Pts. IV and V.

[11]   *Cf.* Chapter III, Sec. 3, in Chatterjee, *The Nyāya Theory of Knowledge.*

between the two, which does not correspond to a real relation between them.[12]

While truth consists in correspondence, the criterion of truth is, for the Nyāya, coherence in a broad sense (*saṁvāda*). But coherence does not here mean anything of the kind that objective idealism means by it. The Nyāya coherence is a practical test and means the harmony between cognitive and conative experiences (*pravṛttisāmarthya*) or between different kinds of knowledge (*tajjātīyatva*). That there is truth in the sense of correspondence cannot, as a general rule, be known directly by intuition. We know it indirectly from the fact that the knowledge in question coheres with other experiences of the same object as also with the general system of our knowledge. Thus the perception of water is known to be valid when different ways of reaction or experiment give us experience of the same water. It is this kind of coherence that Alexander accepts as a test of truth when he says: "If truth is tested by reference to other propositions, the test is not one of correspondence to reality but of whether the proposition tested is consistent or not with other propositions."[13] Hobhouse[14] also means the same thing by 'consilience' as a measure of validity. According to him, validity belongs to judgments as forming a consilient system. Of course, he admits that such validity is relative and not absolute, since the ideal of a complete system of consilient judgments is unattainable. The Nyāya idea of *saṁvāda* or coherence may be better explained as a combination of Reid's methods of correspondence and coherence. If we take the judgment 'that is the light of a ship,' we can test its truth by what Reid calls the correspondence method 'of approaching the light and seeing a ship.' This is exactly what the Nyāya means by *pravṛttisāmarthya* or successful activity. Or, we can employ, so says Reid, the cheaper coherence method "of comparing this knowledge with other kinds of knowledge and see if it is consistent with them."[15] In this we have the Nyāya method of testing one knowledge by reference to some other valid knowledge (*tajjātīyatva*). But the Nyāya goes further than this and accepts practical utility also as a test of truth. Thus the validity of the perception of water may be known from correspondence and coherence in the above sense. But it may be further known from the satisfaction of our practical needs or the fulfilment of our practical purposes in relation to water, such as drinking, bathing, washing, etc. But the Nyāya never admits the pragmatist contention that the truth of any knowledge is constituted by its utility or serviceableness. Knowledge is made true by its correspondence to some reality or objective fact. It is true not because it is useful, but it is useful because it is already true. Hence truth consists in correspondence and is tested by coherence and practical efficiency.

But from the standpoint of the modern Nyāya, all truths do not require to be tested. Some truths are known as such without any test or confirmation. These are manifestly necessary and so self-evident truths. Here the Nyāya view has some affinity with Russell's theory of truth.[16] In both, truth is defined by correspondence to fact, but in different ways. Although truth is thus externally conditioned, some truths are admitted by both to be self-evident. For the Nyāya, however, such truths are only necessary truths or what Russell calls *a priori* principles. Of the different kinds of knowledge by acquaintance—sensation, memory, introspection, etc.—which are admitted by Russell to have self-evident truth, it is only introspection or self-consciousness (*anuvyavasāya*) that is admitted by the Nyāya as having self-evident validity. The validity of self-consciousness is self-evident because there is a necessary relation between consciousness and its contents. When I become conscious of a desire for food, I find that my consciousness is necessarily related to the desire, it is the desire itself as it becomes explicit.[17] Here I not only know something, but know that I am knowing it, *i.e.*, the truth of my knowledge is self-evident.

The different theories of truth discussed above may be shown to supplement one another and be reconciled as complementary aspects of a comprehensive theory. The first requisite of such a theory is the independent existence of a world of objects. If there were no such world, there would be no ground for the distinction between truth and falsehood. Some of our beliefs are true or false accord-

---

[12] *Cf.* "Smith's judgment that it is the light of a ship is true just because 'it,' the light, is in fact so related to a real ship. Jones' judgment (that it is the light of a star), on the other hand, is false, because this thought is not an apprehension of the existing present complex fact, light-belonging-to-ship."—Reid, *Knowledge and Truth*, pp. 209–10.

[13] *Space, Time and Deity*, Vol. II, p. 252.

[14] *The Theory of Knowledge*, pp. 499–500.

[15] *Knowledge and Truth*, pp. 203–04, 211–12.

[16] *The Problems of Philosophy.* Chaps. XI, XII, XIII.

[17] *Cf.* C. Hartshorne's article in *The Monist* (Vol. XLIV, No. 2, p. 171): "Must this (feeling) not be admitted to present an obvious dual aspect of being at once subjective and yet a content or object of consciousness, at once a mode and a datum of awareness?"

ing as they are or are not borne out by independent objects or facts. It is because there are certain independent objects, to which our beliefs may or may not conform, that we distinguish between truth and error. Hence we say that truth consists in the correspondence of our knowledge with independent objects or facts. The difficulty on this view, it is generally remarked, is that if the objects are independent of knowledge, we cannot know whether our knowledge corresponds with them or not. How can we know what is outside and beyond knowledge, and see that true knowledge agrees with it? The reply to this is that in the case of external objects, physical things and other minds, we cannot straightway know the correspondence between our knowledge and its objects. Still, we cannot deny the reality of these external objects. But for the independent existence of other things and minds we cannot explain the order and uniformity of our experiences and the similarity of the experiences that different individuals may have under similar circumstances. That some of our experiences represent the real qualities of things may then be known from the fact that they are given in the same way to different persons, or to the same persons through different senses. As Professor Price has shown, "sense-data cohere together in families, and families are coincident with physical occupants."[18] On the other hand, some of our experiences are not taken to represent the qualities of things, because they do not cohere with other experiences of the same individual or of different individuals. The first kind of experiences is considered to be true and objective, while the second is judged to be false and subjective. Similarly, our knowledge of other minds is true when it correctly represents the contents of those minds. It will be false, if what we impute to them forms no part of their actual contents. This shows that it is correspondence to facts that constitutes the nature of truth, although we cannot directly *know* such correspondence in the case of physical things and other minds. To know this we have to consider if one knowledge coheres with others or the whole body of human knowledge, and also consider if we can successfully act on our knowledge. What is true works, although whatever works is not true. Thus we know the correspondence of knowledge with facts from its coherence and pragmatic value. But to know that a certain knowledge corresponds with facts is to *know* its truth. It does not

constitute its truth. The knowledge becomes true if, and only if, it corresponds with facts. We know or test its truth when we find that it is coherent with other parts of our knowledge and our practical activities. So truth is constituted by correspondence with facts and is tested by coherence and practical activity.

The Vedānta view of truth as uncontradicted experience logically implies the coherence theory of truth. That some experience is uncontradicted means that it is different from the contradicted. But to be different from the contradicted means to belong to the body of coherent knowledge. We do not and cannot rightly judge an experience to be uncontradicted unless we relate it to other experiences and find that it is congruous with them. A dream experience is wrongly judged by the dreamer to be uncontradicted and true, because he cannot relate it to his waking experiences. It cannot be said that a dream experience is true for the time being and becomes false afterwards. What is once true is always true. A dream experience may sometimes be *judged* to be true, but it is really false for all time. And its falsity appears from its incoherence with waking experience. Hence we are to say that an experience is really uncontradicted when it is related to other experiences and is found to be coherent with them.

It may be urged against the above view that truth consists in correspondence and is tested by coherence, that it either assumes the truth of the testing knowledge, or must go on testing knowledge *ad infinitum*. If knowledge is true when it corresponds with facts, and if the correspondence cannot be directly known, then the truth of every knowledge must be tested by its coherence with others. This, however, means that there can be no end of the process of proving knowledge and, therefore, no final proof of any knowledge. To solve this difficulty we must admit that there is at least one case in which knowledge is, by itself, known to be true. We have such a case in self-consciousness. While the truth of all other knowledge is to be tested by coherence, the truth of self-consciousness is self-evident and requires no extraneous test. The self is a self-manifesting reality. Hence the contents of our mind or the self are manifested by themselves. They are at once existent facts and contents of consciousness. To become conscious of the contents of one's mind is just to make them explicit. What we are here conscious of are not outside or beyond consciousness. Mental contents not only *are*, but are conscious of

---

[18]   Cf. *Perception*, p. 302.

themselves. The state of knowledge and the object of knowledge being identical, we cannot strictly speak of a correspondence of the one with the other. Or, if we speak of a correspondence between them, we are to say that it is directly known and so need not be known or tested in any other way. When we feel pain, or know something, or resolve to do anything, we may be conscious of feeling it, or knowing it, or resolving to do it. What we are here conscious of as objects are the objects themselves as they become explicit or conscious of themselves. Similarly, necessary truths and *a priori* principles like the laws of thought, logical and mathematical truths seem to have self-evident validity. The reason for this is that these truths are or express the forms and contents of our own consciousness. They are inherent in or arise out of the nature of our own thought and consciousness, and in knowing them consciousness knows itself, *i.e.* its own forms. They are at once modes and objects of consciousness. In any judgment or knowledge of them, the content and object of consciousness are the same and directly known to be the same. Such knowledge is, therefore, not only true, but also known to be true by itself. Hence we admit that the truth of self-consciousness is self-evident, while all other truths are evidenced by external tests like coherence and pragmatic utility or verification.

W. P. Montague (1873–1953)
PRAGMATISM AS RELATIVISM

In this work, Montague criticizes the view that all truth is relative to what individuals believe. He argues that the apparent strength of this view rests on the ambiguousness of the term "truth," which may mean either (1) whatever is believed or (2) whatever is real or a fact. Montague argues that when truth is construed according to the first meaning, relativism is a truism, while when it is construed according to the second meaning, relativism is paradoxical. Montague's views are discussed at the end of Section A in the introductory essay to Part II.

READING QUESTIONS

As you read the selection, try to answer the following questions and identify the passages that support your answers:

1. What is epistemological relativism?
2. Why does Montague think that epistemological relativism is popular?
3. What are Montague's criticisms of epistemological relativism?
4. Suppose one responds to Montague: "That's true for you, but not for me." Does his article address this possibility?
5. How could one deal with such a response?

PRAGMATISM AS RELATIVISM

The third of the major phases or tendencies of pragmatism I have called, for want of a better name, Relativism. Like Futurism and Practicalism, it is to be found in some form and to a greater or less extent in all who call themselves pragmatists. But while futurism is mainly significant for ethics, education, and social philosophy, and while practicalism in all of its three phases is mainly significant for genetic psychology and for the problem as to the proper criteria for attaining truth, relativism, in distinction from the other parts of the philosophy of pragmatism, is concerned primarily with epistemology, *i.e.* the branch of methodology that addresses itself to the problem, not of how knowledge is and should be attained, but of how the meaning of knowledge or truth when once attained should be interpreted. And . . . the question as to the meaning of truth turns upon the question as to the manner in which the objects of knowledge are related to the minds that know them. . . . Because of the intimate manner in which the practicalist logic of pragmatism is bound up with its relativistic epistemology, it seems best to discuss them together. This somewhat irregular procedure is further justified by the arrogant claim of the epistemological relativist that his interpretation of the meaning of truth is so superior as to render meaningless and artificial all of the traditional answers to the epistemological problem. And this attitude of arrogance is carried so far by the relativist that he does not even like to call his particular species of epistemology by the generic name. He prefers to regard his doctrine as a substitute for epistemology rather than as a form of it, and as a means of escaping the whole set of puzzles involved in the relation of the knowing subject to the objects known.

This relativistic epistemology of pragmatism can be best understood if we treat it as an outgrowth of its practicalistic logic. Hence, before criticizing the relativistic conception of the meaning of truth, I should like to say something about the manner in which it has developed from the practicalist conception of the method of attaining and testing truth. At the outset, let us remember that at least one of the beginnings of pragmatism was the attempt to apply evolutionary biology to the domain of psychology. This results in what James called a "teleological" interpretation of mental processes. And if every phase of mental life is interpreted teleologically, as a dynamic process aimed at the satisfaction of individual needs, it is natural to take the further step of subsuming the logical interest in attaining cognitive satisfaction under the ethical interest in attaining practical satisfaction.

Now, the empirically-minded founders of pragmatism were naturally in strong sympathy with the ethical Utilitarianism of Mill; hence their affiliation of logic with ethics meant that logical value or truth was to be interpreted by the utilitarian principle of expediency. If the morally good is the expedient or satisfactory in the way of conduct, then also the logically true is the expedient or satisfactory in the way of belief. And as utilitarianism in ethics means a relativistic conception of the good, the pragmatic extension of Utilitarianism to logic will mean a relativistic conception of the true. William James's dedication of his *Pragmatism* to the memory of John Stuart Mill voiced with beautiful precision the mission of the new philosophy. The Utilitarians had abolished the notion of a Good that was absolute and independent of the changing desires of individuals. The pragmatists were to abolish the conception of a Truth that was absolute and independent of the changing beliefs of individuals. The utilitarians had substituted for the absolutistic conception of an independent good the relativistic theory that whatever satisfied desires was in so far forth good. The pragmatists would substitute for the absolutistic conception of the true the relativistic theory that whatever satisfies individual beliefs is in so far forth true. And as the utilitarians had answered the charge that their theory meant mere anarchy in ethics, by declaring that the highest good was what was most satisfactory to the desires of the greatest number, so the pragmatists can answer the charge that their theory means mere anarchy in logic by declaring that the highest truth is what proves most satisfactory to the beliefs of the greatest number. *It is the essence of each theory to deny that the good and the true, respectively, possesses any absolute content apart from the interests of individuals.*

It has been customary in recent years for various groups of philosophers to criticize the utilitarians for their somewhat artificial hedonistic psychology; but at least among the empirically-minded of such critics there can be found few if any who will deny the tremendous service which utilitarianism rendered to the whole vast domain of the moral sciences. So much of the spiritual energies of men had been spent in devotion to abstract rules and principles of conduct which had lost their relevance to actual human wants, that there was need for a new ethical gospel which should sweep away antiquated taboos and fine-sounding slogans and call on all lovers of the good for a single-hearted devotion to such measures and only such measures as would increase human well-being. These advocates of the new dispensation appraised any and all codes of morality by the sole criterion of their efficacy to satisfy human needs; and to the service of that supreme ideal they unhesitatingly conscripted the resources of organized knowledge, physical and psychological. Their aim in brief was to make ethics a science, and to substitute the co-operative and experimental methods of intelligence for the sterile competitions of sentiment and dialectic.

Now, the inheritors of this great and clarifying movement of utilitarianism are the pragmatists of to-day. And we cannot properly estimate the strength and weakness of their doctrine of epistemological relativism unless we keep in mind their inheritance of ethical relativism from Bentham and Mill. All pragmatists are in a broad sense utilitarians, and because their relativism in the theory of values is useful and valid they and their friends have assumed that their relativism in the theory of knowledge must be equally useful and valid. I feel sure that it is this extension of relativity from the field of the good to the field of the true that constitutes the principal cause for the success of pragmatism to-day. And I feel equally sure that this contention of pragmatism, that relativity of value implies relativity of truth, is as false in reality as it is plausible in appearance. It is plausible in appearance because the methods applicable to the moral and social sciences seem to be and in many cases actually are the same as those applicable to the other branches of science. The leaders of pragmatism deserve much credit in the fields of law, education, and political and economic reform, for making the methods of procedure more flexible and efficient and more relevant to the concrete questions at issue. Hence it is natural enough to suppose that their principles will be equally sound in other fields. If it has proved beneficial to conceive the ethically desirable or good as relative to individuals, why should it not prove equally beneficial to conceive the cognitively desirable or true as equally relative to individuals? But this identification, though plausible in appearance, is false in reality because of that profound contrast between the good and the true which we have noted above. We can only express once more our conviction that the adjustment between the individual and his environment, which is the goal of the cognitive interest in truth, is an adjustment in which the environment is the primary and inde-

pendent variable, the individual's ideas and judgments being secondary and dependent for their validity upon their agreement with objective facts. On the other hand, the goal of the conative interest in the good is an adjustment between the individual and the environment in which individual desires and sentiments constitute the primary and independent variables, the environment being secondary and dependent for its goodness on its agreement with individual needs. The cognitive equilibrium of truth is cosmocentric and absolute, while the conative equilibrium of goodness is anthropocentric and relative. Because of this contrast, to recognize that what is really and not merely apparently good for one may be really and not merely apparently bad for another is very sound ethics; while for the same reason, to claim that what is really and not merely apparently true for one may be really and not merely apparently false for another is very unsound logic. Ideas are *true* only when they conform to objective facts; but facts are *good* only when they conform to subjective needs.

In explaining the manner in which the relativism of the pragmatists has developed from their practicalism we were led to a statement and criticism of the first and principal argument in support of that relativism, *viz.* the apparent similarity between the cognitive satisfaction of human beliefs and the conative satisfaction of human needs. The latter being relative to individuals, it was falsely argued that the former was equally relative; and that consequently pragmatism could clarify the concept of *truth* in the same fashion that utilitarianism had clarified the concept of *good*.

In addition to its supposed agreement with utilitarianism, there are, I believe, three further reasons for the growth of pragmatic relativism: (1) its apparent connection with the doctrine of evolution; (2) its apparent connection with the attitude of scepticism; (3) an ambiguity of the term "truth." Let us consider these reasons in turn.

The theory of evolution has made us familiar with the extent to which the universe is pervaded by change; even the things that appear to be most permanent, such as the heavenly bodies, the seas and mountains, and the species of plants and animals, are in a process of change. Human institutions and human beliefs that at one time seemed eternal are now being revised. It is natural for us to suppose that this evolutionary process to which all existing things are subject should extend to the realm of logical meaning; and consequently we tend to regard the notion of an unchangeable system of truth as a relic of the pre-Darwinian age. Yet while the extension of the notion of change from the things of physics to the things of logic may be natural, it is absolutely unjustifiable and leads only to confusion. In the first place, change itself has no meaning unless the terms of the process remain fixed. I cannot speak of a man changing from youth to age, or of a species changing from simian to human, unless the terms "youth," "age," "simian," "human," are supposed to preserve their meanings unchanged. What holds true of logical terms holds true equally of propositions which are relations between terms. If the proposition that the earth has been spherical for the ten billion years prior to the year 1900 is true at this moment, then that proposition will always be true on pain of losing its meaning as a proposition. The earth might change to-morrow from a globe to a disc without changing the truth of the above proposition. In short, the maxims: *True for one, true for all,* and *once true, always true,* apply not only to all abstract or non-existential propositions, but to all other propositions in so far as they are made thoroughly unambiguous with respect to the time and space of the facts asserted. Change resides only in physical processes and in the psychological processes by which we become aware of physical processes. But between those processes and the logical relations which they reveal there is fixed a gulf which no change can cross.

Let us turn now to the second of the three causes for the spread of the doctrine of relativism, *viz.* its connection with scepticism. And here the relativistic pragmatist can make out a somewhat better case. We may imagine him to speak to us as follows: "You talk about an absolute truth, independent of anyone's belief in it or knowledge of it. Well, supposing that there were such a thing, we could never attain it; or at least if we did attain it, we could never recognize it for what it was. All that we can know in the way of truth is something that is believed. Each man calls his own belief by the eulogistic name of *truth,* and with respect to this as an absolute standard, he describes his neighbour's opinions by such uncomplimentary names as 'apparent truths' or 'subjective beliefs.' Consequently, we pragmatists, recognizing this universal shortcoming of human nature, are frank enough to say that there is no truth with a capital T; no absolute impersonal objective reality, not even our own, and that whether we like it or not we have to put up with *the best in the way of belief.* We may still use the word truth in this semi-subjective sense, and it is in this sense that truth is relative to different persons and subject to change."

Now, the only trouble with this reply of the pragmatist is that it is a virtual confession that the relativistic feature of his doctrine, when freed from ambiguities, reduces to pure scepticism. For scepticism is the theory that truth in its objective sense is unattainable by any means within our power. The only difference between pragmatic relativism and scepticism is that the former doctrine uses the word "truth" in a purely subjective sense that is different from the sense in which it is used by the other methodological theories. The thoroughgoing sceptic believes with the relativist that we possess beliefs which we prefer to those of our neighbours, but he gives himself no false verbal comfort by calling these preferred beliefs "truth." He reserves that word for the objective reality which he thinks lies beyond the reach of our knowledge. But whether he is right or wrong in holding to his pessimistic and negative attitude towards the methodological problem, we cannot discuss [here].

The third of the reasons for the popularity of Epistemological relativism may be stated as follows: *All truth depends upon or is in part created by individuals. It is, therefore, inseparable from them and relative to them; and as such, it changes as they change.* Now there are two meanings involved in this statement of relativism which depend upon the two meanings that can be given to the word truth. By "truth" may be meant (1) whatever is believed, or (2) whatever is real or is a fact. If the word is taken in the first or subjective sense, then the relativistic principle that truth changes becomes a truism, for it means only that *people's beliefs change as people's minds change.* If truth is taken in the second or objective sense, the relativistic principle ceases to be a truism and becomes a paradox, for it then means that *the facts or realities of the world change as people's minds change.* We may illustrate the difference by the following example: "'That the earth is flat' was for the ancients an obvious truth; 'that the earth is round' is for us an established truth. Their truth was not our truth. Truth, therefore, is relative and changing, and what is true for one may be false for another." These statements sound pretty well, and we should probably pass them over unchallenged, because we should take for granted that the word "truth" was being used in its subjective sense as a synonym of belief. It is a truism that people's beliefs can differ, that one can believe what another disbelieves; and it is a commonplace that a change in beliefs took place with regard to the shape of the earth. The ancients believed it to be flat, and we believe it to be round. But if we were told that the author of the statements cited meant "truth" to be taken in the objective sense, we should suppose that he had been indulging in either a geological or a logical paradox. If he meant that the flatness of the earth was a truth (fact) in ancient times and also that its roundness was a truth (fact) in modern times, we should assume that he believed that the earth's shape had undergone a marvellous geological change from a disc to a globe. If in still adhering to the objective meaning of the term "truth" he denied that he intended any such geological absurdity as the above, we should have to assume that he was committing the still greater logical absurdity of supposing that the shape of the earth could be both flat and spherical at once.

The pragmatic doctrine of the relativity of truth is thus seen to owe some of its plausibility to an ambiguity. Before the ambiguity is revealed, the truism and the paradox conceal one another and unite to produce the appearance of a novel and important discovery. In exactly the same way a black cardboard seen through white tissue paper appears to be a single surface of grey. When we look at the thing edgewise, however, the effect of grey disappears and we see only the black and the white. So, when once we recognize the ambiguity of the term "truth," and insist upon the relativistic pragmatist using the word in one sense or the other, we find only an ill-looking juxtaposition of the paradox that facts depend upon people believing them, and the truism that our beliefs about facts change and vary. In case the illustration chosen fails to satisfy the reader, I would suggest that he make up for himself examples of statements which can loosely be regarded as cases of "truth changing" or of "true for one but false for another," and see for himself whether a little analysis of the meanings involved in all such statements will not disclose the above-mentioned ambiguity or duplicity of the "truth" in question.

In concluding this analysis of the relativistic epistemology of pragmatism I should like to call attention to a very real disaster which threatens the study and teaching of philosophy, and which is likely to be brought nearer by the spread of the doctrine we have been considering.

There is a certain type of "up-to-date" student to whom the humility involved in honourable scepticism is intolerable. These students, eager, earnest, and not consciously insincere, will study for a time the problems of Being and Knowing which have been raised by the great philosophers. They do their best, but they become confused. They disagree with

the idealistic conclusions of Berkeley and Kant, but cannot refute the reasoning on which those conclusions are based. They are piqued and stirred by such vitalistic criticisms of the current scientific naturalism as are made by Driesch and Bergson, but they lack the knowledge of the elements of natural science that would make possible even a tentative appraisal of those criticisms. It is inevitable that the less scrupulous and more confused of these students, when placed in such a situation, will seize with avidity upon any device, no matter how hollow, which will serve to conceal their failure even from themselves, and enable them to gain a sense of superiority over the great philosophers of the past. There is grave danger that the relativistic form of pragmatism will be adopted to meet such needs. For to the relativist with his covert suggestion that "truth" is only the best that we attain in the way of belief, all questions about the nature of objective reality will appear as "artificial." And if there is no objective reality apart from human interests and beliefs, it may seem unnecessary to bother oneself about the problems of traditional philosophy. Philistine minds will be tempted to mask their incompetency with the boast that the puzzles that they have failed to solve were "unreal," "old-fashioned," "dialectical" subtleties with which a practical man in a practical age need not concern himself. Like the fox in the fable, if we fail to get the grapes we can save our face by calling them sour.

We have now completed our survey of Pragmatism as a methodological theory. We have sketched briefly its origin in the Principle of Peirce, and its development at the hands of James, Dewey, and Schiller, and we have discussed separately its three principal aspects: I. Futurism; II. Practicalism in its three senses: (1) empirical, (2) humanistic, (3) biological; and III. Relativism. Of these three aspects of Pragmatism, Futurism seems by far the most valuable. Indeed, it is difficult to estimate the revolutionary changes in human society which may result from a substitution of a prospective for a retrospective attitude in science and culture. We cannot, of course, give exclusive credit to pragmatism for this interest in the future. Futurism existed before pragmatism in the philosophy of Nietzsche, and, independently of pragmatism, in the philosophy of Bergson. Moreover, it has touched with its influence fields of activity which are indifferent to the utterances of official philosophers. As has been said, the broader spirit of futurism is, like pragmatism itself, the outcome of the doctrine of evolution. Evolution taught us to think of all things as in process of change and growth. The first realization of this view was touched with sadness. We could see in evolution only its negative side. It robbed us of our golden age, of our god-like ancestors, and of the various mythical glories which in one form or another have been attributed by all races and nations to their own past. The primordial aristocrat in each of us grieved at the evolutionist's debasement of human origins. It is only lately that this aristocrat's shame in the fact of having sub-men for ancestors has given way to a democrat's pride in the possibility of having supermen for descendants. Moreover, this modern effort to attain emancipation from the past differs in its spirit from the spirit of previous revolutionary movements, and especially from that of the great revolution in France, in that it is permeated with a biological and historical spirit. It is voluntaristic rather than rationalistic, and is constructive as well as destructive. Futurism is not mere opposition to the past. It is not even an eighteenth-century attempt to put the Goddess of Reason in the place of all lesser idols and to impose upon future generations a Utopia of our own. It is a more positive but less dogmatic, a more experimental and less metaphysical attempt to prepare the world for whatever may turn up. And while pragmatism has not created this movement, it has expressed in technical philosophical form the character and the essence of it.

As for pragmatism as practicalism, here too we find in all three of its phases an expression of modern tendencies, especially as they are at work in America. Practicalism as empiricism is voiced in the popular demand for concrete facts rather than for abstract laws, for the expert knowledge of the specialist rather than for the old-fashioned general culture. Practicalistic humanism, too (though often in partial conflict with practicalistic empiricism), is expressed in the familiar demands for a more ample recognition of personal needs and human sentiment in such subjects as economics, and for a view of physical nature more intuitive and impassioned than that which the cold-blooded pronouncements of natural science would seem to warrant. As for pragmatic practicalism in its third or biological sense, the best examples of it are to be found in the movement for functional rather than formal education, and in the growing feeling that for the old contemplative ideal of truth for truth's sake should be substituted the Baconian ideal of knowledge as a means to the practical control of material conditions.

In addition to these manifestations of futurism and practicalism, the pragmatic doctrine of relativism is also embodied in current movements. The notion that truth is changeable and relative to individuals is, as we have already seen, congenial to a society that is imbued with the spirit of utilitarianism and that feels itself to be in a stage of transition. Moreover, the practicalist's relegation of theoretical learning to the status of an instrument for obtaining practical results fits in well with the view that the essence of all truth is relative.

In conclusion we may note a certain congruity of pragmatism, particularly of pragmatic relativism, with the general attitude of anti-intellectualism which is so prevalent in social philosophy to-day. It was a long time ago that Thrasymachus proclaimed that justice was only the interest of the stronger. But from Thrasymachus down to the latest disciples of Nietzsche, Marx, or Freud, there has existed a sort of Macchiavellian tradition of political "realism" and anti-liberalism. The upholders of this tradition are characterized by two attitudes: (1) a negative attitude of disillusionment as to the capacity of the human mind for a disinterested pursuit of ethical ideals; (2) a positive attitude of a somewhat cynical but wholesome curiosity as to the concrete and interested motives which are the real causes of man's actions. That the practice of hypocrisy is an acknowledgment of the efficacy of virtue is not admitted by these political realists. Nor do they perceive that unless there were a genuine and effective sensitiveness to ideals on the part of the herd, it would be impossible for the herd's leaders to mask their selfish interests by proclaiming high ideals. How could the profession of justice be to the interest of the stronger unless real justice were actually operative as an ideal in the minds of men generally?

Having discarded the validity of the professed ideals for social action on the ground that they are abused, our political "realist" feels that he has reached a standpoint that is "beyond good and evil"—terms which to him as to Nietzsche are merely names, complimentary or the reverse, for selfish interests. And since there are no logical or ethical *reasons* for human actions, but only physical and psychological *causes,* he sets to work to discover just what these causes are. The cynically motivated search for the non-rational factors in social evolution has proved painfully rich. Hobbes, Buckle, Marx, Nietzsche, and Freud, with the aid of troops of investigators in the field of natural science, have unearthed case after case in which man figures not as a rational animal ordering his life according to principles, but only as a complicated animal driven this way and that by the reflexes which constitute what he eulogistically calls his "will." As for his "reason," it fills the otiose and epi-phenomenal rôle of apologist and ratifier of action after the fact.

Knowledge of the psychological mechanisms of logical and ethical processes is bitter and hard to digest. To keep one's faith in the reasons for an action when one understands its causes is difficult at best. And in the face of the present-day onset of the anti-intellectualists it is helpful to recall two earlier and classic protests against misinterpreting man's discovery of his own mechanism.

The first of these protests was the clarion call of Huxley in his *Evolution and Ethics,* warning us not to enthrone nature in place of the old supernature as a source of moral authority. The meaning of ideal right is unaffected by existential might, and we are to hold fast our faith in the values of the human spirit even in the very teeth of nature. For no matter how blind or cruel we may discover nature to be, she and her laws are morally irrelevant except as instruments to be used by us in pursuit of our own ends. This proclamation that moral values do not depend for their sanctions upon physical existence, though it came from a mechanist, was thoroughly Platonic in its wisdom and beauty.

A second warning of similar significance is to be found in the essay by William James entitled *Reflex Action and Theism.* James protested against the then current tendency to belittle intense spiritual experiences merely because they were found to possess certain regular physiological correlates. That a derangement of the digestive or reproductive system occurs in connection with an experience of religious emotion must not be interpreted as a reduction of the religious to the digestive or reproductive. In other words, the value of an experience is to be judged on its intrinsic merits regardless of its bodily correlates. The anti-intellectualism of the present day is not, as in the time of Huxley's essay, based on the discovery of the physical origin of man; nor, as in the time of James's essay, on a realization of the physiological correlates of human emotion. It derives its new strength from the advance in history, anthropology, and social science generally. The discovery of the humble origins of many of the most cherished elements in our culture, such as art, religion, etc., engenders in the mind of the anti-intellectualist the modern fallacy of *geneticism* which consists in evaluating ethical ideals in terms of their

historical origins, or even in depriving them of value altogether merely because they have origins. It is the same naturalistic and pragmatistic irrelevance, though in a new form, as that which called forth the protest of Huxley the naturalist and James the pragmatist. That nature shows no preferences for courage or love is no reason for us to lessen our regard for these virtues. That our highest emotions are conditioned by changes in our blood and sweat in no-wise diminishes their value. And no more should the deluge of new historical discoveries concerning the practical and interested origins of our theoretical and disinterested attitudes cause distrust of *their* value. Our values are what they are irrespective of their physical environment, physiological conditions, or historic origins.

Now, pragmatic relativism in its repudiation of logical validity and in its substitution of the new interest in psychological genesis for the old interest in objective truth and falsity voices accurately and in the language of technical philosophy the anti-intellectualism that dominates the new school of political and social science. This confusion of the genesis of a belief with its truth and of the genesis of a virtue with its value is as morally dangerous as it is intellectually fallacious. In theory it means the deliberate and systematic repudiation of that disinterested faith in ideals which, however imperfectly practised in the past, has been the inspiration of human greatness. In its political program it means the interest of the stronger, the repudiation of democracy, and the adoption of class-dictatorship, whether "red" or "white," as the goal to be sought. In its tactic it means the substitution of bullets for ballots; "direct action," and the unashamed use of force replacing the painfully acquired devices of parliamentary procedure. If the new knowledge of the origins of man's culture is to be purchased at the price of abandoning that for which his culture is most significant, it will turn out to be the worst bargain in history.

The need to-day is for a return to the revolutionary idealism of the eighteenth century. But in returning to the Age of Reason, we need not abandon what the age of intelligence has taught us.

Now, it is the self-appointed task of Pragmatism to make articulate in philosophy these world-wide modern interests in cultural origins and human mechanisms. If it uses them as a substitute for the old devotion to objective truth, it will prove a curse and a blight; but if, on the other hand, it makes of them a new instrument for the realization of human ideals, it will rank among the greatest of philosophies.

Vasubandhu (Fourth Century A.D.)
ALL IS REPRESENTATION

Vasubandhu, a leading representative of the Yogacara school of Buddhist thought, argues for the view that all objects thought to exist in the external world are really consciousness. He challenges his opponents to prove how, when the impression is in our consciousness, its source can be somewhere else, and attempts to meet their various objections. A discussion of Vasubandhu's and related views can be found at the beginning of Section B of the introductory essay to Part II.

READING QUESTIONS

In reading the selection, try to answer the following questions and identify the passages that support your answers:

1. What view does Vasubandhu defend?
2. What does Vasubandhu mean by "consciousness"?
3. Does he indicate any reasons in support of his view?
4. Are they good reasons?
5. Suppose for the moment that idealism is true because it is internally coherent. Is that a good enough reason to accept idealism? Why or why not?

In the Mahāyāna it is established that the three worlds are representation-only. According to the scriptures it is said that the three worlds are only mind. Mind, thought, consciousness, discernment are different names. What is here spoken of as mind includes mental activities also in its meaning. "Only" excludes external objects; it does not do away with mental associates. When inner representations arise, seemingly external objects appear; as [persons] having bad eyes see hairs and flies. [But] herein is no particle of truth.

To this doctrine there are supposed objections. The stanza says:

I

If representations are without real objects,

Then their spatial and temporal determination,

The indetermination of the [perceiving] stream of consciousness,

And their action, must be unfounded.

What does this mean? If we abandon [the notion] that representations have colored etc. outer objects, then when a sense representation arises it does not correspond to a sense object. Why (then) does this representation arise in a certain place, not in all places? Why, in this place, does the representation arise at a certain time, not at all times? When many streams of consciousness are together at one time and place why is the representation not determined to arise according to one of them; just as a person with defective eyes sees hairs and flies while those with good eye-sight do not have these representations arise? Again, why is it that the hairs etc. seen by persons with defective eyes do not function as hairs etc.? In a dream what drink, food, knives, cudgels, poison, medicines, clothes etc. are obtained are without the functions of drink etc. A city of the Gandharvas cannot be used as a city. But other hair and things [of ordinary waking experience] are not without use. If they [i.e. dream and waking] are truly the same in having no outer sense objects and there is only an appearance of external objects arising in consciousness; then (1) their determination in space, (2) their determination in time, (3) the indetermination of the stream of consciousness (doing the perceiving), and (4) the existence of functioning things are all without foundation.

[Reply] They are not without foundation, for the Stanza says:

II

Place and time are determined as in a dream;
The selves are not determined, just as the ghosts [in their abode]
Together behold the same river of pus etc. [and]
As in dreams there is function in the loss of [semen].

When we say "as in a dream" we mean what is seen in a dream. That is, as in a dream although there are no real objects yet it is in a certain place that such things as a village, a garden, a man, or a woman are seen, not in all places; and in this place it is at a certain time that this village, garden, etc., are seen, not at all times. From this, although there are no real objects apart from consciousness, spatial and temporal determination are not unfounded.

The words "as the ghosts" clearly mean "as the hungry ghosts." The river, because it is full of pus, is called the pus river, as we speak of a ghee-bottle meaning that it is full of ghee [i.e. clarified butter]. That is, just as the hungry ghosts through ripening the same kind of deeds assemble together as many selves and all see the pus river; in this it is not determined that only one sees. The "etc." [of the verse] signifies other things seen [by the hungry ghosts] such as ordure etc. and creatures holding swords and clubs, warding them off and standing guard, not allowing them to eat [of the pus]. From this [we see that] though there are no real objects apart from consciousness yet the principle of the indetermination of the stream [which perceives] is explained.

Again as in dream, although the objects are unreal, they yet have function such as the loss of semen etc. From this, although there are no real objects apart from consciousness, yet the principle that there is functioning of unrealities is established.

Thus also, relying upon diverse examples we make it evident that the four principles, spatial determination etc., may be established.

Again, it is said in a further stanza:

III

All [are exemplified] as [those] in hell
Together behold the infernal guards etc.,
And their ability to inflict torments;
Therefore the fo.r principles are all established.

It must be understood that here one example of hell illustrates how spatial determination etc. are all established. The words "as in hell" signify all classes of creatures suffering the bitterness of torments in hell. That is to say, although in hell there are no really actual sentient beings whose lot is to play the part of infernal guards etc., yet because of the force of ripening the same kind of deeds the sentient beings [who are there as sinners] in the same place, at the same time, and as many streams of consciousness, collectively behold infernal guards, dogs, crows, iron hills, and other things coming to inflict their torments upon them. From this, although there are no objects apart from consciousness the four principles of spatial determination and so on are all established.

[Question] For what reason do you not admit that the class of infernal guards etc. are real sentient beings?

[Answer] Because it is not fitting. Now these ought not to be grouped with sinners in hell since they do not suffer the bitterness which the latter suffer. Mutual punishing of each other cannot be proved between the sinners on the one hand and the infernal guards etc. on the other since being equal in form, size and power they ought not greatly to frighten each other. They ought not themselves to be able to endure the fiery heat of the iron earth and the misery from the fierce flames continually burning. How can we say that there they are able to torment others? Those not destined for hell [i.e. nonsinners] should not be born there.

[Objector] How is it that animals are evidently in heaven? In hell, likewise, there are animals and ghosts who act as infernal guards etc.

[Answer] This doctrine is not so, for the Stanza says:

IV

As the animals in heaven
Those in hell are not, indeed;
For the asserted animals and ghosts
Suffer not that bitterness.

All the animals born in heaven must have [performed] deeds capable of leading on to the joys of that realm. Being born there they are certain to sustain the happiness which the realm produces. Not so do the infernal guards etc. sustain in hell the misery which the realm produces. Therefore it is inadmissible that those belonging to the animal and ghost abodes are born in hell.

[Objection] That being the case, you ought to admit that the sovereign strength of deeds [formerly done] by the denizens of hell produces special elements which give rise to superior shapes, color, size, and power, on which we bestow the name of infernal guards etc. In order to frighten the sinners they change their appearance with all kinds of gestures of hands, feet, and so on, and different actions such as the separating and coming together of the ram mountains and the thorns of the steel forest turning now down, now up.

[Answer] These things are not wholly false, but [your argument] does not accord with reason. The Stanza says:

V

If you grant that from the force of deeds
Special elements are born
Which produce such transformations,
Why not admit [the process to be] in consciousness?

Why do you not admit that consciousness by the strength of deeds changes thus, instead of assuming elements? And again, the Stanza says:

VI

The impression of the deed is in one place;
You assert its fruit to be in another;
That the consciousness which is impressed has the fruit
You deny. What is the reason?

You assert that the denizens of hell, owing to the force of their own deeds, produce special elements which give rise to transformations in shape etc. The impression of those deeds reason must admit to be in the continuity of consciousness, not elsewhere. In the place which has the impression you then deny the development of the fruit. Where there is no impression, on the other hand, you assert there is fruit. What is the reason?

[Objector] There is a doctrine which is the reason. That is, if it is only consciousness which appears as if colored etc. and there is no separate colored etc. [object], then the Buddha ought not to have said that there are "bases" (of cognition), visual, [auditory,] and so on.

[Answer] This teaching is not a reason, for it has a different meaning. The Stanza says,

VII

Conforming to the creatures to be converted
The World-honored One with secret intention
Said there are bases of cognition, visual etc.,
Just as [there are] beings of apparitional birth.

Just as Buddha said that there are beings of apparitional birth but spoke relying upon the secret intention that the continuity of mind, unbroken, can proceed on into a future world; he did not say that creatures of apparitional birth really exist, because he said "There is neither creature nor self but only elements and causes." The scriptures which speak of bases, visual and so on, are in like case. In accordance with the creatures to be converted who ought to receive that teaching he speaks with a secret intention. [The bases] are not really existent apart.

[Question] In accordance with what inner meaning does he speak of ten [bases], visual etc.? The Stanza says:

VIII

[Answer]

[Perceptive] consciousness is born from its own seed
And develops into an apparent object aspect.
To establish [the distinction of] inner and outer bases of cognition,
Buddha says there are ten of these.

What is the meaning of this saying? [Since] the immediate consciousness of an apparent color is born from its own seed at the effective moment in its development due to a complex of causes, Buddha with reference to that seed and the apparent color, speaks of them respectively as the eye-base and color-base [i.e. of visual cognition]. Thus on [through the series of the senses] until [we say]: The immediate consciousness of an apparent tangible object is born from its own seed at the effective moment in its development due to a complex of causes; and Buddha with reference to that seed and the apparent tangible object, speaks of them respectively as the body-base and the tangible-base. It is in keeping with this inner meaning that we speak of the ten bases of sense cognition.

[Question] What advantage is there in this teaching of an inner meaning? The Stanza says [in answer]:

IX

By reason of this teaching one enters into

[The doctrine of] the egolessness of the individual:

The asserted non-substantiality of elements

One enters again by reason of the remainder of the teaching,

Those who are converted through trusting to this doctrine of the so-called twelve bases are able to enter into the doctrine of the egolessness of the individual. That is, if it is clearly understood that the six consciousnesses develop from six pairs of elements, and that there is no seer [nor hearer, taster etc.] down to no knower, then those who ought to receive the doctrine of the egolessness of sentient beings will be able to realize the egolessness of sentient beings. [The words], "Again by reason of the remainder of this [teaching]," say that he who is converted to the doctrine of representation-only is able to enter [i.e., realize] the asserted non-substantiality of elements. That is, if it is clearly understood that representations-only arise as images of apparently colored etc. elements, [and that] in all these there are no elements having the qualities of color etc., [then] those who ought to receive the doctrine that all elements are without substantial entity are able to realize the insubstantiality of all elements.

[Objection] If by knowing that all elements of every kind are nonexistent we enter into the insubstantiality of elements, then representation-only is also, in the end, non-existent. How can [representation-only] be sustained?

[Answer] It is not [the man] who knows that all elements of every kind are non-existent who obtains the name of having "entered the insubstantiality of elements"; but [he] who penetrates the insubstantiality of the elements of the "self-natures" and the "special characters" conceived by the imagination of the ignorant, is thus named [he who] has "en-

tered the insubstantiality of elements." It is not because the inexpressible nature of the elements which is the domain of Buddha is also wholly non-existent that we indicate the "insubstantiality of elements." As conceived by another consciousness the substance of the nature of this pure representation is also non-existent; [and this] we call "insubstantiality of elements." Otherwise, the object conceived by this other consciousness exists, and then the doctrine of representation-only could not be established, because it is admitted that all other consciousnesses have real objects. By this reasoning we say that the doctrine of representation-only is established, leading in every way to the realization of the non-substantiality of all elements; and not because we deny the existence of every kind of nature.

[Question] Again, how do we know that Buddha intended such an inner meaning when he said there are bases of sense cognition? Are there not separate, really existing outer elements, having color-and-form etc., which become severally the objects of visual etc. consciousness?

[Answer] The Stanza says:

X

That realm is neither one (thing),

Nor is it many atoms;

Again, it is not an agglomeration etc.,

Because the atom is not proved.

How can this be said? The meaning is that if there really are external bases of sense cognition which respectively become objects of sense representation, then such an outer realm must either be one, as in the assertion of the Vaiśeṣikas that there is form having parts; or it must be many, as in the affirmation that there are very many real atoms acting separately as objects; or it must be many atoms agglomerated and combined, as in the affirmation that there are many real atoms which in agglomeration and combination act together as objects. But the external object cannot logically be one, because we cannot grasp the substance of the whole apart from the parts. Also it logically is not many, because we cannot apprehend the atoms separately. Again logically, they do not in agglomeration or combination make objects, because the theory of single real atoms is not proved.

[Question] How can you say it is not proved? The Stanza says:
[Answer]

XI

One atom joined with six [others]

Must consist of six parts.

If it is in the same place with six

The aggregate must be as one atom.

If one atom on each of its six sides joins with another atom it must consist of six parts, because the place of one does not permit of being the place of the others. If there are six atoms in one atom's place then all the aggregates must be as one atom in quantity, because [though] revolving in mutual confrontation they do not exceed that quantity; and so aggregates also must be invisible.

[Objection] The Vaibhāṣikas of Kaśmir say: The theory that atoms join together is wrong because they do not have spatial divisions—dismiss such an error as the above—but aggregates have the principle of joining together because they do have spatial divisions.

[Answer] This also is not so, for the Stanza says:

XII

Since [it is stated] that atoms do not join

Of what, [then] is the joining of the aggregates?

If joining is not proved [of the latter]

It is not because they have no spatial divisions.

Now we must examine the principle and tendency of their statement. Since apart from atoms there are no aggregates, and there is no joining of atoms, [then] of what is the joining of the aggregates? If you change the statement to save your position and say that aggregates also do not join one another, then you should not say that atoms are without combination because of having no spatial divisions. Aggregates have spatial divisions and yet you do not grant their combination. Therefore the non-combining of atoms is not due to their lack of spatial division. For this reason the single real atom is not proved. Whether atomic combination is or is not admitted the mistake is still as we have said. Whether spatial division of atoms is or is not admitted both views are greatly in error.

[Question] For what reason?
[Answer] The Stanza says:

XIII

If the atom has spatial divisions

It logically should not make a unity.

If it has none, there should be neither shadow nor occultation;

Aggregates being no different [would likewise be] without these two.

If the six spatial divisions of the single atom are different, several parts making up the body, how can unity be proven? If the single atom is without different spatial divisions then when the light of the rising sun strikes upon it how does a shadow occur on the other side, since there is no other part where the light does not reach? Again, if we assert that atoms are without spatial divisions, how can there be mutual occultation of one by another, since there is no remaining portion [of the one] to which the other does not go, by which we may speak of mutual obstruction of one by another? Since they do not mutually obstruct, then all the atoms must revolve in the same place; and the quantity of all aggregates is the same as one atom. The error is as we have said above.

[Question] Why do you not admit that shadow and occultation pertain to aggregates but not to atoms?

[Answer] Can it be that different from the atoms you admit aggregates which cast shadows and cause occultation?

[Objector] Not so!

[Answer] If that is the case, the aggregates must be without these two [phenomena]. That is, if aggregates are not different from the atoms, then shadow and occultation must not belong to the aggregates. The intelligence analyzes, arranges and distinguishes, [but] whether it sets up atoms or aggregates both are unrealities.

[Question] Of what use is it to consider and choose between atoms and aggregates when you still cannot get rid of external sense quality?

[Answer] Here again, what is this quality?

[Objector] I mean that the object of vision is also the real nature of the color, green etc.

[Answer] We must judge whether this "object of vision etc.," which is the "real nature of green etc.," is one or many.

[Objector] Suppose we say, what is the error?

[Answer] Both views are in error. The fault of multiplicity is as explained before. Unity also is irrational. The Stanza says:

XIV

[Assuming] unity, there must be no walking progressively,

At one time, no grasping and not grasping,

And no plural, disconnected condition;

Moreover no scarcely perceptible, tiny things.

If there is no separation and difference and all colored things which the eye can reach are asserted to be one thing, then there can be no reason in walking progressively on the ground, for if one step is taken it reaches everywhere: again there cannot be simultaneously a grasping here and a not grasping there, for the reason that a unitary thing cannot at one time be both obtained and not obtained. A single place, also, ought not to contain disconnected things [such as] elephants, horses, etc. If the place contains one, it also contains the rest. How can we say that one is distinguished from another? Granting two [things present], how comes it that in one place there can be both occupancy and non-occupancy, that there can be a seeing of emptiness between? Moreover there should also be no such scarcely perceptible tiny things as water animalcules, because being in the same single space with the coarse things they should be of equal measure. If you say it is by characteristic aspect that one object differs from another and that they do not become different things from any other reason, then you certainly must admit that this discriminated thing repeatedly divided becomes many atoms. [Now] it has already been argued that an atom is not a single real thing. Consequently, apart from consciousness sense organs such as the eye and sense objects such as color are all unprovable. From these [considerations] we best prove the doctrine that only representations exist.

[Question] The existence or non-existence of anything is determined by means of proof. Among all means of proof immediate perception is the most excellent. If there are no external objects how is there this awareness of objects such as are now immediately evident to me?

[Answer] This evidence is inadequate, for the Stanza says:

XV

Immediate awareness is the same as in dreams etc.

At the time when immediate awareness has arisen,

Seeing and its object are already non-existent;

How can it be admitted that perception exists?

Just as in time of dreaming etc., although there are no outer objects, such immediate awareness may yet be had, so also must the immediate awareness at other times be understood. Therefore to adduce this as evidence is inadequate. Again, if at a certain time there is this immediate awareness, such as the color etc. now evident to me, at that time [along] with the object the seeing is already non-existent: (1) because [such awareness] necessarily belongs to the discriminative action of the intellective consciousness, and (2) because at that time the visual and other [sense consciousnesses] have already faded out. [According to] those who hold the doctrine of momentariness, at the time when this awareness arises the immediate objects, visible [tangible, audible] etc. are already destroyed. How can you admit that at this time there is immediate perception?

[Objection] But a past immediate experience is required before intellective consciousness can remember; for this reason we decide that there is a previously experienced object. The beholding of this object is what we concede to be immediate perception. From this the doctrine that external objects truly exist is established.

[Answer] If you wish thus to prove the existence of external objects from "first experiencing, later remembering," this theory also fails.

[Objector] Why so?

[Answer] The Stanza says:

XVI [*FIRST PART*]

As has been said, the apparent object is a representation.

It is from this that memory arises.

As we have said earlier, although there is no external object, a sense representation, visual etc., appears as an outer object. From this comes the later state with its memory associate, the discriminated mental representation, appearing as a seeming former object. Then we speak of this as a memory of what has been already experienced. Therefore to use a later memory to prove the real existence of a previously seen external object cannot in principle be maintained.

[Question] If, in waking time as well as in a dream, representations may arise although there are no true objects, then, just as the world naturally knows that dream objects are non-existent, why is it not naturally known [of the objects] in waking time, since they are the same? Since it is not naturally known that waking objects are non-existent, how, as in dream consciousness, are the real objects all nothing?

[Answer] This also is no evidence, [for] the Stanza says:

XVI [*SECOND PART*]

Before we have awakened we cannot know

That what is seen in the dream does not exist.

Just as in the unawakened state we do not know dream objects are not externally real, but do know it on awaking, even so the world's falsely discriminated recurrent impressions are confused and fevered as in the midst of a dream, all that is seen being wholly unreal; before the true awakening is attained [this] cannot be naturally known. [But] if there is a time when we attain that world-transcending knowledge, emancipatory and non-discriminative, then we call it the true awakening. After this, the purified knowledge of the world which is obtained takes precedence; according to the truth it is clearly understood that those objects are unreal. The principle is the same.

[Objection] If for all sentient beings representations arise as apparent objects because of transformation and differentiation in their own streams of consciousness, and are not born from external things acting as objects, then how explain [the fact] that those sentient beings through contact with good or evil friends, or through hearing true or false doctrines, are determined to two kinds of representation since there are neither friends nor teaching?

[Answer] It can be explained. The Stanza says:

XVII [*FIRST PART*]

By the power of reciprocal influence

The two representations become determined.

In all sentient beings it is by the reciprocal influence of representations in one another's stream of consciousness that [any] two representations, according to the case, are determined. That is to say, because a distinct representation in one stream of consciousness occasions the arising of a distinct representation in another stream of consciousness, each becomes determined, but not by external objects.

[Question] If just as in dreams, although the objects are unreal, representations may arise, and in waking time likewise, how is it that good and evil conduct performed in dreams and waking do not receive the same due retribution, agreeable or disagreeable?

[Answer] The Stanza says:

XVII [*SECOND PART*]

The mind by sleep is weakened:

Dream and waking retributions are not the same.

In the dream state the power of the mind, weakened by sleep, is reduced; but in the waking state it is not so. Therefore the acts which are performed ought to receive matured consequences, superior and inferior, which are not the same. [The difference] is not because of external objects.

[Question] If only representations exist, and there is no body nor speech etc. how are sheep etc. killed by anybody? If the death of the sheep is not because another has injured them, how can butchers commit the crime of murder. The Stanza says:

[Answer]

XVIII

Because of transformation in another's representation

The act of killing and injury occurs;

Just as the mental power of a demon etc.

Causes another to lose his memory.

As, for example, the thought power of a demon etc. causes another sentient being to lose his memory, to have a dream, or to be possessed of a four-legged devil and other such strange alterations. Every magician by the power of his thought [may] cause another to behold all sorts of things in a dream, just as Mahākātyāyana by the power of his wish caused King Sāraṇa to see strange things in a dream: and again, just as the forest rishis by the power of anger caused King Vemacitra to see strange things in a dream. Thus by a transformation in one person's representations a condition inimical and injurious to the very life of another is caused to arise. It must be understood that death denotes the discontinuance of the homogeneous stream of consciousness by means of alteration of representations. Again, the Stanza says:

XIX

The emptiness of Daṇḍaka forest etc.

How [came it] from a rishi's anger?

"Mental punishment is a great crime"

How can this, again, be proved?

If you do not admit that a sentient being may die because of the power of change in the representation of another, why did the World-honored One, in order to prove that mental punishment is the greatest crime, ask the householder Upāli saying, "Hast thou ever heard it said by what cause the forests of Daṇḍaka, of Mātaṅga, and Kaliṅga became empty and solitary? The householder answered Buddha saying, "Gautama, I have heard it said that it was because of the mental rage of rishis." If you assert that spirits and demons, respecting the rishis and knowing their animosity, acted for them in killing the race of creatures—that it was not merely by virtue of the rishis' mental rage—why then did [Buddha] adduce that [matter of the forests] in order to prove that mental punishment is of the nature of a great crime beyond those of body and speech? From this it must be understood that only through the rishis' anger did those sentient beings die, [which is] rationally the best proof.

[Question] If only representations exist, does knowledge of another's mind know another's mind or not?

[Answer] Suppose we assent [either way]? What is the error?

[Question] If it cannot know, why speak of knowledge of another's mind? If it can know, representation-only is of necessity not proved.

[Answer] Although it knows the mind of another it does not [know it] exactly. The Stanza says:

XX

How does knowledge of another's mind

Know its object inexactly?

Just as the knowledge in knowing one's own mind

Does not know [it] as the Buddha's object.

[Question] How is all knowledge of another's mind not an exact knowing of its object?

[Answer] Just as the knowledge of one's own mind.

[Question] Why is this knowledge of one's own mind not an exact knowing of its object?

[Answer] Because of ignorance. Both knowledges of the object, because each is covered over and darkened by ignorance, do not know [it] as the ineffable object reached by the pure knowledge of a Buddha. These two, in their objects, do not know exactly because of the false appearing of seemingly external objects; and because the distinction between what is apprehended and the apprehender is not yet discontinued.

[Conclusion]

The doctrines and implications of representation-only are of kinds infinitely diverse for decision and selection; difficult is it to fathom their profundities. Without being a Buddha who is able to comprehend their total extent? The Stanza says:

XXI

I, according to my ability,

Have briefly demonstrated the principles of representation-only;

Among these all [other] kinds,

Difficult to think, are reached by Buddhas [alone].

The doctrines and implications of representation-only are of kinds infinite. I, according to my ability, have briefly demonstrated [a few]. All the other kinds have not been thought and discussed [by me] because they transcend the realm which reflection attains. Such doctrinal implications only Buddhas attain unto, because the knowledge of the Buddhas, World-honored Ones, is in all realms and in all kinds without obstacle.

René Descartes (1596–1650)
MEDITATIONS OF FIRST PHILOSOPHY

Descartes sought to establish a firm and abiding basis for the sciences by discovering what could be known beyond the possibility of a doubt. His method leads him to doubt those things we come to know through the senses, those we know based on our memory, and such universal objects as the color red and the truths of mathematics. He finds, however, that he cannot doubt that he exists and is a thinking thing. Descartes' philosophy and its historical significance in Western philosophy are discussed in Section B of the introductory essay to Part II.

READING QUESTIONS

As you read the selection, try to answer the following questions and identify the passages that support your answers:

1. What is Descartes' motivation for writing the selection?
2. What are the wider and the narrower aims of this selection?
3. What is Descartes' method for attaining these aims?
4. How does he put the method to work?
5. Is Descartes' position sound? Why or why not?

Reprinted from E. S. Haldane and G. R. T. Ross (eds.), *The Philosophical Works of Descartes* (Cambridge, England: Cambridge University Press, 1969), pp. 144–157. Copyright © 1969. Reprinted with the permission of Cambridge University Press.

MEDITATION I

Of the Things Which May Be Brought Within the Sphere of the Doubtful

It is now some years since I detected how many were the false beliefs that I had from my earliest youth admitted as true, and how doubtful was everything I had since constructed on this basis; and from that time I was convinced that I must once for all seriously undertake to rid myself of all the opinions which I had formerly accepted, and commence to build anew from the foundation, if I wanted to establish any firm and permanent structure in the sciences. But as this enterprise appeared to be a very great one, I waited until I had attained an age so mature that I could not hope that at any later date I should be better fitted to execute my design. This reason caused me to delay so long that I should feel that I was doing wrong were I to occupy in deliberation the time that yet remains to me for action. Today, then, since very opportunely for the plan I have in view I have delivered my mind from every care [and am happily agitated by no passions] and since I have procured for myself an assured leisure in a peaceable retirement, I shall at last seriously and freely address myself to the general upheaval of all my former opinions.

Now for this object it is not necessary that I should show that all of these are false—I shall perhaps never arrive at this end. But inasmuch as reason already persuades me that I ought no less carefully to withhold my assent from matters which are not entirely certain and indubitable than from those which appear to me manifestly to be false, if I am able to find in each one some reason to doubt, this will suffice to justify my rejecting the whole. And for that end it will not be requisite that I should examine each in particular, which would be an endless undertaking; for owing to the fact that the destruction of the foundations of necessity brings with it the downfall of the rest of the edifice, I shall only in the first place attack those principles upon which all my former opinions rested.

All that up to the present time I have accepted as most true and certain I have learned either from the senses or through the senses; but it is sometimes proved to me that these senses are deceptive, and it is wiser not to trust entirely to any thing by which we have once been deceived.

But it may be that although the senses sometimes deceive us concerning things which are hardly perceptible, or very far away, there are yet many others to be met with as to which we cannot reasonably have any doubt, although we recognise them by their means. For example, there is the fact that I am here, seated by the fire, attired in a dressing gown, having this paper in my hands and other similar matters. And how could I deny that these hands and this body are mine, were it not perhaps that I compare myself to certain persons, devoid of sense, whose cerebella are so troubled and clouded by the violent vapours of black bile, that they constantly assure us that they think they are kings when they are really quite poor, or that they are clothed in purple when they are really without covering, or who imagine that they have an earthenware head or are nothing but pumpkins or are made of glass. But they are mad, and I should not be any the less insane were I to follow examples so extravagant.

At the same time I must remember that I am a man, and that consequently I am in the habit of sleeping, and in my dreams representing to myself the same things or sometimes even less probable things, than do those who are insane in their waking moments. How often has it happened to me that in the night I dreamt that I found myself in this particular place, that I was dressed and seated near the fire, whilst in reality I was lying undressed in bed! At this moment it does indeed seem to me that it is with eyes awake that I am looking at this paper; that this head which I move is not asleep, that it is deliberately and of set purpose that I extend my hand and perceive it; what happens in sleep does not appear so clear nor so distinct as does all this. But in thinking over this I remind myself that on many occasions I have in sleep been deceived by similar illusions, and in dwelling carefully on this reflection I see so manifestly that there are no certain indications by which we may clearly distinguish wakefulness from sleep that I am lost in astonishment. And my astonishment is such that it is almost capable of persuading me that I now dream.

Now let us assume that we are asleep and that all these particulars, e.g. that we open our eyes, shake our head, extend our hands, and so on, are but false delusions; and let us reflect that possibly neither our hands nor our whole body are such as they appear to us to be. At the same time we must at least confess that the things which are represented to us in sleep are like painted representations which can only have been formed as the counterparts of something real and true, and that in this way those general things at least, i.e. eyes, a head, hands, and a whole body, are not imaginary things, but things really existent. For, as a matter of fact, painters, even when they study with the greatest skill to represent sirens and satyrs by forms the most strange and extraordinary, cannot give them natures which are entirely new, but merely make a certain medley of the members of different animals; or if their imagination is extravagant enough to invent something so novel that nothing similar has ever before been seen, and that then their work represents a thing purely fictitious and absolutely false, it is certain all the same that the colours of which this is composed are necessarily real. And for the same reason, although these general things, to wit, [a body], eyes, a head, hands, and such like, may be imaginary, we are bound at the same time to confess that there are at least some other objects yet more simple and more universal, which are real and true; and of these just in the same way as with certain real colours, all these images of things which dwell in our thoughts, whether true and real or false and fantastic, are formed.

To such a class of things pertains corporeal nature in general, and its extension, the figure of extended things, their quantity or magnitude and number, as also the place in which they are, the time which measures their duration, and so on.

That is possibly why our reasoning is not unjust when we conclude from this that Physics, Astronomy, Medicine and all other sciences which have as their end the consideration of composite things, are very dubious and uncertain; but that Arithmetic, Geometry and other sciences of that kind which only treat of things that are very simple and very general, without taking great trouble to ascertain whether they are actually existent or not, contain some measure of certainty and an element of the indubitable. For whether I am awake or asleep, two and three together always form five, and the square can never have more than four sides, and it does not seem possible that truths so clear and apparent can be suspected of any falsity [or uncertainty].

Nevertheless I have long had fixed in my mind the belief that an all-powerful God existed by whom I have been created such as I am. But how do I know that He has not brought it to pass that there is no earth, no heaven, no extended body, no magnitude, no place, and that nevertheless [I possess the perceptions of all these things and that] they seem to me to exist just exactly as I now see them? And, besides, as I sometimes imagine that others deceive themselves in the things which they think they know best, how do I know that I am not deceived every time that I add two and three, or count the sides of a square, or judge of things yet simpler, if anything simpler can be imagined? But possibly God has not desired that I should be thus deceived, for He is said to be supremely good. If, however, it is contrary to His goodness to have made me such that I constantly deceive myself, it would also appear to be contrary to His goodness to permit me to be sometimes deceived, and nevertheless I cannot doubt that He does permit this.

There may indeed be those who would prefer to deny the existence of a God so powerful, rather than believe that all other things are uncertain. But let us not oppose them for the present, and grant that all that is here said of a God is a fable; nevertheless in whatever way they suppose that I have arrived at the state of being that I have reached—whether they attribute it to fate or to accident, or make out that it is by a continual succession of antecedents, or by some other method—since to err and deceive oneself is a defect, it is clear that the greater will be the probability of my being so imperfect as to deceive myself ever, as is the Author to whom they assign my origin the less powerful. To these reasons I have certainly nothing to reply, but at the end I feel constrained to confess that there is nothing in all that I formerly believed to be true, of which I cannot in some measure doubt, and that not merely through want of thought or through levity, but for reasons which are very powerful and maturely considered; so that henceforth I ought not the less carefully to refrain from giving credence to these opinions than to that which is manifestly false, if I desire to arrive at any certainty [in the sciences].

But it is not sufficient to have made these remarks, we must also be careful to keep them in mind. For these ancient and commonly held opinions still revert frequently to my mind, long and familiar custom having given them the right to occupy my mind against my inclination and rendered them almost masters of my belief; nor will I ever lose the habit of deferring to them or of placing my confidence in them, so long as I consider them as they really are, i.e. opinions in some measure doubtful, as I have just shown, and at the same time highly probable, so that there is much more reason to believe in than to deny them. That is why I consider that I shall not be acting amiss, if, taking of set purpose a contrary belief, I allow myself to be deceived, and for a certain time pretend that all these opinions are entirely false and imaginary, until at last, having thus balanced my former prejudices with my latter [so that they cannot divert my opinions more to one side than to the other], my judgment will no longer be dominated by bad usage or turned away from the right knowledge of the truth. For I am assured that there can be neither peril nor error in this course, and that I cannot at present yield too much to distrust, since I am not considering the question of action, but only of knowledge.

I shall then suppose, not that God who is supremely good and the fountain of truth, but some evil genius not less powerful than deceitful, has employed his whole energies in deceiving me; I shall consider that the heavens, the earth, colours, figures, sound, and all other external things are nought but the illusions and dreams of which this genius has availed himself in order to lay traps for my credulity; I shall consider myself as having no hands, no eyes, no flesh, no blood, nor any senses, yet falsely believing myself to possess all these things; I shall remain obstinately attached to this idea, and if by this means it is not in my power to arrive at the knowl-

edge of any truth, I may at least do what is in my power [i.e. suspend my judgment], and with firm purpose avoid giving credence to any false thing, or being imposed upon by this arch deceiver, however powerful and deceptive he may be. But this task is a laborious one, and insensibly a certain lassitude leads me into the course of my ordinary life. And just as a captive who in sleep enjoys an imaginary liberty, when he begins to suspect that his liberty is but a dream, fears to awaken, and conspires with these agreeable illusions that the deception may be prolonged, so insensibly of my own accord I fall back into my former opinions, and I dread awakening from this slumber, lest the laborious wakefulness which would follow the tranquillity of this repose should have to be spent not in daylight, but in the excessive darkness of the difficulties which have just been discussed.

MEDITATION II

Of the Nature of the Human Mind; and That It Is More Easily Known Than the Body

The Meditation of yesterday filled my mind with so many doubts that it is no longer in my power to forget them. And yet I do not see in what manner I can resolve them; and, just as if I had all of a sudden fallen into very deep water, I am so disconcerted that I can neither make certain of setting my feet on the bottom, nor can I swim and so support myself on the surface. I shall nevertheless make an effort and follow anew the same path as that on which I yesterday entered, i.e. I shall proceed by setting aside all that in which the least doubt could be supposed to exist, just as if I had discovered that it was absolutely false; and I shall ever follow in this road until I have met with something which is certain, or at least, if I can do nothing else, until I have learned for certain that there is nothing in the world that is certain. Archimedes, in order that he might draw the terrestrial globe out of its place, and transport it elsewhere, demanded only that one point should be fixed and immoveable; in the same way I shall have the right to conceive high hopes if I am happy enough to discover one thing only which is certain and indubitable.

I suppose, then, that all the things that I see are false; I persuade myself that nothing has ever existed of all that my fallacious memory represents to me. I consider that I possess no senses; I imagine that body, figure, extension, movement and place are but the fictions of my mind. What, then, can be esteemed as true? Perhaps nothing at all, unless that there is nothing in the world that is certain.

But how can I know there is not something different from those things that I have just considered, of which one cannot have the slightest doubt? Is there not some God, or some other being by whatever name we call it, who puts these reflections into my mind? That is not necessary, for is it not possible that I am capable of producing them myself? I myself, am I not at least something? But I have already denied that I had senses and body. Yet I hesitate, for what follows from that? Am I so dependent on body and senses that I cannot exist without these? But I was persuaded that there was nothing in all the world, that there was no heaven, no earth, that there were no minds, nor any bodies: was I not then likewise persuaded that I did not exist? Not at all; of a surety I myself did exist since I persuaded myself of something [or merely because I thought of something]. But there is some deceiver or other, very powerful and very cunning, who ever employs his ingenuity in deceiving me. Then without doubt I exist also if he deceives me, and let him deceive me as much as he will, he can never cause me to be nothing so long as I think that I am something. So that after having reflected well and carefully examined all things, we must come to the definite conclusion that this proposition: I am, I exist, is necessarily true each time that I pronounce it, or that I mentally conceive it.

But I do not yet know clearly enough what I am, I who am certain that I am; and hence I must be careful to see that I do not imprudently take some other object in place of myself, and thus that I do not go astray in respect of this knowledge that I hold to be the most certain and most evident of all that I have formerly learned. That is why I shall now consider anew what I believed myself to be before I embarked upon these last reflections; and of my former opinions I shall withdraw all that might even in a small degree be invalidated by the reasons which I have just brought forward, in order that there may be nothing at all left beyond what is absolutely certain and indubitable.

What then did I formerly believe myself to be? Undoubtedly I believed myself to be a man. But what is a man? Shall I say a reasonable animal? Certainly not; for then I should have to inquire what an animal is, and what is reasonable; and thus from a single question I should insensibly fall into an infinitude of others more difficult; and I should not wish to waste the little time and leisure remaining to me

in trying to unravel subtleties like these. But I shall rather stop here to consider the thoughts which of themselves spring up in my mind, and which were not inspired by anything beyond my own nature alone when I applied myself to the consideration of my being. In the first place, then, I considered myself as having a face, hands, arms, and all that system of members composed of bones and flesh as seen in a corpse which I designated by the name of body. In addition to this I considered that I was nourished, that I walked, that I felt, and that I thought, and I referred all these actions to the soul: but I did not stop to consider what the soul was, or if I did stop, I imagined that it was something extremely rare and subtle like a wind, a flame, or an ether, which was spread throughout my grosser parts. As to body I had no manner of doubt about its nature, but thought I had a very clear knowledge of it; and if I had desired to explain it according to the notions that I had then formed of it, I should have described it thus: By the body I understand all that which can be defined by a certain figure: something which can be confined in a certain place, and which can fill a given space in such a way that every other body will be excluded from it; which can be perceived either by touch, or by sight, or by hearing, or by taste, or by smell: which can be moved in many ways not, in truth, by itself, but by something which is foreign to it, by which it is touched [and from which it receives impressions]: for to have the power of self-movement, as also of feeling or of thinking, I did not consider to appertain to the nature of body: on the contrary, I was rather astonished to find that faculties similar to them existed in some bodies.

But what am I, now that I suppose that there is a certain genius which is extremely powerful, and, if I may say so, malicious, who employs all his powers in deceiving me? Can I affirm that I possess the least of all those things which I have just said pertain to the nature of body? I pause to consider, I revolve all these things in my mind, and I find none of which I can say that it pertains to me. It would be tedious to stop to enumerate them. Let us pass to the attributes of soul and see if there is any one which is in me? What of nutrition or walking [the first mentioned]? But if it is so that I have no body it is also true that I can neither walk nor take nourishment. Another attribute is sensation. But one cannot feel without body, and besides I have thought I perceived many things during sleep that I recognised in my waking moments as not having been experienced at all. What of thinking? I find here that thought is an attribute that belongs to me; it alone cannot be separated from me. I am, I exist, that is certain. But how often? Just when I think; for it might possibly be the case if I ceased entirely to think, that I should likewise cease altogether to exist. I do not now admit anything which is not necessarily true: to speak accurately I am not more than a thing which thinks, that is to say a mind or a soul, or an understanding, or a reason, which are terms whose significance was formerly unknown to me. I am, however, a real thing and really exist; but what thing? I have answered: a thing which thinks.

And what more? I shall exercise my imagination [in order to see if I am not something more]. I am not a collection of members which we call the human body: I am not a subtle air distributed through these members, I am not a wind, a fire, a vapour, a breath, nor anything at all which I can imagine or conceive; because I have assumed that all these were nothing. Without changing that supposition I find that I only leave myself certain of the fact that I am somewhat. But perhaps it is true that these same things which I supposed were non-existent because they are unknown to me, are really not different from the self which I know. I am not sure about this, I shall not dispute about it now; I can only give judgment on things that are known to me. I know that I exist, and I inquire what I am, I whom I know to exist. But it is very certain that the knowledge of my existence taken in its precise significance does not depend on things whose existence is not yet known to me; consequently it does not depend on those which I can feign in imagination. And indeed the very term *feign* in imagination[1] proves to me my error, for I really do this if I image myself a something, since to imagine is nothing else than to contemplate the figure or image of a corporeal thing. But I already know for certain that I am, and that it may be that all these images, and, speaking generally, all things that relate to the nature of body are nothing but dreams [and chimeras]. For this reason I see clearly that I have as little reason to say, 'I shall stimulate my imagination in order to know more distinctly what I am,' than if I were to say, 'I am now awake, and I perceive somewhat that is real and true: but because I do not yet perceive it distinctly enough, I shall go to sleep of express purpose, so that my dreams may represent the perception with greatest truth and evidence.' And, thus, I know for certain that nothing of all that I can understand by means of my imagi-

nation belongs to this knowledge which I have of myself, and that it is necessary to recall the mind from this mode of thought with the utmost diligence in order that it may be able to know its own nature with perfect distinctness.

But what then am I? A thing which thinks. What is a thing which thinks? It is a thing which doubts, understands, [conceives], affirms, denies, wills, refuses, which also imagines and feels.

Certainly it is no small matter if all these things pertain to my nature. But why should they not so pertain? Am I not that being who now doubts nearly everything, who nevertheless understands certain things, who affirms that one only is true, who denies all the others, who desires to know more, is averse from being deceived, who imagines many things, sometimes indeed despite his will, and who perceives many likewise, as by the intervention of the bodily organs? Is there nothing in all this which is as true as it is certain that I exist, even though I should always sleep and though he who has given me being employed all his ingenuity in deceiving me? Is there likewise any one of these attributes which can be distinguished from my thought, or which might be said to be separated from myself? For it is so evident of itself that it is I who doubts, who understands, and who desires, that there is no reason here to add anything to explain it. And I have certainly the power of imagining likewise; for although it may happen (as I formerly supposed) that none of the things which I imagine are true, nevertheless this power of imagining does not cease to be really in use, and it forms part of my thought. Finally, I am the same who feels, that is to say, who perceives certain things, as by the organs of sense, since in truth I see light, I hear noise, I feel heat. But it will be said that these phenomena are false and that I am dreaming. Let it be so; still it is at least quite certain that it seems to me that I see light, that I hear noise and that I feel heat. That cannot be false; properly speaking it is what is in me called feeling[2]; and used in this precise sense that is no other thing than thinking.

From this time I begin to know what I am with a little more clearness and distinction than before; but nevertheless it still seems to me, and I cannot prevent myself from thinking, that corporeal things, whose images are framed by thought, which are tested by the senses, are much more distinctly known than that obscure part of me which does not come under the imagination. Although really it is very

---

[1] Or "form an image" (effingo).

[2] Sentire.

strange to say that I know and understand more distinctly these things whose existence seems to me dubious, which are unknown to me, and which do not belong to me, than others of the truth of which I am convinced, which are known to me and which pertain to my real nature, in a word, than myself. But I see clearly how the case stands: my mind loves to wander, and cannot yet suffer itself to be retained within the just limits of truth. Very good, let us once more give it the freest rein, so that, when afterwards we seize the proper occasion for pulling up, it may the more easily be regulated and guided.

Let us begin by considering the commonest matters, those which we believe to be the most distinctly comprehended, to wit, the bodies which we touch and see; not indeed bodies in general, for these general ideas are usually a little more confused, but let us consider one body in particular. Let us take, for example, this piece of wax: it has been taken quite freshly from the hive, and it has not yet lost the sweetness of the honey which it contains; it still retains somewhat of the odour of the flowers from which it has been culled; its colour, its figure, its size are apparent; it is hard, cold, easily handled, and if you strike it with the finger, it will emit a sound. Finally all the things which are requisite to cause us distinctly to recognise a body, are met with in it. But notice that while I speak and approach the fire what remained of the taste is exhaled, the smell evaporates, the colour alters, the figure is destroyed, the size increases, it becomes liquid, it heats, scarcely can one handle it, and when one strikes it, no sound is emitted. Does the same wax remain after this change? We must confess that it remains; none would judge otherwise. What then did I know so distinctly in this piece of wax? It could certainly be nothing of all that the senses brought to my notice, since all these things which fall under taste, smell, sight, touch, and hearing, are found to be changed, and yet the same wax remains.

Perhaps it was what I now think, viz. that this wax was not that sweetness of honey, nor that agreeable scent of flowers, nor that particular whiteness, nor that figure, nor that sound, but simply a body which a little while before appeared to me as perceptible under these forms, and which is now perceptible under others. But what, precisely, is it that I imagine when I form such conceptions? Let us attentively consider this, and, abstracting from all that does not belong to the wax, let us see what remains. Certainly nothing remains excepting a certain extended thing which is flexible and movable. But what is the mean-

ing of flexible and movable? Is it not that I imagine that this piece of wax being round is capable of becoming square and of passing from a square to a triangular figure? No, certainly it is not that, since I imagine it admits of an infinitude of similar changes, and I nevertheless do not know how to compass the infinitude by my imagination, and consequently this conception which I have of the wax is not brought about by the faculty of imagination. What now is this extension? Is it not also unknown? For it becomes greater when the wax is melted, greater when it is boiled, and greater still when the heat increases; and I should not conceive [clearly] according to truth what wax is, if I did not think that even this piece that we are considering is capable of receiving more variations in extension than I have ever imagined. We must then grant that I could not even understand through the imagination what this piece of wax is, and that it is my mind[3] alone which perceives it. I say this piece of wax in particular, for as to wax in general it is yet clearer. But what is this piece of wax which cannot be understood excepting by the [understanding or] mind? It is certainly the same that I see, touch, imagine, and finally it is the same which I have always believed it to be from the beginning. But what must particularly be observed is that its perception is neither an act of vision, nor of touch, nor of imagination, and has never been such although it may have appeared formerly to be so, but only an intuition[4] of the mind, which may be imperfect and confused as it was formerly, or clear and distinct as it is at present, according as my attention is more or less directed to the elements which are found in it, and of which it is composed.

Yet in the meantime I am greatly astonished when I consider [the great feebleness of mind] and its proneness to fall [insensibly] into error; for although without giving expression to my thoughts I consider all this in my own mind, words often impede me and I am almost deceived by the terms of ordinary language. For we say that we see the same wax, if it is present, and not that we simply judge that it is the same from its having the same colour and figure. From this I should conclude that I knew the wax by means of vision and not simply by the intuition of the mind; unless by chance I remember that, when looking from a window and saying I see men who pass in the street, I really do not see them, but infer that what I see is men, just as I say that I see

---

[3] entendement F., mens L.

[4] inspectio.

wax. And yet what do I see from the window but hats and coats which may cover automatic machines? Yet I judge these to be men. And similarly solely by the faculty of judgment which rests in my mind, I comprehend that which I believed I saw with my eyes.

A man who makes it his aim to raise his knowledge above the common should be ashamed to derive the occasion for doubting from the forms of speech invented by the vulgar; I prefer to pass on and consider whether I had a more evident and perfect conception of what the wax was when I first perceived it, and when I believed I knew it by means of the external senses or at least by the common sense[5] as it is called, that is to say by the imaginative faculty, or whether my present conception is clearer now that I have most carefully examined what it is, and in what way it can be known. It would certainly be absurd to doubt as to this. For what was there in this first perception which was distinct? What was there which might not as well have been perceived by any of the animals? But when I distinguish the wax from its external forms, and when, just as if I had taken from it its vestments, I consider it quite naked, it is certain that although some error may still be found in my judgment, I can nevertheless not perceive it thus without a human mind.

But finally what shall I say of this mind, that is, of myself, for up to this point I do not admit in myself anything but mind? What then, I who seem to perceive this piece of wax so distinctly, do I not know myself, not only with much more truth and certainty, but also with much more distinctness and clearness? For if I judge that the wax is or exists from the fact that I see it, it certainly follows much more clearly that I am or that I exist myself from the fact that I see it. For it may be that what I see is not really wax, it may also be that I do not possess eyes with which to see anything; but it cannot be that when I see, or (for I no longer take account of the distinction) when I think I see, that I myself who think am nought. So if I judge that the wax exists from the fact that I touch it, the same thing will follow, to wit, that I am; and if I judge that my imagination, or some other cause, whatever it is, persuades me that the wax exists, I shall still conclude the same. And what I have here remarked of wax may be applied to all other things which are external to me [and which are met with outside of me]. And further, if the [notion or] perception of wax has seemed to me clearer and more distinct, not only after the sight or the touch, but also after many other causes have rendered it quite manifest to me, with how much more [evidence] and distinctness must it be said that I now know myself, since all the reasons which contribute to the knowledge of wax, or any other body whatever, are yet better proofs of the nature of my mind! And there are so many other things in the mind itself which may contribute to the elucidation of its nature, that those which depend on body such as these just mentioned, hardly merit being taken into account.

But finally here I am, having insensibly reverted to the point I desired, for, since it is now manifest to me that even bodies are not properly speaking known by the senses or by the faculty of imagination, but by the understanding only, and since they are not known from the fact that they are seen or touched, but only because they are understood, I see clearly that there is nothing which is easier for me to know than my mind. But because it is difficult to rid oneself so promptly of an opinion to which one was accustomed for so long, it will be well that I should halt a little at this point, so that by the length of my meditation I may more deeply imprint on my memory this new knowledge.

[5] sensus communis.

George Berkeley (1685–1753)
OF THE PRINCIPLES OF HUMAN KNOWLEDGE

Berkeley characterizes realism as the doctrine that physical objects have an existence independent of our experience of them. He argues that this doctrine is contradictory because whatever we perceive, we perceive by sense, and is therefore a sensation or an idea derived from a sensation; hence, objects are merely collections of sensations and have no existence outside of our experience. Berkeley's position is discussed in Section B of the introductory essay to Part II.

READING QUESTIONS

In reading the selection, try to answer the following questions and identify the passages that support your answers:

1. What philosophic view does Berkeley uphold?
2. Does he give any reasons in support of this view?
3. Are they good reasons?
4. Does idealism involve a commitment to the coherence theory of truth?
5. Is idealism a good theory? Why or why not?

1. It is evident to anyone who takes a survey of the *objects* of human knowledge that they are either ideas actually imprinted on the senses, or else such as are perceived by attending to the passions and operations of the mind, or lastly, ideas formed by help of memory and imagination—either compounding, dividing, or barely representing those originally perceived in the aforesaid ways. By sight I have the ideas of light and colors, with their several degrees and variations. By touch I perceive, for example, hard and soft, heat and cold, motion and resistance, and of all these more and less either as to quantity or degree. Smelling furnishes me with odors, the palate with tastes, and hearing conveys sounds to the mind in all their variety of tone and composition. And as several of these are observed to accompany each other, they come to be marked by one name, and so to be reputed as one thing. Thus, for example, a certain color, taste, smell, figure, and consistence having been observed to go together, are accounted one distinct thing signified by the name "apple"; other collections of ideas constitute a stone, a tree, a book, and the like sensible things—which as they are pleasing or disagreeable excite the passions of love, hatred, joy, grief, and so forth.

2. But, besides all that endless variety of ideas or objects of knowledge, there is likewise something which knows or perceives them and exercises divers operations, as willing, imagining, remembering, about them. This perceiving, active being is what I call "mind," "spirit," "soul," or "myself." By which words I do not denote any one of my ideas, but a thing entirely distinct from them, wherein they exist or, which is the same thing, whereby they are perceived—for the existence of an idea consists in being perceived.

3. That neither our thoughts, nor passions, nor ideas formed by the imagination exist without the mind is what everybody will allow. And it seems no less evident that the various sensations or ideas imprinted on the sense, however blended or combined together (that is, whatever objects they compose), cannot exist otherwise than in a mind perceiving them.—I think an intuitive knowledge may be obtained of this by anyone that shall attend to what is meant by the term "exist" when applied to sensible things. The table I write on I say exists, that is, I see and feel it; and if I were out of my study I should say it existed—meaning thereby that if I was in my study I might perceive it, or that some other spirit actually does perceive it. There was an odor, that is, it was smelled, there was a sound, that is to say, it was heard; a color or figure, and it was perceived by sight or touch. This is all that I can understand by these and the like expressions. For as to what is said of the absolute existence of unthinking things without any relation to their being perceived, that seems perfectly unintelligible. Their *esse* is *percipi*, nor is it possible they should have any existence out of the minds or thinking things which perceive them.

4. It is indeed an opinion strangely prevailing amongst men that houses, mountains, rivers, and, in a word, all sensible objects have an existence, natural or real, distinct from their being perceived by the understanding. But with how great an assurance and acquiescence soever this principle may be entertained in the world, yet whoever shall find in his heart to call it in question may, if I mistake not, perceive it to involve a manifest contradiction. For what are the forementioned objects but the things we perceive by sense? And what do we perceive besides our own ideas or sensations? And is it not plainly repug-

nant that any one of these, or any combination of them, should exist unperceived?

5. If we thoroughly examine this tenet it will, perhaps, be found at bottom to depend on the doctrine of *abstract ideas*. For can there be a nicer strain of abstraction than to distinguish the existence of sensible objects from their being perceived, so as to conceive them existing unperceived? Light and colors, heat and cold, extension and figures—in a word, the things we see and feel—what are they but so many sensations, notions, ideas, or impressions on the sense? And is it possible to separate, even in thought, any of these from perception? For my part, I might as easily divide a thing from itself. I may, indeed, divide in my thoughts, or conceive apart from each other, those things which, perhaps, I never perceived by sense so divided. Thus I imagine the trunk of a human body without the limbs, or conceive the smell of a rose without thinking on the rose itself. So far, I will not deny, I can abstract—if that may properly be called "abstraction" which extends only to the conceiving separately such objects as it is possible may really exist or be actually perceived asunder. But my conceiving or imagining power does not extend beyond the possibility of real existence or perception. Hence, as it is impossible for me to see or feel anything without an actual sensation of that thing, so it is impossible for me to conceive in my thoughts any sensible thing or object distinct from the sensation or perception of it.

6. Some truths there are so near and obvious to the mind that a man need only open his eyes to see them. Such I take this important one to be, to wit, that all the choir of heaven and furniture of the earth, in a word, all those bodies which compose the mighty frame of the world, have not any subsistence without a mind—that their *being* is to be perceived or known, that, consequently, so long as they are not actually perceived by me or do not exist in my mind or that of any other created spirit, they must either have no existence at all or else subsist in the mind of some eternal spirit—it being perfectly unintelligible, and involving all the absurdity of abstraction, to attribute to any single part of them an existence independent of a spirit. To be convinced of which, the reader need only reflect, and try to separate in his own thoughts, the *being* of a sensible thing from its *being perceived*.

7. From what has been said it follows there is not any other substance than *spirit*, or that which perceives. But, for the fuller proof of this point, let it be considered the sensible qualities are color, figure, motion, smell, taste, and such like—that is, the ideas perceived by sense. Now, for an idea to exist in an unperceiving thing is a manifest contradiction, for to have an idea is all one as to perceive; that, therefore, wherein color, figure, and the like qualities exist must perceive them; hence it is clear there can be no unthinking substance or *substratum* of those ideas.

8. But, say you, though the ideas themselves do not exist without the mind, yet there may be things like them, whereof they are copies or resemblances, which things exist without the mind in an unthinking substance. I answer, an idea can be like nothing but an idea; a color or figure can be like nothing but another color or figure. If we look but ever so little into our thoughts, we shall find it impossible for us to conceive a likeness except only between our ideas. Again, I ask whether those supposed originals or external things, of which our ideas are the pictures or representations, be themselves perceivable or no? If they are, then they are ideas and we have gained our point; but if you say they are not, I appeal to anyone whether it be sense to assert a color is like something which is invisible; hard or soft, like something which is intangible; and so of the rest.

9. Some there are who make a distinction betwixt *primary* and *secondary* qualities.[1] By the former they mean extension, figure, motion, rest, solidity or impenetrability, and number; by the latter they denote all other sensible qualities, as colors, sounds, tastes, and so forth. The ideas we have of these they acknowledge not to be the resemblances of anything existing without the mind, or unperceived, but they will have our ideas of the primary qualities to be patterns or images of things which exist without the mind, in an unthinking substance which they call "matter." By "matter," therefore, we are to understand an inert, senseless substance, in which extension, figure, and motion do actually subsist. But it is evident from what we have already shown that extension, figure, and motion are only ideas existing in the mind, and that an idea can be like nothing but another idea, and that consequently neither they nor their archetypes can exist in an unperceiving substance. Hence it is plain that the very notion of what is called "matter" or "corporeal substance" involves a contradiction in it.

10. They who assert that figure, motion, and the rest of the primary or original qualities do exist without the mind in unthinking substances do at the same time acknowledge that colors, sounds, heat,

---

[1] [E.g., Locke, *Essay*, Bk. II, chap. 8.]

cold, and suchlike secondary qualities do not—which they tell us are sensations existing in the mind alone, that depend on and are occasioned by the different size, texture, and motion of the minute particles of matter. This they take for an undoubted truth which they can demonstrate beyond all exception. Now, if it be certain that those original qualities are inseparably united with the other sensible qualities, and not, even in thought, capable of being abstracted from them, it plainly follows that they exist only in the mind. But I desire anyone to reflect and try whether he can, by any abstraction of thought, conceive the extension and motion of a body without all other sensible qualities. For my own part, I see evidently that it is not in my power to frame an idea of a body extended and moved, but I must withal give it some color or other sensible quality which is acknowledged to exist only in the mind. In short, extension, figure, and motion, abstracted from all other qualities, are inconceivable. Where therefore the other sensible qualities are, there must these be also, to wit, in the mind and nowhere else.

11. Again, *great* and *small, swift* and *slow* are allowed to exist nowhere without the mind, being entirely relative, and changing as the frame or position of the organs of sense varies. The extension, therefore, which exists without the mind is neither great nor small, the motion neither swift nor slow: that is, they are nothing at all. But, say you, they are extension in general, and motion in general: thus we see how much the tenet of extended movable substances existing without the mind depends on that strange doctrine of *abstract ideas*. And here I cannot but remark how nearly the vague and indeterminate description of matter or corporeal substance, which the modern philosophers are run into by their own principles, resembles that antiquated and so much ridiculed notion of *materia prima,* to be met with in Aristotle and his followers. Without extension, solidity cannot be conceived; since, therefore, it has been shown that extension exists not in an unthinking substance, the same must also be true of solidity.

12. That number is entirely the creature of the mind, even though the other qualities be allowed to exist without, will be evident to whoever considers that the same thing bears a different denomination of number as the mind views it with different respects. Thus the same extension is one, or three, or thirty-six, according as the mind considers it with reference to a yard, a foot, or an inch. Number is so visibly relative and dependent on men's understand-

ing that it is strange to think how anyone should give it an absolute existence without the mind. We say one book, one page, one line; all these are equally units, though some contain several of the others. And in each instance it is plain the unit relates to some particular combination of ideas arbitrarily put together by the mind.

13. Unity I know some will have to be a simple or uncompounded idea accompanying all other ideas into the mind.[2] That I have any such idea answering the word "unity" I do not find; and if I had, methinks I could not miss finding it; on the contrary, it should be the most familiar to my understanding, since it is said to accompany all other ideas and to be perceived by all the ways of sensation and reflection. To say no more, it is an *abstract idea.*

14. I shall further add that, after the same manner as modern philosophers prove certain sensible qualities to have no existence in matter, or without the mind, the same thing may be likewise proved of all other sensible qualities whatsoever. Thus, for instance, it is said that heat and cold are affections only of the mind, and not at all patterns of real beings existing in the corporeal substances which excite them, for that the same body which appears cold to one hand seems warm to another. Now, why may we not as well argue that figure and extension are not patterns or resemblances of qualities existing in matter, because to the same eye at different stations, or eyes of a different texture at the same station, they appear various and cannot, therefore, be the images of anything settled and determinate without the mind? Again, it is proved that sweetness is not really in the sapid thing, because, the thing remaining unaltered, the sweetness is changed into bitter, as in case of a fever or otherwise vitiated palate. Is it not as reasonable to say that motion is not without the mind, since if the succession of ideas in the mind become swifter, the motion, it is acknowledged, shall appear slower without any alteration in any external object?

15. In short, let anyone consider those arguments which are thought manifestly to prove that colors and tastes exist only in the mind, and he shall find they may with equal force be brought to prove the same thing of extension, figure, and motion. Though it must be confessed this method of arguing does not so much prove that there is no extension or color in an outward object as that we do not know by sense which is the true extension or color

---

2 [E.g., Locke, *Essay,* Bk. II, chap. 16, sec. 1: "Amongst all the ideas we have, there is none more simple than that of unity."]

of the object. But the arguments foregoing plainly show it to be impossible that any color or extension at all, or other sensible quality whatsoever, should exist in an unthinking subject without the mind, or, in truth, that there should be any such thing as an outward object.

16. But let us examine a little the received opinion.—It is said extension is a mode or accident of matter, and that matter is the *substratum* that supports it. Now I desire that you would explain what is meant by matter's "supporting" extension. Say you, I have no idea of matter and, therefore, cannot explain it. I answer, though you have no positive, yet, if you have any meaning at all, you must at least have a relative idea of matter; though you know not what it is, yet you must be supposed to know what relation it bears to accidents, and what is meant by its supporting them. It is evident "support" cannot here be taken in its usual or literal sense—as when we say that pillars support a building; in what sense therefore must it be taken?

17. If we inquire into what the most accurate philosophers[3] declare themselves to mean by "material substance," we shall find them acknowledge they have no other meaning annexed to those sounds but the idea of being in general together with the relative notion of its supporting accidents. The general idea of being appears to me the most abstract and incomprehensible of all other; and as for its supporting accidents, this, as we have just now observed, cannot be understood in the common sense of those words; it must, therefore, be taken in some other sense, but what that is they do not explain. So that when I consider the two parts or branches which make the signification of the words "material substance," I am convinced there is no distinct meaning annexed to them. But why should we trouble ourselves any further in discussing this material *substratum* or support of figure and motion and other sensible qualities? Does it not suppose they have an existence without the mind? And is not this a direct repugnancy and altogether inconceivable?

18. But, though it were possible that solid, figured, movable substances may exist without the mind, corresponding to the ideas we have of bodies, yet how is it possible for us to know this? Either we must know it by sense or by reason. As for our senses, by them

we have the knowledge only of our sensations, ideas, or those things that are immediately perceived by sense, call them what you will; but they do not inform us that things exist without the mind, or unperceived, like to those which are perceived. This the materialists themselves acknowledge. It remains therefore that if we have any knowledge at all of external things, it must be by reason, inferring their existence from what is immediately perceived by sense. But what reason can induce us to believe the existence of bodies without the mind, from what we perceive, since the very patrons of matter themselves do not pretend there is any necessary connection betwixt them and our ideas? I say it is granted on all hands (and what happens in dreams, frenzies, and the like, puts it beyond dispute) that it is possible we might be affected with all the ideas we have now, though no bodies existed without resembling them. Hence it is evident the supposition of external bodies is not necessary for the producing our ideas; since it is granted they are produced sometimes, and might possibly be produced always in the same order we see them in at present, without their concurrence.

19. But though we might possibly have all our sensations without them, yet perhaps it may be thought easier to conceive and explain the manner of their production by supposing external bodies in their likeness rather than otherwise; and so it might be at least probable there are such things as bodies that excite their ideas in our minds. But neither can this be said, for, though we give the materialists their external bodies, they by their own confession are never the nearer knowing how our ideas are produced, since they own themselves unable to comprehend in what manner body can act upon spirit, or how it is possible it should imprint any idea in the mind. Hence it is evident the production of ideas or sensations in our minds can be no reason why we should suppose matter or corporeal substances, since that is acknowledged to remain equally inexplicable with or without this supposition. If therefore it were possible for bodies to exist without the mind, yet to hold they do so must needs be a very precarious opinion, since it is to suppose, without any reason at all, that God has created innumerable beings that are entirely useless and serve to no manner of purpose.

20. In short, if there were external bodies, it is impossible we should ever come to know it; and if there were not, we might have the very same reasons to think there were that we have now. Suppose—what no one can deny possible—an intelligence without

---

[3] [E.g., Locke, *Essay*, Bk. II, chap. 23, sec. 2: "If anyone will examine himself concerning his notion of pure substance in general, he will find he has no other idea of it all but only a supposition of he knows not what support of such qualities which are capable of producing simple ideas in us: which qualities are commonly called accidents."]

the help of external bodies, to be affected with the same train of sensations or ideas that you are, imprinted in the same order and with like vividness in his mind. I ask whether that intelligence has not all the reason to believe the existence of corporeal substances, represented by his ideas and exciting them in his mind, that you can possibly have for believing the same thing? Of this there can be no question—which one consideration is enough to make any reasonable person suspect the strength of whatever arguments he may think himself to have for the existence of bodies without the mind.

21. Were it necessary to add any further proof against the existence of matter after what has been said, I could instance several of those errors and difficulties (not to mention impieties) which have sprung from that tenet. It has occasioned numberless controversies and disputes in philosophy, and not a few of far greater moment in religion. But I shall not enter into the detail of them in this place as well because I think arguments a posteriori are unnecessary for confirming what has been, if I mistake not, sufficiently demonstrated a priori, as because I shall hereafter find occasion to speak somewhat of them.

22. I am afraid I have given cause to think me needlessly prolix in handling this subject. For to what purpose is it to dilate on that which may be demonstrated with the utmost evidence in a line or two to anyone that is capable of the least reflection? It is but looking into your own thoughts, and so trying whether you can conceive it possible for a sound, or figure, or motion, or color to exist without the mind or unperceived. This easy trial may make you see that what you contend for is a downright contradiction. Insomuch that I am content to put the whole upon this issue: if you can but conceive it possible for one extended movable substance, or, in general, for any one idea, or anything like an idea, to exist otherwise than in a mind perceiving it, I shall readily give up the cause. And, as for all that compages of external bodies which you contend for, I shall grant you its existence, though you cannot either give me any reason why you believe it exists, or assign any use to it when it is supposed to exist. I say the bare possibility of your opinion's being true shall pass for an argument that it is so.

23. But, say you, surely there is nothing easier than to imagine trees, for instance, in a park, or books existing in a closet, and nobody by to perceive them. I answer you may so, there is no difficulty in it; but what is all this, I beseech you, more than framing in your mind certain ideas which you call books and trees, and at the same time omitting to frame the idea of anyone that may perceive them? But do not you yourself perceive or think of them all the while? This therefore is nothing to the purpose: it only shows you have the power of imagining or forming ideas in your mind: but it does not show that you can conceive it possible the objects of your thought may exist without the mind. To make out this, it is necessary that you conceive them existing unconceived or unthought of, which is a manifest repugnancy. When we do our utmost to conceive the existence of external bodies, we are all the while only contemplating our own ideas. But the mind, taking no notice of itself, is deluded to think it can and does conceive bodies existing unthought of or without the mind, though at the same time they are apprehended by or exist in itself. A little attention will discover to anyone the truth and evidence of what is here said, and make it unnecessary to insist on any other proofs against the existence of *material substance.*

24. It is very obvious, upon the least inquiry into our own thoughts, to know whether it be possible for us to understand what is meant by "the absolute existence of sensible objects in themselves, or without the mind." To me it is evident those words mark out either a direct contradiction or else nothing at all. And to convince others of this, I know no readier or fairer way than to entreat they would calmly attend to their own thoughts; and if by this attention the emptiness or repugnancy of those expressions does appear, surely nothing more is requisite for their conviction. It is on this, therefore, that I insist, to wit, that "the absolute existence of unthinking things" are words without a meaning, or which include a contradiction. This is what I repeat and inculcate, and earnestly recommend to the attentive thoughts of the reader.

25. All our ideas, sensations, or the things which we perceive, by whatsoever names they may be distinguished, are visibly inactive—there is nothing of power or agency included in them. So that one idea or object of thought cannot produce or make any alteration in another. To be satisfied of the truth of this, there is nothing else requisite but a bare observation of our ideas. For since they and every part of them exist only in the mind, it follows that there is nothing in them but what is perceived; but whoever shall attend to his ideas, whether of sense or reflection, will not perceive in them any power or activity; there is, therefore, no such thing contained

in them. A little attention will discover to us that the very being of an idea implies passiveness and inertness in it, insomuch that it is impossible for an idea to do anything or strictly speaking, to be the cause of anything; neither can it be the resemblance or pattern of any active being, as is evident from sec. 8. Whence it plainly follows that extension, figure, and motion cannot be the cause of our sensations. To say, therefore, that these are the effects of powers resulting from the configuration, number, motion, and size of corpuscles must certainly be false.

26. We perceive a continual succession of ideas, some are anew excited, others are changed or totally disappear. There is, therefore, some cause of these ideas, whereon they depend and which produces and changes them. That this cause cannot be any quality or idea or combination of ideas is clear from the preceding section. It must therefore be a substance; but it has been shown that there is no corporeal or material substance: it remains, therefore, that the cause of ideas is an incorporeal, active substance or spirit.

27. A spirit is one simple, undivided, active being—as it perceives ideas it is called "the understanding," and as it produces or otherwise operates about them it is called "the will." Hence there can be no *idea* formed of a soul or spirit; for all ideas whatever, being passive and inert (*vide* sec. 25), they cannot represent unto us, by way of image or likeness, that which acts. A little attention will make it plain to anyone that to have an idea which shall be like that active principle of motion and change of ideas is absolutely impossible. Such is the nature of *spirit,* or that which acts, that it cannot be of itself perceived, but only by the effects which it produces. If any man shall doubt of the truth of what is here delivered, let him but reflect and try if he can frame the idea of any power or active being, and whether he has ideas of two principal powers marked by the names "will" and "understanding," distinct from each other as well as from a third idea of substance or being in general, with a relative notion of its supporting or being the subject of the aforesaid powers—which is signified by the name "soul" or "spirit." This is what some hold; but, so far as I can see, the words "will," "soul," "spirit" do not stand for different ideas or, in truth, for any idea at all, but for something which is very different from ideas, and which, being an agent, cannot be like unto, or represented by, any idea whatsoever. [Though it must be owned at the same time that we have some notion of soul, spirit, and the operations of the mind, such as will-

ing, loving, hating—in as much as we know or understand the meaning of those words.][4]

28. I find I can excite ideas in my mind at pleasure, and vary and shift the scene as oft as I think fit. It is no more than willing, and straightway this or that idea arises in my fancy; and by the same power it is obliterated and makes way for another. This making and unmaking of ideas does very properly denominate the mind active. Thus much is certain and grounded on experience; but when we talk of unthinking agents or of exciting ideas exclusive of volition, we only amuse ourselves with words.

29. But, whatever power I may have over my own thoughts, I find the ideas actually perceived by sense have not a like dependence on my will. When in broad daylight I open my eyes, it is not in my power to choose whether I shall see or no, or to determine what particular objects shall present themselves to my view; and so likewise as to the hearing and other senses; the ideas imprinted on them are not creatures of my will. There is therefore some *other* will or spirit that produces them.

30. The ideas of sense are more strong, lively, and distinct than those of the imagination; they have likewise a steadiness, order, and coherence, and are not excited at random, as those which are the effects of human wills often are, but in a regular train or series, the admirable connection whereof sufficiently testifies the wisdom and benevolence of its Author. Now the set rules or established methods wherein the mind we depend on excites in us the ideas of sense are called "the laws of nature"; and these we learn by experience, which teaches us that such and such ideas are attended with such and such other ideas in the ordinary course of things.

31. This gives us a sort of foresight which enables us to regulate our actions for the benefit of life. And without this we should be eternally at a loss; we could not know how to act anything that might procure us the least pleasure or remove the least pain of sense. That food nourishes, sleep refreshes, and fire warms us; that to sow in the seedtime is the way to reap in the harvest; and in general that to obtain such or such ends, such or such means are conducive—all this we know, not by discovering any necessary connection between our ideas, but only by the observation of the settled laws of nature, without which we should be all in uncertainty and confusion, and a

---

[4] [This sentence, added to the second edition of 1734, introduces the technical term "notion," but it is doubtful whether it marks a change of doctrine. Similar changes were made in *Principles*, secs. 89, 140, 142; and *Dialogues*, III, sec. 4.]

grown man no more know how to manage himself in the affairs of life than an infant just born.

32. And yet this consistent, uniform working which so evidently displays the goodness and wisdom of that Governing Spirit whose Will constitutes the laws of nature, is so far from leading our thoughts to Him that it rather sends them awandering after second causes. For when we perceive certain ideas of sense constantly followed by other ideas, and we know this is not of our own doing, we forthwith attribute power and agency to the ideas themselves and make one the cause of another, than which nothing can be more absurd and unintelligible. Thus, for example, having observed that when we perceive by sight a certain round, luminous figure, we at the same time perceive by touch the idea or sensation called "heat," we do from thence conclude the sun to be the cause of heat. And in like manner perceiving the motion and collision of bodies to be attended with sound, we are inclined to think the latter an effect of the former.

33. The ideas imprinted on the senses by the Author of Nature are called "real things"; and those excited in the imagination, being less regular, vivid, and constant, are more properly termed "ideas" or "images of things" which they copy and represent. But then our sensations, be they never so vivid and distinct, are nevertheless ideas, that is, they exist in the mind, or are perceived by it, as truly as the ideas of its own framing. The ideas of sense are allowed to have more reality in them, that is, to be more strong, orderly, and coherent than the creatures of the mind; but this is no argument that they exist without the mind. They are also less dependent on the spirit, or thinking substance which perceives them, in that they are excited by the will of another and more powerful spirit; yet still they are *ideas;* and certainly no idea, whether faint or strong, can exist otherwise than in a mind perceiving it.

34. Before we proceed any further it is necessary to spend some time in answering objections which may probably be made against the principles hitherto laid down. In doing of which, if I seem too prolix to those of quick apprehensions, I hope it may be pardoned, since all men do not equally apprehend things of this nature, and I am willing to be understood by everyone.

First, then, it will be objected that by the foregoing principles all that is real and substantial in nature is banished out of the world, and instead thereof a chimerical scheme of *ideas* takes place. All things that exist, exist only in the mind, that is, they are purely notional. What therefore becomes of the sun, moon, and stars? What must we think of houses, rivers, mountains, trees, stones, nay, even of our own bodies? Are all these but so many chimeras and illusions on the fancy? To all which, and whatever else of the same sort may be objected, I answer that by the principles premised we are not deprived of any one thing in nature. Whatever we see, feel, hear, or anywise conceive or understand remains as secure as ever, and is as real as ever. There is a *rerum natura,* and the distinction between realities and chimeras retains its full force. This is evident from secs. 29, 30, and 33, where we have shown what is meant by "real things" in opposition to "chimeras" or ideas of our own framing; but then they both equally exist in the mind, and in that sense they are alike *ideas.*

35. I do not argue against the existence of any one thing that we can apprehend either by sense or reflection. That the things I see with my eyes and touch with my hands do exist, really exist, I make not the least question. The only thing whose existence we deny is that which philosophers call matter or corporeal substance. And in doing of this there is no damage done to the rest of mankind, who, I dare say, will never miss it. The atheist indeed will want the color of an empty name to support his impiety; and the philosophers may possibly find they have lost a great handle for trifling and disputation.

36. If any man thinks this detracts from the existence or reality of things, he is very far from understanding what has been premised in the plainest terms I could think of. Take here an abstract of what has been said: there are spiritual substances, minds, or human souls, which will or excite ideas in themselves at pleasure, but these are faint, weak, and unsteady in respect of others they perceive by sense—which, being impressed upon them according to certain rules or laws of nature, speak themselves the effects of a mind more powerful and wise than human spirits. These latter are said to have more *reality* in them than the former—by which is meant that they are more affecting, orderly, and distinct, and that they are not fictions of the mind perceiving them. And in this sense the sun that I see by day is the real sun, and that which I imagine by night is the idea of the former. In the sense here given of "reality" it is evident that every vegetable, star, mineral, and in general each part of the mundane system, is as much a *real being* by our principles as by any other. Whether others mean anything by the term "reality" different from what I do, I entreat them to look into their own thoughts and see.

37. It will be urged that this much at least is true, to wit, that we take away all corporeal substances. To this my answer is that if the word "substance" be taken in the vulgar sense—for a combination of sensible qualities, such as extension, solidity, weight, and the like—this we cannot be accused of taking away;but if it be taken in a philosophic sense—for the support of accidents or qualities without the mind—then indeed I acknowledge that we take it away, if one may be said to take away that which never had any existence, not even in the imagination.

Charles Sanders Peirce (1839–1914)
THE FIXATION OF BELIEF

Peirce argues that real doubt involves three features: it creates a feeling of uneasiness, it provokes a struggle to get rid of this feeling, and it has no action-guiding function. By contrast, belief creates a feeling of satisfaction, produces no struggle, and has action-guiding functions. Peirce sees inquiry as the struggle to get rid of doubt and fix belief. His position is discussed in Section B of the introductory essay to Part II.

READING QUESTIONS

As you read the selection, try to answer the following questions and identify the passages that support your answers:

1. What are Peirce's conceptions of doubt, belief, and inquiry?
2. Are these conceptions sound? Why or why not?
3. What is fixing belief according to Peirce?
4. What is Peirce's conception of the fact with which our opinion, if true, must agree?
5. Is Peirce committed to the ultimate convergence of inquirers' opinions? Is his position sound? Why or why not?

Reprinted with the permission of Dover Publications, Inc., from Philip P. Wiener (ed.), *Charles S. Peirce: Selected Writings* (New York: Dover, 1958), pp. 98–112. Copyright © 1958.

I

We generally know when we wish to ask a question and when we wish to pronounce a judgment, for there is a dissimilarity between the sensation of doubting and that of believing.

But this is not all which distinguishes doubt from belief. There is a practical difference. Our beliefs guide our desires and shape our actions. The Assassins, or followers of the Old Man of the Mountain, used to rush into death at his least command, because they believed that obedience to him would insure everlasting felicity. Had they doubted this, they would not have acted as they did. So it is with every belief, according to its degree. The feeling of believing is a more or less sure indication of there being established in our nature some habit which will determine our actions. Doubt never has such an effect.

Nor must we overlook a third point of difference.

Doubt is an uneasy and dissatisfied state from which we struggle to free ourselves and pass into the state of belief;[1] while the latter is a calm and satisfactory state which we do not wish to avoid, or to change to a belief in anything else.[2] On the contrary, we cling tenaciously, not merely to believing, but to believing just what we do believe.

Thus, both doubt and belief have positive effects upon us, though very different ones. Belief does not make us act at once, but puts us into such a condition that we shall behave in a certain way, when the occasion arises. Doubt has not the least effect of this sort, but stimulates us to action until it is destroyed. This reminds us of the irritation of a nerve and the reflex action produced thereby; while for the analogue of belief, in the nervous system, we must look to what are called nervous associations—for example, to that habit of the nerves in consequence of which the smell of a peach will make the mouth water.

II

The irritation of doubt causes a struggle to attain a state of belief.[3] I shall term this struggle *inquiry*, though it must be admitted that this is sometimes not a very apt designation.

The irritation of doubt is the only immediate motive for the struggle to attain belief. It is certainly best for us that our beliefs should be such as may truly guide our actions so as to satisfy our desires; and this reflection will make us reject any belief which does not seem to have been so formed as to insure this result. But it will only do so by creating a doubt in the place of that belief. With the doubt, therefore, the struggle begins, and with the cessation of doubt it ends. Hence, the sole object of inquiry is the settlement of opinion. We may fancy that this is not enough for us, and that we seek not merely an opin-

ion, but a true opinion. But put this fancy to the test, and it proves groundless; for as soon as a firm belief is reached we are entirely satisfied, whether the belief be false or true. And it is clear that nothing out of the sphere of our knowledge can be our object, for nothing which does not affect the mind can be a motive for a mental effort. The most that can be maintained is that we seek for a belief that we shall *think* to be true. But we think each one of our beliefs to be true, and, indeed, it is mere tautology to say so.[4]

That the settlement of opinion is the sole end of inquiry is a very important proposition. It sweeps away, at once, various vague and erroneous conceptions of proof. A few of these may be noticed here.

1. Some philosophers have imagined that to start an inquiry it was only necessary to utter a question or set it down on paper, and have even recommended us to begin our studies with questioning everything! But the mere putting of a proposition into the interrogative form does not stimulate the mind to any struggle after belief. There must be a real and living doubt, and without all this, discussion is idle.

2. It is a very common idea that a demonstration must rest on some ultimate and absolutely indubitable propositions. These, according to one school, are first principles of a general nature; according to another, are first sensations. But, in point of fact, an inquiry, to have that completely satisfactory result called demonstration, has only to start with propositions perfectly free from all actual doubt. If the premises are not in fact doubted at all, they cannot be more satisfactory than they are.[5]

3. Some people seem to love to argue a point after all the world is fully convinced of it. But no further advance can be made. When doubt ceases, mental action on the subject comes to an end; and, if it did go on, it would be without a purpose, except that of self-criticism.

---

[1] "In this, it [doubt] is like any other stimulus. It is true that just as man may, for the sake of the pleasures of the table, like to be hungry and take means to make themselves so, although hunger always involves a desire to fill the stomach, so for the sake of the pleasures of inquiry, men may like to seek out doubts. Yet for all that, doubt essentially involves a struggle to escape it." Peirce's note of 1903.

[2] I am not speaking of secondary effects occasionally produced by the interference of other impulses.

[3] "Doubt, however, is not usually hesitancy about what is to be done then and there. It is anticipated hesitancy about what I shall do hereafter, or a feigned hesitancy about a fictitious state of things. It is the power of making believe we hesitate, together with the pregnant fact that the decision upon the make-believe dilemma goes toward forming a bona fide habit that will be operative in a real emergency." Peirce's note of 1893.

[4] "For truth is neither more nor less than that character of a proposition which consists in this, that belief in the proposition would, with sufficient experience and reflection, lead us to such conduct as would tend to satisfy the desires we should then have. To say that truth means more than this is to say that it has no meaning at all." Peirce's note of 1903.

[5] "Doubts about them [the premises] may spring up later; but we can find no propositions which are not subject to this contingency." This note, of 1893, indicates Peirce's view of the probability and fallibility of any particular assertion about reality, without denying that some common-sense assertions about reality must be taken as certain even while questioning the others. For example, I may doubt that I see a bent stick in the water without doubting that it seems bent. Thus Peirce called himself a "critical common-sensist" and "fallibilist."

III

If the settlement of opinion is the sole object of inquiry, and if belief is of the nature of a habit, why should we not attain the desired end, by taking any answer to a question, which we may fancy, and constantly reiterating it to ourselves, dwelling on all which may conduce to that belief, and learning to turn with contempt and hatred from anything which might disturb it? This simple and direct method is really pursued by many men. I remember once being entreated not to read a certain newspaper lest it might change my opinion upon free-trade. "Lest I might be entrapped by its fallacies and misstatements" was the form of expression. "You are not," my friend said, "a special student of political economy. You might, therefore, easily be deceived by fallacious arguments upon the subject. You might, then, if you read this paper, be led to believe in protection. But you admit that free-trade is the true doctrine; and you do not wish to believe what is not true." I have often known this system to be deliberately adopted. Still oftener, the instinctive dislike of an undecided state of mind, exaggerated into a vague dread of doubt, makes men cling spasmodically to the views they already take. The man feels that if he only holds to his belief without wavering, it will be entirely satisfactory. Nor can it be denied that a steady and immovable faith yields great peace of mind. It may, indeed, give rise to inconveniences, as if a man should resolutely continue to believe that fire would not burn him, or that he would be eternally damned if he received his *ingesta* otherwise than through a stomach-pump. But then the man who adopts this method will not allow that its inconveniences are greater than its advantages. He will say, "I hold steadfastly to the truth and the truth is always wholesome." And in many cases it may very well be that the pleasure he derives from his calm faith overbalances any inconveniences resulting from its deceptive character. Thus, if it be true that death is annihilation, then the man who believes that he will certainly go straight to heaven when he dies, provided he have fulfilled certain simple observances in this life, has a cheap pleasure which will not be followed by the least disappointment. A similar consideration seems to have weight with many persons in religious topics, for we frequently hear it said, "Oh, I could not believe so-and-so, because I should be wretched if I did." When an ostrich buries its head in the sand as danger approaches, it very likely takes the happiest course. It hides the danger, and then

calmly says there is no danger; and, if it feels perfectly sure there is none, why should it raise its head to see? A man may go through life, systematically keeping out of view all that might cause a change in his opinions, and if he only succeeds—basing his method, as he does, on two fundamental psychological laws—I do not see what can be said against his doing so. It would be an egotistical impertinence to object that his procedure is irrational, for that only amounts to saying that his method of settling belief is not ours. He does not propose to himself to be rational, and indeed, will often talk with scorn of man's weak and illusive reason. So let him think as he pleases.

But this method of fixing belief, which may be called the method of tenacity, will be unable to hold its ground in practice. The social impulse is against it. The man who adopts it will find that other men think differently from him, and it will be apt to occur to him in some saner moment that their opinions are quite as good as his own, and this will shake his confidence in his belief. This conception, that another man's thought or sentiment may be equivalent to one's own, is a distinctly new step, and a highly important one. It arises from an impulse too strong in man to be suppressed, without danger of destroying the human species. Unless we make ourselves hermits, we shall necessarily influence each other's opinions; so that the problem becomes how to fix belief, not in the individual merely, but in the community.

Let the will of the state act, then, instead of that of the individual. Let an institution be created which shall have for its object to keep correct doctrines before the attention of the people, to reiterate them perpetually, and to teach them to the young; having at the same time power to prevent contrary doctrines from being taught, advocated, or expressed. Let all possible causes of a change of mind be removed from men's apprehensions. Let them be kept ignorant, lest they should learn of some reason to think otherwise than they do. Let their passions be enlisted, so that they may regard private and unusual opinions with hatred and horror. Then, let all men who reject the established belief be terrified into silence. Let the people turn out and tar-and-feather such men, or let inquisitions be made into the manner of thinking of suspected persons, and, when they are found guilty of forbidden beliefs, let them be subjected to some signal punishment. When complete agreement could not otherwise be reached, a general massacre of all who have not thought in a certain way has proved a very effective means of settling opinion in a country. If the power to do this be wanting, let a list of opinions be drawn up, to which no man of the least independence of thought can assent, and let the faithful be required to accept all these propositions, in order to segregate them as radically as possible from the influence of the rest of the world.

This method has, from the earliest times, been one of the chief means of upholding correct theological and political doctrines, and of preserving their universal or catholic character. In Rome, especially, it has been practiced from the days of Numa Pompilius to those of Pius Nonus. This is the most perfect example in history; but wherever there is a priesthood—and no religion has been without one—this method has been more or less made use of. Wherever there is aristocracy, or a guild, or any association of a class of men whose interests depend or are supposed to depend on certain propositions, there will be inevitably found some traces of this natural product of social feeling. Cruelties always accompany this system; and when it is consistently carried out, they become atrocities of the most horrible kind in the eyes of any rational man. Nor should this occasion surprise, for the officer of a society does not feel justified in surrendering the interests of that society for the sake of mercy, as he might his own private interests. It is natural, therefore, that sympathy and fellowship should thus produce a most ruthless power.

In judging this method of fixing belief, which may be called the method of authority, we must, in the first place, allow its immeasurable mental and moral superiority to the method of tenacity. Its success is proportionally greater; and in fact it has over and over again worked the most majestic results. The mere structures of stone which it has caused to be put together—in Siam, for example, in Egypt, and in Europe—have many of them a sublimity hardly more than rivaled by the greatest works of nature. And, except the geological epochs, there are no periods of time so vast as those which are measured by some of these organized faiths. If we scrutinize the matter closely, we shall find that there has not been one of their creeds which has remained always the same; yet the change is so slow as to be imperceptible during one person's life, so that individual belief remains sensibly fixed. For the mass of mankind, then, there is perhaps no better method than this. If it is their highest impulse to be intellectual slaves, then slaves they ought to remain.

But no institution can undertake to regulate opinions upon every subject. Only the most important ones can be attended to, and on the rest men's minds must be left to the action of natural causes. This imperfection will be no source of weakness so long as men are in such a state of culture that one opinion does not influence another—that is, so long as they cannot put two and two together. But in the most priest-ridden states some individuals will be found who are raised above that condition. These men possess a wider sort of social feeling; they see that men in other countries and in other ages have held to very different doctrines from those which they themselves have been brought up to believe; and they cannot help seeing that it is the mere accident of their having been taught as they have, and of their having been surrounded with the manners and associations they have, that has caused them to believe as they do and not far differently. And their candor cannot resist the reflection that there is no reason to rate their own views at a higher value than those of other nations and other centuries; and this gives rise to doubts in their minds.

They will further perceive that such doubts as these must exist in their minds with reference to every belief which seems to be determined by the caprice either of themselves or of those who originated the popular opinions. The willful adherence to a belief, and the arbitrary forcing of it upon others, must, therefore, both be given up and a new method of settling opinions must be adopted, which shall not only produce an impulse to believe, but shall also decide what proposition it is which is to be believed. Let the action of natural preferences be unimpeded, then, and under their influence let men conversing together and regarding matters in different lights, gradually develop beliefs in harmony with natural causes. This method resembles that by which conceptions of art have been brought to maturity. The most perfect example of it is to be found in the history of metaphysical philosophy. Systems of this sort have not usually rested upon observed facts, at least not in any great degree. They have been chiefly adopted because their fundamental propositions seemed "agreeable to reason." This is an apt expression; it does not mean that which agrees with experience, but that which we find ourselves inclined to believe. Plato, for example, finds it agreeable to reason that the distances of the celestial spheres from one another should be proportional to the different lengths of strings which produce harmonious chords. Many philosophers have been led to their main conclusions by considerations like this; but this is the lowest and least developed form which the method takes, for it is clear that another man might find Kepler's [earlier] theory, that the celestial spheres are proportional to the inscribed and circumscribed spheres of the different regular solids, more agreeable to *his* reason. But the shock of opinions will soon lead men to rest on preferences of a far more universal nature. Take, for example, the doctrine that man only acts selfishly—that is, from the consideration that acting in one way will afford him more pleasure than acting in another. This rests on no fact in the world, but it has had a wide acceptance as being the only reasonable theory.

This method is far more intellectual and respectable from the point of view of reason than either of the others which we have noticed.[6] But its failure has been the most manifest. It makes of inquiry something similar to the development of taste; but taste, unfortunately, is always more or less a matter of fashion, and accordingly, metaphysicians have never come to any fixed agreement, but the pendulum has swung backward and forward between a more material and a more spiritual philosophy, from the earliest times to the latest. And so from this, which has been called the *a priori* method, we are driven, in Lord Bacon's phrase, to a true induction. We have examined into this *a priori* method as something which promised to deliver our opinions from their accidental and capricious element. But development, while it is a process which eliminates the effect of some casual circumstances, only magnifies that of others. This method, therefore, does not differ in a very essential way from that of authority. The government may not have lifted its finger to influence my convictions; I may have been left outwardly quite free to choose, we will say, between monogamy and polygamy, and appealing to my conscience only, I may have concluded that the latter practice is in itself licentious. But when I come to see that the chief obstacle to the spread of Christianity among a people of as high culture as the Hindoos has been a conviction of the immorality of our way of treating women, I cannot help seeing that, though governments do not interfere, sentiments in their development will be very greatly determined by acciden-

tal causes. Now, there are some people, among whom I must suppose that my reader is to be found, who, when they see that any belief of theirs is determined by any circumstance extraneous to the facts, will from that moment not merely admit in words that that belief is doubtful, but will experience a real doubt of it, so that it ceases in some degree at least to be a belief.

To satisfy our doubts, therefore, it is necessary that a method should be found by which our beliefs may be caused by nothing human, but by some external permanency—by something upon which our thinking has no effect. Some mystics imagine that they have such a method in a private inspiration from on high. But that is only a form of the method of tenacity, in which the conception of truth as something public is not yet developed. Our external permanency would not be external, in our sense, if it was restricted in its influence to one individual. It must be something which affects, or might affect, every man. And, though these affections are necessarily as various as are individual conditions, yet the method must be such that the ultimate conclusion of every man shall be the same, or would be the same if inquiry were sufficiently persisted in. Such is the method of science. Its fundamental hypothesis, restated in more familiar language, is this: There are real things, whose characters are entirely independent of our opinions about them; those realities affect our senses according to regular laws, and, though our sensations are as different as our relations to the objects, yet, by taking advantage of the laws of perception, we can ascertain by reasoning how things really are, and any man, if he have sufficient experience and reason enough about it, will be led to the one true conclusion. The new conception here involved is that of reality. It may be asked how I know that there are any realities. If this hypothesis is the sole support of my method of inquiry, my method of inquiry must not be used to support my hypothesis. The reply is this: (1) If investigation cannot be regarded as proving that there are real things, it at least does not lead to a contrary conclusion; but the method and the conception on which it is based remain ever in harmony. No doubts of the method, therefore, necessarily arise from its practice, as is the case with all the others. (2) The feeling which gives rise to any method of fixing belief is a dissatisfaction at two repugnant propositions. But here already is a vague concession that there is some *one* thing to which a proposition should conform. Nobody, therefore, can really doubt that there are realities, or, if

---

[6] "Indeed, as long as no better method can be applied, it [the *a priori* method] ought to be followed, since it is then the expression of instinct which must be the ultimate cause of belief in all cases."—Peirce's note of 1910. Compare F. H. Bradley's view that metaphysics consists in finding bad reasons for what we believe on instinct, but the giving of such reasons is itself an instinct.

he did, doubt would not be a source of dissatisfaction. The hypothesis, therefore, is one which every mind admits. So that the social impulse does not cause men to doubt it. (3) Everybody uses the scientific method about a great many things, and only ceases to use it when he does not know how to apply it. (4) Experience of the method has not led us to doubt it, but, on the contrary, scientific investigation has had the most wonderful triumphs in the way of settling opinion. These afford the explanation of my not doubting the method or the hypothesis which it supposes; and not having any doubt, nor believing that anybody else whom I could influence has, it would be the merest babble for me to say more about it. If there be anybody with a living doubt upon the subject, let him consider it.

To describe the method of scientific investigation is the object of this series of papers. At present I have only room to notice some points of contrast between it and other methods of fixing belief.

This is the only one of the four methods which presents any distinction of a right and a wrong way. If I adopt the method of tenacity and shut myself out from all influences, whatever I think necessary to doing this is necessary according to that method. So with the method of authority: the state may try to put down heresy by means which, from a scientific point of view, seems very ill-calculated to accomplish its purposes; but the only test *on that method* is what the state thinks, so that it cannot pursue the method wrongly. So with the *a priori* method. The very essence of it is to think as one is inclined to think. All metaphysicians will be sure to do that, however they may be inclined to judge each other to be perversely wrong. The Hegelian system recognizes every natural tendency of thought as logical, although it is certain to be abolished by countertendencies. Hegel thinks there is a regular system in the succession of these tendencies, in consequence of which, after drifting one way and the other for a long time, opinion will at last go right. And it is true that metaphysicians get the right ideas at last; Hegel's system of Nature represents tolerably the science of his day; and one may be sure that whatever scientific investigation has put out of doubt will presently receive *a priori* demonstration on the part of the metaphysicians. But with the scientific method the case is different. I may start with known and observed facts to proceed to the unknown; and yet the rules which I follow in doing so may not be such as investigation would approve. The test of whether I am truly following the method is not an immediate appeal to my

feelings and purposes, but, on the contrary, itself involves the application of the method. Hence it is that bad reasoning as well as good reasoning is possible; and this fact is the foundation of the practical side of logic.

It is not to be supposed that the first three methods of settling opinion present no advantage whatever over the scientific method. On the contrary, each has some peculiar convenience of its own. The *a priori* method is distinguished for its comfortable conclusions. It is the nature of the process to adopt whatever belief we are inclined to, and there are certain flatteries to one's vanities which we all believe by nature, until we are awakened from our pleasing dream by rough facts. The method of authority will always govern the mass of mankind; and those who wield the various forms of organized force in the state will never be convinced that dangerous reasoning ought not to be suppressed in some way. If liberty of speech is to be untrammeled from the grosser forms of constraint, then uniformity of opinion will be secured by a moral terrorism to which the respectability of society will give its thorough approval. Following the method of authority is the path of peace. Certain non-conformities are permitted; certain others (considered unsafe) are forbidden. These are different in different countries and in different ages; but, wherever you are let it be known that you seriously hold a tabooed belief, and you may be perfectly sure of being treated with a cruelty no less brutal but more refined than hunting you like a wolf. Thus, the greatest intellectual benefactors of mankind have never dared, and dare not now, to utter the whole of their thought; and thus a shade of *prima facie* doubt is cast upon every proposition which is considered essential to the security of society. Singularly enough, the persecution does not all come from without; but a man torments himself and is oftentimes most distressed at finding himself believing propositions which he has been brought up to regard with aversion. The peaceful and sympathetic man will, therefore, find it hard to resist the temptation to submit his opinions to authority. But most of all I admire the method of tenacity for its strength, simplicity, and directness. Men who pursue it are distinguished for their decision of character, which becomes very easy with such a mental rule. They do not waste time in trying to make up their minds to what they want, but, fastening like lightning upon whatever alternative comes first, they hold to it to the end, whatever happens, without an instant's irresolution. This is one of the splendid qualities which generally accompany brilliant, unlasting success. It is impossible not to envy the man who can dismiss reason, although we know how it must turn out at last.

Such are the advantages which the other methods of settling opinions have over scientific investigation. A man should consider well of them; and then he should consider that, after all, he wishes his opinions to coincide with the fact, and that there is no reason why the results of those first three methods should do so. To bring about this effect is the prerogative of the method of science. Upon such considerations he has to make his choice—a choice which is far more than the adoption of any intellectual opinion, which is one of the ruling decisions of his life, to which when once made he is bound to adhere. The force of habit will sometimes cause a man to hold on to old beliefs after he is in a condition to see that they have no sound basis. But reflection upon the state of the case will overcome these habits, and he ought to allow reflection full weight. People sometimes shrink from doing this, having an idea that beliefs are wholesome which they cannot help feeling rest on nothing. But let such persons suppose an analogous though different case from their own. Let them ask themselves what they would say to a reformed Mussulman who should hesitate to give up his old notions in regard to the relations of the sexes; or to a reformed Catholic who should still shrink from the Bible. Would they not say that these persons ought to consider the matter fully, and clearly understand the new doctrine, and then ought to embrace it in its entirety? But, above all, let it be considered that what is more wholesome than any particular belief is integrity of belief; and that to avoid looking into the support of any belief from a fear that it may turn out rotten is quite as immoral as it is disadvantageous. The person who confesses that there is such a thing as truth, which is distinguished from falsehood simply by this, that if acted on it should, on full consideration, carry us to the point we aim at and not astray, and then, though convinced of this, dares not know the truth and seeks to avoid it, is in a sorry state of mind, indeed.

Yes, the other methods do have their merits: a clear logical conscience does cost something—just as any virtue, just as all that we cherish, costs us dear. But, we should not desire it to be otherwise. The genius of a man's logical method should be loved and reverenced as his bride, whom he has chosen from all the world. He need not condemn the others; on the contrary, he may honor them deeply, and in doing so he only honors her the more. But she is the one that he has chosen, and he knows that he was right in making that choice. And having made it, he will work and fight for her, and will not complain that there are blows to take, hoping that there may be as many and as hard to give, and will strive to be the worthy knight and champion of her from the blaze of whose splendors he draws his inspiration and his courage.

Ernest Nagel (1901–1985)
SCIENCE AND COMMON SENSE

Nagel states that there is no sharp line separating commonsense beliefs from scientific beliefs. Yet science has a characteristic core of features, most notably a desire for explanations that are at once systematic and controllable by factual evidence. This leads to a concern with consistency, precision, systematic scrutiny of its own tenets, and an awareness of the limits of its generalizations. A discussion of Nagel's views can be found at the end of Section B in the introductory essay to Part II.

READING QUESTIONS

In reading the selection, try to answer the following questions and identify the passages that support your answers:

1.   Is science sharply different from common sense? Why or why not?
2.   What distinguishes science from common sense according to Nagel?

3. Is Nagel correct in drawing the line where he does? Why or why not?
4. Is science value free? Why or why not?
5. Is there a difference between the way common sense and science are concerned with values? If so, what is it and why? If not, why not?

Reprinted with the permission of Hackett Publishing Company, Inc., Indianapolis, IN, and Cambridge, MA, from Ernest Nagel, *The Structure of Science* (New York: Harcourt, Brace and World, 1961), pp. 1–14. Copyright © 1961.

Long before the beginnings of modern civilization, men acquired vast funds of information about their environment. They learned to recognize substances which nourished their bodies. They discovered the uses of fire and developed skills for transforming raw materials into shelters, clothing, and utensils. They invented arts of tilling the soil, communicating, and governing themselves. Some of them discovered that objects are moved more easily when placed on carts with wheels, that the sizes of fields are more reliably compared when standard schemes of measurement are employed, and that the seasons of the year as well as many phenomena of the heavens succeed each other with a certain regularity. John Locke's quip at Aristotle—that God was not so sparing to men as to make them merely two-legged creatures, leaving it to Aristotle to make them rational—seems obviously applicable to modern science. The acquisition of reliable knowledge concerning many aspects of the world certainly did not wait upon the advent of modern science and the self-conscious use of its methods. Indeed, in this respect, many men in every generation repeat in their own lives the history of the race: they manage to secure for themselves skills and competent information, without benefit of training in the sciences and without the calculated adoption of scientific modes of procedure.

If so much in the way of knowledge can be achieved by the shrewd exercise of native gifts and "common-sense" methods, what special excellence do the sciences possess, and what do their elaborate intellectual and physical tools contribute to the acquisition of knowledge? The question requires a careful answer if a definite meaning is to be associated with the word 'science.'

The word and its linguistic variants are certainly not always employed with discrimination, and they are frequently used merely to confer an honorific distinction on something or other. Many men take pride in being "scientific" in their beliefs and in living in an "age of science." However, quite often the sole discoverable ground for their pride is a conviction that, unlike their ancestors or their neighbors, they are in possession of some alleged final truth. It is in this spirit that currently accepted theories in physics or biology are sometimes described as scientific, while all previously held but no longer accredited theories in those domains are firmly refused that label. Similarly, types of practice that are highly successful under prevailing physical and social conditions, such as certain techniques of farming or industry, are occasionally contrasted with the allegedly "unscientific" practices of other times and places. Perhaps an extreme form of the tendency to rob the term 'scientific' of all definite content is illustrated by the earnest use that advertisers sometimes make of such phrases as 'scientific haircutting,' 'scientific rug cleaning,' and even 'scientific astrology.' It will be clear, however, that in none of the above examples is a readily identifiable and differentiating characteristic of beliefs or practices associated with the word. It would certainly be ill-advised to adopt the suggestion, implicit in the first example, to limit the application of the adjective 'scientific' to beliefs that are indefeasibly true—if only because infallible guaranties of truth are lacking in most if not all areas of inquiry, so that the adoption of such a suggestion would in effect deprive the adjective of any proper use.

The words 'science' and 'scientific' are nevertheless not quite so empty of a determinate content as their frequently debased uses might indicate. For in fact the words are labels either for an identifiable, continuing enterprise of inquiry or for its intellectual products, and they are often employed to signify traits that distinguish those products from other things. In the present chapter we shall therefore survey briefly some of the ways in which "prescientific" or "common-sense" knowledge differs from the intellectual products of modern science. To be sure, no sharp line separates beliefs generally subsumed under the familiar but vague rubric of "common sense" from those cognitive claims recognized as "scientific." Nevertheless, as in the case of other words whose fields of intended application have notoriously hazy boundaries (such as the term 'democracy'), absence of precise dividing lines is not incompatible with the presence of at least a core of firm meaning for each of these words. In their more sober uses, at any rate, these words do in fact connote important and recognizable differences. It is these differences that we must attempt to identify, even if we are compelled to sharpen some of them for the sake of expository emphasis and clarity.

1. No one seriously disputes that many of the existing special sciences have grown out of the practical concerns of daily living: geometry out of problems of measuring and surveying fields, mechanics out of problems raised by the architectural and military arts, biology out of problems of human health and animal husbandry, chemistry out of problems raised by metallurgical and dyeing industries, economics out of problems of household and political management, and so on. To be sure, there have been other stimuli to the development of the sciences than those provided by problems of the practical arts; nevertheless, these latter have had, and still continue to have, important roles in the history of scientific inquiry. In any case, commentators on the nature of science who have been impressed by the historical continuity of common-sense convictions and scientific conclusions have sometimes proposed to differentiate between them by the formula that the sciences are simply "organized" or "classified" common sense.

It is undoubtedly the case that the sciences are organized bodies of knowledge and that in all of them a classification of their materials into significant types or kinds (as in biology, the classification of living things into species) is an indispensable task. It is clear, nonetheless, that the proposed formula does not adequately express the characteristic differences between science and common sense. A lecturer's notes on his travels in Africa may be very well organized for the purposes of communicating information interestingly and efficiently, without thereby converting that information into what has historically been called a science. A librarian's card catalogue represents an invaluable classification of books, but no one with a sense for the historical association of the word would say that the catalogue is a science. The obvious difficulty is that the proposed formula does not specify what *kind* of organization or classification is characteristic of the sciences.

Let us therefore turn to this question. A marked feature of much information acquired in the course of ordinary experience is that, although this information may be accurate enough within certain limits, it is seldom accompanied by any explanation of why the facts are as alleged. Thus societies which have discovered the uses of the wheel usually know nothing of frictional forces, nor of any reasons why goods loaded on vehicles with wheels are easier to move than goods dragged on the ground. Many peoples have learned the advisability of manuring their agricultural fields, but only a few have concerned themselves with the reasons for so acting. The medicinal properties of herbs like the foxglove have been recognized for centuries, though usually no account was given of the grounds for their beneficent virtues. Moreover, when "common sense" does attempt to give explanations for its facts—as when the value of the foxglove as a cardiac stimulant is explained in terms of the similarity in shape of the flower and the human heart—the explanations are frequently without critical tests of their relevance to the facts. Common sense is often eligible to receive the well-known advice Lord Mansfield gave to a newly appointed governor of a colony who was unversed in the law: "There is no difficulty in deciding a case—only hear both sides patiently, then consider what you think justice requires, and decide accordingly; but never give your reasons, for your judgment will probably be right, but your reasons will certainly be wrong."

It is the desire for explanations which are at once systematic and controllable by factual evidence that generates science; and it is the organization and classification of knowledge on the basis of explanatory principles that is the distinctive goal of the sciences. More specifically, the sciences seek to discover and to formulate in general terms the conditions under which events of various sorts occur, the statements of such determining conditions being the explanations of the corresponding happenings. This goal can be achieved only by distinguishing or isolating certain properties in the subject matter studied and by ascertaining the repeatable patterns of dependence in which these properties stand to one another. In consequence, when the inquiry is successful, propositions that hitherto appeared to be quite unrelated are exhibited as linked to each other in determinate ways by virtue of their place in a system of explanations. In some cases, indeed, the inquiry can be carried to remarkable lengths. Patterns of relations may be discovered that are pervasive in vast ranges of fact, so that with the help of a small number of explanatory principles an indefinitely large number of propositions about these facts can be shown to constitute a logically unified body of knowledge. The unification sometimes takes the form of a deductive system, as in the case of demonstrative geometry or the science of mechanics. Thus a few principles, such as those formulated by Newton, suffice to show that propositions concerning the moon's motion, the behavior of the tides, the paths of projectiles, and the rise of liquids in thin tubes are intimately related, and that all these propositions can be rigorously deduced from those principles conjoined with various special assumptions of fact. In this way a systematic explanation is achieved for the diverse phenomena which the logically derived propositions report.

Not all the existing sciences present the highly integrated form of systematic explanation which the science of mechanics exhibits, though for many of the sciences—in domains of social inquiry as well as in the various divisions of natural science—the idea of such a rigorous logical systematization continues to function as an ideal. But even in those branches of departmentalized inquiry in which this ideal is not generally pursued, as in much historical research, the goal of finding explanations for facts is usually always present. Men seek to know why the thirteen American colonies rebelled from England while Canada did not, why the ancient Greeks were able to repel the Persians but succumbed to the Roman armies, or why urban and commercial activity developed in medieval Europe in the tenth century and not before. To explain, to establish some relation of dependence between propositions superficially unrelated, to exhibit systematically connections between apparently miscellaneous items of information are distinctive marks of scientific inquiry.

2. A number of further differences between common sense and scientific knowledge are almost direct consequences of the systematic character of the latter. A well-recognized feature of common sense is that, though the knowledge it claims may be accurate, it seldom is aware of the limits within which its beliefs are valid or its practices successful. A community, acting on the rule that spreading manure preserves the fertility of the soil, may in many cases continue its mode of agriculture successfully. However, it may continue to follow the rule blindly, in spite of the manifest deterioration of the soil, and it may therefore be helpless in the face of a critical

problem of food supply. On the other hand, when the reasons for the efficacy of manure as a fertilizer are understood, so that the rule is connected with principles of biology and soil chemistry, the rule comes to be recognized as only of restricted validity, since the efficiency of manure is seen to depend on the persistence of conditions of which common sense is usually unaware. Few who know them are capable of withholding admiration for the sturdy independence of those farmers who, without much formal education, are equipped with an almost endless variety of skills and sound information in matters affecting their immediate environment. Nevertheless, the traditional resourcefulness of the farmer is narrowly circumscribed: he often becomes ineffective when some break occurs in the continuity of his daily round of living, for his skills are usually products of tradition and routine habit and are not informed by an understanding of the reasons for their successful operation. More generally, common-sense knowledge is most adequate in situations in which a certain number of factors remain practically unchanged. But since it is normally not recognized that this adequacy does depend on the constancy of such factors—indeed, the very existence of the pertinent factors may not be recognized—common-sense knowledge suffers from a serious incompleteness. It is the aim of systematic science to remove this incompleteness, even if it is an aim which frequently is only partially realized.

The sciences thus introduce refinements into ordinary conceptions by the very process of exhibiting the systematic connections of propositions about matters of common knowledge. Not only are familiar practices thereby shown to be explicable in terms of principles formulating relations between items in wide areas of fact; those principles also provide clues for altering and correcting habitual modes of behavior, so as to make them more effective in familiar contexts and more adaptable to novel ones. This is not to say, however, that common beliefs are necessarily mistaken, or even that they are inherently more subject to change under the pressure of experience than are the propositions of science. Indeed, the age-long and warranted stability of common-sense convictions, such as that oaks do not develop overnight from acorns or that water solidifies on sufficient cooling, compares favorably with the relatively short life span of many theories of science. The essential point to be observed is that, since common sense shows little interest in systematically explaining the facts it notes, the range of valid application of its beliefs, though in fact narrowly circumscribed, is not of serious concern to it.

3. The ease with which the plain man as well as the man of affairs entertains incompatible and even inconsistent beliefs has often been the subject for ironic commentary. Thus, men will sometimes argue for sharply increasing the quantity of money and also demand a stable currency; they will insist upon the repayment of foreign debts and also take steps to prevent the importation of foreign goods; and they will make inconsistent judgments on the effects of the foods they consume, on the size of bodies they see, on the temperature of liquids, and the violence of noises. Such conflicting judgments are often the result of an almost exclusive preoccupation with the immediate consequences and qualities of observed events. Much that passes as common-sense knowledge certainly is about the effects familiar things have upon matters that men happen to value; the relations of events to one another, independent of their incidence upon specific human concerns, are not systematically noticed and explored.

The occurrence of conflicts between judgments is one of the stimuli to the development of science. By introducing a systematic explanation of facts, by ascertaining the conditions and consequences of events, by exhibiting the logical relations of propositions to one another, the sciences strike at the sources of such conflicts. Indeed, a large number of extraordinarily able minds have traced out the logical consequences of basic principles in various sciences; and an even larger number of investigators have repeatedly checked such consequences with other propositions obtained as a result of critical observation and experiment. There is no iron-clad guaranty that, in spite of this care, serious inconsistencies in these sciences have been eliminated. On the contrary, mutually incompatible assumptions sometimes serve as the bases for inquiries in different branches of the same science. For example, in certain parts of physics atoms were at one time assumed to be perfectly elastic bodies, although in other branches of physical science perfect elasticity was not ascribed to atoms. However, such inconsistencies are sometimes only apparent ones, the impression of inconsistency arising from a failure to note that different assumptions are being employed for the solution of quite different classes of problems. Moreover, even when the inconsistencies are genuine, they are often only temporary, since in-

compatible assumptions may be employed only because a logically coherent theory is not yet available to do the complex job for which those assumptions were originally introduced. In any event, the flagrant inconsistencies that so frequently mark common beliefs are notably absent from those sciences in which the pursuit of unified systems of explanation has made considerable headway.

4. As has already been noted, many everyday beliefs have survived centuries of experience, in contradistinction to the relatively short life span that is so often the fate of conclusions advanced in various branches of modern science. One partial reason for this circumstance merits attention. Consider some instance of common-sense beliefs, such as that water solidifies when it is sufficiently cooled; and let us ask what is signified by the terms 'water' and 'sufficiently' in that assertion. It is a familiar fact that the word 'water,' when used by those unacquainted with modern science, generally has no clear-cut meaning. It is then frequently employed as a name for a variety of liquids despite important physicochemical differences between them, but is frequently rejected as a label for other liquids even though these latter liquids do not differ among themselves in their essential physicochemical characteristics to a greater extent than do the former fluids. Thus, the word may perhaps be used to designate the liquids falling from the sky as rain, emerging from the ground in springs, flowing in rivers and roadside ditches, and constituting the seas and oceans; but the word may be employed less frequently if at all for liquids pressed out of fruits, contained in soups and other beverages, or evacuated through the pores of the human skin. Similarly, the word 'sufficiently' when used to characterize a cooling process may sometimes signify a difference as great as that between the maximum temperature on a midsummer day and the minimum temperature of a day in midwinter; at other times, the word may signify a difference no greater than that between the noon and the twilight temperatures on a day in winter. In short, in its common-sense use for characterizing temperature changes, the word 'sufficiently' is not associated with a precise specification of their extent.

If this example can be taken as typical, the language in which common-sense knowledge is formulated and transmitted may exhibit two important kinds of indeterminacy. In the first place, the terms of ordinary speech may be quite vague, in the sense that the class of things designated by a term is not sharply and clearly demarcated from (and may in fact overlap to a considerable extent with) the class of things not so designated. Accordingly, the range of presumed validity for statements employing such terms has no determinate limits. In the second place, the terms of ordinary speech may lack a relevant degree of specificity, in the sense that the broad distinctions signified by the terms do not suffice to characterize more narrowly drawn but important differences between the things denoted by the terms. Accordingly, relations of dependence between occurrences are not formulated in a precisely determinate manner by statements containing such terms.

As a consequence of these features of ordinary speech, experimental control of common-sense beliefs is frequently difficult, since the distinction between confirming and contradicting evidence for such beliefs cannot be easily drawn. Thus, the belief that "in general" water solidifies when sufficiently cooled may answer the needs of men whose interest in the phenomenon of freezing is circumscribed by their concern to achieve the routine objectives of their daily lives, despite the fact that the language employed in codifying this belief is vague and lacks specificity. Such men may therefore see no reason for modifying their belief, even if they should note that ocean water fails to freeze although its temperature is sensibly the same as that of well water when the latter begins to solidify, or that some liquids must be cooled to a greater extent than others before changing into the solid state. If pressed to justify their belief in the face of such facts, these men may perhaps arbitrarily exclude the oceans from the class of things they denominate as water; or, alternatively, they may express renewed confidence in their belief, irrespective of the extent of cooling that may be required, on the ground that liquids classified as water do indeed solidify when cooled.

In their quest for systematic explanations, on the other hand, the sciences must mitigate the indicated indeterminacy of ordinary language by refashioning it. For example, physical chemistry is not content with the loosely formulated generalization that water solidifies if it is sufficiently cooled, for the aim of that discipline is to explain, among other things, why drinking water and milk freeze at certain temperatures although at those temperatures ocean water does not. To achieve this aim, physical chemistry must therefore introduce clear distinctions between

various kinds of water and between various amounts of cooling. Several devices reduce the vagueness and increase the specificity of linguistic expressions. Counting and measuring are for many purposes the most effective of these techniques, and are perhaps the most familiar ones. Poets may sing of the infinity of stars which stud the visible heavens, but the astronomer will want to specify their exact number. The artisan in metals may be content with knowing that iron is harder than lead, but the physicist who wishes to explain this fact will require a precise measure of the difference in hardness. Accordingly, an obvious but important consequence of the precision thus introduced is that statements become capable of more thorough and critical testing by experience. Prescientific beliefs are frequently incapable of being put to definite experiential tests, simply because those beliefs may be vaguely compatible with an indeterminate class of unanalyzed facts. Scientific statements, because they are required to be in agreement with more closely specified materials of observation, face greater risks of being refuted by such data.

This difference between common and scientific knowledge is roughly analogous to differences in standards of excellence which may be set up for handling firearms. Most men would qualify as expert shots if the standard of expertness were the ability to hit the side of a barn from a distance of a hundred feet. But only a much smaller number of individuals could meet the more rigorous requirement of consistently centering their shots upon a three-inch target at twice that distance. Similarly, a prediction that the sun will be eclipsed during the autumn months is more likely to be fulfilled than a prediction that the eclipse will occur at a specific moment on a given day in the fall of the year. The first prediction will be confirmed should the eclipse take place during any one of something like one hundred days; the second prediction will be refuted if the eclipse does not occur within something like a small fraction of a minute from the time given. The latter prediction could be false without the former being so, but not conversely; and the latter prediction must therefore satisfy more rigorous standards of experiential control than are assumed for the former.

This greater determinacy of scientific language helps to make clear why so many common-sense beliefs have a stability, often lasting for many centuries, that few theories of science possess. It is more difficult to devise a theory that remains unshaken by repeated confrontation with the outcome of painstaking experimental observation, when the standards are high for the agreement that must obtain between such experimental data and the predictions derived from the theory, than when such standards are lax and the admissible experimental evidence is not required to be established by carefully controlled procedures. The more advanced sciences do in fact specify almost invariably the extent to which predictions based on a theory may deviate from the results of experiment without invalidating the theory. The limits of such permissible deviations are usually quite narrow, so that discrepancies between theory and experiment which common sense would ordinarily regard as insignificant are often judged to be fatal to the adequacy of the theory.

On the other hand, although the greater determinacy of scientific statements exposes them to greater risks of being found in error than are faced by the less precisely stated common-sense beliefs, the former have an important advantage over the latter. They have a greater capacity for incorporation into comprehensive but clearly articulated systems of explanation. When such systems are adequately confirmed by experimental data, they codify frequently unsuspected relations of dependence between many varieties of experimentally identifiable but distinct kinds of fact. In consequence, confirmatory evidence for statements belonging to such a system can often be accumulated more rapidly and in larger quantities than for statements (such as those expressing common-sense beliefs) not belonging to such a system. This is so because evidence for statements in such a system may be obtainable by observations of an extensive class of events, many of which may not be explicitly mentioned by those statements but which are nevertheless relevant sources of evidence for the statements in question, in view of the relations of dependence asserted by the system to hold between the events in that class. For example, the data of spectroscopic analysis are employed in modern physics to test assumptions concerning the chemical structure of various substances; and experiments on thermal properties of solids are used to support theories of light. In brief, by increasing the determinacy of statements and incorporating them into logically integrated systems of explanation, modern science sharpens the discriminating powers of its testing procedure and augments the sources of relevant evidence for its conclusions.

5. It has already been mentioned in passing that, while common-sense knowledge is largely concerned with the impact of events upon matters of special value to men, theoretical science is in general not so provincial. The quest for systematic explanations requires that inquiry be directed to the relations of dependence between things irrespective of their bearing upon human values. Thus, to take an extreme case, astrology is concerned with the relative positions of stars and planets in order to determine the import of such conjunctions for the destinies of men; in contrast, astronomy studies the relative positions and motions of celestial bodies without reference to the fortunes of human beings. Similarly, breeders of horses and of other animals have acquired much skill and knowledge relating to the problem of developing breeds that will implement certain human purposes; theoretical biologists, on the other hand, are only incidentally concerned with such problems, and are interested in analyzing among other things the mechanisms of heredity and in obtaining laws of genetic development.

One important consequence of this difference in orientation between theoretical and common-sense knowledge, however, is that theoretical science deliberately neglects the immediate values of things, so that the statements of science often appear to be only tenuously relevant to the familiar events and qualities of daily life. To many people, for example, an unbridgeable chasm seems to separate electromagnetic theory, which provides a systematic account of optical phenomena, and the brilliant colors one may see at sunset; and the chemistry of colloids, which contributes to an understanding of the organization of living bodies, appears to be an equally impossible distance from the manifold traits of personality exhibited by human beings.

It must certainly be admitted that scientific statements make use of highly abstract concepts, whose pertinence to the familiar qualities which things manifest in their customary settings is by no means obvious. Nevertheless, the relevance of such statements to matters encountered in the ordinary business of life is also indisputable. It is well to bear in mind that the unusually abstract character of scientific notions, as well as their alleged "remoteness" from the traits of things found in customary experience, are inevitable concomitants of the quest for systematic and comprehensive explanations. Such explanations can be constructed only if the familiar qualities and relations of things, in terms of which individual objects and events are usually identified and differentiated, can be shown to depend for their occurrence on the presence of certain other pervasive relational or structural properties that characterize in various ways an extensive class of objects and processes. Accordingly, to achieve generality of explanation for qualitatively diverse things, those structural properties must be formulated without reference to, and in abstraction from, the individualizing qualities and relations of familiar experience. It is for the sake of achieving such generality that, for example, the temperature of bodies is defined in physics not in terms of directly felt differences in warmth, but in terms of certain abstractly formulated relations characterizing an extensive class of reversible thermal cycles.

However, although abstractness in formulation is an undoubted feature in scientific knowledge, it would be an obvious error to suppose that common-sense knowledge does not involve the use of abstract conceptions. Everyone who believes that man is a mortal creature certainly employs the abstract notions of humanity and mortality. The conceptions of science do not differ from those of common sense merely in being abstract. They differ in being formulations of pervasive structural properties, abstracted from familiar traits manifested by limited classes of things usually only under highly specialized conditions, related to matters open to direct observation only by way of complex logical and experimental procedures, and articulated with a view to developing systematic explanations for extensive ranges of diverse phenomena.

6. Implicit in the contrasts between modern science and common sense already noted is the important difference that derives from the deliberate policy of science to expose its cognitive claims to the repeated challenge of critically probative observational data, procured under carefully controlled conditions. As we had occasion to mention previously, however, this does not mean that common-sense beliefs are invariably erroneous or that they have no foundations in empirically verifiable fact. It does mean that common-sense beliefs are not subjected, as a matter of established principle, to systematic scrutiny in the light of data secured for the sake of determining the accuracy of those beliefs and the range of their validity. It also means that evidence admitted as competent in science must be obtained by procedures instituted with a view to eliminating known sources of error; and it means, furthermore, that the weight of the available evidence for any hypothesis proposed as an answer to the problem under inquiry is assessed with the help of canons of evaluation whose authority is itself based on the performance of those canons in an extensive class of inquiries. Accordingly, the quest for explanation in science is not simply a search for any *prima facie* plausible "first principles" that might account in a vague way for the familiar "facts" of conventional experience. On the contrary, it is a quest for explanatory hypotheses that are genuinely testable, because they are required to have logical consequences precise enough not to be compatible with almost every conceivable state of affairs. The hypotheses sought must therefore be subject to the possibility of rejection, which will depend on the outcome of critical procedures, integral to the scientific quest, for determining what the actual facts are.

The difference just described can be expressed by the dictum that the conclusions of science, unlike common-sense beliefs, are the products of scientific method. However, this brief formula should not be misconstrued. It must not be understood to assert, for example, that the practice of scientific method consists in following prescribed rules for making experimental discoveries or for finding satisfactory explanations for matters of established fact. There are no rules of discovery and invention in science, any more than there are such rules in the arts. Nor must the formula be construed as maintaining that the practice of scientific method consists in the use in all inquiries of some special set of techniques (such as the techniques of measurement employed in physical science), irrespective of the subject matter or the problem under investigation. Such an interpretation of the dictum is a caricature of its intent; and in any event the dictum on that interpretation is preposterous. Nor, finally, should the formula be read as claiming that the practice of scientific method effectively eliminates every form of personal bias or source of error which might otherwise impair the outcome of the inquiry, and more generally that it assures the truth of every conclusion reached by inquiries employing the method. But no such assurances can in fact be given; and no antecedently fixed set of rules can serve as automatic safeguards against unsuspected prejudices and other causes of error that might adversely affect the course of an investigation.

The practice of scientific method is the persistent critique of arguments, in the light of tried canons for judging the reliability of the procedures by which evidential data are obtained, and for assessing the probative force of the evidence on which conclusions are based. As estimated by standards prescribed by those canons, a given hypothesis may be strongly supported by stated evidence. But this fact does not guarantee the truth of the hypothesis, even if the evidential statements are admitted to be true—unless, contrary to standards usually assumed for observational data in the empirical sciences, the degree of support is that which the premises of a valid deductive argument give to its conclusion. Accordingly, the difference between the cognitive claims of science and common sense, which stems from the fact that the former are the products of scientific method, does not connote that the former are invariably true. It does imply that, while common-sense beliefs are usually accepted without a critical evaluation of the evidence available, the evidence for the conclusions of science conforms to standards such that a significant proportion of conclusions supported by similarly structured evidence remains in good agreement with additional factual data when fresh data are obtained.

Further discussion of these considerations must be postponed. However, one brief addendum is required at this point. If the conclusions of science are the products of inquiries conducted in accordance with a definite policy for obtaining and assessing evidence, the rationale for confidence in those conclusions as warranted must be based on the merits of that policy. It must be admitted that the canons for assessing evidence which define the policy have, at best, been explicitly codified only in part, and operate in the main only as intellectual habits manifested by competent investigators in the conduct of their inquiries. But despite this fact the historical record of what has been achieved by this policy in the way of dependable and systematically ordered knowledge leaves little room for serious doubt concerning the superiority of the policy over alternatives to it.

This brief survey of features that distinguish in a general way the cognitive claims and the logical method of modern science suggests a variety of questions for detailed study. The conclusions of science are the fruits of an institutionalized system of inquiry which plays an increasingly important role in the lives of men. Accordingly, the organization of that social institution, the circumstances and stages of its development and influence, and the consequences of its expansion have been repeatedly explored by sociologists, economists, historians, and moralists. However, if the nature of the scientific enterprise and its place in contemporary society are to be properly understood, the types and the articulation of scientific statements, as well as the logic by which scientific conclusions are established, also require careful analysis. This is a task—a major if not exclusive task—that the philosophy of science undertakes to execute. Three broad areas for such an analysis are in fact suggested by the survey just concluded: the logical patterns exhibited by explanations in the sciences; the construction of scientific concepts; and the validation of scientific conclusions.

Traditional Buddhist Text
THE FIVE CARDINAL VIRTUES AND THE DEFINITION OF FAITH

This Mahayana text briefly characterizes the nature, objects, and function of faith in Buddhism. Faith is characterized as a condition in which one has left behind all doubts concerning Buddha's teachings, which are the objects of faith. With the help of the remaining four virtues—vigor, mindfulness, concentration, and wisdom—faith guides the individual in acquiring and developing the qualities of a Buddha. A discussion of this selection can be found at the beginning of Section C of the introductory essay to Part II.

READING QUESTIONS

As you read the selection, try to answer the following questions and identify the passages that support your answers:

1. What is faith according to the selection?
2. What is the purpose of such faith and how is it attained?
3. Is faith thus understood a good thing? Why or why not?
4. Are there other kinds of faith?
5. Does every belief system (e.g., science) involve faith? Why or why not?

Reprinted with permission from the Philosophical Library from Edward Conze (ed.), *Buddhist Texts* (New York: Philosophical Library, 1954), pp. 185–186. Copyright © 1954.

The five faculties are Faith, Vigour, Mindfulness, Concentration and Wisdom. Here what is *Faith*? By this faith one has faith in four dharmas. Which four? He accepts the right view which assumes a transmigration in the world of birth-and-death; he puts his trust in the ripening of karma, and knows that he will experience the fruit of any karma that he may have done; even to save his life he does not do any evil deed. He has faith in the mode of life of a Bodhisattva, and, having taken up this discipline, he does not long for any other vehicle. He believes when he hears all the doctrines which are characterized by the true, clear and profound knowledge of conditioned co-production, by such terms as lack of self, absence of a being, absence of a soul, absence of a person, and by emptiness, the signless and the wishless. He follows none of the false doctrines, and believes in all the qualities (dharmas) of a Buddha, his powers, grounds of self-confidence and all the rest; and when in his faith he has left behind all doubts, he brings about in himself those qualities of a Buddha. This is known as the virtue of faith. His *vigour* consists in his bringing about (in himself) the dharmas in which he has faith. His *mindfulness* consists in his preventing the qualities which he brings about by vigour from being destroyed by forgetfulness. His *concentration* consists in his fixing his one-pointed attention on these very same qualities. With the faculty of *wisdom* he contemplates those dharmas on which he has fixed his one-pointed attention, and penetrates to their reality. The cognition of those dharmas which arises in himself and which has no outside condition is called the virtue of wisdom. Thus these five virtues, together, are sufficient to bring forth all the qualities of a Buddha.

Śikshāsamuccaya, 316 (Akshayamati Sūtra)

W. K. Clifford (1845–1879)
THE ETHICS OF BELIEF

Clifford argues that it is wrong always, everywhere, and for everyone to believe anything on insufficient evidence. He gives three reasons for this position; first, fair inquiry is necessary to do one's duty; second, no belief is insignificant; and third, no belief is merely a private matter. Clifford's views are discussed in Section C of the introductory essay to Part II.

READING QUESTIONS

While reading the selection, try to answer the following questions and identify the passages that support your answers:

1. What are Clifford's theses?
2. What reasons does he give in support of these theses?

3. Are they good reasons? Why or why not?

4. Are there other kinds of faith?

5. Does every belief system (e.g., science) involve faith? Why or why not?

Reprinted from W. K. Clifford, *Lectures and Essays* (London: Macmillan, 1879), pp. 177–188.

I. THE DUTY OF INQUIRY

A shipowner was about to send to sea an emigrant-ship. He knew that she was old, and not over-well built at the first; that she had seen many seas and climes, and often had needed repairs. Doubts had been suggested to him that possibly she was not seaworthy. These doubts preyed upon his mind, and made him unhappy; he thought that perhaps he ought to have her thoroughly overhauled and refitted, even though this should put him to great expense. Before the ship sailed, however, he succeeded in overcoming these melancholy reflections. He said to himself that she had gone safely through so many voyages and weathered so many storms that it was idle to suppose she would not come safely home from this trip also. He would put his trust in Providence, which could hardly fail to protect all these unhappy families that were leaving their fatherland to seek for better times elsewhere. He would dismiss from his mind all ungenerous suspicions about the honesty of builders and contractors. In such ways he acquired a sincere and comfortable conviction that his vessel was thoroughly safe and seaworthy; he watched her departure with a light heart, and benevolent wishes for the success of the exiles in their strange new home that was to be; and he got his insurance-money when she went down in mid-ocean and told no tales.

What shall we say of him? Surely this, that he was verily guilty of the death of those men. It is admitted that he did sincerely believe in the soundness of his ship; but the sincerity of his conviction can in no wise help him, because *he had no right to believe on such evidence as was before him*. He had acquired his belief not by honestly earning it in patient investigation, but by stifling his doubts. And although in the end he may have felt so sure about it that he could not think otherwise, yet inasmuch as he had knowingly and willingly worked himself into that frame of mind, he must be held responsible for it.

Let us alter the case a little, and suppose that the ship was not unsound after all; that she made her voyage safely, and many others after it. Will that diminish the guilt of her owner? Not one jot. When an action is once done, it is right or wrong for ever; no accidental failure of its good or evil fruits can possibly alter that. The man would not have been innocent, he would only have been not found out. The question of right or wrong has to do with the origin of his belief, not the matter of it; not what it was, but how he got it; not whether it turned out to be true or false, but whether he had a right to believe on such evidence as was before him.

There was once an island in which some of the inhabitants professed a religion teaching neither the doctrine of original sin nor that of eternal punishment. A suspicion got abroad that the professors of this religion had made use of unfair means to get their doctrines taught to children. They were accused of wresting the laws of their country in such a way as to remove children from the care of their natural and legal guardians; and even of stealing them away and keeping them concealed from their friends and relations. A certain number of men formed themselves into a society for the purpose of agitating the public about this matter. They published grave accusations against individual citizens of the highest position and character, and did all in their power to injure these citizens in the exercise of their professions. So great was the noise they made, that a Commission was appointed to investigate the facts; but after the Commission had carefully inquired into all the evidence that could be got, it appeared that the accused were innocent. Not only had they been accused on insufficient evidence, but the evidence of their innocence was such as the agitators might easily have obtained, if they had attempted a fair inquiry. After these disclosures the inhabitants of that country looked upon the members of the agitating society, not only as persons whose judgment was to be distrusted, but also as no longer to be counted honourable men. For although they had sincerely and conscientiously believed in the charges they had made, yet *they had no right to believe on such evidence as was before them*. Their sincere convictions, instead of being honestly earned by patient inquiring, were stolen by listening to the voice of prejudice and passion.

Let us vary this case also, and suppose, other things remaining as before, that a still more accurate investigation proved the accused to have been really guilty. Would this make any difference in the guilt of the accusers? Clearly not; the question is not whether their belief was true or false, but whether they entertained it on wrong grounds. They would no doubt say, 'Now you see that we were right after all; next time perhaps you will believe us.' And they might be believed, but they would not thereby become honourable men. They would not be innocent, they would only be not found out. Every one of them, if he chose to examine himself *in foro conscientiæ*, would know that he had acquired and nourished a belief, when he had no right to believe on such evidence as was before him; and therein he would know that he had done a wrong thing.

It may be said, however, that in both of these supposed cases it is not the belief which is judged to be wrong, but the action following upon it. The shipowner might say, 'I am perfectly certain that my ship is sound, but still I feel it my duty to have her examined, before trusting the lives of so many people to her.' And it might be said to the agitator, 'However convinced you were of the justice of your cause and the truth of your convictions, you ought not to have made a public attack upon any man's character until you had examined the evidence on both sides with the utmost patience and care.'

In the first place, let us admit that, so far as it goes, this view of the case is right and necessary; right, because even when a man's belief is so fixed that he cannot think otherwise, he still has a choice in regard to the action suggested by it, and so cannot escape the duty of investigating on the ground of the strength of his convictions; and necessary, because those who are not yet capable of controlling their feelings and thoughts must have a plain rule dealing with overt acts.

But this being premised as necessary, it becomes clear that it is not sufficient, and that our previous judgment is required to supplement it. For it is not possible so to sever the belief from the action it suggests as to condemn the one without condemning the other. No man holding a strong belief on one side of a question, or even wishing to hold a belief on one side, can investigate it with such fairness and completeness as if he were really in doubt and unbiassed; so that the existence of a belief not founded on fair inquiry unfits a man for the performance of this necessary duty.

Nor is that truly a belief at all which has not some influence upon the actions of him who holds it. He who truly believes that which prompts him to an ac-

tion has looked upon the action to lust after it, he has committed it already in his heart. If a belief is not realized immediately in open deeds, it is stored up for the guidance of the future. It goes to make a part of that aggregate of beliefs which is the link between sensation and action at every moment of all our lives, and which is so organized and compacted together that no part of it can be isolated from the rest, but every new addition modifies the structure of the whole. No real belief, however trifling and fragmentary it may seem, is ever truly insignificant; it prepares us to receive more of its like, confirms those which resembled it before, and weakens others; and so gradually it lays a stealthy train in our inmost thoughts, which may some day explode into overt action, and leave its stamp upon our character for ever.

And no one man's beliefs is in any case a private matter which concerns himself alone. Our lives are guided by that general conception of the course of things which has been created by society for social purposes. Our words, our phrases, our forms and processes and modes of thought, are common property, fashioned and perfected from age to age; an heirloom which every succeeding generation inherits as a precious deposit and a sacred trust to be handed on to the next one, not unchanged but enlarged and purified, with some clear marks of its proper handiwork. Into this, for good or ill, is woven every belief of every man who has speech of his fellows. An awful privilege, and an awful responsibility, that we should help to create the world in which posterity will live.

In the two supposed cases which have been considered, it has been judged wrong to believe on insufficient evidence, or to nourish belief by suppressing doubts and avoiding investigation. The reason of this judgment is not far to seek: it is that in both these cases the belief held by one man was of great importance to other men. But forasmuch as no belief held by one man, however seemingly trivial the belief, and however obscure the believer, is ever actually insignificant or without its effect on the fate of mankind, we have no choice but to extend our judgment to all cases of belief whatever. Belief, that sacred faculty which prompts the decisions of our will, and knits into harmonious working all the compacted energies of our being, is ours not for ourselves, but for humanity. It is rightly used on truths which have been established by long experience and waiting toil, and which have stood in the fierce light of free and fearless questioning. Then it helps to bind men together, and to strengthen and direct their common action. It is desecrated when given to unproved and unquestioned statements, for the solace and private pleasure of the believer; to add a tinsel splendour to the plain straight road of our life and display a bright mirage beyond it; or even to drown the common sorrows of our kind by a self-deception which allows them not only to cast down, but also to degrade us. Whoso would deserve well of his fellows in this matter will guard the purity of his belief with a very fanaticism of jealous care, lest at any time it should rest on an unworthy object, and catch a stain which can never be wiped away.

It is not only the leader of men, statesman, philosopher, or poet, that owes this bounden duty to mankind. Every rustic who delivers in the village alehouse his slow, infrequent sentences, may help to kill or keep alive the fatal superstitions which clog his race. Every hard-worked wife of an artisan may transmit to her children beliefs which shall knit society together, or rend it in pieces. No simplicity of mind, no obscurity of station, can escape the universal duty of questioning all that we believe.

It is true that this duty is a hard one, and the doubt which comes out of it is often a very bitter thing. It leaves us bare and powerless where we thought that we were safe and strong. To know all about anything is to know how to deal with it under all circumstances. We feel much happier and more secure when we think we know precisely what to do, no matter what happens, than when we have lost our way and do not know where to turn. And if we have supposed ourselves to know all about anything, and to be capable of doing what is fit in regard to it, we naturally do not like to find that we are really ignorant and powerless, that we have to begin again at the beginning, and try to learn what the thing is and how it is to be dealt with—if indeed anything can be learnt about it. It is the sense of power attached to a sense of knowledge that makes men desirous of believing, and afraid of doubting.

This sense of power is the highest and best of pleasures when the belief on which it is founded is a true belief, and has been fairly earned by investigation. For then we may justly feel that it is common property, and holds good for others as well as for ourselves. Then we may be glad, not that *I* have learned secrets by which I am safer and stronger, but that *we men* have got mastery over more of the world; and we shall be strong, not for ourselves, but in the name of Man and in his strength. But if the belief has been accepted on insufficient evidence, the pleasure is a stolen one. Not only does it deceive ourselves by giving us a sense of power which we do not really possess, but it is sinful, because it is stolen in defiance of our duty to mankind. That duty is to guard ourselves from such beliefs as from a pestilence, which may shortly master our own body and then spread to the rest of the town. What would be thought of one who, for the sake of a sweet fruit, should deliberately run the risk of bringing a plague upon his family and his neighbours?

And, as in other such cases, it is not the risk only which has to be considered; for a bad action is always bad at the time when it is done, no matter what happens afterwards. Every time we let ourselves believe for unworthy reasons, we weaken our powers of self-control, of doubting, of judicially and fairly weighing evidence. We all suffer severely enough from the maintenance and support of false beliefs and the fatally wrong actions which they lead to, and the evil born when one such belief is entertained is great and wide. But a greater and wider evil arises when the credulous character is maintained and supported, when a habit of believing for unworthy reasons is fostered and made permanent. If I steal money from any person, there may be no harm done by the mere transfer of possession; he may not feel the loss, or it may prevent him from using the money badly. But I cannot help doing this great wrong towards Man, that I make myself dishonest. What hurts society is not that it should lose its property, but that it should become a den of thieves; for then it must cease to be society. This is why we ought not to do evil that good may come; for at any rate this great evil has come, that we have done evil and are made wicked thereby. In like manner, if I let myself believe anything on insufficient evidence, there may be no great harm done by the mere belief; it may be true after all, or I may never have occasion to exhibit it in outward acts. But I cannot help doing this great wrong towards Man, that I make myself credulous. The danger to society is not merely that it should believe wrong things, though that is great enough; but that it should become credulous, and lose the habit of testing things and inquiring into them; for then it must sink back into savagery.

The harm which is done by credulity in a man is not confined for the fostering of a credulous character in others, and consequent support of false beliefs. Habitual want of care about what I believe leads to habitual want of care in others about the truth of

what is told to me. Men speak the truth to one another when each reveres the truth in his own mind
and in the other's mind; but how shall my friend re-
vere the truth in my mind when I myself am careless
about it, when I believe things because I want to believe them, and because they are comforting and
pleasant? Will he not learn to cry, 'Peace,' to me,
when there is no peace? By such a course I shall surround myself with a thick atmosphere of falsehood
and fraud, and in that I must live. It may matter little to me, in my cloudcastle of sweet illusions and
darling lies; but it matters much to Man that I have
made my neighbours ready to deceive. The credulous man is father to the liar and the cheat; he lives
in the bosom of this his family, and it is no marvel if
he should become even as they are. So closely are
our duties knit together, that whoso shall keep the
whole law, and yet offend in one point, he is guilty
of all.

To sum up: it is wrong always, everywhere, and for
anyone, to believe anything upon insufficient evidence.

If a man, holding a belief which he was taught in
childhood or persuaded of afterwards, keeps down
and pushes away any doubts which arise about it
in his mind, purposely avoids the reading of books
and the company of men that call in question or
discuss it, and regards as impious these questions
which cannot easily be asked without disturbing
it—the life of that man is one long sin against
mankind.

If this judgment seems harsh when applied to
those simple souls who have never known better, who
have been brought up from the cradle with a horror
of doubt, and taught that their eternal welfare depends on *what* they believe, then it leads to the very
serious question, *Who hath made Israel to sin?*

It may be permitted me to fortify this judgment
with the sentence of Milton[1]—

'A man may be a heretic in the truth; and if he
believe things only because his pastor says so, or the
assembly so determine, without knowing other reason, though his belief be true, yet the very truth he
holds becomes his heresy.'

And with this famous aphorism of Coleridge[2]—

'He who begins by loving Christianity better than
Truth, will proceed by loving his own sect or Church
better than Christianity, and end in loving himself
better than all.'

Inquiry into the evidence of a doctrine is not to
be made once for all, and then taken as finally settled. It is never lawful to stifle a doubt; for either it
can be honestly answered by means of the inquiry
already made, or else it proves that the inquiry was
not complete.

'But,' says one, 'I am a busy man; I have no time
for the long course of study which would be necessary to make me in any degree a competent judge of
certain questions, or even able to understand the nature of the arguments.' Then he should have no time
to believe.

[1]   *Areopagitica.*
[2]   *Aids to Reflection.*

William James (1842–1910)
THE WILL TO BELIEVE

*James holds that we are justified in believing as we please if three main conditions are satisfied.
First, we face a genuine option—that is, we face an option between alternative beliefs that is
forced, live, and momentous. Second, the matter is undecidable on intellectual grounds. Third,
the consequences to us depend on what we believe. He argues for this view on the grounds that,
otherwise, in order to avoid risk of error, we would as a rule forsake believing certain truths and
that this would be irrational. A discussion of James's views can be found in Section C of the introductory essay to Part II.*

READING QUESTIONS

In reading the selection, try to answer the following questions and identify the passages that support your answers:

1. What is James's thesis?
2. Does it mean that we are always entitled to believe as we please?
3. Should we be thus entitled? Why or why not?
4. If we are entitled to believe something, does it then follow that we are entitled to act on the basis of our belief? Why or why not?
5. Is James's position sound? Why or why not?

Reprinted with permission from Dover Publications from William James, *The Will to Believe and Other Essays in Popular Philosophy, and Human Immortality* (New York: Dover, 1956), pp. 2, 3, 11, 19–20, 22–31. Copyright © 1956.

. . . Let us give the name of *hypothesis* to anything that may be proposed to our belief; and just as the electricians speak of live and dead wires, let us speak of any hypothesis as either *live* or *dead*. A live hypothesis is one which appeals as a real possibility to him to whom it is proposed. If I ask you to believe in the Mahdi, the notion makes no electric connection with your nature,—it refuses to scintillate with any credibility at all. As an hypothesis it is completely dead. To an Arab, however (even if he be not one of the Mahdi's followers), the hypothesis is among the mind's possibilities: it is alive. This shows that deadness and liveness in an hypothesis are not intrinsic properties, but relations to the individual thinker. They are measured by his willingness to act. The maximum of liveness in an hypothesis means willingness to act irrevocably. Practically, that means belief; but there is some believing tendency wherever there is willingness to act at all.

Next, let us call the decision between two hypotheses an *option*. Options may be of several kinds. They may be—1, *living* or *dead;* 2, *forced* or *avoidable;* 3, *momentous* or *trivial;* and for our purposes we may call an option a *genuine* option when it is of the forced, living, and momentous kind.

1. A living option is one in which both hypotheses are live ones. If I say to you: "Be a theosophist or be a Mohammedan," it is probably a dead option, because for you neither hypothesis is likely to be alive. But if I say: "Be an agnostic or be a Christian," it is otherwise: trained as you are, each hypothesis makes some appeal, however small, to your belief.

2. Next, if I say to you: "Choose between going out with your umbrella or without it," I do not offer you a genuine option, for it is not forced. You can easily avoid it by not going out at all. Similarly, if I say, "Either love me or hate me," "Either call my theory true or call it false," your option is avoidable. You may remain indifferent to me, neither loving nor hating, and you may decline to offer any judgment as to my theory. But if I say, "Either accept this truth or go without it," I put on you a forced option, for there is no standing place outside of the alternative. Every dilemma based on a complete logical disjunction, with no possibility of not choosing, is an option of this forced kind.

3. Finally, if I were Dr. Nansen and proposed to you to join my North Pole expedition, your option would be momentous; for this would probably be your only similar opportunity, and your choice now would either exclude you from the North Pole sort of immortality altogether or put at least the chance of it into your hands. He who refuses to embrace a unique opportunity loses the prize as surely as if he tried and failed. *Per contra,* the option is trivial when the opportunity is not unique, when the stake is insignificant, or when the decision is reversible if it later prove unwise.

. . . The thesis I defend is, briefly stated, this: *Our passional nature not only lawfully may, but must, decide an option between propositions, whenever it is a genuine option that cannot by its nature be decided on intellectual grounds; for to say, under such circumstances, "Do not decide, but leave the question open," is itself a passional decision,—just like deciding yes or no,—and is attended with the same risk of losing the truth.* The thesis thus abstractly expressed will, I trust, soon become quite clear.

. . . Wherever the option between losing truth and gaining it is not momentous, we can throw the chance of *gaining truth* away, and at any rate save ourselves from any chance of *believing falsehood,* by not making up our minds at all till objective evidence has come. In scientific questions, this is almost always the case; and even in human affairs in general, the need of acting is seldom so urgent that a false belief to act on is better than no belief at all. Law courts, indeed, have to decide on the best evidence attainable for the moment, because a judge's duty is to make law as well as to ascertain it, and (as a learned judge once said to me) few cases are worth spending much time over: the great thing is to have them decided on *any* acceptable principle, and got out of the way. But in our dealings with objective nature we obviously are recorders, not makers, of the truth; and decisions for the mere sake of deciding promptly and getting on to the next business would be wholly out of place. Throughout the breadth of physical nature facts are what they are quite independently of us, and seldom is there any such hurry about them that the risks of being duped by believing a premature theory need be faced. The questions here are always trivial options, the hypotheses are hardly living (at any rate not living for us spectators), the choice between believing truth or falsehood is seldom forced. The attitude of sceptical balance is therefore the absolutely wise one if we would escape mistakes. What difference, indeed, does it make to most of us whether we have or have not a theory of the Röntgen rays, whether we believe or not in mind-stuff, or have a conviction about the causality of conscious states? It makes no difference. Such options are not forced on us. On every account it is better not to make them, but still keep weighing reasons *pro et contra* with an indifferent hand.

. . . The question next arises: Are there not somewhere forced options in our speculative questions, and can we (as men who may be interested at least as much in positively gaining truth as in merely escaping dupery) always wait with impunity till the coercive evidence shall have arrived? It seems *a priori* improbable that the truth should be so nicely adjusted to our needs and powers as that. In the great boarding-house of nature, the cakes and the butter and the syrup seldom come out so even and leave the plates so clean. Indeed, we should view them with scientific suspicion if they did.

Moral questions immediately present themselves as questions whose solution cannot wait for sensible proof. A moral question is a question not of what sensibly exists, but of what is good, or would be good if it did exist. Science can tell us what exists; but to compare the *worths,* both of what exists and of what does not exist, we must consult not science, but what Pascal calls our heart. Science herself consults her heart when she lays it down that the infinite ascertainment of fact and correction of false belief are the supreme goods for man. Challenge the statement, and science can only repeat it oracularly, or else prove it by showing that such ascertainment and correction bring man all sorts of other goods which man's heart in turn declares. The question of having moral beliefs at all or not having them is decided by our will. Are our moral preferences true or false, or are they only odd biological phenomena, making things good or bad for *us,* but in themselves indifferent? How can your pure intellect decide? If your heart does not *want* a world of moral reality, your head will assuredly never make you believe in one. Mephistophelian scepticism, indeed, will satisfy the head's play-instincts much better than any rigorous idealism can. Some men (even at the student age) are so naturally cool-hearted that the moralistic hypothesis never has for them any pungent life, and in their supercilious presence the hot young moralist always feels strangely ill at ease. The appearance of knowingness is on their side, of *naïveté* and gullibility on his. Yet, in the inarticulate heart of him, he clings to it that he is not a dupe, and that there is a realm in which (as Emerson says) all their wit and intellectual superiority is no better than the cunning of a fox. Moral scepticism can no more be refuted or proved by logic than intellectual scepticism can. When we stick to it that there *is* truth (be it of either kind), we do so with our whole nature, and resolve to stand or fall by the results. The sceptic with his whole nature adopts the doubting attitude; but which of us is the wiser, Omniscience only knows.

Turn now from these wide questions of good to a certain class of questions of fact, questions concerning personal relations, states of mind between one man and another. *Do you like me or not?*—for example. Whether you do or not depends, in countless instances, on whether I meet you half-way, am willing to assume that you must like me, and show you trust and expectation. The previous faith on my part in your liking's existence is in such cases what makes your liking come. But if I stand aloof, and refuse to budge an inch until I have objective evidence, until you shall have done something apt, as the absolutists say, *ad extorquendum assensum meum,* ten to one your liking never comes. How many women's hearts are vanquished by the mere sanguine insistence of some man that they *must* love him! he will not consent to the hypothesis that they cannot. The desire for a certain kind of truth here brings about that special truth's existence; and so it is in innumerable cases of other sorts. Who gains promotions, boons, appointments, but the man in whose life they are seen to play the part of live hypotheses, who discounts them, sacrifices other things for their sake before they have come, and takes risks for them in advance? His faith acts on the powers above him as a claim, and creates its own verification.

A social organism of any sort whatever, large or small, is what it is because each member proceeds to his own duty with a trust that the other members will simultaneously do theirs. Wherever a desired result is achieved by the co-operation of many independent persons, its existence as a fact is a pure consequence of the precursive faith in one another of those immediately concerned. A government, an army, a commercial system, a ship, a college, an athletic team, all exist on this condition, without which not only is nothing achieved, but nothing is even attempted. A whole train of passengers (individually brave enough) will be looted by a few highwaymen, simply because the latter can count on one another, while each passenger fears that if he makes a movement of resistance, he will be shot before any one else backs him up. If we believed that the whole carfull would rise at once with us, we should each severally rise, and train-robbing would never even be attempted. There are, then, cases where a fact cannot come at all unless a preliminary faith exists in its coming. *And where faith in a fact can help create the fact,* that would be an insane logic which should say that faith running ahead of scientific evidence is the 'lowest kind of immorality' into which a thinking being can fall. Yet such is the logic by which our scientific absolutists pretend to regulate our lives!

In truths dependent on our personal action, then, faith based on desire is certainly a lawful and possibly an indispensable thing.

But now, it will be said, these are all childish human cases, and have nothing to do with great cosmical matters, like the question of religious faith. Let us then pass on to that. Religions differ so much in their accidents that in discussing the religious question we must make it very generic and broad. What then do we now mean by the religious hypothesis? Science says things are; morality says some things are better than other things; and religion says essentially two things.

First, she says that the best things are the more eternal things, the overlapping things, the things in the universe that throw the last stone, so to speak, and say the final word. "Perfection is eternal,"—this phrase of Charles Secrétan seems a good way of putting this first affirmation of religion, an affirmation which obviously cannot yet be verified scientifically at all.

The second affirmation of religion is that we are better off even now if we believe her first affirmation to be true.

Now, let us consider what the logical elements of this situation are *in case the religious hypothesis in both its branches be really true.* (Of course, we must admit that possibility at the outset. If we are to discuss the question at all, it must involve a living option. If for any of you religion be a hypothesis that cannot, by any living possibility be true, then you need go no farther. I speak to the 'saving remnant' alone.) So proceeding, we see, first, that religion offers itself as a *momentous* option. We are supposed to gain, even now, by our belief, and to lose by our nonbelief, a certain vital good. Secondly, religion is a *forced* option, so far as that good goes. We cannot escape the issue by remaining sceptical and waiting for more light, because, although we do avoid error in that way *if religion be untrue,* we lose the good, *if it be true,* just as certainly as if we positively chose to disbelieve. It is as if a man should hesitate indefinitely to ask a certain woman to marry him because he was not perfectly sure that she would prove an angel after he brought her home. Would he not cut himself off from that particular angel-possibility as decisively as if he went and married some one else? Scepticism, then, is not avoidance of option; it is option of a certain particular kind of risk. *Better risk loss of truth than chance of error,*—that is your faith-vetoer's exact position. He is actively playing his stake as much as the believer is; he is backing the field against the religious hypothesis, just as the believer is backing the religious hypothesis against the field. To preach scepticism to us as a duty until 'sufficient evidence' for religion be found, is tantamount therefore to telling us, when in presence of the religious hypothesis, that to yield to our fear of its being error is wiser and better than to yield to our hope that it may be true. It is not intellect against all passions, then; it is only intellect with one passion laying down its law. And by what, forsooth, is the supreme wisdom of this passion warranted? Dupery for dupery, what proof is there that dupery through hope is so much worse than dupery through fear? I, for one, can see no proof; and I simply refuse obedience to the scientist's command to imitate his kind of option, in a case where my own stake is important enough to give me the right to choose my own form of risk. If religion be true and the evidence for it be still insufficient, I do not wish, by putting your extinguisher upon my nature (which feels to me as if it had after all some business in this matter), to forfeit my sole chance in life of getting upon the winning side,— that chance depending, of course, on my willingness to run the risk of acting as if my passional need of taking the world religiously might be prophetic and right.

All this is on the supposition that it really may be prophetic and right, and that, even to us who are discussing the matter, religion is a live hypothesis which may be true. Now, to most of us religion comes in a still further way that makes a veto on our active faith even more illogical. The more perfect and more eternal aspect of the universe is represented in our religions as having personal form. The universe is no longer a mere *It* to us, but a *Thou*, if we are religious; and any relation that may be possible from person to person might be possible here. For instance, although in one sense we are passive portions of the universe, in another we show a curious autonomy, as if we were small active centres on our own account. We feel, too, as if the appeal of religion to us were made to our own active good-will, as if evidence might be forever withheld from us unless we met the hypothesis half-way. To take a trivial illustration: just as a man who in a company of gentlemen made no advances, asked a warrant for every concession, and believed no one's word without proof, would cut himself off by such churlishness from all the social rewards that a more trusting spirit would earn,—so here, one who should shut himself up in snarling logicality and try to make the gods extort his recognition willy-nilly, or not get it at all, might cut himself off forever from his only opportunity of making the god's acquaintance. This feeling, forced on us we know not whence, that by obstinately believing that there are gods (although not to do so would be so easy both for our logic and our life) we are doing the universe the deepest service we can, seems part of the living essence of the religious hypothesis. If the hypothesis *were* true in all its parts, including this one, then pure intellectualism, with its veto on our making willing advances, would be an absurdity; and some participation of our sympathetic nature would be logically required. I, therefore, for one, cannot see my way to accepting the agnostic rules for truth-

seeking, or wilfully agree to keep my willing nature out of the game. I cannot do so for this plain reason, that *a rule of thinking which would absolutely prevent me from acknowledging certain kinds of truth if those kinds of truth were really there, would be an irrational rule.* That for me is the long and short of the formal logic of the situation, no matter what the kinds of truth might materially be.

I confess I do not see how this logic can be escaped. But sad experience makes me fear that some of you may still shrink from radically saying with me, *in abstracto,* that we have the right to believe at our own risk any hypothesis that is live enough to tempt our will. I suspect, however, that if this is so, it is because you have got away from the abstract logical point of view altogether, and are thinking (perhaps without realizing it) of some particular religious hypothesis which for you is dead. The freedom to 'believe what we will' you apply to the case of some patent superstition; and the faith you think of is the faith defined by the schoolboy when he said, "Faith is when you believe something that you know ain't true." I can only repeat that this is misapprehension. *In concreto,* the freedom to believe can only cover living options which the intellect of the individual cannot by itself resolve; and living options never seem absurdities to him who has them to consider. When I look at the religious question as it really puts itself to concrete men, and when I think of all the possibilities which both practically and theoretically it involves, then this command that we shall put a stopper on our heart, instincts, and courage, and *wait*—acting of course meanwhile more or less as if religion were *not* true[1]—till doomsday, or till such time as our intellect and senses working together may have raked in evidence enough,—this command, I say, seems to me the queerest idol ever manufactured in the philosophic cave. Were we scholastic absolutists, there might be more excuse. If we had an infallible intellect with its objective certitudes, we might feel ourselves disloyal to such a perfect organ of knowledge in not trusting to it exclusively, in not waiting for its releasing word. But if we are empiri-

---

[1] Since belief is measured by action, he who forbids us to believe religion to be true, necessarily also forbids us to act as we should if we did believe it to be true. The whole defence of religious faith hinges upon action. If the action required or inspired by the religious hypothesis is in no way different from that dictated by the naturalistic hypothesis, then religious faith is a pure superfluity, better pruned away, and controversy about its legitimacy is a piece of idle trifling, unworthy of serious minds. I myself believe, of course, that the religious hypothesis gives to the world an expression which specifically determines our reactions, and makes them in a large part unlike what they might be on a purely naturalistic scheme of belief.

cists, if we believe that no bell in us tolls to let us know for certain when truth is in our grasp, then it seems a piece of idle fantasticality to preach so solemnly our duty of waiting for the bell. Indeed we *may* wait if we will,—I hope you do not think that I am denying that,—but if we do so, we do so at our peril as much as if we believed. In either case we *act*, taking our life in our hands. No one of us ought to issue vetoes to the other, nor should we bandy words of abuse. We ought, on the contrary, delicately and profoundly to respect one another's mental freedom: then only shall we bring about the intellectual republic; then only shall we have that spirit of inner tolerance without which all our outer tolerance is soulless, and which is empiricism's glory; then only shall we live and let live, in speculative as well as in practical things.

. . . Let me end by a quotation from Fitz James Stephen. "What do you think of yourself? What do you think of the world? . . . These are questions with which all must deal as it seems good to them. They are riddles of the Sphinx, and in some way or other we must deal with them. . . . In all important transactions of life we have to take a leap in the dark. . . . If we decide to leave the riddles unanswered, that is a choice; if we waver in our answer, that, too, is a choice: but whatever choice we make, we make it at our peril. If a man chooses to turn his back altogether on God and the future, no one can prevent him; no one can show beyond reasonable doubt that he is mistaken. If a man thinks otherwise and acts as he thinks, I do not see that any one can prove that *he* is mistaken. Each must act as he thinks best; and if he is wrong, so much the worse for him. We stand on a mountain pass in the midst of whirling snow and blinding mist, through which we get glimpses now and then of paths which may be deceptive. If we stand still we shall be frozen to death. If we take the wrong road we shall be dashed to pieces. We do not certainly know whether there is any right one. What must we do? 'Be strong and of a good courage.' Act for the best, hope for the best, and take what comes. . . . If death ends all, we cannot meet death better."[2]

[2]   Liberty, Equality, Fraternity, p. 353, 2d edition. London, 1874.

Annette Baier (contemporary)
SECULAR FAITH

Baier argues that there is a secular equivalent of faith in God that we need for morality, science, and, generally, the acquisition of knowledge. She defines this as faith in the human community and its evolving procedures, where it converges with hope and trust in people, and is understood to involve belief on grounds other than deductive or inductive reasons for its truth. A discussion of Baier's views can be found at the end of Section C in the introductory essay to Part II.

READING QUESTIONS

In reading the selection, try to answer the following questions and identify the passages that support your answers:

1.   What is Baier's thesis?
2.   How is faith related to hope and trust according to Baier?
3.   Can we do without such a faith? Why or why not?
4.   How, if at all, may this faith be limited and why?
5.   Is Baier's position sound? Why or why not?

Reprinted with the permission of University of Calgary Press and the author from Annette Baier, "Secular Faith," *Canadian Journal of Philosophy 10* (1980): 131–148. Copyright © 1980. Reprinted in Annette Baier, *Postures of the Mind: Essays on Mind and Morals* (Minneapolis, MN: University of Minnesota Press, and Methuen, 1985), pp. 292–308.

I. THE CHALLENGE

Both in ethics and in epistemology one source of skepticism in its contemporary version is the realization, often belated, of the full consequences of atheism. Modern nonmoral philosophy looks back to Descartes as its father figure, but disowns the *Third Meditation*. But if God does not underwrite one's cognitive powers, what does? The largely unknown evolution of them, which is just a version of Descartes' unreliable demon? "Let us . . . grant that all that is here said of God is a fable, nevertheless in whatever way they suppose that I have arrived at the state of being that I have reached, whether they attribute it to fate or to accident, or make out that it is by a continual succession of antecedents, or by some other method—since to err and deceive oneself is a defect, it is clear that the greater will be the probability of my being so imperfect as to deceive myself ever, as is the Author to whom they assign my being the less powerful" (*Meditation* I, Haldane and Ross, trans.). Atheism undermines a solitary thinker's single-handed cognitive ambitions, as it can undermine his expectation that unilateral virtue will bring happiness. The phenomenon of atheism in unacknowledged debt to theism can be seen both in ethical theory and in epistemology, and the threat of skepticism arises in a parallel manner.

In a provocative article, David Gauthier[1] has supported the charge made two decades ago by Anscombe,[2] that modern secular moral philosophers retain in their theories concepts which require a theological underpinning. "The taking away of God . . . in thought dissolves all," said Locke, and Gauthier agrees that it dissolves all those duties or obligations whose full justification depends upon a general performance of which one has no assurance. He quotes Hobbes: "He that would be modeste and tractable and perform all he promises in such time and place where no man els should do so, should but make himself the prey to others, and procure his own ruin, contrary to the ground of all Lawes of Nature, which tend to Nature's preservation"

(*Leviathan,* ch. 15). The problem arises not merely when "no man els" does his[3] duty, but when a significant number do not, so that the rest, even a majority, make themselves prey to the immoral ones, and procure their own exploitation, if not their own ruin. The theist can believe, in his cool hour, that unilateral, or minority, or exploited majority morality will not procure his ultimate ruin, that all things work together for good, but what consolation can a secular philosopher offer for the cool thoughtful hour, in the absence of God? If Gauthier is right, either false or insufficient consolation. He says that in those modern theories which preserve some vestige of a duty to do what others are not known to be doing, or known to be failing to do, "God is lurking unwanted, even unconceived, but not unneeded."[4]

I shall suggest that the secular equivalent of faith in God, which we need in morality as well as in science or knowledge acquisition, is faith in the human community and its evolving procedures—in the prospects for many-handed cognitive ambitions and moral hopes. Descartes had deliberately shut himself away from other thinkers, distrusting the influence of his teachers and the tradition in which he had been trained. All alone, he found he could take no step beyond a sterile self-certainty. Some other mind must come to his aid before he could advance. Descartes sought an absolute assurance to replace the human reassurance he distrusted, and I suggest that we can reverse the procedure. If we distrust the theist's absolute assurance we can return to what Descartes spurned, the support of human tradition, of a cross-generational community. This allows us to avoid the narrow and self-destructive self-seeking which is the moral equivalent of solipsism. But Gauthier's challenge is precisely to the reasonableness of community-supportive action when we have no guarantee of reciprocal public-spirited or communally minded action from others. Not only may we have no such guarantee, we may have evidence which strongly *dis*confirms the hypothesis that others are doing their part. We may have neither knowledge nor inductively well-based belief that others are doing their part. Faith and hope I take to involve acceptance of belief on grounds other than deductive

---

[1] "Why Ought One Obey God, Reflections on Hobbes and Locke," *Canadian Journal of Philosophy* 7 (1977): 425–46.

[2] G. E. M. Anscombe, in "Modern Moral Philosophy" (*Philosophy* (1958): 1–18; reprinted in *The Definition of Morality,* ed. G. Wallace and A. D. M. Walker (London: Methune, 1970), claimed that all deontological moral concepts are empty words unless there is a divine lawgiver and duty-determiner. Gauthier's thesis concerns not *all* moral laws and duties, but only those involving "moral convention," where mutual benefits depend upon general observance. I accept his assumption that all moral duties require some rational basis, that we do not simply intuit moral absolutes.

[3] Throughout this paper I use "his" to mean "his or her" and sometimes use "man" to mean "person." This is especially regrettable in a paper about justice, but needed allusions to the words of Hobbes and other sexists dictated my usage. I am not, it seems, willing to make the sacrifices in communication needed to help gain as much currency for 'the one just woman' as already gained for the one just man.

[4] Gauthier, "Why Ought One Obey God," p. 428.

or inductive evidence of its truth. Faith is the evidence of things unseen. It will be faith, not knowledge, which will replace religious faith. I shall try to make clear exactly what that faith is faith in, and what it would be for it to be (a) ill-founded or unreasonable, (b) reasonable, but in vain. I shall be defending the thesis that the just must live by faith, faith in a community of just persons.

II. FAITH: THE SUBSTANCE OF THINGS HOPED FOR

Faith, not knowledge, was and is needed to support those "plain duties" whose unilateral observation sometimes appears to procure the dutiful person's ruin. But faith, for rational persons, must appear reasonable before it can be attained. If it is to be reasonable, it must not fly in the face of inductive evidence, but it may go beyond it, when there are good reasons of another sort to do so. We may have such good reasons to hope for an empirically very unlikely but not impossible eventuality. Reasonableness is relative to the alternative beliefs or policies one might adopt, or be left with, if one rejected the candidate for the status of reasonable belief. One of the chief arguments for the moral faith I shall present is the great unreasonableness of any alternative to it. The *via negativa* which leads to secular faith has been clearly indicated in Hobbes' description of the state of nature, the state of persons without the constraint of justice. Hobbes' modern commentators, including Gauthier, have underlined the futility of the alternatives to morality. Yet if everyone insisted on knowing in advance that any sacrifice of independent advantage which they personally make, in joining or supporting a moral order, will be made up for by the returns they will get from membership in that moral order, that order could never be created nor, if miraculously brought about, sustained. Only by conquest could a Hobbesian *Leviathan* ever be created, if the rational man must have secure knowledge that others are doing likewise before he voluntarily renounces his right to pursue independent advantage. How, except by total conquest, could one ever know for sure that other would-be war makers will lay down their arms when one does so?

In fact Hobbes' first Law of Nature requires every man to endeavor peace, not when he has certainty of attaining it, but "as fare as he has *hope* of attaining it" (*Leviathan*, ch. 14, emphasis added). Hope had been previously defined as "appetite with opinion of attaining" (op. cit., chap. 6) and opinion is con-

trasted with science (op. cit., ch. 7), which alone is the outcome of correct reckoning or calculation. It is then, for Hobbes, a Law of Nature, or a counsel of rational prudence, to act on hope when what is at stake is escape from the Hobbesian state of nature.

Faith, Hobbes tells us "is in the man, Beleefe both of the man and of the truth of what he says" (ibid.). It is faith in its Hobbesian sense, in men, not merely belief in the truth of what they say which I shall argue is the only 'substance' of the hoped-for cooperation which avoids the futility and self-destructiveness of its alternatives. Faith, in a non-Hobbesian sense, that is a belief which runs beyond the inductive evidence for it, when it is faith in the possibility of a just cooperative scheme being actualized, is the same as that hope whose support is trust "in the man."

Trust in people, and distrust, tends to be self-fulfilling. Faith or lack of faith in any enterprise, but especially one requiring trust in fellow-workers, can also be self-fulfilling. Confidence can produce its own justification, as William James[5] persuasively argued. The question whether to support a moral practice without guarantee of full reciprocity is, in James' terminology, live, momentous, and forced, and the choice made can be self-verifying whichever way we choose. Every new conversion to moral skepticism strengthens the reason for such skepticism, since, if acted on, it weakens the support of moral practices and so diminishes their returns to the morally faithful. Similarly, every person who continues to observe those practices provides some reason for belief that they are supported, and so strengthens the foundation for his own belief that their support is sufficient, and provides some justification for his own dependence on that support. *Some* justification, but not enough, surely, to be decisive, since he is unlikely to be the critical straw to save or break the camel's back. The case for the self-confirmation of moral faith is less clear than for the self-confirmation, the band wagon effect, of moral skepticism. Immorality breeds immorality, but need moral action, especially if *unilateral,* breed more of the same? The sense in which the exemplary unilateral act *does* provide its own support, even if the example it gives is not fol-

---

[5] William James, "The Will to Believe," in *The Will to Believe and Other Essays in Popular Philosophy* (New York and London, 1897). In this paper I am really saying no more than James said about moral faith. I suppose the justification for saying it again, and adapting it to a Hobbesian context, is the perennial character of the issue. I have benefited from discussion with Richard Gale on James' position, and from his comments on an earlier version of this paper.

lowed by one's contemporaries, will be explored later. For the moment the best one can say for the reasonableness of willing to believe in the value of (possibly) unilateral moral action is that the alternative, giving up on that crucial part of the moral enterprise which secures cooperation, must lead eventually to an outcome disastrous to all, although those with a taste for gun-running may make a good profit before doomsday dawns. There are different styles of shoring fragments against one's ruin, and some choose to exploit the presumed failure of morality, while others, or even the same ones, retreat into a narrow circle where virtues can still be cultivated. But when, even granted the badness of its alternatives, would it be unreasonable to keep faith in the moral enterprise, in particular in the attempt to achieve a fair scheme of human cooperation? I turn next to consider the coherence of the ideal of justice.

III. MORE OR LESS JUST SOCIETIES

When would an actual cooperative scheme between persons be a just one, one which gave its participants the *best reasons* to support it? When the goods, for each, gained by cooperation outweigh the individual advantage any sacrificed, and where all partakers in the benefits make their fair contribution, pay their dues, observe the rules which ensure production and fair distribution of benefits. Even in a society where this was true, there would still be a place for a descendant of Hobbes' *Leviathan,* to enforce rules, since there may still be persons who acted irrationally, and who have a perverse taste for bucking the system, whatever the system. A stable, efficient, equitable[6] and democratic scheme of cooperation would give its conforming members security, delectation, nonexploitation and freedom, but some may still try to get a free ride, or to break the rules out of what Hobbes called "the stubbornness of their passions." His fifth Law of Nature commands "compleasance," that every man strive to accommodate himself to the rest, and unilateral breach of this rule is contrary to Hobbesian reason whose dictates include the laws of nature, since it cal-

culates that the individual can count on preserving himself only if steps are taken to ensure the conservation of men in multitudes, and so to ensure peace. "He that having sufficient security, that others observe the same laws towards him, observes them not himself, seeketh not peace, but war; and consequently the destruction of his own nature by violence" (*Leviathan,* ch. 15, immediately following the passage quoted by Gauthier, which points out the folly of unilateral conformity to the laws of nature).

Both unilateral conformity and unilateral nonconformity are, according to Hobbes, contrary to reason, but man's natural intractability inclines him to the latter. In any state of affairs short of perfect and perfectly secure justice such intractability provides a healthy challenge to an imperfect *status quo,* but if a satisfactory form of cooperation were attained such a character trait would serve no useful function. And even if Hobbes is wrong in claiming that one who refuses to do his part thereby irrationally seeks his own violent destruction, his claim that only a fool believes he can profit by breaking the rules his fellows keep is plausible to this extent, that if those rules were just in a stronger sense than any Hobbes can provide, then however attractive the promised gains of a free ride, or of exploiting others, only a fool would believe that he has more to gain by risking the enmity of his fellows by such a policy than by cultivating a taste for the pleasures of cooperation and regulated fair competition. It may not be positively irrational to break the fifth Law of Nature, especially in a would-be totalitarian Leviathan state, but it would be against reason to think one would do better by breaking the rules of a decent just scheme of cooperation. There is no reason *not* to be sociable in a decent society, and nothing to be gained there by nonirrational unsociability, by going it alone, by entering into a state of war with one's fellows. But some will act contrary to reason, "by asperity of Nature," and be "Stubborn, Insociable, Froward, Intractable." Such stubbornness is perversity, not superior rationality, when the rules are just. We could define a perfectly just society as one where it takes such intractability to motivate disobedience.

How do we measure how close an actual society is to the adequately just society? Unless we can do this it would seem impossible ever to judge a society so unjust that its institutions merit disrespect, or to have confidence that any change made in existing institutions is a change for the better. Yet there are grave problems in establishing any coherent meas-

---

[6] It is not an easy matter to formulate an acceptable criterion of the equitable, but I have assumed that we can get a stronger test for justice than that provided by Hobbes—"What all men have accepted, no man can call unjust." If we cannot, then maybe only the fool says in his heart that there is more to justice than fidelity to possibly forced agreement. If the ideal of the equitable or fair is empty or incoherent, then the more inclusive ideal of justice in a strong sense, which I am invoking, will also be empty or incoherent.

ure of comparative justice. These problems arise because of the tension between two ways in which an existing state of things may approximate the just society. In one sense an institution is just to the extent that it *resembles* one we expect to be part of the adequately just society. In another sense an institution is better to the extent that it is instrumental in moving the society closer in time to that adequacy. But the institutions a society needs, to change itself, may be quite other than those it needs, once improvement is no longer needed. Yet if we opt for this dynamic measure of relative justice, and say that institutions are good to the extent that they facilitate movement towards adequate justice, we run up against the possibility, explored by Hegel and developed by Marx, that historical movement towards a social ideal may be dialectical, that the institutions which best facilitate movement towards an ideal may be ones which least embody that ideal.

The ideal of *justice,* however, is one which cannot generate a sense of "more just than" in which intolerable exploitation is counted more just than a lesser degree of exploitation, merely because it is more likely to precipitate rebellion and change. Those who advocate making things worse in order that they may get better cannot claim that what their strategies increase is justice. Is justice then an ideal which is committed to a perhaps groundless liberal faith in progress, faith in its own gradual attainment by moves, each of which represents *both* an increase in qualitative approximation to the ideal, and *also* a step closer, historically and causally, to its attainment? If these two measures of approximation are both proper, yet can come apart, can come into irresolvable conflict with one another, then the ideal of justice may be confused and incoherent,[7] may rest on a faith which is false. I think there is genuine issue here, but it is not one which I shall discuss further. Social science, not philosophy, would shore up the liberal's faith, or show it to be false. If it is false, if there is no coherent measure of relative justice, then the modern moral philosophy Gauthier criticizes is in even worse straits than he claims. But I shall proceed within the limits of the comforting liberal faith which I take Gauthier to share, faith that some in-

stitutions can be judged less just than others, and that improving them can count as progress towards a just society. It is worth pointing out that this is part of the *faith* the just live by, but it is not the part of it which is controversial to Gauthier and those he criticizes, none of whom embrace the radical moral skepticism to which the Marxist argument leads, nor the new nonmoral revolutionary faith which can fill the vacuum it creates.

Where else does faith enter into the motivation to act, in a less than fully just society, for the sake of justice, to conform to more or less just institutions which not all conform to, or to act, possibly unilaterally, to reform salvageable institutions, and to protest corrupt ones? What must the just person believe, which must turn out to be true if his action is not to be pointless or futile? Before we can discuss the question of whether and when personal advantage is pointlessly sacrificed, we must first discuss the nature and varieties of advantage and personal good. I shall in this discussion adopt a hedonist terminology, to stay as close as possible to the Hobbesian point of departure.

IV. GOODS: SECURE AND INSECURE

Hobbes speaks not of advantage but of *power,* namely "present means to obtain some future apparent good." Advantage strictly is advantage over, or against, others, and Hobbes' emphasis on man's "diffidence" or need to assure himself that there is "no other power great enough to endanger him" (op.cit., ch. 13) turns power-seeking into the attempt to attain advantage, competitive edge, a position superior to one's fellows, since even in civil society he believes that men "can relish nothing but what is eminent" (op.cit., ch. 17). I shall keep the term "advantage" for this competitive good, superiority over others, and use Hobbes' word "power" for the more generic concept of possession of present means to obtain some future, apparent, possibly noncompetitive, good. (I think that when Gauthier speaks of "advantage" he is using it in a looser way, more equivalent simply to "good," that is to a combination of possession of present good and power or present means to attain a future good, whether or not these goods are scarce and competed for.)

Hobbes says that prudence, the concern for power rather than for immediate good, is concern for the future, which is "but a fiction of the mind" (op. cit., ch. 3), and moreover is based on an uncertain presumption that we can learn, from the past,

---

[7] As has been pointed out by a reader for this journal, coherence could be preserved by letting one test apply on some occasions, the other on others, whenever the two tests would give conflicting decisions if both were applied. This would preserve only a weak formal coherence, unless some clear principle could be formulated which selects which test is applicable, and unless this principle itself expressed some component element in our hazy intuitive idea of justice.

what to expect in the future. "And though it be called Prudence, when the Event answereth our Expectation; yet in its own nature is but Presumption" (ibid.). Hobbes is surely correct in pointing out the risks inherent in prudence. One may invest in a form of power which turns out to be a passing not a lasting one. Hobbes (op. cit., ch. 10) catalogues the many forms power takes, and it is fairly obvious that accidents of chance and history may add to, and subtract from, this list, as well as determine the relative importance of different items on it. Even if one's choice of a form of power to obtain is a lucky one, one may not live into that future where the power could be spent in delectation, or even in misery-avoidance. At some point, in any case, the restless pursuit of power after power must end in death, so *some* future good for which the prudent person saved is bound, if he remains prudent to the end, not to be enjoyed by him. In theory one might, when imminent death is anticipated, make a timely conversion to imprudence, cash one's power in for delectation, and die gratified and powerless, but persons with Hobbesian, or with our actual, psychology are not likely to be capable of such a feat. One may have advantage, and have power, which is no good to one, or no longer any good to one, if to be good it must be cashed in delectation.

How are we to judge what is and what is not good to a person? Must good, to be such, be converted, eventually, from apparent good into real indubitable good, and from future into present good? These are hard questions, and it would take a full theory of the good of a person, the place in it of pleasure, interest, power, advantage to answer them. I have no such theory,[8] and will offer only a few remarks about the complexity of all goods other than present simple pleasures. In all human motivation, other than the gratification of current appetite, there is a potential multitier structure. In the case of action designed to make possible the gratification of future desires, that is in prudent action, the good for the sake of which one acts is the expected future gratification, but usually also, derivatively, the present satisfaction of feeling secure, of believing that one has taken thought for the future, secured its needs. So even if the prudent investor does not live into that future for which he provided, he may still enjoy a sense of security while he lives. Prudence, like virtue, may be, and sometimes has to be, its own reward. It is possible, but unlikely, that prudent persons take no present satisfaction in their prudent action, that they develop no taste for a sense of security. The normal accompaniment of prudence is the pleasure of a sense of security. I shall call such pleasures, which make reference to other, possibly nonpresent pleasures, "higher" pleasures (Hobbes' "pleasures of the mind"). By calling these pleasures "higher" I do not mean to imply that they should necessarily be preferred to lower ones. The special class of them which makes reference to future pleasures are power-derivative higher pleasures (Hobbes' "glory"). Such pleasures can coexist with regret that the cost of prudence was renunciation of a present available lower pleasure, and even with doubt whether such costs were unavoidable, and whether one will live to enjoy the future for which one has saved. It would be incorrect to say that the prudent person trades in present lower pleasure for higher pleasure—the higher pleasure is merely a bonus which can come with the power for which the lower pleasure was traded. But hedonic bonuses count for *something,* when the rationality of the action is to be judged.

When one acts for the sake of some good for others, be that good pleasure or power, present or future, there is a similar immediate bonus or "glory" possible, the pleasure of believing that someone else's present or future is improved by one's action. Persons who perform such altruistic acts usually do develop a taste for altruism, a fellow-feeling whereby they share in the good they do others. Just as the sense of personal security usually pleases the prudent person, the awareness of others' pleasure and the sense of their security usually pleases the altruist. It may be possible to do good to others because the moral law is thought to require it, without thereby getting any satisfaction for oneself, but such bonus-refusing psychology seems neither likely nor desirable. It is best if virtue is at least *part* of its own reward, and a waste if it is not.

V. ARTIFICES TO SECURE THE INSECURE

To be a normal person is to be capable of higher pleasures, both self-derived and other-derived, to be able to make the remote in time and the remote from oneself close enough in thought and concern not merely to affect present action but to give present

---

[8] Although in what follows I try to depart as little as possible from the hedonism of Hobbes and Locke (not because I agree with it, but because of the context of the present discussion), I do however depart very significantly from Hobbes in accepting, as rational motivation, not only self-preservation of the natural man, or "nature's preservation" but also preservation, not of Leviathan, but of a moral community, and of the very idea of such a community. A special "pleasure of the mind" would have to be added to Hobbes' list to accommodate such Kantian motivation.

pleasure. Hume explored the mechanisms whereby concern for the remote, both from the present, and from oneself and one's family, can be strengthened by its coincidence with concern for the contiguous, so that the "violent propension to prefer the contiguous to the remote," (*Treatise,* p. 537), may be combated, its unfortunate and sometimes violent effects avoided. These mechanisms include not merely psychological ones, imagination and sympathy, which turn the useful into the also agreeable, and the agreeable for others into the agreeable for oneself also, but also social practices of training and education and social artifices. Such artifices—promise, property, allegiance—turn the useful for people in general into what is useful for oneself, and this requires both convention, or agreement between people as to *what* the artifice is, and general conformity to its constitutive rules. Convention requires both communication and coordination. Hume believed, perhaps wrongly, that all of justice was in this sense artificial and that only with respect to the artificial virtues did a person risk being "the cully of his integrity" (*Treatise,* p. 535) if he acted unilaterally, without assurance that others were similarly virtuous. Since the actions of a kind or a generous person do the good they do, to individual others, case by case, whereas just or honest actions *need* do no good to any specified individual, and do what good they do, for people in general, for the public interest, only when they are supported by other just acts, it is an easy but false move from this valid contrast between the ways the natural and the artificial virtues do good, to a contrast at the level of motivation for the agent, and to the claim that an individual always has good reason to display a natural virtue whether or not others do, while one has no reason to display an artificial virtue, unless others are displaying the same version of it. Nonviolence, or gentleness, is a natural virtue, but nonviolence toward the violent can be as self-destructive as unilateral promise-keeping. Moreover, the higher pleasure of knowing that one's attacker has not suffered at one's hands is not merely insufficient to outweigh the loss of life or limb, it will also be lessened by the awareness that, when violence is the rule, the good to the violent man done by one's own nonviolence is short-lived and insignificant, unless it inspires others to nonviolence.

The natural virtues can, in individual cases, lose most of their point if the degree of nonvirtuousness of others is great enough. They still contrast with the artificial virtues, however, in that their good-

promoting power will vary from case to case, given the same degree of general conformity. When there is general conformity to nonviolence, one may still have reason not to trust individual persons, if there is reason to believe that those ones reciprocate nonviolence with violence. When there is general violence, one may still have reason to expect a nonviolent response to nonviolence in selected cases, so that isolated pockets of gentleness and mutual trust can grow up within a climate of general violence. The same is true, up to a point, of the artificial virtues, in that respect for property rules, or promise-keeping, or allegiance, may be dependable within a restricted circle—say among members of the Mafia—although they do not observe rules outside that group. The artificial virtues differ from the natural ones, however, in that there is never excuse for *selective nonobservance,* within a generally conforming circle, as there can be reason for selective nonobservance of nonviolence, generosity, helpfulness. A debt owed to a vicious man, a miser, a profligate debauchee, or a dishonest man, is still owed. "Justice, in her decisions, never regards the fitness or unfitness of objects to particular persons, but conducts herself by more extensive views. Whether a man be generous, or a miser, he is equally well receiv'd by her, and obtains with the same facility or decision in her favor, even for what is entirely useless to him" (Hume, *Treatise,* p. 502). To grant that the conformity of others does affect the value of the natural as well as the artificial virtues is not to deny Hume's point here, that selective nonobservance, based on "fitness or unfitness of objects to particular persons," is reasonable with natural but not with artificial virtues. "Taking any single act, my justice may be pernicious in every respect; and 'tis only on the supposition, that others are to imitate my example, that I can be persuaded to embrace that virtue; since nothing but this combination can render justice advantageous or afford me any motives to conform myself to its rules" (op. cit., p. 498).

VI. THE PLEASURES OF CONFORMITY

One must suppose, then, that enough others will imitate one's just action if a just act is to be "advantageous," is to advance any interest, or give anyone, however altruistic or public-spirited, rational motive to perform it. When that supposition or faith is reasonable, then there will be a new higher pleasure obtainable by virtuous persons, the satisfaction of knowing that they have contributed to the preservation of the condition of general conformity needed for justice to deliver its utility. The higher pleasure of conformity will be obtained not only from acts conforming to established more or less just artifices, but also from acts displaying those natural virtues whose full point requires the reasonable expectation that others will not return vice for virtue. The higher pleasure of conformity can, in those latter cases, be added to those of altruism and prudence, and it exceeds them in "height." As prudence and altruism facilitate delectation, so conformity facilitates prudence and altruism, as well as extending their range through artifices.

There are, then, a series of hedonic bonus pleasures which we can enjoy, if we cultivate our spiritual palates and develop a relish for them, as Locke puts it (*Essay*, bk. II, 21, 69). They can accompany the nonhedonic goods which are powers, the non-self-directed goods, and conformity to those artifices which create public "powers" to increase the powers and pleasures of individuals. Such present occurrent pleasures, once obtained, cannot be taken away from the prudent man, the altruist, or the conformist, even if the nonpresent or other-dependent good *in* which the pleasure is taken does not eventuate. Bonus pleasures are non-negligible contributors to the goodness of a life. As pains are indicators of other ills, these pleasures are indicators, not guarantees, of other presumed goods, and they add to them as well as indicate them. But the indication may be false, and the glory may be vainglory. Only in so far as one can reasonably hope for the success of one's prudent policy, altruistic project, or for the successful achievement of *general* conformity to an institution, can one derive a higher pleasure from prudent, altruistic, or conforming action. Should the hopes on which they were, reasonably, based become later known to be false, the already obtained bonus pleasures may be devalued. They cannot be canceled, but they may count for less, perhaps count negatively, in the person's proper assessment of the goodness of the life. If hopes turn out to have been what Hobbes calls vain "presumptions," the pleasures dependent on them may come to have been vainglory. If, on one's deathbed, one were persuaded that the person whose apparent love and devotion had given one much pleasure had really been uncaring, perhaps even had despised one, it would not, I think, be reasonable to react with the thought "thank God I didn't know till now." False pleasures, pleasures based on

what comes to be seen as a lie, can, if the lie is serious and has reverberating implications for many of one's concerns, be worse than the absence of pleasure. Better no glory than vainglory.

Would the prudent man's bonus pleasure of feeling secure come to have been, like the friend's trusting pleasure, fool's gold, if he comes to realize that he will not live into the future for which he saved? If the bonus pleasure had been pleasure in the anticipated spendings of his savings, it would certainly be degraded by realization that he will not spend it, but to the extent that his bonus pleasure in his sense of security was in that which freed him from anxiety about his future, that bonus pleasure is not devalued by any knowledge he may acquire about his imminent early death. The power he had was a good, even if not exercised, because its absence would have been an ever-present felt evil. One might say, of the trusting friend, that his trust that his love was reciprocated was a good similar to the prudent man's security, in that its absence would have been an evil for him. But could the evil of suspicion or distrust, or of the absence of affection, be as great as the evil the friend suffers if he bases his life on a false trust? The difference, I think, lies in the fact that the unnecessarily prudent man is not *betrayed* by events, as the friend is by the false friend. The prudent man saves, because of the *possibility* that he may live long, but the friend loved in the confidence that love was returned. Prudence is, and knows itself to be, a reaction to risk and uncertainty, so its goods are not devalued if the possibility the prudent man provided for does not come about. But friendship does not, typically, see itself as content with the mere *possibility* of returned trust and love.

Can the man who acts for the sake of justice, when he knows or suspects that others are *not* conforming, get any bonus pleasures which are not fool's gold? We need to distinguish the cases where most but not all others are conforming from the cases where the conformists are in a minority, and, within the latter class, between the few who are trying to *inaugurate* a needed practice, and the few who are clinging to a once accepted but now imperiled institution. The last case, of fidelity to a once supported practice, faces less severe problems than those of the moral innovator, who must both get agreement on what should be conformed to, and also try to get sufficient conformity to it to secure the rewards of conformity. At least the moral conservative, the would-be supporter of a once established practice, does not face what have been called[9] the isolation and coordination problems, he faces only the problem of assurance of compliance. I shall not discuss the problems, faced by Hobbesian natural men, of simultaneously achieving communication, agreeing on what institutions are desirable (what coordination scheme to adopt) and also getting assured compliance to them. Let us, optimistically, assume that we have got, by the fact of past established conventions, their later reform, and their agreed need for specific further reforms, a solution to the isolation and coordination problems, that is, we have agreement on how we *should* all be acting. The compliance problem then arises—namely whether to act as we all should if we all are to get the best state of things for us, when there is no assurance that the rest of us are going to comply. If I comply and the rest of you don't, then the main good, for the sake of which that cooperative scheme was seen to be acceptable, will not be fully obtained, by any of us. To the extent it is partially attained it will be attained by noncompliers as well as compliers. I will have been the cully of my integrity. So, it seems, the pleasure of conformity is fool's gold unless others do in fact conform in sufficient numbers.

One thing which might save those pleasures from becoming false is the psychological taste of the individual for conformity. Not everyone can enjoy gun-running. Just as the prudent man who doesn't live to enjoy his savings may nevertheless have been saved by his prudence from unpleasant anxiety, so conformity to the old ways may soothe the timid who would be alarmed, not gratified, by the immoralists' life style.

But suppose I *could* develop a relish for gun-running, would it be irrational for me to decide to stick by, not to abandon, the threatened moral practices? Can unilateral (or minority-wide) conformity to just, or potentially just, institutions have any genuine lure for me?

VII. THE HIGHER PLEASURE OF QUALIFYING FOR MEMBERSHIP IN THE KINGDOM OF ENDS

Hume's point, a valid one, is that only a fool supports widely unsupported institutions whose only

good depends on their getting wide support. But support from whom? My contemporaries and only them? It is fairly evident, I think, that the support of the majority of his contemporaries is not *sufficient* to guard the conformist from being taken in by fool's gold, especially when the institution is one which *conserves* goods for future generations. Whole generations can be retroactively made into cullies of their joint integrity by later generations' waste and destruction. What I want to stress is that conformity by the majority of one's contemporaries is not *necessary* to save the moral man from having been a fool.

Here, at least, I turn to the obvious source of a reply to Gauthier: Kant. He spelled out more clearly than any other modern philosopher the wholly secular basis for a strong set of plain duties. It is wholly secular, and it is also faith-requiring.

Kant says that although a rational being, when he acts on the maxim he can will as a universal law, "cannot for that reason expect every other rational being to be true to it; nor can he expect the realm of nature and its orderly design to harmonize with him as a fitting member of a realm of ends which is possible through himself. That is, he cannot count on its favoring his expectation of happiness. Still the law: Act according to the maxims of a universally legislative member of a merely potential realm of ends, remains in full force, because it commands categorically. And just in this lies the paradox, that merely the dignity of humanity as rational nature without any end or advantage to be gained by it, and thus respect for a mere idea, should serve as the inflexible precept of the will. There is the further paradox that the sublimity and worthiness of every rational subject to be a legislative member in the realm of ends consists precisely in independence of maxims from all such incentives" (Kant, *Foundation of the Metaphysics of Morals,* trans. Lewis White Beck). In this remarkable passage Kant appears to be claiming that the willingness to act as *if* one were a member of an actual kingdom of ends, when one knows that one is in fact a member of a society which falls short of this ideal, alone makes one worthy to be a legislating member of an actual kingdom of ends, or just society. But unless there can be such sublime and worthy persons, no just society is possible. The kingdom of ends is "possible through oneself." The existence of persons with the ability to act from respect for that "mere idea," is, then, the condition of the idea's actualization. Apparently just institutions would not guarantee a just society, if those persons living under them fail Kant's motivational test. A just

9   Kurt Baier, "Rationality and Morality," *Erkenntnis 11* (1977): 197, where the "isolation," "coordination," and "assurance" problems are distinguished.

society must be comprised of just men whose lives are ordered by just institutions.

On this account, apparently futile unilateral and possibly self-sacrificing action is neither futile nor unilateral. Not futile, because it keeps alive the assurance of the possibility of qualified members for a just society. Not unilateral, because the one just man has a "cloud of witnesses," all those others whose similar acts in other times kept alive the same hope. The actions of individuals who, unsupported by their contemporaries, act for the sake of justice do not necessarily hasten the coming of a just society, but they do rule out one ground on which it might be feared impossible. In this very modest way the just man's actions confirm his faith, demonstrate that *one* condition of the existence of a just society can be met, that human psychology can be a psychology for sovereigns. And the one just man is not alone, his isolation problem is solved if he recalls that enough others have already acted as he is acting. Thus every action in conformity to a just but threatened institution, or in protest against an unjust but supported one, furthers the cause, keeps the faith. The highest pleasure or "relish" of all is that of qualifying for membership in the kingdom of ends.[10] It is not just a priggish pleasure if the demonstration that there are and can be qualified members has the role which Kant as I interpret him claimed for it. (The blood of the martyrs is the seed of the church.)

VIII. THE FAITH THE JUST LIVE BY

The secular faith which the just live by is, then, a faith in the possibility of a society for membership in which their just action theoretically qualifies them. They believe, in part, because of the previous demonstration that there can be such qualified members, so they join a movement already started. Each new member gives other potential members new assurance that the faith is not in vain, and it also confirms the faith of that new member himself, in that, after his act, the club of which he is an "honorary" member is the larger by one, and its point depends on the size and persistence of its membership.

The qualified, so honorary, member of the kingdom of ends, usually hopes that some actual society, perhaps long after his death, will embody the kingdom of ends on earth, that the possible will become

actual. Such a society would, in general intention, honor all those who acted for the sake of justice, who qualified for membership but did not survive to be members. They would be participants in the secular variant of the communion of the saints. This higher pleasure is a variant of that pleasure of imagination, delight in the prospect of a posthumous recognition, which even Hobbes allows as a real pleasure. "Though after death there be no sense of the praise given us on earth, as being joys that are either swallowed up in the unspeakable joys of heaven or extinguished in the extreme torments of hell, yet is not such fame vain; because men have a present delight therein from the foresight of it and of the benefit that may redound thereby to their prosperity, which though they see not, yet they imagine; and anything that is pleasure to the sense, the same is also pleasure in the imagination" (*Leviathan*, ch. 11). Hobbes would not be content with anonymous recognition—presumably only the foresight that one's name will live on, preserved on some honor roll, could give Hobbesian man this pleasure of imagination. Fame is one thing, membership in the faceless communion of the saints quite another for one who values nothing but what is eminent. Still, the qualification for praise and recognition by a posterity to whom benefits redound is at least part of what the Hobbesian can glory in, and for a Kantian it suffices for glory.

Does this pleasure of imagination require expectation that posterity *will* benefit? Does the faith the just live by include confidence that some society on earth will some day actually be just? As already acknowledged, the ideal of justice includes a demand, which may be utopian, that its historical approximation coincide with its qualitative approximation. In addition to this demand, which the just person must, for the moment at least, merely *hope* can be met, there is another more serious difficulty in the idea of an actual just society which would meet the Kantian requirements. This is that, to the extent that there *is* conformity among one's contemporaries to apparently just practices, to precisely that extent none of the conformers can be assured that they, each of them, qualify for membership in the kingdom of ends. If they are acting, not for a mere idea, but in support of an actual practice, they cannot be sure they meet Kant's paradoxical test for qualification for membership in a just society, that is they cannot be sure how they *would* act if there were not general conformity. But the apparently just conforming society will not *be* just, in Kant's sense, if

---

[10] I have not discussed the question, raised by Gauthier's example of unilateral abstention from preemptive nuclear strike, of what should be done when the decision taken may commit others besides the decision-maker to the higher pleasures of martyrdom for a good cause. This is the *really* difficult question.

its sovereign-subjects are not qualified to be members. Kant's paradox is real, and so, once again, the ideal of a just society threatens to become incoherent. The threat, this time, is not one which can be allayed by sociological and historical findings, but is more fundamental—a *necessary* conflict between the criteria for qualification as the just society comprised of qualified members, and the criteria for its actualization.

Must the just man then conclude "credo quia absurdum est?" He might—as he might develop a relish for acting for necessarily lost causes—but he can keep his faith from being the absurd hope for the impossible, by acceptance of the fact that one can live without certainty. As the just man *now,* in an unjust world, has no certainty, only faith and hope, that

there really can and will be a just society of the living, so, in any apparently attained just society, that is in one with just institutions, its members will rely on the faith and hope that they could if necessary act for a mere idea, and so that they really qualify for membership. A new variant of Hobbesian faith in man will be needed. Both in the absence and in the presence of an actual just society, then, the just will live by faith.[11]

---

[11] I have tried, throughout this paper, to evoke some Biblical echoes, to show how the secular faith I describe parallels its theological forerunners. The effort to speak both the language of Hobbes and that of the King James Bible has resulted in a style which some readers have found obscure. This I regret, but I do want to keep, for those in a position to recognize them, allusions to, e.g., St. Paul's Epistle to the Hebrews, chs. 10 and 11.

QUESTIONS FOR REVIEW AND FURTHER THOUGHT

1. What theories of truth are discussed in Part II? Which of these various theories are you inclined to believe and why? What reasons might others give for disagreeing with you, and what would be the shortcomings of their reasons?

2. Consider the following statement: "Nothing is true or false, but only true or false for some individual." What can this statement mean? Is it ever true? Is it ever false? Why or why not? How would you defend your answers against some plausible objections?

3. Is it true that when, under ordinary circumstances, you hear birds' singing, there are birds out there, outside of your experience, whose singing you experience? Why or why not? How would you defend your answer against some plausible objections?

4. Compare and contrast Vasubandhu's and Berkeley's positions on the existence of an external world.

5. According to his *Meditation I,* what sorts of things does Descartes conclude he can doubt and why? Are his reasons sound? Why or why not?

6. What is Peirce's conception of doubt? Does it implicitly criticize Descartes' position in his *Meditations of First Philosophy*? How could Descartes respond to the criticisms?

7. Identify the methods for fixing belief followed in these examples:
   a. Redoubling your efforts when you have forgotten your aim.
   b. Consulting the experts in deciding how to deal with environmental problems.
   c. Following a local person's directions in looking for the town railroad station.
   d. Consulting an oracle in deciding how to deal with environmental problems.
   e. Believing that the orbits of the planets are perfectly circular because this is the best shape they could have.
   f. Believing that 2+2=4 because we cannot conceive it to be otherwise.

    g. Believing that physical space is three dimensional because that is the only way in which we can experience it.

    h. Believing, on the basis of empirical studies, that untreated high blood pressure will eventually cause a heart condition.

8. What conception of explanation offered by the authors in Part II do you find most convincing and why?

9. What are laws of nature and what is the cost of not believing that there are any?

10. Compare and contrast the positions of Clifford and James on the will to believe. Which one do you find most convincing and why?

11. Compare and contrast the conception of faith formulated in the traditional Buddhist text included in Part II with that formulated in Annette Baier's selection. Which one do you think preferable? Why? Can you formulate an even better characterization of faith? If not, why not? If you can, what is it and why is it better?

12. Why does Baier hold that a secular faith is necessary for morals and science? Are her arguments sound? If so, what objections could be advanced against them and why would these objections be flawed? If not, what makes the arguments unsound and how would you address some plausible objections to your position that they are unsound?

13. Do any authors in Part II engage in cross-cultural reflection and dialogue to any extent? Do they, for example, try to adapt categories used in other cultures to their own cultural context? Who, how, and how fruitfully?

14. Could those authors in Part II who do not engage in cross-cultural reflection have done so while being faithful to the views they espouse?

III

What Is The Universe Really Like?

A. IS THERE A GOD?

Ideas about deities are about as varied as people's circumstances. For example, the *Popol Vuh* ("Sacred Book") of the ancient Quiché Maya, written by a member of the Quiché in the middle of the sixteenth century, says:

> This is the account of how all was in suspense, all calm, in silence; all motionless, still, and the expanse of the sky was empty.
>
> . . . There was only immobility and silence in the darkness, in the night. Only the Creator, the Maker, Tepeu, Gucumatz, the Forefathers, were in the water surrounded with light. They were hidden under green and blue feathers, and were therefore called Gucumatz. By nature they were great sages and great thinkers. In this manner the sky existed and also the Heart of Heaven, which is the name of God and thus He is called.
>
> . . . Then came the word. Tepeu and Gucumatz came together in this darkness, in the night, and Tepeu and Gucumatz talked together. They talked then, discussing and deliberating; they agreed, they united their words and their thoughts.
>
> . . . Then they planned the creation, and the growth of the trees and the thickets and the birth of life and the creation of man. Thus it was arranged in the darkness and in the night by the Heart of Heaven who is called Huracán.[1]

This story of creation involves a belief in more than one god deliberating and coming to a joint decision on the world's creation. Another Mayan book, however, the *Chilam Balam of Chumayel*, espouses a monotheistic view:

> Where there was neither heaven nor earth sounded the first word of God. And He unloosed Himself from His stone, and declared His divinity. And all the vastness of eternity shuddered. And His word was a measure of grace, and He broke and pierced the backbone of the mountains. Who was borne there? Who? Father, Thou knowest: He who was tender in Heaven came into Being.[2]

Among western South American Indians, whose cultures were significantly agrarian, a predominant deity was (and still is) the Pachamama (Mother Earth), a female goddess associated with fertility. This conception of a female goddess is also found among many North American peoples. In Judaism, Christianity, and Islam, which originated among the Arabian desert's nomadic clans and their settled descendants, God is a male. His authoritarianism—very much like that of a chieftain—has been moderated to some degree by Jesus' message of love.

As we saw in Part II, people sometimes believe in their deities simply as a matter of faith. At other times, however, they argue for their existence. In the Judeo-Christian tradition, for example, many attempts have been made to prove, inductively or deductively, the existence of God. The first selection in Part III "Proslogium" by Anselm (1033–1109), is one such attempt.

Anselm gives two arguments in this selection: one for God's existence, and the other for the impossibility of conceiving that God does not exist. Both arguments are partly based on a presumed distinction between two conceptions of God. In one conception, God is characterized by the following properties: omnipotence, omniscience, personhood, absolute benevolence and justice, uniqueness, and eternalness. In the second conception, God has all these features plus existence. To be sure, these features are not explicitly mentioned by Anselm, but they were commonly ascribed to God in his religious environment, and Anselm was a nondissenting member of that environment. Thus, we can then plausibly say that, for Anselm, an omnipotent, omniscient, personal, absolutely benevolent and just, unique, and eternal God that exists is greater—that is, more perfect—than a God who has all these properties except existence. Let us call this view, which assumes existence is a property, the *perfection hypothesis*. Anselm's first argument, then, can be formulated as follows:

Statement	*Justification*
1. God is that than which nothing greater can be conceived.	Definition of "God."
2. God exists in the understanding.	Because we understand the definition of "God."
3. If God exists only in the understanding and not also in reality, then something greater than God can be conceived.	By the perfection hypothesis.
4. God exists only in the understanding and not also in reality.	Hypothesis.
5. Something greater than God can be conceived.	From steps 3 and 4, by a valid rule of inference (*modus ponens*).
6. Something greater than that than which nothing greater can be conceived, can be conceived.	From steps 1 and 5, by replacing the definition of "God" for the term "God."
7. God exists not only in the understanding but also in reality.	Because step 6 is a contradiction. Hence, step 4, which led to it, is false, and so, step 6 is true.

Anselm's second argument parallels the first:

Statement	*Justification*
1. God is that than which nothing greater can be conceived.	Definition of "God."
2. God exists in the understanding and can be conceived to exist in the understanding.	Because we understand the definition of "God."
3. If God can be conceived to exist only in the understanding and not also in reality, then something greater than God can be conceived.	By the perfection hypothesis.

4. God can be conceived to exist only in the understanding and not also in reality.	Hypothesis.
5. Something greater than God can be conceived.	From steps 3 and 4, by a valid rule of inference (*modus ponens*).
6. Something greater than that than which nothing greater can be conceived, can be conceived.	From steps 1 and 5, by replacing the definition of "God" for the term "God."
7. God cannot be conceived to exist only in the understanding and not also in reality.	Because step 6 is a contradiction. Hence, step 4, which led to it, is false, and so, step 6 is true.

The second selection in Part III, "In Behalf of the Fool" by Gaunilon de Marmoutier (?–1083), is a reply to Anselm. Gaunilon argues that the mere fact that I understand what is said does not by itself entail that what I understand is in my understanding. For if it were, then all sorts of vague and unreal things would be in my understanding. But they are not. Besides, "an object can hardly or never be conceived according to the word alone," because in such a case, it is conceived only as a meaningless sound, not as the meaning of that sound. To this, Anselm might reply that there is nothing mysterious in the meaning of God as that than which nothing greater can be thought. Yet one might object that this is not the concept of *God*, but merely the concept of a *property* (understood as any feature, attribute, or characteristic) that the concept of God must have, if there is such a concept. This property is that nothing greater than this concept can be thought.

Moreover, concerning the perfection hypothesis, which presupposes existence is a property, the question arises: Is existence a defining property? Suppose it is, and also suppose we say that Mount Everest does not exist. To be sure, it is false—but not a contradiction—that Mount Everest does not exist. But if existence is a defining property, then it would be contradictory. And to say that Mount Everest exists, which is true—but not necessarily true—would be necessarily true. These implications go against both common sense and logic. Of course, Anselm could reply that existence is a defining property only in the case of God. But then we would ask: Why only in this case? Until this point has been explained, Anselm's arguments have to be considered ad hoc.

Some of these criticisms are taken into account in the next selection, "The Existence of God" by St. Thomas Aquinas (c. 1224–1274). After criticizing Anselm's and other arguments for God's existence, Aquinas argues that the existence of God can be proved inductively "from those of His effects which are known to us." He outlines five arguments: the argument from motion, that from the nature of efficient cause, that from possibility and necessity, that from gradation, and that from the governance of the world. The first three of these arguments are forms of the *cosmological argument*, which rests on at least two suppositions. The first—dating back to Aristotle's *Metaphysics*—is that change implies an ultimate, unchanging source of change. The second is that the fact that there is a world at all demands an explanation. But at least the latter supposition begs the question, for it is precisely what an agnostic or an atheist will deny.[3]

Aquinas's fourth argument involves the supposition that "*more* and *less* are predicated of different things according as they resemble in their different ways something which is the maximum." It also involves the supposition that the maximum of every genus is its cause ("fire . . . is the cause of all hot things"). From these suppositions and the fact that "more" and "less" are predicated with regard to every perfection and being, Aquinas concludes that there must be a maximum that is the cause of every being and all perfections of all beings, and this maximum is God.

This argument can be interpreted as an *argument to the best explanation* of our judgments of degree. It raises the question: Why believe that in our judgments of degree the predicates "more" and "less" are applied by reference to a maximum resembled by the items to which they apply? They could as well be applied by comparison with other items to which the predicates apply to different degrees. But suppose that our judgments of degree are best explained by a maximum that is the standard of comparison and cause of all things' perfections and being. This in no way entails that such a maximum is the omniscient, omnipotent, eternal, personal, unique, all-benevolent, and just God of the Judeo-Christian tradition.

Concerning this argument and, especially, Aquinas's fifth argument, the *argument from design* (one version of which is that the world's intricate structure can be explained only by appeal to a God that designed it), David Hume (1711–1776) makes the same point in the next selection, 'Design, Evil, and God's Existence.'' Aquinas could have answered that he was well aware of the arguments' limitations, but that they at least commit us to believing in the existence of such a being. (For a modern version of this argument, see Selection 23 by Ernest Nagel and the discussion of this piece at the end of Section A of this essay.) Hume also argues that the arguments for God's existence cannot be based on probabilities soundly understood:

> When two *species* of objects have always been observed to be conjoined together, I can *infer*, by custom, the existence of one wherever I *see* the existence of the other: And this I call an argument from experience. But how this argument can have place, where the objects, as in the present case, are single, individual, without parallel, or specific resemblance, may be difficult to explain. And will any man tell me with a serious countenance, that an orderly universe must arise from some thought and art, like the human; because we have experience of it? To ascertain this reasoning, it were requisite, that we had experience of the origin of worlds; and it is not sufficient surely, that we have seen ships and cities arise from human contrivance. . . .

One might respond that Hume's objection proves that the concept of probability that operates in the theistic arguments is not cogent, except when it is interpreted as the ordinary notion of likelihood. According to this notion, to say that something is probable or likely is to say that it is reasonable to believe it because, given the alternatives and our entrenched beliefs, it provides the best available explanation of the matter thought to need an explanation; while to say that it is improbable or unlikely is to say that it is unreasonable to believe it because, given the alternatives and our entrenched beliefs, it does not provide the best available explanation. But is God's existence the best explanation for our judgments of degree, or for the intricate world structure? Hume discusses an argument for the opposite conclusion: the *argument from evil.* The argument can be formulated as follows:

> *If God were omniscient, omnipotent, and absolutely benevolent and just, then there would be no evil in the world. But there is evil in the world. Hence, God is not omnipotent, or not omniscient, or not absolutely benevolent and just.*

One could respond to this argument in various ways. First, one could argue that some evil is necessary so that we may recognize the good. Hume might respond:

Why so much? Do we need a long night to appreciate the light of day? Second, one could argue that what we take to be evil is actually good. Hume might respond: That is a possibility we human beings cannot understand or even find plausible; hence, it cannot serve as a reason for us. Third, one could argue that this is the best of all possible worlds in that, though all possible worlds involve some evil, this world involves the least possible evil. One response to this argument resembles the response to the previous one. It is implausible that there could not be a better world than the present one. We can easily imagine another world better than this one in that an infant murdered in this world would not be murdered, but would live happily and make others happier. Fourth, one could argue that it is not God, but we ourselves, acting on our own free will, who bring about evil in the world. Yet this argument does not explain the widespread death and suffering brought about by floods, earthquakes, and other natural disasters many of whose victims are innocent children.

These objections and replies could continue indefinitely, but we have said enough to establish Hume's point, which is that the argument from design raises a serious question concerning the view that the Judeo-Christian God is the best explanation for the features of the world we experience. Hume does not conclude that such a God does not exist, but says:

> There is no view of human life, or the condition of mankind, from which, without the greatest violence, we can infer the moral attributes, or learn that infinite benevolence, conjoined with infinite power and infinite wisdom, which we must discover by the eyes of faith alone.

Whatever position one takes on this matter, the best explanation must do more than explain in an enlightening manner. It must either fit well with our ordinary beliefs— say, with our beliefs about the extent of evil in the world—or it must overwhelmingly show that these beliefs are false or highly doubtful.[4]

Our next selection is "Philosophical Concepts of Atheism" by Ernest Nagel (1901–1985). By "atheism," Nagel means "a critique and a denial of the major claims of all varieties of theism." By "theism," he means the doctrine that the entire universe owes its existence and persistence "to the wisdom and will of a supreme, self-consistent, omnipotent, omniscient, righteous, and benevolent being, who is distinct from, and independent of, what he has created." By this definition, as Nagel makes plain, early Buddhism is atheistic, because it "does not subscribe to any doctrine about a god." So is pantheism, because it denies that God is separate and independent of the world.

Nagel deals with the cosmological and ontological arguments for the existence of God in a manner that restates some points we made in the preceding discussion. After discussing the traditional version of the argument from design, which postulates God to explain the variety of biological species, he proposes what seems to him a better explanation. This is the Darwinian theory, which explains biological diversity "in terms of chance variations in the structure of organisms, and of a mechanism of selection which retains those variant forms that possess some advantages for survival."

Nagel then discusses a second form of the argument from design, one recently revived in the speculations of some physicists. This is the argument that since the laws of nature are best formulated in mathematical language, they must have been created by a divine mathematician. As Nagel states, this version of the argument assumes that mathematical language can be thus used only if the world has a *special* kind of order. On the contrary, Nagel argues, mathematical language can be used whatever order the world has and however chaotic it turns out to be.

Nagel's refutations of both forms of the argument from design shift the burden of proof to those who believe in God's existence. They are faced with showing that the Darwinian explanation and Nagel's point about mathematical language are false or irrelevant to the topic of discussion. But current scientific evidence indicates that they are not false. Neither are they irrelevant, because the argument from design is meant to use rather than exclude scientific results.

In addition, Nagel discusses an argument formulated by Kant, which was also discussed by Annette Baier in Part II (Selection 18). One version is this:

> *If God exists, morality and the fact that the highest human good is the realization of happiness commensurate with one's virtue are justified. But they are justified, and no alternative other than God appears to guarantee that the highest human good is realizable, hence justified. Therefore, God must exist.*

Nagel correctly criticizes this argument by stating: "No postulation carries with it any assurance that what is postulated is actually the case." The best we can say for this argument is that, as James stated in Selection 17, those people who desire happiness commensurate with their virtue are justified in believing that God exists.

Nagel also considers the argument from religious experience, which roughly says: Since there are certain distinctive religious experiences, and God makes sense of these experiences, God exists. To this Nagel replies that though the experience itself may be genuine, the report that God caused it cannot be taken seriously. In response, one might say, with the comedian Lily Tomlin: "Why is it when we talk to God, we're said to be praying—but when God talks to us, we're schizophrenic?"[5] Nagel never deals with the genuine point raised here, but could reply that though the experience of praying may be real, praying makes as much sense as talking to the walls, and insisting that we are talking to God is as nonsensical as insisting that God is talking to us. As for the argument from evil, Nagel argues that it shows the glaring inconsistencies in the traditional Judeo-Christian conception of God.

What is perhaps most interesting about Nagel's position is his thesis that atheism, rather than being merely a negative standpoint, is characterized by a certain type of "intellectual temper" and involves a tragic view of life. This brings us back to Annette Baier's discussion of secular faith (see Part II, Selection 18). Is it possible to rely, not on a religious or secular faith, but on one's presence of mind, sense of rightness (even if virtue is not rewarded with happiness), and determination, in order to give morality a chance? These conditions may constitute all that is required—and, indeed, permitted—by the intellectual temper characteristic of the form of atheism Nagel describes. But the attempt to live a moral life under such conditions involves a fundamental risk: that morality that is not based on some kind of faith, religious or secular, may become as outmoded as Nagel and others believe that faith is. This thought prompts anxiety, and for many people, their passional nature (as James put it) would have to decide what to believe for the sake of dealing with such anxiety. Others, however, could try to curb their passions by means of reasoning and reflection.

This discussion brings up a variety of questions about mental life. We will discuss them next.

B. ARE THERE MINDS BESIDE MATTER?

This section's first selection, "From *Spiritual Physick*" by Rhazes (864–925), provides an account of how and how far one should restrain one's passions in order to reform one's character. Rhazes, a Persian philosopher, physician, and scientist, acknowledges the views of Socrates and Plato on this matter, but then proceeds to distance himself from them and to adopt a worldly standpoint. He writes:

> Besides all this, there is neither any purely mundane view whatsoever that does not necessitate some reining of passion and appetite, or that gives them free head and rope altogether.

His criterion for establishing the extent to which passion should be restrained is expressed as follows:

> This then will suffice as to the amount the appetites should be suppressed: they may only be indulged where it is known that the consequence will not involve a man in pain and temporal loss equivalent to the pleasure thereby obtained—much less discomfort superior to and exceeding the pleasure and temporal loss that is momentarily experienced.

In other words, restraint should aim at increasing individual happiness (in the pleasure oriented sense of "happiness") overall. Why does Rhazes use such a largely hedonistic criterion? This is an ethical criticism and, accordingly, will be addressed in Part IV. Here we will focus on some questions his position raises about the nature of mental life. Rhazes says:

> . . . our passion and instinct, see nothing else but the actual state in which they happen to be, and only seek to get rid of the pain that hurts them at that very moment. In this way a child suffering from ophthalmia will rub its eyes and eat dates and play in the sun.

In this passage, passion and instinct are treated as merely episodic reactions to particular stimuli, like thirst, hunger, and panic. In other passages, however, Rhazes holds that some passions become habitual, and then they are character traits. Of those who are constantly having intercourse with women, or drinking, or listening to music, for example, he says: "these passions become for them . . . commonplace and habitual," and "it is not within their power to leave off these pursuits because they have turned into something of the nature of a necessity of life for them, instead of being a luxury and a relish."

Are these passages compatible with the previous one, which treats passion and instinct as episodic? Although Rhazes himself does not address this question, one could argue that they are compatible on the grounds that all it takes for a passion to become a habit is for the behavioral episodes displaying it to become more frequent. By this explanation, a habit is statistical in nature. This position, however, raises several questions worth pursuing: What is it to have a passion—say, cruelty or vindictiveness—over and above one's particular displays of this passion? Is there a difference between having a habitual passion—for example, callousness—and having a character trait? Do these have a causal or theoretical component (like charm particles in physics), or are they merely statistical in nature? Are all personality traits—liveliness, charm, wit, and so forth—also character traits, or are character traits a subset of personality traits? If so, what are the latter?

We will return to some of these questions later. Here we point out that philosophical and commonsense answers to some of them have often presupposed that minds are distinct from bodies, and that if minds are subject to laws, these are not the same laws as those governing bodies. That is, such traits as cruelty, vindictiveness, and callousness belong to the mind, which, by contrast with bodies, is supposed to exist in time, but not in space, and to be governed by different laws than those governing the physical world in which bodies exist. In the next selection, "The Ghost in the Machine," Gilbert Ryle (1900–1976) describes the view that involves these and related presuppositions:

> A person . . . lives through two collateral histories, one consisting of what happens in and to his body, the other consisting of what happens in and to his mind. The first is public, the second private. . . .
>
> It is customary to express this bifurcation of his two lives and of his two worlds by saying that the things and events which belong to the physical world, including his own body, are external, while the workings of his own mind are internal.

Ryle thinks that this external-internal distinction is a metaphor that has led some to make significant philosophical errors:

> Underlying this partly metaphorical representation of the bifurcation of a person's two lives there is a seemingly more profound and philosophical assumption. It is assumed that there are two kinds of existence or status. What exists or happens may have the status of physical existence, or it may have the status of mental existence. . . . It is a necessary feature of what has physical existence that it is in space and time, it is a necessary feature of what has mental existence that it is in time but not in space. What has physical existence is composed of matter, or else is a function of matter; what has mental existence consists of consciousness, or else is a function of consciousness.

Ryle's name for this theory is "the dogma of the Ghost in the Machine." He argues that this dogma amounts to a category mistake. One example of a category mistake is to think that a university is a building, in addition to its library, administration, science, and museum buildings and its playing fields. Another example is to think that the average taxpayer is one of the many taxpayers. In general, a category mistake is representing something as if it belonged to one logical type or category (or range of logical types or categories), when it actually belongs to another.

According to Ryle, the category mistake made concerning minds consists in thinking that the *occurrence* of mental processes belongs in the same category with the *occurrence* of physical processes. Ryle does not deny that mental processes and physical processes occur. He denies that their occurrence is of the same sort and says that the dogma of the ghost in the machine presupposes it is of the same sort.

To hold, against Ryle, that these occurrences are of the same sort would amount to holding that the same type of change goes on when I change my mind and when I change my shirt. Obviously, to claim that both changes are of the same type is preposterous, and Ryle would explain why it is preposterous by saying that it involves a category mistake.

C.   DO ALL EVENTS HAVE CAUSES?

Our discussions in Sections A and B abounded in references to causes and effects. These notions are discussed in the next selection, "From *The Incoherence of the Incoherence*" by Averroes (1126–1198), an Islamic philosopher who was born in Córdoba (in the southern part of modern Spain). This selection is a good example of philosophical dialogue because in it Averroes formulates and criticizes views presented by the Persian philosopher Ghazali (1058–1111) in his *The Incoherence of the Philosophers*. According to Averroes's initial quotation from Ghazali's work, the philosophers assert that the "connexion observed between causes and effects is of logical necessity." This is an assertion Ghazali criticizes. He makes his motivation clear:

> . . . it is necessary to contest it, for on its negation depends the possibility of affirming the existence of miracles which interrupt the usual course of nature, like the changing of the rod into a serpent or the resurrection of the dead or the cleavage of the moon, and those who consider the ordinary course of nature a logical necessity regard all this as impossible.

Averroes's own criticisms focus on Ghazali's arguments about causality. Ghazali formulates his thesis as follows: "the connexion between what is usually believed to be a cause and what is believed to be an effect is not a necessary connexion." In assessing this thesis, one should keep in mind that neither Ghazali nor Averroes clearly drew the distinction that some modern philosophers draw—especially since Hume (see Selection 27)—and others deny, between logical and physical necessity. Yet they were talking about matters relevant to this distinction.

Logical necessity is said to be a feature of tautologies and analytic statements. (See the discussion of necessary and empirical statements in Selection 7 by Churchill in Part I.) A *tautology*—for example, "Either it is raining here and now, or it is not raining here and now"—is a statement that is true just by virtue of its form. In our example, the statement is true regardless of the meaning of the phrase "raining here and now." Were we to replace it in both places where it occurs in the statement with the phrase "snowing here and now" (or, for that matter, with "the French Revolution" or "the moon"), the statement would remain true. Indeed, the statement itself would be true whether or not the phrase "it is raining here and now" (or "it is snowing here and now" or "it is the French Revolution" or "it is the moon") is true or false.

Analytic statements—for example, "Bachelors are unmarried"—are statements that are true just by virtue of the meaning of their terms. That is, by contrast with tautologies, the meaning of the terms (like "bachelors" and "unmarried") makes a difference to the truth of analytic statements. Indeed, it suffices to establish it.

By contrast with tautologies and analytic statements, the form and meanings of the terms in "Whenever water is heated up to 100 degrees centigrades at one atmosphere of pressure, it boils," do not by themselves make the statement true. It is logically possible that the statement is true, and it is also logically possible that the statement is false. Whether the statement turns out to be true depends on the physical world: on actual water behaving as the statement says under the conditions the statement specifies. As a matter of fact, the statement is true according to current physics. It is a particular case of a law of nature concerning the boiling of water relative to given temperatures and pressures. Accordingly, some philosophers would hold that, though logical necessity is not a feature of the above statement, *physical necessity* is.

Ghazali seems to deny both the logical and the physical necessity of causal connections when he says:

> According to us the connexion between what is usually believed to be a cause and what is believed to be an effect is not a necessary connexion; each of two things has its own individuality and is not the other, and neither the affirmation nor the negation, neither the existence nor the nonexistence of the one is implied in the affirmation, negation, existence, and non-existence of the other. . . .

That is, to use Ghazali's own example, it is neither tautological nor analytic that when cotton is placed in fire, cotton burns. Neither is it a physical law that whenever cotton is placed in fire, fire causes cotton to burn. All one observes in that circumstance is the simultaneity of cotton's contact with fire and cotton's burning. The causation itself is not observed. Ghazali says:

> For fire is a dead body which has no action, and what is the proof that it is the agent? Indeed, the philosophers have no other proof than the observation of the occurrence of the burning, when there is contact with fire, but observation proves only a simultaneity, not a causation. . . .

To this Averroes replies:

> To deny the existence of efficient causes which are observed in sensible things is sophistry. . . . For he who denies this can no longer acknowledge that every act must have an agent. . . . And if the theologians had doubts about the efficient causes which are perceived to cause each other, because there are also effects whose cause is not perceived, this is illogical. Those things whose causes are not perceived are still unknown and must be investigated, precisely because their causes are not perceived; and since everything whose causes are not perceived is still unknown by nature and must be investigated, it follows necessarily that what is not unknown has causes which are perceived.

Regarding the first of Averroes's arguments—that if there are no observed efficient causes, then some acts have no agents—Ghazali would say, as he does in the extract Alverroes was refuting in the above quotation, "in reality, there is no other cause but God." Note that this reply need not deny natural causality, but only subordinate it to God's will, thus making room for divine intervention and miracles. This position no doubt entails that the acts of those who carry out God's particular interventions do not involve individual responsibility, but these sorts of acts would not be the rule in human life.

Averroes's second argument appears to be this: Take any item. If its cause is not perceived, then the item is unknown. Hence, if it is not the case that the item is unknown—that is, if the item is known—then it is not the case that its cause is not perceived—that is, its cause is perceived. But some items are known. Hence, their causes are perceived. Ghazali could respond that this argument begs the question, for at least two things are at issue here. One is whether *there is a cause of the unknown item,* and the first premise presupposes it. The other is whether *there is a cause of any known item whose perception makes the item known,* and using the second premise to infer the conclusion presupposes it.

Averroes's argument, however, is based on the assumption that "it is self-evident that all events have four causes, agent, form, matter, and end, and that they are necessary for the existence of the effects." This, he postulates, is an assumption shared by philosophers and theologians alike, and using it, he attempts to show that Ghazali's position is self-defeating:

> Now intelligence is nothing but the perception of things with their causes, and in this it distinguishes itself from all the other faculties of apprehension, and he who denies causes must deny the intellect. Logic implies the existence of causes and effects, and knowledge of these effects can only be rendered perfect through knowledge of their causes. Denial of causes implies the denial of knowledge, and denial of knowledge implies that nothing in this world can be really known. . . . The man who denies the necessity of any item of knowledge must admit that even this, his own affirmation, is not necessary knowledge.

Averroes accepts the existence of knowledge that is not necessary but is based "on slight evidence," yet is imagined to be necessary; this he calls "habit." However, he cautions that if this were the only kind of knowledge, it would yield nothing but regularities, and this would have some unacceptable implications. For example, it would allow us to know how someone will act most of the time, but we could not infer the person's traits from these behavioral regularities: "there would be no wisdom in the world from which it might be inferred that its agent was wise" (see Selections 24 and 25, and the relevant discussions in Section B).

Our next selection, "Of Probability; and the Idea of Cause and Effect" by David Hume (1711–1776), deals with the topic just discussed. Hume argues that causation amounts to two relations between objects: contiguity and succession. Thus, he denies causation-at-a-distance and asserts that the cause always precedes the effect—at least in the sense that the cause begins to happen before its effect begins to happen. Concerning the need for a connection between the objects, Hume writes:

> . . . I turn the object on all sides, in order to discover the nature of this necessary connexion, and find the impression, or impressions, from which its idea may be deriv'd. When I cast my eye on the *known qualities* of objects, I immediately discover that the relation of cause and effect depends not in the least on *them*. When I consider their *relations*, I can find none but those of contiguity and succession.

Unlike Ghazali, Hume is hesitant to let "the despair of success" make him assert that the idea of a necessary connection in causality is not based on experience. His search leads him to assess the various arguments that have been offered to prove that every event has a cause. He concludes that the causal law "Every event has a cause" is not intuitive. Nor can it be deductively proven. Hume's suggestion is that the idea of a necessary connection in causality can be explained by explaining our inference of such a necessary connection. Accordingly, we should answer such questions as the following: What makes us infer that there is a necessary connection between two events when we observe particular instances of one event related by contiguity and succession to particular instances of the other?

Hume's suggestion points to the problem of induction, which can be formulated by asking: What is the justification for our inferring that features observed among the items of a sample—say, the color red observed to cover three balls taken out of a box—are features of all the items in the general class—that is, that red covers all the balls in the box? Incidentally, discussion of this problem here confirms a point made at the outset of this book: that the various areas of philosophy we have used to structure this book sometimes overlap. Notice how the idea of cause and effect, which is characteristic of this part of the book (What Is the Universe Really Like?) leads to the problem of induction, which connects with the investigation of knowledge undertaken in Part II (What Are Truth, Knowledge, and Faith, and How Are They Related?).

But let us return to our discussion of induction as related to the idea of cause and effect. As Hume, who was an empiricist, understands it, the laws of nature that make sense of the necessary connection presumably involved in causality are to be established by induction in the narrow sense of generalization from examination of particular instances. This view is rightly questioned by the contemporary Latin American physicist and philosopher Mario Bunge in our next selection, "Induction in Science." Bunge argues that scientific research follows "a *via media* between the extremes of inductivism and deductivism." Concerning the proper place of induction in science, he concludes that

> induction—which is but one of the kinds of plausible reasoning—contributes modestly to the framing of scientific hypotheses, but is indispensable for their test, or rather at the empirical stage of their test.

Bunge equates induction with generalization on the basis of case examination and points out that it would exclude the following from strictly inductive reasoning: arguments by analogy; generalizations involving new concepts; induction by elimination (i.e., the refutation of hypotheses because their observational implications do not match the available empirical evidence); interpolation (i.e., specification); and reduction (i.e., the acceptance of a conditional's antecedent because its consequent has been repeatedly verified). Yet all these are plausible forms of inference in science.

Besides, Bunge argues, induction in the strict sense (enumerative induction) does not serve as a form of reasoning leading to inventions, elementary generalizations involving dispositions such as that of sugar to dissolve in water, and hypotheses containing theoretical predicates such as "attraction" and "energy." He says:

> The hypothesis "Copper is a good conductor" . . . contains the class terms "copper" and "conductor" (a dispositional term). Its generalization "All metals are good conductors" . . . refers . . . to the conceptually open class of metals known and knowable. We do not accept the latter generalization just because of its inductive support, weighty as it is, but also—perhaps mainly—because the theoretical study of the crystal structure of metals and the electron gas inside them shows us that the predicate "metal" . . . is functionally associated with the predicate "conductor." This association, which transcends the Humean juxtaposition of properties, is expressed in law statements belonging to the theory of solid state.

In addition, Bunge points out the significant role of deduction in testing hypotheses, that of theorification (or the inclusion of a hypothesis into a hypothetico-deductive system) and the involvement of other noninductive forms of reasoning in establishing hypotheses.

Now, given all this, there are good reasons to question Hume's contention that the necessary connections presumably involved in causal relations must be established inductively. A plausible alternative is to say that such necessary connections (where the necessity involved is not logical but scientific or physical) are established through the confirmation of scientific laws. And those laws are confirmed using various forms of reasoning, of which inductive reasoning is only one minor, albeit significant, form.

D.   ARE WE EVER FREE TO DO AS WE CHOOSE?

Section C of this essay centers on the notion that every event has a cause—that is, that whenever an event occurs, there is a cause for its occurrence. Those who hold this notion are called "determinists." Determinism raises the following questions: Given any act an individual performs, and supposing that the act is an event, could the individual have acted differently? Are we ever in control of our conduct, or is our conduct always caused by factors beyond our control? These questions formulate the problem of free will, and various answers have been given to them.

Some argue that we have free will and are sometimes in control of our actions, because even though our actions are events, they do not have causes; that is, determinism is false. Yet: If determinism is false and, at least concerning our actions, ours is a world of sheer chance, how can we ever be in control of our actions?

Others argue that determinism is true and we are never in control of our conduct. This doctrine is called "incompatibilism." It says that determinism and free will are incompatible; that is, they are mutually exclusive. Still others uphold a doctrine called "compatibilism," which says that though determinism is true (that is, all our acts are determined), some of us are sometimes in control of our conduct (that is, some of our acts are also free). In other words, as its name indicates, compatibilism is the view that free will is compatible with determinism.

Our next selection, written during the Italian Renaissance by Lorenzo Valla (1405–1457), discusses a point related to the ones just raised. The "Dialogue on Free Will" between Lorenzo Valla and Antonio Glarea puts the problem as follows:

> *Lor.* What do you ask me to explain to you?
>
> *Ant.* Whether the foreknowledge of God stands in the way of free will and whether Boethius has correctly argued this question.

We can state the problem thus: If everything we do is predictable—if God can foresee it all—how can we ever do anything other than what we do? And if we cannot, then how can we have free will, for a necessary feature of free will is the ability to do something other than what one does. As Glarea puts it, "if [God] sees that Judas will be a traitor, it is impossible for him not to become a traitor, that is, it is necessary for Judas to betray."

Valla's reply suggests one solution to the problem: "You say God foresaw that Judas would be a traitor, but did He on that account induce him to betrayal?" Glarea objects that if, as assumed, Judas's betrayal was foreknown, then it must have been necessary. In response, Valla argues that from the fact that our volitions are foreknown, it does not follow that they are necessary. For if knowing that something will happen makes it come about, "surely knowing something *is* just as easily makes the same thing *be*." Indeed, Valla argues, this also applies to the past.

Glarea's response is that where the future is concerned, things are different. Perhaps the best way to describe his position is by a modern analogy. Imagine that God is a moviemaker and our actions are those of characters in the movie as the movie rolls. By this analogy, foreknowledge of what we will do is like having already seen the movie. And given that this is the movie it is, having already seen it amounts to having seen that there is no way in which we, the characters, could ever do anything but what we do in the movie. Yet, if we have free will, the future should be alterable.

Valla questions the distinction between an unalterable past and present and an alterable future. No doubt, whatever will happen will indeed happen. Yet, he argues, it could happen otherwise. He says:

> Something that can happen and something that will happen are very different. . . . Though I can do otherwise than will happen, nevertheless I shall not do otherwise; and it was in Judas' power not to sin even though it was foreseen that he would, but he preferred to sin, which it was foreseen would happen. Thus foreknowledge is valid and free will abides.

In addition, the dialogue suggests the view that we are not responsible for our inborn nature, but only for what, given our nature, we choose to do.

One might object that if we do not choose our nature, then we do not have free will. But does the notion of free will that this objection presupposes make sense? It calls for one to be already existing in order to be able to choose the initial features of one's nature at the same time that, since one is supposed to be choosing *initial* features—that is, those with which one will come into existence—one is nonexistent. This contradiction makes the notion of choice of one's own nature nonsensical, and therefore not a good basis for the objection stated above.

Our next selection, Roderick W. Chisholm's "Responsibility and Avoidability," focuses on the particular choices that we make in life and argues that, if determinism is true, then every choice we make could not have been avoided. Hence, we have no responsibility for any of our choices. In other words, we have no free will. Chisholm considers various objections to this argument, but finds them all wanting.

An objection that he fails to consider could take the following form. Certainly, if determinism is true, given the circumstances—meaning such things as our wants, preferences, and inclination to reflect at a given time—we could not at this time choose anything other than what we choose. But does the notion of free will or responsibility involved in this objection make any sense? A reason to believe it does not is that it calls for our being someone other than who we are at choosing time so that we can choose otherwise, while remaining the same person all along. This contradiction makes the notion nonsensical, and hence, not a good basis for an objection like the one stated above.

One could object that such a defense of free will amounts to denying it, not to showing how it is compatible with determinism. However, the defense only denies absurd notions of free will. It does not deny, for example, that given our current psychological makeup, we can decide to change some of its elements (e.g., irritability) by relying on other of its elements (e.g., reflectiveness and a desire to avoid unjustified conflicts), so as to make better choices in the future. What is nonsensical is to say that free will requires the ability to choose ourselves in advance of our existence or to be someone other than we are at the time we are making any particular choice.

E.   WHAT IS IT TO BE A PERSON?

Section D examined the notion that persons have free will and responsibility concerning moral, legal, and lifestyle matters. Indeed, being a person who has moral responsibility is crucial to accountability for everything from making a business or governmental decision to committing a crime. It is also crucial to everything about ourselves that we are proud of—say, doing a job well, improving our character through the years, or acquiring an education painstakingly. As these examples make plain, the concepts of *person* and *personal identity* are central to our lives. Without them, free will and responsibility would be inapplicable or of little value. Accordingly, various questions arise: What is it to be the person I am? What features are involved in having a personal identity? These, and related questions, are discussed in "Personal Identity" by John Locke (1632–1704). He characterizes a person at the outset of this selection:

> . . . we must consider what *person* stands for;—which, I think, is a thinking intelligent being, that has reason and reflection, and can consider itself as itself, the same thinking thing, in different times and places; which it does only by that consciousness which is inseparable from thinking, and, as it seems to me, essential to it: it being impossible for anyone to perceive without *perceiving* that he does perceive.

But, as Locke realizes, though this is an account of what it is to be the same person through time and space, it does not characterize what it is to be this particular person rather than any other—that is, to have personal identity, not simply personhood. Accordingly, he writes that

> since consciousness always accompanies thinking, and it is that which makes everyone to be what he calls self, and thereby distinguishes himself from all other thinking things, in this alone consists personal identity, i.e. the sameness of a rational being: and as far as this consciousness can be extended backwards to any past action or thought, so far reaches the identity of that person; it is the same self now it was then; and it is by the same self with this present one that now reflects on it, that that action was done.

A difficulty with this account is that our awareness lacks continuity. After all, we forget, we do not always reflect on our past, and we fall asleep. In any of these cases, as Locke acknowledges, the consciousness crucial to being one and the same person is interrupted. He meets this problem by saying that

> as far as any intelligent being *can* repeat the idea of any past action with the same consciousness it had of it at first, and with the same consciousness it has of any present action; so far it is the same personal self.

This position has the consequence that "if it be possible for the same man to have distinct incommunicable consciousness at different times, it is past doubt the same man would at different times make different persons." Locke argues for this view on the grounds that it is presupposed in our laws, which do not punish individuals for acts they performed when they were not themselves, or "beside themselves."

The obvious objection here is that our laws punish the sober for what they did while drunk, even if they cannot recall what they did while drunk. Locke attempts to explain this objection away by saying that we punish such people because we cannot know for sure that they were indeed unaware of what they were doing and have no recollection of it afterward. If we could know for sure that they knew nothing of what they had done, then we would not punish them. But is this so? Some would reply that people are legally punished for what they did when drunk because they are held responsible for having allowed themselves to get drunk, regardless of whether they can recall what they did while in that state or how they got there. Thus, the legal system presupposes that, throughout the process, these people are persons—and responsible—regardless of whether they are conscious of having done that for which they are being punished.

Another objection is that Locke overstated his case to begin with by saying that in order to be the same person who performed a certain act in the past, one must be able to recall it *with the same consciousness one has of any present action.* Since the ability to recall in this manner is uncommon, many an individual who is, and has steadily been, one and the same person according to the standards of ordinary people and the law, would turn out to be many persons according to Locke's standard.

One might grant that Locke's point is overstated, but argue that being the same person, and different from other persons through time and space, is a matter of psychological connectedness. This conception makes room for degrees of personhood, in which consciousness plays a significant, though not the only, role. Consciousness, then, will be involved in whether, and to what extent, an individual undergoes such things as character changes, loss of memory, and the entanglement of memories with the products of imagination.[6]

Various questions arise in trying to explain the notion of psychological connectedness: Is it of a causal nature? Is it an association of atomic psychological components? Does it involve emergent properties? Our next selection, "The Nature of the Self" by the Latin American philosopher Risieri Frondizi (1910–1983), provides some material for addressing these questions. The author agrees with Locke in not focusing on the category of substance. His reason for this is that none of the three classic characteristics of this concept—immutability, simplicity, and independence—belong to the self. Frondizi also finds wanting atomistic accounts that consider the self to be a collection of experiences. First, the notion of a psychic atom—say, a given instant's consciousness of a past act—is "a mere arbitrary instant in an uninterrupted process." And second, "the aggregation of atoms, which can have only a relationship of juxtaposition one to another, looks like a grotesque caricature of the real organic unity of the self."

Having taken this position, Frondizi is faced with explaining the organic unity he attributes to the self and showing why this sort of unity is preferable to that involved in atomistic accounts. He explains the organic unity of the self by appealing to the notion of Gestalt used in Gestalt psychology. First, the self is a structural whole with qualities not possessed by any of its elements, just as a melody "possesses qualities which cannot be found in any of the notes, for it can be transposed without being changed into another melody." Indeed, a melody can be transposed, not just an octave higher or lower, but from one scale to another, and the latter transposition, to use musicians' language, gives it a different character. Second, the self (like the melody), though not reducible to its members (notes), is dependent on them. For without them, it ceases to exist, and the removal of one member changes the whole thing as well as the member removed.

An objector might argue that the member removed is not changed, for though removing it (a note) changes the structural whole (the melody), it does not change the member itself. Frondizi, however, could reply that though it is still the same member (note); it is not what it was in the context of the structural whole (the melody). In other words, it has lost certain functions characteristic of its being part of that whole. In any case, what is at issue here is the unity of the self, not what would happen to individual elements of the self were they to cease being parts of the self.

Frondizi relies on these features to explain why the organic unity of the self is best understood as the concrete dynamic structure of a Gestalt ("a symphony rather than a painting"). He further relies on our ordinary experiences:

> . . . our daily experiences supply all the material we require—the sound and sight of the sea is exhilarating one day and depressing the next; the same piece of music arouses in us different reactions according to the situation in which we hear it; . . . the memory of a disagreement with a friend, which irritated us so much when it happened, may now provoke only an indifferent smile. . . .
>
> These undeniable data of the psychic life are founded on the fact that the self is not a sum of experiences or an aggregate of parts in juxtaposition but a structure. . . . The self is not departmentalized—like modern bureaucracy—but constitutes an organic unity with intimate, complex, and varied interrelations.

Frondizi holds that the immediate components of this structure are substructures rather than psychic atoms, and that changes in the self result not just in rearrangements among its components but also in "the *tensions* produced by the reciprocal play of influences." Some of these influences are our past experiences. Others are traits or steady attitudes we may have developed:

> Thus, the perceptions which we have at this moment depend on our former state. . . . What is more, the stable nature of the self colors the transitory state. There are people who give the impression of seeing the world in the rosiest colors, whatever the tint of the spectacles they wear, and there are others who see clouds in the clearest sky.

Frondizi argues that this account of the self, unlike atomistic accounts, helps solve various paradoxes. One paradox he claims it helps solve is that of the supposed permanence and obvious mutability of the self. If so, then Frondizi's account of the self should also help solve the previously discussed problems of personal identity. It should, for example, account for psychological connectedness as a structural connectedness that is concrete, dynamic, and involves causal interactions. In order to assess the extent to which Frondizi's account helps solve this problem, we would have to analyze and integrate some notions previously discussed—individual character, personality, and physique—with current psychological studies. No doubt this would be a worthwhile line of inquiry, but we cannot pursue it here. In Part IV, however, we will discuss some of these concepts in a moral context.[7]

NOTES

[1] Delia Goetz and Sylvanus G. Morley (trans.), *Popol Vuh* (Norman: University of Oklahoma Press, 1950, 1975), p. 81. This is a translation from Adrián Recinos's Spanish translation.

[2] Irene Nicholson, *Mexican and Central American Mythology* (London and New York: Paul Hamlyn, 1967), p. 20.

[3] For a discussion of this point, see John Hick, *The Existence of God* (London: Macmillan, 1964), pp. 6–7 and 80–82.

[4] For a discussion of these and related points see Ibid., pp. 7–12.

[5] Robert Andrews, *The Concise Columbia Dictionary of Quotations* (New York: Columbia University Press, 1987, 1989), p. 111.

[6] For a discussion of this notion as it relates to contemporary problems of personal identity, see Derek Parfit, "Personal Identity," *Philosophical Review* vol. 80, no 1 (January 1971), pp. 3–27.

[7] For an initial outline of the topics that need to be addressed, see my *Character Traits*, Ph.D. diss. (Madison: University of Wisconsin-Madison, 1975).

St. Anselm (1033–1109)
PROSLOGIUM

The author formulates two deductive arguments, one for God's existence and the other for the impossibility of conceiving that God does not exist. Anselm's arguments are discussed in Section A of the introductory essay to Part III.

READING QUESTIONS

In reading the selection, try to answer the following questions and identify the passages that support your answers:

1. What theses does Anselm defend in the selection?
2. What arguments does he give for these theses?
3. Are the arguments valid?
4. Are they sound?
5. Can the arguments be modified so as to make them sound?

Reprinted from *St. Anselm Basic Writings,* trans. S. N. Deane, (La Salle, IL.: Open Court, 1968), 2nd. ed., pp. 47–50; 52–57, by permission of Open Court Publishing Company, La Salle, Illinois. Copyright © 1968 Open Court Publishing Company.

PREFACE

In this brief work the author aims at proving in a single argument the existence of God, and whatsoever we believe of God.—The difficulty of the task.—The author writes in the person of one who contemplates God, and seeks to understand what he believes. To this work he had given this title: Faith Seeking Understanding. He finally named it Proslogium,—that is, A Discourse.

After I had published, at the solicitous entreaties of certain brethren, a brief work (the *Monologium*) as an example of meditation on the grounds of faith, in the person of one who investigates, in a course of silent reasoning with himself, matters of which he is ignorant; considering that this book was knit together by the linking of many arguments, I began to ask myself whether there might be found a single argument which would require no other for its proof than itself alone; and alone would suffice to demonstrate that God truly exists, and that there is a supreme good requiring nothing else, which all other things require for their existence and well-being; and whatever we believe regarding the divine Being.

Although I often and earnestly directed my thought to this end, and at some times that which I sought seemed to be just within my reach, while again it wholly evaded my mental vision, at last in despair I was about to cease, as if from the search for a thing which could not be found. But when I wished to exclude this thought altogether, lest, by busying my mind to no purpose, it should keep me from other thoughts, in which I might be successful; then more and more, though I was unwilling and shunned it, it began to force itself upon me, with a kind of importunity. So, one day, when I was exceedingly wearied with resisting its importunity, in the very conflict of my thoughts, the proof of which I had despaired offered itself, so that I eagerly embraced the thoughts which I was strenuously repelling.

Thinking, therefore, that what I rejoiced to have found, would, if put in writing, be welcome to some readers, of this very matter, and of some others, I have written the following treatise, in the person of one who strives to lift his mind to the contemplation of God, and seeks to understand what he believes. In my judgment, neither this work nor the other, which I mentioned above, deserved to be called a book, or to bear the name of an author; and yet I thought they ought not to be sent forth without some title by which they might, in some sort, invite one into whose hands they fell to their perusal. I accordingly gave each a title, that the first might be known as, An Example of Meditation on the Grounds of Faith, and its sequel as, Faith Seeking Understanding. But, after both had been copied by many under these titles, many urged me, and especially Hugo, the reverend Archbishop of Lyons, who discharges the apostolic office in Gaul, who instructed me to this effect on his apostolic authority— to prefix my name to these writings. And that this might be done more fitly, I named the first, *Monologium*, that is, A Soliloquy; but the second, *Proslogium,* that is, A Discourse.

CHAPTER I

Exhortation of the mind to the contemplation of God.—It casts aside cares, and excludes all thoughts save that of God, that it may seek Him. Man was created to see God. Man cannot seek God, unless God himself teaches him; nor find him, unless he reveals himself. God created man in his image, that he might be mindful of him, think of him, and love him. The believer does not seek to understand, that he may believe, but he believes that he may understand: for unless he believed he would not understand.

Up now, slight man! flee, for a little while, thy occupations; hide thyself, for a time, from thy disturbing thoughts. Cast aside, now, thy burdensome cares, and put away thy toilsome business. Yield room for some little time to God; and rest for a little time in him. Enter the inner chamber of thy mind; shut out all thoughts save that of God, and such as can aid thee in seeking him; close thy door and seek him. Speak now, my whole heart! speak now to God, saying, I seek thy face; thy face, Lord, will I seek (Psalms xxvii.8). And come thou now, O Lord my God, teach my heart where and how it may seek thee, where and how it may find thee.

Lord, if thou art not here, where shall I seek thee, being absent? But if thou art everywhere, why do I not see thee present? Truly thou dewllest in unapproachable light. But where is unapproachable light, or how shall I come to it? Or who shall lead me to that light and into it, that I may see thee in it? Again, by what marks, under what form, shall I seek thee? I have never seen thee, O Lord, my God; I do not know thy form. What, O most high Lord, shall this man do, an exile far from thee? What shall thy servant do, anxious in his love of thee, and cast out afar from thy face? He pants to see thee, and thy face is too far from him. He longs to come to thee, and thy dwelling-place is inaccessible. He is eager to find

thee, and knows not thy place. He desires to seek thee, and does not know thy face. Lord, thou art my God, and thou art my Lord, and never have I seen thee. It is thou that has made me, and has made me anew, and hast bestowed upon me all the blessings I enjoy; and not yet do I know thee. Finally, I was created to see thee, and not yet have I done that for which I was made.

. . . Be it mine to look up to the light, even from afar, even from the depths. Teach me to seek thee, and reveal thyself to me, when I seek thee, for I cannot seek thee, except thou teach me, nor find thee, except thou reveal thyself. Let me seek thee in longing, let me long for thee in seeking; let me find thee in love, and love thee in finding. Lord, I acknowledge and I thank thee that thou hast created me in this thine image, in order that I may be mindful of thee, may conceive of thee, and love thee; but that image has been so consumed and wasted away by vices, and obscured by the smoke of wrong-doing, that it cannot achieve that for which it was made, except thou renew it, and create it anew. I do not endeavor, O Lord, to penetrate thy sublimity, for in no wise do I compare my understanding with that; but I long to understand in some degree thy truth, which my heart believes and loves. For I do not seek to understand that I may believe, but I believe in order to understand. For this also I believe,—that unless I believed, I should not understand.

CHAPTER II

Truly there is a God, although the fool hath said in his heart, There is no God.

And so, Lord, do thou, who dost give understanding to faith, give me, so far as thou knowest it to be profitable, to understand that thou art as we believe; and that thou art that which we believe. And, indeed, we believe that thou art a being than which nothing greater can be conceived. Or is there no such nature, since the fool hath said in his heart, there is no God? (Psalms xiv. I). But, at any rate, this very fool, when he hears of this being of which I speak—a being than which nothing greater can be conceived—understands what he hears, and what he understands is in his understanding; although he does not understand it to exist.

For, it is one thing for an object to be in the understanding, and another to understand that the object exists. When a painter first conceives of what he will afterwards perform, he has it in his understanding, but he does not yet understand it to be, because he has not yet performed it. But after he has made the painting, he both has it in his understanding, and he understands that it exists, because he has made it.

Hence, even the fool is convinced that something exists in the understanding, at least, than which nothing greater can be conceived. For, when he hears of this, he understands it. And whatever is understood, exists in the understanding. And assuredly that, than which nothing greater can be conceived, cannot exist in the understanding alone. For, suppose it exists in the understanding alone: then it can be conceived to exist in reality; which is greater.

Therefore, if that, than which nothing greater can be conceived, exists in the understanding alone, the very being, than which nothing greater can be conceived, is one, than which a greater can be conceived. But obviously this is impossible. Hence, there is no doubt that there exists a being, than which nothing greater can be conceived, and it exists both in the understanding and in reality.

CHAPTER III

God cannot be conceived not to exist.—God is that, than which nothing greater can be conceived.—That which can be conceived not to exist is not God.

And it assuredly exists so truly, that it cannot be conceived not to exist. For, it is possible to conceive of a being which cannot be conceived not to exist; and this is greater than one which can be conceived not to exist. Hence, if that, than which nothing greater can be conceived, can be conceived not to exist, it is not that, than which nothing greater can be conceived. But this is an irreconcilable contradiction. There is, then, so truly a being than which nothing greater can be conceived to exist, that it cannot even be conceived not to exist; and this being thou art, O Lord, our God.

So truly, therefore, dost thou exist, O Lord, my God, that thou canst not be conceived not to exist; and rightly. For, if a mind could conceive of a being better than thee, the creature would rise above the Creator; and this is most absurd. And, indeed, whatever else there is, except thee alone, can be conceived not to exist. To thee alone, therefore, it belongs to exist more truly than all other beings, and hence in a higher degree than all others. For, whatever else exists does not exist so truly, and hence in a less degree it belongs to it to exist. Why, then, has the fool said in his heart, there is no God (Psalms xiv. I), since it is so evident, to a rational mind, that

thou dost exist in the highest degree of all? Why, except that he is dull and a fool?

CHAPTER IV

How the fool has said in his heart what cannot be conceived.—A thing may be conceived in two ways: (I) when the word signifying it is conceived; (2) when the thing itself is understood. As far as the word goes, God can be conceived not to exist; in reality he cannot.

But how has the fool said in his heart what he could not conceive; or how is it that he could not conceive what he said in his heart? since it is the same to say in the heart, and to conceive.

But, if really, nay, since really, he both conceived, because he said in his heart; and did not say in his heart, because he could not conceive; there is more than one way in which a thing is said in the heart or conceived. For, in one sense, an object is conceived, when the word signifying it is conceived; and in another, when the very entity, which the object is, is understood.

In the former sense, then, God can be conceived not to exist; but in the latter, not at all. For no one who understands what fire and water are can conceive fire to be water, in accordance with the nature of the facts themselves, although this is possible according to the words. So, then, no one who understands what God is can conceive that God does not exist; although he says these words in his heart, either without any, or with some foreign, signification. For, God is that than which a greater cannot be conceived. And he who thoroughly understands this, assuredly understands that this being so truly exists, that not even in concept can it be non-existent. Therefore, he who understands that God so exists, cannot conceive that he does not exist.

I thank thee, gracious Lord, I thank thee; because what I formerly believed by thy bounty, I now so understand by thine illumination, that if I were unwilling to believe that thou dost exist, I should not be able not to understand this to be true.

CHAPTER V

God is whatever it is better to be than not to be; and he, as the only self-existent being, creates all things from nothing.

What art thou, then, Lord God, than whom nothing greater can be conceived? But what art thou, except that which, as the highest of all beings, alone exists through itself, and creates all other things from nothing? For, whatever is not this is less than a thing which can be conceived of. But this cannot be conceived of thee. What good, therefore, does the supreme Good lack, through which every good is? Therefore, thou art just, truthful, blessed, and whatever it is better to be than not to be. For it is better to be just than not just; better to be blessed than not blessed.

CHAPTER VI

How God is sensible (*sensibilis*) although he is not a body.—God is sensible, omnipotent, compassionate, passionless; for it is better to be these than not be. He who in any way knows, is not improperly said in some sort to feel.

But, although it is better for thee to be sensible, omnipotent, compassionate, passionless, than not to be these things; how art thou sensible, if thou art not a body; or omnipotent, if thou hast not all powers; or at once compassionate and passionless? For, if only corporeal things are sensible, since the senses encompass a body and are in a body, how art thou sensible, although thou art not a body, but a supreme Spirit, who is superior to body? But, if feeling is only cognition, or for the sake of cognition,—for he who feels obtains knowledge in accordance with the proper functions of his senses; as through sight, of colors; through taste, of flavors,—whatever in any way cognises is not inappropriately said, in some sort, to feel.

Therefore, O Lord, although thou art not a body, yet thou art truly sensible in the highest degree in respect of this, that thou dost cognise all things in the highest degree; and not as an animal cognises, through a corporeal sense.

Gaunilon de Marmoutier (?–1083)
IN BEHALF OF THE FOOL

In this reply to Anselm, Gaunilon argues that the mere fact that I understand what is said does not entail that what I understand is in my understanding. In particular, the fact that I understand the definition of God does not entail that God exists in my understanding. If so, a crucial premise of Anselm's arguments is false, and hence, his arguments are unsound. A discussion of Gaunilon's position can be found in Section A of the introductory essay to Part III.

READING QUESTIONS

In reading the selection, try to answer the following questions and identify the passages that support your answers:

1. What thesis does Gaunilon defend in the selection?
2. What reasons does he give for this thesis?
3. Are the reasons good?
4. Why or why not?
5. Can existence be a defining property of God?

AN ANSWER TO THE ARGUMENT OF ANSELM IN THE PROSLOGIUM, BY GAUNILON, A MONK OF MARMOUTIER

1. If one doubts or denies the existence of a being of such a nature that nothing greater than it can be conceived, he receives this answer:

The existence of this being is proved, in the first place, by the fact that he himself, in his doubt or denial regarding this being, already has it in his understanding; for in hearing it spoken of he understands what is spoken of. It is proved, therefore, by the fact that what he understands must exist not only in his understanding, but in reality also.

And the proof of this is as follows.—It is a greater thing to exist both in the understanding and in reality than to be in the understanding alone. And if this being is in the understanding alone, whatever has even in the past existed in reality will be greater than this being. And so that which was greater than all beings will be less than some being, and will not be greater than all: which is a manifest contradiction.

And hence, that which is greater than all, already proved to be in the understanding, must exist not only in the understanding, but also in reality: for otherwise it will not be greater than all other beings.

2. The fool might make this reply:

This being is said to be in my understanding already, only because I understand what is said. Now could it not with equal justice be said that I have in my understanding all manner of unreal objects, having absolutely no existence in themselves, because I understand these things if one speaks of them, whatever they may be?

Unless indeed it is shown that this being is of such a character that it cannot be held in concept like all unreal objects, or objects whose existence is uncertain: and hence I am not able to conceive of it when I hear of it, or to hold it in concept; but I must understand it and have it in my understanding; because, it seems, I cannot conceive of it in any other way than by understanding it, that is, by comprehending in my knowledge its existence in reality.

But if this is the case, in the first place there will be no distinction between what has precedence in time—namely, the having of an object in the understanding—and what is subsequent in time—namely, the understanding that an object exists; as in the example of the picture, which exists first in the mind of the painter, and afterwards in his work.

Moreover, the following assertion can hardly be accepted: that this being, when it is spoken of and heard of, cannot be conceived not to exist in the way in which even God can be conceived not to exist. For if this is impossible, what was the object of this argument against one who doubts or denies the existence of such a being?

Finally, that this being so exists that it cannot be perceived by an understanding convinced of its own indubitable existence, unless this being is afterwards conceived of—this should be proved to me by an indisputable argument, but not by that which you have advanced: namely, that what I understand, when I hear it, already is in my understanding. For thus in my understanding, as I still think, could be all sorts of things whose existence is uncertain, or which do not exist at all, if some one whose words I should understand mentioned them. And so much the more if I should be deceived, as often happens, and believe in them: though I do not yet believe in the being whose existence you would prove.

3. Hence, your example of the painter who already has in his understanding what he is to paint cannot agree with this argument. For the picture, before it is made, is contained in the artificer's art itself; and any such thing, existing in the art of the artificer, is nothing but a part of his understanding itself. A joiner, St. Augustine says, when he is about to make a box in fact, first has it in his art. The box which is made in fact is not life; but the box which exists in his art is life. For the artificer's soul lives, in which all these things are, before they are produced. Why, then, are these things life in the living soul of the artificer, unless because they are nothing else than the knowledge or understanding of the soul itself?

With the exception, however, of those facts which are known to pertain to the mental nature, whatever, on being heard and thought out by the understanding, is perceived to be real, undoubtedly that real object is one thing, and the understanding itself, by which the object is grasped, is another. Hence, even if it were true that there is a being than which a greater is inconceivable: yet to this being, when heard of and understood, the not yet created picture in the mind of the painter is not analogous.

4. Let us notice also the point touched on above, with regard to this being which is greater than all which can be conceived, and which, it is said, can be none other than God himself. I, so far as actual knowledge of the object, either from its specific or general character, is concerned, am as little able to conceive of this being when I hear of it, or to have

it in my understanding, as I am to conceive of or understand God himself: whom, indeed, for this very reason I can conceive not to exist. For I do not know that reality itself which God is, nor can I form a conjecture of that reality from some other like reality. For you yourself assert that that reality is such that there can be nothing else like it.

For, suppose that I should hear something said of a man absolutely unknown to me, of whose very existence I was unaware. Through that special or general knowledge by which I know what man is, or what men are, I could conceive of him also, according to the reality itself, which man is. And yet it would be possible, if the person who told me of him deceived me, that the man himself, of whom I conceived, did not exist; since that reality according to which I conceived of him, though a no less indisputable fact, was not that man, but any man.

Hence, I am not able, in the way in which I should have this unreal being in concept or in understanding, to have that being of which you speak in concept or in understanding, when I hear the word *God* or the words, *a being greater than all other beings*. For I can conceive of a man according to a fact that is real and familiar to me: but of God, or a being greater than all others, I could not conceive at all, except merely according to the word. And an object can hardly or never be conceived according to the word alone.

For when it is so conceived, it is not so much the word itself (which is, indeed, a real thing—that is, the sound of the letters and syllables) as the signification of the word, when heard, that is conceived. But it is not conceived as by one who knows what is generally signified by the word; by whom, that is, it is conceived according to a reality and in true conception alone. It is conceived as by a man who does not know the object, and conceives of it only in accordance with the movement of his mind produced by hearing the word, the mind attempting to image for itself the signification of the word that is heard. And it would be surprising if in the reality of fact it could ever attain to this.

Thus, it appears, and in no other way, this being is also in my understanding, when I hear and understand a person who says that there is a being greater than all conceivable beings. So much for the assertion that this supreme nature already is in my understanding.

5. But that this being must exist, not only in the understanding but also in reality, is thus proved to me:

If it did not so exist, whatever exists in reality would be greater than it. And so the being which has been already proved to exist in my understanding, will not be greater than all other beings.

I still answer: if it should be said that a being which cannot be even conceived in terms of any fact, is in the understanding, I do not deny that this being is, accordingly, in my understanding. But since through this fact it can in no wise attain to real existence also, I do not yet concede to it that existence at all, until some certain proof of it shall be given.

For he who says that this being exists, because otherwise the being which is greater than all will not be greater than all, does not attend strictly enough to what he is saying. For I do not yet say, no, I even deny or doubt that this being is greater than any real object. Nor do I concede to it any other existence than this (if it should be called existence) which it has when the mind, according to a word merely heard, tries to form the image of an object absolutely unknown to it.

How, then, is the veritable existence of that being proved to me from the assumption, by hypothesis, that it is greater than all other beings? For I should still deny this, or doubt your demonstration of it, to this extent, that I should not admit that this being is in my understanding and concept even in the way in which many objects whose real existence is uncertain and doubtful, are in my understanding and concept. For it should be proved first that this being itself really exists somewhere; and then, from the fact that it is greater than all, we shall not hesitate to infer that it also subsists in itself.

6. For example: it is said that somewhere in the ocean is an island, which, because of the difficulty, or rather the impossibility, of discovering what does not exist, is called the lost island. And they say that this island has an inestimable wealth of all manner of riches and delicacies in greater abundance than is told of the Islands of the Blest; and that having no owner or inhabitant, it is more excellent than all other countries, which are inhabited by mankind, in the abundance with which it is stored.

Now if some one should tell me that there is such an island, I should easily understand his words, in which there is no difficulty. But suppose that he went on to say, as if by logical inference: "You can no longer doubt that this island which is more excellent than all lands exists somewhere, since you have no doubt that it is in your understanding. And since it is more excellent not to be in the understanding alone, but to exist both in the understanding and in reality, for this reason it must exist. For if it does not exist, any land which really exists will be more excellent than it; and so the island already understood by you to be more excellent will not be more excellent."

If a man should try to prove to me by such reasoning that this island truly exists, and that its existence should no longer be doubted, either I should believe that he was jesting, or I know not which I ought to regard as the greater fool: myself, supposing that I should allow this proof; or him, if he should suppose that he had established with any certainty the existence of this island. For he ought to show first that the hypothetical excellence of this island exists as a real and indubitable fact, and in no wise as any unreal object, or one whose existence is uncertain, in my understanding.

7. This, in the mean time, is the answer the fool could make to the arguments urged against him. When he is assured in the first place that this being is so great that its non-existence is not even conceivable, and that this in turn is proved on no other ground than the fact that otherwise it will not be greater than all things, the fool may make the same answer, and say:

When did I say that any such being exists in reality, that is, a being greater than all others?—that on this ground it should be proved to me that it also exists in reality to such a degree that it cannot even be conceived not to exist? Whereas in the first place it should be in some way proved that a nature which is higher, that is, greater and better, than all other natures, exists; in order that from this we may then be able to prove all attributes which necessarily the being that is greater and better than all possesses.

Moreover, it is said that the non-existence of this being is inconceivable. It might better be said, perhaps, that its non-existence, or the possibility of its non-existence, is unintelligible. For according to the true meaning of the word, unreal objects are unintelligible. Yet their existence is conceivable in the way in which the fool conceived of the non-existence of God. I am most certainly aware of my own existence; but I know, nevertheless, that my non-existence is possible. As to that supreme being, moreover, which God is, I understand without any doubt both his existence, and the impossibility of his non-existence. Whether, however, so long as I am most positively aware of my existence, I can conceive of my non-existence, I am not sure. But if I can, why can I not conceive of the non-existence of whatever else I know with the same certainty? If, however, I cannot, God will not be the only being of which it can be said, it is impossible to conceive of his non-existence.

8. The other parts of this book are argued with such truth, such brilliancy, such grandeur; and are so replete with usefulness, so fragrant with a certain perfume of devout and holy feeling, that though there are matters in the beginning which, however rightly sensed, are weakly presented, the rest of the work should not be rejected on this account. The rather ought these earlier matters to be reasoned more cogently, and the whole to be received with great respect and honor.

St. Thomas Aquinas (c. 1224–1274)
THE EXISTENCE OF GOD

Aquinas advances various criticisms against Anselm's arguments and argues that the existence of God can be proved inductively. He offers five inductive proofs for God's existence: from motion, from the nature of an efficient cause, from possibility and necessity, from gradation, and from the governance of the world. Aquinas's proofs are discussed in Section A of the introductory essay to Part III.

READING QUESTIONS

In reading the selection, try to answer the following questions and identify the passages that support your answers:

1. What thesis does Aquinas defend in the selection?
2. What arguments does he give for this thesis?
3. Are the arguments sound?
4. Why or why not?
5. If Aquinas's arguments are good, do they prove with certainty that God exists?

Reprinted from Anton C. Pegis (ed.), *Writings of Saint Thomas Aquinas* (New York: Random House, 1945), "The Summa Theologica," Part I, Question II: "The Existence of God." Reprinted by permission of Richard J. Pegis.

FIRST ARTICLE

Whether the Existence of God Is Self-Evident?

We proceed thus to the First Article:—

Objection 1. It seems that the existence of God is self-evident. For those things are said to be self-evident to us the knowledge of which exists naturally in us, as we can see in regard to first principles. But as Damascene says, *the knowledge of God is naturally implanted in all.*[1] Therefore the existence of God is self-evident.

Obj. 2. Further, those things are said to be self-evident which are known as soon as the terms are known, which the Philosopher says is true of the first principles of demonstration.[2] Thus, when the nature of a whole and of a part is known, it is at once recognized that every whole is greater than its part. But as soon as the signification of the name *God* is understood, it is at once seen that God exists. For by this name is signified that thing than which nothing greater can be conceived. But that which exists actually and mentally is greater than that which exists only mentally. Therefore, since as soon as the name *God* is understood it exists mentally, it also follows that it exists actually. Therefore the proposition *God exists* is self-evident.

Obj. 3. Further, the existence of truth is self-evident. For whoever denies the existence of truth grants that truth does not exist: and, if truth does not exist, then the proposition *Truth does not exist* is true: and if there is anything true, there must be truth. But God is truth itself: *I am the way, the truth, and the life (Jo.* xiv. 6). Therefore *God exists* is self-evident.

On the contrary, No one can mentally admit the opposite of what is self-evident, as the Philosopher states concerning the first principles of demonstration.[3] But the opposite of the proposition *God is* can be mentally admitted: *The fool said in his heart, There is no God (Ps.* lii. 1). Therefore, that God exists is not self-evident.

I answer that, A thing can be self-evident in either of two ways: on the one hand, self-evident in itself, though not to us; on the other, self-evident in itself, and to us. A proposition is self-evident because the predicate is included in the essence of the subject: *e.g., Man is an animal,* for animal is contained in the essence of man. If, therefore, the essence of the predicate and subject be known to all, the proposition will be self-evident to all; as is clear with regard to the first principles of demonstration, the terms of which are certain common notions that no one is ignorant of, such as being and non-being, whole and part, and the like. If, however, there are some to whom the essence of the predicate and subject is unknown, the proposition will be self-evident in itself, but not to those who do not know the meaning of the predicate and subject of the proposition. Therefore, it happens, as Boethius says, that there are some notions of the mind which are common and self-evident only to the learned, as that incorporeal substances are not in space.[4] Therefore I say

---

[1]   *De Fide Orth.,* I, 1; 3 (PG 94, 789: 793).

[2]   *Post. Anal.,* I, 3 (72b 18).

[3]   *Metaph.,* III, 3 (1005b 11); *Post. Anal.,* I, 10 (76b 23).

[4]   *De Hebdom.* (PL 64, 1311).

that this proposition, *God exists,* of itself is self-evident, for the predicate is the same as the subject, because God is His own existence as will be hereafter shown.[5] Now because we do not know the essence of God, the proposition is not self-evident to us, but needs to be demonstrated by things that are more known to us, though less known in their nature—namely, by His effects.

Reply Obj. 1. To know that God exists in a general and confused way is implanted in us by nature, inasmuch as God is man's beatitude. For man naturally desires happiness, and what is naturally desired by man is naturally known by him. This, however, is not to know absolutely that God exists; just to know that someone is approaching is not the same as to know that Peter is approaching, even though it is Peter who is approaching; for there are many who imagine that man's perfect good, which is happiness, consists in riches, and others in pleasures, and others in something else.

Reply Obj. 2. Perhaps not everyone who hears this name *God* understands it to signify something than which nothing greater can be thought, seeing that some have believed God to be a body.[6] Yet, granted that everyone understands that by this name *God* is signified something than which nothing greater can be thought, nevertheless, it does not therefore follow that he understands that what the name signifies exists actually, but only that it exists mentally. Nor can it be argued that it actually exists, unless it be admitted that there actually exists something than which nothing greater can be thought; and this precisely is not admitted by those who hold that God does not exist.

Reply Obj. 3. The existence of truth in general is self-evident, but the existence of a Primal Truth is not self-evident to us.

SECOND ARTICLE

Whether It Can Be Demonstrated That God Exists?

We proceed thus to the Second Article:—

Objection 1. It seems that the existence of God cannot be demonstrated. For it is an article of faith that God exists. But what is of faith cannot be demonstrated, because a demonstration produces scientific

knowledge, whereas faith is of the unseen, as is clear from the Apostle (*Heb.* xi. 1). Therefore it cannot be demonstrated that God exists.

Obj. 2. Further, essence is the middle term of demonstration. But we cannot know in what God's essence consists, but solely in what it does not consist, as Damascene says.[7] Therefore we cannot demonstrate that God exists.

Obj. 3. Further, if the existence of God were demonstrated, this could only be from His effects. But His effects are not proportioned to Him, since He is infinite and His effects are finite, and between the finite and infinite there is no proportion. Therefore, since a cause cannot be demonstrated by an effect not proportioned to it, it seems that the existence of God cannot be demonstrated.

On the contrary, The Apostle says: *The invisible things of Him are clearly seen, being understood by the things that are made* (*Rom.* i. 20). But this would not be unless the existence of God could be demonstrated through the things that are made; for the first thing we must know of anything is, whether it exists.

I answer that, Demonstration can be made in two ways: One is through the cause, and is called *propter quid,* and this is to argue from what is prior absolutely. The other is through the effect, and is called a demonstration *quia;* this is to argue from what is prior relatively only to us. When an effect is better known to us than its cause, from the effect we proceed to the knowledge of the cause. And from every effect the existence of its proper cause can be demonstrated, so long as its effects are better known to us; because, since every effect depends upon its cause, if the effect exists, the cause must preexist. Hence the existence of God, in so far as it is not self-evident to us, can be demonstrated from those of His effects which are known to us.

Reply Obj. 1. The existence of God and other like truths about God, which can be known by natural reason, are not articles of faith, but are preambles to the articles; for faith presupposes natural knowledge, even as grace presupposes nature and perfection the perfectible. Nevertheless, there is nothing to prevent a man, who cannot grasp a proof, from accepting, as a matter of faith, something which in itself is capable of being scientifically known and demonstrated.

Reply Obj. 2. When the existence of a cause is demonstrated from an effect, this effect takes the place of the definition of the cause in proving the

---

[5] Q. 3, a. 4.
[6] Cf. *C. G.,* I, 20.—Cf. also Aristotle, *Phys.,* I, 4 (187a 12); St. Augustine, *De Civit. Dei,* VIII, 2; 5 (PL 41, 226; 239); *De Haeres.,* 46, 50, 86 (PL 42, 35; 39; 46); *De Genesi ad Litt.,* X, 25 (PL 34, 427); Maimonides, *Guide,* I, 53 (p. 72).

[7] *De Fide Orth.,* I, 4 (PG 94, 800).

cause's existence. This is especially the case in regard to God, because, in order to prove the existence of anything, it is necessary to accept as a middle term the meaning of the name, and not its essence, for the question of its essence follows on the question of its existence. Now the names given to God are derived from His effects, as will be later shown.[8] Consequently, in demonstrating the existence of God from His effects, we may take for the middle term the meaning of the name *God*.

Reply Obj. 3. From effects not proportioned to the cause no perfect knowledge of that cause can be obtained. Yet from every effect the existence of the cause can be clearly demonstrated, and so we can demonstrate the existence of God from His effects; though from them we cannot know God perfectly as He is in His essence.

THIRD ARTICLE

Whether God Exists?

We proceed thus to the Third Article:—

Objection 1. It seems that God does not exist; because if one of two contraries be infinite, the other would be altogether destroyed. But the name *God* means that He is infinite goodness. If, therefore, God existed, there would be no evil discoverable; but there is evil in the world. Therefore God does not exist.

Obj. 2. Further, it is superfluous to suppose that what can be accounted for by a few principles has been produced by many. But it seems that everything we see in the world can be accounted for by other principles, supposing God did not exist. For all natural things can be reduced to one principle, which is nature; and all voluntary things can be reduced to one principle, which is human reason, or will. Therefore there is no need to suppose God's existence.

On the contrary, It is said in the person of God: *I am Who am* (*Exod.* iii. 14).

I answer that, The existence of God can be proved in five ways.

The first and more manifest way is the argument from motion. It is certain, and evident to our senses, that in the world some things are in motion. Now whatever is moved is moved by another, for nothing can be moved except it is in potentiality to that towards which it is moved; whereas a thing moves inas-

much as it is in act. For motion is nothing else than the reduction of something from potentiality to actuality. But nothing can be reduced from potentiality to actuality, except by something in a state of actuality. Thus that which is actually hot, as fire, makes wood, which is potentially hot, to be actually hot, and thereby moves and changes it. Now it is not possible that the same thing should be at once in actuality and potentiality in the same respect, but only in different respects. For what is actually hot cannot simultaneously be potentially hot; but it is simultaneously potentially cold. It is therefore impossible that in the same respect and in the same way a thing should be both mover and moved, *i.e.,* that it should move itself. Therefore, whatever is moved must be moved by another. If that by which it is moved be itself moved, then this also must needs be moved by another, and that by another again. But this cannot go on to infinity, because then there would be no first mover, and, consequently, no other mover, seeing that subsequent movers move only inasmuch as they are moved by the first mover; as the staff moves only because it is moved by the hand. Therefore it is necessary to arrive at a first mover, moved by no other; and this everyone understands to be God.

The second way is from the nature of efficient cause. In the world of sensible things we find there is an order of efficient causes. There is no case known (neither is it, indeed, possible) in which a thing is found to be the efficient cause of itself; for so it would be prior to itself, which is impossible. Now in efficient causes it is not possible to go on to infinity, because in all efficient causes following in order, the first is the cause of the intermediate cause, and the intermediate is the cause of the ultimate cause, whether the intermediate cause be several, or one only. Now to take away the cause is to take away the effect. Therefore, if there be no first cause among efficient causes, there will be no ultimate, nor any intermediate, cause. But if in efficient causes it is possible to go on to infinity, there will be no first efficient cause, neither will there be an ultimate effect, nor any intermediate efficient causes; all of which is plainly false. Therefore it is necessary to admit a first efficient cause, to which everyone gives the name of God.

The third way is taken from possibility and necessity, and runs thus. We find in nature things that are possible to be and not to be, since they are found to be generated, and to be corrupted, and consequently, it is possible for them to be and not to be. But it is impossible for these always to exist, for that

---

[8] Q. 13, a, I.

which can not-be at some time is not. Therefore, if everything can not-be, then at one time there was nothing in existence. Now if this were true, even now there would be nothing in existence, because that which does not exist begins to exist only through something already existing. Therefore, if at one time nothing was in existence, it would have been impossible for anything to have begun to exist; and thus even now nothing would be in existence—which is absurd. Therefore, not all beings are merely possible, but there must exist something the existence of which is necessary. But every necessary thing either has its necessity caused by another, or not. Now it is impossible to go on to infinity in necessary things which have their necessity caused by another, as has been already proved in regard to efficient causes. Therefore we cannot but admit the existence of some being having of itself its own necessity, and not receiving it from another, but rather causing in others their necessity. This all men speak of as God.

The fourth way is taken from the gradation to be found in things. Among beings there are some more and some less good, true, noble, and the like. But *more* and *less* are predicated of different things according as they resemble in their different ways something which is the maximum, as a thing is said to be hotter according as it more nearly resembles that which is hottest; so that there is something which is truest, something best, something noblest, and, consequently, something which is most being, for those things that are greatest in truth are greatest in being, as it is written in *Metaph.* ii.[9] Now the maximum in any genus is the cause of all in that genus,

as fire, which is the maximum of heat, is the cause of all hot things, as is said in the same book.[10] Therefore there must also be something which is to all beings the cause of their being, goodness, and every other perfection; and this we call God.

The fifth way is taken from the governance of the world. We see that things which lack knowledge, such as natural bodies, act for an end, and this is evident from their acting always, or nearly always, in the same way, so as to obtain the best result. Hence it is plain that they achieve their end, not fortuitously, but designedly. Now whatever lacks knowledge cannot move towards an end, unless it be directed by some being endowed with knowledge and intelligence; as the arrow is directed by the archer. Therefore some intelligent being exists by whom all natural things are directed to their end; and this being we call God.

Reply Obj. 1. As Augustine says: *Since God is the highest good, He would not allow any evil to exist in His works, unless His omnipotence and goodness were such as to bring good even out of evil.*[11] This is part of the infinite goodness of God, that He should allow evil to exist, and out of it produce good.

Reply Obj. 2. Since nature works for a determinate end under the direction of a higher agent, whatever is done by nature must be traced back to God as to its first cause. So likewise whatever is done voluntarily must be traced back to some higher cause other than human reason and will, since these can change and fail; for all things that are changeable and capable of defect must be traced back to an immovable and self-necessary first principle, as has been shown.

---

[9]   *Metaph.* Ia, I (993b 30).

[10]   *Ibid.* (993b 25).

[11]   *Enchir.*, XI (PL 40, 236).

David Hume (1711–1776)
DESIGN, EVIL, AND GOD'S EXISTENCE

Hume argues that probabilistic arguments for God's existence cannot be based strictly on scientific probability. He also says that if such arguments prove anything, it is not the existence of the omnipotent, omniscient, absolutely benevolent and just personal God of the Judeo-Christian tradition. Rather, they prove, at best, the existence of an intelligent being who could be other than omniscient, omnipotent, just, or benevolent. Hume's positions are discussed in Section A of the introductory essay to Part III.

READING QUESTIONS

In reading the selection, try to answer the following questions and identify the passages that support your answers:

1. What thesis does Hume defend in the selection?
2. What arguments does he give for this thesis?
3. Are the arguments sound?
4. Why or why not?
5. Are Aquinas's arguments open to Hume's criticisms?

Reprinted with the permission of Macmillan Publishing Company from David Hume, *Dialogues Concerning Natural Religion*, ed. by Norman Kemp Smith (Indianapolis, IN: Bobbs-Merrill, 1965), Part II, pp. 141–151, and Part X, pp. 193–202. Copyright © 1947 by Thomas Nelson & Sons, Ltd.

. . . , CLEANTHES, said DEMEA, I hope, is not by any means a question among us. No man; no man, at least, of common sense, I am persuaded, ever entertained a serious doubt with regard to a truth so certain and self-evident. The question is not concerning the *being* but the *nature of God*. This, I affirm, from the infirmities of human understanding, to be altogether incomprehensible and unknown to us. The essence of that supreme mind, his attributes, the manner of his existence, the very nature of his duration; these and every particular, which regards so divine a Being, are mysterious to men. Finite, weak, and blind creatures, we ought to humble ourselves in his august presence, and, conscious of our frailties, adore in silence his infinite perfections, which eye hath not seen, ear hath not heard, neither hath it entered into the heart of man to conceive them. They are covered in a deep cloud from human curiosity: It is profaneness to attempt penetrating through these sacred obscurities: And next to the impiety of denying his existence, is the temerity of prying into his nature and essence, decrees and attributes.

But lest you should think, that my *piety* has here got the better of my *philosophy*, I shall support my opinion, if it needs any support, by a very great authority. I might cite all the divines almost, from the foundation of Christianity, who have ever treated of this or any other theological subject: But I shall confine myself, at present, to one equally celebrated for piety and philosophy. It is FATHER MALEBRANCHE, who, I remember, thus expresses himself.[1] "One ought not so much (says he) to call God a spirit, in order to express positively what he is, as in order to signify that he is not matter. He is a Being infinitely perfect: Of this we cannot doubt. But in the same manner as we ought not to imagine, even supposing him corporeal, that he is cloathed with a human body, as the ANTHROPOMORPHITES asserted, under colour that that figure was the most perfect of any; so neither ought we to imagine, that the Spirit of God has human ideas, or bears *any* resemblance to our spirit; under colour that we know nothing more perfect than a human mind. We ought rather to believe, that as he comprehends the perfections of matter without being material . . . he comprehends also the perfections of created spirits, without being spirit, in the manner we conceive spirit: That his true name is, *He that is,* or in other words, Being without restriction, All Being, the Being infinite and universal."

After so great an authority, DEMEA, replied PHILO, as that which you have produced, and a thousand more, which you might produce, it would appear ridiculous in me to add my sentiment, or express my approbation of your doctrine. But surely, where reasonable men treat these subjects, the question can

[1] *Recherche de la vérité, liv.* 3, chap. 9

never be concerning the *being,* but only the *nature* of the Deity. The former truth, as you well observe, is unquestionable and self-evident. Nothing exists without a cause; and the original cause of this universe (whatever it be) we call GOD; and piously ascribe to him every species of perfection. Whoever scruples this fundamental truth deserves every punishment, which can be inflicted among philosophers, to wit, the greatest ridicule, contempt and disapprobation. But as all perfection is entirely relative, we ought never to imagine, that we comprehend the attributes of this divine Being, or to suppose, that his perfections have any analogy or likeness to the perfections of a human creature. Wisdom, thought, design, knowledge; these we justly ascribe to him; because these words are honourable among men, and we have no other language or other conceptions, by which we can express our adoration of him. But let us beware, lest we think, that our ideas any wise correspond to his perfections, or that his attributes have any resemblance to these qualities among men. He is infinitely superior to our limited view and comprehension; and is more the object of worship in the temple, than of disputation in the schools.

In reality, CLEANTHES, continued he, there is no need of having recourse to that affected scepticism, so displeasing to you, in order to come at this determination. Our ideas reach no farther than our experience: We have no experience of divine attributes and operations: I need not conclude my syllogism: You can draw the inference yourself. And it is a pleasure to me (and I hope to you too) that just reasoning and sound piety here concur in the same conclusion, and both of them establish the adorably mysterious and incomprehensible nature of the supreme Being.

Not to lose any time in circumlocutions, said CLEANTHES, addressing himself to DEMEA, much less in replying to the pious declamations of PHILO; I shall briefly explain how I conceive this matter. Look round the world: Contemplate the whole and every part of it: You will find it to be nothing but one great machine, subdivided into an infinite number of lesser machines, which again admit of subdivisions, to a degree beyond what human senses and faculties can trace and explain. All these various machines, and even their most minute parts, are adjusted to each other with an accuracy, which ravishes into admiration all men, who have ever contemplated them. The curious adapting of means to ends, throughout all nature, resembles exactly, though it much ex-

ceeds, the productions of human contrivance; of human design, thought, wisdom, and intelligence. Since therefore the effects resemble each other, we are led to infer, by all the rules of analogy, that the causes also resemble; and that the Author of nature is somewhat similar to the mind of man; though possessed of much larger faculties, proportioned to the grandeur of the work, which he has executed. By this argument *a posteriori,* and by this argument alone, we do prove at once the existence of a Deity, and his similarity to human mind and intelligence.

I shall be so free, CLEANTHES, said DEMEA, as to tell you, that from the beginning, I could not approve of your conclusion concerning the similarity of the Deity to men; still less can I approve of the mediums, by which you endeavor to establish it. What! No demonstration of the being of a God! No abstract arguments! No proofs *a priori!* Are these, which have hitherto been so much insisted on by philosophers, all fallacy, all sophism? Can we reach no farther in this subject than experience[2] and probability? I will not say, that this is betraying the cause of a Deity: But surely, by this affected candour, you give advantage to atheists, which they never could obtain, by the mere dint of argument and reasoning.

What I chiefly scruple in this subject, said PHILO, is not so much, that all religious arguments are by CLEANTHES reduced to experience, as that they appear not to be even the most certain and irrefragable of that inferior kind. That a stone will fall, that fire will burn, that the earth has solidity, we have observed a thousand and a thousand times; and when any new instance of this nature is presented, we draw without hesitation the accustomed inference. The exact similarity of the cases gives us a perfect assurance of a similar event; and a stronger evidence is never desired nor sought after. But wherever you depart, in the least, from the similarity of the cases, you diminish proportionably the evidence; and may at last bring it to a very weak *analogy,* which is confessedly liable to error and uncertainty. After having experienced the circulation of the blood in human creatures, we make no doubt that it takes place in Titius and Mævius: But from its circulation in frogs and fishes, it is only a presumption, though a strong one, from analogy, that it takes place in men and other animals. The analogical reasoning is much weaker, when we infer the circulation of the sap in vegetables from our experience that the blood cir-

---

[2] [moral evidence *substituted for* experience, and *then* experience *restored*]

culates in animals; and those, who hastily followed that imperfect analogy, are found, by more accurate experiments, to have been mistaken.

If we see a house, CLEANTHES, we conclude, with the greatest certainty, that it had an architect or builder; because this is precisely that species of effect, which we have experienced to proceed from that species of cause. But surely you will not affirm, that the universe bears such a resemblance to a house, that we can with the same certainty infer a similar cause, or that the analogy is here entire and perfect. The dissimilitude is so striking, that the utmost you can here pretend to is a guess, a conjecture, a presumption concerning a similar cause; and how that pretension will be received in the world, I leave you to consider.

It would surely be very ill received, replied CLEANTHES; and I should be deservedly blamed and detested, did I allow that the proofs of a Deity amounted to no more than a guess or conjecture. But is the whole adjustment of means to ends in a house and in the universe so slight a resemblance? The œconomy of final causes? The order, proportion, and arrangement of every part? Steps of a stair are plainly contrived, that human legs may use them in mounting; and this inference is certain and infallible. Human legs are also contrived for walking and mounting; and this inference, I allow, is not altogether so certain, because of the dissimilarity which you remark; but does it, therefore, deserve the name only of presumption or conjecture?

Good God! cried DEMEA, interrupting him, where are we? Zealous defenders of religion allow, that the proofs of a Deity fall short of perfect evidence! And you, PHILO, on whose assistance I depended, in proving the adorable mysteriousness of the divine nature, do you assent to all these extravagant opinions of CLEANTHES? For what other name can I give them? Or why spare my censure, when such principles are advanced, supported by such an authority, before so young a man as PAMPHILUS?

You seem not to apprehend, replied PHILO, that I argue with CLEANTHES in his own way; and by showing him the dangerous consequences of his tenets, hope at last to reduce him to our opinion. But what sticks most with you, I observe, is the representation which CLEANTHES has made of the argument *a posteriori;* and finding that that argument is likely to escape your hold and vanish into air, you think it so disguised that you can scarcely believe it to be set in its true light. Now, however much I may dissent, in other respects, from the dangerous principles of

CLEANTHES, I must allow, that he has fairly represented that argument; and I shall endeavour so to state the matter to you, that you will entertain no farther scruples with regard to it.

Were a man to abstract from every thing which he knows or has seen, he would be altogether incapable, merely from his own ideas, to determine what kind of scene the universe must be, or to give the preference to one state or situation of things above another. For as nothing, which he clearly conceives, could be esteemed impossible or implying a contradiction, every chimera of his fancy would be upon an equal footing; nor could he assign any just reason, why he adheres to one idea or system, and rejects the others, which are equally possible.

Again; after he opens his eyes, and contemplates the world, as it really is, it would be impossible for him, at first, to assign the cause of any one event; much less, of the whole of things or of the universe. He might set his fancy a rambling; and she might bring him in an infinite variety of reports and representations. These would all be possible; but being all equally possible, he would never, of himself, give a satisfactory account for his preferring one of them to the rest. Experience alone can point out to him the true cause of any phenomenon.

Now according to this method of reasoning, DEMEA, it follows (and is, indeed, tacitly allowed by CLEANTHES himself) that order, arrangement, or the adjustment of final causes is not, of itself, any proof of design; but only so far as it has been experienced to proceed from that principle. For aught we can know *a priori,* matter may contain the source or spring of order originally, within itself, as well as mind does; and there is no more difficulty in conceiving, that the several elements, from an internal unknown cause, may fall into the most exquisite arrangement, than to conceive that their ideas, in the great, universal mind, from a like internal, unknown cause, fall into that arrangement. The equal possibility of both these suppositions is allowed. By experience we find (according to CLEANTHES), that there is a difference between them. Throw several pieces of steel together, without shape or form; they will never arrange themselves so as to compose a watch: Stone, and mortar, and wood, without an architect, never erect a house. But the ideas in a human mind, we see, by an unknown, inexplicable œconomy, arrange themselves so as to form the plan of a watch or house. Experience, therefore, proves, that there is an original principle of order in mind, not in matter. From similar effects we infer similar causes. The adjustment of means to ends[3] is alike in the universe, as in a machine of human contrivance. The causes, therefore, must be resembling.

I was from the beginning scandalised, I must own, with this resemblance, which is asserted, between the Deity and human creatures; and must conceive it to imply such a degradation of the supreme Being as no sound theist could endure. With your assistance, therefore, DEMEA, I shall endeavour to defend what you justly call the adorable mysteriousness of the divine nature, and shall refute this reasoning of CLEANTHES; provided he allows, that I have made a fair representation of it.

When CLEANTHES had assented, PHILO, after a short pause, proceeded in the following manner.

That all inferences, CLEANTHES, concerning fact, are founded on experience, and that all experimental reasonings are founded on the supposition, that similar causes prove similar effects, and similar effects similar causes; I shall not, at present, much dispute with you. But observe, I entreat you, with what extreme caution all just reasoners proceed in the transferring of experiments to similar cases. Unless the cases be exactly similar, they repose no perfect confidence in applying their past observation to any particular phenomenon. Every alteration of circumstances occasions a doubt concerning the event; and it requires new experiments to prove certainly, that the new circumstances are of no moment or importance. A change in bulk, situation, arrangement, age, disposition of the air, or surrounding bodies; any of these particulars may be attended with the most unexpected consequences: And unless the objects be quite familiar to us, it is the highest temerity to expect with assurance, after any of these changes, an event similar to that which before fell under our observation. The slow and deliberate steps of philosophers, here, if any where, are distinguished from the precipitate march of the vulgar, who, hurried on by the smallest similitude, are incapable of all discernment or consideration.

But can you think, CLEANTHES, that your usual phlegm and philosophy have been preserved in so wide a step as you have taken, when you compared to the universe houses, ships, furniture, machines; and from their similarity in some circumstances inferred a similarity in their causes? Thought, design, intelligence, such as we discover in men and other

animals, is no more than one of the springs and principles of the universe, as well as heat or cold, attraction or repulsion, and a hundred others, which fall under daily observation. It is an active cause, by which some particular parts of nature, we find, produce alterations on other parts. But can a conclusion, with any propriety, be transferred from parts to the whole? Does not the great disproportion bar all comparison and inference? From observing the growth of a hair, can we learn any thing concerning the generation of a man? Would the manner of a leaf's blowing, even though perfectly known, afford us any instruction concerning the vegatation of a tree?

But allowing that we were to take the *operations* of one part of nature upon another for the foundation of our judgment concerning the *origin* of the whole (which never can be admitted) yet why select so minute, so weak, so bounded a principle as the reason and design of animals is found to be upon this planet? What peculiar privilege has this little agitation of the rain which we call thought, that we must thus make it the model of the whole universe? Our partiality in our own favour does indeed present it on all occasions: But sound philosophy ought carefully to guard against so natural an illusion.

So far from admitting, continued PHILO, that the operations of a part can afford us any just conclusion concerning the origin of the whole, I will not allow any one part to form a rule for another part, if the latter be very remote from the former. Is there any reasonable ground to conclude, that the inhabitants of other planets possess thought, intelligence, reason, or any thing similar to these faculties in men? When nature has so extremely diversified her manner of operation in this small globe; can we imagine, that she incessantly copies herself throughout so immense a universe? And if thought, as we may well suppose, be confined merely to this narrow corner, and has even there so limited a sphere of action; with what propriety can we assign it for the original cause of all things? The narrow views of a peasant, who makes his domestic œconomy the rule for the government of kingdoms, is in comparison a pardonable sophism.

But were we ever so much assured, that a thought and reason, resembling the human, were to be found throughout the whole universe, and were its activity elsewhere vastly greater and more commanding than it appears in this globe: Yet I cannot see, why the operations of a world, constituted, arranged, ad-

---

[3] [means to ends *for* final causes]

justed, can with any propriety be extended to a world, which is in its embryo-state, and is advancing towards that constitution and arrangement. By observation, we know somewhat of the œconomy, action, and nourishment of a finished animal; but we must transfer with great caution that observation to the growth of a fœtus in the womb, and still more, to the formation of an animalcule in the loins of its male parent. Nature, we find, even from our limited experience, possesses an infinite number of springs and principles, which incessantly discover themselves on every change of her position and situation. And what new and unknown principles would actuate her in so new and unknown a situation as that of the formation of a universe, we cannot, without the utmost temerity, pretend to determine.

[A very small part of this great system, during a very short time, is very imperfectly discovered to us: And do we thence pronounce decisively concerning the origin of the whole?][4]

Admirable conclusion! Stone, wood, brick, iron, brass have not, at this time, in this minute globe of earth, an order or arrangement without human art and contrivance: Therefore the universe could not originally attain its order and arrangement, without something similar to human art. But is a part of nature a rule for another part very wide of the former? Is it a rule for the whole?[5] Is a very small part a rule for the universe? Is nature in one situation, a certain rule for[6] nature in another situation, vastly different from the former?

And can you blame me, CLEANTHES, if I here imitate the prudent reserve of SIMONIDES, who, according to the noted story,[7] being asked by HIERO, *What God was?* desired a day to think of it, and then two days more; and after that manner continually prolonged the term, without ever bringing in his definition or description? Could you even blame me, if I had answered at first, *that I did not know,* and was sensible that this subject lay vastly beyond the reach of my faculties? You might cry out sceptic and raillier as much as you pleased: But having found, in so many other subjects, much more familiar, the imperfections and even contradictions of human reason, I never should expect any success from its feeble conjectures, in a subject, so sublime, and so remote from

the sphere of our observation. When two *species* of objects have always been observed to be conjoined together, I can *infer,* by custom, the existence of one wherever I *see* the existence of the other: And this I call an argument from experience. But how this argument can have place, where the objects, as in the present case,[8] are single, individual, without parallel, or specific resemblance, may be difficult to explain. And will any man tell me with a serious countenance, that an orderly universe must arise from some thought and art, like the human; because we have experience of it? To ascertain this reasoning, it were requisite, that we had experience of the origin of the worlds; and it is not sufficient surely, that we have seen ships and cities arise from human art and contrivance. . . .

PHILO was proceeding in this vehement manner, somewhat between jest and earnest, as it appeared to me; when he observed some signs of impatience in CLEANTHES, and then immediately stopped short. What I had to suggest, said CLEANTHES, is only that you would not abuse terms, or make use of popular expressions to subvert philosophical reasonings. You know, that the vulgar often distinguish reason from experience, even where the question relates only to matter of fact and existence; though it is found, where that *reason* is properly analysed, that it is nothing but a species of experience. To prove by experience the origin of the universe from mind is not more contrary to common speech than to prove the motion of the earth from the same principle. And a caviller might raise all the same objections to the COPERNICAN system, which you have urged against my reasonings. Have you other earths, might he say, which you have seen to move? Have. . . .

Yes! cried PHILO, interrupting him, we have other earths. Is not the moon another earth, which we see to turn round its centre? Is not Venus another earth, where we observe the same phenomenon? Are not the revolutions of the sun also a confirmation, from analogy, of the same theory? All the planets, are they not earths, which revolve about the sun? Are not the satellites moons, which move round Jupiter and Saturn, and along with these primary planets, round the sun? These analogies and resemblances, with others, which I have not mentioned, are the sole proofs of the COPERNICAN system: And to you it belongs to consider, whether you have any analogies of the same kind to support your theory.

---

[4] [This paragraph transferred from p. 135 in the original]

[5] [whole *for* world]

[6] [a certain rule for *for* precisely similar to]

[7] [*Cf.* Cicero, *De Natura Deorum,* Bk. 1, 22]

[8] [concerning the origin of the world *omitted*]

In reality, CLEANTHES, continued he, the modern system of astronomy is now so much received by all enquirers, and has become so essential a part even of our earliest education, that we are not commonly very scrupulous in examining the reasons upon which it is founded. It is now become a matter of mere curiosity to study the first writers on that subject, who had the full force of prejudice to encounter, and were obliged to turn their arguments on every side, in order to render them popular and convincing. But if we peruse GALILÆO's famous Dialogues concerning the system of the world, we shall find, that that great genius, one of the sublimest that ever existed, first bent all his endeavours to prove, that there was no foundation for the distinction commonly made between elementary and celestial substances. The schools, proceeding from the illusions of sense, had carried this distinction very far; and had established the latter substances to be ingenerable, incorruptible, unalterable, impassible; and had assigned all the opposite qualities to the former. But GALILÆO, beginning with the moon, proved its similarity in every particular to the earth; its convex figure, its natural darkness when not illuminated, its density, its distinction into solid and liquid, the variations of its phases, the mutual illuminations of the earth and moon, their mutual eclipses, the inequalities of the lunar surface, &c. After many instances of this kind, with regard to all the planets, men plainly saw, that these bodies became proper objects of experience; and that the similarity of their nature enabled us to extend the same arguments and phenomena from one to the other.

In this cautious proceeding of the astronomers, you may read your own condemnation, CLEANTHES; or rather may see, that the subject in which you are engaged exceeds all human reason and enquiry. Can you pretend to show any such similarity between the fabric of a house, and the generation of a universe? Have you ever seen nature in any such situation as resembles the first arrangement of the elements? Have worlds ever been formed under your eye? and have you had leisure to observe the whole progress of the phenomenon, from the first appearance of order to its final consummation? If you have, then cite your experience, and deliver your theory. . . .

It is my opinion, I own, replied DEMEA, that each man feels, in a manner, the truth of religion within his own breast; and from a consciousness of his imbecility and misery, rather than from any reasoning, is led to seek protection from that Being, on whom he and all nature is dependent. So anxious or so tedious are even the best scenes of life, that futurity is still the object of all our hopes and fears. We incessantly look forward, and endeavour, by prayers, adoration, and sacrifice, to appease those unknown powers, whom we find, by experience, so able to afflict and oppress us. Wretched creatures that we are! What resource for us amidst the innumerable ills of life, did not religion suggest some methods of atonement, and appease those terrors, with which we are incessantly agitated and tormented?

I am indeed persuaded, said PHILO, that the best and indeed the only method of bringing every one to a due sense of religion is by just representations of the misery and wickedness of men. And for that purpose a talent of eloquence and strong imagery is more requisite than that of reasoning and argument. For is it necessary to prove, what every one feels within himself? It is only necessary to make us feel it, if possible, more intimately and sensibly.

The people, indeed, replied DEMEA, are sufficiently convinced of this great and melancholy truth. The miseries of life, the unhappiness of man, the general corruptions of our nature, the unsatisfactory enjoyment of pleasures, riches, honours; these phrases have become almost proverbial in all languages. And who can doubt of what all men declare from their own immediate feeling and experience?

In this point, said PHILO, the learned are perfectly agreed with the vulgar; and in all letters, *sacred* and *profane,* the topic of human misery has been insisted on with the most pathetic eloquence that sorrow and melancholy could inspire. The poets, who speak from sentiment, without a system, and whose testimony has therefore the more authority, abound in images of this nature. From HOMER down to Dr. YOUNG, the whole inspired tribe have ever been sensible, that no other representation of things would suit the feeling and observation of each individual.

As to authorities, replied DEMEA, you need not seek them. Look round this library of CLEANTHES. I shall venture to affirm, that, except authors of particular sciences, such as chemistry or botany, who have no occasion to treat of human life, there scarce is one of those innumerable writers, from whom the sense of human misery has not, in some passage or other, extorted a complaint and confession of it. At least, the chance is entirely on that side; and no one author has ever, so far as I can recollect, been so extravagant as to deny it.

There you must excuse me, said PHILO: LEIBNITZ has denied it; and is perhaps the first,[9] who ventured upon so bold and paradoxical an opinion; at least, the first, who made it essential to his philosophical system.

And by being the first, replied DEMEA, might he not have been sensible of his error? For is this a subject in which philosophers can propose to make discoveries, especially in so late an age? And can any man hope by a simple denial (for the subject scarcely admits of reasoning) to bear down the united testimony of mankind, founded on sense and consciousness?

And why should man, added he, pretend to an exemption from the lot of all other animals? The whole earth, believe me, PHILO, is cursed and polluted. A perpetual war is kindled amongst all living creatures. Necessity, hunger, want, stimulate the strong and courageous: Fear, anxiety, terror, agitate the weak and infirm. The first entrance into life gives anguish to the new-born infant and to its wretched parent: Weakness, impotence, distress, attend each stage of that life: And it is at last finished in agony and horror.

Observe too, says PHILO, the curious artifices of nature, in order to embitter the life of every living being. The stronger prey upon the weaker, and keep them in perpetual terror and anxiety. The weaker too, in their turn, often prey upon the stronger, and vex and molest them without relaxation. Consider that innumerable race of insects, which either are bred on the body of each animal, or flying about infix their stings in him. These insects have others still less than themselves, which torment them. And thus on each hand, before and behind, above and below, every animal is surrounded with enemies, which incessantly seek his misery and destruction.

Man alone, said DEMEA, seems to be, in part, an exception to this rule. For by combination in society, he can easily master lions, tigers, and bears, whose greater strength and agility naturally enable them to prey upon him.

On the contrary, it is here chiefly, cried PHILO, that the uniform and equal maxims of nature are most apparent. Man, it is true, can, by combination, surmount all his *real* enemies, and become master of the whole animal creation: But does he not immediately raise up to himself *imaginary* enemies, the daemons of his fancy, who haunt him with superstitious terrors, and blast every enjoyment of life? His pleasure, as he imagines, becomes, in their eyes, a crime: His food and repose give them umbrage and offence: His very sleep and dreams furnish new materials to anxious fear: And even death, his refuge from every other ill, presents only the dread of endless and innumerable woes. Nor does the wolf molest more the timid flock, than superstition does the anxious breast of wretched mortals.

Besides, consider, DEMEA; this very society, by which we surmount those wild beasts, our natural enemies; what new enemies does it not raise to us? What woe and misery does it not occasion? Man is the greatest enemy of man. Oppression, injustice, contempt, contumely, violence, sedition, war, calumny, treachery, fraud; by these they mutually torment each other: And they would soon dissolve that society which they had formed, were it not for the dread of still greater ills, which must attend their separation.

But though these external insults, said DEMEA, from animals, from men, from all the elements, which assault us, form a frightful catalogue of woes, they are nothing in comparison of those, which arise within ourselves, from the distempered condition of our mind and body. How many lie under the lingering torment of diseases? Hear the pathetic enumeration of the great poet.

> Intestine stone and ulcer, colic-pangs,
> Daemoniac frenzy, moping melancholy,
> And moon-struck madness, pining atrophy,
> Marasmus and wide-wasting pestilence.
> Dire was the tossing, deep the groans: DESPAIR
> Tended the sick, busiest from couch to couch.
> And over them triumphant DEATH his dart
> Shook, but delay'd to strike, tho' oft invok'd
> With vows, as their chief good and final hope.[10]

The disorders of the mind, continued DEMEA, though more secret, are not perhaps less dismal and vexatious. Remorse, shame, anguish, rage, disappointment, anxiety, fear, dejection, despair; who has ever passed through life without cruel inroads from these tormentors? How many have scarcely ever felt any better sensations? Labour and poverty, so abhorred by every one, are the certain lot of the far greater number: And those few privileged persons, who enjoy ease and opulence, never reach contentment or true felicity. All the goods of life united

---

[9] That sentiment had been maintained by Dr. King [*De Origine Mali*, 1702] and some few others, before LEIBNITZ, though by none of so great fame as that German philosopher.

[10] [Milton: *Paradise Lost*, XI]

would not make a very happy man: But all the ills united would make a wretch indeed; and any one of them almost (and who can be free from every one), nay often the absence of one good (and who can possess all) is sufficient to render life ineligible.

Were a stranger to drop, in a sudden, into this world, I would show him, as a specimen of its ills, an hospital full of diseases, a prison crowded with malefactors and debtors, a field of battle strowed with carcases, a fleet floundering in the ocean, a nation languishing under tyranny, famine, or pestilence. To turn the gay side of life to him, and give him a notion of its pleasures; whither should I conduct him? to a ball, to an opera, to court? He might justly think, that I was only showing him a diversity of distress and sorrow.

There is no evading such striking instances, said PHILO, but by apologies, which still farther aggravate the charge. Why have all men, I ask, in all ages, complained incessantly of the miseries of life? . . . They have no just reason, says one: These complaints proceed only from their discontented, repining, anxious disposition . . . And can there possibly, I reply, be a more certain foundation of misery, than such a wretched temper?

But if they were really as unhappy as they pretend, says my antagonist, why do they remain in life? . . .

Not satisfied with life, afraid of death.

This is the secret chain, say I, that holds us. We are terrified, not bribed to the continuance of or existence.

It is only a false delicacy, he may insist, which a few spirits indulge, and which has spread these complaints among the whole race of mankind. . . . And what is this delicacy, I ask, which you blame? Is it any thing but a greater sensibility to all the pleasures and pains of life? and if the man of a delicate, refined temper, by being so much more alive than the rest of the world, is only so much more unhappy; what judgment must we form in general of human life?

Let men remain at rest, says our adversary; and they will be easy. They are willing artificers of their own misery. . . . No! reply I; an anxious languor follows their repose: Disappointment, vexation, trouble, their activity and ambition.

I can observe something like what you mention in some others, replied CLEANTHES: But I confess, I feel little or nothing of it in myself; and hope that it is not so common as you represent it.

If you feel not human misery yourself, cried DEMEA, I congratulate you on so happy a singularity.

Others, seemingly the most prosperous, have not been ashamed to vent their complaints in the most melancholy strains. Let us attend to the great, the fortunate Emperor, CHARLES V, when, tired with human grandeur, he resigned all his extensive dominions into the hands of his son. In the last harangue, which he made on that memorable occasion, he publicly avowed, *that the greatest prosperities which he had ever enjoyed, had been mixed with so many adversities, that he might truly say he had never enjoyed any satisfaction or contentment.* But did the retired life, in which he sought for shelter, afford him any greater happiness? If we may credit his son's account, his repentance commenced the very day of his resignation.

CICERO's fortune, from small beginnings, rose to the greatest lustre and renown; yet what pathetic complaints of the ills of life do his familiar letters, as well as philosophical discourses, contain? And suitably to his own experience, he introduces CATO, the great, the fortunate CATO, protesting in his old age, that, had he a new life in his offer, he would reject the present.

Ask yourself, ask any of your acquaintance, whether they would live over again the last ten or twenty years of their life. No! but the next twenty, they say, will be better:

And from the dregs of life, hope to receive
What the first sprightly running could not give.[11]

Thus at last they find (such is the greatness of human misery; it reconciles even contradictions) that they complain, at once, of the shortness of life, and of its vanity and sorrow.

And it is possible, CLEANTHES, said PHILO, that after all these reflections, and infinitely more, which might be suggested, you can still persevere in your anthropomorphism, and assert the moral attributes of the Deity, his justice, benevolence, mercy, and rectitude, to be of the same nature with these virtues in human creatures? His power we allow infinite: Whatever he wills is executed: But neither man nor any other animal are happy: Therefore he does not will their happiness. His wisdom is infinite: He is never mistaken in choosing the means to any end: But the course of nature tends not to human or animal felicity: Therefore it is not established for that purpose. Through the whole compass of human knowledge, there are no inferences more certain and infallible than these. In what respect, then, do

---

[11] Dryden, *Aurengzebe*, Act IV, sc. 1. Hume has written 'hope' *for* 'think']

his benevolence and mercy resemble the benevolence and mercy of men?

EPICURUS's old questions are yet unanswered. Is he willing to prevent evil, but not able? then is he impotent. Is he able, but not willing? then is he malevolent. Is he both able and willing? whence then is evil?

You ascribe, CLEANTHES (and I believe justly) a purpose and intention to nature. But what, I beseech you, is the object of that curious artifice and machinery, which she has displayed in all animals? The preservation alone of individuals and propagation of the species. It seems enough for her purpose, if such a rank be barely upheld in the universe, without any care or concern for the happiness of the members that compose it. No resource for this purpose: No machinery, in order merely to give pleasure or ease: No fund of pure joy and contentment: No indulgence without some want or necessity accompanying it. At least, the few phenomena of this nature are overbalanced by opposite phenomena of still greater importance.

Our sense of music, harmony, and indeed beauty of all kinds, gives satisfaction, without being absolutely necessary to the preservation and propagation of the species. But what racking pains, on the other hand, arise from gouts, gravels, megrims, tooth-aches, rheumatisms; where the injury to the animal-machinery is either small or incurable? Mirth, laughter, play, frolic, seem gratuitous satisfactions, which have no further tendency: Spleen, melancholy, discontent, superstition, are pains of the same nature. How then does the divine benevolence display itself, in the sense of you anthropomorphites? None but we mystics, as you were pleased to call us, can account for this strange mixture of phenomena, by deriving it from attributes, infinitely perfect, but incomprehensible.

And have you at last, said CLEANTHES smiling, betrayed your intentions, PHILO? Your long agreement with DEMEA did indeed a little surprise me; but I find you were all the while erecting a concealed battery against me. And I must confess, that you have now fallen upon a subject worthy of your noble spirit of opposition and controversy. If you can make out the present point, and prove mankind to be unhappy or corrupted, there is an end at once of all religion. For to what purpose establish the natural attributes of the Deity, while the moral are still doubtful and uncertain?

You take umbrage very easily, replied DEMEA, at opinions the most innocent, and the most generally received even amongst the religious and devout themselves: And nothing can be more surprising than to find a topic like this, concerning the wickedness and misery of man, charged with no less than atheism and profaneness. Have not all pious divines and preachers, who have indulged their rhetoric on so fertile a subject: have they not easily, I say, given a solution of any difficulties which may attend it? This world is but a point in comparison of the universe: This life but a moment in comparison of eternity. The present evil phenomena, therefore, are rectified in other regions, and in some future period of existence. And the eyes of men, being then opened to larger views of things, see the whole connection of general laws, and trace, with adoration, the benevolence and rectitude of the Deity, through all the mazes and intricacies of his providence.

No! replied CLEANTHES, No! These arbitrary suppositions can never be admitted, contrary to matter of fact, visible and uncontroverted. Whence can any cause be known but from its known effects? Whence can any hypothesis be proved but from the apparent phenomena? To establish one hypothesis upon another is building entirely in the air; and the utmost we ever attain, by these conjectures and fictions, is to ascertain the bare possibility of our opinion; but never can we, upon such terms, establish its reality.

The only method of supporting divine benevolence (and it is what I willingly embrace) is to deny absolutely the misery and wickedness of man. Your representations are exaggerated: Your melancholy views mostly fictitious: Your inferences contrary to fact and experience. Health is more common than sickness: Pleasure than pain: Happiness than misery. And for one vexation which we meet with, we attain, upon computation, a hundred enjoyments.

Admitting your position, replied PHILO, which yet is extremely doubtful, you must, at the same time, allow, that, if pain be less frequent than pleasure, it is infinitely more violent and durable. One hour of it is often able to outweigh a day, a week, a month of our common insipid enjoyments: And how many days, weeks, and months are passed by several in the most acute torments? Pleasure, scarcely in one instance, is ever able to reach ecstasy and rapture: And in no one instance can it continue for any time at its highest pitch and altitude. The spirits evaporate; the nerves relax; the fabric is disordered; and the enjoyment quickly degenerates into fatigue and uneasiness. But pain often, Good God, how often! rises to torture and agony; and the longer it continues, it becomes still more genuine agony and torture.

Patience is exhausted; courage languishes; melancholy seizes us; and nothing terminates our misery but the removal of its cause, or another event, which is the sole cure of all evil, but which, from our natural folly, we regard with still greater horror and consternation.

But not to insist upon these topics, continued PHILO, though most obvious, certain, and important; I must use the freedom to admonish you, CLEANTHES, that you have put this controversy upon a most dangerous issue, and are unawares introducing a total scepticism into the most essential articles of natural and revealed theology. What! no method of fixing a just foundation for religion, unless we allow the happiness of human life, and maintain a continued existence even in this world, with all our present pains, infirmities, vexations, and follies, to be eligible and desirable! But this is contrary to every one's feeling and experience: It is contrary to an authority so established as nothing can subvert: No decisive proofs can ever be produced against this authority; nor is it possible for you to compute, estimate, and compare all the pains and all the pleasures in the lives of all men and of all animals: And thus by your resting the whole system of religion on a point, which, from its very nature, must for ever be uncertain, you tacitly confess, that that system is equally uncertain.

But allowing you, what never will be believed; at least, what you never possibly[12] can prove, that animal, or at least, human happiness,[13] in this life, exceeds its misery; you have yet done nothing: For this is not, by any means, what we expect from infinite power, infinite wisdom, and infinite goodness. Why is there any misery at all in the world? Not by chance surely. From some cause then. Is it from the intention of the Deity? But he is perfectly benevolent. Is it contrary to his intention? But he is almighty. Nothing can shake the solidity of this reasoning, so short, so clear, so decisive; except we assert, that these

subjects exceed all human capacity, and that our common measures of truth and falsehood are not applicable to them; a topic, which I have all along insisted on, but which you have, from the beginning, rejected with scorn and indignation.

But I will be contented to retire still from this intrenchment:[14] For I deny that you can ever force me in it: I will allow, that pain or misery in man is *compatible* with infinite power and goodness in the Deity, even in your sense of these attributes: What are you advanced by all these concessions? A mere possible compatibility is not sufficient. You must *prove* these pure, unmixed, and uncontrollable attributes from the present mixed and confused phenomena, and from these alone. A hopeful[15] undertaking! Were the phenomena ever so pure and unmixed, yet being finite, they would be insufficient for that purpose. How much more, were they also so jarring and discordant?

Here, CLEANTHES, I find myself at ease in my argument. Here I triumph. Formerly, when we argued concerning the natural attributes of intelligence and design, I needed all my sceptical and metaphysical subtilty to elude your grasp. In many views of the universe, and of its parts, particularly the latter, the beauty and fitness of final causes strike us with such irresistible force, that all objections appear (what I believe[16] they really are) mere cavils and sophisms; nor can we then imagine how it was ever possible for us to repose any weight on them. But there is no view of human life, or of the condition of mankind, from which, without the greatest violence, we can infer the moral attributes, or learn that infinite benevolence, conjoined with infinite power and infinite wisdom, which we must discover by the eyes of faith alone. It is your turn now to tug the labouring oar, and to support your philosophical subtilities against the dictates of plain reason and experience.

---

[12]   [possibly *omitted and then restored*]

[13]   [animal, or at least *added*]

[14]   [retrenchment *for* defence: *altered to* intrenchment *by Hume's nephew*]

[15]   [hopeful *for* strange]

[16]   [I believe *for* perhaps. This alteration may have been made in 1776. *Cf.* above, Appendix C, p. 95.]

Ernest Nagel (1901–1985)
PHILOSOPHICAL CONCEPTS OF ATHEISM

Nagel characterizes atheism as a critique and a denial of the major claims of all varieties of theism. He understands theism as the doctrine that the entire universe owes its existence and persistence to the wisdom and will of a supreme, self-consistent, omnipotent, omniscient, righteous, and benevolent being, who is distinct from, and independent of, what he has created. Nagel criticizes various arguments for the existence of such a being, then argues that atheism is not a merely negative position, but is characterized by a specific sort of intellectual temper and involves a tragic conception of life. A discussion of Nagel's views can be found at the end of Section A in the introductory essay to Part III.

READING QUESTIONS

In reading the selection, try to answer the following questions and identify the passages that support your answers:

1. Is Nagel's conception of atheism sound?
2. What arguments about God's existence does Nagel criticize?
3. Are his criticisms sound?
4. What is their effect on discussions about God's existence?
5. What are the positive features of atheism according to Nagel?

The essays in this section are devoted in the main to the exposition of major religious creeds of humanity. It is a natural expectation that this paper, even though its theme is so radically different from nearly all of the others, will show how atheism belongs to the great tradition of religious thought. Needless to say, this expectation is difficult to satisfy, and did anyone succeed in doing so he would indeed be performing the neatest conjuring trick of the week. But the expectation nevertheless does cause me some embarrassment, which is only slightly relieved by an anecdote Bertrand Russell reports in his recent book, *Portraits from Memory.* Russell was imprisoned during the First World War for pacifistic activities. On entering the prison he was asked a number of customary questions about himself for the prison records. One question was about his religion. Russell explained that he was an agnostic. "Never heard of it," the warden declared. "How do you spell it?" When

Russell told him, the warden observed "Well, there are many religions, but I suppose they all worship the same God." Russell adds that this remark kept him cheerful for about a week. Perhaps philosophical atheism also is a religion.

1

I must begin by stating what sense I am attaching to the word "atheism," and how I am construing the theme of this paper. I shall understand by "atheism" a critique and a denial of the major claims of all varieties of theism. And by theism I shall mean the view which holds, as one writer has expressed it, "that the heavens and the earth and all that they contain owe their existence and continuance in existence to the wisdom and will of a supreme, self-consistent, omnipotent, omniscient, righteous, and benevolent being, who is distinct from, and independent of, what he has created." Several things immediately follow from these definitions.

In the first place, atheism is not necessarily an irreligious concept, for theism is just one among many views concerning the nature and origin of the world. The denial of theism is logically compatible with a religious outlook upon life, and is in fact characteristic of some of the great historical religions. For example, early Buddhism is a religion which does not subscribe to any doctrine about a god; and there are pantheistic religions and philosophies which, because they deny that God is a being separate from and independent of the world, are not theistic in the sense of the word explained above.

The second point to note is that atheism is not to be identified with sheer unbelief, or with disbelief in some particular creed of a religious group. Thus, a child who has received no religious instruction and has never heard about God, is not an atheist—for he is not denying any theistic claims. Similarly in the case of an adult who, if he has withdrawn from the faith of his fathers without reflection or because of frank indifference to any theological issue, is also not an athiest—for such an adult is not challenging theism and is not professing any views on the subject. Moreover, though the term "atheist" has been used historically as an abusive label for those who do not happen to subscribe to some regnant orthodoxy (for example, the ancient Romans called the early Christians atheists, because the latter denied the Roman divinities), or for those who engage in conduct regarded as immoral it is not in this sense that I am discussing atheism.

One final word of preliminary explanation. I propose to examine some *philosophic* concepts of atheism, and I am not interested in the slightest in the many considerations atheists have advanced against the evidences for some particular religious and theological doctrine—for example, against the truth of the Christian story. What I mean by "philosophical" in the present context is that the views I shall consider are directed against any form of theism, and have their origin and basis in a logical analysis of the theistic position, and in a comprehensive account of the world believed to be wholly intelligible without the adoption of a theistic hypothesis.

Theism as I conceive it is a theological proposition, not a statement of a position that belongs primarily to religion. On my view, religion as a historical and social phenomenon is primarily an institutionalized *cultus* or practice, which possesses identifiable social functions and which expresses certain attitudes men take toward their world. Although it is doubtful whether men ever engage in religious practices or assume religious attitudes without some more or less explicit interpretation of their ritual or some rationale for their attitude, it is still the case that it is possible to distinguish religion as a social and personal phenomenon from the theological doctrines which may be developed as justifications for religious practices. Indeed, in some of the great religions of the world the profession of a creed plays a relatively minor role. In short, religion is a form of social communion, a participation in certain kinds of ritual (whether it be a dance, worship, prayer, or the like), and a form of experience (sometimes, though not invariably, directed to a personal confrontation with divine and holy things). Theology is an articulated and, at its best, a rational attempt at understanding these feelings and practices, in the light of their relation to other parts of human experience, and in terms of some hypothesis concerning the nature of things entire.

2

As I see it, atheistic philosophies fall into two major groups: 1) those which hold that the theistic doctrine is meaningful, but reject it either on the ground that, (a) the positive evidence for it is insufficient, or (b) the negative evidence is quite overwhelming; and 2) those who hold that the theistic thesis is not even meaningful, and reject it (a) as just nonsense or (b) as literally meaningless but interpreting it as a symbolic rendering of human ideals, thus reading the theistic thesis in a sense that most believers in theism would disavow. It will not be possible in the limited space at my disposal to discuss the second category of atheistic critiques; and in any event, most of the traditional atheistic critiques of theism belong to the first group.

But before turning to the philosophical examination of the major classical arguments for theism, it is well to note that such philosophical critiques do not quite convey the passion with which atheists have often carried on their analyses of theistic views. For historically, atheism has been, and indeed continues to be, a form of social and political protest, directed as much against institutionalized religion as against theistic doctrine. Atheism has been, in effect, a moral revulsion against the undoubted abuses of the secular power exercised by religious leaders and religious institutions.

Religious authorities have opposed the correction of glaring injustices, and encouraged politically and socially reactionary policies. Religious institutions have been havens of obscurantist thought and centers for the dissemination of intolerance. Religious creeds have been used to set limits to free inquiry, to perpetuate inhumane treatment of the ill and the underprivileged, and to support moral doctrines insensitive to human suffering.

These indictments may not tell the whole story about the historical significance of religion; but they are at least an important part of the story. The refutation of theism has thus seemed to many as an indispensable step not only towards liberating men's minds from superstition, but also towards achieving a more equitable reordering of society. And no account of even the more philosophical aspects of atheistic thought is adequate, which does not give proper recognition to the powerful social motives that actuate many atheistic arguments.

But however this may be, I want now to discuss three classical arguments for the existence of God, arguments which have constituted at least a partial basis for theistic commitments. As long as theism is defended simply as a dogma, asserted as a matter of direct revelation or as the deliverance of authority, belief in the dogma is impregnable to rational argument. In fact, however, reasons are frequently advanced in support of the theistic creed, and these reasons have been the subject of acute philosophical critiques.

One of the oldest intellectual defenses of theism is the cosmological argument, also known as the argument from a first cause. Briefly put, the argument runs as follows. Every event must have a cause. Hence an event A must have as cause some event B, which in turn must have a cause C, and so on. But if there is no end to this backward progression of causes, the progression will be infinite; and in the opinion of those who use this argument, an infinite series of actual events is unintelligible and absurd. Hence there must be a first cause, and this first cause is God, the initiator of all change in the universe.

The argument is an ancient one, and is especially effective when stated within the framework of assumptions of Aristotelian physics; and it has impressed many generations of exceptionally keen minds. The argument is nonetheless a weak reed on which to rest the theistic thesis. Let us waive any question concerning the validity of the principle that every event has a cause, for though the question is important its discussion would lead us far afield. However, if the principle is assumed, it is surely in-

congruous to postulate a first cause as a way of escaping from the coils of an infinite series. For if everything must have a cause, why does not God require one for His own existence? The standard answer is that He does not need any, because He is self-caused. But if God can be self-caused, why cannot the world itself be self-caused? Why do we require a God transcending the world to bring the world into existence and to initiate changes in it? On the other hand, the supposed inconceivability and absurdity of an infinite series of regressive causes will be admitted by no one who has competent familiarity with the modern mathematical analysis of infinity. The cosmological argument does not stand up under scrutiny.

The second "proof" of God's existence is usually called the ontological argument. It too has a long history going back to early Christian days, though it acquired great prominence only in medieval times. The argument can be stated in several ways, one of which is the following. Since God is conceived to be omnipotent, he is a perfect being. A perfect being is defined as one whose essence or nature lacks no attributes (or properties) whatsoever, one whose nature is complete in every respect. But it is evident that we have an idea of a perfect being, for we have just defined the idea; and since this is so, the argument continues, God who is the perfect being must exist. Why must he? Because his existence follows from his defined nature. For if God lacked the attribute of existence, he would be lacking at least one attribute, and would therefore not be perfect. To sum up, since we have an idea of God as a perfect being, God must exist.

There are several ways of approaching this argument, but I shall consider only one. The argument was exploded by the 18th century philosopher Immanuel Kant. The substance of Kant's criticism is that it is just a confusion to say that existence is an attribute, and that though the *word* "existence" may occur as the grammatical predicate in a sentence no attribute is being predicated of a thing when we say that the thing exists or has existence. Thus, to use Kant's example, when we think of $100 we are thinking of the nature of this sum of money; but the nature of $100 remains the same whether we have $100 in our pockets or not. Accordingly, we are confounding grammar with logic if we suppose that some characteristic is being attributed to the nature of $100 when we say that a hundred dollar bill exists in someone's pocket.

To make the point clearer, consider another example. When we say that a lion has a tawny color, we are predicating a certain attribute of the animal, and similarly when we say that the lion is fierce or is hungry. But when we say the lion exists, all that we are saying is that something is (or has the nature of) a lion; we are not specifying an attribute which belongs to the nature of anything that is a lion. In short, the word "existence" does not signify any attribute, and in consequence no attribute that belongs to the nature of anything. Accordingly, it does not follow from the assumption that we have an idea of a perfect being that such a being exists. For the idea of a perfect being does not involve the attribute of existence as a constituent of that idea, since there is no such attribute. The ontological argument thus has a serious leak, and it can hold no water.

3

The two arguments discussed thus far are purely dialectical, and attempt to establish God's existence without any appeal to empirical data. The next argument, called the argument from design, is different in character, for it is based on what purports to be empirical evidence. I wish to examine two forms of this argument.

One variant of it calls attention to the remarkable way in which different things and processes in the world are integrated with each other, and concludes that this mutual "fitness" of things can be explained only by the assumption of a divine architect who planned the world and everything in it. For example, living organisms can maintain themselves in a variety of environments, and do so in virtue of their delicate mechanisms which adapt the organisms to all sorts of environmental changes. There is thus an intricate pattern of means and ends throughout the animate world. But the existence of this pattern is unintelligible, so the argument runs, except on the hypothesis that the pattern has been deliberately instituted by a Supreme Designer. If we find a watch in some deserted spot, we do not think it came into existence by chance, and we do not hesitate to conclude that an intelligent creature designed and made it. But the world and all its contents exhibit mechanisms and mutual adjustments that are far more complicated and subtle than are those of a watch. Must we not therefore conclude that these things too have a Creator?

The conclusion of this argument is based on an inference from analogy: the watch and the world are alike in possessing a congruence of parts and an adjustment of means to ends: the watch has a watch-maker; hence the world has a world-maker. But is the analogy a good one? Let us once more waive some important issues, in particular the issue whether the universe is a unified system such as the watch admittedly is. And let us concentrate on the question what is the ground for our assurance that watches do not come into existence except through the operations of intelligent manufacturers. The answer is plain. We have never run across a watch which has not been deliberately made by someone. But the situation is nothing like this in the case of the innumerable animate and inanimate systems with which we are familiar. Even in the case of living organisms, though they are generated by their parent organisms, the parents do not "make" their progeny in the same sense in which watchmakers make watches. And once this point is clear, the inference from the existence of living organisms to the existence of a supreme designer no longer appears credible.

Moreover, the argument loses all its force if the facts which the hypothesis of a divine designer is supposed to explain can be understood on the basis of a better supported assumption. And indeed, such an alternative explanation is one of the achievements of Darwinian biology. For Darwin showed that one can account for the variety of biological species, as well as for their adaptations to their environments, without invoking a divine creator and acts of special creation. The Darwinian theory explains the diversity of biological species in terms of chance variations in the structure of organisms, and of a mechanism of selection which retains those variant forms that possess some advantages for survival. The evidence for these assumptions is considerable; and developments subsequent to Darwin have only strengthened the case for a thoroughly naturalistic explanation of the facts of biological adaptation. In any event, this version of the argument from design has nothing to recommend it.

A second form of this argument has been recently revived in the speculations of some modern physicists. No one who is familiar with the facts, can fail to be impressed by the success with which the use of mathematical methods has enabled us to obtain intellectual mastery of many parts of nature. But some thinkers have therefore concluded that since the book of nature is ostensibly written in mathematical language, nature must be the creation of a divine mathematician. However, the argument is most dubious. For it rests, among other things, on the assumption that mathematical tools can be successfully used only if the events of nature exhibit some *special* kind of order, and on the further assumption that if the structure of things were different from what they are mathematical language would be inadequate for describing such structure. But it can be shown that no matter what the world were like—even if it impressed us as being utterly chaotic—it would still possess some order, and would in principle be amenable to a mathematical description. In point of fact, it makes no sense to say that there is absolutely *no* pattern in any conceivable subject matter. To be sure, there are differences in complexities of structure, and if the patterns of events were sufficiently complex we might not be able to unravel them. But however that may be, the success of mathematical physics in giving us some understanding of the world around us does not yield the conclusion that only a mathematician could have devised the patterns of order we have discovered in nature.

4

The inconclusiveness of the three classical arguments for the existence of God was already made evident by Kant, in a manner substantially not different from the above discussion. There are, however, other types of arguments for theism that have been influential in the history of thought, two of which I wish to consider, even if only briefly.

Indeed, though Kant destroyed the classical intellectual foundations for theism, he himself invented a fresh argument for it. Kant's attempted proof is not intended to be a purely theoretical demonstration, and is based on the supposed facts of our moral nature. It has exerted an enormous influence on subsequent theological speculation. In barest outline, the argument is as follows. According to Kant, we are subject not only to physical laws like the rest of nature, but also to moral ones. These moral laws are categorical imperatives, which we must heed not because of their utilitarian consequences, but simply because as autonomous moral agents it is our duty to accept them as binding. However, Kant was keenly aware that though virtue may be its reward, the virtuous man (that is, the man who acts out of a sense of duty and in conformity with the moral law) does not always receive his just desserts in this world; nor did he shut his eyes to the fact that evil men frequently enjoy the best things this world has to offer. In short, virtue does not always reap happiness. Nevertheless, the highest human good is the realization of happiness commensurate with one's virtue; and Kant believed that it is

a practical postulate of the moral life to promote this good. But what can guarantee that the highest good is realizable? Such a guarantee can be found only in God, who must therefore exist if the highest good is not to be a fatuous ideal. The existence of an omnipotent, omniscient, and omnibenevolent God is thus postulated as a necessary condition for the possibility of a moral life.

Despite the prestige this argument has acquired, it is difficult to grant it any force. It is easy enough to postulate God's existence. But as Bertrand Russell observed in another connection, postulation has all the advantages of theft over honest toil. No postulation carries with it any assurance that what is postulated is actually the case. And though we may postulate God's existence as a means to guaranteeing the possibility of realizing happiness together with virtue, the postulation establishes neither the actual realizability of this ideal nor the fact of his existence. Moreover, the argument is not made more cogent when we recognize that it is based squarely on the highly dubious conception that considerations of utility and human happiness must not enter into the determination of what is morally obligatory. Having built his moral theory on a radical separation of means from ends, Kant was driven to the desperate postulation of God's existence in order to relate them again. The argument is thus at best a *tour de force*, contrived to remedy a fatal flaw in Kant's initial moral assumptions. It carries no conviction to anyone who does not commit Kant's initial blunder.

One further type of argument, pervasive in much Protestant theological literature, deserves brief mention. Arguments of this type take their point of departure from the psychology of religious and mystical experience. Those who have undergone such experiences, often report that during the experience they feel themselves to be in the presence of the divine and holy, that they loose their sense of self-identity and become merged with some fundamental reality, or that they enjoy a feeling of total dependence upon some ultimate power. The overwhelming sense of transcending one's finitude which characterizes such vivid periods of life, and of coalescing with some ultimate source of all existence, is then taken to be compelling evidence for the existence of a supreme being. In a variant form of this argument, other theologians have identified God as the object which satisfies the commonly experienced need for integrating one's scattered and conflicting impulses into a coherent unity, or as the subject which is of ultimate concern to us. In short, a proof of God's existence is found in the occurrence of certain distinctive experiences.

It would be flying in the face of well-attested facts were one to deny that such experiences frequently occur. But do these facts constitute evidence for the conclusion based on them? Does the fact, for example, that an individual experiences a profound sense of direct contact with an alleged transcendent ground of all reality, constitute competent evidence for the claim that there is such a ground and that it is the immediate cause of the experience? If well-established canons for evaluating evidence are accepted, the answer is surely negative. No one will dispute that many men do have vivid experiences in which such things as ghosts or pink elephants appear before them; but only the hopelessly credulous will without further ado count such experiences as establishing the existence of ghosts and pink elephants. To establish the existence of such things, evidence is required that is obtained under controlled conditions and that can be confirmed by independent inquirers. Again, though a man's report that he is suffering pain may be taken at face value, one cannot take at face value the claim, were he to make it, that it is the food he ate which is the cause (or a contributory cause) of his felt pain—not even if the man were to report a vivid feeling of abdominal disturbance. And similarly, an overwhelming feeling of being in the presence of the Divine is evidence enough for admitting the genuineness of such feeling; it is no evidence for the claim that a supreme being with a substantial existence independent of the experience is the cause of the experience.

5

Thus far the discussion has been concerned with noting inadequacies in various arguments widely used to support theism. However, much atheistic criticism is also directed toward exposing incoherencies in the very thesis of theism. I want therefore to consider this aspect of the atheistic critique, though I will restrict myself to the central difficulty in the theistic position which arises from the simultaneous attribution of omnipotence, omniscience, and omnibenevolence to the Deity. The difficulty is that of reconciling these attributes with the occurrence of evil in the world. Accordingly, the question to which I now turn is whether, despite the existence of evil, it is possible to construct a theodicy which will justify the ways of an infinitely powerful and just God to man.

Two main types of solutions have been proposed for this problem. One way that is frequently used is to maintain that what is commonly called evil is only an illusion, or at worst only the "privation" or absence of good. Accordingly, evil is not "really real," it is only the "negative" side of God's beneficence, it is only the product of our limited intelligence which fails to plumb the true character of God's creative bounty. A sufficient comment on this proposed solution is that facts are not altered or abolished by rebaptizing them. Evil may indeed be only an appearance and not genuine. But this does not eliminate from the realm of appearance the tragedies, the sufferings, and the iniquities which men so frequently endure. And it raises once more, though on another level, the problem of reconciling the fact that there is evil in the realm of appearance with God's alleged omnibenevolence. In any event, it is small comfort to anyone suffering a cruel misfortune for which he is in no way responsible, to be told that what he is undergoing is only the absence of good. It is a gratuitous insult to mankind, a symptom of insensitivity and indifference to human suffering, to be assured that all the miseries and agonies men experience are only illusory.

Another gambit often played in attempting to justify the ways of God to man is to argue that the things called evil are evil only because they are viewed in isolation; they are not evil when viewed in proper perspective and in relation to the rest of creation. Thus, if one attends to but a single instrument in an orchestra, the sounds issuing from it may indeed be harsh and discordant. But if one is placed at a proper distance from the whole orchestra, the sounds of that single instrument will mingle with the sounds issuing from the other players to produce a marvellous bit of symphonic music. Analogously, experiences we call painful undoubtedly occur and are real enough. But the pain is judged to be an evil only because it is experienced in a limited perspective—the pain is there for the sake of a more inclusive good, whose reality eludes us because our intelligences are too weak to apprehend things in their entirety.

It is an appropriate retort to this argument that of course we judge things to be evil in a human perspective, but that since we are not God this is the only proper perspective in which to judge them. It may indeed be the case that what is evil for us is not evil for some other part of creation. However, we are not this other part of creation, and it is irrelevant to argue that were we something other than what we are, our evaluations of what is good and bad would be different. Moreover, the worthlessness of the argument becomes even more evident if we remind ourselves that it is unsupported speculation to suppose that whatever is evil in a finite perspective is good from the purported perspective of the totality of things. For the argument can be turned around: what we judge to be a good is a good only because it is viewed in isolation; when it is viewed in proper perspective, and in relation to the entire scheme of things, it is an evil. This is in fact a standard form of the argument for a universal pessimism. Is it any worse than the similar argument for a universal optimism? The very raising of this question is a *reductio ad absurdum* of the proposed solution to the ancient problem of evil.

I do not believe it is possible to reconcile the alleged omnipotence and omnibenevolence of God with the unvarnished facts of human existence. In point of fact, many theologians have concurred in this conclusion; for in order to escape from the difficulty which the traditional attributes of God 0present, they have assumed that God is not all powerful, and that there are limits as to what He can do in his efforts to establish a righteous order in the universe. But whether such a modified theology is better off, is doubtful; and in any event, the question still remains whether the facts of human life support the claim that an omnibenevolent Deity, though limited in power, is revealed in the ordering of human history. It is pertinent to note in this connection that though there have been many historians who have made the effort, no historian has yet succeeded in showing to the satisfaction of his professional colleagues that the hypothesis of a Divine Providence is capable of explaining anything which cannot be explained just as well without this hypothesis.

6

This last remark naturally leads to the question whether, apart from their polemics against theism, philosophical atheists have not shared a common set of positive views, a common set of philosophical convictions which set them off from other groups of thinkers. In one very clear sense of this query the answer is indubitably negative. For there never has been what one might call a "school of atheism," in the way in which there has been a Platonic school or even a Kantian school. In point of fact, atheistic critics of theism can be found among many of the conventional groupings of philosophical thinkers—

even, I venture to add, among professional theologians in recent years who in effect preach atheism in the guise of language taken bodily from the Christian tradition.

Nevertheless, despite the variety of philosophic positions to which at one time or another in the history of thought atheists have subscribed, it seems to me that atheism is not simply a negative standpoint. At any rate, there is a certain quality of intellectual temper that has characterized, and continues to characterize, many philosophical atheists. (I am excluding from consideration the so-called "village atheist," whose primary concern is to twit and ridicule those who accept some form of theism, or for that matter those who have any religious convictions.) Moreover, their rejection of theism is based not only on the inadequacies they have found in the arguments for theism, but often also on the positive ground that atheism is a corollary to a better supported general outlook upon the nature of things. I want therefore to conclude this discussion with a brief enumeration of some points of positive doctrine to which by and large philosophical atheists seem to me to subscribe. These points fall into three major groups.

In the first place, philosophical atheists reject the assumption that there are disembodied spirits, or that incorporeal entities of any sort can exercise a causal agency. On the contrary, atheists are generally agreed that if we wish to achieve any understanding of what takes place in the universe, we must look to the operations of organized bodies. Accordingly, the various processes taking place in nature, whether animate or inanimate, are to be explained in terms of the properties and structures of identifiable and spatio-temporally located objects. Moreover, the present variety of systems and activities found in the universe is to be accounted for on the basis of the transformations things undergo when they enter into different relations with one another—transformations which often result in the emergence of novel kinds of objects. On the other hand, though things are in flux and undergo alteration, there is no all-encompassing unitary pattern of change. Nature is ineradicably plural, both in respect to the individuals occurring in it as well as in respect to the processes in which things become involved. Accordingly, the human scene and the human perspective are not illusory; and man and his works are no less and no more "real" than are other parts or phases of the cosmos. At the risk of using a possibly misleading characterization, all of this can be summarized by saying that an atheistic view of things is a form of materialism.

In the second place, atheists generally manifest a marked empirical temper, and often take as their ideal the intellectual methods employed in the contemporaneous empirical sciences. Philosophical atheists differ considerably on important points of detail in their account of how responsible claims to knowledge are to be established. But there is substantial agreement among them that controlled sensory observation is the court of final appeal in issues concerning matters of fact. It is indeed this commitment to the use of an empirical method which is the final basis of the atheistic critique of theism. For at bottom this critique seeks to show that we can understand whatever a theistic assumption is alleged to explain, through the use of the proved methods of the positive sciences and without the introduction of empirically unsupported *ad hoc* hypotheses about a Deity. It is pertinent in this connection to recall a familiar legend about the French mathematical physicist Laplace. According to the story, Laplace made a personal presentation of a copy of his now famous book on celestial mechanics to Napoleon. Napoleon glanced through the volume, and finding no reference to the Deity asked Laplace whether God's existence played any role in the analysis. "Sire, I have no need for that hypothesis," Laplace is reported to have replied. The dismissal of sterile hypotheses characterizes not only the work of Laplace; it is the uniform rule in scientific inquiry. The sterility of the theistic assumption is one of the main burdens of the literature of atheism both ancient and modern.

And finally, atheistic thinkers have generally accepted a utilitarian basis for judging moral issues, and they have exhibited a libertarian attitude toward human needs and impulses. The conceptions of the human good they have advocated are conceptions which are commensurate with the actual capacities of mortal men, so that it is the satisfaction of the complex needs of the human creature which is the final standard for evaluating the validity of a moral ideal or moral prescription.

In consequence, the emphasis of atheistic moral reflection has been this-worldly rather than other-worldly, individualistic rather than authoritarian. The stress upon a good life that must be consummated in this world, has made atheists vigorous opponents of moral codes which seek to repress human impulses in the name of some unrealizable other-worldly ideal. The individualism that is so pronounced a strain in many philosophical atheists has made them tolerant of human limitations and sensitive to the plurality of legitimate moral goals. On the other hand, this individualism has certainly not prevented many of them from recognizing the crucial role which institutional arrangements can play in achieving desirable patterns of human living. In consequence, atheists have made important contributions to the development of a climate of opinion favorable to pursuing the values of a liberal civilization and they have played effective roles in attempts to rectify social injustices.

Atheists cannot build their moral outlook on foundations upon which so many men conduct their lives. In particular, atheism cannot offer the incentives to conduct and the consolations for misfortune which theistic religions supply to their adherents. It can offer no hope of personal immortality, no threats of Divine chastisement, no promise of eventual recompense for injustices suffered, no blueprints to sure salvation. For on its view of the place of man in nature, human excellence and human dignity must be achieved within a finite life-span, or not at all, so that the rewards of moral endeavor must come from the quality of civilized living, and not from some source of disbursement that dwells outside of time. Accordingly, atheistic moral reflection at its best does not culminate in a quiescent ideal of human perfection, but is a vigorous call to intelligent activity—activity for the sake of realizing human potentialities and for eliminating whatever stands in the way of such realization. Nevertheless, though slavish resignation to remediable ills is not characteristic of atheistic thought, responsible atheists have never pretended that human effort can invariably achieve the heart's every legitimate desire. A tragic view of life is thus an uneliminable ingredient in atheistic thought. This ingredient does not invite or generally produce lugubrious lamentation. But it does touch the atheist's view of man and his place in nature with an emotion that makes the philosophical atheist a kindred spirit to those who, within the frameworks of various religious traditions, have developed a serenely resigned attitude toward the inevitable tragedies of the human estate.

Rhazes (864–925)
FROM *SPIRITUAL PHYSICK*

Rhazes, a Persian philosopher, physician, and scientist, argues that no plausible philosophy fails to recognize the need to rein in human passion and appetite. His criterion for how much these should be restrained is based on happiness understood as a favorable balance of pleasure over pain and temporal loss: passion and appetite may be indulged only when it is known that this will not lead to as much or more pain and temporal loss than the pleasure thereby obtained. A discussion of Rhazes's conception of psychology appears in Section B of the introductory essay to Part III.

READING QUESTIONS

In reading the selection, try to answer the following questions and identify the passages that support your answers:

1. What is Rhazes's conception of human psychology?
2. What arguments does he give in support of this conception?
3. Are they sound?
4. Are passions merely episodic? Why or why not?
5. What, if any, are the differences between passions and character traits?

CHAPTER 1

Of the Excellence and Praise of Reason

THE Creator (Exalted be His Name) gave and bestowed upon us Reason to the end that we might thereby attain and achieve every advantage, that lies within the nature of such as us to attain and achieve, in this world and the next. It is God's greatest blessing to us, and there is nothing that surpasses it in procuring our advantage and profit. By Reason we are preferred above the irrational beasts, so that we rule over them and manage them, subjecting and controlling them in ways profitable alike to us and them. By Reason we reach all that raises us up, and sweetens and beautifies our life, and through it we obtain our purpose and desire. For by Reason we have comprehended the manufacture and use of ships, so that we have reached unto distant lands divided from us by the seas; by it we have achieved medicine with its many uses to the body, and all the other arts that yield us profit. By Reason we have comprehended matters obscure and remote, things that were secret and hidden from us; by it we have learned the shape of the earth and the sky, the dimension of the sun, moon and other stars, their distances and motions; by it we have achieved even the knowledge of the Almighty, our Creator, the most majestic of all that we have sought to reach and our most profitable attainment. In short, Reason is the thing without which our state would be the state of wild beasts, of children and lunatics; it is the thing whereby we picture our intellectual acts before they become manifest to the senses, so that we see them exactly as though we had sensed them, then we represent these pictures in our sensual acts so that they correspond exactly with what we have represented and imagined.

Since this is its worth and place, its value and significance, it behoves us not to bring it down from its high rank or in any way to degrade it, neither to make it the governed seeing that it is the governor, or the controlled seeing that it is the controller, or the subject seeing that it is the sovereign; rather must we consult it in all matters, respecting it and relying upon it always, conducting our affairs as it dictates and bringing them to a stop when it so commands. We must not give Passion the mastery over it, for Passion is the blemish of Reason, clouding it and diverting it from its proper path and right purpose, preventing the reasonable man from finding the true guidance and the ultimate salvation of all his affairs. Nay, but we must discipline and subject our Passion, driving and compelling it to obey the every dictate of Reason. If we do thus, our Reason will become absolutely clear and will illuminate us with all its light, bringing us to the achievement of all that we desire to attain; and we shall be happy in God's free gift and grace of it.

CHAPTER II

Of Suppressing and Restraining the Passion, with a Summary of the Views of Plato the Philosopher

Now following on this we will proceed to speak about Spiritual Physick, the goal of which is the reformation of the soul's character; and we propose to be extremely concise, going straight forward to deal with those points, principles and ideas which are the foundations of this entire object. We state that our intention in prefixing our views on Reason and Passion was because we considered this to be as it were the starting-point of our whole purpose; we shall now follow it up with a discussion of the most important and loftiest fundamentals of this matter.

The loftiest and most important of these fundamentals, and that most helpful in reaching our object in the present book, is the suppression of passion, the opposing of natural inclinations in most circumstances, and the gradual training of the soul to that end. For this is the first point of superiority of man over the beasts—I mean the faculty of will, and the release of action after deliberation. This is because the beasts are undisciplined, and do whatever their natural inclinations dictate, acting without restraint or deliberation. You will not find that any undisciplined animal will refrain from defecating, or from seizing upon its food whenever it is there at hand and it feels the need of it, in the way you find a man leaving that on one side and compelling his inclinations to obedience at the dictate of various intellectual ideas; on the contrary, the beasts act exactly as their instincts urge, without restraint or conscious choice.

This degree of superiority over the beasts, in the way of reining the natural impulses, belongs pretty well to the majority of men, even if it be as a result of training and education. It is general and universal, and may readily be observed on all hands, and in fact every child is accustomed to it and is brought up accordingly; the point requires no labouring. At the same time there is a great difference and a wide range of variety between the different peoples in this respect. However, to reach the highest summit of this virtue attainable by human nature is scarcely open to any but the supreme philosopher; such a man must be accounted as superior to the common run of humanity, as mankind as a whole excels the beasts in reining the natural instincts and controlling the passion. From this we realize that whosoever desires to adorn himself with this ornament, and to perfect this virtue in his soul, is upon a hard and difficult quest; he needs to acclimatize himself to controlling and opposing and wrestling with his passion. And because there is a great difference and a wide range of variety between men as regards their temperaments, the acquisition of certain virtues rather than others and the getting rid of certain vices rather than others will prove a harder or an easier task for some men rather than the rest.

Now I will begin by mentioning how this virtue may be acquired—I mean the suppression and opposing of the passion—seeing that it is the loftiest and most important of these virtues, and its position relative to this entire purpose is similar to that of the element which immediately succeeds the origin.

Passion and instinct are always inciting and urging and pressing us to follow after present pleasures and to choose them without reflection or deliberation upon the possible consequence, even though this may involve pain hereafter and prevent us from attaining a pleasure many times greater than that immediately experienced. This is because they, our passion and instinct, see nothing else but the actual state in which they happen to be, and only seek to get rid of the pain that hurts them at that very moment. In this way a child suffering from ophthalmia will rub its eyes and eat dates and play in the sun. It therefore behoves the intelligent man to restrain and suppress his passion and instinct, and not to let them have their way except after careful and prudent consideration of what they may bring in their train; he will represent this to himself and weigh the matter accurately, and then he will follow the course of greater advantage. This he will do, lest he should suffer pain where he supposed he would experience pleasure, and lose where he thought he would gain. If in the course of such representation and balancing he should be seized by any doubt, he will not give his appetite free play, but will continue to restrain and suppress it; for he cannot be sure that in gratifying his appetite he will not involve himself in evil consequences very many times more painful and distressing than the labour of resolutely suppressing it. Prudence clearly dictates that he should deny such a lust. Again, if the two discomforts—that of suppression, and that consequent upon gratification—seem exactly balanced, he will still continue to suppress his appetite; for the immediate bitterness is easier and simpler to taste than that which he must inevitably expect to swallow in the great majority of cases.

Nor is this enough. He ought further to suppress his passion in many circumstances even when he foresees no disagreeable consequence of indulgence, and that in order to train and discipline his soul to endure and become accustomed to such denial (for then it will be far less difficult to do so when the consequences are bad), as much as to prevent his lusts getting control of him and dominating him. The lusts in any case have sufficient hold, in the ordinary way of nature and human disposition, without needing to be reinforced by habit as well, so that a man will find himself in a situation where he cannot resist them at all.

You must know also that those who persistently indulge and gratify their appetites ultimately reach a stage where they no longer have any enjoyment of them, and still are unable to give them up. For instance, those who are forever having intercourse with women, or drinking, or listening to music—though these are the strongest and deepest-rooted of all the lusts—do not enjoy these indulgences so much as men who do not incessantly gratify them; for these passions become for them exactly the same as any other passion with other men—that is to say, they become commonplace and habitual. Nevertheless it is not within their power to leave off these pursuits because they have turned into something of the nature of a necessity of life for them, instead of being a luxury and a relish. They are in consequence affected adversely in their religious life as well as their mundane situation, so that they are compelled to employ all kinds of shifts, and to acquire money by risking their lives and precipitating themselves into any sort of danger. In the end they find they are miserable where they expected to be happy, that they are sorrowful where they expected to rejoice, that they are pained where they expected to experience pleasure. So what difference is there between them and the man who deliberately sets out to destroy himself? They are exactly like animals duped by the bait laid

for them in the snares; when they arrive in the trap, they neither obtain what they had been duped with nor are they able to escape from what they have fallen into.

This then will suffice as to the amount the appetites should be suppressed: they may only be indulged where it is known that the consequence will not involve a man in pain and temporal loss equivalent to the pleasure thereby obtained—much less discomfort superior to and exceeding the pleasure that is momentarily experienced. This is the view and assertion and recommendation even of those philosophers who have not considered the soul to have an independent existence, but to decay and perish with the body in which it is lodged. As for those who hold that the soul has an individual identity of its own, and that it uses the body as it would an instrument or an implement, not perishing simultaneously with it, they rise far, far beyond the mere reining of the instincts, and combating and opposing the passions. They despise and revile exceedingly those who allow themselves to be led by and who incline after their lower nature, considering them to be no better than beasts. They believe that by following and indulging their passion, by inclining after and loving their appetites, by regretting anything they may miss, and inflicting pain on animals in order to secure and satisfy their lusts, these men will experience, after the soul has left the body, pain and regret and sorrow for the evil consequences of their actions alike abundant and prolonged.

These philosophers can put forward the very physique of man to prove that he is not equipped to occupy himself with pleasures and lusts, seeing how deficient he is in this respect compared with the irrational animals, but rather to use his powers of thought and deliberation. For a single wild beast experiences more pleasure in eating and having intercourse than a multitude of men can possibly achieve; while as for its capacity for casting care and thought aside, and enjoying life simply and wholly, that is a state of affairs no man can ever rival. This is because that is the animal's entire be-all and end-all; we may observe that a beast at the very moment of its slaughter will still go on eating and drinking with complete absorption. They further argue that if the gratification of the appetites and the indulgence of the calls of nature had been the nobler part, man would never have been made so deficient in this respect or been more meanly endowed than the animals. The very fact that man is so deficient—in spite of his being the noblest of mortal animals—in his share of these things, whereas he possesses such an ample portion of deliberation and reflection, is enough to teach us that it is nobler to utilize and improve the reason, and not to be slave and lackey of the calls of nature.

Moreover, they say, if the advantage lay in gratifying carnal pleasure and lust, the creature furnished by nature to that end would be nobler than that not so equipped. By such a standard the bull and the ass would be superior not only to man, but also to the immortal beings, and to God Himself, Who is without carnal pleasure and lust.

It may be (they go on) that certain undisciplined men unused to reflect and deliberate upon such matters will not agree with us that the beasts enjoy greater pleasure than men. Those who argue thus may quote against us such an instance as that of a king who, having triumphed over an opposing foe, thenceforward sits at his amusement, and summons together and displays all his pomp and circumstance, so that he achieves the ultimate limit of what a man may reach. "What," they ask, "is the pleasure of a beast in comparison with the pleasure of such a man? Can so great a pleasure be measured or related with any other?" Those who speak in this fashion should realize that the perfection or imperfection of such pleasures must not be judged by comparing one pleasure with another, but in relation to the need felt for such a pleasure. Consider the case of a man who requires 1,000 dinars to put his affairs in order: if he is given 999, that will not completely restore his position for him. On the other hand suppose a man needs a single dinar: his situation will be perfectly amended by obtaining that one dinar. Yet the former has been given many times more than the latter, and still his state is not completely restored. When a beast has enjoyed full satisfaction of the call of its instincts, its pleasure therein is perfect and complete; it feels no pain or hurt at missing a still greater gratification because such an idea never occurs to its mind at all. Yet in any case the beast always experiences the superior pleasure; for there is no man who can ever attain all his hopes and desires, since his soul being endowed with the faculties of reflection, deliberation, and imagination of what he yet lacks, and it being in its nature always to consider that the state enjoyed by another is bound to be superior, never under any circumstances is it free from yearning and gazing after what it does not itself possess, and from being fearful and anxious lest it lose what it has possessed; its pleasure and desire are therefore always in a state of imperfect realization. If any man should possess half the world, his soul would still wrestle with him to acquire the remainder, and would be anxious and fearful of losing hold of as much as it has already gotten; and if he possessed the entire world, nevertheless he would yearn for perpetual well-being and immortality, and his soul would gaze after the knowledge of all the mysteries in heaven and earth. One day, as I have heard tell, someone spoke in the presence of a great-souled king of the splendid and immortal joys of Paradise, whereupon the king remarked, "Such bliss seems to me wholly bitter and wearisome, when I reflect that if I were granted it, I should be in the position of one on whom a favour and a kindness had been conferred." How could such a man ever know perfect pleasure and enjoyment of his lot? And who is there that rejoices within himself, save only the beasts and those who live like beasts? So the poet says:

> Can any man be truly blest,
> Save him immortally possessed
> Of fortune, who has scarce a care
> And never goes to bed with fear?

This sect of philosophers soar beyond the mere reining and opposing of passion, even beyond the contempt and mortification thereof, unto a matter exceedingly sublime. They partake of a bare subsistence of food and drink; they acquire not wealth or lands or houses; and some advance so far in this opinion that they go apart from other men, and withdraw into waste places. Such are the arguments they put forward in support of their views regarding the things that are present and seen. As for their reasonings about the state of the soul after it has left the body, to speak of this would take us far beyond the scope of the present book, alike in loftiness, length and breadth: in loftiness because this involves research into the nature of the soul, the purpose of its association with and separation from the body, and its state after it has gone out of it; in length, because each of these several branches of research requires its own interpretation and explanation, to an extent many times the discourse contained in this book; and in breadth, because the purpose of such researches is the salvation of the soul after it has left the body, though it is true that the discourse involves a major consideration of the reformation of character. Still, there will be no harm in giving a very brief account of these matters, without however involving ourselves in an argument for or against their opinions;

what we have particularly in view are those ideas which we think will assist and enable us to fulfil the purpose of our present book.

Plato, the chief and greatest of the philosophers, held that there are three souls in every man. The first he called the rational and divine soul, the second the choleric and animal, and the third the vegetative, incremental and appetitive soul. The animal and vegetative souls were created for the sake of the rational soul. The vegetative soul was made in order to feed the body, which is as it were the instrument and implement of the rational soul; for the body is not of an eternal, indisoluble substance, but its substance is fluid and soluble, and every soluble object only survives by leaving behind it something to replace that element which is dissolved. The choleric soul's function is to be of assistance to the rational soul in suppressing the appetitive soul and in preventing it from preoccupying the rational soul with its manifold desires so that it is incapable of using its reason. If the rational soul employed its reason completely, this would mean that it would be delivered from the body in which it is enmeshed. These two souls—the vegetative and the choleric—possess in Plato's view no special substance that survives the corruption of the body, such as that which belongs to the rational soul. On the contrary one of them, the choleric, is the entire temperament of the heart, while the other, the appetitive, is the entire temperament of the liver. As for the temperament of the brain, this he said is the first instrument and implement used by the rational soul.

Man is fed and derives his increase and growth from the liver, his heat and pulse-movement from the heart, his sensation, voluntary movement, imagination, thought and memory from the brain. It is not the case that this is part of its peculiar property and temperament; it belongs rather to the essence dwelling within it and using it after the manner of an instrument or implement. However, it is the most intimate of all the instruments and implements associated with this agent.

Plato taught that men should labour by means of corporeal physick (which is the well-known variety) as well as spiritual physick (which is persuasion through arguments and proofs) to equilibrate the actions of the several souls so that they may neither fail nor exceed what is desired of them. Failure in the vegetative soul consists in not supplying food, growth and increase of the quantity and quality required by the whole body; its excess is when it surpasses and transgresses that limit so that the body is furnished with an abundance beyond its needs, and plunges into all kinds of pleasures and desires. Failure in the choleric soul consists in not having the fervour, pride and courage to enable it to rein and vanquish the appetitive soul at such times as it feels desire, so as to come between it and its desires; its excess is when it is possessed of so much arrogance and love of domination that it seeks to overcome all other men and the entire animal kingdom, and has no other ambition but supremacy and domination—such a state of soul as affected Alexander the Great. Failure in the rational soul is recognized when it does not occur to it to wonder and marvel at this world of ours, to meditate upon it with interest, curiosity and a passionate desire to discover all that it contains, and above all to investigate the body in which it dwells and its form and fate after death. Truly, if a man does not wonder and marvel at our world, if he is not moved to astonishment at its form, and if his soul does not gaze after the knowledge of all that it contains, if he is not concerned or interested to discover what his state will be after death, his portion of reason is that of the beasts—nay, of bats and fishes and worthless things that never think or reflect. Excess in the rational soul is proved when a man is so swayed and overmastered by the consideration of such things as these that the appetitive soul cannot obtain the food and sleep and so forth to keep the body fit, or in sufficient quantity to maintain the temperament of the brain in a healthy state. Such a man is forever seeking and probing and striving to the utmost of his powers, supposing that he will attain and realize these matters in a shorter time than that which is absolutely necessary for their achievement. The result is that the temperament of the whole body is upset, so that he falls a prey to depression and melancholia, and he misses his entire quest through supposing that he could quickly master it.

Plato held that the period which has been appointed for the survival of this dissoluble and corruptible body, in a state the rational soul can make use of to procure the needs of its salvation after it leaves the body—the period that is from the time a man is born until he grows old and withers—is adequate for the fulfilment of every man, even the stupidest; provided he never gives up thinking and speculating and gazing after the matters we have mentioned as proper to the rational soul, and provided he despises this body and the physical world altogether, and loathes and detests it, being aware that the sentient soul, so long as it is attached to any part of it, continues to pass through states deleterious and painful because generation and corruption are forever succeeding each other in the body; provided further that he does not hate but rather yearns to depart out of the body and to be liberated from it. He believed that when the time comes for the sentient soul to leave the body in which it is lodged, if it has acquired and believed firmly in these ideas it will pass immediately into its own world, and will not desire to be attached to any particle of the body thereafter; it will remain living and reasoning eternally, free from pain, and rejoicing in its place of abode. For life and reason belong to it of its own essence; freedom from pain will be the consequence of its removal from generation and corruption; it will rejoice in its own world and place of abiding because it has been liberated from association with the body and existence in the physical world. But if the soul leaves the body without having acquired these ideas and without having recognized the true nature of the physical world, but rather still yearning after it and eager to exist therein, it will not leave its present dwelling-place but will continue to be linked with some portion of it; it will not cease—because of the succession of generation and corruption within the body in which it is lodged—to suffer continual and reduplicated pains, and cares multitudinous and afflicting.

Such in brief are the views of Plato, and of Socrates the Divine Hermit before him.

Besides all this, there is neither any purely mundane view whatsoever that does not necessitate some reining of passion and appetite, or that gives them free head and rope altogether. To rein and suppress the passion is an obligation according to every opinion, in the view of every reasoning man, and according to every religion. Therefore let the reasoning man observe these ideals with the eye of his reason, and keep them before his attention and in his mind; and even if he should not achieve the highest rank and level of this order described in the present book, let him at least cling hold of the meanest level. That is the view of those who advocate the reining of the passion to the extent that will not involve mundane loss in this present life; for if he tastes some bitterness and unpleasantness at the beginning of his career through reining and suppressing his passion, this will presently be followed by a consequent sweetness and a pleasure in which he may rejoice with great joy and gladness; while the labour he endures in wrestling with his passion and suppressing his appetites will grow easier by habit, especially if this be effected gradually—by accustoming himself to the discipline and leading on his soul gently, first to deny trifling appetites and to forgo a little of its desires at the requirement of reason and judgment, and then to seek after further discipline until it becomes associated with his character and habit. In this way his appetitive soul will become submissive and will grow accustomed to being subject to his rational soul. So the process will continue to develop; and the discipline will be reinforced by the joy he has in the results yielded by this reining of his passion, and the profit he has of his judgment and reason and of controlling his affairs by them; by the praise men lavish upon him, and their evident desire to emulate his achievement.

Gilbert Ryle (1900–1976)
THE GHOST IN THE MACHINE

Ryle argues that the common belief that mental occurrences are of the same sort as physical occurrences is a category mistake, like thinking that changing one's mind is the same type of occurrence as changing one's shirt. As a consequence, he argues, it is false to say that we have an internal psychological history that parallels the external physical history of our body. Ryle's views are discussed in Section B of the introductory essay to Part III.

READING QUESTIONS

In reading the selection, try to answer the following questions and identify the passages that support your answers:

1. What does Ryle mean by a "category mistake"?
2. How does he think this mistake arises concerning the conception of mind and body?
3. What reasons does he give in support of his position?
4. Are they good? Why or why not?
5. How does Ryle's position help us in the study of motives, intentions, and psychological traits?

(1) THE OFFICIAL DOCTRINE

THERE is a doctrine about the nature and place of minds which is so prevalent among theorists and even among laymen that it deserves to be described as the official theory. Most philosophers, psychologists and religious teachers subscribe, with minor reservations, to its main articles and, although they admit certain theoretical difficulties in it, they tend to assume that these can be overcome without serious modifications being made to the architecture of the theory. It will be argued here that the central principles of the doctrine are unsound and conflict with the whole body of what we know about minds when we are not speculating about them.

The official doctrine, which hails chiefly from Descartes, is something like this. With the doubtful exceptions of idiots and infants in arms every human being has both a body and a mind. Some would prefer to say that every human being is both a body and a mind. His body and his mind are ordinarily harnessed together, but after the death of the body his mind may continue to exist and function.

Human bodies are in space and are subject to the mechanical laws which govern all other bodies in space. Bodily processes and states can be inspected by external observers. So a man's bodily life is as much a public affair as are the lives of animals and reptiles and even as the careers of trees, crystals and planets.

But minds are not in space, nor are their operations subject to mechanical laws. The workings of one mind are not witnessable by other observers; its career is private. Only I can take direct cognisance of the states and processes of my own mind. A person therefore lives through two collateral histories, one consisting of what happens in and to his body, the other consisting of what happens in and to his mind. The first is public, the second private. The events in the first history are events in the physical world, those in the second are events in the mental world.

It has been disputed whether a person does or can directly monitor all or only some of the episodes of his own private history; but, according to the official doctrine, of at least some of these episodes he has direct and unchallengeable cognisance. In consciousness, self-consciousness and introspection he is directly and authentically apprised of the present states and operations of his mind. He may have great or small uncertainties about concurrent and adjacent episodes in the physical world, but he can have none about at least part of what is momentarily occupying his mind.

It is customary to express this bifurcation of his two lives and of his two worlds by saying that the things and events which belong to the physical world, including his own body, are external, while the workings of his own mind are internal. This antithesis of outer and inner is of course meant to be construed as a metaphor, since minds, not being in space, could not be described as being spatially inside anything else, or as having things going on spatially inside themselves. But relapses from this good intention are common and theorists are found speculating how stimuli, the physical sources of which are yards or miles outside a person's skin can generate mental responses inside his skull, or how decisions framed inside his cranium can set going movements of his extremities.

Even when 'inner' and 'outer' are construed as metaphors, the problem how a person's mind and body influence one another is notoriously charged with theoretical difficulties. What the mind wills, the legs, arms and the tongue execute; what affects the ear and the eye has something to do with what the mind perceives; grimaces and smiles betray the mind's moods and bodily castigations lead, it is hoped, to moral improvement. But the actual transactions between the episodes of the private history and those of the public history remain mysterious, since by definition they can belong to neither series. They could not be reported among the happenings described in a person's autobiography of his inner life, but nor could they be reported among those described in some one else's biography of that person's overt career. They can be inspected neither by introspection nor by laboratory experiment. They are theoretical shuttlecocks which are forever being bandied from the physiologist back to the psychologist and from the psychologist back to the physiologist.

Underlying this partly metaphorical representation of the bifurcation of a person's two lives there is a seemingly more profound and philosophical assumption. It is assumed that there are two different kinds of existence or status. What exists or happens may have the status of physical existence, or it may have the status of mental existence. Somewhat as the faces of coins are either heads or tails, or somewhat as living creatures are either male or female, so, it is supposed, some existing is physical existing, other existing is mental existing. It is a necessary feature of what has physical existence that it is in space and time, it is a necessary feature of what has mental existence that it is in time but not in space. What has physical existence is composed of matter, or else is a function of matter; what has mental existence consists of consciousness, or else is a function of consciousness.

There is thus a polar opposition between mind and matter, an opposition which is often brought out as follows. Material objects are situated in a common field, known as 'space', and what happens to one body in one part of space is mechanically connected with what happens to other bodies in other parts of space. But mental happenings occur in insulated fields, known as 'minds', and there is, apart maybe from telepathy, no direct causal connection between what happens in one mind and what happens in another. Only through the medium of the public physical world can the mind of one person make a difference to the mind of another. The mind is its own place and in his inner life each of us lives the life of a ghostly Robinson Crusoe. People can see, hear and jolt one another's bodies, but they are irremediably blind and deaf to the workings of one another's minds and inoperative upon them.

What sort of knowledge can be secured of the workings of a mind? On the one side, according to the official theory, a person has direct knowledge of the best imaginable kind of the workings of his own mind. Mental states and processes are (or are normally) conscious states and processes, and the consciousness which irradiates them can engender no illusions and leaves the door open for no doubts. A person's present thinkings, feelings and willings, his perceivings, rememberings and imaginings are intrinsically 'phosphorescent'; their existence and their nature are inevitably betrayed to their owner. The inner life is a stream of consciousness of such a sort that it would be absurd to suggest that the mind whose life is that stream might be unaware of what is passing down it.

True, the evidence adduced recently by Freud seems to show that there exist channels tributary to this stream, which run hidden from their owner. People are actuated by impulses the existence of which they vigorously disavow; some of their thoughts differ from the thoughts which they acknowledge; and some of the actions which they think they will to perform they do not really will. They are thoroughly gulled by some of their own hypocrisies and they successfully ignore facts about their mental lives which on the official theory ought to be patent to them. Holders of the official theory tend, however, to maintain that anyhow in normal circumstances a person must be directly and authentically seized of the present state and workings of his own mind.

Besides being currently supplied with these alleged immediate data of consciousness, a person is also generally supposed to be able to exercise from time to time a special kind of perception, namely inner perception, or introspection. He can take a (non-optical) 'look' at what is passing in his mind. Not only can he view and scrutinize a flower through his sense of sight and listen to and discriminate the notes of a bell through his sense of hearing; he can also reflectively or introspectively watch, without any bodily organ of sense, the current episodes of his inner life. This self-observation is also commonly supposed to be immune from illusion, confusion or doubt. A mind's reports of its own affairs have a certainty superior to the best that is possessed by its reports of matters in the physical world. Sense-perceptions can, but consciousness and introspection cannot, be mistaken or confused.

On the other side, one person has no direct access of any sort to the events of the inner life of another. He cannot do better than make problematic inferences from the observed behaviour of the other person's body to the states of mind which, by analogy from his own conduct, he supposes to be signalised by that behaviour. Direct access to the workings of a mind is the privilege of that mind itself; in default of such privileged access, the workings of one mind are inevitably occult to everyone else. For the supposed arguments from bodily movements similar to their own to mental workings similar to their own would lack any possibility of observational corroboration. Not unnaturally, therefore, an adherent of the official theory finds it difficult to resist this consequence of his premisses, that he has no good reason to believe that there do exist minds other than his own. Even if he prefers to believe that to other human bodies there are harnessed minds not unlike his own, he cannot claim to be able to discover their individual characteristics, or the particular things that they undergo and do. Absolute solitude is on this showing the ineluctable destiny of the soul. Only our bodies can meet.

As a necessary corollary of this general scheme there is implicitly prescribed a special way of construing our ordinary concepts of mental powers and operations. The verbs, nouns and adjectives with which in ordinary life we describe the wits, characters and higher-grade performances of the people with whom we have do are required to be construed as signifying special episodes in their secret histories, or else as signifying tendencies for such episodes to occur. When someone is described as knowing, believing or guessing something, as hoping, dreading, intending or shirking something, as designing this or being amused at that, these verbs are supposed to denote the occurrence of specific modifications in his (to us) occult stream of consciousness. Only his own privileged access to this stream in direct awareness and introspection could provide authentic testimony that these mental-conduct verbs were correctly or incorrectly applied. The onlooker, be he teacher, critic, biographer or friend, can never assure himself that his comments have any vestige of truth. Yet it was just because we do in fact all know how to make such comments, make them with general correctness and correct them when they turn out to be confused or mistaken, that philosophers found it necessary to construct their theories of the nature and place of minds. Finding mental-conduct concepts being regularly and effectively used, they properly sought to fix their logical geography. But the logical geography officially recommended would entail that there could be no regular or effective use of these mental-conduct concepts in our descriptions of, and prescriptions for, other people's minds.

(2) THE ABSURDITY OF THE OFFICIAL DOCTRINE

Such in outline is the official theory. I shall often speak of it, with deliberate abusiveness, as 'the dogma of the Ghost in the Machine'. I hope to prove that it is entirely false, and false not in detail but in principle. It is not merely an assemblage of particular mistakes. It is one big mistake and a mistake of a special kind. It is, namely, a category-mistake. It represents the facts of mental life as if they belonged to one logical type or category (or range of types or categories), when they actually belong to another. The dogma is therefore a philosopher's myth. In attempting to explode the myth I shall probably be taken to be denying well-known facts about the mental life of human beings, and my plea that I aim at doing nothing more than rectify the logic of mental-conduct concepts will probably be disallowed as mere subterfuge.

I must first indicate what is meant by the phrase 'Category-mistake'. This I do in a series of illustrations.

A foreigner visiting Oxford or Cambridge for the first time is shown a number of colleges, libraries, playing fields, museums, scientific departments and administrative offices. He then asks 'But where is the University? I have seen where the members of the Colleges live, where the Registrar works, where the scientists experiment and the rest. But I have not yet seen the University in which reside and work the members of your University.' It has then to be explained to him that the University is not another collateral institution, some ulterior counterpart to the colleges, laboratories and offices which he has seen. The University is just the way in which all that he has already seen is organized. When they are seen and when their co-ordination is understood, the University has been seen. His mistake lay in his innocent assumption that it was correct to speak of Christ Church, the Bodleian Library, the Ashmolean Museum *and* the University, to speak, that is, as if 'the University' stood for an extra member of the class of which these other units are members. He was mistakenly allocating the University to the same category as that to which the other institutions belong.

The same mistake would be made by a child witnessing the march-past of a division, who, having had pointed out to him such and such battalions, batteries, squadrons, etc., asked when the division was going to appear. He would be supposing that a division was a counterpart to the units already seen, partly similar to them and partly unlike them. He would be shown his mistake by being told that in watching the battalions, batteries and squadrons marching past he had been watching the division marching past. The march-past was not a parade of battalions, batteries, squadrons *and* a division; it was a parade of the battalions, batteries and squadrons *of* a division.

One more illustration. A foreigner watching his first game of cricket learns what are the functions of the bowlers, the batsmen, the fielders, the umpires and the scorers. He then says 'But there is no one left on the field to contribute the famous element of team-spirit. I see who does the bowling, the batting and the wicketkeeping; but I do not see whose role it is to exercise *esprit de corps.*' Once more, it would have to be explained that he was looking for the wrong type of thing. Team-spirit is not another cricketing-operation supplementary to all of the other special tasks. It is, roughly, the keenness with which each of the special tasks is performed, and performing a task keenly is not performing two tasks. Certainly exhibiting team-spirit is not the same thing as bowling or catching, but nor is it a third thing such that we can say that the bowler first bowls *and* then exhibits team-spirit or that a fielder is at a given moment *either* catching *or* displaying *esprit de corps.*

These illustrations of category-mistakes have a common feature which must be noticed. The mistakes were made by people who did not know how to wield the concepts *University, division* and *team-spirit.* Their puzzles arose from inability to use certain items in the English vocabulary.

The theoretically interesting category-mistakes are those made by people who are perfectly competent to apply concepts, at least in the situations with which they are familiar, but are still liable in their abstract thinking to allocate those concepts to logical types to which they do not belong. An instance of a mistake of this sort would be the following story. A student of politics has learned the main differences between the British, the French and the American Consitutions, and has learned also the differences and connections between the Cabinet, Parliament, the various Ministries, the Judicature and the Church of England. But he still becomes embarrassed when asked questions about the connections between the Church of England, the Home Office and the British Constitution. For while the Church and the Home Office are institutions, the British Constitution is not another institution in the same sense of that noun. So inter-institutional relations which can be asserted or denied to hold between the Church and the Home Office cannot be asserted or denied to hold between either of them and the British Constitution. 'The British Constitution' is not a term of the same logical type as 'the Home Office' and 'the Church of England'. In a partially similar way, John Doe may be a relative, a friend, an enemy or a stranger to Richard Roe; but he cannot be any of these things to the Average Taxpayer. He knows how to talk sense in certain sorts of discussions about the Average Taxpayer, but he is baffled to say why he could not come across him in the street as he can come across Richard Roe.

It is pertinent to our main subject to notice that, so long as the student of politics continues to think of the British Constitution as a counterpart to the other institutions, he will tend to describe it as a mysteriously occult institution; and so long as John Doe continues to think of the Average Taxpayer as a fellow-citizen, he will tend to think of him as an elusive insubstantial man, a ghost who is everywhere yet nowhere.

My destructive purpose is to show that a family of radical category-mistakes is the source of the double-life theory. The representation of a person as a ghost mysteriously ensconced in a machine derives from this argument. Because, as is true, a person's thinking, feeling and purposive doing cannot be described solely in the idioms of physics, chemistry and physiology, therefore they must be described in counterpart idioms. As the human body is a complex organised unit, so the human mind must be another complex organised unit, though one made of a different sort of stuff and with a different sort of structure. Or, again, as the human body, like any other parcel of matter, is a field of causes and effects, so the mind must be another field of causes and effects, though not (Heaven be praised) mechanical causes and effects.

(3) THE ORIGIN OF THE CATEGORY-MISTAKE

One of the chief intellectual origins of what I have yet to prove to be the Cartesian category-mistake seems to be this. When Galileo showed that his methods of scientific discovery were competent to provide a mechanical theory which should cover every occupant of space, Descartes found in himself two conflicting motives. As a man of scientific genius he could not but endorse the claims of mechanics, yet as a religious and moral man he could not accept, as Hobbes accepted, the discouraging rider to those claims, namely that human nature differs only in degree of complexity from clockwork. The mental could not be just a variety of the mechanical.

He and subsequent philosophers naturally but erroneously availed themselves of the following escape-route. Since mental-conduct words are not to be construed as signifying the occurrence of mechanical processes, they must be construed as signifying the occurrence of non-mechanical processes; since mechanical laws explain movements in space as the effects of other movements in space, other laws must explain some of the non-spatial workings of minds as the effects of other non-spatial workings of minds. The difference between the human behaviours which we describe as intelligent and those which we describe as unintelligent must be a difference in their causation; so, while some movements of human tongues and limbs are the effects of mechanical causes, others must be the effects of non-mechanical causes, i.e., some issue from movements of particles of matter, others from workings of the mind.

The differences between the physical and the mental were thus represented as differences inside the common framework of the categories of 'thing', 'stuff', 'attribute', 'state', 'process', 'change', 'cause', and 'effect'. Minds are things, but different sorts of things from bodies; mental processes are causes and effects, but different sorts of causes and effects from bodily movements. And so on. Somewhat as the foreigner expected the University to be an extra edifice, rather like a college but also

considerably different, so the repudiators of mechanism represented minds as extra centres of causal processes, rather like machines but also considerably different from them. Their theory was a para-mechanical hypothesis.

That this assumption was at the heart of the doctrine is shown by the fact that there was from the beginning felt to be a major theoretical difficulty in explaining how minds can influence and be influenced by bodies. How can a mental process, such as willing, cause spatial movements like the movements of the tongue? How can a physical change in the optic nerve have among its effects a mind's perception of a flash of light? This notorious crux by itself shows the logical mould into which Descartes pressed his theory of the mind. It was the self-same mould into which he and Galileo set their mechanics. Still unwittingly adhering to the grammar of mechanics, he tried to avert disaster by describing minds in what was merely an obverse vocabulary. The workings of minds had to be described by the mere negatives of the specific descriptions given to bodies; they are not in space, they are not motions, they are not modifications of matter, they are not accessible to public observation. Minds are not bits of clockwork, they are just bits of not-clockwork.

As thus represented, minds are not merely ghosts harnessed to machines, they are themselves just spectral machines. Though the human body is an engine, it is not quite an ordinary engine, since some of its workings are governed by another engine inside it—this interior governor-engine being one of a very special sort. It is invisible, inaudible and it has no size or weight. It cannot be taken to bits and the laws it obeys are not those known to ordinary engineers. Nothing is known of how it governs the bodily engine.

A second major crux points the same moral. Since, according to the doctrine, minds belong to the same category as bodies and since bodies are rigidly governed by mechanical laws, it seemed to many theorists to follow that minds must be similarly governed by rigid non-mechanical laws. The physical world is a deterministic system, so the mental world must be a deterministic system. Bodies cannot help the modifications that they undergo, so minds cannot help pursuing the careers fixed for them. *Responsibility, choice, merit* and *demerit* are therefore inapplicable concepts—unless the compromise solution is adopted of saying that the laws governing mental processes, unlike those governing physical processes, have the congenial attribute of being only rather rigid. The problem of the Freedom of the Will was the problem how to reconcile the hypothesis that minds are to be described in terms drawn from the categories of mechanics with the knowledge that higher-grade human conduct is not of a piece with the behaviour of machines.

It is an historical curiosity that it was not noticed that the entire argument was broken-backed. Theorists correctly assumed that any sane man could already recognise the differences between, say, rational and non-rational utterances or between purposive and automatic behaviour. Else there would have been nothing requiring to be salved from mechanism. Yet the explanation given presupposed that one person could in principle never recognise the difference between the rational and the irrational utterances issuing from other human bodies, since he could never get access to the postulated immaterial causes of some of their utterances. Save for the doubtful exception of himself, he could never tell the difference between a man and a Robot. It would have to be conceded, for example, that, for all that we can tell, the inner lives of persons who are classed as idiots or lunatics are as rational as those of anyone else. Perhaps only their overt behaviour is disappointing; that is to say, perhaps 'idiots' are not really idiotic, or 'lunatics' lunatic. Perhaps, too, some of those who are classed as sane are really idiots. According to the theory, external observers could never know how the overt behaviour of others is correlated with their mental powers and processes and so they could never know or even plausibly conjecture whether their applications of mental-conduct concepts to these other people were correct or incorrect. It would then be hazardous or impossible for a man to claim sanity or logical consistency even for himself, since he would be debarred from comparing his own performances with those of others. In short, our characterisations of persons and their performances as intelligent, prudent and virtuous or as stupid, hypocritical and cowardly could never have been made, so the problem of providing a special causal hypothesis to serve as the basis of such diagnoses would never have arisen. The question, 'How do persons differ from machines?' arose just because everyone already knew how to apply mental-conduct concepts before the new causal hypothesis was introduced. This causal hypothesis could not therefore be the source of the criteria used in those applications. Nor, of course, has the causal hypothesis in any degree improved our handling of

those criteria. We still distinguish good from bad arithmetic, politic from impolitic conduct and fertile from infertile imaginations in the ways in which Descartes himself distinguished them before and after he speculated how the applicability of these criteria was compatible with the principle of mechanical causation.

He had mistaken the logic of his problem. Instead of asking by what criteria intelligent behaviour is actually distinguished from non-intelligent behaviour, he asked 'Given that the principle of mechanical causation does not tell us the difference, what other causal principle will tell it us?' He realised that the problem was not one of mechanics and assumed that it must therefore be one of some counterpart to mechanics. Not unnaturally psychology is often cast for just this role.

When two terms belong to the same category, it is proper to construct conjunctive propositions embodying them. Thus a purchaser may say that he bought a left-hand glove and a right-hand glove, but not that he bought a left-hand glove, a right-hand glove and a pair of gloves. 'She came home in a flood of tears and a sedan-chair' is a well-known joke based on the absurdity of conjoining terms of different types. It would have been equally ridiculous to construct the disjunction 'She came home either in a flood of tears or else in a sedan-chair'. Now the dogma of the Ghost in the Machine does just this. It maintains that there exist both bodies and minds; that there occur physical processes and mental processes; that there are mechanical causes of corporeal movements and mental causes of corporeal movements. I shall argue that these and other analogous conjunctions are absurd; but, it must be noticed, the argument will not show that either of the illegitimately conjoined propositions is absurd in itself. I am not, for example, denying that there occur mental processes. Doing long division is a mental process and so is making a joke. But I am saying that the phrase 'there occur mental processes' does not mean the same sort of thing as 'there occur physical processes', and, therefore, that it makes no sense to conjoin or disjoin the two.

If my argument is successful, there will follow some interesting consequences. First, the hallowed contrast between Mind and Matter will be dissipated, but dissipated not by either of the equally hallowed absorptions of Mind by Matter or of Matter by Mind, but in quite a different way. For the seeming contrast of the two will be shown to be as illegitimate as would be the contrast of 'she came home in a flood of tears' and 'she came home in a sedan-chair'. The belief that there is a polar opposition between Mind and Matter is the belief that they are terms of the same logical type.

It will also follow that both Idealism and Materialism are answers to an improper question. The 'reduction' of the material world to mental states and processes, as well as the 'reduction' of mental states and processes to physical states and processes, presuppose the legitimacy of the disjunction 'Either there exist minds or there exist bodies (but not both)'. It would be like saying, 'Either she bought a left-hand and a right-hand glove or she bought a pair of gloves (but not both)'.

It is perfectly proper to say, in one logical tone of voice, that there exist minds and to say, in another logical tone of voice, that there exist bodies. But these expressions do not indicate two different species of existence, for 'existence' is not a generic word like 'coloured' or 'sexed'. They indicate two different senses of 'exist', somewhat as 'rising' has different senses in 'the tide is rising', 'hopes are rising', and 'the average age of death is rising'. A man would be thought to be making a poor joke who said that three things are now rising, namely the tide, hopes and the average age of death. It would be just as good or bad a joke to say that there exist prime numbers and Wednesdays and public opinions and navies; or that there exist both minds and bodies. In the succeeding chapters I try to prove that the official theory does rest on a batch of category-mistakes by showing that logically absurd corollaries follow from it. The exhibition of these absurdities will have the constructive effect of bringing out part of the correct logic of mental-conduct concepts.

(4) HISTORICAL NOTE

It would not be true to say that the official theory derives solely from Descartes' theories, or even from a more widespread anxiety about the implications of seventeenth century mechanics. Scholastic and Reformation theology had schooled the intellects of the scientists as well as of the laymen, philosophers and clerics of that age. Stoic-Augustinian theories of the will were embedded in the Calvinist doctrines of sin and grace; Platonic and Aristotelian theories of the intellect shaped the orthodox doctrines of the immortality of the soul. Descartes was reformulating already prevalent theological doctrines of the soul in the new syntax of Galileo. The theologian's privacy of conscience became the philosopher's privacy of consciousness, and what had been the bogy of Predestination reappeared as the bogy of Determinism.

It would also not be true to say that the two-worlds myth did no theoretical good. Myths often do a lot of theoretical good, while they are still new. One benefit bestowed by the paramechanical myth was that it partly superannuated the then prevalent parapolitical myth. Minds and their Faculties had previously been described by analogies with political superiors and political subordinates. The idioms used were those of ruling, obeying, collaborating and rebelling. They survived and still survive in many ethical and some epistemological discussions. As, in physics, the new myth of occult Forces was a scientific improvement on the old myth of Final Causes, so, in anthropological and psychological theory, the new myth of hidden operations, impulses and agencies was an improvement on the old myth of dictations, deferences and disobediences.

Averroes (1126–1198)
FROM *THE INCOHERENCE OF THE INCOHERENCE*

The author, an Islamic philosopher born in Córdoba (in present-day Spain), formulates and criticizes the views that Ghazali (1058–1111), an Islamic philosopher from Tus, Persia, held on causality. Ghazali holds that there is no necessary connection between what is believed to be a cause and what is believed to be its effect. Averroes objects that if there are no observed efficient causes, then, contrary to what is commonly supposed, some acts must have no agents. Moreover, we could not infer someone's traits from that person's behavioral patterns. But we can. So causes are necessarily—even if, to use a modern expression, not "logically"—connected to their effects. This philosophical dialogue on cause and effect is discussed in Section C of the introductory essay to Part III.

READING QUESTIONS

In reading the selection, try to answer the following questions and identify the passages that support your answers:

1. What are Ghazali's views on causality according to Averroes?
2. What reasons does Ghazali give in support of his views?
3. What criticisms does Averroes formulate against Ghazali's position?
4. Which position, Ghazali's or Averroes's, is better and why?
5. What does the view that we can only know regularities entail?

Reprinted with the permission of the Gibb Memorial Trust from Averroes, *Tahafut al-Tahafut (The Incoherence from the Incoherence)*, trans. Simon Van den Bergh (London: Luzac & Co., 1954), pp. 312–333. Copyright © 1954.

We shall treat the four points Ghazali mentions one after the other.

Ghazali says:

The first point is their assertion that this connexion observed between causes and effects is of logical necessity, and that the existence of the cause without the effect or the effect without the cause is not within the realm of the contingent and possible. The second point is their assertion that human souls are substances existing by themselves, not imprinted on the body, and that the meaning of death is the end of their attachment to the body and the end of their direction of the body; and that otherwise the soul would exist at any time by itself. They affirm that this is known by demonstrative proof. The third point is their assertion that these souls cannot cease to exist, but that when they exist they are eternal and their annihilation cannot be conceived. The fourth point is their assertion that these souls cannot return to their bodies.

As to the first point, it is necessary to contest it, for on its negation depends the possibility of affirming the existence of miracles which interrupt the usual course of nature, like the changing of the rod into a serpent or the resurrection of the dead or the cleavage of the moon, and those who consider the ordinary course of nature a logical necessity regard all this as impossible. They interpret the resurrection of the dead in the Koran by saying that the cessation of the death of ignorance is to be understood by it, and the rod which conceived the arch-deceiver, the serpent, by saying that it means the clear divine proof in the hands of Moses to refute the false doctrines of the heretics; and as to the cleavage of the moon they often deny that it took place and assert that it does not rest on a sound tradition; and the philosophers accept miracles that interrupt the usual course of nature only in three cases.

First: in respect to the imaginative faculty they say that

when this faculty becomes predominant and strong, and the senses and perceptions do not submerge it, it observes the Indelible Tablet, and the forms of particular events which will happen in the future become imprinted on it; and that this happens to the prophets in a waking condition and to other people in sleep, and that this is a peculiar quality of the imaginative faculty in prophecy.

Secondly: in respect of a property of the rational speculative faculty i.e. intellectual acuteness, that is rapidity in passing from one known thing to another; for often when a problem which has been proved is mentioned to a keen-sighted man he is at once aware of its proof, and when the proof is mentioned to him he understands what is proved by himself, and in general when the middle term occurs to him he is at once aware of the conclusion, and when the two terms of the conclusion are present in his mind the middle term which connects the two terms of the conclusion occurs to him. And in this matter people are different; there are those who understand by themselves, those who understand when the slightest hint is given to them, and those who, being instructed, understand only after much trouble; and while on the one hand it may be assumed that incapacity to understand can reach such a degree that a man does not understand anything at all and has, although instructed, no disposition whatever to grasp the intelligibles, it may on the other hand be assumed that his capacity and proficiency may be so great as to arrive at a comprehension of all the intelligibles or the majority of them in the shortest and quickest time. And this difference exists quantitatively over all or certain problems, and qualitatively so that there is an excellence in quickness and easiness, and the understanding of a holy and pure soul may reach through its acuteness all intelligibles in the shortest time possible; and this is the soul of a prophet, who possesses a miraculous speculative faculty and so far as the intelligibles are concerned is not in need of a teacher; but it is as if he learned by himself, and he it is who is described by the words 'the oil of which would well-nigh give light though no fire were in contact with it, light upon light.'

Thirdly: in respect to a practical psychological faculty which can reach such a pitch as to influence and subject the things of nature: for instance, when our soul imagines something the limbs and the potencies in these limbs obey it and move in the required direction which we imagine, so that when a man imagines something sweet of taste the corners of his mouth begin to water, and the potency which brings forth the saliva from the places where it is springs into action, and when coitus is imagined the copulative potency springs into action, and the penis extends; indeed, when a man walks on a plank between two walls over an empty space, his imagination is stirred by the possibility of falling and his body is impressed by this imagination and in fact he falls, but when the plank is on the earth, he walks over it without falling. This happens because the body and the bodily faculties are created to be subservient and subordinate to the soul, and there is a difference here according to the purity and the power of the souls. And it is not impossible that the power of the soul should reach such a degree that also the natural power of things outside a man's body obeys it, since the soul of man is not impressed on his body although there is created in man's nature a certain impulse and desire to govern his body. And if it is possible that the limbs of his body should obey him, it is not impossible that other things besides his body should obey him and that his soul should control the blasts of the wind or the downpour of rain, or the striking of a thunderbolt or the trembling of the earth, which causes a land to be swallowed up with its inhabitants. The same is the case with his influence in producing cold or warmth or a movement in the air; this warmth or cold comes about through his soul, all these things occur without any apparent physical cause, and such a thing will be a miracle brought about by a prophet. But this only happens in matters disposed to receive it, and cannot attain such a scale that wood could be changed into an animal or that the moon, which cannot undergo cleavage, could be cloven. This is their theory of miracles, and we do not deny anything they have mentioned, and that such things happen to prophets; we are only opposed to their limiting themselves to this, and to their denial of the possibility that a stick might change into a serpent, and of the resurrection of the dead and other things. We must occupy ourselves with this question in order to be able to assert the existence of miracles and for still another reason, namely to give effective support to the doctrine on which the Muslims base their belief that God can do anything. And let us now fulfil our intention.

I say:

The ancient philosophers did not discuss the problem of miracles, since according to them such things must not be examined and questioned; for they are the principles of the religions, and the man who inquires into them and doubts them merits punishment, like the man who examines the other general religious principles, such as whether God exists or blessedness or the virtues. For the existence of all these cannot be doubted, and the mode of their existence is something divine which human apprehension cannot attain. The reason for this is that these are the principles of the acts through which man becomes virtuous, and that one can only attain knowledge after the attainment of virtue. One must not investigate the principles which cause virtue before the attainment of virtue, and since the theoretical sciences can only be perfected through assumptions and axioms which the learner accepts in the first place, this must be still more the case with the practical sciences.

As to what Ghazali relates of the causes of this as they are according to the philosophers, I do not know anyone who asserts this but Avicenna. And if such facts are verified and it is possible that a body could be changed qualitatively through something which is neither a body nor a bodily potency, then the reasons he mentions for this are possible; but not everything which in its nature is possible can be done by man, for what is possible to man is well known. Most things which are possible in themselves are impossible for man, and what is true of the prophet, that he can interrupt the ordinary course of nature, is impossible for man, but possible in itself; and because of this one need not assume that things logically impossible are possible for the prophets, and if you observe those miracles whose existence is confirmed, you will find that they are of this kind. The clearest of miracles is the Venerable Book of Allah, the existence of which is not an interruption of the course of nature assumed by tradition, like the changing of a rod into a serpent, but its miraculous nature is established by way of perception and consideration for every man who has been or who will be till the day of resurrection. And so this miracle is far superior to all others.

Let this suffice for the man who is not satisfied with passing this problem over in silence, and may he understand that the argument on which the learned base their belief in the prophets is another, to which Ghazali himself has drawn attention in another place, namely the act which proceeds from that quality through which the prophet is called prophet, that is the act of making known the mysterious and establishing religious laws which are in accordance with the truth and which bring about acts that will determine the happiness of the totality of mankind. I do not know anyone but Avicenna who has held the theory about dreams Ghazali mentions. The ancient philosophers assert about revelation and dreams only that they proceed from God through the intermediation of a spiritual incorporeal being which is according to them the bestower of the human intellect, and which is called by the best authors the active intellect and in the Holy Law angel. We shall now return to Ghazali's four points.

THE FIRST DISCUSSION

Ghazali says:

According to us the connexion between what is usually believed to be a cause and what is believed to be an effect is not a necessary connexion; each of two things has its own individuality and is not the other, and neither the affirmation nor the negation, neither the existence nor the non-existence of the one is implied in the affirmation, negation, existence, and non-existence of the other—e.g. the satisfaction of thirst does not imply drinking, nor satiety eating, nor burning contact with fire, nor light sunrise, nor decapitation death, nor recovery the drinking of medicine, nor evacuation the taking of a purgative, and so on for all the empirical connexions existing in medicine, astronomy, the sciences, and the crafts. For the connexion in these things is based on a prior power of God to create them in a successive order, though not because this connexion is necessary in itself and cannot be disjoined—on the contrary, it is in God's power to create satiety without eating, and death without decapitation, and to let life persist notwithstanding the decapitation, and so on with respect to all connexions. The philosophers, however, deny this possibility and claim that that is impossible. To investigate all these innumerable connexions would take us too long, and so we shall choose one single example, namely the burning of cotton through contact with fire; for we regard it as possible that the contact might occur without the burning taking place, and also that the cotton might be changed into ashes without any contact with fire, although the philosophers deny this possibility. The discussion of this matter has three points.

The first is that our opponent claims that the agent of the burning is the fire exclusively; this is a natural, not a voluntary agent, and cannot abstain from what is in its nature when it is brought into contact with a receptive substratum. This we deny, saying: The agent of the burning is God, through His creating the black in the cotton and the disconnexion of its parts, and it is God who made the cotton burn and made it ashes either through the intermediation of angels or without intermediation. For fire is a dead body which has no action, and what is the proof that it is the agent? Indeed, the philosophers have no other proof than the observation of the occurrence of the burning, when there is contact with fire, but observation proves only a simultaneity, not a causation, and, in reality, there is no other cause but God. For there is unanimity of opinion about the fact that the union of the spirit with the perceptive and moving faculties in the sperm of animals does not originate in the natures contained in warmth, cold, moistness, and dryness, and that the father is neither the agent of the embryo through introducing the sperm into the uterus, nor the agent of its life, its sight and hearing, and all its other faculties. And although it is well known that the same faculties exist in the father, still nobody thinks that these faculties exist through him; no, their existence is produced by the First either directly or through the intermediation of the angels who are in charge of these events. Of this fact the philosophers who believe in a creator are quite convinced, but it is precisely with them that we are in dispute.

It has been shown that coexistence does not indicate causation. We shall make this still more clear through an example. Suppose that a man blind from birth, whose eyes are veiled by a membrane and who has never heard people talk of the difference between night and day, has the membrane removed from his eyes by day and sees visible things, he will surely think then that the actual perception in his eyes of the forms of visible things is caused by the opening of his eyelids, and that as long as his sight is sound and in function, the hindrance removed and the object in front of him visible, he will, without doubt, be able to see, and he will never think that he will not see, till, at the moment when the sun sets and the air darkens, he will understand that it was the light of the sun which impressed the visible forms on his sight. And for what other reason do our opponents believe that in the principles of existence there are causes and influences from which the events which coincide with them proceed, than that they are constant, do not disappear, and are not moving bodies which vanish from sight? For if they disappeared or vanished we should observe the disjunction and understand then that behind our perceptions there exists a cause. And out of this there is no issue, according to the very conclusions of the philosophers themselves.

The true philosophers were therefore unanimously of the opinion that these accidents and events which occur when there is a contact of bodies, or in general a change in their positions, proceed from the bestower of forms who is an angel or a plurality of angels, so that they even said that the impression of the visible forms on the eye occurs through the bestower of forms, and that the rising of the sun, the soundness of the pupil, and the existence of the visible object are only the preparations and dispositions which enable the substratum to receive the forms; and this theory they applied to all events. And this refutes the claim of those who profess that fire is the agent of burning, bread the agent of satiety, medicine the agent of health, and so on.

I say:

To deny the existence of efficient causes which are observed in sensible things is sophistry, and he who defends this doctrine either denies with his tongue what is present in his mind or is carried away by a sophistical doubt which occurs to him concerning this question. For he who denies this can no longer acknowledge that every act must have an agent. The question whether these causes by themselves are sufficient to perform the acts which proceed from them, or need an external cause for the perfection of their act, whether separate or not, is not self-evident and requires much investigation and research. And if the theologians had doubts about the efficient causes which are perceived to cause each other, because there are also effects whose cause is not perceived, this is illogical. Those things whose causes are not perceived are still unknown and must be investigated, precisely because their causes are not perceived; and since everything whose causes are not perceived is still unknown by nature and must be investigated, it follows necessarily that what is not unknown has causes which are perceived. The man who reasons like the theologians does not distinguish between what is self-evident and what is unknown and everything Ghazali says in this passage is sophistical.

And further, what do the theologians say about the essential causes, the understanding of which alone can make a thing understood? For it is self-evident that things have essences and attributes which determine the special functions of each thing and through which the essences and names of things are differentiated. If a thing had not its specific nature, it would not have a special name nor a definition, and all things would be one—indeed, not even one; for it might be asked whether this one has a special act or one special passivity or not, and if it had a special act, then there would indeed exist special acts proceeding from special natures, but if it had no single special act, then the one would not be one. But if the nature of oneness is denied, the nature of

being is denied, and the consequence of the denial of being is nothingness.

Further, are the acts which proceed from all things absolutely necessary for those in whose nature it lies to perform them, or are they only performed in most cases or in half the cases? This is a question which must be investigated, since one single action-and-passivity between two existent things occurs only through one relation out of an infinite number, and it happens often that one relation hinders another. Therefore it is not absolutely certain that fire acts when it is brought near a sensitive body, for surely it is not improbable that there should be something which stands in such a relation to the sensitive thing as to hinder the action of the fire, as is asserted of talc and other things. But one need not therefore deny fire its burning power so long as fire keeps its name and definition.

Further, it is self-evident that all events have four causes, agent, form, matter, and end, and that they are necessary for the existence of the effects—especially those causes which form a part of the effect, namely that which is called by the philosophers matter, by the theologians condition and substratum, and that which is called by the philosophers form, by the theologians psychological quality. The theologians acknowledge that there exist conditions which are necessary to the conditioned, as when they say that life is a condition of knowledge; and they equally recognize that things have realities and definitions, and that these are necessary for the existence of the existent, and therefore they here judge the visible and the invisible according to one and the same scheme. And they adopt the same attitude towards the consequences of a thing's essence, namely what they call 'sign', as for instance when they say that the harmony in the world indicates that its agent possesses mind and that the existence of a world having a design indicates that its agent knows this world. Now intelligence is nothing but the perception of things with their causes, and in this it distinguishes itself from all the other faculties of apprehension, and he who denies causes must deny the intellect. Logic implies the existence of causes and effects, and knowledge of these effects can only be rendered perfect through knowledge of their causes. Denial of cause implies the denial of knowledge, and denial of knowledge implies that nothing in this world can be really known, and that what is supposed to be known is nothing but opinion, that neither proof nor definition exist, and that the essential attributes which compose definitions are void. The man who denies the necessity of any item of knowledge must admit that even this, his own affirmation, is not necessary knowledge.

As to those who admit that there exists, besides necessary knowledge, knowledge which is not necessary, about which the soul forms a judgement on slight evidence and imagines it to be necessary, whereas it is not necessary, the philosophers do not deny this. And if they call such a fact 'habit' this may be granted, but otherwise I do not know what they understand by the term 'habit'—whether they mean that it is the habit of the agent, the habit of the existing things, or our habit to form a judgement about such things? It is, however, impossible that God should have a habit, for a habit is a custom which the agent acquires and from which a frequent repetition of his act follows, whereas God says in the Holy Book: 'Thou shalt not find any alteration in the course of God, and they shall not find any change in the course of God.' If they mean a habit in existing things, habit can only exist in the animated; if it exists in something else, it is really a nature, and it is not possible that a thing should have a nature which determined it either necessarily or in most cases. If they mean our habit of forming judgements about things, such a habit is nothing but an act of the soul which is determined by its nature and through which the intellect becomes intellect. The philosophers do not deny such a habit; but 'habit' is an ambiguous term, and if it is analysed it means only a hypothetical act; as when we say 'So-and-so has the habit of acting in such-and-such a way', meaning that he will act in that way most of the time. If this were true, everything would be the case only by supposition, and there would be no wisdom in the world from which it might be inferred that its agent was wise.

And, as we said, we need not doubt that some of these existents cause each other and act through each other, and that in themselves they do not suffice for their act, but that they are in need of an external agent whose act is a condition of their act, and not only of their act but even of their existence. However, about the essence of this agent or of these agents the philosophers differ in one way, although in another they agree. They all agree in this, that the First Agent is immaterial and that its act is the condition of the existence and acts of existents, and that the act of their agent reaches these existents through the intermediation of an effect of this agent, which is different from these existents and which, according to some of them, is exclusively the heavenly sphere, whereas others assume besides this sphere another immaterial existent which they call the bestower of forms.

But this is not the place to investigate these theories, and the highest part of their inquiry is this; and if you are one of those who desire these truths, then follow the right road which leads to them. The reason why the philosophers differed about the origin of the essential forms and especially of the forms of the soul is that they could not relate them to the warm, cold, moist, and dry, which are the causes of all natural things which come into being and pass away, whereas the materialists related everything which does not seem to have an apparent cause to the warm, cold, moist, and dry, affirming that these things originated through certain mixtures of those elements, just as colours and other accidents come into existence. And the philosophers tried to refute them.

Ghazali says:

Our second point is concerned with those who acknowledge that these events proceed from their principles, but say that the disposition to receive the forms arises from their observed and apparent causes. However, according to them also the events proceed from these principles not by deliberation and will, but by necessity and nature, as light does from the sun, and the substrata differ for their reception only through the differentiations in their disposition. For instance, a polished body receives the rays of the sun, reflects them and illuminates another spot with them, whereas an opaque body does not receive them; the air does not hinder the penetration of the sun's light, but a stone does; certain things become soft through the sun, others hard; certain things, like the garments which the fuller bleaches, become white through the sun, others like the fuller's face become black: the principle is, however, one and the same, although the effects differ through the differences of disposition in the substratum. Thus there is no hindrance or incapacity in the emanation of what emanates from the principles of existence; the insufficiency lies only in the receiving substrata. If this is true, and we assume a fire that has the quality it has, and two similar pieces of cotton in the same contact with it, how can it be imagined that only one and not the other will be burned, as there is here no voluntary act? And from this point of view they deny that Abraham could fall into the fire and not be burned notwithstanding the fact that the fire remained fire, and they affirm that this could only be possible through abstracting the warmth from the fire (through which it would, however, cease to be fire) or through changing the essence of Abraham and making him a stone or something on which fire has no influence, and neither the one nor the other is possible.

I say:

Those philosophers who say that these perceptible existents do not act on each other, and that their agent is exclusively an external principle, cannot affirm that their apparent action on each other is totally illusory, but would say that this action is limited to preparing the disposition to accept the forms from the external principle. However, I do not know any philosopher who affirms this absolutely; they assert this only of the essential forms, not of the forms of accidents. They all agree that warmth causes warmth, and that all the four qualities act likewise, but in such a way that through it the elemental fire and the warmth which proceeds from the heavenly bodies are conserved. The theory which Ghazali ascribes to the philosophers, that the separate principles act by nature, not by choice, is not held by any important philosophers; on the contrary, the philosophers affirm that that which possesses knowledge must act by choice. However, according to the philosophers, in view of the excellence which exists in the world, there can proceed out of two contraries only the better, and their choice is not made to perfect their essences—since there is no imperfection in their essence—but in order that through it those existents which have an imperfection in their nature may be perfected.

As to the objection which Ghazali ascribes to the philosophers over the miracle of Abraham, such things are only asserted by heretical Muslims. The learned among the philosophers do not permit discussion or disputation about the principles of religion, and he who does such a thing needs, according to them, a severe lesson. For whereas every science has its principles, and every student of this science must concede its principles and may not interfere with them by denying them, this is still more obligatory in the practical science of religion, for to walk on the path of the religious virtues is necessary for a man's existence, according to them, not in so far as he is a man, but in so far as he has knowledge; and therefore it is necessary for every man to concede the principles of religion and invest with authority the man who lays them down. The denial and discussion of these principles denies human existence, and therefore heretics must be killed. Of religious principles it must be said that they are divine things which surpass human understanding, but must be acknowledged although their causes are unknown.

Therefore we do not find that any of the ancient philosophers discusses miracles, although they were known and had appeared all over the world, for they are the principles on which religion is based and religion is the principle of the virtues; nor did they discuss any of the things which are said to happen after death. For if a man grows up according to the religious virtues he becomes absolutely virtuous, and if time and felicity are granted to him, so that he becomes one of the deeply learned thinkers and it happens that he can explain one of the principles of religion, it is enjoined upon him that he should not divulge this explanation and should say 'all these are the terms of religion and the wise', conforming himself to the Divine Words, 'but those who are deeply versed in knowledge say: we believe in it, it is all from our Lord'.

Ghazali says:

There are two answers to this theory. The first is to say: 'We do not accept the assertion that the principles do not act in a voluntary way and that God does not act through His will, and we have already refuted their claim in treating of the question of the temporal creation of the world. If it is established that the Agent creates the burning through His will when the piece of cotton is brought in contact with the fire, He can equally well omit to create it when the contact takes place.

I say:

Ghazali, to confuse his opponent, here regards as established what his opponent refuses to admit, and says that his opponent has no proof for his refusal. He says that the First Agent causes the burning without an intermediary He might have created in order that the burning might take place through the fire. But such a claim abolishes any perception of the existence of causes and effects. No philosopher doubts that, for instance, the fire is the cause of the burning which occurs in the cotton through the fire—not, however, absolutely, but by an external principle which is the condition of the existence of fire, not to speak of its burning. The philosophers differ only about the quiddity of this principle—whether it is a separate principle, or an intermediary between the event and the separate principle besides the fire.

Ghazali says, on behalf of the philosophers:

But it may be said that such a conception involves reprehensible impossibilities. For if you deny the necessary dependence of effects or their causes and relate them to the will of their Creator, and do not allow even in the will a particular definite pattern, but regard it as possible that it may vary and change in type, then it may happen to any of us that there should be in his presence beasts of pray and flaming fires and immovable mountains and enemies equipped with arms, without his seeing them, because God had not created in him the faculty of seeing them. And a man who had left a book at home might find it on his return changed into a youth, handsome, intelligent, and efficient, or into an animal; or if he left a youth at home, he might find him turned into a dog; or he might leave ashes and find them changed into musk; or a stone changed into gold, and gold changed into stone. And if he were asked about any of these things, he would answer: 'I do not know what there is at present in my house; I only know that I left a book in my house, but perhaps by now it is a horse which has soiled the library with its urine and excrement, and I left in my house a piece of bread which has perhaps changed into an apple-tree.' For God is able to do all these things, and it does not belong to the necessity of a horse that it should be created from a sperm, nor is it of the necessity of a tree that it should be created from a seed; no, there is no necessity that it should be created out of anything at all. And perhaps God creates things which never existed before; indeed, when one sees a man one never saw before and is asked whether this man has been generated, one should answer hesitantly: 'It may be that he was one of the fruits in the market which has been changed into a man, and that this is that man.' For God can do any possible thing, and this is possible, and one cannot avoid being perplexed by it; and to this kind of fancy one may yield *ad infinitum*, but these examples will do.

But the answer is to say: If it were true that the existence of the possible implied that there could not be created in man any knowledge of the non-occurrence of a possible, all these consequences would follow necessarily. But we are not at a loss over any of the examples which you have brought forward. For God has created in us the knowledge that He will not do all these possible things, and we only profess that these things are not necessary, but that they are possible and may or may not happen, and protracted habit time after time fixes their occurrence in our minds according to the past habit in a fixed impression. Yes, it is possible that a prophet should know in such ways as the philosophers have explained that a certain man will not come tomorrow from a journey, and although his coming is possible the prophet knows that this possibility will not be realized. And often you may observe even ordinary men of whom you know that they are not aware of anything occult, and can know the intelligible only through instruction, and still it cannot be denied that nevertheless their soul and conjecturing power can acquire sufficient strength to apprehend what the prophets apprehend in so far as they know the possibility of an event, but know that it will not happen. And if God interrupts the habitual course by causing this unusual event to happen this knowledge of the habitual is at the time of the interruption removed from their hearts and He no longer creates it. There is, therefore, no objection to admitting that a thing may be possible for God, but that He had the previous knowledge that although He might have done so He would not carry it out during a certain time, and that He has created in us the knowledge that He would not do it during that time.

I say:

When the theologians admit that the opposite of everything existing is equally possible, and that it is such in regard to the Agent, and that only one of these opposites can be differentiated through the will of the Agent, there is no fixed standard for His will either constantly or for most cases, according to which things must happen. For this reason the theologians are open to all the scandalous implications with which they are charged. For true knowledge is the knowledge of a thing as it is in reality. And if in reality there only existed, in regard both to the substratum and to the Agent, the possibility of the two opposites, there would no longer, even for the twinkling of an eye, be any permanent knowledge of anything, since we suppose such an agent to rule existents like a tyrannical prince who has the highest power, for whom nobody in his dominion can deputize, of whom no standard or custom is known to which reference might be made. Indeed, the acts of such a prince will undoubtedly be unknown by nature, and if an act of his comes into existence the continuance of its existence at any moment will be unknown by nature.

Ghazali's defence against these difficulties that God created in us the knowledge that these possibilities would be realized only at special times, such as at the time of the miracle, is not a true one. For the knowledge created in us is always in conformity with the nature of the real thing, since the definition of truth is that a thing is believed to be such as it is in reality. If therefore there is knowledge of these possibles, there must be in the real possibles a condition to which our knowledge refers, either through these possibles themselves or through the agent, or for both reasons—a condition which the theologians call habit. And since the existence of this condition which is called habit is impossible in the First Agent, this condition can only be found in the existents, and this, as we said, is what the philosophers call nature.

The same congruity exists between God's knowledge and the existents, although God's knowledge of existents is their cause, and these existents are the consequence of God's knowledge, and therefore reality conforms to God's knowledge. If, for instance, knowledge of Zaid's coming reaches the prophet through a communication of God, the reason why the actual happening is congruous with the knowledge is nothing but the fact that the nature of the actually existent is a consequence of the eternal knowledge, for knowledge *qua* knowledge can only refer to something which has an actualized nature. The knowledge of the Creator is the reason why this nature becomes actual in the existent which is attached to it. Our ignorance of these possibles is brought about through our ignorance of the nature which determines the being or non-being of a thing. If the opposites in existents were in a condition of equilibrium, both in themselves and through their efficient causes, it would follow that they neither existed nor did not exist, or that they existed and did not exist at the same time, and one of the opposites must therefore have a preponderance in existence. And it is the knowledge of the existence of this nature which causes the actualization of one of the opposites. And the knowledge attached to this nature is either a knowledge prior to it, and this is the knowledge of which this nature is the effect, namely eternal knowledge, or the knowledge which is consequent on this nature, namely non-eternal knowledge. The attainment of the occult is nothing but the vision of this nature, and our acquisition of this knowledge not preceded by any proof is what is called in ordinary human beings a dream, and in prophets inspiration. The eternal will and eternal knowledge are the causes of this nature in existents. And this is the meaning of the Divine Words: 'Say that none in the heavens or on the earth know the occult but God alone. This nature is sometimes necessary and sometimes what happens in most cases. Dreams and inspiration are only, as we said, the announcement of this nature in possible things, and the sciences which claim the prognostication of future events possess only rare traces of the influences of this nature or constitution or whatever you wish to call it, namely that which is actualized in itself and to which the knowledge attaches itself.

Ghazali says:

The second answer—and in it is to be found deliverance from these reprehensible consequences—is to agree that in fire there is created a nature which burns two similar pieces of cotton which are brought into contact with it and does not differentiate between them, when they are alike in every respect. But still we regard it as possible that a prophet should be thrown into the fire and not burn, either through a change in the quality of the fire or through a change in the quality of the prophet, and that either through God or through the angels there should arise a quality in the fire which limited its heat to its own body, so that it did not go beyond it, but remained confined to it, keeping, however, to the form and reality of the fire, without its heat and influence extending beyond it; or that there should arise in the body of the person an attribute, which did not stop the body from being flesh and bone, but still defended it against the action of the fire. For we can see a man rub himself with talc and sit down in a lighted oven and not suffer from it; and if one had not seen it, one would deny it, and the denial of our opponents that it lies in God's power to confer on the fire or to the body an attribute which prevents it from being burnt is like the denial of one who has not seen the talc and its effect. For strange and marvellous things are in the power of God, many of which we have not seen, and why should we deny their possibility and regard them as impossible?

And also the bringing back to life of the dead and the changing of a stick into a serpent are possible in the following way: matter can receive any form, and therefore earth and the other elements can be changed into a plant, and a plant, when an animal eats it, can be changed into blood, then blood can be changed into sperm, and then sperm can be thrown into the womb and take the character of an animal. This, in the habitual course of nature, takes place over a long space of time, but why does our opponent declare it impossible that matter should pass through these different phases in a shorter period than is usual, and when once a shorter period is allowed there is no limit to its being shorter and shorter, so that these potencies can always become quicker in their action and eventually arrive at the stage of being a miracle of a prophet.

And if it is asked: 'Does this arise through the soul of the prophet or through another principle at the instigation of the prophet?'—we answer: 'Does what you acknowledge may happen through the power of the prophet's soul, like the downpour of rain or the falling of a thunderbolt or earthquakes—does that occur through him or through another principle? What we say about the facts which we have mentioned is like what you say about those facts which you regard as possible. And the best method according to both you and us is to relate these things to God, either immediately or through the intermediation of the angels. But at the time these occurrences become real, the attention of the prophet turns to such facts, and the order of the good determines its appearance to ensure the duration of the order of religion, and this gives a preponderance to the side of existence. The fact in itself is possible, and the principle in God is His magnanimity; but such a fact only emanates from Him when necessity gives a preponderance to its existence and the good determines it, and the good only determines it when a prophet needs it to establish his prophetic office for the promulgation of the good.

And all this is in accordance with the theory of the philosophers and follows from it for them, since they allow to the prophet a particular characteristic which distinguishes him from common people. There is no intellectual criterion for the extent of its possibility, but there is no need to declare it false when it rests on a good tradition and the religious law states it to be true. Now, in general, it is only the sperm which accepts the form of animals—and it receives its animal potencies only from the angels, who according to the philosophers, are the principles of existents—and only a man can be created from the sperm of a man, and only a horse from the sperm of a horse, in so far as the actualization of the sperm through the horse determines the preponderance of the analogous form of a horse over all other forms, and it accepts only the form to which in this way the preponderance is given, and therefore barley never grows from wheat or an apple from a pear. Further, we see that certain kinds of animal are only produced by spontaneous generation from earth and never are generated by procreation—e.g., worms, and some which are produced both spontaneously and by procreation like the mouse, the serpent, and the scorpion, for their generation can come also from earth. Their disposition to accept forms varies through causes unknown to us, and it is not in human power to ascertain them, since those forms do not, according to the philosophers, emanate from the angels by their good pleasure or haphazard, but in every substratum only in such a way that a form arises for whose acceptance it is specially determined through its own disposition. These dispositions differ, and their principles are, according to the philosophers, the aspects of the stars and the different relative positions of the heavenly bodies in their movements. And through this the possibility is open that there may be in the principles of these dispositions wonderful and marvellous things, so that those who understand talismans through their knowledge of the particular qualities of minerals and of the stars succeed in combining the heavenly potencies with those mineral peculiarities, and make shapes of these earthly substances, and seek a special virtue for them and produce marvellous things in the world through them. And often they drive serpents and scorpions from a country, and sometimes bugs, and they do other things which are known to belong to the science of talismans.

And since there is no fixed criterion for the principles of these dispositions, and we cannot ascertain their essence or limit them, how can we know that it is impossible that in certain bodies dispositions occur to change their phases at a quicker rhythm, so that such a body would be disposed to accept a form for the acceptance of which it was not prepared before, which is claimed to be a miracle? There is no denying this, except through a lack of understanding and an unfamiliarity with higher things and oblivion of the secrets of God in the created world and in nature. And he who has examined the many wonders of the sciences does not consider in any way impossible for God's power what is told of the wonders of the prophets.

Our opponents may say: 'We agree with you that everything possible is in the power of God, and you theologians agree with us that the impossible cannot be done and that there are things whose impossibility is known and things which are known to be possible, and that there are also things about which the understanding is undecided and which it does not hold to be either impossible or possible. Now what according to you is the limit of the impossible? If the impossible includes nothing but the simultaneous affirmation and negation of the same thing, then say that of two things the one is not the other, and that the existence of the one does not demand the existence of the other. And say then that God can create will without knowledge of the thing willed, and knowledge without life, and that He can move the hand of a dead man and make him sit and write volumes with his hand and engage himself in sciences while he has his eye open and his looks are fixed on his work, although he does not see and there is no life in him and he has no power, and it is God alone who creates all these ordered actions with the moving of the dead man's hand, and the movement comes from God. But by regarding this as possible the difference between voluntary action and a reflex action like shivering is destroyed, and a judicious act will no longer indicate that the agent possesses knowledge or power. It will then be necessary that God should be able to change genera and transform the substance into an accident and knowledge into power and black into white and a voice into an odour, just as He is able to change the inorganic into an animal and a stone into gold, and will then follow that God can also bring about other unlimited impossibilities.'

The answer to this is to say that the impossible cannot be done by God, and the impossible consists in the simultaneous affirmation and negation of a thing, or the affirmation of the more particular with the negation of the more general, or the affirmation of two things with the negation of one of them, and what does not refer to this is not impossible and what is not impossible can be done. The identification of black and white is impossible, because by the affirmation of the form of black in the substratum the negation of the form of white and of the existence of white is implied; and since the negation of white is implied by the affirmation of black, the simultaneous affirmation and negation of white is impossible. And the existence of a person in two places at once is only impossible because we imply by his being in the house that he cannot be in another place, and it cannot be understood from the denial that he is in another place that he can be simultaneously both in another place and in the house. And in the same way by will is implied the seeking of something that can be known, and if we assume a seeking without knowledge there cannot be a will and we would then deny what we had implied. And it is impossible that in the inorganic knowledge should be created, because we understand by inorganic that which does not perceive, and if in the organic perception was created it would become impossible to call it inorganic in the sense in which this word is understood.

As to the transformation of one genus into another, some theologians affirm that it is in the power of God, but we say that for one thing to become another is irrational; for, if for instance, the black could be transformed into power, the black would either remain or not, and if it does not exist any more, it is not changed but simply does not exist any more and something else exists; and if it remains existent together with power, it is not changed, but something else is brought in relation to it, and if the black remains and power does not exist, then it does not change, but remains as it was before. And when we say that blood changes into sperm, we mean by it that this identical matter is divested of one form and invested with another; and it amounts to this, that one form becomes nonexistent and another form comes into existence while the matter remains, and that two forms succeed one another in it. And when we say that water becomes air through being heated, we mean by it that the matter which had received the form of the water is deprived of this form and takes another, and the matter is common to them but the attribute changes. And it is the same when we say that the stick is changed into a serpent or earth into an animal. But there is no matter common to the accident and the substance, nor to black and to power, nor to the other categories, and it is impossible for this reason that they should be changed into each other.

As to God's moving the hand of a dead man, and raising this man up in the form of a living one who sits and writes, so that through the movement of his hand a well-ordered script is written, this in itself is not impossible as long as we refer events to the will of a voluntary being, and it is only to be denied because the habitual course of nature is in opposition to it. And your affirmation, philosophers, that, if this is so, the judiciousness of an act no longer indicates that the agent possesses knowledge is false, for the agent in this case is God; He determines the act and He performs it. And as to your assertion that if this is so there is no longer any difference between shivering and voluntary motion, we answer that we know this difference only because we experience in ourselves the difference between these two conditions, and we find thereby that the differentiating factor is power, and know that of the two classes of the possible the one happens at one time, the other at another; that is to say, we produce movement with the power to produce it at one time, and a movement without this power at another. Now, when we observe other movements than ours and see many well-ordered movements, we attain knowledge of the power behind them, and God creates in us all these different kinds of knowledge through the habitual course of events, through which one of the two classes of possibility becomes known, though the impossibility of the second class is not proved thereby.

I say:

When Ghazali saw that the theory that things have no particular qualities and forms from which particular acts follow, for every thing is very objectionable, and contrary to common sense, he conceded this in this last section and replaced it by the denial of two points: first that a thing can have these qualities but that they need not act on a thing in the way they usually act on it, e.g. fire can have its warmth but need not burn something that is brought near to it, even if it is usually burnt when fire is brought near to it; secondly that the particular forms have not a particular matter in every object.

The first point can be accepted by the philosophers, for because of external causes the procession of acts from agents may not be necessary, and it is not impossible that for instance fire may sometimes be brought near cotton without burning it, when something is placed with the cotton that makes it non-inflammable, as Ghazali says in his instance of talc and a living being.

As to the point that matter is one of the conditions for material things, this cannot be denied by the theologians, for, as Ghazali says, there is no difference between our simultaneous negation and affirmation of a thing and our simultaneous denial of part of it and affirmation of the whole. And since things consist of two qualities, a general and a particular—and this is what the philosophers mean by the term 'definition', a definition being composed according to them of a genus and a specific difference—it is indifferent for the denial of an existent which of its two qualities is denied. For instance, since man consists of two qualities, one being a general quality, viz. animality, and the second a particular, viz. rationality, man remains man just as little when we take away his animality as when we take away his rationality, for animality is a condition of rationality and when the condition is removed the conditioned is removed equally.

On this question the theologians and the philosophers agree, except that the philosophers believe that for particular things the general qualities are just as much a condition as the particular, and this the theologians do not believe; for the philosophers, for instance, warmth and moisture are a condition of life in the transient, because they are more general than life, just as life is a condition of rationality. But the theologians do not believe this, and so you hear them say: 'For us dryness and moisture are not a condition of life.' For the philosophers shape, too, is one of the particular conditions of life in an organic being; if not, one of two following cases might arise: either the special shape of the animal might exist without exercising any function, or this special shape might not exist at all. For instance, for the philosophers the hand is the organ of the intellect, and by means of it man performs his rational acts, like writing and the carrying on of the other arts; now if intelligence were possible in the inorganic, it would be possible that intellect might exist without performing its function, and it would be as if warmth could exist without warming the things that are normally warmed by it. Also, according to the philosophers, every existent has a definite quantity and a definite quality, and also the time when it comes into existence and during which it persists are determined, although in all these determinations there is, according to the philosophers, a certain latitude.

Theologians and philosophers agree that the matter of existents which participate in one and the same matter sometimes accepts one of two forms and sometimes its opposite, as happens, according to them, with the forms of the four elements, fire, air, water, and earth. Only in regard to the things which have no common matter or which have different matters do they disagree whether some of them can accept the forms of others—for instance, whether something which is not known by experience to accept a certain form except through many intermediaries can also accept this ultimate form without intermediaries. For instance, the plant comes into existence through composition out of the elements; it becomes blood and sperm through being eaten by an animal and from sperm and blood comes the animal, as is said in the Divine Words: 'We created man from an extract of clay, then We made him a clot in a sure depository' and so on till His words 'and blessed be God, the best of creators'. The theologians affirm that the soul of man can inhere in earth

without the intermediaries known by experience, whereas the philosophers deny this and say that, if this were possible, wisdom would consist in the creation of man without such intermediaries, and a creator who created in such a way would be the best and most powerful of creators; both parties claim that what they say is self-evident, and neither has any proof for its theory. And you, reader, consult your heart; it is your duty to believe what it announces, and this is what God—who may make us and you into men of truth and evidence—has ordained for you.

But some of the Muslims have even affirmed that there can be attributed to God the power to combine the two opposites, and their dubious proof is that the judgement of our intellect that this is impossible is something which has been impressed on the intellect, whereas if there had been impressed on it the judgement that this is possible, it would not deny this possibility, but admit it. For such people it follows as a consequence that neither intellect nor existents have a well-defined nature, and that the truth which exists in the intellect does not correspond to the existence of existing things. The theologians themselves are ashamed of such a theory, but if they held it, it would be more consistent with their point of view than the contradictions in which their opponents involve them on this point. For their opponents try to find out where the difference lies between what as a matter of fact the theologians affirm on this point and what they deny, and it is very difficult for them to make this out—indeed they do not find anything but vague words. We find, therefore, that those most expert in the art of theological discussion take refuge in denying the necessary connexion between condition and conditioned, between a thing and its definition, between a thing and its cause and between a thing and its sign. All this is full of sophistry and is without sense, and the theologian who did this was Abu-l-Ma'ali. The general argument which solves these difficulties is that existents are divided into opposites and correlates, and if the latter could be separated, the former might be united, but opposites are not united and correlates therefore cannot be separated. And this is the wisdom of God and God's course in created things, and you will never find in God's course any alteration. And it is through the perception of this wisdom that the intellect of man becomes intellect, and the existence of such wisdom in the eternal intellect is the cause of its existence in reality. The intellect therefore is not a possible entity which might have been created with other qualities, as Ibn Hazm imagined.

David Hume (1711–1776)
OF PROBABILITY; AND THE IDEA OF CAUSE AND EFFECT

Hume argues that no necessary connection can be observed between any cause and its supposed effect, nor can the connection be deductively proved. He suggests that our idea of a necessary connection can be explained by explaining our inference of such a connection. Hume's views are discussed in Section C of the introductory essay to Part III.

READING QUESTIONS

In reading the selection, try to answer the following questions and identify the passages that support your answers:

1. What are Hume's views on causality?
2. What reasons does Hume give in support of his views?
3. Are there any similarities between Hume's and Ghazali's views on causality?
4. Are Hume's views on causality open to any of the criticisms Averroes formulated against Ghazali's views on causality?
5. What are the differences between Hume's and Ghazali's motivations in formulating their views on causality?

Reprinted from David Hume, *A Treatise of Human Nature,* ed. L. A. Selby-Bigge (London: Oxford University Press, 1888, 1967), pp. 73–82.

. . . All kinds of reasoning consist in nothing but a *comparison,* and a discovery of those relations, either constant or inconstant, which two or more objects bear to each other. This comparison we may make, either when both the objects are present to the senses, or when neither of them is present, or when only one. When both the objects are present to the senses along with the relation, we call *this* perception rather than reasoning; nor is there in this case any exercise of the thought, or any action, properly speaking, but a mere passive admission of the impressions thro' the organs of sensation. According to this way of thinking, we ought not to receive as reasoning any of the observations we may make concerning *identity,* and the *relations* of *time* and *place;* since in none of them the mind can go beyond what

is immediately present to the senses, either to discover the real existence or the relations of objects. 'Tis only *causation,* which produces such a connexion, as to give us assurance from the existence or action of one object, that 'twas follow'd or preceded by any other existence or action; nor can the other two relations be ever made use of in reasoning, except so far as they either affect or are affected by it. There is nothing in any objects to perswade us, that they are either always *remote* or always *contiguous;* and when from experience and observation we discover, that their relation in this particular is invariable, we always conclude there is some secret *cause,* which separates or unites them. The same reasoning extends to *identity.* We readily suppose an object may continue individually the same, tho' several times absent from and present to the senses; and ascribe to it an identity, notwithstanding the interruption of the perception, whenever we conclude, that if we had kept our eye or hand constantly upon it, it wou'd have convey'd an invariable and uninterrupted perception. But this conclusion beyond the impressions of our senses can be founded only on the connexion of *cause and effect;* nor can we otherwise have any security, that the object is not chang'd upon us, however much the new object may resemble that which was formerly present to the senses. Whenever we discover such a perfect resemblance, we consider, whether it be common in that species of objects; whether possibly or probably any cause cou'd operate in producing the change and resemblance; and according as we determine concerning these causes and effects, we form our judgment concerning the identity of the object.

Here then it appears, that of those three relations, which depend not upon the mere ideas, the only one, that can be trac'd beyond our senses, and informs us of existences and objects, which we do not see or feel, is *causation*. This relation, therefore, we shall endeavour to explain fully before we leave the subject of the understanding.

To begin regularly, we must consider the idea of *causation*, and see from what origin it is deriv'd. 'Tis impossible to reason justly, without understanding perfectly the idea concerning which we reason; and 'tis impossible perfectly to understand any idea, without tracing it up to its origin, and examining that primary impression, from which it arises. The examination of the impression bestows a clearness on the idea; and the examination of the idea bestows a like clearness on all our reasoning.

Let us therefore cast our eye on any two objects, which we call cause and effect, and turn them on all sides, in order to find that impression, which produces an idea of such prodigious consequence. At first sight I perceive, that I must not search for it in any of the particular *qualities* of the objects; since, which-ever of these qualities I pitch on, I find some object, that is not possest of it, and yet falls under the denomination of cause or effect. And indeed there is nothing existent, either externally or internally, which is not to be consider'd either as a cause or an effect; tho' 'tis plain there is no one quality, which universally belongs to all beings, and gives them a title to that denomination.

The idea, then, of causation must be deriv'd from some *relation* among objects; and that relation we must now endeavour to discover. I find in the first place, that whatever objects are consider'd as causes or effects, are *contiguous;* and that nothing can operate in a time or place, which is ever so little remov'd from those of its existence. Tho' distant objects may sometimes seem productive of each other, they are commonly found upon examination to be link'd by a chain of causes, which are contiguous among themselves, and to the distant objects; and when in any particular instance we cannot discover this connexion, we still presume it to exist. We may therefore consider the relation of CONTIGUITY as essential to that of causation; at least may suppose it such, according to the general opinion, till we can find a more[1] proper occasion to clear up this matter, by examining what objects are or are not susceptible of juxtaposition and conjunction.

The second relation I shall observe as essential to causes and effects, is not so universally acknowledg'd, but is liable to some controversy. 'Tis that of PRIORITY of time in the cause before the effect. Some pretend that 'tis not absolutely necessary a cause shou'd precede its effect; but that any object or action, in the very first moment of its existence, may exert its productive quality, and give rise to another object or action, perfectly co-temporary with itself. But beside that experience in most instances seems to contradict this opinion, we may establish the relation of priority by a kind of inference or reasoning. 'Tis an establish'd maxim both in natural and moral philosophy, that an object, which exists for any time in its full perfection without producing another, is not its sole cause; but is assisted by some other principle, which pushes it from its state of inactivity, and makes it exert that energy, of which it was secretly possest. Now if any cause may be perfectly co-temporary with its effect, 'tis certain, according to this maxim, that they must all of them be so; since any one of them, which retards its operation for a single moment, exerts not itself at that very individual time, in which it might have operated; and therefore is no proper cause. The consequence of this wou'd be no less than the destruction of that succession of causes, which we observe in the world; and indeed, the utter annihilation of time. For if one cause were co-temporary with its effect, and this effect with *its* effect, and so on, 'tis plain there wou'd be no such thing as succession, and all objects must be co-existent.

If this argument appear satisfactory, 'tis well. If not, I beg the reader to allow me the same liberty,

---

[1] Part IV. sect. 5.

which I have us'd in the preceding case, of supposing it such. For he shall find, that the affair is of-no great importance.

Having thus discover'd or suppos'd the two relations of *contiguity* and *succession* to be essential to causes and effects, I find I am stopt short, and can proceed no farther in considering any single instance of cause and effect. Motion in one body is regarded upon impulse as the cause of motion in another. When we consider these objects with the utmost attention, we find only that the one body approaches the other; and that the motion of it precedes that of the other, but without any sensible interval. 'Tis in vain to rack ourselves with *farther* thought and reflexion upon this subject. We can go no *farther* in considering this particular instance.

Shou'd any one leave this instance, and pretend to define a cause, by saying it is something productive of another, 'tis evident he wou'd say nothing. For what does he mean by *production?* Can he give any definition of it, that will not be the same with that of causation? If he can; I desire it may be produc'd. If he cannot; he here runs in a circle, and gives a synonimous term instead of a definition.

Shall we then rest contented with these two relations of contiguity and succession, as affording a compleat idea of causation? By no means. An object may be contiguous and prior to another, without being consider'd as its cause. There is a NECESSARY CONNEXION to be taken into consideration; and that relation is of much greater importance, than any of the other two above-mention'd.

Here again I turn the object on all sides, in order to discover the nature of this necessary connexion, and find the impression, or impressions, from which its idea may be deriv'd. When I cast my eye on the *known qualities* of objects, I immediately discover that the relation of cause and effect depends not in the least on *them.* When I consider their *relations,* I can find none but those of contiguity and succession; which I have already regarded as imperfect and unsatisfactory. Shall the despair of success make me assert, that I am here possest of an idea, which is not preceded by any similar impression? This wou'd be too strong a proof of levity and inconstancy; since the contrary principle has been already so firmly establish'd, as to admit of no farther doubt; at least, till we have more fully examin'd the present difficulty.

We must, therefore, proceed like those, who being in search of any thing that lies conceal'd from them, and not finding it in the place they expected, beat about all the neighbouring fields, without any

certain view or design, in hopes their good fortune will at last guide them to what they search for. 'Tis necessary for us to leave the direct survey of this question concerning the nature of that *necessary connexion,* which enters into our idea of cause and effect; and endeavour to find some other questions, the examination of which will perhaps afford a hint, that may serve to clear up the present difficulty. Of these questions there occur two, which I shall proceed to examine, *viz.*

First, For what reason we pronounce it *necessary,* that every thing whose existence has a beginning, shou'd also have a cause?

Secondly, Why we conclude, that such particular causes must *necessarily* have such particular effects; and what is the nature of that *inference* we draw from the one to the other, and of the *belief* we repose in it?

I shall only observe before I proceed any farther, that tho' the ideas of cause and effect be deriv'd from the impressions of reflexion as well as from those of sensation, yet for brevity's sake, I commonly mention only the latter as the origin of these ideas; tho' I desire that whatever I say of them may also extend to the former. Passions are connected with their objects and with one another; no less than external bodies are connected together. The same relation, then, of cause and effect, which belongs to one, must be common to all of them.

Why a Cause Is Always Necessary

To begin with the first question concerning the necessity of a cause: 'Tis a general maxim in philosophy, that *whatever begins to exist, must have a cause of existence.* This is commonly taken for granted in all reasonings, without any proof given or demanded. 'Tis suppos'd to be founded on intuition, and to be one of those maxims, which tho' they may be deny'd with the lips, 'tis impossible for men in their hearts really to doubt of. But if we examine this maxim by the idea of knowledge above-explain'd, we shall discover in it no mark of any such intuitive certainty; but on the contrary shall find, that 'tis of a nature quite foreign to that species of conviction.

All certainty arises from the comparison of ideas, and from the discovery of such relations as are unalterable, so long as the ideas continue the same. These relations are *resemblance, proportions in quantity and number, degrees of any quality, and contrariety;* none of which are imply'd in this proposition, *Whatever has a beginning has also a cause of existence.* That proposition therefore is not intuitively certain. At least any one, who wou'd assert it to be intuitively certain, must deny these to be the only infallible relations, and must find some other relation of that kind to be imply'd in it; which it will then be time enough to examine.

But here is an argument, which proves at once, that the foregoing proposition is neither intuitively nor demonstrably certain. We can never demonstrate the necessity of a cause to every new existence, or new modification of existence, without shewing at the same time the impossibility there is, that any thing can ever begin to exist without some productive principle; and where the latter proposition cannot be prov'd, we must despair of ever being able to prove the former. Now that the latter proposition is utterly incapable of a demonstrative proof, we may satisfy ourselves by considering, that as all distinct ideas are separable from each other, and as the ideas of cause and effect are evidently distinct, 'twill be easy for us to conceive any object to be non-existent this moment, and existent the next, without conjoining to it the distinct idea of a cause or productive principle. The separation, therefore, of the idea of a cause from that of a beginning of existence, is plainly possible for the imagination; and consequently the actual separation of these objects is so far possible, that it implies no contradiction nor absurdity; and is therefore incapable of being refuted by any reasoning from mere ideas; without which 'tis impossible to demonstrate the necessity of a cause.

Accordingly we shall find upon examination, that every demonstration, which has been produc'd for the necessity of a cause, is fallacious and sophistical. All the points of time and place,[2] say some philosophers, in which we can suppose any object to begin to exist, are in themselves equal; and unless there be some cause, which is peculiar to one time and to one place, and which by that means determines and fixes the existence, it must remain in eternal suspence; and the object can never begin to be, for want of something to fix its beginning. But I ask; Is there any more difficulty in supposing the time and place to be fix'd without a cause, than to suppose the existence to be determin'd in that manner? The first question that occurs on this subject is always, *whether* the object shall exist or not: The next, *when* and *where* it shall begin to exist. If the removal of a cause be intuitively absurd in the one case, it must be so in the other: And if that absurdity be not clear without a proof in the one case, it will equally require one in the other. The absurdity, then, of the one supposition can never be a proof of that of the other; since they are both upon the same footing, and must stand or fall by the same reasoning.

The second argument,[3] which I find us'd on this head, labours under an equal difficulty. Every thing, 'tis said, must have a cause; for if any thing wanted a cause, *it* wou'd produce *itself;* that is, exist before it existed; which is impossible. But this reasoning is plainly unconclusive; because it supposes, that in our denial of a cause we still grant what we expressly deny, *viz.* that there must be a cause; which therefore is taken to be the object itself; and *that,* no doubt, is an evident contradiction. But to say that any thing is produc'd, or to express myself more properly, comes into existence, without a cause, is not to affirm, that 'tis itself its own cause; but on the contrary in excluding all external causes, excludes *a fortiori* the thing itself which is created. An object, that exists absolutely without any cause, certainly is not its own cause; and when you assert, that the one follows from the other, you suppose the very point in question, and take it for granted, that 'tis utterly impossible any thing can ever begin to exist without a cause, but that upon the exclusion of one productive principle, we must still have recourse to another.

'Tis exactly the same case with the[4] third argument, which has been employ'd to demonstrate the necessity of a cause. Whatever is produc'd without any cause, is produc'd by *nothing;* or in other words, has nothing for its cause. But nothing can never be a cause, no more than it can be something, or equal to two right angles. By the same intuition, that we perceive nothing not to be equal to two right angles, or not to be something, we perceive, that it can never be a cause; and consequently must perceive, that every object has a real cause of its existence.

I believe it will not be necessary to employ many words in shewing the weakness of this argument, after what I have said of the foregoing. They are all of them founded on the same fallacy, and are deriv'd from the same turn of thought. 'Tis sufficient only to observe, that when we exclude all causes we really do exclude them, and neither suppose nothing nor the object itself to be the causes of the existence; and consequently can draw no argument from the absurdity of these suppositions to prove the absurdity of that exclusion. If every thing must have a cause, it follows, that upon the exclusion of other causes we

---

[2] Mr. *Hobbes.*

[3] Dr. *Clarke* and others.

[4] Mr. *Locke.*

must accept of the object itself or of nothing as causes. But 'tis the very point in question, whether every thing must have a cause or not; and therefore, according to all just reasoning, it ought never to be taken for granted.

They are still more frivolous, who say, that every effect must have a cause, because 'tis imply'd in the very idea of effect. Every effect necessarily presupposes a cause; effect being a relative term, of which cause is the correlative. But this does not prove, that every being must be preceded by a cause; no more than it follows, because every husband must have a wife, that therefore every man must be marry'd. The true state of the question is, whether every object, which begins to exist, must owe its existence to a cause; and this I assert neither to be intuitively nor demonstratively certain, and hope to have prov'd it sufficiently by the foregoing arguments.

Since it is not from knowledge or any scientific reasoning, that we derive the opinion of the necessity of a cause to every new production, that opinion must necessarily arise from observation and experience. The next question, then, shou'd naturally be, *how experience gives rise to such a principle?* But as I find it will be more convenient to sink this question in the following, *Why we conclude, that such particular causes must necessarily have such particular effects, and why we form an inference from one to another?* we shall make that the subject of our future enquiry. 'Twill, perhaps, be found in the end, that the same answer will serve for both questions.

Mario Bunge (contemporary)
INDUCTION IN SCIENCE

Bunge is a Latin American philosopher and physicist. In this selection, he questions the view that the laws of nature can be established by induction in the narrow sense of inferring from a sample to the whole class of which the sample is a representative. He argues that scientific research actually follows a via media *between the extremes of inductivism and deductivism. Besides inductive arguments, it uses arguments by analogy, generalizations involving new concepts, induction by elimination, prediction, interpolation, and reduction. Bunge's views are discussed at the end of Section C of the introductory essay to Part III.*

READING QUESTIONS

In reading the selection, try to answer the following questions and identify the passages that support your answers:

1. What are Bunge's views on induction?
2. What reasons does he give in support of his views?
3. Are they sound? Why or why not?
4. What implications does Bunge's position have for Hume's views on causality?
5. What implications does it have for the views of Ghazali and Averroes?

Reprinted with the permission of the author and publisher from Mario Bunge, *The Myth of Simplicity* (Englewood Cliffs, NJ: Prentice Hall, 1963), pp. 137–152. Copyright © 1963.

Laws, the vertebrae of science, are sometimes believed to be established by induction (empiricist tradition, as represented by Bacon), and at other times to be the product of reason and free imagination (rationalist tradition, as exemplified by Einstein). The first belief is frequent among field and laboratory workers, the second among theoreticians. When the *establishment* of a law statement is mentioned, either of two entirely different inferential procedures may be meant: the *inception* or introduction of the statement, or its *test*. In either case it is accepted that inferences are involved, rather than direct and immediate apprehensions. The question is whether the inferences are inductive, deductive, or perhaps neither exclusively inductive nor exclusively deductive, but a combination of the two with the addition of analogy and of some kind of invention or creation.

In the present chapter we shall investigate the question of whether scientific inference is predominantly inductive, as claimed by inductivist metascience,[1] or predominantly deductive, as maintained by deductivism[2]—or, finally, whether it actually goes along a third way of its own. The discussion will be confined to factual statements, usually called empirical sentences, without thereby denying the great heuristic value that case examination also has in mathematical invention and problem-solving.[3]

1. INDUCTION PROPER

Before approaching the problem let us clear the ground. By *induction stricto sensu* I shall understand the type of nondemonstrative reasoning consisting in *obtaining or validating general propositions on the basis of the examination of cases.* Or, as Whewell put it long ago, "by *Induction* is to be understood that process of collecting general truths from the examination of particular facts."[4] This linguistic convention makes no appeal to epistemological categories such as 'new knowledge,' which are often used in the characterization of inductive inference, although the enlargement of knowledge is the purpose of both inductive and deductive inference.

The proposed equation of induction and generalization on the basis of case examination leaves the following kinds of inference *out* of the domain of inductive inference: (1) *analogy*, which is a certain reasoning from particular to particular, or from general to general, and which probably underlies inductive inference; (2) generalization involving the introduction of *new* concepts, that is, of concepts absent in the evidential basis; (3) the so-called *induction by elimination*, which is nothing but the refutation of hypotheses found unfit because their observable consequences, derived by deduction, do not match with the empirical evidence at hand; (4) scientific *prediction*, which is clearly deductive, since it consists in the derivation of singular or existential propositions from the conjunction of law statements and specific information; (5) *interpolation* in the strict sense (not, however, curve fitting), which is deductive as well, since it amounts to specification; (6) *reduction*, or assertion of the antecedent of a conditional on the ground of the repeated verification of the consequent.

With the above definition of induction in mind, let us inquire into the role of induction in the formation and testing of the hypotheses that are dignified with the name of laws of nature or of culture.

2. INDUCTION IN THE FRAMING OF HYPOTHESES

The premises of induction may be singular or general. Let us distinguish the two cases by calling *first degree induction* the inference leading from the examination of observed instances to general statements of the lowest level (e.g., "All men are mortal"), and *second degree induction* the inference consisting in the widening of such empirical generalizations (leading, e.g., from such statements as "All men are mortal," "All lobsters are mortal," "All snakes are mortal," to "All metazoans are mortal"). First degree induction starts from singular propositions, whereas second degree induction is the generalization of generalizations.

[1] J. M. Keynes, *A Treatise on Probability* (London: Macmillan, 1921 and 1929); H. Reichenbach, *The Theory of Probability* (Berkeley and Los Angeles: University of California Press, 1949); R. Carnap, *Logical Foundations of Probability* (Chicago: The University of Chicago Press, 1950); H. Jeffreys, *Scientific Inference* (Cambridge: University Press, 1931 and 1957); G. H. von Wright, *The Logical Problem of Induction*, 2nd ed. (Oxford: Blackwell, 1957).

[2] P. Duhem, *La théorie physique*, 2nd ed. (Paris: Rivière, 1914); K. R. Popper, *The Logic of Scientific Discovery*, 2nd ed. (London: Hutchinson 1959); J. O. Wisdom, *Foundations of Inference in Natural Science* (London: Methuen, 1952). Actually two of the earliest anti-Baconian works were clad in a predominantly inductivist language, as required by the "spirit of the times": I mean J. F. W. Herschel's *Preliminary Discourse on the Study of Natural Philosophy* (London: Longmans, 1830), and W. Whewell's *Novum Organum Renovatum*, 3rd ed. (London: Parker, 1858), where the first revindication of the method of hypothesis is to be found.

[3] G. Polya, *Mathematics and Plausible Reasoning* (Princeton: Princeton University Press, 1954), 2 vols. Analogy and induction in the factual sciences are still waiting for a study as masterful as Polya's.

[4] W. Whewell, *History of the Inductive Sciences*, 3rd ed. (New York: Appleton, 1858), I, p. 43.

Empirical generalizations of the type of "Owls eat mice" are often reached by first degree induction. Necessary, though not sufficient, conditions for performing a first degree induction are: (*a*) the facts referred to by the singular propositions that are to be generalized must have been observed, must be actual phenomena, never merely possible facts like the burning of this book or the establishment of a democratic government in Argentina; (*b*) the predicates contained in the generalization must be observable *stricto sensu,* such as predicates designating the color and size of perceptible bodies. Hence the "observables" of atomic theory, such as the variables representing the instantaneous position or angular momentum of an electron, will not do for this purpose, since they are actually theoretical predicates (constructs).

Condition (*a*) excludes from the range of induction all inventions, and countless elementary generalizations, such as those involving dispositions or potential properties. Condition (*b*) excludes from the domain of induction all the more important scientific hypotheses: those which have been called transcendent[5] or non-instantial,[6] because they contain non-observable, or theoretical predicates, such as 'attraction,' 'energy,' 'stable,' 'adaptation,' or 'mental.' Transcendent hypotheses—that is, assumptions going beyond experience—are most important in science because, far from merely enabling us to colligate or summarize empirical data, they enter into the explanation of data.

The hypothesis "Copper is a good conductor" is a second degree inductive generalization. It contains the class terms 'copper' and 'conductor' (a dispositional term). Its generalization "All metals are good conductors" is, a fortiori, another second degree induction: it refers not only to the class of metals known at the moment it was framed, but to the conceptually open class of metals known and knowable. We do not accept the latter generalization just because of its inductive support, weighty as it is, but also—perhaps mainly—because the theoretical study of the crystal structure of metals and the electron gas inside them shows us that the predicate 'metal' or, if preferred, 'solid,' is functionally associated with the predicate 'conductor.' This association, which transcends the Humean juxtaposition of properties, is expressed in law statements belonging to the theory of solid state. We accept the generalization with some confidence because we have succeeded in understanding it, by subsuming it under a theory. Similarly, we know since Harvey that "There are no heartless vertebrates" is true, not because this statement has been found and verified inductively, but because we understand the function of the heart in the maintenance of life.

Compare the above examples with the low-level generalization "All ravens are black," the stock-in-trade example of inductivists. Ornithology has not yet accounted for the constant conjunction of the two properties occurring in this first degree induction. The day animal physiology hits upon an explanation of it, we shall presumably be told something like this: "All birds having the biological properties $P, Q, R, \ldots$ are black." And then some ornithologist may inquire whether ravens do possess the properties $P, Q, R, \ldots$, in order to ascertain whether the old generalization fits in the new systematic body of knowledge.

In summary, enumerative induction does play a role in the framing of general hypotheses, though certainly not as big a role as the one imagined by inductivism. Induction, important as it is in daily life and in the more backward stages of empirical science, has not led to finding a single important scientific law, incapable as it is of creating new and transempirical (transcendent) concepts, which are typical of theoretical science. In other words: induction may lead to framing *low-level, pre-theoretical, ad hoc* and *ex post facto* general hypotheses; the introduction of comprehensive and deep hypotheses requires a leap beyond induction.

3. INDUCTION IN THE TEST OF HYPOTHESES

Scientific hypotheses are empirically tested by seeking *both* positive instances (according to the inductivist injunction) and unfavorable ones (deductivist rule). In other words, the empirical test of hypotheses includes both confirmations and unsuccessful attempts at refutation. . . . But only first degree inductive generalizations *have* instances; hence they are the only ones that can be directly checked against empirical evidence. Statements expressing empirical evidence— i.e. basic statements—do not contain theoretical predicates such as 'mass,' 'recessive character,' or 'population pressure.' Hence, case examination by itself is irrelevant both to the framing and to the testing of transcendent hypotheses.

[5]   W. Kneale, *Probability and Induction* (Oxford: University Press, 1949 and 1952).

[6]   J. O. Wisdom, *op. cit.,* (fn. 2).

However, we do perform inductive inferences when stating plausible "conclusions" (i.e., guesses) from the examination of observed consequences of our theories. Granted, we cannot examine instances of transcendent hypotheses such as "The intensity of the electric current is proportional to the potential difference," because they are non-instantial. But hypotheses of this kind, which are the most numerous in the advanced chapters of science, do have observable consequents when conjoined with lower-level hypotheses containing both unobservable and observable predicates, such as "Electric currents deflect the magnetic needle." (The deflections can literally be observed, even though electricity and magnetism are unobservable.) And, if we wish to validate transcendent hypotheses, we must examine instances of such end-points of the piece of theory to which they belong.

To sum up, in the factual sciences the following rule of method seems to be accepted at least tacitly: "All hypotheses, even the epistemologically most complex ones, must entail—through inferential chains as long and twisted as is necessary—instantial hypotheses, so that they can be inductively confirmed." This rule assigns induction a place in scientific method, the over-all pattern of which is admittedly hypothetico-deductive.

Inductivism rejects the deductivist thesis that what is put to the test is always some (often remote) observable consequence of theories, and that we never test isolated hypotheses but always some *pot-pourri* of fragments of various theories—eventually including those involved in the building and reading of instruments and in the performing of computations. Inductivism maintains that this description of scientific procedure might square only with very high level hypotheses, such as the postulates of quantum mechanics. However, an analysis of elementary scientific hypotheses, even of existential ones—like "There is an air layer around the Earth"—confirms the deductivist description, with the sole though important exception of the contact line between the lowest level theorems and the empirical evidence.

Consider, for instance, the process that led to the establishment of the existence of the atmosphere. An analysis of this process[7] will show that Torricelli's basic hypotheses ("We live at the bottom of a sea of elemental air," and "Air is a fluid obeying the laws

of hydrostatics") were framed by analogy, not by induction, and that the remaining process of reasoning was almost entirely deductive. Induction occurred neither in the formulation nor in the elaboration of the hypotheses: it was equally absent in the design of the experiments that put them to the test. Nobody felt the need of repeating the simple experiments imagined by Torricelli and Pascal, nor of increasing their poor precision. Rather on the contrary, Torricelli's hypotheses were employed to explain further known facts and were instrumental in suggesting a number of new spectacular experiments, such as Guericke's and Boyle's. Induction did appear in the process, but only in the *final* estimate of the whole set of hypotheses and experimental results—namely, when it was concluded that the former had been confirmed by a large number and, particularly, by a great variety of experiments—whereas the rival peripatetic hypothesis of the abhorrence of void had been conclusively refuted.

To sum up, enumerative induction plays a role in the test of scientific hypotheses, but only in their *empirical* checking, which is not the sole test to which they are subjected.

4. INDUCTIVE CONFIRMATION AND DEDUCTIVE REFUTATION

Deductivists may object to the above concessions to induction, by stating that confirming instances have no value as compared with negative ones, since the rule of *modus tollens* ("If p, then q. Now, not—q; hence, not—p.") shows that a single definitely unfavorable case is conclusive, whereas no theorem of inductive logic could warrant a hypothesis through the mere accumulation of favorable instances. But this objection does not render the examination of cases worthless and does not invalidate our "concluding" something about them; hence it does not dispose of induction by enumeration.

Consider, in fact, a frequent laboratory situation, like the one described by the following sentence: "The results of n measurements of the property P of system S by means of the experimental set-up E agree, to within the experimental error ϵ, with the values x_i predicted by the theory T." Certainly, ninety favorable instances will have little value in the face of ten definitely unfavorable measured values, at least if high precision is sought. (On the other hand, a single unfavorable case against ninety-nine favorable ones would pose the question of the reliability of the

---

[7] M. Bunge, "¿Cómo sabemos que existe la atmósfera?," *Revista de la Universidad de Buenos Aires,* IV (1959), 246.

anomalous measurement value itself rather than rendering the theory suspect.) But how do we know that an instance is definitely unfavorable to the central hypothesis of the theory we are examining, and not to some of the background hypotheses, among which the usual assumption may occur, that no external perturbations are acting upon our system? Moreover, do not we call "negative" or "unfavorable" precisely those instances which, if relevant at all, *fail to confirm* the theory under examination?

Confirmation and refutation are unsymmetrical to each other, and the latter is weightier than the former; moreover, a theory that can only be confirmed, because no conceivable counterexample would ruin it, is not a scientific theory. But confirmation and refutation cannot be separated, because the very concept of negative instance is meaningful only in connection with the notion of favorable case, just as 'abnormality' is meaningless apart from 'normality.' To say that hypotheses, such as natural laws (or, rather, the corresponding statements), are only refutable, but not confirmable by experiment,[8] is as misleading as to maintain that all men are abnormal.

How do we know that a skilled and sincere attempt to refute a hypothesis has failed, if not because the attempt has *confirmed* some of the lowest-level consequences of the theory to which the given hypothesis belongs? How do we know that an attempt has succeeded—thereby forcing us to abandon the hypothesis concerned provided we are able to isolate it from the piece of theory to which it belongs, and provided better ones are in sight—if not because we have obtained no positive instances of its low-level consequences, or even because the percentage of positive instances is too poor?

The falsifiabilist rule enables us to discard certain hypotheses even *before* testing them; in fact, it commands us to reject as nonscientific all those conjectures that admit of no possible refutation, as is the case, e.g., with "All dreams are wish fulfilments, even though in some cases the wishes are repressed and consequently do not show up." But refutability, a necessary condition for a hypothesis to be *scientific,* is not a criterion of *truth:* to establish a proposition as at least partially true we must confirm it. Confirmation is insufficient, but it is necessary.

The falsifiabilist rule *supplements* the characteri-

zation of the difficult notion of positive instance, or favorable case, but provides no substitute for it. Refutation enables us to (provisionally) eliminate the less fitted assumptions—which are those that fit the data less adequately—but it does not enable us to justify alternative hypotheses. And, if we wish to resist irrationalism, if we believe that science and scientific philosophy constitute bulwarks against obscurantism, we cannot admit that scientific hypotheses are altogether unfounded but happy guesses, as deductivism claims. Law statements do not hang in the air: they are both *grounded* on previous knowledge and successfully *tested* by fresh evidence, both empirical and theoretical.

The attitude of attempting to refute a theory by subjecting it to severe empirical tests belongs to the pragmatic and methodological level, and pertains even to the ethical code of the modern scientist. The problem of confirmation and, consequently, the problem of the degree of validation and hence of acceptability of factual theories, belong both to the methodological and the epistemological levels. There is no conflict between the procedure that aims at refuting a theory, and the assignment to it of a degree of validation, or corroboration, on the basis of an examination of positive instances: they are complementary, not incompatible operations. Yet none of them is sufficient: pure experience has never been the supreme court of science.

5. THEORIFICATION

Neither unsuccessful attempts to refute a hypothesis nor heaps of positive instances of its observable consequents are enough to establish the hypothesis for the time being. We usually do not accept a conjecture as a full member of the body of scientific knowledge unless it has passed a further test which is as exacting as the empirical one or perhaps even more so: to wit, the rational test of *theorification,* an ugly neologism that is supposed to suggest the transformation of an isolated proposition into a statement belonging to a hypothetico-deductive system. We make this requirement, among other reasons, because the hypothesis to be validated acquires in this way the support of allied hypotheses in the same or in contiguous fields.

Consider the hypothesis "All men live less than 200 years." In order to test it, a confirmationist would accumulate positive instances, whereas a refutabilist would presumably establish an enrolling office for

---

[8] See K. R. Popper, *op. cit.* (fn. 2), and B. Russell, *Human Knowledge* (London: Allen & Unwin, 1948).

bicentenaries—the simplest and cheapest but not the most enlightening procedure. Old age medicine does not seem to pay much attention to either procedure, but tends on the other hand to explain or deduce the given statement from higher-level propositions, such as "The arteries of all men harden in time," "All cells accumulate noxious residues," "Neurons decrease in number after a certain age," "After youth every vertebrate ceases to employ certain organs, which consequently begin to atrophy," and so on.

The day physiology, histology and cytology succeed in explaining the empirical generalization, "All men live less than 200 years," in terms of higher-level laws, we shall judge it as established in a much better way than by the addition of another billion deaths fitting the low-level law. At the same time, the hypothesis will, after theorification, offer a larger target to refutation—which is, after all, a desideratum of geriatry—since it will become connected with a host of basic laws and may consequently contact with a number of new contiguous domains of experience.

The degree of support or sustenance of scientific hypotheses—which is not a quantitative but a comparative concept (among other reasons because hypotheses have philosophical supports besides empirical ones)—increases enormously upon their insertion into nomological systems, i.e., upon their inclusion in a theory or development into a theory.

No inference can even provisionally be justified outside the context of some theory, including, of course, one or more chapters of formal logic. Factual hypotheses can be justified up to a certain point if they are grounded on deep (non-phenomenological) laws that, far from being just summaries of phenomenal regularities, enable us to explain them by some "mechanism" (often nonmechanical). Thus, the age-long recorded succession of days and nights does not warrant the inference that the sun will "rise" tomorrow—as Hume rightly saw. But a study of the dynamic stability of the solar system, and of the thermonuclear stability of the sun, as well as a knowledge of the present positions and velocities of other neighboring celestial bodies, renders our expectation highly probable. Theory affords the validation refused by plain experience: not *any* theory but a theory including deep laws transcending first degree inductive generalizations. In this way inductivism is inverted: *we may trust inductions to the extent that they are justified by noninductive theories.*

In summary, empirical confirmation is but one phase, though an indispensable, of the complex and unending process of inventing, checking, mending, and replacing scientific hypotheses.

6. INDUCTIVIST METHODOLOGY AND THE PROBLEMS OF INDUCTION

According to inductivism, empirical knowledge (*a*) is obtained by inductive inference alone, (*b*) is tested only by enumerative induction, (*c*) is more reliable as it is closer to experience (epistemologically simpler), (*d*) is more acceptable as it is more probable, and consequently (*e*) its logic—inductive logic—is an application or an interpretation of the calculus of probability. Deductivists[9] have shown that these claims are untenable, particularly in connection with theoretical laws, which are neither obtained nor directly tested by induction, and which have exactly zero probability in any universe that is infinite in some respect. They and a few others[10] have also conclusively shown that the theory of probability does not solve the riddles of induction and does not provide a warrant for inductive leaps.

All this, however, does not prove the vanity of the cluster of problems concerning induction, conceived as the set of questions connected with both the inductive inception and, particularly, the inductive confirmation of hypotheses; hence, those arguments do not establish the impossibility of *every* logic of induction, even though they considerably deflate the claims of available systems of inductive logic. It is, indeed, a fact that induction is employed in the formulation of some hypotheses both in formal and in factual science, even though it is true that such hypotheses are rarely impressive and deep. And it is a fact, too (or rather a metascientific induction!) that induction is employed in the validation of all factual theories. The mere mention of statistical inference should suffice. Now, if a subject exists, scientific philosophy suggests that the corresponding scientific (or metascientific) approach should be attempted. And why should induction be left in the hands of inductivists?

Granted, there is no inductive *method*,[11] either in the context of invention or in the context of valida-

9   Particularly K. R. Popper, *op. cit.* (fn. 2); see also "Probability Magic or Knowledge out of Ignorance," *Dialectica*, 11 (1957), 354, and "Probabilistic Independence and Corroboration by Empirical Tests," *The British Journal for the Philosophy of Science*, 10 (1960), 315.

10   W. Kneale, *op. cit.* (fn. 5).

11   The existence of an inductive method, claimed by empiricism from Bacon to Reichenbach, is difficulty to prove because it has never been clearly described. The safest would be to say that the method of science is not inductive.

tion; at least, there is no inductive method in the sense of a set of secure rules or recipes guaranteeing once and for ever the jump to true general conclusions out of case examination. Nor is there an intuitive method or a hypnotic method. Yet induction, intuition, and hypnosis do exist and deserve to be studied scientifically. An analysis of scientific research shows the current employment of various patterns of plausible inference,[12] such as analogy, reduction, weakened reduction, and weakened *modus tollens;* it also shows the operation of inductive policies, such as those connected with sampling, and which are after all designed to provide the best possible inductions. Why should we disregard these various kinds of nondemonstrative inference, especially knowing as we do that successful patterns tend to be accepted as rules admitted uncritically unless they are critically examined?

The rules of deductive inference, to which we all pay at least lip service, were not arbitrarily posited by some inspired genius in the late Neolithic: they were first *recognized* in sound discourse and then explicitly adopted because they lead from accepted statements to accepted statements—and statements are accepted, in turn, if they are deemed to be at least partially true. Conversely, statements that are not postulated by convention are regarded as true if they are obtained by procedures respecting accepted rules of inference. Such a *mutual and progressive adjustment* of statements and rules is apparently the sole ultimate justification of either.[13] Analogously, the belief in the possibility of a logic of plausible (nondemonstrative) reasoning rests not only on a false theory of knowledge which minimizes the role of constructs, and on a history of science biased against the theoretical, but also on the plain observation that some nondemonstrative inferences *are* crowned with success. (Usually this is the case with recorded inferences, because men, as Bacon pointed out, mark when they hit.) This is what entitles us to adopt as (fallible) rules of inference, and as inductive policies, those patterns that in good research lead from accepted propositions to accepted propositions.

Of course, the theory of plausible inference should not restrict itself to a *description* of the types of argument found in everyday life and in science: it should also refine them, devising *ideal* (least dirty) patterns of inference.[14] However, such a rational reconstruction should be preceded by a realistically oriented investigation into patterns of *actual* scientific inference, rather than by another study of the opinions of distinguished philosophers concerning the nature and role of induction.

Furthermore, ideal patterns of plausible reasoning should be regarded neither as binding rules nor as inference tickets, but rather as more or less successful, hence advisable, patterns. This, at least in the constructive stage, when the greatest freedom to imagine is needed, since creative imagination alone is able to bridge the gap separating precepts from concepts,[15] first degree inductions from transcendent hypotheses, and isolated generalizations from theoretical systems. Logic, whether formal or informal, deductive or inductive, is not supposed to concoct recipes for jumping to happy conclusions—jumps without which there is as little science as there is without careful test—but it may show which are the best patterns that can be discerned in the test of hypotheses framed in whatever way.

7. CONCLUSION

As must have been suspected by many, scientific research seems to follow a *via media* between the extremes of inductivism and deductivism. In this middle course induction is instrumental both heuristically and methodologically, by taking part in the framing of some hypotheses and in the empirical validation of all sorts of hypotheses. Induction is certainly powerless without the invention of audacious transcendent hypotheses which could not possibly be suggested by the mere examination of experiential data. But the deepest hypotheses are idle speculation unless their lower-level consequents receive instantial confirmation. Induction plays scarcely a role in the design of experiments, which involves theories and demands creative imagination; but experiment is useless unless its results are interpreted in terms of theories that are partly validated by the in-

[12] See J. M. Keynes, reference 1; G. Polya, reference 3; G. H. von Wright, reference 1; Z. Czerwinski, "Statistical Inference, Induction and Deduction," *Studia Logica,* 7 (1958), 243.

[13] See M. Bôcher, "The Fundamental Conceptions and Methods of Mathematics," *Bulletin of the American Mathematical Society,* 11 (1905), 115, and N. Goodman, *Fact, Fiction, & Forecast* (London: Athlone Press 1954; Cambridge, Mass.: Harvard University Press, 1955).

[14] See S. F. Barker, *Induction and Hypothesis* (Ithaca, New York: Cornell University Press, 1957).

[15] A. Einstein, "Remarks on the Theory of Knowledge of Bertrand Russell," in P. A. Schilpp (Ed.), *The Philosophy of Bertrand Russell* (New York: Tudor Publishing Co., 1944 and 1951). See also M. Bunge, *Intuition and Science* (Englewood Cliffs, N. J.: Prentice Hall, Inc., 1962).

ductive processing of their empirically testable consequences.

To sum up, induction—which is but one of the kinds of plausible reasoning—contributes modestly to the framing of scientific hypotheses, but is indispensable for their test, or rather at the empirical stage of their test. Hence a noninductivist logic of induction should be welcome.

Lorenzo Valla (1405–1457)
DIALOGUE ON FREE WILL

The author, who lived during the Italian Renaissance, argues that foreknowledge is compatible with free will, for to know in advance what we, given our nature, will choose to do is in no way to make us do it. He also suggests that having the nature we have does not preclude us from freely choosing each time we choose. Valla's dialogue is discussed in Section D of the introductory essay to Part III.

READING QUESTIONS

In reading the selection, try to answer the following questions and identify the passages that support your answers:

1. What are Valla's views on free will?
2. What reasons does he give in support of his views?
3. Are they sound? Why or why not?
4. What implications does Valla's position have for moral responsibility?
5. Can one sensibly argue that we have no free will if we cannot choose our nature? Why or why not?

Reprinted with the permission of The University of Chicago Press from Lorenzo Valla, "Dialogue on Free Will," in E. Cassirer, P. O. Kristeller, and J. H. Randall, Jr. (eds.), *The Renaissance Philosophy of Man* (Chicago: University of Chicago Press, 1948), pp. 155–182. Copyright © 1948.

DIALOGUE ON FREE WILL[1]

I would prefer, O Garsia,[2] most learned and best of bishops, that other Christians and, indeed, those who are called theologians would not depend so much on philosophy or devote so much energy to it, making it almost an equal and sister (I do not say patron) of theology. For it seems to me that they have a poor opinion of our religion if they think it needs the protection of philosophy. The followers of the Apostles, truly columns in the temple of God, whose works have now been extant many centuries, used this protection least of all. In fact, if we look carefully, the heresies of those times, which we understand were many and not insignificant, derived al-

[1] [*Laurentii Vallae De libero arbitrio edidit Maria Anfossi* ("Opusculi filosofici: testi e documenti inediti o rari pubblicati da Giovanni Gentile," Vol. VI [Firenze, 1934]), was used for the following translation. Anfossi's edition, based on Codices Monacensis 3561, 78, and 17523 and on the editions of Louvain, 1483, and Basel, 1543, seemed clear and reliable. For the most part the variations, deriving from two families of texts (Clm 3561, 78 and Louvain: Clm 17523 and Basel), are in spelling, word order, and grammatical form; rarely is meaning involved. Valla's style is relatively direct, and, for a Humanist, not too intricate. There are very few places where his meaning is obscure. The aim in the translation was to secure a simple, clear, informal rendering of the Latin. Where this has succeeded, it is in keeping with the spirit of Valla's own efforts to treat serious matters on a familiar level.]

[2] [Garzia Asnarez de Añon was bishop of Lerida from 1435 to 1449 (Girolamo Mancini, *Vita di Lorenzo Valla* [Florence, 1891], p. 111, and Gams, *Series episcoporum*, p. 44). As Valla was secretary to Alfonso in Gaeta from 1435 to 1443, and his contact with Garzia was through the Aragonese connection, the dialogue would seem to have been written between the latter dates.]

most entirely from philosophic sources, so that philosophy not only profited our most sacred religion little but even violently injured it.[3] But they of whom I speak consider [philosophy] a tool for weeding out heresies, when actually it is a seedbed of heresy. They do not realize that the most pious antiquity, which lacked the arm of philosophy in combating heresies, and which often fought bitterly against philosophy itself—driving it forth like Tarquin into exile, never to allow its return—is thus accused of ignorance. Were those men ignorant and weaponless? And how did they reduce so much of the world to their authority? You who are fortified by such armament are not able to guard what they have left you as a patrimony, ah, lamentable and unworthy thing!

Why, therefore, do you not walk in the footsteps of your ancestors? If not their reason, certainly their authority and example ought to persuade that they should be followed instead of your entering upon some new path. I consider the physician who tries out new and experimental medicines on the sick rather than time-tested ones to be mean and contemptible. So is the sailor who prefers to hold an uncharted course to one upon which others safely sail their ships and cargoes. You have likewise reached such a degree of insolence that you believe no one can become a theologian unless he knows the precepts of philosophy and has learned them, most diligently and thoroughly, and you also suppose those of former times who either did not know or did not wish to know them to be stupid. O times! O customs! Formerly neither citizen nor stranger was allowed to speak in a foreign tongue in the Roman state, and only the dialect of that city could be used. However, you who could be called senators of the Christian commonwealth are better pleased to hear and employ pagan speech than ecclesiastical.

As time will be given to criticism of others elsewhere, in this present work we have wished to show that Boethius (for no other reason than that he loved philosophy excessively) argued incorrectly about free will in the fifth book of his *Consolation of Philosophy*.[4] We have replied to the first four books in our work on *True Good*.[5] Now I will exert myself as far as possible in the discussion and solution of this

problem, and, so that it will not seem purposeless after so many other writers have held forth on this subject, I shall add something of my own.[6] Although I was anxious myself to do this, I was further driven by an argument I recently held with Antonio Glarea,[7] a very well-read and keen man, long dear to me both because of his habits and because he is a countryman of San Lorenzo. I have reported the words of our argument in this little book, recounting them as if the affair were proceeding and not narrated, so that "I said" and "he said" does not need to be so frequently interpolated. I fail to see why Marcus Tullius, that man of immortal genius, claims to have done this in his book the *Laelius*,[8] for where an author does not report what he himself said, but what was reported by others, how, pray, can he interpose "I said"? Such is the case in the *Laelius* of Cicero, which contains a debate held by Laelius with two sons-in-law, Gaius Fannius and Quintus Scaevola. It is related by Scaevola, himself, with Cicero and some of his friends listening, and because of his youth he scarcely dares to argue and contend with Scaevola, who inspired a certain veneration either of age or of dignity.

But let us return to our subject. Antonio, therefore, had come to visit me at midday and finding me unoccupied and sitting with some servants in the hall, made a few introductory remarks concerning the subject and then continued as follows:

Ant. To me the question of free will seems very difficult and extremely arduous; on it depends all human action, all right and wrong, all reward and punishment, in this life and in the future as well. It is not easy for us to say whether any question either needs more understanding or is less understood than this. I repeatedly inquire about it, by myself and with others, and have not so far been able to find any way out of its ambiguity. So much so that I am sometimes disturbed, as well as confused, within myself because of it. Nevertheless, I never shall weary of wondering about it, nor shall I despair of being able to perceive, although I know many were frustrated in the same hope. Therefore I should also like to hear your opinion on this question, because by thor-

[3] [An allusion to the early Fathers' war against classicism consistent with remarks in the Introduction.]

[4] [Anicii Manlii Severini Boethii, *Philosophiae consolationis libri v*, with the English translation of "I.T." (1609) revised by H. F. Stewart ("Loeb Classical Library" [New York, 1926]). The fifth book of the *Consolations* also takes up in its first section the question of the relation of chance to providence.]

[5] [*De voluptate ac vero bono libri tres* (Basel, 1519).]

[6] [The "something of my own" apparently is Valla's distinction between the operation of divine foreknowledge and divine will below, pp. 169 ff.]

[7] [Mancini (*op. cit.*, p. 111) thinks that Glarea was a native of Huesca in Aragon, one of the birthplaces claimed for San Lorenzo.]

[8] [The *Laelius* or *De amicitia* of Cicero begins with a description of the setting and personages as Valla describes it, and continues with some remarks about the impressiveness of the dialogue form. Cf. the translation by W. Melmoth in the Everyman's edition, pp. 167–69.]

ough investigation and survey I may perhaps arrive at that which I seek, and also because I have known how sharp and exact you are in judgment.

Lor. As you say, this question is very difficult, and I scarcely know whether it has been understood by anyone. But that is no reason for you to be disturbed or confused, even if you never understand it. For what just complaint is there if you do not measure up to that which you see none has come up to? Even if others may have much that we have not, nevertheless we should bear it gladly and calmly. One may be endowed with nobility, another with high office, another with wealth, another with genius, another with eloquence, another with many of these, another with all. Nevertheless, no levelheaded person who is aware of his own efforts would think of mourning because he himself does not have those things. Besides, how much less ought he to mourn because he lacks the wings of a bird, which no one has? For if we were sorrowed by all we do not know, we would make life hard and bitter for ourselves. Would you like me to list for you how many things are unknown to us, not only divine and supernatural things such as this of which we are talking, but also the human ones which can enter our knowledge? In brief, there are many more things which are unknown. For this reason the Academics, though wrongly, nevertheless said nothing is fully known to us.[9]

Ant. To be sure, I admit that what you say is true, but somehow I am so impatient and greedy that I cannot control the impulse of my mind. For I hear what you have said about the wings of a bird, that I should not regret it if I don't have them; yet why should I forswear wings if I could possibly obtain them by Daedalus' example? And indeed how much finer wings do I long for? With them I might fly not from the prison of walls but from the prison of errors and fly away and arrive not in the fatherland, which breeds bodies as did Daedalus, but in the one where souls are born. Let us dismiss the Academics with their point of view, who, although they would put all in doubt, certainly could not doubt of their own doubts; and, although they argued nothing is known, nevertheless they did not lose their zeal for investigation. Furthermore, we know that later thinkers added much to what was previously found

out; their precept and example ought to spur us to discovering other things also. Wherefore, I pray, do not wish to take this worry and burden from me, for, having removed the burden, you will at the same time have removed desire for inquiry, unless, perhaps, as I hope and would prefer, you will satisfy my greedy appetite.

Lor. Might I satisfy what no one else could? For what should I say about books? Either you agree with them, then nothing further is demanded; or you do not agree with them, and then there is nothing which I can put better. Yet you will see how pious and tolerable it is for you to declare war on all books, including the wisest, and not to side with any of them.

Ant. Of course I know it seems intolerable and almost a sacrilege not to agree with books already tested by custom, but you also mark that in many things it is usual for them to differ among themselves and to support divergent views and that there are very few whose authority is too great for their sayings to be questioned. Indeed, on other questions I do not completely reject writers, thinking now this one, now that one, speaks with greater probability. Yet in this question on which I am about to speak with you, with your leave and that of others, I agree absolutely with no one. For what might I say of the others when Boethius, to whom all give the palm in explaining this question, is himself unable to complete what he undertakes and at certain points takes refuge in the imaginary and fictitious? For he says God, through an intelligence which is beyond reason, both knows all things for eternity and holds all things present.[10] But can I, who am rational and know nothing outside of time, aspire to the knowledge of intelligence and eternity? I suspect Boethius himself did not understand them, even if the things he said were true, which I do not believe. For he should not be thought to speak truly whose speech not he himself or anyone else understands. And so although he began this

---

[9] [This counsel of humility and the succeeding passage where Antonio expresses a wish for wings of knowledge and praises the stimulating effects of the pursuit of the unknown symbolize the new and old attitudes. Valla, however, in contrast to Pico on the *Dignity of Man* (cf. pp. 176 ff.) seems definitely on the conservative side both in his own statement and in the disbelief of Antonio in any possible solution to his question.]

[10] [Boethius, *op. cit.* "Wherefore, since every judgment comprehendeth those things which are subject unto it, according to its own nature, and God hath always an everlasting and present state, His knowledge also surpassing all notions of time, remaineth in the simplicity of His presence, and comprehending the infinite spaces of that which is past and to come, considereth all things in his simple knowledge as though they were now in doing. So that, if thou will weigh His foreknowledge with which He discerneth all things, thou wilt more rightly esteem it to be the knowledge of a never fading instant than a foreknowledge as of a thing to come" (pp. 403 and 405). "But God beholdeth those future things which proceed from free will present. These things, therefore, being referred to the divine sight are necessary by the condition of the divine knowledge, and considered by themselves, they lose not absolute freedom of their own nature. Wherefore doubtless all those things come to pass which God foreknoweth shall come, but some of them proceed from free will . . . ." (p. 407). Cf. also pp. 396 and 397, ll. 46–56.]

argument correctly, he did not correctly conclude it. If you agree with me on this, I shall rejoice in my own opinion; if not, because of your humanity [i.e., eloquence and culture of language], you will not refuse to express more lucidly what he said obscurely; in either case, you will reveal your opinion.

Lor. See what a fair demand you make, ordering me, either by damning or amending, to insult Boethius!

Ant. But do you call it an insult to have a true opinion about another or to interpret his obscure statements more clearly?

Lor. Well, it is unpleasant to do this to great men.

Ant. It is certainly more unpleasant not to show the way to the erring and to him who asks you to show it.

Lor. What if I do not know the way?

Ant. To say "I do not know the way" is to have no desire to show the way; therefore, do not refuse to reveal your opinion.

Lor. What if I should say that I agree with you about Boethius, that I do not understand him, and that I have nothing else by which I might explain this question?

Ant. If you say this truly, I am not such a fool that I would ask for more than you are able to give; but beware lest you discharge poorly the office of friendship and show yourself begrudging and false to me.

Lor. What do you ask me to explain to you?

Ant. Whether the foreknowledge of God stands in the way of free will and whether Boethius has correctly argued this question.

Lor. I shall attend to Boethius later; but if I satisfy you in this matter, I want you to make a promise.

Ant. What sort of a promise?

Lor. That if I serve you splendidly in this luncheon, you will not want to be entertained again for dinner.

Ant. What do you mean as lunch for me and what as dinner, for I do not understand?

Lor. That contented after discussing this one question, you will not ask for another afterward.

Ant. You say another? As if this one will not be sufficient and more! I freely promise that I will ask no dinner from you.

Lor. Go ahead then and get into the very heart of the question.

Ant. You advise well. If God foresees the future, it cannot happen otherwise than He foresaw. For example, if He sees that Judas will be a traitor, it is impossible for him not to become a traitor, that is, it is necessary for Judas to betray, unless—which should be far from us—we assume God to lack providence.

Since He has providence, one must undoubtedly believe that mankind does not have free will in its own power; and I do not speak particularly of evil men, for as it is necessary for these to do evil, so conversely it is necessary for the good to do good,[11] provided those are still to be called good or evil who lack will or that their actions are to be considered right or wrong which are necessary and forced. And what now follows you yourself see: for God either to praise this one for justice or accuse that of injustice and to reward the one and punish the other, to speak freely, seems to be the opposite of justice, since the actions of men follow by necessity the foreknowledge of God.[12] We should therefore abandon religion, piety, sanctity, ceremonies, sacrifices; we may expect nothing from Him, employ no prayers, not call upon his mercy at all, neglect to improve our mind, and, finally, do nothing except what pleases us, since our justice or injustice is foreknown by God. Consequently, it seems that either He does not foresee the future if we are endowed with will or He is not just if we lack free will. There you have what makes me inclined to doubt in this matter.

Lor. You have indeed not only pushed into the middle of the question but have even more widely extended it. You say God foresaw that Judas would be a traitor, but did He on that account induce him to betrayal? I do not see that, for, although God may foreknow some future act to be done by man, this act is not done by necessity because he may do it willingly. Moreover, what is voluntary cannot be necessary.

Ant. Do not expect me to give in to you so easily or to flee without sweat and blood.

Lor. Good luck to you; let us contend closely in hand-to-hand and foot-to-foot conflict. Let the decision be by sword, not spear.

Ant. You say Judas acted voluntarily and on that account not by necessity. Indeed, it would be most shameless to deny that he did it voluntarily. What do I say to that? Certainly this act of will was necessary since God foreknew it; moreover, since it was foreknown by Him, it was necessary for Judas to will and

11 [The moral (or psychological) determinism raised by Antonio here as an obstacle to foreknowledge may be compared with the speech Lorenzo attributes to Apollo when he tells Sextus that his evil nature, created by Jupiter, will make him sin. Cf. p. 173.]

12 [Cf. Boethius, *op. cit.,* p. 379: "For in vain are rewards and punishments proposed to good and evil, which no free and voluntary motion of their minds hath deserved. And that will seem most unjust which now is judged most just, that either the wicked should be punished or the good rewarded, since their own will leadeth them to neither, but they are compelled by the certain necessity of that which is to come," etc.]

do it lest he should make the foreknowledge in any way false.

Lor. Still I do not see why the necessity for our volitions and actions should derive from God's foreknowledge. For, if foreknowing something *will be* makes it come about, surely knowing something *is* just as easily makes the same thing *be*. Certainly, if I know your genius, you would not say that something *is* because you *know* it is. For example, you know it is now day; because you know it is, is it on that account also day? Or, conversely, because it is day, do you for that reason know it is day?[13]

Ant. Indeed, continue.

Lor. The same reasoning applies to the past. I know it was night eight hours ago, but my knowledge does not make that it was night; rather I know it was night because it was night. Again, that I may come closer to the point, I know in advance that after eight hours it will be night; and will it be on that account? Not at all, but because it will be night, for that reason I foreknew it; now if the foreknowledge of man is not the cause of something occurring, neither is the foreknowledge of God.

Ant. Believe me, that comparison deceives us; it is one thing to know the present and past, another to know the future. For when I know something is, it cannot be changed, as that day, which now is, cannot be made not to be. Also the past does not differ from the present, for we did not notice the day when it was past but while it was occurring as the present; I learned it was night not then when it *had passed* but when it was. And so for these times I concede that something *was,* or *is,* not because I know it but that I know it because it *is* or *was*. But a different reasoning applies to the future because it is subject to change. It cannot be known for certain because it is uncertain. And, in order that we may not defraud God of foreknowledge, we must admit that the future is certain and on that account necessary; this is what deprives us of free will. Nor can you say what you said just now that the future is not preordained merely because God foresees it but that God foresees it because the future is preordained; you thus wound God by implying that it is necessary for him to foreknow the future.

Lor. You have come well armed and weaponed for the fight, but let us see who is deceived, you or I. First, however, I would meet this latter point where you say that, if God foresees the future because it is

to be, He labors under the necessity to foresee the future. Indeed this should not be attributed to necessity but to nature, to will, to power, unless it is an attribute of weakness perchance that God cannot sin, cannot die, cannot give up His wisdom rather than an attribute of power and of divinity. Thus, when we said He is unable to escape foresight, which is a form of wisdom, we inflicted no wound on Him but did Him honor. So I shall not be afraid to say that God is unable to escape foreseeing what is to be. I come now to your first point: that the present and the past are unalterable and therefore knowable; that the future is alterable and therefore not capable of being foreknown. I ask if it can be changed that at eight hours from now night will arrive, that after summer there will be autumn, after autumn winter, after winter spring, after spring summer?

Ant. Those are natural phenomena always running the same course; I speak, however, of matters of the will.

Lor. What do you say of chance things? Can they be foreseen by God without necessity being imputed to them? Perchance today it may rain or I may find a treasure, would you concede this could be foreknown without any necessity?[14]

Ant. Why should I not concede it? Do you believe I think so ill of God?

Lor. Make sure that you do not think ill when you say you think well. For if you concede in this case, why should you doubt in matters of the will, for both classes of events can happen in two different ways?

Ant. The matter is not that way. For these chance things follow a certain nature of their own, and for this reason doctors, sailors, and farmers are accustomed to foresee much, since they reckon consequences out of antecedents, which cannot happen in affairs of the will.[15] Predict which foot I will move first, and, whichever you have said, you will lie, since I shall move the other.

Lor. I ask you, who was ever found so clever as this Glarea? He thinks he can impose on God like the man in Aesop who consulted Apollo whether the sparrow he held under his coat was dead for the sake

---

[13] [Cf. *ibid.,* pp. 387 and 405, where a parallel argument is employed.]

[14] [Boethius (pp. 367 and 369, citing Aristotle *Physics* ii. 4) makes use of the same example of a buried treasure to prove that providence and chance events are compatible.]

[15] [Valla has thus classified events into "natural phenomena always running the same course," "chance things" which "follow a certain nature of their own," and "affairs of the will." Since he later argues that human action follows man's individual nature (p. 173), he would seem to be a natural determinist, leaving freedom as a gift of grace. This is what Barozzi, *Lorenzo Valla . . . .* (Florence, 1891), meant when he called Valla a positivist.]

of deceiving him. For you have not told me to predict, but God. Indeed, I have not the ability to predict whether there will be a good vintage, such as you ascribe to farmers. But by saying and also believing that God does not know which foot you will move first, you involve yourself in great sin.

Ant. Do you think I affirm something rather than raise the question for the sake of the argument? Again you seem to seek excuses by your speech and, giving ground, decline to fight.

Lor. As if I fought for the sake of victory rather than truth! Witness how I am driven from my ground; do you grant that God now knows your will even better than you yourself do?

Ant. I indeed grant it.

Lor. It is also necessary that you grant that you will do nothing other than the will decides.

Ant. Of course.

Lor. How then can He not know the action if He knows the will which is the source of the action?

Ant. Not at all, for I myself do not know what I shall do even though I know what I have in my will. For I do not will to move this foot or that foot, in any case, but the other than He will have announced. And so, if you compare me with God, just as I do not know what I will do, so He does not know.

Lor. What difficulty is there in meeting this sophism of yours? He knows that you are prepared to reply otherwise than He will say and that you will move the left first if the right is named by Him; whichever one He should say therefore, it is certain to Him what will happen.

Ant. Yet which of the two will He say?

Lor. Do you speak of God? Let me know your will and I will announce what will happen.

Ant. Go ahead, you try to know my will.

Lor. You will move the right one first.

Ant. Behold, the left one.

Lor. How have you shown my foreknowledge to be false, since I knew you would move the left one?

Ant. But why did you say other than you thought?

Lor. In order to deceive you by your own arts and to deceive the man willing to deceive.

Ant. But God Himself would not lie nor deceive in replying, nor did you do rightly in replying for Another as He would not reply.

Lor. Did you not tell me to "predict"? Therefore, I should not speak for God but for myself whom you asked.

Ant. How changeable you are. A little while ago you were saying I told God to "predict," not you; now on the contrary you say the opposite. Let God reply

which foot I will move first.

Lor. How ridiculous, as if He would answer you!

Ant. What? Can He not indeed reply truly if He wishes?

Lor. Rather He can lie who is the Truth itself.

Ant. What would He reply then?

Lor. Certainly what you will do, but, you not hearing, He might say to me, He might say to one of those other people, He might say it to many; and, when He has done that, do you not think He will truly have predicted?[16]

Ant. Yea, indeed, He will have truly predicted, but what would you think if He predicted it to me?

Lor. Believe me, you who thus lie in wait to deceive God, if you should hear or certainly know what He said you would do, either out of love or out of fear you would hasten to do what you knew was predicted by Him. But let us skip this which has nothing to do with foreknowledge. For it is one thing to foreknow and another to predict the future. Say whatever you have in mind about foreknowledge, but leave prediction out of it.

Ant. So be it, for the things that I have said were spoken not so much for me as against you. I return from this digression to where I said it was necessary for Judas to betray, unless we entirely annul providence, because God foresaw it would be thus. So if it was possible for something to happen otherwise than it was foreseen, providence is destroyed; but if it is impossible, free will is destroyed, a thing no less unworthy to God than if we should cancel His providence. I, in what concerns me, would prefer Him to be less wise rather than less good. The latter would injure mankind; the other would not.

Lor. I praise your modesty and wisdom. When you are not able to win, you do not fight on stubbornly but give in and apply yourself to another defense, which seems to be the argument of what you set forth a while back. In reply to this argument, I deny that foreknowledge can be deceived as the consequence of the possibility that something might turn out otherwise than as it has been foreseen. For what prevents it from also being true that something can turn out otherwise than it will immediately happen? Something that can happen and something that will happen are very different. I can be a husband, I can

---

[16] [Boethius, *op. cit.*, p. 409, also uses this argument: "But thou wilt say, 'If it is in my power to change my purpose, shall I frustrate providence if I chance to alter things which she foreknoweth?' I answer that thou mayest indeed change thy purpose, but because the truth of providence, being present, seeth that thou canst do so or not, and what thou purposest anew, thou canst not avoid the divine foreknowledge...."]

be a soldier or a priest, but will I right away? Not at all. Though I can do otherwise than will happen, nevertheless I shall not do otherwise; and it was in Judas' power not to sin even though it was foreseen that he would, but he preferred to sin, which it was foreseen would happen. Thus foreknowledge is valid and free will abides. This will make a choice between two alternatives, for to do both is not possible, and He foreknows by His own light which will be chosen.

Ant. Here I have you. Are you unaware of the philosophical rule that whatever is possible ought to be conceded as if it were? It is possible for something to happen otherwise than it is foreknown; it may be granted it will happen that way, through which it is now manifest that foreknowledge is deceived since it happens otherwise than foreknowledge had believed.

Lor. Are you using formulas of philosophers on me? Indeed, as if I would not dare to contradict them! Certainly I think that precept you mention, whose ever it is, most absurd, for I can concede it to be possible to move the right foot first, and we may concede it will be so, and I can also concede it possible for me to move the left foot first, and we may concede this will be as well; I will move therefore both the left before the right and the right before the left, and through your concession of the possible I arrive at the impossible. Therefore, know that it is not to be conceded that whatever is possible will likewise happen. It is possible for you to do otherwise than God foreknows, nevertheless you will not do otherwise, nor will you therefore deceive Him.

Ant. I will not object further, nor, since I smashed all my weapons, will I fight with tooth and nail as is said; but, if there is any other point through which you can explain it to me more amply and plainly persuade, I wish to hear it.[17]

Lor. You covet the praise of wisdom and modesty again, since you are your true self. And so I will do as you ask because I was doing it anyway of my own will. For what has been said so far is not what I had decided to say but what need of defense itself demanded. Now attend to what persuades me and perhaps it will even persuade you that foreknowledge is no impediment to free will. However, would you prefer me to touch on this subject briefly or to explain it more clearly at greater length?

Ant. It always seems to me, indeed, that those who speak lucidly speak most briefly, while those who speak obscurely, though in the fewest words, are always more lengthy. Besides, fulness of expression has itself a certain appropriateness and aptness for persuasion. Wherefore, since I asked you from the start that this matter be more lucidly stated by you, you should not doubt my wishes; nevertheless, do whatever is more agreeable to you. For I would never put my judgment ahead of yours.

Lor. Indeed, it is of importance to me to follow your wish, and whatever you think more convenient I do also. Apollo, who was so greatly celebrated among the Greeks, either through his own nature or by concession of the other gods, had foresight and knowledge of all future things, not only those which pertained to men but to the gods as well; thus, if we may believe the tradition, and nothing prevents our accepting it just for the moment, Apollo rendered true and certain prophecies about those consulting him. Sextus Tarquinius consulted him as to what would happen to himself. We may pretend that he replied, as was customary, in verse as follows:

> An exile and a pauper you will fall,
> Killed by the angry city.

To this Sextus: "What are you saying, Apollo? Have I deserved thus of you that you announce me a fate so cruel, that you assign me such a sad condition of death? Repeal your response, I implore you, predict happier things; you should be better disposed toward me who so royally endowed you." In reply Apollo: "Your gifts, O youth, certainly are agreeable and acceptable to me; in return for which I have rendered a miserable and sad prophecy, I wish it were happier, but it is not in my power to do this. I know the fates, I do not decide them; I am able to announce Fortune, not change her; I am the index of destinies, not the arbiter; I would reveal better things if better things awaited. Certainly this is not my fault who cannot prevent even my own misfortune that I foresee. Accuse Jupiter, if you will, accuse the fates, accuse Fortune whence the course of events descends. The power and decision over the fates are seated with them; with me, mere foreknowledge and prediction. You earnestly besought an oracle; I gave it. You inquired after the truth; I was unable to tell a lie. You have come to my temple from a far-distant region, and I ought not to send you away without a reply. Two things are most alien to me: falsehood

---

[17] [Valla breaks off at this point from where he was essentially reworking Boethius' arguments to begin the "something of my own" he mentioned above, p. 157.]

and silence." Could Sextus justly reply to this speech: "Yea, indeed, it is your fault, Apollo, who foresee my fate with your wisdom, for, unless you had foreseen it, this would not be about to happen to me"?

Ant. Not only would he speak unjustly but he should never reply thus.

Lor. How then?

Ant. Why do you not say?

Lor. Should he not reply in this way: "Indeed, I give thanks to you, holy Apollo, who have neither deceived me with falsehood nor spurned me in silence. But this also I ask you to tell me: Why is Jupiter so unjust, so cruel, to me that he should assign such a sad fate to me, an undeserving, innocent worshiper of the gods"?

Ant. Certainly I would reply in this way if I were Sextus, but what did Apollo reply to him?

Lor. "You call yourself undeserving and innocent, Sextus? You may be sure that the crimes that you will commit, the adulteries, betrayals, perjuries, the almost hereditary arrogance are to blame." Would Sextus then reply this way: "The fault for my crimes must rather be assigned to you, for it is necessary for me, who you foreknow will sin, to sin"?

Ant. Sextus would be mad as well as unjust if he replied in that way.

Lor. Do you have anything that you might say on his behalf?

Ant. Absolutely nothing.

Lor. If therefore Sextus had nothing which could be argued against the foreknowledge of Apollo, certainly Judas had nothing either which might accuse the foreknowledge of God. And, if that is so, certainly the question by which you said you were confused and disturbed is answered.

Ant. It is indeed answered and, what I scarcely dared to hope, fully solved, for the sake of which I both give you thanks and have, I would say, an almost immortal gift. What Boethius was unable to show me you have shown.[18]

Lor. And now I shall try to say something about him because I know you expect it and I promised to do it.[19]

Ant. What are you saying about Boethius? It will be agreeable and pleasant to me.

Lor. We may follow the line of the fable we started. You think Sextus had nothing to reply to Apollo; I ask you what would you say to a king who refused to offer an office or position to you because he says you would commit a capital offense in that function.

Ant. "I would swear to you, King, by your most strong and faithful right hand that I will commit no crime in this magistracy."

Lor. Likewise perhaps Sextus would say to Apollo, "I swear to you, Apollo, that I will not commit what you say."

Ant. What does Apollo answer?

Lor. Certainly not in the way the king would, for the king has not discovered what the future is, as God has. Apollo therefore might say: "Am I a liar, Sextus? Do I not know what the future is? Do I speak for the sake of warning you, or do I render a prophecy? I say to you again, you will be an adulterer, you will be a traitor, you will be a perjurer, you will be arrogant and evil."

Ant. A worthy speech by Apollo! What was Sextus able to muster against it?

Lor. Does it not occur to you what he could argue in his own defense? Is he with a meek mind to suffer himself to be condemned?

Ant. Why not, if he is guilty?

Lor. He is not guilty but is predicted to be so in the future. Indeed, I believe that if Apollo announced this to you, you would flee to prayer, and pray not to Apollo but to Jupiter that he would give you a better mind and change the fates.

Ant. That I would do, but I would be making Apollo a liar.

Lor. You speak rightly, because if Sextus cannot make him a liar, he employs prayers in vain. What should he do? Would he not be offended, angered, burst forth in complaints? "Thus, Apollo, am I unable to restrain myself from offenses, am I unable to accept virtue, do I not avail to reform the mind from wickedness, am I not endowed with free will?"

Ant. Sextus speaks bravely and truly and justly. What does the god reply?

Lor. "That is the way things are, Sextus. Jupiter as he created the wolf fierce, the hare timid, the lion brave, the ass stupid, the dog savage, the sheep mild, so he fashioned some men hard of heart, others soft, he generated one given to evil, the other to virtue, and, further, he gave a capacity for reform to one and made another incorrigible. To you, indeed, he assigned an evil soul with no resource for reform. And so both you, for your inborn character, will do

---

[18] [Thus foreknowledge is relieved of responsibility for human actions, but, in so doing, Valla has conceived of human nature as acting according to predetermined conditioning rather than as possessed of free will. The succeeding passage will make this even more clear.]

[19] [What follows seems to have little relation to Boethius.]

evil, and Jupiter, on account of your actions and their evil effects, will punish sternly, and thus he has sworn by the Stygian swamp it will be."[20]

Ant. At the same time that Apollo neatly excuses himself, he accuses Jupiter the more, for I am more favorable to Sextus than Jupiter. And so he might best protest justly as follows: "And why is it my crime rather than Jupiter's? When I am not allowed to do anything except evil, why does Jupiter condemn me for his own crime? Why does he punish me without guilt? Whatever I do, I do not do it by free will but of necessity. Am I able to oppose his will and power?"

Lor. This is what I wished to say for my proof. For this is the point of my fable, that, although the wisdom of God cannot be separated from His power and will, I may by this device of Apollo and Jupiter separate them. What cannot be achieved with one god may be achieved with two, each having his own proper nature—the one for creating the character of men, the other for knowing—that it may appear that providence is not the cause of necessity but that all this whatever it is must be referred to the will of God.

Ant. See, you have thrown me back into the same pit whence you dug me; this doubt is like that which I set forth about Judas. There necessity was ascribed to the foreknowledge of God, here to the will; what difference is it how you annul free will? That it is destroyed by foreknowledge, you indeed deny, but you say it is by divine will, by which the question goes back to the same place.

Lor. Do I say that free will is annulled by the will of God?

Ant. Is it not implied unless you solve the ambiguity?

Lor. Pray who will solve it for you?

Ant. Indeed I will not let you go until you solve it.

Lor. But that is to violate the agreement, and not content with luncheon you demand dinner also.

Ant. Is it thus you have defrauded me and coerced me through a deceitful promise? Promises in which deceit enters do not stand, nor do I think I have received luncheon from you if I am forced to vomit up whatever I have eaten, or, to speak more lightly, you send me away no less hungry than you received me.

Lor. Believe me, I didn't want to make you promise in such a way that I would cheat you, for what advantage would there have been to me, since I not even have been allowed to give you luncheon? Since you received it willingly and since you gave me thanks for it, you are ungrateful if you say you were forced by me to vomit it or that I send you away as hungry as you came. That is asking for dinner, not luncheon, and wanting to find fault with luncheon and to demand that I spread before you ambrosia and nectar, the food of the gods, not men. I have put my fish and fowl from my preserves and wine from a suburban hill before you. You should demand ambrosia and nectar from Apollo and Jupiter themselves.

Ant. Are not ambrosia and what you call nectar poetic and fabulous things? Let us leave this emptiness to the empty and fictitious gods, Jupiter and Apollo. You have given luncheon from these preserves and cellars; I ask dinner from the same.

Lor. Do you think I am so rude that I would send away a friend coming to me for dinner? But since I saw how this question was likely to end, I consulted my own interests back there and compelled you to promise that afterward you would not exact from me anything besides the one thing that was asked. Therefore, I proceed with you not so much from right as from equity. Perhaps you will obtain this dinner from others which, if friendship can be trusted, is not entirely in my possession.

Ant. I will give you no further trouble lest I seem ungrateful to a benefactor and distrustful of a friend; but, still, from whom do you suggest I seek this out?

Lor. If I were able, I would not send you away for dinner, but I would go there for dinner together with you.

Ant. Do you suppose no one has these divine foods, as you call them?

Lor. Why should I not think so.[21] Have you not read the words of Paul about the two children of Rebecca and Isaac? There he said:

---

[20] [To Setus' question, "Am I not endowed with free will?" Valla has Apollo reply, "You, for your inborn character, will do evil." It is interesting to compare this treatment with Leibniz' extension of the fable, *Opera*, ed. Erdmann, ¶¶ 413–17. "This dialogue of Valla is fine," he said, "although there is something to revise here and there. The principal fault, however, is that . . . . he seems to condemn providence under the name of Jupiter whom he makes almost the author of sin." Leibniz goes on to say, contrary to what Valla left possible, that Sextus had the choice of reforming or going his way and chose the latter. Thereafter continuing the fable he shows all of the possible futures open to Sextus through the additional figure of Pallas. This point of view is more like the doctrine of multiple possibility and rational freedom that is usually expected in the Humanists and is found in the case of Pico, certainly. But it is very different from that of Valla, who views man as a much less flexible creature. Leibniz goes on (¶ 417): "It seems to me that this continuation of the fiction can clear up the difficulty which Valla did not at all want to touch on. If Apollo has well represented the divine knowledge of vision (which concerns existences), I hope Pallas would not badly make the personage called the knowledge of simple intelligence (which concerns all possibilities) where it is ultimately necessary to search for the origin of things."]

[21] [In the preceding passage, and the succeeding citations from Paul, Valla seems to be stating his position as essentially agnostic. He thus limits his conception of human powers even further.]

For the children being not yet born, neither having done any good or evil, that the purpose of God according to election might stand, not of works, but of him that calleth; it was said unto her, The elder shall serve the younger. As it is written, Jacob have I loved, but Esau have I hated. What shall we say then? Is there unrighteousness with God? God forbid. For he saith to Moses, I will have mercy on whom I will have mercy, and I will have compassion on whom I will have compassion. So then it is not of him that willeth, nor of him that runneth, but of God that showeth mercy. For the scripture saith unto Pharaoh, Even for this same purpose have I raised thee up, that I might show my power in thee, and that my name might be declared throughout all the earth. Therefore hath he mercy on whom he will have mercy, and whom he will he hardeneth. Thou wilt say then unto me, Why doth he yet find fault? For who hath resisted his will? Nay but, O man, who art thou that repliest against God? Shall the thing formed say to him that formed it, Why hast thou made me thus? Hath not the potter power over the clay, of the same lump to make one vessel unto honor, and another unto dishonor? [Rom. 9:11–21 (King James Version)].

And a little later, as if the excessive splendor of the wisdom of God darkened his eyes, he proclaimed (Rom. 11:33): "O the depth of the riches both of the wisdom and knowledge of God! how unsearchable are his judgments, and his ways past finding out!" For if that vessel of election who, snatched up even to the third heaven, heard the secret words which man is not permitted to speak, nevertheless was unable to say or even to perceive them, who at length would hope that he could search out and comprehend? Carefully notice, however, free will is not said to be impeded in the same way by the will of God as by foreknowledge, for the will[22] has an antecedent cause which is seated in the wisdom of God. Indeed the most worthy reason may be adduced as to why He hardens this one and shows mercy to that, namely, that He is most wise and good. For it is impious to believe otherwise than that, being absolutely good. He does rightly. Yet, in foreknowledge there is no antecedent or any cause at all of justice and goodness. We do not ask: Why has He foreknown this or why does He wish it? We rather ask this only: How is God good if He takes away free will? For He would take it away if it were not possible for something to happen otherwise than is foreknown. Now, indeed, He brings no necessity, and His hardening one and showing another mercy does not deprive us of free will, since He does this most wisely and in full holiness.[23] He has placed the hidden reason of this cause in a certain secret sort of treasury. I will not hide the fact that certain men have dared to inquire into this purpose, saying, those who are hardened and reprobated are justly hardened and reprobated, for we come out of that lump polluted and converted into clay by the guilt of the first parent. Now, if I may cut across much and reply by one argument, why was Adam, made of unpolluted matter as he was, himself hardened for sin and why did he make the universal lump of his offspring of clay?

What was done to the angels was similar. Some of them were hardened, some obtained mercy, although all were of the same substance, from the same unpolluted lump which up to this point, if I may say so boldly, remained in the nature of a substance and in the quality of a material that is, so to speak, golden. Neither were some changed into better matter through election nor others into worse by reprobation. Some, as if chosen vessels for ministering to the divine table, received grace; others indeed could be thought vessels hidden from sight because, more despicable than if they became clay, they caught up every collection of obscenity! For that reason their damnation is more to be mourned than men's. For gold, from which angels are made, receives more outrage than silver, from which men are made, if filled with filth. Therefore the silver, or if you prefer to call it clay, matter in Adam is not changed but remained the same as it was before. And so, just as it was with him, so is it with us. Does not Paul say that from the same lump of clay one vessel was made unto honor and the other indeed unto dishonor? Nor ought it to be said that the vessels of honor were made of polluted matter. We are, therefore, vessels of silver, I would say, rather than of clay, and we have long been vessels of dishonor, damnation, and of death rather than hardness. For God poured into us, on account of the disobedience of the first parent in whom all of us have sinned, the penalty of death, not the guilt which comes from hardening. Paul says the same (Rom. 5:14): "Nevertheless death reigned from Adam to Moses, even over them that had not sinned after the similitude of Adam's transgression."

---

[22] [It is unclear whether this is divine or human will, but it seems to make better sense as divine.]

[23] [This would seem to leave it that man does have free will, but not only can God's wisdom not be questioned, but free will itself is left in an ambiguous situation if we are either hardened and, therefore, unable not to sin, or shown mercy and thereby enabled to do good. The latter state would seem to be the nearest to freedom, which becomes in this way not a natural possession of man but a gift of grace—a position extremely close to Luther.]

If we really had been hardened because of Adam's sin, then freed by the grace of Christ, we would no longer be hardened, which is not the case for many of us are hardened. Therefore, all who are baptized in the death of Christ are freed from that original sin and from that death. Baptism not having been sufficient, some of them receive mercy; and others are hardened just as Adam and the angels were hardened. Let him who wishes reply why He hardens one and shows mercy to the other, and I will confess he is an angel rather than a man, if this is even known to angels, which I do not believe, since it was not known to Paul (see how much I attribute to him). If the angels, therefore, who always see the face of God, do not know this, how great is our boldness to wish to know it at all? But before we conclude we should say something of Boethius.

Ant. You have opportunely mentioned him. In truth I was concerned about the man who hoped that he knew this matter himself and could teach others, not along the same road as Paul, yet tending in the same direction.

Lor. He not only trusted himself more than ought to be, and attempted things too great for his capacities, but he does not pursue the same road or complete the path entered upon.

Ant. Why is that?

Lor. Listen, for this is what I wished to say: Paul first said, "So then it is not of him that willeth, nor of [man] that runneth, but of God that showeth mercy." But Boethius in his whole argument concludes, not actually in words but in substance: It is not of God who forseeth, but of man who willeth and runneth.[24] Thence it is not enough to dispute about the providence of God unless the will (of God) is also discussed. This in short can be proved from your behavior. Not content with the explanation of the first question, you thought also to ask about the next.

Ant. If I consider your arguments deeply, you have expressed a most true opinion of Boethius from which not even he should appeal.

Lor. And what cause was there for a Christian man to depart from Paul and never remember him when dealing with the same matter he had dealt with? What is more, in the entire work of *Consolation* nothing at all is found about our religion—none of the precepts leading to a blessed life, no mention and hardly a hint of Christ.

Ant. I believe it was because he was too ardent an admirer of philosophy.

Lor. You are of a good opinion, or rather of understanding, for I also think that no such ardent admirer of philosophy can please God. And therefore Boethius, sailing north instead of south, did not bring the fleet laden with wine into the port of the fatherland but dashed it on barbarian coasts and on foreign shores.

Ant. You prove all that you say.

Lor. Let us therefore come to the conclusion and make some sort of finish, since I judge I have satisfied you on the foreknowledge, the will of God, and Boethius. I say what remains for the sake of exhortation rather than teaching, although, as you have a well-constituted soul, you do not need exhortation.

Ant. Indeed, go ahead. Exhortation is always fitting and useful, and I am accustomed to accept it gladly both from others and the most intimate and serious friends, such as I have always regarded you.

Lor. Indeed, I shall exhort not you alone but the others present here and myself among the first. I said that the cause of the divine will which hardens one and shows mercy to another is known neither to men nor to angels. If because of ignorance on this matter and on many others the angels do not lose their love of God, do not retreat from their service, and do not consider their own blessedness diminished on that account, should we for this same reason depart from faith, hope, and charity and desert as if from a commander? And if we have faith in wise men, even without reason, because of authority, should we not have faith in Christ who is the Power and Wisdom of God? He says He wishes to save all and that He does not wish the death of the sinner but rather that he be converted and live. And if we loan money to good men without a surety, should we require a guarantee from Christ in Whom no fraud may be found? And if we intrust our life to friends, should we not dare to intrust it to Christ, who for our salvation took on both the life of the flesh and the death of the cross? We do not know the cause of this matter; of what consequence is it? We stand by faith not by the probability of reason. Does knowledge do much for the corroboration of faith? Humility does more. The Apostle says (Rom. 12:16): "Mind not high (wise) things, but condescend to men of low estate." Is the foreknowledge of divine things useful? Charity is more useful. For the Apostle likewise says (I Cor. 8:1): "Knowledge puffeth us, but charity edifieth." And lest you think so much was said about the knowledge of human affairs, he says (II Cor. 12:7): "And lest I should be exalted above measure through the abundance of the revelations, there was given to me a

---

[24] [A clear enough repudiation of the doctrine of human independence.]

thorn in the flesh." Let us not wish to know the height, but let us fear lest we become like the philosophers who, calling themselves wise, are made foolish; who, lest they should appear ignorant of anything, disputed about everything. Raising their own mouths to heaven, and wishing to scale it—I do not say tear it apart—like proud and rash giants, they were hurled to earth by the strong forearm of God and buried in Hell as Typhoeus in Sicily. Among the chief of these was Aristotle, in whom the best and greatest God revealed and at length damned the arrogance and boldness of not only this same Aristotle but of the other philosophers as well. For when he (Aristotle) could not discover the nature of Euripus, throwing himself into its depth, he was swallowed up, but before that he testified with this sentence:

'Επειδή Ἀριστοτέλης οὐχ εἵλετο Εὔριπον Εὔριπος εἵλετο Ἀριστοτέλην

("Since Aristotle did not grasp Euripus, Euripus grasped Aristotle").[25] What is more arrogant or mad than this, or how could God by more manifest judgment condemn his cleverness and that of others like him than by letting him be turned into a madman by immoderate greed for knowledge and thus bring his own death on himself, a death, I say, far more

horrible than that of the most wicked Judas? Let us therefore shun greedy knowledge of high things, condescending rather to those of low estate. For nothing is of greater avail for Christian men than to feel humble. In this way we are more aware of the magnificence of God, whence it is written (I Pet. 5:5): "God resisteth the proud and giveth grace to the humble." To attain this grace I will no longer be anxious about this question lest by investigating the majesty of God I might be blinded by His light. I hope you also will do this. Here you have what I had to say by way of an exhortation, which I said not so much that I might move you and them as that I might show my own disposition of mind.

Ant. Indeed, this exhortation both showed the persuasion of your mind very well and, if I may reply for the others, has deeply moved us. Will you not commit this debate which we have had between us to writing and make a report of it so that you may have others share this good?

Lor. That is good advice. Let us make others judges in this matter, and, if it is good, sharers. Above all, let us send this argument, written and, as you say, made into a report, to the Bishop of Lerida, whose judgment I would place before all I know, and if he alone approves, I would not fear the disapproval of others. For I attribute more to him than Antimachus to Plato or Cicero to Cato.

Ant. You could say or do nothing more correct, and I beg you to do this as soon as possible.

Lor. So it will be done.

---

[25] Gregory Nazianzen, *Oratio IV, Contra Iulianum* (Migne, *Patro logia Graeca*, XXXV, 597), refers to this same legend.]

Roderick W. Chisholm (contemporary)
RESPONSIBILITY AND AVOIDABILITY

Chisholm formulates an argument, based on determinism, that we have no responsibility for our choices. He considers various objections to the argument and finds them all wanting. Yet he states that he is certain that the conclusion is false, and hence, at least one of its premises must be false. A discussion of Chisholm's and related positions can be found in Section D of the introductory essay to Part III.

READING QUESTIONS

In reading the selection, try to answer the following questions and identify the passages that support your answers:

1. What are Chisholm's views on free will?
2. What reasons does he give in support of his views?
3. Are they sound? Why or why not?
4. What implications does his position have for moral responsibility?
5. Can one sensibly argue that we have no free will if we cannot choose the wants, desires, or preferences that make us choose as we do? Why or why not?

Reprinted with the permission of New York University Press from Roderick W. Chisholm, "Avoidability and Responsibility," in Sidney Hook (ed.), *Determinism and Freedom in the Age of Modern Science* (New York: New York University Press, 1958), pp. 145–147. Copyright © 1958.

Edwards and Hospers hold that there is an important sense in which we may be said *not* to be morally responsible for any of our acts or choices. I propose the following as an explicit formulation of their reasoning:

1. If a choice is one we could not have avoided making, then it is one for which we are not morally responsible.

2. If we make a choice under conditions such that, given those conditions, it is (causally but not logically) impossible for the choice not to be made, then the choice is one we could not have avoided making.

3. Every event occurs under conditions such that, given those conditions, it is (causally but not logically) impossible for that event not to occur.

4. The making of a choice is the occurrence of an event.

5. We are not morally responsible for any of our choices.

If we wish to reject the conclusion (5)—and for most of us (5) is difficult to accpet—we must reject at least one of the premises.

Premise (1), I think, may be interpreted as a logical truth. If a man is responsible for what he did, then we may say, "He *could* have done otherwise." And if we may say, "He couldn't help it," then he is not responsible for what he did.

Many philosophers would deny (2), substituting a weaker account of *avoidability*. A choice is avoid-able, they might say, provided only it is such that, *if* the agent had reflected further, or had reflected on certain things on which in fact he did not reflect, he would *not* have made the choice. To say of a choice that it "could *not* have been avoided," in accordance with this account, would be to say that, even if the agent *had* reflected further, on anything you like, he would all the same have made the choice. But such conditional accounts of *avoidability* ("An act or choice is avoidable provided only it is such that, *if* the agent were to do so-and-so, the act or choice would not occur") usually have this serious defect: the antecedent clause ("if the agent were to do so-and-so") refers to some act or choice, or to the failure to perform some act or to make some choice; hence we may ask, concerning the occurrence or nonoccurrence of this act or choice, whether or not *it* is avoidable. Thus one who accepted (5) could say that, if the agent's failure to reflect further was itself unavoidable, his choice was also unavoidable. And no such conditional account of *avoidability* seems adequate to the use of "avoidable" and "unavoidable" in questions and statements such as these.

If we accept a conditional account of avoidability, we may be tempted to say, of course, that it would be a *misuse* of "avoidable" to ask whether the nonoccurrence of the antecedent event ("the agent does so-and-so") is avoidable. But the philosopher who accepts (5) may well insist that, since the antecedent clause refers to an act or a choice, the use of "avoidable" in question is *not* a misuse.

What, then, if we were to deny (3)? Suppose that some of our choices do not satisfy (3)—that when they are made they are *not* made under any conditions such that it is (causally) impossible (though logically possible) for them not to be made. If there are choices of this sort, then they are merely fortuitous or capricious. And if they are merely fortuitous or capricious, if they "just happen," then, I think, we may say with Blanshard that we are *not* morally responsible for them. Hence denying (3) is not the way to avoid (5).

We seem confronted, then, with a dilemma: either our choices have sufficient causal conditions or they do not; if they do have sufficient causal conditions they are not avoidable; if they do not, they are fortuitous or capricious; and therefore, since our choices are either unavoidable or fortuitous, we are not morally responsible for them.

There are philosophers who believe that by denying the rather strange-sounding premise (4) we can escape the dilemma. Insisting on something like "the primacy of practical reason," they would say that since we are certain that (5) is false we must construct a metaphysical theory about the self, a theory

denying (4) and enabling us to reconcile (3) and the denial of (5). I say "metaphysical" because it seems to be necessary for the theory to replace (4) by sentences using such terms as "active power," "the autonomy of the will," "prime mover," or "higher levels of causality"—terms designating something to which we apparently need not refer when expressing the conclusions of physics and the natural sciences. But I believe we cannot know whether such theories enable us to escape our dilemma. For it seems impossible to conceive what the relation is that, according to these theories, holds between the "will," "self," "mover," or "active power," on the one hand, and the bodily events this power is supposed to control, on the other—the relation between the "activities" of the self and the events described by physics.

I am dissatisfied, then, with what philosophers have proposed as alternatives to premises (1) through (4) above, but since I feel certain that (5) is false I also feel certain that at least one of the premises is false.

John Locke (1632–1704)
PERSONAL IDENTITY

Locke argues that what makes an individual one and the same person through time and space, and different from every other person, is consciousness. He uses forensic and commonsense evidence to support this thesis. Locke's views are discussed in Section E of the introductory essay to Part III.

READING QUESTIONS

In reading the selection, try to answer the following questions and identify the passages that support your answers:

1. How does Locke characterize the concept of person?
2. What reasons does he give in support of his characterization?
3. Are they good? Why or why not?
4. What implications does Locke's position have for moral and legal responsibility?
5. Should these implications be accepted or should Locke's characterization be rejected, and why?

This being premised, to find wherein personal identity consists, we must consider what *person* stands for;—which, I think, is a thinking intelligent being,[1] that has reason and reflection, and can consider itself as itself, the same thinking thing, in different times and places; which it does only by that consciousness[2] which is inseparable from thinking, and, as it seems to me, essential to it: it being impossible for any one to perceive without *perceiving* that he does perceive. When we see, hear, smell, taste, feel, meditate, or will anything, we know that we do so. Thus it is always as to our present sensations and perceptions: and by this every one is to himself that which he calls *self:*—it not being considered, in this case, whether the same self be continued in the same or divers substances. For, since consciousness always accompanies thinking, and it is that which makes every one to be what he calls self,[3] and thereby distinguishes himself from all other thinking things, in this alone consists personal identity,[4] i.e. the sameness of a rational being: and as far as this consciousness can be extended backwards to any past action or thought, so far reaches the identity of that person;[5] it is the same self now it was then; and it is by the same self with this present one that now reflects on it, that that action was done.[6]

But it is further inquired, whether it be the same identical substance. This few would think they had reason to doubt of, if these perceptions, with their consciousness, always remained present in the mind, whereby the same thinking thing would be always consciously present, and, as would be thought, evidently the same to itself. But that which seems to make the difficulty is this, that this consciousness being interrupted always by forgetfulness, there being no moment of our lives wherein we have the whole train of all our past actions before our eyes in one view, but even the best memories losing the sight of one part whilst they are viewing another[7]; and we sometimes, and that the greatest part of our lives, not reflecting on our past selves, being intent on our present thoughts, and in sound sleep having no thoughts at all, or at least none with that consciousness which remarks our waking thoughts,[8]—I say, in all these cases, our consciousness being interrupted, and we losing the sight of our past selves, doubts are raised whether we are the same thinking thing, i.e. the same *substance* or no. Which, however reasonable or unreasonable, concerns not *personal* identity at all. The question being what makes the same person; and not whether it be the same identical substance, which always thinks in the same person, which, in this case, matters not at all: different substances, by the same consciousness (where they do partake in it) being united into one person, as well as different bodies by the same life are united into one animal, whose identity is preserved in that change of substances by the unity of one continued life.[9] For, it being the same consciousness that makes a man be himself to himself, personal identity de-

---

[1] '*Being* and *substance* in this place stand for the same idea.' (Butler.)

[2] To the French version the following note on 'consciousness' (*conscience*) is appended: 'Le mot Anglais est *consciousness*, qu'on pourroit exprimer en Latin par celui de *conscientia*, si sumatur pro actu illo hominis qui *sibi* est conscius. Et c'est en ce sens que les Latins ont souvent employé ce mot, témoin cet endroit de Cicéron (*Epist*. Lib. vi. Epist. 4). En François nous n'avons à nos avis que les mots de *sentiment* et de *conviction* qui respondent en quelque sorte à cette idée. Mais, en plusieurs endroits de ce chapitre, ils ne peuvent qu'exprimer fort imperfectement la pensée de M. Locke.' The term 'consciousness,' in the sense of apprehension by the *ego* of its operations and other states as its own, came into use in the seventeenth century, among the Cartesians and in Locke, who sometimes confuses direct consciousness with the reflex act in which self is *explicitly* recognised. Although recently in almost as constant use with some psychologists as the term 'idea' is with Locke, 'consciousness,' so often introduced in this chapter, hardly occurs in any other part of the *Essay*. See, however, ch. i. §§ 10–19.

[3] 'Self consciousness,' says Ferrier, '*creates the ego*'—'a being *makes itself* I by thinking itself I.' Locke and Ferrier so far regard the *cogito* as the presupposition of the *sum,* instead of the *sum* as presupposed in the *cogito;* but in the *Essay* the presupposition refers to the order of experience, according to which our idea of continued identity of person is formed.

[4] That is, any positive idea we have of what identity of person means is that given in memory.

[5] Here identity of person is limited to what is remembered—potentially as well as actually (?) 'Wherein,' asks Berkeley, 'consists identity of person? Not in *actual* consciousness; for then I am not the same person I was this day twelvemonth, but only while I think of what I then did. Not in *potential;* for then all persons may be the same, for ought we know.' (*C. P. B. Works,* vol. iv. p. 481.)

[6] 'All attempts to define personal identity would but perplex it. Yet there is no difficulty at all in ascertaining the *idea*. For as upon two triangles being compared together, there arises to the mind the idea of *similitude;* or upon twice two and four the idea of *equality;* so likewise upon comparing the consciousness of oneself in any two moments, there as immediately arises to the mind the idea of *personal identity*. . . . By reflecting on that which is myself now, and that which was myself twenty years ago, I *discern* that they are not two, but one and the same self. (Bp. Butler, *Dissertation on Personal Identity*.) And it is the 'idea,' or 'what makes personal identity to ourselves' that Locke is concerned with, in this Book, which deals with ideas, not with knowledge.

[7] Cf. ch. x. § 9.

[8] Cf. ch. i. §§ 10–17.

[9] In thus pressing a distinction between identity of *substance* and identity of *person*, he seeks to show that the latter is independent of the former, and that the personality is continuous as far as memory (latent as well as patent?) can go, whatever changes of annexed bodily or spiritual substances may take place; especially if (as he elsewhere suggests) the substance of a man is perhaps 'material'—as it may 'have pleased God to make' consciousness one of the qualities or powers of organised matter. All that is essential to the idea of personal identity is, that memory *can* bridge over the apparent interruptions in self-conscious life, whatever substance may be united with that life.

pends on that only,[10] whether it be annexed solely to one individual substance, or can be continued in a succession of several substances.[11] For as far as any intelligent being *can* repeat the idea of any past action with the same consciousness it had of it at first, and with the same consciousness it has of any present action; so far it is the same personal self. For it is by the consciousness it has of its present thoughts and actions, that it is *self to itself* now, and so will be the same self, as far as the same consciousness can extend to actions past or to come;[12] and would be by distance of time, or change of substance, no more two persons, than a man be two men by wearing other clothes to-day than he did yesterday, with a long or a short sleep between: the same consciousness uniting those distant actions into the same person, whatever substances[13] contributed to their production.[14]

That this is so, we have some kind of evidence in our very bodies, all whose particles, whilst vitally united to this same thinking conscious self, so that *we feel* when they are touched, and are affected by, and conscious of good or harm that happens to them, are a part of ourselves; i.e. of our thinking conscious self. Thus, the limbs of his body are to every one a part of himself; he sympathizes and is concerned for them. Cut off a hand, and thereby separate it from that consciousness he had of its heat, cold, and other affections, and it is then no longer

a part of that which is himself, any more than the remotest part of matter. Thus, we see the *substance* whereof personal self consisted at one time may be varied at another, without the change of personal identity; there being no question about the same person, though the limbs which but now were a part of it, be cut off.[15]

But the question is, Whether if the same substance which thinks be changed, it can be the same person; or, remaining the same, it can be different persons?

And to this I answer: First, This can be no question at all to those who place thought in a purely material animal constitution, void of an immaterial substance. For, whether their supposition be true or no, it is plain they conceive personal identity preserved in something else than identity of substance; as animal identity is preserved in identity of life, and not of substance.[16] And therefore those who place thinking in an immaterial substance only, before they can come to deal with these men, must show why personal identity cannot be preserved in the change of immaterial substances, or variety of particular immaterial substances, as well as animal identity is preserved in the change of material substances, or variety of particular bodies: unless they will say, it is one immaterial spirit that makes the same life in brutes, as it is one immaterial spirit that makes the same person in men; which the Cartesians at least will not admit, for fear of making brutes thinking things too.

But next, as to the first part of the question, Whether, if the same thinking substance (supposing immaterial substances only to think) be changed, it can be the same person? I answer, that cannot be resolved but by those who know what kind of substances they are that do think;[17] and whether the

---

[10] Here 'depends on,' not 'is constituted by,' as in other passages. It is the *terms* which contribute to the relation of personal identity—i.e. self now, and self in the past—in which this relation 'terminates,' that Locke has in view. As to our conviction of the identity of those terms, Butler remarks, 'But though we are certain that we are the same agents, living beings, or substances, now, which we were as far back as our remembrance reaches; yet it is asked whether we may not be deceived in it? And this question may be asked at the end of any demonstration whatever; because it is a question concerning the truth of perception by memory. And he who can doubt whether *perception by memory* may in this case be depended upon, may doubt also whether *perception by deduction and reasoning* which also include memory, or indeed whether *intuitive perception* can. Here then we can go no further. For it is ridiculous to attempt to prove the truth of those perceptions, whose truth we can no otherwise prove than by other perceptions of exactly the same kind with them, and which there is just the same ground to suspect.' (*Dissertation on Personal Identity*.)

[11] As in a change from the 'natural body' to a 'spiritual body'—the person, and his accountability for his past conscious experience, remaining unchanged.

[12] Making itself the same by its memory of itself, and thus in memory *creating*, and not merely discovering, itself—if the expressions in the text are strictly interpreted; the thinking substance 'contributing to the production' of the successive acts, which acts memory 'unites' in one person. (Cf. p. 415, note 2.)

[13] 'change of substance,' e.g. by transmigration into another body— 'whatever substances'—whatever organised body, or other substance.

[14] Can the *same personality*—accountability—be 'annexed' to *two or more substances,* which all contribute to the production of the memory by which the personality is constituted?

[15] 'Je suis aussi de cette opinion, que la conscience, ou le sentiment du moi, *prouve* une identité morale ou personnelle. Je ne voudrais point dire que *l'identité personnelle* et même le *soi* ne demeurent point en nous, et que je ne suis point le *moi* qui ait été dans le berceau, sous prétexte que je ne me souviens plus de rien de tout ce que j'ai fait alors. Il suffit, pour trouver l'identité morale par soimême, qu'il y ait une *moyenne liaison de consciosité* d'un état voisin, ou même un peu éloigné à l'autre, quand quelque saut ou intervalle oublié y serait mêlé.' (Leibniz.) When Locke makes personal i.e. moral identity depend on memory, this may include *potential* memory, in which our whole past conscious experience is possibly retained; and when he suggests the transmigration of one man's memory into the bodies of other men, or even of brutes, this may be taken as an emphatic illustration of the essential dependence of the idea of our personality upon self-consciousness *only*, but not as affirming that this transmigration actually occurs under the present order of things.

[16] The animal organism is continually changing its particles, and this, according to Locke, is change of the 'material substance.' Consciousness that he is the same *person*, cannot be consciousness that he is the same *substance*, to one who makes his body his substance.

[17] He maintains (ch. xxiii. §§ 5, 15, &c.) that we have as clear (or as obscure) an idea of what spiritual substances are as of material substances.

consciousness of past actions can be transferred from one thinking substance to another.[18] I grant were the same consciousness the same individual action it could not: but it being a present representation of a past action, why it may not be possible, that that may be represented to the mind to have been which really never was, will remain to be shown. And therefore how far the consciousness of past actions is annexed to any individual agent, so that another cannot possibly have it, will be hard for us to determine, till we know what kind of action it is that cannot be done without a reflex act of perception accompanying it, and how performed by thinking substances, who cannot think without being conscious of it. But that which we call the same consciousness, not being the same individual act, why one intellectual substance may not have represented to it, as done by itself, what *it* never did, and was perhaps done by some other agent—why, I say, such a representation may not possibly be without reality of matter of fact, as well as several representations in dreams are, which yet whilst dreaming we take for true—will be difficult to conclude from the nature of things.[19] And that it never is so, will by us, till we have clearer views of the nature of thinking substances, be best resolved into the goodness of God; who, as far as the happiness or misery of any of his sensible creatures is concerned in it, will not, by a fatal error of theirs, transfer from one to another that consciousness which draws reward or punishment with it.[20] How far this may be an argument against those who would place thinking in a system of fleeting animal spirits, I leave to be considered. But yet, to return to the question before us, it must be allowed, that, if the same consciousness (which, as has been shown, is quite a different thing from the same numerical figure or motion in body) can be transferred from one thinking substance to another, it will be possible that two thinking substances may make but one person. For the same consciousness being preserved, whether in the same or different substances, the personal identity is preserved.[21]

As to the second part of the question, Whether the same immaterial substance remaining, there may be two distinct persons; which question seems to me to be built on this,—Whether the same immaterial being, being conscious of the action of its past duration, may be wholly stripped of all the consciousness of its past existence, and lose it beyond the power of ever retrieving it again:[22] and so as it were beginning a new account from a new period, have a consciousness that *cannot* reach beyond this new state. All those who hold pre-existence are evidently of this mind; since they allow the soul to have no remaining consciousness of what it did in that pre-existent state, either wholly separate from body, or informing any other body; and if they should not, it is plain experience would be against them.[23] So that personal identity, reaching no further than consciousness[24] reaches, a pre-existent spirit not having continued so many ages in a state of silence, must needs make different persons. Suppose a Christian Platonist or a Pythagorean should, upon God's having ended all his works of creation the seventh day, think his soul hath existed ever since; and should imagine it has revolved in several human bodies; as I once met with one, who was persuaded his had been the *soul* of Socrates (how reasonably I will not dispute; this I know, that in the post he filled, which was no inconsiderable one, he passed for a very rational man, and the press has shown that he wanted not parts or learning;)—would any one say, that he, being not conscious of any of Socrates's actions or thoughts, could be the same *person* with Socrates?[25] Let any one reflect upon himself, and conclude that he has in himself an immaterial spirit, which is that which thinks in him, and, in the constant change of

---

[18]   How does Locke thus distinguish the spiritual substance from the self that is given in consciousness? Is not a person a spiritual substance manifested? Here again he uses words which seem to imply that a substance, material or spiritual, is one thing, and its manifestations of itself another and different thing, by which to the substance is concealed rather than revealed. But is not our idea of personality rather the highest form in which substance can be conceived by us? On this subject see Lotze's *Metaphysics*, Bk. III. ch. i. *passim*, especially the reference to Kant, § 244.

[19]   In other words, we cannot be deceived in our presentative, but we may in our representative experience.

[20]   Under the natural order of things, which we are obliged to accept in faith, the identity apparent to the person who feels himself the same, with its implied moral responsibility, is intransferable in fact.

[21]   'According to Mr. Locke, we may always be sure that we are the same persons, that is, the same accountable agents or beings, now which we were as far back as our remembrance reaches: or as far as a perfectly just and good God will cause it to reach.' (Perronet's *Vindication of Locke*, p. 21.) The last clause suggests a conscious revival of the latent stores of memory, which may include all the past experience of the person.

[22]   There being in that case not only no actual, but no potential memory of a past conscious life.

[23]   Hardly so, if the Platonic interpretation of the universal ideas of reason, as reminiscence of what we were conscious of, in a pre-existing state, is taken literally, as rendered in Wordsworth's 'Ode on Intimations of Immortality.'

[24]   'Consciousness,' i.e. memory, including its latent possibilities.

[25]   But what if the conscious experience of Socrates, is all the while *latent* in him, and capable of being recollected by him, as on the thread of *his* consciousness? When the recollection occurs, Locke would say, he finds himself the same person who then went under that name. Locke, is satirised in Martinus Scriblerus for his paradoxical illustrations of the idea of personal identity.

his body keeps him the same: and is that which he calls *himself:* let him also suppose it to be the same soul that was in Nestor or Thersites, at the siege of Troy, (for souls being, as far as we know anything of them, in their nature indifferent to any parcel of matter, the supposition has no apparent absurdity in it,) which it may have been, as well as it is now the soul of any other man: but he now having no consciousness of any of the actions either of Nestor or Thersites, does or can he conceive himself the same person with either of them? Can he be concerned in either of their actions? attribute them to himself, or think them his own, more than the actions of any other men that ever existed? So that this consciousness, not reaching to any of the actions of either of those men, he is no more one *self* with either of them than if the soul or immaterial spirit that now informs him had been created, and began to exist, when it began to inform his present body; though it were never so true, that the same *spirit* that informed Nestor's or Thersites' body were numerically the same that now informs his.[26] For this would no more make him the same person with Nestor, than if some of the particles of matter that were once a part of Nestor were now a part of this man; the same immaterial substance, without the same consciousness, no more making the same person, by being united to any body, than the same particle of matter, without consciousness, united to any body, makes the same person. But let him once find himself conscious of any of the actions of Nestor, he then finds himself the same person with Nestor.

And thus may we be able, without any difficulty, to conceive the same person at the resurrection,[27]

though in a body not exactly in make or parts the same which he had here,—the same consciousness going along with the soul that inhabits it. But yet the soul alone, in the change of bodies, would scarce to any one but to him that makes the soul the man, be enough to make the same man. For should the soul of a prince, carrying with it the consciousness of the prince's past life, enter and inform the body of a cobbler, as soon as deserted by his own soul, every one sees he would be the same *person* with the prince, accountable only for the prince's actions: but who would say it was the same *man?* The body too goes to the making the man, and would, I guess, to everybody determine the man in this case, wherein the soul, with all its princely thoughts about it, would not make another man: but he would be the same cobbler to every one besides himself.[28] I know that, in the ordinary way of speaking, the same person, and the same man, stand for one and the same thing. And indeed every one will always have a liberty to speak as he pleases, and to apply what articulate sounds to what ideas he thinks fit, and change them as often as he pleases. But yet, when we will inquire what makes the same *spirit, man,* or *person,* we must fix the ideas of spirit, man, or person in our minds; and having resolved with ourselves what we mean by them, it will not be hard to determine, in either of them, or the like, when it is the same, and when not.[29]

But though the same immaterial substance or soul does not alone, wherever it be, and in whatsoever state, make the same *man;* yet it is plain, consciousness, as far as ever it can be extended—should it be to ages past—unites existences and actions very remote in time into the same *person,* as well as it does the existences and actions of the immediately preceding moment: so that whatever[30] has the con-

---

[26] That is, he cannot have the *idea* of himself now, as one and the same with either of them; being unable, by memory, to connect his present consciousness with theirs. The supposed identity of 'spiritual substance' does not carry with it the idea of personal responsibility for the actions of Nestor, or of Thersites, unless he also finds himself conscious of their actions as having been once his own. But is memory the only means for testing or discovering one's personal identity?

[27] One of Stillingfleet's charges against the *Essay* was, that its doctrine regarding personality and personal identity was inconsistent with the Christian doctrine of the resurrection of the body. For sameness of person, in Locke's account of our idea of personal identity, is indifferent to sameness of body. 'My idea of personal identity,' Locke replies, 'makes the same body not to be necessary to making the same person, either here or after death; and even in this life the particles of the bodies of the same persons change every moment, and there is thus no such identity in the *body* as in the *person.*' Moreover, while the resurrection of the dead is revealed in scripture, we find 'no such express words there as that the body shall rise, or the resurrection of the body; and though I do not question that the dead shall be raised with bodies, as matter of revelation, I think it our duty to keep close to the words of the scripture.' (Cf. Bk. IV. ch. xviii. § 7.) The question of the identity of the risen body, with any or all the ever fluctuating bodies with which the person has been connected in this life, is irrelevant to Christianity.

[28] Because sameness of person is directly revealed only to the person, or spiritual substance, whose identity is in question; but to all others only indirectly, by those visible signs from which we infer the existence and continued identity of other men.

[29] 'No identity (other than perfect likeness) in any individuals besides persons,' says Berkeley (*C. P. B.* p. 486); but by 'person' he means spiritual substance, and not merely (as Locke) a consciousness that is (actually or potentially) aware of its own past, and can more or less anticipate its future.

[30] 'whatever.' Does this mean, whatever *being* or *substance*—as that on which the 'consciousness' depends? 'One should really think it self-evident,' says Bishop Butler, 'that consciousness of personal identity presupposes, and therefore cannot constitute, personal identity, any more than knowledge in any other case can constitute the reality which it presupposes.' But the presented facts in which the presuppositions of reason are primarily embodied are, throughout the *Essay,* always apt to throw in the background the metaphysical presuppositions which they imply. Concrete examples supersede their principles. Locke prefers the practical consideration of particular facts given in consciousness to elaboration of abstract theories about their 'substance.'

sciousness of present and past actions, is the same person to whom they both belong. Had I the same consciousness that I saw the ark and Noah's flood, as that I saw an overflowing of the Thames last winter, or as that I write now, I could no more doubt that I who write this now, that saw the Thames overflowed last winter, and that viewed the flood at the general deluge, was the same *self,*—place that self in what *substance* you please—than that I who write this am the same *myself* now whilst I write (whether I consist of all the same substance, material or immaterial, or no) that I was yesterday. For as to this point of being the same self, it matters not whether this present self be made up of the same or other substances—I being as much concerned, and as justly accountable[31] for any action that was done a thousand years since, appropriated to me now by this self-consciousness, as I am for what I did the last moment.

Self is that conscious thinking thing,—whatever substance made up of, (whether spiritual or material, simple or compounded, it matters not)—which is sensible or conscious of pleasure and pain, capable of happiness or misery, and so is concerned for itself, as far as that consciousness extends.[32] Thus every one finds that, whilst comprehended under that consciousness, the little finger is as much a part of himself as what is most so. Upon separation of this little finger, should this consciousness go along with the little finger, and leave the rest of the body, it is evident the little finger would be the person, the same person; and self then would have nothing to do with the rest of the body. As in this case it is the consciousness that goes along with the substance, when one part is separate[33] from another, which makes the same person, and constitutes this inseparable self: so it is in reference to substances remote in time. That with which the consciousness of this present thinking thing *can* join itself, makes the same person, and is one self with it, and with nothing else; and so attributes to itself, and owns all the actions of that thing,[34] as its own, as far as that consciousness

reaches, and no further; as every one who reflects will perceive.[35]

In this personal identity is founded all the right and justice of reward and punishment; happiness and misery being that for which every one is concerned for *himself,* and not mattering what becomes of any *substance,* not joined to, or affected with that consciousness. For, as it is evident in the instance I gave but now, if the consciousness went along with the little finger when it was cut off, that[36] would be the same self which was concerned for the whole body yesterday, as making part of itself, whose actions then it cannot but admit as its own now. Though, if the same body should still live, and immediately from the separation of the little finger have its own peculiar consciousness, whereof the little finger knew nothing, it would not at all be concerned for it, as a part of itself, or could own any of its actions, or have any of them imputed to him.

This may show us wherein personal identity consists: not in the identity of substance, but, as I have said, in the identity of consciousness, wherein if Socrates and the present mayor of Queinborough agree, they are the same person: if the same Socrates[37] waking and sleeping do not partake of the same consciousness, Socrates waking and sleeping is not the same person. And to punish Socrates waking for what sleeping Socrates thought, and waking Socrates was never conscious of, would be no more of right,[38] than to punish one twin for what his brother-twin did, whereof he knew nothing, because their outsides were so like, that they could not be distinguished; for such twins have been seen.

But yet possibly it will still be objected,—Suppose I wholly lose the memory of some parts of my life, beyond a possibility of retrieving them, so that perhaps I shall never be conscious of them again; yet am I not the same person that did those actions, had

---

[31] 'Accountability' is with Locke a criterion of personality. We are 'persons' only in respect to what is necessary for this. Person is a 'forensic term.' (Cf. § 26.) It does not mean a man, or any other living agent, merely as such, but only an ego that actually (or potentially?) appropriates past actions. No being that is not capable of recognising his own past answers this description. So that a madman, though he is living and a man, is not, in Locke's forensic sense, a person. For he cannot be justly punished for what the sane man did. Therefore more is necessary to the idea of a person than to the idea of a man; and that, Locke argues, is intelligent recognition of a past as his own past.

[32] What is this but a definition of a *spiritual substance?*

[33] 'separate,' i.e. in place.

[34] 'that thing,' i.e. that substance, whether material or spiritual.

[35] Facts alleged by physiologists in evidence of inherited memory, through which, under abnormal conditions, a person becomes conscious of acts and thoughts of an ancestor, as his own, are, so far, in analogy with the suggestion that, in a sense, all men may constitute one person.

[36] 'that,' i.e. that finger-consciousness. Appropriation of organ is with Locke determined by consciousness. But consciousness, Leibniz remarks, is not the only means of determining the identity of a person. It can be proved, sufficiently for practical purposes, by certain external appearances, which sufficiently signify that the person continues to be the same, as in questions of personal identity in courts of justice.

[37] 'same Socrates,' i.e. the same bodily appearance which signifies the *man* Socrates.

[38] Because, although outwardly Socrates, he is not really Socrates, either man or person, if the apparent Socrates has ceased to partake of the same 'consciousness.' Disease sometimes deprives persons of consciousness of their identity.

those thoughts that I once was conscious of, though I have now forgot them? To which I answer, that we must here take notice what the word *I* is applied to; which, in this case, is the *man* only. And the same man being presumed to be the same person, I is easily here supposed to stand also for the same person. But if it be possible for the same man to have distinct incommunicable consciousness at different times,[39] it is past doubt the same man would at different times make different persons; which, we see, is the sense of mankind in the solemnest declaration of their opinions, human laws not punishing the mad man for the sober man's actions, nor the sober man for what the mad man did,—thereby making them two persons: which is somewhat explained by our way of speaking in English when we say such an one is 'not himself,' or is 'beside himself'; in which phrases it is insinuated, as if those who now, or at least first used them, thought that self was changed; the self-same person was no longer in that man.

But yet it is hard to conceive that Socrates, the same individual man, should be two persons. To help us a little in this, we must consider what is meant by Socrates, or the same individual *man*.

First, it must be either the same individual, immaterial, thinking substance; in short, the same numerical soul, and nothing else.

Secondly, or the same animal, without any regard to an immaterial soul.

Thirdly, or the same immaterial spirit united to the same animal.

Now, take which of these suppositions you please, it is impossible to make personal identity to consist in anything but consciousness; or reach any further than that does.

For, by the first of them, it must be allowed possible that a man born of different women, and in distant times, may be the same man.[40] A way of speaking which, whoever admits, must allow it possible for the same man to be two distinct persons, as any two that have lived in different ages without the knowledge of one another's thoughts.

By the second and third, Socrates, in this life and after it, cannot be the same man any way, but by the same consciousness;[41] and so making human identity to consist in the same thing wherein we place personal identity, there will be no difficulty to allow

the same man to be the same person. But then they who place human identity in consciousness only, and not in something else, must consider how they will make the infant Socrates the same man with Socrates after the resurrection.[42] But whatsoever to some men makes a man, and consequently the same individual man, wherein perhaps few are agreed, personal identity can by us be placed in nothing but consciousness, (which is that alone which makes what we call *self,*) without involving us in great absurdities.[43]

But is not a man drunk and sober the same person? why else is he punished for the fact he commits when drunk, though he be never afterwards conscious of it? Just as much the same person as a man that walks, and does other things in his sleep, is the same person, and is answerable for any mischief he shall do in it. Human laws punish both, with a justice suitable to *their* way of knowledge;—because, in these cases, they cannot distinguish certainly what is real, what counterfeit: and so the ignorance in drunkenness or sleep is not admitted as a plea. [[44]For, though punishment be annexed to person-

---

[39] For curious cases of double, and of alternate personality, see James's *Psychology*, vol. i. pp. 379–92.

[40] Because the same thinking *substance* might conceivably be joined to the different organisms.

[41] Because the animal organism is changed.

[42] This sentence may have suggested the following by Sir James Mackintosh:—'When the mind is purified from gross notions, it is evident that belief in a future state can no longer rest on the merely selfish idea of preserving its own individuality. When we make a further progress, it becomes indifferent whether the *same* individuals who now inhabit the universe, or others who do not yet exist, are to reach that superior degree of virtue and happiness of which human nature seems to be capable. The object of desire is, the quantity of virtue and happiness, not the identical beings who are to act and enjoy. Even those who distinctly believe in the continued existence (after death) of their fellow men are unable to pursue their opinion through its consequences. The dissimilarity between Socrates at his death, and Socrates in a future state, ten thousand years after death, is so very great, that to call these two beings by the same name is rather consequence of the imperfection of language than of exact views in philosophy. There is no practical identity. The Socrates of Elysium can feel no interest in recollecting what befel the Socrates at Athens. He is infinitely more removed from his former state than Newton was in this world from his infancy.' (*Life,* vol. ii. p. 120.) But is this so, if the thread of self-consciousness is still maintained, and perhaps with the potential memory transformed into an actual consciousness in which all past experience is revived?

[43] According to Locke, our idea of the identity of a *man* includes participation in the same life by constantly changing particles of matter. Our idea of the identity of a *person*, on the other hand, is *independent of particles of matter, organised or unorganised;* and involves only a conception of the self-conscious being or person as the same, *as far back as memory extends,* and without implying that connection with the same material or other substance is also continued. The same person might thus be incarnated in succession in a series of bodies. Locke's curious speculations on identity of person may have suggested to Jonathan Edwards his paradoxical vindication of the responsibility of all men for Adam's sin, on the ground that personality is a consciousness arbitrarily sustained, by divine will, in a constant creation, so that all men, by divine appointment might make one person, all thus, in a revived consciousness, participating in the act by which mankind rebelled against God. (See Edwards on *Original Sin.*) (Cf. p. 415, note 2.)

[44] Added in fourth edition.

ality, and personality to consciousness, and the drunkard perhaps be not conscious of what he did, yet human judicatures justly punish him; because the fact is proved against him, but want of consciousness cannot be proved for him.[45]] But in the Great Day, wherein the secrets of all hearts shall be laid open, it may be reasonable to think, no one shall be made to answer for what he knows nothing of; but shall receive his doom, his conscience accusing or excusing him.[46]

Nothing but consciousness can unite remote existences into the same person: the identity of substance will not do it; for whatever substance there is, however framed, without consciousness there is no person: and a carcass may be a person, as well as any sort of substance be so, without consciousness.

Could we suppose two distinct incommunicable consciousnesses acting the same body, the one constantly by day, the other by night; and, on the other side, the same consciousness, acting by intervals, two distinct bodies: I ask, in the first case, whether the day and the night—man would not be two as distinct persons as Socrates and Plato? And whether, in the second case, there would not be one person in two distinct bodies, as much as one man is the same in two distinct clothings? Nor is it at all material to say, that this same, and this distinct consciousness, in the cases above mentioned, is owing to the same and distinct immaterial substances, bringing it with them to those bodies; which, whether true or no, alters not the case: since it is evident the personal identity would equally be determined by the consciousness, whether that consciousness were annexed to some individual immaterial substance or no. For, granting that the thinking substance in man must be necessarily supposed immaterial, it is evident that immaterial thinking thing may sometimes part with its past consciousness, and be restored to it again: as appears in the forgetfulness men often have of their past actions; and the mind many times recovers the memory of a past consciousness, which it had lost for twenty years together. Make these intervals of memory and forgetfulness to take their turns regularly by day and night, and you have two persons with the same immaterial spirit, as much as in the former instance two persons with the same body. So that self is not determined by identity or diversity of substance, which it cannot be sure of,[47] but only by identity of consciousness.

Indeed it may conceive the substance whereof it is now made up to have existed formerly, united in the same conscious being: but, consciousness removed, that substance is no more itself, or makes no more a part of it, than any other substance; as is evident in the instance we have already given of a limb cut off, of whose heat, or cold, or other affections, having no longer any consciousness, it is no more of a man's self than any other matter of the universe. In like manner it will be in reference to any immaterial substance, which is void of that consciousness whereby I am myself to myself: [[48]if there be any part of its existence which] I cannot upon recollection join with that present consciousness whereby I am now myself, it is, in that part of its existence, no more *myself* than any other immaterial being. For, whatsoever any substance has thought or done, which I cannot recollect, and by my consciousness make my own thought and action, it will no more belong to me, whether a part of me[49] thought or did it, than if it

<hr>

[45] 'A man may be punished for any crime which he committed when drunk, *whereof he is not conscious.*' Locke allows, in reply to an objection of Molyneux to the statement in the text, that if a man may be justly punished for a crime committed when he was drunk, his theory of personal identity fails. 'You doubt whether my answer be full in the case of the drunkard. To try whether it be or no, we must consider what I am there doing. As I remember (for I have not that chapter here by me) I am there showing that *punishment* is annexed to *personality*, and *personality* to *consciousness:* how then can a drunkard be punished for what he did whereof he is not conscious? To this I answer: human judicatures justly punish him, because the *fact* is proved against him; but *want of consciousness* cannot be proved for him. This you think not sufficient, but would have me add the common reason,—that drunkenness being a crime, one crime cannot be alleged in excuse for another. This reason, how good soever, cannot I think be used by me, as not reaching my case; for what has this to do with consciousness? Nay, it is an argument against me; for if a man may be punished for any crime which he committed when drunk, whereof he is allowed not to be conscious, it overturns my hypothesis' (19th Jan. 1694). In reply to this, Molyneux asks (Feb. 17, 1694), 'How it comes to pass that want of consciousness cannot be proved for a drunkard, as well as for a frantic? One methinks is as manifest as the other: if drunkenness may be counterfeit, so may a frenzy. Wherefore to me it seems that the law has made a difference in these two cases, on this account, viz. that drunkenness is commonly incurred voluntarily and premeditately; whereas a frenzy is commonly without our consent, or impossible to be prevented.' In the end, Locke replies (May 26, 1694):—'I agree with you that drunkenness, being a voluntary defect, want of consciousness ought not to be presumed in favour of the drunkard. But frenzy, being involuntary and a misfortune, not a fault, has a right to that excuse, which certainly is a just one, where it is truly a frenzy. And all that lies upon human justice is, to distinguish carefully between what is real, and what counterfeit in the case.'

[46] His accountability depending upon the possibility of awakening his latent memory of all that he was ever conscious of; which is thus capable of being brought out of latency, so as to become, as suggested by Coleridge, the Book of Judgment, 'in the mysterious hieroglyphics of which every idle word is recorded.'

[47] Locke cannot mean, by this humorous illustration, to suggest the probability of a double personality in the same body being ever exemplified in fact, which would be a 'fatal error' (§ 13), God thereby putting our reason to confusion.

[48] 'so that,' in second edition.

[49] I.e. my substance.

had been thought or done by any other immaterial being anywhere existing.

I agree, the more probable opinion is, that this consciousness is annexed to, and the affection of, one individual immaterial substance.[50]

But let men, according to their diverse hypotheses, resolve of that as they please. This every intelligent being, sensible of happiness or misery, must grant—that there is something that is *himself*, that he is concerned for, and would have happy; that this self has existed in a continued duration more than one instant, and therefore it is possible may exist, as it has done, months and years to come, without any certain bounds to be set to its duration; and may be the same self, by the same consciousness continued on for the future. And thus, by this consciousness he finds himself to be the same self which did such and such an action some years since, by which he comes to be happy or miserable now. In all which account of self, the same numerical *substance* is not considered as making the same self; but the same continued *consciousness*, in which several substances may have been united, and again separated from it, which, whilst they continued in a vital union with that wherein this consciousness then resided, made a part of that same self. Thus any part of our bodies, vitally united to that which is conscious in us, makes a part of ourselves: but upon separation from the vital union by which that consciousness is communicated, that which a moment since was part of ourselves, is now no more so than a part of another man's self is a part of me: and it is not impossible but in a little time may become a real part of another person. And so we have the same numerical substance become a part of two different persons; and the same person preserved under the change of various substances. Could we suppose any spirit[51] wholly stripped of all its memory or consciousness of past actions,[52] as we find our minds always are of a great part of ours, and sometimes of them all;[53] the union or separation of such a spiritual substance would make no variation of personal identity, any more

than that of any particle of matter does. Any substance vitally united to the present thinking being is a part of that very same self which now is; anything united to it by a consciousness of former actions, makes also a part of the same self, which is the same both then and now.

Person, as I take it, is the name for this self. Wherever a man finds what he calls himself, there, I think, another may say is the same person.[54] It is a forensic term, appropriating actions and their merit; and so belongs only to intelligent agents, capable of a law, and happiness, and misery. This personality extends itself beyond present existence to what is past, only by consciousness,—whereby it becomes concerned and accountable; owns and imputes to itself past actions, just upon the same ground and for the same reason as it does the present.[55] All which is founded in a concern for happiness, the unavoidable concomitant of consciousness; that which is conscious of pleasure and pain, desiring that that self that is conscious should be happy. And therefore whatever past actions it cannot reconcile or *appropriate* to that present self by consciousness, it can be no more concerned in than if they had never been done: and to receive pleasure or pain, i.e. reward or punishment, on the account of any such action, is all one as to be made happy or miserable in its first being,[56] without any demerit at all. For, supposing a

---

[50] Is it only 'probable' that in 'consciousness' the spiritual substance is manifesting itself to itself? Berkeley, on the other hand, sees in 'persons' the *only* substances—personality and substantiality being identified. 'Nothing properly but persons, i.e. conscious things, do exist. All other things are not so much (independent?) existences as modes of the existence of persons.' (*C. P. B.* p. 469.) In this philosophy personality and its identity is the ultimate basis of all actual existence.

[51] Spirit, i.e. spiritual substance.

[52] So that its past actions were all *incapable* of being recollected—neither patent nor latent in memory.

[53] For a time, e.g. in sleep.

[54] Throughout this discussion, what Locke means by 'person' must be kept in view. If person means the living agent, or the man, then appropriation of past actions by present consciousness is not necessary to sameness of personality; since they are the same living agents, whether conscious or not of past and present actions. But a 'person' with Locke means an agent who is *accountable for past actions*. Although present 'appropriation' by consciousness of past actions is not implied in a living agent, it is necessary, according to the *Essay*, to our being persons, i.e. the proper objects of reward or punishment on account of them. If a man is not justly responsible for a past act, he is not the *person* by whom it was done, although he is the *man* or *living agent* through whom it was done; as no man can justly be punished for an action that cannot be brought home to his consciousness and conscience, as in a Book of Judgment. We are thus responsible only for voluntary actions which can by consciousness be appropriated to ourselves; consciousness uniting the most distant actions in one and the same personality. Consciousness that I am the same *person* cannot, Locke would say, be consciousness that I am the same *substance*, to any one who makes his body his substance. In short, we need not, he implies, for determining personality, embarrass ourselves with subtle questions about 'substances': they are irrelevant to the practical certainty that we are the same accountable agents, as far back as our remembrance of actions *as ours* can be *made* to reach, by a just and good God. Cf. § 11.

[55] The character of the self in former times and places, as it appears in the memory, is thereby appropriated, i.e. *personified*. The name 'person' (*persona*) was given originally to the mask worn by actors, through the mouthplace of which the voice sent forth its sounds (*personuit*); then to the mask itself; to the wearer of it, the actor; to the character acted; and at last to any assumed character.

[56] 'first being,' i.e. inasmuch as he could not *personify*, or appropriate them to himself, as *formerly* his.

man punished now for what he had done in another life, whereof he could be made to have no consciousness at all, what difference is there between that punishment and being *created* miserable?[57] And therefore, conformable to this, the apostle tells us, that, at the great day, when every one shall 'receive according to his doings, the secrets of all hearts shall be laid open.' The sentence shall be justified by the consciousness all persons shall have, that *they themselves*, in what bodies soever they appear, or what substances soever that consciousness adheres to, are the *same* that committed those actions, and deserve that punishment for them.[58]

I am apt enough to think I have, in treating of this subject, made some suppositions that will look strange to some readers, and possibly they are so in themselves.[59] But yet, I think they are such as are pardonable, in this ignorance we are in of the nature of that thinking thing that is in us, and which we look on as *ourselves*.[60] Did we know what it was; or how it was tied to a certain system of fleeting animal spirits; or whether it could or could not perform its operations of thinking and memory out of a body organized as ours is; and whether it has pleased God that no one such spirit shall ever be united to any but one such body, upon the right constitution of whose organs its memory should depend; we might see the absurdity of some of those suppositions I have made. But taking, as we ordinarily now do (in the dark concerning these matters,) the soul of a man for an immaterial substance, independent from matter, and indifferent alike to it all; there can, from the nature of things, be no absurdity at all to suppose that the same *soul* may at different times be united to different *bodies,* and with them make up for that time one *man:* as well as we suppose a part of a sheep's body yesterday should be a part of a man's body to-morrow, and in that union make a vital part of Melibœus himself, as well as it did of his ram.[61]

To conclude: Whatever substance begins to exist, it must, during its existence, necessarily be the same: whatever compositions of substances begin to exist, during the union of those substances, the concrete must be the same: whatsoever mode begins to exist, during its existence it is the same: and so if the composition be of distinct substances and different modes,[62] the same rule holds. Whereby it will appear, that the difficulty or obscurity that has been about this matter rather rises from the names ill-used, than from any obscurity in things themselves. For whatever makes the specific idea to which the name is applied, if that idea be steadily kept to, the distinction of anything into the same and divers will easily be conceived, and there can arise no doubt about it.

For, supposing a rational spirit be the idea of a *man,*[63] it is easy to know what is the same man, viz. the same spirit—whether separate or in a body—will be the *same man.* Supposing a rational spirit vitally united to a body of a certain conformation of parts to make a man;[64] whilst that rational spirit, with that vital conformation of parts, though continued in a fleeting successive body, remains, it will be the *same man.* But if to any one the idea of a man be but the vital union of parts in a certain shape; as long as that vital union and shape remain in a concrete, no otherwise the same but by a continued succession of fleeting particles, it will be the *same man.* For, whatever be the composition whereof the complex idea is made, whenever existence makes it one particular thing under any denomination,[65] *the same existence*

---

[57] The past consciousness having been finally or for ever obliterated. This implies that his own consciousness in memory is the only means by which he could in reason be satisfied that the action was his.

[58] See § 18, in which it is implied that a murderer for example is not accountable for a murder of which his organism was the instrument, if a consciousness of it, as his own past act, *cannot* be awakened in him! It follows (unless conscious experience is ultimately indelible) that any man who has forgotten that he committed a murder, did not *personally* commit it. Who, in that case, was the murderer?

[59] They called forth a host of critics, Sergeant, Stillingfleet, Lee, Clarke in controversy with Collins, Butler, and Reid, with Vincent Perronet and others in defence. The main objection is thus put by Butler:—'One should think it self-evident that consciousness *presupposes,* and cannot *constitute* personal identity.' But Locke, it must be remembered, defines personality from the forensic point of view. He also views its identity as manifested in consciousness, and not in the mystery of its ultimate constitution, the *conscious manifestations* concealing rather than revealing the *substance* on which they depend.

[60] Cf. Bk. IV. ch. ix.—On our certainty of 'our own existence.' We are apt to take for granted that the idea man can form of his own personality, and that of God, is more adequate to the reality than consists with the necessary limitations of our knowledge. That the personality of men *somehow* rests on the personality of God is the language of religion, according to which God is all, and man can do nothing that is *good* without God.

[61] In all this the connection between the soul, or the self-conscious person, and the body is assumed to be accidental or contingent; so that the loss of the body by death or otherwise, is irrelevant to the immortality of the soul, or to that continued *appropriation* by consciousness of past experience on which responsibility or personality depends.

[62] As in man, supposed to comprehend spiritual and also material substance—soul and body.

[63] That is, if we exclude the body, as an accident and not of the essence of man, and mean by 'man' only the soul or 'rational spirit.'

[64] And this is what Locke means by 'a man.'

[65] The nominalism of Locke, who is apt to make questions of this sort questions about the meaning of words only, appears in all this.

continued preserves it the *same* individual under the same denomination.[66]

[66] In the foregoing argument, Locke emphatically distinguishes the person from the man, and from the bodily substance. Should we not rather say that it is in his personality and personal agency that *man* finds what is deepest and truest in himself; and, by analogy, in the constitution of the universe? Locke, working from sensation upward, makes his Book of Ideas culminate in the complex idea of our concrete continuous personality, and in the moral relations to which persons ought to conform,—in this and the following chapter. Transcendental philosophy, from Descartes to Hegel, working from thought downward, ends by making abstract self-consciousness the key to the mysteries of existence.

By implication Locke appears to make the idea of our personal existence a simple idea of reflection, which gives its meaning to the personal pronoun 'I,' in the 'perception' that I am. (Cf. Bk. IV. ch. ix.) The idea of our *continuous* personality, or personal identity, is a complex idea of relation between *myself now* and *myself in the past*, which 'terminates,' and is made concrete in actual consciousnesses, past and present. The identity of myself now with myself in the past; and my separateness from all that is not myself, in a private consciousness in which no other finite person can mingle, afford the unique experience of the spirit as distinguished from the mere animal in man. This experience of identical personal life and moral agency is thus the occasion of the most significant ideas in the human mind.

Risieri Frondizi (1910–1983)
THE NATURE OF THE SELF

Frondizi, a Latin American philosopher, argues that the self's unity is concrete and dynamic, like that of a Gestalt. He supports his argument with appeals to commonsense evidence; then he suggests the kind of scientific research, along the lines of Gestalt psychology, that could bolster his position. A discussion of Frondizi's views can be found in Section E of the introductory essay to Part III.

READING QUESTIONS

In reading the selection, try to answer the following questions and identify the passages that support your answers:

1. How does Frondizi characterize the concept of person?
2. What reasons does he give in support of his characterization?
3. Are they good? Why or why not?
4. What implications does Frondizi's position have for moral and legal responsibility?
5. Should these implications serve as a basis for accepting Frondizi's rather than Locke's characterization of the self? Why or why not?

Reprinted with the permission of Risieri Frondizi's widow, Mrs. Josefina Barbat de Frondizi, from Risieri Frondizi, *The Nature of the Self* (Carbondale, Il.: Southern Illinois University Press, 1971), pp. 163, 173–177, 181–184, 188–193, and 197–200. Copyright © 1953.

3. THE CONCEPT OF GESTALT

What is the self before its unity has been broken down by analysis? In what does its organic or structural unity consist?

Let us first make clear that this unity is not one that transcends the empirical world, the world of experiences. It is a unity derived from the very experiences themselves. There is nothing under or above the totality of experiences. If one overlooks the word "totality" or interprets it in an atomistic sense, this statement would be equivalent of subscribing to Hume's theory. But we should never interpret the totality or structure of experiences as a mere sum or aggregate of the same. The experiential totality has qualities which are not possessed by the members which constitute it. Consequently the characteristics of the total structure of the self cannot be deduced, necessarily, from the characteristics of each of the experiences taken separately. . . .

So far we have stated only that the self is a structure. We need now to examine the concept of Gestalt in order to show how it may be applied to the self.

What is it that characterizes a Gestalt? Like any other fundamental concept, that of Gestalt presents a degree of complexity which does not allow one to enunciate in a few words all the richness of its content.[1] Nevertheless, there are certain characteristics which seem to be fundamental. First, there is the one that has already been emphasized: a structural whole—a Gestalt—has qualities not possessed by any of the elements which form it. In this sense, a Gestalt or structure is set in contrast with a mere sum of elements. The physical and chemical qualities of a cubic yard of water are the same as those of each gallon that makes it up. The whole, in this case, is no more than the mere sum of its parts. In the case of a structure, on the other hand, this is not so, as . . . in . . . the character of a melody; it possesses qualities which cannot be found in any of the notes, for it can be transposed without being changed into another melody.

The above-mentioned characteristic does not mean, of course, that a Gestalt is completely independent of the members which constitute it. In the first place, there can be no structure without members. But the dependence of structure upon members does not stop here—the removal, addition, or fundamental alteration of a member modifies the whole structure, as can be seen in the case of an organism.[2] Any important alteration or suppression of a member alters the totality of an organism and may

even cause its disappearance. This does not happen in the case of a sum. We can remove one, two, thirty, or forty gallons of water without causing the rest to undergo any important change in quality.

But not only does the structural whole suffer alteration when one of its members is taken away, the member that is taken away is also basically altered. A hand separated from the body is unable to feel or to seize an object—it ceases to be a hand—whereas the gallon of water separated from the rest retains practically all of its properties. This characteristic, taken along with the foregoing one, will suffice for the definition of a member of a structure. A member of a structure is that which cannot be removed without affecting the whole structure and losing its own nature when separated from the "whole." Conversely, we can characterize the "mere sum" as something made up of "parts" or "elements" that undergo no change when joined to other "parts" and which can be removed without producing any change either in itself or in what remains. The relationship between the parts is that of mere juxtaposition.

The difference between structure and mere sum does not stem solely from the fact that the parts of the latter are independent of the whole and that the members of the former are conditioned by the structure. There is also the fact that the parts may be homogeneous, whereas the members must offer diversity and even opposition of characteristics. One gallon of water is just as much water as any other gallon or measure. The same is true of one brick in a pile of bricks or of each grain of sand in the desert. On the contrary, in an organism each member has its own specific nature—the heart is the heart and cannot perform the functions of the liver or kidneys. There is not only diversity among the members but also opposition; and this opposition is subsumed into the unity which organizes them. The unification and organization of the members which make up a structure do not come about at the expense of the peculiar and distinctive qualities of each member. Organization is not the equivalent of homogenization, and unity does not contradict the multiplicity and diversity of the elements. This multiplicity and diversity must always be maintained as absolutely essential. Thus we find structure to be the result of a dialectic play of opposites, of a struggle between the members; it seems to hang by the thread which establishes a dynamic balance. But this unity is not of an abstract sort. A concept which organizes different members into a unity by grouping them in agree-

---

[1] It is a notable fact that in all the extensive bibliography on the Gestalttheorie there are few worth-while studies of the Gestalt concept itself. Perhaps this is due to the fact that the theory arose as the result of concrete psychological investigations and that those who advocated it did not want to appear to be "metaphysicians." Cf. Koffka, *Principles of Gestalt Psychology*, p. 683.

The briefest and best work that I know of on the concept of Gestalt is Wertheimer's article, "Gestalt Theory," *Social Research*, 11, No. 1 (Feb. 1944), which is a version of a lecture given in Berlin in 1924. Of the three original proponents of the movement, Wertheimer seems to be the one who has the greatest interest and ability with regard to philosophy. Koffka devotes less than one page (pp. 682–3) to an examination of the concept of Gestalt in his *Principles of Gestalt Psychology*. Chap. vi of Köhler's *Gestalt Psychology*, which promises to expound the theory of the concept, actually restricts itself to the examination of concrete problems of the psychology of perception.

[2] Lewin defines a Gestalt in his *Principles of Topological Psychology* (p. 208) as a "system whose parts are dynamically connected in such a way that a change of one part results in a change of all the other parts."

ment with a common note does not constitute a structure. One essential aspect of the structure is lacking: its unity must be concrete. For that reason I use the term "structure" rather than "form" or "configuration" to translate the German word Gestalt, which, besides carrying the connotation of these two latter concepts, designates a unity that is *concrete*.[3]

THE STRUCTURAL UNITY OF THE SELF

When we consider the applicability of the category of substance to the self, we notice that none of the three classic characteristics of this concept—immutability, simplicity, and independence—belong to the self. We obtain a similarly negative result from the consideration of the atomistic conception. In the first place, the supposed psychic atom is a poorly defined unit which, when one attempts to fix it with any precision, vanishes into thin air, becoming a mere arbitrary instant in an uninterrupted process. In the second place, the aggregation of atoms, which can have only a relationship of juxtaposition one to another, looks like a grotesque caricature of the real organic unity of the self. Let us now see if the category which we have called Gestalt or structure is any more successful.[4]

It seems unquestionable that the psychic life is not chaotic, that each state or experience is connected to all the rest. This connection, however, is not of experience to experience, like the links of a chain, for if this were so there would be a fixed order of connections and in order to get to one link we should necessarily have to go by way of the preceding ones. But in the same way that Köhler showed that there is no constant relation between stimulus and response, it would be easy to show that in like manner there is no constant relation between one experience and another. No laboratory experiment is needed to prove this, for our daily experiences supply all the material we require—the sound and sight of the sea is exhilarating one day and depressing the next; the same piece of music arouses in us different reactions according to the situation in which we hear it; our arrival at the same port and in the same ship can start altogether different trains of reflection in us, depending on whether we have arrived to stay for the rest of our life or only for a short vacation; the memory of a disagreement with a friend, which irritated us so much when it happened, may now provoke only an indifferent smile. The relations of experiences to each other resemble the relations between stimuli and responses in the fact that they arise within a given context.

These undeniable data of the psychic life are founded on the fact that the self is not a sum of experiences or an aggregate of parts in juxtaposition but a structure—in the sense defined above; whatever happens to one of its elements affects the whole, and the whole in turn exerts an influence upon each element. It is because the whole reacts as a structural unity and not as a mechanism that a stimulus can provoke consequences in an altogether different field from the one in which it has arisen. Thus, a strictly intellectual problem can give rise to emotional torment, and a fact of an emotional sort can have far-reaching volitional consequences. The self is not departmentalized—like modern bureaucracy—but constitutes an organic unity with intimate, complex, and varied interrelations.

The self presents itself, then, as an organized whole, an integrated structure, and experiences are related to one another not through but within the whole. For that reason, when the structure is modified the nature of the experiences and of the relationships between them are also modified. The interdependence of the different experiential groups shows that the self is a structure which is organized and "makes sense" and that each member occupies its proper place within the structure.

This does not mean, of course, that the structure which constitutes the self cannot be analyzed and broken down, theoretically, into less complex structures. It does mean, however, that we are in fact dealing with a unity that is formed upon substructures and the intimate and complex interrelation of these substructures.[5]

---

[3] Cf. Köhler, *Gestalt Psychology*, p. 192.

[4] [Editor's Note: Some changes of tense have been made in this paragraph.] An exposition of the Gestalt theory of the Ego may be found in Koffka's work, *Principles of Gestalt Psychology*, especially pp. 319–42. If one compares Koffka's theory with the one which I am here proposing, he will see that although I have taken the concept of structure from the Gestalttheorie I am not subscribing to the theory of the German psychologist. In the first place, Koffka defines psychology as the science of behavior (*ibid.*, p. 25)—though not in Watson's sense of the word—and faces the problem of the self or Ego as a problem of *segregation* from its field (pp. 319–33). The procedure that I am following is just the reverse: my problem is that of the *integration*. This fundamental difference in our points of departure and the philosophical attitude which I have adopted (which obliges me to transcend the limits of experimental psychology, a thing which Koffka never does since he has adopted a strictly scientific attitude) allow me more freedom in my thesis. What is more, in my opinion the categories of function, process, and intentionality are just as important as that of structure in the interpretation of the self.

[5] By substructure I mean any of the structural parts that constitute the total Gestalt that makes up the self.

And here we notice another characteristic of the concept of structure which is directly applicable to the self: the members of a structure are heterogeneous in contrast with the homogeneity of the parts of a nonstructural unity. Let us state, first of all, that the structure which constitutes the self, being a very complex structure, is made up not of "simple members" but of substructures; it is consequently to the heterogeneity of these substructures that we are referring. It must also be kept in mind that the substructures are not of an abstract nature, like concepts, and that we are not trying to reconstruct a reality by juxtaposing abstractions such as the so-called "faculties of the soul."

The complexity and heterogeneity of the structure are twofold: on the one hand there is the complexity which we may call transversal; on the other there is the horizontal or, better, the temporal complexity. In actuality the self embraces the combination of both complexes, which do not and cannot exist in separation. . . .

This diversity and opposition among the elements which constitute the self should not lead us to forget the unity which characterizes every structure. The self is no exception. Its multiplicity does not exclude its unity or vice versa. And this is not the abstract unity of a concept which points to what is common; it is a concrete unity, of "flesh and blood" as Unamuno would say, for there is nothing more real and concrete than our self. Diversity underlies the structure but is in turn lost within it, for the elements uphold each other mutually in an intimate sort of interweaving in which it is impossible to distinguish warp from woof. This is not because the three types of substructure have equivalent strength and no one of them dominates the other two—as in the theory of the so-called balance of power—but because they vary constantly. At a given moment one element stands forth as the figure and the others form the ground; after a while there is a change of roles. These changes are explained by the fact that the self is a dynamic structure and thus resembles a symphony rather than a painting.

We should perhaps stress the point that the changes undergone by the self are not due exclusively to a different distribution of the members, for the members themselves are of a dynamic nature. Moreover, the self is constituted not only of members but also of the *tensions* produced by the reciprocal play of influences. The breakdown of the equilibrium of tensions is what generally produces the most important changes.

It now appears obvious that the relations between the experiences are not fixed, for each experience as it is incorporated into the structure modifies its former state. This member in turn undergoes the influence of the whole, which is another characteristic of a Gestalt easy to find in the self. Thus, the perceptions which we have at this moment depend upon our former state. The new experience immediately acquires the coloration given it both by the basic structure of the self and by the particular situation in which it finds itself at that moment. If we are happy and in pleasant company, for example, the color of the spectacles we happen to be wearing has very little effect upon the emotive state of our spirit. This is not because visual perception ceases to have emotional tonality but because a greater affective tone—the happiness which results from a different cause—completely overshadows it. What is more, the stable nature of the self colors the transitory state. There are people who give the impression of seeing the world in the rosiest colors, whatever the tint of the spectacles they wear, and there are others who see clouds in the clearest sky.

This is the influence of the whole upon the member which is incorporated, but there is also an influence of the member upon the whole. We must not forget that a structure is not suspended in thin air but rests solely upon the members which constitute it. A symphonic orchestra is something more than the sum of the musicians that go to form it, but it cannot exist without the musicians. A self without the experiential structures that go to make it up would be the same as an orchestra without musicians, that is, a pure fantasy, the fantasy of a spiritual entity that would be unable to love, hate, decide, want, perceive, etc., and would pretend to be immutable substance. Such a concept would be immutable without doubt, but it would have the immutability of nothingness.

In the same way that the total suppression of the experiential structures would mean the suppression of the self, any change or alteration of a member has repercussions on the whole structure. By this I do not mean a man lacking in emotional life, for example, for it is obvious that he would not be a man but a mere caricature, or projection on a plane of two dimensions, of a three-dimensional reality. I am referring to the alteration of a structural subcomplex. Abulia, for example, is a disease of the will, but the changes which it provokes are not limited to the volitional—it has immediate repercussions in the emotive and intellectual spheres and consequently in the total structure. Its intellectual repercussions are easily seen, for the person suffering from abulia is unable to concentrate his attention, and thus his intellectual processes break down completely. And the emotional sphere is impaired too, for the sufferer is unable, by an act of the will, to get rid of the emotion which has taken control of him, so he lets himself be so possessed by this emotion that it changes his whole personality.

Of the characteristics of the structure that are applicable to the self we have only to consider now the first and most important, that is, the fact that the structure possesses qualities not possessed by the members that make it up. At this stage in our inquiry it seems a waste of time to insist that this is one of the characteristics of the self. Let us consider only the most obvious reasons. The self has a permanence—in the sense of constant presence—and a stability that the experiences and experiential groups do not have. Experiences are totally unstable; transiency is their characteristic. The self, on the other hand, remains stable in the face of the coming and going of experiences. If experiences do not have stability, even less can they have permanence, which is the fundamental characteristic of the self. And this is not all. The structure of the self is such that the members that make it up cannot exist in separation from it. There is no experience that does not belong to a particular self. The self depends, then, upon the experiences, but it is not equivalent to their sum. It is a structural quality. . . .

PROBLEMS SOLVED BY THE STRUCTURAL CONCEPTION[6]

A. Permanence and Mutability of the Self

. . . Both substantialism and atomism were unable to give an adequate picture of the self because they could not comprehend how its permanence and continuity could be compatible with the changes that it undergoes. Substantialism emphasized the permanence and atomism the mutability.

The structural conception that we are here proposing allows us to see that the two characteristics are not only compatible but also complementary. . . . Substantialism could not understand the changing nature of the self because it held fast to an irreducible and immutable nucleus and that Hume's atomism, in its effort to destroy the doctrine of a sub-

stantial nucleus, confused it with the very real permanence and continuity of the self.

If we free ourselves of the limitations of both historical positions and observe reality just as it presents itself, we shall see that the permanence and continuity of the self are based upon its structural character, for it is a dynamic structure made up not only of the elements which we can isolate in a cross section of our life but also of the substructures that form the complex longitudinal bundles that constitute the self. And change occurs each time a new element is taken in, which alters but does not destroy the structure.

In this way the constant alteration of the self insures its stability. It is undeniable that a new experience modifies, or can modify, the structure of the self. The loss of a child or a friend, a war, a religious experience, etc. can produce such an inner commotion that they may alter the total structure. From that time on we are not the same person as before. We act in a different way, we see life in a different perspective, and it may be that not only the future but also the past is colored by the new attitude. But it is just this experience causing us to change which gives endurance to the self. From now on we shall be the man who has lost his son or his friend or who had this or that religious experience. Other children that we may have or the new friends which we may take into our hearts may cover up but can never completely obliterate the existence of an experience that at one time shook us deeply and persists in the structure of our spirit despite all that may happen to us in the future.

What happens on a large scale in the case of experiences that are profoundly moving happens on a smaller scale in all the other experiences of our life. Each new experience alters the structure or substructure to which it is connected, and thus it is incorporated "definitively," so to speak. Whatever happens afterward may alter the meaning of the experience within the whole—increasing it or diminishing it—but it can never erase the experience completely.

An analogy of a physical sort, even though inadequate to characterize our psychic life, may perhaps make clear the meaning of what I am trying to put across. The self resembles, in this respect, a mixture of colors. If we add to the mixture a new color—for example, blue—the mixture will be altered to a degree that will depend upon the quantity and shade of blue added and upon the combination of colors that were there before. This quantity of blue which

---

[6] What follows should be regarded as an illustration of the doctrine of the self as a functional Gestalt.

produces a change in the former mixture is incorporated definitively into the whole, and however many more colors we add we shall never be able completely to counteract its presence.

The nature of the whole and the influence of the element incorporated into it are controlled, in the case of the analogy, by certain stable physical laws in which quantity plays an important role. This is not the case with psychic structures, in which quantity gives way to equality. Psychic structures obey certain principles, carefully studied by the Gestalt psychologists in the case of visual perception, which also exist in all the other orders of life and in the constitution of the total structure of the self. These general principles governing the organization of our total personality are what the most psychologically acute educators use as the basis for their choice of one type of experience rather than another in their endeavor to devise a system of corrective education for an aberrant personality.

Every self has a center or axis around which its structure is organized. When the personality has already developed, this axis is what gives direction and organization to our life, not only in that new experiences do not succeed in dislodging it from its route but also in that it chooses the type of experience that it finds to be in tune with it. But it is not a nucleus immutable in itself or fixed in relation to the rest of the structure. In the first place it undergoes an evolution which we can consider normal. The axis that predominates changes at the different stages of our life. In our earliest childhood the predominant experiential substructure is that related to alimentation, later it is play, and so on through life.

What is more, the center undergoes sudden displacements caused by new experiences that shake and modify the total structure. This is the case with the soldier who, according to war records, after devoting his life to the acquisition or intensification of his capacity for destruction and after exercising this capacity for years at the cost of many lives, suddenly discovers "the truth," "finds himself," decides that "we are all brothers." The center of his personality is completely displaced. His technical capacity as a killer, in which he formerly took pride—and centered his whole personality—is now a source of humiliation and shame. His personality must retrace its steps and choose another route.

These changes are due to many varied and complex reasons. Usually they have a long period of germination, as it were, in the world of the subconscious and burst forth full blown at a propitious moment. I recall the case of an American pilot who fought for several years in the Pacific; all of a sudden "the truth was revealed to him" while he was reading, more or less by chance, certain passages in the Bible. At other times the change comes about because of the intensification of the means of destruction; the explosion of the atomic bomb produced a psychological shock in many of those who had launched 200-pound bombs under the same flag. Most commonly it comes about because of the shock of contrast; the soldier, in the midst of hatred, destruction, and death, comes across people who are devoting their lives to healing, in a spirit of disinterested love, the physical and moral wounds that other men cause. These external situations usually act as the immediate cause for the eruption of subterranean currents; at other times they stir up for the first time currents that burst forth later on, if a propitious situation presents itself.

We should not be surprised that an apparently insignificant fact may be able to change the total structure of our personality after it has been stable for many years; in the psychological realm quantities are of no great importance. The principle, *causa aequat effectum,* is not valid in the interrelations of the different elements. Gestalt psychology has shown us how the constitution of the structure and its alteration are governed by principles that have nothing to do with the principle of causality in its simplistic interpretation as the equal of cause and effect. . . .

B. Immanence and Transcendence of the Self

Another apparent paradox—similar to that of permanence and mutability—which is resolved by the structural conception is that of the immanence and transcendence of the self. For both atomism and substantialism, immanence and transcendence are incompatible. Either the self is equivalent to the totality of experiences—and in this sense is immanent to them—or it is something that transcends the experiences. Atomism holds the first position and substantialism the second.

According to the theory that I am proposing, the self is immanent and transcends experiences at the same time, though admittedly the terms have different meanings from those attributed to them both by atomism and by substantialism. The self is immanent because it is, indeed, equivalent to the totality of experiences; but this totality, in turn, should be interpreted not as the sum or aggregate of the experiences but as a structure that has properties that cannot be found in its parts. According to this interpretation of the concept of totality, the self transcends the experiences and becomes a structural quality, in the sense in which Ehrenfels used this expression. Nevertheless, this is not the transcendence defended by the substantialists when they affirm the existence of a being that supports states or experiences. Mine is a transcendence that not only does not exclude immanence but actually takes it for granted.

Let us look at the problem from another point of view. The relation between the self and its experiences is so intimate that every experience reveals some aspect of the self; what is more, every experience forms part of the self. In this sense, the self seems to be represented in each one of the experiences, to be nothing but them. No experience, however, is able to reveal to us the self in its entirety. Not even the sum of all the experiences can do that. The self is able to transcend its autobiography; hence the possibility of a true repentance, a conversion, a new life. In the first instance the self seems to be immanent; in the second it is seen to be something that transcends its experiences.

The problem is clarified considerably if one turns his attention to those two propositions which Hume, and many others after him, considered to be incompatible: *a*) that the self is nothing apart from its experiences; *b*) that the self cannot be reduced to its experiences. I, of course, affirm that both propositions are true. When Hume maintained that the self should be reduced to a bundle of perceptions because it could not exist without them, he let himself be misled by the substantialist prejudice in favor of the so-called independence of the self. But the self, though not independent of the perceptions, is not reducible to the mere sum of them.

The paradox of the immanence and transcendence of the self, just like the paradox which we examined before, has arisen as a consequence of the way in which substantialists stated the problem of the self, a statement that the atomists accepted without realizing its consequences. The problem, as stated, presupposes a metaphysics and a logic which our conception rejects. First, it conceives of real existence as substance, independent and immutable; and second, it interprets the principles of identity and of noncontradiction in a very rigid way. My concept, on the other hand, gives a very dynamic interpretation to both principles, to the point of seeing in contradiction much of the essence of the real. What is more, I believe that there is nothing independent and immutable. I can hardly believe, therefore, in the independence and immutability of the self, the stuff of which is relationship and the essence of which is creative process.

C. Unity and Multiplicity

A variant of the preceding paradoxes is that of unity and multiplicity. When atomism took over the analysis of the self, its unity was destroyed forever and the self was turned into a great mosaic of loose pieces. Each perception became a reality in itself, independent, separable, sharply delimited. With this conception of the elements it proved impossible to rewin the lost unity. Atomists maintained, therefore, the plurality of the self, even though they sighed from time to time for the unity that they themselves had destroyed. When atomists—and men like William James who criticized atomism without being able to free themselves from the source of its confusion— ask what unites the different parts constituting the self, one must simply answer that the self never ceased to constitute a unity. Atomism's difficulties in reaching the unity of the self are merely a consequence of the arbitrary way in which it was dismembered. First they build a wall; then they complain they cannot see beyond the wall.

Substantialism, on the other hand, takes as its point of departure the postulate of unity and relegates multiplicity to accidents. The self is only one, although many different things happen to it.

With the importance that these "happenings" have for us—the self is made up of what it does—the whole statement of the problem collapses; the self is one or multiple according to how one looks at it. It is one if one focuses on the whole; it is multiple if one focuses on the members that constitute it. The self is the unity of the multiplicity of its experiences. . . .

QUESTIONS FOR REVIEW AND FURTHER THOUGHT

1. What are Anselm's arguments in the *Proslogium?* Are they sound? If you think they are, what reasons might there be for thinking otherwise and why would these reasons be inadequate? If, on the other hand, you think Anselm's arguments are unsound, say why and defend your position against any plausible objections you can imagine.

2. What are Aquinas's arguments concerning God's existence? Are they sound? If you think they are, why might someone else think they are not and why would these reasons be inadequate? If, on the other hand, you think Aquinas's arguments are unsound, say why and defend your position against those objections you find plausible.

3. What are Hume's arguments concerning God's existence? Are they sound? If you think they are, what reasons might there be for thinking they are not and why would these reasons be inadequate? If, on the other hand, you think Hume's arguments are unsound, say why and defend your position against any objections you think plausible.

4. How does Nagel characterize atheism? What arguments for God's existence does he consider? Does he think the argument from evil is sound? Critically compare and contrast Nagel's position on the argument from evil with that of Hume.

5. Characterize Rhazes's conception of character and the role that he attributes to reason in character development. Is his position sound? If you think it is, what reasons might someone else advance against it and why would these reasons be inadequate? If, on the other hand, you think Rhazes's position is unsound, say why and defend your position against those objections you consider plausible.

6. What does Ryle mean by "the ghost in the machine"? What are his views about it and why? Is his position sound? Why or why not? Defend your position against any objections you think plausible.

7. Compare and contrast Hume's views on causality with those of Ghazali as formulated in Averroes's "From *The Incoherence of the Incoherence.*" Are Averroes's criticisms of Ghazali's position sound? Why or why not? To what extent, if any, do his criticisms also apply to Hume's position? Explain your answer and defend it against any plausible objections you can imagine.

8. What is Bunge's position concerning the use of induction in science? What, if any, implications does it have for Hume's position on causality? Explain your answer and defend it against plausible objections.

9. What is Lorenzo Valla's position on free will? Is it sound? In assessing it, compare and contrast it with Chisholm's position on free will.

10. What is Locke's position on personal identity? Is it sound? If you think it is, what reasons might there be for thinking it unsound and why would these reasons fail to establish that it is? On the other hand, if you think Locke's position is unsound, say why and defend your position against plausible objections.

11. What is Frondizi's view of the self? What reasons does he give to support this view? Is his view adequate and are his reasons good? Why or why not? Defend your position against plausible objections.

12. Do any authors in Part III engage in cross-cultural reflection and dialogue to any extent? Do they, for example, try to adapt categories used in other cultures to their own cultural context? Who, how, and how fruitfully?

13. Consider those authors in Part III who do not engage in cross-cultural reflection. How could they have done so while remaining faithful to the views they espouse?

14. Which of the selections in Part III include discussions that overlap with matters discussed in Part II?

IV

What Is Morally Justified?

A. WHAT IS THE MORAL SIGNIFICANCE OF LIVING IN A COMMUNITY?

A twenty-nine-year-old unmarried professional woman finds herself pregnant again four months after giving birth to her third child. She asks her physician whether there are any health reasons why it is not advisable for her to have this child, and the physician tells her there are none. She discusses her pregnancy with some close friends and relatives, all of whom tell her that they love her and will support her whether she decides to have an abortion or not. She believes that abortion is the taking of a potential human life and that, except when there are overriding moral reasons, it is wrong. Yet the recent birth of her third child has created some financial strains in her family. She must work full days to make ends meet, and after putting in an eight-hour day, she hardly has the time and energy to take care of the newborn, plus the two older children. In addition, she does not at all feel ready to have still another baby. She thinks: "An abortion is taking a life; but I also ought to think of the lives of my three-month-old, and my older children, and of my own life. And these would be shortchanged, if not harmed, were I to have another child now." Would she be justified in having an abortion?

Some people say that abortion is killing an innocent human being, and therefore always wrong. Others hold that although it is killing an innocent human being, it is sometimes permissible; but they differ on the conditions under which it is permissible. Still others deny that abortion is the taking of a human life at all, and hold that it is always morally permissible. Conflicting positions on moral questions are not unusual. One individual often holds beliefs about right and wrong, good and bad, justified and unjustified, that conflict with those of other individuals. That is, personal ethics—morals—vary. This does not settle the question of what action is right, but it does provide an example of one of the ways in which the term "ethics" is used: the *personal* sense, in which ethics is a particular person's beliefs and presuppositions about right and wrong, good and bad, justified and unjustified. This—a person's *morals*—is something a particular person *has*.

In our abortion example, one individual's personal ethics may include the belief that under the conditions described, it would be morally permissible for the woman to have an abortion. This individual's personal ethics may also include the presupposition that some considerations are so personal and private that they are best judged by those directly involved—in this instance, the pregnant woman. The belief here is that the woman herself is the best judge of whether, in the circumstances, the well-being of her children, as well as her own, should take precedence over the life of the fetus. This is not an unusual view and it, or something very much like it, is reflected in *Roe v. Wade* and related abortion decisions by the United States Supreme Court.[1]

Of course, the fact that an opinion is reflected in the law does not make it right. What the law says in no way settles the question of what it *ought* to say. Yet what the law says is not irrelevant to the moral description of both a problem and conduct in addressing that problem. Nor is it irrelevant for evaluating conduct. For what the law says—what it permits and forbids—may both contribute to creating a problem and form part of the circumstances in which the problem must be addressed. With this in mind, let us return to our case.

> Aware of the conflicting opinions different people hold about abortion and, partly for this reason, feeling uneasy about it, the woman proceeds to take a look at the codes of conduct of various religious and professional groups involved in abortion discussions. Some religious codes strictly prohibit all, or nearly all, abortions. Others are somewhat permissive. The professional codes she finds tend to be somewhat noncommittal.

The woman soon realizes that whatever guidance a certain group's code of conduct may provide, it is, like the law's guidance, criticized by disagreeing members of the group or some of the public. A group's code of conduct—its *mores*—cannot by itself settle the question of what actions are right. However, such a code does constitute an example of ethics in the *social* or *group* sense of the term. In this sense, ethics is a particular group's predominant beliefs and presuppositions about right and wrong, good and bad, justified and unjustified. Accordingly, ethics in the social sense is something a group—rather than a particular individual—*has,* in that the group has explicitly, though perhaps only partially, formulated these beliefs or predominantly holds them.

When the beliefs and presuppositions constituting one person's or group's ethics conflict with those of others, giving rise to disagreements between individuals, between groups, or between groups and some of their members, the question of who is right can become a heated one. Indeed, when, as in our example, the issue concerns abortion, disagreements are often sharp, resulting in controversies and even confrontations, which creates an urgency to resolve the disagreement by establishing who is right. When people engage in critical inquiry such matters of disagreement, they *do* ethics, rather than simply *have* ethics, as in the personal and social senses of the terms. In the sense in which people do ethics, ethics is an activity rather than simply a set of beliefs and presuppositions. The activity is not identical with, but is *about,* beliefs and presuppositions, and is often prompted by conflicts among them. Thus, ethics in this sense is a branch of inquiry variously called *moral philosophy, ethical theory, moral theory,* or *reflection on morality.* It is a critical study with the goal of soundly dealing with problems of right and wrong, good and bad, and justified and unjustified that arise in people's lives.[2]

The abortion case we have presented raises the question of whether it would be right for the woman described to have an abortion. This is a question about the rightness or wrongness of a particular individual's action under specified circumstances. It poses an ethical problem—a moral problem—that is behavioral in that it is about an action or piece of conduct. *Behavioral* ethical problems—ethical problems of conduct—deal with the rightness or wrongness of actions. They occur quite frequently in life.

In discussing the rightness or wrongness of this woman's having an abortion, the question may arise whether actions of this type should be permitted by law. The focus of this question is not an action, but a social policy. The problem it poses is not one of behavioral, but of *institutional,* ethics. This brings up questions of justifiability concerning policies, practices, and institutions.[3] *Socio-political philosophy* significantly, if not entirely, overlaps with institutional ethics, for it deals with problems that concern institutions: authority, obedience to the law and to rulers, the rights of groups to act in self-defense against members or outsiders, how the interests of a group relate to those of their members and outsiders, and how social decisions should be made and policy making carried out. In fact, both ethics and socio-political philosophy are often considered branches of moral philosophy, and they will be so considered in what follows.

There is yet a third kind of ethical problem that can be raised in discussing the abortion case. The woman who is considering the option of abortion may ask herself: What is having an abortion going to do to me? What kind of character traits would such an action tend to instill in me? Are they good traits? The focus of these questions is not a policy, a practice, or an institution. Neither is it primarily action. Rather, these questions center on character traits specific to a person, such as courage and kindness (creditable traits) and cowardice and callousness (discreditable traits). A person's character is made up of various character traits. Questions about character traits such as those we just formulated raise *ethical problems of character:* problems about the goodness or badness of a person's traits, motives, and attitudes.

To say that we can distinguish three kinds of ethical problems does not mean that the three are not interconnected. They are, and various selections and discussions in Part IV illustrate how various kinds of ethical problems are often raised in an interrelated manner. Yet the kinds *are* different, and one task of moral philosophy is to investigate what makes them different. Another is to examine whether the kinds of considerations relevant for dealing with moral problems of one kind—say, institutional—are the same as those relevant for dealing with moral problems of another kind—say, behavioral.

These two examples of tasks pursued in doing moral philosophy as a branch of inquiry illustrate how this branch of philosophy, though concerned with particular, concrete moral problems, is also concerned with *kinds* of moral problems that are relatively general in nature. Moral philosophy at this level is associated with the development of moral theories, a task that individuals, busy pursuing the pressing concerns of their everyday lives, must often put aside. Yet a sound moral theory is often immensely helpful in dealing with the ethical problems encountered in daily living, some of which turn out to be complex, difficult, and urgent.

As the selections in Part IV make plain, there is more than one moral theory, and sometimes one moral theory enjoins what another moral theory proscribes. This raises the question: Which theory is better and why? Our discussion here is meant to encourage and guide you to decide this question by addressing the following, more specific one: What relative weights do the various considerations at the core of the theories contrasted have for a specific moral problem?

Though advocacy is not part of our discussion, we make no pretense to moral neutrality. Our discussion is guided by a theory that combines considerations of consequences, rights, and the pragmatic, rather than by a unilateral approach that relies solely on one of these in dealing with moral problems. Thus, our survey of the selections in Part IV is informed by what can be called the *range hypothesis,* according to which ethical problems constitute a range of problems with the following characteristics. At one extreme are problems for which individual rights carry much more weight than any other considerations because (for example) natural rights are unequivocally at stake. At the other extreme are problems for which consequences carry the most weight because (for example) the very existence and well-being of reasonably good societies is at stake. In between are problems for which rights and consequences have less decisive weight. In many of these cases, fortunately, considerations of rights and consequences reinforce each other. Sometimes, however, they conflict, making the cases hard to deal with. All along the range of problems, pragmatic considerations put limits on alternatives.[4] Let us now examine the selections in this part in the light of this hypothesis.

As we noted in the General Introduction, ethical reflection did not appear abruptly with advanced civilization. Such reflection is evident in preliterate societies in both storytelling and tribal customs. Among the earliest written codes of conduct are the *Laws of Manu* which, according to some scholars, appeared in India between the eighth and the fifth centuries B.C., and the *Dharma Sutras,* written between the sixth and third centuries B.C.[5] In China, a significantly developed ethical theory was formulated during the fifth century B.C. It can be found in the first selection in this part, "Universal Love." Its author, Mo Tzu (479–438 B.C.), writes:

> It is the business of the benevolent man to try to promote what is beneficial to the world and to eliminate what is harmful.

Mo Tzu argues that the greatest harms come from partiality; hence, "Partiality should be replaced by universality." What does Mo Tzu mean by "universality"? From his discussion of what things would be like if universality replaced partiality, one gathers that universality is treating the states, cities, and families of others as one would treat one's own.

We might be tempted to interpret Mo Tzu's conception of universality as a version of the Golden Rule of the Judeo-Christian tradition, usually phrased as: "Do unto others as you would have them do unto you." Yet the touchstone of the Golden Rule is what the *individual* would have others do *to himself or herself.* This is not so in Mo Tzu's universality. Here the touchstone is what the *individual* would have others do *to the state, city, and family to which the individual belongs.* In others words, Mo Tzu's concept of morality is community-oriented rather than individualistic.

This conception of moral behavior, universal beneficence, raises certain questions: Is universality thus understood a source of good? And who should be the judge of universal beneficence—someone attached to his own state, city, or family, or just anyone? Given Mo Tzu's discussion, we may presume that people with such attachments are supposed to be the judges. Yet this raises the questions: Do such people exist? Can universal beneficence ever be actualized? Or is universal beneficence so difficult as to be unattainable? Mo Tzu argues that this ideal "can be put to use"— that is, it is attainable—by pointing to cases in which, according to historical accounts, much more difficult things were achieved by entire societies. One example he mentions is that when King Ling of the state of Ching expressed a preference for slender people, the people of Ching went on a diet and lost weight. His conclusion is that "within the space of a single generation the ways of the people can be changed, for they will strive to ingratiate themselves with their superiors."

It could be objected that while the motivation to ingratiate oneself with one's superiors might work in some societies, it would not work in many others. In response to this objection, it could be pointed out that, though motivations may vary with time, culture, and circumstance, wide attitudinal changes are possible. In the late twentieth century, for example, there was a wide attitudinal change concerning the environment, and this is reflected in public policy changes that took place between the early 1960s and the early 1990s.

Of course, the objector might respond that these changes have been insufficient and that environmental problems persist. But all this objection proves is that Mo Tzu's doctrine of universal love may be too simplistic for certain social ills. Indeed, it may need to be supplemented with other motivations, especially in situations where time is of the essence. That is to say, society cannot always wait until new attitudes emerge to address urgent problems (e.g., the depletion of the ozone layer).

This brings us to an important question: How can a society be organized so that social problems are soundly addressed when not all, or even most, members of that society care about finding viable solutions to them? Our next selection, "From *The Republic*" by Plato (428–348 B.C.), partly addresses this question. *The Republic* is a developed example of Western moral philosophy. Moral reflection was already evident in Greek poetry of the seventh and sixth centuries B.C., but it was through the teachings of Socrates (470–399 B.C.) that it acquired a central position in Western thought, which it has never since lost.

As we noted in Part I, Socrates wrote nothing, but his student, Plato, and Plato's student, Aristotle, characterized many of the traditional concepts and problems in philosophy in general and in moral philosophy in particular. Our knowledge of Socrates himself and his teachings is based on the testimony of others. This is abundant, but, unfortunately, inconsistent. Our two main authorities, Xenophon and Plato, do not agree on who the man was or what he taught. Xenophon was an avowed apologist for Socrates, while Plato purported to convey Socrates' teachings through artistic constructions called *dialogues*, which, whatever their reliability in reproducing Socrates' thinking, can hardly be literal reports. Thus, our interpretation here is of what the character Socrates in Plato's dialogue held, not of what the actual Socrates may have held.[6]

The dialogue addresses the question: Is it, without exception, better to be just than unjust? Socrates holds that justice is better than injustice, not simply because of its beneficial effects, but also for its own sake.

In opposition, Glaucon formulates Thrasymachus' arguments. The first one concerns the nature and origin of justice. The argument goes roughly like this: Justice is not better than injustice for its own sake, but only for its effects. For anyone with the power to do injustice will go ahead and do it. Most people, however, have a "lack of vigor to do injustice" and also lack the power to avoid being victimized by injustice. Since in a society, "the excess of evil in being wronged is greater than the excess of good in doing wrong," people approve of justice. They enter into covenants and abide by legislation intended to uphold it only because of its effects: it would help them attain a favorable balance of good over evil.

One might object to the argument's assumption that anyone with the power to do injustice will go ahead and do it because this amounts to saying that all who practice justice "do so reluctantly." But do they? In response to this objection, one might formulate, as Glaucon does, Thrasymachus' second argument. It assumes that one has the power to do as one pleases. This assumption is dramatized by supposing that both a just and an unjust person have a mythical ring that allows them to become invisible at will, and thus never get caught at any wrongdoing. In such a situation, Glaucon adds:

> No one could be found, it would seem, of such adamantine temper as to persevere in justice and endure to refrain his hands from the possessions of others and not touch them, though he might with impunity take what he wished even from the market place, and enter into houses and lie with whom he pleased, and slay and loose from bonds whomsoever he would, and in all other things conduct himself among mankind as the equal of a god.

An objector might say that this argument begs the question. First, it is an empirical matter to be determined by psychological studies whether the ordinary person would commit such unjust actions if he or she knew that detection were impossible. Second, even if the ordinary person would opt for injustice, this does not establish that there is good reason for so opting.

In response, Glaucon could formulate, as he does, Thrasymachus' third argument. It concludes that there are plausible reasons for acting unjustly if one can get away with it. A perfectly clever unjust man would never get caught—indeed, would be esteemed as just—while a perfectly just man would stick to justice even if berated as unjust and made to suffer horribly for it. But the perfectly unjust man would surely be happier than the perfectly just one. Hence, there are plausible reasons of happiness for acting unjustly if one can get away with it.

How much force does this argument have? One might answer that it has little force because it concerns the value of injustice in the rare circumstance that one is *perfectly clever and can always get away with wrongdoing,* versus the value of justice in the also arguably rare circumstances that *everyone* mistakes it for injustice. These circumstances are hardly likely in life, so the argument cannot be said to show the comparative value of justice and injustice for ordinary human beings.

Glaucon might reply that it is necessary to use such extreme cases in order to assess the value of justice for its own sake independently of the value of its effects. This may be true. But, after all, are the effects of justice entirely irrelevant to the value justice has for human beings? This question will be addressed later in this essay. Here let us turn to a cluster of questions raised by Plato's student Aristotle (384–322 B.C.) in the book's next selection, "From the *Nicomachean Ethics*": What, if anything, is the human good? What is happiness? How, if at all, is happiness related to virtue?

While very many of Plato's writings have been preserved, all of Aristotle's have been lost. All we have of his works is class notes by some of his students. The present selection is included among the class notes recorded by Nicomachus—hence the title *Nicomachean Ethics*. Aristotle's initial observation is: "Every art and every inquiry, and similarly every action and pursuit, is thought to aim at some good." He argues that some ends are to be preferred to others because "it is for the sake of the former that the latter are pursued." Given this, he formulates the following hypothesis about the human good:

> If, then, there is some end of the things we do, which we desire for its own sake (everything else being desired for the sake of this), and if we do not choose everything for the sake of something else (for at that rate the process would go on to infinity, so that our desire would be empty and vain), clearly this must be the good and the chief good.

Aristotle argues that finding out what this good is would make us "more likely to hit upon what is right," and therefore this good is worth determining. He conceives of his inquiry into the good as political science.

Aristotle argues that if there is a human good or set of human goods, it is, first, achievable by action, because it is to be found in everything we do. Second, it is final, because sought for its own sake and not for that of something else; and if more than one end is thus sought, the human good is the most final of all. Third, it is self-sufficient—that is, when isolated, it makes life desirable and lacking in nothing. For Aristotle, the human good is not an individual but a community matter, because "man is born for citizenship."

An obvious candidate for having all these characteristics is happiness, yet Aristotle finds the simple equation of the human good with happiness a platitude. It is necessary to characterize happiness. In order to do so, Aristotle formulates another hypothesis. If human beings have a characteristic function or activity—that is, something they do *as humans* just as musicians *as musicians* play music—then performing this function well (or engaging in this activity well) is the human good. He argues that human beings do have a characteristic function: namely, a mental activity that involves acting in accordance with reason and deliberating by appeal to reasons. Hence, the human good is excellence at engaging in this activity. In Aristotle's words, the "human good turns out to be activity of soul in accordance with virtue, and if there are more than one virtue, in accordance with the best and most complete." He adds that such a good can only be attained in a complete life. That is, it cannot be merely episodic, or just a phase in one's life.

As for the relation between human happiness and human good, Aristotle states: "With those who identify happiness with virtue or some one virtue our account is in harmony; for to virtue belongs virtuous activity." As we saw, this activity is central to Aristotle's conception of the good. Yet there are conditions that Aristotle appears to consider external to the human good, though essential to its attainment and part of happiness. He writes:

> Yet evidently, . . . it needs the external goods as well; for it is impossible, or not easy, to do noble acts without the proper equipment. In many actions we use friends and riches and political power as instruments; and there are some things the lack of which takes the lustre from happiness, as good birth, goodly children, beauty. . . . As we said, then, happiness seems to need this sort of prosperity in addition; for which reason some identify happiness with good fortune, though others identify it with virtue.

These statements pose a puzzle. Suppose that, as Aristotle suggests and as seems plausible, attaining the human good through performing noble acts requires such things as friends, riches, and political power—all matters not entirely under our control. Since, according to Aristotle, the human good is "achievable by action," how can it be conditional on things not entirely under our control?

Aristotle might answer that to say the human good is achievable by action does not entail that we are always free to attain it. In fact, there are minimum conditions for attaining the human good, and some of these are not under our control. One might find this answer acceptable, but wonder how far these conditions can sensibly be extended. How much "moral luck" do we need to perform noble acts? And how noble are these acts if we are lucky enough to have friends, inherited riches, and political power partly bestowed on us by others? One answer is that it is still noble to use these fortunate conditions for a noble purpose rather than to frivolously misuse them by simply pursuing a pleasant, but uncaring, good time.

Parallel questions could be asked concerning Aristotle's discussion of happiness. No doubt, many people believe that good birth, good children, and beauty are conducive to happiness. In fact, these things may be crucial to this or that person's happiness; but are they crucial to *human* happiness? Aristotle says "the man who is very ugly in appearance or ill-born or solitary and childless is not very likely to be happy." Is Aristotle here identifying human happiness with the happiness of ordinary people he knew in his culture? Suppose he is. Is this a mistake? Some people today would say that being childless in no way detracts from their happiness; others would claim that being solitary actually makes them happy because they are self-sufficient. But Aristotle is concerned with characterizing the good for humans understood as community members. His notion of self-sufficiency as a feature of the human good is not individualistic:

> Now by self-sufficient we do not mean that which is sufficient for a man by himself, for one who lives a solitary life, but also for parents, children, wife, and in general for his friends and fellow citizens, since man is born for citizenship.

Still, the question remains: Are the features Aristotle considers crucial for human happiness merely crucial in Aristotle's culture? Or are there some features he describes that are cross-cultural and enduring? If so, what are they? These questions were pursued in later centuries. We now turn to some answers other thinkers provided, beginning with two works written in the Middle Ages.

B. WHAT IS THE MORAL SIGNIFICANCE OF HUMAN NATURE?

In his excellent *A Short History of Medieval Philosophy,* Julius Weinberg writes:

> The three great religious systems of the Western world—Judaism, Christianity, and Islam—have employed philosophy as a handmaid of theology. The degree of servitude has varied with time and difference in these religious traditions, but there is no doubt in principle that philosophical investigations were confined within a set of more or less determinate theological commitments. . . . Under these circumstances, it might be asked whether any philosophy, properly so called, could exist. If we take a standard kind of philosophizing with which we have been familiar since the Enlightenment, we might be tempted to deny that philosophy existed under such control of thought and action as we thought existed in the first fifteen centuries of the Christian era. But all these reflections suffer from a completely unhistorical view of the circumstances in which men

act and think. Moreover, to single out the Middle Ages as unique in respect of the control of thought is to be victimized by the propaganda against medieval thought which began in the sixteenth century as a reaction of humanists and reformers against the older ways of thought and action.[7]

In this book's previous parts, we saw definite examples of philosophical investigation pursued within the boundaries of the selections by Rhazes, St. Anselm, Gaunilon de Marmoutier, St. Thomas Aquinas, and Averroes. The next two selections are also examples of medieval philosophizing, and we would do well to keep in mind Weinberg's caution against taking an "unhistorical view of the circumstances in which men act and think" as we read them. The first selection, by St. Thomas Aquinas (1224–1274), is entitled "On Happiness, the Virtues, and the Natural Law."

It starts with certain presuppositions. Aquinas has previously argued that happiness cannot be an act of the will, but is "principally and essentially an act of the intellect." He has given various reasons in support of this thesis. First, happiness is the proper good of the intellectual nature. Second, since the will's object is prior to the will's act, an act of the will cannot be the first thing willed. Third, just as the first thing understood cannot be an act of understanding but some intelligible thing, the first thing willed cannot be an act of the will. Fourth, there is a difference between true happiness and false happiness (or attaining an object mistaken for the supreme good); but this difference cannot be drawn within the confines of an act of the will, which simply aims at an object (as in wanting a drink). Fifth, neither desire nor love nor delight (each a kind of act of the will) can be happiness, for happiness is fulfilled and is the last end; while desire is unfulfilled, since we love even when we do not possess what we love, and we take delight when we possess an object that is a further end. Finally, the intellect moves the will through the object apprehended as good—that is, as an end—while the will moves the intellect to actual operation, and the latter is impossible without the former. In Aquinas's words: "the agent in moving presupposes the end, for the agent does not move except for the sake of the end."

After giving these arguments, Aquinas derives their implications: human happiness is neither carnal pleasure, nor honor, nor glory, nor wealth, nor worldly power, nor the good of the body; neither is it seated in the senses, nor in acts of the moral virtues or of prudence, nor in the practice of art. Rather, he argues, it consists in contemplating God. In the present selection, he goes on to argue that happiness cannot be attained in this life, because human beings are never satisfied until they attain their end perfectly. And he concludes of any human being: "Therefore, he must obtain it after this life."

But is it true that human beings are such perfectionists concerning happiness? Or do they simply aim at what is good enough?[8] Of course, Aquinas could respond that even if human beings do not aim at perfect happiness, they *should* and would be irrational not to do so. But why? We will return to this point later. Let us first take up another objection to Aquinas's argument.

Aquinas's conclusion that every human being must obtain happiness after this life does not follow from his argument. In order for it to follow, he would have to prove that there is an afterlife and a God, and that humans can attain happiness in his sense—that is, in the contemplation of God—in that afterlife. We examined Aquinas's arguments for one of these theses—that God exists—in the introductory essay to Part III. Rather than formulating and assessing his arguments for the existence of an afterlife, we will focus on a different matter here. Even if we supposed that his theses are true—that there is a God and an afterlife, and that humans can attain happiness in it—we would still have this question: Has Aquinas's account totally severed the connection that Aristotle described between human happiness—let us concede, *imperfect* human happiness—in this world and virtue? For one thing, can human beings act virtuously even when they do not believe or have never heard of the God whose contemplation in the afterlife is, in Aquinas's terms, "true happiness"?

Aquinas could address this question by appealing to his theory of the natural law. He writes:

> There belong to the natural law, first, certain most common precepts that are known to all; and secondly, certain secondary and more particular precepts, which are, as it were, conclusions following closely from first principles.

One might agree that there is a natural law that applies to all without agreeing that its most common precepts—let alone the particular ones that follow from those common precepts—are known to all. And even if they were known to all, we would still wonder: What does the natural law enjoin in specifiable circumstances?

Aquinas takes this question to be a valid one and acknowledges the difficulties it involves. He says:

> It is right and true for all to act according to reason, and from this principle it follows, as a proper conclusion, that goods entrusted to another should be restored to their owner. Now this is true for the majority of cases. But it may happen in a particular case that it would be injurious, and therefore unreasonable, to restore goods held in trust; for instance, if they are claimed for the purpose of fighting against one's country. And this principle will be found to fail the more, according as we descend further towards the particular. . . .
>
> Consequently, . . . the natural law, as to the first common principles, is the same for all. . . . But as to certain more particular aspects, . . . it is the same for all in the majority of cases, . . . and yet in some few cases it may fail, both as to rectitude, . . . and as to knowledge. . . .

Under what conditions do the most common precepts of the natural law fail to hold and why? Aquinas suggests one type of case: when the security of one's own country is at stake. As we shall see, more recent discussions pursue this matter further.

Our next selection is by Ibn Khaldun (1332–1406), who was born in Tunis, North Africa. Its title is "Of Natural Groups, Group Feeling, Civilization, and Justice." The question guiding this selection's discussions can be formulated as follows: Why do the most irritable, nasty, and individualistic creatures on Earth—human beings— live in societies?

Ibn Khaldun leaves us in no doubt about his bleak conception of humanity:

> Evil is the quality that is closest to man when he fails to improve his customs and (when) religion is not used as the model to improve him. The great mass of mankind is in that condition, with the exception of those to whom God gives success. Evil qualities in man are injustice and mutual aggression.

This does not mean that injustice and aggression are *inborn*. Indeed, Ibn Khaldun thinks they are acquired:

> The soul in its first natural state of creation is ready to accept whatever good or evil may arrive and leave an imprint upon it. . . . When customs proper to goodness have been first to enter the soul of a good person and his (soul) has thus acquired the habit of (goodness, that person) moves away from evil and finds it difficult to do anything evil. The same applies to the evil person when customs (proper to evil) have been first to affect him.

This view implies that most people are in a condition of injustice and mutual aggression, because most have been initially exposed to unjust and aggressive customs. But did injustice and aggression always exist, even when there were no societies? Or did they develop and become predominant after the development of societies? If they have always existed and predominated, it is hard to imagine how societies could have been formed.

In searching for an explanation, Ibn Khaldun distinguishes between two forms of social organization: rural and urban. The rural groups he was acquainted with lived in the desert. He describes them as "restricting themselves to the necessary in food, clothing, and mode of dwelling, and to the other necessary conditions and customs." Some, "who make their living from animals requiring pasturage, such as sheep and cattle," are nomads; while others, who practice agriculture, are sedentary, living in "small communities, villages, and mountain regions." Ibn Khaldun argues that the nomads—or, as he calls them, the Bedouins—"are the basis of, and prior to, sedentary people," as evidenced by the fact that most inhabitants of the small settlements of his time had originated among the nomads. Eventually, larger urban developments—towns and cities—developed from some small settlements. From these towns and cities came customs "pertaining to luxury and ease," which later spread around.

Ibn Khaldun does not hold that nomads are good and sedentary people are bad, but that "Bedouins are closer to being good than sedentary people":

> Sedentary people are much concerned with all kinds of pleasures. They are accustomed to luxury and success in worldly occupations and to indulgence in worldly desires. . . . Eventually they lose all sense of restraint . . . Bedouins may be as concerned with worldly affairs as (sedentary people are). However, such concern would touch only the necessities of life and not luxuries or anything causing, or calling for, desires and pleasures.

A critic might object that although this account may explain the generalization of injustice and aggression, as well as the appearance of small sedentary settlements and, later on, of large urban settlements, it does not explain why humans live in any kind of society to begin with. It does not explain the existence of the nomadic groups Ibn Khaldun thinks original and basic. Why do humans, including nomads, live in social groups?

Ibn Khaldun's answer is twofold. First, all human beings try, at a very minimum, to make a living, and "social organization enables them to cooperate toward that end." Second, only those who cooperate in groups survive; as Ibn Khaldun puts it, "only tribes held together by group feeling can live in the desert." That is, unless they can make a living, people cannot survive, and without groups, people cannot make a living. Hence, among the groups Ibn Khaldun considers to be basic and original, group loyalty is crucial to survival.

This view echoes Artistotle's tenet that human beings are political animals and provides a natural and historical account of the primacy of the community in human survival. Virtue is characterized from this standpoint. Further, Ibn Khaldun's account provides an unequivocal answer to the question: Can virtue be lost? He argues that it can be, and is, lost when people succumb to the luxuries of civilization, which lead to a lack of restraint, and hence to aggression and injustice. But should civilization necessarily produce aggression and injustice? Why would it not produce peace and justice among a given society's members and between societies? Is Ibn Khaldun's conception of aggression and injustice restricted to the experience of certain social groups?

The answer seems to be affirmative, for Ibn Khaldun describes aggression and injustice within the particular social groups he knows, ranging from attacks on property to expropriations and forced labor. Concerning the relations between different social groups, he writes:

> Once group feeling has established superiority over the people who share (in that particular group feeling), it will, by its very nature, seek superiority over people of other group feelings unrelated to the first. . . . In this way, it goes on until the power of that particular group feeling equals the power of the ruling dynasty. Then, when the ruling dynasty grows senile . . .[a] (new group feeling) takes over and deprives the ruling dynasty of its power, and, thus, obtains complete royal authority.

In this view, the conflict between different groups held together by different loyalties is only resolved through power and conquest. However, once the conflict is resolved, it would be unjust for the new rulers to do such things as take their subjects' property or exploit them. Indeed, such actions would weaken their rule:

> It should be known that attacks on people's property remove the incentive to acquire and gain property. . . . When the incentive to acquire and obtain property is gone, people no longer make efforts to acquire any. . . . Civilization and its well-being as well as business prosperity depend on productivity and people's efforts in all directions in their own interest and profit. When people no longer do business in order to make a living, and when they cease all gainful activity, the business of civilization slumps, and everything decays. . . . The disintegration of (civilization) causes the disintegration of the status of dynasty and ruler. . . .

In Ibn Khaldun's account, this is as far as group feeling and concomitant striving for hegemony support justice and the avoidance of aggression. Can group feeling go no further in supporting justice? Is it true that it naturally strives for hegemony? Could groups trying to attain hegemony come to recognize that they stand to gain from cooperating both in economic and in political stability? Could group feeling be moderated by this recognition? Does our late-twentieth-century vantage point—after two world wars, the end of the cold war and the superpowers' arms race, the continuation of nuclear proliferation, and the evolving power of the United Nations—help us to answer these questions? Does natural law have any role in answering them?

Our next selection, "From *Leviathan*" by Thomas Hobbes (1588–1679), addresses this issue from a secular standpoint, and with a rather political emphasis. He writes:

> To this warre of every man against every man, this also is consequent; that nothing can be Unjust. The notions of Right and Wrong, Justice and Injustice have there no place. Where there is no common Power, there is no Law: where no Law, no Injustice.

Hobbes is not saying here that all is just in a generalized war situation, but that nothing is unjust in such a situation. His position is that right and wrong, justice and injustice, are *irrelevant* in this kind of situation. But notice how he later seems to contradict the view he espoused in the above passage:

> And because the condition of Man . . . is a condition of Warre of every one against every one; in which case every one is governed by his own Reason; and there is nothing he can make use of, that may not be a help unto him, in preserving his life against his enemyes; It followeth, that in such a condition, every man has a Right to every thing; even to one another's body.

This is not an uncommon view. People voice it, or something close to it, when they say "all is fair in love and war." As for the apparent contradiction in Hobbes's position, it is suggested by the following question: How can it be that everyone has any *right* to anything in a situation where justice—hence, presumably, the very notion of a right—is irrelevant?

This apparent inconsistency can be resolved by distinguishing a weak from a strong sense of "right" and of "a right." In the weakest sense of the term "right," to say that it is right for someone to perform an action is to say that it is not wrong for that person to perform it. If you see a twenty-dollar bill on the ground and no one is claiming it, it is right for you to pick it up and it is also right for me to pick it up. You and I are both at liberty to pick it up. In this sense, "right" means the same as "not wrong" or "permissible," and "a right" is a liberty.

If, however, the bill is mine and I have dropped it and want it back, I have a right to the bill and you do not. This conclusion involves two things. First, it is now wrong for you to interfere with my recovering and keeping the bill; that is, you are required to refrain from interfering. Second, I am entitled to demand that you not interfere. This case exemplifies a stronger sense of "right." The two conditions distinguish a right in this sense from what is right in the weak sense of simply not being wrong.

Hobbes, then, can be interpreted as saying that in a generalized war situation, everyone has a *weak right* to everything. In other words, everyone is at liberty to do as he or she sees fit. In this situation, right and wrong and justice and injustice in the strong sense of these terms have no application.

Still, this does not preclude general rules of reason from applying, for Hobbes writes:

> [A]s long as this naturall Right of every man to every thing endureth, there can be no security to any man, (how strong or wise soever he be,) of living out the time, which Nature ordinarily alloweth men to live. And consequently it is a precept, or generall rule

of Reason, *That every man, ought to endeavour Peace, as farre as he has hope of obtaining it; and when he cannot obtain it, that he may seek, and use, all helps, and advantages of Warre.* The first branch of which Rule, containeth that first, and Fundamentall Law of Nature; which is, *to seek Peace, and follow it.* The Second, the summe of the Right of Nature; which is, *By all means we can, to defend our selves.*

It might be objected that the injunction to seek peace can hardly work given Hobbes's account of human nature. For he also writes:

[I]n the nature of man, we find three principall causes of quarrell. First, Competition; Secondly, Diffidence; Thirdly, Glory.

The first, maketh men invade for Gain; the second, for Safety; and the third, for Reputation. . . .

Hereby it is manifest, that during the time men live without a common Power to keep them all in awe, they are in that condition which is called Warre. . . .

Given Hobbes's conception of human nature, how could the first and fundamental law of nature to seek peace ever work? It would not whenever some individual's interests in gain, safety, and reputation conflict with those of others. Even were they to sign a treaty on how these interests should be satisfied, their signing the treaty would amount to a false promise.

One way out of this situation is to question the accuracy of Hobbes's account of human psychology. In fact, if Hobbes's conception of human nature were accurate, there would be no societies, for the covenants supposed to bring human beings out of the state of nature and into civil society would not be meaningful. It might be possible to reach a state beyond the primitive, but this would still be a state of nature, though less overtly so. Yet there are true societies that are not in a merely disguised state of nature. Hence, Hobbes's conception of human nature must be inaccurate.

The previously discussed selection by Ibn Khaldun would seem to provide a more convincing answer to the question: Why do human beings live in societies at all? Ibn Khaldun's answer, as we saw, is that humans *start out* as members of highly cohesive social groups rather than as individuals, because it is only in such groups that they can make a living. Selfishness and individualism come afterward, with urban life and its luxuries, and undermine civilization.[9]

One might also find Hobbes's conception of a law of nature inadequate both for providing moral injunctions and for explaining the rich variety of existing social relations. There is a resemblance between Hobbes's conception and that of traditional natural law theorists. Both purport to derive their basic principles from human nature, and then, from these principles, to derive some rules of government. However, traditional natural law theorists—say, Aquinas—relied on final causes. For them, the natural law stated the conditions of civilized life and were ends—indeed, moral ends—to approximate. By contrast, Hobbes's account relies on efficient causes: the psychological drives (for gain, safety, and reputation) he thinks characteristic of human beings. These yield, at best, prudential injunctions.[10]

Our next selection, "Of the Influencing Motives of the Will" by David Hume (1711–1776), proceeds along the causal lines charted by Hobbes to explain social relations. But Hume disagrees with Hobbes on the specific emotions that move human beings to action. He writes:

> Now 'tis certain, there are certain calm desires and tendencies, which, tho' they be real passions, produce little emotion in the mind, and are more known by their effects than by the immediate feeling or sensation. These desires are of two kinds; either certain instincts originally implanted in our natures, such as benevolence and resentment, the love of life, and kindness to children; or the general appetite to good, and aversion to evil, consider'd merely as such.

Hume's conception of human motives goes far beyond the Hobbesian drives for gain, safety, and reputation by including such things as benevolence and kindness to children. Which of these conceptions of human nature, Hobbes's or Hume's, is more accurate and why? The answer depends on what kind of morality human beings can, and do, have.

Hume's conception of the kind of morality humans can, and do, have involves human sympathies rather than, as in Hobbes's account, merely selfish aims. People have such morality because these sympathies motivate them to act accordingly. Indeed, the existence of such sympathies ties in with Hume's criticism of Hobbes's problem: How can humans ever meaningfully make covenants, thus leaving the state of nature and forming civil societies? Hume rejects this problem as phony, for if an institution of promises is supposed to exist, the problem could not arise, and there would be no need to resolve it historically or through a rational reconstruction based on a social contract.[11]

C. HOW CAN THE DEMANDS OF JUSTICE, UTILITY, AND CULTURE BE BALANCED AGAINST ONE ANOTHER?

In the next selection, "The Categorical Imperative," Immanuel Kant (1724–1804) sharply disagrees with Hume both about the nature of morality and about what can—and does—motivate human beings to act morally:

> Nothing can possibly be conceived in the world, or even out of it, which can be called good without qualification, except a *good will.*

That is, such things as intelligence, wit, and judgment are not good without qualification. After all, a bad person can be intelligent and witty and possess good judgment. The same can be said of such things as power, riches, honor, health, well-being, and contentment. In fact, according to Kant, not even moderation, self-control, and calm deliberation are good without qualification, for, again, a bad person can have these characteristics. Accordingly, he states:

> We have then to develop the notion of a will which deserves to be highly esteemed for itself, and is good without a view to anything further, a notion which exists already in the sound natural understanding. . . . In order to do this, we will take the notion of duty. . . .

A way of characterizing Kant's notion of good will by appeal to the notion of duty is to say that its aim is to do *the right thing,* not to do *good.* In addition, since it is a will, it is a determination to act. And since such a determination cannot be merely episodic but must be a matter of character, it is settled. Thus, Kant's notion of a good will can be characterized as *a settled determination to do the right thing*. Such a will is what gives moral worth to our actions. Kant considers the case of preserving one's life in the face of hopeless adversity:

> . . . if the unfortunate one, strong in mind, indignant at his fate rather than desponding or dejected, wishes for death, and yet preserves his life without loving it—not from inclination or fear, but from duty—then his maxim has a moral worth.
>
> Thus the moral worth of an action does not lie in the effect expected from it, nor in any principle of action which requires to borrow its motive from this expected effect.

But how can one be motivated simply by the thought of the right thing or the thought of duty, regardless of any inclination to do one's duty? In a footnote, Kant says that one can be motivated by a feeling of respect: "What I recognize immediately as a law for me, I recognize with respect. This merely signifies the consciousness that my will is *subordinate* to a law, without the intervention of other influences on my sense."

Now, Hume states in his selection that reason is and ought to be the slave of the passions. This notion seems to be incompatible with Kant's notion that the conception of my duty—what I immediately recognize as a law for me—can by itself move me to act. But is it incompatible? And if so, whose notion is accurate: Hume's or Kant's? Suppose it is Hume's. Then would any criteria of right and wrong that Kant offers be inadequate? Let us turn to Kant's criteria of right and wrong.

Kant first answers the question: What ought I to do? by saying: "I am never to act otherwise than so *that I could also will that my maxim should become a universal law.*" This has been called the *principle of universality*. It can be interpreted in a variety of ways. One interpretation is that I can do only that which meets two conditions: first, it is logically possible for every similar person in similar circumstances to do the same thing; and second, if every similar person in similar circumstances were to do the same thing, the reasons or preconditions for my action would not be undermined.

Consider the case of breaking a business contract because it seems likely to improve my business firm's position. Presumably, everyone who has entered into a business contract and thinks it advantageous to break it could do so. Therefore, my action is not ruled out by the first condition. However, it would be ruled out by the second, for were everyone to break business contracts, no one would believe in contracts; hence no one would enter into them and business could not exist. That is, the institution of business, which my actions presuppose, could not exist under such conditions; or if it did exist, it would be undermined, and in that case, I would not have improved my business firm's position at all.

On this interpretation, the principle of universality would seem to be both too strict and too lenient. It is too strict because the first condition seems to rule out actions that are morally harmless, although eccentric. For example, it would seem to rule out my using English from now on in a manner that conflicts with all English conventions. For any English speaker can cease to use English in accordance with English conventions; but when everybody does, no one can keep on using English in conflict with English conventions, for the conventions have then ceased to exist.

As interpreted, the principle of universality is also too lenient, for it seems to imply that some clearly immoral actions—say, rape—are morally permissible. Suppose that someone is in a position to commit rape and wants to do so for the sake of the power trip it involves, even at the cost of eventual—though unlikely—punishment. This action would meet the first condition—that is, there is no logical inconsistency in a situation where everyone who is in a position to commit rape with such motivation does so. It also meets the second condition. For if every such person were to commit rape, neither the person's reasons for committing rape nor the actions' presuppositions would apparently be undermined. A great deal of human history sadly attests to this.

But Kant provides two additional formulations of the supreme practical principle, which, with regard to human beings, who are imperfect (but not to God, who is perfect), is the *categorical imperative.* One is the *principle of humanity* or *principle of personality:* "*So act as to treat humanity, whether in thine own person or in that of any other, in every case as an end withal, never as a means only.*" The other formulation is that of the *kingdom of ends:* "[A]lways so to act *that the will could at the same time regard itself as giving in its maxims universal laws.*"

Now, the principle of humanity could be interpreted to rule out rape on the grounds that, in raping someone, one is treating that person merely as an object—that is, merely as a means to one's satisfaction—rather than also as a person—that is, in Kant's terms, rather than also as an end. If so, the question arises: Is there more than one supreme practical principle, or are there only various formulations of one and the same principle? The fact that the principle of humanity appears to rule out rape while that of universality does not may be a reason for saying that these are different principles rather than different formulations of one and the same principle.

One might reply, however, that what is mistaken is the previously advanced interpretation of the principle of universality. On a correct interpretation, one might argue, this principle would rule out rape too. Kant's comments concerning the kingdom-of-ends formulation might be of help here. At the very basis of his account is the distinction between market value and dignity and the notion that moral agents have dignity and the moral law rests on it. Along these lines, one might argue that the principle of universality is best interpreted as involving a different second condition: If every similar person in similar circumstances were to do the same thing, the reasons or preconditions for my action—one of which is my dignity, which is equal to that of everyone else—would not be undermined. Is this a better interpretation? Will it do the job it is meant to do? Even if it helps regarding the matter of rape, does it weaken Kant's theory in some other respect? These are questions worth pursuing; but we will next focus on a different one: Why not establish what acts are right, what policies or practices are justified, and even what traits are good by establishing whether, overall, they would bring about the greatest happiness of the greatest number of those affected?

The alternative theory this question suggests is one among a family of theories called *utilitarianism.* It is subject to criticism in a variety of ways. First, it might be argued that it does not help establish how much each individual and group affected by an action should share in the happiness and unhappiness the action tends to promote. Should most of those affected suffer much and enjoy little, while a minority—maybe of one—enjoys much and suffers little? Or should happiness and unhappiness be shared in a fairer manner? The principle itself has nothing to say about this. And since this problem of distribution is a valid moral problem, one might argue that the principle, and hence the theory, is incomplete. We will return to this point later.

Second, it can be argued that the notion of dignity, which, as Kant holds, is crucial in ethics, cannot be accounted for by utilitarianism. For on this theory, the value of anything consists merely in the happiness or unhappiness that accompanies it. Hence, it can be worthwhile to trade off one's dignity, which often calls for sacrifices and pain, for contentment. For example, one's dignity calls for painstaking study to pass a course rather than cheating on an exam. Cheating, assuming one is likely to get away with it, would lead to the contentment of passing the course, provided one could manage to forget about one's dignity. But suppose one has qualms about cheating. There is no decisive utilitarian reason to forgo cheating instead of, say, undergoing therapy to get rid of the qualms and so feel free to cheat. Of course, the therapy might cost money one could use to attain forms of happiness other than that of passing the course. But the point is that in the utilitarian view, dignity is subject to trade-offs. If, however, as Kant thought, dignity has a value that is not subject to trade-offs, then utilitarianism is inadequate.

The third argument that can be made against utilitarianism is that the positive value it assigns to *anything*—from a pig's rolling in the mud to the performance of a musical masterpiece—is merely the value of the happiness that accompanies it. Likewise, the negative value of anything—from having to sell one of one's luxury boats to the victimization of an innocent person for the sake of prejudice—is merely the value of the suffering that accompanies it. Such a position is hedonistic if happiness is defined to equal pleasure and the absence of pain and unhappiness to equal pain and the absence of pleasure. It is not hedonistic otherwise (see Selection 24 in Part III). But in either case, this position seems to put such vastly disparate things as a pig's rolling in the mud and the performance of a musical masterpiece at the same level. This brings up the question: Are there *kinds* of pleasures that are so superior to other kinds of pleasures that the lowest pleasure of the superior kind is higher than the highest pleasure of the other kinds? And how do we rank the kinds of pleasure without introducing a nonutilitarian criterion?

In one solution, no such additional criterion is needed. Happiness and unhappiness are simply ranked as higher and lower by competent judges of happiness. Now, even if we concede this solution resolves the conflict, it raises still another question: Who is a competent judge? What features should competent judges have? Should they, for example, be impartial? Regarding what matters?

The selection by John Stuart Mill (1806–1873), "On the Connection Between Justice and Utility," partly addresses these questions. Mill is out to refute the charge that utilitarianism cannot soundly deal with matters of justice. He begins his argument by analyzing justice:

> [T]he idea of justice supposes two things; a rule of conduct, and a sentiment which sanctions the rule. The first must be supposed common to all mankind, and intended for their good. The other (the sentiment) is a desire that punishment may be suffered by those who infringe the rule. There is involved, in addition, the conception of some definite person who suffers by the infringement; whose rights (to use the expression appropriate to the case) are violated by it.

One might object that this account is incomplete. For if we suppose that the said rule of conduct is indeed intended for the good of humanity, we still need to know: How much good should each person get? Indeed, when all must suffer, we also need to know: How much should each person suffer?

Mill deals with this objection when he discusses the notions of impartiality and equality, which are crucial to justice. He grants that it is a duty to do to each according to his deserts, returning good for good as well as evil for evil. Given this, he concludes that

> it necessarily follows that we should treat all equally well (when no higher duty forbids) who have deserved equally well of *us,* and that society should treat all equally well who have deserved equally well of it. . . . This is the highest abstract standard of social and distributive justice. . . .
>
> But this great moral duty rests upon a still deeper foundation. . . . It is involved in the very meaning of Utility, or the Greatest-Happiness Principle. That principle is a mere form of words without rational justification, unless one person's happiness, supposed equal in degree (with the proper allowance made for kind), is counted for exactly as much as another's.

But what does it mean to say that one person's happiness (with the proper allowances made for kind), is to be counted for exactly as much as another's?

One interpretation is that, in calculating the happiness an action would lead to, one should avoid both double-counting and assigning more weight to one person's happiness than to someone else's, when both happinesses are of the same kind and degree. But this interpretation applies only to the calculation, not to the distribution, of happiness.

Another interpretation—the one Mill seems to favor—adds to the above rules for calculating happiness the notion that everybody has an equal claim to happiness. As Mill remarks in a footnote, it is possible to object that the impartial distribution of happiness involved in this claim is not part of the principle of utility, but something that is smuggled in. Mill meets this objection by saying that perfect impartiality between persons "may be more correctly described as supposing that equal amounts of happiness are equally desirable whether felt by the same or by different persons."

This reply only brings us back to the first interpretation, for it implies that calculations of happiness should neither involve double-counting nor giving more weight to one person's happiness than to another's when the happinesses are of the same kind and degree. Indeed, if equal amounts of happiness are equally desirable whether felt by the same or by different persons, what reason is there for acting so that a given amount goes only to one person rather than being distributed among some or all affected by the action?

Our next selection, "Labor Power, Exchanges, Surplus Value and Exploitation" by Karl Marx (1818–1883), examines the mechanisms by which market and production activities bring about social changes of questionable justice. Marx's analysis goes beyond the sphere of the exchange of commodities, about which he writes:

> This sphere. . . , within whose boundaries the sale and purchase of labour-power goes on, is in fact a very Eden of the innate rights of man. There alone rule Freedom, Equality, Property and Bentham. Freedom, because both buyer and seller of a commodity, say of

labour-power, are constrained only by their own free will. They contract as free agents, and the agreement they come to, is but the form in which they give legal expression to their common will. Equality, because each enters into relation with the other, as with a simple owner of commodities, and they exchange equivalent for equivalent. Property, because each dispenses only of what is his own. And Bentham, because each looks only to himself. . . .

Let us explore Marx's conception of the deeper process of capital production through surplus value. This conception is significant because it has influenced some current interpretations of the role of class in social structures, racism, relations between ethnic groups, and relations between the sexes (see, for example, Selection 45 at the end of Part IV).

Marx's description of the sphere of capital production is morally charged. He writes:

> He, who before was the money-owner, now strides in front as capitalist; the possessor of labour-power follows as his labourer. The one with an air of importance, smirking, intent on business; the other, timid and holding back, like one who is bringing his own hide to market and has nothing to expect but—a hiding.

Why does the laborer (wage earner) have nothing to expect but a hiding? Marx argues that the labor process can be divided into two periods. During the first, workers produce only the value of their labor power—that is, what it costs to buy the skills they use to produce any merchandise (say, a certain amount of yarn). This is what Marx calls "*necessary* labour-time," and the labor expended during this period he calls "*necessary* labour." As for the second period, Marx says:

> During the second period of the labour-process, . . . the workman . . . creates no value for himself. He creates surplus-value which, for the capitalist, has all the charms of a creation out of nothing.

Of course, workers might want to work for only that period of time during which they create value for themselves.

The obvious objection here is that no such jobs are available because capitalists will not invest money in a production process that does not bring them a profit. Marx would respond that this is precisely what is wrong with capitalism: profits come from the surplus value exacted from workers, which involves exploitation and is therefore unjust.

But is it? After all, workers are not slaves. They can freely sell their labor or refrain from selling it. Marx would rejoin that refraining from selling their labor is not a viable choice for those who want to eat. And he would shift the focus to a fact he considers crucial: workers produce surplus value by doing work that they themselves do not need. It does not matter through what social mechanism this is accomplished. He writes:

> The essential difference between the various economic forms of society, between, for instance, a society based on slave-labour, and one based on wage-labour, lies only in the mode in which this surplus-labour is in each case extracted from the actual producer, the labourer.

Marx is saying that in both types of society workers are exploited, for though the wage laborer is legally free to choose not to work, he actually has very little choice. The alternative to working under capitalist conditions is no work at all—and hence, no shelter or food.

What alternative social arrangement would do away with these onerous terms? Would it be one in which workers would produce goods only insofar as they have value for themselves? Or would it be one in which workers produce enough so that some extra value is added and can be shared by all? If the latter arrangement is desirable, how should this extra value be shared: equally; in proportion to each worker's contribution; in proportion to each worker's needs; or in some other way? Supposing such an arrangement could be worked out, would people tend to manipulate it to their own advantage?

Whatever the answers to these questions, Marx's account can be criticized on the grounds that it is significantly incomplete. He utterly disregards competition, which is crucial in market relations. To be sure, competition is not relevant to the socialist mode of production and distribution of goods that Marx promotes, but it should have a prominent place in any discussion of markets under a capitalist mode of production.

Furthermore, some of the extremes of exploitation Marx mentions are eliminated through the competition for labor among firms, so that to attract the best workers, it is necessary to offer them a better deal. Marx could reply that, within capitalism, even the best deal for workers involves having them produce some surplus value, and hence they are being exploited. But one could respond that whether the capitalist appropriation of surplus value is exploitation depends on whether or not such production has value, however indirect, for the workers. For example, it may have the value of keeping the economy viable and business firms opened and employing workers.

Given Marx's notion of exploitation, however, even if workers see value in an arrangement, that does not make it nonexploitative. Mystification, ideology, and false consciousness may lead workers to see value in an arrangement that, in fact, has no value for them. Of course, if empirical evidence should turn out to indicate that mystification, ideology, and false consciousness are not involved in the workers' perceptions of value under the capitalist arrangement, then Marx's characterization would be disconfirmed.

To say that some capitalistic arrangements do not involve as much exploitation as Marx thinks they do is not to say that there is no exploitation or injustice in capitalist societies. On the contrary, exploitation and injustice occur often, and one question is: How can they be eliminated? Marx did not rule out violence as a way of eliminating them, though he saw class struggle largely as a social process in which capitalism destroyed itself through its crises. Others have taken an approach to exploitation and injustice that is both thoroughly nonviolent and much more individualistic than Marx's. An example is provided by our next selection, "Through Non-Violence to God" by the Indian thinker and activist Mohandas K. Gandhi (1869–1948). He says "there is no other god than Truth"; but Truth is something to be realized, and "the only means for the realization of Truth is non-violence." Gandhi's reasons for this view are that truth is universal and all-pervading, and to see it face to face, "one must be able to love the meanest of creations as oneself."

Anything short of identification with everything that lives causes people to fall prey to factionalism; then they do not know the Truth, let alone act so that their lives and institutions reflect it.

In our next selection, "The Ethics of Ambiguity," Simone de Beauvoir (1908–1986) takes a different view of violence. She says that

> violence is justified only if it opens concrete possibilities to the freedom which I am trying to save; by practising it I am willy-nilly assuming an engagement in relation to others and myself. . . .

This poses the problem of determining whether violence—or for that matter, any sort of behavior—opens concrete possibilities for the values one is trying to uphold by so behaving. De Beauvoir says:

> The fact is that no behavior is ever authorized to begin with, and one of the concrete consequences of existentialist ethics is the rejection of all the previous justifications which might be drawn from the civilization, the age, and the culture; it is the rejection of every principle of authority. To put it positively, the precept will be to treat the other . . . as a freedom so that his end may be freedom; in using this conducting-wire one will have to incur the risk, in each case, of inventing an original solution.

How does this principle differ from Kant's principle of humanity? De Beauvoir responds by stating that not abstract acts, but "particular solidarities" matter, so long as they do not contradict the will for universal solidarity. Yet a Kantian might counter that the maxim of an act includes a reference to its particular circumstances, which can include particular solidarities such as those between friends, family members, ethnic group members, and the like. But after acknowledging that "the individual as such is one of the ends at which our action must aim. Here we are at one with the point of view of . . . Kantian moralism," de Beauvoir adds:

> However, it must not be forgotten that there is a concrete bond between freedom and existence; . . . the movement toward freedom assumes its real, flesh and blood figure in the world by thickening into pleasure, into happiness.

That is, moral motives cannot be, as in Kant's account, a matter of abstract respect for the moral law as such. They must be concrete, particular motives aimed at particular individuals or groups. For example, when I perform an act for the sake of my friend, I do, and morally must do, so for *him* or *her.* I do not, and morally cannot, do so merely, or primarily, because he or she happens to belong to the abstract class of people who are friends of mine and the kind of action I perform is one of the things that ought to be done for friends. When these latter reasons motivate us, our acts are based on abstractions and are not acts of friendship. They result from a commitment to an abstract cause, not a person.

This is not simply a difficulty in Kant's account; it is a stumbling block in any account—Mill's, for instance—that includes general principles meant to motivate moral agents to perform moral actions. No doubt, one could hold that all the principles do is to formulate the kinds of reasons that justify moral actions, even though these may not always be the reasons that, logically and factually, can motivate (hence, explain) the actions. In other words, though any of the reasons characterized by a principle can be *a* good reason for performing an action, it sometimes may be impossible for it to be *my* or *your* reason for performing that action. *A* reason, by its very logical nature, is impersonal. In such relationships as friendship and parenthood, impersonal reasons would turn the normally personal relationship into something entirely different. One's actions might be right, but they would not be those of a friend or a parent crucially motivated by care for a child.[12]

Such a position raises a number of questions: If reasons that justify moral actions cannot always serve as motives for those actions, what criteria (beyond clarity, consistency, completeness, and informative power) would be significant for establishing one moral principle rather than another? And what features should moral theories have to be useful as guides for our actions? Could practical applicability and realism still be useful in assessing moral theories? If so, how?

One way in which these criteria could be used is by seeing how a principle fits with the self-understanding of those to whose actions it is supposed to apply. An example of this kind of investigation is provided by our next selection, "Have We Got a Theory for You! Feminist Theory, Cultural Imperialism, and the Demand for 'The Woman's Voice'" by the Latin American philosopher María C. Lugones and the U.S. philosopher Elizabeth V. Spelman. Their introduction states:

> [W]hile part of what feminists want and demand for women is the right to move and to act in accordance with our own wills and not against them, another part is the desire and insistence that we give our *own* accounts of these movements and actions. For . . . part of human life, human living, is talking about it, and we can be sure that being silenced in one's own account of one's life is a kind of amputation that signals oppression. Another reason for not divorcing life from the telling of it or talking about it is that as humans our experiences are deeply influenced by what is said about them, by ourselves or powerful . . . others.

This point goes beyond feminist concerns. The experiences of individuals from various ethnic groups and cultures can also be silenced or misrepresented, resulting in skewed data and therefore in the formulation of unrealistic moral principles and theories. Indeed, as Lugones and Spelman argue concerning feminist theory, principles and theories based on distorted data can hardly lead to sound results. They write:

> Feminist theory—of all kinds—is to be based on, or anyway touch base with, the variety of real life stories women provide about themselves. But in fact, because, among other things, of the structural political and social and economic inequalities among women, the tail has been wagging the dog: feminist theory has not for the most part arisen out of a medley of women's voices; instead, the theory has arisen out of the voices, the experiences, of a fairly small handful of women, and if other women's voices do not sing in harmony with the theory, they aren't counted as women's voices—rather, they are the voices of the woman as Hispana, Black, Jew, etc.

This phenomenon involves what the selection's title calls "cultural imperialism." The authors say: "A non-imperialist feminism requires that you make a real space for our articulating, interpreting, theorizing and reflecting about the connections among" our experiences. This is a difficult task, and the article suggests that only one motive can prompt people to make room for such theorizing: friendship.

Why not other motives also? Lugones and Spelman rule out some other motives that have been suggested. Self-interest will not do, they say, for two reasons. First, it would lead to a sectarian sort of ethical inquiry, which certainly would not be welcomed by members of the cultures studied and, more significantly, would be unlikely to make space for contributions by members of those cultures. Second, it would not be reciprocal and it is doubtful that the task envisioned would lead to self-growth. On the contrary, when interaction with another culture is extensive, the authors suggest, it may well lead to effacing oneself.

Would the motive of duty be any better? Lugones and Spelman reject duty as a motive because "white/Anglos have done people of color wrong," and therefore, people (not just women) of color rightly reject becoming the vehicles of white/Anglos' redemption. But duty need not be based on guilt about past wrongdoing. It could, instead, be based on considerations of fairness. This motive is also ruled out by Lugones and Spelman on the grounds that the members of other cultural groups do not want white/Anglos to inquire into their worlds out of obligation.

This is an empirical claim that, if true, would make the motive of duty, as the selection says, "an inappropriate motive." But is it true that the members of other cultural groups do not want white/Anglos motivated by fairness to listen to and learn about them? No one member of these groups can claim special insight into this matter. Hence, the questions arise: In what way, if any, would the listening and learning process be welcome? Would even asking for a start of such dialogue be inappropriate? Might it not be justified given the greater cultural fragmentation and conflict that lack of dialogue and alienated negligence may lead to?[13]

Whatever the answers to these questions, other motives could be suggested. One is the motive of care. Another, weaker motive is concern for others. Though neither of these motives amounts to friendship, neither would have to be paternalistic or arrogant. Would such motives be inappropriate for leading members of a dominant culture seeking to learn about people of other cultures—even if they strive to jointly engage, on an equal footing, in moral inquiry that is realistic, useful, and significant for all involved? These questions are crucial to this book's task: seeking and, where necessary, building common ground for a sound and fruitful cross-cultural discussion of philosophical problems.

NOTES

[1]   Supreme Court, 410 U.S. 113 (1973).

[2]   A parallel discussion of the senses of the term "ethics" can be found in my *Contemporary Moral Controversies in Technology* (New York and London: Oxford University Press, 1987), pp. 3–4, and *Contemporary Moral Controversies in Business* (New York and London: Oxford University Press, 1989), pp. 3–4. A succinct discussion of the topic that draws distinctions akin to those we are making here is included in *Morals and Values,* ed. Marcus G. Singer (New York: Scribner's Sons, 1977), p. 11. By contrast with Singer's distinctions, however, the ones we are drawing here do not rely on the notion of a code of conduct, but rather on the idea of a person's or group's beliefs and presuppositions about right and wrong, good and bad, justified and unjustified. This wider perspective is capable of explaining a code of conduct. Singer provides a more developed version of his distinctions in terms of rules, principles, and standards of conduct involved in ideas of right and wrong, in his Presidential Address delivered before the Eighty-fourth Annual Meeting of the Western (now Central) Division of the American Philosophical Association, St. Louis, Missouri, May 2, 1986. It is entitled "The Ideal of a Rational Morality," and is published in the American Philosophical Association's *Proceedings and Addresses 60* (September 1986): 15–38, 16–21. By contrast with Singer's later version, the distinctions developed in this and my other books are not restricted to problems of conduct and ideas of right and

wrong. In addition, they leave open the question of whether all ideas of right and wrong involve rules, principles, or standards.

3   As mentioned in my *Contemporary Moral Controversies in Technology,* p. 7, n. 3, and also in my *Contemporary Moral Controversies in Business,* p. 7, n. 3, Marcus G. Singer, in *Morals and Values,* distinguishes between problems of conduct and policy in a way similar to the distinction made here. By contrast with his account, however, the present one rules out neither a concrete, even personal, aspect in at least some problems of policy nor the significant effects of solutions on individual conduct.

4   For arguments in favor of this approach, see my *Contemporary Moral Controversies in Technology* as well as my *Contemporary Moral Controversies in Business.*

5   For the laws of Manu, see F. Max Müller (ed.), *The Sacred Books of the East,* Vol. XXV, trans. G. Bühler. (Oxford: Clarendon Press, 1886) For the *Dharma-Sūtras,* see Louis Renou, *Hinduism* (New York: Braziller, 1961), pp. 108–130.

6   A. R. Lacey, "Our Knowledge of Socrates," in Gregory Vlastos (ed.), *The Philosophy of Socrates* (Garden City, NY: Doubleday, 1971), pp. 22–49.

7   Julius R. Weinberg, *A Short History of Medieval Philosophy,* (Princeton, NJ: Princeton University Press, 1964), p. 3.

8   For a discussion of this alternative, see, for example, my *Philosophy as Diplomacy: Essays in Ethics and Policy Making* (Atlantic Highlands, NJ: Humanities Press International, 1993).

9   For modern corroborating evidence, see G. Simmel, "The Web of Group Affiliation," in *Conflict: The Web of Group Affiliation,* trans. G. Bendix (Glencoe, Il.: The Free Press, 1955). See also David Braybrooke, "The Insoluble Problem of the Social Contract," *Dialogue* Vol. 15 (1976): 3–37.

10 For a contemporary alternative view, see Amitai Etzioni, *The Moral Dimension: Toward a New Economics* (New York and London: The Free Press and Collier Macmillan, 1988).

11 See Hume, *Treatise of Human Nature,* Book III, Section VII.

12 A useful discussion of the differences between *a* reason and *my* reason for action, and their relation to motives and motivation, can be found in R. S. Peters, *The Concept of Motivation* (London and New York: Routledge & Kegan Paul and Humanities Press, 1966), Chaps. 1 and 2, pp. 1–51. An insightful discussion of this topic as it relates to morality and personal relations can be found in María C. Lugones, *Morality and Personal Relations,* Ph.D. diss. (Madison: University of Wisconsin-Madison, 1978).

13 There is an insightful discussion of current intercultural conflicts in Nathan Gardels, "Two Concepts of Nationalism: An Interview with Isaiah Berlin," *The New York Review of Books 38* (November 19, 1991): 19–23.

Mo Tzu (479–438 B.C.)
UNIVERSAL LOVE

The author, a Chinese philosopher, argues that one should try to promote what is beneficial and eliminate what is harmful to the world without being partial to one's own state, city, or family. Indeed, one should treat the states, cities, and families of others as one would treat one's own. Mo Tzu's conception of universality is discussed in Section A of the introductory essay to Part IV.

READING QUESTIONS

In reading the selection, try to answer the following questions and identify the passages that support your answers:

1. What should benevolent people do according to Mo Tzu?
2. What does Mo Tzu mean by "universality"?
3. Is universality as Mo Tzu understands it a good thing?
4. What other conceptions of universality are there?
5. Which conception is better and why?

Reprinted from Mo Tzu, *Basic Writings,* trans. Burton Watson (New York and London: Columbia University Press, 1963), pp. 39–49. Copyright © 1963, Columbia University Press. Reprinted by permission of Columbia University Press.

Mo Tzu said: It is the business of the benevolent man to try to promote what is beneficial to the world, and to eliminate what is harmful. Now at the present time, what brings the greatest harm to the world? Great states attacking small ones, great families overthrowing small ones, the strong oppressing the weak, the many harrying the few, the cunning deceiving the stupid, the eminent lording it over the humble—these are harmful to the world. So too are rulers who are not generous, ministers who are not loyal, fathers who are without kindness, and sons who are unfilial, as well as those mean men who, with weapons, knives, poison, fire, and water, seek to injure and undo each other.

When we inquire into the cause of these various harms, what do we find has produced them? Do they come about from loving others and trying to benefit them? Surely not! They come rather from hating others and trying to injure them. And when we set out to classify and describe those men who hate and injure others, shall we say that their actions are motivated by universality or partiality? Surely we must

answer, by partiality, and it is this partiality in their dealings with one another that gives rise to all the great harms in the world. Therefore we know that partiality is wrong.

Mo Tzu said: Whoever criticizes others must have some alternative to offer them. To criticize and yet offer no alternative is like trying to stop flood with flood or put out fire with fire. It will surely have no effect. Therefore Mo Tzu said: Partiality should be replaced by universality.

But how can partiality be replaced by universality? If men were to regard the states of others as they regard their own, then who would raise up his state to attack the state of another? It would be like attacking his own. If men were to regard the cities of others as they regard their own, then who would raise up his city to attack the city of another? It would be like attacking his own. If men were to regard the families of others as they regard their own, then who would raise up his family to overthrow that of another? It would be like overthrowing his own. Now when states and cities do not attack and make war on each other and families and individuals do not overthrow or injure one another, is this a harm or a benefit to the world? Surely it is a benefit.

When we inquire into the cause of such benefits, what do we find has produced them? Do they come about from hating others and trying to injure them? Surely not! They come rather from loving others and trying to benefit them. And when we set out to classify and describe those men who love and benefit others, shall we say that their actions are motivated by partiality or by universality? Surely we must answer, by universality, and it is this universality in their dealings with one another that gives rise to all the great benefits in the world. Therefore Mo Tzu has said that universality is right.

I have said previously that it is the business of the benevolent man to try to promote what is beneficial to the world and to eliminate what is harmful. Now I have demonstrated that universality is the source of all the great benefits in the world and partiality is the source of all the great harm. It is for this reason that Mo Tzu has said that partiality is wrong and universality is right.

Now if we seek to benefit the world by taking universality as our standard, those with sharp ears and clear eyes will see and hear for others, those with sturdy limbs will work for others, and those with a knowledge of the Way will endeavor to teach others. Those who are old and without wives or children will find means of support and be able to live out their days; the young and orphaned who have no parents will find someone to care for them and look after their needs. When all these benefits may be secured merely by taking universality as our standard, I cannot understand how the men of the world can hear about this doctrine of universality and still criticize it!

And yet the men of the world continue to criticize it, saying, "It may be a good thing, but how can it be put to use?"

Mo Tzu said: If it cannot be put to use, even I would criticize it. But how can there be a good thing that still cannot be put to use? Let us try considering both sides of the question. Suppose there are two men, one of them holding to partiality, the other to universality. The believer in partiality says, "How could I possibly regard my friend the same as myself, or my friend's father the same as my own?" Because he views his friend in this way, he will not feed him when he is hungry, clothe him when he is cold, nourish him when he is sick, or bury him when he dies. Such are the words of the partial man, and such his

actions. But the words and actions of the universal-minded man are not like these. He will say, "I have heard that the truly superior man of the world regards his friend the same as himself, and his friend's father the same as his own. Only if he does this can he be considered a truly superior man." Because he views his friend in this way, he will feed him when he is hungry, clothe him when he is cold, nourish him when he is sick, and bury him when he dies. Such are the words and actions of the universal-minded man.

So the words of these two men disagree and their actions are diametrically opposed. Yet let us suppose that both of them are determined to carry out their words in action, so that word and deed agree like the two parts of a tally and nothing they say is not put into action. Then let us venture to inquire further. Suppose that there is a broad plain, a vast wilderness, and a man is buckling on his armor and donning his helmet to set out for the field of battle, where the fortunes of life and death are unknown; or he is setting out in his lord's name upon a distant mission to Pa or Yüeh, Chi'i or Ching, and his return is uncertain. Now let us ask,[1] to whom would he entrust the support of his parents and the care of his wife and children? Would it be to the universal-minded man, or to the partial man? It seems to me that, on occasions like these, there are no fools in the world. Though one may disapprove of universality himself, he would surely think it best to entrust his family to the universal-minded man. Thus people condemn universality in words but adopt it in practice, and word and deed belie each other. I cannot understand how the men of the world can hear about this doctrine of universality and still criticize it!

And yet the men of the world continue to criticize, saying, "Such a principle may be all right as a basis in choosing among ordinary men, but it cannot be used in selecting a ruler."

Let us try considering both sides of the question. Suppose there are two rulers, one of them holding to universality, the other to partiality. The partial ruler says, "How could I possibly regard my countless subjects the same as I regard myself? That would be completely at variance with human nature! Man's life on earth is as brief as the passing of a team of horses glimpsed through a crack in the wall." Because he views his subjects in this way, he will not feed them when they are hungry, clothe them when

---

[1] The text at this point appears to be corrupt and a few words have been omitted in translation.

they are cold, nourish them when they are sick, or bury them when they die. Such are the words of the partial ruler, and such his actions. But the words and actions of the universal-minded ruler are not like these. He will say, "I have heard that the truly enlightened ruler must think of his subjects first, and of himself last. Only then can he be considered a truly enlightened ruler." Because he views his subjects in this way, he will feed them when they are hungry, clothe them when they are cold, nourish them when they are sick, and bury them when they die. Such are the words and actions of the universal-minded ruler.

So the words of these two rulers disagree and their actions are diametrically opposed. Yet let us suppose that both of them speak in good faith and are determined to carry out their words in action, so that word and deed agree like the two parts of a tally and nothing they say is not put into action. Then let us venture to inquire further. Suppose this year there is plague and disease, many of the people are suffering from hardship and hunger, and the corpses of countless victims lie tumbled in the ditches. If the people could choose between these two types of ruler, which would they follow? It seems to me that, on occasions like this, there are no fools in the world. Though one may disapprove of universality himself, he would surely think it best to follow the universal-minded ruler. Thus people condemn universality in words but adopt it in practice, and word and deed belie each other. I cannot understand how the men of the world can hear about this doctrine of universality and still criticize it!

And yet the men of the world continue to criticize, saying, "This doctrine of universality is benevolent and righteous. And yet how can it be carried out? As we see it, one can no more put it into practice than one can pick up Mount T'ai and leap over a river with it! Thus universality is only something to be longed for, not something that can be put into practice."

Mo Tzu said: As for picking up Mount T'ai and leaping over rivers with it, no one from ancient times to the present, from the beginning of mankind to now, has ever succeeded in doing that! But universal love and mutual aid were actually practiced by four sage kings of antiquity. How do we know that they practiced these?

Mo Tzu said: I did not live at the same time as they did, nor have I in person heard their voices or seen their faces. Yet I know it because of what is written on the bamboo and silk that has been handed down

to posterity, what is engraved on metal and stone, and what is inscribed on bowls and basins.

The "Great Oath" says: "King Wen was like the sun or moon, shedding his bright light in the four quarters and over the western land."[2] That is to say, the universal love of King Wen was so broad that it embraced the whole world, as the universal light of the sun and the moon shines upon the whole world without partiality. Such was the universality of King Wen, and the universality which Mo Tzu has been telling you about is patterned after that of King Wen.

Not only the "Great Oath" but the "Oath of Yü"[3] also expresses this idea. Yü said: "All you teeming multitudes, listen to my words! It is not that I, the little child, would dare to act in a disorderly way. But this ruler of the Miao, with his unyielding ways, deserves Heaven's punishment. So I shall lead you, the lords of the various states, to conquer the ruler of the Miao." When Yü went to conquer the ruler of the Miao, it was not that he sought to increase his wealth or eminence, to win fortune or blessing, or to delight his ears and eyes. It was only that he sought to promote what was beneficial to the world and to eliminate what was harmful. Such was the universality of Yü, and the universality which Mo Tzu has been telling you about is patterned after that of Yü.

And not only the "Oath of Yü" but the "Speech of T'ang"[4] also expresses this idea. T'ang said: "I, the little child, Lü, dare to sacrifice a dark beast and make this announcement to the Heavenly Lord above, saying, 'Now Heaven has sent a great drought and it has fallen upon me, Lü. But I do not know what fault I have committed against high or low. If there is good, I dare not conceal it; if there is evil, I dare not pardon it. Judgment resides with the mind of God. If the myriad regions have any fault, may it rest upon my person; but if I have any fault, may it not extend to the myriad regions.'" This shows that, though T'ang was honored as the Son of Heaven and possessed all the riches of the world, he did not hesitate to offer himself as a sacrifice in his prayers and entreaties to the Lord on High and the spirits. Such was the universality of T'ang, and the universality which Mo Tzu has been telling you about is patterned after that of T'ang.

---

[2] The "Great Oath," supposedly a speech by King Wu, the son of King Wen, was a section of the *Book of Documents*. It was lost long ago, and the text by that name included in the present *Book of Documents* is a forgery of the 3d century A.D., though it includes a passage much like the one quoted here by Mo Tzu.

[3] A section of the *Book of Documents*, now lost.

[4] A section of the *Book of Documents*, now lost. Almost the same quotation is found at the beginning of Book XX of the Confucian *Analects*.

This idea is expressed not only in the "Speech of T'ang" but in the odes of Chou as well. In the odes of Chou it says:

Broad, broad is the way of the king,
Neither partial nor partisan.
Fair, fair is the way of the king,
Neither partisan nor partial.

It is straight like an arrow,
Smooth like a whetstone.
The superior man treads it;
The small man looks upon it.[5]

So what I have been speaking about is no mere theory of action. In ancient times, when Kings Wen and Wu administered the government and assigned each person his just share, they rewarded the worthy and punished the wicked without showing any favoritism toward their own kin or brothers. Such was the universality of Kings Wen and Wu, and the universality which Mo Tzu has been telling you about is patterned after that of Wen and Wu. I cannot understand how the men of the world can hear about this doctrine of universality and still criticize it!

And yet the men of the world continue to criticize, saying, "If one takes no thought for what is beneficial or harmful to one's parents, how can one be called filial?"

Mo Tzu said: Let us examine for a moment the way in which a filial son plans for the welfare of his parents. When a filial son plans for his parents, does he wish others to love and benefit them, or does he wish others to hate and injure them? It stands to reason that he wishes others to love and benefit his parents. Now if I am a filial son, how do I go about accomplishing this? Do I first make it a point to love and benefit other men's parents, so that they in return will love and benefit my parents? Or do I first make it a point to hate and injure other men's parents, so that they in return will love and benefit my parents? Obviously, I must first make it a point to love and benefit other men's parents, so that they in return will love and benefit my parents. So if all of us are to be filial sons, can we set about it any other way than by first making a point of loving and benefiting other men's parents? And are we to suppose

that the filial sons of the world are all too stupid to be capable of doing what is right?

Let us examine further. Among the books of the former kings, in the "Greater Odes" of the *Book of Odes*, it says:

There are no words that are not answered,
No kindness that is not requited.
Throw me a peach,
I'll requite you a plum.[6]

The meaning is that one who loves will be loved by others, and one who hates will be hated by others. So I cannot understand how the men of the world can hear about this doctrine of universality and still criticize it!

Do they believe that it is too difficult to carry out? Yet there are much more difficult things that have been carried out. In the past King Ling of the state of Ching loved slender waists. During his reign, the people of Ching ate no more than one meal a day, until they were too weak to stand up without a cane, or to walk without leaning against the wall. Now reducing one's diet is a difficult thing to do, and yet people did it because it pleased King Ling. So within the space of a single generation the ways of the people can be changed, for they will strive to ingratiate themselves with their superiors.

Again in the past King Kou-chien of Yüeh admired bravery and for three years trained his soldiers and subjects to be brave. But he was not sure whether they had understood the true meaning of bravery, and so he set fire to his warships and then sounded the drum to advance. The soldiers trampled each other down in their haste to go forward, and countless numbers of them perished in the fire and water. At that time, even though he ceased to drum them forward, they did not retreat. The soldiers of Yüeh were truly astonishing. Now consigning one's body to the flames is a difficult thing to do, and yet they did it because it pleased the king of Yüeh. So within the space of a single generation the ways of the people can be changed, for they will strive to ingratiate themselves with their superiors.

Duke Wen of Chin liked coarse clothing, and so during his reign the men of the state of Chin wore robes of coarse cloth, wraps of sheepskin, hats of plain silk, and big rough shoes, whether they were

---

[5] The first four lines are now found, not in the *Book of Odes*, but in the *Hung fan* section of the *Book of Documents*. The last four lines are from the *Book of Odes, Hsiao ya* section, "Ta tung" (Mao text no. 203).

[6] The first two lines are from the poem "Yi" (Mao text no. 256), in the "Greater Odes" or *Ta ya* section of the *Book of Odes*. The last two lines, though not found in exactly this form, bear a close resemblance to lines in the poem "Mu-kua" (Mao text no. 64), in the *Kuo feng* or "Airs from the States" section of the *Odes*.

appearing before the duke in the inner chamber or walking about in the outer halls of the court. Now bringing oneself to wear coarse clothing is a difficult thing to do, and yet people did it because it pleased Duke Wen. So within the space of a single generation the ways of the people can be changed, for they will strive to ingratiate themselves with their superiors.

To reduce one's diet, consign one's body to the flames, or wear coarse clothing are among the most difficult things in the world to do. And yet people will do them because they know their superiors will be pleased. So within the space of a single generation the ways of the people can be changed. Why? Because they will strive to ingratiate themselves with their superiors.

Now universal love and mutual benefit are both profitable and easy beyond all measure. The only trouble, as I see it, is that no ruler takes any delight in them. If the rulers really delighted in them, pro-moted them with rewards and praise, and prevented neglect of them by punishments, then I believe that people would turn to universal love and mutual benefit as naturally as fire turns upward or water turns downward, and nothing in the world could stop them.

The principle of universality is the way of the sage kings, the means of bringing safety to the rulers and officials and of assuring ample food and clothing to the people. Therefore the superior man can do no better than to examine it carefully and strive to put it into practice. If he does, then as a ruler he will be generous, as a subject loyal, as a father kind, as a son filial, as an older brother comradely, and as a younger brother respectful. So if the superior man wishes to be a generous ruler, a loyal subject, a kind father, a filial son, a comradely older brother, and a respectful younger brother, he must put into practice this principle of universality. It is the way of the sage kings and a great benefit to the people.

Plato (428–348 B.C.)
FROM *THE REPUBLIC*

This selection raises the question: Is it, without exception, better to be just than unjust? Socrates holds that justice is always better, both for its own sake and for its effects. In the process of defending this thesis, he deals with the views that justice is better than injustice only because of its effects, that whoever acts justly does so reluctantly, and that there are plausible reasons for acting unjustly if one can get away with it. Plato's formulation of Socrates' arguments in this dialogue is discussed in Section A of the introductory essay to Part IV.

READING QUESTIONS

In reading the selection, try to answer the following questions and identify the passages that support your answers:

1.   What is Socrates' thesis about justice in this dialogue?
2.   What arguments does he give for his thesis?
3.   What arguments does Glaucon give in response?
4.   Whose arguments, Socrates' or Glaucon's, are better and why?
5.   Are the effects of justice relevant to the value of justice? Why or why not?

. . . When I had said this I supposed that I was done with the subject, but it all turned out to be only a prelude. For Glaucon, who is always an intrepid, enterprising spirit in everything, would not on this occasion acquiesce in Thrasymachus' abandonment of his case, but said, Socrates, is it your desire to seem to have persuaded us or really to persuade us that it is without exception better to be just than unjust?

Really, I said, if the choice rested with me.

Well, then, you are not doing what you wish. For tell me, do you agree that there is a kind of good which we would choose to possess, not from desire for its aftereffects, but welcoming it for its own sake? As, for example, joy and such pleasures as are harmless and nothing results from them afterward save to have and to hold the enjoyment.

I recognize that kind, said I.

And again a kind that we love both for its own sake and for its consequences, such as understanding, sight, and health? For these I presume we welcome for both reasons.

Yes, I said.

And can you discern a third form of good under which fall exercise and being healed when sick and the art of healing and the making of money generally? For of them we would say that they are laborious and painful yet beneficial, and for their own sake we would not accept them, but only for the rewards and other benefits that accrue from them.

Why yes, I said, I must admit this third class also. But what of it?

In which of these classes do you place justice? he said.

In my opinion, I said, it belongs in the fairest class, that which a man who is to be happy must love both for its own sake and for the results.

Yet the multitude, he said, do not think so, but that it belongs to the toilsome class of things that must be practiced for the sake of rewards and repute due to opinion but that in itself is to be shunned as an affliction.

I am aware, said I, that that is the general opinion and Thrasymachus has for some time been disparaging it as such and praising injustice. But I, it seems, am somewhat slow to learn.

Come now, he said, hear what I too have to say and see if you agree with me. For Thrasymachus seems to me to have given up to you too soon, as if he were a serpent that you had charmed, but I am not yet satisfied with the proof that has been offered about justice and injustice. For what I desire is to hear what each of them is and what potency and ef-

fect each has in and of itself dwelling in the soul, but to dismiss their rewards and consequences. This, then, is what I propose to do, with your concurrence. I will renew the argument of Thrasymachus and will first state what men say is the nature and origin of justice, secondly, that all who practice it do so reluctantly, regarding it as something necessary and not as a good, and thirdly, that they have plausible grounds for thus acting, since forsooth the life of the unjust man is far better than that of the just man— as they say, though I, Socrates, don't believe it. Yet I am disconcerted when my ears are dinned by the arguments of Thrasymachus and innumerable others. But the case for justice, to prove that it is better than injustice, I have never yet heard stated by any as I desire to hear it. What I desire is to hear an encomium on justice in and by itself. And I think I am most likely to get that from you. For which reason I will lay myself out in praise of the life of injustice, and in so speaking will give you an example of the manner in which I desire to hear from you in turn the dispraise of injustice and the praise of justice. Consider whether my proposal pleases you.

Nothing could please me more, said I, for on what subject would a man of sense rather delight to hold and hear discourse again and again?

That is excellent, he said, and now listen to what I said would be the first topic—the nature and origin of justice.

By nature, they say, to commit injustice is a good and to suffer it is an evil, but that the excess of evil in being wronged is greater than the excess of good in doing wrong, so that when men do wrong and are wronged by one another and taste of both, those who lack the power to avoid the one and take the other determine that it is for their profit to make a compact with one another neither to commit nor to suffer injustice, and that this is the beginning of legislation and of covenants between men, and that they name the commandment of the law the lawful and the just, and that this is the genesis and essential nature of justice—a compromise between the best, which is to do wrong with impunity, and the worst, which is to be wronged and be impotent to get one's revenge. Justice, they tell us, being midway between the two, is accepted and approved, not as a real good, but as a thing honored in the lack of vigor to do injustice, since anyone who had the power to do it and was in reality 'a man' would never make a compact with anybody neither to wrong nor to be wronged, for he would be mad. The nature, then, of justice is this and such as this, Socrates, and such are the conditions in which it originates, according to the theory.

But as for the second point, that those who practice it do so unwillingly and from want of power to commit injustice, we shall be most likely to apprehend that if we entertain some such supposition as this in thought—if we grant to both the just and the unjust license and power to do whatever they please, and then accompany them in imagination and see whither desire will conduct them. We should then catch the just man in the very act of resorting to the same conduct as the unjust man because of the self-advantage which every creature by its nature pursues as a good, while by the convention of law it is forcibly diverted to paying honor to 'equality.' The license that I mean would be most nearly such as would result from supposing them to have the power which men say once came to the ancestor of Gyges the Lydian. They relate that he was a shepherd in the service of the ruler at that time of Lydia, and that after a great deluge of rain and an earthquake the ground opened and a chasm appeared in the place where he was pasturing, and they say that he saw and wondered and went down into the chasm. And the story goes that he beheld other marvels there and a hollow bronze horse with little doors, and that he peeped in and saw a corpse within, as it seemed, of more than mortal stature, and that there was nothing else but a gold ring on its hand, which he took off, and so went forth. And when the shepherds held their customary assembly to make their monthly report to the king about the flocks, he also attended, wearing the ring. So as he sat there it chanced that he turned the collet of the ring toward himself, toward the inner part of his hand, and when this took place they say that he became invisible to those who sat by him and they spoke of him as absent, and that he was amazed, and again fumbling with the ring turned the collet outward and so became visible. On noting this he experimented with the ring to see if it possessed this virtue, and he found the result to be that when he turned the collet inward he became invisible, and when outward visible, and becoming aware of this, he immediately managed things so that he became one of the messengers who went up to the king, and on coming there he seduced the king's wife and with her aid set upon the king and slew him and possessed his kingdom.

If now there should be two such rings, and the just man should put on one and the unjust the other, no one could be found, it would seem, of such adamantine temper as to persevere in justice and en-

dure to refrain his hands from the possessions of others and not touch them, though he might with impunity take what he wished even from the market place, and enter into houses and lie with whom he pleased, and slay and loose from bonds whomsoever he would, and in all other things conduct himself among mankind as the equal of a god. And in so acting he would do no differently from the other man, but both would pursue the same course. And yet this is a great proof, one might argue, that no one is just of his own will but only from constraint, in the belief that justice is not his personal good, inasmuch as every man, when he supposes himself to have the power to do wrong, does wrong. For that there is far more profit for him personally in injustice than in justice is what every man believes, and believes truly, as the proponent of this theory will maintain. For if anyone who had got such a license within his grasp should refuse to do any wrong or lay his hands on others' possessions, he would be regarded as most pitiable and a great fool by all who took note of it, though they would praise him before one another's faces, deceiving one another because of their fear of suffering injustice. So much for this point.

But to come now to the decision between our two kinds of life, if we separate the most completely just and the most completely unjust man, we shall be able to decide rightly, but if not, not. How, then, is this separation to be made? Thus. We must subtract nothing of his injustice from the unjust man or of his justice from the just, but assume the perfection of each in his own mode of conduct. In the first place, the unjust man must act as clever craftsmen do. A first-rate pilot or physician, for example, feels the difference between impossibilities and possibilities in his art and attempts the one and lets the others go, and then, too, if he does happen to trip, he is equal to correcting his error. Similarly, the unjust man who attempts injustice rightly must be supposed to escape detection if he is to be altogether unjust, and we must regard the man who is caught as a bungler. For the height of injustice is to seem just without being so. To the perfectly unjust man, then, we must assign perfect injustice and withhold nothing of it, but we must allow him, while committing the greatest wrongs, to have secured for himself the greatest reputation for justice, and if he does happen to trip, we must concede to him the power to correct his mistakes by his ability to speak persuasively if any of his misdeeds come to light, and when force is needed, to employ force by reason of his manly spirit and vigor and his provision of friends and money. And when we have set up an unjust man of this character, our theory must set the just man at his side—a simple and noble man, who, in the phrase of Aeschylus, does not wish to seem but to be good. Then we must deprive him of the seeming. For if he is going to be thought just he will have honors and gifts because of that esteem. We cannot be sure in that case whether he is just for justice' sake or for the sake of the gifts and the honors. So we must strip him bare of everything but justice and make his state the opposite of his imagined counterpart. Though doing no wrong he must have the repute of the greatest injustice, so that he may be put to the test as regards justice through not softening because of ill repute and the consequences thereof. But let him hold on his course unchangeable even unto death, seeming all his life to be unjust though being just, so that, both men attaining to the limit, the one of injustice, the other of justice, we may pass judgment which of the two is the happier.

Bless me, my dear Glaucon, said I. How strenuously you polish off each of your two men for the competition for the prize as if it were a statue!

To the best of my ability, he replied, and if such is the nature of the two, it becomes an easy matter, I fancy, to unfold the tale of the sort of life that awaits each. We must tell it, then, and even if my language is somewhat rude and brutal, you must not suppose, Socrates, that it is I who speak thus, but those who commend injustice above justice. What they will say is this, that such being his disposition the just man will have to endure the lash, the rack, chains, the branding iron in his eyes, and finally, after every extremity of suffering, he will be crucified, and so will learn his lesson that not to be but to seem just is what we ought to desire. And the saying of Aeschylus was, it seems, far more correctly applicable to the unjust man. For it is literally true, they will say, that the unjust man, as pursuing what clings closely to reality, to truth, and not regulating his life by opinion, desires not to seem but to be unjust,

Exploiting the deep furrows of his wit
From which there grows the fruit of counsels shrewd,[1]

first office and rule in the state because of his reputation for justice, then a wife from any family he chooses, and the giving of his children in marriage to whomsoever he pleases, dealings and partnerships with whom he will, and in all these transactions advantage and profit for himself because he has no squeamishness about committing injustice. And so they say that if he enters into lawsuits, public or private, he wins and gets the better of his opponents, and, getting the better, is rich and benefits his friends and harms his enemies, and he performs sacrifices and dedicates votive offerings to the gods adequately and magnificently, and he serves and pays court to men whom he favors and to the gods far better than the just man, so that he may reasonably expect the favor of heaven also to fall rather to him than to the just. So much better they say, Socrates, is the life that is prepared for the unjust man from gods and men than that which awaits the just.

[1] *Septem* 592 sq.

Aristotle (384–322 B.C.)
FROM *THE NICOMACHEAN ETHICS*

Starting from the observation that every art and inquiry, every action and pursuit, is thought to aim at some good, Aristotle proceeds to characterize what this good is for human beings. By analogy with the characteristic function of certain kinds of humans—for example—musicians,—and their good, Aristotle concludes that human good is an activity of soul in accordance with virtue, and if there is more than one virtue, in accordance with the best and most complete virtue. Aristotle's views of the human good, happiness, and virtue are discussed in Section A of the introductory essay to Part IV.

READING QUESTIONS

In reading the selection, try to answer the following questions and identify the passages that support your answers:

1.   What is the human good according to Aristotle?
2.   What is happiness according to Aristotle, and how does he think that it is related to the human good?
3.   How does he think that virtue is related to happiness?
4.   What reasons does Aristotle give for his views on the human good, happiness, and virtue?
5.   Are they good? Why or why not?

Reprinted from Richard McKeon (ed.), *The Basic Works of Aristotle* (Oxford/New York: Oxford University Press/Random House, 1966), "Nicomachean Ethics," Book I, Chaps. 1, 2, 7, and 8. Reprinted by permission of Oxford University Press.

Every art and every inquiry, and similarly every action and pursuit, is thought to aim at some good; and for this reason the good has rightly been declared[1] to be that at which all things aim. But a certain difference is found among ends; some are activities, others are products apart from the activities that produce them. Where there are ends apart from the actions, it is the nature of the products to be better than the activities. Now, as there are many actions, arts, and sciences, their ends also are many; the end of the medical art is health, that of shipbuilding a vessel, that of strategy victory, that of economics wealth. But where such arts fall under a single capacity—as bridle-making and the other arts concerned with the equipment of horses fall under the art of riding, and this and every military action under strategy, in the same way other arts fall under yet others—in all of these the ends of the master arts are to be preferred to all the subordinate ends; for it is for the sake of the former that the latter are pursued. It makes no difference whether the activities themselves are the ends of the actions, or something else apart from the activities, as in the case of the sciences just mentioned.

If, then, there is some end of the things we do, which we desire for its own sake (everything else being desired for the sake of this), and if we do not choose everything for the sake of something else (for at that rate the process would go on to infinity, so that our desire would be empty and vain), clearly this must be the good and the chief good. Will not the knowledge of it, then, have a great influence on life? Shall we not, like archers who have a mark to aim at, be more likely to hit upon what is right? If so, we must try, in outline at least to determine what it is, and of which of the sciences or capacities it is the object. It would seem to belong to the most authoritative art and that which is most truly the master art. And politics appears to be of this nature; for it is this that ordains which of the sciences should be studied in a state, and which each class of citizens should learn and up to what point they should learn them; and we see even the most highly esteemed of capacities to fall under this, e.g. strategy, economics, rhetoric; now, since politics uses the rest of the sciences, and since, again, it legislates as to what we are to do and what we are to abstain from, the end of this science must include those of the others, so that this end must be the good for man. For even if the end is the same for a single man and for a state, that of the state seems at all events something greater and more complete whether to attain or to preserve; though it is worth while to attain the end merely for one man, it is finer and more godlike to attain it for a nation or for city-states. These, then, are the ends at which our inquiry aims, since it is political science, in one sense of that term.

. . . Let us again return to the good we are seeking, and ask what it can be. It seems different in different actions and arts; it is different in medicine, in strategy, and in other arts likewise. What then is the

---

[1]   Perhaps by Eudoxus; Cf. 1172[b] 9.

good of each? Surely that for whose sake everything else is done. In medicine this is health, in strategy victory, in architecture a house, in any other sphere something else, and in every action and pursuit the end; for it is for the sake of this that all men do whatever else they do. Therefore, if there is an end for all that we do, this will be the good achievable by action, and if there are more than one, these will be the goods achievable by action.

So the argument has by a different course reached the same point; but we must try to state this even more clearly. Since there are evidently more than one end, and we choose some of these (e.g., wealth, flutes, and in general instruments) for the sake of something else, clearly not all ends are final ends; but the chief good is evidently something final. Therefore, if there is only one final end, this will be what we are seeking, and if there are more than one, the most final of these will be what we are seeking. Now we call that which is in itself worthy of pursuit more final than that which is worthy of pursuit for the sake of something else, and that which is never desirable for the sake of something else more final than the things that are desirable both in themselves and for the sake of that other thing, and therefore we call final without qualification that which is always desirable in itself and never for the sake of something else.

Now such a thing happiness, above all else, is held to be; for this we choose always for itself and never for the sake of something else, but honour, pleasure, reason, and every virtue we choose indeed for themselves (for if nothing resulted from them we should still choose each of them), but we choose them also for the sake of happiness, judging that by means of them we shall be happy. Happiness, on the other hand, no one chooses for the sake of these, nor, in general, for anything other than itself.

From the point of view of self-sufficiency the same result seems to follow; for the final good is thought to be self-sufficient. Now by self-sufficient we do not mean that which is sufficient for a man by himself, for one who lives a solitary life, but also for parents, children, wife, and in general for his friends and fellow citizens, since man is born for citizenship. But some limit must be set to this; for if we extend our requirement to ancestors and descendants and friends' friends we are in for an infinite series. Let us examine this question, however, on another occasion; the self-sufficient we now define as that which when isolated makes life desirable and lacking in nothing; and such we think happiness to be; and fur-

ther we think it most desirable of all things, without being counted as one good thing among others—if it were so counted it would clearly be made more desirable by the addition of even the least of goods; for that which is added becomes an excess of goods, and of goods the greater is always more desirable. Happiness, then, is something final and self-sufficient, and is the end of action.

Presumably, however, to say that happiness is the chief good seems a platitude, and a clearer account of what it is is still desired. This might perhaps be given, if we could first ascertain the function of man. For just as for a flute-player, a sculptor, or any artist, and, in general, for all things that have a function or activity, the good and the 'well' is thought to reside in the function, so would it seem to be for man, if he has a function. Have the carpenter, then, and the tanner certain functions or activities, and has man none? Is he born without a function? Or as eye, hand, foot, and in general each of the parts evidently has a function, may one lay it down that man similarly has a function apart from all these? What then can this be? Life seems to be common even to plants, but we are seeking what is peculiar to man. Let us exclude, therefore, the life of nutrition and growth. Next there would be a life of perception, but *it* also seems to be common even to the horse, the ox, and every animal. There remains, then, an active life of the element that has a rational principle; of this, one part has such a principle in the sense of being obedient to one, the other in the sense of possessing one and exercising thought. And, as 'life of the rational element' also has two meanings, we must state that life in the sense of activity is what we mean; for this seems to be the more proper sense of the term. Now if the function of man is an activity of soul which follows or implies a rational principle, and if we say 'a so-and-so' and 'a good so-and-so' have a function which is the same in kind, e.g. a lyre-player and a good lyre-player, and so without qualification in all cases, eminence in respect of goodness being added to the name of the function (for the function of a lyre-player is to play the lyre, and that of a good lyre-player is to do so well): if this is the case, [and we state the function of man to be a certain kind of life, and this to be an activity or actions of the soul implying a rational principle, and the function of a good man to be the good and noble performance of these, and if any action is well performed when it is performed in accordance with the appropriate excellence: if this is the case,] human good turns out to be activity of soul in accordance with virtue, and if there are more than one virtue, in accordance with the best and most complete.

But we must add 'in a complete life'. For one swallow does not make a summer, nor does one day; and so too one day, or a short time, does not make a man blessed and happy.

Let this serve as an outline of the good; for we must presumably first sketch it roughly, and then later fill in the details. But it would seem that any one is capable of carrying on and articulating what has once been well outlined, and that time is a good discoverer or partner in such a work; to which facts the advances of the arts are due; for any one can add what is lacking. And we must also remember what has been said before, and not look for precision in all things alike, but in each class of things such precision as accords with the subject-matter, and so much as is appropriate to the inquiry. For a carpenter and a geometer investigate the right angle in different ways; the former does so in so far as the right angle is useful for his work, while the latter inquires what it is or what sort of thing it is; for he is a spectator of the truth. We must act in the same way, then, in all other matters as well, that our main task may not be subordinated to minor questions. Nor must we demand the cause in all matters alike; it is enough in some cases that the *fact* be well established, as in the case of the first principles; the fact is the primary thing or first principle. Now of first principles we see some by induction, some by perception, some by a certain habituation, and others too in other ways. But each set of principles we must try to investigate in the natural way, and we must take pains to state them definitely, since they have a great influence on what follows. For the beginning is thought to be more than half of the whole, and many of the questions we ask are cleared up by it.

We must consider it, however, in the light not only of our conclusion and our premises, but also of what is commonly said about it; for with a true view all the data harmonize, but with a false one the facts soon clash. Now goods have been divided into three classes,[2] and some are described as external, others as relating to soul or to body; we call those that relate to soul most properly and truly goods, and psychical actions and activities we class as relating to soul. Therefore our account must be sound, at least according to this view, which is an old one and agreed on by philosophers. It is correct also in that we identify the end with certain actions and activities; for

thus it falls among goods of the soul and not among external goods. Another belief which harmonizes with our account is that the happy man lives well and does well; for we have practically defined happiness as a sort of good life and good action. The characteristics that are looked for in happiness seem also, all of them, to belong to what we have defined happiness as being. For some identify happiness with virtue, some with practical wisdom, others with a kind of philosophic wisdom, others with these, or one of these, accompanied by pleasure or not without pleasure; while others include also external prosperity. Now some of these views have been held by many men and men of old, others by a few eminent persons; and it is not probable that either of these should be entirely mistaken, but rather that they should be right in at least some one respect or even in most respects.

With those who identify happiness with virtue or some one virtue our account is in harmony; for to virtue belongs virtuous activity. But it makes, perhaps, no small difference whether we place the chief good in possession or in use, in state of mind or in activity. For the state of mind may exist without producing any good result, as in a man who is asleep or in some other way quite inactive, but the activity cannot; for one who has the activity will of necessity be acting, and acting well. And as in the Olympic Games it is not the most beautiful and the strongest that are crowned but those who compete (for it is some of these that are victorious), so those who act win, and rightly win, the noble and good things in life.

Their life is also in itself pleasant. For pleasure is a state of *soul*, and to each man that which he is said to be a lover of is pleasant; e.g. not only is a horse pleasant to the lover of horses, and a spectacle to the lover of sights, but also in the same way just acts are pleasant to the lover of justice and in general virtuous acts to the lover of virtue. Now for most men their pleasures are in conflict with one another because these are not by nature pleasant, but the lovers of what is noble find pleasant the things that are by nature pleasant; and virtuous actions are such, so that these are pleasant for such men as well as in their own nature. Their life, therefore, has no further need of pleasure as a sort of adventitious charm, but has its pleasure in itself. For, besides what we have said, the man who does not rejoice in noble actions is not even good; since no one would call a man just who did not enjoy acting justly, nor any man liberal who did not enjoy liberal actions; and similarly in all other cases. If this is so, virtuous actions must be in

---

[2] Pl. *Euthyd.* 279 AB, *Phil.* 48 E, *Laws,* 743 E.

themselves pleasant. But they are also *good* and *noble*, and have each of these attributes in the highest degree, since the good man judges well about these attributes; his judgement is such as we have described.[3] Happiness then is the best, noblest, and most pleasant thing in the world, and these attributes are not severed as in the inscription at Delos—

> Most noble is that which is justest, and best is health;
> But pleasantest is it to win what we love.

For all these properties belong to the best activities; and these, or one—the best—of these, we identify with happiness.

[3] i.e., he judges that virtuous actions are good and noble in the highest degree.

Yet evidently, as we said, it needs the external goods as well; for it is impossible, or not easy, to do noble acts without the proper equipment. In many actions we use friends and riches and political power as instruments; and there are some things the lack of which takes the lustre from happiness, as good birth, goodly children, beauty; for the man who is very ugly in appearance or ill-born or solitary and childless is not very likely to be happy, and perhaps a man would be still less likely if he had thoroughly bad children or friends or had lost good children or friends by death. As we said, then, happiness seems to need this sort of prosperity in addition; for which reason some identify happiness with good fortune, though others identify it with virtue.

St. Thomas Aquinas (1224–1274)
ON HAPPINESS, THE VIRTUES, AND THE NATURAL LAW

After having argued that happiness cannot be an act of the will but must, first and foremost, be an act of the intellect, and that happiness is contemplating God, Aquinas argues in this selection that happiness cannot occur in this life. As for acting morally in this life, the natural law guides all human beings. See Section B of the introductory essay to Part IV for a discussion of Aquinas's arguments.

READING QUESTIONS

In reading the selection, try to answer the following questions and identify passages that support your answers:

1. What is Aquinas's conception of happiness?
2. What conceptions of happiness does he rule out and why?
3. Are his reasons good? Why or why not?
4. Are human beings perfectionists concerning happiness? Why or why not?
5. What is Aquinas's conception of the natural law and what function does he suppose the natural law to have?

Reprinted with the permission of Richard J. Pegis from Anton C. Pegis (ed.), *Basic Writings of Saint Thomas Aquinas* (New York: Random House, 1945), *The Summa Contra Gentiles*, Chap. XLVIII, pp. 84–87, and *The Summa Theologica*, Question XCIV, "The Natural Law," pp. 773–781 Copyright © 1945 by Anton C. Pegis.

THE SUMMA CONTRA GENTILES

CHAPTER XLVIII

That Man's Ultimate Happiness Is Not in This Life

Man's ultimate happiness does not consist in that knowledge of God whereby He is known by all or many in a vague kind of opinion, nor again in that knowledge of God whereby He is known in the speculative sciences through demonstration, nor in that knowledge whereby He is known through faith, as we have proved above;[1] and seeing that it is not possible in this life to arrive at a higher knowledge of God in His essence, or at least so that we understand other separate substances, and thus know God through that which is nearest to Him, so to say, as we have proved;[2] and since we must place our ultimate happiness in some kind of knowledge of God, as we have shown:[3]—it is impossible for man's happiness to be in this life.

Again. Man's last end is the term of his natural appetite, so that when he has obtained it, he desires nothing more; because if he still has a movement towards something, he has not yet reached an end wherein to be at rest. Now this cannot happen in this life, since the more man understands, the more is the desire to understand increased in him (for this is natural to man), unless perhaps there be some one who understands all things. Now in this life this never did nor can happen to anyone that was a mere man, seeing that in this life we are unable to know separate substances which in themselves are most intelligible, as we have proved.[4] Therefore man's ultimate happiness cannot possibly be in this life.

Besides. Whatever is in motion towards an end has a natural desire to be established and at rest therein. Hence a body does not move away from the place towards which it has a natural movement, except by a violent movement which is contrary to that appetite. Now happiness is the last end which man naturally desires. Therefore it is his natural desire to be established in happiness. Consequently, unless together with happiness he acquires a state of immobility, he is not yet happy, since his natural desire is not yet at rest. When, therefore, a man acquires happiness, he also acquires stability and rest; so that all agree in conceiving stability as a necessary condition of happiness. Hence the Philosopher says: *We do not look upon the happy man as a kind of chameleon.*[5] Now in this life there is no sure stability, since, however happy a man may be, sickness and misfortune may come upon him, so that he is hindered in the operation, whatever it be, in which happiness consists. Therefore man's ultimate happiness cannot be in this life.

Moreover. It would seem unfitting and unreasonable for a thing to take a long time in becoming, and to have but a short time in being; for it would follow that for a longer duration of time nature would be deprived of its end. Hence we see that animals which live but a short time are perfected in a short time. But if happiness consists in a perfect operation according to perfect virtue,[6] whether intellectual or moral, it cannot possibly come to man except after a long time. This is most evident in speculative matters, wherein man's ultimate happiness consists, as we have proved;[7] for hardly is man able to arrive at perfection in the speculations of science, even though he reach the last stage of life, and then, in the majority of cases, but a short space of life remains to him. Therefore man's ultimate happiness cannot be in this life.

Further. All admit that happiness is a perfect good, or else it would not bring rest to the appetite. Now perfect good is that which is wholly free from any admixture of evil; just as that which is perfectly white is that which is entirely free from any admixture of black. But man cannot be wholly free from evils in this state of life, and not only from evils of the body, such as hunger, thirst, heat, cold and the like, but also from evils of the soul. For there is no one who at times is not disturbed by inordinate passions; who sometimes does not go beyond the mean, wherein virtue consists,[8] either in excess or in deficiency; who is not deceived in some thing or another; or who at least is not ignorant of what he would wish to know, or does not feel doubtful about an opinion of which he would like to be certain. Therefore no man is happy in this life.

Again. Man naturally shuns death, and is sad about it, not only shunning it at the moment when he feels its presence, but also when he thinks about it. But man, in this life, cannot obtain not to die. Therefore it is not possible for man to be happy in this life.

[1] Ch. 38ff.
[2] Ch. 45.
[3] Ch. 37.
[4] Ch. 45.
[5] *Eth.*, I, 10 (1100b 5).
[6] *Op. cit.*, X, 7 (1177a 11).
[7] Ch. 37.
[8] Cf. Aristotle, *Eth.*, II, 6 (1106b 24).

Besides. Ultimate happiness consists, not in a habit, but in an operation, since habits are for the sake of actions. But in this life it is impossible to perform any action continuously. Therefore man cannot be entirely happy in this life.

Further. The more a thing is desired and loved, the more does its loss bring sorrow and pain. Now happiness is most desired and loved. Therefore its loss brings the greatest sorrow. But if there be ultimate happiness in this life, it will certainly be lost, at least by death. Nor is it certain that it will last till death, since it is possible for every man in this life to encounter sickness, whereby he is wholly hindered from the operation of virtue, e.g., madness and the like, which hinder the use of reason. Such happiness therefore always has sorrow naturally connected with it, and consequently it will not be perfect happiness.

But someone might say that, since happiness is a good of the intellectual nature, perfect and true happiness is for those in whom the intellectual nature is perfect, namely, in separate substances, and that in man it is imperfect, and by a kind of participation. For man can arrive at a full understanding of the truth only by a sort of movement of inquiry; and he fails entirely to understand things that are by nature most intelligible, as we have proved. Therefore neither is happiness, in its perfect nature, possible to man; but he has a certain participation of it, even in this life. This seems to have been Aristotle's opinion about happiness. Hence, inquiring whether misfortunes destroy happiness, he shows that happiness seems especially to consist in deeds of virtue, which seem to be most stable in this life, and concludes that those who in this life attain to this perfection are happy *as men*, as though not attaining to happiness absolutely, but in a human way.[9]

We must now show that this explanation does not remove the foregoing arguments. For although man is below the separate substances according to the order of nature, he is above irrational creatures, and so he attains his ultimate end in a more perfect way than they. Now these attain their last end so perfectly that they seek nothing further. Thus a heavy body rests when it is in its own proper place, and when an animal enjoys sensible pleasure, its natural desire is at rest. Much more, therefore, when man has obtained his last end, must his natural desire be at rest. But this cannot happen in this life. Therefore in this life man does not obtain happiness considered as his

proper end, as we have proved. Therefore he must obtain it after this life.

Again. Natural desire cannot be empty, since *nature does nothing in vain*.[10] But nature's desire would be empty if it could never be fulfilled. Therefore man's natural desire can be fulfilled. But not in this life, as we have shown. Therefore it must be fulfilled after this life. Therefore man's ultimate happiness is after this life.

Besides. As long as a thing is in motion towards perfection, it has not reached its last end. Now in the knowledge of truth all men are always in motion and tending towards perfection; because those who follow make discoveries in addition to those made by their predecessors, as is also stated in *Metaph.* ii.[11] Therefore in the knowledge of truth man is not situated as though he had arrived at his last end. Since, then, as Aristotle himself shows,[12] man's ultimate happiness in this life consists apparently in speculation, whereby he seeks the knowledge of truth, we cannot possibly allow that man obtains his last end in this life.

Moreover. Whatever is in potentiality tends to become actual, so that as long as it is not wholly actual, it has not reached its last end. Now our intellect is in potentiality to the knowledge of all the forms of things, and it becomes actual when it knows any one of them. Consequently, it will not be wholly actual, nor in possession of its last end, except when it knows all things, at least all these material things. But man cannot obtain this through speculative sciences, by which we know truth in this life. Therefore man's ultimate happiness cannot be in this life.

For these and like reasons, Alexander and Averroes held that man's ultimate happiness does not consist in that human knowledge obtained through the speculative sciences, but in that which results from a union with a separate substance, which union they deemed possible to man in this life.[13] But as Aristotle realized that man has no knowledge in this life other than that which he obtains through the speculative sciences, he maintained that man attains to a happiness which is not perfect, but a human one.

Hence it becomes sufficiently clear how these great minds suffered from being so straitened on every side. We, however, shall be freed from these

---

[9] *Op. cit.*, I, 10 (1101a 18).

[10] Aristotle, *De Caelo*, II, 11 (291b 13).

[11] Aristotle. *Metaph.*, I a, 1 (993a 31).

[12] *Eth.*, X, 7 (1177a 18).

[13] Cf. ch. 42, 43.

straits if we hold, in accordance with the foregoing arguments, that man is able to reach perfect happiness after this life, since man has an immortal soul; and that in that state his soul will understand in the same way as separate substances understand, as we proved in the Second Book.[14]

Therefore man's ultimate happiness will consist in that knowledge of God which the human mind possesses after this life, a knowledge similar to that by which separate substances know him. Hence our Lord promises us a *reward . . . in heaven* (*Matt.* v. 12) and states (*Matt.* xxii. 30) that the saints *shall be as the angels,* who always see God in heaven (*Matt.* xviii. 10).

THE SUMMA THEOLOGICA
Question XCIV
THE NATURAL LAW
(In Six Articles)

We now consider the natural law, concerning which there are six points of inquiry: (1) What is the natural law? (2) What are the precepts of the natural law? (3) Whether all the acts of the virtues are prescribed by the natural law? (4) Whether the natural law is the same in all? (5) Whether it is changeable? (6) Whether it can be abolished from the mind of man?

First Article
Whether the Natural Law Is a Habit?

We proceed thus to the First Article:—

Objection 1. It would seem that the natural law is a habit. For, as the Philosopher says, *there are three things in the soul, power, habit and passion.*[15] But the natural law is not one of the soul's powers, nor is it one of the passions, as we may see by going through them one by one. Therefore the natural law is a habit.

Obj. 2. Further, Basil says that the *conscience or synderesis is the law of our mind;*[16] which can apply only to the natural law. But *synderesis* is a habit, as was shown in the First Part.[17] Therefore the natural law is a habit.

Obj. 3. Further, the natural law abides in man always, as will be shown further on. But man's reason, which the law regards, does not always think about

the natural law. Therefore the natural law is not an act, but a habit.

On the contrary, Augustine says that a *habit is that whereby something is done when necessary.*[18] But such is not the natural law, since it is in infants and in the damned who cannot act by it. Therefore the natural law is not a habit.

I answer that, A thing may be called a habit in two ways. First, properly and essentially, and thus the natural law is not a habit. For it has been stated above that the natural law is something appointed by reason, just as a proposition is a work of reason.[19] Now that which a man does is not the same as that whereby he does it, for he makes a becoming speech by the habit of grammar. Since, then, a habit is that by which we act, a law cannot be a habit properly and essentially.

Secondly, the term habit may be applied to that which we hold by a habit. Thus *faith* may mean *that which we hold by faith.* Accordingly, since the precepts of the natural law are sometimes considered by reason actually, while sometimes they are in the reason only habitually, in this way the natural law may be called a habit. So, too, in speculative matters, the indemonstrable principles are not the habit itself whereby we hold these principles; they are rather the principles of which we possess the habit.

Reply Obj. 1. The Philosopher proposes there to discover the genus of virtue;[20] and since it is evident that virtue is a principle of action, he mentions only those things which are principles of human acts, viz., powers, habits and passions. But there are other things in the soul besides these three: e.g., acts, as *to will* is in the one that wills; again, there are things known in the knower; moreover its own natural properties are in the soul, such as immortality and the like.

Reply Obj. 2. *Synderesis* is said to be the law of our intellect because it is a habit containing the precepts of the natural law, which are the first principles of human actions.

Reply Obj. 3. This argument proves that the natural law is held habitually; and this is granted.

To the argument advanced in the contrary sense we reply that sometimes a man is unable to make use of that which is in him habitually, because of some impediment. Thus, because of sleep, a man is unable to use the habit of science. In like manner, through

---

[14] C. G., II, 81.

[15] *Eth.,* II, 5 (1105b 20).

[16] Cf. *In Hexaëm.,* hom., VII (PG 29, 158); St. John Damascene, *De Fide Orth.,* IV, 22 (PG 94, 1200).

[17] S. T., I, q. 79, a. 12.

[18] *De Bono Coniug.,* XXI (PL 40, 390).

[19] Q. 90, a.I, ad 2.

[20] *Eth.,* II, 5 (1105b 20).

the deficiency of his age, a child cannot use the habit of the understanding of principles, or the natural law, which is in him habitually.

Second Article
Whether the Natural Law Contains Several Precepts, or Only One?

We proceed thus to the Second Article:—

Objection 1. It would seem that the natural law contains, not several precepts, but only one. For law is a kind of precept, as was stated above.[21] If therefore there were many precepts of the natural law, it would follow that there are also many natural laws.

Obj. 2. Further, the natural law is consequent upon human nature. But human nature, as a whole, is one, though, as to its parts, it is manifold. Therefore, either there is but one precept of the law of nature because of the unity of nature as a whole, or there are many by reason of the number of parts of human nature. The result would be that even things relating to the inclination of the concupiscible power would belong to the natural law.

Obj. 3. Further, law is something pertaining to reason, as was stated above.[22] Now reason is but one in man. Therefore there is only one precept of the natural law.

On the contrary. The precepts of the natural law in man stand in relation to operable matters as first principles do to matters of demonstration. But there are several first indemonstrable principles. Therefore there are also several precepts of the natural law.

I answer that, As was stated above, the precepts of the natural law are to the practical reason what the first principles of demonstrations are to the speculative reason, because both are self-evident principles.[23] Now a thing is said to be self-evident in two ways: first, in itself; secondly, in relation to us. Any proposition is said to be self-evident in itself, if its predicate is contained in the notion of the subject; even though it may happen that to one who does not know the definition of the subject, such a proposition is not self-evident. For instance, this proposition, *Man is a rational being,* is, in its very nature, self-evident, since he who says *man,* says *a rational being;* and yet to one who does not know what a man is, this proposition is not self-evident. Hence it is that, as Boethius says,[24] certain axioms or propositions are universally self-evident to all; and such are the propositions whose terms are known to all, as, *Every whole is greater than its part,* and, *Things equal to one and the same are equal to one another.* But some propositions are self-evident only to the wise, who understand the meaning of the terms of such propositions. Thus to one who understands that an angel is not a body, it is self-evident that an angel is not circumscriptively in a place. But this is not evident to the unlearned, for they cannot grasp it.

Now a certain order is to be found in those things that are apprehended by men. For that which first falls under apprehension is *being,* the understanding of which is included in all things whatsoever a man apprehends. Therefore the first indemonstrable principle is that *the same thing cannot be affirmed and denied at the same time,* which is based on the notion of *being* and *not-being:* and on this principle all others are based, as is stated in *Metaph.* iv.[25] Now as *being* is the first thing that falls under the apprehension absolutely, so *good* is the first thing that falls under the apprehension of the practical reason, which is directed to action (since every agent acts for an end, which has the nature of good). Consequently, the first principle in the practical reason is one founded on the nature of good, viz., that *good is that which all things seek after.* Hence this is the first precept of law, that *good is to be done and promoted, and evil is to be avoided.* All other precepts of the natural law are based upon this; so that all the things which the practical reason naturally apprehends as man's good belong to the precepts of the natural law under the form of things to be done or avoided.

Since, however, good has the nature of an end, and evil, the nature of the contrary, hence it is that all those things to which man has a natural inclination are naturally apprehended by reason as being good, and consequently as objects of pursuit, and their contraries as evil, and objects of avoidance. Therefore, the order of the precepts of the natural law is according to the order of natural inclinations. For there is in man, first of all, an inclination to good in accordance with the nature which he has in common with all substances, inasmuch, namely, as every substance seeks the preservation of its own being, according to its nature; and by reason of this inclina-

---

[21] Q. 92, a. 2.

[22] Q. 90, a. 1.

[23] Q. 91, a. 3.

[24] *De Hebdom.* (PL 64, 1311).

[25] Aristotle, *Metaph.,* III, 3 (1005b 29).

tion, whatever is a means of preserving human life, and of warding off its obstacles, belongs to the natural law. Secondly, there is in man an inclination to things that pertain to him more specially, according to that nature which he has in common with other animals; and in virtue of this inclination, those things are said to belong to the natural law *which nature has taught to all animals*,[26] such as sexual intercourse, the education of offspring and so forth. Thirdly, there is in man an inclination to good according to the nature of his reason, which nature is proper to him. Thus man has a natural inclination to know the truth about God, and to live in society; and in this respect, whatever pertains to this inclination belongs to the natural law: e.g., to shun ignorance, to avoid offending those among whom one has to live, and other such things regarding the above inclination.

Reply Obj. 1. All these precepts of the law of nature have the character of one natural law, inasmuch as they flow from one first precept.

Reply Obj. 2. All the inclinations of any parts whatsoever of human nature, e.g., of the concupiscible and irascible parts, in so far as they are ruled by reason, belong to the natural law, and are reduced to one first precept, as was stated above. And thus the precepts of the natural law are many in themselves, but they are based on one common foundation.

Reply Obj. 3. Although reason is one in itself, yet it directs all things regarding man; so that whatever can be ruled by reason is contained under the law of reason.

Third Article
Whether All the Acts of the Virtues Are Prescribed by the Natural Law?

We proceed thus to the Third Article:—

Objection 1. It would seem that not all the acts of the virtues are prescribed by the natural law. For, as was stated above, it is of the nature of law that it be ordained to the common good.[27] But some acts of the virtues are ordained to the private good of the individual, as is evident especially in regard to acts of temperance. Therefore, not all the acts of the virtues are the subject of natural law.

Obj. 2. Further, every sin is opposed to some virtuous act. If therefore all the acts of the virtues are prescribed by the natural law, it seems to follow that all sins are against nature; whereas this applies to certain special sins.

Obj. 3. Further, those things which are according to nature are common to all. But the acts of the virtues are not common to all, since a thing is virtuous in one, and vicious in another. Therefore, not all the acts of the virtues are prescribed by the natural law.

On the contrary. Damascene says that *virtues are natural.*[28] Therefore virtuous acts are also subject to the natural law.

I answer that, We may speak of virtuous acts in two ways: first, in so far as they are virtuous; secondly, as such and such acts considered in their proper species. If, then, we are speaking of the acts of the virtues in so far as they are virtuous, thus all virtuous acts belong to the natural law. For it has been stated that to the natural law belongs everything to which a man is inclined according to his nature. Now each thing is inclined naturally to an operation that is suitable to it according to its form: e.g., fire is inclined to give heat. Therefore, since the rational soul is the proper form of man, there is in every man a natural inclination to act according to reason; and this is to act according to virtue. Consequently, considered thus, all the acts of the virtues are prescribed by the natural law, since each one's reason naturally dictates to him to act virtuously. But if we speak of virtuous acts, considered in themselves, i.e., in their proper species, thus not all virtuous acts are prescribed by the natural law. For many things are done virtuously, to which nature does not primarily incline, but which, through the inquiry of reason, have been found by men to be conducive to well-living.

Reply Obj. 1. Temperance is about the natural concupiscences of food, drink and sexual matters, which are indeed ordained to the common good of nature, just as other matters of law are ordained to the moral common good.

Reply Obj. 2. By human nature we may mean either that which is proper to man, and in this sense all sins, as being against reason, are also against nature, as Damascene states;[29] or we may mean that nature which is common to man and other animals, and in this sense, certain special sins are said to be against nature: e.g., contrary to sexual intercourse, which is natural to all animals, is unisexual lust, which has received the special name of the unnatural crime.

Reply Obj. 3. This argument considers acts in themselves. For it is owing to the various conditions of

---

[26] *Dig.*, I, i, 1 (I, 29a).—Cf. O. Lottin, *Le droit naturel*, pp. 34, 78.
[27] Q. 90, a. 2.

[28] *De Fide Orth.*, III, 14 (PG 94, 1045).
[29] *Op. cit.*, II, 4; 30; IV, 20 (PG 94, 876; 976; 1196).

men that certain acts are virtuous for some, as being proportioned and becoming to them, while they are vicious for others, as not being proportioned to them.

Fourth Article
Whether the Natural Law Is the Same in All Men?

We proceed thus to the Fourth Article:—

Objection 1. It would seem that the natural law is not the same in all. For it is stated in the *Decretals* that *the natural law is that which is contained in the Law and the Gospel.*[30] But this is not common to all men, because, as it is written (*Rom.* x. 16), *all do not obey the gospel.* Therefore the natural law is not the same in all men.

Obj. 2. Further, *Things which are according to the law are said to be just,* as is stated in *Ethics* v.[31] But it is stated in the same book that nothing is so just for all as not to be subject to change in regard to some men.[32] Therefore even the natural law is not the same in all men.

Obj. 3. Further, as was stated above, to the natural law belongs everything to which a man is inclined according to his nature. Now different men are naturally inclined to different things,—some to the desire of pleasures, others to the desire of honors, and other men to other things. Therefore, there is not one natural law for all.

On the contrary, Isidore says: *The natural law is common to all nations.*[33]

I answer that, As we have stated above, to the natural law belong those things to which a man is inclined naturally; and among these it is proper to man to be inclined to act according to reason. Now it belongs to the reason to proceed from what is common to what is proper, as is stated in *Physics* i.[34] The speculative reason, however, is differently situated, in this matter, from the practical reason. For, since the speculative reason is concerned chiefly with necessary things, which cannot be otherwise than they are, its proper conclusions, like the universal principles, contain the truth without fail. The practical reason, on the other hand, is concerned with contingent matters, which is the domain of human actions; and, consequently, although there is necessity in the common principles, the more we descend towards the

particular, the more frequently we encounter defects. Accordingly, then, in speculative matters truth is the same in all men, both as to principles and as to conclusions; although the truth is not known to all as regards the conclusions, but only as regards the principles which are called *common notions.*[35] But in matters of action, truth or practical rectitude is not the same for all as to what is particular, but only as to the common principles; and where there is the same rectitude in relation to particulars, it is not equally known to all.

It is therefore evident that, as regards the common principles whether of speculative or of practical reason, truth or rectitude is the same for all, and is equally known by all. But as to the proper conclusions of the speculative reason, the truth is the same for all, but it is not equally known to all. Thus, it is true for all that the three angles of a triangle are together equal to two right angles, although it is not known to all. But as to the proper conclusions of the practical reason, neither is the truth or rectitude the same for all, nor, where it is the same, is it equally known by all. Thus, it is right and true for all to act according to reason, and from this principle it follows, as a proper conclusion, that goods entrusted to another should be restored to their owner. Now this is true for the majority of cases. But it may happen in a particular case that it would be injurious, and therefore unreasonable, to restore goods held in trust; for instance, if they are claimed for the purpose of fighting against one's country. And this principle will be found to fail the more, according as we descend further towards the particular, e.g., if one were to say that goods held in trust should be restored with such and such a guarantee, or in such and such a way; because the greater the number of conditions added, the greater the number of ways in which the principle may fail, so that it be not right to restore or not to restore.

Consequently, we must say that the natural law, as to the first common principles, is the same for all, both as to rectitude and as to knowledge. But as to certain more particular aspects, which are conclusions, as it were, of those common principles, it is the same for all in the majority of cases, both as to rectitude and as to knowledge; and yet in some few cases it may fail, both as to rectitude, by reason of certain obstacles (just as natures subject to generation and corruption fail in some few cases because of some obstacle), and as to knowledge, since in

---

30 Gratian, *Decretum,* I, i. prol. (I, 1).

31 Aristotle, *Eth.,* V, 1 (1129b 12).

32 *Op. cit.,* V, 7 (1134b 32).

33 *Etymol.,* V, 4 (PL 82, 199).

34 Aristotle, *Phys.* I, 1 (184a 16).

35 Boethius, *De Hebdom.* (PL 64, 1311).

some the reason is perverted by passion, or evil habit, or an evil disposition of nature. Thus at one time theft, although it is expressly contrary to the natural law, was not considered wrong among the Germans, as Julius Cæsar relates.[36]

Reply Obj. 1. The meaning of the sentence quoted is not that whatever is contained in the Law and the Gospel belongs to the natural law, since they contain many things that are above nature; but that whatever belongs to the natural law is fully contained in them. Therefore Gratian, after saying that *the natural law is what is contained in the Law and the Gospel,* adds at once, by way of example, *by which everyone is commanded to do to others as he would be done by.*[37]

Reply Obj. 2. The saying of the Philosopher is to be understood of things that are naturally just, not as common principles, but as conclusions drawn from them, having rectitude in the majority of cases, but failing in a few.[38]

Reply Obj. 3. Just as in a man reason rules and commands the other powers, so all the natural inclinations belonging to the other powers must needs be directed according to reason. Therefore it is universally right for all men that all their inclinations should be directed according to reason.

Fifth Article
Whether the Natural Law Can Be Changed?

We proceed thus to the Fifth Article:—

Objection 1. It would seem that the natural law can be changed. For on *Ecclus.* xvii. 9 (*He gave them instructions, and the law of life*) the *Gloss* says: *He wished the law of the letter to be written in order to correct the law of nature.*[39] But that which is corrected is changed. Therefore the natural law can be changed.

Obj. 2. Further, the slaying of the innocent, adultery and theft are against the natural law. But we find these things changed by God: as when God commanded Abraham to slay his innocent son (*Gen.* xxii. 2); and when He ordered the Jews to borrow and purloin the vessels of the Egyptians (*Exod.* xii. 35); and when He commanded Osee to take to himself *a wife of fornications* (*Osee* i. 2). Therefore the natural law can be changed.

Obj. 3. Further, Isidore says that *the possession of all things in common, and universal freedom, are matters of natural law.*[40] But these things are seen to be changed by human laws. Therefore it seems that the natural law is subject to change.

On the contrary, It is said in the *Decretals: The natural law dates from the creation of the rational creature. It does not vary according to time, but remains unchangeable.*[41]

I answer that, A change in the natural law may be understood in two ways. First, by way of addition. In this sense, nothing hinders the natural law from being changed, since many things for the benefit of human life have been added over and above the natural law, both by the divine law and by human laws.

Secondly, a change in the natural law may be understood by way of subtraction, so that what previously was according to the natural law, ceases to be so. In this sense, the natural law is altogether unchangeable in its first principles. But in its secondary principles, which, as we have said, are certain detailed proximate conclusions drawn from the first principles, the natural law is not changed so that what it prescribes be not right in most cases. But it may be changed in some particular cases of rare occurrence, through some special causes hindering the observance of such precepts, as was stated above.

Reply Obj. 1. The written law is said to be given for the correction of the natural law, either because it supplies what was wanting to the natural law, or because the natural law was so perverted in the hearts of some men, as to certain matters, that they esteemed those things good which are naturally evil; which perversion stood in need of correction.

Reply Obj. 2. All men alike, both guilty and innocent, die the death of nature; which death of nature is inflicted by the power of God because of original sin, according to *I Kings* ii. 6: *The Lord killeth and maketh alive.* Consequently, by the command of God, death can be inflicted on any man, guilty or innocent, without any injustice whatever.—In like manner adultery is intercourse with another's wife; who is allotted to him by the law emanating from God. Consequently intercourse with any woman, by the command of God, is neither adultery nor fornication.—The same applies to theft, which is the taking of another's property. For whatever is taken by the command of God, to Whom all things belong, is not taken against the will of its owner, whereas it is in this

---

[36] Caesar, *De Bello Gallico*, VI, 23 (I, 348).

[37] *Decretum*, I, i, prol. (I, 1).

[38] *Eth.*, V, 1 (1129b 12).

[39] *Glossa ordin.* (III, 403E).

[40] *Etymol.*, V, 4 (PL 82, 199).

[41] Gratian. *Decretum*, 1, v, prol. (I, 7).

that theft consists.—Nor is it only in human things that whatever is commanded by God is right; but also in natural things, whatever is done by God is, in some way, natural, as was stated in the First Part.[42]

Reply Obj. 3. A thing is said to belong to the natural law in two ways. First, because nature inclines thereto: e.g., that one should not do harm to another. Secondly, because nature did not bring with it the contrary. Thus, we might say that for man to be naked is of the natural law, because nature did not give him clothes, but art invented them. In this sense, *the possession of all things in common and universal freedom* are said to be of the natural law, because, namely, the distinction of possessions and slavery were not brought in by nature, but devised by human reason for the benefit of human life. Accordingly, the law of nature was not changed in this respect, except by addition.

Sixth Article
Whether the Natural Law Can Be Abolished from the Heart of Man?

We proceed thus to the Sixth Article:—

Objection 1. It would seem that the natural law can be abolished from the heart of man. For on *Rom.* ii. 14 (*When the Gentiles who have not the law,* etc.) the *Gloss* says that *the law of justice, which sin had blotted out, is graven on the heart of man when he is restored by grace.*[43] But the law of justice is the law of nature. Therefore the law of nature can be blotted out.

Obj. 2. Further, the law of grace is more efficacious than the law of nature. But the law of grace is blotted out by sin. Much more, therefore, can the law of nature be blotted out.

Obj. 3. Further, that which is established by law is proposed as something just. But many things are enacted by men which are contrary to the law of nature. Therefore the law of nature can be abolished from the heart of man.

On the contrary, Augustine says: *Thy law is written in the hearts of men, which iniquity itself effaces not.*[44] But the law which is written in men's hearts is the natural law. Therefore the natural law cannot be blotted out.

I answer that, As we have stated above, there belong to the natural law, first, certain most common precepts that are known to all; and secondly, certain secondary and more particular precepts, which are, as it were, conclusions following closely from first principles. As to the common principles, the natural law, in its universal meaning, cannot in any way be blotted out from men's hearts. But it is blotted out in the case of a particular action, in so far as reason is hindered from applying the common principle to the particular action because of concupiscence or some other passion, as was stated above.[45] But as to the other, i.e., the secondary precepts, the natural law can be blotted out from the human heart, either by evil persuasions, just as in speculative matters errors occur in respect of necessary conclusions; or by vicious customs and corrupt habits, as, among some men, theft, and even unnatural vices, as the Apostle states (*Rom.* i. 24), were not esteemed sinful.

Reply Obj. 1. Sin blots out the law of nature in particular cases, not universally, except perchance in regard to the secondary precepts of the natural law, in the way stated above.

Reply Obj. 2. Although grace is more efficacious than nature, yet nature is more essential to man, and therefore more enduring.

Reply Obj. 3. This argument is true of the secondary precepts of the natural law, against which some legislators have framed certain enactments which are unjust.

---

[42] *S T.,* I, q. 105, a. 6, ad 1.

[43] *Glossa ordin.* (VI, 7E); Peter Lombard, *In Rom.,* super II, 14 (PL 191, 1345).

[44] *Confess.,* II, 4 (PL 32, 678).

[45] Q. 77, a. 2.

Ibn Khaldun (1332–1406)
OF NATURAL GROUPS, GROUP FEELING, CIVILIZATION, AND JUSTICE

The author, born in Tunis, North Africa, asks: Why is it that individualistic and selfish human beings live in societies at all? He argues that nomadic groups are closer to being good—that is, to acting in a manner that is good for human beings—than sedentary groups, for among nomads, the community and group feeling tend to take precedence over individualistic aims. The more urbanized sedentary groups become, the more luxuries they have and, as a result, injustice and aggression prevail, eventually putting an end to civilization. Ibn Khaldun's conception of humanity is discussed in Section B of the introductory essay to Part IV.

READING QUESTIONS

In reading the selection, try to answer the following questions and identify the passages that support your answers:

1. What is Ibn Khaldun's conception of humanity?
2. What does he think causes human beings to be aggressive?
3. How does he explain the existence of societies?
4. Does he think there is room for justice in the relations between societies?
5. Is Ibn Khaldun's position sound? Why or why not?

Both Bedouins and Sedentary People are Natural Groups

It[1] should be known that differences of condition among people are the result of the different ways in which they make their living. Social organization enables them to co-operate toward that end and to start with the simple necessities of life, before they get to conveniences and luxuries.

Some people adopt agriculture, the cultivation of vegetables and grains, (as their way of making a living). Others adopt animal husbandry, the use of sheep, cattle, goats, bees, and silkworms, for breeding and for their products. Those who live by agriculture or animal husbandry cannot avoid the call of the desert, because it alone offers the wide fields, acres, pastures for animals, and other things that the settled areas do not offer.[2] It is therefore necessary for them to restrict themselves to the desert. Their social organization and co-operation for the needs of life and civilization, such as food, shelter, and warmth, do not take them beyond the bare subsistence level, because of their inability (to provide) for anything beyond those (things). Subsequent improvement of their conditions and acquisition of more wealth and comfort than they need, cause them to rest and take it easy. Then, they co-operate for things beyond the (bare) necessities. They use more food and clothes, and take pride in them. They build large houses, and lay out towns and cities for protection. This is followed by an increase in comfort and ease, which leads to formation of the most

---

[1] Cf. Issawi, pp. 80 f.

[2] Cf. G. E. von Grunebaum, "as-Sakkâkî on Milieu and Thought," *Journal of the American Oriental Society,* LXV (1945), 62.

developed luxury customs. They take the greatest pride in the preparation of food and a fine cuisine, in the use of varied splendid clothes of silk and brocade and other (fine materials), in the construction of ever higher buildings and towers, in elaborate furnishings for the buildings, and the most intensive cultivation of crafts in actuality. They build castles and mansions, provide them with running water, build their towers higher and higher, and compete in furnishing them (most elaborately). They differ in the quality of the clothes, the beds, the vessels, and the utensils they employ for their purposes. Here, now, (we have) sedentary people. "Sedentary people" means the inhabitants of cities and countries, some of whom adopt the crafts as their way of making a living, while others adopt commerce. They earn more and live more comfortably than Bedouins, because they live on a level beyond the level of (bare) necessity, and their way of making a living corresponds to their wealth.

It has thus become clear that Bedouins and sedentary people are natural groups which exist by necessity, as we have stated.

The Arabs[3] are a Natural Group in the World

We have mentioned in the previous section that the inhabitants of the desert adopt the natural manner of making a living, namely, agriculture and animal husbandry. They restrict themselves to the necessary in food, clothing, and mode of dwelling, and to the other necessary conditions and customs. They do not possess conveniences and luxuries beyond (these bare necessities). They use tents of hair and wool, or houses of wood, or of clay and stone, which are not furnished (elaborately). The purpose is to have shade and shelter, and nothing beyond that. They also take shelter in caverns and caves. The food they take is either little prepared or not prepared at all, save that it may have been touched by fire.[4]

For those who make their living through the cultivation of grain and through agriculture, it is better to be stationary than to travel around. Such, therefore, are the inhabitants of small communities, villages, and mountain regions. These people make up the large mass of Berbers and non-Arabs.

Those who make their living from animals re-

quiring pasturage, such as sheep and cattle, usually travel around in order to find pasture and water for their animals, since it is better for them to move around in the land. They are called "sheepmen" (shâwiyah), that is, men who live on sheep and cattle. They do not go deep into the desert, because they would not find good pastures there. Such people include the Berbers, the Turks and their relatives, the Turkomans and the Slavs,[5] for instance.

Those who make their living by raising camels move around more. They wander deeper into the desert, because the hilly[6] pastures with their plants and shrubs do not furnish enough subsistence for camels. They must feed on the desert shrubs and drink the salty desert water. They must move around the desert regions during the winter, in flight from the harmful cold to the warm desert air. In the desert sands, camels can find places to give birth to their young ones. Of all animals, camels have the hardest delivery and the greatest need for warmth in connection with it.[7] (Camel nomads) are therefore forced to make excursions deep (into the desert). Frequently, too, they are driven from the hills by the militia,[8] and they penetrate farther into the desert, because they do not want the militia to mete out justice to them or to punish them for their hostile acts. As a result, they are the most savage human beings that exist. Compared with sedentary people, they are on a level with wild, untamable (animals) and dumb beasts of prey. Such people are the Arabs. In the West, the nomadic Berbers and the Zanâtah are their counterparts, and in the East, the Kurds, the Turkomans, and the Turks. The Arabs, however, make deeper excursions into the desert and are more rooted in desert life (than the other groups), because they live exclusively on camels, while the other groups live on sheep and cattle, as well as camels.

It has thus become clear that the Arabs are a natural group which by necessity exists in civilization. God is "the Creator, the Knowing One."[9]

---

[3]   As a sociological term, "Arab" is always synonymous with "Bedouin, nomad" to Ibn Khaldûn, regardless of racial, national, or linguistic distinctions.

[4]   Ibn Khaldûn was familiar with this phrase for "preparing food in the open fire" through the hadîth literature. Cf. F. Rosenthal, A History of Muslim Historiography, p. 206.

[5]   Though the Arabic text need not be understood as saying that there exists a relationship between the Slavs and the Turks, it is the most natural construction to understand it that way. It has been shown that Muslim geographers did not always mean precisely Slavs when they spoke about the Saqâlibah. (Cf. A. Zeki Validi Togan, Ibn Fadlân's Reisebericht, pp. 295 ff.) However, the above statement should not be taken too literally, and the term used for "relatives" (ikhwân "brethren") may perhaps be translated as "companions" or the like, implying no real relationship.

[6]   Tall, pl. tulûl "hills." The expression reflects the situation in northwestern Africa rather than in Arabia.

[7]   'Ibar, II, 336 f.

[8]   Bulaq, apparently by mistake, has "to humiliate them" for the rest of the sentence.

[9]   Qur'ân 15.86 (86); 36.81 (81).

Bedouins are Prior to Sedentary People. The Desert is the Basis and Reservoir of Civilization and Cities

We[10] have mentioned that the Bedouins restrict themselves to the (bare) necessities in their conditions (of life) and are unable to go beyond them, while sedentary people concern themselves with conveniences and luxuries in their conditions and customs. The (bare) necessities are no doubt prior to the conveniences and luxuries. (Bare) necessities, in a way, are basic, and luxuries secondary and an outgrowth (of the necessities). Bedouins, thus, are the basis of, and prior to, cities and sedentary people. Man seeks first the (bare) necessities. Only after he has obtained the (bare) necessities, does he get to comforts and luxuries. The toughness of desert life precedes the softness of sedentary life. Therefore, urbanization is found to be the goal of the Bedouin. He aspires to (that goal). Through his own efforts, he achieves what he proposes to achieve in this respect. When he has obtained enough to be ready for the conditions and customs of luxury, he enters upon a life of ease and submits himself to the yoke of the city. This is the case with all Bedouin tribes. Sedentary people, on the other hand, have no desire for desert conditions, unless they are motivated by some urgent necessity[11] or they cannot keep up with their fellow city dwellers.

Evidence for the fact that Bedouins are the basis of, and prior to, sedentary people is furnished by investigating the inhabitants of any given city. We shall find that most of its inhabitants originated among Bedouins dwelling in the country and villages of the vicinity. Such Bedouins became wealthy, settled in the city, and adopted a life of ease and luxury, such as exists in the sedentary environment. This proves that sedentary conditions are secondary to desert conditions and that they are the basis of them.[12] This should be understood.

All Bedouins and sedentary people differ also among themselves in their conditions (of life). Many a clan is greater than another, many a tribe greater than another, many a city larger than another, and many a town more populous ('*umrân*) than another.

It has thus become clear that the existence of Bedouins is prior to, and the basis of, the existence of towns and cities. Likewise, the existence of towns and cities results from luxury customs pertaining to luxury and ease, which are posterior to the customs that go with the bare necessities of life.

Bedouins are Closer to Being Good Than Sendentary People

The[13] reason for it is that the soul in its first natural state of creation is ready to accept whatever good or evil may arrive and leave an imprint upon it. Muḥammad said: "Every infant is born in the natural state. It is his parents who make him a Jew or a Christian or a Magian."[14] To the degree the soul is first affected by one of the two qualities, it moves away from the other and finds it difficult to acquire it. When customs proper to goodness have been first to enter the soul of a good person and his (soul) has thus acquired the habit of (goodness, that person) moves away from evil and finds it difficult to do anything evil. The same applies to the evil person when customs (proper to evil) have been first to affect him.

Sedentary people are much concerned with all kinds of pleasures. They are accustomed to luxury and success in worldly occupations and to indulgence in worldly desires. Therefore, their souls are colored with all kinds of blameworthy and evil qualities. The more of them they possess, the more remote do the ways and means of goodness become to them. Eventually they lose all sense of restraint. Many of them are found to use improper language in their gatherings as well as in the presence of their superiors and womenfolk. They are not deterrred by any sense of restraint, because the bad custom of behaving openly in an improper manner in both words and deeds has taken hold of them. Bedouins may be as concerned with worldly affairs as (sedentary people are). However, such concern would touch only the necessities of life and not luxuries or anything causing, or calling for, desires and pleasures. The customs they follow in their mutual dealings are, therefore, appropriate. As compared with those of sedentary people, their evil ways and blameworthy qualities are much less numerous. They are closer to the first natural state and more remote from the evil habits that have been impressed upon the souls (of sedentary people) through numerous and ugly blameworthy customs. Thus, they can more easily be

---

[10] Cf. Issawi, pp. 81 f.

[11] Ibn Khaldûn is probably thinking of political exile and retirement in the country such as he experienced himself when writing the *Muqaddimah*.

[12] The pronouns are as ambiguous in Arabic as they are in English, and, were it not for the context, would be understood to mean the opposite of what they are intended to mean.

[13] Cf. Issawi, pp. 66 f.

[14] Cf., for instance, al-Bukhâri, *Ṣaḥîḥ*, I, 341; *Concordance*, I 7*b*, ll. 5 f.

cured than sedentary people. This is obvious. It will later on become clear that sedentary life constitutes the last stage of civilization and the point where it begins to decay. It also constitutes the last stage of evil and of remoteness from goodness. It has thus become clear that Bedouins are closer to being good than sedentary people. "God loves those who fear God."[15]

This is not contradicted by the statement of al-Ḥajjâj to Salamah b. al-Akwaʻ, which is included among the traditions of al-Bukhârî. When al-Ḥajjâj learned that Salamah was going to live in the desert, he asked him, "You have turned back and become an Arab?" Salamah replied, "No, but the Messenger of God permitted me to go (back) to the desert."[16]

It should be known that at the beginning of Islam, the inhabitants of Mecca were enjoined to emigrate, so as to be with the Prophet wherever he might settle, in order to help him and to aid him in his affairs and to guard him. The Arab Bedouins of the desert were not enjoined to emigrate, because the Meccans were possessed of a strong group feeling for the Prophet to aid and guard him, such as did not exist among the desert Arabs. The emigrants, therefore, used to express an aversion to "becoming Arabs," that is, (to becoming) inhabitants of the desert upon whom emigration was not obligatory. According to the tradition of Saʻd b. Abî Waqqâṣ, Muḥammad said, when (Saʻd) was ill in Mecca: "O God, give success to the emigration of my companions and do not cause them to turn back."[17] That means, God should enable them to stay in Medina and not to have to leave it, so that they would not have to discontinue the emigration they had begun, and return. It is the same meaning as is implied in the expression "turning back" in connection with any enterprise.

It is (also) said that the (prohibition against "turning back") was restricted to the time before the conquest of Mecca, when there was a need for emigration because of the small number of Muslims. After the conquest, when the Muslims had become numerous and strong, and God had guaranteed His Prophet inviolability (ʻiṣmah), emigration was no longer necessary. Muḥammad said: "There is no emigration after the conquest."[18] This has been interpreted as meaning that the injunction to emigrate

was no longer valid for those who became Muslims after the conquest. It has also been interpreted (to mean) that emigration was no longer obligatory upon those who had become Muslims and had emigrated before the conquest. (At any rate,) all agree that emigration was no longer necessary after the Prophet's death, because the men around Muḥammad had by then dispersed and spread in all directions. The only thing that remained was the merit of living in Medina, which constituted emigration.

Thus, al-Ḥajjâj's statement to Salamah, who went to live in the desert: "You have turned back and become an Arab?" is a reproach to Salamah for giving up his residence in Medina. It contains an allusion to the words of the afore-mentioned prayer of the Prophet: "Do not cause them to turn back." The words, "You have become an Arab?" are a reproach, as they imply that Salamah had become one of the Arabs who did not emigrate. In his reply, Salamah denied both insinuations. He said that the Prophet had permitted him to go to the desert. This was a special (permission) in Salamah's case, exactly as, for instance, the testimony of Khuzaymah[19] and Abû Burdah's[20] lamb were special to the cases of Khuzaymah and Abû Burdah. Or, (it may be) al-Ḥajjâj reproached Salamah only because he was giving up his residence in Medina, as he was aware that emigration was no longer necessary after the Prophet's death. Salamah's reply was that it was more proper and better to avail himself of the Prophet's permission, who had distinguished him by this special permission only because (the Prophet) had some motive known to him (self) when he gave it.

In any event, the story does not imply that censure of desert (life) is meant by the expression "to become an Arab." It is known that the legal obligation to emigrate served the purposes of aiding and guarding the Prophet. It did not have the purpose of censuring desert (life). Use of the expression "to become an Arab," to condemn non-fulfillment of the duty (of emigration), is no indication that "becoming an Arab" is something blameworthy. And God knows better.

---

[15] Qurʾân 3.76 (70); 9.4 (4), 7 (7).

[16] Cf. al-Bukhârî, Ṣaḥîḥ, IV, 373; Concordance, II, 247a, ll. 32f.; Ibn Hajar, Tahdhîb, IV, 150 ff.

[17] Cf. al-Bukhârî, Ṣaḥîḥ, I, 326; Condordance, I, 245b, ll. 25 ff.

[18] Cf. the references in Handbook, p. 98b.

[19] Khuzaymah b. Thâbit's testimony was counted by the Prophet as that of two men. Cf. Concordance, III, 198b, l. 4; al-Bukhârî, Taʾrîkh, II¹, 188; Ibn Saʻd, Ṭabaqât, ed. E. Sachau et al. (Leiden, 1905–40), IV², 90 ff.; Ibn Hajar, Tahdhîb, III, 140.

[20] The sacrificial animal should be slaughtered after prayer, but in the case of Abû Burdah Hânìʾ b. Niyâr, the animal he had slaughtered previously was accounted a valid sacrifice by the Prophet. This, however, is stated not to be a precedent. Cf. al-Bukhârî, Ṣaḥîḥ, IV, 21; Concordance, I, 329b, ll. 32 ff.

Bedouins are More Disposed to Courage Than Sedentary People

The[21] reason for this is that sedentary people have become used to laziness and ease. They are sunk in well-being and luxury. They have entrusted defense of their property and their lives to the governor and ruler who rules them, and to the militia which has the task of guarding them. They find full assurance of safety in the walls that surround them, and the fortifications that protect them. No noise disturbs them, and no hunting occupies them. They are carefree and trusting, and have ceased to carry weapons. Successive generations have grown up in this way of life. They have become like women and children, who depend upon the master of the house. Eventually, this has come to be a quality of character that replaces natural (disposition).

The Bedouins, on the other hand, live separate from the community. They are alone in the country and remote from militias. They have no walls and gates. Therefore, they provide their own defense and do not entrust it to, or rely upon others for it. They always carry weapons. They watch carefully all sides of the road. They take hurried naps only when they are together in company or when they are in the saddle. They pay attention to every faint barking and noise. They go alone into the desert, guided by their fortitude, putting their trust in themselves. Fortitude has become a character quality of theirs, and courage their nature. They use it whenever they are called upon or an alarm stirs them. When sedentary people mix with them in the desert or associate with them on a journey, they depend on them. They cannot do anything for themselves without them. This is an observed fact. (Their dependence extends) even to knowledge of the country, the (right) directions, watering places, and crossroads. The reason for this is the thing we have explained. At the base of it is the fact that man is a child of customs and the things he has become used to. He is not the product of his natural disposition and temperament. The conditions to which he has become accustomed, until they have become for him a quality of character and matters of habit and custom, have replaced his natural disposition. If one studies this in human beings, one will find much of it, and it will be found to be a correct (observation).

"God creates whatever he wishes."[22]

The Reliance of Sedentary People upon Laws Destroys Their Fortitude and Power of Resistance

Not everyone is master of his own affairs. Chiefs and leaders who are masters of the affairs of men are few in comparison with the rest. As a rule, man must by necessity be dominated by someone else. If the domination is kind and just and the people under it are not oppressed by its laws and restrictions, they are guided by the courage or cowardice that they possess in themselves. They are satisfied with the absence of any restraining power. Self-reliance eventually becomes a quality natural to them. They would not know anything else. If, however, the domination with its laws is one of brute force and intimidation, it breaks their fortitude and deprives them of their power of resistance as a result of the inertness that develops in the souls of the oppressed, as we shall explain.

'Umar forbade Sa'd (b. Abî Waqqâṣ) to exercise such (arbitrary power) when Zuhrah b. Ḥawîyah took the spoils of al-Jâlinûs. The value of the spoils was 75,000 gold pieces. (Zuhrah) had followed al-Jâlinûs on the day of al-Qâdisîyah, killed him, and taken his spoils. Sa'd took them away from him and said, "Why did you not wait for my permission to follow him?" He wrote to 'Umar and asked 'Umar for permission (to confiscate the spoils). But 'Umar replied, "Would you want to proceed against a man like Zuhrah, who already has borne so much of the brunt (of battle),[23] and while there still remains so much of the war for you (to finish)? Would you want to break his strength and morale?" Thus, 'Umar confirmed (Zuhrah) in possession of the spoils.[24]

When laws are (enforced) by means of punishment, they completely destroy fortitude, because the use of punishment against someone who cannot defend himself generates in that person a feeling of humiliation that, no doubt, must break his fortitude.

When laws are (intended to serve the purposes of) education and instruction and are applied from childhood on, they have to some degree the same effect, because people then grow up in fear and docility and consequently do not rely on their own fortitude.

For this (reason), greater fortitude is found among the savage Arab Bedouins than among people who are subject to laws. Furthermore, those who

---

[21] Cf. Issawi, pp. 67 f.

[22] Qur'ân 3.47 (42); 5.17 (20); 24.45 (44); 28.68 (68); 30.54 (53); 39.4 (6); 42.49 (48).

[23] Or, more generally, "who has shown himself so courageous."

[24] Cf. aṭ-Ṭabarî, *Annales*, I, 2346.

rely on laws and are dominated by them from the very beginning of their education and instruction in the crafts, sciences, and religious matters, are thereby deprived of much of their own fortitude. They can scarcely defend themselves at all against hostile acts. This is the case with students, whose occupation it is to study and to learn from teachers and religious leaders, and who constantly apply themselves to instruction and education in very dignified gatherings. This situation and the fact that it destroys the power of resistance and fortitude must be understood.

It is no argument against the (statement just made) that the men around Muḥammad observed the religious laws, and yet did not experience any diminution of their fortitude, but possessed the greatest possible fortitude. When the Muslims got their religion from the Lawgiver (Muḥammad), the restraining influence came from themselves, as a result of the encouragement and discouragement he gave them in the Qur'ân.[25] It was not a result of technical instruction or scientific education. (The laws) were the laws and precepts of the religion, which they received orally and which their firmly rooted (belief in) the truth of the articles of faith caused them to observe. Their fortitude remained unabated, and it was not corroded by education or authority. 'Umar said, "Those who are not educated (disciplined) by the religious law are not educated (disciplined) by God." (This statement expresses) 'Umar's desire that everyone should have his restraining influence in himself. It also expresses his certainty that the Lawgiver (Muḥammad) knew best what is good for mankind.

(The influence of) religion, then, decreased among men, and they came to use restraining laws. The religious law became a branch of learning and a craft to be acquired through instruction and education. People turned to sedentary life and assumed the character trait of submissiveness to law. This led to a decrease in their fortitude.

It has thus become clear that governmental and educational laws destroy fortitude, because their restraining influence is something that comes from outside. The religious laws, on the other hand, do not destroy fortitude, because their restraining influence is something inherent. Therefore, governmental and educational laws influence sedentary people, in that they weaken their souls and diminish their stamina, because they have to suffer (their authority) both as children and as adults. The Bedouins, on the other hand, are not in the same position, because they live far away from the laws of government, instruction, and education. Therefore, Abû Muḥammad b. Abî Zayd, in his book on the laws governing teachers and students (Aḥkâm al-muʿallimîn wa-l-mutaʿallimîn), said: "The educator must not strike a boy more than three times (in one punishment) as an educational measure."[26] (Ibn Abî Zayd) reported this remark on the authority of Judge Shurayḥ.[27] Certain scholar(s) argued in favor of the procedure mentioned, by referring to the threefold choking mentioned in the tradition concerned with the beginning of revelation.[28] This, however, is a weak argument. (The tradition about the) choking is not suitable proof, because it has nothing to do with ordinary instruction. God "is wise and knowing."[29]

Only Tribes Held Together by Group Feeling Can Live in the Desert

It should be known that God put good and evil into the nature of man. Thus, He said in the Qur'ân: "We led him along the two paths."[30] He further said: "And inspired (the soul) with its wickedness as well as its fear of God."[31]

Evil is the quality that is closest to man when he fails to improve his customs and (when) religion is not used as the model to improve him. The great mass of mankind is in that condition, with the exception of those to whom God gives success. Evil[32] qualities in man are injustice and mutual aggression. He who casts his eye upon the property of his brother will lay his hand upon it to take it, unless there is a

[26]   In the city of Ibn Khaldûn's ancestors, it was prescribed ca. 1100 that "an older child should not be struck more than five times, nor a small one more than three, and the severity of the blows should be according to the strength of the individual children to stand them." Cf. E. Lévi-Provençal, "Le Traité d'Ibn 'Abdûn," *Journal asiatique*, CCXXIV (1934), 214; tr. by the same, *Séville musulmane au début du XIIe siècle* (Islam d'hier et d'aujourd'hui, No. 2) (Paris, 1947), pp. 53 f.

[27]   Shurayḥ. lived in the seventh century and is said to have been appointed judge of al-Kûfah by 'Umar. Cf. J. Schacht, *The Origins of Muhammadan Jurisprudence* (Oxford, 1950), pp. 228 f.

[28]   The story ofè the threefold choking is here understood as an educational measure, serving the purpose of teaching Muḥammad how to read the writing revealed to him by Gabriel.

[29]   Qur'ân 6.18 (18), 73 (73); 34.1 (1).

[30]   Qur'ân 90.10 (10).

[31]   Qur'ân 91.8 (8).

[32]   Cf. Issawi, pp. 105 f.

[25]   *Talâ* "he recited."

restraining influence to hold him back. The poet thus said:

Injustice is a human characteristic. If you find
A moral man,[33] there is some reason why he is not unjust.

Mutual aggression of people in towns and cities is averted by the authorities and the government, which hold back the masses under their control from attacks and aggression upon each other. They are thus prevented by the influence of force and governmental authority from mutual injustice, save such injustice as comes from the ruler himself.

Aggression against a city from outside may be averted by walls, in the event of negligence,[34] a surprise attack at night, or inability (of the inhabitants) to withstand the enemy during the day. (Or,) it may be averted with the help of a militia of government auxiliary troops, if (the inhabitants are otherwise) prepared and ready to offer resistance.

The[35] restraining influence among Bedouin tribes comes from their *shaykhs* and leaders. It results from the great respect and veneration they generally enjoy among the people. The hamlets of the Bedouins are defended against outside enemies by a tribal militia composed of noble youths of the tribe who are known for their courage. Their defense and protection are successful only if they are a closely-knit group[36] of common descent. This strengthens their stamina and makes them feared, since everybody's affection for his family and his group is more important (than anything else). Compassion and affection for one's blood relations and relatives exist in human nature as something God put into the hearts of men. It makes for mutual support and aid, and increases the fear felt by the enemy.

This may be exemplified by the story in the Qur'ân about Joseph's brothers. They said to their father: "If the wolf eats him, while we are a group, then, indeed, we have lost out."[37] This means that one cannot imagine any hostile act being undertaken against anyone who has his group feeling to support him.

Those who have no one of their own lineage (to care for) rarely feel affection for their fellows. If danger is in the air on the day of battle, such a one slinks away and seeks to save himself, because he is afraid of being left without support[38] and dreads (that prospect). Such people, therefore, cannot live in the desert, because they would fall prey to any nation that might want to swallow them up.

If this is true with regard to the place where one lives, which is in constant need of defense and military protection, it is equally true with regard to every other human activity, such as prophecy, the establishment of royal authority, or propaganda (for a cause). Nothing can be achieved in these matters without fighting for it, since man has the natural urge to offer resistance. And for fighting one cannot do without group feeling, as we mentioned at the beginning. This should be taken as the guiding principle of our later exposition.

God gives success.

Group Feeling Results Only From (Blood) Relationship or Something Corresponding to it

(Respect for) blood[39] ties is something natural among men, with the rarest exceptions. It leads to affection for one's relations and blood relatives, (the feeling that) no harm ought to befall them nor any destruction come upon them. One feels shame when one's relatives are treated unjustly or attacked, and one wishes to intervene between them and whatever peril or destruction threatens them. This is a natural urge in man, for as long as there have been human beings. If the direct relationship between persons who help each other is very close, so that it leads to close contact and unity, the ties are obvious and clearly require the (existence of a feeling of solidarity) without any outside (prodding). If, however, the relationship is somewhat distant, it is often forgotten in part. However, some knowledge of it remains and this causes a person to help his relatives for the known motive, in order to escape the shame he would feel in his soul were a person to whom he is somehow related treated unjustly.[40]

Clients and allies belong in the same category. The affection everybody has for his clients and allies results from the feeling of shame that comes to a person when one of his neighbors, relatives, or a blood relation in any degree (of kinship) is humiliated.

---

[33] '*Iffah* is the term picked by translators of Greek texts into Arabic for σωφροσύνη. The verse is by al-Mutanabbî'; cf. the appendix to the edition of his *Dîwân* (Beirut, 1882), II, 630, and ar-Râghib al-Iṣfahânî, *Muhâḍarât*, I, 140.

[34] That is, a general state of unpreparedness.

[35] The remainder of this section was translated by R. A. Nicholson, *Translations of Eastern Poetry and Prose*, pp. 181 f.

[36] Here the text has '*aṣabîyah* "group feeling," though '*uṣbah* "group" would seem better.

[37] Qur'ân 12.14 (14).

[38] Cf. R. Dozy in *Journal asiatique*, XIV[6] (1869), 152 f.

[39] Cf. Issawi, pp. 103f.

[40] Cf. Bombaci, pp. 446 f.

The reason for it is that a client (-master) relationship leads to close contact exactly, or approximately in the same way, as does common descent. . . .

Savage Nations are Better Able to Achieve Superiority than Others

It should be known that since, as we have stated in the Third Prefatory Discussion,[41] desert life no doubt is the reason for bravery, savage groups are braver than others. They are, therefore, better able to achieve superiority and to take away the things that are in the hands of other nations. The situation of one and the same group changes, in this respect, with the change of time. Whenever people settle in the fertile plains and amass[42] luxuries and become accustomed to a life of abundance and luxury, their bravery decreases to the degree that their wildness and desert habits decrease.

This is exemplified by dumb animals, such as gazelles, wild buffaloes (cows), and donkeys, that are domesticated. When they cease to be wild as the result of contact with human beings, and when they have a life of abundance, their vigor and violence undergo change. This affects even their movements and the beauty of their coat. The same applies to savage human beings who become sociable and friendly.

The reason is that familiar customs determine human nature and character. Superiority comes to nations through enterprise and courage. The more firmly rooted in desert habits and the wilder a group is, the closer does it come to achieving superiority over others, if both (parties are otherwise) approximately equal in number, strength, and group (feeling).

In this connection, one may compare the Muḍar with the Ḥimyar and the Kahlân before them, who preceded them in royal authority and in the life of luxury, and also with the Rabîʿah who settled in the fertile fields of the ʿIrâq. The Muḍar retained their desert habits, and the others embarked upon a life of abundance and great luxury before they did. Desert life prepared the Muḍar most effectively for achieving superiority. They took away and appropriated what the other groups had in their hands.

The same was the case also with the Banû Ṭayy,

the Banû ʿÂmir b. S.aʿṣaʿah, and the Banû Sulaym b. Manṣûr[43] later on. They remained longer in the desert than the other Muḍar and Yemenite tribes, and did not have any of their wealth. The desert habits thus preserved the power of their group feeling, and the habits of luxury did not wear it out. They thus eventually became the most powerful (group) among (the Arabs). Thus, wherever an Arab tribe leads a life of luxury and abundance, while another does not, the one holding fast to desert life the longer will be superior to and more powerful than the other, if both parties are (otherwise) equal in strength and number.

This is how God proceeds with His creatures.

The Goal to Which Group Feeling Leads Is Royal Authority

This[44] is because, as we have mentioned before, group feeling gives protection and makes possible mutual defense, the pressing of claims,[45] and every other kind of social activity. We have also mentioned before that according to their nature, human beings need someone to act as a restraining influence and mediator in every social organization, in order to keep the members from (fighting) with each other. That person must, by necessity, have superiority over the others in the matter of group feeling. If not, his power to (exercise a restraining influence) could not materialize. Such superiority is royal authority (*mulk*). It is more than leadership. Leadership means being a chieftain, and the leader is obeyed, but he has no power to force others to accept his rulings. Royal authority means superiority and the power to rule by force.

When a person sharing in the group feeling[46] has reached the rank of chieftain and commands obedience, and when he then finds the way open toward superiority and (the use of) force, he follows that way, because it is something desirable. He cannot completely achieve his (goal) except with the help of the group feeling, which causes (the others) to obey him. Thus, royal superiority is a goal to which group feeling leads, as one can see.

---

[41] In the paragraph called thus, nothing of the sort is said. Ibn Khaldûn mentions the subject in the fifth section of this chapter.

[42] Cf. R. Dozy in *Journal asiatique*, XIV[6] (1869), 153 f.

[43] This refers to the Arab tribes that invaded northwestern Africa in the eleventh century.

[44] Cf. Issawi, pp. 108 f.

[45] *Mutâlabah* might be more simply translated "aggression," but it should be kept in mind that it is a legal term, translatable as "action." Cf. D. Santillana, *Istituzioni di diritto musulmano malichita*, II, 3, 554.

[46] Bulaq adds: "has reached a certain rank, he aspires to the next higher one (and so on). When he then. . . ."

Even if an individual tribe has different "houses" and many diverse group feelings, still, there must exist a group feeling that is stronger than all the other group feelings combined, that is superior to them all and makes them subservient, and in which all the diverse group feelings coalesce, as it were, to become one greater group feeling. Otherwise, splits would occur and lead to dissension and strife. "If God did not keep human beings apart, the earth would perish."[47]

Once group feeling has established superiority over the people who share (in that particular group feeling), it will, by its very nature, seek superiority over people of other group feelings unrelated to the first. If the one (group feeling) is the equal of the other or is able to stave off (its challenge), the (competing people) are even with and equal to each other. (In this case,) each group feeling maintains its sway over its own domain and people, as is the case with tribes and nations all over the earth. However, if the one group feeling overpowers the other and makes it subservient to itself, the two group feelings enter into close contact, and the (defeated) group feeling gives added power to the (victorious) group feeling, which, as a result, sets its goal of superiority and domination higher than before. In this way, it goes on until the power of that particular group feeling equals the power of the ruling dynasty. Then, when the ruling dynasty grows senile and no defender arises from among its friends who share in its group feeling, the (new group feeling) takes over and deprives the ruling dynasty of its power, and, thus, obtains complete royal authority.

The power of (a given group feeling) may (also) reach its peak when the ruling dynasty has not yet reached senility. (This stage) may coincide with the stage at which (the ruling dynasty) needs to have recourse to the people who represent the various group feelings (in order to master the situation). In such a case, the ruling dynasty incorporates (the people who enjoy the powerful group feeling) among its clients whom it uses for the execution of its various projects. This, then, means (the formation of) another royal authority, inferior to that of the controlling royal authority. This was the case with the Turks under the 'Abbâsids,[48] with the Ṣinhâjah and the Zanâtah in their relation to the Kutâmah, and with the Ḥamdânids in their relation to the (Fâṭimid) 'Alids and the 'Abbâsids.

It is thus evident that royal authority is the goal of the group feeling. When (group feeling) attains that goal, the tribe (representing that particular group feeling) obtains royal authority, either by seizing actual control or by giving assistance (to the ruling dynasty). It depends on the circumstances prevailing at a given time (which of the two alternatives applies). If the group feeling encounters obstacles on its way to the goal, as we shall explain, it stops where it is, until God decides what is going to happen to it.

Obstacles on the Way Toward Royal Authority Are Luxury and the Submergence of the Tribe in a Life of Prosperity

The reason for this is that, when a tribe has achieved a certain measure of superiority with the help of its group feeling, it gains control over a corresponding amount of wealth and comes to share prosperity and abundance with those who have been in possession of these things (for a long time). It shares in them to the degree of its power and usefulness to the ruling dynasty. If the ruling dynasty is so strong that no one would think of depriving it of its power or sharing (its power) with it, the tribe in question submits to its rule and is satisfied with whatever share in the dynasty's wealth and tax revenue it is permitted to enjoy. Hopes would not go so high as to (think of) the royal prerogatives or ways to obtain the (royal authority. Members of the tribe) are merely concerned with prosperity, gain, and a life of abundance. (They are satisfied) to lead an easy, restful life in the shadow of the ruling dynasty, and to adopt royal habits in building and dress, a matter they stress and in which they take more and more pride, the more luxuries and plenty they obtain, as well as all the other things that go with luxury and plenty.

As a result, the toughness of desert life is lost. Group feeling and courage weaken. Members of the tribe revel in the well-being that God has given them. Their children and offspring grow up too proud to look after themselves or to attend to their own needs. They have disdain also for all the other things that are necessary in connection with group feeling. This finally becomes a character trait and natural characteristic of theirs. Their group feeling and courage decrease in the next generations. Eventually, group feeling is altogether destroyed. They thus invite (their) own destruction. The greater their luxury

---

[47] Qur'ân 2.251 (252).

[48] While the following two examples concern dynasties that made themselves independent, the first example is not quite of the same order. Ibn Khaldûn himself considers the Turks usurpers of control over the 'Abbâsid rulers. The reference to the 'Alids (Fâṭimids) in connection with the Ḥamdânids also does not appear to be exactly to the point.

and the easier the life they enjoy, the closer they are to extinction, not to mention (their lost chance of obtaining) royal authority. The things that go with luxury and submergence in a life of ease break the vigor of the group feeling, which alone produces superiority. When group feeling is destroyed, the tribe is no longer able to defend or protect itself, let alone press any claims. It will be swallowed up by other nations.

It has thus become clear that luxury is an obstacle on the way toward royal authority. "God gives His kingdom (royal authority) to whomever He wants to give it."[49] . . .

Injustice Brings About the Ruin of Civilization

It[50] should be known that attacks on people's property remove the incentive to acquire and gain property. People, then, become of the opinion that the purpose and ultimate destiny of (acquiring property) is to have it taken away from them. When the incentive to acquire and obtain property is gone, people no longer make efforts to acquire any. The extent and degree to which property rights are infringed upon determines the extent and degree to which the efforts of the subjects to acquire property slacken. When attacks (on property) are extensive and general, extending to all means of making a livelihood, business inactivity, too, becomes (general), because the general extent of (such attacks upon property) means a general destruction of the incentive (to do business). If the attacks upon property are but light, the stoppage of gainful activity is correspondingly slight. Civilization and its well-being as well as business prosperity depend on productivity and people's efforts in all directions in their own interest and profit. When people no longer do business in order to make a living, and when they cease all gainful activity, the business of civilization slumps, and everything decays. People scatter everywhere in search of sustenance, to places outside the jurisdiction of their present government. The population of the particular region becomes light. The settlements there become empty. The cities lie in ruins. The disintegration of (civilization) causes the disintegration of the status of dynasty and ruler, because (their peculiar status) constitutes the *form* of civilization and the form necessarily decays when its *matter* (in this case, civilization), decays.

One may compare (here) the story which al-Mas'ûdî tells in connection with the history of the Persians.[51] In the days of King Bahrâm b. Bahrâm, the Môbedhân, the chief religious dignitary among the Persians, expressed to the King his disapproval of the latter's injustice and neglect for the consequences that his injustice must bring upon the dynasty. He did this through a parable, which he placed in the mouth of an owl. The King, hearing the cry of (an owl), asked (the Môbedhân) whether he understood what it was saying. (The Môbedhân) replied: "A male owl wanted to marry a female owl. The female owl, as a condition prior to consent, asked the male owl for the gift of twenty villages ruined in the days of Bahrâm, that she might hoot in them. (The male owl) accepted her condition and said to her: 'If the King continues to rule, I shall give you a thousand ruined villages. This is of all wishes the easiest to fulfill.'"

The King was stirred out of his negligence by that story. He had a private (talk) with the Môbedhân and asked him what he had in mind. (The Môbedhân) replied: "O King, the might of royal authority materializes only through the religious law, obedience toward God, and compliance with His commands and prohibitions. The religious law persists only through royal authority. Mighty royal authority is achieved only through men. Men persist only with the help of property. The only way to property is through cultivation. The only way to cultivation is through justice. Justice is a balance set up among mankind. The Lord set it up and appointed an overseer of it, and that is the ruler. You, O King, went after the farms and took them away from their owners and cultivators. They are the people who pay the land tax and from whom one gets money. You gave their farms as fiefs to (your) entourage and servants and to sluggards. They did not cultivate (the farms) and did not heed the consequences. (They did not look for the things) that would be good for the farms. They were leniently treated with regard to the land tax (and were not asked to pay it), because they were close to the king. The remaining landowners who did pay the land tax and cultivated their farms had to carry an unjust burden. Therefore, they left their farms and abandoned their settlements. They took refuge in farms that were far away or difficult (of access), and lived on them. Thus, cultivation slackened, and the farms were ruined.

---

[49]   Qur'án 2.247 (248).
[50]   Cf. Issawi, pp. 84 f.

[51]   Cf. the English translation of this story from the Persian of Niẓâmî by E. G. Browne, *A Literary History of Persia* (London, 1902–24), II, 404.

There was little money, and soldiers and subjects perished. Neighboring rulers coveted the Persian realm, because they were aware of the fact that the basic materials that alone maintain the foundation of a realm had been cut off."

When the King heard that, he proceeded to look into (the affairs of) his realm. The farms were taken away from the intimates of the ruler and restored to their owners. They were again treated, as they had formerly been treated. They began to cultivate (their farms). Those who had been weak gained in strength. The land was cultivated, and the country became prosperous. There was much money for the collectors of the land tax. The army was strengthened. The enemies' sources of (strength) were cut off. The frontier garrisons were manned. The ruler proceeded to take personal charge of his affairs. His days were prosperous, and his realm was well organized.

The lesson this (story) teaches is that injustice ruins civilization. The ruin (of civilization) has as its consequence the complete destruction of the dynasty. In this connection, one should disregard the fact that dynasties (centered) in great cities often infringe upon justice and still are not ruined. It should be known that this is the result of a relationship that exists between such infringements and the situation of the urban population. When a city is large and densely populated and unlimited in the variety of its conditions, the loss it suffers from hostile acts and injustice is small, because such losses take place gradually. Because of the great variety of conditions and the manifold productivity of a particular city, any loss may remain concealed. Its consequences will become visible only after some time. Thus, the dynasty which committed the infringements (of justice) may be replaced before the city is ruined. Another dynasty may make its appearance and restore the city with the help of its wealth. Thus, the (previous) loss which had remained concealed, is made up and is scarcely noticed. This, however, happens only rarely. The proven fact is that civilization inevitably suffers losses through injustice and hostile acts, as we have mentioned, and it is the dynasty that suffers therefrom.

Injustice should not be understood to imply only the confiscation of money or other property from the owners, without compensation and without cause. It is commonly understood in that way, but it is something more general than that. Whoever takes someone's property, or uses him for forced labor, or presses an unjustified claim against him, or imposes upon him a duty not required by the religious law, does an injustice to that particular person. People who collect unjustified taxes commit an injustice. Those who infringe upon property (rights) commit an injustice. Those who take away property commit an injustice. Those who deny people their rights commit an injustice. Those who, in general, take property by force, commit an injustice. It is the dynasty that suffers from all these acts, in as much as civilization, which is the substance of the dynasty, is ruined when people have lost all incentive.

It should be known that this is what the Lawgiver (Muḥammad) actually had in mind when he forbade injustice. He meant the resulting destruction and ruin of civilization, which ultimately permits the eradication of the human species. This is what the religious law quite generally and wisely aims at in emphasizing five things as necessary: the preservation of (1) the religion, (2) the soul (life), (3) the intellect, (4) progeny, and (5) property.

Since, as we have seen, injustice calls for the eradication of the (human) species by leading to the ruin of civilization, it contains in itself a good reason for being prohibited. Consequently, it is important that it be forbidden. There is ample evidence for that in the Qur'ân and the Sunnah. It is much too ample to have it accurately or fully presented here.

If injustice were to be committed by every individual, the list of deterring punishments that would then have been given for it (in the religious law) would be as large as that given for the other (crimes) which lead to the destruction of the human species and which everybody is capable of committing, such as adultery, murder, and drunkenness. However, injustice can be committed only by persons who cannot be touched, only by persons who have power and authority. Therefore, injustice has been very much censured, and repeated threats against it have been expressed in the hope that perhaps the persons who are able to commit injustice will find a restraining influence in themselves.

"Your Lord does not do injustice to His servants."[52]

It should not be objected that punishment for highway robbery is provided for in the religious law,[53] and that (highway robbery) is an injustice that

---

[52] Qur'ân 41.46 (46). Cf. also Qur'ân 3.182 (178); 8.51 (53); 22.10 (10); 50.29 (28).

[53] Cf., for instance, Ibn Abî Zayd, *Risâlah*, ed. L. Bercher (3d ed.), pp. 250 ff.

can be committed only by someone who has the ability to commit it, in as much as the highway robber, when he commits the robbery, must have the ability to do it. The reply to that would be twofold:

First, it may be said that the punishment laid down for (highway robbery) is for crimes against life or property that (the highway robber) commits. This is an opinion held by many. The (punishment applies) only after one has gained power over him and brought him to account for his crime.[54] Highway robbery itself has no fixed legal punishment.

Second, it may be said that the highway robber cannot be described as having the ability (to commit injustice), because we understand by ability to commit injustice that the person has a free hand and there is no rival power, which means that he has (a power to) bring about (complete) ruin. The ability of the highway robber is merely an ability to cause fear. (This fear) then enables the highway robber to take away the property of others. Everyone may defend himself against it, according to both the religious and the political law. It is not, then, an ability that could bring about (complete) ruin.

God has power to do what He wishes.

One of the greatest injustices and one which contributes most to the destruction of civilization is the unjustified imposition of tasks and the use of subjects for forced labor. This is so because labor belongs to the things that constitute capital, as we shall explain in the chapter on sustenance. Gain and sustenance represent the value realized from labor among civilized people. All their efforts and all their labors are (means) for them (to acquire) capital and (to make a) profit. They have no other way to make a profit except (through labor). Subjects employed in cultural enterprises gain their livelihood and profit from such activities. Now, if they are obliged to work outside their own field and are used for forced labor unrelated to their (ordinary ways of) making a living, they no longer have any profit and are thus deprived of the price of their labor, which is their capital (asset). They suffer, and a good deal of their livelihood is gone, or even all of it. If this occurs repeatedly, all incentive to cultural enterprise is destroyed, and they cease utterly to make an effort. This leads to the destruction and ruin of civilization.

"God gives sustenance to whomever He wishes to give it, without accounting."[55]

An injustice even greater and more destructive of civilization and the dynasty than (the one just mentioned) is the appropriation of people's property by buying their possessions as cheaply as possible and then reselling the merchandise to them at the highest possible prices by means of forced sales and purchases. Often, people have to accept (high) prices with the privilege of later payment. They console (themselves) for the loss they suffer (at the moment) with the hope that the market will fluctuate in favor of the merchandise that had been sold to them at such a high price, and that their loss will be canceled later on. But then, they are required to make payment at once, and they are forced to sell the merchandise at the lowest possible price. The loss involved in the two transactions affects their capital.

This (situation) affects all kinds of merchants, those resident in town and those who import merchandise from elsewhere. (It also affects) the peddlers and shopkeepers who deal in food and fruit, as well as the craftsmen who deal in the instruments and implements that are in general use. The loss affects all professions and classes quite generally. This goes on from hour to hour.[56] It causes (all) capital funds to dwindle. The only possibility that remains is for the merchants to go out of business, because their capital is gone, as it can no longer be restored by the profits. Merchants who come from elsewhere for the purchase and sale of merchandise are slow to come, because of that situation. Business declines, and the subjects lose their livelihood, which, generally, comes from trading. Therefore, if no (trading) is being done in the markets, they have no livelihood, and the tax revenue of the ruler decreases or deteriorates, since, in the middle (period) of a dynasty and later on, most of the tax revenue comes from customs duties on commerce, as we have stated before.[57] This leads to the dissolution of the dynasty and the decay of urban civilization. The disintegration comes about gradually and imperceptibly.

This happens whenever the ways and means of seizing property described above are used. On the

---

[54] Ergo, it cannot be said that the highway robber still has the special ability to commit his crime, at the time the punishment becomes applicable.

[55] Qur'ân 2.212 (208); 3.37 (32); 24.38 (38).

[56] 'Alâ s-sâ'ât, as in Bulaq and MSS. A, B, and D. (C is supplied by a later hand in this section, indistinctly.) Paris has 'alâ l-bayâ'ât "affects the trading."

[57] Cf. pp. 90 f., above, where it is said that in the later years of a dynasty, customs duties are levied. Cf. also pp. 97 ff., where it is said that only in the middle period of a dynasty are the ruler and his entourage wealthy.

other hand, if (the property) is taken outright and if the hostile acts are extended to affect the property, the wives, the lives, the skins,[58] and the honor of people, it will lead to sudden disintegration and decay and the quick destruction of the dynasty. It will result in disturbances leading to complete destruction.

On account of these evil (consequences), all such (unfair activities) are prohibited by the religious law. The religious law legalizes the use of cunning in trading, but forbids depriving people of the property illegally. The purpose is to prevent such evil (consequences), which would lead to the destruction of civilization through disturbances or the lack of opportunity to make a living.

[58]   This refers to corporal punishment, torture, and the like.

It should be known that all these (practices) are caused by the need for more money on the part of dynasty and ruler, because they have become accustomed to luxurious living. Their expenditures increase, and much spending is done. The ordinary income does not meet (the expenditures). Therefore, the ruler invents new sorts and kinds of taxes, in order to increase the revenues and to be able to balance the budget. But luxury continues to grow, and spending increases on account of it. The need for (appropriating) people's property becomes stronger and stronger. In this way, the authority of the dynasty shrinks until its influence is wiped out and its identity lost and it is defeated by an attacker.

God determines all affairs. There is no Lord except Him.

Thomas Hobbes (1588–1679)
FROM *LEVIATHAN*

The author argues that there is no law, hence no injustice, in a state of nature. Yet general rules of reason apply to such a situation. The first is that every human being aim at peace as far as he or she can attain it, but when its attainment is impossible, war is permissible. The second rule of reason is to defend ourselves by all the means we can muster. See Section B of the introductory essay to Part IV for an analysis of Hobbes's secular view of natural law.

READING QUESTIONS

In reading the selection, try to answer the following questions and identify the passages that support your answers:

1.   What is Hobbes's conception of human nature?
2.   What is his conception of the state of nature?
3.   Does Hobbes think that justice applies in the state of nature?
4.   What reasons does he give for his views?
5.   Are they good? Why or why not?

Reprinted from Thomas Hobbes, *Leviathan* (New York: Dutton, 1914; repr. 1947), Chapters. XIII through XVII, pp. 63–90.

CHAP. XIII

Of the Naturall Condition of Mankind, as concerning their Felicity, and Misery

NATURE hath made men so equall, in the faculties of body, and mind; as that though there bee found one man sometimes manifestly stronger in body, or of quicker mind then another; yet when all is reckoned together, the difference between man, and man, is not so considerable, as that one man can thereupon claim to himselfe any benefit, to which another may not pretend, as well as he. For as to the strength of body, the weakest has strength enough to kill the strongest, either by secret machination, or by confederacy with others, that are in the same danger with himselfe.

And as to the faculties of the mind, (setting aside the arts grounded upon words, and especially that skill of proceeding upon generall, and infallible rules, called Science; which very few have, and but in few things; as being not a native faculty, born with us; nor attained, (as Prudence,) while we look after somewhat els,) I find yet a greater equality amongst men, than that of strength. For Prudence, is but Experience; which equall time, equally bestowes on all men, in those things they equally apply themselves unto. That which may perhaps make such equality incredible, is but a vain conceipt of ones owne wisdome, which almost all men think they have in a greater degree, than the Vulgar; that is, than all men but themselves, and a few others, whom by Fame, or for concurring with themselves, they approve. For such is the nature of men, that howsoever they may acknowledge many others to be more witty, or more eloquent, or more learned; Yet they will hardly beleeve there be many so wise as themselves: For they see their own wit at hand, and other mens at a distance. But this proveth rather that men are in that point equall, than unequall. For there is not ordinarily a greater signe of the equall distribution of any thing, than that every man is contented with his share.

From this equality of ability, ariseth equality of hope in the attaining of our Ends. And therefore if any two men desire the same thing, which neverthelesse they cannot both enjoy, they become enemies; and in the way to their End, (which is principally their owne conservation, and sometimes their delectation only,) endeavour to destroy, or subdue one an another. And from hence it comes to passe, that where an Invader hath no more to feare, than an other mans single power; if one plant, sow, build, or possesse a convenient Seat, others may probably be expected to come prepared with forces united, to dispossesse, and deprive him, not only of the fruit of his labour, but also of his life, or liberty. And the Invader again is in the like danger of another.

And from this diffidence of one another, there is no way for any man to secure himselfe, so reasonable, as Anticipation; that is, by force, or wiles, to master the persons of all men he can, so long, till he see no other power great enough to endanger him: And this is no more than his own conservation requireth, and is generally allowed. Also because there be some, that taking pleasure in contemplating their own power in the acts of conquest, which they pursue farther than their security requires; if others, that otherwise would be glad to be at ease within modest bounds, should not by invasion increase their power, they would not be able, long time, by standing only on their defence, to subsist. And by consequence, such augmentation of dominion over men, being necessary to a mans conservation, it ought to be allowed him.

Againe, men have no pleasure, (but on the contrary a great deale of griefe) in keeping company, where there is no power able to overawe them all. For every man looketh that his companion should value him, at the same rate he sets upon himselfe: And upon all signes of contempt, or undervaluing, naturally endeavours, as far as he dares (which amongst them that have no common power to keep them in quiet, is far enough to make them destroy each other,) to extort a greater value from his contemners, by dommage; and from others, by the example.

So that in the nature of man, we find three principall causes of quarrell. First, Competition; Secondly, Diffidence; Thirdly, Glory.

The first, maketh men invade for Gain; the second, for Safety; and the third, for Reputation. The first use Violence, to make themselves Masters of other mens persons, wives, children, and cattell; the second, to defend them; the third, for trifles, as a word, a smile, a different opinion, and any other signe of undervalue, either direct in their Persons, or by reflexion in their Kindred, their Friends, their Nation, their Profession, or their Name.

Hereby it is manifest, that during the time men live without a common Power to keep them all in awe, they are in that condition which is called Warre; and such a warre, as is of every man, against every man. For WARRE, consisteth not in Battell onely, or the act of fighting; but in a tract of time, wherein the

Will to contend by Battell is sufficiently known: and therefore the notion of *Time*, is to be considered in the nature of Warre; as it is in the nature of Weather. For as the nature of Foule weather, lyeth not in a showre or two of rain; but in an inclination thereto of many dayes together; So the nature of War, consisteth not in actuall fighting; but in the known disposition thereto, during all the time there is no assurance to the contrary. All other time is Peace.

Whatsoever therefore is consequent to a time of Warre, where every man is Enemy to every man; the same is consequent to the time, wherein men live without other security, than what their own strength, and their own invention shall furnish them withall. In such condition, there is no place for Industry; because the fruit thereof is uncertain: and consequently no Culture of the Earth; no Navigation, nor use of the commodities that may be imported by Sea; no commodious Building; no Instruments of moving, and removing such things as require much force; no Knowledge of the face of the Earth; no account of Time; no Arts; no Letters; no Society; and which is worst of all, continuall feare, and danger of violent death; And the life of man, solitary, poore, nasty, brutish, and short.

It may seem strange to some man, that has not well weighed these things; that Nature should thus dissociate, and render men apt to invade, and destroy one another: and he may therefore, not trusting to this Inference, made from the Passions, desire perhaps to have the same confirmed by Experience. Let him therefore consider with himselfe, when taking a journey, he armes himselfe, and seeks to go well accompanied; when going to sleep, he locks his dores; when even in his house he locks his chests; and this when he knowes there bee Lawes, and publike Officers, armed; to revenge all injuries shall bee done him; what opinion he has of his fellow subjects, when he rides armed; of his fellow Citizens, when he locks his dores; and of his children, and servants, when he locks his chests. Does he not there as much accuse mankind by his actions, as I do by my words? But neither of us accuse mans nature in it. The Desires, and other Passions of man, are in themselves no Sin. No more are the Actions, that proceed from those Passions, till they know a Law that forbids them: which till Lawes be made they cannot know: nor can any Law be made, till they have agreed upon the Person that shall make it.

It may peradventure be thought, there was never such a time, nor condition of warre as this; and I believe it was never generally so, over all the world: but there are many places, where they live so now. For the savage people in many places of *America*, except the government of small Families, the concord whereof dependeth on naturall lust, have no government at all; and live at this day in that brutish manner, as I said before. Howsoever, it may be perceived what manner of life there would be, where there were no common Power to feare; by the manner of life, which men that have formerly lived under a peacefull government, use to degenerate into, in a civill Warre.

But though there had never been any time, wherein particular men were in a condition of warre one against another; yet in all times, Kings, and Persons of Soveraigne authority, because of their Independency, are in continuall jealousies, and in the state and posture of Gladiators; having their weapons pointing, and their eyes fixed on one another; that is, their Forts, Garrisons, and Guns, upon the Frontiers of their Kingdomes; and continuall Spyes upon their neighbours; which is a posture of War. But because they uphold thereby, the Industry of their Subjects; there does not follow from it, that misery, which accompanies the Liberty of particular men.

To this warre of every man against every man, this also is consequent; that nothing can be Unjust. The notions of Right and Wrong, Justice and Injustice have there no place. Where there is no common Power, there is no Law: where no Law, no Injustice. Force, and Fraud, are in warre the two Cardinall vertues. Justice, and Injustice are none of the Faculties neither of the Body, nor Mind. If they were, they might be in a man that were alone in the world, as well as his Senses, and Passions. They are Qualities, that relate to men in Society, not in Solitude. It is consequent also to the same condition, that there be no Propriety, no Dominion, no *Mine* and *Thine* distinct; but onely that to be every mans, that he can get; and for so long, as he can keep it. And thus much for the ill condition, which man by meer Nature is actually placed in; though with a possibility to come out of it, consisting partly in the Passions, partly in his Reason.

The Passions that encline men to Peace, are Feare of Death; Desire of such things as are necessary to commodious living; and a Hope by their Industry to obtain them. And Reason suggesteth convenient Articles of Peace, upon which men may be drawn to agreement. These Articles, are they, which otherwise are called the Lawes of Nature: whereof I shall speak more particularly, in the two following Chapters.

CHAP. XIV

Of the first and second Natural Lawes, and of Contracts

THE RIGHT OF NATURE, which Writers commonly call *Jus Naturale,* is the Liberty each man hath, to use his own power, as he will himselfe, for the preservation of his own Nature; that is to say, of his own Life; and consequently, of doing any thing, which in his own Judgement, and Reason, hee shall conceive to be the aptest means thereunto.

By LIBERTY, is understood, according to the proper signification of the word, the absence of externall Impediments: which Impediments, may oft take away part of a mans power to do what hee would; but cannot hinder him from using the power left him, according as his judgement, and reason shall dictate to him.

A LAW OF NATURE, (*Lex Naturalis,*) is a precept, or generall Rule, found out by Reason, by which a man is forbidden to do, that, which is destructive of his life, or taketh away the means of preserving the same; and to omit, that, by which he thinketh it may be best preserved. For though they that speak of this subject, use to confound *Jus,* and *Lex, Right* and *Law;* yet they ought to be distinguished; because RIGHT, consisteth in liberty to do, or to forbeare; Whereas LAW, determineth, and bindeth to one of them: so that Law and Right, differ as much, as Obligation, and Liberty; which in one and the same matter are inconsistent.

And because the condition of Man, (as hath been declared in the precedent Chapter) is a condition of Warre of every one against every one; in which case every one is governed by his own Reason; and there is nothing he can make use of, that may not be a help unto him, in preserving his life against his enemyes; It followeth, that in such a condition, every man has a Right to every thing; even to one anothers body. And therefore, as long as this naturall Right of every man to every thing endureth, there can be no security to any man, (how strong or wise soever he be,) of living out the time, which Nature ordinarily alloweth men to live. And consequently it is a precept, or general rule of Reason, *That every man, ought to endeavour Peace, as farre as he has hope of obtaining it; and when he cannot obtain it, that he may seek, and use, all helps, and advantages of Warre.* The first branch of which Rule, containeth the first, and Fundamentall Law of Nature; which is, *to seek Peace, and follow it.* The Second, the summe of the Right of Nature; which is, *By all means we can, to defend our selves.*

From this Fundamentall Law of Nature, by which men are commanded to endeavour Peace, is derived this second Law; *That a man be willing, when others are so too, as farre-forth, as for Peace, and defence of himselfe he shall think it necessary, to lay down this right to all things; and be contented with so much liberty against other men, as he would allow other men against himselfe.* For as long as every man holdeth this Right, of doing any thing he liketh; so long are all men in the condition of Warre. But if other men will not lay down their Right, as well as he; then there is no Reason for any one, to devest himselfe of his: For that were to expose himselfe to Prey, (which no man is bound to) rather than to dispose himselfe to Peace. This is that Law of the Gospell; *Whatsoever you require that others should do to you, that do ye to them.* And that Law of all men, *Quod tibi fieri non vis, alteri ne feceris.*

To *lay downe* a mans *Right* to any thing, is to *devest* himselfe of the *Liberty,* of hindring another of the benefit of his own Right to the same. For he that renounceth, or passeth away his Right, giveth not to any other man a Right which he had not before; because there is nothing to which every man had not Right by Nature: but onely standeth out of his way, that he may enjoy his own originall Right, without hindrance from him; not without hindrance from another. So that the effect which redoundeth to one man, by another mans defect of Right, is but so much diminution of impediments to the use of his own Right originall.

Right is layd aside, either by simply Renouncing it; or by Transferring it to another. By *Simply* RENOUNCING; when he cares not to whom the benefit thereof redoundeth. By TRANSFERRING; when he intendeth the benefit thereof to some certain person, or persons. And when a man hath in either manner abandoned, or granted away his Right; then is he said to be OBLIGED or BOUND, not to hinder those, to whom such Right is granted, or abandoned, from the benefit of it: and that he *Ought,* and it is his DUTY, not to make voyd that voluntary act of his own: and that such hindrance is INJUSTICE, and INJURY, as being *Sine Jure;* the Right being before renounced, or transferred. So that *Injury,* or *Injustice,* in the controversies of the world, is somewhat like to that, which in the disputations of Scholers is called *Absurdity.* For as it is there called an Absurdity, to contradict what one maintained in the Beginning: so in the world, it is called Injustice, and Injury, voluntarily to undo that, which from the beginning he had voluntarily done. The way by which a man either simply Renounceth, or Transferreth his Right, is a Declaration, or Signification, by some voluntary and sufficient signe, or signes, that he doth so Renounce, or Transferre; or hath so Renounced, or Transferred the same, to him that accepteth it. And these Signes are either Words onely, or Actions onely; or (as it happeneth most often) both Words, and Actions. And the same are the BONDS, by which men are bound, and obliged: Bonds, that have their strength, not from their own Nature, (for nothing is more easily broken then a mans word,) but from Feare of some evill consequence upon the rupture.

Whensoever a man Transferreth his Right, or Renounceth it; it is either in consideration of some Right reciprocally transferred to himselfe; or for some other good he hopeth for thereby. For it is a voluntary act: and of the voluntary acts of every man, the object is some *Good to himselfe*. And therefore there be some Rights, which no man can be understood by any words, or other signes, to have abandoned, or transferred. As first a man cannot lay down the right of resisting them, that assault him by force, to take away his life; because he cannot be understood to ayme thereby, at any Good to himselfe. The same may be sayd of Wounds, and Chayns, and Imprisonment; both because there is no benefit consequent to such patience; as there is to the patience of suffering another to be wounded, or imprisoned: as also because a man cannot tell, when he seeth men proceed against him by violence, whether they intend his death or not. And lastly the motive, and end for which this renouncing, and transferring of Right is introduced, is nothing else but the security of a mans person, in his life, and in the means of so preserving life, as not to be weary of it. And therefore if a man by words, or other signes, seem to despoyle himselfe of the End, for which those signes were intended; he is not to be understood as if he meant it, or that it was his will; but that he was ignorant of how such words and actions were to be interpreted.

The mutuall transferring of Right, is that which men call CONTRACT.

There is difference, between transferring of Right to the Thing; and transferring, or tradition, that is, delivery of the Thing it selfe. For the Thing may be delivered together with the Translation of the Right; as in buying and selling with ready mony; or exchange of goods, or lands: and it may be delivered some time after.

Again, one of the Contractors, may deliver the Thing contracted for on his part, and leave the other to perform his part at some determinate time after, and in the mean time be trusted; and then the Contract on his part, is called PACT, or COVENANT: Or both parts may contract now, to performe hereafter: in which cases, he that is to performe in time to come, being trusted, his performance is called *Keeping of Promise,* or Faith; and the fayling of performance (if it be voluntary), *Violation of Faith.*

When the transferring of Right, is not mutuall; but one of the parties transferreth, in hope to gain thereby friendship, or service from another, or from his friends; or in hope to gain the reputation of Charity, or Magnanimity; or to deliver his mind from the pain of compassion; or in hope of reward in heaven; This is not Contract, but GIFT, FREE-GIFT, GRACE: which words signifie one and the same thing.

Signes of Contract, are either *Expresse,* or *by Inference.* Expresse, are words spoken with understanding of what they signifie: And such words are either of the time *Present,* or *Past;* as, *I Give, I Grant, I have Given, I have Granted, I will that this be yours:* Or of the future; as, *I will Give, I will Grant:* which words of the future, are called PROMISE.

Signes by Inference, are sometimes the consequence of Words; sometimes the consequence of Silence; sometimes the consequence of Actions; sometimes the consequence of Forbearing an Action: and generally a signe by Inference, of any Contract, is whatsoever sufficiently argues the will of the Contractor.

Words alone, if they be of the time to come, and contain a bare promise, are an insufficient signe of a Free-gift and therefore not obligatory. For if they be of the time to Come, as, *To morrow I will Give,* they are a signe I have not given yet, and consequently that my right is not transferred, but remaineth till I transferre it by some other Act. But if the words be of the time Present, or Past, as, *I have given, or do give to be delivered to morrow,* then is my to morrows Right given away to day; and that by the vertue of the words, though there were no other argument of my will. And there is a great difference in the signification of these words, *Volo hoc twum esse cras,* and *Cras dabo;* that is, between *I will that this be thine to morrow,* and, *I will give it thee to morrow:* For the word *I will,* in the former manner of speech, signifies an act of the will Present; but in the later, it signifies a promise of an act of the will to Come: and therefore the former words, being of the Present, transferre a future right; the later, that be of the Future, transferre nothing. But if there be other signes of the Will to transferre a Right, besides Words; then, though the gift be Free, yet may the Right be understood to passe by words of the future: as if a man propound a Prize to him that comes first to the end of a race, The gift is Free; and though the words be of the Future, yet the Right passeth: for if he would not have his words so be understood, he should not have let them runne.

In Contracts, the right passeth, not onely where the words are of the time Present, or Past; but also where they are of the Future: because all Contract is mutuall translation, or change of Right; and therefore he that promiseth onely, because he hath already received the benefit for which he promiseth, is to be understood as if he intended the Right should passe: for unless he had been content to have his words so understood, the other would not have performed his part first. And for that cause, in buying, and selling, and other acts of Contract, a Promise is equivalent to a Covenant; and therefore obligatory.

He that performeth first in the case of a Contract, is said to MERIT that which he is to receive by the performance of the other; and he hath it as *Due.* Also when a Prize is propounded to many, which is to be given to him only that winneth; or mony is thrown amongst many, to be enjoyed by them that catch it; though this be a Free gift; yet so to Win, or so to Catch, is to *Merit,* and to have it as DUE. For the Right is transferred in the Propounding of the Prize, and in throwing down the mony; though it be not determined to whom, but by the Event of the contention. But there is between these two sorts of Merit, this difference, that In Contract, I Merit by vertue of my own power, and the Contractors need; but in this case of Free gift, I am enabled to Merit onely by the benignity of the Giver: In Contract, I merit at the Contractors hand that he should depart with his right; In this case of Gift, I Merit not that the giver should part with his right; but that when he has parted with it, it should be mine, rather than anothers. And this I think to be the meaning of that distinction of the Schooles, between *Meritum congrui,* and *Meritum condigni.* For God Almighty, having promised Paradise to those men (hoodwinkt with carnall desires,) that can walk through this world according to the Precepts, and Limits prescribed by him; they say, he that shall so walk, shall Merit Paradise *Ex congruo.* But because no man can demand a right to it, by his own Righteousnesse, or any other power in himselfe, but by the Free Grace of God onely; they say, no man can Merit Paradise *ex condigno.* This I say, I think is the meaning of that distinction; but because Disputers do not agree upon the signification of their own termes of Art, longer

than it serves their turn; I will not affirme any thing of their meaning: onely this I say; when a gift is given indefinitely, as a prize to be contended for, he that winneth Meriteth, and may claime the Prize as Due.

If a Covenant be made, wherein neither of the parties performe presently, but trust one another; in the condition of meer Nature, (which is a condition of Warre of every man against every man,) upon any reasonable suspition, it is Voyd: But if there be a common Power set over them both, with right and force sufficient to compell performance; it is not Voyd. For he that performeth first, has no assurance the other will performe after; because the bonds of words are too weak to bridle mens ambition, avarice, anger, and other Passions, without the feare of some coerceive Power; which in the condition of meer Nature, where all men are equall, and judges of the justnesse of their own fears, cannot possibly be supposed. And therefore he which performeth first, does but betray himselfe to his enemy; contrary to the Right (he can never abandon) of defending his life, and means of living.

But in a civill estate, where there is a Power set up to constrain those that would otherwise violate their faith, that feare is no more reasonable; and for that cause, he which by the Covenant is to perform first, is obliged so to do.

The cause of feare, which maketh such a Covenant invalid, must be alwayes something arising after the Covenant made; as some new fact, or other signe of the Will not to performe: else it cannot make the Covenant voyd. For that which could not hinder a man from promising, ought not to be admitted as a hindrance of performing.

He that transferreth any Right, transferreth the Means of enjoying it, as farre as lyeth in his power. As he that selleth Land, is understood to transferre the Herbage, and whatsoever growes upon it; Nor can he that sells a Mill turn away the Stream that drives it. And they that give a man the Right of government in Soveraignty, are understood to give him the right of levying mony to maintain Souldiers; and of appointing Magistrates for the administration of Justice.

To make Covenants with bruit Beasts, is impossible; because not understanding our speech, they understand not, nor accept of any translation of Right; nor can translate any Right to another: and without mutuall acceptation, there is no Covenant.

To make Covenant with God, is impossible, but by Mediation of such as God speaketh to, either by Revelation supernaturall, or by his Lieutenants that govern under him, and in his Name: For otherwise we know not whether our Covenants be accepted, or not. And therefore they that Vow any thing contrary to any law of Nature, Vow in vain; as being a thing unjust to pay such Vow. And if it be a thing commanded by the Law of Nature, it is not the Vow, but the Law that binds them.

The matter, or subject of a Covenant, is alwayes something that falleth under deliberation; (For to Covenant, is an act of the Will; that is to say an act, and the last act, of deliberation;) and is therefore alwayes understood to be something to come; and which is judged Possible for him that Covenanteth to performe.

And therefore, to promise that which is known to be Impossible, is no Covenant. But if that prove impossible afterwards, which before was thought possible, the Covenant is valid, and bindeth, (though not to the thing it selfe,) yet to the value; or, if that also be impossible, to the unfeigned endeavour of performing as much as is possible: for to more no man can be obliged.

Men are freed of their Covenants two wayes; by Performing; or by being Forgiven. For Performance, is the naturall end of obligation; and Forgivenesse, the restitution of liberty; as being a re-transferring of that Right, in which the obligation consisted.

Covenants entred into by fear, in the condition of meer Nature, are obligatory. For example, if I Covenant to pay a ransome, or service for my life, to an enemy; I am bound by it. For it is a Contract, wherein one receiveth the benefit of life; the other is to receive mony, or service for it; and consequently, where no other Law (as in the condition, of meer nature) forbiddeth the performance, the Covenant is valid. Therefore Prisoners of warre, if trusted with the payment of their Ransome, are obliged to pay it: And if a weaker Prince, make a disadvantageous peace with a stronger, for feare; he is bound to keep it; unlesse (as hath been sayd before) there ariseth some new, and just cause of feare, to renew the war. And even in Common-wealths, if I be forced to redeem my selfe from a Theefe by promising him mony, I am bound to pay it, till the Civill Law discharge me. For whatsoever I may lawfully do without Obligation, the same I may lawfully Covenant to do through feare: and what I lawfully Covenant, I cannot lawfully break.

A former Covenant makes voyd a later. For a man that hath passed away his Right to one man to day, hath it not to passe to morrow to another: and therefore the later promise passeth no Right, but is null.

A Covenant not to defend my selfe from force, by force, is alwayes voyd. For (as I have shewed before) no man can transferre, or lay down his Right to save himselfe from Death, Wounds, and Imprisonment, (the avoyding whereof is the onely End of laying down any Right, and therefore the promise of not resisting force, in no Covenant transferreth any right; nor is obliging. For though a man may Covenant thus, *Unlesse I do so, or so, kill me;* he cannot Covenant thus, *Unlesse I do so, or so, I will not resist you, when you come to kill me.* For man by nature chooseth the lesser evill, which is danger of death in resisting; rather than the greater, which is certain and present death in not resisting. And this is granted to be true by all men, in that they lead Criminals to Execution, and Prison, with armed men, notwithstanding that such Criminals have consented to the Law, by which they are condemned.

A Covenant to accuse ones selfe, without assurance of pardon, is likewise invalide. For in the condition of Nature, where every man is Judge, there is no place for Accusation: and in the Civill State, the Accusation is followed with Punishment; which being Force, a man is not obliged not to resist. The same is also true, of the Accusation of those, by whose Condemnation a man falls into misery; as of a Father, Wife, or Benefactor.

For the Testimony of such an Accuser, if it be not willingly given, is presumed to be corrupted by Nature; and therefore not to be received: and where a mans Testimony is not to be credited, he is not bound to give it. Also Accusations upon Torture, are not to be reputed as Testimonies. For Torture is to be used but as means of conjecture, and light, in the further examination, and search of truth: and what is in that case confessed, tendeth to the ease of him that is Tortured; not to the informing of the Torturers: and therefore ought not to have the credit of a sufficient Testimony: for whether he deliver himselfe by true, or false Accusation, he does it by the Right of preserving his own life.

The force of Words, being (as I have formerly noted) too weak to hold men to the performance of their Covenants; there are in mans nature, but two imaginable helps to strengthen it. And those are either a Feare of the consequence of breaking their word; or a Glory, or Pride in appearing not to need to breake it. This later is a Generosity too rarely found to be presumed on, especially in the pursuers of Wealth, Command, or sensuall Pleasure; which are the greatest part of Mankind. The Passion to be reckoned upon, is Fear; whereof there be two very generall Objects: one, The Power of Spirits Invisible;

the other, The Power of those men they shall therein Offend. Of these two, though the former be the greater Power, yet the feare of the later is commonly the greater Feare. The Feare of the former is in every man, his own Religion, which hath place in the nature of man before Civill Society. The later hath not so; at least not place enough, to keep men to their promises; because in the condition of meer Nature, the inequality of Power is not discerned, but by the event of Battell. So that before the time of Civill Society, or in the interruption thereof by Warre, there is nothing can strengthen a Covenant of Peace agreed on, against the temptations of Avarice, Ambition, Lust, or other strong desire, but the feare of that Invisible Power, which they every one Worship as God; and Feare as a Revenger of their perfidy. All therefore that can be done between two men not subject to Civill Power, is to put one another to swear by the God he feareth: Which *Swearing*, or OATH, is a *Forme of Speech, added to a Promise; by which he that promiseth, signifieth, that unlesse he performe, he renounceth the mercy of his God, or calleth to him for vengeance on himselfe.* Such was the Heathen Forme, *Let* Jupiter *kill me else, as I kill this Beast.* So is our Forme, *I shall do thus, and thus, so help me God.* And this, with the Rites and Ceremonies, which every one useth in his own Religion, that the feare of breaking faith might be the greater.

By this it appears, that an Oath taken according to any other Forme, or Rite; then his, that sweareth, is in vain; and no Oath: And that there is no Swearing by any thing which the Swearer thinks not God. For though men have sometimes used to swear by their Kings, for feare, or flattery; yet they would have it thereby understood, they attributed to them Divine honour. And that Swearing unnecessarily by God, is but prophaning of his name: and Swearing by other things, as men do in common discourse, is not Swearing, but an impious Custome, gotten by too much vehemence of talking.

It appears also, that the Oath addes nothing to the Obligation. For a Covenant, if lawfull, binds in the sight of God, without the Oath, as much as with it: if unlawfull, bindeth not at all; though it be confirmed with an Oath.

CHAP. XV

Of Other Lawes of Nature

FROM that law of Nature, by which we are obliged to transferre to another, such Rights, as being retained, hinder the peace of Mankind, there followeth a

Third; which is this, *That men performe their Covenants made:* without which, Covenants are in vain, and but Empty words; and the Right of all men to all things remaining, wee are still in the condition of Warre.

And in this law of Nature, consisteth the Fountain and Originall of JUSTICE. For where no Covenant hath preceded, there hath no Right been transferred, and every man has right to every thing; and consequently, no action can be Unjust. But when a Covenant is made, then to break it is *Unjust:* And the definition of INIUSTICE, is no other than *the not Performance of Covenant.* And whatsoever is not Unjust, is *Just.*

But because Covenants of mutuall trust, where there is a feare of not performance on either part, (as hath been said in the former Chapter,) are invalid; though the Originall of Justice be the making of Covenants; yet Injustice actually there can be none, till the cause of such feare be taken away; which while men are in the naturall condition of Warre, cannot be done. Therefore before the names of Just, and Unjust can have place, there must be some coërcive Power, to compell men equally to the performance of their Covenants, by the terrour of some punishment, greater than the benefit they expect by the breach of their Covenant; and to make good that Propriety, which by mutuall Contract men acquire, in recompence of the universall Right they abandon: and such power there is none before the erection of a Common-wealth. And this is also to be gathered out of the ordinary definition of Justice in the Schooles: For they say, that *Justice is the constant Will of giving to every men his own.* And therefore where there is no *Own,* that is, no Propriety, there is no Injustice; and where there is no coërcive Power erected, that is, where there is no Common-wealth, there is no Propriety; all men having Right to all things: Therefore where there is no Common-wealth, there is nothing Unjust. So that the nature of Justice, consisteth in keeping of valid Covenants: but the Validity of Covenants begins not but with the Constitution of a Civill Power, sufficient to compell men to keep them: And then it is also that Propriety begins.

The Foole hath sayd in his heart, there is no such thing as Justice; and sometimes also with his tongue; seriously alleaging, that every mans conservation, and contentment, being committed to his own care, there could be no reason, why every man might not do what he thought conduced thereunto: and therefore also to make, or not make; keep, or not keep Covenants, was not against Reason, when it conduced to ones benefit. He does not therein deny, that there be Covenants; and that they are sometimes broken, sometimes kept; and that such breach of them may be called Injustice, and the observance of them Justice: but he questioneth, whether Injustice, taking away the feare of God, (for the same Foole hath said in his heart there is no God,) may not sometimes stand with that Reason, which dictateth to every man his own good; and particularly then, when it conduceth to such a benefit, as shall put a man in a condition, to neglect not onely the dispraise, and revilings, but also the power of other men. The Kingdome of God is gotten by violence: but what if it could be gotten by unjust violence? were it against Reason so to get it, when it is impossible to receive hurt by it? and if it be not against Reason, it is not against Justice: or else Justice is not to be approved for good. From such reasoning as this, Successfull wickednesse hath obtained the name of Vertue: and some that in all other things have disallowed the violation of Faith; yet have allowed it, when it is for the getting of a Kingdome. And the Heathen that believed, that *Saturn* was deposed by his son *Jupiter,* believed neverthelesse the same *Jupiter* to be the avenger of Injustice: Somewhat like to a piece of Law in *Cokes* Commentaries on *Litleton;* where he sayes, If the right Heire of the Crown be attainted of Treason; yet the Crown shall descend to him, and *eo instante* the Atteynder be voyd: From which instances a man will be very prone to inferre; that when the Heire apparent of a Kingdome, shall kill him that is in possession, though his father; you may call it Injustice, or by what other name you will; yet it can never be against Reason, seeing all the voluntary actions of men tend to the benefit of themselves; and those actions are most Reasonable, that conduce most to their ends. This specious reasoning is neverthelesse false.

For the question is not of promises mutuall, where there is no security of performance on either side; as when there is no Civill Power erected over the parties promising; for such promises are no Covenants: But either where one of the parties has performed already; or where there is a Power to make him performe; there is the question whether it be against reason, that is, against the benefit of the other to performe, or not. And I say it is not against reason. For the manifestation whereof, we are to consider; First, that when a man doth a thing, which notwithstanding any thing can be foreseen, and reckoned on, tendeth to his own destruction, howsoever some accident which he could not expect, arriving may turne it to

his benefit; yet such events do not make it reasonably or wisely done. Secondly, that in a condition of Warre, wherein every man to every man, for want of a common Power to keep them all in awe, is an Enemy, there is no man can hope by his own strength, or wit, to defend himselfe from destruction, without the help of Confederates; where every one expects the same defence by the Confederation, that any one else does: and therefore he which declares he thinks it reason to deceive those that help him, can in reason expect no other means of safety, than what can be had from his own single Power. He therefore that breaketh his Covenant, and consequently declareth that he thinks he may with reason do so, cannot be received into any Society, that unite themselves for Peace and Defence, but by the errour of them that receive him; nor when he is received, be retayned in it, without seeing the danger of their errour; which errours a man cannot reasonably reckon upon as the means of his security: and therefore if he be left, or cast out of Society, he perisheth; and if he live in Society, it is by the errours of other men, which he could not foresee, nor reckon upon; and consequently against the reason of his preservation; and so, as all men that contribute not to his destruction, forbear him onely out of ignorance of what is good for themselves.

As for the Instance of gaining the secure and perpetual felicity of Heaven, by any way; it is frivolous: there being but one way imaginable; and that is not breaking, but keeping of Covenant.

And for the other Instance of attaining Soveraignty by Rebellion; it is manifest, that though the event follow, yet because it cannot reasonbly be expected, but rather the contrary; and because by gaining it so, others are taught to gain the same in like manner, the attempt thereof is against reason. Justice therefore, that is to say, Keeping of Covenant, is a Rule of Reason, by which we are forbidden to do any thing destructive to our life; and consequently a Law of Nature.

There be some that proceed further; and will not have the Law of Nature, to be those Rules which conduce to the preservation of mans life on earth; but to the attaining of an eternall felicity after death; to which they think the breach of Covenant may conduce; and consequently be just and reasonable; (such are they that think it a work of merit to kill, or depose, or rebell against, the Soveraigne Power constituted over them by their own consent.) But, because there is no naturall knowledge of mans estate after death; much lesse of the reward that is then to be given to breach of Faith; but onely a beliefe grounded upon other mens saying, that they know it supernaturally, or that they know those, that knew them, that knew others, that knew it supernaturally; Breach of Faith cannot be called a Precept of Reason, or Nature.

Others, that allow for a Law of Nature, the keeping of Faith, do neverthelesse make exception of certain persons; as Heretiques, and such as use not to performe their Covenant to others: And this also is against reason. For if any fault of a man, be sufficient to discharge our Covenant made; the same ought in reason to have been sufficient to have hindred the making of it.

The names of Just, and Injust, when they are attributed to Men, signifie one thing; and when they are attributed to Actions, another. When they are attributed to Men, they signifie Conformity, or Inconformity of Manners, to Reason. But when they are attributed to Actions, they signifie the Conformity or Inconformity to Reason, not of Manners, or manner of life, but of particular Actions. A Just man therefore, is he that taketh all the care he can, that his Actions may be all Just: and an Unjust man, is he that neglecteth it. And such men are more often in our Language stiled by the names of Righteous, and Unrighteous; then Just, and Unjust; though the meaning be the same. Therefore a Righteous man, does not lose that Title, by one, or a few unjust Actions, that proceed from sudden Passion, or mistake of Things, or Persons: nor does an Unrighteous man, lose his character, for such Actions, as he does, or forbeares to do, for feare: because his Will is not framed by the Justice, but by the apparent benefit of what he is to do. That which gives to humane Actions the relish of Justice, is a certain Noblenesse or Gallantnesse of courage, (rarely found,) by which a man scorns to be beholding for the contentment or his life, to fraud, or breach of promise. This Justice of the Manners, is that which is meant, where Justice is called a Vertue; and Injustice a Vice.

But the Justice of Actions denominates men, not Just, *Guiltlesse:* and the Injustice of the same (which is also called Injury) gives them but the name of *Guilty.*

Again, the Injustice of Manners, is the disposition, or aptitude to do Injurie; and is Injustice before it proceed to Act; and without supposing any individuall person injured. But the Injustice of an Action, (that is to say Injury,) supposeth an individuall person Injured; namely him, to whom the Covenant was

made: And therefore many times the injury is received by one man, when the dammage redoundeth to another. As when the Master commandeth his servant to give mony to a stranger; if it be not done, the Injury is done to the Master, whom he had before Covenanted to obey; but the dammage redoundeth to the stranger, to whom he had no Obligation; and therefore could not Injure him. And so also in Common-wealths, private men may remit to one another their debts; but not robberies or other violences, whereby they are endammaged; because the detaining of Debt, is an Injury to themselves; but Robbery and Violence, are Injuries to the Person of the Common-wealth.

Whatsoever is done to a man, conformable to his own Will signified to the doer, is no Injury to him. For if he that doeth it, hath not passed away his originall right to do what he please, by some Antecedent Covenant, there is no breach of Covenant; and therefore no Injury done him. And if he have; then his Will to have it done being signified, is a release of that Covenant: and so again there is no Injury done him.

Justice of Actions, is by Writers divided into *Commutative,* and *Distributive:* and the former they say consisteth in proportion Arithmeticall; the later in proportion Geometricall. Commutative therefore, they place in the equality of value of the things contracted for; And Distributive, in the distribution of equall benefit, to men of equall merit. As if it were Injustice to sell dearer than we buy; or to give more to a man than he merits. The value of all things contracted for, is measured by the Appetite of the Contractors: and therefore the just value, is that which they be contented to give. And Merit (besides that which is by Covenant, where the performance on one part, meriteth the performance of the other part, and falls under Justice Commutative, not Distributive,) is not due by Justice; but is rewarded of Grace onely. And therefore this distinction, in the sense wherein it useth to be expounded, is not right. To speak properly, Commutative Justice, is the Justice of a Contractor; that is, a Performance of Covenant, in Buying, and Selling; Hiring, and Letting to Hire; Lending, and Borrowing; Exchanging, Bartering, and other acts of Contract.

And Distributive Justice, the Justice of an Arbitrator; that is to say, the act of defining what is Just. Wherein, (being trusted by them that make him Arbitrator,) if he performe his Trust, he is said to distribute to every man his own: and this is indeed Just Distribution, and may be called (though improperly) Distributive Justice; but more properly Equity; which also is a Law of Nature, as shall be shewn in due place.

As Justice dependeth on Antecedent Covenant; so does GRATITUDE depend on Antecedent Grace; that is to say, Antecedent-Free-Gift: and is the fourth Law of Nature; which may be conceived in this Forme, *That a man which receiveth Benefit from another of meer Grace, Endeavour that he which giveth it, have no reasonable cause to repent him of his good will.* For no man giveth, but with intention of Good to himselfe; because Gift is Voluntary; and of all Voluntary Acts, the Object is to every man his own Good; of which if men see they shall be frustrated, there will be no beginning of benevolence, or trust; nor consequently of mutuall help; nor of reconciliation of one man to another; and therefore they are to remain still in the condition of *War;* which is contrary to the first and Fundamentall Law of Nature, which commandeth men to *Seek Peace.* The breach of this Law, is called *Ingratitude;* and hath the same relation to Grace, that Injustice hath to Obligation by Covenant.

A fifth Law of Nature, is COMPLEASANCE; that is to say, *That every man strive to accommodate himselfe to the rest.* For the understanding whereof, we may consider, that there is in mens aptnesse to Society, a diversity of Nature, rising from their diversity of Affections; not unlike to that we see in stones brought together for building of an Ædifice. For as that stone which by the asperity, and irregularity of Figure, takes more room from others, than it selfe fills; and for the hardnesse, cannot be easily made plain, and thereby hindereth the building, is by the builders cast away as unprofitable, and troublesome: so also, a man that by asperity of Nature, will strive to retain those things which to himselfe are superfluous, and to others necessary; and for the stubbornness of his Passions, cannot be corrected, is to be left, or cast out of Society, as combersome thereunto. For seeing every man, not onely by Right, but also by necessity of Nature, is supposed to endeavour all he can, to obtain that which is necessary for his conservation; He that shall oppose himselfe against it, for things superfluous, is guilty of the warre that thereupon is to follow; and therefore doth that, which is contrary to the fundamentall Law of Nature, which commandeth *to seek Peace.* The observers of this Law, may be called SOCIABLE, (the Latines call them *Commodi;*) The contrary, *Stubborn, Insociable, Froward, Intractable.*

A sixth Law of Nature, is this, *That upon caution of the Future time, a man ought to pardon the offences past of them that repenting, desire it.* For PARDON, is nothing but granting of Peace; which though granted to them that persevere in their hostility, be not Peace, but Feare; yet not granted to them that give caution of the Future time, is signe of an aversion to Peace; and therefore contrary to the Law of Nature.

A seventh is, *That in Revenges,* (that is, retribution of Evil for Evil,) *Men look not at the greatnesse of the evill past, but the greatnesse of the good to follow.* Whereby we are forbidden to inflict punishment with any other designe, than for correction of the offender, or direction of others. For this Law is consequent to the next before it, that commandeth Pardon, upon security of the Future time. Besides, Revenge without respect to the Example, and profit to come, is a triumph, or glorying in the hurt of another, tending to no end; (for the End is always somewhat to Come;) and glorying to no end, is vain-glory, and contrary to reason; and to hurt without reason, tendeth to the introduction of Warre; which is against the Law of Nature; and is commonly stiled by the name of *Cruelty.*

And because all signes of hatred, or contempt, provoke to fight; insomuch as most men choose rather to hazard their life, than not to be revenged; we may in the eighth place, for a Law of Nature, set down this Precept, *That no man by deed, word, countenance, or gesture, declare Hatred, or Contempt of another.* The breach of which Law, is commonly called *Contumely.*

The question who is the better man, has no place in the condition of meer Nature; where, (as has been shewn before,) all men are equall. The inequallity that now is, has bin introduced by the Lawes civill. I know that *Aristotle* in the first booke of his Politiques, for a foundation of his doctrine, maketh men by Nature, some more worthy to Command, meaning the wiser sort (such as he thought himselfe to be for his Philosophy;) others to Serve, (meaning those that had strong bodies, but were not Philosophers as he;) as if Master and Servant were not introduced by consent of men, but by difference of Wit: which is not only against reason; but also against experience. For there are very few so foolish, that had not rather governe themselves, than be governed by others: Nor when the wise in their own conceit, contend by force, with them who distrust their owne wisdome, do they alwaies, or often, or almost at any time, get the Victory. If Nature therefore have made men equall, that equalitie is to be acknowledged: or if Nature have made men unequall; yet because men that think themselves equall, will not enter into conditions of Peace, but upon Equall termes, such equalitie must be admitted. And therefore for the ninth law of Nature, I put this, *That every man acknowledge other for his Equall by Nature.* The breach of this Precept is *Pride.*

On this law, dependeth another, *That at the entrance into conditions of Peace, no man require to reserve to himselfe any Right, which he is not content should be reserved to every one of the rest.* As it is necessary for all men that seek peace, to lay down certaine Rights of Nature; that is to say, not to have libertie to do all they list: so is it necessarie for mans life, to retaine some; as right to governe their owne bodies; enjoy aire, water, motion, waies to go from place to place; and all things else without which a man cannot live, or not live well. If in this case, at the making of Peace, men require for themselves, that which they would not have to be granted to others, they do contrary to the precedent law, that commandeth the acknowledgment of naturall equalitie, and therefore also against the law of Nature. The observers of this law, are those we call *Modest,* and the breakers *Arrogant* men. The Greeks call the violation of this law πλεομεξία; that is, a desire of more than their share.

Also if *a man be trusted to judge between man and man,* it is a precept of the Law of Nature, *that he deale Equally between them.* For without that, the Controversies of men cannot be determined but by Warre. He therefore that is partiall in judgment, doth what in him lies, to deterre men from the use of Judges, and Arbitrators; and consequently, (against the fundamentall Lawe of Nature) is the cause of Warre.

The observance of this law, from the equall distribution to each man, of that which in reason belongeth to him, is called EQUITY, and (as I have sayd before) distributive Justice: the violation, *Acception of persons,* προσωπτοληψία.

And from this followeth another law, *That such things as cannot be divided, be enjoyed in Common, if it can be; and if the quantity of the thing permit, without Stint; otherwise Proportionably to the number of them that have Right.* For otherwise the distribution is Unequall, and contrary to Equitie.

But some things there be, that can neither be divided, nor enjoyed in common. Then, The Law of Nature, which prescribeth Equity, requireth, *That the Entire Right; or else, (making the use alternate,) the First Possession, be determined by Lot.* For equall distribution, is of the Law of Nature; and other means of equall distribution cannot be imagined.

Of *Lots* there be two sorts, *Arbitrary,* and *Naturall.* Arbitrary, is that which is agreed on by the Competitors: Naturall is either *Primogeniture,* (which the Greek calls Κληρονομία, which signifies, *Given by Lot;*) or *First Seisure.*

And therefore those things which cannot be enjoyed in common, nor divided, ought to be adjudged to the First Possessor; and in some cases to the First-Borne, as acquired by Lot.

It is also a Law of Nature, *That all men that mediate Peace, be allowed safe Conduct.* For the Law that commandeth Peace, as the *End,* commandeth Intercession, as the *Means;* and to Intercession the Means is safe Conduct.

And because, though men be never so willing to observe these Lawes, there may neverthelesse arise questions concerning a mans action; First, whether it were done, or not done; Secondly (if done) whether against the Law, or not against the Law; the former whereof, is called a question *Of Fact;* the later a question *Of Right;* therefore unlesse the parties to the question, Covenant mutually to stand to the sentence of another, they are as farre from Peace as ever. This other, to whose Sentence they submit, is called an ARBITRATOR. And therefore it is of the Law of Nature, *That they that are at controversie, submit their Right to the judgement of an Arbitrator.*

And seeing every man is presumed to do all things in order to his own benefit, no man is a fit Arbitrator in his own cause: and if he were never so fit; yet Equity allowing to each party equall benefit, if one be admitted to be Judge, the other is to be admitted also; and so the controversie, that is, the cause of War, remains, against the Law of Nature.

For the same reason no man in any Cause ought to be received for Arbitrator, to whom greater profit, or honour, or pleasure apparently ariseth out of the victory of one party, than of the other: for hee hath taken (though an unavoydable bribe, yet) a bribe; and no man can be obliged to trust him. And thus also the controversie, and the condition of War remaineth, contrary to the Law of Nature.

And in a controversie of *Fact,* the Judge being to give no more credit to one, than to the other, (if there be no other Arguments) must give credit to a third; or to a third and fourth; or more: For else the question is undecided, and left to force, contrary to the Law of Nature.

These are the Lawes of Nature, dictating Peace, for a means of the conservation of men in multitudes; and which onely concern the doctrine of Civill Society. There be other things tending to the destruction of particular men; as Drunkenness, and all other parts of Intemperance, which may therefore also be reckoned amongst those things which the Law of Nature hath forbidden; but are not necessary to be mentioned, nor are pertinent enough to this place.

And though this may seem too subtile a deduction of the Lawes of Nature, to be taken notice of by all men; whereof the most part are too busie in getting food, and the rest too negligent to understand; yet to leave all men unexcusable, they have been contracted into one easie sum, intelligible, even to the meanest capacity; and that is, *Do not that to another, which thou wouldest not have done to thy selfe;* which sheweth him, that he has no more to do in learning the Lawes of Nature, but, when weighing the actions of other men with his own, they seem too heavy, to put them into the other part of the ballance, and his own into their place, that his own passions, and selfe-love, may adde nothing to the weight; and then there is none of these Lawes of Nature that will not appear unto him very reasonable.

The Lawes of Nature oblige *in foro interno;* that is to say, they bind to a desire they should take place: but *in foro externo;* that is, to the putting them in act, not alwayes. For he that should be modest, and tractable, and performe all he promises, in such time, and place, where no man els should do so, should but make himselfe a prey to others, and procure his own certain ruine, contrary to the ground of all Lawes of Nature, which tend to Natures preservation. And again, he that having sufficient Security, that others shall observe the same Lawes towards him, observes them not himselfe, seeketh not Peace, but War; & consequently the destruction of his Nature by Violence.

And whatsoever Lawes bind *in foro interno,* may be broken, not onely by a fact contrary to the Law, but also by a fact according to it, in case a man think it contrary. For though his Action in this case, be according to the Law; yet his Purpose was against the Law; which where the Obligation is *in foro interno,* is a breach.

The Lawes of Nature are Immutable and Eternall; For Injustice, Ingratitude, Arrogance, Pride, Iniquity, Acception of persons, and the rest, can never be made lawfull. For it can never be that Warre shall preserve life, and Peace destroy it.

The [same] Lawes, because they oblige onely to a desire, and endeavour, I mean an unfeigned and constant endeavour, are easie to be observed. For in that they require nothing but endeavour; he that endeavoureth their performance, fulfilleth them; and he that fulfilleth the Law, is Just.

And the Science of them, is the true and onely Morall Philosophy. For Morall Philosophy is nothing else but the Science of what is *Good,* and *Evill,* in the conversation, and Society of man-kind. *Good* and *Evill,* are names that signifie our Appetites, and Aversions; which in different tempers, customes, and doctrines of men, are different: And divers men, differ not onely in their judgement, on the senses of what is pleasant, and unpleasant to the tast, smell, hearing, touch, and sight; but also of what is conformable, or disagreeable to Reason, in the actions of common life. Nay, the same man, in divers times, differs from himselfe; and one time praiseth, that is, calleth Good, what another time he dispraiseth, and calleth Evil: From whence arise Disputes, Controversies, and at last War. And therefore so long a man is in the condition of meer Nature, (which is a condition of War,) as private Appetite is the measure of Good, and Evill: And consequently all men agree on this, that Peace is Good, and therefore also the way, or means of Peace, which (as I have shewed before) are *Justice, Gratitude, Modesty, Equity, Mercy,* & the rest of the Laws of Nature, are good; that is to say, *Morall Vertues;* and their contrarie *Vices,* Evill. Now the science of Vertue and Vice, is Morall Philosophie; and therfore the true Doctrine of the Lawes of Nature, is the true Morall Philosophie. But the Writers of Morall Philosophie, though they acknowledge the same Vertues and Vices; Yet not seeing wherein consisted their Goodnesse; not that they come to be praised, as the meanes of peaceable, sociable, and comfortable living; place them in a mediocrity of passions: as if not the Cause, but the Degree of daring, made Fortitude; or not the Cause, but the Quantity of a gift, made Liberality.

These dictates of Reason, men use to call by the name of Lawes; but improperly: for they are but Conclusions, or Theoremes concerning what conduceth to the conservation and defence of themselves; whereas Law, properly is the word of him, that by right hath command over others. But yet if we consider the same Theoremes, as delivered in the word of God, that by right commandeth all things; then are they properly called Lawes.

CHAP. XVI

Of Persons, Authors, and things Personated

A PERSON, is he, *whose words or actions are considered, either as his own, or as representing the words or actions of an other man, or of any other thing to whom they are attributed, whether Truly or by Fiction.*

When they are considered as his owne, then is he called a *Naturall Person:* And when they are considered as representing the words and actions of an other, then is he a *Feigned* or *Artificiall person.*

The word Person is latine: insteed whereof the Greeks have πρόσωπον, which signifies the *Face,* as *Persona* in latine signifies the *disguise,* or *outward appearance* of a man, counterfeited on the Stage; and sometimes more particularly that part of it, which disguiseth the face, as a Mask or Visard: And from the Stage, hath been translated to any Representer of speech and action, as well in Tribunalls, as Theaters. So that a *Person,* is the same that an *Actor* is, both on the Stage and in common Conversation; and to *Personate,* is to *Act,* or *Represent* himselfe, or an other; and he that acteth another, is said to beare his Person, or act in his name; (in which sence *Cicero* useth it where he saies, *Unus sustineo tres Personas; Mei, Adversarii, & Judicis,* I beare three Persons; my own, my Adversaries, and the Judges;) and is called in diverse occasions diversly; as a *Representer,* or *Representative,* a *Lieutenant,* a *Vicar,* an *Attorney,* a *Deputy,* a *Procurator,* an *Actor,* and the like.

Of Persons Artificiall, some have their words and actions *Owned* by those whom they represent. And then the Person is the *Actor;* and he that owneth his words and actions is the AUTHOR: In which case the Actor acteth by Authority. For that which in speaking of goods and possessions, is called an *Owner,* and in latine *Dominus,* in Greeke κύριος; speaking of Actions, is called Author. And as the Right of possession, is called Dominion; so the Right of doing any Action, is called AUTHORITY. So that by Authority, is alwayes understood a Right of doing any act: and *done by Authority,* done by Commission, or Licence from him whose right it is.

From hence it followeth, that when the Actor maketh a Covenant by Authority, he bindeth thereby the Author, no lesse than he had made it himselfe; and no lesse subjecteth him to all the consequences of the same. And therfore all that hath been said formerly, (*Chap.* 14.) of the nature of Covenants between man and man in their naturall capacity, is true also when they are made by their Actors, Representers, or Procurators, that have authority from them so far-forth as is in their Commission, but no farther.

And therefore he that maketh a Covenant with the Actor, or Representer, not knowing the Authority he hath, doth it at his own perill. For no man is obliged by a Covenant, whereof he is not Author; nor consequently by a Covenant made against, or beside the Authority he gave.

When the Actor doth any thing against the Law of Nature by command of the Author, if he be obliged by former Covenant to obey him, not he, but the Author breaketh the Law of Nature: for though the Action be against the Law of Nature; yet it is not his: but contrarily, to refuse to do it, is against the Law of Nature, that forbiddeth breach of Covenant.

And he that maketh a Covenant with the Author, by mediation of the Actor, not knowing what Authority he hath, but onely takes his word; in case such Authority be not made manifest unto him upon demand, is no longer obliged: For the Covenant made with the Author, is not valid, without his Counter-assurance. But if he that so Covenanteth, know before hand he was to expect no other assurance, than the Actors word; then is the Covenant valid; because the Actor in this case maketh himselfe the Author. And therefore, as when the Authority is evident, the Covenant obligeth the Author, not the Actor; so when the Authority is feigned, it obligeth the Actor onely; there being no Author but himselfe.

There are few things, that are uncapable of being represented by Fiction. Inanimate things, as a Church, an Hospital, a Bridge, may be personated by a Rector, Master, or Overseer. But things Inanimate, cannot be Authors, nor therefore give Authority to their Actors: Yet the Actors may have Authority to procure their maintenance, given them by those that are Owners, or Governours of those things. And therefore, such things cannot be Personated, before there be some state of Civill Government.

Likewise Children, Fooles, and Mad-men that have no use of Reason, may be Personated by Guardians, or Curators; but can be no Authors (during that time) of any action done by them, longer then (when they shall recover the use of Reason) they shall judge the same reasonable. Yet during the Folly, he that hath right of governing them, may give Authority to the Guardian. But this again has no place but in a State Civill, because before such estate, there is no Dominion of Persons.

An Idol, or meer Figment of the brain, may be Personated; as were the Gods of the Heathen; which by such Officers as the State appointed, were Personated, and held Possessions, and other Goods, and Rights, which men from time to time dedicated, and consecrated unto them. But Idols cannot be Authors: for an Idol is nothing. The Authority proceeded from the State: and therefore before introduction of Civill Government, the Gods of the Heathen could not be Personated.

The true God may be Personated. As he was; first by *Moses;* who governed the Israelites, (that were not his, but Gods people,) not in his own name, with *Hoc dicit Moses;* but in Gods Name, with *Hoc dicit Dominus.* Secondly, by the Son of man, his own Son, our Blessed Saviour *Jesus Christ,* that came to reduce the Jewes, and induce all Nations into the Kingdome of his Father; not as of himselfe, but as sent from his Father. And thirdly, by the Holy Ghost, or Comforter, speaking, and working in the Apostles: which Holy Ghost, was a Comforter that came not of himselfe; but was sent, and proceeded from them both.

A Multitude of men, are made *One* Person, when they are by one man, or one Person, Represented; so that it be done with the consent of every one of that Multitude in particular. For it is the *Unity* of the Representer, not the *Unity* of the Represented, that maketh the Person *One.* And it is the Representer that beareth the Person, and but one Person: And *Unity,* cannot otherwise be understood in Multitude.

And because the Multitude naturally is not *One,* but *Many;* they cannot be understood for one; but many Authors, of every thing their Representative saith, or doth in their name; Every man giving their common Representer, Authority from himselfe in particular; and owning all the actions the Representer doth, in case they give him Authority without stint: Otherwise, when they limit him in what, and how farre he shall represent them, none of them owneth more, than they gave him commission to Act.

And if the Representative consist of many men, the voyce of the greater number, must be considered as the voyce of them all. For if the lesser number pronounce (for example) in the Affirmative, and the greater in the Negative, there will be Negatives more than enough to destroy the Affirmatives; and thereby the excesse of Negatives, standing uncontradicted, are the onely voyce the Representative hath.

And a Representative of even number, especially when the number is not great, whereby the contradictory voyces are oftentimes equall, is therefore oftentimes mute, and uncapable of Action. Yet in some cases contradictory voyces equall in number, may determine a question; as in condemning, or absolving, equality of votes, even in that they condemne not, do absolve; but not on the contrary condemne, in that they absolve not. For when a Cause is heard; not to condemne, is to absolve: but on the contrary, to say that not absolving, is condemning, is not true.

The like it is in a deliberation of executing presently, or deferring till another time: For when the voyces are equall, the not decreeing Execution, is a decree of Dilation.

Or if the number be odde, as three, or more, (men, or assemblies;) whereof every one has by a Negative Voice, authority to take away the effect of all the Affirmative Voices of the rest, This number is no Representative; because by the diversity of Opinions, and Interests of men, it becomes oftentimes, and in cases of the greatest consequence, a mute Person, and unapt, as for many things else, so for the government of a Multitude, especially in time of Warre.

Of Authors there be two sorts. The first simply so called; which I have before defined to be him, that owneth the Action of another simply. The second is he, that owneth an Action, or Covenant of another conditionally; that is to say, he undertaketh to do it, if the other doth it not, at, or before a certain time. And these Authors conditionall, are generally called SURETYES, in Latine *Fidejussores,* and *Sponsores;* and particularly for Debt, *Prædes;* and for Appearance before Judge, or Magistrate, *Vades.*

PART II: OF COMMON-WEALTH
CHAP. XVII
Of the Causes, Generation, and Definition of a Common-Wealth

THE finall Cause, End, or Designe of men, (who naturally love Liberty, and Dominion over others,) in the introduction of that restraint upon themselves, (in which wee see them live in Common-wealths,) is the foresight of their own preservation, and of a more contented live thereby; that is to say, of getting themselves out from that miserable condition of Warre, which is necessarily consequent (as hath been shewn) to the naturall Passions of men, when there is no visible Power to keep them in awe, and tye them by feare of punishment to the performance of their Covenants, and observation of those Lawes of Nature set down in the fourteenth and fifteenth Chapters.

For the Lawes of Nature (as *Justice, Equity, Modesty, Mercy,* and (in summe) *doing to others, as wee would be done to,*) of themselves, without the terrour of some Power, to cause them to be observed, are contrary to our naturall Passions, that carry us to Partiality, Pride, Revenge, and the like. And Covenants, without the Sword, are but Words, and of no strength to secure a man at all. Therefore notwithstanding the Lawes of Nature, (which every one hath then kept, when he has the will to keep them, when he can do it safely,) if there be no Power erected, or not great enough for our security; every man will, and may lawfully rely on his own strength and art, for caution against all other men. And in all places, where men have lived by small Families, to robbe and spoyle one another, has been a Trade, and so farre from being reputed against the Law of Nature, that the greater spoyles they gained, the greater was their honour; and men observed no other Lawes therein, but the Lawes of Honour; that is, to abstain from cruelty, leaving to men their lives, and instruments of husbandry. And as small Familyes did then; so now do Cities and Kingdomes, which are but greater Families (for their own security) enlarge their Dominions, upon all pretences of danger, and fear of Invasion, or assistance that may be given to Invaders, endeavour as much as they can, to subdue, or weaken their neighbours, by open force, and secret arts, for want of other Caution, justly; and are remembered for it in after ages with honour.

Nor is it the joyning together of a small number of men, that gives them this security; because in small numbers, small additions on the one side or the other, make the advantage of strength so great, as is sufficient to carry the Victory; and therefore gives encouragement to an Invasion. The Multitude sufficient to confide in for our Security, is not determined by any certain number, but by comparison with the Enemy we feare; and is then sufficient, when the odds of the Enemy is not of so visible and conspicuous moment, to determine the event of warre, as to move him to attempt.

And be there never so great a Multitude; yet if their actions be directed according to their particular judgements, and particular appetites, they can expect thereby no defence, nor protection, neither against a common enemy, nor against the injuries of one another. For being distracted in opinions concerning the best use and application of their strength, they do not help, but hinder one another; and reduce their strength by mutuall opposition to nothing: whereby they are easily, not onely subdued by a very few that agree together; but also when there is no common enemy, they make warre upon each other, for their particular interests. For if we could suppose a great Multitude of men to consent in the observation of Justice, and other Lawes of Nature, without a common Power to keep them all in awe; we might as well suppose all Man-kind to do the same; and then there neither would be, nor need to be any Civill Government, or Common-wealth at all; because there would be Peace without subjection.

Nor is it enough for the security, which men desire should last all the time of their life, that they be governed, and directed by one judgement, for a limited time; as in one Battel, or one Warre. For though they obtain a Victory by their unanimous endeavour against a forraign enemy; yet afterwards, when either they have no common enemy, or he that by one part is held for an enemy, is by another part held for a friend, they must needs by the difference of their interests dissolve, and fall again into a Warre amongst themselves.

It is true, that certain living creatures, as Bees, and Ants, live sociably one with another, (which are therefore by *Aristotle* numbered amongst Politicall creatures;) and yet have no other direction, than their particular judgements and appetites; nor speech, whereby one of them can signifie to another, what he thinks expedient for the common benefit: and therefore some man may perhaps desire to know, why Man-kind cannot do the same. To which I answer,

First, that men are continually in competition for Honour and Dignity, which these creatures are not; and consequently amongst men there ariseth on that ground, Envy and Hatred, and finally Warre; but amongst these not so.

Secondly, that amongst these creatures, the Common good differeth not from the Private; and being by nature enclined to their private, they procure thereby the common benefit. But man, whose Joy consisteth in comparing himselfe with other men, can relish nothing but what is eminent.

Thirdly, that these creatures, having not (as man) the use of reason, do not see, nor think they see any fault in the administration of their common businesse: whereas amongst men, there are very many, that thinke themselves wiser, and abler to govern the Publique, better than the rest; and these strive to reforme and innovate one this way, another that way; and thereby bring it into Distraction and Civill warre.

Fourthly, that these creatures, though they have some use of voice, in making knowne to one another their desires, and other affections; yet they want that art of words, by which some men can represent to others, that which is Good, in the likenesse of Evill; and Evill, in the likenesse of Good; and augment, or diminish the apparent greatnesse of Good and Evill; discontenting men, and troubling their Peace at their pleasure.

Fifthly, irrationall creatures cannot distinguish betweene *Injury,* and *Dammage;* and therefore as long as they be at ease, they are not offended with their fellowes: whereas Man is then most troublesome, when he is most at ease: for then it is that he loves to shew his Wisdome, and controule the Actions of them that governe the Common-wealth.

Lastly, the agreement of these creatures is Naturall; that of men, is by Covenant only, which is Artificiall: and therefore it is no wonder if there be somwhat else required (besides Covenant) to make their Agreement constant and lasting; which is a Common Power, to keep them in awe, and to direct their actions to the Common Benefit.

The only way to erect such a Common Power, as may be able to defend them from the invasion of Forraigners, and the injuries of one another, and thereby to secure them in such sort, as that by their owne industrie, and by the fruites of the Earth, they may nourish themselves and live contendedly; is, to conferre all their power and strength upon one Man, or upon one Assembly of men, that may reduce all their Wills, by plurality of voices, unto one Will: which is as much as to say, to appoint one Man, or Assembly of men, to beare their Person; and every one to owne, and acknowledge himselfe to be Author of whatsoever he that so beareth their Person, shall Act, or cause to be Acted, in those things which concerne the Common Peace and Safetie; and therein to submit their Wills, every one to his Will, and their Judgements, to his Judgement. This is more than Consent, or Concord; it is a reall Unitie of them all, in one and the same Person, made by Covenant of every man with every man, in such manner, as if every man should say to every man, *I Authorise and give up my Right of Governing my selfe, to this Man, or to this Assembly of men, on this condition, that thou give up thy Right to him, and Authorise all his Actions in like manner.* This done, the Multitude so united in one Person, is called a COMMON-WEALTH, in latine CIVITAS. This is the Generation of that great LEVIATHAN, or rather (to speake more reverently) of that *Mortall God,* to which wee owe under the *Immortall God,* our peace and defence. For by this Authoritie, given him by every particular man in the Common-Wealth, he hath the use of so much Power and Strength conferred on him, that by terror thereof, he is inabled to forme the wills of them all, to Peace at home, and mutuall ayd against their enemies abroad. And in him consisteth the Essence of the Common-wealth; which (to define it,) is *One person, of whose Acts a great Multitude, by mutuall Covenants one with another, have made themselves every one the Author, to the end he may use the strength and means of them all, as he shall think expedient, for their Peace and Common Defence.*

And he that carryeth this Person, is called SOVERAIGNE, and said to have *Soveraigne Power;* and every one besides, his SUBJECT.

The attaining to this Soveraigne Power, is by two wayes. One, by Naturall force; as when a man maketh his children, to submit themselves, and their children to his government, as being able to destroy them if they refuse; or by Warre subdueth his enemies to his will, giving them their lives on that condition. The other, is when men agree amongst themselves, to submit to some Man, or Assembly of men, voluntarily, on confidence to be protected by him against all others. This later, may be called a Politicall Common-wealth, or Common-wealth by *Institution;* and the former, a Common-wealth by *Acquisition.*

David Hume (1711–1776)
OF THE INFLUENCING MOTIVES OF THE WILL

Hume holds that reason is and ought to be the slave of the passions. He stresses that human beings have such passions as benevolence and kindness to children, which involve sympathy for others, as well as such selfish passions as the drive for gain, safety, or reputation. Hume's views on human nature and morality are explored in Section B of the introductory essay to Part IV.

READING QUESTIONS

In reading the selection, try to answer the following questions and identify the passages that support your answers:

1. What is Hume's conception of human nature?
2. How does his conception differ from that of Hobbes?
3. What reasons does Hume give for his views?
4. Which conception, Hobbes's or Hume's, is preferable and why?
5. How can the existence of societies be better explained: assuming Hobbes's or Hume's conception of human nature?

Reprinted from David Hume, *A Treatise of Human Nature,* ed. L. A. Selby-Bigge (London: Oxford University Press, 1888), Book II, Section III, "Of the Influencing Motives of the Will," pp. 413–418.

SECTION III

Of the Influencing Motives of the Will

NOTHING is more usual in philosophy, and even in common life, than to talk of the combat of passion and reason, to give the preference to reason, and to assert that men are only so far virtuous as they conform themselves to its dictates. Every rational creature, 'tis said, is oblig'd to regulate his actions by reason; and if any other motive or principle challenge the direction of his conduct, he ought to oppose it, 'till it be entirely subdu'd, or at least brought to a conformity with that superior principle. On this method of thinking the greatest part of moral philosophy, ancient and modern, seems to be founded; nor is there an ampler field, as well for metaphysical arguments, as popular declamations, than this suppos'd pre-eminence of reason above passion. The eternity, invariableness, and divine origin of the former have been display'd to the best advantage: The blindness, unconstancy and deceitfulness of the latter have been as strongly insisted on. In order to shew the fallacy of all this philosophy, I shall endeavour to prove *first,* that reason alone can never be a motive to any action of the will; and *secondly,* that it can never oppose passion in the direction of the will.

The understanding exerts itself after two different ways (1) as it judges from demonstration or probability; (2) as it regards the abstract relations of our ideas, or those relations of objects, of which experience only gives us information. I believe it scarce will be asserted, that the first species of reasoning alone is ever the cause of any action. As its proper province is the world of ideas, and as the will always places us

in that of realities, demonstration and volition seem, upon that account, to be totally remov'd, from each other. Mathematics, indeed, are useful in all mechanical operations, and arithmetic in almost every art and profession: But 'tis not of themselves they have any influence. Mechanics are the art of regulating the motions of bodies *to some design'd end or purpose;* and the reason why we employ arithmetic in fixing the proportions of numbers, is only that we may discover the proportions of their influence and operation. A merchant is desirous of knowing the sum total of his accounts with any person: Why? but that he may learn what sum will have the same *effects* in paying his debt, and going to market, as all the particular articles taken together. Abstract or demonstrative reasoning, therefore, never influences any of our actions, but only as it directs our judgment concerning causes and effects; which leads us to the second operation of the understanding.

'Tis obvious, that when we have the prospect of pain or pleasure from any object, we feel a consequent emotion of aversion or propensity, and are carry'd to avoid or embrace what will give us this uneasiness or satisfaction. 'Tis also obvious, that this emotion rests not here but making us cast our view on every side, comprehends whatever objects are connected with its original one by the relation of cause and effect. Here then reasoning takes place to discover this relation; and according as our reasoning varies, our actions receive a subsequent variation. But 'tis evident in this case, that the impulse arises not from reason, but is only directed by it. 'Tis from the prospect of pain or pleasure that the aversion or propensity arises towards any object: And these emotions extend themselves to the causes and effects of that object, as they are pointed out to us by reason and experience. It can never in the least concern us to know, that such objects are causes, and such others effects, if both the causes and effects be indifferent to us. Where the objects themselves do not affect us, their connexion can never give them any influence; and 'tis plain, that as reason is nothing but the discovery of this connexion, it cannot be by its means that the objects are able to affect us.

Since reason alone can never produce any action, or give rise to volition, I infer, that the same faculty is as incapable of preventing volition, or of disputing the preference with any passion or emotion. This consequence is necessary. 'Tis impossible reason cou'd have the latter effect of preventing volition, but by giving an impulse in a contrary direction to our passion; and that impulse, had it operated alone, wou'd have been able to produce volition. Nothing can oppose or retard the impulse of passion, but a contrary impulse; and if this contrary impulse ever arises from reason, that latter faculty must have an original influence on the will, and must be able to cause, as well as hinder any act of volition. But if reason has no original influence, 'tis impossible it can withstand any principle, which has such an efficacy, or ever keep the mind in suspence a moment. Thus it appears, that the principle, which opposes our passion, cannot be the same with reason, and is only call'd so in an improper sense. We speak not strictly and philosophically when we talk of the combat of passion and of reason. Reason is, and ought only to be the slave of the passions, and can never pretend to any other office than to serve and obey them. As this opinion may appear somewhat extraordinary, it may not be improper to confirm it by some other considerations.

A passion is an original existence, or, if you will, modification of existence, and contains not any representative quality, which renders it a copy of any other existence or modification. When I am angry, I am actually possest with the passion, and in that emotion have no more a reference to any other object, than when I am thirsty, or sick, or more than five foot high. 'Tis impossible, therefore, that this passion can be oppos'd by, or be contradictory to truth and reason; since this contradiction consists in the disagreement of ideas, consider'd as copies, with those objects, which they represent.

What may at first occur on this head, is, that as nothing can be contrary to truth or reason, except what has a reference to it, and as the judgments of our understanding only have this reference, it must follow, that passions can be contrary to reason only so far as they are *accompany'd* with some judgment or opinion. According to this principle, which is so obvious and natural, 'tis only in two senses, that any affection can be call'd unreasonable. First, When a passion, such as hope or fear, grief or joy, despair or security, is founded on the supposition of the existence of objects, which really do not exist. Secondly, When in exerting any passion in action, we chuse means insufficient for the design'd end, and deceive ourselves in our judgment of causes and effects. Where a passion is neither founded on false suppositions, nor chuses means insufficient for the end, the understanding can neither justify nor condemn it. 'Tis not contrary to reason to prefer the destruction of the whole world to the scratching of my finger. 'Tis not contrary to reason for me to chuse my total ruin, to prevent the least uneasiness of an *Indian* or person wholly unknown to me. 'Tis as little contrary to reason to prefer even my own acknowledg'd lesser good to my greater, and have a more ardent affection for the former than the latter. A trivial good may, from certain circumstances, produce a desire superior to what arises from the greatest and most valuable enjoyment; nor is there any thing more extraordinary in this, than in mechanics to see one pound weight raise up a hundred by the advantage of its situation. In short, a passion must be accompany'd with some false judgment, in order to its being unreasonable; and even then 'tis not the passion, properly speaking, which is unreasonable, but the judgment.

The consequences are evident. Since a passion can never, in any sense, be call'd unreasonable, but when founded on a false supposition, or when it chuses means insufficient for the design'd end, 'tis impossible, that reason and passion can ever oppose each other, or dispute for the government of the will and actions. The moment we perceive the falshood of any supposition, or the insufficiency of any means our passions yield to our reason without any opposition. I may desire any fruit as of an excellent relish; but whenever you convince me of my mistake, my longing ceases. I may will the performance of certain actions as means of obtaining any desir'd good; but as my willing of these actions is only secondary, and founded on the supposition, that they are causes of the propos'd effect; as soon as I discover the falshood of that supposition, they must become indifferent to me.

'Tis natural for one, that does not examine objects with a strict philosophic eye, to imagine, that those actions of the mind are entirely the same, which produce not a different sensation, and are not immediately distinguishable to the feeling and perception. Reason, for instance, exerts itself without producing any sensible emotion; and except in the more sublime disquisitions of philosophy, or in the frivolous subtilties of the schools, scarce ever conveys any pleasure or uneasiness. Hence it proceeds, that every action of the mind, which operates with the same calmness and tranquillity, is confounded with reason by all those, who judge of things from the first view and appearance. Now 'tis certain, there are certain calm desires and tendencies, which, tho' they be real passions, produce little emotion in the mind, and are more known more by their effects than by the immediate feeling or sensation. These desires are of two kinds; either certain instincts originally implanted in our natures, such as benevolence and resentment, the love of life, and kindness to children; or the general appetite to good, and aversion to evil, consider'd merely as such. When any of these passions are calm, and cause no disorder in the soul, they are very readily taken for the determinations of reason, and are suppos'd to proceed from the same faculty, with that, which judges of truth and falshood. Their nature and principles have been suppos'd the same, because their sensations are not evidently different.

Beside these calm passions, which often determine the will, there are certain violent emotions of the same kind, which have likewise a great influence on that faculty. When I receive any injury from another, I often feel a violent passion of resentment, which makes me desire his evil and punishment, independent of all considerations of pleasure and advantage to myself. When I am immediately threaten'd with any grievous ill, my fears, apprehensions, and aversions rise to a great height, and produce a sensible emotion.

The common error of metaphysicians has lain in ascribing the direction of the will entirely to one of these principles, and supposing the other to have no influence. Men often act knowingly against their interest: For which reason the view of the greatest possible good does not always influence them. Men often counter-act a violent passion in prosecution of their interests and designs: 'Tis not therefore the present uneasiness alone, which determines them. In general we may observe, that both these principles operate on the will; and where they are contrary, that either of them prevails, according to the *general* character or *present* disposition of the person. What we call strength of mind, implies the prevalence of the calm passions above the violent; tho' we may easily observe, there is no man so constantly possess'd of this virtue, as never on any occasion to yield to the sollicitations of passion and desire. From these variations of temper proceeds the great difficulty of deciding concerning the actions and resolutions of men, where there is any contrariety of motives and passions.

Immanuel Kant (1724–1804)
THE CATEGORICAL IMPERATIVE

The author argues that the only thing that gives actions moral worth is a good will—that is, a settled determination to do one's duty. The type of motivation involved in a good will amounts simply to the thought of what is right and the feeling of respect for what the moral law requires. Kant calls the moral law as applied to human beings, the "categorical imperative." He offers various formulations of the categorical imperative, that are known as the principle of universality, the principle of humanity (or personality), and the principle of the kingdom of ends. Kant's conception of morality and the motivations for acting morally are explored in Section C of the introductory essay to Part IV.

READING QUESTIONS

In reading the selection, try to answer the following questions and identify the passages that support your answers:

1. What is Kant's conception of morality?
2. How does his conception of morality differ from those of Hobbes and Hume?
3. What reasons does Kant give for his views?
4. Which conception of morality, Hobbes's, Hume's, or Kant's, is preferable and why?
5. Does Kant's position involve only one moral principle? Why or why not?

NOTHING can possibly be conceived in the world, or even out of it, which can be called good without qualification, except a *good will*. Intelligence, wit, judgment, and the other *talents* of the mind, however they may be named, or courage, resolution, perseverance, as qualities of temperament, are undoubtedly good and desirable in many respects; but these gifts of nature may also become extremely bad and mischievous if the will which is to make use of them, and which, therefore, constitutes what is called *character,* is not good. It is the same with the *gifts of fortune.* Power, riches, honor, even health, and the general well-being and contentment with one's condition which is called *happiness,* inspire pride, and often presumption, if there is not a good will to correct the influence of these on the mind, and with this also to rectify the whole principle of acting, and adapt it to its end. The sight of a being who is not adorned with a single feature of a pure and good will, enjoying unbroken prosperity, can never give pleasure to an impartial rational spectator. [12] Thus a good will appears to constitute the indispensable condition even of being worthy of happiness.

There are even some qualities which are of service to this good will itself, and may facilitate its action, yet which have no intrinsic unconditional value, but always presuppose a good will, and this qualifies the esteem that we justly have for them, and does not permit us to regard them as absolutely good. Moderation in the affections and passions, self-control, and calm deliberation are not only good in many respects, but even seem to constitute part of

the intrinsic worth of the person; but they are far from deserving to be called good without qualification, although they have been so unconditionally praised by the ancients. For without the principles of a good will, they may become extremely bad. . . .

We have then to develop the notion of a will which deserves to be highly esteemed for itself, and is good without a view to anything further, a notion which exists already in the sound natural understanding, requiring rather to be cleared up than to be taught, and which in estimating the value of our actions always takes the first place and constitutes the condition of all the rest. In order to do this, we will take the notion of duty, which includes that of a good will, although implying certain subjective restrictions and hindrances. These, however, far from concealing it or rendering it unrecognizable, rather bring it out by contrast and make it shine forth so much brighter.

I omit here all actions which are already recognized as inconsistent with duty, although they may be useful for this or that purpose, for with these the question whether they are done *from duty* cannot arise at all, since they even conflict with it. I also set aside those actions which really conform to duty, but to which men have *no* direct *inclination,* performing them because they are impelled thereto by some other inclination. For in this case we can readily distinguish whether the action which agrees with duty is done *from duty* or from a selfish view. It is much harder to make this distinction when the action accords with duty, and the subject has besides a *direct* inclination to it. For example, it is always a matter of duty that a dealer should not overcharge an inexperienced purchaser; and wherever there is much commerce the prudent tradesman does not overcharge, but keeps a fixed price for everyone, so that a child buys of him as well as any other. Men are thus *honestly* served; but this is not enough to make us believe that the tradesman has so acted from duty and from principles of honesty; his own advantage required it; it is out of the question in this case to suppose that he might besides have a direct inclination in favor of the buyers, so that, [17] as it were, from love he should give no advantage to one over another. Accordingly, the action was done neither from duty nor from direct inclination, but merely with a selfish view.

On the other hand, it is a duty to maintain one's life; and, in addition, everyone has also a direct inclination to do so. But on this account the often anxious care which most men take for it has no intrinsic worth, and their maxim has no moral import. They preserve their life *as duty requires*, no doubt, but not *because duty requires*. On the other hand, if adversity and hopeless sorrow have completely taken away the relish for life, if the unfortunate one, strong in mind, indignant at his fate rather than desponding or dejected, wishes for death, and yet preserves his life without loving it—not from inclination or fear, but from duty—then his maxim has a moral worth. . . .

Thus the moral worth of an action does not lie in the effect expected from it, nor in any principle of action which requires to borrow its motive from this expected effect. For all these effects—agreeableness of one's condition, and even the promotion of the happiness of others—could have been also brought about by other causes, so that for this there would have been no need of the will of a rational being; whereas it is in this alone that the supreme and unconditional good can be found. The pre-eminent good which we call moral can therefore consist in nothing else than *the conception of law* in itself, *which certainly is only possible in a rational being*, in so far as this conception, and not the expected effect, determines the will. This is a good which is already present in the person who acts accordingly, and we have not to wait for it to appear first in the result.[1]

But what sort of law can that be the conception of which must determine the will, even without paying any regard to the effect expected from it, in order that this will may be called good absolutely and without qualification? As I have deprived the will of every impulse which could arise to it from obedience to any law, there remains nothing but the universal conformity of its actions to law in general, which alone is to serve the will as a principle, that is, I am never to act otherwise than so *that I could also will that my maxim should become a universal law*. Here, now, it is the simple conformity to law in general, without assuming any particular law applicable to certain actions. . . .

If then there is a supreme practical principle or, in respect of the human will, a categorical imperative, it must be one which, [57] being drawn from the conception of that which is necessarily an end for everyone because it is *an end in itself,* constitutes an *objective* principle of will, and can therefore serve as a universal practical law. The foundation of this principle is: *rational nature exists as an end in itself.* Man necessarily conceives his own existence as being so; so far then this is a *subjective* principle of human actions. But every other rational being regards its existence similarly, just on the same rational principle that holds for me; so that it is at the same time an objective principle from which as a supreme practical law all laws of the will must be capable of being deduced. Accordingly the practical imperative will be as follows: *So act as to treat humanity, whether in thine own person or in that of any other, in every case as an end withal, never as means only.* We will now inquire whether this can be practically carried out. . . .

The conception of every rational being as one which must consider itself as giving in all the maxims of its will universal laws, so as to judge itself and its actions from this point of view—this conception

[1] It might be here objected to me that I take refuge behind the word *respect* in an obscure feeling, instead of giving a distinct solution of the question by a concept of the reason. But although respect is a feeling, it is not a feeling *received* through influence, but is *self-wrought* by a rational concept, and, therefore, is specifically distinct from all feelings of the former kind, which may be referred either to inclination or fear. What I recognize immediately as a law for me, I recognize with respect. This merely signifies the consciousness that my will is *subordinate* to a law, without the intervention of other influences on my sense. The immediate determination of the will by the law, and the consciousness of this, is called *respect,* so that this is regarded as an *effect* of the law on the subject, and not as the *cause* of it. Respect is properly the [22] conception of a worth which thwarts my self-love. Accordingly it is something which is considered neither as an object of inclination nor of fear, although it has something analogous to both. The *object* of respect is the *law* only, that is, the law which we impose on *ourselves,* and yet recognize as necessary in itself. As a law, we are subjected to it without consulting self-love; as imposed by us on ourselves, it is a result of our will. In the former aspect it has an analogy to fear, in the latter to inclination. Respect for a person is properly only respect for the law (of honesty, etc.) of which he gives us an example. Since we see in a person of talents, as it were, the *example of a law* (viz. to become like him in this by exercise), and this constitutes our respect. All so-called moral *interest* consists simply in *respect* for the law.

leads to another which depends on it and is very fruitful, namely, that of a *kingdom of ends.*

By a "kingdom" I understand the union of different rational beings in a system by common laws. Now since it is by laws that ends are determined as regards their universal validity, hence, if we abstract from the personal differences of rational beings, and likewise from all the content of their private ends, we shall be able to conceive all ends combined in a systematic whole (including both rational beings as ends in themselves, and also the special ends which each may propose to himself), that is to say, we can conceive a kingdom of ends, which on the preceding principles is possible.

[63] For all rational beings come under the *law* that each of them must treat itself and all others *never merely as means,* but in every case *at the same time as ends in themselves.* Hence results a systematic union of rational beings by common objective laws, that is, a kingdom which may be called a kingdom of ends, since what these laws have in view is just the relation of these beings to one another as ends and means. It is certainly only an ideal.

A rational being belongs as a *member* to the kingdom of ends when, although giving universal laws in it, he is also himself subject to these laws. He belongs to it *as sovereign* when, while giving laws, he is not subject to the will of any other.

A rational being must always regard himself as giving laws either as member or as sovereign in a kingdom of ends which is rendered possible by the freedom of will. He cannot, however, maintain the latter position merely by the maxims of his will, but only in case he is a completely independent being without wants and with unrestricted power adequate to his will.

Morality consists then in the reference of all action to the legislation which alone can render a kingdom of ends possible. This legislation must be capable of existing in every rational being, and of emanating from his will, so that the principle of this will is never to act on any maxim which could not without contradiction be also a universal law, and accordingly, always so to act *that the will could at the same time regard itself as giving in its maxims universal laws.* If now the maxims of rational beings are not by their own nature coincident with this objective principle, then the necessity of acting on it is called practical necessitation [64], that is, *duty.* Duty does not apply to the sovereign in the kingdom of ends, but it does to every member of it and to all in the same degree.

The practical necessity of acting on this principle, that is, duty, does not rest at all on feelings, impulses, or inclinations, but solely on the relation of rational beings to one another, a relation in which the will of a rational being must always be regarded as *legislative,* since otherwise it could not be conceived as *an end in itself.* Reason then refers every maxim of the will, regarding it as legislating universally, to every other will and also to every action towards oneself; and this not on account of any other practical motive or any future advantage, but from the idea of the *dignity* of a rational being, obeying no law but that which he himself also gives.

In the kingdom of ends everything has either *value* or *dignity.* Whatever has a value can be replaced by something else which is *equivalent;* whatever, on the other hand, is above all value, and therefore admits of no equivalent, has a dignity.

Whatever has reference to the general inclinations and wants of mankind has a *market value;* whatever, without presupposing a want, corresponds to a certain taste, that is, to a satisfaction in the mere purposeless play of our faculties, has a *fancy value;* but that which constitutes the condition under which alone anything can be an end in itself, this has not merely a relative worth, that is, value, but an intrinsic worth, that is, *dignity.*

John Stuart Mill (1806–1873)
ON THE CONNECTION BETWEEN JUSTICE AND UTILITY

Mill argues that utilitarianism, properly understood, can deal with all matters crucial to justice. Indeed, he argues that the greatest-happiness principle provides a rational foundation for social and distributive justice. See Section C of the introductory essay to Part IV for a discussion of Mill's views on justice.

READING QUESTIONS

In reading the selection, try to answer the following questions and identify the passages that support your answers:

1. What is Mill's conception of utility?
2. What is his conception of justice?
3. How does Mill think that justice relates to utility?
4. What reasons does Mill give for his views?
5. Are they good? Why or why not?

Reprinted from Max Lerner (ed.), *Essential Works of John Stuart Mill* (New York: Bantam, 1961), "On the Connection Between Justice and Utility," pp. 226–248.

In all ages of speculation one of the strongest obstacles to the reception of the doctrine that Utility or Happiness is the criterion of right and wrong has been drawn from the idea of Justice. The powerful sentiment, and apparently clear perception, which that word recalls with a rapidity and certainty resembling an instinct, have seemed to the majority of thinkers to point to an inherent quality in things; to show that the Just must have an existence in Nature as something absolute, generically distinct from every variety of the Expedient, and, in idea, opposed to it, though (as is commonly acknowledged) never, in the long run, disjoined from it in fact.

In the case of this, as of our other moral sentiments, there is no necessary connexion between the question of its origin, and that of its binding force. That a feeling is bestowed on us by Nature does not necessarily legitimate all its promptings. The feeling of justice might be a peculiar instinct, and might yet require, like our other instincts, to be controlled and enlightened by a higher reason. If we have intellectual instincts, leading us to judge in a particular way, as well as animal instincts that prompt us to act in a particular way, there is no necessity that the former should be more infallible in their sphere than the latter in theirs: it may as well happen that wrong judgments are occasionally suggested by those, as wrong actions by these. But though it is one thing to believe that we have natural feelings of justice, and another to acknowledge them as an ultimate criterion of conduct, these two opinions are very closely connected in point of fact. Mankind are always predisposed to believe that any subjective feeling, not otherwise accounted for, is a revelation of some objective reality.

Our present object is to determine whether the reality, to which the feeling of justice corresponds, is one which needs any such special revelation; whether the justice or injustice of an action is a thing intrinsically peculiar, and distinct from all its other qualities, or only a combination of certain of those qualities, presented under a peculiar aspect.

For the purpose of this inquiry it is practically important to consider whether the feeling itself, of justice and injustice, is *sui generis* like our sensations of colour and taste, or a derivative feeling, formed by a combination of others. And this it is the more essential to examine, as people are in general willing enough to allow, that objectively the dictates of Justice coincide with a part of the field of General Expediency; but inasmuch as the subjective mental feeling of Justice is different from that which commonly attaches to simple expediency, and, except in the extreme cases of the latter, is far more imperative in its demands, people find it difficult to see, in Justice, only a particular kind of branch of general utility, and think that its superior binding force requires a totally different origin.

To throw light upon this question it is necessary to attempt to ascertain what is the distinguishing character of justice, or of injustice: what is the quality, or whether there is any quality, attributed in common to all modes of conduct designated as unjust (for justice, like many other moral attributes, is best defined by its opposite), and distinguishing them from such modes of conduct as are disapproved, but without having that particular epithet of disapprobation applied to them. If in everything which men are accustomed to characterize as just or unjust some one common attribute or collection of attributes is always present, we may judge whether this particular attribute or combination of attributes would be capable of gathering round it a sentiment of that peculiar character and intensity by virtue of the general laws of our emotional constitution, or whether the sentiment is inexplicable, and requires to be regarded as a special provision of Nature. If we find the former to be the case, we shall, in resolving this question, have resolved also the main problem: if the latter, we shall have to seek for some other mode of investigating it.

To find the common attributes of a variety of objects it is necessary to begin by surveying the objects themselves in the concrete. Let us therefore advert successively to the various modes of action, and arrangements of human affairs, which are classed, by universal or widely spread opinion, as Just or as Unjust. The things well known to excite the sentiments associated with those names, are of a very multifarious character. I shall pass them rapidly in review, without studying any particular arrangement.

In the first place, it is mostly considered unjust to deprive any one of his personal liberty, his property, or any other thing which belongs to him by law. Here, therefore, is one instance of the application of the terms just and unjust in a perfectly definite sense, namely that it is just to respect, unjust to violate, the *legal rights* of any one. But this judgment admits of several exceptions, arising from the other forms in which the notions of justice and injustice present themselves. For example, the person who suffers the deprivation may (as the phrase is) have *forfeited* the rights which he is so deprived of: a case to which we shall return presently. But also,

Secondly: the legal rights of which he is deprived, may be rights which *ought* not to have belonged to him; in other words, the law which confers on him these rights, may be a bad law. When it is so, or when (which is the same thing for our purpose) it is supposed to be so, opinions will differ as to the justice or injustice of infringing it. Some maintain that no law, however bad, ought to be disobeyed by an individual citizen; that his opposition to it, if shown at all, should be shown only in endeavouring to get it altered by competent authority.

This opinion (which condemns many of the most illustrious benefactors of mankind and would often protect pernicious institutions against the only weapons which, in the state of things existing at the time, have any chance of succeeding against them)

is defended by those who hold it on grounds of expediency; principally on that of the importance, to the common interest of mankind, of maintaining inviolate the sentiment of submission to law. Other persons, again, hold the directly contrary opinion, that any law, judged to be bad, may blamelessly be disobeyed, even though it be not judged to be unjust, but only inexpedient; while others would confine the license of disobedience to the case of unjust laws: but again, some say, that all laws which are inexpedient are unjust; since every law imposes some restriction on the natural liberty of mankind, which restriction is an injustice, unless legitimated by tending to their good. Among these diversities of opinion, it seems to be universally admitted that there may be unjust laws, and that law, consequently, is not the ultimate criterion of justice, but may give to one person a benefit, or impose on another an evil, which justice condemns. When, however, a law is thought to be unjust, it seems always to be regarded as being so in the same way in which a breach of law is unjust, namely, by infringing somebody's right; which, as it cannot in this case be a legal right, receives a different appellation, and is called a moral right. We may say, therefore, that a second case of injustice consists in taking or withholding from any person that to which he has a *moral right*.

Thirdly: it is universally considered just that each person should obtain that (whether good or evil) which he *deserves;* and unjust that he should obtain a good, or be made to undergo an evil, which he does not deserve. This is, perhaps, the clearest and most emphatic form in which the idea of justice is conceived by the general mind. As it involves the notion of desert, the question arises, what constitutes desert? Speaking in a general way, a person is understood to deserve good if he does right, evil if he does wrong; and in a more particular sense, to deserve good from those to whom he does or has done good, and evil from those in whom he does or has done evil. The precept of returning good for evil has never been regarded as a case of the fulfillment of justice, but as one in which the claims of justice are waived, in obedience to other considerations.

Fourthly: it is confessedly unjust to *break faith* with any one: to violate an engagement, either express or implied, or disappoint expectations raised by our own conduct, at least if we have raised those expectations knowingly and voluntarily. Like the other obligations of justice already spoken of, this one is not regarded as absolute, but as capable of being overruled by a stronger obligation of justice on the other side; or by such conduct on the part of the person concerned as is deemed to absolve us from our obligation to him, and to constitute a *forfeiture* of the benefit which he has been led to expect.

Fifthly: it is, by universal admission, inconsistent with justice to be *partial;* to show favour or preference to one person over another, in matters to which favour and preference do not properly apply. Impartiality, however, does not seem to be regarded as a duty in itself, but rather as instrumental to some other duty; for it is admitted that favour and preference are not always censurable, and indeed the cases in which they are condemned are rather the exception than the rule. A person would be more likely to be blamed than applauded for giving his family or friends no superiority in good offices over strangers, when he could do so without violating any other duty; and no one thinks it unjust to seek one person in preference to another as a friend, connexion, or companion. Impartiality where rights are concerned, is of course obligatory, but this is involved in the more general obligation, of giving to every one his right. A tribunal, for example, must be impartial, because it is bound to award, without regard to any other consideration, a disputed object to the one of two parties who has the right to it. There are other cases in which impartiality means, being solely influenced by desert; as with those who, in the capacity of judges, preceptors, or parents, administer reward and punishment as such. There are cases again, in which it means, being solely influenced by consideration for the public interest; as in making a selection among candidates for a government employment. Impartiality, in short, as an obligation of justice, may be said to mean, being exclusively influenced by the considerations which it is supposed ought to influence the particular case in hand; and resisting the solicitation of any motives which prompt to conduct different from what those considerations would dictate.

Nearly allied to the idea of impartiality, is that of *equality;* which often enters as a component part both into the conception of justice and into the practice of it, and, in the eyes of many persons, constitutes its essence. But in this, still more than in any other case, the notion of justice varies in different persons, and always conforms in its variations to their notion of utility. Each person maintains that equality is the dictate of justice, except where he thinks that expediency requires inequality. The justice of giving equal protection to the rights of all, is maintained by those who support the most outrageous inequality in the rights themselves. Even in slave countries it is theoretically admitted that the rights of the slave, such as they are, ought to be as sacred as those of the master; and that a tribunal which fails to enforce them with equal strictness is wanting in justice; while, at the same time, institutions which leave to the slave scarcely any rights to enforce, are not deemed unjust, because they are not deemed inexpedient. Those who think that utility requires distinctions of rank, do not consider it unjust that riches and social privileges should be unequally dispensed; but those who think this inequality inexpedient, think it unjust also. Whoever thinks that government is necessary, sees no injustice in as much inequality as is constituted by giving to the magistrate powers not granted to other people. Even among those who hold levelling doctrines, there are as many questions of justice as there are differences of opinion about expediency. Some Communists consider it unjust that the produce of the labour of the community should be shared on any other principle than that of exact equality; others think it just that those should receive most whose wants are greatest; while others hold that those who work harder, or who produce more, or whose services are more valuable to the community, may justly claim a larger quota in the division of the produce. And the sense of natural justice may be plausibly appealed to in behalf of every one of these opinions.

Among so many diverse applications of the term Justice, which yet is not regarded as ambiguous, it is a matter of some difficulty to seize the mental link which holds them together, and on which the moral sentiment adhering to the term essentially depends. Perhaps, in this embarrassment, some help may be derived from the history of the word, as indicated by its etymology.

In most, if not in all, languages, the etymology of the word which corresponds to Just, points distinctly to an origin connected with the ordinances of law. *Justum* is a form of *jussum,* that which has been ordered. Δικαιον comes directly from δίκη, a suit at law. *Recht,* from which came *right* and *righteous,* is synonymous with law. The courts of justice, the administration of justice, are the courts and the administration of law. *La justice,* in French, is the established term for judicature. I am not committing the fallacy, imputed with some show of truth to Horne Tooke, of assuming that a word must still continue to mean what it originally meant. Etymology is slight evidence of what the idea now signified is, but the very best evidence of how it sprang up. There can, I think, be no doubt that the *idée mère,* the primitive element, in the formation of the notion of justice, was conformity to law. It constituted the entire idea among the Hebrews, up to the birth of Christianity; as might be expected in the case of a people whose laws attempted to embrace all subjects on which precepts were required, and who believed those laws to be a direct emanation from the Supreme Being. But other nations, and in particular the Greeks and Romans, who knew that their laws had been made originally, and still continued to be made, by men, were not afraid to admit that those men might make bad laws; might do, by law, the same things, and from the same motives, which if done by individuals without the sanction of law, would be called unjust. And hence the sentiment of injustice came to be attached, not to all violations of law, but only to violations of such laws as *ought* to exist, including such as ought to exist, but do not; and to laws themselves, if supposed to be contrary to what ought to be law. In this manner the idea of law and of its injunctions was still predominant in the notion of justice, even when the laws actually in force ceased to be accepted as the standard of it.

It is true that mankind consider the idea of justice and its obligations as applicable to many things which neither are, nor is it desired that they should be, regulated by law. Nobody desires that laws should interfere with the whole detail of private life; yet every one allows that in all daily conduct a person may and does show himself to be either just or unjust. But even here, the idea of the breach of what ought to be law, still lingers in a modified shape. It would always give us pleasure, and chime in with our feelings of fitness, that acts which we deem unjust should be punished, though we do not always think it expedient that this should be done by the tribunals. We forego that gratification on account of incidental inconveniences. We should be glad to see just conduct enforced and injustice repressed, even in the minutest details, if we were not, with reason, afraid of trusting the magistrate with so unlimited an amount of power over individuals. When we think that a person is bound in justice to do a thing, it is an ordinary form of language to say that he ought to be compelled to do it. We should be gratified to see the obligation enforced by anybody who had the power. If we see that its enforcement by law would be inexpedient, we lament the impossibility, we consider the inpunity given to injustice as an evil, and strive to make amends for it by bringing a strong ex-

pression of our own and the public disapprobation to bear upon the offender. Thus the idea of legal constraint is still the generating idea of the notion of justice, though undergoing several transformations before that notion, as it exists in an advanced state of society, becomes complete.

The above is, I think, a true account, as far as it goes, of the origin and progressive growth of the idea of justice. But we must observe, that it contains, as yet, nothing to distinguish that obligation from moral obligation in general. For the truth is, that the idea of penal sanction, which is the essence of law, enters not only into the conception of injustice, but into that of any kind of wrong. We do not call anything wrong, unless we mean to imply that a person ought to be punished in some way or other for doing it; if not by law, by the opinion of his fellow creatures; if not by opinion, by the reproaches of his own conscience. This seems the real turning point of the distinction between morality and simple expediency. It is a part of the notion of Duty in every one of its forms, that a person may rightfully be compelled to fulfill it. Duty is a thing which may be *exacted* from a person, as one exacts a debt. Unless we think that it may be exacted from him, we do not call it his duty. Reasons of prudence, or the interest of other people, may militate against actually exacting it; but the person himself, it is clearly understood, would not be entitled to complain. There are other things, on the contrary, which we wish that people should do, which we like or admire them for doing, perhaps dislike or despise them for not doing, but yet admit that they are not bound to do; it is not a case of moral obligation; we do not blame them, that is, we do not think that they are proper objects of punishment. How we come by these ideas of deserving and not deserving punishment, will appear, perhaps, in the sequel; but I think there is no doubt that this distinction lies at the bottom of the notions of right and wrong; that we call any conduct wrong, or employ, instead, some other term of dislike or disparagement, according as we think that the person ought, or ought not, to be punished for it; and we say, it would be right to do so and so, or merely that it would be desirable or laudable, according as we would wish to see the person whom it concerns, compelled, or only persuaded and exhorted to act in that manner.[1]

---

[1] See this point enforced and illustrated by Professor Bain, in an admirable chapter (entitled *The Ethical Emotions, or the Moral Sense*) of the second of the two treatises composing his elaborate and profound work on the Mind.

This, therefore, being the characteristic difference which marks off, not justice, but morality in general, from the remaining provinces of Expediency and Worthiness; the character is still to be sought which distinguishes justice from other branches of morality. Now it is known that ethical writers divide moral duties into two classes, denoted by the ill-chosen expressions, duties of perfect and of imperfect obligation; the latter being those in which, though the act is obligatory, the particular occasions of performing it are left to our choice; as in the case of charity or beneficence, which we are indeed bound to practise, but not towards any definite person, nor at any prescribed time. In the more precise language of philosophic jurists, duties of perfect obligation are those duties in virtue of which a correlative *right* resides in some person or persons; duties of imperfect obligation are those moral obligations which do not give birth to any right. I think it will be found that this distinction exactly coincides with that which exists between justice and the other obligations of morality.

In our survey of the various popular acceptations of justice, the term appeared generally to involve the idea of a personal right—a claim on the part of one or more individuals, like that which the law gives when it confers a proprietary or other legal right. Whether the injustice consists in depriving a person of a possession, or in breaking faith with him, or in treating him worse than he deserves, or worse than other people who have no greater claims, in each case the supposition implies two things—a wrong done, and some assignable person who is wronged. Injustice may also be done by treating a person better than others; but the wrong in this case is to his competitors, who are also assignable persons. It seems to me that this feature in the case—a right in some person, correlative to the moral obligation—constitutes the specific difference between justice, and generosity or beneficence. Justice implies something which it is not only right to do, and wrong not to do, but which some individual person can claim from us as his moral right. No one has a moral right to our generosity or beneficence, because we are not morally bound to practise those virtues towards any given individual. And it will be found with respect to this as to every correct definition, that the instances which seem to conflict with it are those which most confirm it. For if a moralist attempts, as some have done, to make out that mankind generally, though not any given individual, have a right to all the good we can do them, he at once, by that thesis, includes generosity and beneficence within the category of justice. He is obliged to say that our utmost exertions are *due* to fellow creatures, thus assimilating them to a debt; or that nothing less can be a sufficient *return* for what society does for us, thus classing the case as one of gratitude; both of which are acknowledged cases of justice. Wherever there is a right, the case is one of justice, and not of the virtue of beneficence: and whoever does not place the distinction between justice and morality in general, where we have now placed it, will be found to make no distinction between them at all, but to merge all morality in justice.

Having thus endeavoured to determine the distinctive elements which enter into the composition of the idea of justice, we are ready to enter on the inquiry, whether the feeling which accompanies the idea is attached to it by a special dispensation of nature, or whether it could have grown up, by any known laws, out of the idea itself; and in particular, whether it can have originated in considerations of general expediency.

I conceive that the sentiment itself does not arise from anything which would commonly, or correctly, be termed an idea of expediency; but that, though the sentiment does not, whatever is moral in it does.

We have seen that the two essential ingredients in the sentiment of justice are the desire to punish a person who has done harm, and the knowledge or belief that there is some definite individual or individuals to whom harm has been done.

Now it appears to me, that the desire to punish a person who has done harm to some individual, is a spontaneous outgrowth from two sentiments, both in the highest degree natural, and which either are or resemble instincts; the impulse of self-defence, and the feeling of sympathy.

It is natural to resent, and to repel, or retaliate, any harm done or attempted against ourselves, or against those with whom we sympathize. The origin of this sentiment it is not necessary here to discuss. Whether it be an instinct or a result of intelligence, it is, we know, common to all animal nature; for every animal tries to hurt those who have hurt, or who it thinks are about to hurt, itself or its young. Human beings, on this point, only differ from other animals in two particulars. First, in being capable of sympathizing, not solely with their offspring, or, like some of the more noble animals, with some superior animal who is kind to them, but with all human, and even with all sentient, beings. Secondly, in having a more developed intelligence, which gives a wider range to the whole of their sentiments, whether self-regarding or sympathetic. By virtue of his superior intelligence, even apart from his superior range of sympathy, a human being is capable of apprehending a community of interest between himself and the human society of which he forms a part, such that any conduct which threatens the security of the society generally, is threatening to his own, and calls forth his instinct (if instinct it be) of self-defence. The same superiority of intelligence, joined to the power of sympathizing with human beings generally, enables him to attach himself to the collective idea of his tribe, his country, or mankind, in such a manner that any act hurtful to them, raises his instinct of sympathy, and urges him to resistance.

The sentiment of justice, in that one of its elements which consists of the desire to punish, is thus, I conceive, the natural feeling of retaliation or vengeance, rendered by intellect and sympathy applicable to those injuries, that is, to those hurts, which wound us through, or in common with, society at large. This sentiment, in itself, has nothing moral in it; what is moral is, the exclusive subordination of it to the social sympathies, so as to wait on and obey their call. For the natural feeling would make us resent indiscriminately whatever any one does that is disagreeable to us; but when moralized by the social feeling, it only acts in the directions conformable to the general good: just persons resenting a hurt to society, though not otherwise a hurt to themselves, and not resenting a hurt to themselves, however painful, unless it be the kind which society has a common interest with them in the repression of.

It is no objection against this doctrine to say, that when we feel our sentiment of justice outraged, we are not thinking of society at large, or of any collective interest, but only of the individual case. It is common enough certainly, though the reverse of commendable, to feel resentment merely because we have suffered pain; but a person whose resentment is really a moral feeling, that is, who considers whether an act is blameable before he allows himself to resent it—such a person, though he may not say expressly to himself that he is standing up for the interest of society, certainly does feel that he is asserting a rule which is for the benefit of others as well as for his own. If he is not feeling this—if he is regarding the act solely as it affects him individually—he is not consciously just; he is not concerning himself about the justice of his actions. This is admitted even by anti-utilitarian moralists. When Kant

(as before remarked) propounds as the fundamental principle of morals, 'So act, that thy rule of conduct might, be adopted as a law by all rational beings', he virtually acknowledges that the interest of mankind collectively, or at least of mankind indiscriminately, must be in the mind of the agent when conscientiously deciding on the morality of the act. Otherwise he uses words without a meaning: for, that a rule even of utter selfishness could not *possibly* be adopted by all rational beings—that there is any insuperable obstacle in the nature of things to its adoption—cannot be even plausibly maintained. To give any meaning to Kant's principle, the sense put upon it must be, that we ought to shape our conduct by a rule which all rational beings might adopt *with benefit to their collective interest.*

To recapitulate: the idea of justice supposes two things; a rule of conduct, and a sentiment which sanctions the rule. The first must be supposed common to all mankind, and intended for their good. The other (the sentiment) is a desire that punishment may be suffered by those who infringe the rule. There is involved, in addition, the conception of some definite person who suffers by the infringement; whose rights (to use the expression appropriate to the case) are violated by it. And the sentiment of justice appears to me to be, the animal desire to repel or retaliate a hurt or damage to oneself, or to those with whom one sympathizes, widened so as to include all persons, by the human capacity of enlarged sympathy, and the human conception of intelligent self-interest. From the latter elements, the feeling derives its morality; from the former, its peculiar impressiveness, and energy of self-assertion.

I have, throughout, treated the idea of a *right* residing in the injured person, and violated by the injury, not as a separate element in the composition of the idea and sentiment, but as one of the forms in which the other two elements clothe themselves. These elements are a hurt to some assignable person or persons on the one hand, and a demand for punishment on the other. An examination of our own minds, I think, will show that these two things include all that we mean when we speak of violation of a right. When we call anything a person's right, we mean that he has a valid claim on society to protect him in the possession of it, either by the force of law, or by that of education and opinion. If he has what we consider a sufficient claim, on whatever account, to have something guaranteed to him by society, we say that he has a right to it. If we desire to prove that anything does not belong to him by right, we think this done as soon as it is admitted that society ought not to take measures for securing it to him, but should leave him to chance, or to his own exertions. Thus, a person is said to have a right to what he can earn in fair professional competition; because society ought not to allow any other person to hinder him from endeavouring to earn in that manner as much as he can. But he has not a right to three hundred a-year, though he may happen to be earning it; because society is not called on to provide that he shall earn that sum. On the contrary, if he owns ten thousand pounds three per cent stock, he *has* a right to three hundred a-year; because society has come under an obligation to provide him with an income of that amount.

To have a right, then, is, I conceive, to have something which society ought to defend me in the possession of. If the objector goes on to ask, why it ought? I can give him no other reason than general utility. If that expression does not seem to convey a sufficient feeling of the strength of the obligation, nor to account for the peculiar energy of the feeling, it is because there goes to the composition of the sentiment, not a rational only but also an animal element, the thirst for retaliation; and this thirst derives its intensity, as well as its moral justification, from the extraordinarily important and impressive kind of utility which is concerned. The interest involved is that of security, to every one's feelings the most vital of all interests. All other earthly benefits are needed by one person, not needed by another; and many of them can, if necessary, be cheerfully foregone, or replaced by something else; but security no human being can possibly do without; on it we depend for all our immunity from evil, and for the whole value of all and every good, beyond the passing moment; since nothing but the gratification of the instant could be of any worth to us, if we could be deprived of everything the next instant by whoever was momentarily stronger than ourselves. Now this most indispensable of all necessaries, after physical nutriment, cannot be had, unless the machinery for providing it is kept unintermittedly in active play. Our notion, therefore, of the claim we have on our fellow creatures to join in making safe for us the very groundwork of our existence, gathers feelings around it so much more intense than those concerned in any of the more common cases of utility, that the difference in degree (as is often the case in psychology) becomes a real difference in kind. The claim assumes that character of absoluteness, that apparent infinity, and incommensurability with all other considerations, which constitute the distinction between the feeling of right and wrong and that of ordinary expediency and inexpediency. The feelings concerned are so powerful, and we count so positively on finding a responsive feeling in others (all being alike interested), that *ought* and *should* grow into *must,* and recognized indispensability becomes a moral necessity, analogous to physical, and often not inferior to it in binding force.

If the preceding analysis, or something resembling it, be not the correct account of the notion of justice; if justice be totally independent of utility, and be a standard *per se,* which the mind can recognize by simple introspection of itself, it is hard to understand why that internal oracle is so ambiguous, and why so many things appear either just or unjust, according to the light in which they are regarded.

We are continually informed that Utility is an uncertain standard, which every different person interprets differently, and that there is no safety but in the immutable, ineffaceable, and unmistakable dictates of Justice, which carry their evidence in themselves, and are independent of the fluctuations of opinion. One would suppose from this that on questions of justice there could be no controversy; that if we take that for our rule, its application to any given case could leave us in as little doubt as a mathematical demonstration. So far is this from being the fact, that there is as much difference of opinion, and as much discussion, about what is just, as about what is useful to society. Not only have different nations and individuals different notions of justice, but in the mind of one and the same individual, justice is not some one rule, principle, or maxim, but many, which do not always coincide in their dictates, and in choosing between which, he is guided either by some extraneous standard, or by his own personal predilections.

For instance, there are some who say it is unjust to punish any one for the sake of example to others; that punishment is just, only when intended for the good of the sufferer himself. Others maintain the extreme reverse, contending that to punish persons who have attained years of discretion, for their own benefit, is despotism and injustice, since if the matter at issue is solely their own good, no one has a right to control their own judgment of it; but that they may justly be punished to prevent evil to others, this being the exercise of the legitimate right of self-defence.

Mr. Owen, again, affirms that it is unjust to punish at all; for the criminal did not make his own character; his education, and the circumstances which surrounded him, have made him a criminal, and for these he is not responsible. All these opinions are extremely plausible; and, so long as the question is argued as one of justice simply, without going down to the principles which lie under justice and are the source of its authority, I am unable to see how any of these reasoners can be refuted. For in truth every one of the three builds upon rules of justice confessedly true.

The first appeals to the acknowledged injustice of singling out an individual, and making him a sacrifice, without his consent, for other people's benefit. The second relies on the acknowledged justice of self-defence, and the admitted injustice of forcing one person to conform to another's notions of what constitutes his good. The Owenite invokes the admitted principle that it is unjust to punish any one for what he cannot help. Each is triumphant so long as he is not compelled to take into consideration any other maxims of justice than the one he has selected; but as soon as their several maxims are brought face to face, each disputant seems to have exactly as much to say for himself as the others. No one of them can carry out his own notion of justice without trampling upon another equally binding. These are difficulties; they have always been felt to be such; and many devices have been invented to turn rather than to overcome them. As a refuge from the last of the three, men imagined what they called the freedom of the will; fancying that they could not justify punishing a man whose will is in a thoroughly hateful state, unless it be supposed to have come into that state through no influence of anterior circumstances. To escape from the other difficulties, a favourite contrivance has been the fiction of a contract, whereby at some unknown period all the members of society engaged to obey the laws, and consented to be punished for any disobedience to them; thereby giving to their legislators the right, which it is assumed they would not otherwise have had, of punishing them, either for their own good or for that of society.

This happy thought was considered to get rid of the whole difficulty, and to legitimate the infliction of punishment, in virtue of another received maxim of justice, *Volenti non fit injuria;* that is not unjust which is done with the consent of the person who is supposed to be hurt by it. I need hardly remark that even if the consent were not a mere fiction, this maxim is not superior in authority to the others which it is brought in to supersede. It is, on the contrary, an instructive specimen of the loose and irregular manner in which supposed principles of justice grow up. This particular one evidently came into use as a help to the coarse exigencies of courts of law, which are sometimes obliged to be content with very uncertain presumptions on account of the greater evils which would often arise from any attempt on their part to cut finer. But even courts of law are not able to adhere consistently to the maxim, for they allow voluntary engagements to be set aside on the ground of fraud, and sometimes on that of mere mistake or misinformation.

Again, when the legitimacy of inflicting punishment is admitted, how many conflicting conceptions of justice come to light in discussing the proper apportionment of punishments to offences. No rule on the subject recommends itself so strongly to the primitive and spontaneous sentiment of justice as the *lex talionis,* an eye for an eye and a tooth for a tooth. Though this principle of the Jewish and of the Mahamedan law has been generally abandoned in Europe as a practical maxim, there is, I suspect, in most minds, a secret hankering after it; and when retribution accidentally falls on an offender in that precise shape, the general feeling of satisfaction evinced, bears witness how natural is the sentiment to which this repayment in kind is acceptable. With many the test of justice in penal infliction is that the punishment should be proportioned to the offence; meaning that it should be exactly measured by the moral guilt of the culprit (whatever be their standard for measuring moral guilt): the consideration, what amount of punishment is necessary to deter from the offence, having nothing to do with the question of justice, in their estimation; while there are others to whom that consideration is all in all; who maintain that it is not just, at least for man, to inflict on a fellow-creature, whatever may be his offences, any amount of suffering beyond the least that will suffice to prevent him from repeating, and others from imitating, his misconduct.

To take another example from a subject already once referred to. In a co-operative industrial association is it just or not that talent or skill should give a title to superior remuneration? On the negative side of the question it is argued that whoever does the best he can deserves equally well, and ought not in justice to be put in a position of inferiority for no fault of his own; that superior abilities have already advantages more than enough, in the admiration they excite, the personal influence they command, and the internal sources of satisfaction attending them, without adding to these a superior share of the world's goods; and that society is bound in justice rather to make compensation to the less favoured, for this unmerited inequality of advantages, than to aggravate it. On the contrary side it is contended that society receives more from the efficient labourer; that his services being more useful, society owes him a larger return for them; that a greater share of the joint result is actually his work, and not to allow his claim to it is a kind of robbery; that if he is only to receive as much as others, he can only be justly required to produce as much, and to give a smaller amount of time and exertion, proportioned to his superior efficiency. Who shall decide between these appeals to conflicting principles of justice? Justice has in this case two sides to it, which it is impossible to bring into harmony, and the two disputants have chosen opposite sides; the one looks to what it is just that the individual should receive, the other to what it is just that the community should give. Each from his own point of view is unanswerable; and any choice between them, on grounds of justice, must be perfectly arbitrary. Social utility alone can decide the preference.

How many, again, and how irreconcileable, are the standards of justice to which reference is made in discussing the repartition of taxation. One opinion is that payment to the State should be in numerical proportion to pecuniary means. Others think that justice dictates what they term graduated taxation; taking a higher per-centage from those who have more to spare. In point of natural justice a strong case might be made for disregarding means altogether, and taking the same absolute sum (whenever it could be got) from every one: as the subscribers to a mess, or to a club, all pay the same sum for the same privileges, whether they can all equally afford it or not. Since the protection (it might be said) of law and government is afforded to and is equally required by all, there is no injustice in making all buy it at the same price. It is reckoned justice, not injustice, that a dealer should charge to all customers the same price for the same article, not a price varying according to their means of payment. This doctrine, as applied to taxation, finds no advocates, because it conflicts so strongly with man's feelings of humanity and of social expediency; but the principle of justice which it invokes is as true and as binding as those which can be appealed to against it. Accordingly it exerts a tacit influence on the line of defence employed for other modes of assessing taxation. People feel obliged to argue that the State does more for the rich than for the poor, as a justification for its taking more from them: though this is in reality not true, for the rich would be far better able to protect themselves, in the absence of law or government, than the poor, and indeed would probably be successful in converting the poor into their slaves. Others, again, so far defer to the same conception of justice as to maintain that all should pay an equal capitation tax for the protection of their persons (these being of equal value to all), and an unequal tax for the protection of their property, which is unequal. To this others reply that the all of one man is as valuable to him as the all of another. From these confusions there is no other mode of extrication than the utilitarian.

Is, then, the difference between the Just and the Expedient a merely imaginary distinction? Have mankind been under a delusion in thinking that justice is a more sacred thing than policy, and that the latter ought only to be listened to after the former has been satisfied? By no means. The exposition we have given of the nature and origin of the sentiment, recognizes a real distinction; and no one of those who profess the most sublime contempt for the consequences of actions as an element in their morality, attaches more importance to the distinction than I do. While I dispute the pretensions of any theory which sets up an imaginary standard of justice not grounded on utility, I account the justice which is grounded on utility to be the chief part, and incomparably the most sacred and binding part, of all morality. Justice is a name for certain classes of moral rules, which concern the essentials of human well-being more nearly, and are therefore of more absolute obligation, than any other rules for the guidance of life; and the notion which we have found to be of the essence of the idea of justice, that of a right residing in an individual, implies and testifies to this more binding obligation.

The moral rules which forbid mankind to hurt one another (in which we must never forget to include wrongful interference with each other's freedom) are more vital to human well-being than any maxims, however important, which only point out the best mode of managing some department of human affairs. They have also the peculiarity, that they are the main element in determining the whole of the social feelings of mankind. It is their observance which alone preserves peace among human beings: if obedience to them were not the rule, and disobedience the exception, every one would see in every one else an enemy, against whom he must be perpetually guarding himself. What is hardly less important, these are the precepts which mankind have the strongest and the most direct inducements for impressing upon one another. By merely giving to each other prudential instruction or exhortation, they may gain, or think they gain, nothing: in inculcating on each other the duty of positive beneficence they have an unmistakable interest, but far less in degree: the person may possibly not need the benefits of others; but he always needs that they should not do him hurt.

Thus the moralities which protect every individual from being harmed by others, either directly or by being hindered in his freedom of pursuing his own good, are at once those which he himself has most at heart, and those which he has the strongest interest in publishing and enforcing by word and deed. It is by a person's observance of these that his fitness to exist as one of the fellowship of human beings is tested and decided; for on that depends his being a nuisance or not to those with whom he is in contact. Now it is these moralities primarily, which compose the obligations of justice. The most marked cases of injustice, and those which give the tone to the feeling of repugnance which characterizes the sentiment, are acts of wrongful aggression, or wrongful exercise of power over some one; the next are those which consist in wrongfully withholding from him something which is his due: in both cases, inflicting on him a positive hurt, either in the form of direct suffering, or of the privation of some good which he had reasonable ground, either of a physical or of a social kind, for counting upon.

The same powerful motives which command the observance of these primary moralities enjoin the punishment of those who violate them; and as the impulses of self-defence, of defence of others, and of vengeance, are all called forth against such persons, retribution, or evil for evil, becomes closely connected with the sentiment of justice, and is universally included in the idea. Good for good is also one of the dictates of justice; and this, though its social utility is evident, and though it carries with it a natural human feeling, has not at first sight that obvious connexion with hurt or injury, which, existing in the most elementary cases of just and unjust, is the source of the characteristic intensity of the sentiment. But the connexion, though less obvious, is not less real. He who accepts benefits, and denies a return of them when needed, inflicts a real hurt, by disappointing one of the most natural and reasonable of expectations, and one which he must at least tacitly have encouraged, otherwise the benefits would seldom have been conferred. The important rank, among human evils and wrongs, of the disappointment of expectation, is shown in the fact that it constitutes the principal criminality of two such highly immoral acts as a breach of friendship and a breach of promise. Few hurts which human beings can sustain are greater, and none wound more, than when that on which they habitually and with full assurance relied, fails them in the hour of need; and few wrongs are greater than this mere withholding of good; none excite more resentment, either in the person suffering, or in a sympathizing spectator. The principle, therefore, of giving to each what they deserve, that is, good for good as well as evil for evil, is not only included within the idea of Justice as we have defined it, but is a proper object of that intensity of sentiment, which places the Just, in human estimation, above the simply Expedient.

Most of the maxims of justice current in the world, and commonly appealed to in its transactions, are simply instrumental to carrying into effect the principles of justice which we have now spoken of. That a person is responsible only for what he has done voluntarily, or could voluntarily have avoided; that it is unjust to condemn any person unheard; that the punishment ought to be proportioned to the offence, and the like, are maxims intended to prevent the just principle of evil for evil from being perverted to the infliction of evil without that justification. The greater part of these common maxims have come into use from the practice of courts of justice, which have been naturally led to a more complete recognition and elaboration than was likely to suggest itself to others, of the rules necessary to enable them to fulfill their double function, of inflicting punishment when due, and of awarding to each person his right.

That first of judicial virtues, impartiality, is an obligation of justice, partly for the reason last mentioned; as being a necessary condition of the fulfillment of the obligations of justice. But this is not the only source of the exalted rank, among human obligations, of those maxims of equality and impartiality, which, both in popular estimation and in that of the most enlightened, are included among the precepts of justice. In one point of view, they may be considered as corollaries from the principles already laid down. If it is a duty to do to each according to his deserts, returning good for good as well as repressing evil by evil, it necessarily follows that we should treat all equally well (when no higher duty forbids) who have deserved equally well of *us*, and that society should treat all equally well who have deserved equally well of *it*, that is, who have deserved equally well absolutely. This is the highest abstract standard of social and distributive justice; towards which all institutions, and the efforts of all virtuous citizens, should be made in the utmost possible degree to converge.

But this great moral duty rests upon a still deeper foundation, being a direct emanation from the first principle of morals, and not a mere logical corollary from secondary or derivative doctrines. It is involved in the very meaning of Utility, or the Greatest-Happiness Principle. That principle is a mere form of words without rational signification, unless one person's happiness, supposed equal in degree (with the proper allowance made for kind), is counted for exactly as much as another's. Those conditions being supplied, Bentham's dictum, 'everybody to count for one, nobody for more than one,' might be written under the principle of utility as an explanatory commentary.[2] The equal claim of everybody to happiness in the estimation of the moralist and the legislator, involves an equal claim to all the means of

[2] This implication, in the first principle of the utilitarian scheme, of perfect impartiality between persons, is regarded by Mr. Herbert Spencer (in his *Social Statics*) as a disproof of the pretensions of utility to be a sufficient guide to right; since (he says) the principle of utility presupposes the anterior principle, that everybody has an equal right to happiness. It may be more correctly described as supposing that equal amounts of happiness are equally desirable whether felt by the same or by different persons. This, however, is not a *presupposition;* not a premise needful to support the principle of utility, but the very principle itself; for what is the principle of utility, if it be not that 'happiness' and 'desirable' are synonymous terms? If there is any anterior principle implied, it can be no other than this, that the truths of arithmetic are applicable to the valuation of happiness, as of all other measurable qualities.

[Mr. Herbert Spencer, in a private communication on the subject of the preceding Note, objects to being considered an opponent of Utilitarianism, and states that he regards happiness as the ultimate end of morality; but deems that end only partially attainable by empirical generalizations from the observed results of conduct, and completely attainable only by deducing, from the laws of life and the conditions of existence, what kinds of action necessarily tend to produce happiness, and what kinds to produce unhappiness. With the exception of the word 'necessarily' I have no dissent to express from this doctrine, and (omitting that word) I am not aware that any modern advocate of utilitarianism is of a different opinion. Bentham, certainly, to whom in the *Social Statics* Mr. Spencer particularly referred, is, least of all writers, chargeable with unwillingness to deduce the effect of actions on happiness from the laws of human nature and the universal conditions of human life. The common charge against him is of relying too exclusively upon such deductions, and declining altogether to be bound by the generalizations from specific experience which Mr. Spencer thinks that utilitarians generally confine themselves to. My own opinion (and, as I collect, Mr. Spencer's) is, that in ethics, as in all other branches of scientific study, the consilience of the results of both these processes, each corroborating and verifying the other, is requisite to give to any general proposition the kind and degree of evidence which constitutes scientific proof.]

happiness, except in so far as the inevitable conditions of human life, and the general interest, in which that of every individual is included, set limits to the maxim; and those limits ought to be strictly construed. As every other maxim of justice, so this, is by no means applied or held applicable, universally; on the contrary, as I have already remarked, it bends to every person's ideas of social expediency. But in whatever case it is deemed applicable at all, it is held to be the dictate of justice. All persons are deemed to have a *right* to equality of treatment, except when some recognised social expediency requires the reverse. And hence all social inequalities which have ceased to be considered expedient, assume the character not of simple inexpediency, but of injustice, and appear so tyrannical, that people are apt to wonder how they ever could have been tolerated; forgetful that they themselves perhaps tolerate other inequalities under an equally mistaken notion of expediency, the correction of which would make that which they approve, seem quite as monstrous as what they have at least learnt to condemn. The entire history of social improvement has been a series of transitions, by which one custom or institution after another, from being a supposed primary necessity of social existence, has passed into the rank of an universally stigmatized injustice and tyranny. So it has been with the distinctions of slaves and freemen, nobles and serfs, patricians and plebeians; and so it will be, and in part already is, with the aristocracies of colour, race, and sex.

It appears from what has been said that justice is a name for certain moral requirements, which, regarded collectively, stand higher in the scale of social utility, and are therefore of more paramount obligation, than any others; though particular cases may occur in which some other social duty is so important, as to overrule any one of the general maxims of justice. Thus, to save a life it may not only be allowable, but a duty, to steal, or take by force, the necessary food or medicine, or to kidnap, and compel to officiate, the only qualified medical practitioner. In such cases, as we do not call anything justice which is not a virtue, we usually say, not that justice must give way to some other moral principle, but that what is just in ordinary cases is, by reason of that other principle, not just in the particular case. By this useful accommodation of language, the character of indefeasibility attributed to justice is kept up, and we are saved from the necessity of maintaining that there can be laudable injustice.

The considerations which have now been adduced resolve, I conceive, the only real difficulty in the utilitarian theory of morals. It has always been evident that all cases of justice are also cases of expediency: the difference is in the peculiar sentiment which attaches to the former as contradistinguished from the latter. If this characteristic sentiment has been sufficiently accounted for; if there is no necessity to assume for it any peculiarity of origin; if it is simply the natural feeling of resentment, moralized by being made coextensive with the demands of social good; and if this feeling not only does but ought to exist in all the classes of cases to which the idea of justice corresponds; that idea no longer presents itself as a stumblingblock to the utilitarian ethics. Justice remains the appropriate name for certain social utilities which are vastly more important, and therefore more absolute and imperative, than any others are as a class (though not more so than others may be in particular cases); and which, therefore, ought to be, as well as naturally are, guarded by a sentiment not only different in degree, but also in kind; distinguished from the milder feeling which attaches to the mere idea of promoting human pleasure or convenience, at once by the more definite nature of its commands, and by the sterner character of its sanctions.

Karl Marx (1818–1883)
LABOR POWER, EXCHANGES, SURPLUS VALUE, AND EXPLOITATION

Marx examines the mechanisms by which market and production activities bring about social changes whose justice is questionable. In particular, he focuses on the creation of surplus value, in which workers produce no value for themselves, and suggests that in a nonexploitative society workers would work only insofar as they produced value for themselves. Marx's ideas are discussed in Section C of the introductory essay to Part IV.

READING QUESTIONS

In reading the selection, try to answer the following questions and identify the passages that support your answers:

1. What is Marx's conception of labor power?
2. What is his conception of surplus value?
3. How, if at all, are these conceptions morally relevant?
4. What reasons does Marx give for his views?
5. Are they good? Why or why not?

Reprinted with the permission of the publishers from Karl Marx, *Capital* (New York: International Publishers, 1967; 7th pr.: 1975), Chap. VI, pp. 167–176, and Chap. X, pp. 212–221. Copyright © 1967.

THE BUYING AND SELLING OF LABOUR-POWER

The change of value that occurs in the case of money intended to be converted into capital, cannot take place in the money itself, since in its function of means of purchase and of payment, it does no more than realise the price of the commodity it buys or pays for; and, as hard cash, it is value petrified, never varying.[1] Just as little can it originate in the second act of circulation, the re-sale of the commodity,

---

[1] "In the form of money . . . capital is productive of no profit." (Ricardo: "Princ. of Pol. Econ.," p. 267.)

which does no more than transform the article from its bodily form back again into its money-form. The change must, therefore, take place in the commodity bought by the first act, M − C, but not in its value, for equivalents are exchanged, and the commodity is paid for at its full value. We are, therefore, forced to the conclusion that the change originates in the use-value, as such, of the commodity, i.e., in its consumption. In order to be able to extract value from the consumption of a commodity, our friend, Moneybags, must be so lucky as to find, within the sphere of circulation, in the market, a commodity, whose use-value possesses the peculiar property of being a source of value, whose actual consumption, therefore, is itself an embodiment of labour, and, consequently, a creation of value. The possessor of money does find on the market such a special commodity in capacity for labour or labour-power.

By labour-power or capacity for labour is to be understood the aggregate of those mental and physical capabilities existing in a human being, which he exercises whenever he produces a use-value of any description.

But in order that our owner of money may be able to find labour-power offered for sale as a commodity, various conditions must first be fulfilled. The exchange of commodities of itself implies no other relations of dependence than those which result from its own nature. On this assumption, labour-power can appear upon the market as a commodity, only if, and so far as, its possessor, the individual whose labour-power it is, offers it for sale, or sells it, as a commodity. In order that he may be able to do this, he must have it at his disposal, must be the untrammelled owner of his capacity for labour, i.e., of his person.[2] He and the owner of money meet in the market, and deal with each other as on the basis of equal rights, with this difference alone, that one is buyer, the other seller; both, therefore, equal in the eyes of the law. The continuance of this relation demands that the owner of the labour-power should sell it only for a definite period, for if he were to sell it rump and stump, once for all, he would be selling himself, converting himself from a free man into a slave, from an owner of a commodity into a commodity. He must constantly look upon his labour-power as his own property, his own commodity, and

this he can only do by placing it at the disposal of the buyer temporarily, for a definite period of time. By this means alone can he avoid renouncing his rights of ownership over it.[3]

The second essential condition to the owner of money finding labour-power in the market as a commodity is this—that the labourer instead of being in the position to sell commodities in which his labour is incorporated, must be obliged to offer for sale as a commodity that very labour-power, which exists only in his living self.

In order that a man may be able to sell commodities other than labour-power, he must of course have the means of production, as raw material, implements, &c. No boots can be made without leather. He requires also the means of subsistence. Nobody—not even "a musician of the future"—can live upon future products, or upon use-values in an unfinished state; and ever since the first moment of his appearance on the world's stage, man always has been, and must still be a consumer, both before and while he is producing. In a society where all products assume the form of commodities, these commodities must be sold after they have been produced, it is only after their sale that they can serve in satisfying the requirements of their producer. The time necessary for their sale is superadded to that necessary for their production.

For the conversion of his money into capital, therefore, the owner of money must meet in the market with the free labourer, free in the double sense, that as a free man he can dispose of his labour-power as his own commodity, and that on the other hand he has no other commodity for sale, is short of everything necessary for the realisation of his labour-power.

---

[2]   In encyclopædias of classical antiquities we find such nonsense as this—that in the ancient world capital was fully developed, "except that the free labourer and a system of credit was wanting." Mommsen also, in his "History of Rome," commits, in this respect, one blunder after another.

[3]   Hence legislation in various countries fixes a maximum for labour-contracts. Wherever free labour is the rule, the laws regulate the mode of terminating this contract. In some States, particularly in Mexico (before the American Civil War, also in the territories taken from Mexico, and also, as a matter of fact, in the Danubian provinces till the revolution effected by Kusa), slavery is hidden under the form of *peonage*. By means of advances, repayable in labour, which are handed down from generation to generation, not only the individual labourer, but his family, become, *de facto*, the property of other persons and their families. Juarez abolished *peonage*. The so-called Emperor Maximilian re-established it by a decree, which, in the House of Representatives at Washington, was aptly denounced as a decree for the re-introduction of slavery into Mexico. "I may make over to another the use, for a limited time, of my particular bodily and mental aptitudes and capabilities; because, in consequence of this restriction, they are impressed with a character of alienation with regard to me as a whole. But by the alienation of all my labour-time and the whole of my work, I should be converting the substance itself, in other words, my general activity and reality, my person, into the property of another." (Hegel, "Philosophie des Rechts." Berlin, 1840, p. 104, § 67.)

The question why this free labourer confronts him in the market, has no interest for the owner of money, who regards the labour-market as a branch of the general market for commodities. And for the present it interests us just as little. We cling to the fact theoretically, as he does practically. One thing, however, is clear—Nature does not produce on the one side owners of money or commodities, and on the other men possessing nothing but their own labour-power. This relation has no natural basis, neither is its social basis one that is common to all historical periods. It is clearly the result of a past historical development, the product of many economic revolutions, of the extinction of a whole series of older forms of social production.

So, too, the economic categories, already discussed by us, bear the stamp of history. Definite historical conditions are necessary that a product may become a commodity. It must not be produced as the immediate means of subsistence of the producer himself. Had we gone further, and inquired under what circumstances all, or even the majority of products take the form of commodities, we should have found that this can only happen with production of a very specific kind, capitalist production. Such an inquiry, however, would have been foreign to the analysis of commodities. Production and circulation of commodities can take place, although the great mass of the objects produced are intended for the immediate requirements of their producers, are not turned into commodities, and consequently social production is not yet by a long way dominated in its length and breadth by exchange-value. The appearance of products as commodities pre-supposes such a development of the social division of labour, that the separation of use-value from exchange-value, a separation which first begins with barter, must already have been completed. But such a degree of development is common to many forms of society, which in other respects present the most varying historical features. On the other hand, if we consider money, its existence implies a definite stage in the exchange of commodities. The particular functions of money which it performs, either as the mere equivalent of commodities, or as means of circulation, or means of payment, as hoard or as universal money, point, according to the extent and relative preponderance of the one function or the other, to very different stages in the process of social production. Yet we know by experience that a circulation of commodities relatively primitive, suffices for the production of all these forms. Otherwise with capital.

The historical conditions of its existence are by no means given with the mere circulation of money and commodities. It can spring into life, only when the owner of the means of production and subsistence meets in the market with the free labourer selling his labour-power. And this one historical condition comprises a world's history. Capital, therefore, announces from its first appearance a new epoch in the process of social production.[4]

We must now examine more closely this peculiar commodity, labour-power. Like all others it has a value.[5] How is that value determined?

The value of labour-power is determined, as in the case of every other commodity, by the labour-time necessary for the production, and consequently also the reproduction, of this special article. So far as it has value, it represents no more than a definite quantity of the average labour of society incorporated in it. Labour-power exists only as a capacity, or power of the living individual. Its production consequently pre-supposes his existence. Given the individual, the production of labour-power consists in his reproduction of himself or his maintenance. For his maintenance he requires a given quantity of the means of subsistence. Therefore the labour-time requisite for the production of labour-power reduces itself to that necessary for the production of those means of subsistence; in other words, the value of labour-power is the value of the means of subsistence necessary for the maintenance of the labourer. Labour-power, however, becomes a reality only by its exercise; it sets itself in action only by working. But thereby a definite quantity of human muscle, nerve, brain, &c., is wasted, and these require to be restored. This increased expenditure demands a larger income.[6] If the owner of labour-power works to-day, to-morrow he must again be able to repeat the same process in the same conditions as regards health and strength. His means of subsistence must therefore be sufficient to maintain him in his normal state as a labouring individual. His natural wants, such as food, clothing, fuel, and housing, vary according to

---

[4] The capitalist epoch is therefore characterised by this, that labour power takes in the eyes of the labourer himself the form of a commodity which is his property; his labour consequently becomes wage-labour. On the other hand, it is only from this moment that the produce of labour universally becomes a commodity.

[5] "The value or worth of a man, is as of all other things his price—that is to say, so much as would be given for the use of his power." (Th. Hobbes: "Leviathan" in Works, Ed. Molesworth. Lond. 1839–44, v. iii, p. 76.)

[6] Hence the Roman Villieus, as overlooker of the agricultural slaves, received "more meagre fare than working slaves, because his work was lighter." (Th. Mommsen, Röm. Geschichte, 1856, p. 810.)

the climatic and other physical conditions of his country. On the other hand, the number and extent of his so-called necessary wants, as also the modes of satisfying them, are themselves the product of historical development, and depend therefore to a great extent on the degree of civilisation of a country, more particularly on the conditions under which, and consequently on the habits and degree of comfort in which, the class of free labourers has been formed.[7] In contradistinction therefore to the case of other commodities, there enters into the determination of the value of labour-power a historical and moral element. Nevertheless, in a given country, at a given period, the average quantity of the means of subsistence necessary for the labourer is practically known.

The owner of labour-power is mortal. If then his appearance in the market is to be continuous, and the continuous conversion of money into capital assumes this, the seller of labour-power must perpetuate himself, "in the way that every living individual perpetuates himself, by procreation."[8] The labour-power withdrawn from the market by wear and tear and death, must be continually replaced by, at the very least, an equal amount of fresh labour-power. Hence the sum of the means of subsistence necessary for the production of labour-power must include the means necessary for the labourer's substitutes, i.e., his children, in order that this race of peculiar commodity-owners may perpetuate its appearance in the market.[9]

In order to modify the human organism, so that it may acquire skill and handiness in a given branch of industry, and become labour-power of a special kind, a special education or training is requisite, and this, on its part, costs an equivalent in commodities of a greater or less amount. This amount varies according to the more or less complicated character of the labour-power. The expenses of this education (excessively small in the case of ordinary labour-power), enter pro tanto into the total value spent in its production.

The value of labour-power resolves itself into the value of a definite quantity of the means of subsistence. It therefore varies with the value of these means or with the quantity of labour requisite for their production.

Some of the means of subsistence, such as food and fuel, are consumed daily, and a fresh supply must be provided daily. Others such as clothes and furniture last for longer periods and require to be replaced only at longer intervals. One article must be bought or paid for daily, another weekly, another quarterly, and so on. But in whatever way the sum total of these outlays may be spread over the year, they must be covered by the average income, taking one day with another. If the total of the commodities required daily for the production of labour-power = A, and those required weekly = B, and those required quarterly = C, and so on, the daily average

of these commodities $= \dfrac{365A + 52B + 4C + \&c.}{365}$.

Suppose that in this mass of commodities requisite for the average day there are embodied 6 hours of social labour, then there is incorporated daily in labour-power half a day's average social labour, in other words, half a day's labour is requisite for the daily production of labour-power. This quantity of labour forms the value of a day's labour-power or the value of the labour-power daily reproduced. If half a day's average social labour is incorporated in three shillings, then three shillings is the price corresponding to the value of a day's labour-power. If its owner therefore offers it for sale at three shillings a day, its selling price is equal to its value, and according to our supposition, our friend Moneybags, who is intent upon converting his three shillings into capital, pays this value.

The minimum limit of the value of labour-power is determined by the value of the commodities, without the daily supply of which the labourer cannot renew his vital energy, consequently by the value of those means of subsistence that are physically indispensable. If the price of labour-power fall to this minimum, it falls below its value, since under such circumstances it can be maintained and developed only in a crippled state. But the value of every commodity is determined by the labour-time requisite to turn it out so as to be of normal quality.

It is a very cheap sort of sentimentality which declares this method of determining the value of labour-power, a method prescribed by the very nature of the case, to be a brutal method, and which wails with Rossi that, "To comprehend capacity for

[7]   Compare W. Th. Thornton: "Over-population and its Remedy," Lond., 1846.

[8]   Petty.

[9]   "Its (labour's) natural price . . . consists in such a quantity of necessaries and comforts of life, as, from the nature of the climate, and the habits of the country, are necessary to support the labourer, and to enable him to rear such a family as may preserve, in the market, an undiminished supply of labour." (R. Torrens: "An Essay on the External Corn Trade." Lond. 1815, p. 62.) The word labour is here wrongly used for labour-power.

labour (puissance de travail) at the same time that we make abstraction from the means of subsistence of the labourers during the process of production, is to comprehend a phantom (être de raison). When we speak of labour, or capacity for labour, we speak at the same time of the labourer and his means of subsistence, of labourer and wages."[10] When we speak of capacity for labour, we do not speak of labour, any more than when we speak of capacity for digestion, we speak of digestion. The latter process requires something more than a good stomach. When we speak of capacity for labour, we do not abstract from the necessary means of subsistence. On the contrary, their value is expressed in its value. If his capacity for labour remains unsold, the labourer derives no benefit from it, but rather he will feel it to be a cruel nature-imposed necessity that this capacity has cost for its production a definite amount of the means of subsistence and that it will continue to do so for its reproduction. He will then agree with Sismondi: "that capacity for labour . . . is nothing unless it is sold."[11]

One consequence of the peculiar nature of labour-power as a commodity is, that its use-value does not, on the conclusion of the contract between the buyer and seller, immediately pass into the hands of the former. Its value, like that of every other commodity, is already fixed before it goes into circulation, since a definite quantity of social labour has been spent upon it; but its use-value consists in the subsequent exercise of its force. The alienation of labour-power and its actual appropriation by the buyer, its employment as a use-value, are separated by an interval of time. But in those cases in which the formal alienation by sale of the use-value of a commodity, is not simultaneous with its actual delivery to the buyer, the money of the latter usually functions as means of payment.[12] In every country in which the capitalist mode of production reigns, it is the custom not to pay for labour-power before it has been exercised for the period fixed by the contract, as for example, the end of each week. In all cases, therefore, the use-value of the labour-power is advanced to the capitalist: the labourer allows the

buyer to consume it before he receives payment of the price; he everywhere gives credit to the capitalist. That this credit is no mere fiction, is shown not only by the occasional loss of wages on the bankruptcy of the capitalist,[13] but also by a series of more enduring consequences.[14] Nevertheless, whether money serves as a means of purchase or as a means of payment, this makes no alteration in the nature of the exchange of commodities. The price of the labour-power is fixed by the contract, although it is not realised till later, like the rent of a house. The labour-power is sold, although it is only paid for at a later period. It will, therefore, be useful, for a clear comprehension of the relation of the parties, to assume provisionally, that the possessor of labour-power, on the occasion of each sale, immediately receives the price stipulated to be paid for it.

---

[10] Rossi. "Cours d'Econ. Polit.," Bruxelles, 1842, p. 370.

[11] Sismondi: "Nouv. Princ. etc.," t. I, p. 112.

[12] "All labour is paid after it has ceased." ("An Inquiry into those Principles Respecting the Nature of Demand." &c., p. 104.) "Le crédit commercial a dû commencer au moment où l'ouvrier, premier artisan de la production, a pu, au moyen de ses économies, attendre le salaire de son travail jusqu' à la fin de la semaine, de la quinzaine, du mois, du trimestre, &c." (Ch. Ganilh: "Des Systèmes d'Econ. Polit." 2ème edit. Paris, 1821, t. II, p. 150.)

[13] "L'ouvrier prête son industrie," but adds Storch slyly: he "risks nothing" except "de perdre son salaire . . . l'ouvrier ne transmet rien de matériel." (Storch: "Cours d'Econ. Polit." Pétersbourg, 1815, t. II., p. 37.)

[14] One example. In London there are two sorts of bakers, the "full priced," who sell bread at its full value, and the "undersellers," who sell it under its value. The latter class comprises more than three-fourths of the total number of bakers. (p. xxxii in the Report of H. S. Tremenheere, commissioner to examine into "the grievances complained of by the journeymen bakers," &c., Lond. 1862.) The undersellers, almost without exception, sell bread adulterated with alum, soap, pearl ashes, chalk, Derbyshire stone-dust, and such like agreeable nourishing and wholesome ingredients. (See the above cited Blue book, as also the report of "the committee of 1855 on the adulteration of bread," and Dr. Hassall's "Adulterations Detected," 2nd Ed. Lond. 1861.) Sir John Gordon stated before the committee of 1855, that "in consequence of these adulterations, the poor man, who lives on two pounds of bread a day, does not now get one fourth part of nourishing matter, let alone the deleterious effects on his health." Tremenheere states (l. c., p. xlviii), as the reason, why a very large part of the working-class, although well aware of this adulteration, nevertheless accept the alum, stone-dust, &c., as part of their purchase: that it is for them "a matter of necessity to take from their baker or from the chandler's shop, such bread as they choose to supply." As they are not paid their wages before the end of the week, they in their turn are unable "to pay for the bread consumed by their families, during the week, before the end of the week," and Tremenheere adds on the evidence of witnesses, "it is notorious that bread composed of those mixtures, is made expressly for sale in this manner." In many English and still more Scotch agricultural districts, wages are paid fortnightly and even monthly; with such long intervals between the payments, the agricultural labourer is obliged to buy on credit. . . . He must pay higher prices, and is in fact tied to the shop which gives him credit. Thus at Horningham in Wilts, for example, where the wages are monthly, the same flour that he could buy elsewhere at 1s 10d per stone, costs him 2s 4d per stone. ("Sixth Report" on "Public Health" by "The Medical Officer of the Privy Council, &c., 1864," p. 264.) "The block printers of Paisley and Kilmaruock enforced, by a strike, fortnightly, instead of monthly payment of wages." ("Reports of the Inspectors of Factories for 31st Oct., 1853," p 34.) As a further pretty result of the credit given by the workmen to the capitalist, we may refer to the method current in many English coal mines, where the labourer is not paid till the end of the month, and in the meantime, receives sums on account from the capitalist, often in goods for which the miner is obliged to pay more than the market price (Truck-system). "It is a common practice with the coal masters to pay once a month, and advance cash to their workmen at the end of each intermediate week. The cash is given in the shop" (i.e., the Tommy shop which belongs to the master); "the men take it on one side and lay it out on the other." ("Children's Employment Commission, III. Report," Lond. 1864, p. 38, n. 192.)

We now know how the value paid by the purchaser to the possessor of this peculiar commodity, labour-power, is determined. The use-value which the former gets in exchange, manifests itself only in the actual usufruct, in the consumption of the labour-power. The money-owner buys everything necessary for this purpose, such as raw material, in the market, and pays for it at its full value. The consumption of labour-power is at one and the same time the production of commodities and of surplus-value. The consumption of labour-power is completed, as in the case of every other commodity, outside the limits of the market or of the sphere of circulation. Accompanied by Mr. Moneybags and by the possessor of labour-power, we therefore take leave for a time of this noisy sphere, where everything takes place on the surface and in view of all men, and follow them both into the hidden abode of production, on whose threshold there stares us in the face "No admittance except on business." Here we shall see, not only how capital produces, but how capital is produced. We shall at last force the secret of profit making.

This sphere that we are deserting, within whose boundaries the sale and purchase of labour-power goes on, is in fact a very Eden of the innate rights of man. There alone rule Freedom, Equality, Property and Bentham. Freedom, because both buyer and seller of a commodity, say of labour-power, are constrained only by their own free will. They contract as free agents, and the agreement they come to, is but the form in which they give legal expression to their common will. Equality, because each enters into relation with the other, as with a simple owner of commodities, and they exchange equivalent for equivalent. Property, because each disposes only of what is his own. And Bentham, because each looks only to himself. The only force that brings them together and puts them in relation with each other, is the selfishness, the gain and the private interests of each. Each looks to himself only, and no one troubles himself about the rest, and just because they do so, do they all, in accordance with the preestablished harmony of things, or under the auspices of an all-shrewd providence, work together to their mutual advantage, for the common weal and in the interest of all.

On leaving this sphere of simple circulation or of exchange of commodities, which furnishes the "Free-trader Vulgaris" with his views and ideas, and with the standard by which he judges a society based on capital and wages, we think we can perceive a change in the physiognomy of our dramatis personae. He, who before was the money-owner, now strides in front as capitalist; the possessor of labour-power follows as his labourer. The one with an air of importance, smirking, intent on business; the other, timid and holding back, like one who is bringing his own hide to market and has nothing to expect but— a hiding.

CHAPTER IX
THE RATE OF SURPLUS-VALUE

Section 1. The Degree of Exploitation of Labour-Power

The surplus-value generated in the process of production by C, the capital advanced, or in other words, the self-expansion of the value of the capital C, presents itself for our consideration, in the first place, as a surplus, as the amount by which the value of the product exceeds the value of its constituent elements.

The capital C is made up of two components, one, the sum of money c laid out upon the means of production, and the other, the sum of money v expended upon the labour-power; c represents the portion that has become constant capital, and v the portion that has become variable capital. At first then, C = c + v: for example, if £500 is the capital advanced, its components may be such that the £500 = £410 const. + £90 var. When the process of production is finished, we get a commodity whose value = (c + v) + s, where s is the surplus-value; or taking our former figures, the value of this commodity may be (£410 const. + £90 var.) + £90 surpl. The original capital has now changed from C to C', from £500 to £590. The difference is s or a surplus-value of £90. Since the value of the constituent elements of the product is equal to the value of the advanced capital, it is mere tautology to say, that the excess of the value of the product over the value of its constituent elements, is equal to the expansion of the capital advanced or to the surplus-value produced.

Nevertheless, we must examine this tautology a little more closely. The two things compared are, the value of the product and the value of its constituents consumed in the process of production. Now we have seen how that portion of the constant capital which consists of the instruments of labour, transfers to the production only fraction of its value, while the remainder of that value continues to reside in those instruments. Since this remainder plays no part in the formation of value, we may at present leave it on one side. To introduce it into the calculation would make no difference. For instance, taking our former example, c = £410: suppose this sum to consist of £312 value of raw material, £44 value of auxiliary material, and £54 value of the machinery worn away in the process; and suppose that the total value of the machinery employed is £1,054. Out of this latter sum, then, we reckon as advanced for the purpose of turning out the product, the sum of £54 alone, which the machinery loses by wear and tear in the process; for this is all it parts with to the product. Now if we also reckon the remaining £1,000, which still continues in the machinery, as transferred to the product, we ought also to reckon it as part of the value advanced, and thus make it appear on both sides of our calculation.[15] We should, in this way, get £1,500 on one side and £1,590 on the other. The difference of these two sums, or the surplus-value, would still be £90. Throughout this Book therefore, by constant capital advanced for the production of value, we always mean, unless the context is repugnant thereto, the value of the means of production actually consumed in the process, and that value alone.

This being so, let us return to the formula C = c + v, which we saw was transformed into C′ = (c + v) + s, C becoming C′. We know that the value of the constant capital is transferred to, and merely reappears in the product. The new value actually created in the process, the value produced, or value-product, is therefore not the same as the value of the product; it is not, as it would at first sight appear (c + v) + s or £410 const. + £90 var. + £90 surpl.; but v + s or £90 var. + £90 surpl. not £590 but £180. If c = 0, or in other words, if there were branches of industry in which the capitalist could dispense with all means of production made by previous labour, whether they be raw material, auxiliary material, or instruments of labour, employing only labour-power and materials supplied by Nature, in that case, there would be no constant capital to transfer to the product. This component of the value of the product, i.e., the £410 in our example, would be eliminated, but the sum of £180, the amount of new value created, or the value produced, which contains £90 of surplus-value, would remain just as great as if c represented the highest value imaginable. We should have C = (0 + v) = v or C′ the expanded capital = v + s and therefore C′ − C = s as before. On the other hand, if s = 0, or in other words, if the labour-power, whose value is advanced in the form of variable capital, were to produce only its equivalent, we should have C = c + v or C′ the value of the product = (c + v) + 0 or C − C′. The capital advanced would, in this case, not have expanded its value.

From what has gone before, we know that surplus-value is purely the result of a variation in the value of v, of that portion of the capital which is transformed into labour-power; consequently, v + s = v + v′ or v plus an increment of v. But the fact that it is v alone that varies, and the conditions of that variation, are obscured by the circumstance that in consequence of the increase in the variable component of the capital, there is also an increase in the sum total of the advanced capital. It was originally £500 and becomes £590. Therefore in order that our investigation may lead to accurate results, we must make abstraction from that portion of the value of the product, in which constant capital alone appears, and consequently must equate the constant capital to zero or make c = 0. This is merely an application of a mathematical rule, employed whenever we operate with constant and variable magnitudes, related to each other by the symbols of addition and subtraction only.

A further difficulty is caused by the original form of the variable capital. In our example, C′ = £410 const. + £90 var. + £90 surpl.; but £90 is a given and therefore a constant quantity; hence it appears absurd to treat it as variable. But in fact, the term £90 var. is here merely a symbol to show that this value undergoes a process. The portion of the capital invested in the purchase of labour-power is a definite quantity of materialised labour, a constant value like the value of the labour-power purchased. But in the process of production the place of the £90 is taken by the labour-power in action, dead labour is replaced by living labour, something stagnant by something flowing, a constant by a variable. The result is the reproduction of v plus an increment of v. From the point of view then of capitalist production, the whole process appears as the spontaneous variation of the originally constant value, which is transformed into labour-power. Both the process and its result, appear to be owing to this value. If, therefore, such expressions as "£90 variable capital," or "so much self-expanding value," appear contradictory, this is

---

[15] "If we reckon the value of the fixed capital employed as a part of the advances, we must reckon the remaining value of such capital at the end of the year as a part of the annual returns." (Malthus, "Princ. of Pol. Econ." 2nd ed., Lond., 1836, p. 269.)

only because they bring to the surface a contradiction immanent in capitalist production.

At first sight it appears a strange proceeding, to equate the constant capital to zero. Yet it is what we do every day. If, for example, we wish to calculate the amount of England's profits from the cotton industry, we first of all deduct the sums paid for cotton to the United States, India, Egypt and other countries; in other words, the value of the capital that merely re-appears in the value of the product, is put = 0.

Of course the ratio of surplus-value not only to that portion of the capital from which it immediately springs, and whose change of value it represents, but also to the sum total of the capital advanced is economically of very great importance. We shall, therefore, in the third book, treat of this ratio exhaustively. In order to enable one portion of a capital to expand its value by being converted into labour-power, it is necessary that another portion be converted into means of production. In order that variable capital may perform its function, constant capital must be advanced in proper proportion, a proportion given by the special technical conditions of each labour-process. The circumstance, however, that retorts and other vessels, are necessary to a chemical process, does not compel the chemist to notice them in the result of his analysis. If we look at the means of production, in their relation to the creation of value, and to the variation in the quantity of value, apart from anything else, they appear simply as the material in which labour-power, the value-creator, incorporates itself. Neither the nature, nor the value of this material is of any importance. The only requisite is that there be a sufficient supply to absorb the labour expended in the process of production. That supply once given, the material may rise or fall in value, or even be, as land and the sea, without any value in itself; but this will have no influence on the creation of value or on the variation in the quantity of value.[16]

In the first place then we equate the constant capital to zero. The capital advanced is consequently reduced from c + v to v, and instead of the value of the product (c + v) + s we have now the value produced (v + s). Given the new value produced = £180, which sum consequently represents the whole labour expended during the process, then subtract-ing from it £90 the value of the variable capital, we have remaining £90, the amount of the surplus-value. This sum of £90 or s expresses the absolute quantity of surplus-value produced. The relative quantity produced, or the increase per cent of the variable capital, is determined, it is plain, by the ratio of the surplus-value to the variable capital, or is expressed by $\frac{s}{v}$. In our example this ratio is $\frac{90}{90}$, which gives an increase of 100%. This relative increase in the value of the variable capital, or the relative magnitude of the surplus-value, I call, "The rate of surplus-value."[17]

We have seen that the labourer, during one portion of the labour-process, produces only the value of his labour-power, that is, the value of his means of subsistence. Now since his work forms part of a system, based on the social division of labour, he does not directly produce the actual necessaries which he himself consumes; he produces instead a particular commodity, yarn for example, whose value is equal to the value of those necessaries or of the money with which they can be bought. The portion of his day's labour devoted to this purpose, will be greater or less, in proportion to the value of the necessaries that he daily requires on an average, or, what amounts to the same thing, in proportion to the labour-time required on an average to produce them. If the value of those necessaries represent on an average the expenditure of six hours' labour, the workman must on an average work for six hours to produce that value. If instead of working for the capitalist, he worked independently on his own account, he would, other things being equal, still be obliged to labour for the same number of hours, in order to produce the value of his labour-power, and thereby to gain the means of subsistence necessary for his conservation or continued reproduction. But as we have seen, during that portion of his day's labour in which he produces the value of his labour-power, say three shillings, he produces only an equivalent for the value of his labour-power already advanced[18] by the capitalist; the new value created only replaces the variable capital advanced. It is owing to this fact, that the production of the new value of three shillings takes the semblance of a mere reproduction. That

---

[16] What Lucretius says is self-evident; "nil posse creari de nihilo," out of nothing, nothing can be created. Creation of value is transformation of labour-power into labour. Labour-power itself is energy transferred to a human organism by means of nourishing matter.

[17] In the same way that the English use the terms "rate of profit," "rate of interest." We shall see, in Book III., that the rate of profit is no mystery, so soon as we know the laws of surplus-value. If we reverse the process, we cannot comprehend either the one or the other.

[18] [*Note added in the 3rd German edition.*—The author resorts here to the economic language in current use.

portion of the working-day, then, during which this reproduction takes place, I call "*necessary*" labour-time, and the labour expended during that time I call "*necessary*" labour.[19] Necessary, as regards the labourer, because independent of the particular social form of his labour; necessary, as regards capital, and the world of capitalists, because on the continued existence of the labourer depends their existence also.

During the second period of the labour-process, that in which his labour is no longer necessary labour, the workman, it is true, labours, expends labour-power; but his labour, being no longer necessary labour, he creates no value for himself. He creates surplus-value which, for the capitalist, has all the charms of a creation out of nothing. This portion of the working-day, I name surplus labour-time, and to the labour expended during that time, I give the name of surplus-labour. It is every bit as important, for a correct understanding of surplus-value, to conceive it as a mere congelation of surplus labour-time, as nothing but materialised surplus-labour, as it is, for a proper comprehension of value, to conceive it as a mere congelation of so many hours of labour, as nothing but materialised labour. The essential difference between the various economic forms of society, between, for instance, a society based on slave-labour, and one based on wage-labour, lies only in the mode in which this surplus-labour is in each case extracted from the actual producer, the labourer.[20]

Since, on the one hand, the values of the variable capital and of the labour-power purchased by that capital are equal, and the value of this labour-power determines the necessary portion of the working-day; and since, on the other hand, the surplus-value is determined by the surplus portion of the working-day, it follows that surplus-value bears the same ratio to variable capital, that surplus-labour does to necessary labour, or in other words, the rate of surplus-value, $\frac{s}{v} = \frac{\text{surplus-labour}}{\text{necessary labour}}$. Both ratios, $\frac{s}{v}$ and $\frac{\text{surplus-labour}}{\text{necessary labour}}$, express the same thing in different ways, in the one case by reference to materialised, incorporated labour, in the other by reference to living, fluent labour.

The rate of surplus-value is therefore an exact expression for the degree of exploitation of labour-power by capital, or of the labourer by the capitalist.[21]

We assumed in our example, that the value of the product = £410 const. + £90 var. + £90 surpl., and that the capital advanced = £500. Since the surplus-value = £90, and the advanced capital = £500, we should, according to the usual way of reckoning, get as the rate of surplus-value (generally confounded with rate of profits) 18%, a rate so low as possibly to cause a pleasant surprise to Mr. Carey and other harmonisers. But in truth, the rate of surplus-value is not equal to $\frac{s}{C}$ or $\frac{s}{c+v}$ but to $\frac{s}{v}$: thus it is not $\frac{90}{500}$ but $\frac{90}{90}$ or 100%, which is more than five times the apparent degree of exploitation. Although, in the case we have supposed, we are ignorant of the actual length of the working-day, and of the duration in days or weeks of the labour-process, as also of the number of labourers employed, yet the rate of surplus-value $\frac{s}{v}$ accurately discloses to us, by means of its equivalent expression, $\frac{\text{surplus-labour}}{\text{necessary labour}}$ the relation between the two parts of the working-day. This relation is here one of equality, the rate being 100%. Hence, it is plain, the labourer, in our exam-

---

[19] In this work, we have, up to now, employed the term "necessary labour-time," to designate the time necessary under given social conditions for the production of any commodity. Henceforward we use it to designate also the time necessary for the production of the particular commodity labour-power. The use of one and the same technical term in different senses is inconvenient, but in no science can it be altogether avoided. Compare, for instance, the higher with the lower branches of mathematics.

[20] Herr Wilhelm Thucydides Roscher has found a mare's nest. He has made the important discovery that if, on the one hand, the formation of surplus-value, or surplus-produce, and the consequent accumulation of capital, is now-a-days due to the thrift of the capitalist, on the other hand, in the lowest stages of civilisation it is the strong who compel the weak to economise. (l. c., p. 78.) To economise what? Labour? Or superfluous wealth that does not exist? What is it that makes such men as Roscher account for the origin of surplus-value, by a mere rechauffé of the more or less plausible excuses by the capitalist, for his appropriation of surplus-value? It is, besides their real ignorance, their apologetic dread of a scientific analysis of value and surplus-value, and of obtaining a result, possibly not altogether palatable to the powers that be.

[21] Although the rate of surplus-value is an exact expression for the degree of exploitation of labour-power, it is, in no sense, an expression for the absolute amount of exploitation. For example, if the necessary labour = 5 hours and the surplus-labour = 5 hours, the degree of exploitation is 100%. The amount of exploitation is here measured by 5 hours. If, on the other hand, the necessary labour = 6 hours and the surplus-labour = 6 hours, the degree of exploitation remains, as before, 100%, while the actual amount of exploitation has increased 20%, namely from five hours to six.

ple, works one half of the day for himself, the other half for the capitalist.

The method of calculating the rate of surplus-value is therefore, shortly, as follows. We take the total value of the product and put the constant capital which merely re-appears in it, equal to zero. What remains, is the only value that has, in the process of producing the commodity, been actually created. If the amount of surplus-value be given, we have only to deduct it from this remainder, to find the variable capital. And *vice versâ*, if the latter be given, and we require to find the surplus-value. If both be given, we have only to perform the concluding operation, viz., to calculate $\frac{s}{v}$, the ratio of the surplus-value to the variable capital.

Though the method is so simple, yet it may not be amiss, by means of a few examples, to exercise the reader in the application of the novel principles underlying it.

First we will take the case of a spinning mill containing 10,000 mule spindles, spinning No. 32 yarn from American cotton, and producing 1 lb. of yarn weekly per spindle. We assume the waste to be 6%: under these circumstances 10,600 lbs. of cotton are consumed weekly, of which 600 lbs. go to waste. The price of the cotton in April, 1871, was $7\frac{3}{4}$ d. per. lb.; the raw material therefore costs in round numbers £342. The 10,000 spindles, including preparation-machinery, and motive power, cost, we will assume, £1 per spindle, amounting to a total of £10,000. The wear and tear we put at 10%, or £1,000 yearly = £20 weekly. The rent of the building we suppose to be £300 a year, or £6 a week. Coal consumed (for 100 horse-power indicated, at 4 lbs. of coal per horse-power per hour during 60 hours, and inclusive of that consumed in heating the mill), 11 tons a week at 8s. 6d. a ton, amounts to about £4 $\frac{1}{2}$ a week: gas, £1 a week, oil, &c., £4 $\frac{1}{2}$ a week. Total cost of the above auxiliary materials, £10 weekly. Therefore the constant portion of the value of the week's product is £378. Wages amount to £52 a week. The price of the yarn is 12 $\frac{1}{4}$ d. per lb. which gives for the value of 10,000 lbs. the sum of £510. The surplus-value is therefore in this case £510 − £430 = £80. We put the constant part of the value of the product = 0, as it plays no part in the creation of value. There remains £132 as the weekly value created, which = £52 var. + £80 surpl. The rate of surplus-value is therefore $\frac{80}{52} = 153\frac{11}{13}$%. In a working-day of 10 hours with average labour the result is: necessary labour = $3\frac{31}{33}$ hours, and surplus-labour = $6\frac{2}{33}$.[22]

One more example. Jacob gives the following calculation for the year 1815. Owing to the previous adjustment of several items it is very imperfect; nevertheless for our purpose it is sufficient. In it he assumes the price of wheat to be 8s. a quarter, and the average yield per acre to be 22 bushels.

Value Produced Per Acre

Seed,	£1 9 0		Tithes, Rates, and Taxes,	£1 1 0
Manure,	2 10 0		Rent,	1 8 0
Wages,	3 10 0		Farmer's Profit and Interest,	1 2 0
Total,	£7 9 0		Total,	£3 11 0

Assuming that the price of the product is the same as its value, we here find the surplus-value distributed under the various heads of profit, interest, rent, &c. We have nothing to do with these in detail; we simply add them together, and the sum is a surplus-value of £3 11s. 0d. The sum of £3 19 s. 0d., paid for seed and manure, is constant capital, and we put it equal to zero. There is left the sum of £3 10s. 0d., which is the variable capital advanced: and we see that a new value of £3 10s. 0d. + £3 11s. 0d. has been produced in its place. Therefore $\frac{s}{v} = \frac{£3\ 11s.\ 0d.}{£3\ 10s\ 0d}$ giving a rate of surplus-value of more than 100%. The labourer employs more than one half of his working-day in producing the surplus-value, which different persons, under different pretexts, share amongst themselves.

[22] The above data, which may be relied upon, were given me by a Manchester spinner. In England the horse-power of an engine was formerly calculated from the diameter of its cylinder, now the actual horse-power shown by the indicator is taken.

Mohandas K. Gandhi (1869–1948)
THROUGH NON-VIOLENCE TO GOD

The author, a philosopher and activist from India, holds that there is no other God than Truth, and Truth can only be realized by human beings through nonviolence. Since Truth is universal and all-pervading, those who wish to see it face to face must learn to love even the meanest of creatures as themselves. See Section C of the introductory essay to Part IV for comments on Gandhi's nonviolent and individualistic approach to morality.

READING QUESTIONS

In reading the selection, try to answer the following questions and identify the passages that support your answers:

1. What is Gandhi's conception of God?
2. What is his conception of truth?
3. Why does he think truth can be attained only through nonviolence?
4. Are his reasons good? Why or why not?
5. How would a Marxist criticize Gandhi's position?

Reprinted from Mohandas K. Gandhi, "Through Non-Violence to God," in Louis Renou (ed.), *Hinduism* (New York: George Braziller, 1962), Part B, Chap. XVI, Sections 1 and 2, pp. 233–236. Copyright © 1962 by George Braziller, Inc. Reprinted by permission of George Braziller, Inc.

1. THROUGH AHIMSĀ[1] TO GOD

My uniform experience has convinced me that there is no other God than Truth. And if every page of these chapters does not proclaim to the reader that the only means for the realization of Truth is nonviolence, I shall deem all my labor in writing to have been in vain. And, even though my efforts in this behalf may prove fruitless, let the readers know that the vehicle, not the great principle, is at fault. After all, however sincere my strivings after *Ahimsā* may have been, they have still been imperfect and inadequate. The little fleeting glimpses, therefore, that I have been able to have of Truth can hardly convey an idea of the indescribable luster of Truth, a million times more intense than that of the sun we daily see with our eyes. In fact what I have caught is only the faintest glimmer of that mighty effulgence. But this much I can say with assurance, as a result of all my experiments, that a perfect vision of Truth can only follow a complete realization of *Ahimsā*.

To see the universal and all-pervading Spirit of Truth face to face one must be able to love the meanest of creation as oneself. And a man who aspires after that cannot afford to keep out of any field of life. That is why my devotion to Truth has drawn me into the field of politics; and I can say without the slightest hesitation, and yet in all humility, that those who say that religion has nothing to do with politics do not know what religion means.

Identification with everything that lives is impossible without self-purification; without self-purification the observance of the law of *Ahimsā* must remain an empty dream; God can never be realized by one who is not pure of heart. Self-purification therefore must mean purification in all the walks of life. And purification being highly infectious, purification of oneself necessarily leads to the purification of one's surroundings.

But the path of self-purification is hard and steep. To attain to perfect purity one has to become absolutely passion-free in thought, speech, and action; to rise above the opposing currents of love and hatred, attachment and repulsion. I know that I have

---

[1] Nonviolence.

not in me as yet that triple purity, in spite of constant ceaseless striving for it. That is why the world's praise fails to move me, indeed it very often stings me. To conquer the subtle passions seems to me to be harder far than the physical conquest of the world by the force of arms. Ever since my return to India I have had experiences of the dormant passions lying hidden within me. The knowledge of them has made me feel humiliated though not defeated. The experiences and experiments have sustained me and given me a great joy. But I know that I have still before me a difficult path to traverse. I must reduce myself to zero. So long as a man does not of his own free will put himself last among his fellow creatures, there is no salvation for him. *Ahiṃsā* is the farthest limit of humility.

In bidding farewell to the reader, for the time being at any rate, I ask him to join with me in prayer to the God of Truth that He may grant me the boon of *Ahiṃsā* in mind, word, and deed.

2. GOD'S NAME

It is a sun that has brightened my darkest hours. Rāma's name is no copybook maxim. It is something that has to be realized through experience. One who has had personal experience alone can prescribe it, not any other. The recitation of Rāma's name for spiritual ailments is as old as the hills. But the greater includes the less. And my claim is that the recitation of Rāma's name is a sovereign remedy for our physical ailments also. We want healers of souls rather than of bodies. The multiplicity of hospitals and of medical men is no sign of civilization. The less we and others pamper our body, the better for us and the world. Rāma's name is for the pure in heart and for those who want to attain purity and remain pure. It can never be a means of self-indulgence. Rāma's

name, to be efficacious, must absorb your entire being during its recitation and express itself in your whole life. My Rāma, the Rāma of our prayers, is not the historical Rāma, the son of Daśaratha, the king of Ayodhyā He is the eternal, the unborn, the one without a second. Rāma's name has the terrible power of converting one's sex-desire into a divine longing for the Lord. Rāma's name if recited from the heart charms away every evil thought.

Hindudharma is like a boundless ocean, teeming with priceless gems. The deeper you dive, the more treasures you find; it is the way trodden by some of the greatest sages of India who were men of God, not superstitious men or charlatans: to take Rāma's name from the heart means deriving help from an incomparable power. The atom-bomb is as nothing compared with it. This power is capable of removing all pain; to say this is easy. To attain the Reality is very difficult. Nevertheless it is the biggest thing man can possess.

Reason follows the heart, it does not guide it. A pure heart is thus the most essential requisite for mental and physical health. Tolstoy said that if man dismissed God from his heart even for a single moment, Satan occupied the vacancy. Rāma's name would expel Satan. By ourselves we are insignificant worms. We become great when we reflect His greatness. Men make a fetish of their physical being while neglecting the immortal Spirit. Anyone who bears Him in his or her heart has accession of a marvellous force or energy as objective in its results as, say, electricity, but much subtler. Rāma's name is like a mathematical formula which summed up in brief the result of endless research. What an amount of labour and patience have been lavished by men to acquire the non-existent philosopher's stone. Surely, God's name is of infinitely richer value and always existent.

Simone de Beauvoir (1908–1986)
THE ETHICS OF AMBIGUITY

The author says that no action is justified unless it opens up concrete possibilities for the freedom of others. This involves acting from particular motives, aimed at particular individuals or groups and whatever constitutes their happiness. De Beauvoir's position is discussed in Section C of the introductory essay to Part IV.

READING QUESTIONS

In reading the selection, try to answer the following questions and identify the passages that support your answers:

1. When does de Beauvoir think that violence is justified?
2. What problem does this pose?
3. What is de Beauvoir's position on this problem?
4. How does her position differ from Kant's?
5. Which position, de Beauvoir's or Kant's, is better and why?

Reprinted from Simone de Beauvoir, *The Ethics of Ambiguity* (New York: Citadel Press, 1948), pp. 129–155. Copyright © 1948 by Philosophical Library. Reprinted by permission of Philosophical Library.

The notion of ambiguity must not be confused with that of absurdity. To declare that existence is absurd is to deny that it can ever be given a meaning; to say that it is ambiguous is to assert that its meaning is never fixed, that it must be constantly won. Absurdity challenges every ethics; but also the finished rationalization of the real would leave no room for ethics; it is because man's condition is ambiguous that he seeks, through failure and outrageousness, to save his existence. Thus, to say that action has to be lived in its truth, that is, in the consciousness of the antinomies which it involves, does not mean that one has to renounce it. In *Plutarch Lied* Pierrefeu rightly says that in war there is no victory which can not be regarded as unsuccessful, for the objective which one aims at is the total annihilation of the enemy and this result is never attained; yet there are wars which are won and wars which are lost. So is it with any activity; failure and success are two aspects of reality which at the start are not perceptible. That is what makes criticism so easy and art so difficult: the critic is always in a good position to show the limits that every artist gives himself in choosing himself; painting is not given completely either in Giotto or Titian or Cezanne; it is sought through the centuries and is never finished; a painting in which all pictorial problems are resolved is really inconceivable; painting itself is this movement toward its own reality; it is not the vain displacement of a millstone turning in the void; it concretizes itself on each canvas as an absolute existence. Art and science do not establish themselves despite failure but through it; which does not prevent there being truths and errors, masterpieces and lemons, depending upon whether the discovery or the painting has or has not known how to win the adherence of human consciousnesses; this

amounts to saying that failure, always ineluctable, is in certain cases spared and in others not.

It is interesting to pursue this comparison; not that we are likening action to a work of art or a scientific theory, but because in any case human transcendence must cope with the same problem: it has to found itself, though it is prohibited from ever fulfilling itself. Now, we know that neither science nor art ever leaves it up to the future to justify its present existence. In no age does art consider itself as something which is paving the way for Art: so-called archaic art prepares for classicism only in the eyes of archaeologists; the sculptor who fashioned the Korai of Athens rightfully thought that he was producing a finished work of art; in no age has science considered itself as partial and lacunary; without believing itself to be definitive, it has however, always wanted to be a total expression of the world, and it is in its totality that in each age it again raises the question of its own validity. There we have an example of how man must, in any event, assume his finiteness: not by treating his existence as transitory or relative but by reflecting the infinite within it, that is, by treating it as absolute. There is an art only because at every moment art has willed itself absolutely; likewise there is a liberation of man only if, in aiming at itself, freedom is achieved absolutely in the very fact of aiming at itself. This requires that each action be considered as a finished form whose different moments, instead of fleeing toward the future in order to find there their justification, reflect and confirm one another so well that there is no longer a sharp separation between present and future, between means and ends.

But if these moments constitute a unity, there must be no contradiction among them. Since the liberation aimed at is not a *thing* situated in an unfamiliar time, but a movement which realizes itself by tending to conquer, it can not attain itself if it denies itself at the start; action can not seek to fulfill itself by means which would destroy its very meaning. So much so that in certain situations there will be no other issue for man than rejection. In what is called political realism there is no room for rejection because the present is considered as transitory; there is rejection only if man lays claim in the present to his existence as an absolute value; then he must absolutely reject what would deny this value. Today, more or less consciously in the name of such an ethics, we condemn a magistrate who handed over a communist to save ten hostages and along with him all the Vichyites who were trying "to make the best of things": it was not a matter of rationalizing the present such as it was imposed by the German occupation, but of rejecting it unconditionally. The resistance did not aspire to a positive effectiveness; it was a negation, a revolt, a martyrdom; and in this negative movement freedom was positively and absolutely confirmed.

In one sense the negative attitude is easy; the rejected object is given unequivocally and unequivocally defines the revolt that one opposes to it; thus, all French antifascists were united during the occupation by their common resistance to a single oppressor. The return to the positive encounters many more obstacles, as we have well seen in France where divisions and hatreds were revived at the same time as were the parties. In the moment of rejection, the antinomy of action is removed, and means and end meet; freedom immediately sets itself up as its own goal and fulfills itself by so doing. But the antinomy reappears as soon as freedom again gives itself ends which are far off in the future; then, through the resistances of the given, divergent means offer themselves and certain ones come to be seen as contrary to their ends. It has often been observed that revolt alone is pure. Every construction implies the outrage of dictatorship, of violence. This is the theme, among others, of Koestler's *Gladiators*. Those who, like this symbolic *Spartacus*, do not want to retreat from the outrage and resign themselves to impotence, usually seek refuge in the values of seriousness. That is why, among individuals as well as collectivities, the negative moment is often the most genuine. Goethe, Barres, and Aragon, disdainful or rebellious in their romantic youth, shattered old conformisms and thereby proposed a real, though incomplete, liberation. But what happened later on? Goethe became a servant of the state, Barres of na-

tionalism, and Aragon of Stalinist conformism. We know how the seriousness of the Catholic Church was substituted for the Christian spirit, which was a rejection of dead Law, a subjective rapport of the individual with God through faith and charity; the Reformation was a revolt of subjectivity, but Protestantism in turn changed into an objective moralism in which the seriousness of works replaced the restlessness of faith. As for revolutionary humanism, it accepts only rarely the tension of permanent liberation; it has created a Church where salvation is bought by membership in a party as it is bought elsewhere by baptism and indulgences. We have seen that this recourse to the serious is a lie; it entails the sacrifice of man to the Thing, of freedom to the Cause. In order for the return to the positive to be genuine it must involve negativity, it must not conceal the antinomics between means and end, present and future; they must be lived in a permanent tension; one must retreat from neither the outrage of violence nor deny it, or, which amounts to the same thing, assume it lightly. Kierkegaard has said that what distinguishes the pharisee from the genuinely moral man is that the former considers his anguish as a sure sign of his virtue; from the fact that he asks himself, "Am I Abraham?" he concludes, "I am Abraham"; but morality resides in the painfulness of an indefinite questioning. The problem which we are posing is not the same as that of Kierkegaard; the important thing to us is to know whether, in given conditions, Isaac must be killed or not. But we also think that what distinguishes the tyrant from the man of good will is that the first rests in the certainty of his aims, whereas the second keeps asking himself, "Am I really working for the liberation of men? Isn't this end contested by the sacrifices through which I aim at it?" In setting up its ends, freedom must put them in parentheses, confront them at each moment with that absolute end which it itself constitutes, and contest, in its own name, the means it uses to win itself.

It will be said that these considerations remain quite abstract. What must be done, practically? Which action is good? Which is bad? To ask such a question is also to fall into a naive abstraction. We don't ask the physicist, "Which hypotheses are true?" Nor the artist, "By what procedures does one produce a work whose beauty is guaranteed?" Ethics does not furnish recipes any more than do science and art. One can merely propose methods. Thus, in science the fundamental problem is to make the idea adequate to its content and the law adequate to the facts; the logician finds that in the case where the pressure of the given fact bursts the concept which serves to comprehend it, one is obliged to invent another concept; but he can not define *a priori* the moment of invention, still less foresee it. Analogously, one may say that in the case where the content of the action falsifies its meaning, one must modify not the meaning, which is here willed absolutely, but the content itself; however, it is impossible to determine this relationship between meaning and content abstractly and universally: there must be a trial and decision in each case. But likewise just as the physicist finds it profitable to reflect on the conditions of scientific invention and the artist on those of artistic creation without expecting any ready-made solutions to come from these reflections, it is useful for the man of action to find out under what conditions his undertakings are valid. We are going to see that on this basis new perspectives are disclosed.

In the first place, it seems to us that the individual as such is one of the ends at which our action must aim. Here we are at one with the point of view of Christian charity, the Epicurean cult of friendship, and Kantian moralism which treats each man as an end. He interests us not merely as a member of a class, a nation, or a collectivity, but as an individual man. This distinguishes us from the systematic politician who cares only about collective destinies; and probably a tramp enjoying his bottle of wine, or a child playing with a balloon, or a Neapolitan lazzarone loafing in the sun in no way helps in the liberation of man; that is why the abstract will of the revolutionary scorns the concrete benevolence which occupies itself in satisfying desires which have no morrow. However, it must not be forgotten that there is a concrete bond between freedom and existence; to will man free is to will there to *be* being, it is to will the disclosure of being in the joy of existence; in order for the idea of liberation to have a concrete meaning, the joy of existence must be asserted in each one, at every instant; the movement toward freedom assumes its real, flesh and blood figure in the world by thickening into pleasure, into happiness. If the satisfaction of an old man drinking a glass of wine counts for nothing, then production and wealth are only hollow myths; they have meaning only if they are capable of being retrieved in individual and living joy. The saving of time and the conquest of leisure have no meaning if we are not moved by the laugh of a child at play. If we do not love life on our own account and through others, it is futile to seek to justify it in any way.

However, politics is right in rejecting benevolence to the extent that the latter thoughtlessly sacrifices the future to the present. The ambiguity of freedom, which very often is occupied only in fleeing from itself, introduces a difficult equivocation into relationships with each individual taken one by one. Just what is meant by the expression "to love others"? What is meant by taking them as ends? In any event, it is evident that we are not going to decide to fulfill the will of every man. There are cases where a man positively wants evil, that is, the enslavement of other men, and he must then be fought. It also happens that, without harming anyone, he flees from his own freedom, seeking passionately and alone to attain the being which constantly eludes him. If he asks for our help, are we to give it to him? We blame a man who helps a drug addict intoxicate himself or a desperate man commit suicide, for we think that rash behavior of this sort is an attempt of the individual against his own freedom; he must be made aware of his error and put in the presence of the real demands of his freedom. Well and good. But what if he persists? Must we then use violence? There again the serious man busies himself dodging the problem; the values of life, of health, and of moral conformism being set up, one does not hesitate to impose them on others. But we know that this pharisaism can cause the worst disasters: lacking drugs, the addict may kill himself. It is no more necessary to serve an abstract ethics obstinately than to yield without due consideration to impulses of pity or generosity; violence is justified only if it opens concrete possibilities to the freedom which I am trying to save; by practising it I am willy-nilly assuming an engagement in relation to others and to myself; a man whom I snatch from the death which he had chosen has the right to come and ask me for means and reasons for living; the tyranny practised against an invalid can be justified only by his getting better; whatever the purity of the intention which animates me, any dictatorship is a fault for which I have to get myself pardoned. Besides, I am in no position to make decisions of this sort indiscriminately; the example of the unknown person who throws himself in to the Seine and whom I hesitate whether or not to fish out is quite abstract; in the absence of a concrete bond with this desperate person my choice will never be anything but a contingent facticity. If I find myself in a position to do violence to a child, or to a melancholic, sick, or distraught person the reason is that I also find myself charged with his upbringing, his happiness, and his health: I am a parent, a teacher, a nurse, a doctor, or a friend . . . So, by a tacit agreement, by the very fact that I am solicited, the strictness of my decision is accepted or even desired; the more seriously I accept my responsibilities, the more justified it is. That is why love authorizes severities which are not granted to indifference. What makes the problem so complex is that, on the one hand, one must not make himself an accomplice of that flight from freedom that is found in heedlessness, caprice, mania, and passion, and that, on the other hand, it is the abortive movement of man toward being which is his very existence, it is through the failure which he has assumed that he asserts himself as a freedom. To want to prohibit a man from error is to forbid him to fulfill his own existence, it is to deprive him of life. At the beginning of Claudel's *The Satin Shoe*, the husband of Dona Prouheze, the Judge, the Just, as the author regards him, explains that every plant needs a gardener in order to grow and that he is the one whom heaven has destined for his young wife; beside the fact that we are shocked by the arrogance of such a thought (for how does he know that he is this enlightened gardener? Isn't he merely a jealous husband?) this likening of a soul to a plant is not acceptable; for, as Kant would say, the value of an act lies not in its *conformity* to an external model, but in its internal truth. We object to the inquisitors who want to create faith and virtue from without; we object to all forms of fascism which seek to fashion the happiness of man from without; and also the paternalism which thinks that it has done something for man by prohibiting him from certain possibilities of temptation, whereas what is necessary is to give him reasons for resisting it.

Thus, violence is not immediately justified when it opposes willful acts which one considers perverted; it becomes inadmissible if it uses the pretext of ignorance to deny a freedom which, as we have seen, can be practised within ignorance itself. Let the "enlightened elites" strive to change the situation of the child, the illiterate, the primitive crushed beneath his superstitions; that is one of their most urgent tasks; but in this very effort they must respect a freedom which, like theirs, is absolute. They are always opposed, for example, to the extension of universal suffrage by adducing the incompetence of the masses, of women, of the natives in the colonies; but this forgetting that man always has to decide by himself in the darkness, that he must want beyond what he knows. If infinite knowledge were necessary (even supposing that it were conceivable), then the colonial administrator himself would not have the right

to freedom; he is much further from perfect knowledge than the most backward savage is from him. Actually, to vote is not to govern; and to govern is not merely to maneuver; there is an ambiguity today, and particularly in France, because we think that we are not the master of our destiny; we no longer hope to help make history, we are resigned to submitting to it; all that our internal politics does is reflect the play of external forces, no party hopes to determine the fate of the country but merely to foresee the future which is being prepared in the world by foreign powers and to use, as best we can, the bit of indetermination which still escapes their foresight. Drawn along by this tactical realism, the citizens themselves no longer consider the vote as the assertion of their will but as a maneuver, whether one adheres completely to the maneuvering of a party or whether he invents his own strategy; the electors consider themselves not as men who are consulted about a particular point but as forces which are numbered and which are ordered about with a view to distant ends. And that is probably why the French, who formerly were so eager to declare their opinions, take no further interest in an act which has become a disheartening strategy. So, the fact is that if it is necessary not to vote but to measure the weight of one's vote, this calculation requires such extensive information and such a sureness of foresight that only a specialized technician can have the boldness to express an opinion. But that is one of the abuses whereby the whole meaning of democracy is lost; the logical conclusion of this would be to suppress the vote. The vote should really be the expression of a concrete will, the choice of a representative capable of defending, within the general framework of the country and the world, the particular interests of his electors. The ignorant and the outcast also has interests to defend; he alone is "competent" to decide upon his hopes and his trust. By a sophism which leans upon the dishonesty of the serious, one does not merely argue about his formal impotence to choose, but one draws arguments from the content of his choice. I recall, among others, the naivete of a right-thinking young girl who said, "The vote for women is all well and good in principle, only, if women get the vote, they'll all vote red." With like impudence it is almost unanimously stated today in France that if the natives of the French Union were given the rights of self-determination, they would live quietly in their villages without doing anything, which would be harmful to the higher interests of the Economy. And doubtless the state of stagnation in which they choose to live is not that which a man can wish for another man; it is desirable to open new possibilities to the indolent negroes so that the interests of the Economy may one day merge with theirs. But for the time being, they are left to vegetate in the sort of situation where their freedom can merely be negative: the best thing they can desire is not to tire themselves, not to suffer, and not to work; and even this freedom is denied them. It is the most consummate and inacceptable form of oppression.

However, the "enlightened elite" objects, one does not let a child dispose of himself, one does not permit him to vote. This is another sophism. To the extent that woman or the happy or resigned slave lives in the infantile world of ready-made values, calling them "an eternal child" or "a grown-up child" has some meaning, but the analogy is only partial. Childhood is a particular sort of situation: it is a natural situation whose limits are not created by other men and which is thereby not comparable to a situation of oppression; it is a situation which is common to all men and which is temporary for all; therefore, it does not represent a limit which cuts off the individual from his possibilities, but, on the contrary, the moment of a development in which new possibilities are won. The child is ignorant because he has not yet had the time to acquire knowledge, not because this time has been refused him. To treat him as a child is not to bar him from the future but to open it to him; he needs to be taken in hand, he invites authority, it is the form which the resistance of facticity, through which all liberation is brought about, takes for him. And on the other hand, even in this situation the child has a right to his freedom and must be respected as a human person. What gives *Emile* its value is the brilliance with which Rousseau asserts this principle. There is a very annoying naturalistic optimism in *Emile;* in the rearing of the child, as in any relationship with others, the ambiguity of freedom implies the outrage of violence; in a sense, all education is a failure. But Rousseau is right in refusing to allow childhood to be oppressed. And in practice raising a child as one cultivates a plant which one does not consult about its needs is very different from considering it as a freedom to whom the future must be opened.

Thus, we can set up point number one: the good of an individual or a group of individuals requires that it be taken as an absolute end of our action; but we are not authorized to decide upon this end *a priori*. The fact is that no behavior is ever authorized to begin with, and one of the concrete consequences

of existentialist ethics is the rejection of all the previous justifications which might be drawn from the civilization, the age, and the culture; it is the rejection of every principle of authority. To put it positively, the precept will be to treat the other (to the extent that he is the only one concerned, which is the moment that we are considering at present) as a freedom so that his end may be freedom; in using this conducting-wire one will have to incur the risk, in each case, of inventing an original solution. Out of disappointment in love a young girl takes an overdose of pheno-barbital; in the morning friends find her dying, they call a doctor, she is saved; later on she becomes a happy mother of a family; her friends were right in considering her suicide as a hasty and heedless act and in putting her into a position to reject it or return to it freely. But in asylums one sees melancholic patients who have tried to commit suicide twenty times, who devote their freedom to seeking the means of escaping their jailers and of putting an end to their intolerable anguish; the doctor who gives them a friendly pat on the shoulder is their tyrant and their torturer. A friend who is intoxicated by alcohol or drugs asks me for money so that he can go and buy the poison that is necessary to him; I urge him to get cured, I take him to a doctor, I try to help him live; insofar as there is a chance of my being successful, I am acting correctly in refusing him the sum he asks for. But if circumstances prohibit me from doing anything to change the situation in which he is struggling, all I can do is give in; a deprivation of a few hours will do nothing but exasperate his torments uselessly; and he may have recourse to extreme means to get what I do not give him. That is also the problem touched on by Ibsen in *The Wild Duck*. An individual lives in a situation of falsehood; the falsehood is violence, tyranny: shall I tell the truth in order to free the victim? It would first be necessary to create a situation of such a kind that the truth might be bearable and that, though losing his illusions, the deluded individual might again find about him reasons for hoping. What makes the problem more complex is that the freedom of one man almost always concerns that of other individuals. Here is a married couple who persist in living in a hovel; if one does not succeed in giving them the desire to live in a more healthful dwelling, they must be allowed to follow their preferences; but the situation changes if they have children; the freedom of the parents would be the ruin of their sons, and as freedom and the future are on the side of the latter, these are the ones who must first be taken into account. The Other is multiple, and on the basis of this new questions arise.

One might first wonder for whom we are seeking freedom and happiness. When raised in this way, the problem is abstract; the answer will, therefore, be arbitrary, and the arbitrary always involves outrage. It is not entirely the fault of the district social-worker if she is apt to be odious; because, her money and time being limited, she hesitates before distributing it to this one or that one, she appears to others as a pure externality, a blind facticity. Contrary to the formal strictness of Kantianism for whom the more abstract the act is the more virtuous it is, generosity seems to us to be better grounded and therefore more valid the less distinction there is between the other and ourself and the more we fulfill ourself in taking the other as an end. That is what happens if I am engaged in relation to others. The Stoics impugned the ties of family, friendship, and nationality so that they recognized only the universal form of man. But man is man only through situations whose particularity is precisely a universal fact. There are men who expect help from certain men and not from others, and these expectations define privileged lines of action. It is fitting that the negro fight for the negro, the Jew for the Jew, the proletarian for the proletarian, and the Spaniard in Spain. But the assertion of these particular solidarities must not contradict the will for universal solidarity and each finite undertaking must also be open on the totality of men.

But it is then that we find in concrete form the conflicts which we have described abstractly; for the cause of freedom can triumph only through particular sacrifices. And certainly there are hierarchies among the goods desired by men: one will not hesitate to sacrifice the comfort, luxury, and leisure of certain men to assure the liberation of certain others; but when it is a question of choosing among freedoms, how shall we decide?

Let us repeat, one can only indicate a method here. The first point is always to consider what genuine human interest fills the abstract form which one proposes as the action's end. Politics always puts forward Ideas: Nation, Empire, Union, Economy, etc. But none of these forms has value in itself; it has it only insofar as it involves concrete individuals. If a nation can assert itself proudly only to the detriment of its members, if a union can be created only to the detriment of those it is trying to unite, the nation or the union must be rejected. We repudiate all idealisms, mysticisms, etcetera which prefer a Form to

man himself. But the matter becomes really agonizing when it is a question of a Cause which genuinely serves man. That is why the question of Stalinist politics, the problem of the relationship of the Party to the masses which it uses in order to serve them, is in the forefront of the preoccupations of all men of good will. However, there are very few who raise it without dishonesty, and we must first try to dispel a few fallacies.

The opponent of the U.S.S.R. is making use of a fallacy when, emphasizing the part of criminal violence assumed by Stalinist politics, he neglects to confront it with the ends pursued. Doubtless, the purges, the deportations, the abuses of the occupation, and the police dictatorship surpass in importance the violences practised by any other country; the very fact that there are a hundred and sixty million inhabitants in Russia multiplies the numerical coefficient of the injustices committed. But these quantitative considerations are insufficient. One can no more judge the means without the end which gives it its meaning than he can detach the end from the means which defines it. Lynching a negro or suppressing a hundred members of the opposition are two analogous acts. Lynching is an absolute evil; it represents the survival of an obsolete civilization, the perpetuation of a struggle of races which has to disappear; it is a fault without justification or excuse. Suppressing a hundred opponents is surely an outrage, but it may have meaning and a reason; it is a matter of maintaining a regime which brings to an immense mass of men a bettering of their lot. Perhaps this measure could have been avoided; perhaps it merely represents that necessary element of failure which is involved in any positive construction. It can be judged only by being replaced in the ensemble of the cause it serves.

But, on the other hand, the defender of the U.S.S.R. is making use of a fallacy when he unconditionally justifies the sacrifices and the crimes by the ends pursued; it would first be necessary to prove that, on the one hand, the end is unconditioned and that, on the other hand, the crimes committed in its name were strictly necessary. Against the death of Bukharin one counters with Stalingrad; but one would have to know to what effective extent the Moscow trials increased the chances of the Russian victory. One of the ruses of Stalinist orthodoxy is, playing on the idea of necessity, to put the whole of the revolution on one side of the scale; the other side will always seem very light. But the very idea of a total dialectic of history does not imply that any factor is ever determining; on the contrary, if one admits that the life of a man may change the course of events, it is that one adheres to the conception which grants a preponderant role to Cleopatra's nose and Cromwell's wart. One is here playing, with utter dishonesty, on two opposite conceptions of the idea of necessity: one synthetic, and the other analytic; one dialectic, the other deterministic. The first makes History appear as an intelligible becoming within which the particularity of contingent accidents is reabsorbed; the dialectical sequence of the moments is possible only if there is within each moment an indetermination of the particular elements taken one by one. If, on the contrary, one grants the strict determinism of each causal series, one ends in a contingent and disordered vision of the ensemble, the conjunction of the series being brought about by chance. Therefore, a Marxist must recognize that none of his particular decisions involves the revolution in its totality; it is merely a matter of hastening or retarding its coming, of saving himself the use of other and more costly means. That does not mean that he must retreat from violence but that he must not regard it as justified *a priori* by its ends. If he considers his enterprise in its truth, that is, in its finiteness, he will understand that he has never anything but a finite stake to oppose to the sacrifices which he calls for, and that it is an uncertain stake. Of course, this uncertainty should not keep him from pursuing his goals; but it requires that one concern himself in each case with finding a balance between the goal and its means.

Thus, we challenge every condemnation as well as every *a priori* justification of the violence practised with a view to a valid end. They must be legitimized concretely. A calm, mathematical calculation is here impossible. One must attempt to judge the chances of success that are involved in a certain sacrifice; but at the beginning this judgment will always be doubtful; besides, in the face of the immediate reality of the sacrifice, the notion of chance is difficult to think about. On the one hand, one can multiply a probability infinitely without ever reaching certainty; but yet, practically, it ends by merging with this asymptote: in our private life as in our collective life there is no other truth than a statistical one. On the other hand, the interests at stake do not allow themselves to be put into an equation; the suffering of one man, that of a million men, are incommensurable with the conquests realized by millions of others, present death is incommensurable with the life to come. It would be utopian to want to set up on the one hand

the chances of success multiplied by the stake one is after, and on the other hand the weight of the immediate sacrifice. One finds himself back at the anguish of free decision. And that is why political choice is an ethical choice: it is a wager as well as a decision; one bets on the chances and risks of the measure under consideration; but whether chances and risks must be assumed or not in the given circumstances must be decided without help, and in so doing one sets up values. If in 1793 the Girondists rejected the violences of the Terror whereas a Saint-Just and a Robespierre assumed them, the reason is that they did not have the same conception of freedom. Nor was the same republic being aimed at between 1830 and 1840 by the republicans who limited themselves to a purely political opposition and those who adopted the technique of insurrection. In each case it is a matter of defining an end and realizing it, knowing that the choice of the means employed affects both the definition and the fulfillment.

Ordinarily, situations are so complex that a long analysis is necessary before being able to pose the ethical moment of the choice. We shall confine ourselves here to the consideration of a few simple examples which will enable us to make our attitude somewhat more precise. In an underground revolutionary movement when one discovers the presence of a stool-pigeon, one does not hesitate to beat him up; he is a present and future danger who has to be gotten rid of; but if a man is merely suspected of treason, the case is more ambiguous. We blame those northern peasants who in the war of 1914–18 massacred an innocent family which was suspected of signaling to the enemy; the reason is that not only were the presumptions vague, but the danger was uncertain; at any rate, it was enough to put the suspects into prison; while waiting for a serious inquiry it was easy to keep them from doing any harm. However, if a questionable individual holds the fate of other men in his hands, if, in order to avoid the risk of killing one innocent man, one runs the risk of letting ten innocent men die, it is reasonable to sacrifice him. We can merely ask that such decisions be not taken hastily and lightly, and that, all things considered, the evil that one inflicts be lesser than that which is being forestalled.

There are cases still more disturbing because there the violence is not immediately efficacious; the violences of the Resistance did not aim at the material weakening of Germany; it happens that their purpose was to create such a state of violence that collaboration would be impossible; in one sense, the burning of a whole French village was too high a price to pay for the elimination of three enemy officers; but those fires and the massacring of hostages were themselves parts of the plan; they created an abyss between the occupiers and the occupied. Likewise, the insurrections in Paris and Lyons at the beginning of the nineteenth century, or the revolts in India, did not aim at shattering the yoke of the oppressor at one blow, but rather at creating and keeping alive the meaning of the revolt and at making the mystifications of conciliation impossible. Attempts which are aware that one by one they are doomed to failure can be legitimized by the whole of the situation which they create. This is also the meaning of Steinbeck's novel *In Dubious Battle* where a communist leader does not hesitate to launch a costly strike of uncertain success but through which there will be born, along with the solidarity of the workers, the consciousness of exploitation and the will to reject it.

It seems to me interesting to contrast this example with the debate in John Dos Passos' *The Adventures of a Young Man*. Following a strike, some American miners are condemned to death. Their comrades try to have their trial reconsidered. Two methods are put forward: one can act officially, and one knows that they then have an excellent chance of winning their case; one can also work up a sensational trial with the Communist Party taking the affair in hand, stirring up a press campaign and circulating international petitions; but the court will be unwilling to yield to this intimidation. The party will thereby get a tremendous amount of publicity, but the miners will be condemned. What is a man of good will to decide in this case?

Dos Passos' hero chooses to save the miners and we believe that he did right. Certainly, if it were necessary to choose between the whole revolution and the lives of two or three men, no revolutionary would hesitate; but it was merely a matter of helping along the party propaganda, or better, of increasing somewhat its chances of developing within the United States; the immediate interest of the C.P. in that country is only hypothetically tied up with that of the revolution; in fact, a cataclysm like the war has so upset the situation of the world that a great part of the gains and losses of the past have been absolutely swept away. If it is really *men* which the movement claims to be serving, in this case it must prefer saving the lives of three concrete individuals to a very uncertain and weak chance of serving a little more effectively by their sacrifice the mankind to come. If

it considers these lives negligible, it is because it too ranges itself on the side of the formal politicians who prefer the Idea to its content; it is because it prefers itself, in its subjectivity, to the goals to which it claims to be dedicated. Besides, whereas in the example chosen by Steinbeck the strike is immediately an appeal to the freedom of the workers and in its very failure is already a liberation, the sacrifice of the miners is a mystification and an oppression; they are duped by being made to believe that an effort is being made to save their lives, and the whole proletariat is duped with them. Thus, in both examples, we find ourselves before the same abstract case: men are going to die so that the party which claims to be serving them will realize a limited gain; but a concrete analysis leads us to opposite moral solutions.

It is apparent that the method we are proposing, analogous in this respect to scientific or aesthetic methods, consists, in each case, of confronting the values realized with the values aimed at, and the meaning of the act with its content. The fact is that the politician, contrary to the scientist and the artist, and although the element of failure which he assumes is much more outrageous, is rarely concerned with making use of it. May it be that there is an irresistible dialectic of power wherein morality has no place? Is the ethical concern, even in its realistic and concrete form, detrimental to the interests of action? The objection will surely be made that hesitation and misgivings only impede victory. Since, in any case, there is an element of failure in all success, since the ambiguity, at any rate, must be surmounted, why not refuse to take notice of it? In the first number of the *Cahiers d'Action* a reader declared that once and for all we should regard the militant communist as "the permanent hero of our time" and should reject the exhausting tension demanded by existentialism; installed in the permanence of heroism, one will blindly direct himself toward an uncontested goal; but one then resembles Colonel de la Roque who unwaveringly went right straight ahead of him without knowing where he was going. Malaparte relates that the young Nazis, in order to become insensitive to the suffering of others, practised by plucking out the eyes of live cats; there is no more radical way of avoiding the pitfalls of ambiguity. But an action which wants to serve man ought to be careful not to forget him on the way; if it chooses to fulfill itself blindly, it will lose its meaning or will take on an unforeseen meaning; for the goal is not fixed once and for all; it is defined all along the road which leads to it. Vigilance alone can keep alive the validity of the goals and the genuine assertion of freedom. Moreover, ambiguity can not fail to appear on the scene; it is felt by the victim, and his revolt or his complaints also make it exist for his tyrant; the latter will then be tempted to put everything into question, to renounce, thus denying both himself and his ends; or, if he persists, he will continue to blind himself only by multiplying crimes and by perverting his original design more and more. The fact is that the man of action becomes a dictator not in respect to his ends but because these ends are necessarily set up through his will. Hegel, in his *Phenomenology,* has emphasized this inextricable confusion between objectivity and subjectivity. A man gives himself to a Cause only by making it *his* Cause; as he fulfills himself within it, it is also through him that it is expressed, and the will to power is not distinguished in such a case from generosity; when an individual or a party chooses to triumph, whatever the cost may be, it is their own triumph which they take for an end. If the fusion of the Commissar and the Yogi were realized, there would be a self-criticism in the man of action which would expose to him the ambiguity of his will, thus arresting the imperious drive of his subjectivity and, by the same token, contesting the unconditioned value of the goal. But the fact is that the politician follows the line of least resistance; it is easy to fall asleep over the unhappiness of others and to count it for very little; it is easier to throw a hundred men, ninety-seven of whom are innocent, into prison, than to discover the three culprits who are hidden among them; it is easier to kill a man than to keep a close watch on him; all politics makes use of the police, which officially flaunts its radical contempt for the individual and which loves violence for its own sake. The thing that goes by the name of political necessity is in part the laziness and brutality of the police. That is why it is incumbent upon ethics not to follow the line of least resistance; an act which is not destined, but rather quite freely consented to; it must make itself effective so that what was at first facility may become difficult. For want of internal criticism, this is the role that an opposition must take upon itself. There are two types of opposition. The first is a rejection of the very ends set up by a regime: it is the opposition of anti-fascism to fascism, of fascism to socialism. In the second type, the oppositionist accepts the objective goal but criticizes the subjective movement which aims at it; he may not even wish for a change of power, but he deems it necessary to bring into play a contestation which will make the subjective appear as such. Thereby he exacts a perpetual contestation of the means by the end and of the end by the means. He must be careful himself not to ruin, by the means which he employs, the end he is aiming at, and above all not to pass into the service of the oppositionists of the first type. But, delicate as it may be, his role is, nevertheless, necessary. Indeed, on the one hand, it would be absurd to oppose a liberating action with the pretext that it implies crime and tyranny; for without crime and tyranny there could be no liberation of man; one can not escape that dialectic which goes from freedom to freedom through dictatorship and oppression. But, on the other hand, he would be guilty of allowing the liberating movement to harden into a moment which is acceptable only if it passes into its opposite; tyranny and crime must be kept from triumphantly establishing themselves in the world; the conquest of freedom is their only justification, and the assertion of freedom against them must therefore be kept alive.

María C. Lugones and Elizabeth V. Spelman (Contemporary)
HAVE WE GOT A THEORY FOR YOU! FEMINIST THEORY, CULTURAL IMPERIALISM, AND THE DEMAND FOR "THE WOMAN'S VOICE"

Lugones, a Latin American philosopher, and Spelman, a United States philosopher, argue that sound feminist theory must make room for articulating, interpreting, theorizing, and reflecting about the connections among the experiences of women from various cultural backgrounds. The authors point out that current feminist theory has not done this, and argue that only the motive of friendship provides an appropriate ground for what this task requires. This selection is discussed at the end of Section C of the introductory essay to Part IV.

READING QUESTIONS

In reading the selection, try to answer the following questions and identify the passages that support your answers:

1. What theses do the authors defend?
2. What reasons do they give in support of their theses?
3. Do their views go beyond feminist concerns? Why or why not?
4. What do Lugones and Spelman mean by "cultural imperialism"?
5. Is their position sound? Why or why not?

Reprinted with permission from Pergamon Press, Inc., and the first author, from María C. Lugones and Elizabeth V. Spelman, "Have We Got a Theory for You! Feminist Theory, Cultural Imperialism, and the Demand for 'The Woman's Voice,'" *Women's Studies International Forum 6* (1983): 573–581. Copyright © 1983 by Pergamon Press, Inc.

PROLOGUE

(*In an Hispana voice*) A veces quisiera mezclar en una voz el sonido canyenge, tristón y urbano del porteñismo que llevo adentro con la cadencia apacible, serrana y llena de corage de la hispana nuevo mejicana. Contrastar y unir

el piolín y la cuerda
el traé y el pepéname
el camión y la troca
la lluvia y el llanto

Pero este querer se me va cuando veo que he confundido la solidaridad con la falta de diferencia. La solidaridad requiere el reconocer, comprender, respetar y amar lo que nos lleva a llorar en distintas cadencias. El imperialismo cultural desea lo contrario, por eso necesitamos muchas voces. Porque una sola voz nos mata a las dos.

No quiero hablar por ti sino contigo. Pero si no aprendo tus modos y tu los míos la conversación es sólo aparente. Y la apariencia se levanta como una barrera sin sentido entre las dos. Sin sentido y sin sentimiento. Por eso no me debes dejar que te dicte tu ser y no me dictes el mío. Porque entonces ya no dialogamos. El diálogo entre nosotras requiere dos voces y no una.

Tal vez un día jugaremos juntas y nos hablaremos no en una lengua universal sino que vos me hablarás mi voz y yo la tuya.

PREFACE

This paper is the result of our dialogue, of our thinking together about differences among women and how these differences are silenced. (Think, for example, of all the silences there are connected with the fact that this paper is in English—for that is a borrowed tongue for one of us.) In the process of our talking and writing together, we saw that the differences between us did not permit our speaking in one voice. For example, when we agreed we expressed the thought differently; there were some things that both of us thought were true but could not express as true of each of us; sometimes we could not say "we"; and sometimes one of us could not express the thought in the first person singular, and to express it in the third person would be to present an outsider's and not an insider's perspective. Thus the use of two voices is central both to the process of constructing this paper and to the substance of it. We are both the authors of this paper and not just sections of it but we write together without presupposing unity of expression or of experience. So when we speak in unison it means just that—there are two voices and not just one.

INTRODUCTION

(*In the voice of a white/Anglo woman who has been teaching and writing about feminist theory*) Feminism is, among other things, a response to the fact that women either have been left out of, or included in demeaning and disfiguring ways in what has been an almost exclusively male account of the world. And so while part of what feminists want and demand for women is the right to move and to act in accordance with our own wills and not against them, another part is the desire and insistence that we give our *own* accounts of these movements and actions. For it matters to us what is said about us, who says it, and to whom it is said: having the opportunity to talk about one's life, to give an account of it, to interpret it, is integral to leading that life rather than being led through it; hence our distrust of the male monopoly over accounts of women's lives. To put the same point slightly differently, part of human life, human living, is talking about it, and we can be sure that being silenced in one's own account of one's life is a kind of amputation that signals oppression. Another reason for not divorcing life from the telling of it or talking about it is that as humans our experiences are deeply influenced by what is said about them, by ourselves or powerful (as opposed to significant) others. Indeed, the phenomenon of internalized oppression is only possible because this is so: one experiences her life in terms of the impoverished and degrading concepts others have found it convenient to use to describe her. We can't separate lives from the accounts given of them; the articulation of our experience is part of our experience.

Sometimes feminists have made even stronger claims about the importance of speaking about our own lives and the destructiveness of others presuming to speak about us or for us. First of all, the claim has been made that on the whole men's accounts of women's lives have been at best false, a function of ignorance; and at worst malicious lies, a function of a knowledgeable desire to exploit and oppress. Since it matters to us that falsehood and lies not be told about us, we demand, of those who have been responsible for those falsehoods and lies, or those who continue to transmit them, not just that we speak but that they learn to be able to hear us. It has also been claimed that talking about one's life, telling one's story, in the company of those doing the same (as in consciousness-raising sessions), is constitutive of feminist method.[1]

And so the demand that the woman's voice be heard and attended to has been made for a variety of reasons: not just so as to greatly increase the chances that true accounts of women's lives will be given, but also because the articulation of experience (in myriad ways) is among the hallmarks of a self-determining individual or community. There are not just epistemological, but moral and political reasons for demanding that the woman's voice be heard, after centuries of androcentric din.

But what more exactly is the feminist demand that

the woman's voice be heard? There are several crucial notes to make about it. First of all, the demand grows out of a complaint, and in order to understand the scope and focus of the demand we have to look at the scope and focus of the complaint. The complaint does not specify *which* women have been silenced, and in one way this is appropriate to the conditions it is a complaint about: virtually no women have had a voice, whatever their race, class, ethnicity, religion, sexual alliance, whatever place and period in history they lived. And if it is as women that women have been silenced, then of course the demand must be that women as women have a voice. But in another way the complaint is very misleading, insofar as it suggests that it is women as women who have been silenced, and that whether a woman is rich or poor, Black, brown or white, etc., is irrelevant to what it means for her to be a woman. For the demand thus simply made ignores at least two related points: (1) it is only possible for a woman who does not feel highly vulnerable with respect to other parts of her identity, e.g., race, class, ethnicity, religion, sexual alliance, etc., to conceive of her voice simply or essentially as a "woman's voice"; (2) just because not all women are equally vulnerable with respect to race, class, etc., some women's voices are more likely to be heard than others by those who have heretofore been giving—or silencing—the accounts of women's lives. For all these reasons, the women's voices most likely to come forth and the women's voices most likely to be heard are, in the United States anyway, those of white, middle-class, heterosexual Christian (or anyway not self-identified non-Christian) women. Indeed, many Hispanas, Black women, Jewish women—to name a few groups—have felt it an invitation to silence rather than speech to be requested—if they are requested at all—to speak about being "women" (with the plain wrapper—as if there were one) in distinction from speaking about being Hispana, Black, Jewish, working-class, etc., women.

The demand that the "woman's voice" be heard, and the search for the "woman's voice" as central to feminist methodology, reflects nascent feminist theory. It reflects nascent empirical theory insofar as it presupposes that the silencing of women is systematic, shows up in regular, patterned ways, and that there are discoverable causes of this widespread observable phenomenon; the demand reflects nascent political theory insofar as it presupposes that the silencing of women reveals a systematic pattern of power and authority; and it reflects nascent moral

---

[1] For a recent example, see MacKinnon, Catharine. 1982. Feminism, Marxism, method and the state: An agenda for theory. *Signs* 7 (3): 515–544.

theory insofar as it presupposes that the silencing is unjust and that there are particular ways of remedying this injustice. Indeed, whatever else we know feminism to include—e.g., concrete direct political action—theorizing is integral to it: theories about the nature of oppression, the causes of it, the relation of the oppression of women to other forms of oppression. And certainly the concept of the woman's voice is itself a theoretical concept, in the sense that it presupposes a theory according to which our identities as human beings are actually compound identities, a kind of fusion or confusion of our otherwise separate identities as women or men, as Black or brown or white, etc. That is no less a theoretical stance than Plato's division of the person into soul and body or Aristotle's parcelling of the soul into various functions.

The demand that the "woman's voice" be heard also invites some further directions in the exploration of women's lives and discourages or excludes others. For reasons mentioned above, systematic, sustained reflection on being a woman—the kind of contemplation that "doing theory" requires—is most likely to be done by women who vis-a-vis other women enjoy a certain amount of political, social and economic privilege because of their skin color, class membership, ethnic identity. There is a relationship between the content of our contemplation and the fact that we have the time to engage in it at some length—otherwise we shall have to say that it is a mere accident of history that white middle-class women in the United States have in the main developed "feminist theory" (as opposed to "Black feminist theory," "Chicana feminist theory," etc.) and that so much of the theory has failed to be relevant to the lives of women who are not white or middle class. Feminist theory—of all kinds—is to be based on, or anyway touch base with, the variety of real life stories women provide about themselves. But in fact, because, among other things, of the structural political and social and economic inequalities among women, the tail has been wagging the dog: feminist theory has not for the most part arisen out of a medley of women's voices; instead, the theory has arisen out of the voices, the experiences, of a fairly small handful of women, and if other women's voices do not sing in harmony with the theory, they aren't counted as women's voices—rather, they are the voices of the woman as Hispana, Black, Jew, etc. There is another sense in which the tail is wagging the dog, too: it is presumed to be the case that those who do the theory know more about those who are

theorized than vice versa; hence it ought to be the case that if it is white/Anglo women who write for and about all other women, the white/Anglo women must know more about all other women than other women know about them. But in fact just in order to survive, brown and Black women have to know a lot more about white/Anglo women—not through the sustained contemplation theory requires, but through the sharp observation stark exigency demands.

(*In an Hispana voice*) I think it necessary to explain why in so many cases when women of color appear in front of white/Anglo women to talk about feminism and women of color, we mainly raise a complaint: the complaint of exclusion, of silencing, of being included in a universe we have not chosen. We usually raise the complaint with a certain amount of disguised or undisguised anger. I can only attempt to explain this phenomenon from a Hispanic viewpoint and a fairly narrow one at that: the viewpoint of an Argentinian woman who has lived in the US for 16 years, who has attempted to come to terms with the devaluation of things Hispanic and Hispanic people in "America" and who is most familiar with Hispano life in the Southwest of the US. I am quite unfamiliar with daily Hispano life in the urban centers, though not with some of the themes and some of the salient experiences of urban Hispano life.

When I say "we,"[2] I am referring to Hispanas. I am accustomed to use the "we" in this way. I am also pained by the tenuousness of this "we" given that I am not a native of the United States. Through the years I have come to be recognized and I have come to recognize myself more and more firmly as part of this "we." I also have a profound yearning for this firmness since I am a displaced person and I am conscious of not being of and I am unwilling to make myself of—even if this were possible—the white/Anglo community.

When I say "you" I mean not the non-Hispanic but the white/Anglo women that I address. "We" and "you" do not capture my relation to other non-white women. The complexity of that relation is not ad-

[2] I must note that when I think this "we," I think it in Spanish—and in Spanish this "we" is gendered, "nosotras." I also use "nosotros" lovingly and with ease and in it I include all members of "La raza cosmica" (Spanish-speaking people of the Americas, la gente de colores: people of many colors). In the US, I use "we" contextually with varying degrees of discomfort: "we" in the house, "we" in the department, "we" in the classroom, "we" in the meeting. The discomfort springs from the sense of community in the "we" and the varying degrees of lack of community in the context in which the "we" is used.

dressed here, but it is vivid to me as I write down my thoughts on the subject at hand.

I see two related reasons for our complaint-full discourse with white/Anglo women. Both of these reasons plague our world, they contaminate it through and through. It takes some hardening of oneself, some self-acceptance of our own anger to face them, for to face them is to decide that maybe we can change our situation in self-constructive ways and we know fully well that the possibilities are minimal. We know that we cannot rest from facing these reasons, that the tenderness towards others in us undermines our possibilities, that we have to fight our own niceness because it clouds our minds and hearts. Yet we know that a thoroughgoing hardening would dehumanize us. So, we have to walk through our days in a peculiarly fragile psychic state, one that we have to struggle to maintain, one that we do not often succeed in maintaining.

We and you do not talk the same language. When we talk to you we use your language: the language of your experience and of your theories. We try to use it to communicate our world of experience. But since your language and your theories are inadequate in expressing our experiences, we only succeed in communicating our experience of exclusion. We cannot talk to you in our language because you do not understand it. So the brute facts that we understand your language and that the place where most theorizing about women is taking place is your place, both combine to require that we either use your language and distort our experience not just in the speaking about it, but in the living of it, or that we remain silent. Complaining about exclusion is a way of remaining silent.

You are ill at ease in our world. You are ill at ease in our world in a very different way than we are ill at ease in yours. You are not of our world and again, you are not of our world in a very different way than we are not of yours. In the intimacy of a personal relationship we appear to you many times to be wholly there, to have broken through or to have dissipated the barriers that separate us because you are Anglo and we are raza. When we let go of the psychic state that I referred to above in the direction of sympathy, we appear to ourselves equally whole in your presence but our intimacy is thoroughly incomplete. When we are in your world many times you remake us in your own image, although sometimes you clearly and explicitly acknowledge that we are not wholly there in our being with you. When we are in your world we ourselves feel the discomfort of hav-

ing our own being Hispanas disfigured or not understood. And yet, we have had to be in your world and learn its ways. We have to participate in it, make a living in it, live in it, be mistreated in it, be ignored in it, and rarely, be appreciated in it. In learning to do these things or in learning to suffer them or in learning to enjoy what is to be enjoyed or in learning to understand your conception of us, we have had to learn your culture and thus your language and self-conceptions. But there is nothing that necessitates that you understand our world: understand, that is, not as an observer understands things, but as a participant, as someone who has a stake in them understands them. So your being ill at ease in our world lacks the features of our being ill at ease in yours precisely because you can leave and you can always tell yourselves that you will be soon out of there and because the wholeness of your selves is never touched by us, we have no tendency to remake you in our image.

But you theorize about women and we are women, so you understand yourselves to be theorizing about us, and we understand you to be theorizing about us. Yet none of the feminist theories developed so far seems to me to help Hispanas in the articulation of our experience. We have a sense that in using them we are distorting our experiences. Most Hispanas cannot even understand the language used in these theories—and only in some cases the reason is that the Hispana cannot understand English. We do not recognize ourselves in these theories. They create in us a schizophrenic split between our concern for ourselves as women and ourselves as Hispanas, one that we do not feel otherwise. Thus they seem to us to force us to assimilate to some version of Anglo culture, however revised that version may be. They seem to ask that we leave our communities or that we become alienated so completely in them that we feel hollow. When we see that you feel alienated in your own communities, this confuses us because we think that maybe every feminist has to suffer this alienation. But we see that recognition of your alienation leads many of you to be empowered into the remaking of your culture, while we are paralyzed into a state of displacement with no place to go.

So I think that we need to think carefully about the relation between the articulation of our own experience, the interpretation of our own experience, and theory making by us and other non-Hispanic women about themselves and other "women."

The only motive that makes sense to me for your joining us in this investigation is the motive of friendship, out of friendship. A non-imperialist feminism requires that you make a real space for our articulating, interpreting, theorizing and reflecting about the connections among them—a real space must be a non-coerced space—and/or that you follow us into our world out of friendship. I see the "out of friendship" as the only sensical motivation for this following because the task at hand for you is one of extraordinary difficulty. It requires that you be willing to devote a great part of your life to it and that you be willing to suffer alienation and self-disruption. Self-interest has been proposed as a possible motive for entering this task. But self-interest does not seem to me to be a realistic motive, since whatever the benefits you may accrue from such a journey, they cannot be concrete enough for you at this time and they may not be worth your while. I do not think that you have any obligation to understand us. You do have an obligation to abandon your imperialism, your universal claims, your reduction of us to your selves simply because they seriously harm us.

I think that the fact that we are so ill at ease with your theorizing in the ways indicated above does indicate that there is something wrong with these theories. But what is it that is wrong? Is it simply that the theories are flawed if meant to be universal but accurate so long as they are confined to your particular group(s)? Is it that the theories are not really flawed but need to be translated? Can they be translated? Is it something about the process of theorizing that is flawed? How do the two reasons for our complaint-full discourse affect the validity of your theories? Where do *we* begin? To what extent are our experience and its articulation affected by our being a colonized people, and thus by your culture, theories and conceptions? Should we theorize in community and thus as part of community life and outside the academy and other intellectual circles? What is the point of making theory? Is theory making a good thing for us to do at this time? When are we making theory and when are we just articulating and/or interpreting our experiences?

Some Questionable Assumptions About Feminist Theorizing

(*Unproblematically in Vicky's and Maria's voice*) Feminist theories aren't just about what happens to the female population in any given society or across all societies; they are about the meaning of those experiences in the lives of women. They are about beings who give their own accounts of what is happening to them or of what they are doing, who have culturally constructed ways of reflecting on their lives. But how can the theorizer get at the meaning of those experiences? What should the relation be between a woman's own account of her experiences and the theorizer's account of it?

Let us describe two different ways of arriving at an account of another woman's experience. It is one thing for both me and you to observe you and come up with our different accounts of what you are doing; it is quite another for me to observe myself and others much like me culturally and in other ways and to develop an account of myself and then use that account to give an account of you. In the first case you are the "insider" and I am the "outsider." When the outsider makes clear that she is an outsider and that this is an outsider's account of your behavior, there is a touch of honesty about what she is doing. Most of the time the "interpretation by an outsider" is left understood and most of the time the distance of outsidedness is understood to mark objectivity in the interpretation. But why is the outsider as an outsider interpreting your behavior? Is she doing it so that you can understand how she sees you? Is she doing it so that other outsiders will understand how you *are*? Is she doing it so that *you* will understand how you are? It would seem that if the outsider wants you to understand how she sees you and you have given your account of how you see yourself to her, there is a possibility of genuine dialogue between the two. It also seems that the lack of reciprocity could bar genuine dialogue. For why should you engage in such a one-sided dialogue? As soon as we ask this question, a host of other conditions for the possibility of a genuine dialogue between us arise: conditions having to do with your position relative to me in the various social, political and economic structures in which we might come across each other or in which you may run face to face with my account of you and my use of your account of yourself. Is this kind of dialogue necessary for me to get at the meaning of your experiences? That is, is this kind of dialogue necessary for feminist theorizing that is not seriously flawed?

Obviously the most dangerous of the understanding of what I—an outsider—am doing in giving an account of your experience is the one that describes what I'm doing as giving an account of who and how you are whether it be given to you or to other outsiders. Why should you or anyone else believe me; that is, why should you or anyone else believe that you are as I say you are? Could I be right? What conditions would have to obtain for my being right? That many women are put in the position of not knowing whether or not to believe outsiders' accounts of their experiences is clear. The pressures to believe these accounts are enormous even when the woman in question does not see herself in the account. She is thus led to doubt her own judgment and to doubt all interpretation of her experience. This leads her to experience her life differently. Since the consequences of outsiders' accounts can be so significant, it is crucial that we reflect on whether or not this type of account can ever be right and if so, under what conditions.

The last point leads us to the second way of arriving at an account of another woman's experience, viz., the case in which I observe myself and others like me culturally and in other ways and use that account to give an account of you. In doing this, I remake you in my own image. Feminist theorizing approaches this remaking insofar as it depends on the concept of women as women. For it has not arrived at this concept as a consequence of dialogue with many women who are culturally different, or by any other kind of investigation of cultural differences which may include different conceptions of what it is to be a woman; it has simply presupposed this concept.

Our suggestion in this paper, and at this time it is no more than a suggestion, is that only when genuine and reciprocal dialogue takes place between "outsiders" and "insiders" can we trust the outsider's account. At first sight it may appear that the insider/outsider distinction disappears in the dialogue, but it is important to notice that all that happens is that we are now both outsider and insider with respect to each other. The dialogue puts us both in position to give a better account of each other's and our own experience. Here we should again note that white/Anglo women are much less prepared for this dialogue with women of color than women of color are for dialogue with them in that women of color have had to learn white/Anglo ways, self-conceptions, and conceptions of them.

But both the possibility and the desirability of this dialogue are very much in question. We need to think about the possible motivations for engaging in this dialogue, whether doing theory jointly would be a good thing, in what ways and for whom, and whether doing theory is in itself a good thing at this time for women of color or white Anglo women. In motivating the last question let us remember the hierarchical distinctions between theorizers and those theorized about and between theorizers and doers. These distinctions are endorsed by the same views and institutions which endorse and support hierarchical distinctions between men/women, master race/inferior race, intellectuals/manual workers. Of what use is the activity of theorizing to those of us who are women of color engaged day in and day out in the task of empowering women and men of color face to face with them? Should we be articulating and interpreting their experience for them with the aid of theories? Whose theories?

Ways of Talking or Being Talked About That Are Helpful, Illuminating, Empowering, Respectful

(*Unproblematically in Maria's and Vicky's voice*) Feminists have been quite diligent about pointing out ways in which empirical, philosophical and moral theories have been androcentric. They have thought it crucial to ask, with respect to such theories: who makes them? for whom do they make them? about what or whom are the theories? why? how are theories tested? what are the criteria for such tests and where did the criteria come from? Without posing such questions and trying to answer them, we'd never have been able to begin to mount evidence for our claims that particular theories are androcentric, sexist, biased, paternalistic, etc. Certain philosophers have become fond of—indeed, have made their careers on— pointing out that characterizing a statement as true or false is only one of many ways possible of characterizing it; it might also be, oh, rude, funny, disarming, etc.; it may be intended to soothe or to hurt; or it may have the effect, intended or not, of soothing or hurting. Similarly, theories appear to be the kinds of things that are true or false; but they also are the kinds of things that can be, e.g., useless, arrogant, disrespectful, ignorant, ethnocentric, imperialistic. The immediate point is that feminist theory is no less immune to such characterizations than, say, Plato's political theory, or Freud's theory of female psychosexual development. Of course this is not to say that if feminist theory manages to be respectful or helpful it will follow that it must be true. But if, say, an empirical theory is purported to be about "women" and in fact is only about certain women, it is certainly false, probably ethnocentric, and of dubious usefulness except to those whose position in the world it strengthens (and theories, as we know, don't have to be true in order to be used to strengthen people's positions in the world).

Many reasons can be and have been given for the production of accounts of people's lives that plainly have nothing to do with illuminating those lives for the benefit of those living them. It is likely that both the method of investigation and the content of many accounts would be different if illuminating the lives of the people the accounts are about were the aim of the studies. Though we cannot say ahead of time how feminist theory making would be different if all (or many more) of those people it is meant to be about were more intimately part of the theory-making process, we do suggest some specific ways being talked about can be helpful:

1. The theory or account can be helpful if it enables one to see how parts of one's life fit together, for example, to see connections among parts of one's life one hasn't seen before. No account can do this if it doesn't get the parts right to begin with, and this cannot happen if the concepts used to describe a life are utterly foreign.

2. A useful theory will help one locate oneself concretely in the world, rather than add to the mystification of the world and one's location in it. New concepts may be of significance here, but they will not be useful if there is no way they can be translated into already existing concepts. Suppose a theory locates you in the home, because you are a woman, but you know full well that is not where you spend most of your time? Or suppose you can't locate yourself easily in any particular class as defined by some version of Marxist theory?

3. A theory or account not only ought to accurately locate one in the world but also enable one to think about the extent to which one is responsible or not for being in that location. Otherwise, for those whose location is as oppressed peoples, it usually occurs that the oppressed have no way to see themselves as in any way self-determining, as having any sense of being worthwhile or having grounds for pride, and paradoxically at the same time feeling at fault for the position they are in. A useful theory will help people work out just what is and is not due to themselves and their own activities as opposed to those who have power over them.

It may seem odd to make these criteria of a useful theory, if the usefulness is not to be at odds with the issue of the truth of the theory; for the focus on feeling worthwhile or having pride seems to rule out the possibility that the truth might just be that such-and-such a group of people has been under the control of others for centuries and that the only explanation of that is that they are worthless and weak people, and will never be able to change that. Feminist theorizing seems implicitly if not explicitly

committed to the moral view that women *are* worthwhile beings, and the metaphysical theory that we are beings capable of bringing about a change in our situations. Does this mean feminist theory is "biased"? Not any more than any other theory, e.g., psychoanalytic theory. What is odd here is not the feminist presupposition that women are worthwhile but rather that feminist theory (and other theory) often has the effect of empowering one group and demoralizing another.

Aspects of feminist theory are as unabashedly value-laden as other political and moral theories. It is not just an examination of women's positions, for it includes, indeed begins with, moral and political judgments about the injustice (or, where relevant, justice) of them. This means that there are implicit or explicit judgments also about what kind of changes constitute a better or worse situation for women.

4. In this connection a theory that is useful will provide criteria for change and make suggestions for modes of resistance that don't merely reflect the situation and values of the theorizer. A theory that is respectful of those about whom it is a theory will not assume that changes that are perceived as making life better for some women are changes that will make, and will be perceived as making, life better for other women. This is *not* to say that if some women do not find a situation oppressive, other women ought never to suggest to the contrary that there might be very good reasons to think that the situation nevertheless *is* oppressive. But it is to say that, e.g., the prescription that life for women will be better when we're in the workforce rather than at home, when we are completely free of religious beliefs with patriarchal origins, when we live in complete separation from men, etc., are seen as slaps in the face to women whose life would be better if they could spend more time at home, whose identity is inseparable from their religious beliefs and cultural practices (which is not to say those beliefs and practices are to remain completely uncriticized and unchanged), who have ties to men—whether erotic or not—such that to have them severed in the name of some vision of what is "better" is, at that time and for those women, absurd. Our visions of what is better are always informed by our perception of what is bad about our present situation. Surely we've learned enough from the history of clumsy missionaries, and the white suffragists of the 19th century (who couldn't imagine why Black women "couldn't see"

how crucial getting the vote for "women" was) to know that we can clobber people to destruction with our visions, our versions, of what is better. *But:* this does not mean women are not to offer supportive and tentative criticism of one another. But there is a very important difference between (a) developing ideas together, in a "pre-theoretical" stage, engaged as equals in joint enquiry, and (b) one group developing, on the basis of their own experience, a set of criteria for good change for women—and then reluctantly making revisions in the criteria at the insistence of women to whom such criteria seem ethnocentric and arrogant. The deck is stacked when one group takes it upon itself to develop the theory and then have others criticize it. Categories are quick to congeal, and the experiences of women whose lives do not fit the categories will appear as anomalous when in fact the theory should have grown out of them as much as others from the beginning. This, of course, is why any organization or conference having to do with "women"—with no qualification—that seriously does not want to be "solipsistic" will from the beginning be multi-cultural or state the appropriate qualifications. How we think and what we think about does depend in large part on who is there—not to mention who is expected or encouraged to speak. (Recall the boys in the *Symposium* sending the flute girls out.) Conversations and criticism take place in particular circumstances. Turf matters. So does the fact of who if anyone already has set up the terms of the conversations.

5. Theory cannot be useful to anyone interested in resistance and change unless there is reason to believe that knowing what a theory means and believing it to be true have some connection to resistance and change. As we make theory and offer it up to others, what do we assume is the connection between theory and consciousness? Do we expect others to read theory, understand it, believe it, and have their consciousnesses and lives thereby transformed? If we really want theory to make a difference to people's lives, how ought we to present it? Do we think people come to consciousness by reading? only by reading? Speaking to people through theory (orally or in writing) is a *very* specific context-dependent activity. That is, theory makers and their methods and concepts constitute a community of people and of shared meanings. Their language can be just as opaque and foreign to those not in the community as a foreign tongue or dialect.[3] Why do we engage in *this* activity and what effect do we think it ought

to have? As Helen Longino has asked: "Is 'doing theory' just a bonding ritual for academic or educationally privileged feminist women?" Again, whom does our theory making serve?

Some Suggestions About How to do Theory That is not Imperialistic, Ethnocentric, Disrespectful

(*Problematically in the voice of a woman of color*) What are the things we need to know about others, and about ourselves, in order to speak intelligently, intelligibly, sensitively, and helpfully about their lives? We can show respect, or lack of it, in writing theoretically about others no less than in talking directly with them. This is not to say that here we have a well-worked out concept of respect, but only to suggest that together all of us consider what it would mean to theorize in a respectful way.

When we speak, write, and publish our theories, to whom do we think we are accountable? Are the concerns we have in being accountable to "the profession" at odds with the concerns we have in being accountable to those about whom we theorize? Do commitments to "the profession," method, getting something published, getting tenure, lead us to talk and act in ways at odds with what we ourselves (let alone others) would regard as ordinary, decent behavior? To what extent do we presuppose that really understanding another person or culture requires our behaving in ways that are disrespectful, even violent? That is, to what extent do we presuppose that getting and/or publishing the requisite information requires or may require disregarding the wishes of others, lying to them, wresting information from them against their wills? Why and how do we think theorizing about others provides *understanding* of them? Is there any sense in which theorizing about others is a short-cut to understanding them?

Finally, if we think doing theory is an important activity, and we think that some conditions lead to better theorizing than others, what are we going to do about creating those conditions? If we think it not just desirable but necessary for women of different racial and ethnic identities to create feminist theory jointly, how shall that be arranged for? It may be the case that at this particular point we ought not even

---

[3] See Bernstein, Basil. 1972. Social class, language, and socialization. In Giglioli, Pier Paolo, ed., *Language and Social Context*, pp. 157–178. Penguin, Harmondsworth, Middlesex. Bernstein would probably, and we think wrongly, insist that theoretical terms and statements have meanings *not* "tied to a local relationship and to a local social structure," unlike the vocabulary of, e.g., working-class children.

try to do that—that feminist theory by and for Hispanas needs to be done separately from feminist theory by and for Black women, white women, etc. But it must be recognized that white/Anglo women have more power and privilege than Hispanas, Black women, etc., and at the very least they can use such advantage to provide space and time for other women to speak (with the above caveats about implicit restrictions on what counts as "the woman's voice"). And once again it is important to remember that the power of white/Anglo women vis-a-vis Hispanas and Black women is in inverse proportion to their working knowledge of each other.

This asymmetry is a crucial fact about the background of possible relationships between white women and women of color, whether as political co-workers, professional colleagues, or friends.

If white/Anglo women and women of color are to do theory jointly, in helpful, respectful, illuminating and empowering ways, the task ahead of white/Anglo women because of this asymmetry, is a very hard task. The task is a very complex one. In part, to make an analogy, the task can be compared to learning a text without the aid of teachers. We all know the lack of contact felt when we want to discuss a particular issue that requires knowledge of a text with someone who does not know the text at all. Or the discomfort and impatience that arise in us when we are discussing an issue that presupposes a text and someone walks into the conversation who does not know the text. That person is either left out or will impose herself on us and either try to engage in the discussion or try to change the subject. Women of color are put in these situations by white/Anglo women and men constantly. Now imagine yourself simply left out but wanting to do theory with us. The first thing to recognize and accept is that you disturb our own dialogues by putting yourself in the left-out position and not leaving us in some meaningful sense to ourselves.

You must also recognize and accept that you must learn the text. But the text is an extraordinarily complex one: viz., our many different cultures. You are asking us to make ourselves more vulnerable to you than we already are before we have any reason to trust that you will not take advantage of this vulnerability. So you need to learn to become unintrusive, unimportant, patient to the point of tears, while at the same time open to learning any possible lessons. You will also have to come to terms with the sense of alienation, of not belonging, of having your world thoroughly disrupted, having it criticized and scru-

tinized from the point of view of those who have been harmed by it, having important concepts central to it dismissed, being viewed with mistrust, being seen as of no consequence except as an object of mistrust.

Why would any white/Anglo woman engage in this task? Out of self-interest? What in engaging in this task would be, not just in her interest, but perceived as such by her before the task is completed or well underway? Why should we want you to come into our world out of self-interest? Two points need to be made here. The task as described could be entered into with the intention of finding out as much as possible about us so as to better dominate us. The person engaged in this task would act as a spy. The motivation is not unfamiliar to us. We have heard it said that now that Third World countries are more powerful as a bloc, westerners need to learn more about them, that it is in their self-interest to do so. Obviously there is no reason why people of color should welcome white/Anglo women into their world for the carrying out of this intention. It is also obvious that white/Anglo feminists should not engage in this task under this description since the task under this description would not lead to joint theorizing of the desired sort: respectful, illuminating, helpful and empowering. It would be helpful and empowering only in a one-sided way.

Self-interest is also mentioned as a possible motive in another way. White/Anglo women sometimes say that the task of understanding women of color would entail self-growth or self-expansion. If the task is conceived as described here, then one should doubt that growth or expansion will be the result. The severe self-disruption that the task entails should place a doubt in anyone who takes the task seriously about her possibilities of coming out of the task whole, with a self that is not as fragile as the selves of those who have been the victims of racism. But also, why should women of color embrace white/Anglo women's self-betterment without reciprocity? At this time women of color cannot afford this generous affirmation of white/Anglo women.

Another possible motive for engaging in this task is the motive of duty, "out of obligation," because white/Anglos have done people of color wrong. Here again two considerations: coming into Hispano, Black, Native American worlds out of obligation puts white/Anglos in a morally self-righteous position that is inappropriate. You are active, we are passive. We become the vehicles of your own redemption. Secondly, we couldn't want you to come into our worlds "out of obligation." That is like wanting someone to make love to you out of obligation. So, whether or not you have an obligation to do this (and we would deny that you do), or whether this task could even be done out of obligation, this is an inappropriate motive.

Out of obligation you should stay out of our way, respect us and our distance, and forego the use of whatever power you have over us—for example, the power to use your language in our meetings, the power to overwhelm us with your education, the power to intrude in our communities in order to research us and to record the supposed dying of our cultures, the power to engrain in us a sense that we are members of dying cultures and are doomed to assimilate, the power to keep us in a defensive posture with respect to our own cultures.

So the motive of friendship remains as both the only appropriate and understandable motive for white/Anglo feminists engaging in the task as described above. If you enter the task out of friendship with us, then you will be moved to attain the appropriate reciprocity of care for your and our wellbeing as whole beings, you will have a stake in us and in our world, you will be moved to satisfy the need for reciprocity of understanding that will enable you to follow us in our experiences as we are able to follow you in yours.

We are not suggesting that if the learning of the text is to be done out of friendship, you must enter into a friendship with a whole community and for the purpose of making theory. In order to understand what it is that we are suggesting, it is important to remember that during the description of her experience of exclusion, the Hispana voice said that Hispanas experience the intimacy of friendship with white/Anglo women friends as thoroughly incomplete. It is not until this fact is acknowledged by our white/Anglo women friends and felt as a profound lack in our experience of each other that white/Anglo women can begin to see us. Seeing us in our communities will make clear and concrete to you how incomplete we really are in our relationships with you. It is this beginning that forms the proper background for the yearning to understand the text of our cultures that can lead to joint theory making.

Thus, the suggestion made here is that if white/Anglo women are to understand our voices, they must understand our communities and us in them. Again, this is not to suggest that you set out to make friends with our communities, though you may become friends with some of the members, nor is it to suggest that you should try to befriend us for the purpose of making theory with us. The latter would be a perversion of friendship. Rather, from within friendship you may be moved by friendship to undergo the very difficult task of understanding the text of our cultures by understanding our lives in our communities. This learning calls for circumspection, for questioning of yourselves and your roles in your own culture. It necessitates a striving to understand while in the comfortable position of not having an official calling card (as "scientific" observers of our communities have); it demands recognition that you do not have the authority of knowledge; it requires coming to the task without ready-made theories to frame our lives. This learning is then extremely hard because it requires openness (including openness to severe criticism of the white/Anglo world), sensitivity, concentration, self-questioning, circumspection. It should be clear that it does not consist in a passive immersion in our cultures, but in a striving to understand what it is that our voices are saying. Only then can we engage in a mutual dialogue that does not reduce each one of us to instances of the abstraction called "woman."

QUESTIONS FOR REVIEW AND FURTHER THOUGHT

1. Critically compare and contrast Mo Tzu's views on right conduct with Mill's views and Aristotle's. What does Mo Tzu mean by "universal love"? What does Mill mean by "happiness"? What does Aristotle mean by "happiness"? Do you tend to agree with any of these philosophers on these matters and the moral injunctions that follow from them? Why or why not?

2. What, if anything, does Glaucon's hypothesis about the myth of Gyges' ring establish about people's motives to act justly? In particular, does it establish that whenever people act justly, they do so reluctantly? Why or why not? Defend your position against some objections you consider plausible.

3. Aristotle claims that "human good turns out to be activity of soul in accordance with virtue, and if there is more than one virtue, in accordance with the best and most complete." How does he argue for this statement—out of what concerns, in response to what questions? Is the statement true? If so, why? If not, why not?

4. Critically compare and contrast the views of Ibn Khaldun, Hobbes, and Hume on human psychology. Which one of these views is best suited for explaining the existence and nature of human societies? Why? Defend your position against some objections you consider plausible.

5. Critically compare and contrast the views of Aristotle and Aquinas on human happiness. Which view is better for addressing the questions: How should we live? and What kind of persons should we try to become? Think of some objections to your position and then explain those objections' shortcomings.

6. Consider the statement: "justice, after all, must have something to do with happiness." Could one agree with it from the standpoint of Kant's moral philosophy? Why or why not? Could one agree with this statement from the standpoint of Mill's moral philosophy? Why or why not? Which position—Kant's or Mill's—do you think is sounder? Why?

7. Consider the view that pleasure, and only pleasure, is the good we should promote; and pain, and only pain, the evil we should avoid. Is it sound? Why or why not? If you think it is sound, explain how the pleasures and pains to which one's actions can lead could be predicted and added up. If, on the other hand, you think this view is unsound, formulate an alternative and explain why it is better.

8. What is exploitation? Do Marx's views help account for exploitation in the workplace? If so, how? If not, why not, and how would you account for exploitation? Is exploitation ever permissible? Why or why not? Defend your answers against objections you consider plausible.

9. Compare and contrast the positions of Hobbes, Gandhi, and de Beauvoir on the use of violence. Which one do you think is soundest and why? Is de Beauvoir in accord with Kant's moral philosophy? In what way, to what extent, and why? What reasons does she give for her position? Are they sound? Why or why not? Formulate some objections to your position and explain their shortcomings.

10. How do Lugones and Spelman characterize cultural imperialism? How do they think cultural imperialism applies to current feminist theorizing? Is their analysis sound? Why or why not?

11. What is your characterization of cultural imperialism? Do you think there is a moral duty to avoid it? Why or why not? Would Lugones and Spelman say that there is? Or would they say that avoiding cultural imperialism goes beyond the call of duty?

12. Do any authors of selections in Part IV engage in cross-cultural reflection and dialogue to any extent? Do they, for example, try to adapt categories used in other cultures to their own cultural context? Who, how, and how fruitfully?

13. Consider those authors in Part IV who do not engage in cross-cultural reflection. How could they have done so while being faithful to the views they espouse?

14. Consider the selections in Part IV and try to establish which ones include discussions that overlap with matters discussed in Parts II and III.

V

What Is Aesthetically Valuable?

A natural object, such as the song of a meadowlark, has esthetic qualities; and therefore esthetics, which is the theory of esthetic objects and experiences, applies both to natural objects and to works of art.

Melvin Rader, *A Modern Book of Esthetics*

Part V deals with aesthetics in the wide sense embraced by Rader. Yet, though its selections make reference to the aesthetic qualities of natural objects, they focus on the aesthetic qualities of works of art. Thus, they fall into the category of the philosophy of art. Our first selection, "In Defense of Aesthetic Value" by Monroe C. Beardsley (1915–1985), is largely a discussion of aesthetic value. Beardsley takes note of the increasingly felt problematic character of such value:

> Although the philosophy of art flourishes in our day as never before, and although the word "aesthetics" is widely accepted as a label for this subject, the *concept* of the aesthetic has grown more problematic with the progress of aesthetics.

Beardsley is particularly concerned with challenges to the possibility of soundly appraising—hence, passing value judgments on—artworks. He defends the functional account of art appraisal, "which assigns to the art appraiser the task of estimating how well the artworks that fall under his scrutiny fulfill their primary or central purpose." This poses certain questions: What criteria serve to establish the primary or central purpose of a given artwork? For any given creation, what criteria would establish that it is a work of art? And what criteria would establish what kind of art it is? Beardsley responds by characterizing an *artkind instance* as "anything that belongs to some recognized artkind," and an *artwork* as "an intentional arrangement of conditions for affording experiences with marked aesthetic character." He also comments:

> The terms "artwork" and "artkind-instance" are not coextensive, since some artkind-instances were not produced with the requisite intention, and some things produced with the requisite intention belong to no established artkind.

One may wonder why Beardsley would want to draw such distinction. He says that this distinction allows us to characterize art as having the purpose of providing experiences with a marked aesthetic character: "art as a social enterprise is understood in terms of an aesthetic purpose (while allowing that very many artworks have other purposes as well. . . .")

Who is supposed to have this purpose: the producers of the artwork, those who experience it, those who judge it, all of these, or some other individuals? Beardsley says:

> [I]f and only if the intention to provide an occasion for experiences of this sort plays a notable part in the production of some object, event, or state of affairs will that thing be a work of art.

But why should this be so? Take *Gulliver's Travels*. Its creator meant it to be a political satire; hence, to afford experiences of a specific aesthetic and cognitive sort. Historically, it turned out to be read in such a way that it is a children's book, affording aesthetic experiences of quite another sort. These latter experiences were never intended by the author. Does that mean that *Gulliver's Travels* isn't a work of art?

One might reply that the author's intention must be to afford experiences with marked aesthetic value, even if these should turn out to be of a specific sort unintended by the author. However, such a reply raises a cluster of crucial questions about the relation of experience to aesthetic value. If it does not matter *what* specific aesthetic experiences the author intended to provide, then why should it matter whether the author intended to provide *any* aesthetic experiences? Why would not other intentions do as well? For example, images and icons may be intended as tools for producing social cohesiveness. If such intentions would do, then Beardsley's reliance on the intention to provide an aesthetic experience to distinguish artworks from works that belong to a kind of art but are not artworks would be misguided. For social cohesiveness need not involve aesthetic experiences.[1]

To say this is not to say that there is no such thing as aesthetic value. Nor is it to say that the author's intentions do not matter at all. It is simply to suggest an alternative interpretation: The aesthetic value of items that turn out to be artworks (and, perhaps, the aesthetic value of *any* item, including natural objects) is settled through a social process of critical scrutiny of the items (say, the works and their purposes), as well as interactions between these items and those who interpret them (their authors, if any, included), who sometimes engage in dialogue with each other in the process.

As for the specific nature of this value—whether it lies in its capacity to afford experiences of certain sorts, or whether, as with images and icons, it lies in its social purposes—this interpretation leaves the matter open. We will return to this point later. Now let us see if this interpretation can be undermined by the criticisms of the functional account of art Beardsley mentions. These are five. First, we ought not to judge artworks at all. Second, if we may judge, there is little or no point in doing so. Third, even if there is a point in judging, our judgments cannot be true or false. Fourth, even if they can be true or false, no reasons can support them. Fifth, even if reasons can support them, the judgments can never amount to knowledge.

Some clues useful for addressing these criticisms, as well as for establishing whether providing aesthetic experiences is somehow central to artworks, may be found in our next selection, "Traditional African Aesthetics: A Philosophical Perspective" by the contemporary African philosopher Innocent C. Onyewuenyi. Onyewuenyi criticizes the traditional highly individualistic and static Western approaches to aesthetics. By contrast, he says: "Existence-in-relation, communalism, being-for-self-and-others sum up the African conception of life and reality." And, given this culturally entrenched conception, "African art is functional, community-oriented, depersonalized, contextualized, and embedded." He then defines what he means by two of these terms:

> By functional and community-oriented we mean that African arts—visual, musical, kinetic or poetic—are designed to serve practical, meaningful purpose, beauty of appearance being secondary.

If this account is accurate, the traditional Western distinction between arts and crafts does not apply to African arts:

> A carving, for example, is aesthetically beautiful in the African standard if it functions well as stimulus in the worship of the deity, the community of worshippers being the judges.

Furthermore, the artist's individual purpose "is not to depict his own individual whims and feelings. . . . He performs rather in such a way as to fulfill the ritual and social purposes of his community. . . ."

This leads to the question whether the capacity to provide aesthetic experiences is somehow central to all artworks. The highly practical nature of African artworks and art undermines Beardsley's notion that it is the function of artworks to provide experiences with a certain distinctive, aesthetic character, and that this is central to their aesthetic value. As Onyewuenyi shows, this is not the function of African art. It follows that it is not the function of art in general, if there is one.

On the other hand, by closely connecting the social functions of artworks with a variety of societal needs, from the ritual to the highly practical, African art comes to Beardsley's rescue by undermining the five criticisms of functionalism previously mentioned. These criticisms might make some sense when the aesthetic experiences in artworks are sharply separated from the practical functions of art objects. However, when, as in African art, there is no such separation, the views become questionable. Let us see why.

First, given the social circumstances and roles within which artists work in Africa, one may, and ought to, judge whether an artist's product fills community needs. Hence, it is false to say that one ought not to judge artworks. Second, there is a strong communal reason for judging artworks. Therefore, it is false to say that there is no or little point to judging artworks. Third, judgments of artworks can be true or false—for example, they are true when they state that the artwork meets community needs if indeed it does—so the third criticism of functionalism is also false. Fourth, reasons of a significantly factual nature can often support these judgments. Hence, not only can judgments be true or false, but good reasons can be given for or against them. Finally, when the judgments are true and the judgers are sure of their judgments and their reasons are good, then the judges have knowledge. Hence, it is false to say that aesthetic judgments cannot amount to knowledge.

Returning now to the relation between providing aesthetic experiences and the purpose of art, to say that the capacity to provide such experiences is not the characteristic purpose of art (because not the purpose of all artworks) is not to say that *no* artworks can have this purpose. They can, and some Western artworks have it; but it is an adventitious, albeit culturally entrenched, purpose. It follows that Beardsley's criticism of Nelson Goodman's rejection of aesthetic value is based on wrong reasons. Beardsley says:

> Nelson Goodman's position rejects aesthetic value, as I have been analyzing and defending it, and proposes instead to base art appraisals on the *cognitive* value of artworks—their capacity to contribute to the "creation and comprehension of our worlds." Artworks turn up in this account as characters, or classes of characters, in symbol systems, and like other symbols are to be judged primarily or centrally by their successful functioning as symbols, their "cognitive efficacy."

Beardsley formulates various criticisms against this thesis. First, he argues that instrumental musical works and nonrepresentational paintings—"large and important subclasses" of artworks—have not been shown to be such symbol systems, because it has not been shown that they refer to anything. Second, many natural objects, such as mountains and trees, seem to have a value closely akin to that of artworks; yet they, too, are not characters in any symbol system. Third, cognitive concerns are often sacrificed in the arts for the sake of something else.

Beardsley thinks his refutation of Goodman's thesis gives credence to the notion that "the primary purpose [of artworks] is the aesthetizing of experience." But it does not. Consider Onyewuenyi's quote from an article by Peggy Harper on African masks:

> Through his dance Efe has the power to please the witches and so turn their malevolent self-seeking power into a generous benevolence towards the community.

So it appears that the aesthetizing of experience is not the primary purpose of African artworks. Instead, their main function is the provision of tools for social purposes, such as cohesiveness or safety, that at least some of the time are primarily noncognitive and nonexperiential. As for Goodman's claims, no doubt a mask has to depict a divine power correctly, but its overriding purpose goes beyond this cognitive aim. Indeed, if, as Beardsley claims, cognitive claims are often sacrificed in the arts for the sake of something else, this something else need not be an experience. It may be—and sometimes it definitely is—a social purpose such as cohesiveness or safety.

But is this position undermined by Beardsley's claim concerning natural objects? It would be if we were claiming that social function is *the* primary purpose of all artworks. But we are advancing no such view. Instead, our position is that the particular nature of what has aesthetic value, though not necessarily of aesthetic value itself, *varies across cultures*—and, indeed, may vary also within the Western tradition more than Beardsley admits. Our interpretation of aesthetic value makes room for all these differences between and within cultures. It says that the aesthetic value of an item that turns out to be an artwork (and, perhaps, of any item, including natural objects) is settled through a social process of critical scrutiny of the items (say, the works and their purposes), as well as through interactions between these items and those who interpret them (their authors included), who sometimes engage in dialogue with each other in the process.

Our next selection, "The Intentional Fallacy" by William K. Wimsatt and Monroe C. Beardsley, raises the question: How significant for evaluating an artwork are the author's intentions in creating that artwork? Wimsatt and Beardsley argue that art criticism has rules of evidence different from those of author psychology. Concerning poems, for example, they write:

> The paradox is only verbal and superficial that what is (1) internal is also public: it is discovered through the semantics and syntax of a poem, through our habitual knowledge of the language, through grammars, dictionaries, and all the literature which is the source of dictionaries, in general through all that makes a language and culture; while what is (2) external is private or idiosyncratic; not a part of the work as a linguistic fact: it consists of revelations (in journals, for example, or letters, or reported conversations) about how and why the poet wrote the poem—to what lady, while sitting on what lawn, or at the death of what friend or brother.

They grant that there is "an intermediate kind of evidence about the character of the author or about private or semiprivate meanings attached to words or topics by an author or by a coterie of which he is a member," that is relevant to an understanding of the semantics of a poem. Yet making use of such evidence need not amount to engaging in author psychology:

> The use of biographical evidence need not involve intentionalism, because while it may be evidence of what the author intended, it may also be evidence of the meaning of his words and the dramatic character of his utterance.

In support of this view, Wimsatt and Beardsley reason as follows:

> The meaning of words is the history of words, and the biography of an author, his use of a word, and the associations which the words had for *him,* are part of the word's history and meaning.

A cluster of questions arises here: Are the associations a word has for any person, however peculiar they might be, part of the history and the meaning of that word? Or for this to be true, should the person be a competent user of the language to which the word belongs? Should the person be also an author—even a recognized author? In any case, in what manner is evidence of this kind to be used together with our habitual knowledge of the language in the criticism of the author's poem?

Though Wimsatt and Beardsley use poetry to illustrate their position on critical inquiry, they mean it to apply to artworks generally. How well does it apply to paintings? Take Pablo Picasso's work. Between 1901 and 1905, during his so-called "Blue Period," the tonality of his paintings was predominantly blue, but aside from that peculiarity, he was still working within the constraints of pictorial realism. By 1910, however, his paintings involved basic, simplified forms and a markedly shifting point of view, which soon came to be called "Cubism." Suppose it is 1911 and one is engaging in criticism of Picasso's 1911 painting entitled "Accordionist." How could one fruitfully appeal to the existing habitual knowledge of painting, or even to knowledge of Picasso's previous repertoire, to engage in such criticism? Though he had begun to experiment with breaking up smoothly continuous volumes into separate interlocking planes (e.g., in his 1907 *Les Demoiselles D'Avignon*), one might not even recognize the painting as a Picasso!

Is this a good reason for concluding that the author's intentions are crucial for assessing the author's work? Not by itself. An alternative is this: Until the interpreters presented with a new kind of art object an artist has produced have predominantly settled the matter, the judgment is still out as to whether it is art, let alone good art. Concerning the critical assessment of "Accordionist," one could argue that through a process of dialogue among artists and nonartists, and their interaction with Cubist artworks, the matter was settled; it was not settled by Picasso's intentions, but by those affected by Picasso's work—Picasso included—later in the century. This also applies to the previously cited example of *Gulliver's Travels*. Swift meant it as a political satire, yet through the process of dialogue and interaction that followed its publication, *Gulliver's Travels* became a children's book.

One might object that the position we just formulated only manages to avoid the intentional fallacy by succumbing to the sociological fallacy. For it appears that, according to this view, it is not the author's intentions (the intentional fallacy), but society's interpretations (the sociological fallacy) that determine what is art, what is good art, and what kind of art an artist's particular creation is. Yet how society appraises a work of art at one time often turns out to be quite different from how it appraises the same work of art at some other time.

This objection is exaggerated. First of all, to say that the process of critical scrutiny of and interaction with the products of artistic activities is central for settling aesthetic judgment is not to say that society does all the settling. Artists and their creations are an integral part of the criticism process.

The Argentinian writer Jorgé Luis Borges has provided a good example of what we mean here. In his "Kafka and His Precursors," he considers three very dissimilar writings—Zeno's paradox against movement; a paragraph by Han Yu, a prose writer of the ninth century A.D.; and the works of Kierkegaard—and examines their relation to Kafka's work:

> If I am not mistaken, the heterogeneous pieces I have enumerated resemble Kafka; if I am not mistaken, not all of them resemble each other. This second fact is the more significant. In each of these texts we find Kafka's idiosyncrasy to a greater or lesser degree, but if Kafka had never written a line, we would not perceive this quality; in other words, it would not exist.[2]

That is, the artist's creation provides the referent for, and guides, the process of criticism. What it does not do is to settle matters in and of itself. *Artworks—and, for that matter, many other products of human creativity—are dialogues.*

To be sure, the fact that an artwork is a dialogue does not ensure that the dialogue will always converge on a shared or permanent view about the nature, kind, identity, and value of that artwork. But it often does. And the limited number of instances in which the dialogue fails to attain closure provides no good reason to reject the view that artworks are dialogues. Nonclosure can be a feature of some dialogues, either because the objects prompting them offer insufficient guidance to their interpreters, or because interpreters cannot make up their minds about the objects, or because later generations lose interest in the objects. Indeed, the last possibility has the virtue of pointing out that art, like culture, has to be regained by each generation. Classics can cease to be classics and artforms can cease to be artforms, just as a joke can cease to be a joke, given sufficient cultural changes. By themselves, the objects that become classics—say, Homer's *Odyssey*—are only the referents of the dialogues that turn them into classics. If these dialogues cease, they can start again and bring the classics back to life.

At this point, someone might object that the position taken in this essay entails that artistic appreciation and judgment are entirely subjective—a mere matter of taste. But it does not. For at any point in the dialogue, it is possible for anyone to give reasons for or against the view that a given object is art, or that it is art of a certain kind, or that it has this or that identity or value.

One might still argue that since—as has been made plain by our discussions and selections so far—art is highly fragmented in the twentieth century, such reasons are not always, if ever, possible. In other words, the fragmentation is irreducible. This position is relevant to our next selection, "The Dehumanization of Art" by the Spanish philosopher José Ortega y Gasset (1883–1955), which examines art and changes in artistic style from a sociological point of view.

Ortega acknowledges at the outset that "every newcomer among styles passes through a stage of quarantine." However, he states, the unpopularity of twentieth-century Western art is of a different kind. It does not result from a difference of tastes. "It is not that the majority does not *like* the art of the young and the minority likes it, but that the majority, the masses, do not *understand* it." That is, most people do not merely dislike the new art while feeling superior to it. On the contrary, they feel vaguely humiliated by it.

> Through its mere presence, the art of the young compels the average citizen to realize that he is just this—the average citizen, a creature incapable of receiving the sacrament of art, blind and deaf to pure beauty.

This arouses indignation. Yet, the author argues, "A time must come in which society, from politics to art, reorganizes itself into two orders or ranks: the illustrious and the vulgar." He thinks the new art (Stravinski's music and Pirandello's theater are his examples) is accessible only to a special class of human beings, "who may not be better but who evidently are different."

In what manner are these people different? Ortega argues that, in experiencing artworks, ordinary people have the same focus that they have in ordinary life: people and passions. "By art they understand a means through which they are brought in contact with interesting human affairs. Artistic forms proper—figments, fantasy— are tolerated only if they do not interfere with the perception of human forms and fates." But, Ortega argues, the new art seeks to eliminate these "human realities" in favor of aesthetic elements. Even if pure art is impossible, there can be a tendency toward a purification of art, and this is seen in the new art. Thus, it "is an art for artists." By this, Ortega means "not only those who produce this art but also those who are capable of perceiving purely artistic values." This division, he adds, is insurmountable:

> Modern art . . . will always have the masses against it. It is essentially unpopular. . . . Any of its works automatically produces a curious effect on the general public. It divides the public into two groups: one very small, formed by those who are favorably inclined towards it; another very large—the hostile majority.

According to Ortega, this is so because, in defiance of ordinary people's preferences, modern artists divest their objects of aspects of lived reality. This is not to say that they produce objects that have nothing to do with the ordinary objects of human life. They simply produce objects that, though resembling these ordinary objects, resemble them "as little as possible." As a result, such "ultra-objects" come across to ordinary people as dehumanized—mere deformations of ordinary life. But, Ortega argues, this is unavoidable:

> Perception of "lived" reality and perception of artistic form . . . are essentially incompatible because they call for a different adjustment of our perceptive apparatus.

They are as incompatible as seeing a garden through a window and focusing on the windowpane at one and the same time. We cannot do both things, and according to Ortega, perceiving art is like perceiving the pane rather than the garden visible through it.

One might respond that although one cannot do both things at once, many people—certainly artists—can do one or the other at will. However, Ortega indicates that these are not just *psychologically* incompatible activities at one and the same time. They are *socially* incompatible activities:

> Not many people are capable of adjusting their perceptive apparatus to the pane and the transparency that is the work of art. Instead they look right through it and revel in the human reality with which the work deals. When they are invited to let go of this prey and to direct their attention to the work of art itself they will say that they cannot see such a thing, which indeed they cannot, because it is all artistic transparency and without substance.

This is, no doubt, an accurate description of the fragmentation of art appreciation in the Western world during the first part of the twentieth century, but this fragmentation is not necessarily unavoidable or irreducible. For one thing, the notion of irreducibility is just a hypothesis. The recurrent sharp differences in artistic appreciation between artists and ordinary people is not a good ground for believing such differences are irreducible. As we saw earlier in this essay, they do not appear even to exist for African art. Nor is it clear that they predominated, if they existed at all, during the Italian Renaissance. It may be true that *now*, given current linguistic, conceptual, stylistic, and practical differences among groups in the West, fragmentation is irreducible. But neither languages nor conceptual frameworks nor styles nor practices are static. They can and do change through dialogue and social interaction, so that today's incommensurables are superseded by tomorrow's common ground.

Second, even if the construction of a common ground of aesthetic appreciation is, at least on occasion, impossible, this does not mean that artistic appreciation and judgment are entirely subjective. It might, if appreciation and judgment entailed shared experiences. But they don't. At most they entail that good reasons for judgments be formulated in the process of critical scrutiny. To be sure, without sufficiently interested, thinking, and appreciating individuals, artistic dialogues tend to be unstable or to hit dead ends. But this is really the same as saying that without such individuals, the existence of art and artworks will be unstable and precarious.[3]

Just so, without sufficiently interested, thinking, and appreciating individuals, philosophy tends to be unstable and precarious. Which brings us back to questions raised at the beginning of this book concerning the nature and predicament of philosophy. We take them up again in Part VI.

NOTES

[1] The Argentinian writer Jorgé Luis Borges brings up this example, which had been Kipling's, in discussing what he describes as "the error of supposing that intentions and plans matter a great deal." See "The Argentine Writer and Tradition," in Jorgé Luis Borges, *Labyrinths* (New York: New Directions, 1962), p. 185.

[2] Jorgé Luis Borges, "Kafka and His Precursors," in *Labyrinths,* p. 201.

[3] For a discussion of objectivity as it applies to some institutions other than art, see Iannone, "Informing the Public: Ethics, Policy Making, and Objectivity in News Reporting," *Philosophy in Context 20* (1990): 1–21. See also my *Philosophy as Diplomacy* (Atlantic Highlands, N.J.: Humanities Press, 1993), Essay 4.

Monroe C. Beardsley (1915–1985)
IN DEFENSE OF AESTHETIC VALUE

The author defends the functional account of art appraisal, which assesses artworks in terms of how well they fulfill their primary purpose. He argues that this purpose is not merely cognitive, but includes providing experiences of a certain sort that are called aesthetic and constitute aesthetic value. Beardsley's views are discussed at the beginning of the introductory essay to Part V.

READING QUESTIONS

In reading the selection, try to answer the following questions and identify the passages that support your answers:

1.   What account of aesthetic value does Beardsley defend?
2.   What reasons does he give in support of this account?
3.   What is aesthetic value according to Beardsley?
4.   Is his conception of aesthetic value sound? Why or why not?
5.   Can you think of a better conception? Which is it and why is it better?

Reprinted from Monroe C. Beardsley, "In Defense of Aesthetic Value," *Proceedings and Addresses of the American Philosophical Association* (Newark, DE: APA, 1979), pp. 723–749. Copyright © 1979 American Philosophical Association. Reprinted by permission of the American Philosophical Association.

Although the philosophy of art flourishes in our day as never before, and although the word "aesthetics" is widely accepted as a label for this subject, the *concept* of the aesthetic has grown more problematic with the progress of aesthetics. Some have concluded that the term "aesthetic" marks no distinction, or no distinction of theoretical significance; others have clung to the term but pressed upon us redefinitions that amount to surreptitious substitution of new concepts; still others allow a limited scope for a concept of the aesthetic, but argue that it has nothing to do with art—a view that calls the whole enterprise in question, since it was primarily the existence of artworks that got us into this line of inquiry in the first place.

I should apologize at once for my use of so dubious an expression as "the aesthetic"—a peculiarly philosophic form of nominalization that we have learned to be wary of. It is a temporary verbal expedient to postpone debatable commitments, and this particular adjective (which especially calls for caution) will shortly be reunited with familiar nouns.

The problems to which I address myself are created by our inveterate habit of judging artworks as good or poor, better or worse than others. In recent years there has been a certain amount of complaint on this score, both about the judgmental habit itself and about the tendency of aestheticians to concern themselves with it. Now, I am not one to encourage censoriousness—even in art critics—and I don't doubt that ill-supported, as well as ill-tempered, disparagements of artworks have had deplorable consequences. But since we must select to survive, and must discriminate among degrees of quality in our surroundings in order to lift our lives above the survival level, it is clearly inevitable that we will bring our concern about the better and the worse to artworks, as we do to nearly everything else. It has been wittily suggested[1] that aestheticians' preoccupation with goodness in art has been responsible for a lack

---

[1]   By Nelson Goodman, "Merit and Means," in *Art and Philosophy*, ed. Sidney Hook, N.Y.: New York University Press, 1966, pp. 56–57; cf. *Languages of Art*, Indianapolis: Bobbs-Merrill, 1968, p. 261.

of goodness in aesthetics. But even if we grant the alleged deficiencies in the subject, they can hardly be explained by too much thinking, and in any case the remedy is not to be timid in the face of genuine philosophical challenge.

I

One way of meeting this challenge has developed, over the years, into a well-known account of art appraisals, that is, of judgments about the quality of artworks. This account has roots deep in the past, and we can say that a good many aestheticians have accepted it in general, or substantial parts of it, in one version or another. With some uneasiness, I shall refer to it as the "functional" account of art appraisal (a not very endearing label), which assigns to the art appraiser the task of estimating how well the artworks that fall under his scrutiny fulfill their primary or central purpose. The functional account can be displayed in six stages or steps, which I now propose to call to mind.

It begins with a premise that is well illustrated in a forthright remark by a contemporary writer on literary theory, Lee Lemon:

> We know that "Poor Soul! the center of my sinful earth" is a better poem than "Ozymandias," just as we know that the latter is better than Drayton's "To nothing fitter can I thee compare."[2]

To begin with this exemplary truth takes a good deal for granted. The passage may remind you uncomfortably of a famous sentence of Hume's:

> Whoever would assert an equality of genius and elegance between Ogilby and Milton, or Bunyan and Addison, would be thought to defend no less an extravagance, than if he had maintained a mole-hill to be as high as Teneriffe, or a pond as extensive as the ocean.[3]

Not that the first of Hume's invidious comparisons is likely to excite protest. Although John Ogilby was a pioneer in the printing of road maps (and we are all in his debt), his extant poetical works (largely translation of Vergil and Homer) are held in low esteem by those who have ventured to peruse them. But Bunyan is a different story: he has rightly come to be admired as a prose stylist, and so perhaps a difference of opinion on the comparative merits of his

writing and Addison's would strike us as much less unreasonable than Hume's geographical examples. Still, we understand why Bunyan's outcast state prevented his work from receiving, in Hume's day, the unprejudiced judgment required by Hume's own standard of taste. The functional account of art appraisal affirms only that in the case of some artworks we know one to be better than another, and this of course is not precluded by conceding the possibility of error in other cases. It would still be extravagant to equate Michael Drayton's sonnet with Shelley's or Shelley's with Shakespeare's.

Two philosophical tasks naturally present themselves the moment we accede to the first step of the functional account: to explain how one poem, or other artwork, can be better than another; and to explain how we know that this is true of particular pairs of works. I insert a warning here that I am speaking of artworks in a presystematic sense, that is, a sense anterior to theoretical reflection: they include anything that is a poem or play, or musical composition, or painting, or dance, or sculpture or architectural work, et cetera (the "et cetera" is innocuous, I think, because for my present purpose it doesn't matter how far we carry the list beyond the point which I have left off). In other words, I want to be referring to anything that belongs to some recognized artkind, i.e., it is an artkind instance.

The second step in the development of the functional account is to say that if one artkind-instance can be better than another, there must be some way or manner in which it is better. Two lines of argument, one general and other specific, converge here.

The general argument may be illustrated by a characteristic exchange from the works of P. G. Wodehouse:

> ". . . Of course you have read the Zend Avesta of Zoroaster, Sir Roderick?"
>
> "I'm afraid not. Is it good?"[4]

The gentle absurdity of the reply points up a feature of such bare ascriptions of goodness to particular things: they are incomplete until we let on what manner of goodness is in question. Even if we say only that the Zend-Avesta is good in some manner or other, we concede that where there is goodness there is a way of being good. If this is not evident for goodness, it must be so for betterness: if someone should claim that the Zend-Avesta is better than the

[2]   Lee T. Lemon, *The Partial Critics*, N.Y.: Oxford University Press, 1965, p. 223.
[3]   David Hume, "Of the Standard of Taste," in *Four Dissertations* (1757).

[4]   P. G. Wodehouse, *The Return of Jeeves*, N.Y.: Simon and Schuster, 1954, p. 65.

Bagavadgita, it would certainly be in order to inquire in what respect this is, or is believed to be, true. If X is *in no way* better than Y, then X is not better than Y. Here "X" and "Y" stand for individual things. I shall not pause to dispute with those who find intelligibility in more abstract remarks like "Pleasure is good," though I don't myself know how to make very good sense of them.

The specific argument takes off from the observation that a society does assign (no doubt sometimes haphazardly) the role of making such judgments to those who are assumed to have some expertise in making them. We acknowledge that a literary critic, for example, cannot be expected to have the qualifications required for reliable judgment *in* all the respects in which two poems might be compared in quality. I don't suppose, for example, that Lee Lemon, though doubtless equipped to weigh the comparative merits of many literary works, would claim equal authority to discuss the Zend-Avesta of Zoroaster with respect to its theological, ethical, or homiletic quality. So if there is to be such a specialized activity as art criticism, or any branch of it concerned with a particular art, it seems that there must be some limited, discriminable manner of goodness associated with artkind-instances or with their kinds: there must be something that can properly be called "goodness *as* art" or "goodness *as* literature," and so on.

The third step, then, consists in locating and identifying this artistic manner of goodness (waiving the alternative formulations in terms of artkinds). The connection between ways of being good and groups of things that can be judged more or less good has been much and ably explored. We can, I think, set aside here the view (one that seems to have very few current takers) that artkind-instances are themselves intrinsically good. If the special goodness of artkind-instances is, then, extrinsic, and lies in their connections with other things, the procedure for disclosing it seems clear: we inquire what services they offer—that is, what in general (though in varying degrees) they do, or what can be done with them, that is worth doing. It turns out, obviously enough, that artkind-instances are not characteristically to be counted on in enterprises directed toward making physical changes in the world; but they do quite generally give rise to at least temporary psychological changes—and changes for the better—in those who seek them out and make suitable demands on them. In short, their specialty is affording a kind of experience (i.e., inducing an experience specifically by

becoming the phenomenally objective apprehended content, or focus of attention, in the experience). What else could artkind-instances be good for, speaking generally and noting especially the salient features of outstanding examples?

But the diversity of experiences is far too great to provide a manageable manner of goodness without one further restriction. We must look for a common feature to mark off the relevant experiences: a certain desirable character, simple or compound, that can be found in many experiences, especially in experiences of artkind-instances, but not only in such experiences; and we require a character that has degree, so that experience may have more or less of it. According to the functional account, there is such a character, and must be one in order to make sense of specifically critical judgments of the quality of artkind-instances. And in casting about for a suitable label for this character, it seizes upon the word "aesthetic." It is hard to see what other word could be more appropriate. It then becomes convenient to say that some experiences have an aesthetic character, but some have a more pronounced or marked aesthetic character than others, and some, indeed, have it in a high degree.

Step four consists in the introduction of one more term that is made available by the concept of aesthetic character. If we suppose that the presence of aesthetic character in an experience confers value on that experience, we may define "aesthetic value" in this way: the aesthetic value of anything is its capacity to impart—*through cognition of it*—a marked aesthetic character to experience. The term "cognition" here refers to the apprehension (but not the *mis*apprehension) of the thing's qualities and relations, including its semantic properties, if any—it covers both perception and interpretive understanding, in a broad sense, even where the art work is a literary text or a conceptual "piece." In equivalent words, to say that X has aesthetic value is to say that X has the capacity to afford, through the cognition of it, an experience that has value on account of its marked aesthetic character. And to say that X has greater aesthetic value than Y is to say that X has the capacity to afford an experience that is more valuable, on account of its more marked aesthetic character, than any experience that Y has the capacity to afford. This pair of definitions does not, of course, define "value," but is designed only to distinguish aesthetic value from other kinds of value.

Step five is to note that the concept of aesthetic value as a distinct kind of value enables us to draw a distinction that is indispensable to the enterprise of art criticism: that is, the distinction between relevant and irrelevant reasons that might be given in support of judgments of artistic goodness. Not everything that can truly be said about artkind-instances has a bearing on their quality as art; but it seems that only in terms of an appropriate theory of value can we tell which true statements support critical judgments and which do not. Putting it briefly, a statement is relevant if and only if it ascribes a property the possession of which makes a difference to the thing's capacity to afford experiences with marked aesthetic character.

Step six may be regarded as optional: it is a suggestion for tying these concepts together more systematically. To get the search for the aesthetic character of experiences under way, we needed the concept of *artkind-instance;* loose as it was, it plainly included many objects that are unchallengeably within the purview of our inquiry. Now we may wonder whether the concepts we have acquired will enable us to frame a more formal definition of "work of art" or "artwork" that will be significant for the purpose of building theory. Now a good many things produced by human beings have been produced at least in part (I mean that this was one motive in the mixture) to satisfy a demand for experiences with aesthetic character—whether in fact they were successful. Even when—as with the most narcissistic self-expressionist or with the most humble Sunday painter—there is not plan to make the work widely available to others, there may be an intention to make it at least *capable* of satisfying such a demand. This must be true of vast numbers of artkind-instances. Moreover, the category seems significant, for these things will play a distinct role in society; they ask to be approached and treated and judged in a special way; their production and reception may require special explanation in psychological and social science; they would presumably have a special relationship to other recurrent and persistent elements of human culture, such as religion and science. So an artwork can be usefully defined as an intentional arrangement of conditions for affording experiences with marked aesthetic character. In other words, if and only if the intention to provide an occasion for experiences of this sort plays a notable part in the production of some object, event, or state of affairs will that thing be a work of art.

The terms "artwork" and "artkind-instance" are not coextensive, since some artkind-instances were not produced with the requisite intention, and some things produced with the requisite intention belong to no established artkind. But the overlap is considerable—as it must be, to keep the proposed definition from being wholly arbitrary. Yet, our definition need not, of course, be strictly bound by prevailing usage, if that exists; its advantage is that it marks an important distinction with reasonable definiteness. The concept of art and the concept of the aesthetic become closely linked; art as a social enterprise is understood in terms of an aesthetic purpose (while allowing that very many artworks have other purposes as well), just as the judgment of individual artworks is understood in terms of aesthetic success. And this gives us a bearing on the roles that the arts play in culture for, even though these roles go far beyond the provision of aesthetically marked experience, this particular role may nevertheless be both definitive and fundamental to the others.

I noted the detachability of step six from the other elements of the functional account of art appraisal because it meets with so much opposition, which I cannot deal with here—opposition from those who hold that no intention, but only an official institutional endorsement, converts something into an artwork; from those who hold that avant-garde artists have freed the concept of art from any connection with the concept of the aesthetic, and that since they have rightful authority to decide how art is to be defined, their usage is to be followed; from those who hold that general use is authoritative here and that in general use the concept of art is "open" and "essentially contested," so that any attempt to define it is necessarily unfaithful. My view is that the definition of art in terms of aesthetic intention marks an important distinction which the word "art" is best fitted, by its history and by widespread current use, to preserve.

II

Despite its plausibility and apparent coherence, the functional account of art appraisal has come under severe attack. It has its weak points which some aestheticians have been industriously trying to shore up, while others shake their heads and certify it as a hopeless case. My aim is to present a fresh brief for the functional account against doubts that have been raised or might sensibly be raised. All six steps have been rejected by someone; but it seems to me that vague expressions of discontent and sweeping condemnations are a good deal more common than cogent refutations or constructive alternatives. So it is up to the defense to secure its own Sixth Amendment rights by trying to articulate the nature of the charges as well as to display and increase the strength of its position.

We may begin by reconsidering step one, the critic's claim to knowledge of artistic goodness. It has been said:

1. that we ought not to judge artworks at all (and if we didn't, then the philosophical problem of justifying such judgments would not arise);

2. that even if we are permitted to judge, there is little or no point in doing so;

3. that even if there is a point in judging, our judgments cannot be true or false;

4. that even if critical judgments are true or false, they cannot be supported by reasons in any standard sense of these terms;

5. that even if these judgments can be supported by reasons, such support can never amount to knowledge.

A thorough discussion of even these preliminary theses could evidently take us far, so my brief reply must have a regrettable air of dogmatism. As to the first charge, I have seen no reason to think that freedom from appraisal is an inalienable right; a plea for exemption must be accompanied by a showing of probable harm. This of course can be done in some situations regarding particularly vulnerable human beings—including some artists.

A pervasive atmosphere in which a highly appraisive attitude prevails, and critics are far more given to judging than to sympathetic understanding, is no doubt an unhealthy one for the arts. It is no part of my aim to defend, much less promote, such a situation; I only say (1) it is generally not judgments as such, but unfair or unreasonable judgments, that threaten artworks, and (2) sometimes we must judge, as well as we can, because sometimes we must choose.

The second charge emerges from some of the essays in recent years that have compared aesthetic judgments of artworks with moral judgments of human actions—often to the disparagement of the former. Two distinct contrasts are unfortunately often confused. The first is between moral judgments and value judgments in general. Here there is such a difference of category that we risk nonsense in comparing them; however, we might want to note, for example, as John Rawls has noted, that value judgments

are "advisory" in a way in which moral judgments are not.[5] The second contrast is between aesthetic value judgments and others; and with respect to the charge of pointlessness, I have seen no reason to think that, by their very nature, aesthetic value judgments must be any less useful than others—assuming that we can actually have them. If we can have knowledge of artistic quality, such knowledge is bound to be of use to us on many occasions, as individuals and as citizens—quite apart from its satisfaction of a legitimate curiosity.

In recent years there has been a vigorous advancement of the third objection: that judgments of artistic quality lack truth-value. According to this view—which Joseph Margolis has named "robust relativism" to distinguish it from those forms of relativism which allow truth-value to critical judgments, when properly relativized—other sorts of predicates may properly be applied to critical judgments: they are reasonable, suitable, apt, appropriate, plausible, perhaps, but not true or false.[6] The acceptance of this position would indeed wash away the foundations of the functional account, so it would be good to know of a way to argue against it. I believe we could show at length that to withhold truth-values from critical judgments would be intolerable: we could not manage with what seem to be the clear consequence of such a view, namely, that such judgments could not enter into inductive or deductive reasonings as premises or conclusions. On the inductive side, for example, when some years ago Allen Ginsburg's lurid poem, *Howl,* was tried in a San Francisco court, we should have had to disallow the testimony of those professors of literature who were prepared to swear or affirm that *Howl* was a very good poem, and better than many others. They could not honestly take the required oath if they were robust relativists. But under current constitutional doctrines about obscenity (which, granted, are far from coherent in other respects) such expert testimony concerning literary quality is considered highly germane as evidence of "redeeming social importance." On the deductive side, turning back to the passage from Lee Lemon, it is tempting to say that if he holds that Shakespeare's poem is better than Shelley's and Shelley's than Drayton's, he is logically bound to hold that Shakespeare's is better than Drayton's. This intuition presumes the transitivity of (this kind of) betterness, which can hardly

---

[5] *A Theory of Justice,* Cambridge: Harvard University Press, 1971, p. 448.

[6] Joseph Margolis, "Robust Relativism," *Journal of Aesthetics and Art Criticism,* 35 (Fall 1976): 37–46; see especially p. 41.

be formulated (as a conditional) unless betterness-propositions have truth-value.

Skepticism of the fourth kind, taking another turn than robust relativism, attacks the very idea of reason-giving in art criticism, again sometimes by invidious comparisons with ethics. Consider, for example, a provocative remark by Gilbert Harman: "It is not appropriate to ask someone who admires a painting what his principle is."[7] All right; and it is not appropriate to ask someone who admires Justice Thurgood Marshall what *his* principle is. In these examples, admiring is an attitude. If we are thinking of admiring as an illocutionary act (that is, judging the painting to be good, the Justice to be great), the word is "praising," and there is no absurdity in inquiring about principles on which we praise—in either art or morals. Was Hume confused when he confessed—in a sentence I once chose as an epigraph—"I am uneasy to think I approve of one object, and disapprove of another; call one thing beautiful, and another deform'd; decide concerning truth and falsehood, reason and folly, without knowing upon what principles I proceed?"[8]

If an art appraisal is true or false, its truth-value cannot be utterly unconnected with the truth-value of other propositions that can be independently established and can therefore serve as reasons for accepting or rejecting it. Moreover, if it is true that the painting is a good one, this state of affairs (the painting's being good) invites explanation. Of course *reasons-why* are to be distinguished from *reasons-for-believing,* and (as Gilbert Harman has pointed out) reasons-for-believing something are not always "reasons-for-which-one-believes." But reasons why and reasons for believing appear to be related by a universal principle.[9] Suppose R is a reason why the state of affairs S obtains (that is, R explains that state of affairs, say, painting P's being good); then R will also be a reason for believing that S obtains. Moreover, for someone who does not otherwise know that S obtains, and who possesses certain auxiliary information, R can be a reason *for which* that someone believes that S obtains. I am not summoning up the old question of the symmetry of explanation and prediction; my thesis is that if we grant

that the artistic goodness of a painting is in principle explainable, like other things about it, then we must also grant that belief in its presence could in principle be supported by a reason.

But not everyone will grant the antecedent of this conditional. In the context cited earlier, Gilbert Harman adds: "This is an important difference between morality and aesthetics, since you may think that one melody is good, another banal, without feeling compelled to find aesthetic principles that would distinguish them." "Compelled" needs a gloss here, I think. I can see how there might not be the same degree of stringency or urgency in the aesthetic as in the moral case—but that is true of value judgments in general. A fairer way of posing the issue would be to ask whether, in the aesthetic case, you would feel some obligation to try to explain, if politely requested, what *makes* one melody better than the other. Whether this explanatory difference, if pointed out, can be erected into a general *principle* would be disputed. I am only urging that artistic superiority must be explainable by reasons-why—and therefore, as I have said, that propositions about it must be supportable by reasons-to-believe.

There remains the fifth charge: that art appraisals, however reasonable, cannot be knowledge. The direct argument here is one that need not detain us: it is simply that the reasons, in the special case of art appraisals, cannot ever provide sufficient justification to transform belief into knowledge. Such a view is, I believe, easily refuted by Hume's method of citing extreme cases: *Paradise Lost* is known to be a better poem than *Howl.* After that, we can concede the multifarious difficulties of getting reliable art appraisals.

The more interesting argument we confront here is the attempt to show an inherent defect in critical judgments that prevents them from being strictly knowable. Claims to knowledge about the goodness of artworks are typically expressed in judgments, and such judgments have often been said (since Kant's Third Critique) to be peculiarly tied to firsthand experience: that is, the illocutionary-act conditions for critical judging are said to include direct acquaintance with the artwork judged (or with a reproduction of it). Thus one who has never heard a musical work can *report* a critic's judgment of it, but not *make* a judgment, and therefore can't be said to *know* that the work is good or poor. Alan Tormey has worked out this view ingeniously: his conclusion is that even the critic's so-called knowledge lacks an essential feature of knowledge, namely transmissibility to others,

[7] Gilbert Harman, *The Nature of Morality,* N.Y.: Oxford University Press, 1977, p. 51.

[8] David Hume, *A Treatise of Human Nature,* I, iv, vii; ed. L. A. Selby-Bigge, Oxford: Clarendon Press, 1888, p. 271.

[9] Gilbert Harman, *Thought,* Princeton: Princeton University Press, 1973, p. 26.

as expressed in Hintikka's formula: "If B knows that A knows that p, then B knows that p."[10] A variation of his argument might be put as follows:

1. Expand the Hintikka formula to this: If A knows that Schubert's string quintet in C is magnificent, and B knows that A knows this, then B knows that the quintet is magnificent.

2. But B *could* know that A knows the quintet is magnificent even if he has never heard the quintet himself. Suppose this possibility is true.

3. Assume that B has never heard the quintet.

4. Then B cannot judge, and therefore does not know, that the quintet is magnificent.

5. Then A does not know the quintet is magnificent either, for if he did, his knowledge would be something he could pass on to B.

This argument and its supporting discussion deserve much more attention than I can give them here. My way of escaping its clutches is to concede that there is a sense in which B (who has not heard the music) cannot judge it, but to insist that B can still say that the quintet is magnificent (and this is a judgment in a broader sense), and can justifiably assert this on the authority of A, whom he knows to be an excellent music critic. Thus A's knowledge is transmissible to others, even if the others have to borrow or copy judgments, so to speak, rather than initiate them.

III

We come now to the most direct and serious attack on the functional account, striking at points 2, 3, and 4. It has two parts:

1. Talk of a *kind* of value, in a sense required by the functional account, is not intelligible.

2. Even if there *are* kinds of value, there can be no such thing as aesthetic value, since we cannot isolate a special aesthetic character of experiences.

First as to the genus: how could things that have a value constitute a kind, within which we might mark out subordinate kinds? The most plausible answer can be summarized as follows: Toward anything whatever we may act in a variety of favoring ways, or adopt a variety of positive stances: helping to bring it into existence or to preserve and protect it, seeking it out, choosing or selecting it, making it more accessible to ourselves or others, borrowing or buying, taking advantage of its availability, etc. To act in any of these ways is to *elect* that thing, and anything that is or could be elected by someone is eligible. An act of electing something at some time may be one for which a justification can be given—i.e., there is an adequate reason for that act. Then we can say that the thing in question has *warranted eligibility*. A plausible view of value in general is that it is warranted eligibility.

This proposal may seem too broad. Couldn't there be an adequate reason for electing something despite its total worthlessness—or even because of it, in a fanciful and somewhat allegorical case? Someone, perhaps in training for sainthood, is instructed by his spiritual mentor to fare forth and return with something that has no value. Which he dutifully does. There *is* an adequate reason for him to bring that object (and we can even say he *has* an adequate reason), so the election is warranted, yet by hypothesis the object lacks value. Or is this hypothesis itself incoherent? I think it is: the task is impossible to perform—it turns out to be a Koan. Let the object be whatsoever you choose, however humble; it fulfills a purpose, perhaps even carried a message about the last being first or the least being no less precious than the greatest. It has value after all, so it does not defy the concept of value as warranted eligibility.

The question does arise, however, whether this concept can serve as a *definition* of value. In very many cases, at least, the justifying of an election will take the form of showing that the thing makes a contribution (as cause or condition or part of a whole, or in some other way) to the production of a valuable state of affairs. If this is always and necessarily the case, then this justifying procedure is built into the concept of warranted eligibility, which therefore could not without circularity be used in defining value. It is no use to say "X has value" means "The election of X at some time by someone could be justified, because X contributes to the production of a state of affairs with value." The case of the apprentice-saint seems to offer a convenient exception, showing that a reference to value is not a necessary element in the concept of warranted eligibility. But in bringing back the supposedly valueless object, the saint revealed its hitherto unrecognized value—that it could contribute to the realization of that state of affairs which consists in his duty's having been done. The saint's election of the object did not *confer* value on it, but *exploited* its value—which

[10] Alan Tormey, "Critical Judgments," *Theoria* 39 (1973): 35–49.

no doubt it shared with many other equally negligible things: it had to be something that at least non-saints, in their blindness, would despise or disdain. The object acquired its value when the duty was imposed, not when the duty was done. Its value is therefore dependent upon, is a consequence of, the rightness of the action. So we could argue that the action is justified by its rightness, and this is one way in which eligibility can be warranted; therefore it would not be circular to define "value" as "warranted eligibility." I leave this question for further consideration elsewhere. In any case the view that value always *involves* warranted eligibility, whether definitory or not, is true and worth stating, because it uncovers a significant feature of the concept of value and, if it is sustained, has certain noteworthy advantages.

For one thing (if to mention this is not thought frivolous), it warms us to our world; it invites us to look about us, at least occasionally, with some pleasure and approval; for very many of those things that fall under our notice or lie within our technological reach either certainly or probably have *some* value. Nor can we ever know the limits to what may later be discovered to be of the value-possessing kind. More appealing from a theoretical point of view, at least to me, is that the procedure of justifying an election seems clearly to involve showing how the thing-to-be-elected fits into a pattern of human activities and natural connections—especially since it is comparative, and requires a showing of superiority to alternatives. Even in the case of the apprentice-saint, we have to see how the act of bringing the object back generates (in Alvin Goldman's sense) an act of doing a duty. Thus it is hard to see how there can be any intrinsic value, since the very process of establishing the existence of value in an object makes that value dependent on the object's connections with other things. But the most important advantage, in the present context, is that the warranted-eligibility concept of value provides a rationale for distinguishing kinds of value. Since nothing has value unless its election sometime by someone could be justified, all value is grounded. If we can classify various grounds on which eligibility might be warranted, we will at the same time be classifying kinds of value—or, for short, *values,* in the plural—since two values will differ in that different kinds of reason are associated with them.

By switching terminology in mid-sentence, I did not mean to slip anything by, so I assert again that when we speak individually or severally of *a* value, or

of this or that value (keeping this locution clearly distinct from talk about valuable *things*), we are referring to a kind of value. But we speak properly of *a* value, I think, only when the kind has been articulated, so to speak—when a classification has been effected and the distinction made explicit. Anything that has value has some kind of value—perhaps several kinds. But for many such kinds we have no handy names and no need for them. When we have sorted out a range of reasons as having to do, say, with the restoration of health (on the assumption that health has a value), we can speak of therapeutic value as *a* value. And since the ground of eligibility is the thing's capacity to contribute in some way to the production of value, we can say that this capacity *is* a value that the thing has.

Thus we see how *a* value is a capacity (to contribute to the production of value), and how it is not circular to offer *this* as a definition, since "value" is not in turn defined by means of "a value."

I see no fatal flaw, then, in the conception of value-kinds. So our problem centers on the proposed species: whether one of these kinds can be *aesthetic* value. And this seems to depend on two things: identifying an aesthetic character in experience on which aesthetic value can be grounded, and showing that the possession of such a character is a valuable feature of such experiences.

IV

It is interesting, I think, that in the most extensive classification and analysis of what he calls the "varieties of goodness," G. H. von Wright finds no clear or secure place for judgments of the goodness of art. The judgment that someone is a good *artist* (painter or musician) is placed in the category of "technical goodness," along with the goodness of plumbers and accountants: the good composer is *good at* composing music.[11] Such a judgment would seem to presuppose another kind of judgment concerning the goodness of the music the good composer composes, but von Wright is silent about this problem. He merely invites his readers, as a kind of exercise, to try to find the proper category for the expression "a good book (work of art)," which he is apparently not prepared to assign to any of his varieties or "forms" of goodness: instrumental, technical, utilitarian (including the beneficial), hedonic, moral.[12]

[11] George Henrik von Wright, *The Varieties of Goodness,* N.Y.: Humanities Press, 1963, pp. 38–39.
[12] Ibid., p. 11.

I don't attempt any such broad classification here; von Wright's varieties are not, of course, my kinds. But if a place for aesthetic value is to be found in such a scheme, we must first be clear about the kind. And contemporary aestheticians have reserved much of their sharpest language for casting doubt on the idea that there is a special character of experience that it is the purpose or function of artworks to impart. Artworks are not can-openers that they should be pinned down to a limited task! Both they and the experiences they afford are too varied to allow for the sort of generalization and abstraction required for identifying a function! There can be no restriction on the desiderata we seek in artworks, from moral uplift to entertainment! We must not impose prescriptively a limit on the adventurousness and originality of artists and an end to artistic change! These and similar warnings abound, and of course they are to be heeded. But they do not, in my opinion, rule out the notion of a distinctive aesthetic character. Philippa Foot has noted, judiciously, that "We do not . . . *use* works of literature, or not normally, and could not say that it is by their use that the criteria for their goodness are determined . . ." yet—she adds—"the interest which we have in books and pictures determines the grounds on which their excellence is judged."[13] The objector will be quick to jump on the words "*the* interest," and regale us with a list of various interests that artworks may sustain and satisfy. But of course this is beside the point: we are in search of a value, identified by a distinct character of experience that is worth having— though, of course, part of the justification for calling it "aesthetic" depends on showing that it has a fairly close, regular, dependable relationship to artkind-instances. Those who have doubted or denied the existence of a special aesthetic character tend to rely on two negative arguments: first, that they have not succeeded in finding it, and second, that even its partisans cannot agree on what it is. To the first we may respond with commiseration, to the second with a legitimate excuse. It is fair to plead that to get at the aesthetic character is not necessarily a simple task. It may call for a good deal of subtle phenomenological inquiry, taking into account a wide range of experiences and carefully comparing our introspections with the reports of others. There is a serious problem of finding the right words to discriminate and articulate the noteworthy features of our interaction with outstanding artkind-instances. If there are continuing differences of opinion, or at least in emphasis, as for example about the precise nature of "disinterestedness" and its role in the experience of artworks, the fact is not surprising; and it neither belies the obvious truth that aestheticians have made progress in this direction nor mocks the persistent hope for further progress.

Although I am unready to relinquish more substantial claims concerning the analysis of aesthetic character, I am content here to advance a fairly modest one. Let us treat the aesthetic character as compound and disjunctive. It consists of five discernible features. Experience has an aesthetic character if it has at least four of these five features, including the first one.

1. A willingly accepted guidance over the succession of one's mental states by phenomenally objective properties (qualities and relations) of a perceptual or intentional field on which attention is fixed with a feeling that things are working or have worked themselves out fittingly. Since this awareness is directed *by*, as well as *to*, the object, we may call this feature, for short, *object-directedness.*

2. A sense of freedom, of release from the dominance of some antecedent concerns about past and future, a relaxation and sense of harmony with what is presented or semantically invoked by it or implicitly promised by it, so that what comes has the air of having been freely chosen. For short: *felt freedom.*

3. A sense that the objects of which interest is concentrated are set a little at a distance emotionally—a certain detachment of affect, so that even when we are confronted with dark and terrible things, and feel them sharply, they do not oppress but make us aware of our power to rise above them. For short: *detached affect.*

4. A sense of actively exercising constructive powers of the mind, of being challenged by a variety of potentially conflicting stimuli to try to make them cohere; a keyed-up state amounting to exhilaration in seeing connections between percepts and between meanings, a sense (which may be illusory) of achieved intelligibility. For short: *active discovery.*

5. A sense of integration as a person, of being restored to wholeness from distracting and disruptive impulses (but by inclusive synthesis as well as by exclusion), and a corresponding contentment,

[13]   Philippa Foot, "Goodness and Choice," *Proceedings of the Aristotelian Society*, Supplementary Vol. 35 (1961), p. 52.

even through disturbing feelings, that involves self-acceptance and self-expansion. For short: *a sense of wholeness.*

If I may appropriate—or misappropriate—a colorful term introduced for a contrasting view (which I shall shortly acknowledge), I might call these five properties "symptoms" of the aesthetic in experience.

The limitations of these symptoms, as I have sketched them—object-directedness, felt freedom, detached affect, active discovery, and a sense of wholeness—are perhaps not so obscure that they need to be emphasized by me. (Others will cheerfully accept this labor.) Their vagueness is evident and essential. Yet I believe the descriptions apply to genuine realities, which we find in our experiences of many artworks, as well as other things. The symptoms are common (though not omnipresent) in experience; they are individually often present in play, sport, mathematics, and religion. These activities are sometimes accompanied by experiences with aesthetic character, though this is generally incidental to their central purpose. Here is one aspect of the aesthetic character that has made it difficult to manage—not that it is so rare, but that it turns up so widely, in mild or fleeting forms at least.

Despite their vagueness, these features allow for comparisons of degree among experiences with aesthetic character. The familiar dimensions apply here in usual ways: a feature may be more or less intense, sustained, pervasive, saturating, dominant over other aspects of the experience. More or fewer of the properties may be present, and they may cooperate more or less closely and powerfully. Not all comparisons of aesthetic value that might be attempted can be successful in this pluralistic scheme, so not all possible disputes about aesthetic value can be objectively resolved; but that was never promised. It seems to me, perhaps perversely, a merit of the proposal that it explains the considerable looseness and indeterminacy we actually encounter in the justification of art appraisals. Yet it remains true that the experience a well-qualified reader of poems obtains under favorable conditions, from reading Shakespeare's "Poor Soul! the center of my sinful earth" will have a decidedly more marked aesthetic character (considered all in all) than the experience that same reader, under similar conditions, will obtain from reading Michael Drayton's "To nothing fitter can I thee compare." That is evidence of greater aesthetic value.

One piece is still missing from the positive case for aesthetic value. Although I have argued that objects possess this value in virtue of their capacity to impart marked aesthetic character to experience, I have so far merely assumed that experiences themselves possess value in virtue of having a capacity that is based on their aesthetic character. It may be evident that it is a good thing for an experience to have an aesthetic character—that this is *one* of the ways in which experiences can be worth having. But the question *why* this character confers value calls for a systematic answer—one that I am afraid is too long for this occasion. It calls for consideration of profoundly difficult questions about the nature of human goodness, what constitutes a good life, happiness, well-being and well-doing, and perhaps the meaning of life—though even if we differ in our answers to these questions, we may be able to agree that it is good for us to experience, at least occasionally, and to a degree seldom made possible except by artworks, the immediate sense (say) of inclusive self-integration and complex harmony with phenomenal objects.

I certainly do not wish to follow some ardent defenders of the aesthetic in their attempt to extend aesthetic value to cover all intrinsic value, to make it the *only* thing that is ultimately good. This idea, I think, derives from Charles Peirce, and it was not one of his better ideas. First, I do not believe there is such a thing as intrinsic value; and second, the attempt can lead to such morally outrageous views as that once stated by David Prall:

> It is in their ultimately felt aesthetic quality that men all find such sights [as "the suffering of the poor"] revolting and unendurable. . . . If poverty and disease bore a pleasant aspect to discriminating perception, if injustice were aesthetically and directly satisfying to experience, and to dwell upon, what would there be to condemn it in any rational creature's eyes?[14]

Even if an example of injustice had high aesthetic value (and in fact some thoroughly unjust societies have been noted for their elegance or splendor), there would be plenty to condemn it in a rational creature's mind, if not his eyes.

There is an important sense in which the arts, as specialized bearers of aesthetic value, are "nonexistential," as Aurel Kolnai has written in an essay on "Aesthetic and Moral Experience": threats to their eligibility do not invoke the moral imperatives

---

[14] David W. Prall, *Aesthetic Judgment*, N.Y.: Thomas Y. Crowell, 1957, p. 349.

of injustice and destitution. Yet, as Dewey always insisted, there is something exemplary in an artwork's way of having worth—it is always a reminder of the possibilities of living fully. I find some wisdom in Kolnai's words, though I would not choose them all:

> If certain churches of certain regions or street corners in certain cities I peculiarly admire and love did not exist, it "wouldn't make much difference." Yet it is in their contemplation and tangible nearness, undoubtedly an *aesthetic* experience, that I seem somehow to become aware of the ineffable goodness of existence more deeply and vividly than in any experience of benefit or thriving, or even of moral virtues.[15]

V

Having displayed, as I hope, some merits of the functional account of art appraisal, I would naturally like to make them stand out by contrasting this account with available alternatives. There is really only one serious alternative, I think: that put forward by Nelson Goodman. The present argument would be woefully incomplete without at least some attempt to meet his radical challenge.

Nelson Goodman's position rejects aesthetic value, as I have been analyzing and defending it, and proposes instead to base art appraisals on the *cognitive* value of artworks—their capacity to contribute to the "creation and comprehension of our worlds."[16] Artworks turn up in this account as characters, or classes of characters, in symbol systems, and like other symbols are to be judged primarily or centrally by their successful functioning as symbols, their "cognitive efficacy." In a memorable passage toward the end of *Languages of Art,* Goodman says that the use of symbols in making and meeting artworks "is for the sake of understanding. . . . What compels is the urge to know, what delights is discovery. . . . The primary purpose is cognition in and for itself."[17] And more recently, in *Ways of Worldmaking,* pursuing a related theme, he adds that "The arts must be taken no less seriously than the sciences as modes of discovery, creation, and enlargement of knowledge in the broad sense of advancement of the understanding."[18] Though, strictly speaking, truth is reserved for verbal claims, a broader category, "rightness of rendering," which involves both construing and constructing worlds, comprises the aims of both arts and sciences.

It is no small part of the debt we owe to *Language of Art*—along with a few other books in recent decades—that we now recognize the extent to which the experience of artworks involves cognitive activities of many sorts—activities which do often in fact eventuate in knowledge and understanding. And much can be said for some arts as "modes of discovery." Yet when we bring together the results of many aesthetic inquiries, especially in our time, we cannot accede to these claims as stated. Instead of saying in general terms of artworks or artkind-instances that "the primary purpose is cognition in and for itself," we ought rather to say that the primary purpose is the aestheticizing of experience. In support of this rebuttal, I sketch three lines of argument.

First, it has not yet been shown, to my satisfaction, that instrumental musical works and nonrepresentational paintings are characters in symbol systems; it has not been adequately explained how they refer to anything.[19] So I think their peculiar goodness has to be explained in some other way than by their successful symbol functioning in the service of cognition; what delights may be the discovery of the work itself, but not of other things via the work's reference. It would be temerarious to ascribe the artworks in general a primary purpose that cannot be fulfilled by such large and important subclasses of them.

Second, many natural objects, such as mountains and trees, are not characters in any symbol system, yet they seem to have a value that is closely akin to that of artworks. This kinship can easily be explained in terms of aesthetic value, but hardly in terms of cognitive value.

Third, it is a commonplace (but I think well-placed here) that very widely in the arts, where cognitive concern is or could be present, we observe sacrifices in the cognitive dimension for the sake of other ends. Some aestheticians, of course, have tried to show that these apparent retreats are means to greater cognitive achievement (the novelist alters the newspaper facts that inspired his plot only in order to reveal deeper truths of human nature; and Poussin left the Biblical camels out of his famous painting of *Rebecca and Eleazer* the better to portray the essential human situation). This aiming at a "higher" truth certainly occurs in art, and is important; yet there is much that it will not explain (including the cases where the novelist changes the facts

[15]   Aurel Kolnai, *Ethics, Value, and Reality,* Indianapolis: Hackett, 1978, p. 210.

[16]   *Languages of Art,* p. 265.

[17]   Ibid., p. 258.

[18]   *Ways of Worldmaking,* Indianapolis: Hackett, 1978, p. 102.

[19]   Ibid., p. 68.

simply to make a better story—one that is more unified, or dramatic, or ironic, and thus more capable of fulfilling an aesthetic function; and perhaps Poussin found that he could make a better composition without the camels). The longer literature of this controversy supplies many such examples; they argue that cognition is not generally the overriding or dominant purpose of artworks.

And I will even go so far as to suggest—though with appropriate diffidence—that this point is tacitly conceded in Nelson Goodman's theory. It will be recalled that artworks, according to this theory, differ from other symbols basically in that they belong to symbol systems of a special sort, "aesthetic symbol systems." These systems possess one or more of those properties which he calls "symptoms of the aesthetic"—thus he is the victim of my terminological rip-off a little earlier. The symptoms are (1) syntactic and (2) semantic density, (3) a high degree of repleteness (in that more features of the symbol count), (4) exemplificationality (possession of predicates plus reference to them), and—as he has added in his most recent book—(5) "multiple and complex reference, where a symbol performs several integrated and interacting referential functions"[20] Now on the functional account it is understandable that artists creating artworks should often choose to make them symbols—that some types of symbol are very useful for the purpose of fashioning bearers of aesthetic value. And if we inquire what kinds of symbol lend themselves to this use, there is no better answer than Goodman's. But looking at the matter from within *his* system, it is fair to ask what justifies the selection and classification of these properties as "aesthetic."

To this question Goodman gives significant answers. The first three properties "call for maximum sensitivity of discrimination," since in a dense and replete symbol system minute differences between inscriptions makes a difference in what symbols they are and in what they symbolize. Thus (I would suggest) the use of such symbols stimulates and exercises the cognitive faculties connected with perception to the highest degree and makes possible the construction of artworks of great subtlety and refinement, which are open to endless exploration. In an exemplificational symbol the properties referred to or expressed are "shown forth"—vividly presented for concentrated and prolonged affective apprehension.[21] Replete systems and multiple symbols carry complex meanings and compact them, giving an embracing unity to diverse elements of experience. As Goodman says in *Ways of Worldmaking*, "these [aesthetic] properties tend to focus attention on the symbol rather than, or at least along with, what it refers to"[22]—but to the extent that there is a tension here, it seems that our cognitive interests would tend to call for dominant attention to what is referred to, though our aesthetic interests might not. A symbol that attracts attention to itself, and rewards that attention, helps to detach our feelings from that to which it refers. "This emphasis upon the nontransparency of a work of art, upon the primacy of the work over what it refers to, far from involving denial or disregard of symbolic functions, derives from certain characteristics of a work as a symbol."[23] That's certainly true, and important. But also perfectly acceptable to anyone who maintains that the meanings and references in artworks are essential to their artistic nature. It is clearly consistent to emphasize the nontransparency of artworks while insisting on their symbolic character as well; but it is not so clearly consistent to emphasize the nontransparency of artworks and still insist that their cognitive symbolic function is their *primary* purpose.

It is, I think, some recommendation of aesthetic value (both of its reality and its importance) that the most powerful effort to dispense with it seems, in the end, to be driven back to reliance upon it. But I should not like to conclude with a mere dialectical flourish, even in this serious cause. It is rather the issue itself—underlying as it does so many current and promising controversies, yet, to my mind, still given too little serious discussion—that I wish to emphasize and stir into more active life.[24]

[20] Ibid.

[21] *Languages of Art*, p. 253.

[22] *Ways of Worldmaking*, p. 69.

[23] Loc cit.

[24] I wish to acknowledge Elizabeth L. Beardsley's very helpful comments on this essay.

Innocent C. Onyewuenyi (contemporary)
TRADITIONAL AFRICAN AESTHETICS: A PHILOSOPHICAL PERSPECTIVE

The author, an African philosopher, criticizes the highly individualistic and static traditional Western approaches to aesthetics. By contrast, he describes traditional African art as functional, community-oriented, depersonalized, contextualized, and embedded. Hence, he argues, uniqueness and individuality are not the only bases for theories of aesthetics. Onyewuenyi's comparison of Western and African aesthetics is discussed in the introductory essay to Part V.

READING QUESTIONS

In reading the selection, try to answer the following questions and identify the passages that support your answers:

1. What is Onyewuenyi's characterization of African art?
2. What implications does this conception have for Western conceptions of the relation between aesthetic value and aesthetic experience?
3. How does Onyewuenyi's characterization of African art affect functionalism?
4. Can you think of a conception of aesthetic value that applies to both Western and African art?
5. Is such a conception desirable? Why or why not?

Reprinted by permission of the *International Philosophical Quarterly* from Innocent C. Onyewuenyi, "Traditional African Aesthetics: A Philosophical Perspective," Vol. 24, No. 3 (September 1984), pp. 237–244. Copyright © 1984.

ANCIENT GREECE supplies us with the first important contributions to aesthetic theory. Socrates is the first. We learn from Xenophon's account of him that he regarded the beautiful as coincident with the good. Every beautiful object is so called because it serves some rational end. Plato in his scheme for an ideal republic provided for the most inexorable censorship of poets and artists in general, so as to make art as far as possible an instrument of moral and political training.

Except for the very few dedicated aestheticians who have studied the history of aesthetics as it developed and progressed from Plato through medieval philosophers and then Kant and Hegel to its ramifications in the works of Benedetto Croce, Vico, Dewey, etc., the general run of aestheticians conceives of the artist as a free agent bound by no societal conventions, at liberty and "condemned" to experimentation, whose productions must be judged in their individuality and uniqueness. "It has been argued by some people, that each work of art is unique and individual; that it is the essence of it. If you seek to explain the value of any work of art in terms of some general principles then you are destroying that value."[1]

Such a conception of the artist and his arts is so culturally natural to Europeans and Americans and even evolués in Africa that to interpret art differently would be considered unacceptable and erroneous. It is this conception of art that influenced the colonial ambassadors in Africa—be they missionaries, administrators, merchants, educators—in their interpretation and evaluation of the arts in Africa. It explains the mistaken interpretation of African arts by otherwise outstanding European artists when

[1] P.C. Chatterji, *Fundamental Questions in Aesthetics* (New Delhi:: Indian Institute of Advanced Study, 1968), p. 13.

they made the acquaintance of African visual arts. They even contradicted one another in their professional interpretation by extending their preference for one or another European school to African works of art accidentally resembling their favorite style and judged it accordingly. Janheinz Jahn comments:

> Gluck for example, praises the 'baroquising element of form' in the mask of the Cameroons, the style of which 'has understood so consciously how to master the grotesque', while Kiersmeier ascribes to the same masks 'little artistic value', but predicates of the works of the Boula a 'refined sensibility and technical delicacy' which lifts them far above the works of most African races'. Luschan praises the 'great grace' of certain Benin heads, while Einstein places them in a 'degenerate coastal tradition' which has recovered in the Cameroons in a late primitive rebirth'.[2]

This paper is an attempt to think differently from western aestheticians. It will essay to show that African aesthetic standards are different from the "accepted" standards of uniqueness and individuality; that African works of art, be they visual, musical, kinetic, or poetic are created as an answer to a problem and serve some practical end. It will also delineate the philosophical foundation for such differences, and finally propose the theory of African works of art as the Africans see it.

IS THERE AN AFRICAN AESTHETICS?

Before delving into the problem, we will first of all establish whether there is an African aesthetics or not. By way of definitions, we are told that aesthetics is that branch of philosophy which has tried to answer such questions as "What is Art?" "What is Beauty?" Dagobert Runes defines aesthetics traditionally as the branch of philosophy dealing with beauty or the beautiful, especially in art, and with taste and standards of value in judging art.[3] Accepting the above definitions as universal, there is an intellectual temptation to take the position that it is unnecessary and even futile to ask such a question. If aesthetics is universal, it is as ridiculous to talk of African aesthetics as it is to talk of African physics or African chemistry. The question may even be regarded as racially and nationally loaded, indicating an attempt to narrow the discipline of aes-

thetics in order to satisfy some racial or national whim.

A similar problem arose in my paper "Is There an African Philosophy?" where I showed that philosophizing is a universal experience and that

> What is generally agreed about philosophy is that it seeks to establish order among the various phenomena of the surrounding world and it traces their unity by reducing them to their simplest elements . . . that while these phenomena are the same in all cultures and societies, each culture traces the unity of these, synthesizes, or organizes them into a totality *based* on each culture's concept of life. . . . Hence it is that the order or unity the people of a culture establish is their own order, relative to their own conception of life in which everything around them becomes meaningful.[4]

If the above is accepted as true, then we have the basis for calling a philosophy (and by extension, aesthetics) European, Indian, American, African. We can and should talk of African aesthetics because the African culture has its own "standards of value in judging art"; its own "general principles" in explaining the value of any work of art. Africa has its own view of life which Dilthey regarded as the starting point of philosophy. Georg Misch summarizes Dilthey thus:

> Dilthey regarded life as the starting point of philosophy; life as actually lived and embodied or 'objectified' in the spiritual world we live in . . . Our knowledge of life is above all, contained in certain cultural and personal views of the world—which play a prominent part in philosophy as well as in religion and poetry.[5]

That philosophy of art is universal does not mean that all aestheticians should employ similar standards of value in judging art, similar general principles of explaining the value of any work of art. Neither does it mean that all the rationally warrantable or objectively granted principles or methods must be identical or that they must establish similar truths. Two separate aesthetic standards of value or general principles, both being rational, can be opposed to one another.

Hegel underscores the cultural and relative aspect of philosophy when he said:

> But men do not at certain epochs merely philosophize in general. For there is a definite philosophy which arises among a people and the definite character which

[2] Janheinz Jahn, *Muntu: An Outline of the New African Culture* (New York: Grove Press, 1961), p. 173.

[3] Dagobert D. Runes, *Dictionary of Philosophy* (Totowa, NJ: Littlefield, Adams, 1966), p. 6.

[4] Innocent C. Onyewuenyi, "Is There An African Philosophy?" *Journal of African Studies*, 3 (Winter 1976/77). 513–528.

[5] Georg Misch, *The Dawn of Philosophy* (London, 1950), p. 47.

permeates all the other historical sides of the Spirit of the people, which is most intimately related to them, and which constitutes their foundation. The particular form of a philosophy is thus contemporaneous with a particular constitution of the people amongst whom it makes its appearance, with their institutions and forms of government, their morality, their social life and their capabilities, customs and enjoyments of the same.[6]

From the foregoing one may safely suggest that the general principles or standards of value of aesthetics, which is a branch of philosophy, are bound up intimately with a people's spirit and constitution, and are a factor in their life history, subject to the conditions of race, culture, and civilization.

One function of the arts is making explicit the images by which a society recognizes its own *values* and thus offering a means by which the members of a community may express and evaluate new elements in their lives. Furthermore, the arts afford a perspective on human experience as they are created to channel or express the powers of the super-human world on which men recognize their dependence. The Europeans/Americans and Africans evidently have different views of life here and hereafter; different conceptions of the powers of the super-human world to which they owe their existence, different ethical and moral values, different social institutions and forms of government—in short, different ideas of life and reality. Since the works of art, be they visual, musical, kinetic, or poetic are used "to convey the unfamiliar in the familiar, the abstract in the concrete, the discursive in the intuitive and the spiritual in the physical; in general to communicate the nonsensory through the sensory,"[7] it follows that the symbols must be culturally invested with the contents of their referents. Victor Uchendu may be quoted to round off these arguments in support of the issue of aesthetic relativity. He advised: "To know how a people view the world around them is to understand how they evaluate life, and a people's evaluation of life, both temporal and non-temporal, provides them with a 'charter' of action, a guide to behaviour."[8]

METAPHYSICS AS THE FOUNDATION OF AESTHETIC INTERPRETATION

The ultimate basis for cultural differences in interpreting and appreciating art works rests principally on differences in metaphysics, which is an integral vision of reality as such. Henry Alpern in his *March of Philosophy* highlighted the importance of metaphysics as the groundwork, the basis, the explanation of human behaviour:

> Metaphysics by the very definition that it is the study of reality, of that which does not appear to our senses, of truth in the absolute sense, is the groundwork of any theory concerning all phases of human behaviour. David Hume, whom no one can charge of shutting his eyes to experience, said that metaphysics is necessary for art, morality, religion, economics, sociology; for the abstract sciences, as well as for every branch of human endeavour considered from the practical angle. It is the foundation upon which one builds one's career consciously and unconsciously; it is the guide; the author of human interests; upon its truth or falsity depends what type of man you may develop into.[9]

Researchers in African philosophy have amply shown that there is a difference between Western and African metaphysics and consequently a difference between the two cultures' "groundwork of any theory concerning all phases" of their behaviour vis-à-vis their art, morality, religion. Placid Tempels has clearly expressed the specific difference between the two:

> Christian thought in the West having adopted the terminology of Greek philosophy and perhaps under its influence, has defined the reality of all beings, or as one should say, being as such: 'the reality that is', 'what is'. Its metaphysics has most generally been based upon a fundamentally *static* conception of being.[10]

He goes on to add the crucial point, "Herein is to be seen the fundamental difference between Western thought and that of Bantu and other primitive peoples . . . we hold a *static* conception of 'being', they, a *dynamic*."[11]

If we accept what Henry Alpern and David Hume said about the importance of metaphysics as "the groundwork concerning all phases of human be-

---

[6] Georg Hegel, *Lectures on the History of Philosophy* (London, 1968), 1:53.

[7] Arthur Berndtson, *Art Expression and Beauty* (New York: Holt, Rinehart and Winston, 1969), p. 36.

[8] Victor Uchendu, *The Igbo of Southeast Nigeria* (New York: 1965), p. 12.

[9] Henry Alpern, *The March of Philosophy* (New York, 1934), p. 99.

[10] Placide Tempels, *Bantu Philosophy* (Paris: Présence Africaine, 1969), p. 19.

[11] *Ibid.*, p. 50.

haviour and necessary for art . . . as well as for every branch of human endeavour on the one hand," and the fundamental differences between Western and African ontology as suggested by Tempels on the other, it would follow that the aesthetic interpretation and appreciation of the works of art in the two cultures must necessarily be different. And indeed they are! "For philosophies of art and beauty are as various as the philosophies of human conduct, politics, science, history and ultimate reality,"[12] claimed Albert Hofstadter and Richard Kuhns. They emphasized further the metaphysical dependence of all standards of value in judging art:

> In a philosophy of art or in philosophical aesthetics, more generally speaking, beauty and art are understood in terms of essential philosophical ideas . . . Thus the great philosophies of art have interpreted beauty and art in metaphysical terms. . . ."[13]

INFLUENCES OF METAPHYSICS ON WESTERN AESTHETICS

The concept of *staticity* which connotes the idea of separate beings, of substances, to use a scholastic term, which exist side by side, independent one of another, is a peculiarity of western ontology and explains the emphasis on individuality and uniqueness in the interpretation of works of art. This is what Mundy-Castle calls "'out-of-context' or modern art which is frequently without any specific social function. Its primary aim is to communicate personal experience and individualized intuition."[14] The work of art is often identified with the building, book, painting or status in its existence apart from human experience. I suggest that the dictatorship of the spectator, of the collector, even of the dealer over works of art in recent centuries in Europe and America is a function of individuality of interpretation and subjectivity of tastes and meaning. One can even go so far as to claim that the idea of museums which Nigeria's Uche Okeke describes as "a graveyard of human achievements"[15] in the great cities of Europe and other western countries is metaphysi-

cally influenced by the theory of uniqueness and individuality in aesthetics.

Much emphasis is placed on the "perfection" of art works, the prestige they possess because of a long history of unquestioned admiration. Descriptive terms such as 'lively expression', 'naturalistic', 'disinterested gratification', 'ugly', 'beautiful', etc. characterize European/American evaluation of designs and motifs of art works. Thus they are separated from conditions of history and origin and operation in experience. There is no interpenetration of one art work with another, not to mention their supposed function of making explicit the images by which a society recognizes its own values, of offering a means by which the members of a community may express and evaluate new elements in their lives, of affording a perspective on human experience as they are created to channel or express the powers of the superhuman world on which human beings recognize their dependence.

John Dewey in his book *Art as Experience* criticizes the theory of individuality and uniqueness as standards of art evaluation by citing the example of the Parthenon, the great Athenian work of art which enjoys world-wide prestige because of a long history of unquestioned admiration. He maintains that the aesthetic standing is achieved only when one

> goes beyond personal enjoyment into the formation of a theory about that large republic of art of which the building is one member, and is willing at some point in his reflections to turn from it to the bustling, arguing, acutely sensitive Athenian citizens, with civic sense identified with a civic religion, of whose experience the temple was an expression and who built it not as a work art but as a civic commemoration.[16]

Dewey seems to be saying that until the function of an art work in relation to the members of a community is discovered and appreciated, the full aesthetic dimension cannot be achieved. John Dewey could hold this position because he was a great devotee of Hegel and Plato, who were absolute idealists and for whom sensory objects were moments of the Absolute.

A BRIEF SURVEY OF AFRICAN ONTOLOGY

An adequate understanding of African ontology, especially in its conception of the nature of "reality" or "being" as dynamic, is fundamentally important

[12] Albert Hofstadter and Richard Kuhns, *Philosophies of Art and Beauty* (Chicago: Univ. of Chicago Press, 1964), p. xiii.

[13] *Ibid.*, p. xiv.

[14] A. C. Mundy-Castle, "Art, Psychology and Social Change", *Black Orpheus*, 4, No. 1 (1981), p. 8.

[15] Uche Okeke, "Towards a Rational Policy of Art Patronage in Nigeria," *Black Orpheus*, 4, No. 1 (1981), 64.

[16] Hofstadter and Kuhns, *op. cit.*, p. 580.

to our discussion of African art appreciation. The essence of anything is conceived by the African as force. "There is no idea among Bantu of 'being' divorced from the idea of 'force'. Without the element of 'force', 'being' cannot be conceived. Force is the nature of being; force is being; being is force."[17] The concept of force or dynamism cancels out the idea of separate beings or substances which exist side by side independent one of another and which we have shown in our discussion of Western ontology to be responsible for individuality and uniqueness as standards or essence of art. Existence-in-relation, communalism, being-for-self-and-others sum up the African conception of life and reality.

> The African thought holds that created beings preserve a bond one with another, an intimate ontological relationship. There is an interaction of being with being.... This is more so among rational beings, known as Muntu which includes the living and the dead, Orishas and God.[18]

Because of this ontological relationship among beings, the African knows and feels himself to be in intimate and personal relationship with other forces acting above and below him in the hierarchy of forces.

A corollary to this relationship is the traditional African view of the world as one of extraordinary harmony, which Adebayo Adesanya explains as

> not simply a coherence of fact and faith, nor of reason and traditional beliefs, nor of reason and contingent facts, but a coherence of compatibility among all disciplines. A medical theory, e.g., which contradicted a theological conclusion was rejected as absurd and vice versa. ... Philosophy, theology, politics, social theory, landlaw, medicine, psychology, birth and burial, all find themselves logically concatenated in a system so tight that to subtract one item from the whole is to paralyse the structure of the whole.[19]

INFLUENCES ON AFRICAN AESTHETICS

Traditional African aesthetics, or interpretation, appreciation of works of art as a discipline in the body of African reality, cannot but fall in line with other theories and disciplines which "all find themselves logically concatenated" in the tight system of the African world-view; otherwise it would paralyze the whole structure of African life and being. Works of art, as expressions of ritual and religion, as clues to the temperament of the tribe and society, as language in a culture without writing, must do all these in service to the community whose ritual and religion they express, whose temperament they reveal, the being of whose ancestors they participate in. Its theory or standard of evaluation must conform to the theories of its sister disciplines and stem from identical metaphysical foundations. Hence African art is functional, community-oriented, depersonalized, contextualized, and embedded.

By functional and community-oriented we mean that African arts—visual, musical, kinetic or poetic—are designed to serve practical, meaningful purpose, beauty of appearance being secondary. All the same, "Functional beauty is also beauty,"[20] says Janheinz Jahn. A carving, for example, is aesthetically beautiful in the African standard if it functions well as stimulus in the worship of the deity, the community of worshippers being the judges. A mask, despite its "ugly" appearance, is judged beautiful and good if used correctly in the movement of the dance to depict the divine power with which it is imbued through the rhythmic incantations and sacrificial rites of the communal ceremonies. "Through his dance Efe has the power to please the witches and so turn their malevolent self-seeking power into a generous benevolence towards the community."[21]

If a sculpture of an ancestor for purposes of worship in an Igbo Society is scarified[22] and endowed with all the paraphernalia that combine to make a work aesthetically good, it would not be accepted by the Igbo and would have no aesthetic recognition simply because it is not true and meaningful. It does not fulfill the function which an Igbo society expects of it. For, the Igbos do not scarify their bodies, and the Muntu-face represented in such a sculpture cannot command their respect for a revered ancestor. Rather the same scarified Muntu-face may be aesthetically beautiful to the Yoruba or other tribes who culturally scarify their bodies.

> The various African peoples have coined various basic forms for the 'Muntu-face' but they all express the Muntu-face. Within one people the Muntu-face is constant, for it is derived from their common ancestor, that *muzimu* who formed the physiognomy of his people.

[17]   Tempels, *op. cit.*, p. 37.

[18]   *Ibid.*, p. 104.

[19]   Jahn, *op. cit.*, p. 96.

[20]   *Ibid.*, p. 174.

[21]   Peggy Harper, "The Inter-Relation of the Arts in the Performance of Masquerades as an Expression of Oral Tradition in Nigeria," *Black Orpheus*, 4, No. 1 (1981), 3.

[22]   To "scarify" means to adorn with indentations, scratches, or welts (on the skin).

Thus the artist is not free to think out a Muntu-face for himself, according to his own conception. The Muntu to be represented must belong to his own people.[23]

When we say that African art is depersonalized we mean that the artist's concern is not to depict his own individual whims and feelings. He works from a background diametrically opposed to the Nietzschean expressionist influence about which Benn writes: "Our background was Nietzsche: his drive to tear apart one's inner nature with words, to express oneself, to formulate, to dazzle, to sparkle at any risk and without regard for the results."[24] He performs rather in such a way as to fulfill the ritual and social purposes of his community for whom the arts are meant to regulate the spiritual, political, and social forces within the community.

Speaking specifically about African poets, Janheinz Jahn testifies that

> In reality, the neo-African poet is not primarily concerned about his own ego. He is Muntu man who speaks and through the word conquers the world of things. His word is the more powerful the more he speaks in the name of his people living as well as dead. As a poet he is the representative of all, and as a representative he is a poet.[25]

Whether it is music, dancing, painting, poetry, etc., he cannot draw his own motifs, his themes, his obsessions from the very essence of his arts. The needs of the community determine the artist's production. His art is never "art for art's sake." He is responsible to his society. Hence the artists are "held in high esteem by the society because they supply those design needs as are vital to their spiritual and physical well-being. They are not as a rule separated or differentiated from the generality of their kindred people for whom they fashion tools and objects of belief."[26]

The foregoing emphasis on the depersonalization of the artist does not mean to rule out every professional freedom. While the artist is bound to ad-

here to the basic forms recognizable by the people, "the determinant of the first degree, the Muntu-face for man, or the animal shape for beasts," he has some freedom with "the determinants of the second degree."[27] Thus he may indicate a chief by the coiffures, by the crown, or by the dress, or he may set the figure on a horse—or he may even use foreign European insignia and medals that are proper to kings.

CONCLUSION

An attempt has been made in this paper to show the philosophical foundation of traditional African aesthetics vis-à-vis Western aesthetics and thereby the culturally relative interpretation of works of art. It has been shown that uniqueness and individuality are not, and need not be, the only basis for theories of aesthetics; that African works of art are functional, community-oriented and depersonalized, unlike Western art which is arbitrary, representative of the values and emotions of the artist, without reference to the cultural environment and the historical reality of the people. I would suggest that the misinterpretation of African works of art by western scholars of aesthetics is due to an ignorance of the cultural differences.

In conclusion the words of Philip J. C. Dark are most appropriate and relevant:

> There is a strong tendency among those who write about primitive art, and particularly primitive symbolism, to attach descriptive terms deriving from their own culture to designs and motifs they observe, thus often giving the reader a false impression that such terms carry the meanings attached to them by the people themselves. It should be made clear that for the business of formal analysis of alien art forms such terms are purely tools for the purpose of analysis. The recognition of a design such as a snake, a bird, a part of the body and so on, by an observer does not necessarily mean that the particular design in question represents that for the members of a particular culture.[28]

---

23 *Ibid.*, p. 162.
24 *Ibid.*, p. 148. Ben Gottfried, Ch. 2, pp. 39ff.
25 *Ibid.*, p. 142.
26 Uche Okeke, *op. cit.*, p. 62.

27 Jahn, *op. cit.*, p. 163.
28 Philip J.C. Dark, *Bush Negro Art* (London: Alec Tiranti, 1954), p. 49.

William K. Wimsatt (1907–1975) and Monroe C. Beardsley (1915–1985)
THE INTENTIONAL FALLACY

The authors argue that criticism is not author psychology, that it has rules of evidence different from those of author psychology. See the introductory essay to Part V for a discussion of their views.

READING QUESTIONS

In reading the selection, try to answer the following questions and identify the passages that support your answers:

1. What is the "intentional fallacy"?
2. What reasons are there to believe that there is such a fallacy?
3. Could one attribute a work of art to an author simply by reference to the author's repertoire? Why or why not?
4. If not, must one conclude that the author's intentions are crucial to such an identification? Why or why not?
5. What do your previous answers entail about the nature of a work of art and why?

The claim of the author's "intention" upon the critic's judgment has been challenged in a number of recent discussions, notably in the debate entitled *The Personal Heresy,* between Professors Lewis and Tillyard. But it seems doubtful if this claim and most of its romantic corollaries are as yet subject to any widespread questioning. The present writers, in a short article entitled "Intention" for a *Dictionary*[1] of literary criticism, raised the issue but were unable to pursue its implications at any length. We argued that the design or intention of the author is neither available nor desirable as a standard for judging the success of a work of literary art, and it seems to us that this is a principle which goes deep into some differences in the history of critical attitudes. It is a principle which accepted or rejected points to the polar opposites of classical "imitation" and romantic expression. It entails many specific truths about inspiration, authenticity, biography, literary history and scholarship, and about some trends of contemporary poetry, especially its allusiveness. There is hardly a problem of literary criticism in which the critic's approach will not be qualified by his view of "intention."

"Intention," as we shall use the term, corresponds to *what he intended* in a formula which more or less explicitly has had wide acceptance. "In order to judge the poet's performance, we must know *what he intended.*" Intention is design or plan in the author's mind. Intention has obvious affinities for the author's attitude toward his work, the way he felt, what made him write.

We begin our discussion with a series of propositions summarized and abstracted to a degree where they seem to us axiomatic.

1. A poem does not come into existence by accident. The words of a poem, as Professor Stoll has re-

[1] *Dictionary of World Literature,* Joseph T. Shipley, ed. (New York, 1942), 326–29.

marked, come out of a head, not out of a hat. Yet to insist on the designing intellect as a *cause* of a poem is not to grant the design or intention as a *standard* by which the critic is to judge the worth of the poet's performance.

2. One must ask how a critic expects to get an answer to the question about intention. How is he to find out what the poet tried to do? If the poet succeeded in doing it, then the poem itself shows what he was trying to do. And if the poet did not succeed, then the poem is not adequate evidence, and the critic must go outside the poem—for evidence of an intention that did not become effective in the poem. "Only one *caveat* must be borne in mind," says an eminent intentionalist[2] in a moment when his theory repudiates itself; "the poet's aim must be judged at the moment of the creative act, that is to say, by the art of the poem itself."

3. Judging a poem is like judging a pudding or a machine. One demands that it work. It is only because an artifact works that we infer the intention of the artificer. "A poem should not mean but be." A poem can *be* only through its *meaning*—since its medium is words—yet it *is,* simply *is,* in the sense that we have no excuse for inquiring what part is intended or meant. Poetry is a feat of style by which a complex of meaning is handled all at once. Poetry succeeds because all or most of what is said or implied is relevant; what is irrelevant has been excluded, like lumps from pudding and "bugs" from machinery. In this respect poetry differs from practical messages, which are successful if and only if we correctly infer the intention. They are more abstract than poetry.

4. The meaning of a poem may certainly be a personal one, in the sense that a poem expresses a personality or state of soul rather than a physical object like an apple. But even a short lyric poem is dramatic, the response of a speaker (no matter how abstractly conceived) to a situation (no matter how universalized). We ought to impute the thoughts and attitudes of the poem immediately to the dramatic *speaker,* and if to the author at all, only by an act of biographical inference.

5. There is a sense in which an author, by revision, may better achieve his original intention. But it is a very abstract sense. He intended to write a better work, or a better work of a certain kind, and now has done it. But it follows that his former concrete intention was not his intention. "He's the man we were

in search of, that's true," says Hardy's rustic constable, "and yet he's not the man we were in search of. For the man we were in search of was not the man we wanted."

"Is not a critic," asks Professor Stoll, "a judge, who does not explore his own consciousness, but determines the author's meaning or intention, as if the poem were a will, a contract, or the constitution? The poem is not the critic's own." He has accurately diagnosed two forms of irresponsibility, one of which he prefers. Our view is yet different. The poem is not the critic's own and not the author's (it is detached from the author at birth and goes about the world beyond his power to intend about it or control it). The poem belongs to the public. It is embodied in language, the peculiar possession of the public, and it is about the human being, an object of public knowledge. What is said about the poem is subject to the same scrutiny as any statement in linguistics or in the general science of psychology.

A critic of our *Dictionary* article, Ananda K. Coomaraswamy, has argued[3] that there are two kinds of inquiry about a work of art: (1) whether the artist achieved his intentions; (2) whether the work of art "ought ever to have been undertaken at all" and so "whether it is worth preserving." Number (2), Coomaraswamy maintains, is not "criticism of any work of art *qua* work of art," but is rather moral criticism; number (1) is artistic criticism. But we maintain that (2) need not be moral criticism: that there is another way of deciding whether works of art are worth preserving and whether, in a sense, they "ought" to have been undertaken, and this is the way of objective criticism of works of art as such, the way which enables us to distinguish between a skillful murder and a skillful poem. A skillful murder is an example which Coomaraswamy uses, and in his system the difference between the murder and the poem is simply a "moral" one, not an "artistic" one, since each if carried out according to plan is "artistically" successful. We maintain that (2) is an inquiry of more worth than (1), and since (2) and not (1) is capable of distinguishing poetry from murder, the name "artistic criticism" is properly given to (2).

II

It is not so much a historical statement as a definition to say that the intentional fallacy is a romantic one. When a rhetorician of the first century A.D.

[2]   J. E. Spingarn, "The New Criticism," in *Criticism in America* (New York, 1924), 24–25.

[3]   Ananda K. Coomaraswamy, "Intention," in *American Bookman,* I (1944), 41–48.

writes: "Sublimity is the echo of a great soul," or when he tells us that "Homer enters into the sublime actions of his heroes" and "shares the full inspiration of the combat," we shall not be surprised to find this rhetorician considered as a distant harbinger of romanticism and greeted in the warmest terms by Saintsbury. One may wish to argue whether Longinus should be called romantic, but there can hardly be a doubt that in one important way he is.

Goethe's three questions for "constructive criticism" are "What did the author set out to do? Was his plan reasonable and sensible, and how far did he succeed in carrying it out?" If one leaves out the middle question, one has in effect the system of Croce—the culmination and crowning philosophic expression of romanticism. The beautiful is the successful intuition-expression, and the ugly is the unsuccessful; the intuition or private part of art is *the* aesthetic fact, and the medium or public part is not the subject of aesthetic at all.

> The Madonna of Cimabue is still in the Church of Santa Maria Novella; but does she speak to the visitor of today as to the Florentines of the thirteenth century?
>
> *Historical interpretation* labours . . . to reintegrate in us the psychological conditions which have changed in the course of history. It . . . enables us to see a work of art (a physical object) as its *author saw it* in the moment of production.[4]

The first italics are Croce's, the second ours. The upshot of Croce's system is an ambiguous emphasis on history. With such passages as a point of departure a critic may write a nice analysis of the meaning or "spirit" of a play by Shakespeare or Corneille—a process that involves close historical study but remains aesthetic criticism—or he may, with equal plausibility, produce an essay on sociology, biography, or other kinds of nonaesthetic history.

III

I went to the poets; tragic, dithyrambic, and all sorts. . . . I took them some of the most elaborate passages in their own writings, and asked what was the meaning of them. . . . Will you believe me? . . . there is hardly a person present who would not have talked better about their poetry than they did themselves. Then I knew that not by wisdom do poets write poetry, but by a sort of genius and inspiration.

That reiterated mistrust of the poets which we hear from Socrates may have been part of a rigorously ascetic view in which we hardly wish to participate, yet Plato's Socrates saw a truth about the poetic mind which the world no longer commonly sees—so much criticism, and that the most inspirational and most affectionately remembered, has proceeded from the poets themselves.

Certainly the poets have had something to say that the critic and professor could not say; their message has been more exciting: that poetry should come as naturally as leaves to a tree, that poetry is the lava of the imagination, or that it is emotion recollected in tranquillity. But it is necessary that we realize the character and authority of such testimony. There is only a fine shade of difference between such expressions and a kind of earnest advice that authors often give. Thus Edward Young, Carlyle, Walter Pater:

> I know two golden rules from *ethics,* which are no less golden in *Composition,* than in life. 1. *Know thyself;* 2dly, *Reverence thyself.*
>
> This is the grand secret for finding readers and retaining them: let him who would move and convince others, be first moved and convinced himself. Horace's rule, *Si vis me flere,* is applicable in a wider sense than the literal one. To every poet, to every writer, we might say: Be true, if you would be believed.
>
> Truth! there can be no merit, no craft at all, without that. And further, all beauty is in the long run only *fineness* of truth, or what we call expression, the finer accommodation of speech to that vision within.

And Housman's little handbook to the poetic mind yields this illustration:

> Having drunk a pint of beer at luncheon—beer is a sedative to the brain, and my afternoons are the least intellectual portion of my life—I would go out for a walk of two or three hours. As I went along, thinking of nothing in particular, only looking at things around me and following the progress of the seasons, there would flow into my mind, with sudden and unaccountable emotion, sometimes a line or two of verse, sometimes a whole stanza at once.

This is the logical terminus of the series already quoted. Here is a confession of how poems were written which would do as a definition of poetry just as well as "emotion recollected in tranquillity"—and

---

[4] It is true that Croce himself in his *Ariosto, Shakespeare and Corneille* (London, 1920), chap. VII, "The Practical Personality and the Poetical Personality," and in his *Defence of Poetry* (Oxford, 1933), 24, and elsewhere, early and late, has delivered telling attacks on emotive geneticism, but the main drive of the *Aesthetic* is surely toward a kind of cognitive intentionalism.

which the young poet might equally well take to heart as a practical rule. Drink a pint of beer, relax, go walking, think on nothing in particular, look at things, surrender yourself to yourself, search for the truth in your own soul, listen to the sound of your own inside voice, discover and express the *vraie vérité*.

It is probably true that all this is excellent advice for poets. The young imagination fired by Wordsworth and Carlyle is probably closer to the verge of producing a poem than the mind of the student who has been sobered by Aristotle or Richards. The art of inspiring poets, or at least of inciting something like poetry in young persons, has probably gone further in our day than ever before. Books of creative writing such as those issued from the Lincoln School are interesting evidence of what a child can do.[5] All this, however, would appear to belong to an art separate from criticism—to a psychological discipline, a system of self-development, a yoga, which the young poet perhaps does well to notice, but which is something different from the public art of evaluating poems.

Coleridge and Arnold were better critics than most poets have been, and if the critical tendency dried up the poetry in Arnold and perhaps in Coleridge, it is not inconsistent with our argument, which is that judgment of poems is different from the art of producing them. Coleridge has given us the classic "anodyne" story, and tells what he can about the genesis of a poem which he calls a "psychological curiosity," but his definitions of poetry and of the poetic quality "imagination" are to be found elsewhere and in quite other terms.

It would be convenient if the passwords of the intentional school, "sincerity," "fidelity," "spontaneity," "authenticity," "genuineness," "originality," could be equated with terms such as "integrity," "relevance," "unity," "function," "maturity," "subtlety," "adequacy," and other more precise terms of evaluation—in short, if "expression" always meant aesthetic achievement. But this is not so.

"Aesthetic" art, says Professor Curt Ducasse, an ingenious theorist of expression, is the conscious objectification of feelings, in which an intrinsic part is

the critical moment. The artist corrects the objectification when it is not adequate. But this may mean that the earlier attempt was not successful in objectifying the self, or "it may also mean that it was a successful objectification of a self which, when it confronted us clearly, we disowned and repudiated in favor of another."[6] What is the standard by which we disown or accept the self? Professor Ducasse does not say. Whatever it may be, however, this standard is an element in the definition of art which will not reduce to terms of objectification. The evaluation of the work of art remains public; the work is measured against something outside the author.

IV

There is criticism of poetry and there is author psychology, which when applied to the present or future takes the form of inspirational promotion; but author psychology can be historical too, and then we have literary biography, a legitimate and attractive study in itself, one approach, as Professor Tillyard would argue, to personality, the poem being only a parallel approach. Certainly it need not be with a derogatory purpose that one points out personal studies, as distinct from poetic studies, in the realm of literary scholarship. Yet there is danger of confusing personal and poetic studies; and there is the fault of writing the personal as if it were poetic.

There is a difference between internal and external evidence for the meaning of a poem. And the paradox is only verbal and superficial that what is (1) internal is also public: it is discovered through the semantics and syntax of a poem, through our habitual knowledge of the language, through grammars, dictionaries, and all the literature which is the source of dictionaries, in general through all that makes a language and culture; while what is (2) external is private or idiosyncratic; not a part of the work as a linguistic fact: it consists of revelations (in journals, for example, or letters, or reported conversations) about how or why the poet wrote the poem—to what lady, while sitting on what lawn, or at the death of what friend or brother. There is (3) an intermediate kind of evidence about the character of the author or about private or semiprivate meanings attached to words or topics by an author or by a coterie of which he is a member. The meaning of words is the history of words, and the biography of an author, his use of a word, and the associa-

---

[5] See Hughes Mearns, *Creative Youth* (Garden City, 1925), esp. 10, 27–29. The technique of inspiring poems has apparently been outdone more recently by the study of inspiration in successful poets and other artists. See, for instance, Rosamond E. M. Harding, *An Anatomy of Inspiration* (Cambridge, 1940); Julius Portnoy, *A Psychology of Art Creation* (Philadelphia, 1942); Rudolf Arnheim and others, *Poets at Work* (New York, 1947); Phyllis Bartlett, *Poems in Process* (New York, 1951); Brewster Ghiselin (ed.), *The Creative Process: A Symposium* (Berkeley and Los Angeles, 1952).

[6] Curt Ducasse, *The Philosophy of Art* (New York, 1929), 116.

tions which the word had for *him,* are part of the word's history and meaning.[7] But the three types of evidence, especially (2) and (3), shade into one another so subtly that it is not always easy to draw a line between examples, and hence arises the difficulty for criticism. The use of biographical evidence need not involve intentionalism, because while it may be evidence of what the author intended, it may also be evidence of the meaning of his words and the dramatic character of his utterance. On the other hand, it may not be all this. And a critic who is concerned with evidence of type (1) and moderately with that of type (3) will in the long run produce a different sort of comment from that of the critic who is concerned with (2) and with (3) where it shades into (2).

The whole glittering parade of Professor Lowes' *Road to Xanadu,* for instance, runs along the border between types (2) and (3) or boldly traverses the romantic region of (2). "'Kubla Khan,'" says Professor Lowes, "is the fabric of a vision, but every image that rose up in its weaving had passed that way before. And it would seem that there is nothing haphazard or fortuitous in their return." This is not quite clear—not even when Professor Lowes explains that there were clusters of associations, like hooked atoms, which were drawn into complex relation with other clusters in the deep well of Coleridge's memory, and which then coalesced and issued forth as poems. If there was nothing "haphazard or fortuitous" in the way the images returned to the surface, that may mean (1) that Coleridge could not produce what he did not have, that he was limited in his creation by what he had read or otherwise experienced, or (2) that having received certain clusters of associations, he was bound to return them in just the way he did, and that the value of the poem may be described in terms of the experiences on which he had to draw. The latter pair of propositions (a sort of Hartleyan associationism which Coleridge himself repudiated in the *Biographia*) may not be assented to. There were certainly other combinations, other poems, worse or better, that might have been written by men who had read Bartram and Purchas and Bruce and Milton. And this will be true no matter how many times we are able to add to the brilliant complex of Coleridge's reading. In certain flourishes (such as the sentence we have quoted) and in

chapter headings like "The Shaping Spirit," "The Magical Synthesis," "Imagination Creatrix," it may be that Professor Lowes pretends to say more about the actual poems than he does. There is a certain deceptive variation in these fancy chapter titles; one expects to pass on to a new stage in the argument, and one finds—more and more sources, more and more about "the streamy nature of association."

"Wohin der Weg?" quotes Professor Lowes for the motto of his book. "Kein Weg! Ins Unbetretene." Precisely because the way is *unbetreten,* we should say, it leads away from the poem. Bartram's *Travels* contains a good deal of the history of certain words and of certain romantic Floridian conceptions that appear in "Kubla Khan." And a good deal of that history has passed and was then passing into the very stuff of our language. Perhaps a person who has read Bartram appreciates the poem more than one who has not. Or, by looking up the vocabulary of "Kubla Khan" in the *Oxford English Dictionary,* or by reading some of the other books there quoted, a person may know the poem better. But it would seem to pertain little to the poem to know that *Coleridge* had read Bartram. There is a gross body of life, of sensory and mental experience, which lies behind and in some sense causes every poem, but can never be and need not be known in the verbal and hence intellectual composition which is the poem. For all the objects of our manifold experience, for every unity, there is an action of the mind which cuts off roots, melts away context—or indeed we should never have objects or ideas or anything to talk about.

It is probable that there is nothing in Professor Lowes's vast book which could detract from anyone's appreciation of either *The Ancient Mariner* or "Kubla Khan." We next present a case where preoccupation with evidence of type (3) has gone so far as to distort a critic's view of a poem (yet a case not so obvious as those that abound in our critical journals).

In a well known poem by John Donne appears this quatrain:

> Moving of th' earth brings harmes and feares,
>   Men reckon what it did and meant,
> But trepidation of the spheares,
>   Though greater farre, is innocent.

A recent critic in an elaborate treatment of Donne's learning has written of this quatrain as follows:

> He touches the emotional pulse of the situation by a skillful allusion to the new and the old astronomy. . . . Of the new astronomy, the "moving of the earth" is the most radical principle; of the old, the "trepidation of

---

[7] And the history of words *after* a poem is written may contribute meanings which if relevant to the original pattern should not be ruled out by a scruple about intention.

the spheres" is the motion of the greatest complexity. . . . The poet must exhort his love to quietness and calm upon his departure; and for this purpose the figure based upon the latter motion (trepidation), long absorbed into the traditional astronomy, fittingly suggests the tension of the moment without arousing the "harmes and feares" implicit in the figure of the moving earth.[8]

The argument is plausible and rests on a well substantiated thesis that Donne was deeply interested in the new astronomy and its repercussions in the theological realm. In various works Donne shows his familiarity with Kepler's *De Stella Nova,* with Galileo's *Siderius Nuncius,* with William Gilbert's *De Magnete,* and with Clavius' commentary on the *De Sphaera* of Sacrobosco. He refers to the new science in his *Sermon at Paul's Cross* and in a letter to Sir Henry Goodyer. In *The First Anniversary* he says the "new philosophy calls all in doubt." In the *Elegy on Prince Henry* he says that the "least moving of the center" makes "the world to shake."

It is difficult to answer argument like this, and impossible to answer it with evidence of like nature. There is no reason why Donne might not have written a stanza in which the two kinds of celestial motion stood for two sorts of emotion at parting. And if we become full of astronomical ideas and see Donne only against the background of the new science, we may believe that he did. But the text itself remains to be dealt with, the analyzable vehicle of a complicated metaphor. And one may observe: (1) that the movement of the earth according to the Copernican theory is a celestial motion, smooth and regular, and while it might cause religious or philosophic fears, it could not be associated with the crudity and earthiness of the kind of commotion which the speaker in the poem wishes to discourage; (2) that there is another moving of the earth, an earthquake, which has just these qualities and is to be associated with the tear-floods and sigh-tempests of the second stanza of the poem; (3) that "trepidation" is an appropriate opposite of earthquake, because each is a shaking or vibratory motion; and "trepidation of the spheres" is "greater far" than an earthquake, but not much greater (if two such motions can be compared as to greatness) than the annual motion of the earth; (4) that reckoning what it "did and meant" shows that the event has passed, like an earthquake, not like the incessant celestial move-

ment of the earth. Perhaps a knowledge of Donne's interest in the new science may add another shade of meaning, an overtone to the stanza in question, though to say even this runs against the words. To make the geocentric and heliocentric antithesis the core of the metaphor is to disregard the English language, to prefer private evidence to public, external to internal.

V

If the distinction between kinds of evidence has implications for the historical critic, it has them no less for the contemporary poet and his critic. Or, since every rule for a poet is but another side of a judgment by a critic, and since the past is the realm of the scholar and critic, and the future and present that of the poet and the critical leaders of taste, we may say that the problems arising in literary scholarship from the intentional fallacy are matched by others which arise in the world of progressive experiment.

The question of "allusiveness," for example, as acutely posed by the poetry of Eliot, is certainly one where a false judgment is likely to involve the intentional fallacy. The frequency and depth of literary allusion in the poetry of Eliot and others has driven so many in pursuit of full meanings to the *Golden Bough* and the Elizabethan drama that it has become a kind of commonplace to suppose that we do not know what a poet means unless we have traced him in his reading—a supposition redolent with intentional implications. The stand taken by F. O. Matthiessen is a sound one and partially forestalls the difficulty.

> If one reads these lines with an attentive ear and is sensitive to their sudden shifts in movement, the contrast between the actual Thames and the idealized vision of it during an age before it flowed through a megalopolis is sharply conveyed by that movement itself, whether or not one recognizes the refrain to be from Spenser.

Eliot's allusions work when we know them—and to a great extent even when we do not know them, through their suggestive power.

But sometimes we find allusions supported by notes, and it is a nice question whether the notes function more as guides to send us where we may be educated, or more as indications in themselves about the character of the allusions. "Nearly everything of importance . . . that is apposite to an appreciation of "The Waste Land," writes Matthiessen of Miss

---

[8] Charles M. Coffin, *John Donne and the New Philosophy* (New York, 1927), 97–98.

Weston's book, "has been incorporated into the structure of the poem itself, or into Eliot's Notes." And with such an admission it may begin to appear that it would not much matter if Eliot invented his sources (as Sir Walter Scott invented chapter epigraphs from "old plays" and "anonymous" authors, or as Coleridge wrote marginal glosses for *The Ancient Mariner*). Allusions to Dante, Webster, Marvell, or Baudelaire doubtless gain something because these writers existed, but it is doubtful whether the same can be said for an allusion to an obscure Elizabethan:

> The sound of horns and motors, which shall bring
> Sweeney to Mrs. Porter in the spring.

"Cf. Day, *Parliament of Bees:*" says Eliot,

> When of a sudden, listening, you shall hear,
> A noise of horns and hunting, which shall bring
> Actaeon to Diana in the spring,
> Where all shall see her naked skin.

The irony is completed by the quotation itself; had Eliot, as is quite conceivable, composed these lines to furnish his own background, there would be no loss of validity. The conviction may grow as one reads Eliot's next note: "I do not know the origin of the ballad from which these lines are taken: it was reported to me from Sydney, Australia." The important word in this note—on Mrs. Porter and her daughter who washed their feet in soda water—is "ballad." And if one should feel from the lines themselves their "ballad" quality, there would be little need for the note. Ultimately, the inquiry must focus on the integrity of such notes as parts of the poem, for where they constitute special information about the meaning of phrases in the poem, they ought to be subject to the same scrutiny as any of the other words in which it is written. Matthiessen believes the notes were the price Eliot "had to pay in order to avoid what he would have considered muffling the energy of his poem by extended connecting links in the text itself." But it may be questioned whether the notes and the need for them are not equally muffling. F. W. Bateson has plausibly argued that Tennyson's "The Sailor Boy" would be better if half the stanzas were omitted, and the best versions of ballads like "Sir Patrick Spens" owe their power to the very audacity with which the minstrel has taken for granted the story upon which he comments. What then if a poet finds he cannot take so much for granted in a more recondite context and rather than write informatively, supplies notes? It can be said in

favor of this plan that at least the notes do not pretend to be dramatic, as they would if written in verse. On the other hand, the notes may look like unassimilated material lying loose beside the poem, necessary for the meaning of the verbal symbol, but not integrated, so that the symbol stands incomplete.

We mean to suggest by the above analysis that whereas notes tend to seem to justify themselves as external indexes to the author's *intention,* yet they ought to be judged like any other parts of a composition (verbal arrangement special to a particular context), and when so judged their reality as parts of the poem, or their imaginative integration with the rest of the poem, may come into question. Matthiessen, for instance, sees that Eliot's titles for poems and his epigraphs are informative apparatus, like the notes. But while he is worried by some of the notes and thinks that Eliot "appears to be mocking himself for writing the note at the same time that he wants to convey something by it," Matthiessen believes that the "device" of epigraphs "is not at all open to the objection of not being sufficiently structural." "The *intention,*" he says, "is to enable the poet to secure a condensed expression in the poem itself." "In each case the epigraph is *designed* to form an integral part of the effect of the poem." And Eliot himself, in his notes, has justified his poetic practice in terms of intention.

> The Hanged Man, a member of the traditional pack, fits my purpose in two ways: because he is associated in my mind with the Hanged God of Frazer, and because I associate him with the hooded figure in the passage of the disciples to Emmaus in Part V.... The man with Three Staves (an authentic member of the Tarot pack) I associate, quite arbitrarily, with the Fisher King himself.

And perhaps he is to be taken more seriously here, when off guard in a note, than when in his Norton Lectures he comments on the difficulty of saying what a poem means and adds playfully that he thinks of prefixing to a second edition of *Ash Wednesday* some lines from *Don Juan:*

> I don't pretend that I quite understand
> My own meaning when I would be *very* fine;
> But the fact is that I have nothing planned
> Unless it were to be a moment merry.

If Eliot and other contemporary poets have any characteristic fault, it may be in *planning* too much.

Allusiveness in poetry is one of several critical issues by which we have illustrated the more abstract issue of intentionalism, but it may be for today the most important illustration. As a poetic practice allusiveness would appear to be in some recent poems an extreme corollary of the romantic intentionalist assumption, and as a critical issue it challenges and brings to light in a special way the basic premise of intentionalism. The following instance from the poetry of Eliot may serve to epitomize the practical implications of what we have been saying. In Eliot's "Love Song of J. Alfred Prufrock," toward the end, occurs the line: "I have heard the mermaids singing, each to each," and this bears a certain resemblance to a line in a Song by John Donne, "Teach me to heare Mermaides singing," so that for the reader acquainted to a certain degree with Donne's poetry, the critical question arises: Is Eliot's line an allusion to Donne's? Is Prufrock thinking about Donne? Is Eliot thinking about Donne? We suggest that there are two radically different ways of looking for an answer to this question. There is (1) the way of poetic analysis and exegesis, which inquires whether it makes any sense if Eliot-Prufrock *is* thinking about Donne. In an earlier part of the poem, when Prufrock asks, "Would it have been worth while, . . . To have squeezed the universe into a ball," his words take half their sadness and irony from certain energetic and passionate lines of Marvel "To His Coy Mistress." But the exegetical inquirer may wonder whether mermaids considered as "strange sights" (to hear them is in Donne's poem analogous to getting with child a mandrake root) have much to do with Prufrock's mermaids, which seem to be symbols of romance and dynamism, and which incidentally have literary authentication, if they need it, in a line of a sonnet by Gérard de Nerval. This method of inquiry may lead to the conclusion that the given resemblance between Eliot and Donne is without significance and is better not thought of, or the method may have the disadvantage of providing no certain conclusion. Nevertheless, we submit that this is the true and objective way of criticism, as contrasted to what the very uncertainty of exegesis might tempt a second kind of critic to undertake: (2) the way of biographical or genetic inquiry, in which, taking advantage of the fact that Eliot is still alive, and in the spirit of a man who would settle a bet, the critic writes to Eliot and asks what he meant, or if he had Donne in mind. We shall not here weigh the probabilities—whether Eliot would answer that he meant nothing at all, had nothing at all in mind—a sufficiently good answer to such a question—or in an unguarded moment might furnish a clear and, within its limit, irrefutable answer. Our point is that such an answer to such an inquiry would have nothing to do with the poem "Prufrock"; it would not be a critical inquiry. Critical inquiries, unlike bets, are not settled in this way. Critical inquiries are not settled by consulting the oracle.

José Ortega y Gasset (1883–1955)
THE DEHUMANIZATION OF ART

The author, a Spanish philosopher, argues that the new art developed in the Western world during the twentieth century is primarily concerned, not with lived reality, but with artistic value. As a result, it is accessible only to a small group of people: artists. By "artists," Ortega means not just those who produce the art, but also those who can comprehend it—that is, people capable of appreciating purely artistic value. He argues that such art is doomed to remain inaccessible to the vast majority of people. Ortega's views are discussed toward the end of the introductory essay to Part V.

READING QUESTIONS

In reading the selection, try to answer the following questions and identify the passages that support your answers:

1. What is Ortega's characterization of twentieth-century Western art?
2. What problem does he think this art poses?
3. Is this a real problem? Why or why not?
4. Does Ortega think it has a solution?
5. Should anything be done about the problem? What and why?

UNPOPULARITY OF THE NEW ART

Among the many excellent, though inadequately developed, ideas of the eminent French philosopher J. M. Guyau we must count his intention to study art from a sociological point of view.[1] The subject may at first appear unprofitable. Approaching art from the side of its social effects looks very much like putting the cart before the horse, or studying a man by his shadow. The social effects of art seem such an accidental thing, so remote from the aesthetic essence that it does not quite appear how, starting from them, we can ever hope to penetrate into the inner frame of styles. Guyau doubtless failed to make the best of his ingenious idea. His short life and tragic rushing toward death prevented him from clarifying his insight and distinguishing the obvious aspects from the hidden but more relevant ones. We may almost say that of his book *Art from a Sociological Point of View* only the title exists; the rest is yet to be written.

The fruitfulness of a sociology of art was revealed to me unexpectedly when, a few years ago, I wrote a brief study on the new epoch in music which begins with Debussy.[2] My purpose was to define as clearly as possible the difference of style between the new music and traditional music. The problem was strictly aesthetic, and yet it turned out that the shortest way to tackling it started from a sociological fact: the unpopularity of the new music.

In the following I will speak more in general and consider all the arts that are still somewhat alive in the Western world—that is, not only music, but also painting, poetry, and the theater. It is amazing how compact a unity every historical epoch presents throughout its various manifestations. One and the same inspiration, one and the same biological style, are recognizable in the several branches of art. The young musician—himself unaware of it—strives to realize in his medium the same aesthetic values as his contemporary colleagues—the poet, the painter, the playwright—in theirs. And this identity of artistic purpose necessarily produces identical sociological consequences. In fact, the unpopularity of the new music has its counterpart in a similar unpopularity of the other Muses. All modern art is unpopular, and it is so not accidentally and by chance, but essentially and by fate.

It might be said that every newcomer among styles passes through a stage of quarantine. The battle of *Hernani* comes to mind, and all the other skirmishes connected with the advent of Romanticism. However, the unpopularity of present-day art is of a different kind. A distinction must be made between what is not popular and what is unpopular. A new style takes some time in winning popularity; it is not popular, but it is not unpopular either. The breakthrough of Romanticism, although a frequently cited example, is, as a sociological phenomenon, exactly the opposite of the present situation of art. Romanticism was very quick in winning "the people" to whom the old classical art had never appealed. The enemy with whom Romanticism had to fight it out was precisely a select minority irretrievably sold

[1]   Jean Marie Guyau, *L'art au point de vue sociologique.* Paris: F. Alcan, 1897.

[2]   Cf. the author's essay "Musicalia" in *El Espectador* (Madrid: Calpe, 1921), vol. III, 25.

to the classical forms of the "*ancien régime*" in poetry. The works of the romanticists were the first, after the invention of printing, to enjoy large editions. Romanticism was the prototype of a popular style. First-born of democracy, it was coddled by the masses.

Modern art, on the other hand, will always have the masses against it. It is essentially unpopular; moreover, it is antipopular. Any of its works automatically produces a curious effect on the general public. It divides the public into two groups: one very small, formed by those who are favorably inclined towards it; another very large—the hostile majority. (Let us ignore that ambiguous fauna—the snobs.) Thus the work of art acts like a social agent which segregates from the shapeless mass of the many two different castes of men.

Which is the differentiating principle that creates these two antagonistic groups? Every work of art arouses differences of opinion. Some like it, some don't; some like it more, some like it less. Such disagreements have no organic character, they are not a matter of principles. A person's chance disposition determines on which side he will fall. But in the case of the new art the split occurs in a deeper layer than that on which differences of personal taste reside. It is not that the majority does not *like* the art of the young and the minority likes it, but that the majority, the masses, do not *understand* it. The old bigwigs who were present at the performance of *Hernani* understood Victor Hugo's play very well; precisely because they understood it they disliked it. Faithfully adhering to definite aesthetic norms, they were disgusted at the new artistic values which this piece of art proposed to them.

"From a sociological point of view" the characteristic feature of the new art is, in my judgment, that it divides the public into the two classes of those who understand it and those who do not. This implies that one group possesses an organ of comprehension denied to the other—that they are two different varieties of the human species. The new art obviously addresses itself not to everybody, as did Romanticism, but to a specially gifted minority. Hence the indignation it arouses in the masses. When a man dislikes a work of art, but understands it, he feels superior to it; and there is no reason for indignation. But when his dislike is due to his failure to understand, he feels vaguely humiliated and this rankling sense of inferiority must be counterbalanced by indignant self-assertion. Through its mere presence, the art of the young compels the av-

erage citizen to realize that he is just this—the average citizen, a creature incapable of receiving the sacrament of art, blind and deaf to pure beauty. But such a thing cannot be done after a hundred years of adulation of the masses and apotheosis of the people. Accustomed to ruling supreme, the masses feel that the new art, which is the art of a privileged aristocracy of finer senses, endangers their rights as men. Whenever the new Muses present themselves, the masses bristle.

For a century and a half the masses have claimed to be the whole of society. Stravinski's music or Pirandello's drama have the sociological effect of compelling the people to recognize itself for what it is: a component among others of the social structure, inert matter of the historical process, a secondary factor in the cosmos of spiritual life. On the other hand, the new art also helps the elite to recognize themselves and one another in the drab mass of society and to learn their mission which consists in being few and holding their own against the many.

A time must come in which society, from politics to art, reorganizes itself into two orders or ranks: the illustrious and the vulgar. That chaotic, shapeless, and undifferentiated state without discipline and social structure in which Europe has lived these hundred and fifty years cannot go on. Behind all contemporary life lurks the provoking and profound injustice of the assumption that men are actually equal. Each move among men so obviously reveals the opposite that each move results in a painful clash.

If this subject were broached in politics the passions aroused would run too high to make oneself understood. Fortunately the aforementioned unity of spirit within a historical epoch allows us to point out serenely and with perfect clarity in the germinating art of our time the same symptoms and signals of a moral revision that in politics present themselves obscured by low passions.

"*Nolite fieri*," the evangelist exhorts us, "*sicut equus et mulus quibus non est intellectus*"—do not act like horses and mules that lack understanding. The masses kick and do not understand. Let us try to do better and to extract from modern art its essential principle. That will enable us to see in what profound sense modern art is unpopular.

ARTISTIC ART

If the new art is not accessible to every man this implies that its impulses are not of a generically human kind. It is an art not for men in general but for a special class of men who may not be better but who evidently are different.

One point must be clarified before we go on. What is it the majority of people call aesthetic pleasure? What happens in their minds when they "like" a work of art; for instance, a theatrical performance? The answer is easy. A man likes a play when he has become interested in the human destinies presented to him, when the love and hatred, the joys and sorrows of the personages so move his heart that he participates in it all as though it were happening in real life. And he calls a work "good" if it succeeds in creating the illusion necessary to make the imaginary personages appear like living persons. In poetry he seeks the passion and pain of the man behind the poet. Paintings attract him if he finds on them figures of men or women whom it would be interesting to meet. A landscape is pronounced "pretty" if the country it represents deserves for its loveliness or its grandeur to be visited on a trip.

It thus appears that to the majority of people aesthetic pleasure means a state of mind which is essentially undistinguishable from their ordinary behavior. It differs merely in accidental qualities, being perhaps less utilitarian, more intense, and free from painful consequences. But the object towards which their attention and, consequently, all their other mental activities are directed is the same as in daily life: people and passions. By art they understand a means through which they are brought in contact with interesting human affairs. Artistic forms proper—figments, fantasy—are tolerated only if they do not interfere with the perception of human forms and fates. As soon as purely aesthetic elements predominate and the story of John and Mary grows elusive, most people feel out of their depth and are at a loss what to make of the scene, the book, or the painting. As they have never practiced any other attitude but the practical one in which a man's feelings are aroused and he is emotionally involved, a work that does not invite sentimental intervention leaves them without a cue.

Now, this is a point which has to be made perfectly clear. Not only is grieving and rejoicing at such human destinies as a work of art presents or narrates a very different thing from true artistic pleasure, but preoccupation with the human content of the work is in principle incompatible with aesthetic enjoyment proper.

We have here a very simple optical problem. To see a thing we must adjust our visual apparatus in a certain way. If the adjustment is inadequate the thing is seen indistinctly or not at all. Take a garden seen through a window. Looking at the garden we adjust our eyes in such a way that the ray of vision travels through the pane without delay and rests on the shrubs and flowers. Since we are focusing on the garden and our ray of vision is directed toward it, we do not see the window but look clear through it. The purer the glass, the less we see it. But we can also deliberately disregard the garden and, withdrawing the ray of vision, detain it at the window. We then lose sight of the garden; what we still behold of it is a confused mass of color which appears pasted to the pane. Hence to see the garden and to see the windowpane are two incompatible operations which exclude one another because they require different adjustments.

Similarly a work of art vanishes from sight for a beholder who seeks in it nothing but the moving fate of John and Mary or Tristan and Isolde and adjusts his vision to this. Tristan's sorrows are sorrows and can evoke compassion only in so far as they are taken as real. But an object of art is artistic only in so far as it is not real. In order to enjoy Titian's portrait of Charles the Fifth on horseback we must forget that this is Charles the Fifth in person and see instead a portrait—that is, an image, a fiction. The portrayed person and his portrait are two entirely different things; we are interested in either one or the other. In the first case we "live" with Charles the Fifth, in the second we look at an object of art.

But not many people are capable of adjusting their perceptive apparatus to the pane and the transparency that is the work of art. Instead they look right through it and revel in the human reality with which the work deals. When they are invited to let go of this prey and to direct their attention to the work of art itself they will say that they cannot see such a thing, which indeed they cannot, because it is all artistic transparency and without substance.

During the nineteenth century artists proceeded in all too impure a fashion. They reduced the strictly aesthetic elements to a minimum and let the work consist almost entirely in a fiction of human realities. In this sense all normal art of the last century must be called realistic. Beethoven and Wagner were realistic, and so was Chateaubriand as well as Zola. Seen from the vantage-point of our day Romanticism and Naturalism draw closer together and reveal their common realistic root.

Works of this kind are only partially works of art, or artistic objects. Their enjoyment does not depend upon our power to focus on transparencies and images, a power characteristic of the artistic sensibility; all they require is human sensibility and willingness to sympathize with our neighbor's joys and worries. No wonder that nineteenth century art has been so popular; it is made for the masses inasmuch as it is not art but an extract from life. Let us remember that in epochs with two different types of art, one for minorities and one for the majority, the latter has always been realistic.[3]

I will not now discuss whether pure art is possible. Perhaps it is not; but as the reasons that make me inclined to think so are somewhat long and difficult the subject better be dropped. Besides, it is not of major importance for the matter at hand. Even though pure art may be impossible there doubtless can prevail a tendency toward a purification of art. Such a tendency would effect a progressive elimination of the human, all too human, elements predominant in romantic and naturalistic production. And in this process a point can be reached in which the human content has grown so thin that it is negligible. We then have an art which can be comprehended only by people possessed of the peculiar gift of artistic sensibility—an art for artists and not for the masses, for "quality" and not for hoi polloi.

That is why modern art divides the public into two classes, those who understand it and those who do not understand it—that is to say, those who are artists and those who are not. The new art is an artistic art.

I do not propose to extol the new way in art or to condemn the old. My purpose is to characterize them as the zoologist characterizes two contrasting species. The new art is a world-wide fact. For about twenty years now the most alert young people of two successive generations—in Berlin, Paris, London, New York, Rome, Madrid—have found themselves faced with the undeniable fact that they have no use for traditional art; moreover, that they detest it. With these young people one can do one of two things: shoot them, or try to understand them. As soon as one decides in favor of the latter it appears that they are endowed with a perfectly clear, coherent, and rational sense of art. Far from being a whim, their way of feeling represents the inevitable and fruitful result of all previous artistic achievement. Whimsical, arbitrary, and consequently unprofitable it would be to set oneself against the new style and obstinately remain shut up in old forms that are exhausted and

the worse for wear. In art, as in morals, what ought to be done does not depend on our personal judgment; we have to accept the imperative imposed by the time. Obedience to the order of the day is the most hopeful choice open to the idnividual. Even so he may achieve nothing; but he is much more likely to fail if he insists on composing another Wagnerian opera, another naturalistic novel.

In art repetition is nothing. Each historical style can engender a certain number of different forms within a generic type. But there always comes a day when the magnificent mine is worked out. Such, for instance, has been the fate of the romantico-naturalistic novel and theater. It is a naïve error to believe that the present in-fecundity of these two genres is due to lack of talent. What happens is that the possible combinations within these literary forms are exhausted. It must be deemed fortunate that this situation coincides with the emergence of a new artistic sensibility capable of detecting other untouched veins.

When we analyze the new style we find that it contains certain closely connected tendencies. It tends (1) to dehumanize art, (2) to avoid living forms, (3) to see to it that the work of art is nothing but a work of art, (4) to consider art as play and nothing else, (5) to be essentially ironical, (6) to beware of sham and hence to aspire to scrupulous realization, (7) to regard art as a thing of no transcending consequence.

In the following I shall say a few words about each of these features of modern art.

FIRST INSTALLMENT ON THE DEHUMANIZATION OF ART

With amazing swiftness modern art has split up into a multitude of divergent directions. Nothing is easier than to stress the differences. But such an emphasis on the distinguishing and specific features would be pointless without a previous account of the common fund that in a varying and sometimes contradictory manner asserts itself throughout modern art. Did not Aristotle already observe that things differ in what they have in common? Because all bodies are colored we notice that they are differently colored. Species are nothing if not modifications of a genus, and we cannot understand them unless we realize that they draw, in their several ways, upon a common patrimony.

I am little interested in special directions of modern art and, but for a few exceptions, even less in spe-

---

[3] For instance in the Middle Ages. In accordance with the division of society in the two strata of noblemen and commoners, there existed an aristocratic art which was "conventional" and "idealistic," and a popular art which was realistic and satirical.

cial works. Nor do I, for that matter, expect anybody to be particularly interested in my valuation of the new artistic produce. Writers who have nothing to convey but their praise or dispraise of works of art had better abstain from writing. They are unfit for this arduous task.

The important thing is that there unquestionably exists in the world a new artistic sensibility.[4] Over against the multiplicity of special directions and individual works, the new sensibility represents the generic fact and the source, as it were, from which the former spring. This sensibility it is worth while to define. And when we seek to ascertain the most general and most characteristic feature of modern artistic production we come upon the tendency to dehumanize art. After what we have said above, this formula now acquires a tolerably precise meaning.

Let us compare a painting in the new style with one of, say, 1860. The simplest procedure will be to begin by setting against one another the objects they represent: a man perhaps, a house, or a mountain. It then appears that the artist of 1860 wanted nothing so much as to give to the objects in his picture the same looks and airs they possess outside it when they occur as parts of the "lived" or "human" reality. Apart from this he may have been animated by other more intricate aesthetic ambitions, but what interests us is that his first concern was with securing this likeness. Man, house, mountain are at once recognized, they are our good old friends; whereas on a modern painting we are at a loss to recognize them. It might be supposed that the modern painter has failed to achieve resemblance. But then some pictures of the 1860's are "poorly" painted, too, and the objects in them differ considerably from the corresponding objects outside them. And yet, whatever the differences, the very blunders of the traditional artist point toward the "human" object; they are downfalls on the way toward it and somehow equivalent to the orienting words "This is a cock" with which Cervantes lets the painter Orbanejo enlighten his public. In modern paintings the opposite happens. It is not that the painter is bungling and fails to render the natural (natural = human) thing because he deviates from it, but that these deviations point in a direction opposite to that which would lead to reality.

Far from going more or less clumsily toward reality, the artist is seen going against it. He is brazenly set on deforming reality, shattering its human aspect, dehumanizing it. With the things represented on traditional paintings we could have imaginary intercourse. Many a young Englishman has fallen in love with Gioconda. With the objects of modern pictures no intercourse is possible. By divesting them of their aspect of "lived" reality the artist has blown up the bridges and burned the ships that could have taken us back to our daily world. He leaves us locked up in an abstruse universe, surrounded by objects with which human dealings are inconceivable, and thus compels us to improvise other forms of intercourse completely distinct from our ordinary ways with things. We must invent unheard-of gestures to fit those singular figures. This new way of life which presupposes the annulment of spontaneous life is precisely what we call understanding and enjoyment of art. Not that this life lacks sentiments and passions, but those sentiments and passions evidently belong to a flora other than that which covers the hills and dales of primary and human life. What those ultra-objects[5] evoke in our inner artist are secondary passions, specifically aesthetic sentiments.

It may be said that, to achieve this result, it would be simpler to dismiss human forms—man, house, mountain—altogether and to construct entirely original figures. But, in the first place, this is not feasible.[6] Even in the most abstract ornamental line a stubborn reminiscence lurks of certain "natural" forms. Secondly—and this is the crucial point—the art of which we speak is inhuman not only because it contains no things human, but also because it is an explicit act of dehumanization. In his escape from the human world the young artist cares less for the "*terminus ad quem*," the startling fauna at which he arrives, than for the "*terminus a quo*," the human aspect which he destroys. The question is not to paint something altogether different from a man, a house, a mountain, but to paint a man who resembles a man as little as possible; a house that preserves of a house exactly what is needed to reveal the metamorphosis; a cone miraculously emerging—as the snake from his slough—from what used to be a mountain. For the modern artist, aesthetic pleasure derives from such a triumph over human matter. That is why he

---

4 This new sensibility is a gift not only of the artist proper but also of his audience. When I said above that the new art is an art for artists I understood by "artists" not only those who produce this art but also those who are capable of perceiving purely artistic values.

5 "Ultraism" is one of the most appropriate names that have been coined to denote the new sensibility.

6 An attempt has been made in this extreme sense—in certain works by Picasso—but it has failed signally.

has to drive home the victory by presenting in each case the strangled victim.

It may be thought a simple affair to fight shy of reality, but it is by no means easy. There is no difficulty in painting or saying things which make no sense whatever, which are unintelligible and therefore nothing. One only needs to assemble unconnected words or to draw random lines.[7] But to construct something that is not a copy of "nature" and yet possesses substance of its own is a feat which presupposes nothing less than genius.

"Reality" constantly waylays the artist to prevent his flight. Much cunning is needed to effect the sublime escape. A reversed Odysseus, he must free himself from his daily Penelope and sail through reefs and rocks to Circe's Faery. When, for a moment, he succeeds in escaping the perpetual ambush, let us not grudge him a gesture of arrogant triumph, a St. George gesture with the dragon prostrate at his feet.

INVITATION TO UNDERSTANDING

The works of art that the nineteenth century favored invariably contain a core of "lived" reality which furnishes the substance, as it were, of the aesthetic body. With this material the aesthetic process works, and its working consists in endowing the human nucleus with glamour and dignity. To the majority of people this is the most natural and the only possible setup of a work of art. Art is reflected life, nature seen through a temperament, representation of human destinies, and so on. But the fact is that our young artists, with no less conviction, maintain the opposite. Must the old always have the last word today while tomorrow infallibly the young win out? For one thing, let us not rant and rave. "*Dove si grida,*" Leonardo da Vinci warns us, "*no é vera scienza.*" "*Neque lugere neque indignari sed intelligere,*" recommends Spinoza. Our firmest convictions are apt to be the most suspect, they mark our limits and our bonds. Life is a petty thing unless it is moved by the indomitable urge to extend its boundaries. Only in proportion as we are desirous of living more do we really live. Obstinately to insist on carrying on within the same familiar horizon betrays weakness and a decline of vital energies. Our horizon is a biological line, a living part of our organism. In times of fullness of life it expands, elastically moving in unison almost with our breathing. When the horizon stiffens it is because it has become fossilized and we are growing old.

It is less obvious than academicians assume that a work of art must consist of human stuff which the Muses comb and groom. Art cannot be reduced to cosmetics. Perception of "lived" reality and perception of artistic form, as I have said before, are essentially incompatible because they call for a different adjustment of our perceptive apparatus. An art that requires such a double seeing is a squinting art. The nineteenth century was remarkably cross-eyed. That is why its products, far from representing a normal type of art, may be said to mark a maximum aberration in the history of taste. All great periods of art have been careful not to let the work revolve about human contents. The imperative of unmitigated realism that dominated the artistic sensibility of the last century must be put down as a freak in aesthetic evolution. It thus appears that the new inspiration, extravagant though it seems, is merely returning, at least in one point, to the royal road of art. For this road is called "will to style." But to stylize means to deform reality, to derealize; style involves dehumanization. And vice versa, there is no other means of stylizing except by dehumanizing. Whereas realism, exhorting the artist faithfully to follow reality, exhorts him to abandon style. A Zurbarán enthusiast, groping for the suggestive word, will declare that the works of this painter have "character." And character and not style is distinctive of the works of Lucas and Sorolla, of Dickens and Galdós. The eighteenth century, on the other hand, which had so little character was a past master of style.

MORE ABOUT THE DEHUMANIZATION OF ART

The young set has declared taboo any infiltration of human contents into art. Now, human contents, the component elements of our daily world, form a hierarchy of three ranks. There is first the realm of persons, second that of living beings, lastly there are the inorganic things. The veto of modern art is more or less apodictic according to the rank the respective object holds in this hierarchy. The first stratum, as it is most human, is most carefully avoided.

This is clearly discernible in music and in poetry. From Beethoven to Wagner music was primarily concerned with expressing personal feelings. The composer erected great structures of sound in which to accommodate his autobiography. Art was, more

---

[7] This was done by the dadaistic hoax. It is interesting to note again (see the above footnote) that the very vagaries and abortive experiments of the new art derive with a certain cogency from its organic principle, thereby giving ample proof that modern art is a unified and meaningful movement.

or less, confession. There existed no way of aesthetic enjoyment except by contagion. "In music," Nietzsche declared, "the passions enjoy themselves." Wagner poured into *Tristan and Isolde* his adultery with Mathilde Wesendonck, and if we want to enjoy this work we must, for a few hours, turn vaguely adulterous ourselves. That darkly stirring music makes us weep and tremble and melt away voluptuously. From Beethoven to Wagner all music is melodrama.

And that is unfair, a young artist would say. It means taking advantage of a noble weakness inherent in man which exposes him to infection from his neighbor's joys and sorrows. Such an infection is no mental phenomenon; it works like a reflex in the same way as the grating of a knife upon glass sets the teeth on edge. It is an automatic effect, nothing else. We must distinguish between delight and titillation. Romanticism hunts with a decoy, it tampers with the bird's fervor in order to riddle him with the pellets of sounds. Art must not proceed by psychic contagion, for psychic contagion is an unconscious phenomenon, and art ought to be full clarity, high noon of the intellect. Tears and laughter are, aesthetically, frauds. The gesture of beauty never passes beyond smiles, melancholy or delighted. If it can do without them, better still. "*Toute maîtrise jette le froid*" (Mallarmé).

There is, to my mind, a good deal of truth in the young artist's verdict. Aesthetic pleasure must be seeing pleasure. For pleasures may be blind or seeing. The drunken man's happiness is blind. Like everything in the world it has a cause, the alcohol; but it has no motive. A man who has won at sweepstakes is happy too, but in a different manner; he is happy "about" something. The drunken man's merriment is hermetically enclosed in itself, he does not know why he is happy. Whereas the joy of the winner consists precisely in his being conscious of a definite fact that motivates and justifies his contentment. He is glad because he is aware of an object that is in itself gladdening. His is a happiness with eyes and which feeds on its motive, flowing, as it were, from the object to the subject.[8]

Any phenomenon that aspires to being mental and not mechanical must bear this luminous character of intelligibility, of motivation. But the pleasure aroused by romantic art has hardly any connection with its content. What has the beauty of music—something obviously located without and beyond myself in the realm of sound—what has the beauty of music to do with that melting mood it may produce in me? Is not this a thorough confusion? Instead of delighting in the artistic object people delight in their own emotions, the work being only the cause and the alcohol of their pleasure. And such a *quid pro quo* is bound to happen whenever art is made to consist essentially in an exposition of "lived" realities. "Lived" realities are too overpowering not to evoke a sympathy which prevents us from perceiving them in their objective purity.

Seeing requires distance. Each art operates a magic lantern that removes and transfigures its objects. On its screen they stand aloof, inmates of an inaccessible world, in an absolute distance. When this derealization is lacking, an awkward perplexity arises: we do not know whether to "live" the things or to observe them.

Madame Tussaud's comes to mind and the peculiar uneasiness aroused by dummies. The origin of this uneasiness lies in the provoking ambiguity with which wax figures defeat any attempt at adopting a clear and consistent attitude toward them. Treat them as living beings, and they will sniggeringly reveal their waxen secret. Take them for dolls, and they seem to breathe an irritated protest. They will not be reduced to mere objects. Looking at them we suddenly feel a misgiving: should it not be they who are looking at us? Till in the end we are sick and tired of those hired corpses. Wax figures are melodrama at its purest.

The new sensibility, it seems to me, is dominated by a distaste for human elements in art very similar to the feelings cultured people have always experienced at Madame Tussaud's, while the mob has always been delighted by that gruesome waxen hoax. In passing we may here ask ourselves a few impertinent questions which we have no intention to answer now. What is behind this disgust at seeing art mixed up with life? Could it be disgust for the human sphere as such, for reality, for life? Or is it rather the opposite: respect for life and unwillingness to confuse it with art, so inferior a thing as art? But what do we mean by calling art an inferior function—divine art, glory of civilization, *fine fleur* of culture, and so forth? As we were saying, these questions are impertinent; let us dismiss them.

In Wagner, melodrama comes to a peak. Now, an artistic form, on reaching its maximum, is likely to

---

[8]   Causation and motivation are two completely different relations. The causes of our states of consciousness are not present in these states; science must ascertain them. But the motive of a feeling, of a volition, of a belief forms part of the act itself. Motivation is a conscious relation.

topple over into its opposite. And thus we find that in Wagner the human voice has already ceased to be the protagonist and is drowned in the cosmic din of the orchestra. However, a more radical change was to follow. Music had to be relieved of private sentiments and purified in an exemplary objectification. This was the deed of Debussy. Owing to him, it has become possible to listen to music serenely, without swoons and tears. All the various developments in the art of music during these last decades move on the ground of the new ultraworldly world conquered by the genius of Debussy. So decisive is this conversion of the subjective attitude into the objective that any subsequent differentiations appear comparatively negligible.[9] Debussy dehumanized music, that is why he marks a new era in the art of music.

The same happened in poetry. Poetry had to be disencumbered. Laden with human matter it was dragging along, skirting the ground and bumping into trees and house tops like a deflated balloon. Here Mallarmé was the liberator who restored to the lyrical poem its ethereal quality and ascending power. Perhaps he did not reach the goal himself. Yet it was he who gave the decisive order: shoot ballast.

For what was the theme of poetry in the romantic century? The poet informed us prettily of his private upper-middle-class emotions, his major and minor sorrows, his yearnings, his religious or political preoccupations, and, in case he was English, his reveries behind his pipe. In one way or another, his ambition was to enhance his daily existence. Thanks to personal genius, a halo of finer substance might occasionally surround the human core of the poem—as for instance in Baudelaire. But this splendor was a by-product. All the poet wished to be was human.

"And that seems objectionable to a young man?" somebody who has ceased to be one asks with suppressed indignation. "What does he want the poet to be? A bird, and ichthyosaurus, a dodecahedron?"

I can't say. However, I believe that the young poet when writing poetry simply wishes to be a poet. We shall yet see that all new art (like new science, new politics—new life, in sum) abhors nothing so much as blurred borderlines. To insist on neat distinctions is a symptom of mental honesty. Life is one thing, art is another—thus the young set think or at least feel—

let us keep the two apart. The poet begins where the man ends. The man's lot is to live his human life, the poet's to invent what is nonexistent. Herein lies the justification of the poetical profession. The poet aggrandizes the world by adding to reality, which is there by itself, the continents of his imagination. Author derives from *auctor,* he who augments. It was the title Rome bestowed upon her generals when they had conquered new territory for the City.

Mallarmé was the first poet in the nineteenth century who wanted to be nothing but a poet. He "eschewed"—as he said himself—"the materials offered by nature" and composed small lyrical objects distinct from the human fauna and flora. This poetry need not be "felt." As it contains nothing human, it contains no cue for emotion either. When a woman is mentioned it is "the woman no one"; when an hour strikes it is "the hour not marked on dials." Proceeding by negatives, Mallarmé's verse muffles all vital resonance and presents us with figures so extramundane that merely looking at them is delight. Among such creatures, what business has the poor face of the man who officiates as poet? None but to disappear, to vanish and to become a pure nameless voice breathing into the air the words—those true protagonists of the lyrical pursuit. This pure and nameless voice, the mere acoustic carrier of the verse, is the voice of the poet who has learned to extricate himself from the surrounding man.

Wherever we look we see the same thing: flight from the human person. The methods of dehumanization are many. Those employed today may differ vastly from Mallarmé's; in fact, I am well aware that his pages are still reached by romantic palpitations. Yet just as modern music belongs to a historical unity that begins with Debussy, all new poetry moves in the direction in which Mallarmé pointed. The landmarks of these two names seem to me essential for charting the main line of the new style above the indentations produced by individual inspirations.

It will not be easy to interest a person under thirty in a book that under the pretext of art reports on the doings of some men and women. To him, such a thing smacks of sociology or psychology. He would accept it gladly if issues were not confused and those facts were told him in sociological and psychological terms. But art means something else to him.

Poetry has become the higher algebra of metaphors.

[9] A more detailed analysis of Debussy's significance with respect to romantic music may be found in the author's above quoted essay "Musicalia."

SURREALISM AND INFRAREALISM

But the metaphor, though the most radical instrument of dehumanization, is certainly not the only one. There are many of varying scope.

The simplest may be described as a change of perspective. From the standpoint of ordinary human life things appear in a natural order, a definite hierarchy. Some seem very important, some less so, and some altogether negligible. To satisfy the desire for dehumanization one need not alter the inherent nature of things. It is enough to upset the value pattern and to produce an art in which the small events of life appear in the foreground with monumental dimensions.

Here we have the connecting link between two seemingly very different manners of modern art, the surrealism of metaphors and what may be called infrarealism. Both satisfy the urge to escape and elude reality. Instead of soaring to poetical heights, art may dive beneath the level marked by the natural perspective. How it is possible to overcome realism by merely putting too fine a point on it and discovering, lens in hand, the micro-structure of life can be observed in Proust, Ramón Gómez de la Serna, Joyce.

Ramón can compose an entire book on bosoms—somebody has called him a new Columbus discovering hemispheres—or on the circus, or on the dawn, or on the Rastro and the Puerta del Sol. The procedure simply consists in letting the outskirts of attention, that which ordinarily escapes notice, perform the main part in life's drama. Giraudoux, Morand, etc., employ (in their several ways) the same aesthetic equipment.

That explains Giraudoux's and Morand's enthusiasm for Proust, as it explains in general the admiration shown by the younger set for a writer so thoroughly of another time. The essential trait Proust's amplitudinous novel may have in common with the new sensibility is this change of perspective: contempt for the old monumental forms of the soul and an unhuman attention to the micro-structure of sentiments, social relations, characters.

INVERSION

In establishing itself in its own right, the metaphor assumes a more or less leading part in the poetical pursuit. This implies that the aesthetic intention has veered round and now points in the opposite direction. Before, reality was overlaid with metaphors by way of ornament; now the tendency is to eliminate the extrapoetical, or real, prop and to "realize" the metaphor, to make it the *res poetica*. This inversion of the aesthetic process is not restricted to the use made of metaphors. It obtains in all artistic means and orders, to the point of determining—in the form of a tendency[10]—the physiognomy of all contemporary art.

The relation between our mind and things consists in that we think the things, that we form ideas about them. We possess of reality, strictly speaking, nothing but the ideas we have succeeded in forming about it. These ideas are like a belvedere from which we behold the world. Each new idea, as Goethe put it, is like a newly developed organ. By means of ideas we see the world, but in a natural attitude of the mind we do not see the ideas—the same as the eye in seeing does not see itself. In other words, thinking is the endeavor to capture reality by means of ideas; the spontaneous movement of the mind goes from concepts to the world.

But an absolute distance always separates the idea from the thing. The real thing always overflows the concept that is supposed to hold it. An object is more and other than what is implied in the idea of it. The idea remains a bare pattern, a sort of scaffold with which we try to get at reality. Yet a tendency resident in human nature prompts us to assume that reality is what we think of it and thus to confound reality and idea by taking in good faith the latter for the thing itself. Our yearning for reality leads us to an ingenuous idealization of reality. Such is the innate predisposition of man.

If we now invert the natural direction of this process; if, turning our back on alleged reality, we take the ideas for what they are—mere subjective patterns—and make them live as such, lean and angular, but pure and transparent; in short, if we deliberately propose to "realize" our ideas—then we have dehumanized and, as it were, derealized them. For ideas are really unreal. To regard them as reality is an idealization, a candid falsification. On the other hand, making them live in their very unreality is—let us express it this way—realizing the unreal as such. In this way we do not move from the mind to the world. On the contrary, we give three-dimensional being to mere patterns, we objectify the subjective, we "worldify" the immanent.

---

[10]   It would be tedious to warn at the foot of each page that each of the features here pointed out as essential to modern art must be understood as existing in the form of a predominant propensity, not of an absolute property.

A traditional painter painting a portrait claims to have got hold of the real person when, in truth and at best, he has set down on the canvas a schematic selection, arbitrarily decided on by his mind, from the innumerable traits that make a living person. What if the painter changed his mind and decided to paint not the real person but his own idea, his pattern, of the person? Indeed, in that case the portrait would be the truth and nothing but the truth, and failure would no longer be inevitable. In foregoing to emulate reality the painting becomes what it authentically is: an image, an unreality.

Expressionism, cubism, etc., are—in varying degree—attempts at executing this decision. From painting things, the painter has turned to painting ideas. He shuts his eyes to the outer world and concentrates upon the subjective images in his own mind.

Notwithstanding its crudeness and the hopeless vulgarity of its subject. Pirandello's drama *Six Personages in Search of an Author* is, from the point of view of an aesthetic theory of the drama, perhaps one of the most interesting recent plays. It supplies an excellent example of this inversion of the artistic attitude which I am trying to describe. The traditional playwright expects us to take his personages for persons and their gestures for the indications of a "human" drama. Whereas here our interest is aroused by some personages as such—that is, as ideas or pure patterns.

Pirandello's drama is, I dare say, the first "drama of ideas" proper. All the others that bore this name were not dramas of ideas, but dramas among pseudo persons symbolizing ideas. In Pirandello's work, the sad lot of each of the six personages is a mere pretext and remains shadowy. Instead, we witness the real drama of some ideas as such, some subjective phantoms gesticulating in an author's mind. The artist's intent to dehumanize is unmistakable, and conclusive proof is given of the possibility of executing it. At the same time, this work provides a model instance for the difficulty of the average public to accommodate their vision to such an inverted perspective. They are looking for the human drama which the artist insists on presenting in an offhand, elusive, mocking manner putting in its place—that is, in the first place—the theatrical fiction itself. Average theater-goers resent that he will not deceive them, and refuse to be amused by that delightful fraud of art—all the more exquisite the more frankly it reveals its fraudulent nature.

ICONOCLASM

It is not an exaggeration to assert that modern paintings and sculptures betray a real loathing of living forms or forms of living beings. The phenomenon becomes particularly clear if the art of these last years is compared with that sublime hour when painting and sculpture emerge from Gothic discipline as from a nightmare and bring forth the abundant, worldwide harvest of the Renaissance. Brush and chisel delight in rendering the exuberant forms of the model—man, animal, or plant. All bodies are welcome, if only life with its dynamic power is felt to throb in them. And from paintings and sculptures organic form flows over into ornament. It is the epoch of the cornucopias whose torrential fecundity threatens to flood all space with round, ripe fruits.

Why is it that the round and soft forms of living bodies are repulsive to the present-day artist? Why does he replace them with geometric patterns? For with all the blunders and all the sleights of hand of cubism, the fact remains that for some time we have been well pleased with a language of pure Euclidean patterns.

The phenomenon becomes more complex when we remember that crazes of this kind have periodically recurred in history. Even in the evolution of prehistoric art we observe that artistic sensibility begins with seeking the living form and then drops it, as though affrighted and nauseated, and resorts to abstract signs, the last residues of cosmic or animal forms. The serpent is stylized into the meander, the sun into the swastica. At times, this disgust at living forms flares up and produces public conflicts. The revolt against the images of Oriental Christianism, the Semitic law forbidding representation of animals—an attitude opposite to the instinct of those people who decorated the cave of Altamira—doubtless originate not only in a religious feeling but also in an aesthetic sensibility whose subsequent influence on Byzantine art is clearly discernible.

A thorough investigation of such eruptions of iconoclasm in religion and art would be of high interest. Modern art is obviously actuated by one of these curious iconoclastic urges. It might have chosen for its motto the commandment of Porphyrius which, in its Manichaean adaptation, was so violently opposed by St. Augustine: *Omne corpus fugiendum est*—where *corpus*, to be sure, must be understood as "living body." A curious contrast indeed with Greek culture which at its height was so deeply in love with living forms.

NEGATIVE INFLUENCE OF THE PAST

This essay, as I have said before, confines itself to delineating the new art by means of some of its distinguishing features. However, it is prompted by a curiosity of wider scope which these pages do not venture to satisfy but only wish to arouse in the reader; whereupon we shall leave him to his own meditations.

Elsewhere[11] I have pointed out that it is in art and pure science, precisely because they are the freest activities and least dependent on social conditions, that the first signs of any changes of collective sensibility become noticeable. A fundamental revision of man's attitude towards life is apt to find its first expression in artistic creation and scientific theory. The fine texture of both these matters renders them susceptible to the slightest breeze of the spiritual trade-winds. As in the country, opening the window of a morning, we examine the smoke rising from the chimney-stacks in order to determine the wind that will rule the day, thus we can, with a similar meteorologic purpose, study the art and science of the young generation.

The first step has been to describe the new phenomenon. Only now that this is done can we proceed to ask of which new general style of life modern art is the symptom and the harbinger. The answer requires an analysis of the causes that have effected this strange about-face in art. Why this desire to dehumanize? Why this disgust at living forms? Like all historical phenomena this too will have grown from a multitude of entangled roots which only a fine flair is capable of detecting. An investigation of this kind would be too serious a task to be attacked here. However, what other causes may exist, there is one which, though perhaps not decisive, is certainly very clear.

We can hardly put too much stress on the influence which at all times the past of art exerts on the future of art. In the mind of the artist a sort of chemical reaction is set going by the clash between his individual sensibility and already existing art. He does not find himself all alone with the world before him; in his relations with the world there always intervenes, like an interpreter, the artistic tradition. What will the reaction of creative originality upon the beauty of previous works be like? It may be positive or negative. Either the artist is in conformity with the past and regards it as his heritage which he feels called upon to perfect; or he discovers that he has a spontaneous indefinable aversion against established and generally acclaimed art. And as in the first case he will be pleased to settle down in the customary forms and repeat some of their sacred patterns, thus he will, in the second, not only deviate from established tradition but be equally pleased to give to his work an explicit note of protest against the time-honored norms.

The latter is apt to be overlooked when one speaks of the influence of the past on the present. That a work of a certain period may be modeled after works of another previous period has always been easily recognized. But to notice the negative influence of the past and to realize that a new style has not infrequently grown out of a conscious and relished antagonism to traditional styles seems to require somewhat of an effort.

As it is, the development of art from Romanticism to this day cannot be understood unless this negative mood of mocking aggressiveness is taken into account as a factor of aesthetic pleasure. Baudelaire praises the black Venus precisely because the classical is white. From then on the successive styles contain an ever increasing dose of derision and disparagement until in our day the new art consists almost exclusively of protests against the old. The reason is not far to seek. When an art looks back on many centuries of continuous evolution without major hiatuses or historical catastrophes its products keep on accumulating, and the weight of tradition increasingly encumbers the inspiration of the hour. Or to put it differently, an ever growing mass of traditional styles hampers the direct and original communication between the nascent artist and the world around him. In this case one of two things may happen. Either tradition stifles all creative power—as in Egypt, Byzantium, and the Orient in general—or the effect of the past on the present changes its sign and a long epoch appears in which the new art, step by step, breaks free of the old which threatened to smother it. The latter is typical of Europe whose futuristic instinct, predominant throughout its history, stands in marked contrast to the irremediable traditionalism of the Orient.

A good deal of what I have called dehumanization and disgust for living forms is inspired by just such an aversion against the traditional intepretation of realities. The vigor of the assault stands in inverse proportion to the distance. Keenest contempt is felt for nineteenth century procedures although

---

[11] Cf. The author's book *The Modern Theme* (The C. W. Daniel Company, London: 1931), p. 26.

they contain already a noticeable dose of opposition to older styles. On the other hand, the new sensibility exhibits a somewhat suspicious enthusiasm for art that is most remote in time and space, for prehistoric or savage primitivism. In point of fact, what attracts the modern artist in those primordial works is not so much their artistic quality as their candor; that is, the absence of tradition.

If we now briefly consider the question: What type of life reveals itself in this attack on past art? we come upon a strange and stirring fact. To assail all previous art, what else can it mean than to turn against Art itself? For what is art, concretely speaking, if not such art as has been made up to now?

Should that enthusiasm for pure art be but a mask which conceals surfeit with art and hatred for it? But, how can such a thing come about? Hatred of art is unlikely to develop as an isolated phenomenon; it goes hand in hand with hatred of science, hatred of State, hatred, in sum, of civilization as a whole. Is it conceivable that modern Western man bears a rankling grudge against his own historical essence? Does he feel something akin to the *odium professionis* of medieval monks—that aversion, after long years of monastic discipline, against the very rules that had shaped their lives?[12]

This is the moment prudently to lay down one's pen and let a flock of questions take off on their winged course.

DOOMED TO IRONY

When we discovered that the new style taken in its most general aspect is characterized by a tendency to eliminate all that is human and to preserve only the purely artistic elements, this seemed to betray a great enthusiasm for art. But when we then walked around the phenomenon and looked at it from another angle we came upon an unexpected grimace of surfeit or disdain. The contradiction is obvious and must be strongly stressed. It definitely indicates that modern art is of an ambiguous nature which, as a matter of fact, does not surprise us; for ambiguous have been all important issues of these current years.

[12] It would be interesting to analyze the psychological mechanisms through which yesterday's art negatively affects the art of today. One is obvious: ennui. Mere repetition of a style has a blunting and tiring effect. In his *Principles of Art History; the Problem of the Development of Style in Later Art* (London: Bell, 1932) Heinrich Wölfflin mentions the power of boredom which has ever again mobilized art and compelled it to invent new forms. And the same applies to literature, only more so. Cicero still said *"latine loqui"* for "speaking Latin"; but in the fifth century Apollinaris Sidonius resorted to *"latialiter insusurrare."* For too many centuries the same had been said with the same words.

A brief analysis of the political development in Europe would reveal the same intrinsic ambiguity.

However, in the case of art, the contradiction between love and hatred for one and the same thing will appear somewhat mitigated after a closer inspection of present-day artistic production.

The first consequence of the retreat of art upon itself is a ban on all pathos. Art laden with "humanity" had become as weighty as life itself. It was an extremely serious affair, almost sacred. At times—in Schopenhauer and Wagner—it aspired to nothing less than to save mankind. Whereas the modern inspiration—and this is a strange fact indeed—is invariably waggish. The waggery may be more or less refined, it may run the whole gamut from open clownery to a slight ironical twinkle, but it is always there. And it is not that the content of the work is comical—that would mean a relapse into a mode or species of the "human" style—but that, whatever the content, the art itself is jesting. To look for fiction as fiction—which, we have said, modern art does—is a proposition that cannot be executed except with one's tongue in one's cheek. Art is appreciated precisely became it is recognized as a farce. It is this trait more than any other that makes the works of the young so incomprehensible to serious people of less progressive taste. To them modern painting and music are sheer "farce"— in the bad sense of the word— and they will not be convinced that to be a farce may be precisely the mission and the virtue of art. A "farce" in the bad sense of the word it would be if the modern artist pretended to equal status with the "serious" artists of the past, and a cubist painting expected to be extolled as solemnly and all but religiously as a statue by Michelangelo. But all he does is to invite us to look at a piece of art that is a joke and that essentially makes fun of itself. For this is what the facetious quality of the modern inspiration comes down to. Instead of deriding other persons or things—without a victim no comedy—the new art ridicules art itself.

And why be scandalized at this? Art has never shown more clearly its magic gift than in this flout at itself. Thanks to this suicidal gesture art continues to be art, its self-negation miraculously bringing about its preservation and triumph.

I much doubt that any young person of our time can be impressed by a poem, a painting, or a piece of music that is not flavored with a dash of irony.

Nor is this ironical reflection of art upon itself entirely new as an idea and a theory. In the beginning of the last century a group of German romanticists, under the leadership of the two brothers Schlegel, pronounced irony the foremost aesthetic category, their reasons being much the same as those of our young artists. Art has no right to exist if, content to reproduce reality, it uselessly duplicates it. Its mission is to conjure up imaginary worlds. That can be done only if the artist repudiates reality and by this act places himself above it. Being an artist means ceasing to take seriously that very serious person we are when we are not an artist.

This inevitable dash of irony, it is true, imparts to modern art a monotony which must exasperate patience herself. But be that as it may, the contradiction between surfeit and enthusiasm now appears resolved. The first is aroused by art as a serious affair, the second is felt for art that triumphs as a farce, laughing off everything, itself included—much as in a system of mirrors which indefinitely reflect one another no shape is ultimate, all are eventually ridiculed and revealed as pure images.

ART A THING OF NO CONSEQUENCE

All we have ascertained so far will now appear integrated in the most acute, serious, and deep-seated symptom shown by modern art—a strange feature, indeed, and which requires cautious consideration. What I mean is difficult to express for several reasons, but mainly because it is a matter of accurate formulation.

To the young generation art is a thing of no consequence.—The sentence is no sooner written than it frightens me since I am well aware of all the different connotations it implies. It is not that to any random person of our day art seems less important than it seemed to previous generations, but that the artist himself regards his art as a thing of no consequence. But then again this does not accurately describe the situation. I do not mean to say that the artist makes light of his work and his profession; but they interest him precisely because they are of no transcendent importance. For a real understanding of what is happening let us compare the role art is playing today with the role it used to play thirty years ago and in general throughout the last century. Poetry and music then were activities of an enormous caliber. In view of the downfall of religion and the inevitable relativism of science, art was expected to take upon itself nothing less than the salvation of mankind. Art was important for two reasons: on account of its subjects which dealt with the profoundest problems of humanity, and on account of its own

significance as a human pursuit from which the species derived its justification and dignity. It was a remarkable sight, the solemn air with which the great poet or the musical genius appeared before the masses—the air of a prophet and founder of religion, the majestic pose of a statesman responsible for the state of the world.

A present-day artist would be thunderstruck, I suspect, if he were trusted with so enormous a mission and, in consequence, compelled to deal in his work with matters of such scope. To his mind, the kingdom of art commences where the air feels lighter and things, free from formal fetters, begin to cut whimsical capers. In this universal pirouetting he recognizes the best warrant for the existence of the Muses. Were art to redeem man, it could do so only by saving him from the seriousness of life and restoring him to an unexpected boyishness. The symbol of art is seen again in the magic flute of the Great God Pan which makes the young goats frisk at the edge of the grove.

All modern art begins to appear comprehensible and in a way great when it is interpreted as an attempt to instill youthfulness into an ancient world. Other styles must be interpreted in connection with dramatic social or political movements, or with profound religious and philosophical currents. The new style only asks to be linked to the triumph of sports and games. It is of the same kind and origin with them.

In these last few years we have seen almost all caravels of seriousness founder in the tidal wave of sports that floods the newspaper pages. Editorials threaten to be sucked into the abyss of their headlines, and across the surface victoriously sail the yachts of the regattas. Cult of the body is an infallible symptom of a leaning toward youth, for only the young body is lithe and beautiful. Whereas cult of the mind betrays the resolve to accept old age, for the mind reaches plenitude only when the body begins to decline. The triumph of sport marks the victory of the values of youth over the values of age. Note in this context the success of the motion picture, a preeminently corporeal art.

In my generation the manners of old age still enjoyed great prestige. So anxious were boys to cease being boys that they imitated the stoop of their elders. Today children want to prolong their childhood, and boys and girls their youth. No doubt, Europe is entering upon an era of youthfulness.

Nor need this fact surprise us. History moves in long biological rhythms whose chief phases necessarily are brought about not by secondary causes relating to details but by fundamental factors and primary forces of a cosmic nature. It is inconceivable that the major and, as it were, polar differences inherent in the living organism—sex and age—should not decisively mold the profile of the times. Indeed, it can be easily observed that history is rhythmically swinging back and forth between these two poles, stressing the masculine qualities in some epochs and the feminine in others, or exalting now a youthful deportment and then again maturity and old age.

The aspect European existence is taking on in all orders of life points to a time of masculinity and youthfulness. For a while women and old people will have to cede the rule over life to boys; no wonder that the world grows increasingly informal.

All peculiarities of modern art can be summed up in this one feature of its renouncing its importance—a feature which, in its turn, signifies nothing less than that art has changed its position in the hierarchy of human activities and interests. These activities and interests may be represented by a series of concentric circles whose radii measure the dynamic distances from the axis of life where the supreme desires are operating. All human matters—vital and cultural—revolve in their several orbits about the throbbing heart of the system. Art which—like science and politics—used to be very near the axis of enthusiasm, that backbone of our person, has moved toward the outer rings. It has lost none of its attributes, but it has become a minor issue.

The trend toward pure art betrays not arrogance, as is often thought, but modesty. Art that has rid itself of human pathos is a thing without consequence—just art with no other pretenses.

CONCLUSION

Isis *myrionoma,* Isis of the ten thousand names, the Egyptians called their goddess. And a thing with ten thousand names all reality is, in a way. Its components and its facets are countless. Is it not brazen to attempt a definition of any thing, of the humblest thing, with a few names? A stroke of luck it would be if the attributes here pointed out among an infinite number were in fact the decisive ones. The odds are particularly poor since the object is a nascent reality which just begins its course through space.

Thus chances are that this attempt to analyze modern art is full of errors. Now that I am about to conclude it the place it has been taking up in my mind is filled with the hope that others may tackle these problems more successfully. Among many tongues may be divided the calling of the ten thousand names.

But it would not mean improving upon my errors if one tried to correct them by pointing out this or that particular feature omitted in my analysis. Artists are apt to make this mistake when, speaking of their art, they fail to take the step back that affords an ample view of the facts. There can be no doubt that the best approximation to truth is contrived by a formula that in one unified, harmonious turn encompasses the greatest number of particular facts—like a loom which with one stroke interlaces a thousand threads.

I have been moved exclusively by the delight of trying to understand—and neither by ire nor by enthusiasm. I have sought to ascertain the meaning of the new intents of art and that, of course, presupposes an attitude of preconceived benevolence. But is it possible to approach a subject in another mind and not condemn it to barrenness?

It may be said that the new art has so far produced nothing worth while, and I am inclined to think the same. I have proposed to extract from the work of the young the intention which is the juicy part, and I have disregarded the realization. Who knows what may come out of this budding style? The task it sets itself is enormous; it wants to create from nought. Later, I expect, it will be content with less and achieve more.

But whatever their shortcomings, the young artists have to be granted one point: there is no turning back. All the doubts cast upon the inspiration of those pioneers may be justified, and yet they provide no sufficient reason for condemning them. The objections would have to be supplemented by something positive: a suggestion of another way for art different from dehumanization and yet not coincident with the beaten and wornout paths.

It is easy to protest that it is always possible to produce art within the bounds of a given tradition. But this comforting phrase is of no use to the artist who, pen or chisel in hand, sits waiting for a concrete inspiration.

QUESTIONS FOR REVIEW AND FURTHER THOUGHT

1. Critically compare and contrast the view of Monroe C. Beardsley in "In Defense of Aesthetic Value" with that of Innocent C. Onyewuenyi in "Traditional African Aesthetics: A Philosophical Perspective." What does Beardsley mean by "aesthetic value"? Is this notion applicable to African art, given Onyewuenyi's account of it? Do you agree with either of these philosophers' brand of aesthetics and the artistic implications that follow from it? Why or why not? Defend your position against objections you find plausible.

2. Try to formulate a distinction between arts and crafts. Does your formulation apply to African art as described by Onyewuenyi? Can any such formulation so apply? Why or why not? Raise some plausible objections to your position, and then defend your views against those objections.

3. What is the "intentional fallacy" according to William K. Wimsatt and Monroe C. Beardsley? Do you think there is such a fallacy? Why or why not? Defend your position against objections you consider plausible.

4. Taking account of Onyewuenyi's discussion of African art, do you think that all judgments purporting to assess artworks must be disinterested in the sense that an artwork's usefulness for our individual purposes is irrelevant to its aesthetic value? Why or why not? Formulate some objections to your position that seem plausible to you and critically discuss them.

5. Given Ortega y Gasset's account of modern Western art, do you think emotions can have any role in this art? If you think they can, explain why and address some plausible objections to your position. If you think emotions cannot have any such role, explain why, why someone else might think they can, and why their thinking would be mistaken.

6. Critically compare and contrast Beardsley's own notion of aesthetic value with that which he attributes to Goodman. Which position do you think is sounder? Why? Defend your views against objections you consider plausible.

7. Critically compare and contrast the view that beauty is in the eye of the beholder with the view that beauty is in the object. Can you think of a more defensible view of beauty than either of these? What is it and why do you find it more defensible? Formulate plausible objections to your position and critically discuss them.

8. In making aesthetic judgments, people not only use such adjectives as "beautiful" and "fine"; they also (perhaps more frequently) use such expressions as "This musical passage is incoherent" and "His images are precise." Does this tend to support or undermine functionalism in aesthetics? Give reasons for your answer. In doing so, defend it against objections you find plausible.

9. Suppose a dance student says: "This is how one should dance this piece," and then proceeds to demonstrate it. What sense can one make of the student's remark? Is it a mere expression of the student's taste? Can the student's remark be mistaken? If so, what does that mean for subjectivism in aesthetics? If not, why not, and how would you respond to the objection that your position cannot distinguish between good and bad dancing at all?

10. Consider the following passage from Onyewuenyi's selection:

> If a sculpture of an ancestor for purposes of worship in an Igbo Society is scarified . . . , it would not be accepted by the Igbo and would have no aesthetic recognition simply because it is not true and meaningful. It does not fulfill the function which an Igbo society expects of it. For, the Igbos do not scarify their bodies. . . . Rather the same scarified Muntu-face may be aesthetically beautiful to the Yoruba or other tribes who culturally scarify their bodies.

> Suppose that, after some study, a member of the Igbo culture says of a scarified Muntu-face used by the Yoruba: "I can aesthetically appreciate that mask." What can this person mean in making this statement? Could a member of the Yoruba culture mean the same thing in making the same statement? Is there any aesthetic statement that both could meaningfully make about the mask? What implications does your position have for aesthetic judgments? Can they be cross-cultural? Why or why not? Formulate some objections to your position that seem plausible to you, and critically discuss them.

11. What are the two groups in which, according to Ortega y Gasset, modern Western art separates human beings? Can this separation ever be overcome? Critically discuss your position by reference to its implications for art.

12. What role does irony play in modern Western art according to Ortega y Gasset? What, if anything, does it entail about the nature, aesthetic value, and social significance of modern art? Defend your position against objections you consider plausible.

13. Do any authors in Part V engage in cross-cultural reflection and dialogue to any extent? Do they, for example, try to adapt categories used in other cultures to their own cultural context? Who, how, and how fruitfully?

14. Consider those authors in Part V who do not engage in cross-cultural reflection. How could they have done so while remaining faithful to the views they espouse?

15. Consider the selections in Part V and try to establish which ones include discussions that overlap with matters discussed in Parts II, III, and IV.

PART

VI

What Are Philosophy's Prospects Today?

This book began with a discussion of the nature and conceptions of philosophy that made plain the great variety of motives that guide philosophical inquiry. The intervening parts evidenced the multiplicity and complexity of philosophical problems and pursuits. They also demonstrated the recurrence and seeming universality of some of these problems and pursuits and the culture-bound or historically dictated character of others. These unwieldy features of philosophy have prompted the concern—and sometimes the impatient conclusion—that philosophical problems are intractable and the philosophic enterprise is hopeless. The selections in Part VI address this concern and various positions it has given rise to.

Our first selection, Marjorie Grene's "Puzzled Notes on a Puzzling Profession," sets the tone for our inquiry into philosophy's current prospects. Grene describes five different conceptions of philosophy and formulates predictions about their future. One of these conceptions is philosophy *as a research field*. This she describes as follows:

> For some practitioners, philosophy appears to be a "research" field, left over when all the obvious (and even some non-obvious) sciences have split off from us. On this view, every "trained" "philosopher" can and should contribute to the advance of something called philosophical knowledge.

Against this view, Grene takes the position that "philosophy, whatever it is, is not a research subject." While advances in scientific knowledge are evident from the appearance of new topics that were not present at all before—say, genetic engineering in the 1980s—philosophical topics do not change fundamentally, though discussions of them may become sharper.

One might object that the contrast between science and philosophy is not as sharp as Grene makes it out to be. For one thing, some of philosophy's topics do change, though much more slowly than topics in science. For example, the distinction between analytic and synthetic statements and that between logical and physical possibility were not clear—or even discussed—before Hume and Kant. For another, though many topics in science change rapidly, others that are more theoretical recur or endure. For instance, it took a long time to formulate the theory of evolution and it was many more decades before it was generally accepted and creationism was generally abandoned. To take another instance, there is reason to believe, as we stated in Part I, that the concept of entropy and the problems it poses, which are quite current in twentieth-century science, can be traced back to Anaximander. In fact, this topic has been a recurrent one in science for as long as the topic of free will has been in philosophy. The upshot of these parallelisms is not that philosophy is a research field exactly like science. Rather, it is that much philosophical inquiry approaches scientific inquiry when the latter is highly theoretical. Hence, if philosophy is a research field, it is so in the manner in which theoretical physics and theoretical biology are research fields.[1]

One might respond that a fundamental difference remains: scientific problems, however theoretical, are soluble; while philosophical problems are not. Grene, however, believes that this position is anachronistic:

> This conception corresponds, perhaps, to an old-fashioned view of philosophy as dealing with the big problems: the good, the true, the beautiful. Clearly, it also has some connection with Aristotle's view of first philosophy as treating the principles of the other sciences. But it isn't just the presuppositions of the sciences that we reflect on; it's the presuppositions of everyday life as well.

Indeed, the growing philosophical concern with concrete problems in such areas as the environment, technology, health care, and business supports Grene's position.[2] It also supports her further contention that philosophy minds "other people's business, or everybody's business." This raises the obvious question: How can philosophy specialize in everything, when scientific specializations are increasingly circumscribed?

One might respond to this question in two ways. First, it is more accurate to say that philosophy deals, not with *everything*, but with *anything*. That is, though it aims at comprehensiveness, just as science does, it can branch out into particular areas of inquiry. Second, as the growing philosophical interest in environmental, technological, health-care, and business problems indicates, philosophy (unlike science) often minds everyone's business with a predominantly practical concern. This is in accordance with philosophy's initial, and abiding, search for wisdom, which involves both the grounds on which beliefs are held and the manner in which they are reflected in our actions. In this sense, even if particular philosophical inquiries resemble scientific research, philosophy as an enterprise carried out by a variety of practitioners in various historical periods and cultural settings is, because of its connection with actual practice, closer to an art. Grene says:

> I have thought recurrently . . . that philosophy, being so plainly not a science, is an art: an art that uses for its medium not stone or paint and canvas or sound, but argument. Now if that is correct, we ought to distinguish between philosophers and teachers of philosophy rather as we do between, say, novelists or poets or playwrights and teachers of literature. I think there's a lot in this view; but the trouble is that even we ordinary teaching types want to teach the real philosophers *philosophically*, and what does that mean if we're not philosophers ourselves?

One might respond that to distinguish between novelists or playwrights and teachers of literature is to distinguish, not between two separate groups of people, but between two distinct but not necessarily unconnected roles. That is, the distinction does not entail that teachers of literature do not write literature. Indeed, many do write novels, poems, or plays. Analogously, to distinguish between philosophers and teachers of philosophy does not entail that teachers of philosophy do no philosophy. Granted, some do not, and this may be a reason for saying that they are not good teachers of philosophy: they cannot teach it philosophically. Yet nothing in the above distinction entails that teachers of philosophy cannot teach their subject philosophically. All this requires is engaging in philosophy as a branch of inquiry. It in no way requires philosophical originality or influence, let alone being recognized as original or influential by other original or influential philosophers.

Yet, though philosophy as the love of wisdom is connected with practice and is therefore more an art than a science, it proceeds in accordance with rules of inquiry and practice that are not crucial (or necessarily even present) in any art. These rules concern matters of definition, inference, theory construction, and communication that set constraints, not just on the arguments used in philosophy, but also on the manner in which, and the purposes for which, they are to be used. For example, the manner should be nondogmatic; and the purpose should be not simply to convince, but also to establish what views pass the test of critical scrutiny, how they can be balanced against each other in our overall conception of the world, and how this balance gets reflected in our actions.

This brings up Grene's fourth conception of philosophy:

> We may consider philosophy in our tradition as a dialogue about fundamental problems that has been going on since Thales, a dialogue in which we in our time want to take our place. . . . Reflecting on the character of our particular culture, and when our culture permits it, comparing it with others, we are . . . attempting to criticize and improve our fundamental beliefs. This view . . . supports an emphasis . . . on the history of philosophy in philosophical education and in philosophical reflection.

This position is a cognate of that underlying this book's discussions and exemplified in many of its selections. It makes room for various subdialogues, all informed by the overarching search for wisdom—that is, for a sense of balance, which gives all perspectives and reasons their due, in all that we believe and do. For example, it makes room for highly theoretical dialogues (like those in theoretical physics—e.g., in cosmology), that aim at criticizing and improving our fundamental beliefs concerning such things as causality, free will, and the nature of the universe. This has a bearing on philosophy's characteristic search for wisdom, for it is conducive to the acquisition of a clearer, more balanced conception of our place in the universe, without which we cannot act wisely. It also seems to make room for what Grene calls "the underlaborer view" of philosophy, where philosophers of biology, for example, work with scientists to help them with conceptual difficulties so that they can solve problems in their field (biology). Here again, philosophy approaches science, and there is progressive problem solving.

The underlaborer conception and the foundationalist tradition within which it fits are criticized by the contemporary philosopher Kai Nielsen in the next selection, "Philosophy as Critical Theory." Nielsen describes this conception as follows:

> The underlaborer's conception of philosophy goes well with a commitment to a type of analytic philosophy that has no systematic pretensions but is content instead to dispel conceptual confusions emerging out of everyday life and science. We are to do this, it is often claimed, with the aid of sharp new analytical tools that philosophy as conceptual or logical analysis provides.

He grants that "philosophers with a good analytic training have a developed capacity for drawing distinctions, spotting assumptions, digging out unclarities, seeing relationships between propositions . . . and setting out arguments perspicuously." But this is quite different from granting the existence of a philosophers' consensus on a distinctive philosophical method. In fact, there is no such consensus, and Nielsen notes the abilities he enumerated for philosophers with good analytic training are also displayed by "lawyers, classicists, economists and mathematicians with a good training." That is, these abilities do not amount to true expertise, let alone to distinctly philosophical expertise.

Grene could respond that the difference is not one of abilities, but of manner and purposes for which the abilities are put to use. She could claim that philosophers use these abilities in a nondogmatic manner, not simply to convince, but to establish what views pass the test of critical scrutiny. Yet, though this function is commendable, it is hardly distinctive of philosophy. Other branches of inquiry—economics and mathematics, for example—also display these functions.

Still, by contrast with other branches of inquiry, philosophy aims at as much comprehensiveness as can humanly be attained, or at least at integrating the results and activities of these other branches of inquiry into an overall conception of our world. This is not to say that philosophy aims at providing a privileged view of the universe. It is simply to say that philosophy aims at formulating, clarifying, and dealing with problems about the nature and mutual relations of various areas of our world and about our beliefs, values, and norms.

Nielsen is skeptical of comprehensiveness in philosophy. And he has little, if anything, to say about the philosophical aims just described. His position is more limited:

> I want to suggest that there may be a way that philosophy might transform itself in a way that would answer to our unschooled reflective hopes. It would involve (a) giving up all pretensions to autonomy and instead interlocking philosophy fully with the human sciences and (b) taking the resolution of the problems of human life to be very centrally a part of philosophy's reason for being.

Nielsen indicates that our unschooled reflective hopes are involved "in the nondiscipline-based folk conception of philosophy . . . whose continued existence is not threatened whatever philosophers may do." He construes this folk conception of philosophy "quite professionally" as

> an attempt on the part of human beings to make sense of their lives and to come to see, as far as that is possible, what, in our time and place, with whatever real possibilities we

have before us, would be the best sorts of lives for us to live, including what forms of community would be most desirable, and in turn to place this normative picture in a larger framework of how things hang together.

This conception is not in conflict with that supported in this book's discussions and exemplified in many of its selections. Neither is it in conflict with Nielsen's. In fact, he suggests that professional philosophers pursue the same aims as folk philosophy, and for the same reasons, but be "more rigorous, more argument-based and more discipline-oriented." He says:

> What I am advocating . . . is a holistic social theory which is at once a descriptive-explanatory social theory, an interpretive social theory and a normative critique. Departing radically from the philosophical tradition, it will be an empirical theory. Elements of the social sciences will be a very central part, although, in light of the importance of giving a narrative account of who we were, are, and might become, much of the social science utilized may be historiographical.

As far as it goes, this is sound doctrine. Yet, if the problems of human life are to become central to philosophy, the interlocking Nielsen suggests must involve the nonacademic world as well as the social sciences. Otherwise, philosophy will be unable to address problems thoroughly and realistically. Some concerns will likely fall through the conceptual and methodological cracks of the languages of philosophy, academic disciplines, politics, business, technology, and so on. The general public would be unrepresented and their concerns might well be missed.

Some attempts to bring nonacademics into specific interdisciplinary inquiries including philosophy have been carried out—for example, in health-care ethics through hospitals' ethics committees. The results are instructive and point to problems likely to arise. These concern the process of selecting participants; the perceived incompatibilities between disciplinary loyalties, loyalties to particular traditions, or personal styles; academicians' fears of being coopted by representatives of government, industry, or labor, and their uneasiness about becoming entangled in conflicts among these three factions; and the unwillingness on the part of practitioners of this or that profession or trade to submit their practices to academic or public scrutiny.[3]

These conflicts should be expected. Philosophy, after all, is not an apolitical activity, especially in the highly institutionalized environment in which it is pursued today. Squarely acknowledging and sincerely addressing such conflicts is central to the development of philosophy along the lines suggested in this book. This is even more crucial when the people involved have different cultural or social backgrounds. Then it is not simply necessary to integrate the concepts, methods, and practices of different disciplines, or of academic with nonacademic approaches to problems. It is necessary to establish a fruitful interplay between different—sometimes sharply different—cultures or social sectors.

Our next selection, "The Actual Function of Philosophy in Latin America" by the contemporary Latin American philosopher Leopoldo Zea, discounts nationalistic approaches that attempt to eliminate everything European from Latin American culture. Zea argues as follows:

> This position is wrong because, whether we want it or not, we are the children of European culture. From Europe we have received our cultural framework, what could

be called our structure: language, religion, customs; in a word, our conception of life and world is European.

To say that Latin Americans are the children of Europe does not mean that they should strive to be like Europeans. Indeed, Zea cautions against attempting to do European philosophy in Latin America, for this amounts to trying to "adjust the Latin American circumstance to a conception of the world inherited from Europe, rather than adjusting that conception of the world to the Latin American circumstance." As Zea indicates, this can only result in "a gross imitation."

But what is the Latin American circumstance Zea mentions? Is there some circumstance common to countries as disparate as Mexico and Uruguay, Argentina and Suriname? Zea says that language, religion, and customs are similar throughout Latin America. But one could point out that these are not as homogeneous as Zea makes them out to be. For example, Spanish dialects differ sharply from region to region in Latin America, often even the same country. Brazil's official language is Portuguese, while that of Paraguay is an Indian language: Guaraní. Quechua is a major language in Ecuador, Peru, Bolivia, and northwestern Argentina, and Guaraní, not Spanish, is the predominant language in the Argentinian province of Misiones and in much of the Argentinian province of Corrientes. The main languages of Guyana are English and East Indian; while the language of Suriname is Dutch and that of French Guiana French. Catholicism is the predominant religion throughout the region, but Hinduism and Islam are predominant in Suriname. More significantly, even in those Latin American countries where Catholicism is the officially dominant religion, there is a question of who converted whom. Anthropologists have reported observing Mayan ceremonies in the main area of a Guatemalan Catholic church while mass was being conducted in a corner. In Bolivia, statues of the Pachamama (Mother Earth) have been found together with those of saints in Catholic churches. Finally, customs are immensely varied, not just between countries, but within them. Indeed, there is good reason to think that many, if not all, Latin American countries are not nations in the sense that European countries are. In their pronounced regionalism, they more closely resemble the United States.

Zea could respond that, though varied, the language, religions, and customs of Latin America have a family resemblance that helps distinguish Latin American culture from the cultures of, say, Europe or Africa. However, in his account, these languages, religions, and customs constitute the cultural framework received from Europe, not the circumstance to which this framework must be adjusted.

Another possible answer is that the Latin American circumstance consists of various components—from the geographical and economic to the technological and historical—that are present to different degrees in all Latin American countries. The truth or significance of this answer is a matter for empirical investigation. In any case, it does not tell us exactly what these components are. Still another, historical, answer is one that Zea indicates: Latin American cultures are crucially characterized by an ambivalence concerning Europe—and, one might add, other outside sources of cultural influences.

Now, this ambivalence offers little prospect for Latin American philosophical approaches that are supposed to start by defining the essence of Latin American culture. What can be done is to characterize, as Zea does, some goals for Latin American philosophy. One of these is clarifying the relations between Latin American and

European cultures. Some others are contributing to the formulation, clarification, and resolution of philosophical problems about such things as knowledge, reality, space and time, God, life, death, freedom, and the relations between individuals and society. Zea proposes that these goals be pursued both without attempting to imitate European philosophy and without turning philosophy into a parochial, strictly Latin American affair. He says: "One must attempt to do purely and simply philosophy, because what is Latin American will arise by itself." It is only in this way, he argues, that Latin American philosophers can accomplish their goal: to find new values and new approaches within the context of universal culture.

This position calls for a modicum of understanding in cross-cultural relations and philosophy. But since this understanding is often precisely what is lacking, nationalism and separatism usually prevail. For example, imagine an international congress of philosophy held in Latin America. Suppose it features talks by philosophers from the Americas who use Western categories and concepts, as well as talks by Aymará philosophers from Peru who reject the European conceptual framework and proceed to philosophize out of the Aymará conceptual framework. Given the position developed in this book, according to which philosophy as the search for wisdom is incompatible with parochialism, these philosophers should not be ignored. Rather, their reasons for rejecting the European conceptual framework should be subjected to critical scrutiny. They should not be rejected as people who are not doing philosophy—or even not doing "Latin American philosophy"—simply because they use only Aymará concepts. This would be parochial. And if philosophers working within the Anglo-American and European traditions should refuse to attend talks given by the Aymará philosophers because they devalue them as philosophers without even deigning to hear them out, their parochialism would verge on cultural imperialism. If, in a true philosophical vein, one is determined to avoid parochialism and to overcome cross-cultural misunderstandings, how could a fruitful cross-cultural dialogue be initiated in the case just described?

In our next selection, "Playfulness, 'World'-Travelling, and Loving Perception," the Latin American philosopher María Lugones offers some suggestions for enhancing understanding both in cross-cultural relations and in relations between men and women.

> I am particularly interested here in those many cases in which White/Anglo women do one or more of the following to women of color: they ignore us, ostracize us, render us invisible, stereotype us, leave us completely alone, interpret us as crazy. All of this *while we are in their midst.* The more independent I am, the more independent I am left to be. Their world and their integrity do not require me at all.

Lugones sees that separatism might be a solution to this situation, but, she says, "many of us have to work among White/Anglo folk and our best shot at recognition has seemed to be among White/Anglo women." What, then, could help? Lugones recommends what she calls "'world'-travelling."

This notion needs clarification. The worlds Lugones is talking about cannot be utopias—mere possible worlds in the philosophical sense—but must have some flesh-and-blood people in them right now. However, dead or imaginary people (like Martin Luther King or Davy Crockett) may exist in such a world if they exist in the imaginations of flesh-and-blood people who actually live in that world. Furthermore, a world can, but need not, be a society or a large group. Moreover, it need not be complete, nor do all its members have to understand or hold the particular construction that makes them be what they are.

What does Lugones mean by "construction"? The following example may help to explain it. An Argentinian of Italian descent typically grows up in Argentina believing that he or she is a Caucasian of Italian descent who was born in Argentina. If this person moves to the United States, a process that can be called "racialization" begins to take place as soon as the person must fill out a form asking for his or her ethnicity. In the United States, being from a country where the predominant language is (as in Argentina) Spanish legally makes one into a Hispanic. This is a construction—and one that the Argentinian may have difficulty understanding, let alone accepting.

This example may also help explain what Lugones means by "travelling" between worlds. It is not necessary to go to another country in order to travel between worlds. Nor is it sufficient. Think of those tourists who, camera in hand, visit Naples in Italy or Rio in Brazil, expecting things around them to be like what they had at home. They do not wish to experience the local, "foreign" realities of transportation, bathrooms, and climate. In order to travel in Lugones's sense, one needs to be willing to shift from who one is at home to who one is perceived to be in the different world. Lugones says: "The shift from being one person to being a different person is what I call 'travel.'"

This is something that expatriates characteristically experience, though often unwillingly. As a result of their journey away from their original world, and of the manner in which they are perceived in their new world, they have changed.[4] Anthropologists, too, experience something analogous to what Lugones calls "'world'-travelling." This type of activity may help people deal with some of the problems of developing philosophy along cross-cultural lines. Anthropologists, because of their training, have a great deal to contribute to such a project.

Lugones holds that noncompetitive playfulness is a very helpful attitude for engaging in this activity. But is playfulness equally effective across personality differences and cultural boundaries, or is this a quality bounded by culture and personality type?

Our last selection, "Cultural Philosophy as a Philosophy of Integration and Tolerance" by the African philosopher K. C. Anyanwu, explores some of the problems we have just been discussing. The approach he thinks best suited for dealing with them is the philosophy of culture. Anyanwu sees the main problems facing human beings in the twentieth century as "the product of psychic dissociation and the encounter of different cultural values." He explains:

> The whole world seems to have become united under the metric system as well as the system of "hook-ups" and "plug-ins," but the spiritual distance between nations seems to be increasing enormously. The experience of moral denigration, the intransigence of nationalism and spiritual bereavement is definitely forcing modern people or nations back to their fundamental assumptions as they search for the meaning of existence, of life, and of man. . . . And as students of philosophy, our task in this situation includes the search for or the suggestion of new ideas and new modes of thought that will resolve the present conflicts and tensions.

The philosophy of culture is "an 'open system,' an incessant effort at creating new meanings by adjusting new ideas and working them into some pattern of living and thinking." Yet Anyanwu concurs with our preceding discussions that, in order to be successful, philosophy cannot be almost exclusively concerned with methods, nor can it be addressed only to philosophers or, more generally but still too narrowly, only to academicians. It should also help those who are not professional philosophers to deal with the conflicts and tensions of their times. This is why "the study of culture promises to be the basis of philosophical activities in the 20th century."

No doubt, this should be a crucial component of a cross-cultural approach in philosophy, which, as Anyanwu says, should be "a unitary mode of thought." Yet, as Nielsen's discussion suggested, such an approach cannot be successfully carried out by philosophy on its own. Rather, it is necessary to join forces with the social sciences and, as argued earlier in this essay, with various social sectors.

Among the social sciences, anthropology and history should play a strong role. Anthropology has a lot to contribute toward clarifying the very notion of culture, formulating the distinction between culture and race, and understanding such cultural factors as kinship systems and food-gathering strategies. It would help to free our inquiry from ethnocentric, naive, and romantic notions, such as the idea that Western thought emphasizes reason and non-Western thought is based on tradition. History would play a central role in our inquiry because it enables us to place philosophical problems in the context of the times in which they were formulated. This context is crucial not only for understanding the problems but also for formulating their solutions. The selections in this book and our discussions of them constitute evidence that the philosophical inquiry here envisioned should proceed in this anthropologically and historically informed direction.[5]

The inquiry could proceed by using the framework partially developed through this book's categories and its pragmatic emphasis. Our selections showed that some of this framework's categories (e.g., metaphysics and epistemology) are Western in origin, yet are significantly used by non-Western philosophers. As Zea indicates, non-Westerners tend to adapt these categories to their own cultural context, and many have produced good philosophy doing so (not, as some Western-oriented critics would have it, "bad imitations of Western philosophy"). They have shown how the categories can be used to deal more intelligently, and less parochially, with philosophical problems, especially those that must be addressed through time and culture.[6]

NOTES

[1] Concerning evolutionary biology, examples of the manner in which philosophy overlaps with science at the theoretical level can be found in Elliot Sober, *Conceptual Issues in Evolutionary Biology* (Cambridge, MA, and London: The MIT Press, 1984). Discussions of this overlap can be found in Elliot Sober, *The Nature of Selection* (Cambridge, MA, and London: The MIT Press, 1984). As for theoretical physics, a good example of philosophical reflection by a physicist can be found in Richard Feynman, *The Character of Physical Law* (Cambridge, MA, and London: The MIT Press, 1965).

[2] Though the literature in this area is very extensive, philosophical and practical concerns are still largely unintegrated. For attempts at integrating them, see my *Contemporary Moral Controversies in Technology* (New York and London: Oxford University Press, 1987) and *Contemporary Moral Controversies in Business* (New York and London: Oxford University Press, 1989).

[3] See, for example, Arthur Caplan, "Can Applied Ethics Be Effective in Health Care, and Should It Strive to Be?" *Ethics 93* (1983): pp. 311–312. For whatever it's worth, my modest experience in academia—in philosophy, interdisciplinary studies, and the development of interdisciplinary courses, curricula, and workshops—and outside academia—in various business environments in the United States and abroad—confirms the existence of the conflicts mentioned in the text. But it has also convinced me of the viability of multioccupational approaches and the need for negotiation and other social-decision procedures to play a central role in them.

[4] For a literary attempt at conveying this experience, see my "South," in Fernando Alegría and Jorge Ruffinelli (eds.), *Paradise Lost or Gained? The Literature of Hispanic Exile* (Houston: Arte Público, 1990).

[5] This concern has been expressed by anthropologists. See, for example, Richard J. Perry, "Why Do Multiculturalists Ignore Anthropologists?" *The Chronicle of Higher Education,* March 4, 1992, p. A 52. For interdisciplinary discussions of culture, see Richard A. Shweder and Robert A. LeVine, *Culture Theory: Essays on Mind, Self, and Emotion* (Cambridge, MA, and London: Cambridge University Press, 1984).

[6] A playwright's conception of some of these problems can be found in Colette Brooks's *Democracy in America,* performed between January 24, 1992, and March 7, 1992, at the Yale University Theater.

Marjorie Grene (contemporary)
PUZZLED NOTES ON A PUZZLING PROFESSION

The author describes five conceptions of philosophy: philosophy as a research field; philosophy as a study dealing with insoluble questions about the good, the true, and the beautiful; philosophy as an art; philosophy as a reflection on fundamental tenets of our culture; and philosophy as an underlaborer's task. She argues that the first conception has no future because it is inaccurate, and the second has no future because it is anachronistic. As for the others, she argues that their prospects are good. Grene's inquiry into the future of philosophy is discussed at the beginning of the introductory essay to Part VI.

READING QUESTIONS

In reading the selection, try to answer the following questions and identify the passages that support your answers:

1. How does Grene describe the conceptions of philosophy she distinguishes?
2. Can these conceptions of philosophy be found in this book's selections? Where and why?
3. What prospects does Grene see for philosophy today?
4. Why does she think philosophy has such prospects?
5. Are her reasons good? Why or why not?

Reprinted from Marjorie Grene, "Puzzled Notes on a Puzzling Profession," *Proceedings and Addresses of the American Philosophical Association* (Newark, DE: APA, 1987), Vol. 61, Supp., pp. 75–80. Copyright © 1987 by the American Philosophical Association. Reprinted by permission of the American Philosophical Association.

Ever since I was a graduate student—well over half a century ago—I have wondered (as of course many of us do, but not usually, perhaps, quite as sceptically as I have) what in the world, or out of it, our profession amounts to. I know philosophy is a great undergraduate teaching subject. But what is it about, what are its methods, what makes it different from other disciplines, indeed, what makes it any discipline at all? Since I'm still unsure of the answer to these questions, I can hardly speak in any straightforward way about the future of this strange and possibly even nonexistent discipline. So let me try out very briefly five different concepts of philosophy and then hazard predictions about the future of each of them.

1. For some practitioners, philosophy appears to be a "research" field, left over when all the obvious (and even some non-obvious) sciences have split off from us. On this view, every "trained" "philosopher" can and should contribute to the advance of something called philosophical knowledge. That this concept is patently mistaken, I was convinced very early, and my superficial acquaintance with most contemporary literature in our "field" reinforces this impression. I had been an undergraduate zoology major and gave up, I think, chiefly out of sloth and timidity. Science is hard work! But the point here is just that it is a very different kind of work from ours, whatever ours is. We do have problems that are genuinely philosophical, and the sciences, as they have left us, have not "solved" them. Epistemology has not been naturalized, whether by physics or psychology; the mind-body problem has not been solved, whether by neurophysiology or by linguistics. It is not that, in (allegedly) Wittgensteinian manner, I want to cut off philosophy wholly from the advance of empirical knowledge. The sciences, and history, too, have a bearing on philosophical reflection, al-

though I find it very difficult to specify just what it is. Perhaps they chiefly forbid certain answers to our questions; yet I think there is a positive influence, too. But I won't try to follow that hare here. I want only to stress that philosophy, whatever it is, is not a research subject. Compare, for example, the program of the first meeting of the APA recently reprinted in the *Proceedings and Addresses* with an APA Program today, and contrast that comparison in turn with one between a meeting of those who later came to be called geneticists in 1902 and a genetics congress today. The APA papers may be sharper in 1986, but the topics have not changed fundamentally; in the science of heredity and other adjacent disciplines, there are whole new sciences where nothing was before. We're not in that ball game at all, and neither so-called "cognitive science" nor artificial intelligence research nor anything else is going to put us there.

2. If, then, one rejects the first, "research" concept of philosophy, one may want to say that while the sciences and other "research" fields deal with problems that are soluble, at least in principle, philosophy deals with insoluble problems. Or, in Michael Polanyi's terms, it is an attempt to criticize, and so to improve, one's fundamental beliefs. For it is always partial problems that are soluble—the answers to more global questions, of what there is, or what we can know, are taken for granted in the more manageable disciplines. This conception corresponds, perhaps, to an old-fashioned view of philosophy as dealing with the big problems: the good, the true, the beautiful. Clearly, it also has some connection with Aristotle's view of first philosophy as treating the principles of the other sciences. But it isn't just the presuppositions of the sciences that we reflect on; it's the presuppositions of everyday life as well. That's what makes it such a discomfiting subject: how can one earn a PhD in everybody's business, and therefore nobody's? Still, as against the scandal of the first concept, this one does seem to have something in it. We *are* people who have a perverse habit of minding other people's business, or everybody's business.

3. Usually, however—and this is my third suggestion—my own way of stressing the contrast with the "research" or scientist view has been a rather different one. I have thought recurrently (even though some of my own practice seems to contradict this thought) that philosophy, being so plainly not a science, is an art: an art that uses for its medium not stone or paint and canvas or sound, but argument.

Now if that is correct, we ought to distinguish between philosophers and teachers of philosophy rather as we do between, say, novelists or poets or playwrights and teachers of literature. I think there's a lot in this view; but the trouble is that even we ordinary teaching types want to teach the real philosophers *philosophically*, and what does that mean if we're not philosophers ourselves? Still, in reaction against the triviality of most so-called philosophy, I'm inclined to support this one—up to a point. I know perfectly well that I am a teacher of philosophy, not an original thinker, rather as my son happens to be a teacher of dramatic literature, not a playwright. (I should remark in passing that neither this conception nor the next one I'll mention has any affinity whatsoever, so far as I can tell, with Richard Rorty's view of philosophy as literature. He seems to believe that literature itself is a verbal competition about nothing at all and that is not the thesis I am trying to put forward. I don't believe, as Rorty seems to, that scientists or scientistically inclined philosophers have solved, or can solve, our problems, nor do I believe in the trivial-times-agonistic character of literature, and therefore one supposes of all the arts.)

Professor E.A. Burtt (who has just completed a book on "Philosophy Past Present and Future") suggests that I add another concept to my list: that of philosophers as pioneers. I believe this would be a combination of my second and third concepts rather than an independent one. The great philosophers are pioneers as other great artists are—they provide new visions of what there is, new perspectives on the fundamental or "insoluble" problems.

4. Fourth, however, another way of combining some aspects of (2) and (3) may produce yet another view. We may consider philosophy in our tradition as a dialogue about fundamental problems that has been going on since Thales, a dialogue in which we in our time want to take our place. So perhaps each of us, however unoriginal, can think reflectively about his or her place in this history. This is of course a hermeneutical view. It starts from the recognition that we are in a world, within which, and as expressions of which, we become the persons we become. There is for human beings, as Merleau-Ponty put it, no *survol*, no mountaintop from which, like Lucretius, we can survey the armies doing battle on the plain below. The world we are in, moreover, is both a natural and a cultural one. We are animals, units of nature, who need the mediating structures of a culture in order to orient ourselves in nature. Reflecting on the character of our particular culture,

and when our culture permits it, comparing it with others, we are philosophizing in something like Polanyi's sense: attempting to criticize and to improve our fundamental beliefs. This view fits well with my own strong prejudice in favor of historicism, or if you like, of our self-location within a hermeneutical circle. And it also supports an emphasis, which I celebrate, on the history of philosophy in philosophical education and in philosophical reflection.

5. If the first of the concepts I have presented ought to be cast into outer darkness, the second, third and fourth have all, I believe, something in their favor, and indeed they are all related, perhaps in family fashion. Finally, there is a fifth view that seems, at least at first sight, harder to place with the others. That is, of course, the underlaborer view. Philosophy does consist in a way in minding other people's business, not necessarily globally, as in the second concept I have listed, but in more restricted areas. The philosophy of science, of law, perhaps of religion or of art, can contribute to the clarification of conceptual problems in the domains in question, especially when philosophers work closely with the specialists concerned. I was delighted when I returned to the United States in 1965 after thirteen years' absence to be coming back to a country where there were programs in the history and philosophy of science, partly because of my historicist sympathies—I believe philosophy and history of science need to work closely together—but partly just because it seemed that here there was a domain in which philosophers, just ordinary practitioners of whatever it is we practice, could help to get things done. That attitude certainly conflicts with my third concept, to which part of me also subscribes, and it almost sounds like an endorsement of the first, "research" notion. In the end scientists must solve their problems, while we help them with some of the difficulties that attend their conceptual tools. Yet in the philosophy of biology, at least, work by philosophers has proceeded so closely in interaction with work in the biological sciences themselves that there has sometimes been something perilously akin to "progressive problem solving" in this area. There is a practical problem here, too, to which I shall return: how to train "underlaborers" in the disciplines they are to labor for, with, and in, and at the same time to give them the philosophical perspectives characteristic of the second and fourth concepts of our profession. Lacking it, they are inclined to float, almost like the pseudoscientists.

Now at last to the question of the future of philosophy, or of the several practices I have suggested as possibly or partly identifiable with philosophy. Let me suggest five prospects for the future in terms of the above five concepts.

1. Philosophy as an analogue of a science: this seems to me, unfortunately, what the majority of establishment philosophers pretend to practice. Unlike some of my cheerier colleagues claim, I see no lessening of such activities. The future here seems one of increasing triviality (if that is possible)—a lot of analytical skill expended for absolutely no illumination of any real problems whatsoever. Some of these areas, of course, flourish because of grantsmanship, or because of job availability. It is a dismal scene, but I see no end to it.

2. Philosophy as a concern with "insoluble" problems: for some generations this has been an unfashionable view, but perhaps the popularity of the Continental style in some quarters has some connection with the need some people feel to think about "deep" questions. I don't see any promising new opportunities here, however. What is called "Continental philosophy" has got into some many morasses or dreary dead ends or variants of elaborate word games that I can make no prediction here at all.

3. Third, philosophy as an art: if this is the right concept to follow, then we can only wait for original minds to turn up. Of course there may be some in fields I don't follow—in ethics, for example. Here I must plead ignorance. For some years ethics seemed to be restricted to "metaethics," which lends itself easily to pseudoscientism and triviality. On the other hand, when normative ethics is permitted, I find myself asking the Socratic question: who am I to teach virtue? (Besides, when I came home from Ireland two decades ago every one was debating act vs. rule utilitarianism, a dreary question; so I avoided ethics as I usually have.) In general, however, if one follows this conception of philosophy as an art in the medium of argument, then the future here on principle would be what it always has been. Only the prevalence of the first, pseudoscientistic alternative may turn some potentially original thinkers away from philosophy to science or to other art forms.

4. From the fourth, hermeneutical perspective, the history of philosophy becomes central to the practice of philosophy, and the history of philosophy seems to me to be in a very promising and even exciting condition (apart, I should remark, from

Hegel or Nietzsche revivals and such, which I wish would go away). Ancient philosophy has been flourishing for decades, and early modern seems to me to be taking a turn away from too much preoccupation with contemporary "problems" and toward the kind of philosophical-historical and historical-philosophical work that can be truly illuminating for both students and professionals. Consider recent work on ancient scepticism: here are some really magnificent thinkers who in my graduate days just looked rather dreary. That's an enrichment for our understanding of the tradition and where we stand in it. Or consider the papers in Amelie Rorty's recent collection on the *Meditations*—who would have thought that yet another collection on that familiar text could afford so much really fresh insight? The future here looks wonderful. I only wish I believed that a "training" in philosophy would again include, as it once did, an emphasis on the history of Western philosophy as fundamental to a philosophical education.

5. Finally, the underlaborer concept. Hooray for it as well; here, as in the history of philosophy, both present and future look bright. In the field I know best, the philosophy of biology, I find it exhilarating that there are sessions at APA and PSA meetings at which it is hard to tell the scientists from the philosophers. *They* throw up genuine conceptual problems and *we* give them genuine help in dealing with them. Now admittedly this is in a way a counterexample to my third conception: in this kind of area there is sometimes at least some progress in solving problems. But that is because the problems here connect with the more limited problems of the special sciences. We are working with people who know something about the real world and who ask questions that can on principle be answered. And that gives us solid nourishment for our deliberations, in a way that is strikingly absent from the "fields" characteristic of the first conception. The chief difficulty is one of training, as I have already suggested. A program like Chicago's Conceptual Foundations of Science, for instance, is admirable in requiring its graduate students to follow a science up to M.Sc. level. But so far as I can tell they get very little of what I would think of as a philosophical education. I don't know what the answer is. But there are at least a couple of futures here that look bright in themselves if somewhat schizophrenic when looked at together. Philosophers of X need to know X, and by acquaintance, not merely by description. Philosophers as such, whatever that means, and certainly teachers of philosophy, need a thorough grounding in our philosophical tradition, or in some aspects of it. Maybe nobody can be, or do, both of these at once—although I plead guilty to having tried, albeit spottily, in both cases. But that's the past, not the future.

As far as the future goes, then; to sum up: It's gloomy if (1) persists, as I fear it will; (2) and (3) on their own are beyond my powers of prediction; (4) as a general program may be equally unpredictable, although insofar as it entails taking the history of philosophy seriously, it seems to me to be going full steam ahead; (5) is a promising conception as well, even if the relation between (4) and (5) is a matter for concern.

Kai Nielsen (contemporary)
PHILOSOPHY AS CRITICAL THEORY

The author criticizes traditional conceptions of philosophy and argues that philosophy has a future only as critical theory. This is a branch of inquiry in which philosophy is not autonomous, but fully interlocks with the human sciences, and has the resolution of the problems of human life as its central purpose—indeed, its reason for being. See the introductory essay to Part VI for a discussion of Nielsen's position.

READING QUESTIONS

In reading the selection, try to answer the following questions and identify the passages that support your answers:

1. What conceptions of philosophy does Nielsen criticize and why?
2. Can they be found in this book's selections? Where and why?
3. Are Nielsen's criticisms sound? Why or why not?
4. What conception of philosophy does he propose and why?
5. Can you think of a better one? Which and why?

Reprinted from Kai Nielsen, "Philosophy as Critical Theory," *Proceedings and Addresses of the American Philosophical Association* (Newark, DE: APA, 1987), Vol. 61, Supp., pp. 89–108. Copyright © 1987 by the American Philosophical Association. Reprinted by permission of the American Philosophical Association.

I

In speaking of the future of philosophy I am not trying to make any predictions. 'Philosophy', like 'science', is not the name of a natural kind. A glance at an APA or a CPA program or the program of a World Congress in Philosophy makes it evident how many very diverse things go on under the aegis of philosophy with nothing unplatitudinous standing there in virtue of which we could classify them all as the same or even basically similar activities. Some of us will regard some of these activities with a not inconsiderable irony and, for a few of them, some few of us will hardly think of them as genuine philosophy at all. They may indeed, for a few of us, even be the object of our disdain. What will be left of that motley in a hundred years is anyone's guess. Moreover, and similarly, what will be at the centre of the institutional design of those activities that will be taken to be the core of philosophy will, it is not unreasonable to surmise, look very different from what it is now in a hundred years. But, not aspiring to prophecy, I will not hazard a guess at what philosophy will be then.

I shall be concerned instead with the normative and critical task of characterizing how I think philosophy should deeply transform itself. Indeed the transformation, in my view, should be so extensive, make such a shift away from the dominant tradition, that some will believe that what I am proposing is really a successor subject to philosophy and not philosophy. My response is that within certain limits I couldn't care less what we call things here, though it is important to me that the direction I favor for philosophy in the future should have genuine links to some central activities that have been taken to be philosophy in the past. There are, I believe, such links.

What is important, beyond correct verbalization, is to ascertain whether my substantive points are near to the mark, for, if they are, systematic analytic philosophy and the metaphysical traditions of Continental philosophy are both exhausted. If that is so, perhaps, where we take philosophy to be some kind of professional discipline, we should just close up shop. That, of course, is about as likely as it is likely that North American universities, under fiscal constraints, will unburden themselves of their swollen administrative structures. But I am trying to address myself to what it would be most reasonable to do.

Philosophy, at least in the foreseeable future, is not going to wither away. No matter what we who make our living teaching philosophy do or think, there is a kind of folk-conception of philosophy that will live on. I speak here of philosophy in the broad sense where it is conceived not as a distinctive kind of discipline, the property of a professional caste, but as an attempt on the part of human beings to make sense of their lives, both individually and collectively, and to come to see, if we can, what, in our time and place, and with the live possibilities before us, would be the best sorts of lives to live, including what forms of community would be most desirable and to see this normative picture in turn in the larger framework of how things hang together. Philosophy, on this understanding, is as old as the hills, hardly the property of a profession or discipline and not in the least threatened. In that unproblematic way we just are philosophical animals. But in that way E.M. Forster and Doris Lessing are more clearly philosophers than are David Armstrong and Saul Kripke, and that should be sufficient to indicate that the profession has something rather more determinate in mind when it speaks of philosophy.

My claim is (1) that the major traditions supported by the profession are exhausted and (2) that even so, philosophy need not just close up shop but can and should transform itself.

I shall be somewhat briefer with my nay-saying, tradition-bashing, side, both because I have had to go at it elsewhere and because I believe in essentials that Richard Rorty has made the right points about the tradition in spinning the tale he has about the story of modern and contemporary philosophy, though his recipes for 'post-philosophy philosophy' are something else again.[1] For me to go on at length about how the tradition rests on a mistake would, for the most part, be simply to cover much of the same ground again. If Rorty is substantially wrong here in his setting aside of the tradition (more accurately the traditions) then I am mistaken as well. Even then my proposals about the transformation of philosophy might still be well-taken, but more modestly, as proposing an additional something philosophy might come to be.

So the link between my yea-saying and my nay-saying is not all that tight. You might, of course, want to reject both, but it is also possible to take one and leave the other. However, my claim will be that, while the tradition should come to an end, philosophy need not come to an end with it and 'post-philosophy philosophy' need not be limited to a learned and witty kibitzing. We can and should transform philosophy into some form of critical social theory with an emancipatory intent. I am not suggesting just a replay of Habermas or the Frankfurt school or some more orthodox version of Marxism. I shall, after my nay-saying, give a characterization of what

I have in mind and begin building a defense of taking that turning.

II

Why should we set aside the tradition? The tradition is either foundationalist or lives in a timid shadow of foundationalism. But foundationalism in any significant form rests on a mistake. Nor is there much point in the various attempts to 'naturalize' metaphysics or epistemology. Scientific realism is not any great advance over Platonism or Thomism. It just has a rather more scientistic jargon.

A not inconsiderable number of very diverse philosophers, some of rather major importance, would assent to Isaac Levi's comment that "opposition to foundationalism ought to be the philosophical equivalent of resistance to sin."[2] Moreover, with that anti-foundationalism goes as well anti-representationalism and opposition to glassy essences. And this, in turn, if we think the matter through, comes to a rejection of the whole Cartesian-Lockean-Kantian tradition of epistemology, the essentially Platonic tradition of metaphysics in its many disguises, the ideal language and reductionist accounts of logical positivism, 'scientific empiricism' with its commitment to 'an empiricist language' and, as well, so-called scientific realism with its commitment to a correspondence theory of truth and some kind of 'scientific metaphysics'.

Opposition to these various voices of foundationalism comes not only from the classical pragmatists and from Wittgenstein, Wisdom and Waismann, it has emerged, as well, internally to analytic philosophy itself, from the pragmatization of positivism in Quine, Goodman and Sellars and from the work of such (comparatively speaking) younger-generation analytical philosophers as Putnam and Davidson, to say nothing of such apostates to the analytical tradition as Rorty, Taylor and MacIntyre. On the Continental side, in a different way and in a different idiom, the rejection has been as thorough. In France I refer to Merleau-Ponty, Lyotard, Foucault and Derrida and in Germany, to Heidegger, Gadamer, Adorno, Horkheimer, Habermas, Wellmer and Blumberg.

All of these philosophers in their sometimes rather different ways may, of course, be mistaken, and foundationalism could still be alive and well and

[1] Richard Rorty, *Philosophy and the Mirror of Nature* (Princeton, NJ: Princeton University Press, 1979) and *Consequences of Pragmatism* (Minneapolis, MN: University of Minnesota Press, 1982). Kai Nielsen, "Challenging Analytic Philosophy" in *Free Inquiry*, vol. 4, no. 4 (Fall 1984); "Rorty and the Self-Image of Philosophy" in *International Studies in Philosophy*, vol. 18 (1986), pp. 19–28; "How to be Sceptical about Philosophy" in *Philosophy*, vol. 61, no. 235 (January 1986), pp. 83–93; "Scientism, Pragmatism and the Fate of Philosophy" in *Inquiry*, vol. 29, no. 3 (September 1986), pp. 277–304; "Can There be Progress in Philosophy?" in *Metaphilosophy*, vol. 18, no. 1 (January 1987), pp. 1–30.

[2] Isaac Levi, "Escape from Boredom: Edification According to Rorty" in *Canadian Journal of Philosophy*, vol. XI, no. 4 (December 1981), p. 509.

living in North America. But the list is rather impressive, containing many of the luminaries of contemporary philosophy, and that should give the foundationalist, or the foundationalistically inclined person, pause. Perhaps all of these philosophers are merely caught up in the vicissitudes of the *Weltgeist*. It would not be the first time that has happened in history. But the burden of proof is surely on foundationalists to show that something like that is true.

However, not to just call in the big battalions but to argue, I need first to characterize foundationalism. Foundationalism is a philosophical account which seeks to isolate, by some kind of philosophical method, a set of basic beliefs which are foundational to all the rest of the things that we may justifiably claim to know or reasonably believe. Classical foundationalism holds that the only properly basic beliefs are those that are self-evident, incorrigible reports of experience or are evident to the senses. On such an account, other beliefs can be rationally held only if they are supported either deductively or inductively by such properly basic beliefs. Aside from anything else, for reasons purely internal to the framework, such a classical form of foundationalism would appear at least to be self-refuting for the very proposition asserting what classical foundationalism is, is, on the one hand, neither self-evident, evident to the senses or an incorrigible report of experience nor, on the other, deducible from such propositions or inductively justified by them. In fine, classical foundationalism hoists itself by its own petard.

There are more modest forms of foundationalism around, but they are hardly more successful. Suppose our modest foundationalism claims that a belief is properly basic if and only if it is either self-evident, fundamental, evident to the senses or defensible by argument, careful deliberation or inquiry. We are troubled right off by the undefined use of 'fundamental' so crucially and conveniently used here. The modest foundationalist obligingly helps us by telling us that a belief can correctly be said to be fundamental if it is unavoidably part of the noetic structure of every human being and could not be abandoned without causing havoc to that structure. We can then—and indeed we should—wonder how we decide which beliefs are unavoidably part of the noetic structure of every human being and cannot be set aside without playing havoc with that structure. Examples readily come to mind: 'The Earth has existed for many years past', 'The sun comes up in the morning', 'Dogs cannot fly'. 'Human beings need food and sleep' and the like. But how do we

determine what gets on the list? Modest foundationalists provide us with no criterion. If, G.E. Moore-like, we just *ambulando* have to decide in particular instances what on common sense reflection seems fundamental or basic to us, then we hardly need foundationalism or indeed philosophy or critical theory to provide us with a foundation for belief, a critical canon for assessing the rest of culture. Rather, we just use our reflective common sense to decide what is or is not fundamental. Philosophy then becomes quite superfluous. If, alternatively, we relativize what is taken to be fundamental or properly basic to whatever a given community takes to be fundamental or basic, so that, like Alvin Plantinga, we allow such tendentious beliefs as 'God spoke to me' or 'God protects us' as basic, then we lose any possible advantage that a foundational epistemological or metaphysical tradition might have that would make it intellectually attractive. Instead of affording us a basis for criticizing the idols of the tribe, we refer to the idols of the tribe quite uncritically to determine what is basic or fundamental. This is surely a *reductio* of a foundationalist turn.

Besides such internal arguments, anti-foundationalists press home less internal objections, smoke out very problematic presuppositions of both foundationalists and their scientistic opponents (opponents who unwittingly take in their dirty linen) and offer alternative accounts of how we can justify various of our beliefs that give far fewer hostages to fortune. Anti-foundationalists, for example, deny that we can make epistemological sense of the idea of an experiential input as a theory-free basis of alternative interpretive or explanatory theories, some of which give us radically different conceptualizations of this experiential given, which is just there to be noted or discovered and then conceptualized. In attacking such a position, anti-foundationalists reject the hallowed putative distinction, dear to the tradition, between conceptual scheme and reality, or scheme (schema) and content, with all the possibilities built into that traditional philosophical way of conceptualizing things for radical scepticism or for conceptual relativism.[3] But here, as John Wisdom used to put it, it is the manner and not the matter that mystifies. Indeed, the coherence of such a distinction, and of any conceptual relativism rooted in it, is very much in doubt.

---

[3] Donald Davidson, *Truth and Interpretation* (Oxford, England: Clarendon Press 1984), pp. 183–198.

The foundationalist must show how correct ideas can match up with an external reality or (where she takes a linguistic turn) how words can hook onto the world and how true propositions must correspond to some antecedently-given reality and false ones fail to. But no one has ever been able to give a perspicuous account of such a correspondence or to cash in any of the above metaphors. We have, of course, Tarski and his semantical theory of truth; but that is a long way from a correspondence theory. Talk of correspondence here is just a mystification, and talk of mind as a mirror of nature or of language as a map faithfully representing nature has been shown to be a non-starter.[4]

Reference is not fixed by meaning. What a term refers to is determined not by mental states or intentions but, first, by paradigmatic examples established in some historically extant linguistic community in which the term in question has a use and, second, by historical causal connections that obtain in the extralinguistic world. Nature does not have her own language permitting us to claim correctly, or even coherently, that the "the world consists of some fixed totality of mind-independent objects" and that "there is exactly one true and complete description of the world."[5] There is, in Putnam's phrase, no God's-eye point of view of the relation between words and the world. A commitment to clarity requires that we come to see such a representational model as a myth and that we finally break the powerful hold it has had on us. We cannot as neutral agents and observers of the actual disengage ourselves from the world by objectifying it, that is, by making it the object of accurate representations. We can as embodied social agents acting and interacting with the other parts of the world cope with the world successfully or not, and frequently we use language in doing so. But there is no word-world relation such that words simply represent the world as it is. Language does not in that way hook onto the world. Indeed the very idea of Language being something apart from the world to hook onto the world is a weird conception.

It is surely not unnatural to respond: well, perhaps foundationalism has been shown to rest on a mis-

take, but what about naturalistic metaphysics and naturalized epistemology? And are those not part of the tradition too? Naturalized epistemology, making no foundational claims, seeks to explain or account for our beliefs solely in terms of the natural processes which give rise to them. As both Putnam and Rorty point out, this is a very peculiar conception of epistemology indeed, for it does not explain when beliefs are justified but seeks instead to explain how certain psychological or physiological processes work. But it is not that question but the *justifiability* question—the question of how we are to justify our beliefs—that is the very *raison d'être* of epistemology. Indeed it is hard to understand how such an inquiry as the one Quine characterizes could even be regarded as a bit of philosophy, rather than an abandonment of epistemology for psychology.[6]

It is important to recognize how radical Rorty's critique actually is. In attacking metaphysical philosophy from Plato to scientific realism, the Cartesian-Lockean-Kantian tradition of epistemologically-oriented philosophy as well as systematic analytic philosophy, Rorty rejects the very self-image the tradition has of itself and without which it has little, if any, point. It is an illusion, he is telling us, to pretend as the tradition does that philosophy is or can become a distinct discipline with a distinctive methodology, which if properly employed will at long last enable us to discover the foundations of science and the life-world. There is no strictly philosophical account that will finally enable us correctly to see how things hang together and to make sense of our lives, or at least more reasonably to orient our lives. The promise is that it will, if we finally carry it through successfully, provide us with some philosophical understanding of a very general and fundamental sort which will enable us, free of the vicissitudes of culture and history, to in some comprehensive way understand our social life and to criticize our various forms of life, institutions and ordinary and scientific ways of knowing and doing. We will, it is claimed, finally come to know and to understand, if we can only get the right philosophical accounting of things, in a way no one has ever been able to know or understand before. It all sounds a little too much like a religious conversion, but still it

[4]   Richard Rorty, *Consequences of Pragmatism,* pp. xiii–xlvii and his essay on Davidson's account of truth in Ernest Lepore (editor), *Truth and Interpretation: Perspectives in the Philosophy of Donald Davidson* (New York: Basil Blackwell Limited 1986).

[5]   Hilary Putnam, "After Empiricism" in John Rajchman and Cornell West (editors), *Post-Analytic Philosophy* (New York, NY: Columbia University Press, 1985), p. 49.

[6]   Richard Rorty, "The Unnaturalness of Epistemology" in D.F. Gustafson and B.L. Tapscott (editors), *Body, Mind and Method* (Dordrecht, Holland: D. Reidel, 1979), pp. 77–92; Hilary Putnam, "Why Reason Can't Be Naturalized" in Kenneth Baynes, *et al.* (editors), *After Philosophy: End or Transformation* (Cambridge, MA: The MIT Press, 1987), pp. 239–242.

is, put now bluntly and embarrassingly, the deep underlying rationale of the tradition.

In reality we neither have nor can have anything like that. We have instead concepts such as truth, goodness, rationality, knowledge and the like which *ambulando* we have some mastery of (we know how to use the terms correctly), and in that way have some understanding of them. That is to say, in our mother tongue, and perhaps in some other historically determinate tongues as well, we can use terms expressive of these concepts in most of the ordinary, context-bound, historically determinate settings of their use to say what we want to say. And we also understand something, at least in a working way, of the contexts of their proper employment. But we have no ahistorical, context-independent criteria of rationality, reasonableness, knowledge, goodness or truth with which to construct a philosophical discipline that transcends history or to adumbrate a permanent, culture-transcendent, and impartial matrix for assessing all forms of inquiry and all types of knowledge. We philosophers do not possess such 'super-concepts', or such a super-understanding of concepts, and we do not possess a secure matrix of heuristic concepts or categories which would enable us to classify, comprehend and criticize our forms of life. We have neither a philosophical architectonic nor an Archimedean point here, and it is unclear what it would be like to have one or even to have a good understanding of what we are talking about here. And we are also without any privileged, special philosophical knowledge (assuming we know what that is) of concepts, and again it is anything but clear what it would be like to have such a knowledge.

III

Recognition of the illusion behind the tradition undercuts any appeal to a conception of the role of the philosopher as underlaborer. That surely is not apparent, but—or so I shall argue—that conception is itself undermined with the undermining of foundationalism and 'metaphysical realism'.

The underlaborer's conception of philosophy goes well with a commitment to a type of analytic philosophy that has no systematic pretensions but is content instead to dispel conceptual confusions emerging out of everyday life and science.[7] We are

to do this, it is often claimed, with the aid of sharp new analytical tools that philosophy as conceptual or logical analysis provides.

If what I have said so far is close to the mark, we must give up a number of once popular metaphors and give up hoping for what they suggest. Philosophy cannot be the overseer of culture, the adjudicator of knowledge-claims, and it cannot usher the sciences to their proper places and demarcate them from the rest of culture. It cannot—to put the matter very broadly—be the arbiter of culture, distinguishing between what is rational or reasonable and what is irrational or unreasonable to believe and do.

However, the protagonists of the underlaborer conception might respond that all is not lost, for there is another less arrogant metaphor for the philosopher's work. The philosopher should, on this new conception, help keep us all honest. Where she is doing her job properly, according to the new metaphor, she is the inspector of finance of the academy. Welling out of our everyday life—moral and political lives, the arts and the sciences, and intramural relations between them—are all sorts of conceptual confusions, some of them very distorting and harmful indeed.[8] The role of the philosopher, the underlaborer conception of philosophy has it, is to dispel confusion over our concepts in their living settings and to enable us, in these determinate contexts, to come to command a sufficiently clear view of the workings of our language to dispel such perplexities.

This commitment to clarity is salutory and I do not want to denigrate it. Our very intellectual integrity requires that we must strive for and practice such clarity when we philosophize. Yet this metaphor still gives the philosopher the illusion of having an expertise and a technique that she does not have. Eager analytical philosophers have spoken of our having powerful new analytical tools to use in solving or dissolving philosophical perplexities, finally in a rigorous, scientific manner.[9] However, when we look at the matter carefully we will come to see that there are in reality no such powerful analytical techniques that the philosopher can deploy to solve either the problems of philosophers or for that matter the problems of life, or even to break, in a therapeutic manner, philosophical perplexity. No

---

[7] Alice Ambrose Lazerowitz, "Commanding a Clear View of Philosophy" in *Proceedings and Addresses of the American Philosophical Association*, vol. LXIX (1975–76), pp. 5–21.

[8] Alasdair MacIntyre, "Philosophy and its History" in *Analyse & Kritik*, Jahrgang 4 (1982), pp. 102–113.

[9] Rorty criticizes this account perceptively in his *The Consequences of Pragmatism*, pp. 211–230.

distinctive philosophical method enjoys anything even approximating a consensus, even among Anglo-American analytical philosophers. There is not even, as Rorty puts it, an inter-university paradigm within North America.[10] The new tools rapidly become obsolete, and there is a lot of coming and going of intellectual fashion. Indeed, in this respect things seem to be speeding up. The whirligig goes ever faster, but no one outside philosophy departments pays it any attention. There is little to encourage a belief in progress toward a clearer view of things, setting philosophy on the secure path of science or something science-like and cumulative. What needs to be shown, and hasn't been shown by the defenders of the underlaborer conception, is *how* it is that philosophers have some special expertise with concepts such that they will be better able than others to resolve the conceptual problems that arise in science and in the life-world. The belief that we have anything like this appears to be a piece of philosophical mythology.

It is nevertheless true that philosophers with a good analytic training have a developed capacity for drawing distinctions, spotting assumptions, digging out unclarities, seeing relationships between propositions, noting their implications and setting out arguments perspicuously. But so have lawyers, classicists, economists and mathematicians with a good training. These different disciplines use different jargon, but there is no reason to believe that the philosophers' jargon, a jargon which repeatedly changes, is in general any better. We have, as Wittgenstein has powerfully argued, no conception of 'absolute clarity' in virtue of which we could judge that one or another of these ways of speaking affords the most perspicuous representation or (whatever that means) puts us closest to reality.[11]

The shock of the matter, for philosophers at least, is that philosophers cannot tell us what makes our ideas really clear, what we really mean or what we are justified in believing.[12] To make good the underlaborer undertaking, we philosophers would have to be able to display a philosophical expertise that was distinct from and an improvement on just having a cultivated ability, shared with a goodly number of non-philosophers, to think clearly—an ability which could be cultivated in a number of different ways. A philosopher must be able to show us how we can distinguish clear ideas from unclear ones and to show us how we can distinguish sense from nonsense. But we have very good reasons indeed to believe that we philosophers cannot deliver the goods here. We may in certain contexts (say, with respect to certain kinds of metaphysical talk) be able to assemble reminders which will flush out some rather disguised nonsense; but that is quite distinct from having a general criterion or a special expertise.

In general I have in these first sections tried to argue against the tradition. It is my belief that Putnam is right in holding that the tradition is in shambles.[13] This is particularly evident with foundationalism, but it is also true of non-foundationalist analytic philosophy too. Again the words of Putnam capture what I have been arguing. He remarks that "at the very moment when analytical philosophy is recognized as the 'dominant movement' in world philosophy, analytical philosophy has come to the end of its own project—the dead end, not the completion."[14] There is a tendency among analytic philosophers to see analytic philosophy as philosophy itself. But that is just a conceit. If it is at a dead end, as Putnam, Rorty and I believe, is there anything left for philosophy to be with the demise of the tradition? That is the topic I shall pursue in the next section.

IV

Suppose we see philosophy as social critique or as cultural criticism. If neo-Pragmatist critiques of the tradition are well taken, we may not be able in general to say anything very enlightening about what meaning, truth, knowledge, belief or rationality is, but we can—or so the claim goes—come to grips, as have philosophers throughout history, with the pressing problems of life.[15] For us, standing where we are now, this means examining the problems of abortion, euthanasia, privacy, pornography, the rights of children, animal rights, sexism, racism, nuclear warfare, the ideological uses of science and the media, exploitation, and imperialism. Our questions concern what democracy can come to in our industrial societies, what education should be at various levels in our societies, inequality and autonomy, the choice between socialism and capitalism or reform and revolution, and the ethics of terrorism. At other places and at other times, different questions have

---

[10]   *Ibid.*

[11]   Ludwig Wittgenstein, *Philosophical Investigations*, pp. 13–32.

[12]   Rorty, *op. cit.*

[13]   Putnam, "After Empiricism", p. 28.

[14]   *Ibid.*

[15]   Kai Nielsen, "Scientism, Pragmatism and the Fate of Philosophy" and "Can There be Progress in Philosophy?"

come to the fore, and the agenda no doubt will be different in the future. These questions certainly are not the perennial questions of philosophy, if indeed there are any perennial questions.[16] But there is here, so the claim runs, real work for philosophy to do in examining them intelligently, in using, as Dewey used to say, our creative intelligence.[17]

However, problems that we have discussed before come flooding back like the return of the repressed. How can philosophers as philosophers be of any use here? They might, if they are also reflective, knowledgeable and intelligent persons, have something useful to say, but how does their being philosophers help? If foundationalism is out, moral foundationalism is out, so we cannot expect much help here from the classical ethical theories.[18] There seems to be left no distinctive expertise that philosophers can bring to such pressing human questions.

I want to suggest that there may be a way that philosophy might transform itself in a way that would answer to our unschooled reflective hopes. It would involve (a) giving up all pretensions to autonomy and instead interlocking philosophy fully with the human sciences and (b) taking the resolution of the problems of human life to be very centrally a part of philosophy's reason for being.[19]

What I want can be seen by going back to the non-discipline-based folk conception of philosophy I mentioned initially, whose continued existence is not threatened whatever philosophers may do. Quite unprofessionally, I construed philosophy as an attempt on the part of human beings to make sense of their lives and to come to see, as far as that is possible, what, in our time and place, with whatever real possibilities we have before us, would be the best sorts of lives for us to live, including what forms of community would be most desirable, and in turn to place this normative picture in a larger framework of how things hang together.

Taking this folk conception of philosophy as our benchmark, I want to see if something serving the same ends and with the same overall rationale, but more rigorous, more argument-based and more discipline-oriented, could be articulated and then developed. I shall call it *philosophy-as-critical theory*. I so label it with a certain amount of trepidation, lest it be identified with the critical theory of either Habermas or the earlier Frankfurt school. While I am indebted in certain ways to the German critical theorists, particularly to Habermas, I do not model my conception on their accounts, though I deliberately adopt their phrase 'critical theory'.[20]

What I am advocating in advocating philosophy-as-critical-theory is a holistic social theory which is at once a descriptive-explanatory social theory, an interpretive social theory and a normative critique. Departing radically from the philosophical tradition, it will be an empirical theory.[21] Elements of the social sciences will be a very central part, although, in light of the importance of giving a narrative account of who we were, are and might become, much of the social science utilized may be historiographical.[22]

On such a conception, elements of philosophy as more traditionally conceived, particularly elements of analytical philosophy, will be coordinated with the human sciences, with none of the elements claiming hegemony and with philosophy unequivocally giving up all claim to be the autonomous guardian of reason.

Critical theory will, of course, share the fallibilist attitudes of science and of pragmatism. An underlying rationale for the construction of such a comprehensive holistic theory is to provide a comprehensive critique of culture and society and of

---

[16] The essays by Charles Taylor, Alasdair MacIntyre, Richard Rorty and Ian Hacking in Richard Rorty *et al.* (editors), *Philosophy in History* (Cambridge, England: Cambridge University Press, 1984) importantly challenge the whole idea of there being perennial problems in philosophy.

[17] John Dewey, *Reconstruction in Philosophy* (Boston, MA: The Beacon Press, 1957), *The Quest for Certainty* (New York, NY: G.P. Putnam and Sons, 1960), *Problems of Men* (New York, NY: Philosophical Library), pp. 3–20, 169–179, 211–353, *Essays in Experimental Logic* (New York, NY: Dover Publications Inc., 1953), Chapters I, XII, XIII and XIV and "The Need for a Recovery in Philosophy" in *Creative Intelligence,* John Dewey *et al.* (editors), (New York, NY: Holt, 1917), pp. 3–69.

[18] Bernard Williams, *Ethics and the Limits of Philosophy* (Cambridge, MA: Harvard University Press, 1985), and Kai Nielsen, "On Needing a Moral Theory: Rationality, Considered Judgments and the Grounding of Morality" in *Metaphilosophy*, vol. 13 (April 1982).

[19] Kai Nielsen, "Can There be Progress in Philosophy?"

[20] Jurgen Habermas, *Theorie des Kommunikativen Handelns,* Band I & II (Frankfurt am Main: Suhrkamp Verlag, 1981); Raymond Geuss, *The Idea of a Critical Theory* (Cambridge, MA: Cambridge University Press, 1981); David Ingram, *Habermas and the Dialectic of Reason* (New Haven, CT: Yale University Press, 1987); and Syla Benhabib, *Critique, Norm and Utopia* (New York, NY: Columbia University Press, 1986).

[21] Kai Nielsen, "Emancipatory Social Science and Social Critique" in Daniel Callahan and Bruce Jennings (editors), *Ethics, the Social Sciences and Policy Analysis* (New York, NY: Plenum Press, 1983), pp. 113–157 and "Can There Be Progress in Philosophy?": Jungen Habermas, "Philosophy as Stand-In and Interpreter" in *After Philosophy: End or Transformation?*, pp. 296–315.

[22] Charles Taylor's account here is perceptive. Taylor, "Overcoming Epistemology" in *After Philosophy: End or Transformation?*, pp. 464–485. See also Charles Taylor and Alan Montelione, "From an Analytical Perspective" in Gabris Kortian, *Meta-Critique* (London, England: Cambridge University Press, 1980), pp. 1–21.

ideology. In this way it will not only have both a descriptive-explanatory thrust and an interpretive side but a critically normative emancipatory thrust as well. If such a theory can really be fleshed out in a coherent and convincing manner, it will not only help us better see who we were, are and might become; where there are alternatives, it will also help us see who we might *better* become and what kind of a society would be not only more just but a more humane society conducive to human flourishing.

Such a theory will probably have a narrative structure, but it will not be a meta-narrative—a grand *a prioristic* philosophy of history—but a genuinely empirical-cum-theoretical theory with appropriate empirical testing constraints.[23] It will, among other things, be a descriptive-explanatory theory showing us the structure of society, the range of its feasible transformations and the mechanics or modalities of its transformation. The normative side will provide, with the degree of contextuality appropriate, a rational justification (if that isn't pleonastic) for saying, of the various possible transformations, which are the better.

It is not the case that the Frankfurt School and Habermas provide us with our only paradigms. Dewey and Mead, among our near contemporaries have done something like that, and in the past Vico, Hobbes, Montesquieu, Condorcet, Hume, Ferguson, Herder, and Hegel—in various ways, with various styles of reasoning and various techniques of historical narrative—have also done something like that. Under the dominance of the Cartesian-Kantian epistemological and metaphysical tradition, taking its linguistic turn with logical positivism and later analytical philosophy, such approaches were set aside as at best not being philosophy and at worst as incoherent.

Yet critical theory lived on and attained its best articulations to date, again in various ways, in the great sociological trinity of Marx, Weber and Durkheim, as well as in such lesser lights as Pareto, Mosca, Gramsci and, in a somewhat different way, Freud. Critical theory is a definite project of modernity, growing out of the Enlightenment. It is presently under vigorous post-modernist attack from Lyotard, Derrida, Foucault and Rorty, though the latter two have not abandoned the ideals of the Enlightenment but have rather chastened it in the spirit of pragmatism.[24]

There is the legitimate worry on the part of these post-modernists that critical theory might come to nothing but a grandiose and rather vacuous grand theory with a meta-narrative—a totalizing philosophy of history without empirical or critical grounding. That is not an unreasonable worry, and one need not be a Popperian to have it. We certainly need to have a better understanding of how the elements of a critical theory go together and of the devices within the theory, not only to critique ideology but to guard against ideological distortion in the theory itself. There is the pervasive phenomenon of only seeing ideology in the other. Charles Taylor is surely right in seeing ideology as something which is very pervasive indeed and in seeing, as well, such grand accounts as ideology-prone.[25] But that they are ideology-prone does not mean they are inescapably ideological. We want a genuinely critical theory with an emancipatory thrust as free as possible from ideological distortion, and not just a distorting ideology with a grand meta-narrative.

For a critical theory not to come to that it must meet four conditions: (a) it must be seen to be clearly of help in solving some of what Dewey called the problems of men, problems like the more or less determinate social problems I described; (b) it must develop a theoretical practice that has a clear emancipatory pay-off; (c) its descriptive-explanatory structure must actually provide some explanations which are approximately true; and (d) these explanations, together with the evaluative and normative claims contained in the theoretical practice, must compose a well-matching, interlocking, comprehensive framework which is perspicuously articulated.

Even post-Modernists sympathetic to the Enlightenment project such as Foucault and Rorty will

---

23 Richard Rorty, "Habermas and Lyotard on Postmodernity" and Jurgen Habermas, "Questions and Counter Questions" both in Richard J. Bernstein (editor), *Habermas and Modernity* (Cambridge, MA: The MIT Press, 1985); Kai Nielsen, "Scientism, Pragmatism and the Fate of Philosophy" and "Can There Be Progress After Philosophy?"

24 Richard Rorty, "Solidarity or Objectivity?" in *Post-Analytic Philosophy*, pp. 4–29 and "The Priority of Democracy to Philosophy," in Meryl Patterson and Robert Vaugham (eds.), *The Virginia Statute of Religious Freedom* (Cambridge, MA: Cambridge University Press, 1987); Michael Foucault, *The Foucault Reader* (New York, NY: Pantheon Books, 1984), pp. 32–50, 76–97, 333–390; David Couzens Hoy, "Introduction" and his "Power, Repression, Progress, Foucault, Lukes and the Frankfurt School"; and Hubert L. Dreyfus and Paul Robinow, "What is Maturity? Habermas and Foucault on 'What is Enlightenment?'", all in Hoy (editor). *Foucault: A Critical Reader* (Oxford, England: Basil Blackwell, 1986).

25 Charles Taylor, "Use and Abuse of Theory" and Kai Nielsen, "A Marxist Conception of Ideology" both in A. Parel (editor), *Ideology, Philosophy and Politics* (Waterloo, ON: Wilfrid Laurier University Press, 1983).

be sceptical, as many others will as well, about the scope of critical theory. It is a very daunting enterprise. Critics may grant that such a project is not *a priori* impossible or incoherent, but they will instead (a) be sceptical that we can construct a theory with such a scope which will be able to meet demands that will reasonably be put on it (such as the four listed above) and (b) reject the philosophical accoutrements that they perceive as being an essential part of critical theory, namely some ahistorical, non-contextual, non-social-practice-dependent theory of rationality, truth, warranted belief, or undistorted discourse. These post-modernists are as sceptical about this as they are of foundationalist epistemologies or of metaphysics. They will point out, perfectly correctly, that we can recognize what it is rational or reasonable to do without having any inkling of a theory of rationality or any account of what it is to be reasonable, and likewise we can perfectly well distinguish true statements from false ones without having a theory of what truth is or any general criteria for when beliefs are justified.[26] And similar things can and should be said about our capacities to recognize in concrete situations what we ought to do even without any theory of morality, either normative or meta-ethical.[27]

In what are probably its best current examplications (exemplifications which are themselves quite different), namely, in the critical theory of Habermas and his associates and in analytical Marxism, philosophy-as-critical-theory does have such general conceptions of rationality, truth and knowledge, though this is clearer in Habermas than in analytical Marxism.[28] This *may* be a good thing

and it *may*, as Habermas believes, allow critical theory to transcend relativism and historicism.[29] But then again it may not, and criticisms such as those of Rorty and Hacking may carry the day, and philosophical supplements from Putnam or Davidson may not provide the rationale for transcending such rather more historicized accounts.[30] Moreover, if Rorty's arguments are well-taken, a critical theory would not need such supplementation.

While the present exemplars of critical theory go in this standard Enlightenment direction in this respect, and they may be right to do so, I do not believe that such an account need be part of the core conception of what a critical theory must be—it need not be part of the very idea of a critical theory of society. A critical theory could be far more historicist than Habermas's account or Horkheimer's and still remain a critical theory.

I am not here imputing a critical theory to Rorty or Foucault, who are much too leery of theories for that. But someone with the metaphilosophical beliefs of Rorty (what Foucault's are is less clear) and with Rorty's endorsement of reflective equilibrium could very readily come, without a lapse in consistency or coherence, to construct a historicized version of a critical theory.[31] It could not have the relativism (unacknowledged) or the commitment to incommensurability of Rorty's earlier work. But in two late important essays, he constructs an account that takes him beyond relativism without falling into some form of transcendentalist Absolutism or indeed any Absolutism.[32]

Whether an adequate critical theory must have, as a component part, a *theory* of truth, rationality and knowledge, as Habermas, Putnam and Taylor believe it should, or whether it could and should bracket such considerations, as Rorty and Foucault think, is

---

[26] Richard Rorty, "Pragmatism, Davidson and Truth" in Ernest Lepore (editor), *Truth and Interpretation: Perspective in the Philosophy of Donald Davidson.*

[27] Kai Nielsen, "Moral Theory: Rationality, Considered Judgments and the Grounding of Morality," "Searching for an Emancipatory Perspective: Wide Reflective Equilibrium and the Hermeneutical Circle" in Evan Simpson (editor), *Anti-Foundationalism and Practical Reasoning* (Edmonton, AB: Academic Press, 1987), and "Reflective Equilibrium and the Transformation of Philosophy," forthcoming.

[28] Richard W. Miller, "Marx and Analytic Philosophy: The Story of a Rebirth" in *Social Science Quarterly,* vol. 4, no. 4 (December 1983), pp. 846–861 and his *Analyzing Marx* (Princeton, NJ: Princeton University Press, 1984). John Roemer (editor), *Analytical Marxism* (Cambridge, England: Cambridge University Press, 1986); G.A. Cohen, *Karl Marx's Theory of History: A Defense* (Oxford, England: Clarendon Press, 1978), Jon Elster, *Making Sense of Marx* (Cambridge, England: Cambridge University Press, 1987) and Allen W. Wood, *Karl Marx* (London: England: Routledge and Kegan Paul, 1981).

[29] This comes out clearly in his exchange with Rorty. See references in note 24.

[30] Ian Hacking, "Styles of Scientific Reasoning" in *Post-Analytic Philosophy,* pp. 145–165. Donald Davidson, *Inquiries into Truth and Interpretation* and Hilary Putnam, *Reason, Truth and History* (New York, NY: Cambridge University Press, 1982).

[31] See Rorty's discussion of Rawls and of wide reflective equilibrium in "The Priority of Democracy to Philosophy".

[32] It is important to contrast two very recent (1987) essays, essays which I think are much more satisfactory, with two earlier essays which I think are vulnerable in the way I have argued in "Can There be Progress in Philosophy?". The more recent essays I have in mind are "Solidarity or Objectivity?" and "The Priority of Democracy to Philosophy". The earlier essays are "Postmodern Bourgeois Liberalism," *Journal of Philosophy,* vol. 80 (1983) and "Pragmatism, Relativism and Irrationalism" in *Consequences of Pragmatism* (pp. 160–175).

not a matter to be settled *a priori* or on methodological grounds alone but historically. Alternative theories must be fleshed out to see which account works best or meets the four conditions I have described.

However, if a critical theory is to have any bite, if it is to be a *critical* theory, it cannot issue in what is clearly some form of relativism. I agree with Hacking and MacIntyre that we should take relativism seriously, and I further agree with them that there are plausible forms of it not flattened by Davidson's transcendental argument.[33] I further agree with MacIntyre that we are not likely to be able to refute relativism, though we may be able to provide accounts of society and morality that are more plausible than even the best relativistic ones.

Historicist accounts like Rorty's clearly show that historicism need not add up to relativism.[34] Rorty's ethnocentric starting point in the considered convictions of Enlightenment bourgeois individualism does not entrap him in his own starting point. He could, that is, work his way out of his bourgeois individualism. Moreover, he would hardly be anchored to the moral world or to any community if he did not start with some relatively specific considered judgements, some 'prejudices' in Burke's sense. However, in shuttling back and forth to get them into a coherent pattern, none of these starting points are taken to be sacrosanct. We repair, and indeed can even rebuild, the ship at sea. Nothing is beyond amendment or even rejection, though not everything can be rejected at once. In gaining ever more coherent views, where we fit together ever more comprehensively our reflective beliefs in many domains, rejecting those that square badly with most of our most secure beliefs, we come incrementally to gain a more adequate understanding and a more reasonable set of moral commitments.

Critical theory should add, as an integral methodological component, the method of wide reflective equilibrium linked with some pragmatist methodological addenda taken from Isaac Levi.[35] It is a way of proceeding introduced by Goodman and Quine and later explicitly applied to moral theory by Rawls,

English, Daniels and myself, then again developed in a more generalized form by Putnam and Rorty.[36]

We start with the considered judgements of whatever cultural traditions happen to be socialized into our marrow.[37] We seek first to eliminate those which cannot square with a fair appraisal of the facts, would not be held in a cool hour and when we are not fatigued, drunk, under strain or the like. We also seek to get a consistent set of such winnowed considered judgements, eliminating one or another of whatever conflicting judgements remain by seeing which of them adheres best with our other considered judgements background beliefs, and more generalized factual assessments. We consider which of the considered judgements, when we are aware that they conflict, would continue to have the strongest appeal when we take them to heart and agonize over which to stick with. (It is folly to think that in the domain of the moral we can bypass all appeal to sentiment.[38])

Getting such an initial set (perhaps cluster would be the better word), we try to construct general principles or see if there are extant in our tradition general principles which will account for our holding them and interpret them. (These principles may themselves be higher-level considered judgements.) But these principles will also have a justificatory role. If our considered judgements conflict but one is in accordance with one of these higher-order principles and the other is not, then, *ceterus paribus*, we should accept the judgement that is in accordance with the higher-order principle and reject the other. Moreover, some considered judgements are

[33] Ian Hacking, "Styles of Scientific Reasoning" and Alasdair MacIntyre, "Relativism, Power and Philosophy" in *After Philosophy: End or Transformation*, pp. 385–411.

[34] Richard Rorty, "Solidarity or Objectivity?" or "The Priority of Democracy to Philosophy."

[35] Levi, *op. cit.* See my development of it in "Scientism, Pragmatism and the Fate of Philosophy."

[36] John Rawls, *A Theory of Justice* (Cambridge, MA: Harvard University Press, 1971), pp. 19–21, 48–51, 577–587; "The Independence of Moral Theory" in *Proceedings and Addresses of the American Philosophical Association*, vol. XLVII (1974/75), pp. 7–10. Norman Daniels, "Wide Reflective Equilibrium and Theory Acceptance in Ethics," in *The Journal of Philosophy*, vol. 76 (1979); "Moral Theory and Plasticity of Persons." in *The Monist*, vol. 62 (July 1979); "Some Methods of Ethics and Linguistics" in *Philosophical Studies*, vol. 37 (1980), "Reflective Equilibrium and Archimedean Points" in *Canadian Journal of Philosophy*, vol. 10 (March 1980); "Two Approaches to Theory Acceptance in Ethics" in David Copp and David Zimmerman (editors), *Morality, Reason and Truth* (Totowa, NJ: Rowman & Allanheld, 1985), and "An Argument About the Relativity of Justice" in *Revue Internationale de Philosophie* (1987); Jane English, "Ethics and Science" in *Proceedings of the XVI Congress of Philosophy*; Kai Nielsen, "On Needing a Moral Theory: Rationality, Considered Judgments and the Grounding of Morality," "Considered Judgments Again," in *Human Studies*, vol. 5 (April-June, 1982), and *Equality and Liberty* (Totowa, NJ: Rowman and Allanheld, 1985), Chapter 2.

[37] Kai Nielsen, "Searching For an Emancipatory Perspective: Wide Reflective Equilibrium and the Hermeneutical Circle."

[38] W.D. Falk, *Ought, Reasons and Morality* (Ithaca, NY: Cornell University Press, 1986).

more firmly held than others. Where we have half-considered judgements, judgements that we are tempted to hold on some grounds and to reject on others—judgements that is, that we are less sure of, then we have a very good reason to modify them to cohere with the rest. But if we have a higher-order moral principle that conflicts with a great mass of very deeply entrenched considered judgements, as perhaps the principle of utility does, then, again *ceterus paribus,* we have a good reason to reject the higher-order principle.

We shuttle back and forth, as Rawls puts it, until we get these various elements into equilibrium. We extend this to *wide* reflective equilibrium when we add various background theories and principles such as theories about social structure, social change, the function of morality and ideology, the economy, the person and the like. We seek in a similar way to shuttle back and forth between considered judgements, moral principles, moral theories and social theories (and perhaps other theories as well) until we get a coherent package that meets our reflective expectations and hopes. Thus we achieve for a time a stable reflective equilibrium in the unending dialectical process of weaving and unweaving the patterns of our beliefs in order to make sense of our lives, to see things as comprehensively and connectedly as we reasonably can and to guide our conduct.

We start here from traditions and return to tradition. There can be no stepping out of our societies and traditions to be purely rational agents, moral agents, or political animals *uberhaupt.* Such a notion is not merely utopian, it is incoherent. But we are not imprisoned by our traditions either. No belief is in principle immune to criticism and rejection.

Whole traditions, plank by plank, can be transformed as we repair and even rebuild, in Neurath's famous metaphor, the ship at sea.

Philosophy-as-critical-theory-of-society should use, as an integral element, some such method of wide reflective equilibrium. It would enable it to develop this normative critical side without falling into an overly stringent empiricism or adopting an intuitionism that would surely not fit well with the fallibilism of critical theory or its generalized naturalistic framework. Moreover, it is a method that does not require the taking of any epistemological or metaphysical position. We can be free of such tendentious and arcane matters.

A critical theory, which might even turn out to be a historicist theory, can avoid the relativizing claims of conceptual imprisonment, hermeneutical circles, and incommensurabilities as well as claims that fundamental concepts in its armory are essentially contested concepts.[39] It can do justice to the reality of contestedness, conflict and diversity in social life without imputing *essential* contestedness or incommensurabilities between which we must just choose. We can, in this way, reasonably avoid existentialist high drama or Fideist plunking. We can have an empirical-theoretical-cum-normative theory which can provide guidance in wrestling with the problems of life and which can help inform our understanding of who we are and who we might become. This is a worthy enough task for philosophy after the death of epistemology, metaphysics and the grand tradition of *a priori* assurances of metaphysical comfort.

[39] Kai Nielsen, "Searching for an Emancipatory Perspective: Wide Reflective Equilibrium and the Hermeneutical Circle."

Leopoldo Zea (contemporary)
THE ACTUAL FUNCTION OF PHILOSOPHY IN LATIN AMERICA

The author, a Latin American philosopher, discusses the predicament of Latin America and Latin American philosophy in their relation to European culture and philosophy. He argues that neither nationalistic approaches nor mere imitations of European models can soundly address the problems faced by Latin America in the twentieth century or the philosophical problems that arise out of this situation. What Latin American philosophers should do is simply to do philosophy. The products of their inquiry will be bound to reflect their characteristically Latin American experiences. See the introductory essay to Part VI for a discussion of Zea's arguments for a distinctive Latin American philosophy within a larger, universal philosophy.

READING QUESTIONS

In reading the selection, try to answer the following questions and identify the passages that support your answers:

1. What conceptions of philosophy does Zea criticize?
2. Can they be found in this book? Where and why?
3. Are Zea's criticisms sound? Why or why not?
4. What conception of philosophy does Zea propose for Latin America and why?
5. Can you think of a better one? Which and why?

Reprinted by permission of the author from Leopoldo Zea, "The Actual Function of Philosophy in Latin America," in Jorge J. E. Gracia (ed.), *Latin American Philosophy in the Twentieth Century* (Buffalo, NY: Prometheus, 1986), pp. 219–230; from Leopoldo Zea, *Ensayos sobre filosofia en la historia* (Mexico: Stylo, 1948), pp. 165–177. Originally published in *Cuadernos Americanos* (1942).

1

Some years ago, a young Mexican teacher published a book that caused much sensation. This young teacher was Samuel Ramos and the book was *El perfil del hombre y la cultura en México*. This book was the first attempt at interpreting Mexican culture. In it Mexican culture became the subject of philosophical interpretation. Philosophy came down from the world of ideal entities to a world of concrete entities like Mexico, a symbol of men who live and die in their cities and farms. This daring attempt was derogatorily termed *literature*. Philosophy could not be anything other than a clever game of words taken from an alien culture. These words of course lacked meaning: the meaning they had for that alien culture.

Years later another teacher, this time the Argentinian Francisco Romero, emphasized Ibero-America's need to begin thinking about its own issues, and the need to delve into the history of its culture in order to take from it the issues needed for the development of a new type of philosophical concern. This time, however, Romero's call was based on a series of cultural phenomena that he identified in an essay entitled "Sobre la filosofia en Iberoamerica." In this article he showed how the interest in philosophical issues in Latin America was increasing on a daily basis. The public at large now follows and asks with interest for works of a philosophical character and nature. This has resulted in numerous publications—books, journals, newspaper articles, etc.—and also in the creation of institutes and centers for philosophical studies where philosophy is practiced. This interest in philosophy stands in sharp contrast with periods when such an activity was confined to a few misunderstood men. Their activity did not transcend literary or academic circles. Today, we have reached the level that Romero calls "the period of philosophical normalcy," that is, a period in which the practice of philosophy is seen as a function of culture just as is the case with any other activity of a cultural nature. The philosopher ceases to be an eccentric whom nobody cares to understand and becomes a member of his country's culture. There is what one may call a "philosophical environment," that is, a public opinion that judges philosophical production, thus forcing it to address the issues that concern those who are part of this so-called "public opinion."

Now, there is one particular issue that concerns not only a few men in our continent, but the Latin American man in general. This issue concerns the possibility or impossibility of Latin American culture, and, as an aspect of the same issue, the possibility or impossibility of Latin American philosophy. Latin American philosophy can exist if there is a Latin American culture from which this philosophy may take its issues. The existence of Latin American philosophy depends on whether or not there is Latin American culture. However, the formulation and attempt to solve this problem, apart from the affirmative or negative character of the answer, are already Latin American philosophy, since they are an attempt to answer affirmatively or negatively a Latin American question. Hence, the works of Ramos,

Romero, and others on this issue, whatever their conclusions, are already Latin American philosophy.

The issue involved in the possibility of Latin American culture is one demanded by our time and the historical circumstances in which we find ourselves. The Latin American man had not thought much about this issue before because it did not worry him. A Latin American culture, a culture proper to the Latin American man, was considered to be an irrelevant issue: Latin America lived comfortably under the shadow of European culture. However, the latter culture has been shaken (or is in crisis) today, and it seems to have disappeared from the entire European continent. The Latin American man who had lived so comfortably found that the culture that supported him fails him, that he has no future, and that the ideas in which he believed have become useless artifacts, without sense, lacking value even for their own authors. The man who had lived with so much confidence under a tree he had not planted now finds himself in the open when the planter cuts down the tree and throws it into the fire as useless. The man now has to plant his own cultural tree, create his own ideas. But a culture does not emerge miraculously: the seed of that culture must be taken from somewhere, it must belong to someone. Now—and this is the issue that concerns the Latin American man—where is he going to find that seed? That is, what ideas is he going to develop? To what ideas is he going to give his faith? Will he continue to believe and develop the ideas inherited from Europe? Or is there a group of ideas and issues to be developed that are proper to the Latin American circumstance? Or rather, will he have to invent those ideas? In a word, the problem of the existence, or lack of existence, of ideas that are proper to America, as well as the problem of the acceptance or rejection of ideas belonging to European culture that is now in crisis, comes to the fore. Specifically, the problem of the relationship between Latin America and European culture, and the problem of the possibility for a genuinely Latin American ideology.

2

In light of what has been said it is clear that one of the primary issues involved in Latin American philosophy concerns the relations between Latin America and European culture. Now, the first thing that needs to be asked has to do with the type of relations that Latin America has with that culture. There are some who have compared this relationship to that between Asia and European culture. It is said that Latin America, just as Asia, has assimilated only technology from Europe. But if this is so, what would belong to Latin American culture? For the Asian man, what he has adopted from European culture is regarded as something superimposed that he has had to assimilate owing to the change in his own circumstance caused in turn by European intervention. However, what he has adopted from European culture is not properly the culture, that is, a life-style, a world view, but only its instruments, its technology. Asians know that they have inherited an age-old culture that has been transmitted from generation to generation; they know that they have their own culture. Their view of the world is practically the opposite of the European. From Europeans they have only adopted their technology, and only because they have been forced to do so by the intervention of Europeans and their technology in a circumstance that is properly Asian. Our present day shows what Asians can do with their own world view while using European technology. Asians have little concern for the future of European culture, and they will try to destroy it if they feel that it gets in their way or continues to intervene in what they regard as their own culture. Now, can we Latin Americans think in a similar way about European culture? To think so is to believe that we have our own culture, but that this culture has not perhaps reached full expression yet because Europe has prevented it. In light of this, one could think that this is a good time to achieve cultural liberation. If that were the case, the crisis of European culture would not concern us. More than a problem, such a crisis would be a solution. But this is not the case: we are deeply concerned about the crisis of European culture; we experience it as our own crisis.

This is due to the fact that our relationship with European culture as Latin Americans is different from that of the Asians. We do not feel, as Asians do, the heirs of our own autochthonous culture. There was, yes, an indigenous culture, Aztec, Maya, Inca, etc., but this culture does not represent, for us contemporary Latin Americans, the same thing that ancient Oriental culture represents for contemporary Asians. While Asians continue to view the world as their ancestors did, we Latin Americans do not view the world as the Aztecs or the Mayans did. If we did, we would have the same devotion for pre-Columbian temples and divinities that an Oriental has for his very ancient gods and temples. A Mayan temple is as alien and meaningless to us as a Hindu temple.

What belongs to us, what is properly Latin American, is not to be found in pre-Columbian culture. Is it to be found in European culture? Now, something strange happens to us in relation to European culture: we use it but we do not consider it ours; we feel *imitators* of it. Our way of thinking, our world view, is similar to the European. European culture has a meaning for us that we do not find in pre-Columbian culture. Still, we do not feel it to be our own. We feel as bastards who profit from goods to which they have no right. We feel as if we were wearing someone else's clothes: they are too big for our size. We assimilate their ideas but cannot live up to them. We feel that we should realize the ideals of European culture, but we also feel incapable of carrying out the task: we are content with admiring them and thinking that they are not made for us. This is the knot of our problem: we do not feel heirs of an autochthonous culture, because that culture has no meaning for us; and that which has meaning for us, like the European, does not feel as our own. There is something that makes us lean toward European culture while at the same time resists becoming part of that culture. Our view of the world is European but we perceive the achievements of that culture as alien. And when we try to realize its ideals in Latin America we feel as imitators.

What is properly ours, what is Latin American, makes us lean toward Europe and at the same time resists being Europe. Latin America leans toward Europe as a son to his father, but at the same time it resists becoming like his own father. This resistance is noticeable in that, despite leaning toward European culture, Latin America still feels like an imitator when it seeks to achieve what that culture does. It does not feel that it is realizing what is proper to it but only what Europe alone can achieve. That is why we feel inhibited by and inferior to Europeans. The malaise resides in that we perceive what is Latin American, that is, what is ours, as something inferior. The Latin American man's resistance to being like a European is felt as an incapacity. We think as Europeans, but we do not feel that this is enough; we also want to achieve the same things that Europe achieves. The malaise is that we want to adjust the Latin American circumstance to a conception of the world inherited from Europe, rather than adjusting that conception of the world to the Latin American circumstance. Hence the divorce between ideas and reality. We need the ideas of European culture, but when we bring them into our circumstance we find them to be too big because we do not dare to fit them

to this circumstance. We find them big and are afraid to cut them down; we prefer to endure the ridicule of wearing an oversize suit. Indeed, until recently the Latin American man wanted to forget what he is for the sake of becoming another European. This is similar to the case of a son who wants to forget being a son in order to be his own father: the result has to be a gross imitation. This is what the Latin American man feels: that he has tried to imitate rather than to realize his own personality.

Alfonso Reyes portrays the Latin American man's resistance to being Latin American with great humor. The Latin American man felt "in addition to the misfortune of being human and modern, the very specific misfortune of being Latin American; that is, having been born and having roots in a land that was not the center of civilization, but rather a branch of it."[1] To be a Latin American was until very recently a great misfortune, because this did not allow us to be European. Today it is just the opposite: the inability to become European, in spite of our great efforts, allows us to have a personality; it allows us to learn, in this moment of crisis for European culture, that there is something of our own that can give us support. What this something is should be one of the issues that a Latin American philosophy must investigate.

3

Latin America is the daughter of European culture; it is the product of one of its major crises. The discovery of America[2] was not a matter of chance, but rather the product of necessity. Europe needed America: in every European mind there was the idea of America, the idea of a promised land. A land where the European man could place his ideas, since he could no longer continue to place them in the highest places. He could no longer place them in the heavens. Owing to the emergence of a new physics, the heavens were no longer the home of ideals but rather became something unlimited, a mechanical and therefore dead infinity. The idea of an ideal world came down from heaven and landed in America. Hence the European man came out in search of the land and he found it.

---

[1]   Alfonso Reyes, "Notas sobre la inteligencia americana," *Sur*, no. 24 (September 1936).

[2]   Zea consistently uses "America" and "Americanos" to refer to Latin America and its inhabitants. I use "Latin America" and "Latin Americans" respectively to render these terms throughout the paper, except in the present case, because here Zea is referring to the period of discovery, when there was no distinction between Anglo-Saxon and Latin America. TRANS.

The European needed to rid himself of a world view of which he was tired. He needed to get rid of his past and begin a new life. He needed to build a new history, one that would be well planned and calculated, without excess or wanting. What the European was afraid of openly proposing in his own land, he took for granted in this land called America. America became the pretext for criticizing Europe. What he wanted Europe to be became imaginarily fulfilled in America. Fantastic cities and governments that corresponded to the ideals of the modern man were imagined in America. America was presented as the idea of what Europe should be. America became Europe's utopia. It became the ideal world that the old Western world was to follow to rebuild itself. In a word, America was the ideal creation of Europe.

America was born to history as a land of projects, as a land of the future, but of projects and a future that were not its own. Such projects and such future were Europe's. The European man who put his feet in this America becoming part of the Latin American circumstance and giving rise to the Latin American man has been unable to see what is properly American. He has only seen what Europe wanted America to be. When he did not find what European imagination had placed in the American continent, he was disappointed, and this produced the uprooting of the Latin American man from his own circumstance. The Latin American man feels European by origin, but he feels inferior to the European man by reason of his circumstance. He feels inadequate because he regards himself as superior to his circumstance, but inferior to the culture he comes from. He feels contempt for things Latin American, and resentment toward Europe.

Rather than attempting to achieve what is proper to Latin America, the Latin American man labors to achieve the European utopia and thus stumbles, as it could be expected, into a Latin American reality that resists being anything other than what it is: Latin America. This gives rise to the feeling of inferiority about which we already have spoken. The Latin American man considers his reality to be inferior to what he believes to be his destiny. In Anglo-Saxon America this feeling expresses itself in the desire to achieve what Europe has achieved in order to satisfy its own needs. North America has strived to become a second Europe, a magnified copy of it. Original creation does not matter, what matters is to achieve the European models in a big way and with the greatest perfection. Everything is reduced to numbers: so

many dollars or so many meters. In the end, the only thing that is sought with this is to hide a feeling of inferiority. The North American tries to show that he is as capable as the European. And the way to show it is by doing the same things that Europeans have done, on a bigger scale and with greater technical perfection. But this only demonstrates technical, not cultural ability, because cultural ability is demonstrated in the solution one gives to the problems of man's existence, and not in the technical imitation of solutions that other men found for their own problems.

The Latin American man, however, feels inferior not only to the European, but also to the North American man. Not only does he no longer try to hide his feeling of inferiority, but he also exhibits it through self-denigration. The only thing that he has tried to do so far is to live comfortably under the shadow of ideas he knows are not his own. To him, ideas do not matter as much as the way to benefit from them. That is why our politics have turned into bureaucracy. Politics is no longer an end but an instrument to get a job in the bureaucracy. Banners and ideals do not matter anymore; what matters is how these banners and ideals can help us get the job we want. Hence the miraculous and quick change of banners; whence also that we always plan and project but we never achieve definite results. We are continually experimenting and projecting with always-changing ideologies. There is no single national plan because there is no sense of nation. And there is no sense of nation for the same reason that there is no sense of what is Latin American. He who feels inferior as Latin American also feels inferior as a national, that is, as a member of one of the Latin American nations. This is not to say that the fanatic nationalist who talks about a Mexican, Argentinian, Chilean, or any other Latin American nation's culture, to the exclusion of anything that smacks of foreign, has any better sense of what a nation is. No, in the end he would only try to eliminate what makes him feel inferior. This is the case of those who say that this is the appropriate time to eliminate everything European from our culture.

This position is wrong because, whether we want it or not, we are the children of European culture. From Europe we have received our cultural framework, what could be called our structure: language, religion, customs; in a word, our conception of life and world is European. To become disengaged from it would be to become disengaged from the heart of our personality. We can no more deny that culture than we can deny our parents. And just as we have a personality that makes us distinct from our parents without having to deny them, we should also be able to have a cultural personality without having to deny the culture of which we are children. To be aware of our true relations with European culture eliminates our sense of inferiority and gives us instead a *sense of responsibility*. This is the feeling that animates the Latin American man today. He feels that he has "come of age," and, as any other man who reaches maturity, he acknowledges that he has a past that he does not need to deny, just as no one is ashamed of having had a childhood. The Latin American man knows himself to be the heir of Western culture and now demands a place in it. The place that he demands is that of collaborator. As a son of that culture he no longer wants to live off it but to work for it. Alfonso Reyes, speaking on behalf of a Latin America that feels responsible, demanded from Europe "the right of universal citizenship that we have already conquered," because already "we have come of age."[3] Latin America is at a point in its history when it must realize its cultural mission. To determine this mission constitutes another issue that what we have called Latin American philosophy has to develop.

4

Once we know our cultural relations with Europe, another task for this possible Latin American philosophy would be to continue to develop the philosophical issues of that culture, but most especially the issues that European philosophy regards as universal. That is, issues whose level of abstraction allows them to be valid at any time and at any place. Among such issues are those of being, knowledge, space, time, God, life, death, etc. A Latin American philosophy can collaborate with Western culture by attempting to resolve the problems posed by the issues that European philosophy has not been able to resolve, or to which it has failed to find a satisfactory solution. Now, it could be said, particularly by those who are interested in building up a philosophy with a Latin American character, that this cannot be of interest to a philosophy concerned with what is properly Latin American. This is not true, however, because both the issues that we have called universal and the issues that are peculiar to the Latin American circumstance are very closely linked. When we discuss the former we need also to discuss the latter.

The abstract issues will have to be seen from the Latin American man's own circumstance. Each man will see in such issues what is closest to his own circumstance. He will look at these issues from the standpoint of his own interests, and those interests will be determined by his way of life, his abilities and inabilities, in a word, by his own circumstance. In the case of Latin America, his contribution to the philosophy of such issues will be permeated by the Latin American circumstance. Hence, when we address abstract issues, we shall formulate them as issues of our own. Even though being, God, etc., are issues appropriate for every man, the solution to them will be given from a Latin American standpoint. We may not say what these issues mean for every man, but we can say what they mean for us Latin Americans. Being, God, death, etc., would be what these abstractions mean for us.

It should not be forgotten that all European philosophy has worked on these issues on the assumption that their solutions would be universal. However, the product has been an aggregate of philosophies very different from each other. Despite their universalistic goals, the product has been a Greek philosophy, a Christian philosophy, a French philosophy, a British philosophy, and a German philosophy. Likewise, independently of our attempts to realize a Latin American philosophy and despite our efforts to provide universal solutions, our solutions will bear the mark of our own circumstance.

Another type of issue to be addressed by our possible Latin American philosophy is related to our own circumstance. That is, our possible philosophy must try to resolve the problems posed by our circumstance. This point of view is as legitimate and valid a philosophical issue as the one we have just discussed. As Latin Americans we have a series of problems that arise only in the context of our circumstance and that therefore only we can resolve. The posing of such problems does in no way diminish the philosophical character of our philosophy, because philosophy attempts to solve the problems that man encounters during his existence. Hence the problems encountered by the Latin American man are the problems of the circumstance in which he lives.

Among such issues is that of our history. History is part of man's circumstance: it gives him a configuration and a profile, thus making him capable of some endeavors and incapable of others. Hence we must take our history into account, because it is there that we can find the source of our abilities and in-

[3] Reyes, "Notas."

abilities. We cannot continue to ignore our past and our experiences, because without knowing them we cannot claim to be mature. Maturity, age, is experience. He who ignores his history lacks experience, and he who lacks experience cannot be a mature, responsible man.

With respect to the history of our philosophy, one might think that nothing could be found in it other than bad copies of European philosophical systems. In effect, that is what one will find if one is looking for Latin American philosophical systems that have the same value as European ones. But this is a shortsighted attempt; we must approach the history of our philosophy from a different standpoint. This standpoint is provided by our denials, our inability to do much besides bad copies of European models. It is pertinent to ask the reason why we do not have our own philosophy; perhaps the very answer will be a Latin American philosophy. This may show us a way of thinking that is our own and that perhaps has not needed to express itself through the formulae used by European philosophy.

It is also pertinent to ask why our philosophy is a *bad copy* of European philosophy. Because being a bad copy may very well be part of our Latin American philosophy. To be a bad copy does not necessarily mean to be bad, but simply different. Perhaps our feeling of inferiority has made us consider bad anything that is our own just because it is not like, or equal, to its model. To acknowledge that we cannot create the same European philosophical systems is not to acknowledge that we are inferior to the authors of those philosophies, but simply that we are different. On the basis of this assumption we will not view our philosophers' production as an aggregate of bad copies of European philosophy, but as Latin American interpretations of that philosophy. The Latin American element will be present in spite of our philosophers' attempts at objectivity. It will be present despite our thinkers' attempt to depersonalize it.

5

Philosophy in its universal character has been concerned with one of the problems that has agitated men the most at all times: the problem of the relations between man and society. This problem has been posed as political, asking about the forms of organization of these relations, that is, the organization of human interaction. Since the institution in charge of such relations is the State, philosophy has

asked by whom it should be established and who should govern. The State must take care to maintain the balance between individual and society; it must take care to avoid both anarchy and totalitarianism. Now, in order to achieve this balance a moral justification is necessary. Philosophy attempts to offer such a justification. Hence, every metaphysical abstraction ultimately leads to ethics and politics. Every metaphysical idea provides the foundation for a concrete fact, the justification for any proposed type of political organization.

There is a multitude of philosophical examples in which metaphysical abstractions have provided the basis for a political construct. One example is found in Plato's philosophy, whose theory of ideas provides the basis and the justification for *The Republic*. In Saint Augustine's *The City of God* we find another example: the Christian community, the Church, is supported by a metaphysical being that in this case is God. The *Utopias* of the Renaissance constitute yet other examples where rationalism justifies the forms of government that have given birth to our present democracy. One thinker has said that the French Revolution finds its justification in Descartes's *Discourse on Method*. The Marxist revision of Hegel's dialectics has given way to such forms of government as communism. Even totalitarianism has sought metaphysical justification in the ideas of Nietzsche, Sorel, and Pareto. Many other examples from the history of philosophy can be cited where metaphysical abstraction provides the basis for social and political practices.

What we have just discussed underlines how theory and practice must go together. It is necessary that man's material acts be justified by ideas, because this is what makes him different from animals. But our times are characterized by a schism between ideas and reality. European culture is in crisis because of this schism. Man is now lacking a moral theory to justify his acts and hence has been unable to resolve the problems of human interaction. All that he has achieved is the fall into the extremes of anarchy and totalitarianism.

The various crises of Western culture have been produced by a lack of ideas to justify human acts, man's existence. When some ideas have no longer justified this existence, it has been necessary to search for other sets of ideas. The history of Western culture is the history of the crises that man has endured when the harmony that should exist between ideas and reality has been broken. Western culture has gone from crisis to crisis, finding salvation sometimes in ideas, sometimes in God, other times in reason, up to the present time when it no longer has ideas, God, or reason. Culture is now asking for new foundations of support. But this is, from our point of view, practically impossible. However, this point of view belongs to men who are in a situation of crisis, and this could not be otherwise, since we would not be in a situation of crisis if the problem seemed to us to have an easy solution. The fact that we are in a crisis, and that we do not have the much-wanted solution, still does not mean that the solution does not exist. Men who like us have been in situations of crisis before have had a similar pessimism; however, a solution has always been found. We do not know which values will replace those that we see sinking, but what we do know for certain is that such values will emerge, and it is our task as Latin Americans to contribute to this process.

From this we can infer yet another goal for a possible Latin American philosophy. The Western culture of which we are children and heirs needs new values on which to rest. These new values will have to be derived from new human experiences, that is, from the experiences that result from men being in the new circumstances of today. Because of its particular situation, Latin America can contribute to culture with the novelty of untapped experiences. That is why it is necessary that it tell its truth to the world. But it must be a truth without pretensions, a sincere truth. Latin America should not pretend to be the director of Western culture; what it must aspire to do is to produce culture purely and simply. And that can be accomplished by attempting to resolve the problems that are posed to the Latin American man by his own Latin American perspective.

Latin America and Europe will find themselves in a similar situation after the crisis. Both will have to resolve the same problem: what will be the new way of life that they will have to adopt to deal with the new circumstances? Both will have to continue ahead with the interrupted task of universal culture. But the difference is that Latin America will no longer be under the shadow of Europe's accomplishments, because there is neither a shadow nor a place of support at this point. On the contrary, Latin America finds itself at a vantage point in time—which may not last long—but that must be used to initiate the task that belongs to it as an adult member of Western culture.

A Latin American philosophy must begin the task of searching for the values that will provide the basis for a future type of culture. And this task will be carried out with the purpose of safekeeping the human essence: that which makes a man a man. Now, man is essentially an individual who is at the same time engaged in interaction with others, and hence it is necessary to maintain a balance between these two components of his essence. This is the balance that has been upset to the point of leading man to extremes: individualism to the point of anarchy, and social existence to the point of massification. Hence it is imperative to find values that make social interaction possible without detriment to individuality.

This task, which is universal and not simply Latin American, will be the supreme goal of our possible philosophy. This philosophy of ours cannot be limited to purely Latin American problems, that is, the problems of Latin America's circumstance. It must be concerned with the larger circumstance called humanity, of which we are also a part. It is not enough to attempt to reach a Latin American truth, but we must also attempt to reach a truth that is valid for all men, even if this truth may not in fact be accomplished. What is Latin American cannot be regarded as an end in itself, but as a boundary of a larger goal. Hence the reason why every attempt to make a Latin American philosophy, guided by the sole purpose of being Latin American, is destined to fail. One must attempt to do purely and simply philosophy, because what is Latin American will arise by itself. Simply by being Latin American, philosophers will create a Latin American philosophy in spite of their own efforts at depersonalization. Any attempt to the contrary will be anything but philosophy.

When we attempt to resolve the problems of man in any spatiotemporal situation whatever, we will necessarily have to start with ourselves because we are men; we will have to start with our own circumstances, our limitations, and our being Latin Americans, just as the Greeks started with their own circumstance called Greece. But, just like them, we cannot limit ourselves to stay in our own circumstances. If we do that it will be in spite of ourselves, and we will produce Latin American philosophy, just as the Greeks produced Greek philosophy in spite of themselves.

It is only on the basis of these assumptions that we will accomplish our mission within universal culture, and collaborate with it fully aware of our abilities, and be aware also of our capacities as members of the cultural community called humanity, as well as of our limits as children of a circumstance that is our own and to which we owe our personality: Latin America.

María Lugones (contemporary)
PLAYFULNESS, "WORLD"-TRAVELLING, AND LOVING PERCEPTION

The author focuses on the interplay between women from different cultural backgrounds, especially on those cases in which white/Anglo women do one of the following to women of color: ignore them, ostracize them, render them invisible, stereotype them, leave them completely alone, or interpret them as crazy. She argues that this can be overcome, and a loving perception of those others can be developed, through an empathetic exercise she calls "world"-travelling. She further argues that an attitude conducive to this exercise is noncompetitive playfulness. Lugones's views are discussed in the introductory essay to Part VI.

READING QUESTIONS

In reading the selection, try to answer the following questions and identify the passages that support your answers:

1. What cases does Lugones focus on and why?
2. What is separatism and how, if at all, does Lugones criticize it?
3. What does Lugones mean by "construction"?
4. What does she propose that we do about it?
5. Can you think of other things we could do? Are they better? Why or why not?

Reprinted by permission of the author from María Lugones, "Playfulness, 'World'-Travelling, and Loving Perception," *Hypatia,* Vol. 1, No. 2 (Summer 1987), pp. 3–19.

This paper weaves two aspects of life together. My coming to consciousness as a daughter and my coming to consciousness as a woman of color have made this weaving possible. This weaving reveals the possibility and complexity of a pluralistic feminism, a feminism that affirms the plurality in each of us and among us as richness and as central to feminist ontology and epistemology.

The paper describes the experience of 'outsiders' to the mainstream of, for example, White/Anglo organization of life in the U.S. and stresses a particular feature of the outsider's existence: the outsider has necessarily acquired flexibility in shifting from the mainstream construction of life where she is constructed as an outsider to other constructions of life where she is more or less 'at home.' This flexibility is necessary for the outsider but it can also be willfully exercised by the outsider or by those who are at ease in the mainstream. I recommend this willful exercise which I call "world"-travelling and I also rec-

ommend that the willful exercise be animated by an attitude that I describe as playful.

As outsiders to the mainstream, women of color in the U.S. practice "world"-travelling, mostly out of necessity. I affirm this practice as a skillful, creative, rich, enriching and, given certain circumstances, as a loving way of being and living. I recognize that much of our travelling is done unwillfully to hostile White/Anglo "worlds." The hostility of these "worlds" and the compulsory nature of the "travelling" have obscured for us the enormous value of this aspect of our living and its connection to loving. Racism has a vested interest in obscuring and devaluing the complex skills involved in it. I recommend that we affirm this travelling across "worlds" as partly constitutive of cross-cultural and cross-racial loving. Thus I recommend to women of color in the U.S. that we learn to love each other by learning to travel to each other's "worlds."

On the other hand, the paper makes a connection between what Marilyn Frye has named "arrogant perception" and the failure to identify with persons that one views arrogantly or has come to see as the products of arrogant perception. A further connection is made between this failure of identification and a failure of love, and thus between loving and identifying with another person. The sense of love is not the one Frye has identified as both consistent with arrogant perception and as promoting unconditional servitude. "We can be taken in by this equation of servitude with love," Frye (1983, 73) says, "because we make two mistakes at once: we think, of both servitude and love that they are selfless or unselfish." Rather, the identification of which I speak is constituted by what I come to characterize as playful "world"-travelling. To the extent that we learn to perceive others arrogantly or come to see them only as products of arrogant perception and continue to perceive them that way, we fail to identify with them—fail to love them—in this particularly deep way.

IDENTIFICATION AND LOVE

As a child, I was taught to perceive arrogantly. I have also been the object of arrogant perception. Though I am not a White/Anglo woman, it is clear to me that I can understand both my childhood training as an arrogant perceiver and my having been the object of arrogant perception without any reference to White/Anglo men, which is some indication that the concept of arrogant perception can be used cross-culturally and that White/Anglo men are not the only arrogant perceivers. I was brought up in Argentina watching men and women of moderate and of considerable means graft the substance[1] of their servants to themselves. I also learned to graft my mother's substance to my own. It was clear to me that both men and women were the victims of arrogant perception and that arrogant perception was systematically organized to break the spirit of all women and of most men. I valued my rural 'gaucho' ancestry because its ethos has always been one of independence in poverty through enormous loneliness, courage and self-reliance. I found inspiration in this ethos and committed myself never to be broken by arrogant perception. I can say all of this in this way only because I have learned from Frye's "In and Out of Harm's Way: Arrogance and Love." She

has given me a way of understanding and articulating something important in my own life.

Frye is not particularly concerned with women as arrogant perceivers but as the objects of arrogant perception. Her concern is, in part, to enhance our understanding of women "untouched by phallocratic machinations" (Frye 1983, 53), by understanding the harm done to women through such machinations. In this case she proposes that we could understand women untouched by arrogant perception through an understanding of what arrogant perception does to women. She also proposes an understanding of what it is to love women that is inspired by a vision of women unharmed by arrogant perception. To love women is, at least in part, to perceive them with loving eyes. "The loving eye is a contrary of the arrogant eye" (Frye 1983, 75).

I am concerned with women as arrogant perceivers because I want to explore further what it is to love women. I want to explore two failures of love: my failure to love my mother and White/Anglo women's failure to love women across racial and cultural boundaries in the U.S. As a consequence of exploring these failures I will offer a loving solution to them. My solution modifies Frye's account of loving perception by adding what I call playful "world"-travel.

It is clear to me that at least in the U.S. and Argentina women are taught to perceive many other women arrogantly. Being taught to perceive arrogantly is part of being taught to be a woman of a certain class in both the U.S. and Argentina, it is part of being taught to be a White/Anglo woman in the U.S. and it is part of being taught to be a woman in both places: to be both the agent and the object of arrogant perception. My love for my mother seemed to me thoroughly imperfect as I was growing up because I was unwilling to become what I had been taught to see my mother as being. I thought that to love her was consistent with my abusing her (using, taking for granted, and demanding her services in a far reaching way that, since four other people engaged in the same grafting of her substance onto themselves, left her little of herself to herself) and was to be in part constituted by my identifying with her, my seeing myself in her: to love her was supposed to be of a piece with both my abusing her and with my being open to being abused. It is clear to me that I was not supposed to love servants: I could abuse them without identifying with them, without seeing myself in them. When I came to the U.S. I learned that part of racism is the internalization of the pro-

---

[1] Grafting the substance of another to oneself is partly constitutive of arrogant perception. See M. Frye (1983, 66).

priety of abuse without identification: I learned that I could be seen as a being to be used by White/Anglo men and women without the possibility of identification, i.e. without their act of attempting to graft my substance onto theirs, rubbing off on them at all. They could remain untouched, without any sense of loss.

So, women who are perceived arrogantly can perceive other women arrogantly in their turn. To what extent those women are responsible for their arrogant perceptions of other women is certainly open to question, but I do not have any doubt that many women have been taught to abuse women in this particular way. I am not interested in assigning responsibility. I am interested in understanding the phenomenon so as to understand a loving way out of it.

There is something obviously wrong with the love that I was taught and something right with my failure to love my mother in this way. But I do not think that what is wrong is my profound desire to identify with her, to see myself in her; what is wrong is that I was taught to identify with a victim of enslavement. What is wrong is that I was taught to practice enslavement of my mother and to learn to become a slave through this practice. There is something obviously wrong with my having been taught that love is consistent with abuse, consistent with arrogant perception. Notice that the love I was taught is the love that Frye (1983, 73) speaks of when she says "We can be taken in by this equation of servitude with love." Even though I could both abuse and love my mother, I was not supposed to love servants. This is because in the case of servants one is and is supposed to be clear about their servitude and the "equation of servitude with love" is never to be thought clearly in those terms. So, I was not supposed to love and could not love servants. But I could love my mother because deception (in particular, self-deception) is part of this "loving." Servitude is called abnegation and abnegation is not analyzed any further. Abnegation is not instilled in us through an analysis of its nature but rather through a heralding of it as beautiful and noble. We are coaxed, seduced into abnegation not through analysis but through emotive persuasion. Frye makes the connection between deception and this sense of "loving" clear. When I say that there is something obviously wrong with the loving that I was taught, I do not mean to say that the connection between this loving and abuse is obvious. Rather I mean that once the connection between this loving and abuse has been unveiled, there is something obviously wrong with the loving given that it is obvious that it is wrong to abuse others.

I am glad that I did not learn my lessons well, but it is clear that part of the mechanism that permitted my not learning well involved a separation from my mother: I saw us as beings of quite a different sort. It involved an abandoning of my mother while I longed not to abandon her. I wanted to love my mother, though, given what I was taught, "love" could not be the right word for what I longed for.

I was disturbed by my not wanting to be what she was. I had a sense of not being quite integrated, my self was missing because I could not identify with her, I could not see myself in her, I could not welcome her world. I saw myself as separate from her, a different sort of being, not quite of the same species. This separation, this lack of love, I saw, and I think that I saw correctly as a lack in myself (not a fault, but a lack). I also see that if this was a lack of love, love cannot be what I was taught. Love has to be rethought, made anew.

There is something in common between the relation between myself and my mother as someone I did not use to be able to love and the relation between myself or other women of color in the U.S. and White/Anglo women: there is a failure of love. I want to suggest here that Frye has helped me understand one of the aspects of this failure, the directly abusive aspect. But I also think that there is a complex failure of love in the failure to identify with another woman, the failure to see oneself in other women who are quite different from oneself. I want to begin to analyze this complex failure.

Notice that Frye's emphasis on independence in her analysis of loving perception is not particularly helpful in explaining this failure. She says that in loving perception, "the object of the seeing is another being whose existence and character are logically independent of the seer and who may be practically or empirically independent in any particular respect at any particular time" (Frye 1983, 77). But this is not helpful in allowing me to understand how my failure of love toward my mother (when I ceased to be her parasite) left me not quite whole. It is not helpful since I saw her as logically independent from me. It also does not help me to understand why the racist or ethnocentric failure of love of White/Anglo women—in particular of those White/Anglo women who are not pained by their failure—should leave me not quite substantive among them. Here I am not particularly interested in cases of White women's parasitism onto women of color but more pointedly in cases where the failure of identification is the manifestation of the "relation." I am particularly interested here in those many cases in which White/Anglo women do one or more of the following to women of color: they ignore us, ostracize us, render us invisible, stereotype us, leave us completely alone, interpret us as crazy. All of this *while we are in their midst.* The more independent I am, the more independent I am left to be. Their world and their integrity do not require me at all. There is no sense of self-loss in them for my own lack of solidity. But they rob me of my solidity through indifference, an indifference they can afford and which seems sometimes studied. (All of this points of course toward separatism in communities where our substance is seen and celebrated, where we become substantive through this celebration. But many of us have to work among White/Anglo folk and our best shot at recognition has seemed to be among White/Anglo women because many of them have expressed a *general* sense of being pained at their failure of love.)

Many times White/Anglo women want us out of their field of vision. Their lack of concern is a harmful failure of love that leaves me independent from them in a way similar to the way in which, once I ceased to be my mother's parasite, she became, though not independent from all others, certainly independent from me. But of course, because my mother and I wanted to love each other well, we were not whole in this independence. White/Anglo women are independent from me, I am independent from them, I am independent from my mother, she is independent from me, and none of us loves each other in this independence.

I am incomplete and unreal without other women. I am profoundly dependent on others without having to be their subordinate, their slave, their servant.

Frye (1983, 75) also says that the loving eye is "the eye of one who knows that to know the seen, one must consult something other than one's own will and interests and fears and imagination." This is much more helpful to me so long as I do not understand Frye to mean that I should not consult my own interests nor that I should exclude the possibility that my self and the self of the one I love may be importantly tied to each other in many complicated ways. Since I am emphasizing here that the failure of love lies in part in the failure to identify and since I agree with Frye that one "must consult some-

thing other than one's own will and interests and fears and imagination," I will proceed to try to explain what I think needs to be consulted. To love my mother was not possible for me while I retained a sense that it was fine for me and others to see her arrogantly. Loving my mother also required that I see with her eyes, that I go into my mother's world, that I see both of us as we are constructed in her world, that I witness her own sense of herself from within her world. Only through this travelling to her "world" could I identify with her because only then could I cease to ignore her and to be excluded and separate from her. Only then could I see her as a subject even if one subjected and only then could I see at all how meaning could arise fully between us. We are fully dependent on each other for the possibility of being understood and without this understanding we are not intelligible, we do not make sense, we are not solid, visible, integrated; we are lacking. So travelling to each other's "worlds" would enable us to *be* through *loving* each other.

Hopefully the sense of identification I have in mind is becoming clear. But if it is to become clearer, I need to explain what I mean by a "world" and by "travelling" to another "world."

In explaining what I mean by a "world" I will not appeal to travelling to other women's worlds. Rather I will lead you to see what I mean by a "world" the way I came to propose the concept to myself: through the kind of ontological confusion about myself that we, women of color, refer to half-jokingly as "schizophrenia" (we feel schizophrenic in our goings back and forth between different "communities") and through my effort to make some sense of this ontological confusion.

"WORLDS" AND "WORLD" TRAVELLING

Some time ago I came to be in a state of profound confusion as I experienced myself as both having and not having a particular attribute. I was sure I had the attribute in question and, on the other hand, I was sure that I did not have it. I remain convinced that I both have and do not have this attribute. The attribute is playfulness. I am sure that I am a playful person. On the other hand, I can say, painfully, that I am not a playful person. I am not a playful person in certain worlds. One of the things I did as I became confused was to call my friends, far away people who knew me well, to see whether or not I was playful. Maybe they could help me out of my confusion. They said to me, "Of course you are playful" and they said it with the same conviction that I had about it. Of course I am playful. Those people who were around me said to me, "No, you are not playful. You are a serious woman. You just take everything seriously." They were just as sure about what they said to me and could offer me every bit of evidence that one could need to conclude that they were right. So I said to myself: "Okay, maybe what's happening here is that there is an attribute that I do have but there are certain worlds in which I am not at ease and it is because I'm not at ease in those worlds that I don't have that attribute in those worlds. But what does that mean?" I was worried both about what I meant by "worlds" when I said "in some worlds I do not have the attribute" and what I meant by saying that lack of ease was what led me not to be playful in those worlds. Because you see, if it was just a matter of lack of ease, I could work on it.

I can explain some of what I mean by a "world." I do not want the fixity of a definition at this point, because I think the term is suggestive and I do not want to close the suggestiveness of it too soon. I can offer some characteristics that serve to distinguish between a "world," a utopia, a possible world in the philosophical sense, and a world view. By a "world" I do not mean a utopia at all. A utopia does not count as a world in my sense. The "worlds" that I am talking about are possible. But a possible world is not what I mean by a "world" and I do not mean a world-view, though something like a world-view is involved here.

For something to be a "world" in my sense it has to be inhabited at present by some flesh and blood people. That is why it cannot be a utopia. It may also be inhabited by some imaginary people. It may be inhabited by people who are dead or people that the inhabitants of this "world" met in some other "world" and now have in this "world" in imagination.

A "world" in my sense may be an actual society given its dominant culture's description and construction of life, including a construction of the relationships of production, of gender, race, etc. But a "world" can also be such a society given a non-dominant construction, or it can be such a society or *a* society given an idiosyncratic construction. As we will see it is problematic to say that these are all constructions of the same society. But they are different "worlds."

A "world" need not be a construction of a whole society. It may be a construction of a tiny portion of a particular society. It may be inhabited by just a few people. Some "worlds" are bigger than others.

A "world" may be incomplete in that things in it may not be altogether constructed or some things may be constructed negatively (they are not what 'they' are in some other "world.") Or the "world" may be incomplete because it may have references to things that do not quite exist in it, references to things like Brazil, where Brazil is not quite part of that "world." Given lesbian feminism, the construction of 'lesbian' is purposefully and healthily still up in the air, in the process of becoming. What it is to be a Hispanic in this country is, in a dominant Anglo construction purposefully incomplete. Thus one cannot really answer questions of the sort "What is a Hispanic?", "Who counts as a Hispanic?", "Are Latinos, Chicanos, Hispanos, black dominicans, white cubans, korean-colombians, italian-argentinians hispanic?" What it is to be a 'hispanic' in the varied so-called hispanic communities in the U.S. is also yet up in the air. We have not yet decided whether there is something like a 'hispanic' in our varied "worlds." So, a "world" may be an incomplete visionary non-utopian construction of life or it may be a traditional construction of life. A traditional Hispano construction of Northern New Mexican life is a "world." Such a traditional construction, in the face of a racist, ethnocentrist, money-centered anglo construction of Northern New Mexican life is highly unstable because Anglos have the means for imperialist destruction of traditional Hispano "worlds."

In a "world" some of the inhabitants may not understand or hold the particular construction of them that constructs them in that "world." So, there may be "worlds" that construct me in ways that I do not even understand. Or it may be that I understand the construction, but do not hold it of myself. I may not accept it as an account of myself, a construction of myself. And yet, I may be *animating* such a construction.

One can "travel" between these "worlds" and one can inhabit more than one of these "worlds" at the very same time. I think that most of us who are outside the mainstream of, for example, the U.S. dominant construction or organization of life are "world travellers" as a matter of necessity and of survival. It seems to me that inhabiting more than one "world" at the same time and "travelling" between "worlds" is part and parcel of our experience and our situation. One can be at the same time in a "world" that constructs one as stereotypically latin, for example, and in a "world" that constructs one as latin. Being stereotypically latin and being simply latin are different simultaneous constructions of persons that are part of different "worlds." One animates one or the other or both at the same time without necessarily confusing them, though simultaneous enactment can be confusing if one is not on one's guard.

In describing my sense of a "world," I mean to be offering a description of experience, something that is true to experience even if it is ontologically problematic. Though I would think that any account of identity that could not be true to this experience of outsiders to the mainstream would be faulty even if ontologically unproblematic. Its ease would constrain, erase, or deem aberrant experience that has within it significant insights into non-imperialistic understanding between people.

Those of us who are "world"-travellers have the distinct experience of being different in different "worlds" and of having the capacity to remember other "worlds" and ourselves in them. We can say "That is me there, and I am happy in that "world." So, the experience is of being a different person in different "worlds" and yet of having memory of oneself as different without quite having the sense of there being any underlying "I." So I can say "that is me there and I am so playful in that "world." I say, "That is *me* in that "world" not because I recognize myself in that person, rather the first person statement is non-inferential. I may well recognize that that person has abilities that I do not have and yet the having or not having of the abilities is always an "I have . . ." and "I do not have . . .", i.e. it is always experienced in the first person.

The shift from being one person to being a different person is what I call "travel." This shift may not be willful or even conscious, and one may be completely unaware of being different than one is in a different "world," and may not recognize that one is in a different "world." Even though the shift can be done willfully, it is not a matter of acting. One does not pose as someone else, one does not pretend to be, for example, someone of a different personality or character or someone who uses space or language differently than the other person. Rather one is someone who has that personality or character or uses space and language in that particular way. The "one" here does not refer to some underlying "I." One does not *experience* any underlying "I."

BEING AT EASE IN A "WORLD"

In investigating what I mean by "being at ease in a 'world'," I will describe different ways of being at ease. One may be at ease in one or in all of these ways. There is a maximal way of being at ease, viz. being at ease in all of these ways. I take this maximal way of being at ease to be somewhat dangerous because it tends to produce people who have no inclination to travel across "worlds" or have no experience of "world" travelling.

The first way of being at ease in a particular "world" is by being a fluent speaker in that "world." I know all the norms that there are to be followed, I know all the words that there are to be spoken, I know all the moves. I am confident.

Another way of being at ease is by being normatively happy. I agree with all the norms, I could not love any norms better. I am asked to do just what I want to do or what I think I should do. At ease. Another way of being at ease in a world is by being humanly bonded. I am with those I love and they love me too. It should be noticed that I may be with those I love and be at ease because of them in a "world" that is otherwise as hostile to me as "worlds" get.

Finally one may be at ease because one has a history with others that is shared, especially daily history, the kind of shared history that one sees exemplified by the response to the "Do you remember poodle skirts?" question. There you are, with people you do not know at all. The question is posed and then they all begin talking about their poodle skirt stories. I have been in such situations without knowing what poodle skirts, for example, were and I felt so ill at ease because it was not *my* history. The other people did not particularly know each other. It is not that they were humanly bonded. Probably they did not have much politically in common either. But poodle skirts were in their shared history.

One may be at ease in one of these ways or in all of them. Notice that when one says meaningfully "This is *my* world," one may not be at ease in it. Or one may be at ease in it only in some of these respects and not in others. To say of some "world" that it is "*my* world" is to make an evaluation. One may privilege one or more "worlds" in this way for a variety of reasons: for example because one experiences oneself as an agent in a fuller sense than one experiences "oneself" in other "worlds." One may disown a "world" because one has first person memories of a person who is so thoroughly dominated that she has no sense of exercising her own will or has a sense of having serious difficulties in performing actions that are willed by herself and no difficulty in performing actions willed by others. One may say of a "world" that it is "my world" because one is at ease in it, i.e. being at ease in a "world" may be the basis for the evaluation.

Given the clarification of what I mean by a "world," "world"-travel, and being at ease in a "world," we are in a position to return to my problematic attribute, playfulness. It may be that in this "world" in which I am so unplayful, I am a different person than in the "world" in which I am playful. Or it may be that the "world" in which I am unplayful is constructed in such a way that I could be playful in it. I could practice, even though that "world" is constructed in such a way that my being playful in it is kind of hard. In describing what I take a "world" to be, I emphasized the first possibility as both the one that is truest to the experience of "outsiders" to the mainstream and as ontologically problematic because the "I" is identified in some sense as one and in some sense as a plurality. I identify myself as myself through memory and I retain myself as different in memory. When I travel from one "world" to another, I have this image, this memory of myself as playful in this other "world." I can then be in a particular "world" and have a double image of myself as, for example, playful and as not playful. But this is a very familiar and recognizable phenomenon to the outsider to the mainstream in some central cases: when in one "world" I animate, for example, that "world's" caricature of the person I am in the other "world." I can have both images of myself and to the extent that I can materialize or animate both images at the same time I become an ambiguous being. This is very much a part of trickery and foolery. It is worth remembering that the trickster and the fool are significant characters in many non-dominant or outsider cultures. One then sees any particular "world" with these double edges and sees absurdity in them and so inhabits oneself differently. Given that latins are constructed in Anglo "worlds" as stereotypically intense—intensity being a central characteristic of at least one of the anglo stereotypes of latins—and given that many latins, myself included, are genuinely intense, I can say to myself "I am intense" and take a hold of the double meaning. And furthermore, I can be stereotypically intense or be the real thing and, if you are Anglo, you do not know when I am which *because* I am Latin-American. As Latin-American I am an ambiguous being, a two-imaged self: I can see that gringos see me as stereotypically intense because I am, as a Latin-American, constructed that way but I may or may not *intentionally* animate the stereotype or the real thing knowing that you may not see it in anything other than in the stereotypical construction. This ambiguity is funny and is not just funny, it is survival-rich. We can also make the picture of those who dominate us funny precisely because we can see the double edge, we can see them doubly constructed, we can see the plurality in them. So we know truths that only the fool can speak and only the trickster can play out without harm. We inhabit "worlds" and travel across them and keep all the memories.

Sometimes the "world"-traveller has a double image of herself and each self includes as important ingredients of itself one or more attributes that are *incompatible* with one or more of the attributes of the other self: for example being playful and being unplayful. To the extent that the attribute is an important ingredient of the self she is in that "world," i.e., to the extent that there is a particularly good fit between that "world" and her having that attribute in it and to the extent that the attribute is personality or character central, that "world" would have to be changed if she is to be playful in it. It is not the case that if she could come to be at ease in it, she would be her own playful self. Because the attribute is personality or character central and there is such a good fit between that "world" and her being constructed with that attribute as central, *she* cannot become playful, she is unplayful. To become playful would be for her to become a contradictory being. So I am suggesting that the lack of ease solution cannot be a solution to my problematic case. My problem is not one of lack of ease. I am suggesting that I can understand my confusion about whether I am or am not playful by saying that I am both and that I am different persons in different "worlds" and can remember myself in both as I am in the other. I am a plurality of selves. This is to understand my confusion because *it is to come to see it as a piece* with much of the rest of my experience as an outsider in some of the "worlds" that I inhabit and of a piece with significant aspects of the experience of non-dominant people in the "worlds" of their dominators.

So, though I may not be at ease in the "worlds" in which I am not constructed playful, it is not that I am not playful *because* I am not at ease. The two are compatible. But lack of playfulness is not caused by lack of ease. Lack of playfulness is not symptomatic of lack of ease but of lack of health. I am not a healthy being in the "worlds" that construct me unplayful.

PLAYFULNESS

I had a very personal stake in investigating this topic. Playfulness is not only the attribute that was the source of my confusion and the attitude that I recommend as the loving attitude in travelling across "worlds," I am also scared of ending up a serious human being, someone with no multi-dimensionality, with no fun in life, someone who is just someone who has had the fun constructed out of her. I am seriously scared of getting stuck in a "world" that constructs me that way. A world that I have no escape from and in which I cannot be playful.

I thought about what it is to be playful and what it is to play and I did this thinking in a "world" in which I only remember myself as playful and in which all of those who know me as playful are imaginary beings. A "world" in which I am scared of losing my memories of myself as playful or have them erased from me. Because I live in such a "world," after I formulated my own sense of what it is to be playful and to play I decided that I needed to "go to the literature." I read two classics on the subject: Johan Huizinga's *Homo Ludens* and Hans-Georg Gadamer's chapter on the concept of play in his *Truth and Method*. I discovered, to my amazement, that what I thought about play and playfulness, if they were right, was absolutely wrong. Though I will not provide the arguments for this interpretation of Gadamer and Huizinga here, I understood that both of them have an agonistic sense of 'play.' Play and playfulness have, ultimately, to do with contest, with winning, losing, battling. The sense of playfulness that I have in mind has nothing to do with those things. So, I tried to elucidate both senses of play and playfulness by contrasting them to each other. The contrast helped me see the attitude that I have in mind as the loving attitude in travelling across "worlds" more clearly.

An agonistic sense of playfulness is one in which *competence* is supreme. You better know the rules of the game. In agonistic play there is risk, there is *uncertainty*, but the uncertainty is about who is going to win and who is going to lose. There are rules that inspire hostility. The attitude of *playfulness is conceived as secondary to or derivative from play*. Since play is agon, then the only conceivable playful attitude is an agonistic one (the attitude does not turn an activity into play, but rather presupposes an activity

that is play). One of the paradigmatic ways of playing for both Gadamer and Huizinga is role-playing. In role-playing, the person who is a participant in the game has a *fixed conception of him or herself*. I also think that the players are imbued with *self-importance* in agonistic play since they are so keen on winning given their own merits, their very own competence.

When considering the value of "world"-travelling and whether playfulness is the loving attitude to have while travelling, I recognized the agonistic attitude as inimical to travelling across "worlds." The agonistic traveller is a conqueror, an imperialist. Huizinga, in his classic book on play, interprets Western civilization as play. That is an interesting thing for Third World people to think about. Western civilization has been interpreted by a white western man as play in the agonistic sense of play. Huizinga reviews western law, art, and many other aspects of western culture and sees agon in all of them. Agonistic playfulness leads those who attempt to travel to another "world" with this attitude to failure. Agonistic travellers fail consistently in their attempt to travel because what they do is to try to conquer the other "world." The attempt is not an attempt to try to erase the other "world." That is what assimilation is all about. Assimilation is the destruction of other people's "worlds." So, the agonistic attitude, the playful attitude given western man's construction of playfulness, is not a healthy, loving attitude to have in travelling across "worlds." Notice that given the agonistic attitude one *cannot* travel across "worlds," though one can kill other "worlds" with it. So for people who are interested in crossing racial and ethnic boundaries, an arrogant western man's construction of playfulness is deadly. One cannot cross the boundaries with it. One needs to give up such an attitude if one wants to travel.

So then, what is the loving playfulness that I have in mind? Let me begin with one example: We are by the river bank. The river is very, very low. Almost dry. Bits of water here and there. Little pools with a few trout hiding under the rocks. But mostly is wet stones, grey on the outside. We walk on the stones for awhile. You pick up a stone and crash it onto the others. As it breaks, it is quite wet inside and it is very colorful, very pretty. I pick up a stone and break it and run toward the pieces to see the colors. They are beautiful. I laugh and bring the pieces back to you and you are doing the same with your pieces. We keep on crashing stones for hours, anxious to see the beautiful new colors. We are playing. The playfulness of our activity does not presuppose that there is something like "crashing stones" that is a particular form of play with its own rules. Rather *the attitude that carries us through the activity, a playful attitude, turns the activity into play.* Our activity has no rules, though it is certainly intentional activity and we both understand what we are doing. The playfulness that gives meaning to our activity includes uncertainty, but in this case the uncertainty is an *openness to surprise.* This is a particular metaphysical attitude that does not expect the world to be neatly packaged, ruly. Rules may fail to explain what we are doing. We are not self-important, we are not fixed in particular constructions of ourselves, which is part of saying that we are *open to self-construction.* We may not have rules, and when we do have rules, *there are no rules that are to us sacred.* We are not worried about competence. We are not wedded to a particular way of doing things. While playful we have not abandoned ourselves to, nor are we stuck in, any particular "world." We *are there creatively.* We are not passive.

Playfulness is, in part, an openness to being a fool, which is a combination of not worrying about competence, not being self-important, not taking norms as sacred and finding ambiguity and double edges a source of wisdom and delight.

So, positively, the playful attitude involves openness to surprise, openness to being a fool, openness to self-construction or reconstruction and to construction or reconstruction of the "worlds" we inhabit playfully. Negatively, playfulness is characterized by uncertainty, lack of self-importance, absence of rules or a not taking rules as sacred, a not worrying about competence and a lack of abandonment to a particular construction of oneself, others and one's relation to them. In attempting to take a hold of oneself and of one's relation to others in a particular "world," one may study, examine and come to understand oneself. One may then see what the possibilities for play are for the being one is in that "world." One may even decide to inhabit that self fully in order to understand it better and find its creative possibilities. All of this is just self-reflection and it is quite different from resigning or abandoning oneself to the particular construction of oneself that one is attempting to take a hold of.

CONCLUSION

There are "worlds" we enter at our own risk, "worlds" that have agon, conquest, and arrogance as the main ingredients in their ethos. These are "worlds" that

we enter out of necessity and which would be foolish to enter playfully in either the agonistic sense or in my sense. In such "worlds" *we* are not playful.

But there are "worlds" that we can travel to lovingly and travelling to them is part of loving at least some of their inhabitants. The reason why I think that travelling to someone's "world" is a way of identifying with them is because by travelling to their "world" we can understand *what it is to be them and what it is to be ourselves in their eyes.* Only when we have travelled to each other's "worlds" are we fully subjects to each other (I agree with Hegel that self-recognition requires other subjects, but I disagree with his claim that it requires tension or hostility).

Knowing other women's "worlds" is part of knowing them and knowing them is part of loving them. Notice that the knowing can be done in greater or lesser depth, as can the loving. Also notice that travelling to another's "world" is not the same as becoming intimate with them. Intimacy is constituted in part by a very deep knowledge of the other self and "world" travelling is only part of having this knowledge. Also notice that some people, in particular those who are outsiders to the mainstream, can be known only to the extent that they are known in several "worlds" and as "world"-travellers.

Without knowing the other's "world," one does not know the other, and without knowing the other one is really alone in the other's presence because the other is only dimly present to one.

Through travelling to other people's "worlds" we discover that there are "worlds" in which those who are the victims of arrogant perception are really subjects, lively beings, resistors, constructors of visions even though in the mainstream construction they are animated only by the arrogant perceiver and are pliable, foldable, file-awayable, classifiable. I always imagine the Aristotelian slave as pliable and foldable at night or after he or she cannot work anymore (when he or she dies as a tool). Aristotle tells us nothing about the slave *apart from the master.* We know the slave only through the master. The slave is a tool of the master. After working hours he or she is folded and placed in a drawer till the next morning. My mother was apparent to me mostly as a victim of arrogant perception. I was loyal to the arrogant perceiver's construction of her and thus disloyal to her in assuming that she was exhausted by that construction. I was unwilling to be like her and thought that identifying with her, seeing myself in her necessitated that I become like her. I was wrong both in assuming that she was exhausted by the arrogant perceiver's construction of her and in my understanding of identification, though I was not wrong in thinking that identification was part of loving and that it involved in part my seeing myself in her. I came to realize through travelling to her "world" that she is not foldable and pliable, that she is not exhausted by the mainstream argentinian patriarchal construction of her. I came to realize that there are "worlds" in which she shines as a creative being. Seeing myself in her through travelling to her "world" has meant seeing how different from her I am in her "world."

So, in recommending "world"-travelling and identification through "world"-travelling as part of loving other women, I am suggesting disloyalty to arrogant perceivers, including the arrogant perceiver in ourselves, and to their constructions of women. In revealing agonistic playfulness as incompatible with "world"-travelling, I am revealing both its affinity with imperialism and arrogant perception and its incompatibility with loving and loving perception.

K. C. Anyanwu (Contemporary)
CULTURAL PHILOSOPHY AS A PHILOSOPHY OF INTEGRATION AND TOLERANCE

The author, who is an African philosopher, sees the main problem of the twentieth century as psychic dissociation arising from the encounter of different cultural values. He argues that this problem can be soundly addressed through a philosophy of culture: an incessant effort at creating new meanings by adjusting new ideas and working them into some patterns of living and thinking. Anyanwu's views are considered toward the end of the introductory essay to Part VI.

READING QUESTIONS

In reading the selection, try to answer the following questions and identify the passages that support your answers:

1. What does Anyanwu mean by "psychic dissociation"?
2. What problem does this dissociation pose?
3. What does Anyanwu think philosophy can do about it?
4. What reasons does he give for his views on this matter?
5. Are they good reasons? Why or why not?

Reprinted by permission of the *International Philosophical Quarterly* from K. C. Anyanwu, "Cultural Philosophy as a Philosophy of Integration and Tolerance," *International Philosophical Quarterly*, Vol. 25 (September 1987), pp. 271–287. Copyright © 1987.

1. INTRODUCTION

The whole world seems to have become united under the metric system as well as the system of "hook-ups" and "plug-ins," but the spiritual distance between nations seems to be increasing enormously. The experience of moral denigration, the intransi-gence of nationalism and spiritual bereavement is definitely forcing modern people or nations back to their fundamental assumptions as they search for the meaning of existence, of life, and of man.

The purpose of this essay is not to offer a ready-made philosophical treatise on human experience which may be accepted or rejected *en bloc*. Rather, it is an invitation to examine some of the basic issues of the 20th century (the problems of cultural experience and values, of human dignity and integration, of human coexistence and tolerance) whose absence or denial has, to a certain degree, contributed to fear and tension in the world. And as students of philosophy, our task in this situation includes the search for or the suggestion of new ideas and new modes of thought that will resolve the present conflicts and tensions. This means that we need a new philosophy or a new vision of man because "only when we have a sense of direction do we have a basis for action."[1]

DEFINITION OF PROBLEM

All nations are intensely and profoundly aware of change but they seem to disagree on the meaning and direction of change as well as on the forces responsible for it. This is clearly shown in the ideological interpretation of the 20th century crisis, the crisis of faith and man, because "by common consent we live in an age of crisis."[2] This crisis, whether caused by science and technology, which has accelerated social change throughout the world beyond human adaptation,[3] or by the "capitalists" and the "communists" who wish to "dominate the world," or by the "socialists" and "freedom fighters" who wish to liberate themselves from "colonialism," "imperialism," and "neo-colonialism," points to at least one basic question: the question of man and his values.

The question touches on man's beliefs about himself, the world in which he lives, and his purpose in life. Consequently, it is a question of cultural experience and value. "Cultures differ from one another to the extent to which their experience has differed. . . . By 'experience' I mean anything that an individual or group of individuals has undergone or lived, perceived or sensed."[4] Since human experiences and cultures differ, there will also be differences of values. "Values are attitudes of mind. Values represent

judgements as to the manner in which the best adjustment may be made to certain conditions. All peoples obviously must have values."[5] These conclusions supported by cultural and historical experiences seem obvious to all nations but, in practice, all nations do not seem to acknowledge, respect, and tolerate them. Ideological differences, for example, are nothing but differences of values. And to suppose that all nations will embrace only one ideological doctrine is contrary to the evidence of culture and history. In spite of this, each nation seems to enforce her values on other nations or despise those nations whose values differ from her own.[6] Definitely this attitude of intolerance does not aid human coexistence but creates fear and tension. What all nations have to accept is that "since the conditions of life—the history of each people—have differed, the value system of each people will therefore differ accordingly. Once this concept of historical or cultural relativity is grasped it becomes possible to understand why the values of other peoples differ from ours."[7]

In order to grasp the 20th century crisis we need a shift of perspective from the traditional analysis of historical crisis or conflict. In the past, it was analysed in terms of military, political, economic, religious, or spiritual crisis, that is, in terms of the dualism that was characteristic of modern thought for the past four centuries.

> Ideas are never the sole cause of social change, but thought is part of the social process and may facilitate or inhibit its development. The present confusion in knowledge and behaviour is closely related to the deep-lying errors of analytical thought.[8]

Psychic dissociation, or the fragmentation of man and his cultural experience, led to the split in human consciousness, destroyed the unity of selfhood, gave rise to the lust for power, bred fear and tension, frustration and violence. The incapacity of intellectual dualism to see man, life, and the world as a whole, or the incapacity of the dissociated man to

---

[1] Franz E. Winkler, *Man: A Bridge Between Two Worlds* (New York: Harper and Row Publishers, 1960), p. 251.

[2] Roderick Seidenberg, *Anatomy of the Future* (Chapel Hill: University of North Carolina Press, 1961), p. 7.

[3] The behaviouristic interpretation of the modern crisis maintains that man's frustration stems from his inability to adjust to the scientific and technological environment and recommends the control of man's behaviour as a solution to the crisis. It does not seem to imagine that man's frustration or his lack of adjustment arises from the fact that he does not want to live in a meaningless world.

[4] Ashley Montagu, *Man in Process* (New York: New American Library, 1961), p. 20.

[5] Ibid., p. 38.

[6] If universal suffrage is a desirable thing, it does not follow that it will imply universal intelligence. Modern education may be a desirable thing but it does not follow that wherever it exists there is good sense. If all nations should have representative governments as the ideal of democracy, it does not follow that there will necessarily be justice.

[7] Ashley Montagu, op cit., p 38.

[8] Lancelot Law Whyte, *The Next Development in Man* (London: Cresset Press, 1944), p. 22. Analytic thought had aided European material and mechanical development since 1600. It cannot facilitate human integration, which demands a unitary mode of thought.

face life and the world as a whole, negatively influences man's behaviour. And an attempt to give a partial solution to the problem affecting the whole man (a military, political, economic, technological, or religious solution) merely increases world tension.

"The tendency to organise thought is healthy; where order is lacking man inevitably experiences the need for it."[9] This is especially appropriate in the 20th century and the work of organising thought requires a clear understanding of man's problematic situation. It is for this reason that the reader is invited to consider the 20th-century crisis as the product of psychic dissociation and the encounter of different cultural values. What is required from this perspective is the development of a unitary mode of thought, devoid of all forms of dualism, that will facilitate the integration of man and all levels of his cultural experiences and expressions. William Beck considers the 20th-century crisis as "the crisis of transition between two worlds, the old that is dying and the new that is struggling to be born. Its pain is the pain of uncertainty."[10] But this uncertainty does not mean absolute scepticism or despair. Rather, it stems from man's deep insight into his power and limitation, especially his power of knowledge. For example, "unitary thought postulated a unity of the general form of development. It asserts: form develops, when circumstances permit."[11] It is proper that any fundamental postulate should embody two parts, the first part which claims knowledge and the second which claims ignorance. And furthermore, "when thought passes from universal to particular facts, knowledge becomes conditional. It has to distinguish this system here, whose tendency may be known, from the rest of nature, whose complexity is beyond knowledge."[12] The new mode of thought or the new world "that is struggling to be born" depends on certain factors. First, the crisis or conflict should be viewed positively as a life-force that is creative, provided it is directed and controlled. Second, we have to realise that "our business is not to solve problems beyond mortal powers but to see to it that our thoughts are not unworthy of the great theme."[13]

PROBLEMATIC SITUATION

From the best of our historical knowledge, "man has established a mastery over nature which is unique in the three billion years of this earth's history. He has not, however, established anything like a comparable mastery over himself."[14] He seems to possess infinite obligations but he does not seem to possess the knowledge and the will that may enable him to fulfil such obligations. Intolerance and self-interest, the policy of concealment and the lust for power constitute some of the basic impediments to world peace.

The emergence of independent nations from the colonial rule has, for example, brought about the demand on the part of the newly independent people to play

> . . . an equal role with other peoples in the governments of the world affairs and in their relations with other human beings. Political developments in Africa . . . underscore the pressure of what is no less than a profound moral duty on the part of every thinking citizen to make himself acquainted with the facts concerning the nature of human nature.[15]

New beliefs and ideas are challenging the old assumptions about God, man, nature, good, evil, society, well-being, etc. on which the western nations, for example, justified their religious, political, economic, and military activities at home and abroad. And naturally those who profit by such assumptions as well as institutions based on them would be unwilling to see the triumph of new beliefs and ideas that tend to broaden the scope and the terms of human relationships. But the crisis seems to have produced an awareness that makes it possible today for all nations to look for a common solution to it. In 1907 Meredith Townsend, for example, wrote that "if Europe can avoid internal war or war with a much aggrandized America, she will by A.D. 2000 be mistress in Asia, and at liberty as her people think to enjoy."[16] This mode of thought has no merit today and as history shows, it has never had any merit.

In spite of cultural differences, all nations are becoming aware (especially due to the fear of thermonuclear war) that

> they are bound together, beyond any divisiveness, by a more fundamental unity than any mere agreement in thought and doctrine. They are beginning to know that

[9] Ibid., p. 12.

[10] William S. Beck, *Modern Science and the Nature of Life* (Middlesex, England: Penguin Books, 1961), p. 22.

[11] Lancelot Law Whyte, op. cit., p. 45.

[12] Ibid., p. 45.

[13] W. Macneile Dixon, *The Human Situation* (Harmondsworth, Middlesex, England: Penguin Books, 1958), p. 22.

[14] Ashley Montagu, op. cit., p. ix.

[15] Ibid., p. x.

[16] Meredith Townsend, *Asia and Europe* (New York: Putnam, 1907), p. 4.

all men possess the same primordial desires and tendencies; that the domination of man over man can no longer be justified by an appeal to God or nature; and such consciousness is the fruit of the spiritual and moral revolution through which humanity is now passing.[17]

If we are to use beliefs, ideas, and thoughts to facilitate the development of man we have to know how different people in different cultures understand their world and pursue their goals. This knowledge may prepare the ground for the foundation of true world history, not in terms of nations or race, but in terms of man's relationship to God, man, nature, and the universe. This is the task for the philosophy of culture.

PHILOSOPHY OF CULTURE

"The primary problem of all philosophy is the problem of the most general characters of experience and of reflection. For no object-matter of knowledge can escape the necessity of being given in individual experience and no theory can escape the necessity of being the product of logical reflection."[18] If this primary problem is fully understood, it becomes obvious that

> Modern philosophy must be a philosophy of a world of pure ideas independent of the individual's experience, or a world of pure natural reality independent of reflection; starting with experience or reflection was merely a methodical trick used in order to reach something entirely different. But if we realize that the concrete world is a world of culture, the situation changes.[19]

The change is due to the fact that culture as we know it is only human culture, with reference to concrete human beings who experience it. Culture itself is the product of human experience or a response to it while "experience is determined by the place . . . in which groups and individuals live, and it is for this reason that groups and individuals belonging to different cultures will differ mentally from one another.[20]

The goal of the philosophy of culture within the context of the 20th century crisis includes the liberation of man from fear, the integration of human sensibilities, and the restoration of confidence in the human person. In trying to gain insight into the meaning of man the philosophy of culture cannot ignore the history of man who determines history and is determined by history. "History is to be understood as concerned not only with the life of man on this planet but the including also of such cosmic influences as interpenetrate our human world."[21] From this perspective, philosophy of culture emphasizes "the spiritual sense of convergence toward world unity on the basis of the sacredness of each human person and respect for the plurality of culture."[22] In reorganizing and reinterpreting human experience and ideas, it cannot start from scratch to survey the world but from the interpretation of the existing values which have been challenged by fresh ideas. And the new ideas, when clarified, can serve as a new focus for the interpretation of new experiences. Thus the philosophy of culture is an "open system," an incessant effort at creating new meanings by adjusting new ideas and working them into some pattern of living and thinking. "Philosophical orientation is to a large degree determined by the whole cultural pattern of an era,"[22] and the human realities in the 20th century demand the relaxation of tension through the cultural integration of human sensibilities.

THE PRESENT STATE OF PHILOSOPHY

If philosophy is to help in resolving the present crisis, it has to restore its value in human communities.

> The philosophers must bear a large share of the blame for the low estate of philosophy at the present time. Systems have multiplied, but many of them owe their survival only to subtle distinctions which have no significance for the man in the street.[23]

According to Carl Weizsacker, "philosophy as a university discipline commands no authority today; in continental Europe, it mainly stands guard, in the manner of competent philologists, over a historical treasure of knowledge. Rarely indeed is this knowledge transformed into an alive awareness. . . ."[24] He further indicated that "the current situation is obscure, Existentialism has ebbed away."[25]

---

[17] Lancelot Law Whyte, *Accent on Form* (New York: Harper, 1954), p. ix.

[18] Florian Znaneicki, *Cultural Reality* (Chicago: University of Chicago Press, 1919), p. 24.

[19] Ibid., p. 24.

[20] Ashley Montagu, op. cit., p. 20.

[21] Lancelot Law Whyte, *Accent on Form*, p. ix.

[22] Ibid., p. 24.

[23] Charles Nayer, *In Quest of a New Ethics*, trans. Harold A. Larrabee (Boston: Beacon Press, 1954), p. 6.

[24] Carl Friedrich von Weizsacker, *The Unity of Nature*, trans. Francis J. Zucker (New York: Farrar, Straus and Giroux, 1980), p. 26.

[25] Ibid., p. 27.

Richard Kroner described existentialism as "the last cry of a dying humanistic metaphysics. In its French, atheistic form it sounds a rather hysterical note that no longer rings convincingly."[26] In their preoccupation with methodology, philosophers seem to give the impression that "once you have assured yourself of the worth of the instrument, then you will see how to use it properly. But alas, the moment never comes."[27] Philosophers have invented many methods, but do they know to what subject-matter they are applicable? According to Carnap, "science in principle can say all that can be said."[28] Hans Reichenbach was of the view that "what we know can be said, and what cannot be said cannot be known."[29] In Wittgenstein's view, "whatever can be said at all can be said clearly. . . . Whereof one cannot speak, thereof must one be silent."[30] These philosophers have been accused of "legislating conformity to their rigorous standard (in the manner of Benjamin Jowett, the master of Balliol, who allegedly proclaimed, 'I am master of this College/What I do not know isn't knowledge')."[31] One would have supposed that "dogmatism is out of fashion since Kant or has been out of fashion since we are today facing various forms of dogmatism."[32]

The positivists indicate, for example, that we should "restrict our craving for knowledge to those facts which we may be able to know with certainty. That is easy to assert, but it is extremely difficult to limit oneself in any such fashion, and furthermore it is futile to do so rigorously."[33] Philosophy as an institutionalized activity seems to be speaking to professional philosophers (not even as whole human beings but as specialists) and not to the people who experience the turmoil of life and who need certain schemes of thought to organize their lives. "Many philosophies have been built upon the assumption that the true and the good are one and the same,"[34] and Spinoza's philosophy is a good example. Are we to accept that the true is good even when experience

is vile? Are all kinds of agony, atrocity, and wickedness good because they exist? Hobbes, having limited reality to objects of mathematical understanding, maintained that nothing was real except matter and motion, that reason was the movement of the appropriate parts of the human body, that consciousness was unreal being solely "a phantasmatic accompaniment of matter." Thus he established what was for him a rational system of thought but there was no room for reason in that system.

Reason, in its ordinary usage, means sense, sanity, sound thinking and intelligence. For professional philosophers or in philosophy, "it refers to the process of logical thought and not necessarily to the pursuit of truth."[35] The ideal of logic can be found at work in mathematics. Euclid's geometry, for example, was based on the assumptions that parallel lines never meet. What the mathematician does is to analyze his given premises for their implicit meanings even though his "truth" has no direct connection with the external world. "The difficulty with rationalism arose when men, impressed and awed by the power of reason, came to believe that all questions, even the Big Questions of philosophy, could be made to yield to the reasoning mind, which, in fact, has access to all of the great and ultimate."[36] The rationalists have also made "reasonable" proposals in the world but "the criterion of reasonableness is not so much conformity with the stated premises as conformity with reality. . . . Plato's argument concerning the family is logical enough, but it is made precisely because it is logical."[37] Life is larger than the trammels of logic. To make life a part of logic instead of logic a part of life is to distort the living experience which is life itself. The "reasonable" proposals of Plato are absurd not due to "a failure of logic but the narrowness of initial intuition, narrowness of experience, a lack of scope and generosity in their aims."[38] The contemporary conception of philosophy as "open" thinking arises from the recognition that "our logic must follow reality, not reality our logic."[39] Logic constrains us but philosophy always leaves us free.

[26] Richard Kroner, *Culture and Faith* (Cummington, Mass.: 1949), p. ix. Cf. Jean-Paul Sartre, *Existentialism est un Humanisme*, 1946.

[27] Charles Mayer, op. cit., p. 8. Henri Bergson, *L'Energie Spirituelle* (Paris, 1919), pp. 24–25.

[28] Reuben, Abel, *Man is the Measure* (New York: Free Press, 1976), p. 22.

[29] Ibid.

[30] Ibid.

[31] Ibid.

[32] Clarence Irving Lewis, *Mind and the World Order* (New York: Dover Publications, 1956), p. 8.

[33] Charles Mayer, op. cit., p. 8.

[34] W. Macneile Dixon, op. cit., p. 16.

[35] William S. Beck, op. cit., p. 58.

[36] Ibid., p. 59.

[37] Martin Versfeld, *The Mirror of Philosophers* (London and New York: Sheed and Ward, 1960), p. 18.

[38] Ibid., p. 18.

[39] Ibid., p. 28.

Philosophy cannot ignore the evidence of immediate experience[40] even though it may not take us as far as might be expected. But "we must not however conclude that, because we cannot justify a common-sense belief by argument, that the common-sense belief is necessarily wrong."[41] There is a possibility that "at a common-sense level we have a genuine knowledge or justified belief which can stand in its own right and does not require philosophical justification."[42] Beliefs and ideas have vital functions because "they interpret experience that is meaningful in its own terms because it embodies a functioning pattern of living."[43] If philosophy is to fulfill its function as a guide for action, if it is to enable man in the 20th century to recover his integration, if it is "to reassert its former validity and regain its legitimate place of leadership, it has to undergo an internal reformation." This requires that it weed out "some of the innumerable systems which encumber it, and get rid of much of its present useless luggage. It should become again what it once was: a statement, intelligible to everyone, of clear and simple principles whose interconnections are rationally set forth. Let us, then, restore philosophy to what it was in antiquity, the science of life."[44] Philosophy, in this modest status, enables people

> to think well, to reason practically—neither too much nor too little, because it is the means of living as well as circumstances permit us to live. To see clearly into the causes of things, to analyze our own acts and motives, and to try to understand those of others—that is the best way to approach knowledge.[45]

Philosophy of culture, as a guide of life, shows or brings out to how great an extent the dogmatic claim of many philosophers to be the masters and possessors of reality has collapsed. It rejects any authoritarian method because "the essence of the authoritarian method is that the individual relinquishes, in all but his common-sense belief, his independent efforts to determine what is true or false."[46] An authoritarian method does not tolerate alternative ideas. It must also be realized that interest in philosophy is not just an academic subject-matter but an expression of a people's culture. Therefore, if philosophy becomes "so institutionalized as to serve the profession, but not those whom the profession was supposed to serve,"[47] it loses much of its function as a science of life. "A philosophy which speaks, even indirectly, only to philosophers is not philosophy at all. . . . For the business of philosophy . . . is to articulate the principles by which man can live; not just as a scientist, citizen, religious or whatever, but as the whole man that he is."[48] Let us not forget too that "all men are philosophers and that the academic discipline exists solely for the purpose of purifying and refining that natural philosophy of the common man who is a necessary part of human life."[49] This awareness or fact does not in any way underrate the pursuit of philosophy as a technical discipline by professional philosophers. Rather, philosophy as a technical discipline should be pursued "in order to help men think more clearly and more truly about themselves and the world which they inhabit."[50] Any man who thinks, speaks and lives necessarily needs philosophy and "true philosophy is a therapy for the common intellect of common men, and true therapy does not try to destroy what it is trying to heal or perfect."[51]

The need for understanding man as a meaning-maker and as a product of culture is so important today that philosophers cannot afford to dissipate their energy on methodology. It is important to stress this point because philosophers may presume that if they could agree on one method or invent one perfect method, then they would arrive at one philosophy to end all philosophical differences. It is quite erroneous to suppose that the hindrance to progress in philosophy is due to methodology. It is necessary to understand the assumptions, theories, concepts, and world-view (the methods) in terms of which different cultures interpret the facts of experience. But it does not seem appropriate to suppose that any culture whose standard of interpretation does not meet with the approval of other cultures offends against "the one truth," because philosophy does not pos-

---

[40] People do not normally have immediate experience of any minds but their own. Furthermore, the evidence of immediate experience may not possibly tell us that the physical object we experience exists independently of us.

[41] A. C. Ewing, *The Fundamental Questions of Philosophy* (New York: Macmillan, 1968), p. 27.

[42] Ibid., p. 27.

[43] John Herman Randall Jr. and Justus Buchler, *Philosophy: An Introduction* (New York: Harper and Row, 1971), p. 28.

[44] Charles Mayer, op. cit., p. 7.

[45] Ibid., p. 9.

[46] John Herman Randall, Jr. and Justus Buchler, op. cit., p. 51.

[47] Abraham Kaplan, *The New World of Philosophy* (New York: Knopf, 1961), p. 4.

[48] Ibid., p. 4.

[49] John Wild, *Introduction to Realistic Philosophy* (New York: Harper and Row, 1948), p. 3.

[50] Ibid., pp. 3–4.

[51] Ibid., p. 5.

sess it. Even the "logical norms grounded in scientific practice can no longer claim the certainty and universality which for Plato were the only marks of genuine knowledge as distinguished from mere opinions."[52] Kaplan has pointed out that "a more pervasive trait of American culture is manifested in the overemphasis on what methodology can achieve."[53] Reisman also called attention to "the excessive preoccupation with technique which often sets in when Americans realise that they are not able to do certain things—raise children, . . . make friends—naturally."[54] Methodologists seem to have been acting as "baseball commissioners, writing rules, or at any rate as umpires, with power to thumb an offending player out of the game."[55]

As a result, it appears that philosophers have diverted a great deal of effort from the basic issues of man and his cultural experience to the problem of methodology. They may succeed in perfecting a method but without getting anything done even in an imperfect manner. Methodology, if pressed too far, may even impede the emergence of bold and imaginative ideas that can be beneficial to the knowledge of culture. Furthermore, methodology seems to level all minds by encouraging conformity to its own standard. It impedes productivity, encourages the imitation of colleagues, and stifles the genuine effort to establish a new vision of reality. The study of culture may enable us to realise that the principle of autonomy of inquiry cannot be compromised without a profound distortion of cultural experience. "There are certain philosophers who bravely set out to do battle for truth, when it is they themselves, like Don Quixote, who stand in the need of succour."[56] Michael Scriven warned that methodology should remain alert to "the logicians' perennial temptation to make the portrait neat and perhaps the sitter will become neat. Usually there is more to be learnt from a study of disarray than is gained by intentionally disregarding it."[57] Experience shall therefore be the final judge in the study of cultural philosophy, not logical coherence or strict consistency. "To by-pass experience in the pursuit of truth is to make oneself a God; for only He can say, 'Let there be and there is.'"[58]

PHILOSOPHERS IN THE CULTURAL CONTEXT

Cultural philosophy demands that each culture make explicit its basic assumptions about reality and the standards in terms of which it interprets experience. The understanding of these factors will facilitate the knowledge of the normative theory of each culture. In short, self-understanding may be considered as the highest knowledge that cultural philosophy offers. It entails the knowledge of the knower and his circumstances.

Philosophers whose functions include the reorganization and interpretation of cultural experience are products of culture. They have "different centres of evidences and have intellectual, emotional, perhaps financial interests, in the view-points they hold."[59] This awareness would remind us of the personal and cultural characters of all philosophical thoughts. Since this is the case, it is difficult to be impartial in our judgements about human values, especially the questions of ethics, social relations, politics, etc. In other words, our search for objectivity cannot prescind from the circumstances of the thinker. Each person is inclined to judge things, events, or human behaviour according to his education, feelings, social status, and temperament. Therefore, the philosophy of culture teaches us not to forget the wholly relative character of the principles which philosophers may be tempted to set forth as absolute truths. Once this fact is recognised we can no longer conceal the extent to which our personal predilections influence our views or conclusions on cultural experience and value. Rather, we shall begin to realise that "the first principle of any man's philosophy is the man himself in his concrete, individual personal setting, a contingent being in a flux of historical contingencies."[60] For these reasons it does not seem likely that the differences among different schools of thought are merely differences of basic assumptions and logic. "Profound differences in personality and temperament express themselves in ever changing forms . . . between the worldly and otherworldly types of thought."[61] As a result, countless efforts to resolve philosophical differences or conflicts by adopting certain methods of philosophizing were frustrated. "And it seems likely that this situation in philosophy will continue as long

[52] Abraham Kaplan, op. cit., p. 13.

[53] Ibid., p. 24.

[54] Ibid., pp. 24–25.

[55] Ibid., p. 25.

[56] Ibid., p. 26.

[57] Ibid., p. 27.

[58] Ibid., p. 35.

[59] Martin Versfeld, op. cit., p. 75.

[60] Ibid., p. 75.

[61] Dagobert D. Runes, *Living Schools of Thought* (Paterson, New Jersey: Littlefield, Adams, 1962), p. 325.

as human nature in its relation to its cultural environment remains what it has been for the last three or four thousand years."

The cultural circumstances of philosophers do not mean that a fairly objective knowledge cannot be achieved on certain issues. Rather, those cultural circumstances compel us to doubt that there exists only *One Truth* about the world, life, society, nature, etc. They enable us to suspect that there may be many truths about them depending on man's cultural relationship to them.

> It is equally possible that man may know the world in many and diverse interpretations growing out of different experiences. The realization of the different forms of association and interpretations of the world and meaning of life should set tolerance in the place of intolerance, and sympathy and understanding in the place of impatience and contempt.[62]

The philosophy of culture therefore reveals that "a tolerance based on enriched understanding is indeed one of the priceless fruits brought by acquaintance with man's philosophic thinking, even if its critics' severest complaints be accepted."[63] Due to the cultural circumstances of man, "philosophy rises afresh with every human being who takes responsibility for his own thought, and proclaims the originality of his own being and his situation, a being which is itself and not that of anybody else. Philosophers will have one philosophy when each has his own."[64] This is so because

> The philosophic insights that serve men as principles for interpreting their knowledge and activities spring out of their own experience, and in the last analysis it is that experience which they render meaningful. The vision of life a man proclaims is significant for the experience it expresses, and for all those who in some measure share that experience—perhaps an entire society or age.[65]

Philosophy of culture is therefore the philosophy of tolerance. It shows that "every philosophy belongs to its age and its subject to its limitations."[66] It reveals the intimate relationship between man and the circumstances surrounding his thoughts. Leopardi, for example, thought that "all that exists is evil, that

anything exists is evil, everything exists only to achieve evil, existence itself is evil; and destined to evil. There is no other good than evil."[67] Since man's feelings about the world, whether good or bad, affect his thinking, it is certain that Leopardi's thought cannot be understood unless within the context of his cultural experience. "There is no doubt that all reasoning is in a manner biased, and the bias is due to the nature, surroundings, and education of the thinker."[68] If we take all these and similar cultural observations into consideration, philosophers will undeniably accept that "there are in the realm of thought no absolute authorities, no dictators. No man, living or dead, can claim oracular power. . . . All philosophies are in the end personal. . . . Systems of thought are the shadows cast by different races, epochs and civilizations."[69]

"The starting point of any philosophy," as the study of culture reveals, ". . . is a particular man in particular circumstances. Now, in certain obvious ways this situation does determine how he philosophizes and whether he philosophizes at all."[70] The emphasis on the particular man as the starting point of philosophy does not mean that philosophic experience is just an individual property. "No man can hope to become a good philosopher," Bertrand Russell pointed out, "unless he has certain feelings which are not very common. . . . He must learn to think and feel, not as a member of this or that group, but as just a human being."[71] In other words, a person who desires to be a good philosopher should cultivate a general outlook on life. It is important, Russell indicates, that he learns not to be angry with opinions that are different from his own "but to set to work understanding how they come about."[72] Philosophic experience, as already indicated, is a shared and cooperative experience, not just the property of an individual. It is closely related to religious and social experience hence "a sharing of feeling, attitude, habitual cooperative activity as well as belief and observed fact."[73]

There is a sense in which philosophy can speak about "the communality of human problems. I do

---

[62]   Ibid., p. 325. John Herman Randall Jr. and Justus Buchler, op. cit., p. 19.

[63]   Ibid., p. 19.

[64]   Ibid., p. 92.

[65]   Ibid., pp. 19–20.

[66]   W. Macneile Dixon, op. cit., p. 21.

[67]   Ibid., p. 85.

[68]   Ibid., p. 13.

[69]   Ibid., p. 13.

[70]   Martin Versfeld, op. cit., p. 76.

[71]   Bertrand Russell, *The Art of Philosophizing* (New York: Philosophical Library, 1968), p. 26.

[72]   Ibid., p. 25.

[73]   John Herman Randall Jr. and Justus Buchler, op. cit., p. 20.

not mean to say that the world's philosophies today are at bottom all the same; on the contrary. They could not serve as philosophies to live by if they did not embody within themselves the distinctive traits which differentiate one culture from another."[74] Kaplan further indicated that "a number of themes can be identified as recurring elements in the various world philosophies."[75] But he said: "I am not talking about anything so abstruse as a supposedly perennial and universal philosophy." The philosophy of culture invites us to examine and to call "the bluff on accepted dogmas."[76] It invites all men to take a stand on the great issues of life. And because our emotional interests are involved in those matters to which we commit ourselves, "our thoughts must be full of . . . confusion and prejudice."[77] Our emotional commitments to our values or to matters in which we care most also explain why "when we meet those whose conduct and professed beliefs are markedly different from ours, our accustomed standards are challenged, and we become concerned. In our irritated reaction we may turn away in loathing, or try to exterminate the strange abomination."[77] The study of the philosophy of culture would hopefully enable us to tolerate the differences of cultural values without minimizing the importance of those differences and the complementarity of such values. It would also enable us to realize that "the shock of opinions is the necessary condition for breaking up prejudice, fanaticism and for liberating the mind from the incrustations of custom and tradition."[78]

CULTURAL QUEST

Philosophy of culture shows without doubt that different cultures and different men have given different interpretations to the meaning of life. Since there is no absolute standard for interpreting the meaning of life, it is possible that all the interpretations given by different cultures and men were right or valid under the cultural experiences and circumstances of a people. "The experience out of which

come the insights in terms of which men try to organize their lives and their total world-views is much more complex and subtle if less precise and less capable of exact formulation."[79] However, man's cultural quest is the quest for meaning and self-fulfilment.

"Since its beginning, mankind has been interested in the source of its criticism, the keys to survival, the pursuit of beauty (and more recently truth), and the secret of everlasting life."[80] But, as earlier indicated, different cultures found different meanings in life. These differences explain why "cultural patterns of life differ widely from people to people, from age to age, and from location to location, the physical environment obviously having an important influence in shaping the ways of men."[81] Culture is the function of experience and differences in culture give rise to differences of mentality. Cultural quest takes different forms and "is mirrored in arts, sciences, political activity and moral development."[82] This shows that "man engages in varied activities of building in order to restore something which he either has lost or finds lacking in his fundamental constitution."[83] Cultural activities arise from the fact that man has "an inner life which originates from an experience which itself has an inner meaning and which asks for meaning. The primary function of culture is to communicate an answer to that question and to satisfy the demand for meaning."[83]

The conceptual framework of the philosophy of culture is integrative. This is so because "activities, goals or values do not come isolated or piece-meal, but as integral part of this complex habitual way of doing things."[84] In other words, the philosophy of culture cannot speak of art as if it is detached from religion; religion as if detached from mystical feelings. "The culture which man builds is experienced not as a system but as an actual reality which dominates his life and in which he participates by his con-

---

[74] Abraham Kaplan, *The New World of Philosophy*, p. 7.

[75] Ibid.

[76] Mark B. Woodhouse, *A Preface to Philosophy* (Belmont, Ca.: Wadsworth, 1980), p. 23.

[77] Morris Raphael Cohen, *Reason and Nature: The Meaning of Scientific Method* (New York: Free Press, 1964), p. 20.

[78] Alexander N. Tsambassis, *Human Experience and Its Problems* (Belmont, Ca.: Wadsworth, 1967), p. 2.

[79] John Herman Randall, Jr. and Justus Buchler, op. cit., p. 20.

[80] William S. Beck, *Modern Sciences and the Nature of Life* (Middlesex, England: Penguin Books Ltd., 1961), p. 41.

[81] Ibid., p. 41.

[82] John E. Skinner, *Self and World: Religious Philosophy of Richard Kroner* (Philadelphia: University of Pennsylvania Press, 1962), p. 55.

[83] Ibid., p. 60.

[84] John Herman Randall, Jr., and Justus Buchler, op. cit., p. 28. Lancelot Law Whyte discussed extensively how the fragmentation of cultural experience in the West due to analytic thought led to the mechanical development of the western civilization as well as the impoverishment of man as a whole man. Cf. *The Next Development in Man*.

duct and attitude through active contributions and creativity."[85] Culture is not only the product of man but also, in a sense, the producer of man. This is so because "man experiences everything in the light of his culture, which stamps and molds his experience by generating the conceptions which inform him, when he perceives the world and himself or his fellow-man."[86] Since culture makes man what he is, or almost what he is, it is difficult (if not impossible) to cast off the fetters of culture. "It is not language alone which forms and informs the contents of experience, but it is also the habits and manners, traditions and remembrances, aspirations and results, of a living culture which more or less determine the modes of daily experience."[87]

Though thought strives to organize (classify, systematize, criticize) and evaluate the diverse forms of experience, it is not severed from tradition. That is why in the unitary view of reality offered by culture art, morality, philosophy, etc. do not emancipate themselves as autonomous activities.[88] As a result, "thought, if thought is loyal to its task and solves it rightly, produces nothing which is not preconceived and pre-existent in experience."[89] This implies in a sense that "philosophic reflection . . . does not have to create an organization of experience; experience always comes organized in the institutions of culture. Philosophy does not have to provide all meanings for life; life normally follows some meaningful pattern."[90] Whenever we speak of the philosophy of a culture or age, it should be clear that "it is not philosophic thinking that gives the age its assumptions, its controlling beliefs, and its scale of value and general direction. These must all be implicit in its institutions before they can be consciously formulated and expressed in philosophy."[91] This awareness further strengthens the view that philosophy of culture does not admit of the dissociation of cultural experience, that is, that cultural activities and goals are not isolated experiences, but integral parts of man's "habitual way of doing things." It also indicates that thought follows the route mapped out by experience.

But the role of philosophic thought in cultural activities is still quite important. It gives the mood of a period a systematic expression and even modifies certain of its aspects. And furthermore, it gives a conscious formulation of a world outlook. But it cannot "generate a faith, individual or social, or create values and ideals that will impel men to seek them. Its function is not to generate faiths but to clarify and modify them, to give not driving force and impulse to life, but guidance and direction."[92] Philosophic thought makes a difference in cultural activities because "a society that is conscious of its assumptions, methods and aims is certainly not the same as one in which they are only implicit."[93] However, philosophical thought seen as "a critical reorganization and reconstruction of the beliefs of a culture"[94] presupposes that an organized culture with sets of values and standards, objectives and goals, previously exists. In its cultural setting, thought is the servant of life, because it aids man in establishing some satisfactory or meaningful relation to the world in which man finds himself and in finding some wisdom on the conduct of his affairs.

CULTURAL THEORY OF KNOWLEDGE

Nobody can live without conscious or unconscious assumptions about himself and the universe. The philosophy of culture has to raise to the level of man's consciousness the basic assumptions governing his views about himself and the world. Man's deep insight into Nature and his modes or principles of its understanding show that it is impossible to separate the observer from the observed. According to Bohr, man is both an actor and a spectator in the great drama of existence. Therefore, thought is not something passive but acting and doing.

We now acknowledge the intimate kinship between man and nature as well as the fact that there is no view without a viewer, no measure without the measurer, no knowledge without the knower, no universe without an intelligence to be aware of it. Since the Renaissance, it was assumed that man or mind was not a part of the object known, that man dealt with pure nature unaffected by thought. Today, we accept that mind and its possessions are parts of what is known and affect it. Before man can examine any-

[85] Richard Kroner, *Culture and Faith* (Chicago: University of Chicago Press, 1951), p. 71.

[86] Ibid.

[87] Ibid.

[88] Modern societies, especially in the West, are characterized by the increasing separation and autonomy of cultural realms.

[89] Richard Kroner, op. cit., p. 72.

[90] John Herman Randall, Jr. and Justus Buchler, op. cit., p. 28.

[91] Ibid., p. 29.

[92] Ibid.

[93] Ibid.

[94] The mind is free to imagine anything, but this does not mean that the thing imagined necessarily exists whether in principle or in the concrete world.

thing he must first become aware of it. It means that man is present in the picture of the world that he draws. More significantly, no account of the world, scientific or otherwise, can go beyond the world as experienced by an observing being who brings his mysterious faculty of knowing to bear on it. We cannot know nature apart from ourselves.

All these experiences show that the world is permeated by culture. In other words, since we cannot go beyond the world as experienced by the ego, since man-nature constitutes an inseparable reality, the whole universe of reality is permeated by culture. Therefore, all branches of philosophy, all systems of knowledge, all political, economic and social activities based on the theories of Galileo, Newton, and Darwin have to be completely overhauled to reflect the 20th century structure of reality and the principles of its understanding. The universe in which we live is culturally determined. This includes also our mind, thought, language, and all modes of activities. Since experienced reality has reference to persons (since reality must in some way be experienced by a person in order to be real at all), the cultural theory of knowledge imposes restrictions on the theories of naturalism and rationalism due to the impersonal nature of "objective reason" and "objective nature."

The naturalists, operating with the methods and norms of classical science, delved into the impersonal world of nature said to have existed before the emergence of man. From the cultural view of reality and from our experience of the present state of culture, we cannot know the world, as well as nature which existed before man, in its pure state as uninterpreted by man. Just as the world of the fourth dimension escapes man's imagination, man cannot imagine[94] the world of the ancestors of man, that is, the so-called pre-human world. This is so because imagination, thought, language, reason, tools, etc. are cultural products and culturally determined. With these culturally determined faculties and tools, we cannot grasp or reconstruct the pre-human world as it was in itself in its pure state. To apply the knowledge, thought, idea, imagination and language peculiar to the present awareness of cultural reality to the prehuman world would imply that the present human world and environment correspond to those that existed prior to the advent of man. But this presupposition is false because it amounts to the denial of the obvious reality of change. Reality, as man experiences it, is not static but dynamic in nature. Therefore, the naturalists erred by supposing that the present cultural expressions could be explained

by starting from the unknown and impersonal nature of the prehuman world.

The theory of natural evolution, for example, attributes the success of human adaptation to natural evolution. In other words, it means that success (adaptation) arose from the blind, unconscious, and purposeless nature that is not even aware of man's presence. The cultural theory of knowledge, starting from the undeniable testimony of experience, asserts that man has goals and conscious purposes. Therefore, the success of his adaptation stems not from the world of pure nature but from the world of culture, hence was due to his cultural experience. In other words, the success arose from the active part of man's experience, from his conscious creations and ideals because he is a meaning-maker. The theory of natural evolution also pretended to have unified the organic and the inorganic worlds or to have offered a unitary view of the universe. But it could not explain human consciousness, mind, spiritual values, and cultural creations. Furthermore, it left no room for the application of any other view of history and universe.

The rationalists, on the other hand, established absolute and changeless values and expected such values to apply to the changing world. First, they did not recognize the changing world as a world of reality. Second, they were intolerant of the plurality or diversity of cultural expressions and values. Third, they seemed naive by hoping that changeless values could serve as the best standards for human actions in a culturally changing world. Consequently, the rationalists despaired because the world could not stand still. The cultural view of reality denies the existence of absolute and changeless values in the universe of culture. The universe of culture is not complete and definite like that of the rationalists. Rather, it is indefinite and subject to change. And it is within the universe of culture, not of pure idea or of pure nature, that man lives. "Cultural activity in creating works and institutions produces, as it were, a world within the world, a second world, a world of culture, which differs from the first or natural world in that it is meaningful because it is the effect of man's purpose and mind."[95] Furthermore, "this meaningful world is nevertheless a world like the natural universe, in that it has an existence of its own, apart from the inner will of man, though dependent upon that will and, in the sphere of action and institutional life,

---

95 Richard Kroner, op. cit., p. 162.

even partly overlapping the private exertions of actions of individuals."[96]

We can then picture man as living within the visible universe which is a meaningful universe of culture. Within this cultural universe, "man is an ego, a private person, a secret self, an invisible soul, a striving will; and in this inner sanctuary his morality operates."[97] From the cultural view of the universe, man has no nature but culture. In other words, human nature is human culture. Culture has a historical character because it lives and changes. It follows then that "the philosophy of culture is incomplete if it is not simultaneously a philosophy of history or if it fails at least to include such a philosophy."[98] The cultural theory of knowledge does not deny the existence of an objective reality called nature or the world. Rather, it affirms man's relationship to it or insists that the world or nature cannot be spoken of independently of man. As a result, the nature or the world which man experiences has been modified by culture, by technical inventions, aesthetic, moral and religious activities, social and economic endeavours. Consequently a generalized knowledge based on the existing cultural world may not be true of the remote past as well as the distance future. Our cultural knowledge does not apply to the pre-human world because

> we know culture only as human culture and we think of it only with reference to concrete conscious beings that experience it. Whatever else a cultural object may be, it certainly must be at some time and in some connection experienced by somebody, and thus the fact of experience has a universal importance with regard to the cultural world.[99]

We know that the subject (ego) is the condition of experience and is also conditioned by it. Thus, man's response to experience which is the basis of culture involves active thought. In the world of cultural reality (the world of cultural evolution),

> An individual can reach objectivity, can reconstruct an existing reality or reproduce a subsisting thought in their objective character, not by assimilating them merely, not by changing them into subjective data of associations, but, on the contrary, by depersonalizing his personal experiences, by changing his data into realities and his associations into objective thoughts.[100]

The individual has two ways in which he can include

> . . . any part of the objective world in his personality; the first is making this part of the objective world a part of the subjective experience; the second, identifying a part of his own personality with this part of the objective world. By the first method the individual constructs his own subjective personality as component of the cultural world; by the second method he constructs it as creator or at least reconstructor of the cultural world.[101]

In both cases, man is a meaning-maker or the measure of things.

From the cultural standpoint, the study of reality has to start from experience and proceed

> . . . to more and more objective reality and not vice versa. Instead of assuming, as realism does, a maximum of objectivity and rationality as inherent in the real world and trying to show how this maximum decreases in personal experience, we must start with the minimum of objectivity and rationality which reality must have to exist at all as a plurality of objects transcending present experience and opposed to thought, and then show how this minimum can increase.[102]

It can be said that the present cultural world has relatively developed more than the past cultural worlds. But this value judgement has to be understood within its proper context. If the present cultural world has relatively developed more than the past cultural worlds, "it is not merely because our knowledge is more perfect, but because our whole personalities are richer, better organized and more creative, and because the world contains for us more and means to us more; in a word, because ourselves and our world are products of a longer cultural development."[103]

CONCLUSION

The study of culture promises to be the basis of philosophical activities in the 20th century. And the philosophy of culture does not only accept the existence of the plurality of cultures but also the integrative nature of cultural experience. Self-understanding and the integration of selfhood may be the highest goals that the philosophy of culture may achieve. This achievement, hopefully, will organize human activities and relationships.

[96] Ibid., pp. 162–163.
[97] Ibid., p. 163.
[98] Ibid., p. 73.
[99] Florian Znaneicki, *Cultural Reality* (Chicago: University of Chicago Press, 1919), pp. 24–25.
[100] Ibid., p. 52.

[101] Ibid., p. 52.
[102] Ibid., p. 54.
[103] Ibid., p. 18.

The philosophy of culture sees man as a meaning-maker who is capable of transforming himself and the world in which he lives. To do so meaningfully, he must know his capacities as well as the limitation of his powers. And since man is culturally a finite being, faith is indispensable in the ultimate understanding of culture, man, and the world. In the universe of culture, all cultural groups of people constitute a community of faith. The awareness of the plurality of culture of man as a meaning-maker and of the complementary nature of different cultural views would most likely create an atmosphere of tolerance and sympathetic understanding in the world. The primary concern of cultural philosophy is with meaning, and it aims to produce an awareness of what we are about.

QUESTIONS FOR REVIEW AND FURTHER THOUGHT

1. Formulate the conception of culture you think most suitable for developing a philosophy of culture along the lines suggested by Anyanwu. What objections are likely to be raised against your conception? How would you defend it against these objections?

2. Try to formulate the distinction between theory and practice. To what extent and in what ways does it apply to philosophy? Defend your position against objections you consider plausible.

3. What problems in epistemology are brought to the fore by a philosophy of culture such as that suggested by Anyanwu? Are these the same as the problems brought to the fore by Lugones's suggestions concerning world-travelling and feminism? If they are the same, why might some people think they are different and why would these people be mistaken? If they are different, why might some people think they are the same and why would these people be mistaken?

4. Critically compare and contrast Anyanwu's conception of the problems and tasks of philosophy in the twentieth century with the conception set forth by Arthur E. Murphy in "The Philosophic Mind and the Contemporary World" (see Part I, Selection 5). Are their conceptions mutually compatible? Why or why not? Defend your position against objections you find plausible.

5. Given the various examples of philosophical inquiry you have encountered in this book and the discussion of the present and future of philosophy in Part VI, do you agree with the conceptions of wisdom and philosophy advanced by Aristotle in "Wisdom and Philosophy" (Part I, Selection 3)? Why or why not?

6. From the standpoint of the philosophy of culture proposed by Anyanwu, critically compare and contrast the view that beauty is in the eye of the beholder with the view that beauty is in the object. Can you think of a more defensible view than either of these? What is it and why is it more defensible? How does your position hold up against the position advanced on this topic in the introduction to Part V?

7. Can there be objectively defensible, cross-cultural moral judgments? Why or why not? Formulate some objections to your position and defend it against them.

8. Critically compare and contrast Grene's and Nielsen's positions on philosophy. Which one do you consider sounder and why?

9. Does a cross-cultural approach in philosophy make room for the discussion of metaphysical problems like those examined in Part III? Why or why not? What reasons might others have for disagreeing with you and why would these reasons be weaker than yours?

10. What—if any—conception of truth among those considered in Part II is best suited to a cross-cultural approach in philosophy? Why? What objections could be plausibly advanced against your position, and how would you reply to them?

11. Formulate a philosophical problem other than those examined in this book, explain why it is philosophical, and discuss how—if at all—it relates to problems discussed in this book.

12. Do any authors in Part VI engage in cross-cultural reflection and dialogue to any extent? Do they, for example, try to adapt categories used in other cultures to their own cultural context? Who, how, and how fruitfully?

13. Consider those authors in Part VI who do not engage in cross-cultural reflection. How could they have done so while being faithful to the views they espouse?

14. Consider the selections in Part VI and try to establish which ones include discussions that overlap with matters discussed in other parts of the book.

Glossary

Action: The doing of something or what is done. Characteristically, a performance or an omission, not merely a reflex movement.

Ahimsā: Term used in Hinduism for nonviolence.

Allah: The Muslim name for God.

Ambiguity: A word, phrase, or statement that has more than one definite meaning. For example, "I hope I never experience another fall like this" is ambiguous because in it "fall" can mean either the season or the physical event of falling. Note that ambiguity is *not the same as vagueness*, which is a lack of precision. For example, the term "bald" is vague because there is no particular number of hairs beyond which one ceases to be bald, not because, besides meaning lacking hair, feathers, or some other natural growth where it is typically present, it also means unadorned or undisguised.

Also note that although ambiguity often leads to obscurity, it is *not the same as obscurity*, which means lack of clarity. For example, the statement "Life is like a deep well" is obscure, not because it is ambiguous, but because it includes a strained analogy between life and wells.

Analytic statement: A statement that is true just by virtue of the meaning of its terms. For example, "Bachelors are unmarried" is an analytic statement. So is "Whales are mammals."

Anatta: Buddhist term meaning *no-self*.

Apodictic: A statement containing terms like "necessary" and "must." By contrast, a statement containing terms like "possible" and "may" is called *problematic*. Less frequently, "apodictic" is used to mean "connected with demonstration," and sometimes it is used as a synonym for "necessary." Kant uses "apodictic" to indicate how judgments are thought, not how they are formulated.

A posteriori: A Latin expression that means "after." In philosophy, it is quite typically used in the phrase "a posteriori knowledge" to mean knowledge justified by appeal to sensory experience and, perhaps, introspection. For example, when I have a toothache, I know that I have a toothache for the reason that I am experiencing the toothache. A posteriori knowledge is contrasted with a priori knowledge.

A priori: A Latin expression that means "before." In philosophy, it is quite typically used in the phrase "a priori knowledge" to mean a variety of things. First, it can mean knowledge we can acquire without being presented with an instance in experience. For example, we can know what a flying horse is simply by constructing its concept from our concepts of flying and horse. Second, it can mean knowledge we must so acquire, for there are no such instances. Our knowledge of negation, for example, is a priori in this sense. Third, it can mean knowledge we have always had and, hence, cannot acquire through experience. Some argue that our knowledge of causes is of this sort. Fourth, and perhaps most commonly, it can mean knowledge that is justified without any appeal to our sense experiences. For example, we do not prove a mathematical theorem by appeal to our sense experiences.

Argument: A list of statements, some of which—the premises—are regarded as a basis for accepting one of them—the conclusion.

Asabiyya: Group feeling in Islamic philosophy.

Atman: Self or consciousness in Indian philosophy.

Axiology: Theory of value.

Axiom: A formulation taken as given in a system.

Behavior: What an object, especially a living being, does.

Behaviorism: A family of theories that reduce mental concepts such as indignation, love, and fear to publicly observable behavior.

Being: A term used to mean a property common to everything that there is.

Belief: Assent to the truth of statements.

Buddhism: A religion aimed largely at attaining understanding through reasoning, study, devotion, meditation, selflessness, and love.

Categorial: Having to do with categories.

Categorical: A statement that says something without reference to conditions or alternatives. For example, "This is a table" is categorical. By contrast, *hypothetical* statements refer to conditions and alternatives. For example, "If this is a table, then it is a piece of furniture" is hypothetical.

Categories: Ultimate or fundamental divisions or kinds.

Causation: The connection between two events whereby the occurrence of one is brought about by (or at least could not have happened without) the occurrence of the other.

Class: A term, usually synonymous with "set," used to mean any collection of items whatsoever, or at least, of items that do not thereby lead to contradictions.

Cognitive: Concerning or involving knowledge.

Concept: That which makes us able to distinguish an item from others or to think or reason about it.

Conceptualism: The doctrine that universals are thoughts or ideas in or constructed by the mind.

Conditional: When applied to a statement, it is used to mean a statement of the form "If p, then q," where "p" and "q" are variable letters for other statements.

Consequentialism: A family of theories according to which the moral value of such things as actions, policies, and traits is somehow dependent on the value of their consequences.

Contradiction: A statement that is false just by virtue of its form.

Deontological: Usually applied to a family of theories according to which the moral value of such things as actions, policies, and traits is somehow dependent on features of the actions, policies, and traits, not on the value of their consequences.

Determinism: The doctrine that every event has a cause.

Dharma: A Sanskrit term that means "duty," "teachings," and "doctrines." In Hinduism, it is often used to refer to the moral order in nature.

Dialectic: A term used to refer to debate, to a method of debate, and, in the twentieth century, to an interplay between opposites, not just in language or thought, but also in the world itself.

Double-aspect: An expression applied to those theories that hold that mind and body are two different aspects of one and the same thing.

Dualism: A family of theories that hold that mind and body are two real, different things.

Duty: See **obligation.**

Egoism: A family of theories, some psychological, others ethical. *Ethical egoism* is itself a family of theories whose basic component is some formulation of the principle of ethical egoism. One such formulation is this: An action is right (or a policy is justified or a trait is good) if it tends to maximize the balance of desirable over undesirable consequences for the particular person who performs the action (assesses the policy or has the trait), regardless of how great the overall balance of undesirable over desirable consequences might be for any other person or group, unless this would hinder the overall balance of desirable over undesirable consequences for the said person.

Psychological egoism is a family of psychological theories that hold that people, as a matter of fact, think and act only so as to maximize the overall balance of desirable over undesirable consequences for themselves.

Empiricism: A family of views according to which our knowledge or concepts are, at least partly, based on sense experience or, maybe, introspection.

Essence: A *nominal essence* is a set of terms used to define something. A *real essence* is a set of notions or properties that constitute something independently of our definitions.

Event: Typically, a change of short duration in the qualities or relations of something.

Fact: Usually, that which makes a statement true.

Fallibilism: The doctrine according to which nothing can be known for certain.

False: See **truth values.**

Fatalism: The doctrine according to which the future is fixed and our attempts to change it are pointless.

Formal justice: A conception of justice characterized by the principle of formal justice, which says: No one ought to be treated differently from anyone else, despite various differences among individuals, unless one or more of these differences constitute a good reason for doing so.

Foundationalism: A family of theories that seek self-evident truths on which to base rationality, knowledge, and social institutions.

Hedonism: A family of ethical theories according to which pleasure and the absence of pain are the highest—if not the only—goods.

Heuristic: Anything that concerns discovery.

Hinduism: Primarily a religion of renunciation that considers salvation a strictly personal affair. It developed in India and extended its influence to Cambodia, ancient Champa, Bali, and, to a somewhat lesser extent, Ceylon, Nepal, Pakistan, and Indian enclaves all over the globe.

Historicism: A family of theories emphasizing the importance of seeing things through their historical development.

Hypothesis: A statement, not yet accepted as true, that is proposed as an explanation of something.

Hypothetical: See **categorical.**

Idea: In Plato's philosophy, nature, essence, or kind (usually translated as "Form."). In modern philosophy, something in or involving the mind.

Idealism: A family of theories according to which there are only ideas; or according to which ideas have a greater degree of reality, endurance, or value than material things.

Identity: The feature of being a single particular thing or a single kind of things.

Identity theory: The view that various mental events are identical with states or processes in the brain or central nervous system.

Incorrigible: A property attributed to certain statements whereby whoever believes or disbelieves them cannot be mistaken in doing so.

Individuals: Whatever can be counted or referred to, whatever the subject of a logical expression can refer to, or a particular (see **universals**).

Innate ideas: Ideas with which we are born.

Judgment: Act of judging; sometimes, the content of such an act.

Karma: A Sanskrit term meaning "action." In Indian thought, it is often used to mean the consequences of actions and the moral law that governs actions.

Law: In *logic and mathematics,* laws are formulated by basic statements, such as those formulating the laws of identity, contradiction, and the excluded middle. In *science,* laws are formulated by statements that are, or are associated with, generalizations such as: "All bodies unaffected by forces move with constant velocity on a straight line." In *ethics,* laws, by contrast with rules, are invariable; and, by contrast with principles, they have limited scope. For example, a rule against lying is: Lying is generally wrong; while a law against lying is: Lying is always wrong except when there are good reasons to lie. Though a law, the latter statement is not a principle, because it applies only to lying.

Materialism: A family of theories holding that matter is the only thing that exists. Sometimes it is called *physicalism.*

Monism: Any of a family of theories holding that where there appear to be many things or kinds of things, there is in reality only one thing or one kind.

Naturalism: The view that the universe is all one, in the sense that all its components and aspects are accessible to scientific study.

Necessary: In "necessary condition," pertaining to a condition without which something would not occur or exist. For example, that something has apple in it is a necessary condition for its being apple pie.

Nominalism: The doctrine that there are no universals, only individuals.

Objectivism: The view that, in certain areas, there are truths independent of what individuals or groups happen to believe, wish, or prefer; or that there are independent ways of establishing such truths. It is typically contrasted with **subjectivism.**

Obligation: Ordinarily, what we incur because of such specifics as a promise made or a favor received. It is sometimes distinguished from a *duty* in that a duty is thought to be longer-standing and less ad hoc than an obligation. Like duties, obligations are kinds of things we morally or legally ought to do except when specifiable considerations override or nullify them.

Obscurity: See **ambiguity.**

Occam's razor: A principle advocated by the medieval philosopher William of Occam, which advises against multiplying entities beyond necessity.

Perception: Faculty of apprehending the world through the senses.

Phenomenalism: A theory, primarily about physical objects, according to which these, though real, are merely actual or possible appearances.

Predestination: The doctrine that some or all future events have been predetermined by a personal, divine power.

Premise: A statement supporting the conclusion in an argument.

Principle: In *science,* high-level law. In *ethics,* a generalization that has no exceptions, does not vary with changes in circumstances, and is relevant to a wide range of circumstances (e.g., the Principle of Utility, the Principle of Personality).

Problematic: See **apodictic.**

Proposition: See **sentence.**

Rationalism: Any view basing knowledge and justification on reason.

Realism: The doctrine that universals are nonmental, abstract entities that are shared, but not exhausted, by an indefinite number of instances.

Relativism: A view according to which all standards of value or rationality are relative to particular individuals or groups. That is, none, at any level of abstraction, are invariant across cultures.

Scepticism: A family of positions according to which all, or at least some, knowledge is impossible.

Semantically false: A statement is semantically false when it is false by virtue of the meaning of its terms.

Sentence: A grammatically complete string of symbols in a language. For example, "The dog is barking" is a sentence in English, and "5 > 3" is a sentence in arithmetic. Sentences need not be written or uttered. For example, one can sign sentences in sign language. Nor do sentences need to be true or false. For example, "Did you bring candy?" is a sentence, but it is neither true or false. It is simply a question or a request for information, and requests—like commands and expressions of emotion or desire—are incapable of being true or false.

When sentences are capable of being true or, alternatively, false, they are often called "declarative sentences" and what they mean is called a "proposition." For example, the English sentence "It rains" is capable of being true or false. So is the Spanish sentence "Llueve." They both mean the same thing. Hence, only one proposition is involved.

The term "statement" is often used as synonymous with "proposition." Yet "statement" is sometimes used to refer to the linguistic performance in which a sentence is used. For the performance is sometimes crucial to making the sentence declarative, as in "You" in response to the question "Who told you?" Also, the performance sometimes gives the sentence its definite truth value. For example, the truth or falsity of "I'm not uttering anything right now" depends on whether the sentence's user utters it or not.

Set: See **class.**

Sound: To say that an argument is sound is to say that it has the following two characteristics: (1) it is valid, and (2) it has only true premises.

Statement: See **sentence.**

Subjectivism: See **objectivism.**

Substance: In the sense of *primary substance,* this term refers to a particular concrete object, like Napoleon's hat. In the sense of *secondary substance,* it refers to the essence that makes a primary substance what it is. Thus, Napoleon is the primary substance and human being is the secondary substance. Also, in a third sense, substance refers to matter, substratum, or what remains when one removes the properties of a particular thing.

Sufficient: In "sufficient condition," a condition sufficient for something is a condition given which the thing occurs or exists. For example, that something is apple pie is a sufficient condition for its having apple in it.

Synthetic statement: A statement that is true or false neither just by virtue of its form nor just by virtue of the meaning of its terms, but also by virtue of nonlinguistic facts. For example, "Napoleon had a hat" is synthetic because its truth is not a mere matter of language, but partly depends on the nonlinguistic fact that he had a hat.

Tao: A term (sometimes transliterated as "dao") that means *the way.* In Chinese philosophy, it is used to refer to the way of nature or the way in which the universe works.

Tautology: A statement that is true just by virtue of its form. For example, the statement "Either this is a cat or this is not a cat" is a tautology.

Truth: A property of statements. There are three main Western theories of truth. *Correspondence theory* holds that a statement is true whenever it corresponds to the facts. *Coherence theory* holds that a statement is true when it is logically coherent with a system of statements that is wider than the systems with which its rival statements cohere. *Pragmatic theory* holds that a statement is true if it is one of the statements that would be agreed upon if investigation continued indefinitely.

Truth values: Features of declarative sentences, propositions, or statements. In classical logic, there are two such features: truth if the sentences, propositions, or statements are true; and falsity if they are false.

Universals: Features that can be shared by an indefinite number of things. Universals are often contrasted with *particulars,* which cannot be instantiated, appear as wholes at separate places, or appear as wholes at different times without being somehow linked. Particulars must be identifiable and distinguishable from others; but, like the Industrial Revolution, they can be abstract.

Utilitarianism: A family of moral theories whose central component is some formulation of the principle of utility. One such formulation says that an action is right (or a policy justified or a trait good) if it tends to maximize the balance of desirable over undesirable consequences for those affected. Otherwise, the act is wrong (or the policy unjustified or the trait bad).

Vagueness: See **ambiguity.**

Valid: To say that an argument is valid is to say that it has a form such that, if all of its premises are true, then its conclusion is true.

Vedism: A primarily ritualistic religion of northwestern India in which faith is the believers' conviction in the exactitude and effectiveness of their rites.

Selected Bibliography

This bibliography is a selected list of suggestions for further reading. It includes influential philosophical works, interpretive discussions, and works conducive to reflecting along the cross-disciplinary and cross-cultural lines emphasized in this book.

CULTURAL HISTORIES AND ANTHROPOLOGICAL STUDIES

BURCKHARDT, JACOB. *The Civilization of the Renaissance in Italy.* London: Phaidon, 1955.

BURCKHARDT, JACOB. *History of Greek Culture.* New York: Ungar, 1963.

FITZGERALD, C. P. *China: A Short Cultural History.* New York: Praeger, 1961.

GERNET, JACQUES. *A History of Chinese Civilization.* Cambridge and New York: Cambridge University Press, 1982.

GILSENAN, MICHAEL. *Recognizing Islam: An Anthropologist's Introduction.* London: Croom Helm, 1982.

HAWKES, JAQUETTA, AND SIR LEONARD WOOLLEY. *Prehistory and the Beginnings of Civilization.* New York: Harper and Row, 1963.

JAEGER, WERNER W. *Paideia: The Ideals of Greek Culture.* New York: Oxford University Press, 1939–1944.

KEEN, BENJAMIN (ED.). *Latin American Civilization: History and Society, 1492 to the Present.* Boulder, CO: Westview Press, 1991.

LOCKHART, JAMES, and STUART B. SCHWARTZ. *Early Latin America.* Cambridge, New York: Cambridge University Press, 1983.

LOVEJOY, ARTHUR O. *Primitivism and Related Ideas in Antiquity.* Baltimore: Johns Hopkins Press, 1935.

MASSON-OURSEL, PAUL. *Ancient India and Indian Civilization.* New York: Barnes and Noble, 1967.

MCKAY, JOHN P., ET AL. *A History of Western Society.* Boston: Houghton Mifflin, 1983.

MOKHTAR, G. (ED.). *Ancient Civilizations of Africa.* London and Berkeley: Heinemann and University of California Press, 1981.

MOMMSEN, THEODOR. *The History of Rome.* New York: Meridian Books, 1958.

OLANIYAN, RICHARD. *African History and Culture.* Ikeja, Lagos, Nigeria: Longman Nigeria, 1982.

OLIVER, ROLAND. *The African Experience.* New York: Harper Collins Publishers, 1991.

PICÓN SALAS, MARIANO. *A Cultural History of Spanish America.* Berkeley and Los Angeles: University of California Press, 1968.

RADIN, PAUL. *Primitive Man as Philosopher.* New York: D. Appleton, 1927.

RADIN, PAUL. *The Basic Myth of the North American Indians.* Zürich: Rhein-Verlag, 1950.

RENOU, LOUIS. *Hinduism.* New York: George Braziller, 1962.

SANDMEL, SAMUEL. *Judaism and Christian Beginnings.* New York: Oxford University Press, 1978.

SCHIROKAUER, CONRAD. *A Brief History of Chinese and Japanese Civilizations.* New York: Harcourt Brace Jovanovich, 1978.

SCRIVEN, MICHAEL. *Primary Philosophy.* New York: McGraw-Hill, 1966.

SÉJOURNÉ, LAURETTE. *Burning Water: Thought and Religion in Ancient Mexico.* New York: Vanguard Press, 1956.

SHWEDER, RICHARD A., AND ROBERT A. LEVINE. *Culture Theory.* Cambridge and New York: Cambridge University Press, 1986.

SINNIGEN, WILLIAM G. *Ancient History; From Prehistoric Times to the Death of Justinian.* New York and London: Macmillan and Collier-Macmillan, 1981.

SOYINKA, WOLE. *Myth, Literature, and the African World.* Cambridge and New York: Cambridge University Press, 1976.

WENSINCK, A. J. *The Muslim Creed: Its Genesis and Historical Development.* London: Frank Cass & Co. 1965.

DICTIONARIES AND ENCYCLOPEDIAS

BALDWIN, JAMES MARK. *Dictionary of Philosophy and Psychology.* Gloucester, MA: P. Smith, 1925.

EDWARDS, PAUL (ED.). *The Encyclopedia of Philosophy.* New York: Macmillan, 1972.

LACEY, A. R. *A Dictionary of Philosophy.* New York: Charles Scribner's Sons, 1976.

RUNES, DAGOBERT D. *Dictionary of Philosophy.* New York: Philosophical Library, 1983.

URMSON, J. O., AND JONATHAN RÉE. *The Concise Encyclopedia of Western Philosophy and Philosophers.* London and Boston: Unwin Hyman, 1989.

PART I: WHAT IS PHILOSOPHY?

ARISTOTLE. *Prior Analytics.* Indianapolis, IN: Hacket Publishing Co., 1989.

ARISTOTLE. *Posterior Analytics.* Oxford: The Clarendon Press, 1976.

BACON, FRANCIS. *Novum Organum.* In *The Works of Francis Bacon.* London: J. Cundee, 1802–1803.

BLACKWOOD, R. T., AND A. L. HERMANN. *Problems in Philosophy: West and East.* Englewood Cliffs, NJ: Prentice Hall, 1975.

BRÉHIER, EMILE. *The History of Philosophy.* Chicago: University of Chicago Press, 1963–1969.

BUNGE, MARIO. *Treatise on Basic Philosophy.* Vol. 1: *Sense and Reference.* Dordrecht, Neth.: Reidel, 1974.

CASSIRER, ERNST, P. O. KRISTELLER, AND J. H. RANDALL, JR. *The Renaissance Philosophy of Man.* Chicago and London: The University of Chicago Press, 1975.

COLLINGWOOD, R. G. *An Essay on Philosophical Method.* Oxford: The Clarendon Press, 1977.

COLLINGWOOD, R. G. *Essays in the Philosophy of History.* Austin, TX: University of Texas Press, 1967.

COPLESTON, FREDERICK C. *A History of Philosophy.* New York: Image Books, 1985.

COPLESTON, FREDERICK C. *Contemporary Philosophy: Studies of Logical Positivism and Existentialism.* Westminster, MD.: Newman Press, 1968.

DANTO, ARTHUR C. *What Philosophy Is: A Guide to the Elements.* New York: Harper and Row, 1970.

DANTO, ARTHUR C. *Analytical Philosophy of History.* Cambridge: Cambridge University Press, 1965.

DEBOER, T.J. *The History of Philosophy in Islam.* New York: Dover, 1967.

DEWEY, JOHN. *Freedom and Culture.* New York: G. P. Putnam's Sons, 1939.

DEWEY, JOHN. *Philosophy and Civilization.* New York: Milton, Balch & Co., 1931.

FITT, MARY. *The Pre-Socratic Philosophers: A Companion to Diel's Fragmente der Vorsokratiker.* Oxford: Basil Blackwell, 1946.

GRACIA, JORGE J. E. *Philosophy and Its History.* Albany: State University of New York Press, 1992.

GRACIA, JORGE J. E. *Latin American Philosophy in the Twentieth Century.* Buffalo, NY: Prometheus Books, 1986.

GRACIA, JORGE J. E., AND IVÁN JAKSIĆ. "The Problem of Philosophical Identity in Latin America," *Inter American Review of Bibliography 34* (1984): 53–71.

GRACIA, JORGE J. E., EDUARDO RABOSSI, ENRIQUE VILLANUEVA, AND MARCELO DASCAL (EDS.). *Philosophical Analysis in Latin America.* Dordrecht, Neth.: Reidel Publishing Co., 1984.

HERMAN, A. L. *A Brief Introduction to Hinduism: Religion, Philosophy, and Ways of Liberation.* Boulder, CO: Westview Press, 1991.

JAMES, WILLIAM. *Some Problems of Philosophy.* Cambridge, MA: Harvard University Press, 1979.

KESSLER, GARY E. *Voices of Wisdom.* Belmont, CA: Wadsworth Publishing Co., 1992.

KNEALE, WILLIAM, AND MARTHA KNEALE. *The Development of Logic.* Oxford: The Clarendon Press, 1962.

KRAEMER, JOEL L. *Philosophy in the Renaissance of Islam.* Leiden: E. J. Brill, 1986.

LARSON, GERALD JAMES, AND ELIOT DEUTSCH (EDS.). *Interpreting Across Boundaries: New Essays in Comparative Philosophy.* Princeton, NJ: Princeton University Press, 1988.

MASSON-OURSEL PAUL. *Comparative Philosophy.* London and New York: K. Paul, Trench, Trubner & Co., and Harcourt, Brace and Co., 1926.

MILL, JOHN STUART. *A System of Logic.* London: Longmans, Green, 1949.

MORAVCSIK, J. M. E. (ED.). *Aristotle.* Notre Dame, IN: University of Notre Dame Press, 1968.

NAGEL, ERNEST. *Logic Without Metaphysics.* Glencoe, Il: The Free Press, 1956.

NAHM, MILTON C. *Selections from Early Greek Philosophy.* Englewood Cliffs, NJ: Prentice Hall, 1968.

PASSMORE, JOHN A. *Recent Philosophers.* La Salle, IL: Open Court Publishing Co., 1985.

PASSMORE, JOHN A. *Philosophical Reasoning.* New York: Scribner, 1962.

PLATO. *The Euthydemus of Plato.* New York: Arno Press, 1973.

QUINE, W. V. O. *Elementary Logic.* New York: Harper and Row, 1965.

REID, THOMAS. *Essays on the Intellectual Powers of Man.* New York: Garland Publishing, 1971.

ROGERS, ARTHUR K. *A Student's History of Philosophy.* New York: Macmillan, 1932.

ROGERS, ARTHUR K. *A Brief Introduction to Modern Philosophy.* New York and London: Macmillan, 1899.

SCHARFSTEIN, BEN-AMI, ET AL. *Philosophy East/Philosophy West: A Critical Comparison of Indian, Chinese, Islamic, and European Philosophy.* New York: Oxford University Press, 1978.

SCHOLZ, HEINRICH. *Concise History of Logic.* New York: Philosophical Library, 1961.

STEGMÜLLER, WOLFGANG. *Main Currents in Contemporary German, British, and American Philosophy.* Bloomington: Indiana University Press, 1970.

STRAWSON, P. F. *Introduction to Logical Theory.* London: Methuen, 1964.

SUZUKI, DAISETZ TEITARO. *A Brief History of Early Chinese Philosophy.* London: Probsthain, 1914.

TARSKI, ALFRED. *Introduction to Logic.* New York: Oxford University Press, 1965.

URMSON, J. O. *Philosophical Analysis: Its Development Between the Two World Wars.* Oxford: The Clarendon Press, 1958.

VLASTOS, GREGORY (ED.). *The Philosophy of Socrates.* Notre Dame, IN: University of Notre Dame Press, 1980.

VLASTOS, GREGORY (ED.). *Plato.* Notre Dame, IN: University of Notre Dame Press, 1978.

WAHL, JEAN A. *The Philosopher's Way.* New York: Oxford University Press, 1948.

WALZER, RICHARD. *Greek into Arabic.* Oxford: Bruno Cassirer, 1962.

WEINBERG, JULIUS R. *A Short History of Medieval Philosophy.* Princeton, NJ: Princeton University Press, 1964.

ZEA, LEOPOLDO. "The Interpretation of the Ibero-American and North American Cultures," *Philosophy and Phenomenological Research 9* (1948–49): 538–544.

PART II. WHAT ARE TRUTH, KNOWLEDGE, AND FAITH, AND HOW ARE THEY RELATED?

ACKERMANN, ROBERT. *The Philosophy of Science.* New York: Pegasus, 1970.

AYER, A. J. *The Problem of Knowledge.* Baltimore: Pelican, 1966.

BAIER, ANNETTE. *Postures of the Mind.* Minneapolis: University of Minnesota Press, 1985.

BASALLA, GEORGE. *The Rise of Modern Science.* Lexington, MA: D. C. Heath and Co., 1968.

BERKELEY, GEORGE. *Principles, Dialogues, and Philosophical Correspondence.* Indianapolis, IN: Bobbs-Merrill, 1965.

BOAS, MARIE. *The Scientific Renaissance, 1450–1630.* New York: Harper and Row, 1962.

BODDE, DERK. *Chinese Thought, Society, and Science: The Intellectual and Social Background of Science and Technology in Pre-Modern China.* Honolulu: University of Hawaii Press, 1991.

BORGER, R., AND F. CIOFFI. *Explanation in the Behavioral Sciences.* Cambridge: Cambridge University Press, 1970.

BOSE, D. M. *A Concise History of Science in India.* New Delhi: Indian National Science Academy, 1989.

BRAYBROOKE, DAVID. *Philosophy of Social Science.* Englewood Cliffs, NJ: Prentice Hall, 1987.

BROWN, ROBERT. *Explanation in Social Science.* Chicago: Aldine, 1963.

BUNGE, MARIO. *The Myth of Simplicity.* Englewood Cliffs, NJ: Prentice Hall, 1963.

BUNGE, MARIO. *Treatise on Basic Philosophy.* Vol. 2: *Interpretation and Truth.* Dordrecht, Neth.: Reidel, 1974.

CASSIRER, ERNST. *The Philosophy of the Enlightenment.* Boston: Beacon Press, 1951.

CHAPPELL, V. C. *Hume.* Garden City, NY: Doubleday, 1966.

CLAGETT, MARSHALL. *The Science of Mechanics in the Middle Ages.* Madison: University of Wisconsin Press, 1959.

CLAGETT, MARSHALL. *Greek Science in Antiquity.* New York: Abelard-Schuman, 1955.

COHEN, JONATHAN. *The Faith of a Liberal.* New York: Henry Holt and Co., 1946.

DESCARTES, RENÉ. *The Philosophical Works of Descartes.* Cambridge: Cambridge University Press, 1969.

DONEY, WILLIS. *Descartes.* Garden City, NY: Doubleday, 1967.

DRETSKE, FRED I. *Seeing and Knowing.* London: Routledge and Kegan Paul, 1969.

FARRINGTON, BENJAMIN. *Science in Antiquity.* New York and London: Oxford University Press, 1969.

FARRINGTON, BENJAMIN. *Science and Politics in the Ancient World.* New York: Barnes and Noble, 1968.

FARRUKH, UMAR. *The Arab Genius in Science and Philosophy.* Washington, DC: American Council of Learned Societies, 1954.

FEYNMAN, RICHARD. *The Character of Physical Law.* Cambridge, MA, and London: The MIT Press, 1965.

GOODMAN, NELSON. *Fact, Fiction, and Forecast.* Cambridge, MA: Harvard University Press, 1983.

GRAHAM, LOREN R. *Between Science and Values.* New York: Columbia University Press, 1981.

GRIFFITHS, A. PHILLIPS. *Knowledge and Belief.* London: Oxford University Press, 1967.

HO, PENG YOKE. *Li, Qi, and Shu: An Introduction to Science and Civilization in China.* Hong Kong: Hong Kong University Press, 1985.

HUME, DAVID. *An Inquiry Concerning the Human Understanding.* Indianapolis, IN: W. Hendel, 1955.

HUSSERL, EDMUND. *Cartesian Meditations.* The Hague: Martinus Nijhoff, 1969.

HUSSERL, EDMUND. *Phenomenology and the Crisis of Philosophy.* New York: Harper and Row, 1965.

HUSSERL, EDMUND. *The Idea of Phenomenology.* The Hague: Nijhoff, 1964.

JAMES, WILLIAM. *The Will to Believe and Other Essays in Popular Philosophy, and Human Immortality.* New York: Dover Publications, 1956.

KANT, IMMANUEL. *Critique of Pure Reason.* New York and Toronto: St. Martin's and Macmillan, 1965.

KEMP SMITH, NORMAN. *A Commentary to Kant's Critique of Pure Reason.* New York: Humanities Press, 1962.

KERNEY, HUGH. *Science and Change, 1500–1700.* New York: McGraw-Hill, 1971.

KORNBLITH, HILARY. *Naturalizing Epistemology.* Cambridge, MA, and London: The MIT Press, 1985.

KUHN, THOMAS S. *The Structure of Scientific Revolutions.* Chicago: The University of Chicago Press, 1971.

LAKATOS, IMRE, AND ALAN MUSGRAVE. *Criticism and the Growth of Knowledge.* London: Cambridge University Press, 1974.

LEIBNIZ, GOTTFRIED. *Basic Writings.* La Salle, IL: Open Court, 1968.

LINDBLOM, CHARLES E., AND DAVID K. COHEN. *Usable Knowledge.* New Haven, CT, and London: Yale University Press, 1979.

LOCKE, JOHN. *An Essay Concerning Human Understanding.* New York: Dover Publications, 1959.

LOVEJOY, ARTHUR O. *The Thirteen Pragmatisms and Other Essays.* Baltimore: Johns Hopkins Press, 1963.

MALCOLM, NORMAN. *Knowledge and Certainty.* Englewood Cliffs, NJ: Prentice Hall, 1963.

MASON, STEPHEN F. *A History of the Sciences.* New York: Collier, 1962.

MOLINE, JOHN. *Plato's Theory of Understanding.* Madison: University of Wisconsin Press, 1981.

MOORE, G. E. *Philosophical Studies.* London and New York: K. Paul, Trench, Trubner and Co., and Harcourt, Brace and Co., 1922.

NIDDITCH, P. H. *The Philosophy of Science.* New York: Oxford University Press, 1968.

NOZICK, ROBERT. *Philosophical Explanations.* Cambridge, MA: Harvard University Press, 1981.

PAP, ARTHUR. *An Introduction to the Philosophy of Science.* New York and London: The Free Press and Collier-Macmillan, 1967.

PASSMORE, JOHN. *Science and Its Critics.* New Brunswick, NJ: Rutgers University Press, 1978.

PLATO, "Meno" and "Theaetetus." In E. Hamilton and H. Cairns (eds.), *Plato.* Princeton, NJ: Princeton University Press, 1973. Pp. 353–384 and 845–919.

POINCARÉ, HENRI. *The Foundations of Science.* Lancaster: The Science Press, 1946.

POPPER, KARL R. *The Logic of Scientific Discovery.* New York: Harper and Row, 1968.

PRICE, H. H. *Belief.* London and New York: Allen and Unwin and Humanities Press, 1969.

PRICE, H. H. *Perception.* London: Methuen, 1954.

ROGERS, ARTHUR K. *What Is Truth? An Essay in the Theory of Knowledge.* New Haven, CT: Yale University Press, 1923.

RUSSELL, BERTRAND. *Human Knowledge, Its Scope and Limits.* New York: Simon and Schuster, 1948.

SCHEFFLER, ISRAEL. *Science and Subjectivity.* Indianapolis, IN: Bobbs-Merrill, 1967.

SCHULTZ, DUANE P. *A History of Modern Psychology.* New York and London: Academic Press, 1969.

SESONSKE, ALEXANDER, AND NOEL FLEMING. *Human Understanding.* Belmont, CA: Wadsworth, 1965.

SMART, NINIAN. *Worldviews: Crosscultural Explorations of Human Beliefs.* New York: Scribner's, 1983.

STRAWSON, P. F. *The Bounds of Sense.* London: Methuen, 1966.

STRAWSON, P. F. *Individuals.* London: Methuen, 1959.

SWARTZ, ROBERT J. *Perceiving, Sensing, and Knowing.* Garden City, NY: Doubleday, 1965.

TAYLOR, F. SHERWOOD. *Science and Scientific Thought.* New York: W. W. Norton, 1963.

TUGE, HIDEOMI. *Historical Development of Science and Technology in Japan.* Tokyo: Kokusai Bunka Shinkokai, 1968.

VAN SERTIMA, IVAN. *Blacks in Science: Ancient and Modern.* New Brunswick, NJ: Transaction Books, 1983.

WEINBERG, JULIUS R. "The Novelty of Hume's Philosophy." In *Proceedings and Addresses of the American Philosophical Association.* Chicago: APA Meetings, April 29, 30, May 1, 1965.

WESTFALL, RICHARD S. *The Construction of Modern Science: Mechanisms and Mechanics.* New York: John Wiley and Sons, 1971.

WINTER, HENRY J. J. *Eastern Science: An Outline of Its Scope and Contribution.* London: J. Murray, 1952.

PART III. WHAT IS THE UNIVERSE REALLY LIKE?

ARISTOTLE. *Metaphysics.* Oxford: The Clarendon Press, 1924.

AUGUSTINE, ST. *City of God.* London: Oxford University Press, 1963.

BAIER, ANNETTE. *Postures of the Mind.* Minneapolis: University of Minnesota Press, 1985.

BERGSON, HENRI. *An Introduction to Metaphysics.* New York: Liberal Arts Press, 1950.

BERGSON, HENRI. *The Two Sources of Morality and Religion.* New York: H. Holt and Co., 1935.

BUNGE, MARIO. *Scientific Materialism.* Dordrecht, Neth., and Boston: D. Reidel, 1981.

BUNGE, MARIO. *The Mind-Body Problem.* Oxford and New York: Pergamon Press, 1980.

BUNGE, MARIO. *Treatise on Basic Philosophy.* Vols. 4 and 5. Dordrecht, Neth.: D. Reidel, 1977 and 1977–79.

BUTLER, JOSEPH. *The Analogy of Religion, Natural and Revealed.* London: J. M. Dent and Sons, 1917.

COLLINGWOOD, R. G. *An Essay on Metaphysics.* Oxford: The Clarendon Press, 1948.

DEBOER, T. J. *The History of Philosophy in Islam.* New York: Dover, 1967.

ELIADE, MIRCEA. *The Encyclopedia of Religion.* New York: Macmillan, 1987.

ELIADE, MIRCEA. *A History of Religious Ideas.* Chicago: Chicago University Press, 1978–1985.

ELIADE, MIRCEA. *Occultism, Witchcraft, and Cultural Fashions.* Chicago: University of Chicago Press, 1976.

ELIADE, MIRCEA. *Myth and Reality.* New York: Harper and Row, 1975.

ELIADE, MIRCEA. *Australian Religions: An Introduction.* Ithaca, NY: Cornell University Press, 1973.

ELIADE, MIRCEA. *Cultural Fashions and History of Religions.* Middletown, CT: Center for Advanced Studies, Wesleyan University, 1967.

ELIADE, MIRCEA. *The Sacred and the Profane.* New York: Harper and Row, 1961.

FINDLAY, JOHN N. *Hegel: A Re-examination.* London and New York: Collier, 1958.

FRONDIZI, RISIERI. *The Nature of the Self.* Carbondale, IL: Southern Illinois University Press, 1971.

GLOVER, JONATHAN. *The Philosophy of Mind.* Oxford: Oxford University Press, 1976.

GOODMAN, NELSON. *Problems and Projects.* Indianapolis, IN, and New York: Bobbs-Merrill, 1972.

GUYAU, M. *The Non-Religion of the Future: A Sociological Study.* New York: H. Holt and Co., 1897.

HARTMANN, NICOLAI. *New Ways of Ontology.* Chicago: H. Regnery Co., 1953.

HEGEL, GEORG WILHELM FRIEDRICH. *The Berlin Phenomenology.* Dordrecht, Neth., and Boston: D. Reidel, 1981.

HEIDEGGER, MARTIN. *Hegel's Phenomenology of Spirit.* Bloomington: Indiana University Press, 1988.

HEIDEGGER, MARTIN. *Existence and Being.* Chicago: Henry Regnery Co., 1968.

HEIDEGGER, MARTIN. *Being and Time.* New York: Harper and Row, 1962.

HEIDEGGER, MARTIN. *An Introduction to Metaphysics.* Garden City, NY: Doubleday, 1961.

HICK, JOHN. *Philosophy of Religion.* Englewood Cliffs, NJ: Prentice Hall, 1990.

HUME, DAVID. *The Natural History of Religion and Dialogues Concerning Natural Religion.* Oxford: The Clarendon Press, 1976.

JAMES, WILLIAM. *The Varieties of Religious Experience.* Cambridge, MA: Harvard University Press, 1985.

JASPERS, KARL. *Reason and Existence.* New York: Nobody Press, 1968.

KANT, IMMANUEL. *Anthropology from a Pragmatic Point of View.* Carbondale: Southern Illinois University Press, 1978.

KANT, IMMANUEL. *Lectures on Philosophical Theology.* Ithaca, NY: Cornell University Press, 1978.

KANT, IMMANUEL. *Religion Within the Limits of Reason Alone.* New York: Harper, 1960.

KANT, IMMANUEL. *Prolegomena to Any Future Metaphysics.* Chicago: The Open Court Publishing Co., 1902.

KAUFFMANN, WALTER A. *Hegel: Reinterpretation, Text, and Commentary.* Garden City, NY: Doubleday, 1965.

KAUFFMAN, WALTER A. *From Shakespeare to Existentialism.* Boston: Beacon Press, 1959.

KIERKEGAARD, SÖREN. *Fear and Trembling, and The Sickness Unto Death.* Garden City, NY: Doubleday, 1954.

LEWIS, C. I. *Mind and the World Order.* New York: C. Scribner's Sons, 1929.

LOVEJOY, ARTHUR O. *Reflections on Human Nature.* Baltimore: Johns Hopkins Press, 1961.

LOVEJOY, ARTHUR O. *The Great Chain of Being.* Cambridge, MA: Harvard University Press, 1936.

LYOTARD, JEAN F. *Phenomenology.* Albany: State University of New York Press, 1991.

MAIMONIDES, MOSES. *The Guide for the Perplexed.* London: Routledge and Kegan Paul, 1904.

MERLEAU-PONTY, MAURICE. *Perception, Structure, Language.* Atlantic Highlands, NJ: Humanities Press, 1981.

MERLEAU-PONTY, MAURICE. *The Essential Writings of Merleau-Ponty.* New York: Harcourt, Brace and World, 1969.

MERLEAU-PONTY, MAURICE. *Phenomenology of Perception.* New York: Humanities Press, 1962.

OTTO, RUDOLF. *The Idea of the Holy.* New York and London: Oxford University Press, 1957.

OTTO, RUDOLF. *Mysticism East and West.* New York: The Macmillan Company, 1932.

OTTO, RUDOLF. *India's Religion of Grace and Christianity Compared and Contrasted.* London: Student Christian Movement Press, 1930.

PENNER, TERRY. *The Ascent from Nominalism.* Dordrecht, Neth., and Boston: D. Reidel, 1987.

PLATO. *Plato's Cosmology: The Timaeus of Plato.* London: Routledge and Kegan Paul, 1977.

PLATO. *Plato's Republic.* New York: Arno Press, 1973.

SARTRE, JEAN-PAUL. *Being and Nothingness.* New York: Washington Square Press, 1958.

SCHULTZ, DUANE P. *A History of Modern Psychology.* New York and London: Academic Press, 1969.

SMART, NINIAN. *Religion and the Western Mind.* Albany: State University of New York Press, 1987.

SMART, NINIAN. *Beyond Ideology: Religion and the Future of Western Civilization.* New York: Harper and Row, 1981.

SMART, NINIAN. *The Philosophy of Religion.* New York: Oxford University Press, 1979.

SMART, NINIAN. *Doctrine and Argument in Indian Philosophy.* London: Allen and Unwin, 1964.

SOLL, IVAN. *An Introduction to Hegel's Metaphysics.* Chicago and London: The University of Chicago Press, 1969.

SPRAGUE, ELMER. *Metaphysical Thinking.* New York: Oxford University Press, 1978.

TAYLOR, RICHARD. *Metaphysics.* Englewood Cliffs, NJ: Prentice Hall, 1963.

WATT, W. MONTGOMERY. *The Faith and Practice of Al-Ghazali.* London: George Allen and Unwin, 1967.

WAHL, JEAN. *Philosophies of Existence.* New York: Schocken Books, 1969.

WHITE, ALAN R. *The Philosophy of Action.* London, Oxford, New York: Oxford University Press, 1968.

WHITEHEAD, ALFRED NORTH. *Religion in the Making.* New York: Macmillan, 1926.

WHITELEY, CHARLES H. *An Introduction to Metaphysics.* London: Methuen, 1950.

WITTGENSTEIN, LUDWIG. *Philosophical Investigations.* Oxford: B. Blackwell, 1972.

WITTGENSTEIN, LUDWIG. *The Blue and Brown Books.* Oxford: B. Blackwell, 1958.

PART IV. WHAT IS MORALLY JUSTIFIED?

ANZALDÚA, GLORIA. *Making Face, Making Soul/Haciendo Caras: Creative and Critical Perspectives of Women of Color.* San Francisco: Aunt Lute Foundation, 1990.

APPELL, G. N., AND T. N. MADAN. *Choice and Morality in Anthropological Perspective.* Albany: State University of New York Press, 1988.

AQUINAS, THOMAS. *Summa Theologica* and *Summa Contra Gentiles,* in *Basic Writings of Saint Thomas Aquinas.* New York: Random House, 1945.

ARISTOTLE. *Nicomachean Ethics.* Cambridge, MA, and London: Harvard University Press and William Heinemann Ltd., 1975.

ASCHER, CAROL. *Simone de Beauvoir, A Life of Freedom.* Boston: Beacon, 1981.

BAIER, ANNETTE. *A Progress of Sentiments: Reflections on Hume's Treatise.* Cambridge, MA; Harvard University Press, 1991.

BAIER, KURT. *The Moral Point of View.* Ithaca, NY: Cornell University Press, 1958.

BARRY, BRIAN. *The Liberal Theory of Justice.* Oxford: The Clarendon Press, 1973.

BARRY, BRIAN. *Political Argument.* London: Routledge and Kegan Paul, 1965.

BENTHAM, JEREMY. *Fragment on Government and Introduction to the Principles of Morals and Legislation,* ed. Wilfrid Harrison. Oxford: Blackwell, 1948.

BERGSON, HENRI. *The Two Sources of Morality and Religion.* New York: H. Holt and Co., 1935.

BONEVAC, DANIEL. *Beyond the Western Tradition.* Mountain View, CA: Mayfield Publishing Co., 1992.

BOROWEITZ, EUGENE B. *Exploring Jewish Ethics.* Detroit: Wayne State University Press, 1990.

BRADLEY, F. H. *Ethical Studies.* London: Oxford University Press, 1962.

BRAYBROOKE, DAVID. *Meeting Needs.* Princeton, NJ: Princeton University Press, 1987.

BRAYBROOKE, DAVID, AND CHARLES E. LINDBLOM. *A Strategy of Decision.* New York: The Free Press, 1963.

BREASTED, JAMES HENRY. *The Dawn of Conscience.* New York and London: C. Scribner's Sons, 1934.

BRINTON, CRANE. *A History of Western Morals.* New York: Harcourt, Brace, 1959.

BROAD, C. D. *Five Types of Ethical Theory.* New York and London: Humanities Press and Routledge and Kegan Paul, 1971.

BUNGE, MARIO. *Treatise on Basic Philosophy.* Vol. 8. Dordrecht, Neth., and Boston: D. Reidel, 1989.

CAVALIER, ROBERT J., JAMES GOUINLOCK, AND JAMES STERBA. *Ethics in the History of Western Philosophy.* New York: St. Martin's Press, 1989.

CONFUCIUS. "The Four Books," in *The Chinese Classis.* Vol. I. Oxford: The Clarendon Press, 1893.

COOLIDGE, OLIVIA. *Gandhi.* Boston: Houghton Mifflin, 1971.

DANQUAH, J. B. *The Akan Doctrine of God: A Fragment of Gold Coast Ethics and Religion.* London: Cass, 1968.

DANTO, ARTHUR COLEMAN. *Mysticism and Morality: Oriental Thought and Moral Philosophy.* New York: Basic Books, 1972.

DASGUPTA, SURAMA. *Development of Moral Philosophy in India.* Bombay: Orient Longmans, 1961.

DE BEAUVOIR, SIMONE. *The Ethics of Ambiguity.* New York: The Citadel Press, 1968.

DE BOER, T. J. *The History of Philosophy in Islam.* New York: Dover, 1967.

DEWEY, JOHN, AND JAMES H. TUFTS. *Ethics*. New York: Henry Holt, 1913.

DWORKIN, RONALD. *Taking Rights Seriously*. Cambridge, MA: Harvard University Press, 1977.

DZOBO, N. K. *African Proverbs: The Guide to Conduct*. Vol. I. Cape Coast, Ghana: University of Cape Coast, 1973.

EBERHARD, WOLFRAM. *Guilt and Sin in Traditional China*. Berkeley: University of California Press, 1967.

FERGUSON, JOHN. *Moral Values in the Ancient World*. New York: Arno Press, 1979.

FLANAGAN, OWEN J. *Varieties of Moral Personality*. Cambridge, MA: Harvard University Press, 1991.

FLANAGAN, OWEN, AND AMELIE OKSENBERG RORTY. *Identity, Character, and Morality*. Cambridge, MA: MIT Press, 1990.

FOOT, PHILIPPA. *Theories of Ethics*. New York: Oxford University Press, 1971.

FÜRER-HAIMENDORF, CHRISTOPH VON. *Morals and Merit: A Study of Values and Social Controls in South Asian Societies*. Chicago: Chicago University Press, 1967.

GEWIRTH, ALAN. *Reason and Morality*. Chicago and London: The University of Chicago Press, 1978.

GRAHAM, A.C. *Later Mohist Logic, Ethics, and Science*. Hong Kong and London: Chinese University Press and London School of Oriental and African Studies, 1978.

GREENE, NORMAN N. *Jean-Paul Sartre: The Existentialist Ethic*. Ann Arbor: The University of Michigan Press, 1963.

GRICE, RUSSELL. *The Grounds of Moral Judgement*. Cambridge: Cambridge University Press, 1967.

HAMPSHIRE, STUART. *Morality and Conflict*. Cambridge, MA: Harvard University Press, 1983.

HARE, R. M. *The Language of Morals*. New York and London: Oxford University Press, 1964.

HARE, R. M. *Freedom and Reason*. New York and London: Oxford University Press, 1963.

HARTMANN, NICOLAI. *Ethics*. New York: Macmillan, 1932.

HOBHOUSE, L. T. *Morals in Evolution: A Study in Comparative Ethics*. London: Chapman and Hall, 1951.

HOOK, SIDNEY. *From Hegel to Marx: Studies in the Intellectual Development of Karl Marx*. New York: The Humanities Press, 1950.

HUDSON, W. D. *Modern Moral Philosophy*. Garden City, NY: Doubleday, 1970.

HUME, DAVID. *A Treatise of Human Nature*. Oxford: The Clarendon Press, 1987.

IANNONE, A. PABLO. *Philosophy as Diplomacy*. Atlantic Highlands, NJ: Humanities Press International, 1993.

IANNONE, A. PABLO. *Contemporary Moral Controversies in Business*. London and New York: Oxford University Press, 1989.

IANNONE, A. PABLO. *Contemporary Moral Controversies in Technology*. London and New York: Oxford University Press, 1987.

IZUTSU, TOSHIHIKO. *The Structure of the Ethical Terms in the Koran: A Study in Semantics*. Tokyo: Keio Institute of Philological Studies, 1959.

JONES, HARDY E. *Kant's Principle of Personality*. Madison: The University of Wisconsin Press, 1971.

KAMENKA, E. *Marxism and Ethics*. New York and London: St. Martin's and Macmillan, 1969.

KANT, IMMANUEL. *The Metaphysical Elements of Justice*. Indianapolis, IN: Bobbs-Merrill, 1965.

KANT, IMMANUEL. *The Metaphysical Elements of Virtue*. Indianapolis, IN: Bobbs-Merrill, 1964.

KANT, IMMANUEL. *Groundwork of the Metaphysics of Morals*. New York: Harper, 1964.

KANT, IMMANUEL. *Critique of Practical Reason*. Indianapolis, IN: Bobbs-Merrill, 1956.

KÖRNER, S. *Kant*. Baltimore: Penguin, 1967.

KROPOTKIN, PETR ALEKSEEVICH. *Ethics, Origin, and Development*. New York: L. MacVeagh, The Dial Press, 1924.

LAIRD, JOHN. *An Enquiry into Moral Notions*. London: Allen and Unwin, 1935.

LARMORE, CHARLES. *Patterns of Moral Complexity*. Cambridge, England, and New York: Cambridge University Press, 1987.

LEVI, ISAAC. *Hard Choices*. Cambridge and New York: Cambridge University Press, 1986.

MABBOTT, J. D. *An Introduction to Ethics*. Garden City, NY: Doubleday, 1969.

MACINTYRE, ALASDAIR. *Whose Justice? Which Rationality?* Notre Dame, IN: University of Notre Dame Press, 1988.

MACINTYRE, ALASDAIR. *After Virtue*. Notre Dame, IN: University of Notre Dame Press, 1984.

MACINTYRE, ALASDAIR C. *A Short History of Ethics*. New York: Macmillan, 1966.

MACKIE, J. L. *Ethics: Inventing Right and Wrong*. New York: Penguin, 1977.

MANDELBAUM, MAURICE. *The Phenomenology of Moral Experience*. Baltimore and London: The Johns Hopkins University Press, 1969.

MARTINEAU, JAMES. *Types of Ethical Theory*. Oxford: The Clarendon Press, 1901.

MARX, KARL. *Early Writings*. New York: Vintage Books, 1975.

MARX, KARL. *Capital*. New York: International Publishers, 1967.

MARX, KARL, AND FRIEDRICH ENGELS. *Basic Writings on Politics and Philosophy*. Garden City, NY: Doubleday, 1959.

MENCIUS. "The Works of Mencius," in *The Chinese Classics*. Vol. II. Oxford: The Clarendon Press, 1895.

MILL, JOHN STUART. *Essential Works of John Stuart Mill*, ed. Max Lerner. New York: Bantam, 1961.

MILL, JOHN STUART. *Principles of Political Economy*. London: Parker, 1848.

MOORE, G. E. *Principia Ethica*. Cambridge, Cambridge University Press, 1966.

MOORE, G. E. *Ethics*. New York: Oxford University Press, 1965.

MURPHY, ARTHUR E. *The Theory of Practical Reason*. La Salle, IL: Open Court, 1965.

NELL, ONORA. *Acting on Principle*. New York: Columbia University Press, 1975.

NIETZSCHE, FRIEDRICH. *On the Genealogy of Morals and Ecce Homo*. New York: Vintage Books, 1967.

NIETZSCHE, FRIEDRICH. *Beyond Good and Evil*. New York: Vintage Books, 1966.

NORTON, DAVID. *Democracy and Moral Development*. Berkeley: University of California Press, 1991.

NOZICK, ROBERT. *Anarchy, State, and Utopia*. New York: Basic Books, 1974.

PARADIS, JAMES G., AND GEORGE C. WILLIAMS. *Evolution and Ethics*. Princeton, NJ: Princeton University Press, 1989.

PEARSALL, MARILYN. *Women and Values*. Belmont, CA: Wadsworth Publishing Co., 1986.

PERRY, THOMAS D. *Moral Reasoning and Truth*. Oxford: The Clarendon Press, 1976.

PLATO. *Plato's Republic*. New York: Arno Press, 1973.

PLATO. "Laws," In *Plato*, ed. E. Hamilton and H. Cairns. Princeton, NJ: Princeton University Press, 1973.

PLATO. *The Statesman, Philebus, Ion*. London and Cambridge, MA: W. Heinemann and Harvard University Press, 1962.

QUINTON, ANTHONY. *Utilitarian Ethics*. New York: St. Martin's Press, 1973.

RAPHAEL, D. D. *British Moralists*. Oxford: The Clarendon Press, 1969.

RAPHAEL, D. D. *The Moral Sense*. London: Oxford University Press, 1947.

RASHDALL, HASTINGS. *The Theory of Good and Evil*. London: Oxford University Press, 1904.

RAWLING, F. W. *Gandhi and the Struggle for India's Independence*. Minneapolis: Lerner Publication Co. and Cambridge University Press, 1982.

RAWLS, JOHN. *A Theory of Justice*. Cambridge, MA: Harvard University Press, 1971.

ROSS, DAVID. *The Right and The Good*. Oxford: The Clarendon Press, 1930.

SABINE, GEORGE H. *A History of Political Theory*. New York: Holt, Rinehart and Winston, 1960.

SAUNDERS, KENNETH JAMES. *The Ideals of East and West*. New York and Cambridge: The Macmillan Company and Cambridge University Press, 1934.

SCHEVEN, ALBERT. *Swahili Proverbs*. Lantham, MD: University Press of America, 1981.

SCOTUS, DUNS. *Duns Scotus on the Will and Morality*. Washington, DC: Catholic University of America Press, 1986.

SELBY-BIGGE, L. A. *British Moralists*. New York: Dover, 1965.

SEN, AMARTYA, AND BERNARD WILLIAMS. *Utilitarianism and Beyond*. Cambridge: England: Cambridge University Press, 1982.

SIDGWICK, HENRY. *Outlines of the History of Ethics*. Boston: Beacon, 1968.

SIDGWICK, HENRY. *The Methods of Ethics*. London: Macmillan, 1874; 7th ed. 1962.

SIDGWICK, HENRY. *Practical Ethics*. London: Macmillan, 1898.

SIDGWICK, HENRY. *The Elements of Politics*. London: Macmillan, 1891.

SINGER, MARCUS G. *Morals and Values*. New York: Charles Scribner's Sons, 1977.

SINGER, MARCUS G. *Generalization in Ethics*. New York: Atheneum, 1971.

SMART, J. J. C., AND BERNARD WILLIAMS. *Utilitarianism: For and Against*. London: Cambridge University Press, 1973.

SPELMAN, ELIZABETH V. *Inessential Woman*. Boston: Beacon Press, 1988.

SPENCER, HERBERT. *The Comparative Psychology of Man*. Washington, DC: University Publications of America, 1977.

SPENCER, HERBERT. *Social Statics*. New York: A. M. Kelley, 1969.

SPENCER, HERBERT. *Data of Ethics*. New York: Collier, 1902.

SPINOZA, BENEDICTUS DE. *The Ethics and Selected Letters*. Indianapolis, IN: Hackett Publishing Co., 1982.

SSU SHU. *The Chinese Classical Work Commonly Called The Four Books*. Gainesville, FL: Scholars' Facsimiles and Reprints, 1970.

STACKHOUSE, MAX L. *Creeds, Society, and Human Rights: A Study in Three Cultures*. Grand Rapids, MI: W. B. Eerdmans Publishing Co., 1984.

STENT, GUNTHER S. *Morality as a Biological Phenomenon*. Berkeley: University of California Press, 1980.

STEVENSON, CHARLES L. *Ethics and Language*. New Haven, CT, and London: Yale University Press, 1968.

SUZUKI, DAISETZ, TEITARO. *A Brief History of Early Chinese Philosophy*. London: Probsthain, 1914.

TAWNEY, R. H. *Equality*. London: Unwin Books, 1964.

TAWNEY, R. H. *The Acquisitive Society*. New York: Harcourt, Brace and World, 1920.

TAYLOR, RICHARD. *Good and Evil*. New York and London: Macmillan and Collier Macmillan, 1970.

URMSON, J. O. *The Emotive Theory of Ethics*. London: Hutchinson and Co., 1968.

WARNOCK, J. G. *The Object of Morality*. London: Methuen, 1971.

WARNOCK, G. J. *Contemporary Moral Philosophy*. New York and London: St. Martin's and Macmillan, 1967.

WARNOCK, M. *Existentialist Ethics*. New York and London: St. Martin's and Macmillan, 1967.

WHATELY, RICHARD. *Lessons on Morals*. Cambridge, MA: John Bartlett, 1857.

WILLIAMS, BERNARD. *Ethics and the Limits of Philosophy*. Cambridge, MA: Harvard University Press, 1985.

YEARLEY, LEE H. *Mencius and Aquinas: Theories of Virtue and Conceptions of Courage*. Albany: State University of New York Press, 1990.

PART V. WHAT IS AESTHETICALLY VALUABLE?

ALDRICH, VIRGIL C. *Philosophy of Art.* Englewood Cliffs, NJ: Prentice Hall, 1963.

ARISTOTLE. *Poetics.* Oxford: The Clarendon Press, 1968.

BEARDSLEY, MONROE C. *Aesthetics from Classical Greece to the Present: A Short History.* University, AL: University of Alabama Press, 1966.

BEARDSLEY, MONROE C. *Aesthetics.* New York: Harcourt Brace, 1958.

BOSTON, J. S. *Irenga Figures Among the North-West Igbo and the Igala.* London: Ethnographica, 1977.

BRUYNE, EDGAR DE. *The Esthetics of the Middle Ages.* New York: F. Ungar Publishing Co., 1969.

BURCKHARDDT, TITUS. *Art of Islam: Language and Meaning.* London: World of Islam Festival Publishing, 1976.

CANCEL ORTIZ, RAFAEL. "The Language of Conflict in Puerto Rican Literature," *The Americas Review 18* (Summer 1990): 103–113.

CARROLL, DAVID. *Paraesthetics: Foucault, Lyotard, Derrida.* New York: Methuen, 1987.

CARROLL, KEVIN. *Yoruba Religious Carving: Pagan and Christian Sculpture in Nigeria and Dahomey.* London and Dublin: G. Chapman, 1967.

COLLINGWOOD, R. G. *Essays in the Philosophy of Art.* Bloomington, Indiana University Press, 1964.

CROCE, BENEDETTO. *The Aesthetic as the Science of Expression and of the Linguistic in General.* Cambridge and New York: Cambridge University Press, 1992.

DANTO, ARTHUR. *Art/Artifact.* New York and Munich: Center for African Art and Prestel Verlag, 1988.

DANTO, ARTHUR. *The Philosophical Disenfranchisement of Art.* New York: Columbia University Press, 1986.

DERRIDA, JACQUES. *Acts of Literature.* New York: Routledge, 1992.

DERRIDA, JACQUES. *The Truth in Painting.* Chicago: University of Chicago Press, 1987.

DEWEY, JOHN. *Art as Experience.* New York: Minton, Bach, and Co., 1934.

DEWEY, JOHN. *Art and Education.* Merion, PA: The Barnes Foundation, 1929.

DOXIADIS, CONSTANTINOS A. *Architecture in Transition.* New York: Oxford University Press, 1963.

ECO, UMBERTO. *The Aesthetics of Thomas Aquinas.* Cambridge, MA: Harvard University Press, 1988.

ECO, UMBERTO. *Art and Beauty in the Middle Ages.* New Haven, CT: Yale University Press, 1986.

FOWLER, BARBARA H. *The Hellenistic Aesthetic.* Bristol: British Classical Press, 1989.

GARDNER, HELEN. *Art Through the Ages,* 5th ed., revised by Horst de la Croix and Richard G. Tansey. New York: Hartcourt, Brace & World, 1970.

GOODMAN, NELSON. *Ways of Worldmaking.* Indianapolis, IN: Hackett Publishing Co., 1978.

GOODMAN, NELSON. *Languages of Art.* Indianapolis, IN: Bobbs-Merrill, 1968.

GRAY, ROCKWELL. *The Imperative of Modernity.* Berkeley, Los Angeles, London: University of California Press, 1989.

IANNONE, PABLO. "South." In *Paradise Lost or Gained? The Literature of Hispanic Exile,* ed. Fernando Alegria and Jorge Ruffinelli. Houston, TX: Arte Público Press, 1990. Also in *The Americas Review 18* (Fall–Winter, 1990).

IZUTSU, TOSHIHIKO. *The Theory of Beauty in the Classical Aesthetics of Japan.* The Hague and Boston: Martinus Nijhoff Publishers, 1981.

KANT, IMMANUEL. *Critique of Judgment.* New York: Hafner Publishing Co., 1951.

KEENE, DONALD. *The Pleasures of Japanese Literature.* New York: Columbia University Press, 1988.

KINOSHITA, MASAO. *Japanese Architecture: Suhiya.* Tokyo: Shokokusha, 1964.

LANGER, SUSANNE K. *Feeling and Form: A Theory of Art.* New York: Scribner, 1953.

LI, TSE-HOU. *The Path of Beauty: A Study of Chinese Aesthetics.* Beijing: Morning Glory Publishers, 1988.

LISSARRAGUE, F. *The Aesthetics of the Greek Banquet: Images of Wine and Ritual.* Princeton, NJ: Princeton University Press, 1990.

MATHER, CHRISTINE. *Native America: Arts, Traditions, and Celebrations.* New York: Clarkson Potter, 1990.

MERMALL, THOMAS. *The Rhetoric of Humanism: Spanish Culture After Ortega y Gasset.* Jamaica, NY: Bilingual Press, 1976.

MILL, JOHN STUART. *Mill's Essays on Literature and Society.* New York and London: Collier and Collier-Macmillan, 1965.

MORRISON, KARL FREDERICK. *History as a Visual Art in the Twelfth-Century Renaissance.* Princeton, NJ: Princeton University Press, 1990.

MUELDER EATON, MARCIA. *Basic Issues in Aesthetics.* Belmont, CA: Wadsworth Publishing Co., 1988.

MUNRO, THOMAS. *Oriental Aesthetics.* Cleveland: Press of Western Reserve University, 1965.

PLATO. *Symposium.* Indianapolis, IN: Hackett Publishing Co., 1989.

PLATO. *Phaedrus.* Warminster: Aris and Phillips, 1986.

PLATO. "Ion." In *The Statesman, Philebus, Ion.* Cambridge, MA: Harvard University Press, 1962.

RADIN, PAUL. *African Folktales and Sculpture.* New York: Pantheon Books, 1964.

ROSALES F. ARTURO. "Chicano Art: A Historical Reflection of the Community," *The Americas Review 18* (Summer 1990): 58–70.

SANTAYANA, GEORGE. *The Sense of Beauty.* Cambridge, MA: MIT University Press, 1988.

SCOTT, ROSEMARY E., AND GRAHAM HUTT. *Style in the East Asian Tradition.* London: School of Oriental and African Studies, University of London, 1987.

TANIZAKI, JUNICHIRO. *In Praise of Shadows.* New Haven, CT: Leete's Island Books, 1977.

UEDA, MAKOTO. *Literary and Art Theories in Japan.* Cleveland, OH: Press of Western Reserve University, 1967.

WITTGENSTEIN, LUDWIG. *Lectures and Conversations on Aesthetics, Psychology, and Religious Belief.* Berkeley: University of California Press, 1967.

PART VI. WHAT ARE PHILOSOPHY'S PROSPECTS TODAY?

APEL, KARL-OTTO. *Towards a Transformation of Philosophy.* London and Boston: Routledge & Kegan Paul, 1980.

BAIER, ANNETTE. *Postures of the Mind.* Minneapolis: University of Minnesota Press, 1985.

DERRIDA, JACQUES. *Margins of Philosophy.* Chicago: University of Chicago Press, 1982.

DEUTSCH, ELIOT. *Culture and Modernity.* Honolulu: University of Hawaii Press, 1991.

DEWEY, JOHN. *The Quest for Certainty.* New York: Putnam, 1960.

DEWEY, JOHN. *Reconstruction in Philosophy.* Boston: Beacon Press, 1948.

FAIN, HASKELL. *Between Philosophy and History.* Princeton, NJ: Princeton University Press, 1970.

GOODMAN, NELSON. *Reconceptions in Philosophy and Other Arts and Sciences.* Indianapolis, IN: Hackett Publishing Co., 1988.

GOODMAN, NELSON. *Problems and Projects.* Indianapolis, IN: Bobbs-Merrill, 1972.

HARDIN, SANDRA. *Discovering Reality: Feminist Perspectives on Epistemology, Methodology, and Philosophy of Science.* Dordrecht, Netherlands: Reidel, 1983.

LYOTARD, F. *The Postmodern Condition.* Minneapolis: University of Minnesota Press, 1984.

MCGAA, ED. *Mother Earth Spirituality: Native Americans Paths to Healing Ourselves and Our World.* New York: Harper-Collins, 1990.

MOULTON, JANICE. "A Paradigm of Philosophy: The Adversary Method." In *Discovering Reality: Feminist Perspectives on Epistemology, Metaphysics, Methodology, and Philosophy of Science,* ed. Sandra Hardin. Dordrecht, Neth.: Reidel, 1983). Pp. 149–164.

MURPHY, ARTHUR E. *Reason and the Common Good.* Englewood Cliffs, NJ: Prentice Hall, 1963.

NAGEL, THOMAS. *The View from Nowhere.* New York: Oxford University Press, 1986.

NIETZSCHE, FRIEDRICH. "Twilight of the Idols." In *The Portable Nietzsche,* ed. Walter Kaufmann. New York: The Viking Press, 1954.

RORTY, RICHARD. *Consequences of Pragmatism.* Minneapolis: University of Minnesota Press, 1982.

WHITE, MORTON. *Toward Reunion in Philosophy.* New York: Atheneum, 1963.

WITTGENSTEIN, LUDWIG. *Culture and Value.* Chicago: University of Chicago Press, 1980.